Geographical Indications
Volume I

Critical Concepts in Intellectual Property Law

Series Editor: Robert P. Merges

*Wilson Sonsoni Goodrich & Rosati Professor of Law and Technology
and Director, Berkeley Center for Law and Technology
University of California, Berkeley, USA*

1. Patents
    Joseph Scott Miller

2. Intellectual Property and Competition
    Michael A. Carrier

3. Intellectual Property and Biotechnology
    Arti K. Rai

4. Copyright
    Christopher S. Yoo

5. Intellectual Property and Property Rights
    Adam Mossoff

6. Intellectual Property and Digital Content
    Richard S. Gruner

7. Intellectual Property and Human Rights
    Lawrence R. Helfer

8. Intellectual Property, Innovation and the Environment
    Peter S. Menell and Sarah M. Tran

9. Trademark and Unfair Competition Law
    Graeme B. Dinwoodie and Mark D. Janis

10. Trade Secrets and Undisclosed Information
    Sharon K. Sandeen and Elizabeth A. Rowe

11. Geographical Indications
    Michael Blakeney

Future titles will include:

Intellectual Property and Private International Law
Paul Torremans

China and Intellectual Property Law
Peter Yu

Wherever possible, the articles in these volumes have been reproduced as originally published using facsimile reproduction, inclusive of footnotes and pagination to facilitate ease of reference.

For a list of all Edward Elgar published titles visit our website at
www.e-elgar.com

Geographical Indications
Volume I

Edited by

Michael Blakeney

Winthrop Professor,
The University of Western Australia, Australia
and Visiting Professor in Intellectual Property Law,
Queen Mary University of London, UK

CRITICAL CONCEPTS IN INTELLECTUAL PROPERTY LAW

An Elgar Research Collection
Cheltenham, UK • Northampton, MA, USA

Published by
Edward Elgar Publishing Limited
The Lypiatts
15 Lansdown Road
Cheltenham
Glos GL50 2JA
UK

Edward Elgar Publishing, Inc.
William Pratt House
9 Dewey Court
Northampton
Massachusetts 01060
USA

A catalogue record for this book is available from the British Library

Library of Congress Control Number: 2014959460

ISBN 978 1 78254 775 4 (3 volume set)

Printed and bound in Great Britain by T.J. International Ltd, Padstow

Contents

B   Certification of Product Quality

C Marketing Tool

D Cultural Protection

Acknowledgements

The editors and publishers wish to thank the authors and the following publishers who have kindly given permission for the use of copyright material.

Blackwell Publishing Ltd for articles: Terry Marsden, Jo Banks and Gillian Bristow (2000), 'Food Supply Chain Approaches: Exploring Their Role in Rural Development', *Sociologia Ruralis*, **40** (4), October, 424–38; Angela Tregear (2003), 'From Stilton to Vimto: Using Food History to Re-Think Typical Products in Rural Development', *Sociologia Ruralis*, **43** (2), April, 91–107; William van Caenegem (2003), 'Registered Geographical Indications: Between Intellectual Property and Rural Policy – Part II', *Journal of World Intellectual Property*, **6** (6), November, 861–74; Laurence Bérard and Philippe Marchenay (2006), 'Local Products and Geographical Indications: Taking Account of Local Knowledge and Biodiversity', *International Social Science Journal*, **58** (187), March, 109–16; Anselm Kamperman Sanders (2010), 'Incentives for and Protection of Cultural Expression: Art, Trade and Geographical Indications', *Journal of World Intellectual Property, Special Issue: The Law and Economics of Geographical Indications*, **13** (2), March, 81–93.

Tomer Broude for his own article: (2005), 'Taking "Trade and Culture" Seriously: Geographical Indications and Cultural Protection in WTO Law', *University of Pennsylvania Journal of International Economic Law*, **26** (4), Winter, 623–92.

CAB International for excerpt: Giovanni Belletti, and Andrea Marescotti (2011), 'Origin Products, Geographical Indications and Rural Development', in Elizabeth Barham and Bertil Sylvander (eds), *Labels of Origin for Food: Local Development, Global Recognition*, Chapter 6, 75–91.

Éditions Quæ for excerpt: Christine de Sainte Marie and Laurence Bérard (2005), 'Taking Local Knowledge into Account in the AOC System', in Laurence Bérard, Marie Cegarra, Marcel Djama, Sélim Louafi, Philippe Marchenay, Bernard Roussel and François Verdeaux (eds), *Biodiversity and Local Ecological Knowledge in France*, 181–8.

Elsevier Ltd for article: Angela Tregear, Filippo Arfini, Giovanni Belletti, and Andrea Marescotti (2007), 'Regional Foods and Rural Development: The Role of Product Qualification', *Journal of Rural Studies*, **23** (1), January, 12–22.

Emerald Group Publishing Ltd for articles: Dimitris Skuras and Aleka Vakrou (2002), 'Consumers' Willingness to Pay for Origin Labelled Wine: A Greek Case Study', *British Food Journal*, **104** (11), 898–912; Antonio Stasi, Gianluca Nardone, Rosaria Viscecchia and Antonio Seccia (2011), 'Italian Wine Demand and Differentiation Effect of Geographical

Indications', *International Journal of Wine Business Research*, **23** (1), 49–61; Ramona Teuber (2011), 'Consumers' and Producers' Expectations towards Geographical Indications: Empirical Evidence for a German Case Study', *British Food Journal*, **113** (7), 900–918.

Estey Centre Journal of International Law and Trade Policy for articles: Erik W. Ibele (2009), 'The Nature and Function of Geographical Indications in Law', *Estey Centre Journal of International Law and Trade Policy*, **10** (1), 36–49; Tilman Becker (2009), 'European Food Quality Policy: The Importance of Geographical Indications, Organic Certification and Food Quality Assurance Schemes in European Countries', *Estey Centre Journal of International Law and Trade Policy*, **10** (1), 111–30; Teshager Dagne (2010), 'Law and Policy on Intellectual Property, Traditional Knowledge and Development: Legally Protecting Creativity and Collective Rights in Traditional Knowledge Based Agricultural Products through Geographical Indications', *Estey Centre Journal of International Law and Trade Policy*, **11** (1), 68–117.

Phil Evans for his own excerpt: (2006), 'Geographic Indications, Trade and the Functioning of Markets', in Meir Perez Pugatch (ed.), *The Intellectual Property Debate: Perspectives from Law, Economics and Political Economy*, Chapter 17, 345–60.

Justin Hughes for his own article: (2006), 'Champagne, Feta, and Bourbon: The Spirited Debate about Geographical Indications', *Hastings Law Journal*, **58**, December, 299–386.

Inderscience Enterprises Ltd for article: Michael Blakeney (2009), 'Protection of Traditional Knowledge by Geographical Indications', *International Journal of Intellectual Property Management*, **3** (4), 357–74.

International Trade Centre for excerpt: Daniele Giovannucci, Tim Josling, William Kerr, Bernard O'Connor and May T. Yeung (2009), 'Valuing GIs: Their Pros and Cons', in *Guide to Geographical Indications: Linking Products and Their Origins*, Chapter 2, 19–38.

International Trademark Association for article: Norma Dawson (2000), 'Locating Geographical Indications – Perspectives from English Law', *Trademark Reporter*, **90**, July–August, 590–614.

Oxford University Press via the Copyright Clearance Center's RightsLink Service for articles: Ivo A. van der Lans, Koert van Ittersum, Antonella De Cicco, and Margaret Loseby (2001), 'The Role of the Region of Origin and EU Certificates of Origin in Consumer Evaluation of Food Products', *European Review of Agricultural Economics*, **28** (4), December, 451–77; GianCarlo Moschini, Luisa Menapace, and Daniel Pick (2008), 'Geographical Indications and the Competitive Provision of Quality in Agricultural Markets', *American Journal of Agricultural Economics*, **90** (3), August, 794–812; Shivani Singhal (2008), 'Geographical Indications and Traditional Knowledge', *Journal of Intellectual Property Law and Practice*, **3** (11), November, 732–8; Pierre R. Mérel (2009), 'On the Deadweight Cost of Production Requirements for Geographically Differentiated Agricultural Products', *American Journal of Agricultural Economics*, **91** (3), August, 642–55; Luisa Menapace and GianCarlo Moschini

(2012), 'Quality Certification by Geographical Indications, Trademarks and Firm Reputation', *European Review of Agricultural Economics*, **39** (4), September, 539–66.

Springer Science and Business Media B.V. for article: Stuart Landon and C.E. Smith (1997), 'The Use of Quality and Reputation Indicators by Consumers: The Case of Bordeaux Wine', *Journal of Consumer Policy*, **20** (3), September, 289–323.

Swiss Federal Institute of Intellectual Property for excerpt: Marguerite Paus and Sophie Reviron (2011), 'Evaluating the Effects of Protecting Geographical Indications: Scientific Context and Case Studies', in Giovanni Belletti, Andrea Marescotti, Marguerite Paus, Sophie Reviron, Angela Deppeler, Hansueli Stamm and Erik Thévenod-Mottet (eds), *The Effects of Protecting Geographical Indications: Ways and Means of Their Evaluation*, 11–30.

Taylor and Francis Ltd (www.taylorandfrancis.com) for articles and excerpt: Warren Moran (1993), 'The Wine Appellation as Territory in France and California', *Annals of the Association of American Geographers*, **83** (4), December, 694–717; Ramona Teuber (2010), 'Geographical Indications of Origin as a Tool of Product Differentiation: The Case of Coffee', *Journal of International Food and Agribusiness Marketing*, **22** (3–4), 277–98; Susy Frankel (2011), 'The Mismatch of Geographical Indications and Innovative Traditional Knowledge', *Prometheus*, **29** (3), September, 253–67; Rungsaran Wongprawmas, Maurizio Canavari, Rainer Haas and Daniele Asioli (2012), 'Gatekeepers' Perceptions of Thai Geographical Indication Products in Europe', *Journal of International Food and Agribusiness Marketing*, **24** (3), 185–200; Thierry Coulet (2012), 'Assessing the Economic Impact of GI Protection', in Michael Blakeney, Thierry Coulet, Getachew Mengistie and Marcelin Tonye Mahop (eds), *Extending the Protection of Geographical Indications: Case Studies of Agricultural Products in Africa*, Chapter 5, 101–19.

Thomson Reuters for articles: Stephen Stern (2007), 'Are GIs IP?', *European Intellectual Property Review*, **29** (2), February, 39–42; Rhonda Chesmond (2007), 'Protection or Privatisation of Culture? The Cultural Dimension of the International Intellectual Property Debate on Geographical Indications of Origin', *European Intellectual Property Review*, **29** (9), September, 379–88.

University of Iowa College of Law for article: Alexandra Basak Russell (2010), 'Using Geographical Indications to Protect Artisanal Works in Developing Countries: Lessons from a Banana Republic's Misnomered Hat', *Transnational Law and Contemporary Problems*, **19**, Spring, 705–28.

World Intellectual Property Organization (WIPO) for excerpt: Cerkia Bramley, Estelle Biénabe and Johann Kirsten (2009), 'The Economics of Geographical Indications: Towards a Conceptual Framework for Geographical Indication Research in Developing Countries', in *The Economics of Intellectual Property: Suggestions for Further Research in Developing Countries and Countries with Economies in Transition*, Chapter 4, 109–41.

Every effort has been made to trace all the copyright holders but if any have been inadvertently overlooked the publishers will be pleased to make the necessary arrangement at the first opportunity.

In addition the publishers wish to thank the Library of Indiana University at Bloomington, USA and the Library at the University Warwick, UK for their assistance in obtaining these articles.

Geographical Indications
An Introduction to the Literature

Michael Blakeney

Overview

The subject of geographical indications (GIs) has generated a considerable body of scholarship in recent years. A number of reasons can be advanced to explain the burgeoning popularity of this subject. First, it is a nice discrete subject within the general field of intellectual property (IP) law that can be dealt with fairly comprehensively without too much overlap with other IP topics, other than trade marks. Second, the inclusion of GIs within the World Trade Organization (WTO) Agreement on Trade Related Aspects of Intellectual Property Rights (TRIPS Agreement) is considered to be a European ('Old World') IP agenda item, attracting the ire of the 'New World' both in scholarship and in the WTO dispute brought on by a complaint by Australia and the USA against the EU. This conflict has led to a search for allies among the countries of the 'South' and this has generated a body of scholarship investigating the advantages of GIs for developing countries. This scholarship has generally taken the form of European case studies as exemplars for the South, as well as case studies in a range of developing countries. A separate strain of this scholarship overlaps with analyses of the possibility of extending the special protection for wines and spirits in the TRIPS Agreement to other products such as agricultural products and handicrafts. This scholarship parallels and embraces the inconclusive debates in the TRIPS Council on this subject. A separate inconclusive debate in the TRIPS Council, also reflected in GIs scholarship, concerns the nature of the 'multilateral system of notification and registration' of GIs that is envisaged by Article 23.4 of the TRIPS Agreement. Is this to be a French-style AOC registration system? Is it to extend to products other than wines and spirits? What is to be its legal effect?

This book reproduces the principal English language scholarship on GIs but, as with the institution of origin product labelling itself, it should be acknowledged that the oldest and most comprehensive monographs on this subject are by French scholars (see: Lacour, 1904; Guérillon, 1919; Plaisant and Jacq, 1921; Jaton, 1926; Vivez, 1943; Capus, 1947; Auby and Plaisant, 1974; Guyet, 1983; De Vletian, 1989; Rochard, 2002; Denis, 1995; Olszak, 2001; Rochard, 2002). Also a number of the recent English language books and articles on GIs have been written by French scholars participating in the EU-funded DOLPHINS and SINER-GI projects (for example, Barjolle and Sylvander, 2000; Sylvander, 2004; Barham and Sylvander, 2011). However, in recent years an impressive corpus of English language scholarship on GIs has been published. The first significant monograph, O'Connor (2004), explores geographical indications within English trade marks and passing off law. The most recent text, Gangjee (2012), seeks to locate geographical indications within international intellectual property law.

Given the plethora of recent writings on GIs, particularly in the context of the TRIPS Agreement, it has been necessary to select between some fairly similar items. As will be seen below many authors adopt the same methodology of surveying the international treaties and agreements on GIs before addressing their particular concerns. For this reason in a compendium of writings on GIs there is inevitably some repetition in descriptions of the international landscape, but some selection has been made to avoid too much replication. A comprehensive bibliography is annexed to this outline and mention is made herein of a number of articles that could not be included primarily for reasons of repetition, space and also because they may have contained a large number of photographs that would not work in a book such as this. Also excluded from this compilation are a number of economic analyses of GIs that, because of the large number of mathematical formulae, are probably out of place in a law text.

The close examination that GIs have received since the TRIPS Agreement has raised questions about GIs as a valid category of IP and this is considered in Part I, Volume I of the book. The various functions that have been claimed for GIs are addressed in Part II, Volume I. The evaluation of the effects of GIs is considered in Part III, Volume I. Part I, Volume II contains a number of items that describe the European sui generis system for the registration of GIs and Part II, Volume II contrasts this with the New World trade marks-based systems for the protection of GIs. The international dimension of GIs protection is considered in Part I, Volume III and the particular implications of GIs for developing countries is considered in Part II, Volume III. The book concludes in Part III, Volume III with a number of case studies.

Volume I

GIs as Intellectual Property

The Old World/New World disputation over GIs in the context of the TRIPS Agreement has generated a body of scholarship questioning the jurisprudential basis of GIs protection. Stern (Chapter 3, Volume I) questions whether GIs are IP, pursuing a line of scholarship initiated by van Caenegem (Chapter 4, Volume I) and pursued by Hughes (Chapter 5, Volume I). A number of commentators have commented on the uniqueness of GIs as a category of IP. Jókúti (2009) contrasts the protection of GIs with patents or trade marks whose variants are at least comparable. Dawson (Chapter 2, Volume I, p. 27) explains that GIs are 'an intellectual property right in the making surrounded by a complex debate lacking common terminology'. The terminological confusion surrounding the discussion of GIs is highlighted by Gangjee (2012) as a symptom of the conceptual, institutional and epistemic 'mess' characterising GIs jurisprudence. Distilling the analyses of the ECJ and the WTO Secretariat he identified at least four ways in which GIs are described: as 'signs which indicate (1) merely a product's origin, (2) its reputation associated with a specific origin, (3) its distinctive qualities associated with origin, or (4) its unique qualities that are reliant upon origin' (Gangjee, 2012). This diversity of approaches obviously affects the functions, described in Part II, Volume I of this book, which are ascribed to GIs and the correlative scope of protection. A study commissioned by the European Commission describes the protection of GIs in the 160 countries surveyed (O'Connor & Co, 2007a; 2007b), which can be explained by the disparate terminology and functions that GI protection is intended to achieve. At the same time this diversity confuses the debates in the TRIPS Council on both the extension of protection and the scope of the multilateral register that are described in the extracts in Part I, Volume III of this book.

Functions of GIs

The obligation of WTO members to protect GIs, the possible extension of that protection and the various models for GIs protection that are competing for the attention particularly of developing countries have raised questions about the functions and utility of GIs protection. As authors such as van Caenegem (2003) and Ibele (Chapter 6, Volume I) point out, the principal functions that have been identified for GIs are: promotion of rural development, certification of product quality, marketing and consumer protection, environmental protection and cultural protection. These functions are explored in Part II, Volume I of the book.

A: RURAL DEVELOPMENT
There is a significant corpus of scholarship on the contribution of origin products to rural development (Ray, 1998; Banks and Marsden, 2000; Marsden et al., Chapter 7, Volume I; Ilbery and Kneafsey, 2000a and 2000b; Pacciani et al., 2001; Babcock, 2003, Barham, Chapter 8, Volume II; Tregear, Chapter 8, Volume I; Babcock and Clemens, 2004; Belletti and Marescotti, 2002; Rangnekar, 2004; O'Connor & Co, 2005; Tregear et al., Chapter 9, Volume I; Blakeney and Mengistie, 2011, which is reviewed in Réviron and Paus, 2006, and updated in Belletti and Marescotti, Chapter 10, Volume I). Babcock (2003) criticises this evidence as predominantly theoretical, signifying the need for more empirical evidence. However, the increasing number of case studies, a number of which are extracted in Part III, Volume III of this book, confirms the proposition that GIs assist in the promotion of sustainable rural development. Most of the case studies come from France, Italy, Portugal, Greece and Spain, which until recently accounted for three-quarters of the GIs found in Europe (Morgan et al., 2006). Ilbery and Kneafsey (2000b) contrast this with the UK, dominated by homogenous brands, attributable to the fact that the GI movement in the UK is a recent development.

As Pacciani et al. (2001) and O'Connor & Co (2005) point out, protection of GIs accords with the EU policy on rural development. The preamble to the EU Regulation, 510/2006, governing GIs identifies that:

> The diversification of agricultural production should be encouraged so as to achieve a better balance between supply and demand on the markets. The promotion of products having certain characteristics can be of considerable benefit to the rural economy, particularly in less favoured or remote areas, by improving the incomes of farmers and by retaining the rural population in these areas.[1]

The creation of local jobs through the protection of GIs is a factor influencing rural exodus (O'Connor & Co, 2005). Young people are considered the most disadvantaged in rural areas (Chapman and Shucksmith, 1996) yet their departure from rural areas creates challenges for the sustainability of rural communities (Jentsch, 2006). An increase in employment has, for example, been observed for the Comté cheese industry (Requillart, 2007).

Van de Kop et al. (2006) estimate that the production of Comté cheese generates five times more jobs in processing, maturing, marketing, packing, et cetera than does its generic equivalent Emmental, and that migration away from the countryside in the Comté area is only half that of the origin-protected area. They estimate that at the national level, although Comté cheeses account for only 10 per cent of total French cheese output, they are responsible for 40 per cent of the job offers for students who have been trained in cheese-making in vocational schools. Similar results have been identified for origin-protected cheeses supporting the milk supply from cattle in northern Italy and the sheep of southern Italy (Belletti et al., 2002). Belletti et al. (2002) estimated that origin agro-products in Italy generated around 6 billion euros of GNP and employment for 300,000 persons.

However, as noted by Williams (2007) based on the EU case studies, the potential for job creation is dependent on the labour intensity of the protected products.

GIs also have a wider territorial impact that extends beyond the direct GI stakeholders. GIs can lead to employment creation and agro-tourism within the region (Paus and Reviron, Chapter 35, Volume I). GIs are also likely to stimulate investment and the price of land within the borders of the GI region (Zografos, 2008; Giovannucci et al., 2009) also point to the potential 'complementary effect' a GI may have on other products in the area.

Bessière (1998) states that the specific processes involved with food linked to a particular region can invite tourism. However, the development of tourism in association with local food and gastronomy does hold some fears of 'Disneyfication' (Barham, Chapter 8, Volume II). The Comité Interprofessionnel du Vin de Champagne has requested 'the landscapes of the Champagne region' to be included on UNESCO's World Heritage List.[2] The objective is to protect the famous sites of the Champagne region, which include the great diversity of vineyards and the outstanding character of the area's cellars carved from the surrounding chalk and the unique landscapes of the Champagne region.

Finally, Sylvander (2004) observes that the importance of GIs for sustainable rural development should be assessed by keeping in mind their 'multifactorial' nature, which extends beyond market-related benefits to include positive social and environmental externalities within the region.

B: CERTIFICATION OF PRODUCT QUALITY

Scholarship on the importance of information and information about the quality of products for the proper functioning of markets dates back more than 40 years (see Akerlof, 1970). Klein and Leffler (1981) investigate the causes of and remedies for market failures owing to the lack of information on product quality. It is common in the economics literature to distinguish goods according to whether their quality can be identified by consumers (Antle, 1996; Mojduska and Caswell, 2000; Giannakas, 2002). Kreps and Wilson (1982), Shapiro (1983) and Verbeke and Roosen (2009) have shown that this information search can be improved through labelling, which signals reputation. Zago and Pick (2004) consider the welfare impact of the introduction of EU GIs legislation that allows producers of agricultural commodities with specific characteristics to differentiate and label their products accordingly. They find that both consumers and high-quality producers are unambiguously better off from this labelling, while producers of the low-quality commodity are unambiguously worse off. They note that the impact on economic welfare can be negative when the administrative costs of the regulation are relatively high and quality differences low and relatively expensive to obtain.

GIs can play an important role in signalling the quality of goods (see Becker, Chapter 15, Volume I). Hobbs (2003) and Hobbs and Kerr (2006) explain that the attributes of goods may be classified as: (a) search attributes that can be identified by consumers prior to purchase (for example, ripeness); (b) experience attributes that can only be discerned upon consumption (for example, taste); and (c) credence attributes that cannot be identified by consumers even after consumption (for example, product origin and production methods). Although origin brands may assist in the signalling of search or experience attributes, they are mainly important in signalling credence attributes, particularly where the origin brand is underpinned by a registration and certification system. As Winfree and McCluskey (2005) indicate, it enables producers to signal quality and the associated reputation that has been developed over time. Moschini et al. (Chapter 14, Volume I) claim that producers are incentivised by an origin indication to maintain product quality. The reputation signalled by the origin indication attaches to all stakeholders in the supply chain. Zago and Pick (2004) explain that this signalling of quality improves consumer welfare through lowering the costs of searching for information about products. It should be noted that the influence of origin branding in communicating quality information will differ between products. Landon and Smith (Chapter 11, Volume I) examine the use by consumers of quality and reputation indicators in relation to Bordeaux wine, which is protected by GIs. Van der Lans et al. (Chapter 12, Volume I) analyse the role of the region of origin and EU certificates of origin in consumer evaluation of food products.

In order for the perceived benefits of GI labelling to be realised, such as the promotion of sustainable rural development, there needs to be consumer awareness that origin labelling represents qualities linked to natural and human factors. Since there is already a consumer awareness of value added foods and a consumer demand for traceability in agro-food products (Marsden et al., Chapter 7, Volume I; Murdoch et al., 2000; Van der Ploeg et al., 2000) this awareness can be developed for origin products.

Rural product certification schemes have proliferated since the mid 1990s. They include the certification of organic agriculture, fair-trade certification of products from developing countries and food produced in compliance with sanitary and traceability protocols (Giraud, 2003; Mutersbaugh et al., 2005). For smallholder producers in developing countries certification provides quality market niches at a time of declining agricultural and forest commodity prices (Gonzáles and Nigh, 2005). Consumers have been identified as placing increasing value on the integrity of food, such as the social and environmental standards involved in the production and processing of agri-food products (Giraud and Amblard, 2003; Renting et al., 2003; Hobbs et al., 2005; Murdoch et al., 2000). This is particularly the case following recent food crises. As it is not unusual for food to be grown, processed and packaged in different places, consumer trust in products is eroded, particularly as a consequence of these crises. Studies indicate a willingness of consumers to pay a premium price to producers who offer transparency in relation to the composition and origin of their products. In situations where uncertainty about quality or safety is elevated, such as in a health crisis, origin labelling can become an important means of inferring product quality, for example, meat labels after the BSE crisis in Europe (Verbeke and Viaene, 1999; Lees, 2003) and dairy product labels after the Melamin crisis (Xu and Wu, 2010).

GIs are identified as providing a means for the legal regulation of the use of origin product designations as a means of avoiding the deception of consumers as to the true origin of products, production methods and as to the specific quality of products (O'Connor, 2004; van Caenegem, 2004; Tregear and Giraud, 2011; Barjolle et al., 2011).

In Europe, where GIs have been longest developed, there are some empirically based suggestions that consumers and producers both have expectations about the quality of origin products in the European market (Teuber, Chapter 16, Volume I; Stasi et al., Chapter 17, Volume I). This is discussed in the next section.

C: MARKETING TOOL

Agricultural producers in developing countries have the challenge of ensuring market access by differentiating their products from other agricultural producers in both industrialised and developing countries. Evans (Chapter 19, Volume I) and Bramley and Bienabe (Chapter 27, Volume III) explain that GIs provide mechanisms that facilitate the creation of territorially differentiated niche markets. Part I, Volume III of this book examines the advantage that this presents for developing country producers. They cite the work of Réviron and Paus (2006) and Pacciani et al. (2001) who explain that GIs disconnect the origin product from commodity markets by capturing attributes of the locality such as environmental factors and local knowledge in the GI product. Agarwal and Barone (2005) point out that an understanding by producers of the potential to protect regionally embedded value added products through origin branding allows a sustainable competitive advantage for the future of agricultural firms.

Van Ittersum et al. (2003) have made the point that although origin-based marketing has a long history, its contemporary relevance is increasing, partly as a reaction to globalisation as local producers need to be able to distinguish their product in the eyes of consumers from generic competition. In the newly urbanising developing countries consumers and people from a particular region or ethnic group look to the products from their places of origin as being reliable and known. Gradually, these local products begin to gain a commercial reputation among a wider group of traders and consumers.

A number of researchers have identified the capacity of origin labelling to differentiate otherwise homogeneous commodities as the basis for charging premium prices. Reviron et al. (2009) refer to value addition from a mix of economic, cultural and social characteristics leading to the capturing of a premium. Marette (2005) and Williams (2007) assert the higher value that consumers attach to products differentiated according to their origin. Agarwal and Barone (2005) suggest that the exotic nature of origin products allows their producers to charge premium prices. Reviron et al. (2009) argue that this premium might grow over time as consumer recognition of the origin label increases. Teuber (Chapter 22, Volume I) documents the premium prices that can be charged for coffee in the European market, and in a study of Hessian apple wine, Teuber (Chapter 16, Volume I) indicates that the willingness of consumers to pay a premium price is because of their view of the positive impacts of GIs on the local economy. Wongprawmas et al. (Chapter 23, Volume I) question the extent to which foreign producers such as Thais can rely upon this assumption.

A number of studies of European products refer to the premiums that are charged. Babcock (2003) reports that Bresse poultry in France receives quadruple the commodity price for poultry meat; Italian 'Toscano' oil gains a 20 per cent premium above commodity oil; and milk supplied to produce French Comté cheese sells for a 10 per cent premium. The case study of Comté cheese in France by Gerz and Dupont (2006) indicates that French farmers receive an average of 14 per cent more for milk destined for Comté and that dairy farms in the Comté area have become more profitable since 1990, and now are 32 per cent more profitable than similar farms outside the Comté area. The retail price of Comté has risen by 2.5 per cent per year (against 0.5 per cent for Emmental), while the wholesale price has risen by 1.5 per cent a year (no change for Emmental). The French Ministry of Agriculture claims that part of this added value accrues to producers and other actors in the Comté supply chain, whereas retailers have appropriated all of the 0.5 per cent rise in the retail price of Emmental (MAAPAR, 2004). O'Connor & Co (2005) refer to the protection of 'lentilles vertes du puy', which is said to have increased the production of lentils from 13,600 quintals in 1990 to 34,000 quintals in 1996 and 49,776 quintals in 2002, the number of producers almost tripling from 395 in 1990, to 750 in 1996 and 1,079 in 2002. On the other hand Bonnet and Simioni (2001) in a study of designation of origin labelling find that consumers do not value the quality signal provided by the PDO label. For example, they observe that, at the same price, only a small proportion of consumers prefer to buy a similar Camembert brand with a PDO label than one without it, and that brand appears to be more relevant than information in the consumer's valuation of available products.

There are fewer studies of premium prices for origin products outside Europe. Kireeva et al. (2009) examine a number of examples of the use of certification marks in the People's Republic of China. The price of 'Zhangqiu' scallion per kilogram was raised from 0.2 to 0.6 yuan before the use of the certification mark to 1.2 to 5 yuan in 2009. 'Jianlian' lotus seed was registered as a GI in 2006, leading to a rise in price from 26 to 28 yuan per kilogram to 32 to 34 yuan per kilogram. Babcock and Clemens (2004) mention that although New Zealand lamb is protected indirectly as a geographical indication, although a premier product, it has only managed to reach a premium price for a small percentage of exported produce. Menapace et al. (2011) have observed the willingness of Canadian consumers to pay a premium price for origin branded olive oil.

Aggregation of market power   The proposal that farmers enhance their incomes by the collective marketing of their produce dates back around 100 years (Carver and Wilson, 1916). The proposals to achieve this result have included: producer cooperatives; mandatory government acquisition and marketing; and government supported marketing agencies and boards. Gordon et al. (1999) explain that to escape the commodity trap where each producer of a particular product is a direct competitor with every other producer, farmers need to band together, cooperate, differentiate their products and then commit resources to shifting out their now downward sloping demand curve. Yeung and Kerr (Chapter 26, Volume III, citing Giovannucci et al., 2009) characterise the current popularity of GIs in the EU as the latest manifestation of this theme.

The stronger the product/origin nexus, the greater will be the competitive advantage created by the differentiation of the origin branded product from the general commodity group. By creating grounds for competitive advantage based on territorial specificities and reducing competition with non-differentiated products, GIs potentially assist producers in appropriating a larger income from the production of origin-based goods (Zografos, 2008). Bramley and Bienabe (Chapter 27, Volume III) point out that a niche marketing strategy entails an increase in production and marketing costs, particularly promotional costs to secure consumer recognition. Barjolle and Sylvander (2000) suggest that those promotional costs can be recouped through increased sales volumes and as is indicated below through premium product pricing. Giovannucci et al. (2009) identify some of the pros and cons of establishing GI systems. Mérel (Chapter 21, Volume I) details some of the 'deadweight' cost of production requirements for agricultural products sold under GIs.

Belletti et al. (2007) explain the international success of Tuscan firms producing: Olio Toscano PGI, Olio Chianti Classico PDO, Pecorino Toscano PDO and Prosciutto Toscano PDO in aggregating the market power of a number of small enterprises.

Babcock (2003) and Lence et al. (2007) suggest that the protection of origin brands provides an incentive for producers to develop new origin brands. Stasi et al. (Chapter 17, Volume I) in a study of the Italian wine market establish the existence of a differentiation effect of GIs in terms of magnitude of elasticities and substitution effects. GIs corresponding to higher quality generate lower price sensitivity and product substitution compared with wine without origin protection. Blakeney (Chapter 25, Volume II) describes the process whereby Australia's obligation to respect EU GIs for wines and spirits has created a national impetus to create Australian GIs for the same products.

Redistribution of added value through the product chain The principal justification for origin labelling is the enhancement of profits and their distribution through the supply chain. As a general rule, agri-food producers in long food supply chains obtain a decreasing share of any added value, whereas short food supply chains offer greater chances for added value to be enjoyed by all actors (Marsden et al., Chapter 7, Volume I). There are a number of studies that indicate that the primary beneficiaries from origin labelling are those at the distribution end of the value chain. Ilbery and Kneafsey (2000a) report from a study on GIs in the UK that only a small number of food managing companies and their shareholders benefit from added value from GIs and that most farmers and small businesses involved are unlikely to benefit. Yeung and Kerr (Chapter 26, Volume III) point out that all participants in the value chain must understand and buy into the protection of a GI's quality and/or reputation. Young and Hobbs (2002) advise proactive value chain management where incentives are provided for all persons in the supply chain, as there is no reason for producers in developing countries to go to the trouble of creating an origin product if other supply chain participants capture all the extra value that is created by the origin label.

Bowen and De Master (2011) in case studies of agricultural production in France and Poland note that while quality initiatives create the capacity for maintaining rural livelihoods in the face of the homogenising trends in the global agro-food system, 'they also have the potential to undermine local specificity and privilege powerful extralocal actors at the expense of local communities'. A study by Dentoni et al. (2012) of the 'Prosciutto di Parma Consortium' indicates that the high heterogeneity of size between different members negatively affects members' agreement on the future level of the definition of its GI standard and therefore the effectiveness of collective action.

Sustainable use of natural resources and biodiversity conservation Bramley and Bienabe (Chapter 27, Volume III) observe that while environmental sustainability is not the primary aim of GI development, the fact that GIs derive from local, including natural, resources means that environmental benefits are increasingly seen as a potential GI externality. The codes of practices that are collectively adopted in relation to origin labelling often incorporate biodiversity objectives (Larson, 2007). Bienabe et al. (2010) refer to the Rooibos industry in South Africa as an example of an industry that has explicitly considered biodiversity concerns in designing its product specification. This is because Rooibos production takes place in a biodiverse and environmentally sensitive area. Van de Kop et al. (2006) point out that as the registered Comté PDO specifications limit the intensification of farming, so farmers use fewer inputs and the environment is better protected, contributing to maintaining the open landscape of both pasture and woodland that is typical of the Jura region. Profitable traditional livestock raising in the Comté area has limited the loss of pastureland to 7 per cent in the PDO area, compared with 18 per cent in the non-PDO area.

Producers are encouraged to act in a responsible manner towards the local environment as negative publicity would damage the product's image in the mind of the consumer (Williams, 2007). Thus producers are likely to be concerned with environmental factors such as pollution and sustainable management of natural resources. These environmental considerations are increasingly incorporated into the codes of practice associated with origin products.

As origin labelling increases the value of the product, it may also lead to the continued use of traditional resources that may otherwise have been replaced by otherwise more economically profitable species or breeds (Bérard and Marchenay, Chapter 24, Volume I; Lybbert, 2002). However, it is also important to point out that the success of an origin product may lead to an increase in demand and therefore to increased pressure on local resources. Sustainable production guidelines need to be agreed upon by means of a participatory process in order to prevent pressure being placed on fragile environments and to ensure in particular that the GI does not lead to 'genetic erosion' (Downes and Laird, 1999; Boisvert, 2006).

Rural sustainability achieved through the preservation of biodiversity, landscapes and traditional knowledge may be promoted by the protection of GIs (Barham, 2002). For example, Guerra (2004) observes that in the Mexcal region of Mexico the Agave sugar needed to make Tequila is cultivated and managed from wild or forest Agave species, which encourages the biodiverse Agave species. GIs can also serve as a tool for encouraging sustainable agricultural practice by legally limiting the scale of production and production methods (Guerra, 2004). Penker (2006) notes that origin products impose an increased responsibility of producers to their place of production. Lampkin et al. (1999) note that 'organic standards provide a mechanism by which farmers pursuing sustainability goals can be compensated by the market for internalizing external costs'.

Aiding the preservation of traditional knowledge Bérard and Marchenay (1996, p. 240) describe GIs as a means of 'enabling people to translate their long-standing, collective, and patrimonial knowledge into livelihood and income'. De Sainte Marie and Bérard (Chapter 26, Volume I), Panizzon (2006), Singhal (Chapter 28, Volume I), Blakeney (Chapter 29, Volume I) and Dagne (2010) point out that GIs share many of the characteristics of TK as both seek to preserve communal rights and, like TK, GIs can be held in perpetuity, for as long as a community maintains the practices that guarantee the distinctive quality of a local product. Similarly, in its *Review of Existing Intellectual Property Protection of TK* WIPO's IGC Secretariat observed that 'Goods designated and differentiated by geographical indications, be they wines, spirits, cheese, handicrafts, watches, silverware and others, are as much expressions of local cultural and community identification as other elements of traditional knowledge.'[3] Graber and Lai (2012, p. 97), on the other hand, doubt that origin branding is appropriate for the protection of traditional cultural expressions (TCEs) because it is 'difficult to create standards (particularly those that can be consistently certified) for handicrafts'. Mulik and

Crespi (Chapter 33, Volume III), in an analysis of the potential for GIs to protect Basmati rice against the marketing of similarly trademarked US products, suggest that the extension of TRIPS Article 23 protection to agricultural products could provide more effective assistance for the protection of products incorporating TK.

The GI process, on the other hand, involves documenting specific methods into a code of practice that falls within the public domain. In doing this it prevents the appropriation of the knowledge embedded in the GI product, including potential traditional knowledge components (Rangnekar, 2002). However, despite the *a priori* link between GIs and traditional knowledge, the use of GIs for protecting traditional knowledge is not without limitations. Most notably, GIs protect the collective reputation of a product linked to a specific territory and not the underlying knowledge embedded in the good or production process (Kur and Knaak, 2004). The knowledge as such thus remains available for use by outside parties. The GI does nevertheless allow for a commercial value to be attached to products linked to a specific territory that build on traditional knowledge and thereby allow those local communities that produce the GI to benefit economically from their traditional knowledge. GIs can therefore promote the continued use of the knowledge. As such, Bramley (2011, p. 6) suggests that GIs are thus more a means for 'preserving rather than protecting' traditional knowledge. It should be acknowledged that some academic commentators (Kur and Cocks, Chapter 5, Volume II; Hughes, Chapter 5, Volume I) regard 'the assertions on the part of the EU and other nations with vested interests in a worldwide regime of vigorous GI protections – such as Switzerland – that such a scheme would aid developing countries in expanding their economies by ensuring the maintenance of knowledge bases related to the growth and manufacture of traditional indigenous products are unfounded and inherently flawed' (Chapter 5, Volume II, p. 127). Blakeney (Chapter 29, Volume I) interprets this to mean that mere registration of a GI will not create a premium price, as investment is required in advertising and promotion. He suggests that the advantage of the GI system in this regard is that it provides a mechanism for the aggregation of promotional expenditure on the part of agricultural producers, which can be supported by the national agricultural marketing authorities.

D: CULTURAL PROTECTION

Echols (2008) points out that the 2005 UNESCO Convention on the Protection and Promotion of the Diversity of Cultural Expressions reaffirms as one of its objectives the link between culture and development of all countries, particularly developing countries. By attaching an economic value to locally embedded products, an origin brand allows the local population to sustain its way of life and uphold its cultural heritage. This strengthens the region's identity, which in turn reinforces the origin brand. These mutually fortifying linkages are likely to boost the rural development impact of the brand, while Williams (2007) mentions 'social cohesion' as a positive outcome of the GI process that facilitates greater cooperation and information sharing. Arfini et al. (2003) in a study on 15 specific origin labelled products located in seven European countries find that the GIs Taureau de Camargue, Cherry of Lari and Culatello di Zibello strengthened producer pride and self-esteem, and encouraged local population participation in the creation of a common identity.

Broude (Chapter 25, Volume I) and Zographos (2006) apply the discussion mentioned above on the role of GIs in protecting traditional knowledge to their role in the protection of expressions of culture. This research is updated by Sanders (Chapter 32, Volume I), who considers the role of GIs in protecting traditional cultural expressions consonant with the adoption of UNESCO's Universal Declaration of Cultural Diversity.

Evaluating the Effects of GIs

As will be observed in the writings described in Part II, Volume III of the book, the useful functions performed by GIs that are canvassed above are urged as justifications for the adoption of GIs systems by developing countries and these functions are also advanced in support of the extension of the international regime for GIs protection that is described in the writings in Part I, Volume III of the book. To meet these arguments in support of GIs a body of scholarship has developed that disputes the advantages claimed for GIs and that seeks to identify the disadvantages of GIs. A more general body of scholarship subjects GIs to economic evaluation.

At the heart of the justification for GIs is the assumption that product origin can play a part in consumer preference. Van Ittersum et al. (2003) examine the role that origin plays in consumer preference for beer and potatoes in seven regions in the Netherlands. Their conclusion is that origin plays a larger role in relation to potatoes than to beer. This confirms both earlier and later studies that find that the influence of origin is product-specific (for example, Nagashima, 1970; Gaedeke, 1973; Insch and McBride, 2004). Reviewing the place-of-origin literature, Verlegh and Steenkamp (1999) conclude that although the place of origin can have a large effect on product evaluation, the processes behind this effect are not yet well understood. As Yeung and Kerr (Chapter 26, Volume III) explain, evaluating the financial and economic effects of GIs labelling, even in advanced economies, is not easy, particularly as most GIs are used in association with individual producer brands.

Among the disadvantages identified in establishing GIs are the organisational difficulties in establishing collective producer organisations, and the costs of certification, administration, promotion and enforcement.

COLLECTIVE ORGANISATION

The collective mobilisation of all actors in the supply chain is identified as the key to the success of schemes for origin labelling (Barjolle and Sylvander, 2000). This may require a change to the independent mentality of producers in some countries (Reviron and Chappuis, 2011). This will also require the inculcation of entrepreneurial skills (Arfini et al., 2003) as well as a willingness to accept internal discipline and to entrust decision-making to the collective body (Sylvander, 2004). Reviron and Chappuis (2011), looking at the successful example of the EU, identify inter-professional associations, with representation from various levels in the supply chain as the key to this success (Bérard and Marchenay, 2000; Barjolle and Sylvander, 2002). Replicating this model in countries with different cultural traditions may present a problem.

CERTIFICATION COSTS

Establishing an origin labelling system is inevitably going to involve direct certification costs. The decision taken by firms whether to use such a system or not will depend on the overall balance between costs and benefits (see Raynaud and Sauvée, 2000; Verhaegen and Van Huylenbroeck, 2001). In addition to the direct certification costs are all the costs producers will incur in arranging their structure, organisation and production processes to the contents of the certification code. Belletti et al. (2007) examine the effects of certification costs on the success of EU GIs established for Chianina PGI beef, Pecorino Toscano PDO cheese and Olio Toscano PGI extra virgin olive oil. They find that the reorganisation costs for firms producing Chianina PGI beef are quite high because the certification rules establish strict conditions for exclusive transportation of the PGI livestock (separated from non-PGI livestock) to the slaughterhouses. In relation to the Pecorino Toscano PDO cheese, the rules require use of milk from sheep bred in Tuscany instead of cheaper sheep's milk with other origins. Belletti et al. (2007) find that when producers want to use the certified label only for a part of the whole production, there may be some organisation costs owing to the need to keep the production lines separate, which may cause some inefficiencies in managing processes and require dedicated assets (storage structures, plants, transport vehicles, et cetera), thus increasing the overall costs.

ADMINISTRATIVE COSTS

Opponents of proposals advanced at the WTO to extend the special protection of GIs for wines and spirits to agricultural products and handicrafts have pointed to the additional costs and administrative burdens of implementing these proposals.[4] Yeung and Kerr (Chapter 26, Volume III) distinguish between the costs of a 'greenfield' establishment of a sui generis GI system where none exists and the 'switching costs' incurred where origin labelling is already provided for under trademarks law. In the greenfield situation the costs have to be incurred if GIs are to be protected, whereas switching costs are an extra imposition. Kur and Cocks (Chapter 5, Volume II), looking at the EU example, refer to 'the huge bureaucracy capable of scrutinizing applications for GI protection, verifying GI specifications, and monitoring use of protected GIs' (p. 126). Citing Hughes (Chapter 5, Volume I), they question as 'unfounded and inherently flawed' the assertions on the part of the EU and other supporters of vigorous GI protection 'that such a scheme would aid developing countries in expanding their economies by ensuring the maintenance of knowledge bases related to the growth and manufacture of traditional indigenous products' (Chapter 5, Volume II, p. 127).

PROMOTIONAL EFFORT

Giovannucci et al. (2009) and Teuber (Chapter 22, Volume I) point out that educational and promotional efforts are required even before a GIs labelled product is placed on the market. Obviously promotional efforts will be more profitable in markets such as the EU where origin labelling is a feature, but Josling (Chapter 22, Volume II) comments on the limited success of some GIs even in the EU. In the US, mandatory country of origin labelling for food has been proposed as a means of reducing consumer concerns about quality, safety and production methods. However, much of the literature on the effects of this mandatory labelling suggests that the costs of implementation for producers may very likely outweigh estimated consumer benefits (Brester et al., 2004; Lusk and Anderson, 2004) and constitute a barrier to market entry (Chambolle and Giraud-Héraud, 2005). Suh and MacPherson (Chapter 29, Volume III), in their case study on Boseong tea from South Korea, suggest that since GIs often use already well-known names of regions, marketing costs at the early stage are often not very high. However, Grote (Chapter 22, Volume III) points out that their study also shows that a concerted effort by the government, research institutes and the private sector is needed to promote the development of the GI product.

ENFORCEMENT

As is the case with other IPRs, the greater the value of an origin indication, the greater will be the likelihood of unfair business practices such as free riding at the expense of the reputed origin produce. This will require the establishment of an institutional framework that confers the right of exclusive use to those producers within the designated area who comply with the code of production practices (Belletti et al., 2000; Ilbery and Kneafsey, 2000a; Belletti et al., 2007). On the other hand Teuber (Chapter 16, Volume I) indicates that the most important motivation for producers to apply for a protected GI is to secure the established reputation of Hessian apple wine against misuse by competing producers. Monteverde (2012) provides a brief overview of GIs enforcement issues in Europe.

ECONOMIC ANALYSIS

Viewed from the perspective of neoclassical economic theory, Moran (Chapter 1, Volume I) observes that appellation systems are a type of collective monopoly that impose entry barriers on producers wishing to begin production. This competition analysis reflects the considerable scholarship analysing the economic effects of GIs referred to in Part III of this book.

Conceptually, a geographical indication can be considered as a club asset shared by firms acting on a specific territory in the production of a given and specified good. A club good is characterised by partial excludability, no or partial rivalry of benefits and congestion phenomena (Buchanan, 1965; Thiedig and Sylvander, 2000). The immaterial asset represented by a GI can appreciate or depreciate over time and, in particular as a consequence of the behaviour of its owners, the members of the GI club (Benavente, 2010). Collective action among GI-right holders appears to be critical in order to avoid free riding, which consists in the opportunistic behaviour of one or several members of the GI club, benefiting from the club asset without respecting the constraints attached to it and putting the reputation of the GI good, that is, the value of the club asset, at risk (Coulet, Chapter 36, Volume I). As reputation is at the core of the value of a GI, coordination of club members is essential. However, Paus and Reviron (Chapter 35, Volume I) warn that this coordination may lead to anti-competitive behaviour as the market equilibrium for a GI-labelled product could well be similar to a cartel equilibrium, characterised by a higher producer surplus, a lower consumer surplus and a substantial reduction of the overall surplus, that is, the global economic welfare (see also Winfree and McCluskey, 2005).

Benavente (2010) explores the relationship between the size of the membership to the GI club, the quality of the product and the value of the club asset that the GI protection constitutes. She demonstrates that there could be an inflexion point in the size of the membership to a GI club of producers to an equilibrium level after which product quality decreases. Rangnekar (2009) applies a club analysis to GIs protection for Goan Feni.

Musungu (2008) has surveyed the economic literature to identify the principal advantages and disadvantages of GIs protection. His analysis is amplified by Coulet (Chapter 36, Volume I).

As with other distinctive signs, the economics underlying the protection of localised products is founded on the economic theories of information and reputation. These theories illustrate the importance of (1) preventing the market distortions that arise when there is asymmetry of information between producers and consumers and (2) averting the consequences of such asymmetry of information on the level of output quality (OECD, 2000). Reputation, as used in studies of markets characterised by imperfect information (Stiglitz, 1989; Torole, 1988), aids to an extent in overcoming the market failure associated with asymmetry of information. However, the successful use of reputation to restore efficiency to the market through averting the consequences of information asymmetries requires that reputation be protected through a process that can be viewed as the 'institutionalisation of reputation' (Belletti, 1999). Distinctive signs such as geographical indications can achieve this by institutionalising the relationship between the product and the region and/or tradition through the use of legal instruments that prevent the misappropriation of benefits. Geographical indications can thus be viewed as the result of a process whereby reputation is institutionalised in order to solve certain problems that arise from information asymmetry and free riding on reputation. This highlights a fundamental feature of GIs protection, that is, it functions as both a consumer protection measure (through addressing information asymmetries and quality) and a producer protection measure (through its role in protecting reputation as an asset) (OECD, 2000).

Paus and Reviron (Chapter 35, Volume I) note the difficulties that have been identified in measuring the economic impact of GIs research, but review the leading assessments based upon 'objective methods'; diachronic evaluations (before/after historical approach) and synchronic evaluations 'with/without' approach). They note the particular difficulties of measuring impacts in emerging markets. Bramley et al. (Chapter 34, Volume I) undertake an analysis of the economic impacts of GIs in developing countries.

Volume II

Sui Generis GIs Systems

As will be seen in the writings in Part I, Volume II of this book the international debates on the protection of GIs involve a competition between the European sui generis model and the New World countries' assertion that GIs can be adequately protected by trade mark and consumer protection laws.

A: HISTORICAL ORIGINS

The historical origins of GIs in the 19th century French Appellation d'Origine Contrôlée (AOC) system is traced by Stanziani (Chapter 1, Volume II; 2009). There is a voluminous scholarship on the modern European sui generis system. Van Leeuwen and Seguin (2006) describe 'the concept of terroir in viticulture and relate it to the protection of GIs'. The characteristic uniqueness of products that justifies their protection by GIs is described by French commentators as their 'typicity'. As Allaire et al. (2005) explain, typicity requires a knowledgeable consumer interacting with producers who have an *air de famille*.

Relevant to the portability of the sui generis GIs system outside Europe are Casabianca et al.'s (2005) observations that establishing wine GIs can be a complex process. They mention that identifying the 690 distinctive terroirs in the Burgundy area for Pinot Noir wines took centuries. On the other hand, there is a body of quite detailed scholarship on the recent establishment of wine GIs in Australia (Stern and Fund, 2000; Anderson and Wood, 2006; Aylward, 2008), some with a focus on the Coonawarra wine region in South Australia (Banks and Sharpe, 2006; Edmond, 2006; and Banks and Overton, 2010).

B: EUROPEAN SYSTEMS

Beier and Knaak (1994) contain the first descriptions of the modern European sui generis system. This is advanced by Gutierrez (2005), Kur and Cocks (Chapter 5, Volume II), Teil (2010) and Gragnani (2012). The most recent EU legislation on GIs, particularly in relation to foodstuffs, is described in Evans (Chapter 6, Volume II; Chapter 7, Volume II; Chapter 20, Volume II). The impact of the EU legislation on national rights in EU member states is explored by Bently and Sherman (Chapter 4, Volume II). O'Connor and Kireeva (2004), while Charlier and Ngo (2012) survey the European case law on GIs. Evans (2009) compares the jurisprudence of the European Court of Justice with the WTO Appellate Body.

The extraterritorial effect of the European GIs system is explored by Josel (Chapter 2, Volume II), Barham (Chapter 8, Volume II) and Marette (Chapter 9, Volume II). The specific conflict between European GIs and US brands is examined by Zacher (2005), Hughes (Chapter 5, Volume I) and Evans (Chapter 20, Volume II). As a consequence of these disputes Ricolfi (2009) asks whether the European GIs policy is in need of rethinking.

Relevant to the debate about the appropriate model for GIs systems, particularly in developing countries, is Boisvert (2006) who questions whether the AOC French model can be exported to facilitate the conservation of genetic diversity and the promotion of quality foodstuffs.

Alternatives to Sui Generis GIs Protection

A: GIS AND TRADE MARKS

The discussion about the extraterritorial impacts of the European GIs system and the complaint made to the WTO about the EU foodstuffs legislation by Australia and the US has led to a number of writings on the trade marks system as an effective alternative to sui generis GIs protection. Gevers (Chapter 11, Volume II) is the pioneering piece on geographical names and signs used as trade marks. Corte-Real (2005) uses an analysis of the Budweiser Case in Portugal to consider the tension between trade marks and geographical indications. Stern (Chapter 13, Volume II) looks at the overlap between geographical indications and trade marks in Australia. Ayu (Chapter 16, Volume II) extends this analysis of Australian law to the protection of GIs for products other than wines and spirits. Gangjee (Chapter 18, Volume II) reviews the principal conflicts between trademarks and geographical indications. US discussions of the role of trade marks in protecting GIs mainly focus upon wines (Lenzen, Chapter 10, Volume II; Maher, Chapter 12, Volume II; Silva, 2005; Hughes, Chapter 5, Volume I; Kemp and Forsythe, Chapter 23, Volume II; Brauneis and Schechter, Chapter 15, Volume II).

B: BILATERAL AGREEMENTS AND WINE

The economic significance for the EU of its wine trade is of course at the heart of its concern to have GIs included in the TRIPS Agreement and for the additional protection and multilateral system of protection and registration for wines and spirits included in that agreement. An alternative approach that has been adopted by the EU to protect its wine and spirits industry is the negotiation of wine agreements with those countries with which it has had the greatest difficulties. Vivas Egui and Spennemann (Chapter 21, Volume II) describe the inclusion of GIs within bilateral investment treaties. Josling (Chapter 22, Volume II) and Kemp and Forsythe (Chapter 23, Volume II) describe the wine disputes in the US with Rose (Chapter 24, Volume II) assessing the 2005 wine agreement between the US and the EU. Blakeney (Chapter 25, Volume II) undertakes a similar analysis in relation to the Australian wine industry and explores the opportunity that the Australian wine agreements with the EU provide for the establishment of Australian wine GIs and for their marketing in Europe. Van der Merwe (2009) looks at GIs protection for wines in South Africa with particular reference to the EU.

The interface between trade marks and sui generis protection for GIs in developing countries is explored by Balganesh (Chapter 14, Volume II) (India), Kireeva and Vergano (2006) (China, Thailand and Vietnam), Bashaw (Chapter 19, Volume II) (China) and Ali (2011) (Pakistan).

Volume III

The International Dimension

Unquestionably, a significant impetus has been given to GIs scholarship by the negotiations on the subject in the TRIPS Council. Article 23.4 of the TRIPS Agreement provides that 'In order to facilitate the protection of geographical indications for wines, negotiations shall be undertaken in the Council for TRIPS concerning the establishment of a multilateral system of notification and registration of geographical indications for wines eligible for protection in those Members participating in the system.' Article 24 of TRIPS provides in Article 24.1 that 'Members agree to enter into negotiations aimed at increasing the protection of individual geographical indications under Article 23'. This provision, it will be recalled, provides 'additional protection' for GIs in relation to wines and spirits.

Over the years some overlap has developed between the negotiations on the multilateral register and the so-called extension debate, as it has been argued that the multilateral register for wines and spirits could be extended to products beyond wines and spirits. This proposal was originally made in a submission by Turkey dating from 9 July 1999.[5] This proposal was endorsed by the African group of countries. In a document from 6 August 1999[6] Kenya, on behalf of the African Group, noted that paragraph 26 of the WTO's Singapore Ministerial Declaration relating to Article 23.4 negotiations concerning a multilateral register for wines had been extended to include spirits. Consequently, it was submitted in paragraph 27 of Kenya's communication on behalf of the African Group that since the Ministers made no distinction between wines and spirits the African Group took the position that the negotiations envisaged under Article 23.4 should be extended to 'other products recognizable by their geographical origins (handicrafts, agro-food products)'. In the meetings of the TRIPS Council held on 21 and 22 September 2000 the representative of Switzerland provided an example illustrating why the additional protection under Article 23 'was also needed for geographical indications other than those for wines and spirits', pointing out that:

Rice that was sold under the Indian geographical indication 'Basmati', but which was clearly marked as originating from another region or country, would not mislead the public as to the place of origin of that product; nevertheless, such use would free-ride on the worldwide famous and therefore commercially valuable geographical indication 'Basmati'. The same applied with regard to the famous Swiss cheese 'Vacherin Mont d'Or', for example. There was no systematic or logical explanation for the distinction made in Section 3 of Part II of the TRIPS Agreement and this distinction ignored that geographical indications for categories of goods other than wines and spirits were equally important for trade.[7]

As is pointed out in the writings in Part IB, Volume II of this book, the negotiations on these subjects have been long and vigorously debated and continue without any resolution.

A: TRIPS in the International GIs Landscape

General descriptions locating the TRIPS GIs provisions in the international IP landscape abound. Comprehensive descriptions of these provisions at different stages of the international negotiations are contained in Heald (Chapter 1, Volume III), Agdomar (Chapter 7, Volume III) and Kireeva and O'Connor (Chapter 9, Volume III). Paralleling this scholarship is Conrad (1996), Blakeney (2001), Martín (2004), Cortes (2004a), Zou (2005), Beresford (2007), O'Connor & Co (2007a), Echols (2008), Geuze (2009), Gangjee (2012) and Munzinger (2012). Land (Chapter 6, Volume III) seeks to provide an EU perspective on the TRIPS GIs provisions. Kazmi (2001) relates them to NAFTA and Kongolo (1999) to the agreement establishing ARIPO. Heath (2005) also provides an international, regional and bilateral overview of TRIPS.

De Almeida (2005) locates the TRIPS Agreement within the philosophy of the WTO and Taubman (Chapter 8, Volume III), now a WTO functionary, specifically analyses the negotiations over GIs in a fair trade context.

B: TRIPS Revision

The writings in Part IB, Volume III of the book deal with the tortuous negotiations in the TRIPS Council dealing with the issues of extension and the multilateral register. Adegbonmire and Arnold (Chapter 4, Volume III) attempt to define the unclear boundaries of the debates. Similarly Rangnekar (2002) reviews the GI proposals at the TRIPS Council after the WTO's Doha Ministerial in 2001. Murphy (2003) castigates the 'Conflict, Confusion, and Bias under TRIPs Articles 22–24'. Blakeney (Chapter 2, Volume III; 2006), Rangnekar (2003), Calboli (Chapter 13, Volume III), Creditt (Chapter 15, Volume III) and Blakeney et al. (2012) set out the extension issues. Bowers (Chapter 10, Volume III) and Staten (2005) make the case against extension as opposed to Addor and Grazioli (Chapter 3, Volume III) and Lang (Chapter 11, Volume III) who support the expansion of Article 23. Vincent (Chapter 14, Volume III) identifies the beneficiaries of extension. Evans and Blakeney (Chapter 12, Volume III; 2007) place the negotiations in their post Doha context, while Banerjee and Majumdar (Chapter 17, Volume III) and Gangjee (2012) bring the negotiations more or less up to date. Snyder (Chapter 16, Volume III) identifies potential conflicts under the US constitutional and statutory regimes for TRIPS extension. Musungu (2008) examines the strategic and policy considerations for Africa from the GIs negotiations. Cortes (2004b) characterises the negotiations as Old World/ New World conflict. Cotton (2007) merely considers it a conflict that has not been resolved for in excess of 120 years. Vivas Egui (2001) considers the implications for developing countries of the TRIPS Council negotiations on GIs in light of the WTO agricultural negotiations. Vittori (2010) provides the perspective of the Global Coalition of GI Producers (origin).

C: THE WTO GIS DISPUTE

As mentioned above the EU GIs regime was the subject of a WTO dispute initiated by Australia and the USA. Lindquist (1999), Haight (2000), Hughes (Chapter 5, Volume I) and Nieuwveld (Chapter 19, Volume III) provide the US perspective on this dispute and Handler (2004; Chapter 18, Volume III) and Handler and Burrell (2011) provide an Australian perspective. Kur and Cocks (Chapter 5, Volume II) comment on this dispute from a European viewpoint.

D: REVIVAL OF THE LISBON AGREEMENT

With the impasse in the negotiations to revise the TRIPS Agreement the World Intellectual Property Organization (WIPO) has dusted off its Lisbon Agreement for the Protection of Appellations of Origin and their Registration, 1958, which had primarily been of interest to European wine producing countries. Gervais (Chapter 20, Volume III) has made the case for 're-inventing Lisbon'.

GIs and Developing Countries

In the conflict between the EU and its New World opponents allies have been sought from the developing world and Part II, Volume III of the book identifies part of the body of scholarship that has been produced identifying the potential interests of developing countries in having GIs regimes. Reviron et al. (2009) and Sautier et al. (2011) look at the general role of GIs in the creation and distribution of economic value in developing countries. Zographos (2008), now with WIPO, explores the role of GIs as a development tool, as does Bowen (Chapter 25, Volume III). Hughes (2009) and Anders and Caswell (Chapter 21, Volume III) carry forward Musungu's (2008) review of the benefits and costs of proliferation of GIs for developing countries. Yeung and Kerr (Chapter 26, Volume III) apply an economic analysis to question whether GIs are 'a wise strategy for developing country farmers'. Grote (Chapter 22, Volume III) perceives an economic advantage for developing countries in environmental labelling, while Bramley and Bienabe (Chapter 27, Volume III) survey the 'considerations' around GIs in the developing world'.

    Blakeney et al. (2012) consider 12 African case studies that seek to explore the advantages of GIs for the countries surveyed. One of those countries is Ethiopia, which has opted for a trade marks based system to protect its origin products. Roussel and Verdeaux (Chapter 23, Volume III) and O'Kicki (Chapter 24, Volume III) look at the lessons that might be taken by developing countries from the Ethiopian branding of its high quality coffees. Further case studies are contained in Part III, Volume III of this book. Kolady et al. (2011) examine the economic effects of GIs on developing country producers of Darjeeling and Oolong teas.

Case Studies

An important tool in the evaluation of the benefits or the detriments of GIs protection, particularly in developing countries, is the results of case studies of specific industries in those countries. Indeed, Blakeney et al. (2012) arose out of a project to generate empirical evidence about the value of GIs for countries of the African, Caribbean and Pacific (ACP) Group 'to generate empirical evidence, based on country/sub-regional and product case studies, regarding the benefits that African members of the ACP Group can obtain from enhanced multilateral Geographical Indication (GI) protection as a basis for the African Group to engage in the Doha negotiations on the establishment of the multilateral register for wines and spirits and the proposed extension of protection to products other than wines and spirits under Article 23 of TRIPS'.[8] The project was designed to produce 'a replicable methodology for analysing the dynamics of capturing economic value out of GIs; access to GI-protected products by local populations; the role of government in the GI framework; the costs of establishing and administering a GI regime in a country; and the costs of developing, registering and enforcing individual GIs'.[9] This methodology is intended to be applied in other ACP regions. An ACP–EU Regional Workshop on the protection of GIs held in Cape Town with the collaboration of ARIPO, 10–11 May 2010, in considering 'GIs Experiences in African ACP Member States', received reports on vanilla from Madagascar, bark cloth from Uganda and Argan oil from Morocco. A similar workshop organised under the auspices of OAPI in Douala, Cameroon, 27–28 April 2010 discussed the GIs potential of Penja white pepper, Cameroon (poivre blanc du Penja), onions from Dogon, Mali (Echalote du Pays Dogon), Attiéké from Grand-Lahou, Côte D'Ivoire Korhogo cloth and products of Argan trees in Morocco.[10]

These ACP projects were funded by the EU within its aid programme under the Partnership Agreement between the members of the ACP Group of States and the EU, signed 23 June 2000 (Cotonou Agreement) for a twenty-year period from March 2000 to February 2020. The garnering of political support for the EU's position on GIs in the TRIPS Council and WIPO might be an incidental result of this activism.

A number of case studies have been conducted by European-based research institutes to identify the opportunities and pitfalls related to GIs. The Royal Tropical Institute (KIT), Amsterdam, and the French Agricultural Research Centre for International Development (CIRAD), Montpellier, published case studies of Gari Missè in Benin, Mantecoso cheese in Peru, Rooibos tea in South Africa, Costa Rican Arabica coffee and Comté cheese in France (Van de Kop et al., 2006). Barham and Sylvander (2011) is largely derived from an EU project conducted from 2000 to 2004 – 'the Development of Origin Labelled Products, Innovation and Sustainability (DOLPHINS)' – which looks at the organisation and management of supply chains for GIs. The researchers involved in the DOLPHINS project subsequently collaborated in another EU-funded project, under the punning acronym SINER-GI (Strengthening of International Network Research on GIs) 2005–2008, which sought to examine the global impacts of GIs and particularly their impact in developing countries. The book contains six European case studies that are reproduced in an appendix: Lari cherries (Italy), L'Évitaz cheese (Switzerland), Cariñena wine (Spain), Roquefort cheese (France), Salumi Tipici Piancentini (Italy) and Beacon Fell traditional Lancashire cheese (England). Musungu (2008) reports that through a cooperation agreement between the French National IP Institute and OAPI the following products are being developed as GIs: Oku white honey and njombe pepper from Cameroon; Atcheke of Grand Lahou and the Khorogho garment from Côte d'Ivoire; Diama coffee and the Mafeya pineapple from Guinea; and Massina Kwite butter and the Souflou green beans from Burkina Faso.

Switzerland has played a leading role in urging the extension of the additional protection for GIs for wines and spirits to other products. The Agri-food and Agri-environmental Economic Group (Institute for Environmental Decisions, IED) of ETH Zurich conducted seven case studies in different parts of the world (see El Benni and Reviron, 2009): Argan oil – Morocco; cashmere wool – Mongolia; coffee – Colombia and Costa Rica; Havana cigars – Cuba; Rooibos tea – South Africa; and tequila – Mexico. These case studies were then deployed in a paper supporting GIs for developing countries (Reviron et al., 2009).

Augustin-Jean et al. (2012) edited a recent collection of papers on the implications of GIs protection for Asia. This includes case studies of Japanese sake and Kobe and Matsusaka beef, specialty rice from Ifugao Province of the Phillipines and Jinhua ham from China.

The International Trade Commission (Giovannucci et al., 2009) has sought to demystify GIs with an analysis of the evidence from eight case studies: Antigua coffee, Guatemala; Darjeeling tea, India; Gobi Desert camel wool, Mongolia; Blue Mountain coffee, Jamaica; Kona coffee, Hawaii; Mezcal, Mexico; Café Nariño, Colombia; and Café Veracruz, Mexico. Some of these appear in Part III, Volume III of this book, which contains a selection of the case studies conducted under the auspices of the above projects and case studies by independent scholars. Eliminated from the selection were those case studies prefaced by extensive discussions of the international legal framework for GIs regulation that have already been detailed in other parts of the book and those that are replicated in the studies published here. Two case studies are selected from Europe: Prosciutto di Parma and Parmigiano Reggiano cheese (Arfini, 2000) and French Cassis (Gade, Chapter 28, Volume III) and one from the US: Kona coffee, Hawaii (Giovannucci and Smith, Chapter 30, Volume III). The balance of the case studies is of industries in developing countries: Boseong green tea from Korea (Suh and MacPherson, Chapter 29, Volume III); Jasmine rice from Thailand (Kuanpoth and Robinson, Chapter 31, Volume III); Gobi Desert camel wool (Oosterom and Dévé, Chapter 32, Volume III); Kashmiri handicrafts (Mir and Ain, Chapter 34, Volume III); and Moroccan Argan oil (Réviron and El Benni, Chapter 35, Volume III).

A general review of developing country cases is contained in Russell (Chapter 31, Volume I).

One case study subject that has attracted a good deal of attention is in relation to Basmati rice from the Indian Sub-continent. Blakeney and Lightbourne (2005) first drew attention to the possibility of protecting Basmati as a GI as a means of protecting the traditional knowledge surrounding the product. This was followed up by Chandola (2006) who was concerned about the misappropriation of this indication by US rice producers. Jena and Grote (2012) undertake an 'impact evaluation' of traditional Basmati rice cultivation in Uttarakhand State of Northern India to identify the implications for GIs. Rangnekar and Kumar (2002) consider the dual issues of Basmati genericity and the problems of the GI as a transborder issue between India and Pakistan. Marie-Vivien (2008) glides over this latter problem in her examination of the relationship between the plant variety right designation for Basmati and 'the India/Pakistan' GI. Mulik and Crespi's Basmati case study (Chapter 33, Volume III) has been included because of its particular focus on the rice export trade.

Among other useful case studies covered by extracts in this book are: Parmigiano Reggiano cheese (De Roest and Menghi, 2000); Comté cheese in France (Colinet et al., 2006); tequila (Bowen and Zapata, 2009); and Prosciutto di Parma (Dentoni et al., 2012). Finally, mention should be made of the case studies of Zagora apples from Greece (Foutopolis and Krystallis,

2003), Virovitica pepper from Croatia (Radman et al., 2006) and Ladotyri Mytilinis cheese from Greece. Finally, a comprehensive case study that combines empirical analysis with economic doctrine is Rangnekar (2009), which examines Goan Feni.

Notes

1. *Official Journal* L93/12, 2006.
2. http://www.champagne.fr/en_indx.html, August 2007.
3. WIPO/GRTKF/IC/3/7, 6 May 2002, para. 40.
4. See Communication from Argentina, Australia, Canada, Chile, Ecuador, El Salvador, New Zealand and the United States, TN/IP/W/9, 13 April 2004.
5. WTO WT/GC/W/249, 13 July 1999.
6. *Preparations for the 1999 Ministerial Conference: The TRIPS Agreement Communication from Kenya on Behalf of the African Group*, WTO WT/GC/W/302, 6 August 1999.
7. IP/C/W/204/Rev.1, para. 76, 2 October 2000.
8. Project Ref: 9 ACP RPR 140-011-10.
9. Terms of Reference, Project Ref: 9 ACP RPR 140-011-10.
10. Also as part of the ACP-EU programme a report was commissioned on potential GIs in Côte d'Ivoire. M. Bagal and M. Vittori, *Preliminary Report on the Potential for Geographical Indications in Cote d'Ivoire and the Relevant Legal Framework*. ACP-EU Trade.Com Paper on the ACP Regional Workshops on Geographical Indications, April–May 2010.

References

Agarwal, S. and M. Barone (2005), 'Emerging Issues for Geographical Indication Branding Strategies', MATRIC Research Paper 05-MRP. Ames, IA: Iowa State University.

Akerlof, G. (1970), 'The Market for "Lemons": Quality Uncertainty and the Market Mechanism', *Quarterly Journal of Economics*, **84** (3), 488–500.

Allaire, G., B. Sylvander, G. Belletti, A. Marescotti, D. Barjolle, E. Thévenod-Mottet and A. Tregear (2005), 'Les dispositifs français et européens de protection de la qualité et de l'origine dans le contexte de l'OMC: justifications générales et contextes nationaux'. Paper presented at the international symposium on *Territoires et enjeux du développement régional*, Lyon, France, 9–11 March.

Ali, M.H. (2011), 'The Protection of Geographical Indications in Pakistan: Implementation of the TRIPS Agreement', *Journal of World Intellectual Property*, **14** (6), 467–76.

Anderson, K. and D. Wood (2006), 'What Determines the Future Value of an Icon Wine? New Evidence from Australia', *Journal of Wine Economics*, **1** (2), 141–61.

Antle, J.M. (1996), 'Efficient Food Safety Regulation in the Food Manufacturing Sector', *American Journal of Agricultural Economics*, **78** (5), 1242–7.

Arfini, F. (2000), 'The Value of Typical Products: The Case of Prosciutto di Parma and Parmigiano Reggiano Cheese', in B. Sylvander, D. Barjolle and F. Arfini (eds), 'The Socio-Economics of Origin Labelled Products in Agri-Food Supply Chains: Spatial, Institutional and Co-ordination Aspects', *Actes et Communications*, **17** (1), 77–97.

Arfini, F., A. Tregear, M. Ness, K. Corcoran, A. Marescotti and E. Bertoli (2003), *OLP Characteristics, Evolution Problems and Opportunities: Development of Origin Labeled Products: Humanity, Innovation and Sustainability*, Brussels: DOLPHINS Report WP5.

Augustin-Jean, L., H. Ilbert and N. Saavedra-Rivano (eds) (2012), *Geographical Indications and International Agricultural Trade: The Challenge for Asia*, London: Palgrave Macmillan.

Aylward, D. (2008), 'Towards a Cultural Economy Paradigm for the Australian Wine Industry', *Prometheus*, **26** (4), 373–85.

Babcock, B.A. (2003), 'Geographical Indications, Property Rights, and Value-Added Agriculture', *Iowa*

Agricultural Review, **9** (4). Available at http://www.card.iastate.edu/iowa_ag_review/fall_03/article1. aspx.

Babcock, B. and R. Clemens (2004), 'Geographical Indications and Property Rights: Protecting Value Added Agricultural Products', MATRIC Briefing Paper 04-MBP 7.

Banks, G. and J. Overton (2010), 'Reconceptualising the Worlds of Wine', *Journal of Wine Research*, 21(1), 57–75.

Banks, G. and S. Sharpe (2006), 'Wine, Regions and the Geographic Imperative: The Coonawarra Example', *New Zealand Geographer*, **62** (3), 173–84.

Banks, J. and T.K. Marsden (2000), 'Integrating Agri-Environment Policy, Farming Systems and Rural Development: Tir Cymen in Wales', *Sociologia Ruralis*, **40** (4), 466–80.

Barham, E. (2002), 'Towards a Theory of Value-Based Labeling', *Agriculture and Human Values*, **19** (4), 349–60.

Barham, E. and B. Sylvander (eds) (2011), *Labels of Origin for Food: Local Development, Global Recognition*, Wallingford, UK: CAB International.

Barjolle, D. and B. Sylvander (2000), 'PDO and PGI Products: Market, Supply Chains and Institutions', Final Report FAIR 1-CT95-0306 June, Brussels: European Commission.

Barjolle, D. and B. Sylvander (2002), 'Some Factors of Success for "Origin Labelled Products" in Agro-Food Supply Chains in Europe: Market, Internal Resources and Institutions', *Économies et Sociétés*, **25**, 1441–64.

Barjolle, D., B. Sylvander and E. Thévenod-Mottet (2011), 'Public Policies and Geographical Indications', in E. Barham and B. Sylvander (eds), *Labels of Origin for Food: Local Development, Global Recognition*, Wallingford, UK: CAB International, pp. 92–105.

Beier, F.-K. and R. Knaak (1994), 'The Protection of Direct and Indirect Geographical Indications of Source in Germany and the European Community', *IIC*, **25** (1), 1–84.

Belletti G. (1999), 'Origin Labelled Products, Reputation, and Etherogeneity of Firms', 67 EAAE Seminar, Le Mans, 1999/10/28-1999/10/30, European Association of Agricultural Economists (EAAE), in B. Sylvander, D. Barjolle, F. Arfini (eds), The socio-economics of origin labelled products in agri-food supply chains: spatial, institutional and coordination aspects, 408 p, Actes et Communications, N° 17-1, Paris, INRA Editions, 2000/11, 239–60.

Belletti, G., T. Burgassi, A. Marescotti and S. Scaramuzzi (2007), 'The Effects of Certification Costs on the Success of a PDO/PGI', in L. Theuvsen, A. Spiller, M. Peupert and G. Jahn (eds), *Quality Management in Food Chains*, Wageningen, the Netherlands: Wageningen Academic Publishers, pp. 107–21.

Belletti, G., A. Marescotti, and S. Scaramuzzi (2000), *OLP Sector in Italy*, DOLPHINS, Contract QLK5-2000-00593, http://www.originfood.org/pdf/olp/opl-it.pdf.

Belletti, G., A. Marescotti and S. Scaramuzzi (2002), 'Paths of Rural Development Based on Typical Products: A Comparison between Alternative Strategies'. Paper to the Fifth IFSA European Symposium, *Farming and Rural Systems Research and Extension, Local Identities and Globalisation*, Florence, Italy – April 8–11.

Benavente, D. (2010), 'The Economics of Geographical Indications: GIs Modelled as Club Assets', Working Paper 10/2010, Geneva, Switzerland: Graduate Institute of International and Development Studies.

Bérard, L. and P. Marchenay (1996), 'Tradition, Regulation and Intellectual Property: Local Agricultural Products and Foodstuffs in France', in S.B. Brush and D. Stabinsky (eds), *Valuing Local Knowledge: Indigenous Peoples and Intellectual Property Rights*, Covelo, CA: Island Press, pp. 230–43.

Bérard, L. and P. Marchenay (2000), 'Le Vivant, le Culturel et le Marchand: Les Produits de Terroir', in *Autrement, No. 194: Vives Campagnes: Le Patrimoine Rural, Project de Société*, Paris: J-C Lattès, pp. 191–216.

Beresford, L. (2007), 'Geographical Indications: The Current Landscape', *Fordham Intellectual Property and Entertainment Law Journal*, **17** (4), 979–97.

Bessiére, J. (1998), 'Local Development and Heritage: Traditional Food and Cuisine as Tourist Attractions in Rural Areas', *Sociologia Ruralis*, **38** (1), 21–34.

Bienabe, E., C. Bramley, J.F. Kirsten and D. Troskie (2010), 'Linking Farmers to Markets through Valorisation of Local Resources: The Case for Intellectual Property Rights of Indigenous Resources',

IPR DURAS Project Scientific Report.

Blakeney, M. (2001), 'Geographical Indications and TRIPS', Occasional Paper 8, Geneva, Switzerland: Quaker United Nations Office.

Blakeney, M. (2006), 'Geographical Indications and TRIPS', in M. Pugatch (ed.), *Intellectual Property Debate: Perspectives from Law, Economics and Political Economy*, Cheltenham, UK and Northampton, MA, USA: Edward Elgar, pp. 293–304.

Blakeney, M., T. Coulet, G. Mengistie and M.T. Mahop (eds) (2012), *Extending the Protection of Geographical Indications: Case Studies in the Protection of Agricultural Products in Africa*, London: Earthscan.

Blakeney, M. and M. Lightbourne (2005), 'Geographical Indications, Traditional Knowledge and Basmati Rice', in B. O'Connor (ed.), *Agriculture in WTO Law*, London: Cameron May, pp. 349–76.

Blakeney, M. and G. Mengistie (2011), 'Intellectual Property and Economic Development in Sub-Saharan Africa', *Journal of World Intellectual Property*, **14** (3), 238–64.

Boisvert, V. (2006), 'From the Conservation of Genetic Diversity to the Promotion of Quality Foodstuff: Can the French Model of "Appellation d'Origine Contrôlée" Be Exported?' Collective Action and Property Rights Working Paper 49. Washington, DC: International Food Policy Research Institute (IFPRI).

Bonnet, C. and M. Simioni (2001), 'Assessing Consumer Response to Protected Designation of Origin Labelling: A Mixed Multinomial Logit Approach', *European Review of Agricultural Economics*, **28** (4), 433–9.

Bowen, S.C. and A.V. Zapata (2009), 'Geographical Indications, Terroir, and Socioeconomic and Ecological Sustainability: The Case of Tequila', *Journal of Rural Studies*, **25** (1), 108–19.

Bowen, S. and K. De Master (2011), 'New Rural Livelihoods or Museums of Production? Quality Food Initiatives in Practice', *Journal of Rural Studies*, **27** (1), 73–82.

Bramley, C. (2011), 'A Review of the Socio-Economic Impact of Geographical Indications: Considerations for the Developing World'. Paper presented at the WIPO Worldwide Symposium on Geographical Indications, Lima, Peru, 22–24 June.

Brester, G.W., J.M. Marsh and J.A. Atwood (2004), 'Distributional Impacts of Country-of-Origin Labelling in the U.S. Meat Industry', *Journal of Agricultural and Resource Economics*, **29** (2), 206–27.

Buchanan, J.M. (1965), 'An Economic Theory of Clubs', *Economica*, **32** (125), 1–14.

Carver, E.K. and G.L. Wilson (1916), 'Studies in the Marketing of Farm Products in France and England', in T.N. Carver (ed.), *Selected Readings in Rural Economics*, Boston, MA: Ginn and Company, pp. 851–97.

Casabianca, F., B. Sylvander, Y. Noël, C. Béranger, J.-B. Coulon and F. Roncin (2005), 'Terroir et typicité: deux concepts-clés des appellations d'origine controlée'. Essai de définitions scientifiques et opérationnelles. Paper presented at the international symposium on *Territoires et enjeux du développement régional*, Lyon, France, 9–11 March.

Chambolle, C. and E. Giraud-Héraud (2005), 'Certification of Origin as a Non-Tariff Barrier', *Review of International Economics*, **13** (3), 461–71.

Chandola, H.V. (2006), 'Basmati Rice: Geographical Indication or Mis-Indication?', *Journal of World Intellectual Property*, **9** (2), 166–88.

Chapman, P. and M. Shucksmith (1996), 'The Experience of Poverty and Disadvantage in Rural Scotland', *Scottish Geographical Magazine*, **112** (2), 70–76.

Charlier, C. and M.-A. Ngo (2012), 'Geographical Indications outside the European Regulation on PGIs, and the Rule of the Free Movement of Goods: Lessons from Cases Judged by the Court of Justice of the European Communities', *European Journal of Law and Economics*, **34** (1), 17–30.

Colinet, P., M. Desquilbet, D. Hassan, S. Monier-Dilhan, V. Orozco and V. Requillart (2006), 'Case Study: Comté Cheese in France', Toulouse, France: Institut Nationale de la Recherche Agronomique.

Conrad, A. (1996), 'The Protection of Geographical Indications on the TRIPs Agreement', *Trademark Reporter*, **86**, 11–46.

Corte-Real, A. (2005), 'The Conflict between Trade Marks and Geographical Indications: The Budweiser Case in Portugal', in C. Heath and A.K. Sanders (eds), *New Frontiers of Intellectual Property Law: IP and Cultural Heritage, Geographical Indicators, Enforcement, Overprotection*, Oxford, UK: Hart, pp. 149–60.

Cortes, M.J.M. (2004a), 'TRIPS Agreement: Towards a Better Protection for Geographical Indications', *Brooklyn Journal of International Law*, **30** (1), 117–84.

Cortes, M.J.M. (2004b), 'The WTO TRIPS Agreement – The Battle between the Old World and the New World over the Protection of Geographical Indications', *Journal of World Intellectual Property*, **7** (3), 287–326.

Cotton, A.P. (2007), '123 Years at the Negotiating Table and Still No Dessert? The Case in Support of TRIPS Geographical Indication Protections', *Chicago-Kent Law Review*, **82** (3), 1295–316.

Dagne, T.W. (2010), 'Harnessing the Development Potential of Geographical Indications for Traditional Knowledge-Based Agricultural Products', *Journal of Intellectual Property Law and Practice*, **5** (6), 441–58.

De Almeida, A.F.R. (2005), 'The TRIPS Agreement, the Bilateral Agreements Concerning Geographical Indications and the Philosophy of the WTO', *European Intellectual Property Review*, **27** (4), 150–53.

De Roest, K. and A. Menghi (2000), 'Reconsidering "Traditional" Food: The Case of Parmigiano Reggiano Cheese', *Sociologia Ruralis*, **40** (4), 439–51.

Dentoni, D., D. Menozzi and M.G. Capelli (2012), 'Group Heterogeneity and Cooperation on the Geographical Indication Regulation: The Case of the "Prosciutto di Parma" Consortium', *Food Policy*, **37** (3), 207–16.

Downes, D. and S.A. Laird (1999), *Innovative Mechanisms for Sharing Benefits of Biodiversity and Related Knowledge: Cases Studies on Geographical Indications and Trademarks*, UNCTAD Biotrade Initiative.

Echols, M.A. (2008), *Geographical Indications for Food Products: International Legal and Regulatory Perspectives*, Alphen aan der Rijn, the Netherlands: Kluwer Law International.

Edmond, G. (2006), 'Disorder with Law: Determining the Geographical Indication for the Coonawarra Wine Region', *Adelaide Law Review*, **27** (1), 59–182.

El Benni, N. and S. Reviron (2009), 'Geographical Indications: Review of Seven Case Studies Worldwide', NCCR Trade Regulation Working Paper 2009/15, Zurich, Switzerland: ETH.

Evans, G.E. (2009), 'Substantive Trademark Law Harmonization: On the Emerging Coherence between the Jurisprudence of the WTO Appellate Body and the European Court of Justice', in G. Dinwoodie and M. Janis (eds), *Trademark Law and Theory: A Handbook of Contemporary Research*, Cheltenham, UK and Northampton, MA, USA: Edward Elgar, pp. 177–203.

Evans, G. and M. Blakeney (2007), 'The International Protection of Geographical Indications Yesterday, Today and Tomorrow', in G. Weskamp (ed.), *Emerging Issues in Intellectual Property*, Cheltenham, UK and Northampton, MA, USA: Edward Elgar, pp. 359–441.

Foutopolis, C. and A. Krystallis (2003), 'Quality Labels as a Marketing Advantage: The Case of the "PDO Zagora" Apples in the Greek Market', *European Journal of Marketing*, **37** (10), 1350–74.

Gaedeke, R. (1973), 'Consumer Attitudes toward Products "Made in" Developing Countries', *Journal of Retailing*, **49** (2), 13–24.

Gangjee, D. (2012), *Relocating the Law of Geographical Indications*, Cambridge, UK: Cambridge University Press.

Gerz, A. and F. Dupont (2006), 'Comté Cheese in France: Impact of a Geographical Indication on Rural Development', in P. van de Kop, D. Sautier and A. Gerz (eds), *Origin-Based Products: Lessons for Pro-Poor Market Development*, Amsterdam, the Netherlands: KIT, pp. 75–87.

Geuze, M. (2009), 'The Provisions on Geographical Indications in the TRIPS Agreement', *Estey Centre Journal of International Law and Trade Policy*, **10** (1), 50–64.

Giannakas, R. (2002), 'Information Asymmetries and Consumption Decisions in Organic Food Product Markets', *Canadian Journal of Agricultural Economics*, **50** (1), 35–50.

Giovannucci, D., E. Barham and R. Pirog (2009), 'Defining and Marketing "Local" Foods: Geographical Indications for US Products', *Journal of World Intellectual Property*, **13** (2), 94–120.

Giovannucci, D., T. Josling, W.A. Kerr, B. O'Connor and M.T. Yeung (eds) (2009), *Guide to Geographical Indications: Linking Products and Their Origins*, Geneva, Switzerland: International Trade Centre.

Giraud, G. (2003), 'Organic and Origin-Labelled Products in Europe', in W. Lockeretz (ed.), *Ecolabels and the Greening of the Food Market*, Boston, MA: Tufts University, pp. 41–7.

Giraud, G. and C. Amblard (2003), 'What Does Traceability Mean for Beef Meat Consumers?', *Food Science*, **23** (1), 40–46.

González, A.A. and R. Nigh (2005), 'Certifying Rural Spaces: Quality-Certified Products and Rural Governance in Mexico', *Journal of Rural Studies*, **21** (4), 449–60.

Gordon, D.V., R. Hannesson and W.A. Kerr (1999), 'What Is a Commodity? An Empirical Definition Using Time Series Econometrics', *Journal of International Food and Agribusiness Marketing*, **10** (2), 1–29.

Graber, C.B. and J.C. Lai (2012), 'Indigenous Cultural Heritage and Fair Trade: Voluntary Certification Standards in the Light of WIPO and WTO Law and Policy-making', in P. Drahos and S. Frankel (eds), *Indigenous Peoples' Innovation: Intellectual Property Pathways to Development*, Canberra, Australia: ANU, pp. 95–119.

Gragnani, M. (2012), 'The Law of Geographical Indications in the EU', *Journal of Intellectual Property Law and Practice*, **7** (4), 271–82.

Guerra, J.L. (2004), 'Geographical Indications and Biodiversity: Bridges Joining Distant Territories', *Bridges*, **8** (2), 17–18.

Gutierrez, E. (2005), 'Geographical Indicators: A Unique European Perspective on Intellectual Property', *Hastings International and Comparative Law Review*, **29**, 29–50.

Haight, F.C. (2000), 'Conflicts between U.S. Law and International Treaties Concerning Geographical Indications', *Whittier Law Review*, **22** (1), 73–88.

Handler, M. (2004), 'The EU's Geographical Indications Agenda and Its Potential Impact on Australia', *Australian Intellectual Property Journal*, **15**, 173–95.

Handler, M. and R. Burrell (2011), 'GI Blues: The Global Disagreement over Geographical Indications', in K. Bowrey, M. Handler and D. Nicol (eds), *Emerging Challenges in Intellectual Property*, Melbourne, Australia: Oxford University Press, pp. 126–44.

Heath, C. (2005), 'Geographical Indications: International, Bilateral and Regional Agreements', in C. Heath and A.K. Sanders (eds), *New Frontiers of Intellectual Property Law: IP and Cultural Heritage, Geographical Indicators, Enforcement, Overprotection*, Oxford, UK: Hart, pp. 97–132.

Hobbs, J.E. (2003), 'Information, Incentives and Institutions in the Agri-Food Sector', *Canadian Journal of Agricultural Economics*, **51** (3), 413–29.

Hobbs, J.E., D. Bailey, D.L. Dickinson and M. Haghiri (2005), 'Traceability in the Canadian Red Meat Sector: Do Consumers Care?', *Canadian Journal of Agricultural Economics*, **53** (1), 47–65.

Hobbs, J.E. and W.A. Kerr (2006), 'Consumer Information, Labelling and International Trade in Agri-Food Products', *Food Policy*, **31** (1), 78–89.

Hughes, J. (2009), *Coffee and Chocolate: Can We Help Developing Country Farmers through Geographical Indications?*, Washington, DC: International Intellectual Property Institute.

Ilbery, B. and M. Kneafsey (2000a), 'Registering Regional Speciality Food and Drink Products in the United Kingdom: The Case of PDOs and PGIs', *Area*, **32** (3), 317–25.

Ilbery, B. and M. Kneafsey (2000b), 'Producer Constructions of Quality in Regional Specialty Food Production: A Case Study from Southwest England', *Journal of Rural Studies*, **16** (2), 217–30.

Insch, G.S. and J.B. McBride (2004), 'The Impact of Country-of-Origin Cues on Consumer Perceptions of Product Quality: A Binational Test of the Decomposed Country-of-Origin Construct', *Journal of Business Research*, **57**, 256–65.

Jena, P.R. and U. Grote (2012), 'Impact Evaluation of Traditional Basmati Rice Cultivation in Uttarakhand State of Northern India: What Implications Does It Hold for Geographical Indications?', *World Development*, **40** (9), 1895–907.

Jentsch, B. (2006), 'Youth Migration from Rural Areas: Moral Principles to Support Youth and Rural Communities in Policy Debates', *Sociologia Ruralis*, **46** (3), 229–40.

Jókúti, A. (2009), 'Where Is the What If the What Is in Why? A Rough Guide to the Maze of Geographical Indications', *European Intellectual Property Review*, **31** (3), 118–23.

Kazmi, H. (2001), 'Trademarks in the International Arena: International Conventions and Agreements: Does It Make a Difference Where That Chablis Comes from? Geographic Indications in TRIPs and NAFTA', *Journal of Contemporary Legal Issues*, **12**, 470–74.

Kireeva, I. and P. Vergano (2006), 'Geographical Indications and the Interface between Trade Mark Protection and Sui Generis Protection: The Example of China, Thailand and Vietnam', *International Trade Law and Regulation*, **12** (4), 97–108.

Kireeva, I., W. Xiaobing and Z. Yumin (2009), *Comprehensive Feasibility Study for Possible Negotiations* on a Geographical Indications Agreement between China and the EU, Brussels: EU-China IP2.

Klein, B. and K.B. Leffler (1981), 'Role of Market Forces in Assuring Contractual Performance', *Journal of Political Economy*, **89** (4), 615–41.

Kolady, D., W.H. Lesser and C. Ye (2011), 'The Economic Effects of Geographical Indications on Developing Country Producers: A Comparison of Darjeeling and Oolong Teas', *WIPO Journal*, **2**, 157–72.

Kongolo, T. (1999), 'Trademarks and Geographical Indications within the Frameworks of the African Intellectual Property Organization Agreement and the TRIPS Agreement', *Journal of World Intellectual Property*, **2** (5), 833–44.

Kreps, D.M. and R. Wilson (1982), 'Reputation and Imperfect Information', *Journal of Economic Theory*, **27**, 253–79.

Kur, A. and R. Knaak (2004), 'Protection of Traditional Names and Designations', in S. von Lewinski (ed.), *Indigenous Heritage and Intellectual Property: Genetic Resources, Traditional Knowledge and Folklore*, The Hague, London and New York: Kluwer Law International, pp. 221–58.

Lampkin, N., C. Foster and S.M. Padel (1999), *The Policy and Regulatory Environment for Organic Farming in Europe: Country Reports, Organic Farming in Europe: Economics and Policy, Volume 2*, Hohenheim, Germany: Die Deutsche Bibliothek–CIP-Einheitsaufnahme.

Larson, J. (2007), 'The Relevance of Geographical Indications and Designations of Origin for the Sustainable Use of Genetic Resources', Rome, Italy: Global Facilitation Unit for Underutilised Species.

Lees, M. (2003), *Food Authenticity and Traceability*, Cambridge, UK: Woodhead Publishing.

Lence, S.H., S. Marette, D.J. Hayes and W. Foster (2007), 'Collective Marketing Arrangements for Geographically Differentiated Agricultural Products: Welfare Impacts and Policy Implications', *American Journal of Agricultural Economics*, **89**, 947–63.

Lindquist, L.A. (1999), 'Champagne or Champagne? An Examination of U.S. Failure to Comply with the Geographical Provisions of the TRIPS Agreement', *Georgia Journal of International and Comparative Law*, **27**, 309–44.

Lusk, J.L. and J.D. Anderson (2004), 'Effects of Country-of-Origin Labeling on Meat Producers and Consumers', *Journal of Agricultural and Resource Economics*, **12** (2), 185–205.

Lybbert, T. (2002), 'Commercialising Argan Oil in Southwestern Morocco: Pitfalls on the Pathway to Sustainable Development', in S. Pagiola, J. Bishop and S. Wunder (eds), *Buying Biodiversity: Financing Conservation for Sustainable Development*, Washington, DC: World Bank.

MAAPAR (2004), 'Impact d'une indication géographique sur l'agriculture et le développement rural: le fromage de Comté', Paris, France: Ministère de l'agriculture, de l'alimentation, des pêches et des affaires rurales.

Marette, S. (2005), 'The Collective-Quality Promotion in the Agribusiness Sector: An Overview', Working Paper 05-WP406, Ames, IA: Iowa State University, Centre for Agricultural and Rural Development.

Marie-Vivien, D. (2008), 'From Plant Variety Definition to Geographical Indication Protection: A Search for the Link between Basmati Rice and India/Pakistan', *Journal of World Intellectual Property*, **11** (4), 321–44.

Martín, J.M.C. (2004), 'TRIPS Agreement: Towards a Better Protection for Geographical Indications', *Brooklyn Journal of International Law*, **30** (1), 117–84.

Menapace, L., G. Colson, C. Grebitus and M. Facendola (2011), 'Consumers' Preferences for Geographical Origin Labels: Evidence from the Canadian Olive Oil Market', *European Review of Agricultural Economics*, **38** (2), 193–212.

Modjuska, E. and J. Caswell (2000), 'A Test of Nutritional Quality Signaling in Food Markets Prior to Implementation of Mandatory Labeling', *American Journal of Agricultural Economics*, **82**, 298–309.

Monteverde, P. (2012), 'Enforcement of Geographical Indications', *Journal of Intellectual Property Law and Practice*, **7** (4), 291–7.

Morgan, K., T.K. Marsden and J. Banks (2006), *Worlds of Food: Place, Power, and Provenance in the Food Chain*, Oxford, UK: Oxford University Press.

Munzinger, P. (2012), 'Blue Jeans and Other GIs: An Overview of Protection Systems for Geographical Indications', *Journal of Intellectual Property Law and Practice*, **7** (4), 283–90.

Murdoch, J., T. Marsden and J. Banks (2000), 'Quality, Nature, and Embeddedness: Some Theoretical Considerations in the Context of the Food Sector', *Economic Geography*, **76** (2), 107.

Murphy, K.M. (2003), 'Conflict, Confusion, and Bias under TRIPs Articles 22–24', *American University International Law Review*, **19** (5), 1181–230.

Musungu, S.F. (2008), 'The Protection of the Geographical Indications and the Doha Round: Strategic and Policy Considerations for Africa', QUNO IP Issue Paper 8, Geneva, Switzerland: Quaker United Nations Office.

Mutersbaugh, T., D. Klooster, M.-C. Renard and P. Taylor (2005), 'Editorial: Certifying Rural Spaces: Quality Certified Products and Rural Governance', *Journal of Rural Studies*, **21** (4), 381–8.

Nagashima, A. (1970), 'A Comparison of Japanese and US Attitudes toward Foreign Products', *Journal of Marketing*, **34** (1), 68–74.

O'Connor, B. (2004), *The Law of Geographical Indications*, London: Cameron May.

O'Connor, B. and I. Kireeva (2004), 'Overview of the EC Case Law Protecting Geographical Indications: The Slicing of Parma Ham and the Grating of Grana Padano Cheese', *European Intellectual Property Review*, **26** (7), 312–22.

O'Connor & Co. (2005), 'Geographical Indications and the Challenges for ACP Countries', Agritrade, CTA. Available at http://agritrade.cta.int/.

O'Connor & Co. (2007a), 'Geographical Indications and TRIPs: 10 Years Later... Part I. A Roadmap for EU GI Holders to Get Protection in Other WTO Members', Available at http://trade.ec.europa.eu/doclib/docs/2007/june/tradoc_135088.pdf.

O'Connor & Co. (2007b), 'Geographical Indications and TRIPS: 10 Years Later... Part I. Protection of Geographical Indications in 160 Countries around the World', Available at http://trade.ec.europa.eu/doclib/docs/2007/june/tradoc_135089.pdf.

OECD (2000), 'Appellations of Origin and Geographical Indications in OECD Member Countries: Economic and Legal Implications', COM/AGR/APM/TD/WP(2000)15/final.

Pacciani, A., G. Beletti, A. Marescotti and S. Scaramuzzi (2001), 'The Role of Typical Products in Fostering Rural Development and the Effects of Regulation (EEC) 2081/92', 73rd Seminar of the European Association of Agricultural Economists, Ancona, 28–30 June.

Panizzon, M. (2006), 'Traditional Knowledge and Geographical Indications: Foundations, Interests and Negotiating Positions', NCCR Trade Regulation Working Paper 2005/1, Zurich, Switzerland: ETH.

Penker, M. (2006), 'Mapping and Measuring the Ecological Embeddedness of Food Supply Chains', *Geoforum*, **37**, 368–79.

Radman, M., Ž. Mesic and D. Kovacic (2006), 'Geographical Indications in Croatia: A Case Study of Virovitica Pepper', Paper presented at Food and Territories *ALTER 2006* Baeza (Jaén), Spain, 18–21 October.

Rangnekar, D. (2002), 'Geographical Indications: A Review of Proposals at the TRIPS Council'. UNCTAD/ICTSD capacity building project on intellectual property rights and sustainable development, June.

Rangnekar, D. (2003), 'Geographical Indications: A Review of Proposals at the TRIPS Council: Extending Article 23 to Products Other than Wines and Spirits, Issue Paper 4, Geneva, Switzerland: International Centre for Trade and Sustainable Development (ICTSD) and United Nations Conference on Trade and Development (UNCTAD).

Rangnekar, D. (2004), 'The Socio-Economics of Geographical Indications: A Review of Empirical Evidence from Europe', UNCTAD/ICTSD capacity building project on intellectual property rights and sustainable development.

Rangnekar, D. (2009), *Geographical Indications and Localisation: A Case Study of Feni*, ESRC Report. Available at http://papers.ssrn.com/sol3/papers.cfm?abstract_id=1564624.

Rangnekar, D. and S. Kumar (2002), 'Another Look at Basmati: Genericity and the Problems of a Transborder Geographical Indication', *Journal of World Intellectual Property*, **13** (2), 202–30.

Ray, C. (1998), 'Culture, Intellectual Property and Territorial Rural Development', *Sociologia Ruralis*, **38** (1), 3.

Raynaud, E. and L. Sauvée (2000), 'Signes collectifs de qualité et structures de gouvernance', *Revue Économie rurale*, **258** (1), 101–112

Renting, H., T.K. Marsden and J. Banks (2003), 'Understanding Alternative Food Networks: Exploring the Role of Short Food Supply Chains in Rural Development', *Environment and Planning A*, **35** (3), 393–411.

Requillart, V. (2007), 'On the Economics of Geographical Indications in the EU', Paper presented at a workshop on Geographical Indications, Country of Origin and Collective Brands: Firm Strategies and Public Policies. Toulouse, France, 14–15 June.

Réviron, S. and J.-M. Chappuis (2011), 'Geographical Indications: Collective Organization and Management', in E. Barham and B. Sylvander (eds), *Labels of Origin for Food: Local Development, Global Recognition*, Wallingford, UK: CAB International, pp. 45–62.

Réviron, S. and M. Paus (2006), *Special Report: Impact Analysis Methods: WP2 Social and Economic Issues: SINER-GI Project*, European Commission: 6th Framework Program, February.

Reviron, S., E. Thévenod-Mottet and N. El Benni (2009), 'Geographical Indications: Creation and Distribution of Economic Value in Developing Countries', NCCR Trade Regulations Working Paper 14.

Ricolfi, M. (2009), 'Is the European GIs Policy in Need of Rethinking?', *IIC*, **40** (2), 123–4.

Sautier, D., E. Biénabe and C. Cerdan (2011), 'Geographical Indications in Developing Countries', in E. Barham and B. Sylvander (eds), *Labels of Origin for Food: Local Development, Global Recognition*, Wallingford, UK: CAB International, pp. 138–53.

Shapiro, C. (1983), 'Premiums for High Quality Products as Returns to Reputations', *Quarterly Journal of Economics*, **98** (4), 659–79.

Silva, M. (2005), 'Sour Grapes: The Comprimising [sic] Effect of the United States' Failure to Protect Foreign Geographic Indications of Wine', *Boston College International and Comparative Law Review*, **28** (1), 201–41.

Stanziani, A. (2009), 'Information, Quality and Legal Rules: Wine Adulteration in Nineteenth Century France', *Business History*, **51** (2), 268–91.

Staten, T.L. (2005), 'Geographical Indications under the TRIPS Agreement: Uniformity Not Extension', *Journal of the Patent and Trade Mark Office Society*, **87** (3), 221–45.

Stern, S. and C. Fund (2000), 'The Australian System of Registration and Protection of Geographical Indications for Wines', *Flinders Journal of Law Reform*, **5**, 39–52.

Stiglitz, G. (1989), 'Imperfect Information in the Product Market', in R. Schmalensee and R. Willig (eds), *Handbook of Industrial Organization*, **1**, North Holland: Elsevier Science Publishers, 769–847.

Sylvander, B. (2004), 'Development of Origin Labelled Products: Humanity, Innovation and Sustainability', DOLPHINS WP7 Report, January.

Teil, G. (2010), 'The French Wine "Appellations d'Origine Contrôlée" and the Virtues of Suspicion', *Journal of World Intellectual Property*, **13** (2), 253–74.

Torole, J. (1988), *Theory of Industrial Organization*, Massachusetts: MIT Press.

Tregear, A. and G. Giraud (2011), 'Geographical Indications, Consumers and Citizens', in E. Barham and B. Sylvander (eds), *Labels of Origin for Food: Local Development, Global Recognition*, Wallingford, UK: CAB International, pp. 63–74.

Van Caenegem, W. (2003), 'Registered Geographical Indications: Part 1', *Journal of World Intellectual Property*, **6** (5), 699–719.

Van Caenegem, W. (2004), 'Registered GIs: Intellectual Property, Agricultural Policy and International Trade', *European Intellectual Property Review*, **26** (4), 170–81.

Van de Kop, P., D. Sautier and A. Gerz (2006), *Origin-Based Products. Lessons for Pro-Poor Market Development*, Bulletin 372, Amsterdam, The Netherlands: Royal Tropical Institute (KIT) and Montpellier, France: French Agricultural Research Centre for International Development (CIRAD).

Van der Merwe, A. (2009), 'Geographical Indication Protection in South Africa with Particular Reference to Wines and to the EU', *Estey Centre Journal of International Law and Trade Policy*, **10** (1), 186–95.

Van der Ploeg, J.D., H. Renting, G. Brunori, K. Knickel, J. Mannion, T. Marsden, K. De Roest, E. Sevilla-Guzmán and F. Ventura (2000), 'Rural Development: From Practices and Policies towards Theory', *Sociologia Ruralis*, **40** (4), 391–408.

Van Ittersum, K., M.J.J.M. Candel and M.T.G. Meulenberg (2003), 'The Influence of the Image of a Product's Region of Origin on Product Evaluation', *Journal of Business Research*, **56**, 215–26.

Van Leeuwen, C. and G. Seguin (2006), 'The Concept of Terroir in Viticulture', *Journal of Wine Research*, **17** (1), 1–10.

Verbeke, W. and J. Roosen (2009), 'Market Differentiation Potential of Country-of-Origin, Quality and Traceability Labeling', *Estey Centre Journal of International Law and Trade Policy*, **10** (1), 20–35.

Verbeke, W. and J. Viaene (1999), 'Consumer Attitude to Beef Quality Labeling and Associations with Beef Quality Labels', *Journal of International Food and Agribusiness Marketing*, **10** (3), 45–65.

Verhaegen, I. and G. van Huylenbroeck (2001), 'Costs and Benefits for Farmers Participating in Innovative Marketing Channels for Quality Food Products', *Journal of Rural Studies*, **17** (4), 443–56.

Verlegh, P.W.J. and J.-B.E.M. Steenkamp (1999), 'A Review and Meta-Analysis of Country of Origin Research', *Journal of Economic Psychology*, **20** (5), 521–46.

Vittori, M. (2010), 'The International Debate on Geographical Indications (GIs): The Point of View of the Global Coalition of GI Producers—oriGIn', *Journal of World Intellectual Property*, **13** (2), 304–14.

Vivas Egui, D. (2001), 'Negotiations on Geographical Indications in the TRIPS Council and Their Effect on the WTO Agricultural Negotiations: Implications for Developing Countries and the Case of Venezuela', *Journal of World Intellectual Property*, **4** (5), 703–28.

Williams, R.M. (2007), 'Do Geographical Indications Promote Sustainable Rural Development? Two UK Case Studies and Implications for New Zealand Rural Development Policy', Lincoln University. Available at http://researcharchive.lincoln.ac.nz/dspace/ bitstream/10182/585/1/williams_mnrmee.pdf.

Winfree, J.A. and J. McCluskey (2005), 'Collective Reputation and Quality', *American Journal of Agricultural Economics*, **87** (1), 206–13.

Xu, L. and L. Wu (2010), 'Food Safety and Consumer Willingness to Pay for Certified Traceable Food in China', *Journal of the Science of Food and Agriculture*, **90** (8), 1368–73.

Young, L.M. and J.E. Hobbs (2002), 'Vertical Linkages in Agri-Food Supply Chains: Changing Roles for Producers, Commodity Groups and Government Policy', *Review of Agricultural Economics*, **24** (2), 428–41.

Zacher, F.G. (2005), 'Pass the Parmesan: Geographic Indications in the United States and the European Union: Can There Be Compromise?', *Emory International Law Review*, **19**, 427–42.

Zago, A.M. and D. Pick (2004), 'Labelling Policies in Food Markets: Private Incentives, Public Intervention and Welfare Effects', *Journal of Agricultural and Resource Economics*, **29** (1), 150–65.

Zografos, D. (2008), 'Geographical Indications and Socio-Economic Development', IQSensato Working Paper 3.

Zographos, D. (2006), 'Can Geographical Indications Be a Viable Alternative for the Protection of Traditional Cultural Expressions?', in F. Macmillan and K. Bowrey (eds), *New Directions in Copyright Law*, Vol. 3. Cheltenham, UK and Northampton, MA, USA: Edward Elgar, pp. 37–45.

Zou, J. (2005), 'Rice and Cheese, Anyone? The Fight over TRIPS Geographical Indications Continues', *Brooklyn Journal of International Law*, **30** (3), 1141–74.

Further Reading

Adinolfi, F., M. de Rosa and F. Trabalzi (2011), 'Dedicated and Generic Marketing Strategies: The Disconnection between Geographical Indications and Consumer Behavior in Italy', *British Food Journal*, **113** (3), 419–35.

Al Attar Ahmed, M. (2006), 'Monocultures of the Law: Legal Sameness in Restructuring of Global Agriculture', *Drake Journal of Agricultural Law*, **11**, 139–64.

Albayrak, M. and E. Gunes (2010), 'Implementations of Geographical Indications at Brand Management of Traditional Foods in the European Union', *African Journal of Business Management*, **4** (6), 1059–68.

Albisu, L.M. (2002), 'Work Programme 2: Link between Origin Labelled Products and Local Production Systems, Supply Chain Analysis', Final report, DOLPHINS Concerted Action, European Commission.

Aprile, M., V. Caputo and R.M. Nayga Jr (2012), 'Consumers' Valuation of Food Quality Labels: The Case of the European Geographic Indication and Organic Farming Labels', *International Journal of Consumer Studies*, **36** (2), 158–65.

Arfini, F. and C. Mora Zanetti (1998), 'Typical Products and Local Development: The Case of Parma

Area', in F. Arfini and C. Mora (eds), *Typical and Traditional Products: Rural Effects and Agro-Industrial Problems*, Proceedings of the 52nd Seminar of the European Association of Agricultural Economists, 19–21 June 1997, Parma, Italy: Università di Parma, pp. 11–40.

Armistead, J. (2000), 'Whose Cheese Is It Anyway? Correctly Slicing the European Regulation Concerning Protections for Geographic Indications', *Transnational Law and Contemporary Problems*, **10** (1), 303–24.

Aubard, A. (2010), 'The Use of Geographical Indications to Promote Economic Development: Issues, Opportunities, Policy Options', ACP-EU TradeCom Facility Paper on ACP Regional Workshops on Geographical Indications, April–May.

Auby, J.-M. and R. Plaisant (1974), *Le droit des appellations d'origine: l'appellation Cognac*, Paris, France: Libraires Techniques.

Auer, A. (2008), 'Legal Implications of Accession to the European Union on Geographical Indications and Designations of Origin for Agricultural Products and Foodstuffs', *Croatian Yearbook of European Law and Policy*, **2**, 137–72.

Augustin-Jean, L. (2012), 'Standardization vs. Products of Origins: What Kinds of Agricultural Products Have the Potential to Become a Protected Geographical Indication?, in L. Augustin-Jean, H. Ilbert and N. Saavedra-Rivano (eds), *Geographical Indications and International Agricultural Trade: The Challenge for Asia*, London: Palgrave Macmillan, pp. 48–70.

Augustin-Jean, L. and S. Kae (2012), 'From Products of Origin to Geographical Indications in Japan: Perspectives on the Construction of Quality for the Emblematic Productions of Kobe and Matsusaka Beef', in L. Augustin-Jean, H. Ilbert and N. Saavedra-Rivano (eds), *Geographical Indications and International Agricultural Trade: The Challenge for Asia*, London: Palgrave Macmillan, pp. 139–63.

Avelino, J., J.J. Perriot, B. Guyot, C. Pineda, F. Decazy and C. Cilas (2002), 'Identifying Terroir Coffees in Honduras', in *Research and Coffee Growing*, Montpellier, France: CIRAD, pp. 6–16.

Avelino, J., J. Barbosa, J.C. Arraya, C. Fonseca, F. Davrieux, B. Guyot and C. Cilas (2005), 'Effects of Slope Exposure, Altitude and Yield on Coffee Quality in Two Altitude Terroirs of Costa Rica, Orosi and Santa Maria de Dota', *Journal of the Science of Food and Agriculture*, **85**, 1869–76.

Avelino, J., D. Roman, S. Romero and C. Fonseca (2006), 'Las indicaciones geográficas: algunos fundamentos y metodologías con ejemplos de Costa Rica Sobre Café', CIRAD, ICAFE and IICA-PROMECAFE.

Bagal, M. and M. Vittori (2010), 'Preliminary Report on the Potential for Geographical Indications in Côte d'Ivoire and the Relevant Legal Framework', ACP-EU TradeCom Facility Paper on ACP Regional Workshops on Geographical Indications, April–May.

Bagal, M. and M. Vittori (2011), *Practical Manual on Geographical Indications for ACP Countries*, Paris, France: CTA and oriGIn.

Banerji, M. (2012), 'Geographical Indications: Which Way Should ASEAN Go?', *Boston College Intellectual Property and Technology Forum*, 1–11.

Baram, M. and M. Bourrier (2010), *Governing Risk in GM Agriculture*, Leiden, the Netherlands: Cambridge University Press.

Barjolle D., J.-M. Chappuis and M. Dufour (2000), *Competitive Position of Some PDO Cheeses on Their Own Reference Market: Identification of the Key Success Factors*, Lausanne: ETHZ (Institute of Agricultural Economics).

Barjolle, D., S. Réviron and J.-M. Chappuis (2005), 'Organization and Performance of Origin Labelled Food Alliances', in A.R. Bellows (ed.), *Focus on Agricultural Economics*, New York: Nova Science, pp. 91–126.

Barjolle, D., M. Paus and A. Perret (2009), 'Impact of Geographical Indications: A Review of Methods and Empirical Evidences', Contributed IAAE Conference Paper, Beijing, China, 16–22 August.

Barjolle, D. and E. Thévenod-Mottet (2005), 'Economic Aspects of Geographical Indications', in L. Bérard, M. Cegarra, M. Djama and S. Louafi (eds), *Biodiversity and Local Ecological Knowledge in France*, Paris: INRA-CIRAD, pp. 213–19.

Barrett, H.R., A.W. Browne, P.J.C. Harris and K. Cadoret (2002), 'Organic Certification and the UK Market: Organic Imports from Developing Countries', *Food Policy*, **27**, 301–18.

Baumert, N. (2012), 'The Development of Geographical Standards for Sake in Japan', in L. Augustin-Jean, H. Ilbert and N. Saavedra-Rivano (eds), *Geographical Indications and International Agricultural*

Trade: The Challenge for Asia, London: Palgrave Macmillan, pp. 164–80.

Belletti, G. and A. Marescotti (2002), 'Link between Origin-Labeled Products and Rural Development', DOLPHINS WP Report 3.

Belletti, G., G. Brunori, A. Marescotti and A. Rossi (2003), 'Multifunctionality and Rural Development: A Multilevel Approach', in G. van Huylenbroek and G. Durand (eds), *Multifunctional Agriculture. A New Paradigm for European Agriculture and Rural Development*, Aldershot, UK: Ashgate, pp. 55–80.

Belletti, G., T. Burgassi, E. Manco, A. Marescotti and S. Scaramuzzi (2009), 'The Effects of Certification Costs on the Success of a PDO/PGI', in L. Theuvesen, A. Spiller, M. Peupert and G. Jahn (eds), *Quality Management in Food Chains*, Wageningen, the Netherlands: Wageningen Academic Publishers, pp. 107–23.

Belletti, G., A. Marescotti, M. Paus, S. Reviron, A. Deppeler, H. Stamm and E. Thévenod-Mottet (2011), *The Effects of Protecting Geographical Indications: Ways and Means of Their Evaluation*, 2nd revised edn. Bern, Switzerland: Swiss Federal Institute of Intellectual Property.

Bendekgey, L. and C.H. Mead (1992), 'International Protection of Appellations of Origin and Other Geographic Indications', *Trademark Reporter*, **82**, 765–92.

Bérard, L. and P. Marchenay (2001), 'A Market Culture: "Produits de Terroir" or the Selling of Heritage', in S. Blowen, M. Demossier and J. Picard (eds), *Recollections of France: Memories, Identities and Heritage in Contemporary France*, New York: Oxford University Press. Berghahn Contemporary France series, Vol. 4, pp. 154–67.

Bérard, L. and P. Marchenay (2008), *From Localised Products to Geographical Indications: Awareness and Action*, Centre national de la recherche scientifique, Alimentec, Bourg-en-Bresse.

Bérard, L. and P. Marchenay (2009), 'Geographical Indications: A Contribution to Maintaining Biodiversity?', Biosphere Reserves, Technical Notes, 3-2008, Paris: UNESCO.

Blakeney, M. (2000), 'Geographical Indications in Trade', *International Trade Law and Regulation*, **4**, 48–55.

Blakeney, M. (2002), 'Intellectual Property Aspects of Traditional Agricultural Knowledge', in R.E. Evenson, V. Santaniello and D. Zilberman (eds), *Economic and Social Issues in Agricultural Biotechnology*, Wallingford, UK: CAB International, pp. 43–60.

Blakeney, M. (2009), *Intellectual Property Rights and Food Security*, Wallingford, UK: CAB International.

Blakeney, M. and G. Mengistie (2011), 'Intellectual Property Policy Formulation in LDCs in Sub-Saharan Africa', *African Journal of International and Comparative Law*, **19**, 66–98.

Bocedi, G. (2010), 'Country Paper on Potential GI Products for Kenya', ACP-EU TradeCom Facility Paper on ACP Regional Workshops on Geographical Indications, April–May.

Bolos, M.D. (2011), 'Legal Sources of Trademarks and Geographical Indications', *Bulletin of the Transilvania University of Brasov*, Series VII: Social Sciences, Law, **4** (2), 115–22.

Bouamra-Mechemache, Z. and J. Chaban (2010), 'Determinants of Adoption of Protected Designations of Origin Label: Evidence from French Brie', *Journal of Agricultural Economics*, **61** (2), 225–39.

Bourgois, E. (2007), 'Geographical Indications and Trade in Agricultural Products', in V. Mosoti and A. Gobena (eds), *International Trade Rules and the Agriculture Sector: Selected Implementation Issues*, Rome, Italy: FAO, pp. 167–204.

Bowen, S. and M.S. Gaytan (2012), 'The Paradox of Protection: National Identity, Global Commodity Chains, and the Tequila Industry', *Social Problems*, **59** (1), 70–93.

Bramley, C. and J.F. Kirsten (2007), 'Exploring the Economic Rationale for Protecting Geographical Indicators in Agriculture', *Agrekon*, **46** (1), 69–93.

Brody, P.M. (1999), '"Semi-Generic" Geographical Wine Designations: Did Congress Trip over TRIPS?', *Trademark Reporter*, **89** (6), 979–85.

Brouwer, O. (1991), 'Community Protection of Geographical Indications and Specific Character as a Means of Enhancing Foodstuff Quality', *CML Review*, **28** (3), 615–46.

Bureau, J.C. and E. Valceschini (2003), 'The European Food Labeling Policy: Successes and Limitations', *Journal of Food Distribution Research*, **34** (3), 69–76.

Byrne, P.J., U.C. Toensmeyer, C.L. German and I.R. Muller (1991), 'Analysis of Consumer Attitudes toward Organic Produce and Purchase Likelihood', *Journal of Food Distribution Research*, **22**, 49–62.

Capus, J. (1947), *L'Evolution de la Législation sur les Appellations d'Origine: Genèse des Appellations Contrôlées*, Paris, France: L. Larmat.

Caswell, J. (2008), 'The Benefits and Costs of Proliferation of Geographical Labeling for Developing Countries', Working Paper 2008-7, Department of Resource Economics, University of Massachusetts, Amherst. Available at http://works.bepress.com/julie_caswell/86.

Charlier, C. and M.-A. Ngo (2007), 'An Analysis of the European Communities: Protection of Trademarks and Geographical Indications for Agricultural Products and Foodstuffs Dispute', *Journal of World Intellectual Property*, **10** (3–4), 171–86.

Chen, J. (1996), 'A Sober Second Look at Appellations of Origin: How the United States Will Crash France's Wine and Cheese Party', *Minnesota Journal of Global Trade*, **5** (1), 29–64.

CIRAD (2009), 'The Challenges Relating to Geographical Indications (GIs) for ACP Countries', Joint CTA, AFD and CIRAD Workshop Report, Montpellier, France, 24–27 March.

Craven, E. and C. Mather (2001), 'Geographical Indications and the South Africa–European Union Free Trade Agreement', *Area*, **33** (3), 312–20.

Dagne, T. (2012), 'Intellectual Property, Traditional Knowledge and Biodiversity in the Global Economy: The Potential of Geographical Indications for Protecting Traditional Knowledge-Based Agricultural Products', Doctor in the Science of Law Thesis, Halifax, Nova Scotia: Dalhousie University.

Daniels, J.C. (2009), 'The Branding of America: The Rise of Geographic Trademarks and the Need for a Strong Fair Use Defense', *Iowa Law Review*, **94** (5), 1703–37.

Danner, S. (2009), 'Not Confused? Don't be Troubled: Meeting the First Amendment Attack on Protection of "Generic" Foreign Geographical Indications', *Cardozo Law Review*, **30** (5), 2257–93.

Das, K. (2006), 'Protection of India's "Geographical Indications": An Overview of the Indian Legislation and the TRIPS Scenario', *Indian Journal of International Law*, **46** (1), 39–73.

Das, K. (2007), 'Protection of Geographical Indications: An Overview of Select Issues with Particular Reference to India', Working Paper 8, New Delhi, India: Centre for Trade and Development (CENTAD).

Das, K. (2009), 'Prospects and Challenges of Geographical Indications in India', *Journal of World Intellectual Property*, **13** (2), 148–201.

De Lind, L. (2000), 'Transforming Organic Agriculture into Industrial Organic Products: Reconsidering National Organic Standards', *Human Organization*, **59** (2), 198–208.

De Vletian, A. (1989), *Appellations d'origine: Indications de provenance – Indications d'origine*, Paris: Delmas.

Deffontaines, J.-P. (2005), 'The *Terroir*: A Concept with Multiple Meanings', in L. Bérard, M. Cegarra, M. Djama and S. Louafi (eds), *Biodiversity and Local Ecological Knowledge in France*, Paris: INRA-CIRAD, pp. 38–42.

Denis, D. (1995), *Appellation d'origine et indications de provenance*, Paris: Dalloz.

Doster, I. (2006), 'A Cheese by Any Other Name: A Palatable Compromise to the Conflict over Geographical Indications', *Vanderbilt Law Review*, **59** (3), 874–903.

Dunn, H.A. (2004), 'Geographic Indications at Issue in Idaho Spud Case', *National Law Journal*, **26** (21), 10–12.

Echols, M.A. (2003), 'Geographical Indications for Food, TRIPS, and the Doha Development Agenda', *Journal of African Law*, **47** (2), 199–220.

Escudero, S. (2001), 'International Protection of Geographical Indications and Developing Countries', TRADE Working Paper 10, South Centre Geneva. Available at http://www.southcentre.org.

European Court of Auditors (2011), *Do the Design and Management of the Geographical Indications Scheme Allow It to Be Effective?*, Special Report 11/2011, Luxembourg: Publications Office of the European Union.

Evans, G.E. (2008), 'The Multilateral Register for Geographical Indications and the Doha Mandate', in *Anuario Andino De Derechos Intelectuales (Andean Yearbook of Intellectual Property Rights)*, Lima, Peru: Palestra, pp. 397–419.

Evans, G.E. (2010), 'The Comparative Advantages of Geographical Indications and Trademarks for the Marketing of Agricultural Products', in P. Eeckhout and T. Tridimas (eds), *Yearbook of European*

Law, Oxford: Oxford University Press, pp. 224–60.

Evans, G.E. (2013a), 'A Comparative Analysis of the Protection of Geographical Indications in the European Union and the United States under Sui Generis and Trademark Systems', in T. Takenaka (ed.), *Intellectual Property Systems in Common Law and Civil Law Countries*, Cheltenham, UK and Northampton, MA, USA: Edward Elgar.

Evans, G.E. (2013b), 'Simplification and Codification of European Legislation for the Protection of Geographical Indications', in C. Geiger (ed.), *Constructing European Intellectual Property Law: Achievements and New Perspectives*, Cheltenham, UK and Northampton, MA, USA: Edward Elgar.

Evans, P. (2004), 'Development as Institutional Change: The Pitfalls of Monocropping and the Potentials of Deliberation', *Studies in Comparative International Development*, **38** (4), 30–52.

FAO (Food and Agriculture Organization of the United Nations) (2008), 'Promotion of Traditional Regional Agricultural and Food Products: A Further Step towards Sustainable Rural Development', ERC/08/4, Rome: FAO.

FAO (2012), 'Identification of Origin-Linked Products and Their Potential for Development. A Methodology for Participatory Inventories', Rome: FAO.

FAO and SINER-GI (2009). *Linking People, Places And Products: A Guide for Promoting Quality Linked to Geographical Origin and Sustainable Geographical Indications*, Rome: FAO.

Fautrel, V., S. Sureau, M.C. Thirion and M. Vittori (2009), 'Protected Geographical Indications for ACP Countries: A Solution or a Mirage?', *Trade Negotiations Insight*, **6** (8), July–August. Available at www.icstd.net/news/tni.

Fink, C. and B. Smarzynska (2002), 'Trademarks, Geographical Indications, and Developing Countries', in B. Hoekman, A. Mattoo and P. English (eds), *Development, Trade, and the WTO: A Handbook*, Washington, DC: The World Bank, pp. 403–15.

Fitter, R. and R. Kaplinsky (2001), 'Who Gains from Product Rents as the Coffee Market Becomes More Differentiated? A Value Chain Analysis', *IDS Bulletin Special Issue on the Value of Value Chains*, **32** (3), 69–82.

Fonte, M. (2010), 'The Construction of Origin Certification: Knowledge and Local Food', in M. Fonte and A.G. Papadopoulos (eds), *Naming Food after Places: Food Relocalisation and Knowledge Dynamics in Rural Development*, Farnham, UK: Ashgate, pp. 149–71.

Frayssignes, J. (2011), 'Roquefort Cheese (France)', in E. Barham and B. Sylvander (eds), *Labels of Origin for Food: Local Development, Global Recognition*, Wallingford, UK: CAB International, pp. 177–83.

Fuá, G. (1988), 'Small-Scale Industry in Rural Areas: The Italian Experience', in K.J. Arrow (ed.), *The Balance between Industry and Agriculture in Economic Development*, London: Macmillan, pp. 259–79.

Fusco, S. (2008), 'Geographical Indications: A Discussion of the TRIPS Regulation after the Ministerial Conference of Hong Kong', *Marquette Intellectual Property Law Review*, **12** (2), 197–262.

Galtier, F., G. Belletti and A. Marescotti (2008), 'Are Geographical Indications a Way to "Decommodify" the Coffee Market?', Paper presented at the 12th Congress of the European Association of Agricultural Economists (EAAE 2008) Ghent, Belgium, 26–29 August.

Gangjee, D. (2006), 'Melton Mowbray and the GI Pie in the Sky: Exploring Cartographies of Protection', *Intellectual Property Quarterly*, **3**, 291–309.

Gangjee, D. (2007), 'Say Cheese! A Sharper Image of Generic Use through the Lens of Feta', *European Intellectual Property Review*, **29** (5), 172–9.

Gangjee, D. (2008), 'Geographical Indications and Human Rights', in P. Torremans (ed.), *Intellectual Property and Human Rights: Enhanced Edition of Copyright and Human Rights*, The Hague: Kluwer Law International, pp. 383–95.

Gao, Z. and T.C. Schroeder (2009), 'Effects of Label Information on Consumer Willingness-to-Pay for Food Attributes', *American Journal of Agricultural Economics*, **91** (3), 795–809.

Garcia, C., D. Marie-Vivien, C.G. Kushalappa, P.G. Chengappa and K.M. Nanaya (2007), 'Geographical Indications and Biodiversity in the Western Ghats, India: Can Labeling Benefit Producers and the Environment in a Mountain Agroforestry Landscape?', *Mountain Research and Development*, **27** (3), 206–10.

Geiger, C., D. Gervais, N. Olszak and V. Ruzek (2010), 'Towards a Flexible International Framework for the Protection of Geographical Indications', *WIPO Journal*, **1** (2), 147–58.

Gervais, D. (2012), 'Traditional Innovation and the Ongoing Debate on the Protection of Geographical Indications', in P. Drahos and S. Frankel (eds), *Indigenous Peoples' Innovation: Intellectual Property Pathways to Development*, Canberra, Australia: ANU Press, pp. 121–46.

Giovannucci, D. (ed.) (2008), *Guide to Geographical Indications: Approaches to Value*, Geneva: International Trade Centre.

Giovannucci, D. and L.F. Samper (2009), 'Café Nariño, Colombia', in D. Giovannucci, T. Josling, W.A. Kerr, B. O'Connor and M.T. Yeung (eds), *Guide to Geographical Indications: Linking Products and Their Origins*, Geneva: International Trade Centre, pp. 197–202.

Goebbel, B. (2003), 'Geographical Indications and Trademarks: The Road from Doha', *Trademark Reporter*, **93** (4), 964–95.

Goldberg, S.D. (2001), 'Who Will Raise the White Flag? The Battle between the United States and the European Union over the Protection of Geographical Indications', *University of Pennsylvania Journal of International Economic Law*, **22** (1), 107–51.

Goodman, D. (2004), 'Rural Europe Redux? Reflections on Alternative Agro-Food Networks and Paradigm Change', *Sociologia Ruralis*, **44** (1), 3–16.

Gopalakrishnan, N.S., P.S. Nair and A.K. Babu (2007), 'Exploring the Relationship between Geographical Indications and Traditional Knowledge: An Analysis of the Legal Tools for the Protection of Geographical Indications in Asia', ICTSD Working Paper.

Granich, C.I. (2009), 'Mezcal, Mexico', in D. Giovannucci, T. Josling, W.A. Kerr, B. O'Connor and M.T. Yeung (eds), *Guide to Geographical Indications: Linking Products and Their Origins*, Geneva: International Trade Centre, pp. 183–96.

Guérillon, R. (1919), *Les Appellations d'Origine: Loi du 6 Mai 1919*, Paris: Journal l'Epicier.

Guerra, J.L. (2010), 'Geographical Indications, in Situ Conservation and Traditional Knowledge', ICTSD Policy Brief 3. Available at http://ictsd.org/downloads/2011/12/geographical-indications-in-situ-conservation-and-traditional-knowledge.pdf.

Guihong, W. (2012), 'Geographical Indication and Institutional Organization of Food Market in China: A Case Study of Jinhua Ham', in L. Augustin-Jean, H. Ilbert and N. Saavedra-Rivano (eds), *Geographical Indications and International Agricultural Trade: The Challenge for Asia*, London: Palgrave Macmillan, pp. 204–25.

Guthman, J. (2007), 'The Polanyian Way? Voluntary Food Labels as Neoliberal Governance', *Antipode*, **39** (3), 456–78.

Guyet, J. (1983), *Les indications de provenance et appellations d'origine et droit comparé*, Geneva: Librarie Droz.

Guzman, E. and F. Ventura (2000), 'Rural Development: From Practices and Policies towards Theory', *Sociologia Ruralis*, **40** (4), 391–408.

Hendrickson, M. and W. Heffernan (2002), 'Opening Spaces through Relocalization: Locating Potential Resistance in the Weaknesses of the Global Food System', *Sociologia Ruralis*, **42** (4), 347.

Hess, M. (2004), '"Spatial" Relationships? Towards a Reconceptualization of Embeddedness', *Progress in Human Geography*, **28** (2), 165–86.

Higgins, V., J. Dibden and C. Cocklin (2008), 'Building Alternative Agri-Food Networks: Certification, Embeddedness and Agri-Environmental Governance', *Journal of Rural Studies*, **24** (1), 15–27.

Hinchliffe, S.A. (2009), 'Overlap between Trade Marks and Geographical Indications in Australia', *Intellectual Property Law Bulletin*, **21** (7), 147–9.

Hinrichs, C. (2000), 'Embeddedness and Local Food Systems: Notes on Two Types of Direct Agricultural Market', *Journal of Rural Studies*, **16** (3), 295–303.

Hinrichs, C. (2003), 'The Practice and Politics of Food System Localization', *Journal of Rural Studies*, **19** (1), 33–45.

Hobbs, J.E. (1996), 'A Transaction Cost Approach to Supply Chain Management', *Supply Chain Management: An International Journal*, **1** (2), 15–27.

Hobbs, J.E. (2004), 'Information Asymmetry and the Role of Traceability Systems', *Agribusiness*, **20** (4), 397–415.

Hobbs, J.E., W.A. Kerr and K.K. Klein (1998), 'Creating International Competitiveness through Supply

Chain Management: Danish Pork', *Supply Chain Management: An International Journal*, **3** (2), 68–78.

Hobbs, J.E. and L. Young (2000), 'Closer Vertical Co-ordination in Agri-Food Supply Chains: A Conceptual Framework and Some Preliminary Evidence', *Supply Chain Management: An International Journal*, **5** (3), 131–42.

Huang, C.L. (1996), 'Consumer Preferences and Attitudes towards Organically Grown Produce', *European Review of Agricultural Economics*, **23** (34), 331–42.

Ilbery, B., M. Kneafsey, A. Söderlund and E. Dimara (2001), 'Quality, Imagery and Marketing: Producer Perspectives on Quality Products and Services in the Lagging Rural Regions of the European Union', *Geografiska Annaler*, **83** (1), 27–40.

Ilbert, H. (2012), 'Products with Denominations of Origin and Intellectual Property Rights: The International Bargaining Process', in L. Augustin-Jean, H. Ilbert and N. Saavedra-Rivano (eds), *Geographical Indications and International Agricultural Trade: The Challenge for Asia*, London: Palgrave Macmillan, pp. 91–116.

Insight Consulting, oriGIn and Agridea (2009), 'Study on the Protection of Geographical Indications for Products Other than Wines, Spirits, Agricultural Products or Foodstuffs', Brussels: European Commission.

Jain, S. (2009), 'Effects of the Extension of Geographical Indications: A South Asian Perspective', *Asia-Pacific Development Journal*, **16** (2), 65–86.

Jaton, L. (1926), *La Répression des Fausses Indications de Provenance et les Conventions Internationales*, Paris: Librairie Générale de Droit et de Jurisprudence.

Jena, P.R. and U. Grote (2010), 'Changing Institutions to Protect Regional Heritage: A Case for Geographical Indications in the Indian Agrifood Sector', *Development Policy Review*, **28** (2), 217–36.

Jenkins, T.N. (2000), 'Putting Postmodernity into Practice: Endogenous Development and the Role of Traditional Cultures in the Rural Development of Marginal Regions', *Ecological Economics*, **34**, 301–14.

Josling, T.E. (2006), 'What's in a Name? The Economics, Law and Politics of Geographical Indications for Foods and Beverages', Discussion Paper 109, Trinity College, Dublin: Institute for International Integration Studies.

Juarez, R. (2009), 'Café Veracruz, Mexico', in D. Giovannucci, T. Josling, W.A. Kerr, B. O'Connor and M.T. Yeung (eds), *Guide to Geographical Indications: Linking Products and Their Origins*, Geneva: International Trade Centre, pp. 203–14.

Kailasam, K.C. (2003), *Law of Trademarks and Geographical Indications*, New Delhi, India: Wadhwa and Co.

Kaplinsky, R. and R. Fitter (2001), 'Who Gains from Product Rents as the Coffee Market Becomes More Differentiated? A Value Chain Analysis', Institute of Development Studies (IDS) Working Paper.

Kerr, W.A. (2006), 'Enjoying a Good Port with a Clear Conscience: Geographic Indicators, Rent Seeking and Development', *Estey Centre Journal of International Law and Trade Policy*, **7** (1), 1–14.

Kloppenburg, J., J. Hendrickson and G.W. Stevenson (1996), 'Coming into the Foodshed', *Agriculture and Human Values*, **13** (3), 33–42.

Knaak, R. (1996), 'The Protection of Geographical Indications According to the TRIPS Agreement', in F.-K. Beier and G. Schricker (eds), *From GATT to TRIPS: Agreement on Trade-Related Aspects of Intellectual Property Rights*, IIC Studies, **18**, New York: Weinheim, pp. 117–32.

Lacour, L. (1904), *Les fausses indications de provenance*, Paris: Rousseau.

Lecoent, A., E. Vandecandelaere and J.-J. Cadilhon (2004), *Quality Linked to Geographical Origin and Geographical Indications: Lessons Learned from Six Case Studies in Asia*, Bangkok: FAO Regional Office for Asia and the Pacific.

Lee, K. (1989), 'Food Neophobia: Major Causes and Treatments', *Food Technology*, **43** (12), 62–73.

Lipsey, R. (1998), 'Internationalized Production in Developed and Developing Countries and in Industry Sectors', NBER Working Papers 6405, National Bureau of Economic Research, Inc.

Lorvellec, L. (1996), 'You've Got to Fight for Your Right to Party: A Response to Professor Jim Chen', *Minnesota Journal of Global Trade*, **5**, 65–80.

Loureiro, M.L. and J.J. McCluskey (2000), 'Assessing Consumer Response to Protected Geographical Identification Labeling', *Agribusiness*, **16** (3), 309–20.

Loureiro, M.L. and W.J. Umberger (2003), 'Estimating Consumer Willingness to Pay for Country-of-Origin Labeling', *Journal of Agricultural and Resource Economics*, **28** (2), 287–301.

Lucatelli, S. (2000), 'Appellations of Origin and Geographical Indications in OECD Member Countries: Economic and Legal Implications', OECD, Directorate for Food, Agriculture and Fisheries, Trade Directorate: COM/AGR/APM/TD/WP(2000)15/FINAL, pp. 57–65.

Lukose, L.P. (2007), 'Rationale and Prospects of the Protection of Geographical Indication: An Inquiry', *Journal of Intellectual Property Rights*, **12**, 212–23.

Luykx, D.M.A.M and S.M. van Ruth (2008), 'An Overview of Analytical Methods for Determining the Geographical Origin of Food Products', *Food Chemistry*, **107** (2), 897–911.

MacMaoláin, C. (2006), 'Eligibility Criteria for Protected Geographical Food Names', *European Law Review*, **31**, 579–92.

Marescotti, A. (2000), 'Marketing Channels, Quality Hallmarks and the Theory of Conventions', in B. Sylvander, B. Dominique and A. Filippo (eds), *The Socio-Economics of Origin Labelled Products in Agri-Food Supply Chains: Spatial, Institutional and Co-ordination Aspects*, Proceedings of the 67th EAAE Conference, Le Mans, France, 28–30 October, Versailles, France: INRA Editions, Vol. 2, pp. 103–22.

Marescotti, A. (2011), 'Cherry of Lari', in E. Barham and B. Sylvander (eds), *Labels of Origin for Food: Local Development, Global Recognition*, Wallingford, UK: CAB International, pp. 161–6.

Marie-Vivien, D. (2010), 'The Role of the State in the Protection of Geographical Indications: From Disengagement in France/Europe to Significant Involvement in India', *Journal of World Intellectual Property*, **13** (2), 121–47.

Maskus, K.E. (2003), 'Observations on the Development Potential of Geographical Indications', Paper prepared for the UN Millenium Project Task Force on Trade.

McBride, W.D. (2010), 'GI Joe? Coffee, Location, and Regulatory Accountability', *New York University Law Review*, **85**, 2138–69.

McCarthy, J.T. and V.C. Devitt (1979), 'Protection of Geographical Indications: Domestic and International', *Trademark Reporter*, **69**, 199–213.

Menapace, L., G. Colson, C. Grebitus and M. Facendola (2009), 'Consumer Preferences for Country-of-Origin, Geographical Indication, and Protected Designation of Origin Labels', Working Paper 09021, Ames, IA: Iowa State University, Department of Economics.

Mérel, P. (2009), 'Measuring Market Power in the French Comté Cheese Market', *European Review of Agricultural Economics*, **36** (1), 31–51.

Montanari, C. and K. de Roest (2011), 'Salumi Tipici Piacentini (Italy)', in E. Barham and B. Sylvander (eds), *Labels of Origin for Food: Local Development, Global Recognition*, Wallingford, UK: CAB International, pp. 184–9.

Montén, L. (2006), 'Geographical Indications of Origin: Should They Be Protected And Why? An Analysis of the Issue from the U.S. and EU Perspectives', *Santa Clara Computer and High Technology Law Journal*, **22** (2), 315–49.

Moran, W. (1993), 'Rural Space as Intellectual Property', *Political Geography*, **12** (3), 263–77.

Murray, D.L. and L.T. Raynolds (2000), 'Alternative Trade in Bananas: Obstacles and Opportunities for Progressive Social Change in the Global Economy', *Agriculture and Human Values*, **17** (1), 65–74.

Nair, L. and R. Kumar (2005), *Geographical Indications: A Search for Identity*, New Delhi, India: LexisNexis Butterworths.

O'Connor, B. and I. Kireeva (2003), 'What's in a Name? The "Feta" Cheese Saga', *International Trade Law and Regulation*, **9** (4), 110–21.

O'Connor, B. and I. Kireeva (2004), 'The US Marketing Order System', *Zeitschrift für das gesamte Lebensmittelrecht*, **3**, 359–68.

Olszak, N. (2001), *Droit des appellations d'origine et indications de provenence*, Paris: Tec&Doc.

Parrot, N. and B. van Elzakker (2003), *Organic and Like-Minded Movements in Africa*, Tholey-Theley, Germany: IFOAM.

Parrott, N., N. Wilson and J. Murdoch (2002), 'Spatializing Quality: Regional Protection and the Alternative Geography of Food', *European Urban and Regional Studies*, **9** (3), 241–61.

Parry, B. (2008), 'Geographical Indications: Not All Champagne and Roses', in L. Bently, J.C. Ginsburgh and J. Davis (eds), *Trade Marks and Brands: An Interdisciplinary Critique*, Cambridge, UK:

Cambridge University Press, pp. 361–80.

Paus, M. and S. Reviron (2010), 'Crystallisation of Collective Action in the Emergence of a Geographical Indication System', Paper prepared for the 116th EAAE Seminar on Spatial Dynamics in Agrifood Systems: Implications for Sustainability and Consumer Welfare, Parma, Italy, 27–30 October.

Petit, M. and H. Ilbert (2009), 'Are Geographical Indications a Valid Property Right? Global Trends and Challenges', *Development Policy Review*, **27** (5), 503–28.

Pezzini, M. (2000), 'Rural Policy Lessons from OECD Countries', *Economic Review*, 3rd Quarter, 47–57.

Plaisant, M. and F. Jacq (1921), *Traité des noms et appellations d'origine*, Paris: Rousseau.

Pollack, L. (1962), 'Roquefort: An Example of Multiple Protection for a Designation of Regional Origin under the Lanham Act', *Trademark Reporter*, **52** (7), 755–67.

Profeta, A., R. Balling, V. Schoene and A. Wirsig (2009), 'The Protection of Origins for Agricultural Products and Foods in Europe: Status Quo, Problems and Policy Recommendations for the Green Book', *Journal of World Intellectual Property*, **12** (6), 622–48.

Profeta, A., R. Balling, V. Schoene and A. Wirsig (2010), 'Protected Geographical Indications and Designations of Origin: An Overview of the Status Quo and the Development of the Use of Regulation (EC) 510/06 in Europe, with Special Consideration of the German Situation', *Journal of International Food and Agribusiness Marketing*, **22**, 179–98.

Raith, R. (2009), 'Recent WTO and EC Jurisprudence Concerning the Protection of Geographical Indications', *International Trade Law and Regulation*, **4**, 119.

Rangnekar, D. (2009), 'Darjeeling Tea, India', in D. Giovannucci, T. Josling, W.A. Kerr, B. O'Connor and M.T. Yeung (eds), *Guide to Geographical Indications: Linking Products and Their Origins*, Geneva: International Trade Centre, pp. 153–63.

Rangnekar, D. (2012), 'Re-Making Place: The Social Construction of a Geographical Indication for *Feni*', *Environment and Planning*, **43** (9), 2043–59.

Raustiala, K. and Munzer, S.R. (2007), 'The Global Struggle over Geographic Indications', *European Journal of International Law*, **18** (2), 337–65.

Raynolds, L.T. and D.L. Murray (1998), 'Yes, We Have No Bananas: Re-Regulating Global and Regional Trade', *International Journal of Sociology of Agriculture and Food*, **7**, 7–44.

Renard, M.-C. (1999), 'The Interstices of Globalization: The Example of Fair Coffee', *Sociologia Ruralis*, **39** (4), 484–500.

Renaud, J.R. (2001), 'Can't Get There from Here: How NAFTA and GATT Have Reduced Protection for Geographical Trademarks', *Brooklyn Journal of International Law*, **26** (3), 1097–123.

Resinek, N. (2007), 'Geographical Indications and Trade Marks: Coexistence or "First in Time, First in Right" Principle', *European Intellectual Property Review*, **29** (11), 446–55.

Réviron, S. (2011), 'L'Etivaz Cheese', in E. Barham and B. Sylvander (eds), *Labels of Origin for Food: Local Development, Global Recognition*, Wallingford, UK: CAB International, pp. 167–71.

Réviron, S., J.-M. Chappuis and D. Barjolle (2004), 'Vertical Alliances for Origin Labelled Products: What Is the Most Relevant Economic Model of Analysis?', in G. van Huylenbroeck, W. Verbeke and L. Lauwers (eds), *Role of Institutions in Rural Policies and Agricultural Markets*, Amsterdam, the Netherlands: Elsevier, pp. 239–54.

Reviron, S. and A. Tseelei (2008), 'Which Collective Organizational Pattern for Geographical Indications Dominated by a Leading Processor? Similarities between Case Studies from Mongolia and Switzerland', XIIth EAAE Congress, Ghent, Belgium.

Rice, R.A. (2001), 'Noble Goals and Challenging Terrain: Organic and Fair Trade Coffee Movements in the Global Marketplace', *Journal of Agricultural and Environmental Ethics*, **14** (1), 39–66.

Ricolfi, M. (2009), 'Geographical Symbols in Intellectual Property Law: The Policy Options', in R.M. Hilty et al. (eds), *Festschrift für Ulrich Loewenheim zum 75. Geburtstag*, Munich, Germany: Verlag C.H. Beck, pp. 231–49.

Ritzert, M. (2009), 'Champagne Is from Champagne: An Economic Justification for Extending Trademark-Level Protection to Wine-Related Geographic Indicators', *American Intellectual Property Law Association Quarterly Journal*, **37** (2), 191–226.

Rochard, D. (2002), *La protection internationale des indications géographiques*, Paris: Presses Universitaires de France.

Saavedra-Rivano, N. (2012), 'Geographical Indications and International Trade', in L. Augustin-Jean, H. Ilbert and N. Saavedra-Rivano (eds), *Geographical Indications and International Agricultural Trade: The Challenge for Asia*, London: Palgrave Macmillan, pp. 9–33.

Sanders, A.K. (2005), 'Future Solutions for Protecting Geographical Indications Worldwide', in C. Heath and A.K. Sanders (eds), *New Frontiers of Intellectual Property Law: IP and Cultural Heritage, Geographical Indicators, Enforcement, Overprotection*, Oxford, UK: Hart, pp. 133–45.

Sanjuán-López, A.I. (2011), 'Cariñena Wine (Spain)', in E. Barham and B. Sylvander (eds), *Labels of Origin for Food: Local Development, Global Recognition*, Wallingford, UK: CAB International, pp. 172–6.

Santilli, J. (2012), *Agrobiodiversity and the Law: Regulating Genetic Resources, Food Security and Cultural Diversity*, Abingdon, UK: Earthscan.

Sautier, D. and C. Sarfati (2005), 'Indications géographiques en Afrique francophone: rapport 2004 des actions d'appui INAO-CIRAD auprès de l'OAPI'. Montpellier, France: French Agricultural Research Centre for International Development (CIRAD).

Schricker, G. (1983), 'Protection of Indications of Source, Appellations of Origin and Other Geographic Designations in the Federal Republic of Germany', *IIC*, **14** (3), 307–28.

Schroeder, K. (2009), 'Blue Mountain Coffee, Jamaica', in D. Giovannucci, T. Josling, W.A. Kerr, B. O'Connor and M.T. Yeung (eds), *Guide to Geographical Indications: Linking Products and Their Origins*, Geneva: International Trade Centre, pp. 170–77.

Schroeder, K. and A. Guevara (2009), 'Antigua Coffee, Guatemala', in D. Giovannucci, T. Josling, W.A. Kerr, B. O'Connor and M.T. Yeung (eds), *Guide to Geographical Indications: Linking Products and Their Origins*, Geneva: International Trade Centre, pp. 147–52.

Schüßler, L. (2009), 'Protecting "Single-Origin Coffee" within the Global Coffee Market: The Role of Geographical Indications and Trademarks', *Estey Centre Journal of International Law and Trade Policy*, **10** (1), 149–85.

Sciarra, A.F. and L. Gellman (2012), 'Geographical Indications: Why Traceability Systems Matter and How They Add to Brand Value', *Journal of Intellectual Property Law and Practice*, **7** (4), 264–70.

Segale, A., R. Zanoli and C. Sopranzetti (1998), 'The Determinants of "Typical" Production: An Empirical Investigation on Italian PDO and PGI products', in F. Arfini and C. Mora (eds), *Typical and Traditional Products: Rural Effects and Agro-Industrial Problems*, Proceedings of the 52nd Seminar of the European Association of Agricultural Economists, Parma, Università di Parma, 19–21 June 1997, pp. 365–83.

Sekimoto, S. and L. Augustin-Jean (2012), 'An Export Niche in the Philippines: The Commodification of a Specialty Rice in Ifugao Province', in L. Augustin-Jean, H. Ilbert and N. Saavedra-Rivano (eds), *Geographical Indications and International Agricultural Trade: The Challenge for Asia*, London: Palgrave Macmillan, pp. 181–203.

Shimura, K. (2010), 'How to Cut the Cheese: Homonymous Names of Registered Geographic Indicators of Foodstuffs in Regulation 510/2006', *Boston College International and Comparative Law Journal*, **33** (1), 129–52.

Simon, L.E. (1983), 'Appellations of Origin: The Continuing Controversy', *Northwestern Journal of International Law and Business*, **5**, 132–7.

Skuras, D. and E. Dimara (2004), 'Regional Image and the Consumption of Regionally Denominated Products', *Urban Studies*, **41** (4), 801–16.

Smith, A. (2010), 'Industries as Spaces for the Politics of Territory: The Case of Scotch Whisky', *Regional and Federal Studies*, **20** (3), 389–407.

Soam, S.K. (2005), 'Analysis of Prospective Geographical Indications of India', *Journal of World Intellectual Property*, **8** (5), 679–704.

Sonnino, R. (2007), 'Embeddedness in Action: Saffron and the Making of the Local in Southern Tuscany', *Agriculture and Human Values*, **24** (1), 61–74.

Srivastava, S.C. (2003), 'Geographical Indications and Legal Framework in India', *Economic and Political Weekly*, 4022–33.

Stenrűcken, T. and S. Jaenichen (2007), 'The Fair Trade Idea: Toward an Economics of Social Labels', *Journal of Consumer Policy*, **30**, 201–17.

Sylvander, B., D. Barjolle and F. Arfini (2000), 'The Socio-Economics of Origin Labeled Products in

Agri-Food Supply Chains: Spatial, Institutional and Co-ordination Aspects', Proceedings of 67th EAAE Conference, Le Mans, France, 28–30 October 1999, Versailles, France: INRA Editions.

Ten Kate, K. and S.A. Laird (1999), *The Commercial Use of Biodiversity: Access to Genetic Resources and Benefit-Sharing*, London: Earthscan.

Teuber, R. (2009), 'Café de Marcala: Honduras' GI Approach to Achieving Reputation in the Coffee Market', *Estey Centre Journal of International Law and Trade Policy*, **9** (1), 131–48.

Teuber, R. (2009), 'Producers' and Consumers' Expectations towards Geographical Indications: Empirical Evidence for Hessian Apple Wine', Paper presented for the 113th EAAE Seminar, A Resilient European Food Industry and Food Chain in a Challenging World, Chania, Crete, Greece, 3–6 September.

Thiedig, F. and B. Sylvander (2000), 'Welcome to the Club? An Economical Approach to Geographical Indications in the European Union', *Agrarwirtschaft*, **49** (12), 428–37.

Thienes, M. (1994), 'Tradition and Progress: Registration of Geographic Denominations of Origin', *British Food Journal*, **96** (2), 7–10.

Torres-Moreno, M., A. Tarrega, E. Torrescasana and C. Blanch (2012), 'Influence of Label Information on Dark Chocolate Acceptability', *Appetite*, **58** (2), 665–71.

Torson, M. (2005), 'Apples and Oranges: French and American Models of Geographic Indications Policies Demonstrate an International Lack of Consensus', *Trademark Reporter*, **95** (6), 1415–44.

Tregear, A., S. Kuznesof and A. Moxey (1998), 'Policy Initiatives for Regional Foods: Some Insights from Consumer Research', *Food Policy*, **23** (5), 383–94.

Treagar, A. and M. Ness (2011), 'Beacon Fell Traditional Lancashire Cheese (England)', in E. Barham and B. Sylvander (eds), *Labels of Origin for Food: Local Development, Global Recognition*, Wallingford, UK: CAB International, pp. 190–94.

Trubek, A. (2008), *The Taste of Place: A Cultural Journey into Terroir*, Berkeley, CA: University of California Press.

United Nations Industrial Development Organization (UNIDO) (2020), *Adding Value to Traditional Products of Regional Origin: A Guide to Creating a Quality Consortium*, Vienna, Austria: UNIDO.

Vakoufaris, H. (2010), 'The Impact of Ladotyri Mytilinis PDO Cheese on the Rural Development of Lesvos Island, Greece', *Local Environment*, **15** (1), 27–41.

Vandecandelaere, E., F. Arfini, G. Belletti and A. Marescotti (2009), *Linking People, Places and Products: A Guide for Promoting Quality Linked to Geographical Origin and Sustainable Geographical Indications*, Rome: Food and Agriculture Organization of the United Nations (FAO) and SINER-GI.

Van Ittersum, K., M.T.G. Meulenberg, H.C.M. van Trijp and M.J.J.M. Candel (2007), 'Consumers' Appreciation of Regional Certification Labels: A Pan-European Study', *Journal of Agricultural Economics*, **58** (1), 1–23.

Verbeke, W., V. Demey, W. Bosmans and J. Viaene (2005), 'Consumer versus Producer Expectations and Motivations Related to Superior Quality Meat: Qualitative Research Findings', *Journal of Food Products Marketing*, **11** (3), 27–41.

Vialard, A. (1999), 'Regulating Quality Wines in European and French Laws', *Northern Illinois University Law Review*, **19** (2), 235–53.

Vivez, J. (1943), *Traité des appellations d'origine*, Paris: R. Pichon et R. Durand-Auzias.

Voyce, M. (2007), 'Geographical Indications, the EU and Australia: A Case Study on "Government at a Distance" through Intellectual Property Rights', *Macquarie Law Journal*, **7**, 155–65.

Vroom-Cramer, B.M. (1997), 'PDOs and PGIs: Geographical Denominations Protected', *European Food Law Review*, **3**, 336–75.

Waggoner, J.M. (2008), 'Acquiring a European Taste for Geographical Indications', *Brooklyn Journal of International Law*, **33** (2), 569–96.

Waglé, S. (2007), 'Geographical Indications as Trade-Related Intellectual Property: Relevance and Implications for Human Development in Asia-Pacific', Discussion Paper, Colombo: UNDP Asia-Pacific Regional Centre.

Wang, X. and I. Kireeva (2007), 'Protection of Geographical Indications in China: Conflicts, Causes and Solutions', *Journal of World Intellectual Property*, **10** (2), 79–96.

Wattanapruttipaisan, T. (2009), 'Trademarks and Geographical Indications: Policy Issues and Options in

Trade Negotiations and Implementation', *Asian Development Review*, **26**, 166–205.

Waye, V. (2005), 'Assessing Multilateral vs. Bilateral Agreements and Geographic Indications through International Food and Wine', *Currents: International Trade Law Journal*, **14**, 56–68.

Wilkof, N. and S. Uzrad (2008), 'PDO/GI: In the Matter of the Appellation of Origin for "JAFFA"', *Journal of Intellectual Property Law and Practice*, **3** (1), 17–20.

Williams, R. and M. Penker (2009), 'Do Geographical Indications Promote Sustainable Rural Development?', *Jahrbuch der Österreichischen Gesellschaft für Agrarökonomie*, **18** (3), 147–56.

Williamson, M.E.J.B. (2012), 'Geographical Indications, Biodiversity and Traditional Knowledge: Obligations and Opportunities for the Kingdom of Saudi Arabia', *Arab Law Quarterly*, **26** (1), 99–119.

Winter, M. (2003), 'Embeddedness, the New Food Economy and Defensive Localism', *Journal of Rural Studies*, **19** (1), 23–32.

Xiaobing, W. and I. Kireeva (2007), 'Protection of Geographical Indications in China: Conflicts, Causes and Solutions', *Journal of World Intellectual Property*, **10** (2), 79–96.

Yeung, M.T. and W.A. Kerr (2008), *Increasing Protection for GIs at the WTO: Clawbacks, Greenfields and Monopoly Rents*, CATPRN Working Paper 2008-02, Canadian Agricultural Trade Policy Research Network (CATPRN).

Zago, A.M. (1999), 'Quality and Self-Regulation in Agricultural Markets: How Do Producer Organisations Make the Rules?', *European Review of Agricultural Economics*, **26** (2), 199–218.

Zahn, L.A. (2012), 'Australia Corked Its Champagne and So Should We: Enforcing Stricter Protection for Semi-Generic Wines in the United States?', *Transnational Law and Contemporary Problems*, **21** (2), 477–510.

Part I
GIs as Intellectual Property

The Wine Appellation as Territory in France and California

Warren Moran

Department of Geography, University of Auckland, Private Bag 92019, Auckland, New Zealand

FAX 64.9.3737-434, e-mail geog-wm@geog.aukuni.ac.nz.

Abstract. Conventional explanations of the distribution of winemaking regions emphasize the influence of edaphic and atmospheric environments of the vine. This paper argues that legislation that reflects the political power of the prestigious winemaking areas has had a major impact, especially in France. The appellation legislation of France, and the assumptions underlying it, are established. It is conceptualized as a form of territorialization devised to regulate and capture advantages to some of the participants in the industry. I analyze the influence of the French principles and assumptions in devising the European Community and California legislation. In particular, I consider the manner in which the underlying environmental determinism is used both to explain the distribution of prestigious wines and as criteria to establish wine regions. The distribution of vine varieties in France and California illustrates the tight control evident in France compared with the laissez-faire policies in California. Some evidence of converging patterns in the two territories is apparent.

Key Words: appellations, France, intellectual property, territoriality, wine.

THE regional distribution and legislative control of the wine industry pose problems of interpretation that are eminently geographic. Even the most casual perusal of any data on the geography of the species *Vitis vinifera* shows that despite its widespread distribution, both internationally and within nations, the major wine-producing areas are highly localized. Moreover, each variety of grape also has its own distinctive geographic pattern. That vines for making wine are distributed distinctively would be readily agreed by most geographers. It would be much more difficult to come to any agreement on the interpretation of these patterns. Geographers and viticulturalists have been quick to point to the influence of natural environmental influences on the global patterns of viticulture and winemaking (de Blij 1983; Unwin 1991; Winkler et al. 1974) while a few such as Dion (1959) have stressed the preeminence of cultural controls and the power structure of the industry. But the manner in which assumptions about natural environmental influences are used to assert and justify political and territorial control, and thereby influence the distribution of the industry, has received little attention.

In this paper I discuss the political organization of the wine industry and the legislation by which control is established and maintained. In particular, I use the concepts developed by geographers on territoriality to establish the nature of legislative control in the wine industry and to demonstrate its influence by relating it to the actual patterns of viticulture in France and California, two territories where the wine industries operate under quite different legal rules. Territoriality is one approach to understanding how political influence is exerted within an industry to maintain the economic dominance of the most powerful localities.

Territoriality, Economy, and the Law

The concept of territoriality receives little attention in the work of French geographers on the wine industry, even though control of the localities and regions where vines are grown developed in France and is still powerful there. Their explanations for the existence of special-

Annals of the Association of American Geographers, 83(4), 1993, pp. 694-717
© Copyright 1993 by Association of American Geographers
Published by Blackwell Publishers, 238 Main Street, Cambridge, MA 02142, and 108 Cowley Road, Oxford, OX4 1JF, UK.

ized wine-making regions emphasize the more conventional attributes of the regions where the vines are grown, such as natural environmental influences and elements of culture. Usually they confine their interpretation to one region (Huetz de Lemps, et al. 1977). In taking this approach, they are maintaining something of the Vidal de la Blache tradition of French regional geographers. Gadille's (1967) comprehensive work on Burgundy is an excellent example. She poses the eminently geographic question:

> We approach here the fundamental problems posed by the distinctive origin of the grand crus and of all quality viticulture: original physical determinism or careful and costly human creation, these are the two explanations that may be invoked in order to explain the location of the prestigious viticultures and the internal management of their crus (Gadille 1967, 23, author's translation).

By opposing the influence of attributes of the physical environment to human influences on the location and organization of the industry, Gadille's question is not capable of resolution, although in attempting to answer it, she reveals much about the Burgundian wine industry. Separating people from their natural environment means the real interactions between the two are neglected. Gadille exhaustively considers the association of geological, soil, and climate characteristics with the viticulture and winemaking of the region. The characteristics and evolution of cultural practices in the vineyard and cellar are treated similarly. She discusses both physical and human attributes, using the boundaries of the appellation system, but these appellation territories themselves are not incorporated into the explanation. The question of economic, political, or other control of territory is not considered as part of the explanation despite Burgundy having as detailed a territorial subdivision of space as any viticultural region. An overarching aim of this paper, therefore, is to explore how the physical and human attributes of territory as considered by Gadille and others are related to the definition and legitimacy of the French appellation system and its extension to the U.S. Territoriality as a concept must depend on the characteristics of geographic space as well as the boundaries that define that space.

Territoriality is addressed directly, and the term defined widely, in the work of Sack (1983,

1986). In his attempt to build a theory of the nature of territoriality, he defines it as "the attempt to affect, influence, or control actions and interactions (of people, things, and relationships) by asserting and attempting to enforce control over a geographic area" (Sack 1983, 55). It is this approach to territoriality that I adopt here. Sack identifies a set of essential attributes of territoriality. Influence and control over actions is achieved by both including and excluding actions from the territory. Territories vary in the comprehensiveness of the actions that they control and the intensity and degree to which they organize the actions within their domain. They are, thus, a major force in differentiating the isotropic space of classical rent theory. By restricting action and interaction, they give advantages to some areas and exclude other areas. Territories are also often explicitly hierarchical, and their effects are likely to be complex. They also have a strategic role in both classification and communication. Of special importance is the way in which territory is used to make it appear "as though the control of space controls cause and effect" (Sack 1983, 62). Sometimes they also serve to obfuscate the relationship between the attributes of the territory that they define, and the controller and the controlled.

Sack's discussion of territoriality effectively establishes its importance and some theoretical ideas about its operation. It is less successful in providing concrete examples of its universal importance in establishing the character and competitive advantage of pieces of territory. Sack's discussion has a certain remote quality. Territory is discussed almost separately from the people, politicians, organizations, and industries involved in making decisions about and promoting pieces of territory. To some extent, these deficiencies are offset by the literature on territoriality, which takes a more overtly political point of view. From the 1970s, a considerable empirical and theoretical literature has developed around the manner in which local and other governments have differentiated space, and provided differential opportunities for their citizens and industries, by their taxation and other policies (Bennett 1980; Cox 1979; Cox and McCarthy 1982; Dear 1981; Soja 1971, 1974). But territoriality has a much more general applicability than that asserted by official political organizations. The attributes of territory are constantly used by individuals and organizations to attempt to establish the advantages of places. In particular, various industrial organizations make use of territory to promote their own ends.

Sack (1983, 72) suggests two avenues of research to unravel the complexities of the influence of territoriality. Small, informal groups of people could be investigated to establish the effect of one or two of the tendencies of territoriality, such as enforcement of access or classification of territory. Alternatively, complex organizations may be investigated in order to observe how the tendencies of territoriality work together at particular scales. This paper adopts the latter approach, narrowed to the consideration of a single industry in an attempt to provide concrete evidence of the way in which territoriality is asserted. Four general aspects of territoriality receive particular attention. Control of territory must sometimes depend on the characteristics of the territory that is being controlled. In the case of a particular industry, these characteristics need to be established. A second theme flows from this. Are the arguments legitimate that are used about the characteristics (or attributes) of territory and their influence on the industry? This perspective seems an appropriate way of examining Sack's assertion about obfuscating the reasons for control. Third, by what procedures is the control over territory established? In many cases, these procedures may be informal but, in the case of a single industry with large numbers of agents, formal procedures are likely. Fourth, which organizations are responsible for legitimizing territorial control and how do they relate to legislation and government territorial control?

In this paper, I investigate the influence of territoriality on one industry—winemaking in France and California—using Sack's broad definition of territoriality. The type of territorial regulation of space, referred to here as *sectorial* territorialization, has received little attention in the literature but is a similarly powerful force to the impact of government territorial units in differentiating place. Under this heading of sectorial territorialization are those legal rules and legislation that regulate the practice of specific industries within regional, and often hierarchical, boundaries. By restricting analysis to one industry, it should be possible to link the nature of territorial control to the practices and spatial

distribution of one activity and thus begin to establish the interaction between territorial and nonterritorial control on the industry. Almost every country has examples of government rules and regulations that apply to one or a group of industries and that are based on regional boundaries. The boundaries may coincide with administrative territories, as they usually do with the wine appellation in France, but the legislation has a quite different purpose and result from that regulating the regional and local state. Sack claims that by neglecting territoriality, spatial analysis has left unexamined many of the geographic forces molding human spatial organization. Consideration of the influences of territoriality in a highly regulated industry should reveal connections between territorial control and common explanations for the distribution of the industry, including characteristics such as the natural environment.

The wine industry, especially as it is practiced and organized in France, has several advantages for research on this theme. It is territorially organized and influence is legitimized through the legislation that established the Institut National des Appellations d'Origines (INAO), which has jurisdiction at a variety of scales. The territorial approach of the French wine industry has been emulated in many other countries and jurisdictions, including the U.S., Australia, and New Zealand, as well as largely being adopted by the European Community both internally and in relation to imports from third countries (INAO 1987; Audier 1991). Comparison of France, where the industry is highly regulated, to California, which until recently has had very limited regulation, should make apparent the influence of territorial control on some basic viticultural attributes such as varieties of grapes.

The paper will first examine the international and national laws governing the use of geographic names and the nature of territoriality in the French and European wine industries at the national and regional scales. Examples come mainly from one region of France, Burgundy. Second, the assumptions that underlie the French appellation laws, especially the relationships between yield of grapes and the quality of wine, are scrutinized, and alternative interpretations for the appellation laws are discussed. Transference of the assumptions and interpretation of the French laws to the U.S., and comparison between the spatial distribution of grape varieties in France and California, form the third major theme.

The Law and Indications of Geographic Source

In international law on the vine, the distinction is increasingly being made between "geographic indications" (sometimes referred to, when applied to the whole of a country, as geographic provenance) and *appellations d'origine* (Audier 1991; Bodenhausen 1968; GATT 1992; Niederbacher 1988). Geographic indications are simply the attestation that the grapes from which the wine is made originate from a particular region, locality, or field. A recent definition of recognized geographic indications by the Office International de la Vigne et du Vin is "the name of the country, the region, or the place used in the designation of a product originating from this country region or place and recognized by the competent authorities of the country concerned" (OIV 1991). In comparison, appellations have a series of other agreed restrictions, such as authorized varieties of grapes, yields of grapes or wine per hectare, viticultural methods, and sometimes winemaking techniques to which the producers of each appellation must adhere if they are to use authorized place names. Wine is guaranteed to originate from this appellation, but in addition is guaranteed to be produced by the set of rules agreed to and implemented by the growers. The French have the most comprehensive and detailed set of regulations about their appellations.

These indications of geographic source and appellations of origin have legal backing at three scales. In ascending order, these are legislation applying to a single nation, regional agreements for groups of countries such as the European Community, and international agreements such as the Paris Convention or the General Agreement on Tariffs and Trade (GATT) (Audier 1991; Moran 1993). In addition, bilateral agreements between two nations (or between a nation and another legal entity such as the European Community) are sometimes written. These bilateral agreements bind the two parties to respect each other's indications of geographic source.

Within nations, specific legislation has been

written to protect local and regional place names. In many countries, such legislation comes under the control of the Ministry of Agriculture, although in the U.S., it is administered by the Bureau of Alcohol, Tobacco, and Firearms (ATF). By far the most comprehensively developed national system is the French, which was formalized into law in 1935. Before the formation of the European Community, most other European wine-producing countries also had legislation that regulated the use of geographic origins on their wines. Germany's system remains very detailed and complicated. Nations in other parts of the world have more recently adopted laws to formalize and protect their indications of geographic source. The U.S. regulations on viticultural areas came into force in 1978, while in Australia and New Zealand, they are currently being developed.

The European Economic Community is the best example of a regional agreement on wine. It was almost inevitable that the Community should adopt a common set of rules for their wine industries in order to minimize conflict in a major European industry with a history of periodic overproduction and where national attitudes to the industry were distinctive. Their comprehensive sets of Council Regulations are in two documents: Regulation (EEC) No. 823/87 for quality wines and Regulation (EEC) No. 822/87 for other wines. Although these regulations allow EC countries some individuality in their wine industries, they have an underlying philosophy that is strongly influenced by the French example and encourages countries to adopt a common set of conditions. The regulations for quality wine in the EC involve much more than identification of geographic source. They clearly come within the definition of *appellations d'origine*, because they include demarcation of the area of production, vine varieties to be grown, cultivation methods, wine-making methods, minimum natural alcoholic strength by volume, and yield per hectare. Article 2 of EEC Regulation No. 823/87 specifies the special provisions for quality wines produced in specified regions which shall take "into account the traditional conditions of production insofar as these are not such as to prejudice the policy of encouraging quality production and the creation of a single market." The regulations, like many expressions of European Community agricultural policy, recognize the need for market forces but, at the same time, surround the appellation system with restrictions that limit the operation of the free market.

International agreements and accords on indications of geographic source predate the European Community's regulations. From the late nineteenth century, various international meetings have resulted in agreements over what was called at the time industrial property (Audier 1991). Their general aim was to devise sets of principles on the protection of what would now be referred to as intellectual property. Place names, particularly as they relate to wines, were included in these discussions. Two of the most important accords, the Madrid agreement of 1891 and the Paris Convention of 1883, have been amended a number of times and are still in force. They bind signatories to observe the conventions, but the strength of the accords depends on their wording. In the case of names of wine regions, the Paris Convention with 200 signatories, including the U.S. and Canada, appears to be the most influential, but its effectiveness is limited in law because it is based on the use of false indications of geographic source. These are difficult to prove in law (INAO 1987). The effect of other international agreements is weakened by having many fewer signatories and being dominated by European nations.

Intellectual property, including geographic indications, is one of the main items of discussion in the Uruguay Round of the GATT. If the final draft (January 1992) of the GATT agreement is accepted, geographic indications will have much stronger international protection, including the establishment of a register of their place names. Such a strong statement on geographic indications in the major international agreement on trade is the culmination of an extended period of international discussion and diplomacy by European nations, especially France, to have international acceptance of their philosophy, which sees wine as an expression of the geographic individuality of places.

The French Wine Appellation as Territory

Definition of territory is central to the French wine appellation. Its primary aim is to permit the association of a particular wine with the territory from which it originates. The size of the defined area varies from a region to a group of communes, to a single commune, to a single field. There is no doubt, therefore, that the French wine appellations are a form of control over territory. Moreover, the resolution at which they operate is as detailed as any rural territorial legislation in the developed world. Formal classification, which is recorded on the cadastra, is down to the field level, frequently less than one hectare, but the commune is one fundamental unit and scale of classification. The more than 36,000 communes of France are, of course, political units of local government, but, in the major wine-making regions, their very existence and name cannot be separated from the production that is practiced within their territory.

The unity of political identity and production is apparent in all the regions making wine that are eligible for an appellation, where the name of the commune is often synonymous with the name of the wine. The association is marked in Burgundy, notably in the Côtes de Beaune and Côtes de Nuits, where the number of hyphenated village and commune names results from villages adding the name of their most illustrious vineyard: Chambertin in Gevrey-Chambertin, St. Georges in Nuits-St. Georges, Corton in Aloxe-Corton, and Montrachet in both Chassagne-Montrachet and Puligny-Montrachet, where the vineyard actually straddles the boundary of the two communes (Richard 1978; Landrieu-Lussigny 1983). Place names and production are thus inseparable.

This identification of place names with territory begins at a more detailed scale than the commune. Throughout France, but again at very fine resolution in Burgundy, fields are often named after attributes of their sites. Landrieu-Lussigny (1983) has traced the origins of more than 1000 of these *lieux-dits* in Burgundy (literally translated as named places but more colloquially as simply places) and has classified them into three main groups. Most *lieux-dits* take their name from the physical characteristics of their site—relief, the nature of the soils, climate, or vegetation. Others take their name from human endeavor to raise plants and animals—the agrarian structure of the area—while those in the third and smallest group are named after former occupations that were important in the area, feudal institutions, or church properties. The strong tendency to associate vineyard names with physical environments is clear from both the synonyms used for the *lieux-dits* and from more general descriptors—words such as *climats* and *terroir*. The latter is literally translated as soils by Harrap, although the essence of the French word includes aspects of the human as well as physical environment (Unwin 1991).

The Hierarchy of Appellations

French wine appellations are strongly hierarchical. Although the number of steps in the hierarchy varies from region to region, the notion of a sequence from grand cru at the top through premier cru to village (communal) to regional or generic appellations (e.g. Burgundy or Bordeaux) is represented in both Bordeaux and Burgundy. In Burgundy the Chablis appellation follows the sequence of Grand Cru Chablis (to which seven vineyards have the right), to Premier Cru Chablis, to Chablis, to Petit Chablis (Hanson 1982). Vineyards within the boundary of the appellation, but without right to any of these steps in the hierarchy, are eligible for one of the generic appellations such as the name Burgundy itself. Even with a generic appellation, only those parts of their land surface are eligible that are classified by the INAO as suitable to make wines of satisfactory standard. In general, the more specific the appellation, the higher the price of the wine.

The area of vineyards classified in this sequence is pyramid-like in shape. Less than five percent of French vineyards, with a right to an appellation, are classified as grand crus and each level lower in the hierarchy has a larger area than that above it. The total area in vineyards with no right to an appellation is about 55 percent of the total area in vines in France. These are the areas of bulk wine production, mainly in the south of France. In the last twenty years, an increasingly large area here has been granted appellations as parts of the Midi (south of France) upgrade the quality of their vineyard management and winemaking. In the last ten years, INAO has granted appellation status to much larger areas of France until by 1991, 45 percent of the 909,437 ha of vines had appellation status compared to less than 25 percent in 1981 (INAO 1991). This change has occurred as much of the viticultural areas of the Rhone valley and the Midi have planted better varieties and applied to INAO for the status of

Vin Delimité de Qualité Superieur (VDQS), often a step on the way towards appellation status or appellation. Established regions of large production such as Bordeaux and the *département* of Gironde have also had the proportion of their vines under appellation increased. This increased area in vines classified in appellations has coincided with the European Community schemes to pull out (in their terms, "grub up") grapes of lower quality and not allow them to be replanted in areas deemed suitable to produce only *vins de consommation courante* (for every-day consumption), thereby reducing the overproduction of grape wine in the Community. Thus the total area in vines has been dropping quite rapidly, while the area in appellations has been increasing.

Nature and Organization of Territorial Control

The French grape growing and winemaking industry is regulated to an extent that few farmers of other products in other countries would contemplate. At the hub of the control are the Appellations d'Origines Contrôlées organized by the Institut National des Appellations (INAO) in Paris, which also has offices in each of the main grape-producing regions. Some representatives are elected by members of the industry and others are appointed by the government. It is administered by the Ministry of Agriculture and Fisheries of the central government. Although classifications of winemaking regions existed much earlier, the appellations are a product of this century, with effective control in Champagne and Chateauneuf-du-Pape from the 1920s and the comprehensive French law in 1935 (INAO 1985). Since the late nineteenth century, attempts had been made to regulate French wine production, but these had limited success until the producers themselves had a strong role in the system. The French appellation laws are highly distinctive in that the government is not permitted to modify the proposals of the national committee of INAO. It can reject proposals and send them back for review, but the precise form of each proposal is the responsibility of INAO itself. Day-to-day operation of the appellations is controlled by regional offices of INAO, but the local wine *syndicats* (unions) also have a strong hand in the system (INAO 1985).

Each commune has its own *syndicat* of *vignerons,* represented by their elected chairperson. This group attests to the acceptable quality and typicity of the wines in their appellations for each vintage. They also bring forward proposals on applications for modifications to appellations in their commune and generally take responsibility for developing and expressing local policy. Without the *syndicats'* agreement, the INAO can do very little. These *syndicats* are linked to other organizations in the wine industry, such as the *negotiants,* through interprofessional organizations in each region. The appellation system, therefore, is underpinned by a complicated network of organizations which represent different groups in the industry but which are organized to ensure communication among these different groups. The industry is supported by a highly professional bureaucracy. The regional offices of INAO support, advise, and make final decisions on what goes forward to the national committee, but they act on the research and requests of the grape growers and winemakers themselves. INAO goes to considerable trouble to ensure that all proposals are fully discussed and, in this sense, acts as a type of professional referee for the members of the industry.

Three main aspects of production are controlled—the varieties of grapes to be grown, cultural practices in the vineyard, and yields of grapes or wine. In most regional appellations, the number of authorized varieties is fewer than five, and individual varieties are restricted as to the appellation in which they may be used. The highest number permitted in France is 17 in the appellation Chateaneuf-du-Pape, but this is unusual. In some regions such as Burgundy, a single variety dominates wine production—Pinot Noir, in the case of red wine, and Chardonnay in the case of white. One other red variety is authorized in Burgundy (Gamay), but it is highly localized regionally, being largely restricted to the Beaujolais region. Gamay may also be grown in other communes of the Côte de Beaune and Côte de Nuits as long it is blended with at least one-third of Pinot Noir when the wine has the right to the appellation "Bourgogne Passetoutgrains." The flexibility of the regulation for these prestigious areas helps to provide markets for all grapes grown in the region. Under EC regulations, the use of varietal names and the permitted areas for varieties are being tightened, with two

groups of varieties being recognized: those recommended and those authorized. The French, with the longest and most comprehensive experience of the application of such regulation, have again played a major role in devising these community regulations.

Specifying the varieties that the viticulturalist is permitted to grow in any appellation means that innovation in varieties is prohibited in many vineyard regions of France, notably the most successful ones. The argument commonly advanced is that the viticulturalists have had several centuries to observe, cultivate, and select and that the quality of the premium wines attests to their success. Similar arguments are advanced over winemaking techniques, although these are less regulated. The phylloxera crisis of the late nineteenth century interfered with the distribution of traditional varieties but, not surprisingly, most regions producing quality wine returned to grafted versions of the traditional varieties which had long been the basis of their industry. They have thus continued to produce from varieties that became dominant at a time when growers had access to only a limited number of the set of possible varieties that they could have planted. An opportunity to reassess a wider range of grape varieties was not taken, partly because vignerons wanted to get back into production as quickly as possible and naturally continued with the varieties that they knew and which were readily available to them in their own region.

The appellation laws of France also control the cultural practices in the vineyard. They go as far as specifying the spacing of the vines and the methods of trellising and pruning, and prohibit irrigation. These regulations about cultural practices are an extension of the experience argument. Such practices have been developed after long periods of growing grapes in particular environments, and the appellation laws decree that they should not be modified lightly. The final test of the validity of such rules is the quality of the wine. Given the high international esteem of French wine, such an argument must be given credence. But the rules have also been developed from the perspective of the grands cru, where moisture stress is seldom a problem. Outside France very fine wines have been produced using irrigation, provided that it is carefully monitored and used in conjunction with appropriate vineyard techniques. There is no evidence to suggest that fine wine cannot be produced under irrigation in those parts of France where moisture stress is a problem. In the French experience, irrigation has been associated with production of bulk wines of low quality, and the assumption is made that these two are necessarily associated.

Whereas most systems of agricultural production attempt to produce the largest quantity possible, the wine appellation places strict limits on yield per unit area. This aspect of the territorial control is discussed in detail below. The control of action extends to the practices of industrial production—the winemaking itself. Minimum alcohol content of the wine produced in each appellation is also specified. The wine appellation is, on the surface, less comprehensive than many other types of territoriality because it directly controls only viticulture and winemaking. But it is among the most intensive types of territoriality in the degree of its control, and its effects also extend much further than the primary reason for their existence.

The Appellation as Explanation

The existence of the wine appellation in France has provided an accessible path to explanation for commentators on the industry who are seeking reasons for the high quality of the best French wines. The attributes of the territory defined by the appellation, especially the physical attributes, are generously and often uncritically advanced as explanation. The authoritative wine books are replete with such assertions. Some examples from two of the best-known books that discuss Burgundy and especially the Côte de Beaune and Côte de Nuits illustrate the point.

Marl by itself would be too rich a soil for the highest quality wine, but in combination with the silt and scree washed down from the hard limestone higher up is perfect (Johnson 1971, 54).

The best vineyards of the Côtes face due east, or even a shade north of east in places; it is the morning sun they want, to warm the ground gradually all day and let it cool gently in the evening without a sudden lowering of temperature at sunset. (Johnson 1971, 55).

The vines face south-east; from this position they receive the sunshine from early morning to early evening, without the grapes risking being scorched by any great heat from the sun's rays. (Chidley 1984, 4).

This whole area leads down into the River Saône, which in prehistoric times was a vast inland lake—worth remembering, because the fossils of such enrich the soil, especially the vines. (Chidley 1984, 5).

Le Corton is a long, thin strip of vineyard beneath the Bois de Corton where the northern end will enjoy early sunshine and the southern end will see much more of the late, and possibly, drier hours of sunshine (Chidley 1984, 88).

Not surprisingly there are contradictions in this set of quotations because all are popular assertions based on slim or nonexistent scientific evidence. The wine appellations exist, the wines produced in them are of high quality, so there must be an explanation. The most simple to assert, and one which receives widespread approbation from the public at large because of the latent environmental determinism in many of us, is the physical environment.

In all wine regions, the physical environmental attributes of the defined territory of the appellation have been liberally and uncritically transferred to the wine made there. They are a convenient means of enhancing the regional identity. That the physical environment influences the vine and its production is incontestable. The vine has its roots in the soil and leaves and fruit in the atmosphere. Its juice, musts, and wine inevitably reflect these conditions. But before the physical environment can be envoked reliably as explanation, the causal chain connecting it to quality needs to be established as well as the processes by which characteristics of the wine may be attributed to the territory where it is made.

The causal chain that is used is the direct one connecting the environment with the final product—the wine (Fig. 1). Such assertions are examples of an environmental deterministic philosophy using the relatively weak spatial association mode of explanation (Harvey 1969).

The general approach of the Institut Nationale des Appellations d'Origines encourages a similarly coarse use of the environmental characteristics of the appellation as a form of explanation. The attitude is clearest in their approach to the assessment of new areas that have applied for status (INAO 1985). The quality of the wine is not necessarily the main criterion in defining the new territory. This is, of course, assessed, but the actual boundaries of the appellation are set on the basis of a range of

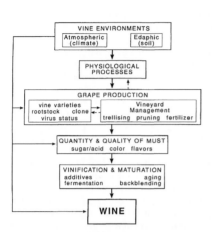

Figure 1. Conceptual diagram of the variables relating vine edaphic and atmospheric environments to the characteristics of wine.

physical environmental variables that are assumed to be the explanation for the characteristics of the wine. The Institut leaves itself plenty of room for maneuver in the criteria that are used in this assessment. Physical homogeneity in soils or even geology is sometimes the unifying factor in the definition of an appellation. At other times, physical heterogeneity is invoked (INAO 1985, 71).

It is important to realize that this method of defining new appellations did not exist until the INAO was created by legislation in 1935. Once it existed, a method had to be found to legitimize the appellations, and it was probably too difficult and controversial to actually classify the wines themselves. Nineteenth-century classifications were on the basis of the wines produced from different *lieux-dits* rather than the assumed relations between the environments and their wines (Pitiot and Poupon 1985). For instance, when the Comité d'Agriculture de Beaune decided in 1860 to produce a map of the Côte d'Or vineyards, the four-level hierarchy that they chose was *Tête de Cuvée, Premier, Deuxième, Troisième* (best of the vintage, first, second, third). The *vignerons* of the Côte de Beaune and the Côte de Nuits were in-

volved in the classification, although those of the Côte de Nuits were hostile towards it, probably because it originated from Beaune (Pitiot and Poupon 1985, 12). But this classification was definitely on the basis of the wines produced from different pieces of land rather than assumed relationships with environment. By this data, viticulture had been established in the Côte d'Or for at least six centuries, and a huge amount of empirical knowledge had developed on those *lieux-dits* that produced the best wines (Dion 1959). Of especial importance were the detailed records on wine quality from different parcels of land kept by the Cistercian monks, who were responsible for the establishment of quality viticulture in much of the Côte d'Or.

The Quantity-Quality Assumptions

The appellation laws themselves make even more specific environmental assumptions that deserve scrutiny. Quality wines, it is contended, cannot be produced if the yield of grapes is too high. Accordingly, accompanying each appellation is a maximum quantity in hectoliters per hectare that is permitted to be produced. The figure is as low as 30 hectoliters per hectare. Since 1974, *vignerons* have been permitted to have this quantity increased after an assessment by a regional committee of the INAO near the time of the vintage.

Most commentators on the French wine industry accept without question the assumed association of quality with low quantity. Lichine (1974, 72) states it unequivocally: "Since quality is inversely proportional to quantity the amount of permissible harvest is specified." Experimental evidence does not support such definite assertions. In a series of experiments at the University of California, Davis from the 1950s, Sinton et al. (1978) and others have demonstrated that the yield of grapes can vary over a very considerable range without discernible effect on the quality of the wine. Researchers at UC-Davis have claimed that by clonal and cultivar selection, they have increased the yield of Chardonnay vines from less than two to an average of more than 15 tons per hectare with no loss of quality (Sinton et al. 1978). Even if there is a relation between quantity and quality, it may well be that intervening variables, that are amenable to manipulation, are the real control. This is the argument advanced in a series of innovative papers by Smart (1985a,b, 1987) and one of the themes in a series of papers by Kliewer (1968, 1971, 1972, 1977). Smart identifies three scales at which the atmospheric environment may be usefully analyzed for its impact on the vine. In his terms, the macroscale is the regional atmospheric environment, the mesoscale the environment of the whole vineyard, and the microscale the immediate environment of the row where the vine is situated. The work of Smart and Kliewer is concerned with identifying the influence of this microatmospheric environment on the nature and quality of the grapes and wine produced. It has implications for the quality-quantity assumptions that are at the heart of the appellation laws.

According to Smart, the intervening variable in the quality-quantity debate may well be the degree of shading of interior leaves, which is strongly influenced by the microclimate of the vine, as he defines it. Vigorous vines, as are those in most countries where the vines are widely spaced, will have more leaves. A wider hedge of leaves in the row may not be able to ripen the grapes to their optimum. In the traditional grapegrowing areas of Bordeaux and Burgundy, the narrow spacing of rows (1 meter) and the close spacing of vines within the row (often <1 meter) restrict the vigor of the vines. The outcome is a narrow hedge of vines and few interior leaves that are shaded, so that maximum use is made of the available solar energy in photosynthesis. Moreover, the rows are less than a meter high. This low size, combined with the rows running north-south (the common practice) provides little shading of one row by another. Furthermore, the shape of the hedges of the Burgundian trellises is controlled in both height and width by several trimmings during the growing season.

Trellising systems for grape vines in cool climates should permit the vine to intercept the maximum amount of incoming solar radiation. Simulation studies have demonstrated that to achieve this in hedge-like trellises, the rows should run north-south and that the minimum ratio of height of trellis to row spacing should be 1:1 in order to avoid shading (Smart 1987). In countries such as Australia, New Zealand,

and the U.S., where the spacing of rows has been driven by the desire to use large machines not developed specifically for viticulture, rows are frequently spaced more widely than is necessary. To make maximum use of available solar radiation for photosynthesis and still use standard machines, the trellises could be higher. One suggested solution for countries in which the rows are widely spaced, for ease of mechanization, is to train the vines in a double-storied higher trellis about 2 meters high. By separating the two sets of foliage, it is possible to achieve a narrower hedge, less shading, and, therefore, effective utilization of total leaf area. Only the outline of Smart's argument is presented here. The original papers contain detailed experimental evidence from a variety of countries which support the contentions. Various trellising systems have been developed that enable increased yields together with high quality of the mature grapes.

The effect of vine vigor and shading may go a long way towards explaining the apparent contradiction between the strongly held views in France and the experimental evidence from the UC-Davis. If vines are vigorous and leaf shading common, it will be difficult for the vine to ripen its fruit to the optimal acid-sugar ratio to produce premium wines. In regions of France such as Burgundy, an appropriate relationship between soil fertility, vine spacing, vine vigor, leaf area and exposure, and yield of grapes has been discovered through centuries of trial and error and informal experimentation. If some of these variables are changed, it may be quite possible to achieve higher yields at similar quality. In the Californian experiments, the higher levels of solar energy compared with the main premium wine areas of France is probably the reason for being able to maintain quality with higher yields.

Certainly, yields have increased through time in many of the French appellations, partly as a result of clonal selection and more healthy vines, although French *vignerons* remain wary of yields that are too high (Moran 1988). The hierarchical nature of appellation law in relation to yield is most effectively illustrated by the laws as they existed until 1974 (INAO 1985). Special regulations existed to dispose of excess production above the yield approved in the appellation laws. If, for instance, 50 hectoliters of wine were produced in a premier cru appellation which permitted only 35 hectoliters, it was possible to market the excess 15 hecto-liters of wine under a lesser appellation—the commune or regional appellation, for example. The wine under the different labels was exactly the same. This aspect of the appellation laws was modified in 1974 because it led to a second, verbally transmitted market for the wines marketed under a lower label but identical to a higher appellation. The practice also undermined the quantity-quality argument that is one basis of the law.

An Alternative Interpretation of the Appellation Laws

Superficially, the wine appellation is relatively uncontentious. For many products, it is considered the consumer's right to know the origin of the product being consumed and the ingredients that it contains. But by tying this production to particular parcels of land, and by recognizing a hierarchy of appellations, the laws introduce a range of other economic effects. Some of the subsidiary, or perhaps even primary, effects of the appellations are evident in their origins. The first steps towards close regulation of the industry occurred after the phylloxera crisis of the late nineteenth century (Bienaymé 1988). As the industry struggled to re-establish vineyards on grafted rootstock, some growers and merchants took advantage of the circumstances by marketing wine under false labels. Wine originating from the Midi was marketed as coming from Bordeaux or Burgundy. The original 1905 regulations were an attempt to control these practices and to protect the regions with an established reputation.

Similarly, the comprehensive law of 1935 emerged during the Depression, at a time when cellars were full from at least two vintages from which little had been sold. Moreover, the wine industry was continuing to face difficulties of overproduction, and producers and marketers had little confidence in the limitations that had been placed on the industry. The 1935 law separated the wine industry of France into two parts, established a structure to administer the appellations, and, although since modified in small ways, remains, in essence, unchanged (INAO 1985). The protection of the existing regions with the reputation

for producing high-quality wines was again at the heart of the legislation.

A strong clue to economic interpretations of the appellations is apparent from the discussions at the time they were formulated (Audier 1991). Baron Le Roy, the strong voice behind the Chateauneuf-du-Pape law, argued strongly for a *politique de qualité* (policy and politics of quality). The region did not have the reputation for premium wine of regions such as Bordeaux and Burgundy and could not be strongly distinguished environmentally from similar parts of the Rhone valley. Establishment of a strong and enduring regional identity was essential if the wines were to sell at the best price on the international market. The appellation laws were one means of achieving this, at the same time ensuring that the best accepted practices of the time were employed in the vineyard and cellar. The international recognition of the name Chateauneuf-du-Pape signifies the success of the strategy.

By restricting the yield of grapes and limiting the production of any wine to a particular area, the appellation laws act as a type of supply control. If this is the only region or locality in which a wine of this type is made, and if the yield is restricted, the price is likely to be higher. The appellation laws establish a type of monopoly rent for those regions that receive the seal of approval (Harvey 1982). The effect of the appellation laws on the rent, value, and competition for land is evident in the inverse relationship between the size of appellations and the price of their wine. Grand cru appellations, especially those, such as Le Montrachet or Chambertin in Burgundy, which are very small, receive the highest prices for their wines and the rent that this yields is capitalized into the value of their vineyards. The general nature of the relationship in Burgundy has been effectively demonstrated by Gadille (1967).

The rent process is circular and self-sustaining over extended periods. Those areas with the highest rents per unit area are able to maintain the best vineyard and winemaking practices. Firms and professional organizations in the elite appellations have the resources to mount comprehensive programs in advertising and public relations to maintain their image and reputation. The laws of the appellations can also be defended in costly international legal battles as has been the case with the name Champagne in the last decade (Audier 1991).

The publicity of the court cases enhances the territorial exclusivity of the appellation and is itself valuable advertising. In the wine industry, of course, much of the publicity for particular appellations is done informally by the wine drinking, writing, and reading public.

Moreover, the control also has a major impact outside the territory regulated by the appellation. The conventional interpretation of the French appellations emphasizes their role as a system of protection for both the consumer and the wine producer. Virtually every serious wine book has a section that takes this point of view (Chidgey 1984; Lichine 1967; Marrison 1973; Hanson 1982; Pitiot and Poupon 1985). Very few such authors consider the political ideology of the appellations and their social and economic impact both within France and internationally. Chidgey expresses a mild criticism (p. 139), and Hanson is more outspoken about the former Chablis appellation, which has long been the butt of vitriolic jokes from some other parts of France.

In sharp contrast is the interpretation of the origins of the localization of French viticulture in the extensive work of Dion (1959), most comprehensively expressed in his *Histoire de la Vigne et du Vin des Origines aux XIX Siècle*. Using historical evidence, he demonstrates that in the long term, the location of the prestigious winemaking areas of France have changed considerably through time, partly as a result of the regional location of political power. For instance, the patronage of the Dukes of Burgundy was extremely important in establishing the reputation of the area and in assuring that its wine was well known among influential buyers. At times in the past, vineyards in the vicinity of Paris were more esteemed than those of Chablis, Montbazillac more highly prized than Sauterne. Dion's (1959) interpretation presents viticulture and winemaking as an integrated agricultural system by attempting to understand the evolution of the human use of the natural environment. Vines have been planted in France for more than 2000 years, and several of the major vineyard regions have been growing grapes for more than a millennium (Dion 1959). Experience and informal experimental evidence on appropriate practices for particular regions has accumulated during this time. Specialized agricultural regions where many producers are engaged in the same activity over a long period have high

probabilities of producing innovations in agricultural practices, processing techniques, and trading methods (Moran and Nason 1981). Through trial and error, successful innovations are adopted and diffused so that regional comparative advantage is enhanced. Such a process is, however, one of adaptation to the environment in which viticulture is being practiced, rather than being incontrovertible evidence that the natural environment is superior in these places. In viticulture, the main arenas in which informal refinement of techniques occurs are varietal and clonal selection, trellising systems, pruning, and other plant-management techniques. These develop at particular times and may even provide a hindrance to later innovation. The appellation laws themselves can be viewed as a legislative and institutional innovation similar in kind to those more mundane production practices.

It is artificial to separate the natural and human components of an agrarian system in the manner of Gadille (1967) when hypothesizing the origins of the prestigious winemaking regions of France. A more appropriate question is, "By what methods have the people of this locality harnessed their natural environment to make fine wines?" The components of an agrarian system are developed through trial and error as well as conscious experimentation to form an integrated system which includes the cultural practices of growing crops and producing livestock. Once a socially and economically successful system is established, its major components are not modified lightly. Such is the case with viticultural practices in Burgundy. The major components of the system have been remarkably constant for long periods, as they have been in many of the prestigious wine regions of France. The extent of the French and Burgundian attachment to established viticultural practices is evident in the persistent efforts over a period of more than thirty years to develop a tractor suited to the existing configuration of the vineyards (Chapuis 1980). Narrow row spacing and restricted headlands at the end of rows made it impossible to use conventional tractors. Burgundian efforts to mechanize vineyard procedures without changing their traditional methods of growing grapes demonstrates two important aspects of the evolution of specialized agricultural regions: the interdependence of elements in an agrarian system and the importance of human agency as intermediary to the physical environment.

U.S. Appellations

The international importance and persistence of the environmental determinism inherent in some interpretations of the French wine appellations is apparent in their uncritical transference into the U.S. legislation on place names in relation to wine (Hutchison and Gay 1981; McCarthy 1980; Lee 1992). Since 1978 the U.S. wine industry has been establishing its own system of wine appellations. They are much less restrictive, being geographic indications rather than *appellations d'origine* as defined in the international agreements; only names of producing areas will be registered. From the 1983 vintage, names of viticultural areas, other than counties and states, have not been permitted on labels unless they have been approved by the ATF.

The U.S. regulations had two main origins. Rules about the use of regional indices were vague and difficult to enforce prior to the establishment of the viticultural areas (Lee 1992). Among these rules was the requirement that 75 percent of the grapes must originate from the locality named on the label; in the regulations of 1978 the requirement became 85 percent for Viticultural Areas and 75 percent for single counties or single states. In order to enforce these rules, it was necessary to define viticultural areas. International pressure was also mounting for countries to protect each other's place names pertaining to wine. Lists of names were necessary. The existing appellation systems provided these names and their boundaries for European countries, but no equivalent existed in non-European nations. In searching for methods to define these viticultural areas, the U.S. and other countries quite naturally turned to European practice. Although the criteria for defining viticultural areas in the U.S. were strongly influenced by the geographic determinism which permeates commentaries on the French industry, other aspects of the French system—such as its hierarchical nature and emphasis on quality—were not included.

The criteria that are to be used to establish the authenticity of a viticultural area in the U.S. include nothing on the wine. Instead, evidence is required "of a geographic nature (climate, elevation, soil, physical features, rainfall) which distinguishes the *viticultures* [my emphasis] of the proposed area as similar within and dissimilar from the surrounding areas" (Hutchison and Gay 1981). All of the environmentally deterministic assumptions that have been developed as interpretations of the French industry are incorporated in, and perpetuated by, the legislation. Rather than classify the wine of the region, or even the viticulture itself, the environment is used as if its effect on the vines and wine of the region were precisely understood. The U.S. system of viticultural areas is only very loosely hierarchical. The following range of names may be used to describe what ATF originally called appellations of origin for American wine: the U.S., a state, two or no more than three states which are all contiguous, a county, two or no more than three counties in the same states, or a viticultural area (BATF 27 CFR §4.25a). The name of more than one viticultural area may be used on a label when the two overlap and certain other conditions are fulfilled (Lee 1992, 3). In California, where state law permits subviticultural areas to describe part of the area within Napa County, provided that Napa Valley also appears on the label, two names may also be used. In this case type-sizes for the two names on the label are also specified. As a result of these rules, and the procedures for petitioning to establish an area, numerous examples exist of viticultural areas which overlap or where one is enclosed within another. Los Carneros, for instance, overlaps both the Sonoma and Napa Valleys, and all three are within the North Coast viticultural area.

A huge range of sizes of viticultural areas also results (Lee 1992). The largest of the viticultural areas, Texas Hill Country, is more than 15,000 sq mi (almost 39,000 km^2) or larger than nine individual American states. The smallest, Cole Ranch in Mendocino County, California, is less than a quarter sq mi (about 63 ha). Of the 115 American Viticultural Areas approved by 1992, 63 are in California. This variability in their size and distribution reflects the quite different scale of the nation compared with France, the variable importance of grape growing in parts of the U.S., together with the federal structure of government. As the California and Napa Valley case illustrates, states are able to impose their own regulations on the definition of viticultural areas and their expression on labels. Nevertheless, the resolution of the viticultural areas, even in California, is much coarser than in France and most other European countries, where the unitary system of government and more dispersed distribution of viticulture permitted a more uniform system to be imposed on the whole country.

The foundation of the entire U.S. system of viticultural areas is to discourage labeling that might mislead the consumer, but the effect of this complicated array of names on consumers is debated within the California wine industry. It seems doubtful that consumers are aware of the location, let alone the boundaries, of the more obscure viticultural areas. Well-known names such as Napa Valley had achieved their fame before their boundaries were formally described for viticultural purposes. Again, few consumers are likely to be aware of their precise boundaries. Although I know of no research on the topic, it seems even less likely that consumers, other than the most ardent wine enthusiasts, would be able to distinguish the nesting of some viticultural areas within others. But from the seller's point of view, the precise location of the viticultural area may not be important. The geographic names act like a trade name or brand, and, like them, do not need precise definition to influence sales. They differ from these commercial marks in that they are the common property of producers or owners of grapes within the viticultural area and cannot be appropriated by any individual who does not own all of the viticultural area. It needs emphasizing that the U.S. definition of viticultural areas has existed for only a decade. As publicity and effective cartographic presentation of them proceed, their recognition and effectiveness are likely to develop.

The effectiveness of the system for consumers and producers also relates to whether recognition of a viticultural area is an endorsement of quality. ATF is quite clear on this point. They claim that they do not wish to "give the impression by approving a viticultural area that it is approving or endorsing the quality of the wine from this area" and that ATF "approves a viticultural area by a finding that the area is distinct from surrounding areas but not better than other areas" (quoted in Lee 1992, 6). In this way the U.S. system is quite different from the EC approach in general and the French in particular. Nevertheless, because parts of the U.S., and notably parts of California, have different reputations for the quality of the wine that they produce, ATF influences both consumers and producers. When ATF defines parcels of land as within or outside a viticultural area (especially those with reputations for producing superior wines), they certainly influence the consumers' perception of quality and the producers' ability to sell.

The U.S. definitions have created regional identity crises. The Napa Valley was the second appellation to receive official designation. During the course of the hearings, the Valley continued to grow. Everyone wanted to be part of the best-known American wine locality. The ATF final definition included all of the watershed of the Napa together with the watersheds of four valleys to the east. Even the Napa Valley itself has considerable variations in soils, with the first three of Amerine and Winkler's temperature regions being represented (Winkler et al. 1974). Variability in the physical environment of the Sonoma Valley's viticultural area is even more obvious. Annual precipitation varies between 600mm–1200mm (Crowley 1982).

In developing the rules for establishing viticultural areas within the U.S., ATF paid some attention to imported wines. Geographic names used in other countries to describe viticultural areas had to be related to the U.S. approach to geographic indications and the legal rules about the protection of what is known in U.S. law as "distinctive designations"—wines that are named after a place which countries such as France also claim as being distinguishable from all other wines. The U.S. protects the names of "viticultural areas" used on imported wines when the boundaries have been "recognized and defined by the country of origin for use on labels of wine available for consumption within the country of origin," (27 CFR §4.25a). The matter of distinctive designations is not as clear-cut because the U.S. regulations do not include any local wines in this category. For foreign wines, ATF is authorized to recognize distinctive designations when the U.S. "consumer and trade know the wine of a particular place or region as distinguishable from all other wines" (Lee 1992, 10). By 1990, ATF had recognized 591 foreign terms which are considered "geographically significant" and a further 128 foreign terms are considered to be "nongeneric names which are also distinctive designations of specific wines" (T.D. ATF-296;

55FR 17960; April 30, 1990). "Non-generic" is important because it signals one of the strong differences of opinion between the U.S. and the EC over geographic indications. The U.S. considers names such as chablis, burgundy, sherry and port as generic, so that names such as "California Chablis" or "North Coast Burgundy" are permitted in the U.S. They are considered by ATF to describe the type of wine rather than its origin and are not in the list of "distinctive designations" and therefore not protected by law. The European Community takes the view that wines with these names must originate from the regions that bear the names. In essence the difference is one of scale and familiarity. The U.S. protects the "distinctive designations" of small areas of European countries, but they claim that the names of the major wine regions of France have been well known for centuries and can be used by the wine industry of California and New York State to describe types of wine.

The French and California Patterns

It seems inevitable that the different degrees of legislative control in the French and California wine industries have resulted in different spatial patterns of production. This hypothesis is tested by comparing the regional patterns of production of grapes for wine in France and California, with particular emphasis on the distribution of one premium red wine-making variety, Cabernet Sauvignon, and one bulk-producing variety, Carignane.

The regional patterns of French viticulture and winemaking are simple but seldom discussed in their entirety because the regions that make high-quality wine are usually separated from what is commonly called *le vignoble de masse* (bulk-production viticulture) (Galtier 1960). The prestigious winemaking areas outline the lineaments of the country (Figs. 2, 3). To the east are Champagne, Burgundy, and the Rhone Valley, to the west the constellation of crus of Bordeaux with Cognac adjoining it to the North. Linking east and west are the vineyards of the Loire valley and the northeastern outlier of Alsace. When measured by the land area in vines, these well-known names are overwhelmed by the viticultural ar-

eas of the Midi, the names of which are much less familiar (Fig. 2). The contrast between production from the premium wine-producing areas and the *vignoble de masse* is well illustrated by comparing the small area in vines in Chablis, one of the best-known wine names in the world, with any of the *départements* of the Midi. When the areas eligible for appellations are considered, the contrast between the south and the rest of France is even more marked (Fig. 2, 3). A very small but quite rapidly increasing proportion of the *vignoble de masse* is entitled to an appellation. Many of those areas that have been accorded the privilege were initially restricted to the lesser VDQS status, a recognition that the wines are close to appellation status. In contrast, most of the vineyards in the other regions have appellation status, with Burgundy having consistently the highest proportion of vineyards in this category (Figs. 2, 3).

In California, the general pattern of the distribution of wine grapes has some broad similarities to France (Fig. 4). It too has its *vignoble de masse*. Its alignment and organizational structure are different, running north-south rather than east-west as in France, with the grapes destined for the large corporations with some cooperatives. These are the Central Valley vineyards of the main producers of "jug" wines in California, the wineries of which are almost unrecognizable from the more mundane industrial plants of the towns and countryside of the region. From these Central Valley vineyards come the table wines that by international standards are of remarkably high quality. The elite wine-making regions of California are further north and closer to the coast, being concentrated in the Napa and Sonoma Valleys. The coastal valleys of Central California also emerged in the 1960s–70s as important winemaking localities. The locational flexibility in the California industry is clearly shown in its changing distribution in the last two decades. During the 1970s–80s major adjustments have taken place in the location of wine grape production (California Grape Acreage 1990). The counties with the largest relative increases in the 1970s were those of Central California—Monterey, San Luis Obispo, and Santa Barbara. The dominant wine-making counties of Napa and Sonoma have also experienced large positive growth rates, especially in the 1980s. Such dynamism and experimentation is rarer until very

Wine Appellation as Territory   709

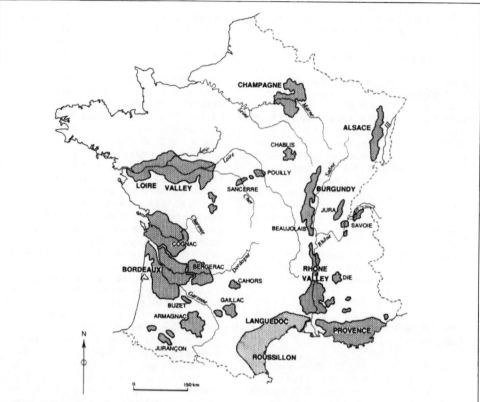

Figure 2. The main wine producing areas of France. Source: *Recensement Général de l'Agriculture 1988.*

recently in the French industry, partly because it would be very difficult for new areas to compete under the appellation laws, even if the quality of wine produced in the new regions were high.

The distribution of wine varieties in France and California illustrates the influence of the appellation laws (Figs. 5, 6). Major wine varieties are much more localized in France. Until the 1980s, Cabernet Sauvignon, for instance, was overwhelmingly localized in Bordeaux (Fig. 5). Recent plantings in regions of southern France (Languedoc-Roussillon and Provence) that are attempting to improve the standing of the viticulture and winemaking have resulted in some dispersion of Cabernet Sauvignon, but Bordeaux still has more than 70 percent of the total French area (Fig. 5). The dispersion of the

variety would have undoubtedly been much quicker had it not been for the restrictions on planting nontraditional grape varieties in many parts of Languedoc-Roussillon (Crowley 1991). Indeed, in the Midi, Cabernet Sauvignon is increasingly being grown in localities which have, or aspire to, no appellation and the grape growers are planting varieties with better winemaking qualities. Between 1968–88 the area in Cabernet Sauvignon also increased substantially in its traditional home in Bordeaux (department of Gironde) where it has displaced other varieties (Fig. 5). In California, Cabernet Sauvignon is much more widely and evenly dispersed, with large areas in Napa and Sonoma Counties, but also significant acreages in more southern counties and in the Central Valley (Fig. 6). The other premium red wine-

710 Moran

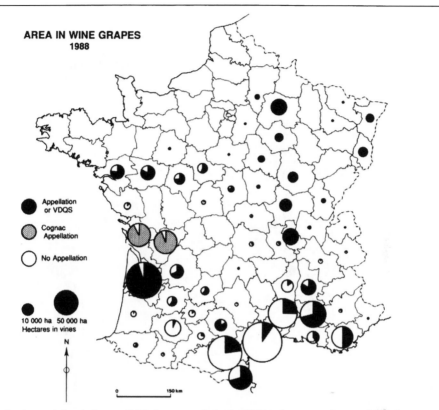

AREA IN WINE GRAPES
1988

Appellation or VDQS

Cognac Appellation

No Appellation

10 000 ha   50 000 ha
Hectares in vines

N

0   150 km

Figure 3. Areas of vines in France eligible for an appellation in 1988 by department. Source of data: *Recensement Général de l'Agriculture 1988*. VDQS means Vin de Qualité Superieur.

making variety, Pinot Noir, shows even stronger localization in France. It remains almost entirely confined to the Champagne and Burgundy regions, whereas in California it is much more widely distributed. If the states of Washington and Oregon were included in the analysis, the variety would be even more dispersed.

The varieties that are the foundation of the *vignoble de masse* in France are also highly localized. Carignane is the mainstay of the bulk-wine industry in southern France, but is not permitted in many other regions of the country (Fig. 5). In California, by contrast, it is more widely distributed and grown even in the prestigious areas of the Sonoma and Napa valleys, although its area there has decreased in recent years as other varieties take precedence (Fig. 6). It remains much more important in the Central Valley counties of San Joaquin, Stanislaus, Merced, Madera and Fresno.

Similar examples can be quoted from the white wine varieties. Until recently Chardonnay was hardly grown outside Champagne and Burgundy. In the 1980s, like Cabernet Sauvignon, it has been planted in many more regions, including the Midi. By contrast, in California, it is one of the varieties that has experienced most rapid growth overall and across a range of regions in the last two decades. For instance,

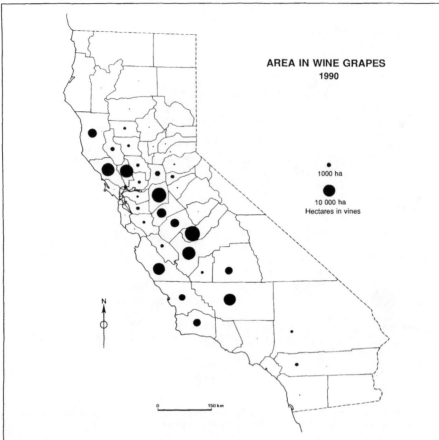

Figure 4. Areas of vines for wine production in California in 1990 by county. Source of data: *California grape acreage 1990.* California Agricultural Statistical Service, Sacramento, 1991.

it has become one of the most important varieties in the valleys of Central and Southern
California, including Monterey and Santa Barbara Counties. Sauvignon Blanc and Chenin
Blanc are similarly widely distributed in California, whereas in France they are highly localized
in Bordeaux and the Loire Valley respectively
(Recensement Général de l'Agriculture 1990;
California Grape Acreage 1990).

   That the French have had a much longer
period to experiment with wine varieties is incontestable, and there is also no question that

a delicate and sensitive balance has developed
between grape varieties, vineyard practices,
and winemaking techniques in the prestigious
regions. There is also no doubt that the appellation laws have ossified this pattern and reduced the flexibility of the French industry. On
probability grounds alone, it seems highly unlikely that a particular variety or combination of
varieties chosen at some time in the past, when
knowledge of other possible varieties was limited, should be the only suitable combination
to produce premium wine in any region. There

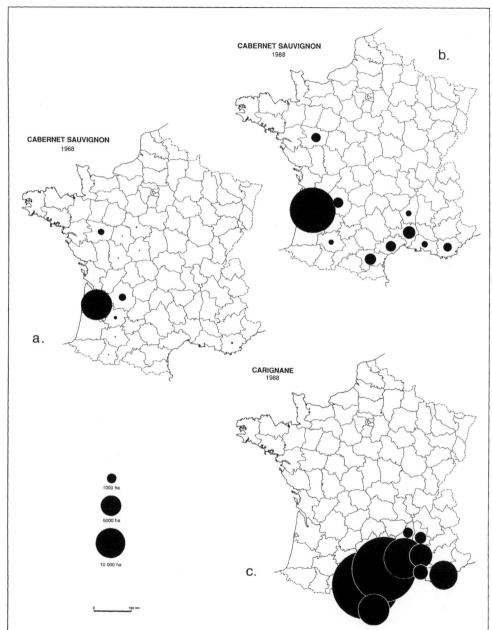

Figure 5. Areas in the varieties Cabernet Sauvignon (a) 1968 and (b) 1988 and (c) Carignane 1988 in France by departments. Source of data: *Recensement Général de l'Agriculture 1968 and 1988.*

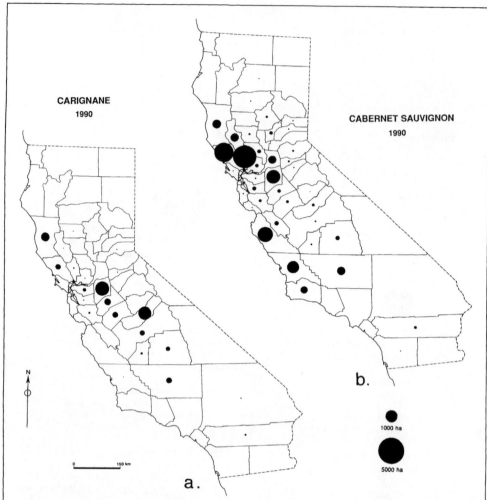

Figure 6. Area in (a) Carignane and (b) Cabernet Sauvignon in California by county in 1990. Source of data: *California grape acreage 1990.* California Agricultural Statistical Service, Sacramento, 1991.

is a high probability that other varieties, especially those that have been clonally selected, combined with other cultural practices and vinification, could produce wines of high quality if the opportunity existed. Under the present French appellation laws, this hypothesis is unlikely to be tested in Bordeaux or Burgundy, Chablis or Champagne, but the evidence from the *vignoble de masse* is that wine of very high quality can be made there using the best varieties (Crowley 1991).

Discussion

The wine appellation laws of France are a powerful example of territorialization of a single industry that has numerous effects on the society and economy in regions where they are practiced as well as outside them. This form of sectorially defined territory is as highly differentiated and influential as the more common definition of territory that is the basis of the organization of government in most nations. The wine appellation certainly fulfills the criteria suggested by Sack and others for territory. Its definitions of territory are detailed, legal, and hierarchical. It proceeds by specifying and controlling comprehensively the actions of the participants in this one industry. Actions and objects are excluded or included in territories according to the rules of the appellations. Practices of agricultural production and of industrial processing are specified in detail. It is, therefore, an intense form of territorialization.

Although the appellation is for wine, the laws have ramifications for other regions and other industries. By specifying territory as having special qualities for the production of wine, they restrict competition from other activities and the land takes on a special value. Fortunately, the vine tolerates natural conditions that are not highly sought after for other types of production. If the vine had been competing for land in demand from other crops yielding high rent, it is less likely that the laws would have come into existence. From reading the appellation regulations of France and California, it is not immediately apparent that they refer to wine. One would expect that the definition of the appellations would be by the quality of the wine. This is certainly an element in the French law and was critical in the definitions of the original appellations. But many of the procedures to establish appellations do not directly consider the wine. Instead, they define aspects of physical characteristics of the territory that are assumed to have an association with the quality of the wine. This paradox is most apparent in U.S. legislation, where both the statements of law and their application in the definition of territory demonstrate an extreme environmental determinism that has a limited physiological foundation.

In France, the original appellations were established by empirical experimentation with grape varieties on different parcels of land and by judging the wine that resulted. Once they had been legally defined, the popular literature and institutional procedures began to appeal more and more to loose scientific explanation for legitimation. The INAO has recently had to define its procedures more carefully because its decisions for territories being included or excluded in appellations is increasingly being appealed by land owners (INAO 1991). In France, the appellations are legitimized by appeal to "scientific explanation" without the definitive evidence of the way in which the characteristics of the edaphic or atmospheric environment influence the wine that results. Myth becomes the conventional wisdom and is legitimated into the dominant ideology. Superficial spatial associations between elements of the physical environment and viticulture derived from a misreading of the French empirical experience were used as the basis of defining the U.S. appellations.

The power of legislation and the INAO in maintaining the dominance of the prestigious winemaking regions of France has been immense. Although the procedures it has used to influence the geography of the industry are clear, its political power structure is deserving of more attention than it has received here. From its inception, the membership of the committee was dominated by members from the prestigious areas who brought with them the attitudes of the grands crus. Procedures for establishing new appellations were very tight, and until the 1970s, few new ones were permitted. In a practical sense, the INAO controlled the dispersion of premium varieties. Champagne, Burgundy and Bordeaux had the premium varieties, and one of the appellation rules was that traditional varieties should be the basis of new appellations. Many of the regions of the Midi were traditionally dependent on lesser varieties of wine grapes. Just as the regions of France with premium appellations are on the treadmill of quality, the Midi has been on the treadmill of quantity.

Considering the intensity and nature of the control, it would be surprising if the appellations did not have an observable effect on elements of the industries that they control. Grape varieties common to both France and California show a quite different spatial pattern and degree of localization. In France, where the appellation laws specify the varieties to be grown, their distribution is localized and highly regionalized. In California, by contrast, all varieties are much more dispersed. California producers have had a much shorter period to experiment and discover the specific environmental and cultural niches that favor particular varieties.

Without the rigid control of the appellations and in a period when knowledge of vine varieties is much less regionally specific, it seems likely that the California patterns will remain more dispersed. Perhaps the most interesting empirical result to emerge is the beginning of what appears to be a converging path for the geographic patterns of the distribution of grape varieties in the French and U.S. industries. The most prestigious wine-grape varieties are beginning to disperse in France whereas there is some evidence that they are beginning to concentrate in California. The power of legislation and the appellation system is weakening in France while in California more knowledge of the characteristics of local environments is seeing some varieties, such as Cabernet Sauvignon in the Napa Valley, becoming more important in particular localities. Some of the forces identified above appear to be central to this process, but the detailed patterns for a wider range of varieties need further investigation.

Conclusion

The wine appellation is certainly used in a strategic role to make it appear as if the "control of territory controls cause and effect" (Sack 1983, 62). Physical attributes of the territory are translated into the reasons for the quality of the wine that they define. The influence of the physical environment on grape production and wine is real, but the mechanisms that connect the two are not established in either the official definitions of the appellation territory or in most commentaries on the industry. The territory becomes the explanation. This tendency is most apparent in one of the contentious aspects of appellation control: the limitations on quantity and the assumed relationship between low yield and high quality. The territories where some of the prestigious appellations are found produce low yields so that this attribute of these territories becomes a direct explanation for quality. The nature of the relationship between the two is much more complex.

French and European attitudes to environment-vine relationships that underlie the appellation laws have been challenged by the growing empirical evidence from New-World countries and Europe itself. The experiences of California, Australia, New Zealand, South Af-

rica, Chile, and Argentina have demonstrated the wide range of environments in which the prestigious grape varieties may grow and produce wines of quality. Variety of grape has become one hallmark of quality. The example of such New-World practices has influenced some French producers. Entrepreneurial producers, often from the prestige winemaking regions, have established large vineyards growing Cabernet Sauvignon, Merlot, Chardonnay or Pinot Noir clonally selected in parts of France which have no right to an appellation. The quality of some of the wines they produce and the price they command are similar to some appellation wines (Crowley 1991). Regions in the south of France, in particular, which have premium grape varieties planted from superior clones, have demonstrated that they are able to produce wines of quality in areas which were formerly considered to be suitable only for producing bulk wines.

Influential in these changes in attitude to different environments are also some fundamental geographic processes of price competition and globalization of production and knowledge. One after another, the non-European winemaking countries have challenged European countries in markets such as the United Kingdom with varietal wines of very high quality. European producers have found it necessary to become much more knowledgeable of these regions. Their recognition of the potential has seen them make direct investments in many parts of the world. As the area of land available from grapes in prestigious appellations of France becomes limited, large companies have also extended their operations internationally. For instance, several Champagne houses have invested in California, Australia, and New Zealand, either alone or in joint ventures. Sparkling wine made from these regions combines grapes of quality with French winemaking experience to produce *methode champenoise* of excellent standard. The globalization of the wine industry deserves further research. It has also had its own influence on the use of place names, as French producers locating in other countries maintain their respect for the European appellation laws and often develop brand names for the local product. Through direct empirical evidence, these geographic processes have challenged the environmental myths about the prestigious winemaking areas being unique. The quality of the wines made outside Europe (or in nontraditional areas of Europe) has demonstrated that environments for making fine and distinctive wines exist in many places.

Paradoxically, the establishment of systems of geographic indications or appellations in many countries has itself contributed to their demystification. Investigation of possible systems for non-European countries has prompted more rigorous analysis of the French and European systems and their assumptions. As the details of their practices have become more widely known, some have increasingly been questioned, the U.S. renunciation of any endorsement of quality in their system of viticultural areas being an example. But the full implications of the adoption of systems of geographic indications has yet to be realized. The definition of viticultural areas used in the U.S. demonstrates that environmentally deterministic ideas are an almost inevitable accompaniment of the French approach to recognizing quality in wine. A philosophy of winemaking that assumes that the best wines come from contiguous small areas is fundamental to geographic indications and appellations. But with modern technology for moving grapes and musts, blending across regions and even vintages is common in many countries. Countries adopting systems of geographic indications which are too rigid or restrictive may find that they undermine the innovation and flexibility that is one foundation of the success of their industries.

Acknowledgments

I wish to acknowledge the assistance of William Crowley of Sonoma State University, of the four anonymous referees who provided helpful comments, the Wine Institute of New Zealand, and Jan Kelly and Jonette Surridge for cartography.

References

Audier, J. 1991. Indications géographiques, marques et autres signes distinctifs: concurrence ou conflits? *Bulletin de l'OIV* 823–24, 406–43.

Bennett, R. J. 1980. *The geography of public finance.* London: Methuen.

Bienaymé, Marie-Hélène. 1988. *La protection internationale des vins et eaux-de-vied, d'appellation d'origine.* Paper presented at a conference organized by the World Office of Industrial Property, Bordeaux.

Bodenhausen, G. H. C. 1968. *Guide to the application of the Paris Convention for the protection of industrial property.* Geneva: United International Bureau for the Protection of Intellectual Property.

California Grape Acreage, 1990. 1991. Sacramento: California Agricultural Statistical Service.

Chapuis, L. 1980. *Vigneron en Bourgogne.* Paris: Robert Lafont.

Chidgey, G. 1984. *The century companion to the wines of Burgundy.* London: Century.

Cox, K. R. 1979. *Location and public problems.* Oxford: Basil Blackwell.

———, and McCarthy, J. J. 1982. Neighborhood activism as a politics of turf: A critical analysis. In *Conflict, politics and the urban scene,* ed. K. R. Cox and R. J. Johnston, pp. 196–219. London: Longmans.

Crowley, W. 1982. Evaluation of geographic appellations for American wine grape regions. Presented at the Annual Meeting of the Association of American Geographers, San Antonio, TX.

Crowley, W. K. 1991. The French wine scene: Fewer vineyards, new regions, varietal expansion and decline. Presented at the Annual Meeting of the Association of Pacific Coast Geographers, 1992.

de Blij, H. J. 1983. *Wine: A geographic appreciation.* Totowa, NJ: Rowman and Allenheld.

Dear, M. 1981. Theory of the local state. In *Political studies from spatial perspectives,* ed. A. Burnett and P. Taylor, pp. 183–200. New York: John Wiley and Sons.

Dion, R. 1959. *Histoire de la vigne et du vin en France des origines au XIX siècle.* Paris: Les Belles Lettres.

Gadille, R. 1967. *La vignoble de la côte bourguignonne: Fondements physiques et humains d'une viticulture de haute qualité.* Paris: Les Belles Lettres.

Galtier, G. 1960. *Le vignoble du Languedoc Mediterranean et du Roussillon. Etude comparative d'un vignoble de masse.* Montpellier, France: Fayard.

General Agreement on Tariffs and Trade (GATT). 1992. EC background. Delegation of the Commission of the European Communities to Australia and New Zealand, Canberra.

Hanson, A. 1982. *Burgundy.* London: Faber and Faber.

Harvey, D. 1969. *Explanation in geography.* London: Edward Arnold.

———. 1982. *The limits to capital.* Oxford: Basil Blackwell.

Huetz de Lemps, A.; Pijassou, R.; and Roudie, P. 1977. *Géographie historiques des vignobles,* Tome 1:

Vignobles français. Paris: Centre National de la Recherche Scientifique.

Hutchison, R. B., and Gay, D. E. 1981. An economic evaluation of geographic appellations for American wine. Presented at the 32nd Annual Meeting of the American Society of Enologists, San Diego.

Institut National des Appellations d'Origine. 1985. *A success story for France: L'appellation d'origine contrôlée*. Paris.

———. 1987. *La protection internationale des appellations d'origine des vins et eaux-de-vie*. Paris.

———. 1991. Composition, fonctionnement et competences de L'INAO. Roneo 91:103, Paris.

Johnson, H. 1971. *World atlas of wine*. London: Mitchell Beazley.

Kliewer, W. M. 1968. Effect of temperature on the composition of grapes grown under field and controlled conditions. *Proceedings of the American Society for Horticultural Science* 93:797–806.

———, and Lider, L. A. 1971. Effects of day temperature and light intensity on growth and composition of *Vitis vinifera* L. fruits. *Journal of the American Society of Horticultural Science* 95:766–69.

———, and Torres, R. E. 1972. Effect of controlled day and night temperatures on grape coloration. *American Journal of Enology and Viticulture* 23:71–77.

———. 1977. Influence of temperature, solar radiation and nitrogen on coloration and composition of Emperor grapes. *American Journal of Enology and Viticulture* 28:96–103.

Landrieu-Lussigny, M-H. 1983. *Le vignobles bourguignon: ses lieux-dits*. Marseille: Jeanne Laffitte.

Lee, W. C. L. 1992. *U.S. viticultural areas*. San Francisco: Wine Institute.

Lichine, A. 1974. *New encyclopedia of wines and spirits*. New York: Alfred Knopf.

Marrison, L. W. 1973. *Wines and spirits*. Harmondsworth, U.K.: Penguin.

McCarthy, J. T. 1980. United States law of geographical denominations. In *Protection of geographic denominations of goods and services*, ed. H. Jehorem, pp. 152–65. Utrecht: Sijthoff and Noordhoff.

Moran, W. 1988. The wine appellation: Environmental description or economic device? In *Proceedings of the second international symposium for cool climate viticulture*, ed. R. E. Smart et al., pp. 356–60. Auckland: New Zealand Society for Viticulture and Oenology.

———, and Nason, S. J. 1981. Spatio-temporal localization of New Zealand dairying. *Australian Geographical Studies* 19:47–66.

———. 1993. Rural space as intellectual property. *Political Geography* 12(3):263–77.

Niederbacher, A. 1988. *Wine in the European Community*. Luxembourg: Office for Official Publications of the European Community.

Office Internationale de la Vigne et du Vin (OIV). 1991. La lettre de L'OIV. N. 55, Paris.

Pitiot, S., and Poupon, P. 1985. *Atlas des grands vignobles de Bourgogne*. Paris: Jaques Legrand.

Recensement Général de l'Agriculture 1968, 1988, 1990. 1970, 1990, 1991. Paris: SCEES.

Richard, J. 1978. Aspects historiques de l'évolution du vignoble bourguignon. In *Géographiques historiques des vignobles*, ed. A. Huetz de Lemps, pp. 187–96. Paris: CNRS.

Sack, R. 1983. Human territoriality: A theory. *Annals of the Association of American Geographers* 73:55–74.

———. 1986. *Human territoriality: Its theory and history*. Cambridge: Cambridge University Press.

Sinton, T. H., et al. 1978. Grape juice indicators for prediction of potential wine quality. I. Relationship between crop level, juice and wine composition, and wine sensory ratings and scores. *American Journal of Enology and Viticulture* 29:267–71.

Smart, R. E. 1985a. Some aspects of climate, canopy microclimate, vine physiology and wine quality. In *Proceedings of the International Symposium on Cool Climate Viticulture and Enology*, Oregon State University Technical Publication 7628, ed. D. A. Heatherbell, et al., pp. 1–19. Eugene, OR.

———. 1985b. Principles of grapevine canopy microclimate manipulation with implications for yield and quality. A review. *American Journal of Enology and Viticulture* 36:230–39.

———. 1987. Influence of light on composition and quality of grapes. *Acta Horticulturae* 206:37–47.

Soja, E. 1971. *The political organization of space*. Washington: Association of American Geographers, Commission on College Geography.

———. 1974. A paradigm for the analysis of political systems. In *Locational approaches to power and conflict*, ed. K. Cox, D. Reynolds, and S. Rokken, pp. 43–71. New York: John Wiley.

Unwin, T. 1991. *Wine and the vine; an historical geography of viticulture and the wine trade*. London: Routledge.

Winkler, A. J., et al. 1974. *General viticulture*. Berkeley: University of California Press.

Submitted 5/92, revised 4/93, 6/93, accepted 7/93.

[2]

Vol. 90 TMR

LOCATING GEOGRAPHICAL INDICATIONS –
PERSPECTIVES FROM ENGLISH LAW

By Norma Dawson*

INTRODUCTION

The protection of industrial property is concerned with patents, utility models, industrial designs, trademarks, trade names, and indications of source or appellations of origin, and the repression of unfair competition.[1]

To the casual inquirer or the student embarking upon the study of intellectual property rights, the law concerning geographical indications is the least accessible. It provokes much less attention and discussion at a general level than its fellows, copyright, design, patent, and its closest kin, the trademark. In the legal literature of some jurisdictions, the geographical indication often leads a shadowy or subterranean existence, rarely emerging in solid form, a state of affairs which, however, may change in the wake of the TRIPS Agreement,[2] considered below. Even among intellectual property lawyers, the geographical indication seems a subject best left to a small group of specialists who drive forward the discussion at WIPO colloquia.[3] This lack of general interest, occasionally tempered by skepticism or even hostility, stems in large measure from the fact that in many countries the geographical indication was rumored as intellectual property right long before it existed. Throughout the twentieth century, the geographical indication has been an intellectual property right in the making surrounded by a complex debate lacking common terminology,[4] ranging between two extreme viewpoints, one of

---

* Professor of Law, Queen's University of Belfast.

1. International Convention for the Protection of Industrial Property 1883 (the Paris Convention), as amended at The Hague, 1925, Article 1[2].

2. Agreement on Trade-Related Aspects of Intellectual Property Rights ("TRIPS"), resulting from the GATT Uruguay Round, adopted in Marrakesh on April 15, 1994, and administered by the Council of TRIPS, an agency of the World Trade Organization (WTO). The TRIPS Agreement prescribes minimum standards concerning the availability, scope and use of intellectual property rights: Articles 22-24 deal with geographical indications.

3. WIPO Symposia on the International Protection of Geographical Indications, Bordeaux, November 3-5, 1988; Santenay, November 9-10, 1989; Geneva, May 28-June 1, 1990; Wiesbaden, October 17-18, 1991; Funchal, Madeira, October 13-14, 1993; Melbourne, April 5-6, 1995; Eger, Hungary, October 24-25, 1997.

4. The Paris Convention refers to two types of geographical indication but defines neither: appellations of origin and indications of source. According to a WIPO definition: "Whereas an indication of source shows only from where a product comes, an appellation of origin indicates, in addition, the characteristic qualities of a product which are determined by the geographical area from which it comes and to which the appellation

Vol. 90 TMR   **591**

which strikes an attitude of supreme indifference to geographical
indications per se and views the problem of their misuse as one
best addressed according to general principles of unfair
competition, while the other, anxious to protect specific
geographical indications of domestic economic and cultural
importance, has argued for exclusive rights in a more absolute
form than is generally accepted in intellectual property law.[5]
Historically, the primary focus of this viewpoint has been the
appellation of origin, such as Roquefort[6] or Champagne,[7] where
a causal link can be established between the geographical origin
and the quality or characteristics of the product, usually foodstuffs,
wine, natural mineral water or other drinks. Complete protection
for specific indications has been achieved most easily as a result
of bilateral agreements, but an early multilateral agreement, the
Madrid Agreement for the Repression of False or Deceptive
Indications of Source 1891, accorded preferential treatment to
products of the vine, granting appellations for such products
protection despite genericness in a manner wholly inimical to first
principles of trademark law. Only thirty-one states have executed
the Madrid Agreement.

The Lisbon Agreement for the Protection of Appellations of
Origin 1958 represents the high watermark of the absolutist
viewpoint, which has been characterized by Frederick Mostert as
representing an Old World philosophy of this commercial
viewpoint,[8] although, in fact, not all Old World nations are Lisbon

refers. . . ." The WIPO definition also distinguishes between indirect and direct indications
of geographical origin: "furthermore, while an expression or sign evoking the geographical
source of a product may constitute an indication of source (e.g., such as a national emblem),
an appellation of origin is always a geographical name." WIPO, The Role of Industrial
Property in the Protection of Consumers (No 648) ¶200 (1983). Article 2 of the Lisbon
Agreement for the Protection of Appellations of Origin and their International Registration
1958 defines "appellation of origin" as "the geographical name of a country, region, or
locality which serves to designate a product originating therein, the quality and
characteristics of which are due exclusively or essentially to the geographical environment,
including natural and human factors." More recent definitions including that contained in
Article 22 of the TRIPS Agreement are considered below.

5. See generally the papers prepared for WIPO symposia, supra note 3, cited as
WIPO/GEO/; Lori Simon, Appellations of Origin: The Continuing Controversy, 5
Northwestern Journal of International Law and Business 132 (1983), and Bryan Harris,
Appellations of Origin and Other Geographical Indications Used in Trade, [1979] EIPR 205.

6. See Lawrence W. Pollack, "Roquefort" — An Example of Multiple Protection for a
Designation of Regional Origin Under the Lanham Act, 52 TMR 755 (1962).

7. The Champagne appellation is semi-generic in the United States. See Louis C.
Lenzen, Bacchus in the Hinterlands: A Study of Denominations of Origin in French and
American Wine-Labeling Laws, 58 TMR 145 (1968), Alfred Phillip Knoll, Federal
Regulation of the Term "Champagne," 60 TMR 285 (1970) and Alfred Phillip Knoll,
Champagne, 19 International and Comparative Law Quarterly 309 (1970).

8. Frederick Mostert, Famous and Well-Known Marks (1997). See also Simon, supra
note 5; Frederick Mostert, Well-Known and Famous Marks: Is Harmony Possible in the
Global Village?, 86 TMR 103 (1996).

adherents. Where its writ runs, the decision of the state of origin to protect an appellation of origin can be given effect in all member states on the basis of registration at the International Bureau of WIPO in Geneva. Over seven hundred appellations of origin have been registered with the International Bureau but only eighteen states are party to the Agreement.[9] The fact that appellations of origin registered under the Lisbon Agreement can never become generic while they are protected in their state of origin is anathema to the laws in those countries which provide a lesser degree of protection, which they contend more accurately reflects actual consumer perceptions. Yet while diverse economic interests or cultural approaches foster differences within the international legal community, the importance of geographical indications in export markets fuels the desire of those states which are home to a significant number of geographical indications to secure greater international cooperation in affording higher standards of protection.

The inclusion of a set of minimum legal standards for the protection of geographical indications within the TRIPS Agreement, concluded as part of the GATT Uruguay Round and adopted at Marrakesh in April 1994, is the first stage of establishing widespread international norms. Section 3 of the TRIPS Agreement, which deals with geographical indications, foreshadows how this emerging intellectual property right may appear in the twenty-first century.[10] The development of enhanced protection for certain indications for wines and spirits or even a fully-developed international wine law are within the contemplation of the somewhat sketchy provisions of Articles 22-24. Article 22 provides that national laws must afford protection against any use of geographical indications which misleads consumers as to the geographical origin of products or which constitutes unfair competition within the meaning of Article 10bis

---

9. Of the 738 appellations of origin which had been registered by 1997, 472 of these had been registered by France, 108 by Czechoslovakia (70 of which were subsequently attributed to the Czech Republic and 37 to Slovakia (one was canceled), 48 by Bulgaria, 28 by Hungary, 26 by Italy, 19 by Algeria, 18 by Cuba, and fewer than 10 each by Tunisia, Portugal, Mexico and Israel. 90 refusals were made. See WIPO/GEO/EGR/97/1 Rev (information supplied by the WIPO International Bureau).

10. Michael Blakeney, A Concise Guide to the TRIPS Agreement, ch 6 (1997); David Gervais, The TRIPS Agreement: Drafting History and Analysis, pp 119-38 (T.P. Stewart (ed)) (1998); Volume 2 of The GATT Uruguay Round: A Negotiating History, pp 2241-2335 (1993); Peter M. Brody, Protection of Geographical Indications in the Wake of TRIPS: Existing United States Laws and the Administration's Proposed Legislation, 84 TMR 520 (1994); Albrecht Conrad, The Protection of Geographical Indications in the TRIPS Agreement, 86 TMR 11 (1996), and Jim Chen, A Sober Second Look at Appellations of Origin: How the United States Will Crash France's Wine and Cheese Party, 5 Minneapolis Journal of Global Trade 29 (1996).

of the Paris Convention.[11] WTO members need not, however, protect geographical indications which have become generic terms either where the alleged infringement takes place or in their country of origin.[12] For intellectual property lawyers, while the adequacy of protection afforded acquired trademark rights under the TRIPS Agreement causes some concern, at the most fundamental level, the TRIPS definition of "geographical indication" is subject to debate.

In the wake of the TRIPS Agreement, one can expect WTO preoccupation with national compliance with TRIPS and WIPO preoccupation with what remains of the Madrid and Lisbon arrangements following the adoption of TRIPS. The more important agenda for the intellectual property community, however, is to influence the continuing debate on the scope of protection of geographical indications in a manner which is consistent with intellectual property law generally. The issues to be debated are which indications should be protected in principle and when should the question of acquired rights and genericness be brought into account?

Through the lens of English law, this article examines the issues surrounding Section 3 of the TRIPS Agreement and the post-TRIPS agenda. At first sight, English law is a hostile environment for the legal protection of geographical indications to flourish. In a jurisdiction lacking any tailor-made legislative framework for their protection with no general law of unfair competition and possessing few native geographical indications of major economic significance, there is little impetus for a strong legal response. Despite this, it was said in the English High Court in 1997 that "the law has advanced in effect to give rise to a civilly enforceable right similar to an appellation contrôlée."[13]

Many commentators view the Spanish Champagne case of 1959, J. Bollinger and others v. Costa Brava Wine Co. Ltd.,[14] as signaling the origin of the legal protection of geographical indications of origin in English law. Indeed when the High Court in that case granted twelve champagne producers and shippers an injunction restraining the sale in England of "Spanish

---

11. TRIPS, Article 22.2. This provision actually extends the scope of Article 10bis. The misuse of geographical indications had been deliberately omitted from the specific cases set out in Article 10bis(3) at the Lisbon Revision Conference of 1958. See Conrad, supra note 10. As to Article 10bis generally, see G.C.H. Bodenhausen, Guide to the Application of the Paris Convention for the Protection of Industrial Property, pp 142-46 (1968).

12. TRIPS, Articles 24.6 and 24.9.

13. Chocosuisse Union des Fabricants Suisses de Chocolat v. Cadbury Ltd., [1998] RPC 117, 127 (Laddie, J. (High Ct)).

14. (No 1) [1959] 3 All ER 800 (High Ct), and (No 2) [1961] 1 All ER 561 (High Ct) discussed by Paul Abel at 51 TMR 466 (1961).

Champagne," Justice Danckwerts, describing the defendants' conduct as "reprehensible" and "dishonest trading," could not have made a plainer statement of legal policy:

> There seems to be no reason why . . . licence should be given to a person, competing in trade, who seeks to attach to his product a name or description with which it has no natural association so as to make use of the reputation and goodwill which has been gained by a product genuinely indicated by the name or description.[15]

While the decision was clear in terms of its contribution to legal precedent, it was doctrinally weak and for some years the Spanish Champagne case was vulnerable to attack. One typical criticism was: "[I]t seems to be based on the premise that a remedy should exist ergo it does exist."[16] But, before we consider the extent to which Justice Danckwerts' statement has become entrenched in English law, it is necessary to consider two earlier phases of development in English law which have contributed to the legal debate concerning geographical indications and have influenced the commercial environment within which they operate.

I. GEOGRAPHICAL TRADEMARKS

The legal protection of geographical indications has its conceptual roots in the law of trademarks. Geographical indications flourish or fail in market conditions created in part by trademark law. It could have been otherwise: as Florent Gevers has wryly observed, a thoroughly hard-line approach restricting the registration of geographical trademarks would have avoided many current legal problems because:

> [A] geographical name [would] never be registered as a trademark:
>
> - if the product is not manufactured in the place described by the geographical name, such name deceives the public; or
>
> - if the product is manufactured in the place described by the geographical name, the name must be left free for use by existing and future competing firms.[17]

---

15. Id at 811.

16. John Walker & Sons Ltd. v. Henry Ost & Co. Ltd., [1970] RPC 489 (High Ct), comment of counsel during argument.

17. Florent Gevers, Geographical Names Used as Trade Marks, WIPO Symposium on the International Protection of Geographical Indications, November 9-10, 1989, Santenay, France (WIPO No 676), 109-28, 121 (1990).

The practical reality, of course, is quite different. The issue of registrability of geographical names as trademarks has involved a much more complex and fluid analysis. The English cases at the turn of the century involving the APOLLINARIS trademark[18] are illustrative of the forces which create a legal policy on that issue and provide the commercial and legal context for the development of geographical indications.

On January 1, 1876, the day on which the United Kingdom Trade Marks Registry first opened its doors, The London Times carried a notice on behalf of the Apollinaris Company, sole importers into the United Kingdom of Apollinaris Water, "incomparably the best of effervescent table waters" and "the sworn enemy of gout, rheumatism and indigestion."[19] The therapeutic powers of the mineral water, drawn from a spring discovered in 1852 at Neuenahr in Rhenish Prussia and named after Apollinaris Berg, a nearby hill, were not, however, the main message of the notice. The company wanted to impress upon trade rivals and consumers the fact that its trademark comprising the words APOLLINARIS BRUNNEN around an anchor was protected against imitations "by perpetual injunction of the Court of Chancery." At that time, notices appeared daily in The London Times alerting consumers to the existence of worthless imitations of many well-known brands and warning imitators of the risk of a passing-off action. The Trade Marks Registration Act 1875[20] was intended to provide a speedy means of establishing title to trademarks through the registration process. Within six weeks of the opening of the Registry, the Apollinaris Company sought and later obtained registration of the word mark APOLLINARIS and the device mark described above, both for natural mineral water. The only marks registrable under the 1875 Act were those already in use before the passing of the Act, provided they were "special and distinctive."[21] Although the Registry examiner must have concluded that APOLLINARIS was such a word, the Apollinaris Company had not used the word APOLLINARIS alone as a trademark prior to the enactment of the 1875 Act. As a result, this registration remained vulnerable to attack.

Fate now intervened to link the registrability of the geographical name APOLLINARIS to the development of legislative

---

18. See Apollinaris Co. Ltd. v. Duckworth, 23 RPC 540 (1906) (High Ct), infra note 27; Re Apollinaris Co.'s trademark, [1891] 2 Ch 186, 8 RPC 137 (High Ct and CA), infra note 31; and Re Apollinaris trademark, [1907] 2 Ch 178, 24 RPC 436 (High Ct), infra note 37.

19. Under the Trade Marks Registration Act 1875, 38 and 39 Vict, ch 91.

20. Ibid.

21. Id at §10.

policy. The Patents, Designs and Trade Marks Act 1883[22] permitted the registration of "fancy words not in common use" but it was short-lived. According to one account, it "caused nothing but trouble," being interpreted too generously by the Registry and too strictly by the courts.[23] The "fancy words" interpretation problem masked the more fundamental issue of language monopolies and was referred in 1887 to the Trade Marks and Designs Inquiry Committee, chaired by Lord Herschell.[24] Using language familiar to trademark lawyers today but quite fresh in 1888, the Herschell Report described a spectrum of registrability at one end of which were invented word marks to which no objection could be made and at the other end of which were words which described the quality, character or geographical origin of the goods, which were "open to obvious objection."[25] Yet, the Committee clearly recognized that word marks could move from the objectionable end of the spectrum as they gained another significance in the minds of consumers: "geographical names ought only to be [registered] where they clearly could not be regarded as indicative of the place of manufacture or sale."[26]

In this respect, the Herschell Report reflected the common law wisdom concerning geographical and other descriptive words. The English law of passing off attempted to facilitate commerce by keeping words which indicate the place of manufacture or sale in the public domain while recognizing that words could acquire secondary meaning through use. In order to prevent consumer deception, the courts were bound to protect geographical names which had acquired reputation as the marks of individual traders. The Apollinaris Company had benefitted from the passing-off action, securing an injunction against a rival trader even before the registration system began.[27]

In 1864, Lord Westbury L. C. stated in the Anatolia Liquorice case:

> But—it is urged on behalf of the defendants—this word Anatolia is a general expression; is, in point of fact, the geographical designation of a whole tract of country [in Turkey] wherein liquorice-root is largely grown, and is therefore a word common to all, and in it there can be no

---

22. 46 and 47 Vict, ch 57, §64.

23. Patent Office, A Century of Trade Marks 1876-1976, 10-11 (1976).

24. Volume 81 Sessional Papers, C.5350 (1888).

25. Id at ¶26.

26. Ibid.

27. See also Apollinaris Co. Ltd. v. Duckworth, 23 RPC 540 (1906) (High Ct). See generally Christopher Wadlow, The Law of Passing-Off ¶¶5.47 and 6.36 (2d ed 1995) and the cases cited there.

property . . . property in the word for all purposes cannot exist; but property in that word . . . does exist the moment the article goes into the market as stamped and there obtains acceptance and reputation.[28]

Yet, the Patents, Designs and Trade Marks Act 1888, enacted to effect the Herschell Committee's recommendations, omitted any reference to the secondary meaning basis for registrability. Instead, it merely allowed registration of "invented words" and words "having no reference to the character or quality of the goods and not being a geographical name."[29] It, therefore, appeared that geographical names as a class were excluded from registration in the United Kingdom even though they enjoyed common law protection.

The timing of the 1888 Act was perfect from the viewpoint of the Vichy Company of France, one of the Apollinaris Company's competitors. Vichy had acquired an English firm which sold natural mineral water, chiefly supplied by the Apollinaris Company. When Vichy asked Apollinaris to continue to supply mineral water, Apollinaris refused. Vichy then opposed pending registration applications made in 1885 for APOLLINARIS BRUNNEN and the word APOLLINARIS alone.[30] Vichy also moved to expunge the 1876 registrations. In the legal proceedings which ensued,[31] the Apollinaris Company admitted that the 1876 registration of APOLLINARIS had been invalid for want of prior use, but argued that even if it was expunged, it could be re-registered under the 1888 Act.

Justice Kekewich disagreed and held that APOLLINARIS was a "thoroughly well known" geographical name and therefore expressly excluded from registrability by the terms of the 1888 Act.[32] It may seem unlikely that the name of a spring or hill in Prussia should be well known to the British public but it had become obvious to consumers that APOLLINARIS was an indication of the geographical source of the water as the result of popularizing the product.

An appeal to the Court of Appeal failed. One member of the court, Lord Justice Lindley, stated: "it is impossible to say that this . . . is not a geographical word."[33] Thus, the 1876 registra-

---

28. M'Andrew v. Bassett, 4 De G J & S 380, 386 (1864) (Ct of Chancery) (injunction granted restraining the defendants' use of ANATOLIA in respect of licorice).

29. Patents, Designs and Trade Marks Act 1888, 51 and 52 Vict, ch 50, §10, amending §64 of the 1883 Act, see supra note 22.

30. The applications were for registration in class 3 for mineral salts.

31. Re Apollinaris Co.'s trademark, [1891] 2 Ch 186, 8 RPC 137 (High Ct and CA).

32. Id at 204 (High Ct).

33. Id at 221 (CA).

tion was expunged, the 1885 application was rejected because APOLLINARIS was not a "fancy word" as required by the 1883 Act in force when the application was made, and the mark fell afoul of the express ban on geographical names in the 1888 Act, which applied at the date of decision.

At the same time as the Court of Appeal was settling the question of the ineligibility of geographical names for registration under the prevailing legislation, the House of Lords was in the process of reaffirming the common law approach in the Stone Ale case, Montgomery v. Thompson,[34] where the defendant's ability to describe beer brewed in the town of Stone as "Stone Ale" was circumscribed by the plaintiffs' century-old reputation as the sole makers and vendors of "Stone Ale."

Eventually, commercial reality, common law and legislative policy were reconciled. The Trade Marks Act 1905 brought the statutory provisions into line with both the common law and the Herschell Committee's recommendations, permitting registration of geographical and other descriptive words upon proof of distinctiveness.[35] In most cases this would be established by evidence of secondary meaning acquired through use but the registration of fanciful or arbitrary geographical names which would cause other traders no inconvenience also was permitted because there was no legitimate business reason for using such names in relation to their products.

Furthermore, the issue of distinctiveness is governed by whether the applicant has a natural or de facto monopoly over the production of the goods in question, removing any need to keep the name free for others in relation to such goods. This has been a consideration in cases involving natural springs[36] and was relevant to the registrability of APOLLINARIS. Shortly after the 1905 Act was passed, the Apollinaris Company again sought to register APOLLINARIS for natural mineral water. The company at the time was—as the sole Apollinaris consignee and proprietor in the United Kingdom—the sole commercial source of the mineral water bearing the APOLLINARIS mark. The issue of distinctive-

---

34. [1891] AC 217 (HL).

35. Trade Marks Act 1905, 5 Edw 7, ch 15, §9 (5).

36. See, eg, the English cases, Karlsbader Wasser, 29 RPC 162 (1912), and the unreported Buxton case noted in Kerly's Law of Trade Marks and Trade Names, at 100n (11th ed 1983), and the decision of the German Federal Patent Court in respect of water from Vittel springs, noted at 23 IIC 416 (1992). Conversely, where the applicant for registration lacked a monopoly of natural springs, see the Irish case of Wheeler v. Johnston, 3 LR Ir 284 (1879) (High Ct) and in the English courts, Grand Hotel of Caledonia Springs Ltd. v. Wilson, [1904] AC 103 (Privy Council). In such cases, any injunction secured by the plaintiff leaves other traders free to use the geographical name to denote the origin of their products provided they avoid confusion with the plaintiff's goods.

Vol. 90 TMR   **599**

ness was referred to the High Court, where Justice Kekewich held that even though the mark was still a geographical name it had come through use to denote only the applicants' goods. He declared that APOLLINARIS should be deemed distinctive and accepted for registration under the 1905 Act, subject to an undertaking that the mark only be used for water drawn from the Apollinaris Spring.[37]

All national trademark laws represent a compromise between the need to preserve commonly used words in the public domain and the ability of descriptive words, including geographical names, to function as effective trademarks. Yet the story of APOLLINARIS, a mark caught in the vortex of the development of common law and legislative policy governing registrability of geographical indications as trademarks, demonstrates how trademark law creates a market place replete with legally protected geographical marks despite public domain concerns. A significant number of geographical marks are not just geographical names but also indicate the geographical origin of products. Any attempt to devise a legal policy for the protection of such indications must take into account not only the existence of prior trademark rights but also the underlying elements of the legal policy. State sponsorship of particular appellations has created pressure to treat geographical indications as a sui generis intellectual property right taking precedence over acquired trademark rights. To succumb to such pressure is to ignore the fact that geographical indications may compete with geographical trademarks for consumer recognition and that the warp and weft of trademark law — prevention from deception and unfair competition, both of which are essentially linked to consumer perceptions — underpin the legal protection of geographical indications.

One of the worst examples of succumbing to such pressures is the European Community (EC) Wine Regulation 1989,[38] drafted by the Commission Directorate-General responsible for agriculture, not intellectual property. The initial failure to address the conflict between geographical indications for wines and earlier trademarks has resulted in three amendments of the Regulation.[39] In the end,

---

37. Re Apollinaris trademark, [1907] 2 Ch 178, 24 RPC 436 (High Ct).

38. Council Regulation No. 2392/89, July 24, 1989, Official Journal (EC) ("OJ") L368, General Rules for the Description and Presentation of Wines and Grape Musts.

39. Most recently, Council Regulation No. 3897/91 of December 16, 1991, OJ L232. Only brand names registered at least 25 years before the official recognition of the geographical name by the producer Member State are permitted to continue in use but they may not be invoked to prevent the use of the (later) geographical name for wines. The amendment was prompted by the Torres case (see amended Article 43B of the EC wine regulations, OJ, No 232/35, August 9, 1989) where a well-known Spanish trademark for wine (whose owner was unaware of the geographical significance of his name) was

some established trademarks with a geographical significance have been permitted to co-exist with, but not take priority over, subsequently-recognized geographical indications. A more serious attempt has been made to address this issue in the EC Foodstuffs Regulation[40] which establishes a system of registration of protected designations of origin ("PDO") and protected geographical indications ("PGI") for agricultural products and foodstuffs. Co-existence of registered trademarks and similar registered PDOs and PGIs is contemplated where the trademark was registered in good faith and there are no grounds for invalidity or revocation of the mark under harmonized European trademark law.[41] In some cases, however, priority will be given to well-known marks. The Regulation provides that registration of a PDO/PGI will be refused where "in the light of a trademark's reputation and renown and the length of time it has been used," the indication is liable to mislead consumers as to the true identity of the product.[42] This at least acknowledges the relevance of consumer perceptions.

The TRIPS Agreement approach is less satisfactory. Article 24.5 provides that:

> Where a trademark has been applied for or registered in good faith, or where rights to a trademark have been acquired through use in good faith either:
>
> (a) before the date of application of these provisions in that member . . .; or
>
> (b) before the geographical indication is protected in its country of origin;
>
> measures adopted to implement this Section shall not prejudice eligibility for or the validity of the registration of a trademark, or the right to use a trademark, on the basis that

threatened with subordination to an unknown newly-adopted Portuguese geographical indication (TORRES VEDRAS) for wine.

40. Council Regulation No. 2081/92 of July 14, 1992, OJ L182, on the Protection of Geographical Indications and Designations of Origin for Agricultural Products and Foodstuffs.

41. Id at Article 14(2), which has recently been considered by the European Court of Justice in the Gorgonzola case, Consorzio per la tutela del formaggio Gorgonzola v. Kaserei Champignon Hofmeister GmbH & Co. KG and Eduard Bradrarz GmbH, Case C-87/97, March 4, 1999 (unreported), a reference to the Court from the Austrian Handelsgericht under Article 177 of the Treaty of Rome. The case concerned the compatibility of the registered trademark CAMBOZOLA in use in Austria since 1977 and the registered PDO Gorgonzola, protected under the EC Foodstuffs Regulation since 1996 and protected in Austria under international conventions. The Court considered that the CAMBOZOLA mark evoked in consumers' minds the GORGONZOLA designation and that it had not been registered in good faith because its registration was precluded under the terms of a bilateral agreement between Austria and Italy. Its continued use as a trademark therefore was not permitted.

42. Id at Article 14(3).

such a trademark is identical with, or similar to, a geographical indication.

While this approach is more satisfactory than that adopted in the EC Wine Regulation, it falls short of the protection afforded by the EC Foodstuffs Regulation for acquired trademark rights, and provides for coexistence rather than priority. It is possible, but by no means clear, that priority can be asserted under Article 16 of the TRIPS Agreement which permits the owner of a trademark to prevent the use of a similar sign. Whether geographical indications will be considered a "sign" for these purposes remains to be seen. To achieve compatibility with the private and public interests promoted by trademark law, geographical indications should be regarded as a "sign."[43]

II. GENERICNESS

Although trademark law places geographical indications within the public domain, it has been clear for many years that some geographical indications could acquire, whether by accident or design, a reputation surrounding particular products originating from the place in question which could serve the same trademark function as the reputation of a privately-owned trademark by acting as a convenient means of advertising and selling products. Such geographical indications do more than just describe geographical origin, as explained by Justice Laddie in the recent Swiss Chocolate case, Chocosuisse Union des Fabricants Suisses de Chocolat v. Cadbury Ltd.:

> If a trader used the expression "French ball-bearings" or "Italian pencils" neither would convey to most members of the public anything other than that the ball-bearings and the pencils came from France and Italy respectively. There is . . . no public perception that ball bearings from France or pencils from Italy form a discrete group of products having any particular reputation. . . . On the other hand a number of cases have held that the word Champagne [a non-generic term in the United Kingdom],[44] when put on a bottle of sparkling wine, is not merely descriptive of a group of products but that those products have a communal reputation . . . which

---

43. Equally, prior geographical indications should take precedence over subsequently-adopted marks. H. Poliner, Appellations of Origin in Israel Pursuant to the Lisbon Agreement, [1999] EIPR 149 (BUDWEISER). This is reflected in Article 14(1) of the EC Foodstuffs Regulation, supra note 40.

44. Unlike the position in the United States where champagne is considered a semi-generic name under the Bureau of Alcohol, Tobacco and Firearms (BATF) regulations. 27 CFR §4.24(b) and 27 CFR §24.257(c).

distinguishes them in the eyes of the public from wines not carrying that word.[45]

The commercial significance of the latter type of geographical name is encapsulated in Justice Laddie's comment that "the fact that . . . Champagne still had a cachet which made products sold under that word attractive to the customer is the hallmark of a particularly valuable mark."[46]

The economic significance of some geographical indications has prompted the formation of juristic entities, some state-sponsored and others created on the initiative of traders, tasked with preserving and promoting the reputation of specific marks. The Irish Linen Guild, English Vineyards Association, Chocosuisse Union, Swiss Embroidery Association, and Consorzio per la tutela del formaggio Gorgonzola, are examples of this type of concerted effort, much of which often occurs outside the country where the products originate. Such organizations create an added dynamic not only in the market place but also in the debate surrounding the proper scope of legal protection for geographical indications.[47]

Two organizations active decades before the Spanish Champagne case are Sherry Shippers' Association formed in 1910 and Harris Tweed Association formed in 1906. At that time, the United Kingdom's adherence to the Paris Convention of 1883,[48] reflected in the Merchandise Marks Act 1887, made it a criminal offense to sell goods bearing a false trade description, including an indication of the place or country of origin.[49] Under a proviso, however, no offense would be committed where the false indication of origin was accompanied by an indication of the actual place of origin.[50] The Sherry Shippers' Association brought a number of prosecutions in the 1920s and 1930s against non-Spanish fortified

---

45. Supra note 13 at 129-30 (High Ct).

46. Id at 128.

47. For example, such agencies provide a convenient means for the registration, exploitation and enforcement of collective and certification trademarks. Milo G. Coerper has advocated the use of the certification trademark system to facilitate focussed, aggressive programs of systematic assertion of ownership of geographical indications in order to prevent their degeneration into generic terms. Paper delivered at the Symposium on the International Protection of Geographical Indications, Madeira, October 13-14, 1993, WIPO/GEO/MA/93/5.

48. The Convention merely requires that goods bearing false indications of source should be seized on importation. Paris Convention, supra note 1, Articles 9 and 10. An obligation to provide effective protection against unfair competition, introduced in general form in Article 10bis at the London Revision Conference and subsequently amended to include specific acts of unfair competition, did not include misuse of geographical indications. Paris Convention, id Article 10bis(3).3. See Knoll, supra note 7, and Simon, supra note 5 at 150. Article 22.2(b) of the TRIPS Agreement, supra note 2, has the effect of extending Article 10 bis(3).3 of the Paris Convention to cover geographical indications.

49. 50 and 51 Vict, ch 28, §2(1)(d) and §18.

50. Id at §18 (proviso).

wines using the word "sherry," a term which one magistrate found to mean wine produced in the Jerez district of Spain. The same magistrate, however, indicated that the proviso "British Sherry" was unobjectionable and would not deceive consumers.[51] Whether or not influenced by the magistrate's view, the Association never brought a prosecution under the Merchandise Marks Act against any trader using the term "Sherry" qualified by the actual place of origin. After the Spanish Champagne case took the British legal community by surprise, sherry producers and shippers threatened passing-off proceedings to restrain the use of the term "British Sherry," "Cyprus Sherry," "Australian Sherry" and "South African Sherry" in England. Some of the defending producers and importers argued that members of the Sherry Shippers Association had by acquiescence over many years lost their right to object to the use of "Sherry" qualified by an accurate indication of origin:

> But whatever might have been the result had this action been brought 100 years ago, and the Courts had appreciated that the law laid down by Danckwerts J. in the Spanish Champagne case, can the [sherry producers] object to the use of these expressions now after so long a user as has been proved?[52]

The court emphatically answered this question in the negative and granted a declaration of entitlement to continue use of these qualified indications of source.

The Harris Tweed Association had more difficulty but ultimately was more successful against those who sought to undermine the meaning of HARRIS TWEED in the pre-Bollinger era. This appellation of origin was adopted in 1909 to certify the trademarked goods regulated by the Harris Tweed Association:

> "Harris Tweed" means a tweed made from pure virgin wool produced in Scotland, spun, dyed, and finished in the Outer Hebrides and hand woven by the Islanders at their own homes in the Islands of Lewis, Harris, Uist, Barra and their several purtenances and all known as the Outer Hebrides.[53]

The human element in the cottage industry which makes HARRIS TWEED traditionally has been a selling point but it has also limited the supply of this popular product. Since the last century, woolen mills in mainland Scotland or England had exploited this shortage by selling cloth which had been hand-

---

51. Vine Products Ltd. v. Mackenzie & Co. Ltd., [1969] RPC 1 (High Ct), referring to *Corke v. Pipers Ltd.* (unreported), id at 18-19.

52. Ibid. The "Sherry" case is discussed by Paul Abel at 58 TMR 188 (1968).

53. Argyllshire Weavers Ltd. and others v. A. Macauley (Tweeds) Ltd. and others, [1964] RPC 477, 522 (Ct of Session, Scotland).

woven on the islands of the Outer Hebrides but which had been spun, dyed or finished elsewhere as "Harris Tweed."[54] As counsel put it: "While a mainland thread has run through the industry for 60 years, it is a thread of deception which has all along been concealed from the public."[55] For several decades, the activities of these mainland traders threatened to dilute the reputation of HARRIS TWEED. Despite the registration of a certification trademark, an orb with the words HARRIS TWEED, the gradual descent into genericness was at times a real prospect in the 1930s and the 1940s. Private prosecutions in England under the Merchandise Marks Act 1887 had met with limited success. But in Scotland where prosecution could only be initiated by the Crown, none was ever brought because it was feared that the consequences of an adverse decision would hasten the degradation of HARRIS TWEED into a purely generic term.[56] It was only after the Spanish Champagne case that the manufacturers of HARRIS TWEED put an end to the generic use of "Harris Tweed" by bringing a passing-off action.[57]

In most intellectual property systems, it is possible to identify a time when the law affords no remedy for misuse of geographical indications or, as in the United Kingdom, a remedy which cannot be availed of without incurring considerable risk including the loss of trademark rights through acquired genericness. Should the effects of lost time and a failure of action due to uncertainties in the law ever be reversible? The failure of English law to protect collective reputation in geographical indications at a time of significant development of other intellectual property rights is remarkable. But a strict application of the principles of public domain, consumer protection and unfair competition militates against the artificial re-creation of the reputation of geographical indications for the purpose of reversing genericness. The process of "rollback" of generic terms is the most difficult issue surrounding the legal protection of geographical indications. The Madrid and Lisbon Agreements required member states to recognize and protect geographical indications which had become generic in their territories because they continued to be valid and non-generic in other member states. The fact that these Agreements attracted so few adherents indicates that, although genericness often can be

---

54. Indeed, English or Welsh wool was used sometimes. When Selfridges of Oxford Street discovered that cloth which they had bought as Harris Tweed was not the genuine article, the supplier "blandly replied that unless we sold these goods as Harris Tweed we would not sell any." Argyllshire Weavers Ltd., supra note 53.

55. Id at 480 (McIlwraith, Q.C.).

56. Id at 494-95, 517, 532 and 538.

57. Argyllshire Weavers, supra note 53.

explained on the basis of legal failure,[58] many states are reluctant to engage in the process of rollback except under bilateral or multilateral arrangements which offer trade advantages in other jurisdictions.[59] Thus, public domain concerns are often set aside to achieve specific economic or political gains. Within Europe, in the Sekt/Weinbrand case,[60] the European Court of Justice (ECJ) disapproved of one member state's attempt to re-create generic terms as geographical indications. The European Council of Ministers, however, has adopted a system of registering protected designations of origin and geographical indications for foodstuffs and agricultural products by the Commission. On the face of this scheme, a geographical indication could in theory be registered and protected throughout the European Union (EU), despite being generic in some areas. Once registered, these names can never become generic, whatever the consumer perception, unless they cease to be actively enforced. It has been argued that the process of rollback within the EU should be seen as a consequence of cultural integration,[61] but the recent hostilities within Europe surrounding the decision to grant the mark FETA protected status as a designation of origin to be used only on such cheese made in Greece, clearly show that domestic economic considerations continue to exert at least as great an influence on the actions of member states as their desire for closer integration. Some comfort may be taken from the recent decision of the ECJ annuling the Commission Regulation of 1996 under which FETA had become a protected designation of origin, at the instigation of Denmark, France and Germany, on the ground that the European Commission had failed to take account of evidence of genericness in some member states. The ECJ stressed the importance of consumer perceptions in the markets of EU countries other than Greece. In several of these countries, non-Greek Feta cheese had circulated lawfully for many years prior to the registration of the PDO.[62]

---

58. Robert Benson in Towards a New Treaty for the Protection of Geographical Indications, Industrial Property 127, 129 (1978), went so far as to say that "today's generic terms are the fossils of past consumer deception." But this is not necessarily the case.

59. Lori Simon reports that the United States offered strict protection to "Cognac," "Armagnac" and "Calvados" in return for similar protection in France for "Bourbon," supra note 5 at 153. In the state of Oregon, on the other hand, where there was a small wine industry, the administrative authorities unilaterally abandoned generic use of a number of foreign appellations for wines. See Benson, supra note 58 at 30.

60. 1977 GRUR Int 25, analyzed by Friedrich-Karl Beier, The Need for Protection of Indications of Source and Appellations of Origin in the Common Market, Industrial Property 152 (1977).

61. See, eg, Beier, ibid.

62. Denmark, Germany and France v. Commission of the European Communities, Joined Cases C-289/96, 293-96 and 299-96, March 16, 1999 (ECJ): 1999 ECJ CELEX LEXIS 210. Feta cheese had been made in Denmark since 1963 and had even been exported to

The jurisprudence of the ECJ, however, permits an individual member state to protect indications which continue to have geographical significance within its territory although they may have become generic in other member states. The resulting restriction on the freedom of movement of goods within the EU is justified on the basis of intellectual property protection.[63]

Under the TRIPS Agreement, a rollback of generic terms is not required at present. Article 24.6 provides that members are not required to protect indications which have become "customary in common language as the common name" for products in their territories.[64] But for the customary name for grape varieties, this exclusion from rollback is limited; only those which have become generic as of the date of entry into force of the agreement establishing the WTO are excluded from the rollback process.[65]

Ultimately, states surrender the freedom of their nationals to use generic terms in trade only when it is politically or commercially expedient. As Ryan has cogently argued in relation to the EC/Australia Wine Agreement,[66] the rollback of generics is not morally mandated; indeed, the fundamental principles of trademark law and unfair competition militate against the artificial reversal of genericness. The real issue in the genericness debate is whether the multilateral system of trade discipline established by TRIPS and related WTO Agreements gives all countries an equal chance to maintain the trading freedom which genericness confers, a question which is beyond the scope of this article.

III. THE MEANING AND ROLE OF "REPUTATION"

A [consumer] who does not know where Champagne comes from can have not the slightest reason for thinking that a bottle labelled "Spanish Champagne" contains a wine produced in France.[67]

The doctrinal weakness of the Spanish Champagne case was that the decision in essence prevented unfair competition caused by the

---

Greece.

63. As provided for in Article 36 of the Treaty of Rome: see Canadane Cheese Trading AMBA and Adelfi G. Kouri Anonymos Emoriki Lai Viomichaniki Etaireia v. Greece, Case C-317/95, June 24, 1997: 1997 ECJ CELEX LEXIS 4638.

64. See also Article 24.9: where the indication becomes generic in its state of origin, the obligation to protect it in other states ceases.

65. Id Article 24.6.

66. Des Ryan, The Protection of Geographical Indications in Australia, [1994] EIPR 521, 523.

67. Vine Products, supra note 51 at 23 (Cross, J.).

dilution of the term "Champagne" but was founded upon a
passing-off theory even though any actual consumer deception was
highly unlikely. This difficulty has been deftly overcome by
recognizing that the reputation of geographical indications
operates at two levels, the specific and the general. A clearly
definable specific reputation determines whether there is a
protectible geographical indication and defines the class of
plaintiffs who may bring a passing-off action to prevent its misuse.
Thus, the use of "Spanish Champagne,"[68] "Elderflower
Champagne"[69] and "Champagne Cider"[70] has been found actionable on the initiative of those who make or ship "Champagne,"
which has a specific meaning in England as a sparkling wine
made in the Champagne district of France. Similarly, specific
meanings have been proved in evidence in cases involving alleged
misuse of the terms "Sherry,"[71] "Scotch Whisky,"[72] "Harris
Tweed,"[73] "Advocaat,"[74] and "Parma ham."[75] General
reputation, on the other hand, refers to the fact that consumers
know of the indication without necessarily understanding its
specific meaning. Thus, the consumer perception of "Champagne"
as "the wine with the great reputation,"[76] possessing "nuances
of quality and celebration, a sense of something privileged and
special,"[77] was considered a sufficient basis for the action in the
Spanish Champagne and Elderflower Champagne cases.[78] A
consumer who is aware that the geographical indication has a
reputation but is unsure as to the precise nature of that
reputation, on seeing products inaccurately marked with the
indication "may very well think . . . that he is buying the genuine
article – real Champagne."[79] This approach effectively guarantees

---

68. J. Bollinger, supra note 14.

69. Taittinger and others v. Allbev Ltd., [1994] 4 All ER 75 (CA).

70. H. P. Bulmer Ltd. and Showerings Ltd. v. J. Bollinger and Champagne Lanson
Pere et Fils, [1976] RPC 97 (CA) (an appeal by the second plaintiff asserting a right to
continue to use Champagne Perry was successful on the basis of the defendants'
acquiescence in the use of that term over many years).

71. Vine Products, supra note 51.

72. John Walker & Sons, supra note 16. See also Matthew Gloag & Son Ltd. v. Welsh
Distillers Ltd., [1998] FSR 718 (High Ct), where it was held that the plaintiffs had an
arguable case of reverse passing off where the defendants sold Scotch whisky as "Welsh
Whisky."

73. Argyllshire Weavers, supra note 53.

74. Erven Warnink B.V. v. J. Townend & Sons (Hull) Ltd., [1979] 2 All ER 927 (HL).

75. Consorzio del Prosciutto di Parma v. Marks & Spencer plc, [1991] RPC 351 (CA),
and Consorzio del Prosciutto di Parma v. Asda Stores Ltd., [1999] 1 CMLR 696 (CA).

76. J. Bollinger (No 2), supra note 14.

77. Taittinger, supra note 69.

78. J. Bollinger, supra note 14, and Taittinger, supra note 69.

79. Vine Products, supra note 51 at 23 (Cross, J.).

a finding of deception in cases of misuse of well-known geographical indications, yet if there is any deception at all, it is deception as to the genuineness of the article and not as to its geographical origin. This suffices as a basis for the passing-off action.

Two further aspects of the case law precedent reinforce the impression that an action for passing off is often used in English law to pursue broader policy goals. In some of the cases cited, the defendant's conduct has been considered particularly relevant to the Court's determination. In the Champagne Cider case,[80] for example, the Court relied upon the cider makers' attempts in advertising to associate their own product with the glamour surrounding the champagne indication. Second, the relevant test of damage in English decisions protecting geographical indications is dilution of the mark's reputation, whether by acquired genericness or otherwise. In the Elderflower Champagne case, Sir Thomas Bingham, Master of the Rolls, recognized that dilution of the name Champagne was the principal type of harm at issue when he stated that:

> Any product which is not Champagne but is allowed to describe itself as such must inevitably, in my view, erode the singularity and exclusiveness of the description "Champagne" and so cause the . . . plaintiffs damage of an insidious but serious kind.[81]

That dilution is at the heart of the matter was also recently acknowledged by Justice Laddie in the Swiss Chocolate case, where he said that "what can be protected by this form of action is the accuracy and exclusivity of the descriptive term." He considered damage of this nature "more or less inevitable" once the other elements of the action have been established.[82]

In the development of the doctrine of specific and general reputation, the English courts have expressly rejected any limitation of the scope of the action for passing off to appellations of origin. While Champagne, Sherry and Parma ham are appella-

---

80. H. P. Bulmer, supra note 70 at 134.

81. Taittinger, supra note 69. See also Vine Products, supra note 51; Erven Warnink B.V. v. J. Townend & Sons (Hull) Ltd., [1980] RPC 31 (High Ct), and Scotch Whisky Assn. v. Glen Kella Distillers Ltd., [1997] ETMR 470 (High Ct), ("whisky"). The English courts have not yet considered diluting uses which clearly avoid confusion, such as "The Cognac of Fine Beer" considered in the Canadian case, Institut National des Appellations d'Origine v. Brick Brewing Co. Ltd., 66 CPR 351 (1995). See also the German case involving the advertisement "A Champagne among Mineral Waters," [1988] EIPR D-177 (Fed Sup Ct). It is submitted that the Spanish Champagne, Champagne cider and Elderflower Champagne cases reveal a willingness to prevent such uses under the law of passing off. The position under English law of diluting uses on wholly dissimilar goods—such as Champagne for perfume or bubble bath—remains unclear.

82. Chocosuisse, supra note 13 at 126 and 143.

tions of origin due to natural factors and *Harris Tweed* is arguably an appellation of origin because of human factors, Scotch whisky is primarily a geographical indication. It has a specific meaning – a blend of whiskys distilled in Scotland – but its reputation does not rest on product characteristics essentially attributable to its geographical origin.[83]

The application of this line of authority to mere geographical indications was explained in the Swiss Chocolate case. The Chocosuisse Union des Fabricants Suisses de Chocolat (Chocosuisse) objected to Cadbury's use of the brand name SWISS CHALET for chocolate not made in Switzerland on the basis that it deceived consumers and diluted the good will in the geographical indication SWISS CHOCOLATE. They, however, could not establish that SWISS CHOCOLATE possessed any objectively verifiable or recognizable distinctive qualities which were not possessed by chocolate made elsewhere, but the evidence established that the public believed or perceived that SWISS CHOCOLATE had special qualities. To many consumers, SWISS CHOCOLATE meant more than just a geographical origin, conveying "a reputation for quality, expense and exclusivity."[84] In the High Court, Justice Laddie found for the plaintiffs, a result confirmed on appeal. He drew an analogy between geographical indications and a famous trademark used in a particular market where there is no inherent difference between the products bearing the mark and rival products (such as the market for cola drinks), where the reputation of a famous brand becomes the only basis upon which to build market share. The reputation of well-known geographical indications, no less than that of appellations of origin, exerts strong commercial magnetism – "the hallmark of a particularly valuable mark" – and deserves to be protected on that basis. He went on to state that reputation should be protected whether it is developed by accident or the result of good "husbandry" by those who shared in the good will or their trade association.[85]

Where, however, the reputation of a geographical indication rests on perceived rather than actual distinctive qualities, it is more difficult to define the class of persons who may bring an

---

83. In the Advocaat case, a more restrictive view taken in the Court of Appeal, [1978] FSR 473, was rejected on appeal to the House of Lords. The view that the earlier "drinks" cases (champagne and sherry) concerned "a class of local products . . . regarded as having acquired a distinctive character by reason of some unique quality . . . in consequence of the geographical circumstances of their manufacture," id at 485 (Buckley, L.J.), could not survive the House of Lords' decision that passing off lies even where the trade indication has no geographical significance whatever, as with "advocaat."

84. Chocosuisse, supra note 13 at 130.

85. Id at 144.

action for passing off. In Chocosuisse, Justice Laddie concluded that:

> Where a designation has a clear meaning in accordance with common usage of the English language, it is reasonable to start from the position that the person and products which can take the benefit of that designation are all those who comply or are made in accordance with that meaning. Prima facie, Swiss chocolate means chocolate made in Switzerland. Of course the circumstances of the trade may show that the class has to be more narrowly defined than that.[86]

The Justice resisted a narrower definition suggested by Chocosuisse on the ground that it would have excluded some of its members from bringing an action for passing off. At the very least, the definition of the class must be broad enough to embrace the membership of the trade association defending the reputation of the geographical indication in question. He resolved the issue by defining the class of products entitled to be called SWISS CHOCOLATE (and therefore the class of persons entitled to seek to protect the geographical indication) as chocolate made in Switzerland in accordance with Swiss food regulations, a finding which was upheld by the Court of Appeal, subject to one further qualification excluding chocolate containing vegetable fat.[87]

This review of case law demonstrates that under English law, all geographical indications known to the relevant public can be subject to protection by an action for passing off to prevent deception as to origin and unfair competition, in recognition of their ability to develop a reputation which operates as an "attractive force which brings in custom."[88]

The concept of the reputation of geographical indications is incorporated into the TRIPS Agreement in an ambiguous way. Article 22.1 provides that:

> geographical indications are, for the purposes of this Agreement, indications which identify a good as originating in the territory of a member, or a region or locality in that territory, where a given quality, reputation or other characteristic of

---

86. Id at 135.

87. Chocosuisse Union des Fabricants Suisses de Chocolat v. Cadbury Ltd., [1999] RPC 826 (CA). None of the Swiss chocolate manufacturers used any vegetable fat in their chocolate (although Swiss food regulations permitted them to do so subject to a five percent limit).

88. Chocosuisse, supra note 13 at 128, Justice Laddie quoting the words of Lord MacNaghten in Commissioners of Inland Revenue v. Muller's Margarine Co. Ltd., [1901] AC 217, 227 (HL). Justice Laddie also stated that it was "a matter of semantics whether the Champagne type of action is called a separate or new tort [unfair competition] . . . or merely a new breach of the existing tort [passing off]." Id at 127. See also Vine Products, supra note 51 and Erven Warnink, supra note 74.

the good is essentially attributable to its geographical origin.[89]

To the extent that the TRIPS Agreement requires member states to protect geographical indications for goods where a causal link can be established between geographical origin and an objectively verifiable quality or characteristic of the product, it closely follows the narrow policy of the Lisbon Agreement.

The effect of the addition of "reputation" is unclear. Gervais gauged that the TRIPS definition was pitched between the Lisbon Agreement (appellations of origin) and the Madrid Agreement (direct or indirect indications of source) but this leaves the exact parameters undefined.[90] Beier and Knaak[91] and Conrad[92] have taken the view that the TRIPS Agreement does not require protection of "quality-neutral" geographical indications. According to this view, the scope of Article 22.1 is limited by the reference to the causal link ("essentially attributable") between product characteristics and geographical origin. More recently, however, the International Bureau of WIPO has taken the position that the TRIPS Agreement is applicable to "products which have a certain reputation due to their geographical origin even if they do not have a particular quality or characteristic because of that geographical origin."[93]

Clearly, clarification is needed as to the precise scope of the current TRIPS provisions relating to geographical indications. The late Professor Beier's view was that while the limited provisions of the TRIPS Agreement were initially an adequate basis for minimum global standards, they were wholly inadequate for the developed market economies of the European Union. Contrasting, on the one hand, the case law of the ECJ[94] which now recognizes that, on both legal and economic grounds, all geographical indications including those which are quality-neutral, deserve to

---

89. An earlier draft, the Brussels Draft 1990, omitted the word "reputation." See Gervais, *supra note* 10 at 120. *The agreed text of Article 22.1 is virtually identical to the* equivalent NAFTA provision, id at 123.

90. Ibid.

91. Friedrich-Karl Beier and Roland Knaak, The Protection of Direct and Indirect Geographical Indications of Source in Germany and the European Community, 25 IIC 1, 34 (1994).

92. Conrad, *supra note* 10 at 32.3.

93. Protection of Geographical Indications under WIPO Treaties and Questions Concerning the Relationship between those Treaties and the TRIPS Agreement, document prepared by the International Bureau for the WIPO Symposium on the Protection of Geographical Indications, Eger, Hungary, October 24-25, 1997: WIPO/GEO/EGR/97/1 Rev, 3.

94. The Turron case: Exportur S.A. v. LOR S.A. and Confiserie du Tech S.A., ECJ, November 10, 1992, 1993 GRUR Int 76, contrary to dicta in the much-criticized Sekt/Weinbrand case, *supra note* 60. See Beier, *supra note* 60 at 158-59.

be protected as intellectual property rights, and, on the other hand, the EC Foodstuffs Regulation[95] which does not protect quality-neutral geographical indications, Beier argued for a consistent policy of high level protection within the EU for all geographical indications, with due regard being had to acquired trademark rights.[96] English law protects appellations of origin and quality-neutral geographical indications on an equal basis provided that they are known to the relevant public (in the sense that they have a general reputation).[97] Justice Laddie's statement that a well-known quality-neutral geographical indication exerts a force in the market place which "is the hallmark of a particularly valuable [trade] mark" describes a policy which is consistent with the holding of the ECJ in the Turron case,[98] where the Court held that, where no causal connection exists between product characteristics and geographical origin, geographical indications:

> . . . may nevertheless be very highly regarded by consumers and constitute for producers established in the places referred to by such designations a vital means of attracting custom. Those designations therefore have to be protected. . . .[99]

IV. "INTERESTED PARTIES"

The TRIPS Agreement provides in Article 22.2 for "interested parties" to have the power to prevent the use of geographical indications in such a way as to cause deception as to origin or to constitute unfair competition. At the very least, these should include those who trade in products legitimately sold under the geographical indication and their trade representatives. The former are referred to in Article 10 of the Paris Convention while the latter are included in Article 10ter(2) of the Convention in relation to acts described in Articles 9, 10 and 10bis, suppression of unfair competition or seizure on importation of goods bearing false indications of source. However, under Article 10ter(2), trade federations and associations are rendered competent only to the

---

95. Supra note 40, Articles 2.2(a) and (b) and Article 4(2)(f).

96. Beier and Knaak, supra note 91.

97. There is no reason to believe that indirect geographical indications will be given a lesser degree of protection under English law than direct geographical indications. The requirement of reputation in the law of passing off, however, may identify one potential shortcoming of English law in that the broad scope of the line of authority from the Champagne case to the Swiss Chocolate case could not embrace mere indications of source which have no current reputation in the jurisdiction. It may be that "indication of source," as referred to in the Madrid Agreement, is broader. See WIPO paper, supra note 93 at 4.

98. Turron, supra note 94 at 79.

99. Turron, supra note 94.

Vol. 90 TMR   613

extent that they are competent to maintain such actions in the country where protection is sought.[100] It does not appear that state agencies such as the Institut National des Appellations d'Origine are within the scope of Article 10ter(2) of the Paris Convention. The status of such agencies under the TRIPS Agreement is unclear.[101] Under English law, traders who share in the reputation surrounding a geographical indication may bring a passing-off action either in their own right or in a representative capacity, seeking an injunction and/or damages.[102] Until recently, the right of trade associations to sue has been unclear. In the Parma ham case, it was decided that the Consorzio del Prosciutto di Parma could not sue in a representative capacity as it did not share a common interest or grievance with its members, but it was held that it could sue for passing off in its own right.[103] In Scotch Whisky Assn. v. J. D. Vinters Ltd., however, where the Association sought to restrain the defendants from passing off "Light Canadian Rye" as "whisky," the court indicated a contrary opinion. Sir Richard Scott V.C. considered that trade associations could not sue in their own right but could bring passing off proceedings in a representative capacity on behalf of their members.[104] Most recently, in the Chocosuisse case, the Court of Appeal held that the Chocosuisse Union des Fabricants Suisses de Chocolat could not sue either in its own right or in a representative action on behalf of its own members.[105] Counsel for Cadbury relied upon the fact that as Chocosuisse had no reputation in the jurisdiction and no actual or potential members there, it was not likely to suffer damage by reason of reduction in membership. The court considered that the association had no legitimate business interest which it could protect by means of a passing off action, and since it lacked any protectible interest of its own, it could not show that it shared a common interest with its

---

100. See Gervais, supra note 10 at 127 and Conrad, supra note 10 at 36-38.

101. See Conrad, supra note 10 at 37-38 describing the United States position; INAO has been found to have locus standi in a United States case involving the alleged misuse of "Chablis" ("Chablis with a Twist"): INAO v. Vintners International Co. Inc., 958 F2d 1574, 22 USPQ2d 1190 (CAFC 1992). Conrad doubts, however, whether this would be the position under Article 22.2 of the TRIPS Agreement.

102. J. Bollinger, supra note 14 and all subsequent "drinks" cases. Where the alleged wrongdoer commences "reverse" proceedings for passing off, seeking a declaration of entitlement to continue to use a geographical indication in a generic (non-geographical) sense, such proceedings may also be instituted on a representative basis. Bulmer Ltd. and Showerings Ltd. v. Bollinger, [1971] RPC 412 (High Ct) but claims of estoppel are not appropriate in representative actions. Ibid.

103. Consorzio del Prosciutto di Parma, supra note 75.

104. [1997] EULR 446. See also Scotch Whisky v. Glen Kella, supra note 81, where the point was not decided.

105. Chocosuisse, supra note 87.

members. It remains to be seen whether, following the Chocosuisse decision, the class of interested parties who may invoke the protection of the action for passing-off by obtaining an injunction to restrain the misuse of geographical indications is more restricted than was originally contemplated by those who framed Article 22.2 of the TRIPS Agreement. The difficulty caused by excluding trade associations may be overcome by employing leading traders as plaintiffs in representative actions but the result is nonetheless inconvenient and contrary to the spirit of the registered certification trademark system.

V. CONCLUSION

English law treats geographical indications as a sui generis intellectual property right only to the extent of related ownership issues. Beyond this, a law of geographical indications has been forged by the same forces which operate within trademark law. Drawing from the lessons of English law—which decisions are remarkably consistent with developing European jurisprudence affecting not only a common market but also a blend of cultures— this article argues for the development of internationally agreed upon principles to protect geographical indications which (1) properly reflect the commercial reality of acquired trademark rights in the market place, (2) view genericness as a bargaining position, not a crime (still less a sin), and (3) afford the same level of protection to all geographical indications which enjoy a significant reputation because they perform the same function and can be misused to deceive or unfairly compete (whether or not there is a causal connection between product characteristics and place of product origin). In the TRIPS Agreement, the dominant trademark law themes—the prevention of consumer deception and of unfair competition—are in evidence in the provisions for the protection of geographical indications. But, while the mischief is identified, the scope of this intellectual property right will remain obscure until the exact significance of "reputation" under Article 22.2 is clarified. Thus, it remains to be seen whether the TRIPS Agreement consistently will be interpreted and applied in a way which recognizes that all geographical indications with reputation bear "the hallmark of a particularly valuable mark" and should be afforded appropriate protection.

[3]

Are GIs IP?

OPINION

Stephen Stern

⊔ Geographical indications; Intellectual property; International law

> "If you call a dog's tail a leg, how many legs does it have? The answer is, of course, 'four', as calling the tail a leg doesn't make it a leg."

At the March 2004 AIDV[1] Conference on the Conflict between Geographical Indications (GIs) and trade marks, held in Reims, Champagne, the question was raised as to whether GIs are really intellectual property. While this is a simple question with a seemingly straightforward answer, the author is far from convinced that the answer is clear.

The first matter is to debunk the suggestion that GIs must be IP simply because they are so treated by a number of international treaties. It is true that at least one form of GI, namely appellations of origin, are referred to and first received IP-like protection under the Paris Convention of 1883, and that they have since been the subject of independent treatment both in treaties and in legislation. The TRIPs Agreement signed in Marrakech in 1994 also treats GIs as if they are IP. Indeed, that Agreement deals only with IP rights. Thus the question must be "how can it be argued that GIs are not a form of IP, if they are dealt with in TRIPs?".

The answer is that calling GIs a form of IP, and dealing with GIs in IP treaties, does not make GIs a form of IP. Rather, one must ask the basic question as to whether GIs fit the traditional description of IP.

What is intellectual property?

IP can be defined as intangible rights, protected at law, and created by the mind. While many legal dictionaries choose to define IP by reference to the traditional forms thereof, such as patents, trade marks, copyright and so forth, examples of the genus should not, of course, constitute the definition. They are mere instances that fit the description. By way of example, plant variety rights and printed circuit rights did not exist two decades ago. Thus the list of types of rights that meet the criteria of being an IP right is expanding, which demonstrates that GIs cannot be defined by a mere list.

"Intellectual Property" can be variously defined as:

- ".. any product of the human intellect that is unique, novel and unobvious . . ."[2];
- "intangible property that is the result of creativity . . ."[3];
- "the property of (the) mind or intellect"[4];
- "property that derives from the work of the mind or intellect".[5]

These are merely sample definitions. Leaving aside the obvious problems with the first definition,[6] the common denominator of each is the involvement of intellectual input.

Article 2(viii) of the Convention which established the World Intellectual Property Organization defined "intellectual property" as including rights relating to:

- "literary, artistic and scientific works
- performances of performing artists, phonograms and broadcasts;
- inventions in all fields of human endeavour;
- scientific discoveries;
- industrial designs;
- trade marks, service marks and commercial names and designation;
- protection against unfair competition
  and all other rights resulting from intellectual activity in the industrial, scientific, literary or artistic fields".

Even taking into account that this definition is an inclusionary and not an exhaustive definition, there is no manner in which geographical indications

---

1 Association Internationale des Juristes du Droit de la Vigne et du Vin.
2 *www.uta.edu.*
3 *http://web.ask.com.*
4 IP Australia definition on its website, *www.ipaustralia.gov.au.*
5 FindLaw definition on its website, *http://dictionary.lp.findlaw.com.*
6 The requirement that the product be "unique, novel and unobvious" is a curious blend of patent law with something else and which would not encompass copyright or trade marks!

40 OPINION: [2007] E.I.P.R.

can fit within the scope of either the WIPO definition or of any of the earlier cited definitions. They are simply not products of intellectual input. The geographical name inevitably pre-existed the product that subsequently became known by that name.

What are geographical indications?

What are GIs? They are defined in a number of treaties in similar language. The TRIPs definition is probably the most current, and is certainly the definition with the greatest level of international currency. Thankfully we do not have any dilemma as the TRIPs definition is entirely consistent with the commonly accepted understanding of the term. TRIPs provides as follows:

> "Geographical indications are, for the purposes of this Agreement, indications which identify a good as originating in the territory of a Member, or a region or locality in that territory, where a given quality, reputation or other characteristic of the good is essentially attributable to its geographical origin."

What then makes a name a "geographical indication"? Can this be created just be drawing lines on a map (or in the soil) and applying a name? The author's view is certainly not, and here is the very core of why GIs are not IP—they cannot be and are not created by an intellectual process.

If that is the case, then how are GIs created? Herein lies the answer as to why GIs are not IP. GIs are generally if not virtually always the name of a region or locality. There are of course some limited exceptions such as "Feta" or "Basmati". However, as the very name GI suggests, the indication or term must function to designate some region or locality, and this is done by the adoption of the geographic name itself as the designator of the product. Thus, at this basic level, there is nothing conceived or invented by the so-called IP owner. At best there is a public recognition that the place name has taken on a secondary meaning. There is no originality or creation involved. There is not even the application of a name or word to an unrelated product or service. Rather the name of the region or location is used to also refer to the product originating from that region or location.

Although one might think of exceptions, the author cannot bring to mind any GI where the name of the product preceded the name of the region or locality. The latter almost certainly invariably existed before it started to be applied to the product, which again is inconsistent with GIs being a form of IP. There is simply no creativity that can be deserving of the form or type of protection to which intellectual creations are accorded.

There is the related and interesting question as to when it can be said that a name has become to truly be a GI. If we take the language from the TRIPs definition, there must be a "name . . . which identifies a good". This suggests that while one needs to use the noun which describes the product when using the so-called GI, then the name of the region or locality has not become a GI. In other words, if one needs to add the product type as a descriptor, such as "Bordeaux wine" or "Parmigiano cheese", then the name of the region or locality is not a real GI. The author acknowledges, however, that this is an extreme view. The fact that the word "ham" follows the GI "Parma" does not in any way derogate from the fact that "Parma" is a GI for ham.

By way of example, the author suggests that the evolution of GIs would follow the following pattern, where wine from Burgundy is used as the example.

    (1) Early in the genesis of the creation of the GI Burgundy, these wines would, when described by reference to their origin, probably have been called "wines from Burgundy", a simple and accurate description.

    (2) The second stage was probably when the reputation of wines from this region or locality had started to be established. At that time, the contracted description of "Burgundy wines" would probably have been used.[7]

    (3) By the time the name had become a true GI, the word "Burgundy" had acquired a secondary meaning and now "identified a good" in

7 Of course this example is, certainly in so far as the distinction between the first two "levels" is concerned, totally fictional as the French for "wines from Burgundy" is exactly the same as the French for "Burgundy wines", namely "vins de Bourgogne".

OPINION: [2007] E.I.P.R. 41

the terms of the current definition of GIs. At this stage, the name was clearly a GI and the wines were merely called "Burgundy".

(4) Perhaps such GIs that do not need to have added to them the noun which describes the product are extreme cases.

A simple test of this thesis suggests that it might be accurate. If you hear something spoken of as a "Bordeaux" or as "Roquefort", you do not need the nouns "wine" or "cheese" to be added to the name of the region or locality to be able to identify the product. Rather the name alone now identifies the good.

As a second stage to this thesis, apply the same test to many of Australia's emerging wine regions. While it makes sense to talk about a "Barossa" or a "Coonawarra", it makes little sense to talk of an "Orange" or of a "Canberra" and expect the listener to have any idea what is being discussed.[8] This is, in the author's view, simply because the names have not taken on a secondary meaning and thus do not, of themselves, identify any product.

How can it be said that GIs are IP?

The fact that GIs are names, just as some forms of trade marks are names, is one obvious similarity between GIs and one form of IP. Indeed, there are other similarities that readily spring to mind.

- GIs are collective rights, just as collective trade marks or, at a stretch, certification trade marks, are collective rights. The English House of Lords held in 1961 in *Bollinger v Costa Brava Wine Co*[9] that the Champagne appellation or origin was capable of protection at a suit brought by some of those persons entitled to use it.
- Concomitant with this, it might be asserted that GIs are a form of property right as are IP rights.
- Each of GIs and trade marks can, in many jurisdictions, be defended or protected by consumer protection law, whether by statute or by passing off or unfair competition type actions.
- Each of GIs and trade marks indicate a source of products, the former the geographical source, and the latter the trade mark owner (or its licensee).

However, the fact that there are similarities in the nature of GIs and IP does not necessarily lead to the conclusion that the two rights are the same, or, more particularly, that GIs are a form or subset of IP. There are a number of crucial distinctions between GIs and every other type of IPR.

Distinctions between GIs and IP

The differences listed below are by no means exhaustive, but demonstrate why the seduction of labelling GIs as IPRs needs to be avoided. Bear in mind that bicycles, like motor cars, are a means of transportation of people and, to a limited extent, products. Both use wheels, are commonly ridden on the road and follow the same road laws. However, there the similarities end and not even these would allow a person to say that bicycles and motor vehicles are the same. While both can be described by the genus "transportation", this is not an answer. Certainly both GIs and IPRs are forms of legal rights, but there are convincing reasons why one is not a subset of the other.

GIs, while having property-like characteristics, are not in fact property. They cannot be:

- sold;
- licensed;
- dealt with independently of the region or locality to which they append;
- used in an exclusionary manner in that they are open to use by all persons in the region or locality making the product in compliance with local laws or customs.

8 These are also the names of Australian wine geographical indications.
9 [1961] R.P.C. 123.

In addition, GIs are physically "appended" to the region or locality they describe and indeed their existence as place names invariably predates their adoption as the name of a product.

Registration of a GI is not of any relevance. Like trade mark registrations (but unlike patents or registered designs), a GI registration system is, in some cases, established merely to facilitate easy recognition and protection while in others, to ensure that the local customs and usages are recorded and faithfully followed by those wishing to have the right to use the GI.

It has been suggested that the creation by a state or country of an administrative system for the recognition and protection of GIs is the establishment of a *sui generis* set of rules or regulations that deprives GIs of the "ability" to be IPRs. This is not a view with which the author agrees, as the *sui generis* legislation that recognises and protects printed circuits and plant breeder rights was not determinative of such rights not being IPRs. Rather the author believes that the issue is a basic one of comparing the characteristics of GIs with the definition of IPRs.

Conclusion

The IP world is fast rushing down the path of accepting that GIs are intellectual property. For the reasons above, the author is far from convinced that this is correct. The ramifications of such a categorisation do not appear to be enormous although the categorisation is relevant to an issue that has received much debate, namely the conflict between GIs and trade marks. Without exploring that topic in this article, the first paragraph above makes it clear that the policy decision as to how to resolve conflicts between GIs and trade marks by using IP principle of "first in time, first in line" may be proceeding on a false assumption, namely that GIs are intellectual property rights and should be dealt with using intellectual property principles. That is not to say whether such a policy decision is incorrect. However, it is certainly called into question. The purpose of this article is not intended to counter the implementation of such a policy determination (which in fact the author supports) but rather to ensure that, before IP world continues too much further down the path, it considers carefully whether the underlying presumption as to the nature of GIs is in fact correct.

STEPHEN STERN
Partner, Corrs Chambers Westgarth, Melbourne, Australia

[4]

Registered Geographical Indications

Between Intellectual Property and Rural Policy—Part II

William van CAENEGEM*

Part I of this article dealt with some of the theoretical issues underlying registration systems for geographical indications (GIs). Part II considers some aspects of the historical development in France and present regulatory structures of GI registration in Europe and the New World.

I. HISTORY AND DEVELOPMENT OF REGISTERED GIs

A. *The History of GIs in France: Reclamation of Lost Property?*

Since so much of the impetus for the expansion of GIs emanates from France, it is useful to delve into some of the history of GI protection in that country. This aids a proper evaluation of the French and European positions in the global GI debate, in the light of the theoretical discussion in Part I of this article. The current struggle to regain some control over French (and other EU Member country) GIs around the world is a geographic extension of a process that began at a more local level.

Of further interest is the fact that in the history of the privileges of French wine-growers, as illustrated by Bordeaux and Champagne, one finds that combination of elements of rural policy, guarantees of authenticity and the search for competitive advantage which marks today's debate about global expansion of GI registration. The historical background provided below is not intended to be comprehensive, but rather illustrative. It focuses on wine, and in particular on the two wine-growing regions of Bordeaux and of Champagne.

1. BORDEAUX'S EARLY HISTORY: PRIVILEGES, IDENTIFYING MARKS AND RURAL POLICY[1]

In the Middle Ages in the South-West of France, and also in other French wine-producing regions, the sale and consumption of wines from other regions were prohibited. Only wines originating in the region were allowed entry into its towns.

---

* Associate Professor of Law, Bond University, Gold Coast, Queensland, Australia.

For acknowledgements relating to research and writing of this article, see Part I, which appeared in the September 2003 issue of The J.W.I.P.

The author may be contacted at: «william_van_caenegem@bond.edu.au».

[1] The information in this part is largely drawn from A. Richard, *De la protection des appellations d'origine en matière vinicole*, Imprimeries Gounouilhou, Bordeaux, 1918.

Right up until the time of the French Revolution of 1789, the Bordeaux region[2] also benefitted from two additional privileges:

(a) the *privilège de la descente*; and
(b) the *privilège de la barrique*.

The latter is said to have been akin to a mark of origin, and thus an early manifestation of the use of such marks to prevent confusion between wines from different regions. Nonetheless, both actually had protectionist motives and effects.

Most, if not all, transport of wine in that region of France was by river. The *privilège de la descente* meant that wines from outlying regions, not being part of the Bordeaux area, were not to be brought down by river to Bordeaux for sale before 11 November of each year, and some even later. This gave the Bordeaux wines a valuable window of monopoly over the sale of wines into the lucrative markets of England and Holland, whence transport became very difficult later in the year because of weather conditions and the icing up of northerly ports. When the wines from outside Bordeaux were brought into the city, they were held in discrete cellars in a specific area of the city. The effect of this privilege, although its intent was predominantly to stifle competition, was also "*l'authentification à peu près absolue des vins de la sénéchaussée pendant une période de l'année.*"[3]

As to privilege (b), the wines of Bordeaux (*vins de ville*) were the only ones entitled to a *barrique* (barrel) of a special form and dimensions. This differentiated them from wines from other regions; hence Richard says:

"*Nous trouvons ici la première manifestation de la protection des appellations de provenance en matière vinicole; il s'agissait bien d'une véritable marque d'origine. D'autres villes ont eu elles aussi une barrique spéciale.*" (emphasized in the original).[4]

But although the special shape was intended to prevent confusion, it also resulted in further trading privileges for the Bordelais: bigger *barriques*, made of better wood, which the Bordelais succeeded in preventing other regions from using, meant that the wine travelled better during export.[5] Because freight was the same whatever the size of the *barrique*, transport costs were also lower than for those who were forced to use smaller *barriques*. This was a distinct advantage in the all-important export trade to England.

A significant development occurred when, in 1764, to prevent the illicit use of the Bordeaux *barrique*, each wine-grower was compelled to identify, by way of a red brand on the bottom of each *barrique*, his name and that of the *paroisse* (parish) of origin.[6] This move was, in fact, opposed by the dealers of Bordeaux. They argued that rather than

---

[2] The *Sénéchaussée de Guyenne*.
[3] "... the well nigh absolute authentication of the wines of the Bordeaux region during a certain time of the year." (all translations made by the author): see Richard, *supra*, footnote 1, at 50.
[4] Id.: "We see here the first appearance of the protection of appellations of origin in relation to wines; it did amount to a true mark of origin. Other towns also had a special barrel."
[5] This monopoly over barrel shapes brings to mind one of the contentious issues in the contemporary debate concerning the extension of rights to the shape of bottles, e.g. Champagne bottles.
[6] *Arrêt de la Cour du Parlement concernant la police des vins*, 18 July 1764, Article 3.

prevent fraud, this measure would encourage it. Nothing would stop dishonest traders from sending poor wine in casks with the most desirable brands, and keeping the best wines for themselves in casks with the less-favoured brands.[7] The ability to hide true origin by misuse was to bedevil the use of marks. In the wine industry, where adulteration, cutting, admixing and other unsavoury practices were rife, and difficult to detect and control, this takes on additional significance.

But another significant problem was that the branding requirement would render illegal certain established practices of mixing and deriving supplemental wine from neighbouring, sometimes better-quality-producing parishes. Much wine was sold under the well-regarded name of a certain parish or vineyard location, but was, in fact, derived from contiguous parishes which were considered to have similar, if not even better characteristics. Again, this is illustrative of a modern problem—that of imposition of rigid regional delimitations and the resulting impossibility of dealing flexibly with varying levels of production within the area of demarcation or, more generally, to meet demand while effectively maintaining quality. The GI can act as a brake on growers' genuine attempts at maintaining consistent quality and supply of wine.

As well as enjoying other privileges, in Bordeaux (as in some other regions) wine sales were also protected against the sale of other beverages, such as beer and cider. Neighbouring regions constantly fought to deprive Bordeaux of its privileges, but in a sense were swimming against the swelling tide of monopolies in the period of the _Ancien Régime_.[8] Although in an edict of April 1776 free trade in wine was declared in the whole of France, Bordeaux was able to maintain most of its privileges, in practice at least. By November 1776 most of the effects of the edict of April 1776 were suspended. It was only with the abolition of all privileges of towns on 4 August 1789, during the Revolutionary period, that Bordeaux's privileged position came to an end.

It was at the time of the struggles about abolition that an interesting shift in argumentation occurred. In fighting for its privileges, Bordeaux emphasized that they were justified for the purpose of guaranteeing the genuineness of the _crus_ (vintages) for foreigners. It also emphasized, invoking agricultural policy, that the land of Bordeaux was not amenable to the growing of other crops; therefore the growing of vines deserved encouragement.[9] Protectionist measures also allowed the people of

---

[7] One should remember that this was during a time when such crude impostures could not readily be exposed through chemical analysis and testing, as would now be possible. And, in the words of Thomas Barton who, on behalf of the traders, drew up a Memorandum to be presented to the _Conseil du Roy_: "_On ne juge point de la qualité du vin, ny de pas une liqueur quelconque, à l'aspect de la futaille ou du tonneau qui le contient; c'est par le goût qu'on en décide, et c'est une vague illusion de penser qu'une marque empreinte sur un tonneau puisse faire trouver le vin qu'il contient de meilleure qualité qu'il ne l'est en effet._" ("One does not judge the quality of wine by its container's appearance; one determines it by taste, and it is an illusion to think that the mark on the outside of a cask will make the quality of the wine contained any better than it actually is.") As quoted in Richard, _supra_, footnote 1, at 55.

[8] Richard argues that Bordeaux went so far in its protection of its wines that it managed to turn every other region against it, contributing to the eventual demise of the privileges; see Richard, _supra_, footnote 1, at 60.

[9] It was well recognized that where soil was poor, the growth of vines was often one of the few options open, and deserved to be encouraged, by the grant of monopolies.

Bordeaux to build up a financial surplus so they could afford to import grain to feed the population.[10]

The injection into the debate of rural and agricultural policy considerations deserves attention. It was for the purpose of ensuring that poor soil areas were indirectly protected or subsidized in relation to growing vines that much of the original geographically-based protection systems were devised. The fact that GIs are an instrument of rural policy is still in evidence today—as mentioned in Part I of this article—and the Preamble to Regulation 2081/92 of the European Union states, in part:

> "... whereas the promotion of products having certain characteristics could be of considerable benefit to the rural economy, in particular to less-favoured or remote areas, by improving the incomes of farmers and by retaining the rural population in these areas;".[11]

2.   CHAMPAGNE: REGULATION FROM PAST TO PRESENT

Champagne has a somewhat different history.[12] In 1670 the sparkling *"mousse"* style was accidentally discovered by Dom Perignon, a Benedictine monk, cellar master at the Abbey of Hautvillers near Epernay in France. Initially the new style came under vigorous attack. But the reputation of Champagne grew steadily both in France and, importantly, also abroad. By 1854-1855 nearly 2.5 million bottles of wine were sold in France and nearly 7 million abroad; in 1872-1873 19 million were sold abroad, and just before World War I total sales were about 30 million bottles, two-thirds of which was abroad.[13]

The Champagne appellation in the modern sense was initially delineated in 1908 over an area of 15,000 hectares. In 1927 it was definitively circumscribed for an area of 34,000 hectares. A set of thirty-five rules controls every aspect of the production of Champagne:

- the grape varieties used;
- planting and pruning of vines;
- limited yields;
- harvest by hand;
- minimum ageing periods.[14]

---

[10] In fact, in the seventeenth and eighteenth centuries, much of the central attack on Bordeaux's privileges was inspired by the desire to encourage the growing of wheat; authorities wanted to prevent the substitution of vines for wheat to ensure a sufficient supply of the latter. The Bordelais twisted this argument to their advantage: giving Bordeaux more privileges would turn others off planting vines, thus maintaining wheat production!

[11] Council Regulation (EEC) No. 2081/92 of 14 July 1992 on the protection of geographical indications and designations of origin for agricultural products and foodstuffs, O.J. L. 208, 24 July 1992; see also D. Hangard, *Protection of Trademarks and Geographical Indications in France and in the European Union*, Symposium of the International Protection of Geographical Indications 65, 75, 1999.

[12] The information provided in this part is largely derived from R. Hodez, *Du droit à l'appellation Champagne*, Presses Universitaires de France, 1923.

[13] See Hodez, ibid., at 12.

[14] Recently, the minimum ageing period was increased to fifteen months for non-vintage and three years for vintage Champagnes. The use of vintage and non-vintage Champagnes adds vital flexibility to the system and allows some balancing out *qua* production levels over time.

Vineyards are not allowed to be planted just anywhere in the Champagne region, but are restricted to hillsides with particular soil characteristics. *Négociants* (merchants) buy grapes to augment their own vineyard's production and then go through the complex and labour-intensive production processes required.

The result is said to have a unique character, notwithstanding the fact that there are numerous imitations around the world. The system of regulation and control is *the* model of an *Appellation d'Origine Contrôlée* (AOC); wine production is heavily regulated, in an endeavour to guarantee its close connection with both the human and the physical characteristics of a narrowly circumscribed region. Stringent quality and production control ensures stability over time, to a degree at least. In the result, as Hodez says:

> "*Le vin de Champagne correspond à des qualités obtenues avec les plus grandes difficultés et à grand frais; il est donc nécessaire de protéger le mot qui sert à le désigner.*"[15]

3.   NATIONAL REGULATION TO PREVENT ABUSES

Regulation in the *Ancien Régime* was piecemeal and adapted to local political and historical privileges and conditions, rather than based on a uniform national approach. It was very much inspired by the fear of fraudulent admixtures and false attachment of names. At that time, since it was not possible to test adulteration chemically, a very high degree of specific regulation and supervision of production was required to prevent subterfuge. This obviously imposed enormous costs and resulted in regulatory constraints whose effect was anti-competitive. It was only with difficulty that the notion of appellation of origin managed to emerge from this regulatory morass once the privileges were later abolished, and to become the focus of regulatory efforts:

> "*Pendant la grande partie du XIXième siècle, les abus en matière de marques et d'appellations étaient généralement considérés comme des faits normaux ... Quant au respect de l'appellation d'origine, il n'a pu s'obtenir que progressivement et avec beaucoup de peine.*"[16]

Early twentieth-century France saw the start of an era of more general regulation of production and trade in foodstuffs, and of wines in particular. Uncertainty about the delimitation of wine-producing regions, and adjacent frauds, was finally removed by the Law of 6 May 1919 concerning *Appellations d'Origine*. This Law fixed the principles of delimitation of regions, and defined the characteristics that the products had to have, as

---

[15] "The wine of Champagne has characteristics that are obtained at very great cost and with great difficulty; therefore it is necessary to protect the word that identifies it."

[16] "During the greater part of the nineteenth century, abuses of marks and appellations were generally considered to be par for the course ... Respect for appellations of origin only emerged gradually and with great effort.": see Hodez, *supra*, footnote 12, at 18–19. This despite several general measures aimed at protecting regional names against imitation and against uses such as "in the style of ..."; see Law of 22 Germinal XI, 12 April 1803. General provisions of Napoleon's *Code Civil* (Article 1382) and *Code Pénal* (Article 423) were applicable but the Law of 28 July 1824 was a complementary and more specific measure expressly making Article 423 applicable to false indications on goods, *inter alia* concerning the place where they were made. Other laws were directed specifically at fraudulent adulteration and admixture, culminating in the law of 1 August 1905 "Concerning fraud in the sale of goods and falsification of foodstuffs and agricultural products."

well as the protection measures afforded them.[17] In 1935, the general system of establishment of AOCs, under the supervision of a Committee that, from 1947 onwards, became the INAO (*Institut National des Appellations d'Origine*), was set up under the Law (*Loi-décret*) of 30 July.

Nonetheless, a well-protected AOC such as Champagne, with all its attendant goodwill, naturally encouraged rival traders if not actually to use the same name to make their goods more attractive, then at least to attempt to ride on its coat-tails "*tantôt par d'adroits subterfuges ou de déformations de mots qui leur permettent parfois d'éviter de tomber sous le coup de la loi*".[18] The modern-day approach to registered GIs for wines, which is very strict and does not permit the use of the GI in combination with other terms, in translations, in the form of "… -style", etc., or with clear disclaimers, originates in earlier recognition of, and attempts to stamp out, this kind of duplicity.

4. FROM NATIONAL TO INTERNATIONAL PROTECTION

Although the protection of GIs, as it emerged during the nineteenth century and then evolved from piecemeal regulation to generally applicable administration, was gradually strengthened and the use of names such as Champagne brought under control within France, unrestrained use of French names continued abroad. International treaties such as Paris 1883 and Madrid 1891[19] did contain provisions against false indications of origin. But neither these nor more specific treaties signed during the twentieth century— in particular Lisbon—had much effect outside a small number of jurisdictions that already favoured registered GIs.[20] Thus, before the Agreement on Trade-Related Aspects of Intellectual Property Rights (TRIPS) and recent bilateral agreements, it fell to non-State actors to pursue the cause of the protection of GIs around the globe.

The actions of the *Comité Interprofessionnel du Vin de Champagne (CIVC)* are well known in this regard. However, the efforts of the CIVC did not meet with universal success,[21] and in any case they were of little or no assistance to owners of other registered GIs. Hence, the international treaty negotiations in the context of TRIPS offered proponents an opportunity to make uniform advances favouring all producers using GIs, continuing the expansion of protection by registration from the local, to the national, to the regional and finally to the global arena. In France, historical developments have culminated in the current system combining the pre-existing system of AOCs with the

---

[17] See Hodez, *supra*, footnote 12, at 20.

[18] Ibid., at 21: "… by cunning subterfuge or modification of terms which sometimes allowed them to escape the effect of the law."

[19] The Paris Convention for the Protection of Industrial Property, 1883; The Madrid Agreement for the Repression of False or Deceptive Indications of Source on Goods, 1891.

[20] The Lisbon Agreement for the Protection of Appellations of Origin and their International Registration, 1958; the World Trade Organization Agreement on Trade-Related Aspects of Intellectual Property Rights (TRIPS), Articles 22–24.

[21] See, for instance, in Australia, *Comité Interprofessionel du Vin de Champagne v. N.L. Burton Pty Ltd.*, (1981) 57 FLR 434.

superimposed structure of PDO/PGIs (protected designations of origin/protected GIs) resulting from European Council Regulation 2081/92, which deals with such protection (see further below). Olszak points out that:

> "*Malgré le souci habituel de précision que l'on connait en droit, la terminologie employée dans notre domaine demeure malheureusement assez fluctuante.*"[22]

Terminological confusion abounds in this area of the law, but there is no doubt that the system of AOCs is universally recognized as the high water mark of protection for registered GIs. The description below illustrates the complexity and pervasiveness of such a high-level system of registration of GIs. Together with the EU PDO/PGI model, it is a significant model in terms of the global expansion of GI protection by registration proposed by the EU in the context of TRIPS.

5.   THE CURRENT SYSTEM OF GI REGISTRATION IN FRANCE

Leaving registered trade-marks law issues aside, French law relating to GIs in general has three levels of regulation; one general, aimed at preventing misleading conduct in relation to geographical names, and two relating to the registration of geographical indications with varying levels of quality significance. As a general principle, geographical indications can be used freely,[23] subject to the general prohibition on the use of false indications of origin, by virtue of Section L 217-6 of the *Code de la Consommation.* Any person who attaches or knowingly uses any indication on or in relation to any goods, in a manner that causes others to believe that they have an origin other than their true origin, is in breach of the Code. However, the law expressly provides that if the true origin is clearly marked on the product, no liability will ensue, unless the false indication of origin is a protected (i.e. registered) regional designation.[24]

---

[22] The current system of protection of geographical indications in France is well described in N. Olszak, *Droit des Appellations d'Origine*, Tec&Doc, Chapter III, *Le droit français des indications Geographiques*, 2001. For a recent precis of the protection of GIs in the broad sense, see also F. Pollaud-Dulian, *Droit de la propriété industrielle*, Montchrestien, 1999. For this passage, see Olszak, at 69: "Despite the usual desire for precision in law, the terminology in our area of study [i.e. that of GIs in general] unfortunately remains fluid."

[23] See Olszak, ibid., at 152.

[24] For all products in general, Article L 115-2 to 4C of the *Code de la Consommation* does provide for an administrative procedure for the registration of designations of origin. A prescribed process of public inquiry and consultation with affected industry groups results in a decree of the *Conseil d'Etat*. Only very few registrations have been granted by this method, and now it is only relevant for industrial products, as procedures for agricultural produce and foodstuffs are now integrated in the regular procedure for PDOs (or AOPs, to use the French acronym), AOCs for wines, and PGIs (or IGPs), paralleling the European Union system (see further below). The administrative procedure is an alternative to the longer established judicial procedure, finding its origins in the Law of 6 May 1919 and now codified in Article L 115-8 to L 115-15 of the *Code de la Consommation*. This procedure allows conflicts concerning the legitimate use of denominations to be referred to a court, which can resolve the conflict and determine for the future the delimitation of an area and the characteristics of the product concerned. This process was previously mainly used in relation to wine, and only rarely in relation to industrial products; according to Olszak, *supra*, footnote 22 at p. 15, it was last used in 1986. *Décision Grenoble, 1re Ch.*, 14 February 1989, PIBD, 1989, III, 118, relating to the term *Raviole du Dauphiné.*

But agricultural produce and foodstuffs, including wines, are far more prescriptively regulated than products in general. As Olszak puts it:

"... *les produits agricoles et les denrées alimentaires font l'objet d'une politique particulièrement détaillée et complexe, en raison de l'importance évidente des terroirs dans leur cas.*"[25]

This level of regulation is so extensive and pervasive that Olszak argues that the exercise of the theoretical right/freedom to employ simple indications of provenance is now liable, in almost every case, to fall foul of the protection afforded to AOCs and PGIs (the French acronym is IGP). In other words, the system of registered GIs has progressively become more predominant and virtually displaced reliance on unfair competition torts.

6.   ADMINISTRATION OF THE GI REGISTRATIONS BY THE INAO

The registration system for food and wine GIs is administered through the *Institut National des Appellations d'Origine*, which previously (before 1990) was only responsible for wines and spirits and in relation to the grant of AOCs, but now is responsible also for the grant of PGIs, and for all agricultural products and food. The system administered by the INAO, which itself is a complex body constituted of numerous national and local committees, is the apogee of regulation, enforcing the closest connection between origin and quality control.

Although this, according to Olszak, is not essential,[26] the registration process is normally instigated by an interested local syndicate.[27] The request is examined by INAO officials and then, after consultation of the relevant regional committee, by the national committee responsible for the produce category in question. This committee then opens an inquiry and commissions experts' reports (which are submitted to the national committee). The committee then rejects, adjourns or approves the proposed project, in the latter case appointing a delimitation committee to determine the definition of the *terroirs* (soils) within the denomination. This, in turn, is incorporated in a draft Decree which, once approved, is submitted for promulgation to the Minister for Agriculture. The Minister cannot amend but can refuse to promulgate, and thus the process is subject to an ultimate exercise of political rather than administrative control. The whole process is subject to review by the *Conseil d'Etat*. According to Olszak, applications for review to the *Conseil* are now more common, in particular with respect to anti-competitiveness and procedural conformity.[28] When the Decree is promulgated, the INAO is responsible, through its inspection system, for the supervision and control required by the Decree's provisions. It is also competent, both nationally and internationally, to pursue infringers, as are the relevant syndicates.

---

[25] "... agricultural produce and foodstuffs are subject to a particularly detailed and complex policy approach, because of the evident importance of *terroirs* [soils]."

[26] See Olszak, *supra*, footnote 22, at 158.

[27] Indeed, in order to obtain EU registration under Regulation 2081/92 this is mandatory—a process instigated by the INAO itself would result in a registration ineligible for European notification.

[28] See Olszak, *supra*, footnote 22.

The AOC corresponds to the Community PDO, and the EU definition is said by Olszak to be applicable. He summarizes the characteristics of the AOC in the following terms:

> "*C'est d'abord une appellation d'origine encadrée par un ensemble complexe de contrôles administratifs et syndicaux, dans la reconnaissance, la délimitation et la production.*"[29]

Whereas the AOC system pre-dates European Regulation 2081/92, the grant of PGIs represents a systematization of previously disparate approaches. As such, it is a relative novelty in the French legal landscape. The pre-existing system of "*labels*"[30] and "*Certification de Conformité*" forms the exclusive basis for the grant of PGIs via the INAO processes. In other words, PGIs cannot be granted unless they incorporate a "*label*" or a certificate of conformity which has been granted in accordance with the relevant administrative procedure. Not all labels or certifications, of course, incorporate a geographical element.[31]

As illustrated above, the French system is partly the inspiration for, and partly based on, the EU Regulation 2081/92 system of registration of PDOs and PGIs. It is therefore opportune to examine the EU rules for registration of GIs more closely as to their substantive requirements and rights. The EU-wide registration system for the protection of GIs also illustrates the steady expansion of high-level registration: from local, to national, to regional, to global.

B.   *The European System of Registration*

It is not the case that there was strong universal support for the expansion of high-level GI protection beyond its heartland by way of adoption of an EU regional system of registered GIs.[32] Certain northern-European countries, although recognizing actions for unfair competition and the like in relation to place names, did not provide for registration for products at all, or only for wine.[33] Nonetheless, European harmonisation

---

[29] Ibid., at 162–163: "It is above all a designation of origin surrounded by a complex set of administrative and syndicate controls, both in its recognition, its delimitation and in production."

[30] The English term "label" is the term used in France in this context.

[31] Labels will only be granted where the product to be labelled (with what is known as a *label rouge*, i.e. a red label) is an edible or other unprocessed agricultural product, which itself is different from the currently commercialized product, in either production, processing or geographical origin. This implies a quality at least different from, if not better than, the norm, usually due to its artisanal and local production. The Certificate of Conformity, on the other hand, implies no more than that the goods are produced in conformity with certain certified requirements in relation to production, processing or geographical origin. In truth, Certificates only indicate conformity to certain rules of production, which does not necessarily imply greater quality than the norm. But, according to Olszak, they are usually promoted as importing guarantees of better quality. Again, only recognized Certificates incorporating a geographical indication will be able to be registered as PGIs.

[32] The EU system is not the only regional registration system for GIs; e.g. Decision 486 of the Andean Community concerning a Common Intellectual Property Regime, which entered into force on 1 December 2000. Note that by virtue of Article 212 of that Decision, there is no limitation as to type of product for which appellations of origin can be protected, whether natural, agricultural, handicraft or industrial.

[33] Germany, incidentally, undertook, in the Treaty of Versailles, to protect a large number of French GIs. Another example of a country without registration for goods in general is Austria; as pointed out in the Opinion of the Advocate-General in the *Spreewalder Gurken* case (see Opinion of the Advocate-General, 5 April 2001, in *Carl Kuhne GmbH & Co. v. Jutro Konservenfabrik GmbH & Co. KG*, Case C-269/99), the northern Member States in general did not have registration systems, relying on legislation relating to misleading and deceptive conduct. This caused some difficulty, since these States did not dispose of established lists from which to notify names to the Commission when Regulation 2081/92 came into force—they had to draw up such lists and determine which names would qualify as registrable indications.

was achieved by the introduction of an EU-wide registration system for GIs for all foodstuffs, in 1992.[34] Partially, the Register consists of notified GIs emanating from national Registers pre-dating the EU-wide system, and partly it consists of applications made since. This Register excludes wines,[35] which are the subject of a separate system by virtue of Council Regulation 1493/99 of 17 May 1999 on the Common Organisation of the Market in Wine.

The most celebrated case under Regulation 2081/92 is, arguably, the *Feta cheese* decision.[36] The long process, which ultimately resulted in the registration of *feta*, illustrates some of the difficulties faced with the introduction of new levels of protection for GIs across still disparate jurisdictions, and the disruption to well-established practices and uses that can result. The European Commission ultimately recognized *"feta"* as a registered GI, rejecting arguments that the term was a generic descriptor of a style of cheese. As a result the term can only be used by producers in certain areas in Greece in accordance with strict product standards. Well-established producers of cheese who employed the denomination as a generic will be compelled to convert to alternative names or alternative products, or cease production altogether.

1. REGULATION 2081/92: PDOS AND PGIS

EC Regulation 2081/92 provides for two categories of registered GIs: protected designations of origin and protected geographical indications.[37] The essential difference between the two categories is that for a PDO, all the production, processing, and preparation must occur within the designated area. For a PGI, only one of either production, processing or preparation must take place within the designated area.[38] Further, whereas indirect GIs can be registered as PDOs, they cannot be registered as PGIs. The PDO category equates to the previously established AOC system for wines in France.[39]

As well, for a PDO, the quality or characteristics of the product must be "essentially or exclusively due to a particular geographical environment with its inherent natural and human factors", whereas for a PGI, "a specific quality, reputation or other characteristics [must be] attributable to that geographical origin" (Article 2(a) and (b)). So, even if a

[34] Council Regulation (EEC) No. 2081/92, 14 July 1992, *supra* footnote 11, 1–8.

[35] Ibid., Article 1.

[36] See Council Regulation (EC) No. 1829/2002 of 14 October 2002. Subject to the fulfilment of certain conditions, producers in other States of the European Union dispose of a five-year transition period before they have to change the name of their product or cease production.

[37] In this sense, and in the statutory definitions of Regulation 2081, the European model and categorizations parallel the French AOC system; see G. Schricker, *Recht der Werbung in Europa*, Nomos (Looseleaf), at 47.

[38] So, for example, ham may be processed and prepared in the designated area, but if the pork is derived from pigs imported from outside the area, the resulting ham may be entitled to a "protected geographical indication" but not to a "protected designation of origin". Nonetheless, by virtue of Article 2(4) of Regulation 2081, if the raw material comes from a different, but defined area, production there is under special conditions, and the conditions are enforced by an inspection system, then the product concerned is entitled to a "protected designation of origin" rather than a mere "protected geographical indication".

[39] See F. Addor and A. Grazioli, *Geographical Indications beyond Wines and Spirits—A Roadmap for a Better Protection for Geographical Indications in the WTO TRIPS Agreement*, 5 J.W.I.P. 6, November 2002, at 865.

product emanates from within an area and is entirely processed and prepared there, it may not be entitled to a PDO if it cannot be established that its quality or characteristics are "essentially or exclusively" due to the geographical environment which includes both human and natural characteristics.[40] In the *Spreewalder Gurken* case the Advocate-General, in his Opinion, touched upon the essential distinction: the Spreewalder gherkins were known to consumers to originate from the Spreewald area and therefore have certain qualities, hence they would be entitled to registration as a PDO, rather than just as a PGI, which would have been appropriate had the term been regarded by consumers as simply referring to the style of processing or recipe of the gherkins.[41]

All applications for PDO or PGI registration must be accompanied by specifications, including details concerning geographical limits, production methods, "and, if appropriate, the authentic and unvarying local methods" (Article 4(2)(e)), and the link between geography and qualities of the product. Member States must police the continued application of the specifications in the relevant area.

2. THE SCOPE OF PROTECTION

Although more stringent criteria apply to the grant of PDO status, there is no difference in the protection enjoyed by both PDOs and PGIs. A registered GI cannot be used in relation to products that do not comply with the specification—producers within the designated area are thus compelled to use the specified processes and sources, etc. By virtue of Article 13 of Regulation 2081/92, the protection has all the typical characteristics of high-level GI registration:[42]

- prohibiting any use of the name on comparable products;

- prohibiting use in any circumstances—i.e. also in relation to unrelated products—if using the name exploits the reputation of the protected GI;

- prohibiting imitations, evocations, translations or use with certain qualifying terms such as "imitation";

- prohibiting false or misleading indications of any kind on containers, packaging, advertising, etc., and use of containers liable to convey a false impression as to origin; or

- anything else that is liable to mislead the public as to the true origin of the product (see Article 13(1)).

Registered names also cannot become generic (Article 13(3)), but as seen above, a name that is generic cannot be registered.

---

[40] The differences between the French and English versions are the source of some uncertainty. The French text being clearer, I have preferred that.
[41] See Opinion of the Advocate-General in the *Spreewalder Gurken* case, *supra*, footnote 33.
[42] As analysed in Part I of this article.

The term "evocation"—which is weaker than "imitation" and thus further extends the scope of protection of the registered name—was considered in the *Cambozola* decision of the European Court of Justice (ECJ). Because "Cambozola" has the same number of syllables, and the same ending (-ola) as the registered term "Gorgonzola", the phonetic and visual similarity would conjure up a mental association in the minds of consumers, given the similarity between the products. It was not necessary to establish a likelihood of confusion.[43]

The scope of protection under Regulation 2081/92 is thus undoubtedly very broad. One would expect the threshold for registration to be concomitantly high. This is clearly the case for PDOs, but the requirements for registration of a PGI are less stringent. Nonetheless, the two requirements of geographical origin and enforceable product standards are present to some degree for both categories. If one accepts that the level of geographical connection required for the grant of a PGI is sufficient, the EU system has the characteristics, identified above, of a system with a sound theoretical basis. However, it emerges clearly from the foregoing discussion of the associated administrative, regulatory and supervisory structures that such a system comes at a high cost, both in financial terms and in terms of administrative constraints on agricultural and commercial decision-making.

By contrast, under the Australian system of registered GIs for wines, which is briefly outlined below, such costs and constraints are much reduced, because it imposes minimal product standards. The guarantee of consistent quality is almost exclusively indirect, i.e. it is derived from a requirement of geographical origin only, without any additional requirements to follow more- or less-elaborate specifications. This Australian wine system (there is no general product equivalent) parallels the U.S. approach as, for instance, employed in the wine-growing areas of California, and is thoroughly different from the EU system.[44] While more flexible, it is arguably less sound in theory, although it does have the incidental benefit of reducing future transaction costs by *a priori* delineation of geographical boundaries.

C. THE AUSTRALIAN MODEL: REGISTERED GIS FOR WINE

The Australian system was established in the wake of the signature of the Australia–EU Wine Agreement.[45] This Agreement bound Australia to providing registered GI-type protection for European registered wine GIs; for that purpose an Australian Register of some sort was required. Because the Agreement also

---

[43] *Gorgonzola/Cambozola*, ECJ, 4 March 1999, (1999) ECR I, 1301, as commented upon by R. Knaak, *Case-Law of the ECJ on the Protection of Geographical Indications and Designations of Origin Pursuant to EC Regulation No. 2081/92*, IIC 32, 375–484, 2001, at 383.

[44] The Australian system approximates the Californian system much more closely; see W. Moran, *Wine Appellations as Territory in France and California*, 83 Annals of the Association of American Geographers, Vol. 4, 1993, at 706 *et seq.*

[45] By way of amendment of the Australian Wine and Brandy Corporation Act, 1980 (Cth).

incorporates an undertaking by the EU to protect Australian registered GIs, the legislation also provides for a mechanism for assessment and registration of Australian wine GIs.[46]

In contrast to the European model, the connection between geography and quality required under the Australian provisions is tenuous; as long as the wine concerned contains 85 percent or more of grapes grown in the designated area, the registered GI can be used.[47] It does not matter how or where the wine is processed. The only guarantee of consistent quality or character lies in the fact that the area of the designation is determined on the basis of statutory factors that should ensure a certain degree of homogeneity of geographical features and conditions.[48] But in truth, the designated area can be quite large and because there is such a multitude of factors that the Act requires to be considered, it can also be geographically heterogenous.[49] Not one single further requirement is imposed: no specifications, no restrictions *qua* varietals, production or processing methods, colour or style of wine, etc. Although an Australian registered GI may thus have a reputation predominantly for certain varietals—for example, Barossa for Cabernet Sauvignon—there is no legal restriction on different varietals being sold under the same GI as long as 85 percent of the grapes are from within the designated area.[50]

Contrast this with French AOCs, or the requirements to be met for European PDOs. It is immediately apparent that the Australian system is based on a rather different philosophy. Partly, of course, it is not based on any philosophy at all, but was simply a minimal response to the exigencies of the EU Agreement. Some have argued that the connection between geography and quality of wines is unproven at the best of times, and

---

[46] The complexities involved in administering a system even as relatively simple as this are well illustrated by the case concerning the Coonawarra GI; see *Coonawarra Penola Wine Industry Association, Inc. & Others and Geographical Indications Committee*, [2001] Aata 844, 5 October 2001.

[47] Regulation 21 of the Australian Wine and Brandy Corporation Regulations, 1981, provides that at least 85 millilitres per litre must originate from grapes within the designated region; see also Section 5D of the Australian Wine and Brandy Corporation Act, 1980 (Cth): *Where Wine Originates*.

[48] It has been advocated that it may make sense in some cases to restrict the types of grape variety grown in a GI: "*Restrict the use of a GI to wines that are made only from limited grape varieties? 'Never!' we say. However, we know that there is a much greater value to the name or description 'Coonawarra Cabernet' than to 'Coonawarra Riesling'.* Perhaps that is only because of a lack of adequate experimentation to date, but the concept of particular regions being best suited to particular grapes is well acknowledged in Australia. That is, of course, the first step on the path." (emphasis added): see S. Stern and C. Fund, *The Australian System of Registration and Protection of Geographical Indications for Wines*, Flinders Journal of Law Reform, Vol. 5, Issue 1, 2000, on page accompanying footnote 7. The term "GI" in Australia does "not necessarily mean, or imply anything unique about the location's climate or environment.": id. Yet, further in the same article, the authors say: "Our system of wine GIs is, at the present time, no more informative to consumers than the indication of source 'Carrera [sic] Marble'. This is because they tell consumers nothing about the product save the source of the raw materials, namely, the grapes. There is nothing said even about the quality of the grapes themselves let alone about the wine that incorporates them. It is this omission that I believe needs to be addressed, if not now, at some time in the near future. Certainly I hope that this can happen before consumers see that our system gives little useful information about the wine bearing the GI.": text on page accompanying footnotes 10 and 11.

[49] See Australian Wine and Brandy Corporation Regulations, 1981, Regulation 25.

[50] In California, where a very similar system exists, the Atf, which is the responsible administrative body, stresses that they do not wish to "give the impression by approving a viticultural area that it is approving or endorsing the quality of the wine from this area", and that granting an area status implies it is different but not better than surrounding areas: as quoted in Moran, *supra*, footnote 44, at 707.

the Australian system seems to implicitly endorse this scepticism.[51] With areas of provenance that are both large and geographically diverse, the system requires little real connection between local conditions and quality characteristics of the wine.[52] It may well be that the Australian system of GI registration, therefore, given the conclusions arrived at above, has little to commend it in theory. But it is an unsurprising adaptation of a European registration model to manifestly different Australian agricultural and industrial policies, conditions and practices. Legitimacy is traded off in favour of flexibility.

II.   CONCLUSION

This trade-off illustrates the conundrum faced when considering policy in relation to GI registration systems. On the one hand, to justify the strong rights granted, not subject to any defence of genericness—and with a strict prohibition on use even in good faith or in the absence of consumer deception—a system of registered GIs should require an intimate geographical connection and high and pervasive product standards. On the other hand, if a system with such characteristics is adopted, restraints on competition, grave rigidities in terms of land use, production levels and innovation, and considerable private and social costs are imposed.

Some might question whether GI registration really should be regarded as a branch of intellectual property at all, and belonging in TRIPS. In many ways, it is a system which contributes to the implementation of rural and agricultural policies. Whether or not a system of GI registration should be adopted, and the shape it should have, is therefore largely a question determined by the nature of rural industries in a given jurisdiction, the broader agricultural and rural policy framework, and historical conditions. It is certainly the case that where some regulatory framework does not already exist, and regional reputation is less pervasively used in the market for foodstuffs, the arguments for and against the introduction of a GI Register should be very carefully weighed.

Furthermore, GI registration does not in itself result in a valuable reputation. While some geographical terms from European countries may benefit from an established worldwide reputation—whether enhanced by imitation or not—the investment required to generate positive consumer recognition for little-known terms is very considerable. Such efforts at differentiation can only generate adequate returns in the long run. It may also be that there are more flexible alternatives available for the promotion of local reputation, such as certification trade marks, or that reliance on corporate brands is a perfectly effective tool for the promotion of rural and agricultural produce, just as it is for other products.

---

[51] See Section IV.C in Part I of this article.
[52] See Moran, *supra*, footnote 44.

[5]

Champagne, Feta, and Bourbon: The Spirited Debate About Geographical Indications

Justin Hughes*

It should be borne in mind that, as is the case with trademarks, an unduly high level of protection of geographical indications and designations of origin would impede the integration of national markets by imposing unjustified restrictions on the free flow of goods.

—European Union Advocate General Francis Jacobs[1]

Tell me what you eat and I will tell you what you are.

—Anthelme Brillat-Savarin[2]

INTRODUCTION

Not so long ago, exotic goods came from exotic places if they came at all. People grew, cured, and cooked local foods; they built with local materials. The people in the village of Roquefort-sur-Salzon ate their cheese because that was what they produced, not because they insisted

---

* Associate Professor and Director, Intellectual Property Law Program, Cardozo School of Law, New York. Over time, elements of this manuscript have benefited from comments received at the WTO Public Symposium, Geneva (2005); the AIPPI Japan International IP Symposium, Tokyo (2004); the Queen Mary's College, London-Fordham University Intellectual Property Conference, London (2003); and the Chicago Intellectual Property Colloquium, Loyola University Chicago/Chicago-Kent (2003). On the legal side, thanks to Barton Beebe, Lynne Beresford, Denis Croze, Lynn LoPucki, Nuno Rocha de Carvalho, Pam Samuelson, and Chrystel Garipuy for comments and suggestions, as well as to Cameron Lambright, Shinji Niioka, and Xiaomin Zhang for research assistance. On the terroir side, I benefited from discussions with Christian Butzke (Sakonnet Vineyards, Rhode Island), David Campbell (Clos du Val, Napa), Susan Hubbard (Lawrence Livermore Labs), Etienne Malan (Rust en Vrede, Stellenbosch), Anthony Truchard (Truchard Vineyards, Napa), and John Williams (Frog's Leap, Napa). The remaining errors are the exclusive intellectual property of the author.

1. Constanze Schulte, Presentation at Lovell Madrid, Similarities and Differences in the Enforcement of Trademarks and Designations of Origin, *available at* http://www.mie.org.hu/conferenceo5/eloadasok/Schulte.ppt (last visited Nov. 5, 2006) (quoting the Opinion of Advocate General Jacobs).

2. THE ANCHOR BOOK OF FRENCH QUOTATIONS 242 (Norbert Guterman ed., 1963) (quoting JEAN ANTHELME BRILLAT-SAVARIN, PHYSIOLOGIE DU GOUT, at IV (1825) ("Dis-moi ce que tu manges, je te dirai ce que tu es.")).

on Roquefort cheese. Over time, trade de-localized consumption and, in the process, established reputations for goods produced in distant places.[3] The trade of Phoenician sailors made purple-hued Phoenician cloth widely known and coveted in the ancient world. In the fifteenth century, swords from Bizen became known among the samurai class in Japan for their impressive strength and suppleness,[4] just as the violins from Cremona became celebrated in Europe for the "warmth" of their sound. In each case, a geographic name became associated, far beyond the borders of that geographic location, with a product known for highly desirable and seemingly unique characteristics.[5]

This accretion of meaning occurred in a similar fashion with trademarks. Trademarks represent the commercially, organizationally, and legally circumscribed group (the "house") that became identified with a specific desirable product. Frequently the two processes happen in tandem. The town of Cremona became famous for violins, as did Stradivarius, Amati, and Guarneri, each name designating a single Cremona violinmaker, and later, a production house.[6] In fact, some assume that geographic designations were an historic precursor of trademarks.[7]

In both cases, geographic designation and organizational source, people may try to free-ride on the meaning of a particular word. The law offers radically different responses to this free-riding, dependent on the effects of the third party usage up to that moment. If the third party use of the word(s) is so extensive that it has already eliminated the geographical or organizational source from the meaning of the word, the use will typically be allowed to stand. This is "genericization" and it works the same way with geographical designations and trademarks: escalator, cellophane, English muffins, camembert, thermos, and Swiss cheese are several uncontroverted examples.

---

3. For a discussion of the development of the global spice trade, see CHRISTIAN BOUDAN, GÉOPOLITIQUE DU GOUT 39–42, 46–51 (2004).

4. *See* NUBUO OGASAWARA, JAPANESE SWORDS 9–10 (1970); JOHN M. YUMOTO, THE SAMURAI SWORD, A HANDBOOK 29–30 (1958).

5. *See generally* CAROLINE BUHL, LE DROIT DES NOMS GEOGRAPHIQUES 323 (1997).

6. Stradivari Antonio (1644–1737); Stradivari Francesco (1671–1743); and Stradivari Omobono (1679–1742). Amati Antonio (1555–1640); Amati Francesco (1640–?); Amati Hieronymus (1556–1630); Amati Hieronymus (1649–1740); Amati Nicolo (1596–1684); and Amati Antonio Hieronymus (1555–1630). ENCYCLOPÆDIA BRITANNICA (2006).

7. For example:

In antiquity, geographic indications were the prevailing type of designation for products. With the development of the productive forces and production relationships, the use of other types of designation, intended to distinguish the goods of one manufacturer from the similar goods of other manufacturers, tended to spread. Thus, certain manufacturers' names have progressively become trade names.

M.C. Coerper, *The Protection of Geographical Indications in the United States of America*, 29 INDUS. PROP. 232, 232 (1990) (Dr. Grigoriev speaking at the Symposium on the International Protection of Geographical Indications, Santenay, France, November 9–10, 1989).

If the law intervenes earlier, while the word still means a specific geographic or organizational source, the third party use is likely to be judged harshly against two concerns: protecting consumers from misinformation and protecting producers from activities we judge "unfair." These two concerns provide, in varying degrees, the justifications for unfair competition and trademark laws on both sides of the Atlantic. These concerns also gave rise in Europe to separate law limiting the use of certain geographic words to designated producers in designated producing regions. Historically, the most important of such laws has been France's system of *appellations d'origine contrôlées.*

Appellation laws are traditionally justified by the idea of terroir: that a particular land is a key input for a particular product. There is no direct English translation of "terroir," but the idea is that the product's qualities "come with the territory." Terroir is the idea of an "essential land/qualities nexus": the local producers are entitled to exclusive use of a product name because no one outside the locale can *truly* make the same product. Of course, when the geographic name has great cachet (e.g., Bordeaux, Napa, or Swiss chocolate) exclusive control produces economic benefits for local producers, regardless of whether there is really anything unique about the local products.

Continental European countries, especially Mediterranean countries, have traditionally followed France's lead in seeking (or accepting) strong protection for geographical indications (GIs).[8] However, it was not until the Trade-Related Aspects of Intellectual Property Rights (TRIPS) Agreement[9] that geographical indication protection joined the ranks of copyright, patents, and trademarks as the subject of a broad-based multilateral agreement with detailed obligations. For geographical indications, the TRIPS Agreement forged a complex substantive compromise between European and "New World" interests. Unsurprisingly, the compromise included an agreement to put off the full battle for another day. This agreement took the form of precise commitments to continue discussions about further, increased protection for geographical indications.

So, in recent years, New World agricultural producers (Australia, Canada, Chile, the United States, and others)[10] have squared off against

---

8. *See, e.g.,* Bruce Lehman, *Intellectual Property under the Clinton Administration,* 27 G.W. J. INT'L L. & ECON. 395, 409 (1993–94) (attributing the TRIPS provisions to "strong French interest in appellations such as Champagne, Burgundy, and Chablis").

9. *See* Agreement on Trade-Related Aspects of Intellectual Property Rights, Apr. 15, 1994, Marrakesh Agreement Establishing the World Trade Organization, Annex 1C, THE LEGAL TEXTS: THE RESULTS OF THE URUGUAY ROUND OF MULTILATERAL TRADE NEGOTIATIONS 320 (1999), 1869 U.N.T.S. 299, 33 I.L.M. 1125, 1197 [hereinafter TRIPS].

10. The New World producers are largely an informal group of industrialized nations that typically include Japan, the U.S., Canada, Australia, and New Zealand ("JUSCANZ") with a few wine producers from the developing world. JUSCANZ sometimes works in tandem and sometimes in

the European Union about how to fulfill these commitments. The European Union advocates an international registration system that provides mandatory, very strong protection of Old World agricultural production names.[11] It also insists that certain words like "Parmesan" (as in cheese), "Parma" (as in ham), and "Chablis" be "returned" to Europe. The European Commission says this is a matter of fairness.[12] The New World producers advocate a less centralized, more market-driven approach and show no enthusiasm to return words that have become generic product names in many countries. Australia and the United States have also successfully argued before the World Trade Organization (WTO) that the European Union has failed to abide by its *existing* obligations to protect the geographical indications of non-EU countries.

The debates about geographical indications are more than just intellectual property arcana; they take place in the context of long-standing, high-stakes negotiations over trade in agricultural goods.[13] Indeed, until the Doha Round negotiations collapsed in the summer of 2006,[14] one EU ambassador identified the geographical indications issue as "one of the few offensive interests" of the European Union in those talks.[15] In a possible world of reduced agricultural subsidies, control of

---

opposition to EU proposals over a wide range of issues from intellectual property to climate change. *See* George Archibald, *'Sexual Rights' Battle Looms: Women's Session to Be Contentious*, WASH. TIMES, June 5, 2000, at A1 (describing EU and JUSCANZ working together to oppose the "G-77" developing countries voting bloc at the UN); Terry Hall, *EU Move Leaves a Sour Taste: New Labeling Rules Raise Concerns for New Zealand Wine Producers*, FIN. TIMES, July 19, 2002, at 18 (describing how 2002 EU Wine Regulations, which touch upon all aspects of wine production for wines imported into the European Union, raised protests from New Zealand, Brazil, the U.S., Australia, and Canada); Tonya Barnes et al., EARTH NEGOTIATIONS BULL., (Int'l Inst. for Sustainable Dev., Winnipeg, Canada), Mar. 10, 2000, at 1, http://www.iisd.ca/linkages/vol14/enb1429e.html (describing comparative EU and JUSCANZ proposals on micro-financing for developing countries).

11. Tobias Buck & Guy de Jonqieres, *Name-Calling over Europe's Delicacies*, FIN. TIMES, May 5, 2003, at 10.

12. James Cox, *What's in a Name*, USA TODAY, Sept. 9, 2003, at 1B.

13. *See, e.g.*, William Drozdiak, *French Winemakers See Themselves as 'Hostages' to Politics*, WASH. POST, Nov. 10, 1992, at A19 (describing pre-WTO U.S.-EU disagreement over oil seed subsidies and possible retaliatory U.S. tariffs against French winemakers); Editorial, *Fair Spirit*, FIN. TIMES, Nov. 8, 1999, at 12 (describing the European Union's strong stand against South Africa on wine geographical indications as "another example of the conflict between the European Union rhetoric of free trade and the continuing protectionism in agriculture").

14. Blame for the collapse flew like mud at a rainy rodeo. *See* Alan Beattie, *Several Suspects in Frame for Doha Murder*, FIN. TIMES, July 26, 2006, at 5; Alan Beattie, *US Hits Back at EU Countries Over Collapse of Doha Round*, FIN. TIMES, July 26, 2006, at 1; Scott Kilman & Roger Thurow, *U.S Farm-Subsidy Cuts a Long Shot as Doha Falters*, WALL ST. J., July 26, 2006, at 19 (discussing how the collapse of free-trade talks is likely to eliminate any chance of overhauling America's farm-subsidy program); *Les aides agricoles provoquent l'échec de la libéralisation du commerce*, LE MONDE, July 26, 2006, at 9 (describing how European Commission officials blamed the U.S. and the U.S. countered).

15. *Hearing on Geographic Indications Before the H. Comm. on Agriculture*, 108th Cong. 4 (2003) (testimony of Michael Pellegrino, Vice President of Marketing & Strategy, Kraft Cheese Division, Kraft Foods North America) [hereinafter Testimony of Michael Pellegrino].

valuable geographical indications would at least allow European farmers to compete better in high-end food categories and secure at least some monopoly rents from well-known food names. Although geographical indications laws technically apply to all kinds of products from Botswanan baskets to Selangor pewter, for all practical purposes, the law of geographical indications is about foodstuffs.[16] Within foodstuffs, geographical indications predominantly concern wine and spirits.[17] This is a debate about the law of the names of what we eat and drink.

There has been relatively little systematic, scholarly analysis of geographical indications in Europe and almost none, or none, on the New World side of the Atlantic.[18] Yet potentially at stake is commercial control of a dizzying array of words and symbols: champagne, port, bourbon, camembert, Idaho potatoes, Swiss cheese, sherry, sake, pictures of the Eiffel Tower or Golden Gate Bridge, Dutch chocolate, shapes of bottles, Budweiser, jasmine rice, Coney Island hot dogs, Neapolitan pizza, perhaps even images of Mozart and Benjamin Franklin.[19] Based on ideas advocated in some quarters, the list is disturbingly long.

This Article proposes that geographical words in product names (that is, labeling and advertising) have three basic purposes. These are (1) to communicate geographic source, (2) to communicate (non-geographic) product qualities, and (3) to create evocative value. The first of these is simple. "Industria Argentina" or "Made in England" communicate a product's geographic origins. Second, geographic words are often used to communicate product characteristics other than geographic origin. This second use often leads to the geographic words

---

16. *See, e.g.,* DOMINIQUE DENIS, APPELLATION D'ORIGINE ET INDICATION DE PROVENANCE I (1995) ("Les appellations d'origine hors de ce secteur [agroalimentaire] sont négligeables sur le plan pratique.") [The appellations of origin outside of this sector (agro-alimentary) are negligible on the practical level.].

17. According to another report, "[t]here are some 4200 registered [geographical indications] for wines and spirits and 600 [geographical indications] for other food products." Bernard O'Connor, *The Legal Protection of Geographical Indications,* 2004 INTELL. PROP. Q. 1, 35. But O'Connor's numbers look suspect because this country break-down produces only 1136 GIs for France, Italy, and Spain together. *Id.* at 35–36.

18. Worthwhile exceptions exist. *See* Jim Chen, *A Sober Second Look at Appellations of Origin: How the United States Will Crash France's Wine and Cheese Party,* 5 MINN. J. GLOBAL TRADE 29 (1996); Albrecht Conrad, *The Protection of Geographic Indications in the TRIPS Agreement,* 86 TRADEMARK REP. 11 (1996); *see also* Robert Brauneis & Roger E. Schechter, *Geographic Trademarks and the Protection of Competitor Communication,* 96 TRADEMARK REP. 782 (2006) (discussing the recent direction geographic trademark law has taken in the U.S.).

19. NORBERT OLSZAK, LES APPELLATIONS D'ORIGINE ET INDICATIONS DE PROVENANCE 34 (2001) (giving the image of William Tell and the Cathedral at Strasbourg as examples of indirect GIs, the latter the subject of a litigation in France in 1968); *see also* L. Wichers Hoeth, *Protection of Geographic Denominations in the Netherlands, in* PROTECTION OF GEOGRAPHIC DENOMINATIONS OF GOODS AND SERVICES 75 (Herman Cohen Jehoram ed., 1980) (giving the Eiffel Tower (France), Cologne Cathedral (Germany), and Tower Bridge (England) as examples).

becoming "generic."[20] The word loses its geographic meaning and acquires another meaning based on non-geographic qualities of the product, as when people go into a *restaurant chinois* off the Champs-Elysées or, nine time zones away, Californians order *French fries* with their *hamburger*.

A third, more overlooked, category for use of geographical words in product names is their use for evocative and aesthetic purposes. These are typically uses of words which, in American trademark doctrine, would be "fanciful" or "arbitrary."[21] The evocative value of geographic words is most evident with geographic names of fictional or no-longer existent places: ATLANTIS waterproofing services,[22] POMPEII game machines,[23] and SHANGRI-LA hotels.[24]

Armed with this framework, we will see that the classical justification for geographical indications is that they serve a special combination of (1) and (2): to communicate a product's geographical source *and* non-geographic qualities of the product that are related to its geographic origin. This is the idea of terroir: that the *particular geography* produces *particular* product characteristics that cannot be imitated by other regions. The idea of terroir undergirds the European Union claim for stronger protection of geographical indications. This

---

20. *See* Black Hills Jewelry Mfg. v. Gold Rush, Inc., 633 F.2d 746, 751 (8th Cir. 1980) ("For 'Black Hills Gold Jewelry' to be generic, it must be applied to three-color gold grape and leaf design wherever produced."). *See generally* Abercrombie & Fitch Co. v. Hunting World, Inc., 537 F.2d 4, 9 (2d Cir. 1976); King-Seeley Thermos Co. v. Aladdin Indus., 321 F.2d 577, 579 (2d Cir. 1963); ANDRÉ BERTRAND, LE DROIT DES MARQUES, DES SIGNES DISTINCTIFS ET DES NOMS DE DOMAINE 146 (CEDAT, 2002) ("Comme en matière de marques ou des indications de provenance, il est admis qu'une appellation d'origine peut perdre ce caractère par usage généralisé.") [As with trademarks and indications of provenance, some appellations of origin admittedly lose their character by falling into general use.]; OLSZAK, *supra* note 19, at 16 ("Certains termes géographiques sont parfois perdu dans l'usage cette signification précise pour deviner un nom commun désignant un type de produit. L 'utilisation de ce nom est alors nécessaire pour identifier un produit et ne peut donc pas être restreinte aux seuls produits originaires de lieu géographique que correspondant au nom propre initial, mais il n'est pas impossible de songer à rétablir la situation en régénérant la valeur géographique du signe.") [Some geographic terms lose their first signification and become a common word used by people to designate a type of product. The use of this term then becomes necessary to identify a product and therefore cannot be restricted to products that originally come from the geographical place that the initial proper name designates.].

21. A classic example from trademark law might be "Alaska brand bananas" because almost no adult would think that bananas can be or would be grown in Alaska. *See In re* Nantucket, Inc., 677 F.2d 95, 97 n.5 (C.C.P.A. 1982). But use of geographic words for evocative purposes could include geographic words which are considered "suggestive" in U.S. trademark doctrine.

22. U.S. Trademark Registration No. 1,212,225 (filed Jan. 26, 1981) (ATLANTIS in stylized form certification mark owned by Rockhopper Group LLC).

23. U.S. Trademark Registration No. 2,539,104 (filed Jan. 6, 2006) (POMPEII certification mark owned by Aristocrat Tech. Austl. Pty. Ltd.).

24. U.S. Trademark Serial No. 7,4148,286 (filed Mar. 18, 1991) (SHANGRI-LA HOTEL & RESORT certification mark abandoned by applicant Nakash Bros. Realty P'ship N.Y. on Jan. 18, 1992).

concept helps justify the European Union's demand, since 2004, for the "return" of over forty words that have become generic names for foodstuffs in other countries (e.g., Parmesan cheese, Champagne, Chablis, Gorgonzola cheese, Parma ham, etc.). Although terroir and a claim for a unique communications function for geographical indications is the European Union's public rhetoric, this Article concludes that the European Commission has a simpler goal: control of geographic words for their *evocative value in the marketplace.* The monopoly rents available from exclusive control of this evocative value drive the EU position in the debates over geographical indications.

Part I provides the reader with the two basic approaches in national law protecting GIs, either a free-standing appellations law or the use of certification marks within trademark law. Part II describes international obligations to protect GIs as they now exist in the TRIPS Agreement, the TRIPS mechanisms mandating further negotiations, the major proposals that have been made, and the 2005 WTO decision concluding that the European Union discriminated against other countries in its own GI law. Part III explores the "popular" parameters of the debate and how the European Union reasonably sees strong GI protection as a way to gain monopoly rents. Part IV turns to the weakness of terroir as a justification for the EU appellation theory behind GIs, and Part V describes the slow process by which geographical words that have become generic can be repropertized. Finally, Part V explores the dangers to evocative and descriptive uses of geographical words from any strengthened protection of GIs against "usurpation."

I. Geographical Indications in National Law

A "geographic identifier" could be any word, phrase, or symbol that designates the place where a product was produced regardless of reputation.[25] So, "made in Patagonia" on ROM chips would be a *geographical identifier* even though Patagonia has no particular reputation for semiconductors. In contrast, a geographical indication designates the place where a product was produced *and* that the place is known to produce that item with particular desirable qualities. In the case of GIs there is a known *land/qualities* nexus. It follows that every geographical indication is a geographical identifier, but not vice versa.

Geographical indications are often geographic words coupled with the generic term for the product (e.g., Irish whiskey). Sometimes the geographic word stands alone (e.g., Scotch). Typically, the places are

---

25. These are sometimes called "indications of source," but I am not using that phrase because "indication of source" is often used in distinction to "geographical indication." *See, e.g.,* Leigh Ann Lindquist, *Champagne or Champagne: An Examination of U.S. Failure to Comply with the Geographical Provisions of the TRIPS Agreement,* 27 Ga. J. Int'l & Comp. L. 309, 312 (1998).

either towns (Roquefort, Chablis), or sub-national regions such as states (Idaho potatoes), departments (Cognac), or counties (Bourbon). The larger the region, the less likely it is that production factors will be both (a) consistent across the region and (b) unique to that region. Nonetheless, and despite resistance to the idea historically,[26] names of countries can be protected as geographical indications one way or another in most legal systems, for example, Canadian whiskey, Colombian coffee, or Swiss chocolate.

Finally, geographical indications are occasionally *not* names of places.[27] For example, in Britain, "claret" has come to refer to red Bordeaux wines. Similarly, the European Union has spent years arguing over whether "feta" is a geographical indication belonging to Greece.[28] A bottle style that has been historically used for, and identified with, a wine or spirit from one particular region might also be claimed as a geographical indication. Some commentators believe that such indirect geographical indications might even include "depictions of landmarks, familiar landscapes, heraldic signs, [and] well-known persons,"[29] a disturbing extension of the concept for anyone concerned about either evocative use of symbols in advertising or free expression in general.

With these basics in mind, it is useful to sketch out the two most divergent approaches to protecting geographical indications.

A. THE FRENCH SYSTEM OF *APPELLATIONS D'ORIGINE CONTRÔLÉES*

Although there were some laws in France, Portugal, and Tuscany controlling wine labeling as early as the fourteenth and fifteenth centuries,[30] appellations law is a modern phenomenon. In 1855, the Médoc vineyards of Bordeaux were classified.[31] This move coincided, not incidentally, with the opening of the railroad between Bordeaux and

---

26. For example in 1975, the European Communities argued against Germany's claim that "Sekt" was an indirect geographical indication, partly on the grounds that "the Federal Government gave no example demonstrating that the territory of a whole country may also be the subject of indirect indications of origin." Case 12/74, Comm'n v. Germany, 1975 E.C.R. 181 ¶ 3. French law does not permit country names to be protected *appellations d'origine* and, according to the California Wine Export Program, country names like "American" do not qualify as geographical indications under EU wine doctrine. *See* CAL. WINE EXP. PROGRAM, EUROPEAN UNION WINE LABELING REGULATIONS 2–3 (Oct. 20, 2000) (on file with author).

27. Case 12/74, Comm'n v. Germany, 1975 E.C.R. 181 ¶ 12.

28. *See* Joined Cases C-465/02 & C-466/02, F.R.G. v. Comm'n, 2005 E.C.R. I-09115.

29. Conrad, *supra* note 18, at 11–12 (giving examples of the Eiffel Tower (France), the Matterhorn (Switzerland), and Mozart (Austria)).

30. BUHL, *supra* note 5, at 331; OLSZAK, *supra* note 19, at 51. Many claim that there existed in ancient Palestine a "hierarchy of crus [wines]" recognized by local connoisseurs. JEAN-ROBERT PITTE, LE VIN ET LE DIVIN 45 (2004). And, of course, Falernian wines were renowned in the Roman era. *See* ANDREW DALBY, FOOD IN THE ANCIENT WORLD FROM A TO Z 138 (2003).

31. A.J. LIEBLING, BETWEEN MEALS: AN APPETITE FOR PARIS 158 (1995); OLSZAK, *supra* note 19, at 6.

Paris. The first modern French law to combat fraudulently labeled wines was passed in 1905, but France's first government committee on appellations of origin for wines and *eaux de vie* was not established until 1935. In 1947, that committee became the *Institut National des Appellations d'Origine* (INAO),[32] now part of the Ministry of Agriculture.

The French system of *appellations d'origine contrôlées* (AOC) is founded on the idea of terroir.[33] Terroir has no direct English translation, but the notion behind the Latinate word is simple: the product's qualities *come with the territory.* As one Australian wine critic describes it: "terroir ... translates roughly as 'the vine's environment[,]' but has connotations that extend right into the glass: in other words, if a wine tastes of somewhere, if the flavours distinctly make you think of a particular place on the surface of this globe, then that wine is expressing its terroir."[34]

To put it less poetically, terroir is the idea of an "essential land/qualities nexus": French law defines an AOC as a region or locality name "that serves to designate a product of that origin whose qualities or characteristics are due to the geographic milieu, which includes natural and human elements."[35]

Beliefs about terroir run deep in France, but not too deep, for if they did there might not be a justification for the elaborate regulatory structure governing production of AOC foodstuffs. The INAO regulates not just the geographic boundaries for each AOC, but all "conditions of production," including, for wine, the grape varietals, hectare production quotas, natural alcohol content during vinification, permitted irrigation, etc.[36] The INAO regulations for AOC cheese place varying legal

---

32. *See* CODE DE LA CONSOMMATION [C. CON.] art. L. 115-19 (establishing INAO); *see also* OLSZAK, *supra* note 19, at 10. A national committee on *appellations d'origine* for cheese was not established until 1955. *Id.* at 11.

33. *See* INAO, History and Genesis of the AOC, http://www.inao.gouv.fr/public/textesPages/ History_and_concepts350.php?mnu=350 (last visited Nov. 5, 2006).

34. MAX ALLEN, SNIFF SWIRL & SLURP: HOW TO GET MORE PLEASURE OUT OF EVERY GLASS OF WINE 24, 29 (2002) (explaining that between Alsatian Pinot Gris and Italian Pinot Grigio white wines "[t]he difference, of course, comes almost solely from the terroir"). For a cyberspace version of the terroir story, see Chateau de Beaucastel, Terroir, http://www.beaucastel.com/ang/terroir/ (last visited Nov. 5, 2006).

35. CODE DE LA PROPRIÉTÉ INTELLECTUELLE [C. PROP. INTELL.] art. L. 721-1 (citing C. CON. art. L. 115-1 (defining AOC as "la dénomination d'un pays, d'une région, ou d'une localité servant à désigner un produit qui en est originaire et dont la qualité ou les caractères sont dus au milieu géographique, comprenant des facteurs naturels et des facteurs humains") [the denomination of a country, a region, or a locality serving to indicate a product which originates from it and to which the quality or characteristics are due to the geographical environment, including natural factors and personal elements]). With implementation of the "Origins Regulation" France also protects "indications of source," which do not require this nexus. *See* discussion *infra* note 99.

36. JAMES E. WILSON, TERROIR 60 (Blue Island Publishing 2005) (1999).

requirements on rennet used in coagulation, curd drainage, milk temperature at different points in curing, salting, and the use of lactic proteins.[37] The INAO works with "interprofessional" committees organized around specific products.[38] Based on committee recommendations, the INAO also establishes new *appellations controlées*.[39]

French statutory law protects an AOC not just against unauthorized uses on products in the same category, but also against any commercial use of the indication "likely to divert or weaken the renown of the appellation d'origine."[40] This standard seems roughly similar to the protection accorded famous trademarks under U.S. federal dilution law. In perhaps the best known application of this broad protection, the producers of sparkling wine from the Champagne region were able to stop Yves St. Laurent from marketing a perfume called "Champagne."[41]

B. The American System of Certification and Collective Marks

In contrast to a separate system for protecting *appellations*, some countries, like the United States, subsume protection of geographical indications under trademark law. This is achieved through the categories of "certification marks" and "collective marks." Under U.S. law, a collective mark is a trademark "used by the members of a cooperative, an association, or other collective group or organization,"[42] a definition that could easily include a foodstuff producers' cooperative or trade association which imposes its own standards.[43] Certification marks are

---

37. Kazuko Masui & Tomoko Yamada, French Cheeses 50, 92, 108 (1996); *see also L'adjonction d'eau ou de colorants est interdite*, Le Monde, Aug. 20, 2002, at 8 (noting requirements for the "calvados domfrontais" AOC issued on December 21, 1997).

38. *E.g.*, "Le Comité Interprofessionnel du Vin de Champagne" was organized in 1941. *See* Decree No. 86-242 of Feb. 21, 1986, Journal Officiel de la République Française [J.O.] [Official Gazette of France], Feb. 25, 1986. The "Interprofession des appellations cidricoles" organizes producers of cider, calvados, and other apple-based spirits. *See* Jean-Jacques Lerosier, *En Normandie, des pommes, des poires et des appellations controlees*, Le Monde, Aug. 20, 2002, at 8. There are committees organized for various types of wines, cheeses, "fragrant plants, " beets, flax, cider, tartar, semolina, etc. *See Le Comité Interprofessionnel du Vin de Champagne* (paper on file with the author).

39. Lerosier, *supra* note 38 (noting that the town of Domfrontais was given AOC for calvados on December 31, 1997 and AOC for poiré (apple and pear-based spirit) on December 12, 2001).

40. C. Con. art. L. 115-5. ("[L]e nom qui constitue l'appellation d'origine ... ne peuvent être employés pour aucun produit similaire.... Ils ne peuvent être employés pour aucun établissement et aucun autre produit ou service, lorsque cette utilisation est susceptible de détourner ou d'affaiblir la notoriété d'appellation d'origine.") [The name that constitutes the *appellation d'origine* cannot be used for any similar product. They cannot be used for establishment or any other product or service, when this use is likely to divert from or weaken the reputation of the *appellation d'origine*.].

41. Yves St. Laurent Parfums S.A. v. Institut National des Appellations d'Origin, Cour d'appel, [CA] [regional court of appeal], Paris, Dec. 15, 1993, 1994 E.C.C. 385 (holding that the use of Champagne as a title for a scent "usurped the prestige" of the appellation).

42. 15 U.S.C. § 1127 (2006).

43. *See* McCarthy on Trademarks and Unfair Competition § 19:99 (4th ed. 2006). In fact, McCarthy gives as one example of a likely collective mark holder "an agricultural cooperative of

used to "certify regional or other origin, material, mode of manufacture, quality, accuracy, or other characteristics of . . . [the] goods or services."[44] Examples include the "Good Housekeeping" seal of approval, the "UL" mark (Underwriters Laboratory),[45] and various trademarks used to designate kosher foods.

A certification mark protects a geographical indication when it is used to "certify regional . . . origin."[46] For example, the state government of Idaho has three registered certification marks at the United States Patent and Trademark Office (USPTO) protecting different versions of "IDAHO POTATOES."[47] Other examples of registered certification marks in the United States include PARMIGIANO-REGGIANO,[48] ROQUEFORT,[49] STILTON,[50] REAL CALIFORNIA[51] for cheese, PARMA for ham,[52] DARJEELING for tea,[53] WASHINGTON for apples,[54] and the FLORIDA SUNSHINE TREE for citrus.[55]

To maintain USPTO registration of a certification mark, the mark holder must meet several standards. The holder must control use of the mark.[56] The holder *cannot* be a producer of the certified products.[57] The holder must *not* allow it to be used for anything but certification of the relevant products; and must not discriminately "refuse[] to certify . . .

---

sellers of farm produce." *Id.*

44. 15 U.S.C. § 1127.

45. RESTATEMENT (THIRD) OF UNFAIR COMPETITION § 11 reporters' note (1995).

46. 15 U.S.C. § 1127.

47. U.S. Trademark Registration No. 2,403,069 (filed Mar. 17, 1997) (FAMOUS IDAHO POTATOES FAMOUS POTATOES GROWN IN IDAHO certification mark owned by Idaho Potato Commission); U.S. Trademark Registration No. 1,735,559 (filed July 21, 1991) (GROWN IN IDAHO IDAHO POTATOES certification mark owned by State of Idaho Potato Commission); U.S. Trademark Registration No. 943,815 (filed June 7, 1971) (PREMIUM PACKED IDAHO POTATOES certification mark owned by State of Idaho).

48. U.S. Trademark Registration No. 1,896,683 (filed June 7, 1993) (PARMIGIANO-REGGIANO certification mark owned by Consorzio del Formaggio Parmigiano-Reggiano).

49. U.S. Trademark Registration No. 571,798 (filed Feb. 13, 1952) (ROQUEFORT certification mark owned by community of Roquefort).

50. U.S. Trademark Registration No. 1,959,589 (filed Jan. 18, 1994) (STILTON certification mark owned by Stilton Cheese Makers' Association).

51. U.S. Trademark Registration No. 1,285,675 (filed Apr. 11, 1993) (REAL CALIFORNIA CHEESE certification mark owned by California Milk Producers Advisory Board).

52. U.S. Trademark Registration No. 2,014,628 (filed Aug. 7, 1984) (PARMA certification mark owned by Consorzio del Prosciutto di Parma).

53. U.S. Trademark Registration No. 1,632,726 (filed July 1, 1998) (DARJEELING certification mark owned by the Tea Board of India).

54. U.S. Trademark Registration No. 1,528,514 (filed Dec. 30, 1985) (WASHINGTON certification mark owned by Washington State Apple Advertising Commission).

55. U.S. Trademark Registration No. 932,033 (filed Oct. 14, 1970) (THE FLORIDA SUNSHINE TREE certification mark owned by Florida Department of Citrus); U.S. Trademark Registration No. 1,559,414 (filed May 11, 1987) (FRESH FROM THE FLORIDA SUNSHINE TREE certification mark owned by Florida Department of Citrus).

56. 15 U.S.C. § 1064(5)(A) (2006).

57. *Id.* § 1064(5)(B).

goods or services . . . [that] maintain[] the standards or conditions which such mark certifies."[58] But, unlike the INAO,[59] as long as the certification standards are applied in a non-discriminatory fashion, the USPTO does not care *what* the certification standards are. Even less government oversight is involved in a "collective mark" which is owned by an association to which all the relevant producers belong.[60] Collective marks are treated like regular trademarks, subject only to traditional trademark doctrines against abandonment, naked licensing, attachment to goodwill, and the like. In short, government involvement with this kind of geographical indication is no different than it is with the trademarks HILTON HOTELS or PEPSI.

Like other trademarks, certification marks can develop as a matter of common law without USPTO registration.[61] Presumably, the same is true for collective marks. In a seminal case concerning COGNAC as an unregistered certification mark, the Trademark Trial and Appeal Board concluded that the critical issue is whether *control* is being exercised over the use of the word.[62] The certification mark exists at common law "if the use of a geographic designation is controlled and limited in such a manner that it reliably indicates to purchasers that the goods bearing the designation come exclusively from a particular region."[63] Thus, if an appellation or *denominazione* is controlled locally in France or Italy, the producers market in the United States, and *no one else in the United States is using the GI for the same product*, there are probably common law trademark rights under U.S. trademark doctrine. This means that a European producer can gain common law protection of its geographical indication in the United States without regard to whether the GI is protected under an EU member state's trademark law, geographical indications law, or both.[64] The ability of certification mark rights to arise

---

58. *Id.* § 1064(5)(C)–(D).

59. *See supra* text accompanying note 36.

60. McCarthy, *supra* note 43. And in many circumstances, "the only possible distinction" between the two kinds of marks "is one of form":

> That is, as to a collective trade or service mark, the sellers are members of an organization with standards of admission, while as to a certification mark, sellers are not members of an organization, but their products are certified according to set standards. This means that creating an "association" and calling a mark a "collective" mark may be a way to avoid the strict duties which Lanham Act § 14(e) applies to certification marks.

Id. § 19:99.

61. *See* Florida v. Real Juices, Inc., 330 F. Supp. 428, 430 (M.D. Fla. 1971) (unregistered SUNSHINE TREE valid certification mark for citrus from Florida); Institut National des Appellations d'Origine v. Brown-Forman Corp., 47 U.S.P.Q.2d (BNA) 1875, 1883 (T.T.A.B. 1998) (COGNAC valid unregistered certification mark for purposes of opposing trademark registration using "Cognac"); RESTATEMENT (THIRD) OF UNFAIR COMPETITION § 18 (1995).

62. *See Brown-Forman*, 47 U.S.P.Q.2d at 1885.

63. *Id.*

64. It is unclear whether GI registration at the EU level "preempts" registration as a certification mark at the national level. For a thorough discussion of the uncertainties on this issue, see Lionel

without any *ex ante* government role further distinguishes the American approach from a real AOC system.

II. The TRIPS Provisions on Geographical Indications

From the late nineteenth century forward, concern for geographical identifiers made its way into many bilateral agreements. In 1910, the United States entered into a bilateral agreement with Portugal on the use of *Porto*; by 1930, there was a complex web of such treaties among European states.[65] Indications of source and geographical indications also made their way into a few multilateral agreements. Two of these multilateral agreements concern us[66]: the Paris Convention on Industrial Property (1883)[67] and the Lisbon Agreement on the Protection of Appellations of Origin and their International Registration (1958).[68]

Established in 1883, the Paris Convention was revised several times in the twentieth century[69] and it is better known for its provisions on patents and trademarks than for anything it says about geographical indications. Although Article 1 provides that the Convention includes "indications of source or appellations of origin"[70] those terms are undefined and the actual treaty obligations are cast at a very general level. Article 10(1) of the Convention requires countries to seize "on importation" or "inside the country" any goods bearing a "direct or indirect use of a false indication of the source of the goods."[71] Article 10bis(3), added in 1958, also prohibits "indications or allegations the use of which in the course of trade is liable to mislead the public as to the

---

Bentley & Brad Sherman, *The Impact of European Geographical Indications on National Rights in Member States*, 96 TRADEMARK REP. 850 (2006).

65. BUHL, *supra* note 5, at 340–41 (listing some of France's bilateral treaties prior to EU competence in this area).

66. Another multilateral agreement on geographical indications—as unsuccessful as it is amusing named—is the Stresa Convention. Convention internationale sur l'emploi des appellations d'origine et dénominations de fromages [The International Convention for the Use of Appellations of Origin and Denominations of Cheeses], June 1, 1951, http://www.admin.ch/ch/f/rs/i8/0.817.142.1.fr.pdf.

67. Paris Convention for the Protection of Industrial Property, *opened for signature* Mar. 20, 1883, 21 U.S.T. 1583, 828 U.N.T.S. 305 [hereinafter Paris Convention] (revised at Brussels on Dec. 14, 1900, at Washington on June 2, 1911, at The Hague on Nov. 6, 1925, at London on June 2, 1934, at Lisbon on Oct. 31, 1958, and at Stockholm on July 14, 1967, and as amended on Sept. 28, 1979).

68. Lisbon Agreement for the Protection of Appellations of Origin and their International Registration, Oct. 31, 1958, 923 U.N.T.S. 189 (English text of Stockholm revision begins at 215), *available at* http://www.wipo.int/lisbon/en/legal_texts/lisbon_agreement.htm [hereinafter Lisbon Agreement] (revised at Stockholm on July 14, 1967, and as amended on September 28, 1979).

69. For an account of the origins of the Paris Convention, see I STEPHEN P. LADAS, PATENTS, TRADEMARKS, AND RELATED RIGHTS: NATIONAL AND INTERNATIONAL PROTECTION 59–94 (1975).

70. Paris Convention, *supra* note 67, art. 1(2).

71. *Id.* art. 10(1). Article 10(1) extends Article 9's seizure obligations for false trademark to false indications of "source." The "source" phrase apparently means geographic origin because it is the first half of a disjunctive in which the other phrase is "the identity of the producer, manufacturer, or merchant." *Id.*

nature, the manufacturing process, [or] the characteristics" of the goods.[72] The drafting history of this provision indicates that it was *not* intended to apply to geographic identifiers,[73] but Article 10bis(3) is nonetheless important because it became a launching point for the current TRIPS provisions on GIs.

The second relevant pre-TRIPS effort is the Lisbon Agreement of 1958. The Lisbon Agreement established an international registration system for *appellations of origin*.[74] Article 2(1) of the agreement provides: "'[A]ppellation of origin' means the geographical name of a country, region, or locality, which serves to designate a product originating therein, the quality and characteristics of which are due exclusively or essentially to the geographical environment, including natural and human factors."[75]

The Lisbon system is both simple and rigorous. Each country decides how its domestic law will determine that an appellation is protected (i.e., judicial or administrative processes).[76] Once an appellation is protected in its country of origin and registered with the World Intellectual Property Organization (WIPO), each member country of the Lisbon Agreement is required to protect that appellation within its own borders—subject to a one year window in which the country "may declare that it cannot ensure the protection of an appellation of origin whose registration has been notified to it."[77] The scope of protection under the Lisbon Agreement is broad. Article 3 expressly provides: "Protection shall be ensured against any usurpation or imitation, even if the true origin of the product is indicated or if the appellation is used in translated form or accompanied by terms such as 'kind', 'type', 'make', 'imitation', or the like."[78]

Thus, the holder of an appellation as such (a certification trademark will not do)[79] has the right to stop *any* use in a descriptive phrasing such

---

72. *Id.* art. 10bis(3)(3).

73. Article 10bis generally binds treaty members "to assure to nationals of [other treaty countries] effective protection against unfair competition." The specific language of Article 10bis(3) then prohibits "indications or allegations the use of which in the course of trade is liable to mislead the public as to the nature, the manufacturing process, the characteristics, the suitability for their purpose, or the quantity, of the goods." The original proposal for this provision included "the origin" between "nature" and "the manufacturing process," but this reference to source was dropped at the insistence of the United States during the 1958 revision of the Convention. *See* J. Thomas McCarthy & Veronica Colby Devitt, *Protection of Geographic Denominations: Domestic and International*, 69 TRADEMARK REP. 199, 202–03 (1979).

74. Lisbon Agreement, *supra* note 68, art. 1.

75. *Id.* art 2(1).

76. *Id.* art. 8.

77. *Id.* art. 5(3).

78. *Id.* art. 3.

79. The Lisbon Agreement leaves no room for anything short of an "appellation" system. Article 1(2) makes it clear that the treaty obligation extends only to "appellations of origin of products . . .

as "Port-like fortified wine," "imitation Chianti," or "Roquefort-style cheese."

As of August 1, 2006, only twenty-five states were parties to the Lisbon Agreement.[80] Five countries have joined the Lisbon Agreement since 2001, but the new signatory list hardly suggests that the treaty is enjoying a second wind of mainstream acceptance (Georgia (2004), North Korea (2005), Peru (2005), Iran (2006), Nicaragua (2006)).[81] Among EU member states, only France, Hungary, Italy, and Portugal belong to the Lisbon system.

Lack of participation in the Lisbon system probably gave GI advocates added incentive to seek inclusion of GI provisions in TRIPS.[82] The negotiation history of these provisions will not be reviewed here,[83] except to say that (a) the contours of the debate crystallized with the

---

recognized and protected *as such* in the country of origin." *Id.* art. 1(2) (emphasis added). The official French text is arguably more demanding, requiring that the protected appellations of origin be "reconnues et protégées à ce titre dans le pays d'origine," arguably meaning that the phrase "appellations d'origine" or a close linguistic translation must be used in the country's domestic legal regime. *See* Arrangement de Lisbonne concernant la protection des appellations d'origine et leur enregistrement international, http://www.wipo.int/lisbon/fr/legal_texts/lisbon_agreement.htm (last visited Nov. 5, 2006). The Spanish text seems to more closely follow the "as such" construction in English ("[D]enominaciones de origen de los productos de los otros países de la Unión particular, reconocidas y protegidas como tales en el país de origen."). *See* Arreglo de Lisboa relativo a la Protección de las Denominaciones de Origen y su Registro Internacional Lisbon Agreement, http://www.wipo.int/treaties/es/registration/lisbon/pdf/trtdocs_woo12.pdf (last visited Nov. 5, 2006).

80. *See* THE WORLD INTELLECTUAL PROPERTY ORGANIZATION, LISBON AGREEMENT STATUS ON OCT. 13, 2006 (2006), http://www.wipo.int/treaties/en/documents/pdf/lisbon.pdf (for a current signatory list).

81. *Id.*

82. The European Union sought inclusion of GI provisions early in the Uruguay Round negotiations. *See* Communication, *European Community—Guidelines Proposed for the Negotiation of Trade-Related Aspects of Intellectual Property Rights,* MTN.GNG/NG11/W/16 (Nov. 20, 1987); Submissions, *European Communities, Japan & United States—Trade Problems Encountered in Connection with Intellectual Property Rights* 2–3, MTN.GNG/NG11/W/7 (May 29, 1987) (European Union submitted that "[t]he protection of appellations of origin and of other geographical indications is of fundamental importance" and that "the wine and spirit sector is one which is particularly vulnerable to imitation, counterfeit and usurpation [which causes] damage not only to producers . . . but also to consumers").

83. The TRIPS Agreement has been described and dissected in detail by several writers and commentators, although the GI provisions have not been scrutinized fully. *See generally* CARLOS M. CORREA, INTELLECTUAL PROPERTY RIGHTS, THE WTO AND DEVELOPING COUNTRIES 3 (noting that "[i]ndustrialized countries forced developing countries to initiate negotiation of an agreement on TRIPS with the clear objective of universalizing the standards of IPRs protection that the former had incorporated in their legislation . . . ."); MICHAEL P. RYAN, KNOWLEDGE DIPLOMACY: GLOBAL COMPETITION AND THE POLITICS OF INTELLECTUAL PROPERTY (1998); SUSAN K. SELL, POWER AND IDEAS: NORTH-SOUTH POLITICS OF INTELLECTUAL PROPERTY AND ANTITRUST (1998); 2 THE GATT URUGUAY ROUND, A NEGOTIATING HISTORY 1986–1992, at 2245–2313 (Terence P. Stewart ed., 1993) (chapter on TRIPs); JAYASHREE WATAL, INTELLECTUAL PROPERTY RIGHTS IN THE WTO AND DEVELOPING COUNTRIES 9–47 (2001) (detailing the North-South negotiation process); Conrad, *supra* note 18, at 29–46; Marci A. Hamilton, *The TRIPS Agreement: Imperialistic, Outdated, and Overprotective,* 29 VAND. J. TRANSNAT'L L. 613 (1996); Roland Knaack, *The Protection of Geographical Indications According to the TRIPS Agreement, in* FROM GATT TO TRIPS—THE AGREEMENT ON TRADE-RELATED ASPECTS OF INTELLECTUAL PROPERTY RIGHTS 117, 127–40 (Freidrich-Karl Beier & Gerhard Schricker eds., 1996).

introduction of divergent U.S. and EU draft treaty texts in 1990[84]; and (b) the final merger/compromise of these conflicting approaches was presented by GATT Director Arthur Dunkel on December 20, 1991.[85] The Dunkel Draft provisions on geographical indications became Article 22–24 of the final TRIPS text.

It may be easiest to think of the TRIPS GI provisions as having four components: (1) a "floor" of unfair competition norms for all geographical indications[86]; (2) special, additional protection for wine and spirit GIs[87]; (3) complex exceptions to GI protection[88]; and (4) obligations to conduct further negotiations to increase protection of wine and spirit GIs.[89] Throughout these provisions, TRIPS is silent as to the mechanism of protection and it is understood that each country may fulfill these obligations through its own particular domestic law tools.

A. Article 22(1)

Article 22 provides the "floor" protection for all GIs. Article 22(1) gives a definition of geographical indications and has three elements that warrant our attention. First, Article 22(1) provides the definition of a geographical indication: "Geographical indications are for purposes of this Agreement, indications which identify a good as originating in the territory of a Member, or a region or locality in that territory, where a given quality, reputation, or other characteristic of the good is essentially attributable to its geographical origin."

This definition is not limited to *words*, so images and packaging are potentially included. Nor is the definition limited to foodstuffs,[90] although

---

84. The critical texts were the Communication, *European Community—Draft Agreement on Trade-Related Aspects of Intellectual Property Rights*, MTN.GNG/NG11/W/68 (Mar. 29, 1990), *reprinted in* 10 World Intell. Prop. Rev. 128 (1990) [hereinafter EU Draft] and Communication, *United States—Draft Agreement on the Trade-Related Aspects of Intellectual Property Rights*, MTN.GNG/NG11/W/70 (May 11, 1990), *reprinted in* 10 World Intell. Prop. Rev. 128 (1990) [hereinafter U.S. Draft].

85. *Draft Final Act Embodying the Results of the Uruguay Round of Multilateral Trade Negotiations*, MTN.TNC/W/FA (Dec. 20, 1991) [hereinafter Dunkel Draft]. There was also a draft treaty text submitted to the GATT Brussels Ministerial meeting in December 1990 which had some bearing on the GI issue. *See Agreement on Trade-Related Aspects of Intellectual Property Rights, Including Trade in Counterfeit Goods* in *Draft Final Act Embodying the Results of the Uruguay Round of Multilateral Trade Negotiations* 193–237, MTN.TNC/W/35/Rev.1 (Dec. 3, 1990) [hereinafter Brussels Draft]. In 1990, there were three other draft treaty texts introduced by Switzerland, Japan, and a coalition of developing countries (including Argentina, Brazil, Nigeria, Egypt, China, Chile, and Tanzania), but those three additional drafts were not central to the geographical indications issues.

86. *See* TRIPS, *supra* note 9, art. 22.

87. *See id.* art. 23(1)–(3).

88. *See id.* art. 24(4)–(9).

89. *See id.* arts. 23(4), 24 (1).

90. *See* Communication, *New Zealand—Geographical Indications and the Article 24.2 Review*, 2, IP/C/W/205 (Sept. 18, 2000) [hereinafter *New Zealand TRIPS Council Submission*] (wording of TRIPS Agreement "cover[s] geographical indications for *all* goods, including industrial goods").

THE SPIRITED DEBATE

it apparently excludes services.[91] But there are other aspects of the definition that warrant our attention.

First, the definition is ambiguous on whether human production factors may be part of the tally of "quality, reputation, or other characteristic of the good."[92] In contrast, the Lisbon Agreement specifies "natural *and* human factors"[93] and the EU Draft in 1991 had proposed this same construction.[94] The lack of this language has led some commentators to conclude that Article 22(1) *excludes* human factors in the consideration of GIs,[95] but that interpretation is not warranted since neither the 1990 U.S. Draft nor any of the other TRIPS proposals expressly attempted to exclude "human factors" of production.

Second, we should note the standard Article 22(1) adopts for the relationship between the product's qualities and the geographic source. The Lisbon Agreement states that the product's "characteristics" must be "due exclusively *or* essentially to the geographical environment."[96] TRIPS Article 22(1) requires that the "given quality, reputation, or other characteristic of the good is *essentially* attributable to its geographical origin."[97] No one knows whether there is any difference between qualities being "essentially" or "exclusively" due to the land. Since we should not multiply legal distinctions needlessly, I think it is reasonable to see the same standard being generated by both terms: an *essential land/qualities connection.*

Third, there is the word "reputation" in the Article 22(1) definition—something absent from the Lisbon Agreement. TRIPS

---

91. *See* Conrad, *supra* note 18, at 33–34. *But see* Carolina Hungria de San Juan Paschoal, *Geography, Source, and Origin: The Legal Framework,* 152 TRADEMARK WORLD 38, 38 (Nov. 2002) (U.K.) ("[I]t is possible to have services protected by a geographical indication, such as 'Swiss Banking Services.'").

92. TRIPS, *supra* note 9, art. 22.

93. Lisbon Agreement, *supra* note 68, art. 2 (emphasis added).

94. *See* EU Draft, *supra* note 84, art. 19 ("Geographic indications are, for the purposes of this agreement, those which designate a product as originating from a country, region or locality where a given quality, reputation or other characteristic of the product is attributable to its geographic origin, including natural and human factors."). WIPO's model law in the 1990s on geographical indications also expressly referred to "the geographical environment, including natural factors, human factors, or both natural and human factors."

95. *See* Lee Bendekgey & Caroline H. Mead, *International Protection of Appellations of Origin and Other Geographical Indications,* 82 TRADEMARK REP. 765, 785 (1992); Conrad, *supra* note 18, at 33. Arguably, this limitation was acceptable to the European Union because French law had already developed in this direction and the United States simply would not have cared.

96. Lisbon Agreement, *supra* note 68, art. 2 (emphasis added).

97. TRIPS, *supra* note 9, art. 22(1) (emphasis added). The "essentially attributable" standard appears in at least one treaty before TRIPS: Article 2(2)(b) of the Australia-European Community Agreement, which entered into force on March 1, 1994. Agreement Between the European Community and Australia on Trade in Wine, Eur.-Austl., *opened for signature* Jan. 26, 1994, 1994 O.J. (L 86) 3, 3. But this bilateral treaty itself was negotiated while TRIPS was being negotiated and, in fact, was largely completed.

Article 22(1) arguably leads to protection of geographic products names "where a given ... reputation ... of the good is essentially attributable to its geographic origin." Broadly read, this could obviate any land/qualities connection of the sort that has been fundamental to the notion of appellations.[98] The addition of "reputation" probably reflects the two-tier system of protecting geographical indications in the European Union, something discussed further below.[99]

B. ARTICLE 22(2)

Article 22(2) then provides the two basic treaty obligations applicable to *all* geographical indications:

> Members shall provide the legal means for interested parties to prevent:
>
> (a) the use of any means in the designation or presentation of a good that indicates or suggests that the good in question originates in a geographical area other than the true place of origin in a manner which misleads the public as to the geographical origin of the good;
>
> (b) any use which constitutes an act of unfair competition within the meaning of Article 10*bis* of the Paris Convention (1967).[100]

Broad enough to include all communications concerning a product, Article 22(2)(a) has three requirements: (1) that a word, phrase, or symbol "indicates or suggests" that a product comes from a geographic region; (2) that the product does *not* come from that producing region, and (3) that the public is misled by (1) and (2). This does not address situations where a word or symbol could fail (3) or even (1). A geographic name's failure to indicate or suggest a particular geographic origin could be because the word, phrase, or symbol is being used for evocative purposes (DARJEELING bras in France[101]) or has become generically descriptive of the product (French fries in Washington, D.C.).

---

98. *See* O'Connor, *supra* note 17, at 52 ("This definition expands the concept of appellation of origin contained in Art. 2 of the Lisbon Agreement to protect goods which merely derive a reputation from their place of origin without possessing a given quality or other characteristics which are due to that place.").

99. The EEC Origins Regulation does allow that its second tier protection can extend to products "which possess[] a specific ... reputation ... attributable to that geographical origin" without an exclusivity or essentiality requirement. *See* Council Regulation 2081/92, art. 2(b), Protection of Geographical Indications and Designations of Origin for Agricultural Products and Foodstuffs, July 14, 1992, 1992 O.J. (L 208) 1, 2 (EC) [hereinafter Origins Regulation]. Nonetheless, the Regulation Preamble says "the scope of this Regulation is limited to certain agricultural products and foodstuffs for which a link between product or foodstuff characteristics and geographical origin exists." *Id.* pmbl.; *see also* Joerg W. Rieke, Attorney-at-Law, German Dairy Association, Presentation at the IDFA 2004 Diary Forum in Boca Raton, Florida, at 15–21, (January 18–21, 2004) http://www.idfa.org/meetings/presentations/reike_df2004.ppt.

100. TRIPS, *supra* note 9, art. 22(2)(a)–(b).

101. U.S. Trademark Registration No. 2,043,112 (filed Dec. 21, 1995) (DARJEELING typed drawing certification owned by Delta Lingerie, a French Corporation).

As for subsection (b), Article 10bis of the Paris Convention provides that member countries of that treaty are generally "bound to assure to nationals of such countries effective protection against unfair competition."[102] Most definitively, TRIPS Article 22(2)(b) "extends" Paris 10bis(3)—which was described above—so that WTO members must prohibit the use of any geographical indication which "in the course of trade is liable to mislead the public as to the nature, the manufacturing process, the characteristics, the suitability for their purpose, or the quantity, of the goods."[103] Obviously, there will be substantial overlap in the coverage of Articles 22(2)(a) and 22(2)(b).

While TRIPS Article 22(2) addresses use in commerce, Article 22(3) bars registration of any trademark that includes a geographical indication "if use of the indication in the trademark for such goods in that Member is of such a nature as to mislead the public as to the true place of origin." This provision is compatible with American law barring geographic terms in trademarks where the term would be "primarily geographically deceptively misdescriptive,"[104] but not barring registration where the public is not misled as to the product's place of origin. For example, Pepperidge Farms has a "distinctive" line of U.S.-made cookies named BORDEAUX, GENEVA, MILANO, ST. TROPEZ, VERONA, etc.[105] Such evocative marks can be registered on the grounds that American consumers do not expect the cookies to come from these places.

C. ARTICLE 23'S ADDITIONAL PROTECTION OF WINES AND SPIRITS

If Article 22's deception-based provisions stood alone, GI protection in TRIPS would be unremarkable. But Article 23 adds another layer of obligations in relation to wines and spirits and these are, at present, the bulk of the world's "appellations."[106] Whereas Article 22 patrols use of

---

102. Paris Convention, *supra* note 67, art. 10bis(1). Article 10bis(2) then provides that "[a]ny act of competition contrary to honest practices in industrial or commercial matters constitutes an act of unfair competition." *Id.*

103. *Id.* art. 10bis(3)(3). Article 10bis(3) appears generally aimed at false or misleading advertising vis-à-vis competitors, i.e., "allegations" in 10bis(3)(2) and (3) and "acts [that] . . . create confusion . . . with the establishment, the goods, or the . . . activities, of a competitor," *id.* art. 10bis(3)(1), but the 10bis(3)(3) inclusion of "indications" seems to return to issues of product labeling.

104. 15 U.S.C. § 1052(e)(3) (2006).

105. *See* Pepperidge Farms, Cookies, http://www.pepperidgefarm.com/indulgent_treats_cookies.asp (last visited Nov. 5, 2006).

106. According to the European Commission in 2003, the "European Communities have registered some 4800 geographical indications (4200 for wines and spirits; 600 for other products)." *See* European Commission, *Intellectual Property—Why Do Geographical Indications Matter to Us?*, July 30, 2003, http://europa.eu.int/comm/trade/issues/sectoral/intell_property/argu_en.htm [hereinafter *Why Do Geographical Indications Matter to Us?*]. But something seems wrong about these numbers because the same document lists France as having "593 GIs (466 for wines and spirits and 127 for other products)"; Italy as having "420 GIs (300 for wines and spirits and 120 on other products)"; and 123 GIs for Spain. *Id.* Since these three countries have the strongest GI traditions, it is hard to believe that they are, together, only 24% of the EU GI total. *See id.*

GIs that would mislead or deceive the consumer, Article 23 eliminates *any* confusion requirement for wines and spirits.[107] Regardless of consumer confusion, a trademark embodying an inaccurate geographical indication for wines or spirits must be denied registration under Article 23(2)[108] and must be eliminated from commerce generally under Article 23(1).[109] In the words of one TRIPS delegate, this "effectively constitutes a departure from the general rule laid down in Article 22" requiring deception or unfair competition.[110]

Article 23(1) also explicitly expands the scope of protection for the wine and spirit geographical indication to bar a whole range of commercial practices:

> Each member shall provide the legal means for interested parties to prevent use of a geographical indication identifying wines for wines not originating in the place indicated by the geographical indication in question or identifying spirits for spirits not originating in the place indicated by the geographical indication in question, even where the true origin of the goods is indicated or the geographical indication is used in translation or accompanied by expressions such as "kind," "type," "style," "imitation," or the like.[111]

As will be discussed further below, this standard eliminates many labeling and advertising possibilities that would actually increase consumer information. At the same time, this is neither as expansive as the protection for GIs in the Lisbon Agreement nor is it what was originally sought by the European Union in the TRIPS negotiations. Recall the language of Article 3 of the Lisbon Agreement: "Protection shall be ensured against any usurpation or imitation, even if the true origin of the product is indicated or if the appellation is used in translated form or accompanied by terms such as 'kind,' 'type,' 'make,' 'imitation,' or the like."[112]

---

107. The United States implemented this TRIPS obligation by making changes to § 2(a) of the Lanham Act in Uruguay Round Agreements Act, Pub. L. No. 103-465, § 522, 108 Stat. 4809, 4982 (1994).

108. The agreement provides:

> The registration of a trademark for wines which contains or consists of a geographical indication identifying wines or for spirits which contains or consists of a geographical indication identifying spirits shall be refused or invalidated, *ex officio* if domestic legislation so permits or at the request of an interested party, with respect to such wines or spirits not having this origin.

TRIPS, *supra* note 9; *accord New Zealand TRIPS Council Submission, supra* note 90, at 3 (stating that under Article 23(1), "[t]here is *no* requirement that the public be misled or that the use constitutes an act of unfair competition").

109. Conrad, *supra* note 18, at 39.

110. *New Zealand TRIPS Council Submission, supra* note 90, at 3. A departure that is acknowledged as "essentially the result of the demands of a number of wine-producing countries during the Uruguay Round, notably in the European Union." *Id.*

111. TRIPS, *supra* note 9, art. 23(1).

112. Lisbon Agreement, *supra* note 68, art. 3.

The European Union's original TRIPS proposal similarly provided that all GIs would be protected from "usurpation" by *any* product or commercial use — a standard drawn from French law and most easily understood by American lawyers as a dilution or "dilution plus" standard of protection for all GIs. In contrast, TRIPS Article 23(1) limits its confusion-less protection to uses *within* the wine or spirit product category (that is, it bars "a geographical indication identifying wines for wines not originating in the place indicated").

D.   ARTICLE 24: LIMITATIONS AND EXCEPTIONS

Article 24 houses an array of limitations[113] to the geographical indication obligations in Articles 22 and 23, but the two limitations that are the most important are the provisions on grandfathering for established trademarks and the provision on genericity. The grandfathering provisions are complex, but, essentially, a country does not have to invalidate any trademark containing a GI if rights in that trademark (including under the common law) developed prior to (a) the date of TRIPS coming into force in that country, or (b) the protection of the GI in its country of origin, whichever comes later.[114] Subsection (6) of Article 24 then provides the general exception for geographic words that have become generic in a WTO country. The obligations of Articles 22 and 23 do not apply if "the relevant indication is identical with the term customary in common language as the common name for such goods or services in the territory of that Member."[115]

Obviously, these provisions on grandfathering and genericity are disliked by some European foodstuff producers. The grandfathering of pre-existing trademarks allows a Canadian producer to continue to use its PARMA ham trademark in Canada. It also allows BUDWEISER to continue to be marketed in countries where it was already trademarked even if the Czech Republic succeeds in its argument, always a bit of a stretch, that the beer-producing town of Budvar is entitled to the German adjectival version of its name. The limitation on generic words allows Argentine vintners to continue to make "Champagne" sparkling wine and South African farmers to continue to sell "Camembert" cheese.

---

113. *See* TRIPS, *supra* note 9, art. 24(4)–(9). Article 24(3) establishes a prohibition on back-tracking, stating that the TRIPS obligations are not a justification to "diminish the protection of geographical indications that existed in that Member immediately prior to the date of entry into force of the WTO Agreement." *Id.*; *see infra* Part II.E (discussing Article 24(1)–(2)).

114. TRIPS, *supra* note 9, art. 24(5)(a)–(b). And Article 65(1) provides that no WTO member is bound by the TRIPS obligations "before the expiry of a general period of one year following the date of entry into force of the WTO Agreement." The date of entry into force for original signatories of TRIPS was January 1, 1995. Article 24(4) also provides a grandfathering clause specific to a geographical indication for wine or spirits.

115. *Id.* art. 24(6).

E. ARTICLES 23 AND 24: COMMITMENTS FOR FURTHER NEGOTIATIONS

The TRIPS Agreement calls for continued discussion of geographical indications in three separate TRIPS provisions: Article 23(4), Article 24(1), and Article 24(2). This contrasts sharply with the TRIPS provisions on copyrights and patents, which were written as complete and final.[116]

One of these, Article 23(4), mandates further negotiations for "the establishment of a multilateral system of notification and registration of geographical indications for wines eligible for protection in those members participating in the system." The goal is limited to wines and is expressed as a system in which participation is completely optional, i.e., a registration "system" establishing "protection in those Members participating in the system."[117] Yet even if this optional system is limited to wine (which is now unlikely) it would essentially reinvigorate the Lisbon Agreement system and move it into the WTO framework. A more open-ended obligation is created by Article 24(1), stating that "[m]embers agree to enter into negotiations aimed at increasing the protection of individual geographical indications under Article 23." As a result of the reference to Article 23, this obligation extends to spirits as well as wines.[118]

The remainder of Article 24(1) shows the level of distrust over these negotiation commitments. The French hope to reclaim key viticultural words is embodied in the second sentence of 24(1), which says that the limitations built into the existing TRIPS system cannot be used by a Member to refuse to engage in negotiations toward increased protection that might eliminate those exceptions. The next sentence then splashes New World cold water on that hope: "Members shall be willing to consider the continued applicability of these provisions to individual geographical indications whose use was the subject of such

116. For that reason, discussion of further development of international legal norms in the copyright and patent fields has returned principally to the World Intellectual Property Organization. *See, e.g.*, WIPO Copyright Treaty, Dec. 20, 1996, 36 I.L.M. 65; WIPO Performances and Phonograms Treaty, Dec. 20, 1996, 36 I.L.M. 76.

117. Eleanor K. Meltzer, *TRIPs and Trademarks, or—GATT Got Your Tongue?*, 83 TRADEMARK REP. 18, 33 (1994) ("Article 23(4) indicates that participation would be discretionary.").

118. At least one commentator believes that the EU intent (or France's intent, in particular) with the Article 24(1) negotiations is the re-propertization of "Burgundy," "Chablis," and "Champagne" instead of countries being able to treat these terms as generic under Article 24(4). *See* Roland Knaak, *The Protection of Geographical Indications According to the TRIPS Agreement, in* FROM GATT TO TRIPs—THE AGREEMENT ON TRADE-RELATED ASPECTS OF INTELLECTUAL PROPERTY RIGHTS, *supra* note 83, at 135–39. Countries advocating a widening of the negotiations to include all foodstuffs usually, if not always, have a specific issue in mind, as with the Czech Republic's *Budweis* beer or India's *basmati* rice. The third and most benign commitment for further discussions, not discussed here, is in Article 24(2), which establishes a special mechanism for dialog and review of both the substantive GI commitments and the procedural commitments for further negotiations.

negotiations."[119] The point-counterpoint reminds one of Francis Walder's observation about diplomacy: no position "can be considered irrevocable or the word 'discussion' would make no sense."[120]

F. THE NEGOTIATIONS BEGIN

The TRIPS-mandated discussions began in earnest in June 1998 when the European Union made its first proposal for a notification and registration system under Article 23(4).[121] The 1998 EU proposal called for a binding system on all WTO members in which country A would designate a geographical indication and any country that did not object to the GI within one year would be obligated to protect the GI, regardless of the Article 24 exceptions.[122] The method for resolving objections was not elaborated. It appears that WTO members who failed to object would be obligated to protect the geographical indication.[123] In other words, if France sought to register "Chablis" and only Australia objected, all WTO members besides Australia would *lose* all Article 24 exceptions vis-à-vis "Chablis" regardless of the outcome of the France-Australia dispute. The European Union modified and elaborated this proposal in June 2000, but it maintained its object-or-be-bound basis and its application to all WTO members.[124]

At the WTO Ministerial meeting in Doha, Qatar in November 2001, the European Union pressed for expedited negotiations on geographical indications and WTO members agreed to expand discussion of the Article 23(4) notification and registration system to include spirits.[125] In response to this renewed pressure, the JUSCANZ+ group with

---

119. TRIPS, *supra* note 9, art. 24(1).

120. FRANCIS WALDER, SAINT-GERMAIN OU LA NÉGOCIATION 60 (1958) ("Elle ne peut être considérée comme irrévocable, ou le mot discussion n'aurait plus de sens.").

121. WTO Proposal, *Multilateral Register of Geographical Indications for Wines and Spirits Based On Article 23.4 of the TRIPS Agreement*, IP/C/W/107 (July 28, 1998) [hereinafter *1998 EU Proposal*].

122. *Id.* at 2–3.

123. *Id.* at 3. While the proposal stated that an international registration could potentially be "refused," it described no mechanism for such refusal and no ramifications for such refusal in non-objecting countries. *Id.* But the clear goal of the 1998 proposal was a system binding on all WTO countries: "One year after notification by the WTO Secretariat, geographical indications will become fully and indefinitely protected in all WTO Members." *Id.*

124. WTO Proposal, *Implementation of Article 23.4 of the TRIPS Agreement Relating to the Establishment of a Multilateral System of Notification and Registration of Geographical Indications*, IP/C/W/107/Rev.1 (June 22, 2000) [hereinafter *2000 EU Proposal*]. Under the modified EU proposal, when country A submits a GI for international registration, country B would have eighteen months (instead of twelve) to ask questions and/or challenge country A's registration. *Id.* at 4–5.

125. World Trade Organization, Ministerial Declaration of 14 November 2001, WT/MIN(01)/DEC/1, at 4, 41 I.L.M. 746 (2002) ("With a view to completing the work started in the Council for Trade-Related Aspects of Intellectual Property Rights (Council for TRIPS) on the implementation of Article 23.4, we agree to negotiate the establishment of a multilateral system of notification and registration of geographical indications for wines and spirits by the Fifth Session of the Ministerial Conference.").

additional countries from Asia and the Americas formally proposed a simple, streamlined registration system: a notification system with a searchable, online database that creates no new rights or obligations.[126] The proposal implicitly contrasted itself with the EU proposal, noting that it more closely hones to the Article 23 mandate to provide a voluntary "notification and registration" system that "facilitate[s]" the protection of GIs.[127] Although simple and non-binding, even this proposal has been criticized in some corners as (unintentionally) doing too much.[128] The core group of New World wine producers (Argentina, Australia, Canada, Chile, New Zealand, and the United States) followed up the proposal with a "communication," implicitly criticizing the EU proposal in diplomatically pointed language.[129]

In the spring of 2003, additional proposals were put forward by Hong Kong, China,[130] and the International Trademark Association (INTA).[131] Hong Kong's proposal would also establish a registration database, an entry on which would be prima facie evidence of GI protection in the country of origin,[132] with challenges to the registered GI occurring in national courts.[133] INTA's proposal goes further. Consciously modeled on the Patent Co-operation Treaty and the Madrid System for Marks, the INTA proposal would require the applicant to designate the jurisdictions in which it is seeking GI protection with examination in each such country. Private parties would be able to challenge the application before the national offices or courts in any country where GI protection is sought[134]; in other words, a trademark owner—faced with a

---

126. WTO Proposal, *Proposal for a Multilateral System for Notification and Registration of Geographical Indications for Wines and Spirits based on Article 23.4 of the TRIPS Agreement*, TN/IP/W/5 (Oct. 23, 2002) (Communication from Argentina, Australia, Canada, Chile, Colombia, Costa Rica, Dominican Republic, Ecuador, El Salvador, Guatemala, Honduras, Japan, Namibia, New Zealand, Philippines, Chinese Taipei, and the United States).

127. *Id.* at 3-4. The proponents emphasize that it fulfills this goal "without undue cost or complexity." *Id.* at 4.

128. Burkhart Goebel, *Geographical Indications and Trademarks—the Road from Doha*, 93 TRADEMARK REP. 964, 978 (2003) (criticizing the American proposal on the grounds that "it is quite likely that the courts of the Member States will presume that designations contained in the WTO data base indeed constitute GIs which will—in many cases—shift the burden of proof to the trademark owner . . . .").

129. WTO Proposal, *Multilateral System of Notification and Registration of Geographical Indications for Wines (and Spirits)*, TN/IP/W/6 (Oct. 29, 2002) (Communication from Argentina, Australia, Canada, Chile, New Zealand, and the United States).

130. WTO Proposal, *Multilateral System of Notification and Registration of Geographical Indications Under Article 23.4 of the TRIPS Agreement*, TN/IP/W/8 (Apr. 23, 2003) [hereinafter 2003 WTO Proposal] (Communication from Hong Kong, China).

131. Int'l Trademark Ass'n [INTA], *Establishment of a Multilateral System of Notification and the Registration of Geographical Indications for Wines and Spirits pursuant to TRIPS Article 23 (4)*, (Apr. 2003), *available at* http://www.wto.org/english/forums_e/ngo_e/posp31_e.htm.

132. 2003 WTO Proposal, *supra* note 130, at 2.

133. Goebel, *supra* note 128, at 981.

134. *Id.* at 983. If the proposal has one overarching principle, it is that "[c]onflicts between . . .

potentially conflicting GI—could defend itself without having to convince one or more WTO member governments to object to the GI.[135] The INTA proposal would allow countries to charge application fees, reducing the burden for governments, but increasing it for GI owners. In contrast, under the EU proposal the GI owner would get free, (fairly) global protection.

In 2003, Brussels upped the stakes. In anticipation of the WTO's September 2003 Cancun meeting, the European Union released a list of forty-one geographical indications that it wanted all WTO members to accept as non-generic, protected terms. According to the EU press release, the forty-one names are all "well established European quality products whose names are being abused today."[136] The Commission characterized its efforts as "recuperation" of the names, although the forty-one names quickly became more colloquially dubbed the "claw back" list.

The claw back list includes familiar cheese terms (Gorgonzola, Mozzarella [di Bufala Campana], Roquefort, etc.) and a few well-known meats (various kinds of Prosciutto), but the list is dominated by twenty-two names for wines and spirits, including all the usual suspects— Bordeaux, Chablis, Champagne, Chianti, Cognac, Porto, etc. Then-EU Farm Commissioner Franz Fischler reiterated that the Commission considers that "[t]his is not about protectionism. It is about fairness."[137] At the time the 2003 claw back list was published, the Commission made it clear that its demands included all translations, so that the list's inclusion of "Porto" would include "Port," "Champagne" would cover "Champaña," and "Prosciutto di Parma" would cover "Parma ham."[138]

G. THE ANGLOS OPEN A SECOND FRONT

While the European Union was pressing for increased protection of

---

rights should be resolved pursuant to the well-established intellectual property principles of territoriality, exclusivity, and priority." *Id.*

135. As Goebel notes, under the EU proposal, "[t]he owner of a medium-sized company who owns a trademark registration conflicting with a geographical indication in 50 countries would have to persuade the governments of 50 countries to raise an objection with the WTO in order to defend the exclusivity of his prior mark." *Id.* And all this would have to be done in eighteen months. *Id.* at 984.

136. Press Release, European Comm'n, WTO Talks: EU Steps up Bid for Better Protection for Regional Quality Products (Aug. 28, 2003), *available at* http://www.fas.usda.gov/gainfiles/200308/145985850.doc.

137. *Id.*

138. *Id.* The entire list of wines and spirits includes: Beaujolais, Bordeaux, Bourgogne, Chablis, Champagne, Chianti, Cognac, Grappa [seven variations], Graves, Liebfrau(en)milch, Malaga, Marsala, Madeira, Médoc, Moselle, Ouzo, Porto, Rhin, Rioja, Saint-Emilion, Sauternes, and Xerez [Sherry]; other products: Asiago, Azafrán de la Mancha, Comté, Feta, Fontina, Gorgonzola, Grana Padano, Jijona y Turrón de Alicante, Manchego, Mortadella Bologna, Mozzarella di Bufala Campana, Parmigiano Reggiano, Pecorino Romano, Prosciutto (di Parma, di San Daniele, and Toscano), Queijo São Jorge, Reblochon, and Roquefort. *Id.*

geographical indications, the WTO dispute settlement system was being used by Australia and the United States to establish that the European Union was not abiding by its existing Article 22 and 23 obligations. To understand this high profile irony, we must first sketch the then-EU system for protecting GIs, the parties' arguments, and, finally, the WTO Panel's conclusions.[139]

The EU rules for wine and spirit GIs are embedded in a web of broader industry regulations. The most important piece of that regulatory framework for our purposes is Council Regulation No. 1493/1999 of May 17, 1999 (1999 Wine Regulation),[140] recently supplemented by 2002 Wine Regulations.[141] Protection of all other GIs is based on European Community Council Regulation (EEC) No. 2081/92—commonly called the "1992 Origins Regulation"[142]—and its recent successor, the 2006 Origins Regulation.[143]

Article 2(2) of the Origins Regulation uses two concepts: the "designations of origin" and the "geographical indication." Both are defined as "the name of a region, a specific place, or, in exceptional cases, a country, used to describe an agricultural product or a foodstuff."[144] A designation of origin applies only to products where "the quality or characteristics of *which are essentially or exclusively due* to a particular geographical environment with its inherent natural and human factors, and the production, processing and preparation of which takes

---

139. Panel Report, *European Communities—Protection of Trademarks and Geographical Indications for Agricultural Products and Foodstuffs*, WT/DS174/R (Mar. 15, 2005) [hereinafter WTO Panel Report on Origins Regulations].

140. Council Regulation 1493/1999, On the Common Organisation of the Market in Wine of 17 May 1999, 1999 O.J. (L 179) 1 (EC) [hereinafter 1999 Wine Regulation], *available at* http://europa.eu.int/eur-lex/en/lif/reg/en_register_036055.html.

141. Commission Regulation 753/2002, Laying Down Certain Rules for Applying Council Regulation (EC) No 1493/1999 as Regards the Description, Designation, Presentation and Protection of Certain Wine Sector Products, 2002 O.J. (L 118) 1.

142. Council Regulation 2081/91, On the Protection of Geographical Indications and Designations of Origin for Agricultural Products and Foodstuffs, 1992 O.J. (L 208) 1 (EC) [hereinafter 1992 Origins Regulation].

143. Council Regulation 510/2006, On the Protection of Geographical Indications and Designations of Origin for Agricultural Products and Foodstuffs, 2006 O.J. (L 93) 12 (EC) [hereinafter 2006 Origins Regulation]. The 2006 Origins Regulation replaces the 1992 Origins Regulation, 2006 O.J. (L 93) at 13, and almost completely duplicates the 1992 regulation language except for revisions made to meet the WTO decision discussed in this part. Citations in text and footnotes of this Article are to the 2006 Origins Regulation unless otherwise noted. The 1992 and 2006 Origins Regulations harmonize EU law for: beer, natural mineral waters and spring waters, beverages made from plant extracts, bread, pastry, cakes, confectionery, biscuits and other baker's wares, natural gums and resins, hay, and "essential oils." *See* 1992 Origins Regulation, *supra* at 8; 2006 Origins Regulation, *supra* at 22–23. The 2006 Origins Regulation does not "apply to wine-sector products, except wine vinegars, or to spirit drinks." 2006 Origins Regulation, *supra* at 13, art. 1(1). The actual list of EU-protected GIs is found in Commission Regulation 2400/96, On the Register of Some Geographical Indications and Appellations of Origin, 1996 O.J. (L 327) 11.

144. 2006 Origins Regulation, *supra* note 143, art. 2(1).

place in the defined geographical area."[145] Thus, designations of origin require an essential connection between the land and the product's qualities, i.e., the French notion of terroir.[146]

In contrast, a "geographical indication" under the Origins Regulation does *not* have the "essentiality" requirement and requires only that "the production and/or processing and/or preparation of [the foodstuff] takes place in the defined geographical area."[147] The result is that under EU GI law the first category, a "designation of origin," is close to, but arguably tighter than, the TRIPS definition of a GI.[148] The second definition, a "geographical indication," is much looser than the TRIPS definition of a GI, albeit no looser than a geography-based certification mark in the United States.

Article 5 of the Origins Regulation provides that registrations are to be given to groups or associations of "producers and/or processors working with the same agricultural product or foodstuff," although in exceptional circumstances a natural or legal person can apply. Successful registration results in a "protected designation of origin" (or "PDO") or a "protected geographical indication" (or "PGI"), both of which enjoy the same protection against:

> (a) any direct or indirect commercial use in respect of products not covered by the registration insofar as those products are comparable to the products registered under that name or insofar as using the name exploits the reputation of the protected name;

> (b) any misuse, imitation or evocation, even if the true origin of the product is indicated or if the protected name is translated or accompanied by an expression such as "style," "type," "method," "as produced in," "imitation" or similar.[149]

So while there are two defined types of GIs, they receive the same protection. According to the Regulation's recitals, this two-tier system

---

145. *Id.* art. 2(1)(a) (emphasis added).

146. Professor André Bertrand reasons that the more restrictive definition of a "protected designation of origin" modified French law vis-à-vis the definition of an *appellation d'origine*, transferring the *essentiality* requirement into French law. BERTRAND, *supra* note 20, § 3.44, at 145.

147. 2006 Origins Regulation, *supra* note 143, art. 2(1)(b). Article 2(3) also allows for some geographical indications to be protected even "where the raw materials for the products concerned come from a geographical area larger than, or different from, the processing area." This is a grandfathering provision and such designations "must have been recognized as designations of origin in the country of origin before 1 May 2004." *Id.* In the 1992 version of the Origins Regulation, this grandfathering provision was Article 2(4). 1992 Origins Regulation, *supra* note 142, at 2. Article 2(7) limited the exception to applications lodged "within two years of the entry into force of this Regulation." *Id.*

148. The EU definition of a "designation of origin" is arguably narrower than the TRIPS definition of a geographical indication because it does not include the ambiguous "reputation" language in TRIPS Article 22(1). *See* discussion *supra* Part II.B.

149. 2006 Origins Regulation, *supra* note 143, art. 13(1). The Origins Regulation also prohibits origin-misleading packaging, containers, and advertising as well as having some catch-all language against misleading origin identifications. *Id.* art. 13(1)(c)–(d).

was appropriate because of "existing practices" in EU member states,[150] i.e., neither the French[151] nor the Germans would give up their own definitional approach.

In contrast, EU regulations concerning wine GIs exist in a very different environment, in which, by Commission admission, "the rules governing the common organisation of the market in wine are extremely complex."[152] Article 50 of the 1999 Wine Regulation gives EU member states more general directions to "take all necessary measures" to protect geographical indications for wine from "third countries" in accordance with Articles 23 and 24 of TRIPS. Articles 51 through 53, in combination with Annexes VII and VIII, then create a system that leaves most control in the hands of the member states to use "the name of a specified region" to designate wines from that region.[153] This allows the French, Italian, and other appellation systems to apply to wines along the same lines as the framework provided by the Origins Regulation.

As originally promulgated, the Origins Regulation required any application for GI protection to be made via an EU member state's government to the Commission.[154] Producers from geographic regions outside the European Union have no EU member national government to make an application on their behalf to the Commission. As a result, they were locked out of the system. This exclusion was either intentional or the product of a belief held by European officials that no one outside the European Union had GIs worthy of protection. It is hard to say which explanation would be worse.

The Origins Regulation was then amended to add Article 12, which provided the sole means for the registration of non-EC GIs. Article 12(1) offered protection on the condition that the non-EC country "adopt[ed] a system for GI protection that is equivalent to that in the European

---

150. 2006 Origins Regulation, *supra* note 143, at 12.

151. As originally formulated, the Origins Regulation would only have covered the stricter protected designation of origin (PDO) definition, rooted in French law. *See* Marina Kolia, *Monopolizing Names of Foodstuffs: The New Legislation*, 4 Eur. Intell. Prop. Rev. 333 (1992) (discussing potential effects of the 1992 Origins Regulation); Opinion on the Proposal for a Council Regulation on the Protection of Geographical Indications and Designations of Origin for Agricultural Products and Foodstuffs, 1991 O.J. (C 269) 62, para. 1.2 (EC). But German officials lobbied for an inclusion of their own approach. For a discussion of the compromise between the French appellations system and the more informal German system for protecting geographical indications, see Dav Gangjee, *Melton Mowbray and the GI Pie in the Sky: Exploring Cartographies of Protection*, 3 Intell. Prop. Q. 291 (2006).

152. 1999 Wine Regulation, *supra* note 140, at 2.

153. *Id.* at 27.

154. 1992 Origins Regulation, *supra* note 143, art. 5. For example, in the United Kingdom, applications go to the Department for the Environment, Food and Rural Affairs (DEFRA). *See* Gangjee, *supra* note 151, at 294. After an application is received, the Commission will then entertain an objection from any Member States or "any 'legitimately concerned natural or legal person.'" Joined Cases C-321/94 & C-324/94, *In re* Pistre, 1997 E.C.R. I-2343, 1997 C.M.L.R. 565, 573.

Communities and provide[s] reciprocal protection to products from the European Communities."[155] Thus, without their own "equivalent" appellation laws, Ethiopians were left with no means to register Yergacheffe as a coffee GI[156]; Ecuadorians had no means to register cocoa/chocolate GIs; and Americans had no means to register Idaho potatoes.

In June 1999, the United States initiated dispute-settlement consultations with the European Union, noting that "[t]he European Communities' Regulation 2081/92, as amended, does not provide national treatment with respect to geographical indications, and does not provide sufficient protection to preexisting trademarks that are similar or identical to a geographical indication."[157] Shortly thereafter, at a 2000 meeting of the TRIPS Council, New Zealand submitted a paper demanding a full analysis of national implementation of existing GI provisions under the Article 24(2) process. This served as a not too subtle warning to the European Union over the same issue.[158] Over time, Canada,[159] Australia,[160] Argentina,[161] and Sri Lanka[162] also joined the consultations on the U.S. side.[163] In 2003 the WTO consolidated the U.S. complaint with a parallel Australian complaint against the European Union and established a three member dispute panel on February 23, 2004.[164] Twelve countries reserved the right to participate in the dispute settlement proceedings on the U.S./Australia side.[165] After submissions

---

155. WTO Panel Report on Origins Regulations, *supra* note 139, ¶ 7.38.

156. Yergacheffe (or Yirgacheffe) is a small town in the Sidamo district of Ethiopia. Joan Reis Nielson, *World Class Cafes*, TEA & COFFEE TRADE J., Feb. 20, 2004, at 64.

157. Request for Consultations by the United States, *European Communities—Protection of Trademarks and Geographical Indications for Agricultural Products and Foodstuffs*, WT/DS174/1/IP/D/19 (June 7, 1999).

158. *See New Zealand TRIPS Council Submission, supra* note 90, *passim*.

159. Request to Join Consultations from Canada, *European Communities—Protection of Trademarks and Geographical Indications for Agricultural Products and Foodstuffs*, WT/DS174/3 (June 22, 1999).

160. Request to Join Consultations from Australia, *European Communities—Protection of Trademarks and Geographical Indications for Agricultural Products and Foodstuffs*, WT/DS174/4 (Apr. 23, 2003).

161. Request to Join Consultations from Argentina, *European Communities—Protection of Trademarks and Geographical Indications for Agricultural Products and Foodstuffs*, WT/DS174/9 (Apr. 24, 2004).

162. Request to Join Consultations from Sri Lanka, *European Communities—Protection of Trademarks and Geographical Indications for Agricultural Products and Foodstuffs*, WT/DS174/7 (Apr. 24, 2003).

163. Others also joined the consultations, i.e., India, Mexico, Hungary, the Czech Republic, Bulgaria, Slovenia, and Turkey. But the wording of the documents cited *supra* notes 159–62 expresses objection or concern with the EU regulations.

164. Constitution of the Panel Established at the Requests of the United States and Australia, *European Communities—Protection of Trademarks and Geographical Indications for Agricultural Products and Foodstuffs*, WT/DS290/19, ¶¶ 1, 3 (Feb. 24, 2004).

165. *Id.* ¶ 5 ("Argentina, Australia (in respect of the United States' complaint), Brazil, Canada,

and hearing, the Panel issued its interim report to the parties on November 16, 2004 and its final report on March 15, 2005.[166]

The U.S. case made two basic types of claims. First, that the Origins Regulation violates national treatment obligations under TRIPS and the General Agreement on Tariffs and Trade (GATT); second, that the Origins Regulation violates TRIPS trademark protection obligations by giving GI holders rights that effectively limit the rights of owners of pre-existing trademarks.

The national treatment claim was founded on the fact that Article 12(1) of the Origins Regulation permits a national from a WTO country to register a GI in the European Union only if the WTO country adopts an "equivalent" system and offers "reciprocal protection." The Panel agreed with the United States that these equivalence and reciprocity provisions denied "national treatment" to citizens of other WTO members.[167] The Panel cited a wide range of evidence that the Origins Regulation excludes WTO countries from GI protection absent these equivalence and reciprocity conditions, including a letter from EC Commissioner Pascal Lamy saying "it is true that U.S. GIs cannot be registered in the EU."[168] On these grounds, the Panel concluded that the 1992 Origins Regulation violated TRIPS and Article III:4 of the GATT.[169] The March 2006 revision of the Origins Regulation addressed this finding, eliminating this reciprocity requirement.[170]

The Panel also embraced the U.S. claim that the Origins Regulation denies national treatment procedurally because non-EU nationals filing applications for EU GI protection must petition their own national government to apply to Brussels, a more uncertain mechanism than the procedure used by EU nationals.[171] In contrast, the Panel declined to find

China, Colombia, Guatemala, India, Mexico, New Zealand, Norway, Chinese Taipei, Turkey, and the United States (in respect of Australia's complaint) have reserved their rights to participate in the Panel proceedings as a third party.").

166. WTO Panel Report on Origins Regulations, *supra* note 139, ¶ 6.1.

167. *Id.* ¶¶ 7.72, .74, .102.

168. *Id.* ¶ 7.83.

169. *Id.* ¶¶ 7.213, .238. Related to this, the Panel concluded that the 1992 Origins Regulation's requirement that a foreign government participate in the "inspection structures" for that foreign country's GI was also an effective *equivalence* requirement in violation of GATT. *Id.* ¶¶ 7.441(b), .463.

170. Under the 2006 regulation, "[w]here the registration application relates to a geographical area in a given Member State," the application goes through the member state's national government in a procedure sketched out in Article 5(4) and (5), whereas Article 5(9) provides that

> [w]here the registration application concerns a geographical area situated in a third country, [the application] shall comprise the elements provided for in paragraph 3 and also proof that the name in question is protected in its country of origin. The application shall be sent to the Commission, either directly or via the authorities of the third country concerned.

2006 Origins Regulation, *supra* note 143, at 16. Although the geographical name must be "protected in its country of origin," it can be protected under a certification mark system and a separate geographical indications law is presumably no longer required.

171. WTO Panel Report on Origins Regulations, *supra* note 139, ¶¶ 7.244–.307. "The [Origins]

that the Origins Regulation procedure for filing objections to GI applications was prejudicial to non-EU nationals.[172]

On the trademark side, the Panel sided with the European Union in concluding that a prior trademark holder's inability to stop the use of a subsequently registered GI was not a violation of TRIPS.[173] The Panel concluded that while a few trademarks involve geographical terms that might one day have GI protection,[174] some limitation on trademark rights arising from such overlap[175] constitutes an acceptable "exception" to trademark protection under TRIPS Article 17.[176] This was an important point for the European Union because it legitimates, to some (as yet unknown) degree, a legal system in which new GIs can adversely impact established trademarks.

The United States also achieved something important in the trademark area: a Commission acknowledgment and Panel finding that GI registration in the European Union extends only to the words registered and *not* to translations.[177] This issue of translations of GIs became quite contentious in the final stages with the United States accusing the European Union of trying to "back away from factual findings that the European Communities itself repeatedly encouraged the Panel to make."[178] This issue has both broad implications and an extremely sharp focal point. The political focal point has been the Czech town Budvar's claim to the German adjectival word *Budweiser*, a dispute with the American Anheuser-Busch Brewing Company that has littered the globe with inconclusive litigations. On the other hand, the broad implications of the translation issue go to the very nature of genericity. In the United States, "Parmesan" is a generic term while PARMIGIANO-REGGIANO is a protected certification mark. In contrast, the European Union's 2003 "claw back" list demands the "return" of forty-one geographic terms and all their translations, i.e., both "Parmigiano" and

---

Regulation does not accord equal treatment because third country governments only comply voluntarily whereas EC member States have a legal obligation to do so." *Id.* ¶ 7.244. The Panel accepted that this procedural difference violated TRIPS, *id.* at ¶ 7.281, and the GATT, *id.* at ¶¶ 7.306–7.307.

172. *Id.* ¶ 7.384. The Panel also declined to find that EU practices regarding labeling of non-EU GIs were prejudicial. *Id.* ¶¶ 7.499, .509.

173. *Id.* ¶ 7.533. The United States' argument was that EU law was asymmetrical in the sense that a registered GI prevails over a later trademark, but a registered trademark only *may* prevail over a later GI. The United States reasoned that "[t]rademarks can incorporate certain geographical elements. If the geographical name subsequently qualifies for GI protection under the Regulation, it will inhibit the ability of the trademark owner from preventing confusing uses." *Id.*

174. *Id.* ¶ 7.565.

175. *Id.* ¶¶ 7.567, .573, .575.

176. *Id.* ¶ 7.661.

177. *Id.* ¶ 7.548 ("The right conferred by registration does not extend to other names or signs not in the registration. Registration does not cover translations.").

178. WTO Panel Report on Origins Regulations, *supra* note 139, ¶ 6.37.

its translations, i.e., "Parmesan," "Parmesano," etc.

To placate both sides, the Panel carefully honed its factual conclusions to EU statements on the issue of translations, then made a Panel finding favorable to the United States[179]:

> [T]he European Communities has emphasized that . . . the positive right to use the GI extends only to the linguistic versions that have been entered in the register and not to other names or signs which have not been registered. Accordingly, on the basis of the terms of the GI Regulation and of the Community Trademark Regulation, and the explanation of them provided by the European Communities, the Panel finds that not only may the trademark continue to be used, but that the trademark owner's right to prevent confusing uses, is unaffected except with respect to the use of a GI as entered in the GI register in according with the registration.[180]

The most reasonable interpretation of this finding is that until the Budvar brewery successfully registers the German adjective "Budweiser" as a GI for Budvar, BUDWEISER beer from the United States should be able to prevent confusing uses of the word by the Budvar brewery (and anyone else).

It will be interesting to watch how the 2005 WTO decision does or does not modify the EU position in TRIPS talks. In light of having repeatedly told the WTO Panel that EU GI registration does not extend to translations, and having the Panel make a finding to this effect—can the Commission comfortably insist that its claw back list include all translations? Thus demanding "recuperation" of "Parmesan" in English and "Champaña" in Spanish?

Until the WTO decision, the European Union was promoting GIs as a tool for developing countries to exploit markets. In their August 2003 press release, the Commission repeatedly mentioned developing world GIs—"India's Darjeeling tea, Sri Lanka's Ceylon tea, Guatemala's Antigua coffee, [and] Morocco's argan oil,"[181] but the WTO decision raises serious questions as to whether Brussels has ever had any genuine interest in giving developing countries the GI tool *within* the European Union. Indeed, the Commission press release was a little clueless: "Darjeeling" has been used as the trademark for a French brand of lingerie sold in the European Union since 1995,[182] an arguably tarnishing use of the geographic word that the Champagne producers would never have to endure.

Will the adverse WTO decision curb the European Union's agenda?

---

179. *Id.* ¶ 6.38.

180. *Id.* ¶ 7.659 (emphasis added).

181. Press Release, European Comm'n, WTO Talks: EU Steps Up Bid for better Protection of Regional Quality Products (Aug. 28, 2003), *available at* http://europe.eu.int/rapid/pressReleasesAction.do?reference=IP/03/1178.

182. *See* Darjeeling Lingerie, http://www.darjeeling.fr/home.php (last visited Nov. 5, 2006).

Perhaps not. If and when there are renewed international negotiations to open global agricultural markets, strong geographical indications protection is likely to remain on the agenda.

III. POPULAR PARAMETERS OF THE DEBATE AND THE AMBITIOUS EU AGENDA

North Americans have thought little about geographical indications and, when they do, their thoughts orbit around a few basic motifs: that European-style geographical indications law is unduly bureaucratic and imposes unneeded transaction costs; that geographical indications are a static kind of entitlement, in contrast to the incentive-based structure of most intellectual property law; and that almost all advantages from strengthened geographical indications would accrue to European countries. This Part explores the validity of these points, adding some nuances and concluding that European negotiators may irrationally overvalue GIs.

Part IV then turns to the deeper question of whether there is any truth to the notion of "terroir" and, if not, what justifications for GI laws remain available. Exploring what we do and do not understand about terroir helps us see the similarity between GIs and high-end trademarks. Like these trademarks, GIs are partly about "myth maintenance" and the extraction of monopoly rents from such myths.

A. HOW MANY REGULATORS? HOW MUCH CONTROL?

Any system for registration of intellectual property claims requires bureaucracy, but an appellations system as used in France involves more bureaucratic intervention in the economy than the certification/collective mark system used in the United States or the geographical indications committee approach used in Australia. In this sense, the geographical indications debate is an instantiation of the larger debate about government versus markets and about how much decision-making is given to government officials and what is left to market signals.

European bureaucracies are criticized and lampooned with both regularity and vigor,[183] perhaps even more so than their American counterparts. Although the law at issue was not a GI law per se, it might be hard to find a more unintentionally damning description of bureaucratic control of words than the European Court of Justice's 1997 description of a French law governing commercial use of the word "mountain":

> Section 4 provided in essence that the products had to comply with manufacturing methods determined by joint ministerial orders of the

---

183. *See, e.g.,* Alphonse Allais, *L'Excessive Bureaucratie, in* ALPHONSE ALLAIS, LECTURE SUBSTANTIELLE 132–36 (1992).

Minister for Agriculture and the Minister for Consumer Affairs. Those orders were to be adopted following advice from the National Labeling Commission and the Regional Commissions for Quality Food Products. In relation to cooked meats, those orders were to specify the choice of raw materials; the method of cutting up, boning, mincing and trimming; the method of salting, drying, or smoking; the mixture of ingredients and the cooking method.[184]

With actual *appellations d'origine contrôlées*, the French government has similarly elaborate rules. Regulations for most AOC wine regions strictly control what grape varieties can be used; for example, only Pinot Noir grapes can be used in red wines from Burgundy. When multiple varietals are permitted (five varietals are permitted for red wines from Bordeaux, fourteen for the Châteauneuf-du-Pape AOC),[185] the maximum percentages for each varietal are designated. As mentioned above, AOC designations for cheese place varying legal requirements on rennet used in coagulation, curd drainage, milk temperature at different points, salting, use of lactic proteins,[186] and the exact size of cheese rounds down to a few millimeters.[187]

Early in the twentieth century, French wine producers themselves had *"réactions d'horreur"* over the amount of bureaucracy involved in the first proposals to protect wine quality in France.[188] The reaction of New World winemakers today is much the same. Discussing the degree of government involvement in an *appellations* system, Australian wine critic Max Allen says "[i]n newer wine-producing countries ... such laws are seen as affronts to the very basic human rights of every winemaker."[189] On the other hand, the more bureaucratic approach theoretically has the upside of stabilizing *meaning* to the geographical indications, a point discussed below.

In contrast, subsuming geographical indications in a regular trademark system[190] means that the *obligatory* bureaucratic role is reduced to a single trademark examiner. The certification mark issues after an application process in which the application must be accompanied by certification standards, but "[t]here is no government control over what are the standards that the certifier uses."[191] Subsequent

---

184. Cases C-321-324/94, *In re* Pistre, 2 C.M.L.R. 565, 570–71 (1997).

185. Richard Nalley, *The Feudal System*, EXPEDIA TRAVELS, Mar./Apr. 2001, at 71, 74.

186. MASUI & YAMADA, *supra* note 37, at 28, 56, 66, 80–81.

187. DENIS, *supra* note 16, at 8 (describing exact size and weights required for AOC *grand pont-l'évêque*, AOC *pont-l'évêque*, AOC *pouligny-saint-pierre*, and AOC *petit pouligny saint-pierre*).

188. OLSZAK, *supra* note 19, at 8.

189. ALLEN, *supra* note 34, at 30.

190. *See, e.g.*, Meltzer, *supra* note 117, at 31 n.61 ("Marks of geographical indication are given their own section, not because they could not be addressed by trademark law, but because the specific concerns of European Community wine growers demanded that unique attention be given to certain regional indicators for wines and spirits.").

191. McCARTHY, *supra* note 43, § 19:91.

issues (like non-discriminatory application of the private standards) can be hammered out before administrative and judicial tribunals.

Nonetheless, both the United States and Australia have additional bureaucracies dedicated to geographical indications for wine. In the United States, beginning in 1978, the Bureau of Alcohol, Tobacco and Firearms (ATF) began establishing "American Viticultural Areas" (AVAs). Petitions (with extensive informational requirements) to designate geographic areas as AVAs were filed with the ATF—and now its post-9/11 successor agency, the Alcohol and Tobacco Tax and Trade Bureau (ATTTB). The U.S. government understands these AVAs to be "approved . . . appellations of origin" for American wines.[192] There are presently over 150 of these AVAs, ranging from "San Francisco Bay" to "Northern Neck George Washington Birthplace" to "Mississippi Delta," giving the impression of a process less concerned with terroir and more concerned with political constituencies. Most importantly, ATTTB makes no attempt to limit acceptable varietals or regulate *production methods* per AVA, activities which might make it a genuine counterpart to INAO.[193] In other words, the AVA system is primarily a marketing tool, and accomplishes little else.

Australia similarly has a national "geographical indications committee" (GIC), whose mandate is principally to determine "the boundaries of the various regions and localities in Australia in which wines are produced" and "the varieties of grapes that may be used in the manufacture of wine in Australia."[194] But, again, the GIC does not dictate mandatory (or forbidden) varietals per region and does not control production conditions.[195] For both countries, imposing GI "quality

---

192. 27 C.F.R. § 9.21 (2006) ("The viticultural areas listed in this subpart are approved for use as appellations of origin in accordance with part 4 of this chapter."); *see also id.*. § 4.25(a)(1) ("(i) The United States; (ii) a State; (iii) two or no more than three States which are all contiguous; (iv) a county (which must be identified with the word 'county,' in the same size of type, and in letters as conspicuous as the name of the county); (v) two or no more than three counties in the same States; or (vi) a viticultural area (as defined in paragraph (e) of this section).").

193. The AVAs are also distinguished by the fact that only 85% of the grapes in the wine have to come from the AVA designated on the label, *id.* § 4.25(e)(3)(ii), a questionable practice from a consumer information point of view and a practice criticized by Europeans. Although practical for vintners, this permissiveness means, in effect, that a "Napa" label means "mainly Napa."

194. Australian Wine and Brandy Corp. Act 1980, § 3(1)(f)(iii), http://scaletext.law.gov.au/html/pasteact/0/155/0/PA000070.htm (last visited Nov. 5, 2006).

195. According to the Australian Wine and Brandy Corporation, the government authority that regulates wine,

> [a] Geographic Indication can be likened to the Appellation naming system used in Europe (eg [sic] Bordeaux, Burgundy) but is much less restrictive in terms of viticultural and winemaking practices. In fact the only restriction is that wine which carries the regional name must consist of a minimum of 85% of fruit from that region. This protects the integrity of the label and safeguards the consumer.

Australian Wine and Brandy Corporation, Wine Region Overview, http://www.awbc.com.au/Content.aspx?p=16 (last visited Nov. 5, 2006). The Australian GIC follows the American 85% rule. *Id.*

controls" is principally a job for market forces.[196]

In contrast, European wine AOCs exist in a rigorous bureaucratic framework that controls almost *all* labeling vocabulary — and in ways that look suspiciously like non-tariff barriers to trade. In addition to geographical indications, there are controls on words such as "reserve," "private cellars," "private," and "select."[197] Wine labels cannot mention any competitions in which the wine has garnered prizes unless the competition is officially recognized by the European Union, and competitions in the United States, New Zealand, Australia, and Argentina are not recognized.[198] The European Union also reserves to its own producers the term "table wine" ("vin de table"),[199] which is a broad category of lesser, but still quality wine. There cannot be Australian or Argentine "table wine" sold in the European Union. Table wines are, in turn, prohibited not just from using protected appellations and confusing similar *names*, they are also prohibited from using many general terms. For example, in France, a table wine cannot use "clos," "tour," "mont," or "moulin" in its name because these are considered evocative of appellation or high-end wines.[200]

The European Union's 2002 Wine Regulations went further, effectively obliging non-EU countries to establish government registries of grape varieties authorized to be used in wine production in those countries even though the European Union would not police or try to control other countries' lists. As the chief executive of the New Zealand Winegrowers said, "the EU wants us to have a register of grape varieties. Where do we keep it?"[201] Retaliatory legislation passed the U.S. House of Representatives in 2002.[202]

B. Static or Dynamic?

Americans view intellectual property principally as an *ex ante*

---

196. *Peel v. Attorney Registration & Disciplinary Comm'n*, 496 U.S. 91, 102 (1990) ("Much like a trademark, the strength of a certification mark is measured by the quality of the organization for which it stands.").

197. *See* Cal. Wine Exp. Program, *supra* note 26, at 2, 12.

198. *Id.* at 11.

199. The European Union reserves the term for its own winemakers in an apparent attempt to keep the lower-end market for domestic producers. *Id.* at 2.

200. Olszak, *supra* note 19, at 45.

201. Hall, *supra* note 10, at 20.

202. The legislation would have required wine importers to provide official certifications and laboratory analyses to prove that wines being brought into the U.S. meet U.S. regulatory standards. These provisions were included in the Miscellaneous Trade and Technical Corrections Act of 2004, H.R. Res. 1047, 108th Cong. (2004) (amending subsection (a) of section 5382 of the IRS code); *see also* Daniel Sogg, *Trade Bill Could Limit Rare-Wine Imports*, Wine Spectator, Jan. 31–Feb. 28, 2003, at 17. On the Senate side, the bill did not get out of the Senate Finance Committee, but because of other, non-wine provisions in the proposed act. *Id.*

incentive structure for wealth-creation.[203] Continental jurists more comfortably embrace intellectual property as an entitlement arising from pre-existing status of the individual, particularly the *auteur*.[204] This difference may connect to broader social differences, the American leaning toward meritocracy and living in a future-oriented society while Europeans hold more to tradition, history, and established hierarchy.[205]

Most intellectual property rewards "doing," but emphasis on "status" arguably manifests itself in moral rights as well as protection of folklore and traditional knowledge. At first blush, geographical indications seem akin to "status" rights. Like rights to folklore or traditional knowledge, geographical indications crystallize protection around traditional purveyors/creators[206] without regard to recent originality or creativity, the hallmarks of copyright and patent law.

At the same time, geographical indications have much of the same incentive function of trademarks[207] because geographical indications can provide the same information feedback loops that trademarks provide.

---

203. *See generally* William W. Fisher, III, *Theories of Intellectual Property*, *in* NEW ESSAYS IN THE LEGAL AND POLITICAL THEORY OF PROPERTY (S. Munzer ed., 2001); Justin Hughes, *The Philosophy of Intellectual Property*, 77 GEO. L.J. 287 (1988) (describing, among other theories, incentive-based, instrumental theory as the vision of intellectual property informing U.S. Constitution); William M. Landes & Richard A. Posner, *An Economic Analysis of Copyright Law*, 18 J. LEG. STUD. 325 (1989).

204. Continental intellectual property law is very much oriented toward "incentives," but they are more likely to turn to status, natural rights, or personality based views of IP law. And those views are not completely unfamiliar to Americans. *See* William W. Fisher III, *Geistiges Eigentum-ein ausufernder Rechtsbereich: Die Geschichte des Ideenschutzes in den Vereinigten Staaten*, *in* EIGENTUM IM INTERNATIONALEN VERGLEICH 265 (Vandenhoeck & Ruprecht 1999), *translated in The Growth of Intellectual Property: A History of the Ownership of Ideas in the United States* 22, *available at* http://cyber.law.harvard.edu/people/tfisher/iphistory.pdf (last visited Nov. 5, 2006); Justin Hughes, *Copyright and incomplete historiographies: of Piracy, Propertization, and Thomas Jefferson*, 79 So. CAL. L. REV. 993, 1058 (2006) (discussing presence of natural rights perspectives in American copyright law); *see also* Thomas B. Nachbar, *Constructing Copyright's Mythology*, 6 GREEN BAG 37, 44 (2002) (noting that in state copyright acts preceding the 1790 federal law "author's natural rights are mentioned as frequently as society's benefits as the justification for protection").

205. One is reminded of the Benjamin Franklin pamphlet, *To Those Who Would Remove to America*, which advised would-be European immigrants that in America "[p]eople do not enquire concerning a Stranger, What is he? But What can he DO?" Edmund S. Morgan, *Poor Richard's New Year*, N.Y. TIMES, Dec. 31, 2002 (quoting BENJAMIN FRANKLIN, TO THOSE WHO WOULD REMOVE TO AMERICA (1784)). Two centuries later, observers like Luigi Barzini were still drawing the same difference between Americans and Europeans. *See, e.g.*, LUIGI BARZINI, THE EUROPEANS 219–53 (Michael Curtis ed., Penguin Books 1984) (1983).

206. *See generally* Christine Haight Farley, *Protecting Folklore of Indigenous Peoples: Is Intellectual Property the Answer?*, 30 CONN. L. REV. 1 (1997); Paul Kuruk, *Protecting Folklore Under Modern Intellectual Property Regimes: A Reappraisal of the Tensions Between Individual and Communal Rights in Africa and the United States*, 48 AM. U. L. REV. 769 (1999); Angela R. Riley, *Recovering Collectivity: Group Rights to Intellectual Property in Indigenous Communities*, 18 CARDOZO ARTS & ENT. L.J. 175 (2000); Susan Scafidi, *Intellectual Property and Cultural Products*, 81 B.U. L. REV. 793 (2001).

207. William M. Landes & Richard A. Posner, *Trademark Law: An Economic Perspective*, 30 J.L. & ECON. 265 (1987).

Some consumers come to recognize Margaux as having desirable characteristics among red wines; they seek out Margaux wines, expecting them to continue to have those characteristics. If enough consumers do this, the Margaux producers are motivated to maintain and enhance the consumer-desired characteristics. In this way, the GI rewards both product quality control and product differentiation. This is no different than the way the SNICKERS and BABY RUTH trademarks give their respective owners incentives to maintain different recipes for similar peanut/caramel/chocolate candies.[208] Additionally, where production is predominantly spread among small and medium sized enterprises, the appellation or certification mark allows marketing on a scale that individual enterprises cannot attempt,[209] providing economies of scale for information transfer from producers to consumers.

If a country's appellations regime recertifies individual producers on a regular basis, this too is an incentive system for quality control arising from the GI. In theory, a certification mark system polices itself on these quality controls. In each case, the principal incentive is to maintain quality. Again, this is not categorically different than regular trademarks. All three, privately-held regular trademarks, certification marks, and appellations, create a pressure for quality maintenance in order to retain consumer loyalty. All three will be subject to market pressures to improve their quality, whether (a) in response to other competitors' improvements or (b) to gain new market share. The preferred way to gain new market share is to gain new customers while retaining old customers, hence the frequent labels on established, trademarked brands: "NEW" and "IMPROVED." In terms of flexibility in efforts to gain new market share, there is a descending order here. Privately-held trademarks offer more flexibility than certification marks; certification marks offer more flexibility than appellations—if only because the appellation criteria is only changed after the government agency is convinced to make the change.

Conversely, by being the least flexible, appellations are arguably the most prone to stability in meaning. Greater meaning-stability in the

---

208. *Id.* at 270 (explaining the incentive "to invest in developing and maintaining . . . a strong mark depends on [the] ability to maintain consistent product quality"); *see also* Friedrich-Karl Beier, *The Need for Protection of Indications of Source and Appellations of Origin in the Common Market: The* Sekt/Weinbrand *Decision of the European Court of Justice of 20 February 1975, in* Protection of Geographic Denominations of Goods and Services 183, 195 (Herman Cohen Jehoram ed., 1980) (explaining the product differentiation function of geographical indications).

209. Beier, *supra* note 208, at 195; *see also* Yves Rousset-Rouard & Thierry Desseauve, La France face aux vins du Nouveau Monde 54 (2002) ("[C]ette notion d'appellation contrôlée est une notion de marque en commun. Je prends un exemple facile. Il y a quatre cents producteurs de chablis, qui se partagent la marque de chablis.") [Jacques Berthomeau, author of a report on French viticulture, remarked that the notion of an *appellation contrôlée* is the idea of a mark held in common, and provided a simple example of four hundred producers of Chablis who share the mark Chablis.].

appellation could be of benefit to consumers.[210] Because information seeps into the consumer base slowly, greater meaning-stability theoretically allows *more* meaning for *more* consumers which furthers the information function that Professor Landes and Judge Posner identified. More rigid controls in wine labeling may increase the payoff of "*savoir lire l'etiquette*" (how to read the label).[211] The rigid controls on wine labeling arguably create an environment where it is more logical for a consumer to invest time learning what certain terms used on wine labels mean. Bordeaux's *classement* (classification) system was, from its inception, a system to stabilize meaning not that different from trademark law. As Laurence Osborne notes, the *classement* system was "a commercial ploy intended to make Bordeaux wines more rationally intelligible to brokers and buyers" during the nineteenth century and "a kind of brand-creation system."[212]

But this is theoretical—or past tense. According to Thierry Desseauve, editor of *La Revue du vin de France*, one of the loudest complaints currently about the appellation system is that it is (at least now) "incomprehensible" for French consumers and even worse for consumers in global markets.[213] A 2005 survey found that Americans find French wines "intimidating,"[214] a feeling that may be connected to wine labeling. There seems to be a wide consensus that New World wine producers have tapped into a simpler, more efficient system of communicating wine characteristics through varietal names, such that any stability advantages for the appellation system have not made up for its daunting complexity.[215]

---

210. *See* Justin Hughes, *Recoding Intellectual Property and Overlooked Audience Interests*, 77 TEX. L. REV. 923 (1999) (discussing even passive audiences' interest in stability in protection of cultural objects by copyright and trademark laws).

211. JACQUELINE GARDAN, LIVRE DE CAVE: PRÉCIS A L'USAGE DE L'AMATEUR ÉCLAIRÉ 13–14 (Porphyre ed., 1991).

212. LAWRENCE OSBORNE, THE ACCIDENTAL CONNOISSEUR: AN IRREVERENT JOURNEY THROUGH THE WINE WORLD 74 (2004).

213. ROUSSET-ROUARD & DESSEAUVE, *supra* note 209, at 45 ("Nous entendons souvent dire que ces appellations sont incompréhensibles pour le consommateur français déjà, à plus forte raison dans le monde entier.").

214. Pascal Galinier, *Le vin français "intimide" les consommateurs américains*, LE MONDE, June 21, 2005, at 17.

215. ROUSSET-ROUARD & DESSEAUVE, *supra* note 209, at 42 ("L'un des axes principaux de ce développement des vis du Nouveau Monde a été le développement de vins dits de cépage, reconnaissables par le consommateur au nom du cépage principal qui le compose.") [One of the principal successes of development for New World wines was to develop varietal wines, recognized by the consumer by the name of the principal varietal of which it is composed.]. In the same panel discussion, Michel LaRoche, a Chablis region winemaker noted that the approach of the New World wines has an enormous advantage in simplifying wine labeling. *Id.* at 44–45. Also among those who acknowledge that the labeling of French wines is too complex is René Renou, president of the Wine Committee of INAO, and Christian Berger, Agricultural Counselor of the French Embassy to the United States, who bluntly states: "Our labels are difficult to read." Corie Brown, *Who's Killing the*

That is the information stability side. On the production side, there is widespread agreement among wine industry experts (but not extensive, hard-nosed empirical work) that the appellations system stifles innovation.[216] Reliable empirical data on this issue may now be impossible because the common wisdom on this point has been so widely repeated that any survey of winemakers would likely be contaminated. There are plenty of reports of innovation in French, Spanish, and Italian vineyards,[217] but there is anecdotal evidence that this is happening more *outside* the appellation-controlled production environments. For example, there are a number of European winemakers who have stayed outside the appellation system as a way of protecting their freedom to innovate.[218]

The adverse impact on innovation and quality improvement appears to be grave enough that, René Renou, the head of INAO's wine committee, was prompted to propose a series of reforms that would permit all but the very top end AOC wine producers to recommend extensive changes in "grape-growing and winemaking protocols."[219] But even this proposal shows the difference between French and New World vineyards. The New World winemaker is free to try all kinds of new techniques, but Renou's proposal is only that the centralized French

---

Great Wines of France?, L.A. TIMES, Mar. 2, 2005, at F5. Charlotte Selles-Simmons, a Beaujolais vintner, agrees with that and recommends putting grape varietals on wine labels so consumers "don't have to get out their reading glasses" and "don't have to ask for help." *Id.; see also* Sarah Nassauer & Christopher Lawton, *French Whine*, WALL ST. J., Mar. 2, 2005, at B1 (attributing decline in sales of French wine partly to "France's complicated labeling system, which obscures what casual drinkers want to know most about a wine—its grape varietal").

216. *See, e.g.*, ROUSSET-ROUARD & DESSEAUVE, *supra* note 209, at 41 (Jérôme Quiot explaining Ricard's opposition to making an appellation of their Jacob's Creek region in Australia); *id.* at 89 ("Le seul problème de l'AOC est que cela a peut-être bridé les structures des entreprises françaises.") [Thierry Desseuve remarking that the AOC's only problem is that it has potentially constrained the structures of French companies.]; *id.* at 109–10 ("Le vrai débat pour l'AOC est de savoir pourquoi les gens les plus novateurs dans la viticulture française se sentent bridés par ce système. S'ils essaient de changer ou d'améliorer, ils sont bloqués.") [William Echikson, wine reporter for the *Wall Street Journal*, noted that the true debate for the AOC system is to understand why the most innovative people in French viticulture feel constrained by the system, and that if they want to change or improve, they are blocked.].

217. *See, e.g.*, Jancis Robinson, *The Grapes of War*, FIN. TIMES, Sept. 16, 1995, at I (reporting on Australian techniques being used in French vineyards); *Les crus du Médoc, d'hier et d'aujourd'hui*, VINS MAG., Winter 2002, at 85 (describing new clonal varieties of grapes being used and research on plant vines); *Les vins de pays d'Oc: diversification, exportation, et communication*, VINS MAG., Winter 2002, at 78 (describing new varietal mixes in Languedoc region).

218. ROUSSET-ROUARD & DESSEAUVE, *supra* note 209, at 29–30 ("Il y avait déjà un choix délibéré dans cette région de rester autour du concept du vin de pays, parce que l'appellation d'origine contrôlée semblait beaucoup trop contraignante, en particulier en n'autorisant pas l'utilisation de cépages que je juge qualitatifs.") [Speaking about Languedoc, Michel Larouche noted that a deliberate choice in this region to stay with the concept of the *"vin de pays"* because the *appellation d'origine contrôlée* appears much too constraining, particularly in not authorizing the use of varietals that he judged appropriate.].

219. Brown, *supra* note 215.

system *consider* recommendations for particular new techniques that could be included under the AOC system: "[w]inemakers would propose their ideas to the National Committee on Wines, and we would decide if those ideas would be permitted."[220]

C. Static Entitlements, IP Monopoly Rents, and Agricultural Subsidies

To the degree that European-style appellations law is less prone to innovation and more prone to safeguarding the status quo, we need to recognize this is not a flaw in appellations law; it is a characteristic, if not the goal. Indeed, Brussels may have made a strategic error in the early 1990s when it pressed for GIs to be enfolded into the TRIPS intellectual property framework when, in fact, GIs are really part of EU agricultural policy.[221]

The European Union's strong position on GIs is an understandable strategy to use monopoly rents from GIs to subsidize European agricultural production at a time when direct subsidies are becoming less tenable and direct competition with New World agriculture is becoming more likely, even with the 2006 collapse of the Doha round. With that logic in mind, it becomes clear why the European Union seeks strong GIs laws far beyond protection against consumer confusion.

1. A Partially Traditional Status Quo

One of the leitmotifs of European advocacy of strong GIs is that European agriculture is "traditional" while agricultural production in North America, Australia, and other New World countries is "industrial." Typical of this kind of thinking is Professor Norbert Olszak, one of the few French legal academics to write at length about geographical indications. He characterizes New World agriculture with the following: "The vast spaces and the recourse to technology permitted the development of very large enterprises producing standard wines for the consumption of the masses."[222] This is after Olszak baldly claims, without a stitch of evidence, that "terroirs" in the "New World" "are less identifiably distinct because the geological and climatological particularities are less diverse."[223] In the same vein, a few years ago, a

---

220. *Id.* Substantively, and to his credit, Renou foresees permitting a wider range of blending of grape varietals in more AOCs, allowing some cross-regional blending for AOC wines and "relax[ing] AOC labeling rules to allow varietal names and other New World conventions." *Id.*

221. O'Connor, *supra* note 17, at 35 ("The protection of GIs, both domestically and internationally, has been at the heart of the EC's agricultural policy for some time.").

222. Olszak, *supra* note 19, at 4 ("Les vastes espaces et le recours à la technologie permettent le développement d'entreprises de très grande taille produisant des vins standards pour une consommation de masse.").

223. *Id.* Olszak's comments may be linked to a French tendency to believe the French territory is uniquely rich and varied compared to other countries. *See, e.g.,* Fernand Braudel, The Identity of France 63–65 (Siân Reynolds trans., 1988) (comparing the rich "micro-climates" and "micro-

French government official notoriously told an assembled convention of French winemakers, "here, you have the products of terroir; elsewhere they have industrial products."[224] In this kind of narrative, as Professor Tomer Broude has observed, terroir is "the epitomic opposite of globalization: a exemplary reflection of place and people."[225]

For many regions in Europe, this idea of family-based, traditional farming is, in the words of Professor Dominique Denis, a "near caricature ... that no longer corresponds to reality."[226] In many European regions both the scale and the methods of production are increasingly industrial. For example, in 2001, the Champagne district vintner Veuve Cliquot produced and sold one million cases of sparkling wine; Piper-Heidsieck sold 455,000 cases.[227] The largest champagne company, LVMH, ships over four *million* cases of its mainline sparkling wines annually.[228] Production of sparkling wines in "industrial quantities"[229] by the big Champagne firms has been true for decades.[230]

---

environments" of France with the "monotony" of northern Europe, Brazil, Madagascar, and the Argentine Pampas). Of course, Americans are no stranger to their own self-absorbed "exceptionalism" narratives. *See generally* SEYMOUR MARTIN LIPSET, AMERICAN EXCEPTIONALISM: A DOUBLE-EDGED SWORD (1997).

224. ROUSSET-ROUARD & DESSEAUVE, *supra* note 209, at 34 ("[Au] congrès national de la CNAOC ... un représentant du ministre . . . a dit tout simplement : 'Ici, vous êtes des produits de terroir; ailleurs, ce sont des produits industriels.'"). We should add to this Christian Boudan who wrote in 2004 that the general usage of freezing (food) at the end of the 1950s, permitted productivity gains for factory-made meals to be served (directly) to the table, announcing the beginning of the end for common, by-hand food preparation in the United States. BOUDAN, *supra* note 3, at 424. But the "end" has not come, and a more careful observer of culinary arts in the United States might have noted just the opposite sort of trends over the past twenty years.

225. Tomer Broude, *Taking "Trade and Culture" Seriously: Geographical Indications and Cultural Protection in WTO Law*, 26 U. PA. J. INT'L ECON. L. 623, 651–52 (2005). Broude insightfully elaborates on the argument: "As such [terroir] arguably deserves protection, even enhanced protection, from commercial forces that threaten to compel homogenization and obliterate local terroir-ist cultures of production. GIs are ostensibly a targeted way of achieving this, since they grant each terroir, as officially defined and delimited, a separate legal source of protection." *Id.* at 652.

226. DENIS, *supra* note 16, at 3 (describing the idea of *exploitation familiale* as almost a carcature which no longer corresponds with the varied number of regions). *See generally* Broude, *supra* note 225 (questioning a variety of assumptions that strengthening GI law would help preserve traditional or local culture).

227. *Uncorking Success*, THE ECONOMIST, Dec. 21, 2002, at 46 (note that these are figures for *brands*, not companies).

228. *Id.* (4,350,000 cases worldwide for 2001 not including smaller selling LVMH brands like Dom Perignon); *see also* Michael Franz, *Boutique Champagnes*, WASH. POST, Dec. 29, 2004, at F7 ("Moet & Chandon reportedly produces 24 million bottles each year"—which would be four million cases).

229. *Uncorking Success*, *supra* note 227, at 47.

230. ALEXIS LICHINE ET AL., ALEXIS LICHINE'S ENCYCLOPEDIA OF WINES & SPIRITS 173, 185, 187 (Alfred A. Knopf, Inc., 1968) (1967) ("Almost all Champagne is made sparkling in the cellars of the big shipping firms . . . . Only in a few isolated cases does the grower in Champagne vinify his own grapes—they are nearly always sold to one of the shipping firms . . . ."). Similar market concentration is true of the Cognac AOC, where, even a handful of companies has controlled production of Cognac exported to the United States. *See* Terry Robards, *The Mystique of Brandies*, N.Y. TIMES MAG., Dec. 26, 1982, at 34 (noting that at that time four companies produced 85% of Cognac exports to the U.S.).

As Thierry Desseauve notes, "[a] generic Bordeaux at 2 euros is an industrial product like any other. Sold on a large scale, it is no more and no less than another varietal wine at 2 euros, except that it is an AOC."[231]

As for production methods, as Professor Denis recognizes, in some viticultural regions farmers control the production process while in others there is a "near total separation, legal and physical, between the raising of grapes and the making of wine."[232] In the Châteauneuf-du-Pape AOC, the production methods range from "ancient oak cooperage with little or no stainless steel" to one vintner that "sends its grapes through stainless-steel pipes, where the skins are flash-heated by steam entering the outer jacket of the pipes."[233]

European cheese production presents the same complicated picture. In Italy, many of the production facilities for *Parmigiano-Reggiano* are "gleaming laborator[ies] in every sense of the word, with white tiles, chrome fixtures and work tables, and great copper cauldrons."[234] One commentator characterized production of the region's famed cheese as "ha[ving] the feel of big business, with more cooperatives and fewer small farms."[235] In France, AOC cheeses are actually classified into four production types: *fermier*, *artesanal*, *cooperative*, and *industriel*.[236] Many AOC cheeses are available in several of these four types.[237] For example, of the more than 3700 tons of *Pont l'Eveque* cheese produced in 1991, only 2% were classified as *fermier* (by the farmer.) The rest was *artisanal*, *cooperative*, or *industriel*. Of the more than three million cheeses cured in the caves of Roquefort-sur-Soulzon (and thus qualifying for the AOC *Roquefort*), 60% are made by one company.[238] Total production of AOC cheeses in France went from 152,411 tons in 1991 to over 172,561 tons in 1997.[239] Given agricultural population trends—flat and falling—it seems very likely that such an increase resulted principally from increasingly larger scale production, not new small farmers.

This is not to deny that there are many small-farm producers in the hills of Burgundy and Reggio Emilia. There are almost certainly more

---

231. ROUSSET-ROUARD & DESSEAUVE, *supra* note 209, at 133.

232. DENIS, *supra* note 16, at 5 ("Dans d'autres pays viticoles, il existe au contraire une séparation presque totale, physique et juridique, entre la production du raisin, et l'élaboration du vin.").

233. Nalley, *supra* note 185, at 71, 73.

234. PAMELA SHELDON JOHNS, PARMIGIANO! 16 (1997).

235. *Id.* at 13.

236. *See* MASUI & YAMADA, *supra* note 37, at 28.

237. *Id.* at 20–21, 48, 51, 187, 188, 196–97, 208 (Abondance AOC from Rhône-Alpes; Beaufort AOC from Rhône-Alps; Bleu d'Auvergne AOC from Auvergne; Livarot AOC from Basse-Normandie; Maroilles AOC from Picardie; Neuchâtel AOC from Haute-Normandie; and Pont-l'Evêque from Basse-Normandie).

238. *See* MASUI & YAMADA, *supra* note 37, at 217 (the Société des Caves et des Producteurs Réunis); *see also* Roquefort Société, http://www.roquefort-societe.com (last visited Nov. 5, 2006).

239. *See* MASUI & YAMADA, *supra* note 37, at 77.

per capita than in California, New South Wales, or Mendoza province. Although France has western Europe's largest farms, French farms are still considerably smaller than their American counterparts.[240] The Bordeaux region is full of vintners like Francois Mitjavile, who produces only a couple thousand cases of his TERTRE ROTEBOEUF Saint-Emilion each year,[241] a yield in the same ballpark with the annual Napa production of Sean Thackrey's legendary wines.[242]

The point of all this is not to say that European farming is as or more "industrial" than Australian and North American farming. On average, it almost certainly is not. But the point is that a "homogenized" average is largely non-sensical. The truth, as French cheese regulations recognize, is that all sorts of food production are happening in both Europe and New World countries, including very much that is industrial.[243] Even the writer Christian Boudan, intent on showing France's unique resistance to the industrialization of food production,[244] recognizes that artisanal food products have generally been pushed to the margins in developed countries (European countries included) and that France has been following these production and consumption trends.[245]

2. *Political Reality and the Pressure to Curtail Agricultural Subsidies*

Although we are familiar with concerns about the "family farm" in American politics, agricultural interests remain more politically potent in the European Union than in the United States. Both western Europe and the United States have experienced a steep decline in their agricultural workforces since World War II, but the population statistics remain different. In France, "about 4% of the total working population" is

---

240. Comparing average farm size, American farming does appear much more "large scale." The average U.S. farm is 199 hectares (491 acres) versus the average French farm of 42 hectares and an average EU farm of 21 hectares. Embassy of France in the United States, http://www.info-france-usa.org/atoz/agriculture.asp (last visited Nov. 5, 2006). But these are difficult numbers to compare. The large American farms are dedicated to grain and beef production, not the core of geographical indications issues. In France, 43% of the agricultural land is in farms larger than 100 hectares—presumably, these are also used for grain and livestock. *Id.*

241. JAY MCINERNEY, BACCHUS & ME: ADVENTURES IN THE CELLAR 124 (2002).

242. *Id.* at 189 (describing production of Thackrey's Orion wine—just 500 cases—and his non-vintage Pleiades Syrah-based blend—around 1500 cases).

243. *See, e.g.*, *L'industrie du sans saveur*, GAULT-MILAU MAG., June/July 2006, at 78 (describing and reviewing nine "industrial" *jambon supérieur au torchon*—"superior" classification ham aged in a sackcloth).

244. BOUDAN, *supra* note 3, at 231 ("Mais en France ce régime avait bien résisté grâce à la suivie tardive du monde rural et aux produits d'une agriculture diversifiée.") [But in France this system had resisted, thanks to the late following of the rural world and to the products of a diversified agriculture.].

245. *Id.* ("[I]l semble qu'on assiste en France même à un effritement sérieux du régime alimentaire et culinaire traditionnel, régime encore suivie par les personnes âgées, mais rejeté par les jeunes générations.") [It seems that one is witnessing in France a serious crumbling of the traditional diet and cuisine still followed by the older people that is rejected by the younger generations.].

occupied in agricultural production and another 2.7% in "food processing."[246] This group produces approximately 4.6% of France's GDP.[247] In contrast, "farming employs only about 1 percent of the U.S. workforce and accounts for less than 1 percent of gross domestic product."[248] By these measures, agricultural or *agroalimentaire* interests should have significantly more political influence in France than in North America.

As in other developed countries, French agriculture continues to decline as a percentage of the country's total GDP. This trend is "mainly attributable to the steady deterioration in agricultural prices relative to prices in general with the saturation of the European single market."[249] Two decades ago, Luigi Barzini pinpointed this problem in his own analysis of French motivations within the European community. He concluded that French political leaders were motivated by a belief that they must "sell their agricultural products at a price high enough to keep the *paysans* happy."[250] Barzini pointed to a systematic French effort to support "its costly patriarchal agriculture, . . . the very expensive and excellent wines, the wonderful cheeses . . . ."[251]

Barzini wrote these words in the 1980s, but since then agricultural subsidies in the European Union have grown. Beginning at the inception of the European Community in the late 1950s, the "Common Agricultural Policy" (CAP) was intended as an income support structure for farmers and a means to ensure self-sufficiency in food products.[252] Rapid increases in production converted western Europe to a net exporter of foodstuffs during the 1960s[253] and, because agricultural subsidies were tied to production, as farm efficiencies improved, subsidies rose dramatically. The cost of EU agricultural subsidies trebled between 1981 and 1991.[254] Efforts in the late 1990s to reform the CAP actually triggered a substantial increase in projected costs: by one estimate from 40.92 billion euros in 2000 to a projected 45.8 billion euros

---

246. BERNARD VIAL, FRENCH AGRICULTURE IN THE CONTEXT OF EUROPE (2001), http://www.info-france-usa.org/atoz/agriculture.asp. Historically the differences were even greater. According to Christian Boudan, in 1900, less than 10% of the English population were engaged in agriculture, 25% in Germany, 35% in the United States, and 45% in France. *See* BOUDAN, *supra* note 3, at 221–22.

247. *See* VIAL, *supra* note 246.

248. KATHRYN L. LIPTON, WILLIAM EDMONDSON & ALDEN MANCHESTER, THE FOOD AND FIBER SYSTEM: CONTRIBUTING TO THE U.S. AND WORLD ECONOMIES 1 (1998), *available at* http://www.ers.usda.gov/publications/aib742/AIB742.pdf.

249. VIAL, *supra* note 246.

250. BARZINI, *supra* note 205.

251. *Id.* at 124; *see also* DENIS, *supra* note 16, at 5.

252. *See* SCOTTISH EXECUTIVE, HISTORY OF THE COMMON AGRICULTURAL POLICY (2004), http://www.scotland.gov.uk/Resource/Doc/1037/0003475.pdf.

253. *Id.* at 3, ¶ 10.

254. *Id.*

in 2006.[255] The present system "decouples" subsidies and production levels, so that farmers get fixed payments and are "able to choose what they want to produce according to what will be the most profitable for them whilst still having the necessary income stability."[256] Unfortunately the market distortion is still enormous. According to one EU Minister, the level of subsidization remains at two euros *per cow, per day.*[257]

There is enormous pressure to curb this system of subsidization. Americans tend to think of the pressure as occurring internationally, but the fiscal pressures *within* the European Union are as, or more, important. The unequal distribution of these subsidies is a bone of contention. In fiscal 2003, France received 10.4 billion euros of subsidies, approximately one quarter of the total.[258] France's share was twice as much as Germany and more than what was received by the UK, Ireland, and all the Nordic EU countries combined.[259] The European Commission admits that by the early 1990s the CAP "did not always serve the best interests of farmers and became unpopular with consumers and taxpayers."[260] In 2004 Lawrence Osborne more colorfully noted, "[t]he French farmer, who is largely subsidized by the urban taxpayers of all the other countries in the European Union, can smell the end of his golden age. The Germans and the British, for one thing, are tired of paying for him."[261] Such predictions became reality in 2005 as the British sought "fundamental" changes in the CAP[262] and Prime Minister Tony Blair pointedly attacked the subsidies as supporting old forms of production

---

255. Interinstitutional Agreement of 6 May 1999 between the European Parliament, the Council and the Commission on Budgetary Discipline and Improvement of the Budgetary Procedure, 1999 O.J. (C 172) 1. There were such efforts again in 2003, but to mixed reviews. *EU Agrees "Radical" Farm Reform*, BBC NEWS, June 26, 2003, http://news.bbc.co.uk/1/hi/business/3021728.stm. According to the Scottish Executive the figure for 2003 was 44.3 billion euros. *See* Scottish Executive, *supra* note 252, ¶ 2.

256. EUROPEAN COMMISSION, AGRICULTURE AND RURAL DEVELOPMENT, THE COMMON AGRICULTURAL POLICY—A POLICY EVOLVING WITH THE TIMES 3 (2004), http://europa.eu.int/comm/agriculture/publi/capleaflet/cap_en.pdf.

257. Daniel Wortmann, *Zwei Euro pro Tag für jede Kuh, Zwei Euro pro Tag für jede Kuh*, DEUTSCHE WELLE, June 18, 2005, *available at* http://.www.dw-world.de/dw/article/0,1564,1619380,00.html. Commission of the European Communities, *33rd Financial Report on the European Agricultural Guidance and Guarantee Fund, Guarantee Section, 2003 Financial Year*, COM (2004) 715 final (Oct. 27, 2004).

258. Commission of the European Communities, *33rd Financial Report on the European Agricultural Guidance and Guarantee Fund, Guarantee Section, 2003 Financial Year*, COM (2004) 715 final (Oct. 27, 2004).

259. *Id.*

260. EUROPEAN COMMISSION, *supra* note 256, at 2.

261. OSBORNE, *supra* note 212, at 156. France has increasingly found itself isolated on these issues. *See Réforme de la PAC, grogne des agriculteurs*, LE FIGARO, June 27, 2003, at 1 (describing France as the principal opponent of efforts to reform the CAP). The farmers' political clout within France may also be weakening. *See* Robert Graham, *The French Love Affair With Farming Life Starts to Wither*, FIN. TIMES, Mar. 6–7, 2004, at 4 (describing how French "politicians seem more interested in the votes of urban middle class" than those of French farmers).

262. David Rennie & Toby Helm, *Now Blair Gives Up Pounds 7bn for Nothing in Return*, DAILY TELEGRAPH (London), Dec. 17, 2005, at 1.

while Europe is not investing enough in new technologies and education.[263] German Chancellor Angela Merkel has supported Prime Minister Blair's efforts to scale down the CAP.[264]

3. GI Monopoly Rents as the New Agricultural Subsidies

If you were a European policymaker and realized that reduction of agricultural subsidies is probable over the long-haul, you would look for means to gain added revenue for European farmers. If you realized that increased opening of your agricultural markets was also, for independent reasons, increasingly likely, you would look for ways to preserve as much of your agricultural employment as possible. One answer would be to migrate your production to *high-end products*, to cultivate and maintain consumer demand for these high-end products, and to control the names of these high-end products as widely as possible in an effort to prevent product substitution and/or consumer defection.[265]

This has been the European Union's consistent strategy, although Brussels has been more circumspect in stating it. The preamble of the 1992 Origins Regulation talks of improving the income of farmers and supporting rural economies through GI protection,[266] while a July 2003 communication from the Commission argues:

> GIs provide added value to our producers. French GI cheeses are sold at a premium of 2 euro. Italian "Toscano" oil is sold at a premium of 20% since it has been registered as a GI in 1998. Many of these products whose names are protected, are exported. 85% of French wine exports use GIs. 80% of EU exported spirits use GIs. GIs are a lifeline for 138[,]000 farms in France and 300[,]000 Italian employees.[267]

---

263. *See* Anthony Browne, *A Wind of Change Starts to Blow Across Europe*, TIMES (London), June 25, 2005, at 30 (describing Blair's address before the European Parliament calling for CAP funds to be moved to "industries of the future"). Blair is correct that the farm subsidies dwarf EU support for education and science. *See* Wortmann, *supra* note 257 (noting EU support for education and science is only 10% of the amount of EU subsidies for agriculture). During this period, the inequitable distribution of the CAP has fed into traditional Anglo-French antipathy. One British writer humorously predicted of his summer vacation in the south of France: "and they will say: 'Non, mais , enfin, dites-nous la vérité, qu'est-ce qu'il mijote la, ce Tony Blair?' ['Oh, come on, don't be chicken, tell us the truth, what does Tony Blair think he is up to?'], and then I will explain to them very gently and carefully why the Common Agricultural Policy may be good for France but it is very bad for the rest of Europe, and they will beat me up in a friendly but meaningful way." Miles Kingston, *A Traveller's Guide to Anglo-French Dialogue*, INDEP. (London), July 7, 2005, at 40.

264. Heather Stewart, *For George Bush, a Fair Deal Means What American Farmers Demand*, GUARDIAN, July 30, 2006, at 5 ("Tony Blair and German Chancellor Angela Merkel have formed a liberalizing alliance, helping to isolate French President Jacques Chirac and drag the European Union toward an agreement that would pare back the CAP to make it palatable to developing countries.").

265. Testimony of Michael Pellegrino, *supra* note 15, at 5 ("The EU sees new rules on GIs as a way of softening the impact on European farmers of further cuts in agricultural protection and support.").

266. 1992 Origins Regulation, *supra* note 142, pmbl. ("[W]hereas the promotion of products having certain characteristics could be of considerable benefit to the rural economy, in particular to less-favoured or remote areas, by improving the incomes of farmers . . . .").

267. *Why Do Geographical Indications Matter to Us?*, *supra* note 106, at 1.

This communiqué is evidence of the European Commission's strategy but belies the wisdom of that strategy. For example, while 85% of French wine exports use GIs, French wines have been *losing market share* in North America and Britain during the past few years to wine producing countries that do not have strict GI systems.[268] The communiqué implies that a GI system by itself increases a product's value (Italian "Toscano" oil is sold at a premium of 20% since it has been registered as a GI in 1998). This assumption is not supported. The mechanism for creating value is not the "GI" or "AOC" label. The AOC wines growing fastest in international markets are Champagnes, but the bottles marketed in North America and Japan are not labeled as *appellations d'origine contrôlées* (the Champagne companies are market savvy and the AOC labeling adds little or no information for an American, Canadian, or Japanese consumer). The same is true for Scotch and Irish whiskey—*none* of the brands marketed in the United States even bother to say they are protected geographical indications.

This communiqué may be for domestic political consumption as much as international persuasion; part of the effort to convince EU farmers that reduced subsidies from liberalization of agricultural trade will be (more) tolerable if European farmers can migrate to high-end foodstuffs. The next step in the reasoning is that exclusive use of their geographical indication names will secure (monopolize) those high-end markets:

> [A]n essential part of the value of many agricultural products is the geographical indication which, if not protected, seriously erodes this value.... The EC's objective is to negotiate fair market access opportunities to those wines, spirits, and other agricultural and foodstuff products whose quality, reputation, or other characteristics are essentially attributable to their geographic origin and traditional know-how.[269]

The Commission then tells EU farmers that "GIs are a unique asset for our producers in an increasingly liberalized world."[270]

As anyone who shops in high-end grocery, wine, and liquor stores can attest, the issue is not really "fair market access" for European

---

268. See Brown, *supra* note 215 (excluding Champagne, French wine exports fell 9.2% in value between 2003 and 2004, after a 2003 year in which sales had been "dismal"); Nassauer & Lawton, *supra* note 215 ("Exports of French wine to the U.S., excluding champagne, dropped 17% by volume in 2003 and a further 4.1% in 2004.").

269. Commission Proposal 625/02 of Dec. 16, 2002, Modalities in the WTO Agriculture Negotiations 4, *available at* http://trade.ec.europa.eu/doclib/docs/2005/september/tradoc_111447.pdf; *accord Why Do Geographical Indications Matter to Us?, supra* note 106, at 3.

270. *Why Do Geographical Indications Matter to Us?, supra* note 106, at 4; *see also* Antonio Fernandez-Martos, European Commission Directorate-General Trade, Powerpoint Presentation, Nov. 21, 2003, slide 5 (on file with author) (showing the Commission publicly acknowledging that strengthened GI protection is perceived as means of offsetting reductions in CAP subsidies under slide entitled "The EC's objectives on GIs" heading "GIs in a wider context" lists "CAP reform").

foodstuffs. A geographical indication is an "essential part of the value" of a foodstuff for the same reasons and in the same ways that a trademark is valuable: it causes people to pay a premium for the labeled product. In this respect, Brussels' drive to capitalize on the value of its geographical names is no different than two California beach towns dueling over who is "Surf City, U.S.A."[271]; New York City trying to "acquire the rights to everything that says 'New York'"[272]; and Hollywood and West Hollywood battling over who has the real "Sunset Strip."[273]

Maximizing monopoly rents from the "unique asset" of geographical indications is a completely rational EU goal, a goal which manifests itself in (a) the European Union wanting to strengthen global protection for all GIs to a product specific usurpation standard (as is already the case with wines and spirits), (b) the European Union seeing GIs as having primacy over trademarks (where North Americans tend to enjoy more monopoly rents globally in the *agroalimentaire* sector), and (c) the European Union wanting to reclaim a substantial set of geographic words that have become generic in many countries. Each of these points is addressed below.

a.   To Maximize Monopoly Rents, GIs Should Have a Broad Penumbra of Protection, Including Against Trademarks

If you believed that you had a unique advantage in geographical indications over your trading partners, who have relied on trademarks for marketing, you would want GIs to have some kind of primacy over trademarks. Not surprisingly, as one commentator reports, "the European Communities traditionally pursue a concept of geographical indication protection which assumes a certain element of superiority of geographical indications over trademarks."[274] First, the law in at least some EU jurisdictions gives GIs protection at least equal to, and arguably beyond, the dilution protection for famous marks in the United States. This protection appears to preclude non-confusing commercial uses of the geographic word.

For example, French law forbids use of the appellation not just on similar products, but on "any other product or service where the use is susceptible of diverting or weakening the notoriety of the appellation d'origine."[275] Thus, Yves St. Laurent could not use Champagne as the

---

271. Kimi Yoshino, *Two Surf Cities Claim the Same Wave of PR*, L.A. TIMES, Jan. 31, 2005, at A1 (Huntington Beach and Santa Cruz, California, competing for trademark rights to "Surf City, USA" and "Original Surf City, USA"). Although in this dispute, the two municipalities are, to some degree, free-riding off the Beach Boys as much as they are trying to capitalize on a geographic designation.

272. Thomas S. Mulligan, *The Big Apple Wants Its Slice*, L.A. TIMES, Feb. 22, 2005, at A9.

273. Bob Pool, *W. Hollywood Stakes Claim to Sunset Strip*, L.A. TIMES, Aug. 16, 2004, at B1.

274. Goebel, *supra* note 128, at 973.

275. C. CON. art. L. 115-5; BERTRAND, *supra* note 20, at 147. In contrast, at least one Belgian court has permitted a beer called "Bourgogne des Flandres" [Burgundy of Flanders] on the grounds that,

name for a high-end perfume,[276] although the haut couture company had believed that with a "luxury product commercialized by a company with a global reputation, there was no diminishment or weakening" of the Champagne name.[277] Under Belgian law, once an appellation is recognized, the use of the word on any "products not covered" by the appellation is forbidden — again, without regard to consumer confusion.[278]

If the same breadth of dilution-like or "dilution-plus" protection were implemented in other countries, Champagne district wine producers could theoretically shut down the CHAMPAGNE café chain in California, TEXAS CHAMPAGNE hot sauce,[279] the CHAMPAGNE POWDER ski resort in Steamboat Springs,[280] BUBBLES-THE CHAMPAGNE OF CAR WASHES in Canada,[281] CHAMPAGNE ROSE as a Yardley of London trademark for bath soaps,[282] and SCHAUMPAGNER bubble bath in Switzerland. (The Champagne

---

although the beer trademark incorporated a protected *appellation d'origine*, consumers know that Belgium does not produce wine and would not be confused. BERTRAND, *supra* note 20, at 147.

276. Cour d'appel [CA] [regional court of appeal] Paris, 1e ch., Dec. 15, 1993, D. 1994, 145, note le Tourneau (finding that YSL's use of the word had "diverted the notoriety which only the producers and marketers in Champagne could exploit in commercializing wine . . . .").

277. OLSZAK, *supra* note 19, at 46.

278. Loi du 14 juillet 1991 sur les pratiques du commerce et sur l'information et la protection du consommateur [Law of July 14, 1991 on Trade Practices and Consumer Information and Protection], Chapitre III, art. 20(3), *available at* http://www.wipo.int/clea/docs_new/fr/be/be054fr.html ("Il est interdit . . . (3) de fabriquer, d'offrir en vente et de vendre sous une appellation d'origine des produits non couverts par une attestation d'origine lorsqu'une telle attestation est requise."). Belgian law also explicitly forbids all translations of the protected appellation, *id.* art. 21(3) ("L'emploi abusif d'une appellation d'origine reste interdit nonobstant . . . l'utilisation de mots étranger lorsque ces mots ne sont que la traduction d'une appellation d'origine ou sont susceptibles de créer une confusion avec une appellation d'origine."), as well as the use of "style" or "type" terms with the appellation, i.e., the TRIPS Article 23 standard expanded to apply to all products. *Id.* art. 21(1) ("L'emploi abusif d'une appellation d'origine reste interdit nonobstant . . . l'adjonction de termes quelconques à ladite appellation d'origine notamment de termes rectificatifs, tels que 'genre,' 'type,' 'façon,' 'similaire.'"). Article 13(1)(a) of the Origins Regulation itself requires the PDOs and PGIs be protected in national law both against "any direct or indirect commercial use of a name registered in respect of products not covered by the registration in so far as those products are comparable to the products registered . . . *or* insofar as using the exploits the reputation of the protected name." Article 13(1)(b) of the Origins Regulation requires that all PDOs and PGIs be protected broadly against "any misuse, imitation or evocation, even if the true origin of the product is indicated or if the protected name is translated or accompanied by an expression such as 'style', 'type', 'method', 'as produced in', 'imitation' or 'similar.'"

279. U.S. Trademark Registration No. 1,526,014 (filed Feb. 21, 1989) (TEXAS CHAMPAGNE certification mark owned by Texxstar Resources (USA), Inc.).

280. U.S. Trademark Registration No. 2,456,466 (filed May 29, 2001) (CHAMPAGNE POWDER certification mark owned by Steamboat Ski & Resort Corp.).

281. Canadian Trademark Registration No. TMA375924 (filed Nov. 16, 1990) (BUBBLES THE CHAMPAGNE OF CAR WASHES AND DESIGN certification mark owned by Bubbles International Car Wash Corp.).

282. Canadian Trademark Registration No. TMA430664 (filed July 22, 1994) (CHAMPAGNE ROSE certification mark owned by Muelhens GMBH & Co.).

district producers lost this last claim in a Geneva court action in 1990.[283]) Potentially they could prevent the use of the word "Champagne" to name a rich yellow wall paint color, or a Vegas showgirl, without consumer confusion in any of these cases. In the strong, French, version of GI law the geographical indication is protected from all *similar* commercial uses. This increases the number of friction points between GI law and trademark law, points of engagement where the GI is likely to prevail. As Professor Olszak notes, "this absolutism of the appellation contrasts with a greater flexibility in the law of trademarks."[284]

Such strong protection of a geographical indication, giving it a very wide penumbra to prevent "usurpation" or dilution, borders on the view that a protected appellation should never be used in a trademark.[285] In contrast, barring dilution protection, a geographic word protected as a certification mark could be used commercially by third parties as long as there is no risk of consumer confusion, i.e., the trademark IDAHO SCIENTIFIC is not confusingly similar to Idaho when used as a certification mark for potatoes. COGNAC can be a common law certification mark and not interfere with a house paint company naming one of its golden colors "cognac." Even where the certification mark achieves sufficient famousness for dilution protection, pre-existing trademarks and trade uses are protected; there is no "priority" for the now-famous certification mark.

To be clear, the European Union has *not* proposed that TRIPS Article 23(1) be strengthened to the wide usurpation standard provided in French law and Article 3 of the Lisbon Agreement. The European Union's present position seeks to increase all GI protection to what I have called the "product specific usurpation standard," i.e., primacy within its product classification only.[286] But the view from Brussels also

283. OLSZAK, *supra* note 19, at 37–38. The Swiss product's counterpart in the United States might be something like ROYAL BAIN DE CHAMPAGNE. U.S. Trademark Registration No. 0856169 (filed Apr. 4, 1967) (ROYAL BAIN DE CHAMPAGNE certification mark owned by Parfums Caron Joint Stock Co.).

284. OLSZAK, *supra* note 19, at 46.

285. BERTRAND, *supra* note 20, at 147 ("L'antinomie des notions de marque et d'appellation d'origine conduit à la prohibition du dépôt de l'appellation d'origine à titre de marque.").

286. Although Article 23(1) does not say "usurpation," that is clearly how the European Union understands it. *See* General Council Trade Negotiations Committee, *Doha Work Programme—The Extension of the Additional Protection for Geographic Indications to Products Other than Wines and Spirits*, WT/GC/W/540/Rev.1, TN/C/W/21/Rev.1, at 3 (Dec. 14 2004) (Communication from Bulgaria, the European Communities, Guinea, India, Kenya, Liechtenstein, Madagascar, Moldova, Romania, Switzerland, Thailand, and Turkey) ("'GI-extension will save litigation costs to legitimate producers of GI products through an easier burden of proof in enforcement procedures to end usurpation and illegitimate use of a geographical indication."); Trade Negotiations Committee, *Statement by Switzerland-Joint Statement by the GI-Friends Group*, TN/C/4 (July 13, 2004) (urging extension of Article 23(1) to all products because GIs "of products other than wines and spirits can be usurped and free-ridden upon by products not having the respective origin or quality").

seems to be that a new GI recognized by a government should displace a pre-existing trademark, at least within that GI's product classification.

This makes the disruptive cost of the EU proposal difficult to calculate because we do not know the full range of future GIs. In fact, GIs are a fairly recent tool of agricultural policy in the European Union. Even as venerable a wine as Chianti did not become a protected *denominazione* in Italy until 1967.[287] In France, there seems to be a slow, but steady stream of new GIs. Of the more than thirty-five protected appellations for cheese in France, only eleven are more than thirty years old.[288] Camembert did not become part of a protected AOC (*Camembert de Normandie*) until 1983.[289] Similarly, although Cantal cheese has been produced in the Auvergne region of France for over a thousand years, it was not granted *appellation* status until 1980.[290] New French AOCs are created fairly regularly for wine[291] and spirits.[292] Uncertainty about how GIs would develop as a policy tool in different countries heightens concern about any proposals in which GIs trump trademarks.

A system that gives geographical indications primacy over trademarks is especially unacceptable if GI status is simply a decision by one national government that is then imposed on all other WTO members, without independent review within each member's national legal system available to trademark holders. This is the essence of the European Union's proposal in TRIPS negotiations.

b. To Maximize Monopoly Rents, the EU Must "Claw Back" Geographic Terms that Have Become Generic

The desire to generate GI monopoly rents for the agricultural sector also explains the European Union's "claw back" list of forty-one geographic terms. There is some irony in this list in that it includes at

---

287. Osborne, *supra* note 212, at 219.

288. Masui & Yamada, *supra* note 37, at 28. In addition to *Camembert*, cheese appellations that have been granted in the past twenty-five years include *Bleu de Haut Jura* from Rhône-Alps, France (1977); *Bleu des Causses* from Midi-Pyrénées, France (1979); *Cantal* from Auvergne, France (1980); *Brie de Melun* from Ile-de-France, France (1990); and *Rocamadour* from Midi-Pyrénées, France (1996). *Id.*

289. *Id.* at 92. Actually, "camembert" by itself was declared generic in 1926 by the Court of Orleans and the AOC only governs *Camembert de Normandie*, leaving "camembert" generic. *See* Olszak, *supra* note 19, at 20 n.23.

290. Masui & Yamada, *supra* note 37, at 94–96.

291. Just in 1990–1991, France added at least five new appellations for wine. Gardan, *supra* note 211, at 135 (*Vacqueyras* (Languedoc, 1990), *Cremant de Limoux* (Sud-Ouest, 1990), *Floc de Gascogne* (Sud-Ouest, 1990), *Marcillac* (Sud-Ouest, 1990), and *Pommeau de Normandie* (Normandie, 1991)). In 2002, at least one new wine AOC was created. *See Une A.O.C. pour les rouges de Limoux*, Vins Mag., Winter 2002, at 10; *see also* McInerney, *supra* note 241, at 37. Discussing the Mâcon area of Burgundy, he notes "[t]he appellation of Viré-Clessé was finally approved and appeared on wines from these special villages for the first time in 1999." *Id.*

292. Lerosier, *supra* note 38 (town of Domfrontais given AOC for calvados on December 31, 1997 and AOC for *poiré* [apple and pear-based spirit] on December 12, 2001).

least two terms, "Feta" and "Parmesan," that have substantial generic use *within* the European Union. In the case of "feta," the Greek government's 2002 registration of the term as a PDO under the Origins Regulation was contested by the German, Danish, French, and British governments. Greece finally prevailed at the European Court of Justice in 2005.[293]

The generic use of "Parmesan" is also widespread in Europe. In April 2004, the European Commission issued an "opinion" (avis motive) to Germany that its continued failure to protect the word, and its use by German cheese manufacturers, would result in the Commission launching a case against the German government at the European Court of Justice.[294] The court decided that "feta" had not become generic, while recognizing that the production of feta cheese in "other countries has been large and of substantial duration (since 1931 in France, since the 1930s in Denmark and since 1972 in Germany)."[295]

What would happen if the cheese-makers of Parmigiano-Reggiano were given global control of commercial use of "Parmesan"? Makers of cheese and cheese products presently labeled "Parmesan" would not stop selling their products; they would re-label and re-brand. This process would impose quantifiable costs on these producers and, during the process, engender a great deal of consumer confusion that is of a less quantifiable cost. The confusion would be augmented if Article 23 protection (the product-specific usurpation standard for wines and spirits) extended to cheese GIs because these producers would not be able to label their products "parmesan-like," "parmesan-style," or anything that would similarly offer efficient communication of product characteristics to the consumer. Similarly, a wide range of dishes, whether in restaurants or commercially-available, prepared food, might be barred from using "parmesan" in their names ("eggplant parmesan," "chicken parmesan," etc.). This might be true even where the prepared food used authentic Parmigiano-Reggiano cheese.[296]

---

293. Press Release No. 92/05, Eur. Court of Justice, Judgment of the Court of Justice in Joined Cases C-465/02 and C-466/02, The Court of Justice Upholds the Name 'Feta' as a Protected Designation of Origin For Greece (Oct. 25, 2005), *available at* http://curia.europa.eu/en/actu/communiques/cpo5/aff/cpo50092en.pdf.

294. Consortium du fromage Parmigiano-reggiano, *Le Parmesan: plus qu'un patrimoine national,* VINS & GASTRONOMIE (Dec. 2004), at 88.

295. Press Release No. 92/05, *supra,* note 293, at 2.

296. The scope of this problem would depend on whether a jurisdiction adopted GI protection as strong as that recognized by the European Court of Justice. Case C-469/00, Ravil S.A.R.L. v. Bellon Imp. S.A.R.L., 2003 E.C.R. I-5053; Case C-108/01, Consorzio del Prosciutto di Parma and Salumificio S. Rita SpA v. Asda Stores Ltd., 2003 E.C.R. I-5121. In *Ravil,* the Court ruled that Grana Padano cheese and Parma ham could impose grating, slicing, and packaging conditions on use of the PDO. As a result, Ravil, a French company which bought the Grana Padano cheese and grated the cheese itself, could be prevented from using the "Grana Padano" name. Similarly, a British supermarket chain that bought boned Parma ham and sliced and packaged the ham itself could be prevented from labeling the

IV. A DEBATE ABOUT COMMERCIAL LINGUISTICS, MYTH-MAINTENANCE, AND COMPARATIVE ADVANTAGE

While the politics of GIs are intriguing, at heart the debate about geographical indications is a struggle about commercial linguistics, myth maintenance, and who will extract the monopoly rents from those myths. This is what makes the geographical indications debate both so interesting and so parallel to conventional trademark law.

The introduction described three basic functions for geographic words in labeling products: (a) to tell us a product's geographic provenance; (b) to tell us about non-geographic characteristics of a product; or (c) for evocative purposes. The European Union's *public* argument for strong GI protection is that GIs serve a *fourth* purpose which is a hybrid combination of (a) and (b): the European Union contention is that GIs are supposed to tell us *non-geographic characteristics of the product linked to the product's geographic provenance.* This is the "terroir" theory, i.e., there is an essential land/qualities nexus. The terroir theory allows the European Union to argue that although words like Parmesan and Chablis have become generic descriptors of products from many locales, such genericity should not have happened because the non-EU products lack the true product's qualities and, therefore, are mis-described, mislabeled, and, thereby, competing unfairly.

This Part will first examine how the essential land/qualities nexus is needed to justify the strong GI protection advocated by the European Union. Then we will turn to the question of whether there is an essential land/qualities nexus across a broad spectrum of products at a sufficient level for strong GI protection to make sense. While winemakers and artisanal farmers are completely justified in their concern for terroir, what we know—and are learning—about terroir does not fit our appellations laws very well and does not justify GI protection beyond protection from consumer confusion. On the other hand, preserving descriptive and evocative uses of geographic words is an important goal counseling us to *limit* such protection.

A. THE MIGRATION OF GEOGRAPHIC WORDS TOWARD NON-GEOGRAPHIC MEANING

Of the three basic uses I have proposed for geographic words in labeling products, the first two are in some opposition to each other: to communicate a product's *geographic origins* as opposed to

---

ham "Parma." *Ravil,* 2003 E.C.R. at I-5119. The Court required that the PDO expressly impose such limitations and that the limitations be relevant to maintaining the quality and, therefore, reputation of the PDO. *Id.* at I-5106. Grating, slicing, and packaging were found to be relevant to the maintenance of the quality and the authenticity of the PDOs at issue. *Id.* at I-5104.

communicating a product's *non-geographic characteristics*. Yet many geographic words naturally drift from geographic source identification toward non-geographic product identification. This genericity drift is all around us, whether one encounters *sauce mexicaine* in a Paris *supermarché* or locally-baked French bread in Beijing.

In the 1992 *Exportur SA v. LOR SA* case before the European Court of Justice, French candy makers contended that two Spanish candy names, "turron de Alicante" and "turron de Jijona," had become generic.[297] The British Government intervened on the side of the French producers, agreeing that the two candy names had come to represent only "certain recipes for confections, whose principal distinctive ingredients, namely honey and almonds, originate in different regions or even different countries."[298] The British Government elegantly summarized the issue:

> [I]t is not unusual for successful foodstuffs produced in one Member state to be imitated in other Member states. If appropriate labeling ensures that 'imitations' are clearly distinguishable from the originals on whose recipes they are based, there is no risk of fraud or deception and so the original name becomes generic.[299]

Although the French candy makers lost this case, their side's arguments nicely capture the problem. Broad-based progress requires both innovation *and* imitation. Imitation of technology (in the broadest sense) is often accompanied by imitation of the relevant terminology. So we get *computador* (Spanish), *televisi* (Malaysian), and *croissant* (English).[300] As the French candy makers argued in the *Exportur* case, "in so far as [the words] indicate certain types of tourons and constitute generic terms, they are necessary in order to identify the products in question for the benefit of consumer[s], so that to reserve them solely for Spanish producers is unlawful."[301]

As recipes (the "technology") migrate, they often retain their original names; generally speaking, it is efficient for them to do so. The original name comes to stand for the results of the technology. This is a

---

297. Case C-3/91, Exportur SA v. LOR SA, 1992 E.C.R. I-5529, I-5535, ¶ 23; *see also* BRAUDEL, *supra* note 223, at 208 (describing how the Roannais wine-producing region 240 miles from Paris lost out to more distant Midi vineyards as railways expanded).

298. *Exportur*, 1992 E.C.R. at I-5539, ¶ 47.

299. *Id.* at I-5534 to 35, ¶ 23. The candy makers argued that "touron Jijona" had come to mean a honey nougat candy "containing ground almonds and being of a soft consistency" while "touron Alicante" was a "brittle specialty made with whole almonds." *Id.*

300. For example, "the Turkish words for parliament and senate are *parlamento* and *senato*, both obviously Italian .... Similarly, the Arabic term for parliament is *barlaman*, clearly from the French *parlement*." BERNARD LEWIS, WHAT WENT WRONG? 144 (2002). And similar terminology makes reporting about techniques easier, as when Professeur Jean-Robert Pitte of the Sorbonne writes about Armenia having a specialty "cognac" that was a favorite of Stalin's. PITTE, *supra* note 30, at 37.

301. *Exportur*, 1992 E.C.R. at I-5535, ¶ 25.

general process—we only call it "genericization" when a geographic word (or trademark) is involved. That is the difference between Caesar salad and Swiss cheese, between honey mustard and Dijon mustard, between crepes Suzette and Chicago pizza. All are general recipes, however, the second in each pair became so through a process of genericization of a geographic word.

In fact, geographic words are sometimes *added* during the migration to describe the supposed source of the technique. We call those delicious cholesterol delivery systems "French fries," although the French just call them "frites." If you buy a waffle in Liege, it is called a "*gaufre.*" In the Brussels train station, the same product is called a "*gaufre,*" "*gaufre de Liege,*" or "*gaufre liegoise*" even though it is baked in front of you. On the streets of Paris, the same product might be called any of these names, or, a "*gaufre Belge,*" although, again, it is prepared before your eyes. By this process, food technologies migrate and geographic words migrate toward non-geographic meaning.

B. Tokay, but not Travertine or Tiramisu

A curious thing about the idea of terroir is that it did not develop to cover the kinds of products that most obviously qualify for an "essential" land/qualities nexus. An essential land/qualities nexus makes the most sense with the *least* processed products. Stone is a good example. In the fifteenth century, the Florentines imported lustrous *biachi marmi* from Carrara for Brunelleschi's construction of the Duomo.[302] In the twentieth century, Angelenos imported glistening Travertine marble from outside Bagni di Tivoli for the walls of the J. Paul Getty Museum complex.[303] Stone from particular places has been coveted throughout history, whether for building or human ornamentation. If the key is *essentiality*, should not GI protection have arisen in relation to various kinds of marble or Afghan lapis lazuli or Jerusalem limestone products whose characteristics are not convincingly reproduced beyond a single geographic area? These are the most unimpeachable examples of desirable final product qualities being intrinsically linked to a single geographic production area.

Of course, marble and lapis lazuli are not foodstuffs. More importantly, it might be said that stone does not reflect terroir, it literally *is* the terroir. But there are plenty of minimally-processed foodstuffs produced in western European countries where geographical indications did not arise originally and where GIs remain practically or completely absent. Four such products historically produced in France are mineral

---

302. Ross King, Brunelleschi's Dome 108–11 (2000) (*biachi marmi* refers to white marble).

303. *See* Richard Meier, Building the Getty 94 (1997). Travertine from the same quarry was used to face the Coliseum, the Trevi Fountain, and the colonnade of St. Peter's Basilica in Rome.

waters, honey, oysters, and sea salt.[304] Generally speaking, these minimally-processed, minimally-transformed foodstuffs have not given rise to appellations laws.

At the other extreme, *more* processed, transformed foods also have not been fertile territory for appellations of origin. Many well-known dishes or preparations, for example, pannetone, have distinct regional origins, but this "cuisine level" of foodstuffs has not lent itself to geographical indications claims.

Geographical indications arose to cover a range of *intermediately* processed foodstuffs. At one level, the rise of appellations for wine and cheese was the result of contingent events like the widespread wine labeling fraud that France experienced in the late nineteenth entury. At another level, geographical indications seem to have arisen for processed products (a) with a single dominant ingredient; (b) where the processing was done in roughly the same location as the ingredient was produced before processing; (c) where the dominant ingredient had multiple producers (at the farming level) that are citizens of the polity creating the protection; and (d) where the processing made the product transportable to distant markets.

Thus, tea, coffee, and chocolate did not give rise to GI protection in Europe because all three lacked characteristics (b) and (c), the latter meaning there was no domestic producer constituency to be served with GI regulations. Mineral waters lacked (c) as most "sources" are controlled by individual landholders, so there is no need for tools to coordinate marketing. Characteristic (d) explains why GIs would not develop for a product like bread. Although made of wheat with some water and salt, its processing did not make it especially transportable until recently, with the development of flash-frozen dough and par baking.[305] Characteristic (d) also subsumes the experience the French had with fraudulent Bordeaux and Burgundy wines in the late nineteenth and early twentieth centuries: the fraud was possible because the product had eager buyers at a distant market, newly serviceable from the expanding railway system in France.[306]

---

304. As for oysters, one WIPO official thought aquatic terroir was certainly a new idea, but French gastronomes speak in such terms concerning these two ocean products. *See, e.g.,* Hélène Lacas, *Reines des coquillages, les huitres,* CUISINES ET VINS DE FRANCE, Feb.–Mar. 2005, at 101 (describing oysters as "des terroirs et des goûts" [regions and tastes]); Hélène Lacas, *Le sel, toutes les saveurs de l'or blanc,* CUISINES ET VINS DE FRANCE, June-July-Aug. 2005, at 30 (describing land and sea salts as "des sels de terroir" [the salts of the region]).

305. *See, e.g.,* La Brea Bakery, http://www.labreabakery.com/store_baked.html (last visited Nov. 5, 2006).

306. By the end of the eighteenth century, France had an excellent system of national roads, perhaps the best in Europe, which had substantially cut down travel times from just twenty-five years earlier and, in that sense, started creating a national market for regional French agricultural products. *See* BOUDAN, *supra* note 3, at 285 (comparing substantially reduced Paris/regional city travel times

But perhaps we must add one other condition for the rise of robust, GI-like law: *that the local product can be imitated and consumers cannot by themselves, at least not enough of them, distinguish the imitations.* If the techniques and ingredients to make delicious foodstuffs get imitated well enough to make sufficiently convincing counterfeits, and the first producers of delicious foodstuffs now face stiff competition, what should the first producers do? This is just an instantiation of the broader problem of what a producer should do when he faces stiff competition from people who have (lawfully) imitated his production technology. One thing to do is continue to improve the technology, hence how often we are told our favorite toothpaste or detergent is "new" and "improved." But that route is partially closed to high-end European farmers by the rigidity of the appellations system itself. Another thing to do is to give brand value to the name—and protect it fiercely, whether by trademark law or a separate GI law.

In the past few decades, three things have intensified this kind of competition between original producers and imitators for intermediate-processed foodstuffs. First, transportation has made international trade in foodstuffs much more viable, opening distant markets that a producer could serve in the past only precariously. Second, consumers in these distant markets have become significantly wealthier. This is true everywhere from the American Midwest to Hyderabad. Third, on top of the initial wave of food technology migration (which often was the result of immigration or colonization), food preparation and processing techniques are being carefully studied and widely shared.

This last trend has attracted much attention in wine. As a Canadian journalist notes, blind taste tests

> [have] become more difficult in the last decade with the globalization of wine varieties, styles, and winemaking. They're making Aussie 'shiraz' and Italian-style pinot grigios in California, Burgundian pinot noirs in Oregon and New Zealand, California-dreaming chardonnays in France and Lotusland zinfandels in Italy.... The Balkans are awash with North American big-flavoured wines, Bordeaux-style blends are sculpted everywhere, even in Austria, zippy Germanic rieslings are sprouting in Ontario and New York.[307]

---

from 1765 to 1789). Nonetheless, it is generally agreed that the expansion of the railway system dramatically affected wine marketing in France. *See, e.g.,* BRAUDEL, *supra* note 223, at 208 (describing how the Roannais wine-producing region 240 miles from Paris lost out to more distant Midi vineyards as railways expanded).

307. Gordon Stimmell, *Seeing Red Over White Blindness,* TORONTO STAR, Jan. 22, 2003, at D04. Australian wine critic Max Allen describes the same process Stimmel noted, but optimistically as creating new variations: "for every bland, internationalized wine, there is an exciting alternative: a South Australian Shiraz, for example, that has been made using ancient techniques developed in Burgundy and has an extra level of texture and structure; or a Spanish Tempranillo made using Australian technology that has an extra layer of pure, varietal fruit flavor." ALLEN, *supra* note 34, at 66.

Another writer puts it more colorfully: "blow me if the[se] new top-notch burgundies don't often taste disarmingly like top-notch Pinot Noir from Oregon . . . or Martinborough (New Zealand)."[308] In this sense, the crisis for French winemakers has been caused, at least partially, by the French companies that export tens of thousands of French oak barrels to California, South Africa, and Australia each year.

How to respond to these new competitors? One answer is to promote the idea of terroir, of an *essential land/qualities connection* (and with it, the idea of appellations law). British writer Andrew Barr puts it fairly directly: "The response that French wine-makers have now offered to the results of tastings such as these has been to introduce an element of mysticism into the equation—to talk up their soil (terroir)."[309]

If the product's non-geographic qualities arise *only* from the product's geographic origins, then imitators of the technique still cannot truly reproduce the product. And if this essential land/qualities connection is real, it justifies extending the intellectual property control to include *all* quality descriptive uses of a protected geographic word. In other words, if the terroir is actually needed for the process, then "Chianti-style wine" and "méthode champenoise" (for sparkling wine) make no sense for products produced outside those respective regions. If the recipe really requires that particular land, you arguably protect consumers by forbidding such "style" or "method" terminology.

C.   DISENTANGLING TERROIR FROM APPELLATIONS

The idea of terroir is an input/output idea: some unique inputs (the terroir elements) produce unique outputs in the same way that individual artisans might produce stylistically unique outputs. The particular input is *necessary* for the particular output: no other input produces that output. Let us consider each side of this equation.

1. Difficulties with the Input Side

As to the input side, terroir is a claim that the product's qualities come uniquely from some combination of inputs specific to that

---

308. ALLEN, *supra* note 34, at 73. Closer to home, a French culinary magazine jocularly characterized the perspective of French Jura cheesemakers to their Alpine neighbor: "Switzerland is a friendly country for sure, but guilty of making a cheese too similar to the local [Jura] glory, le vacherin." Sophie Denis, *Vacherin mont-d'or, la crème du Jura*, CUISINES ET VINS DE FRANCE, Feb.–Mar. 2005, at 82.

309. ANDREW BARR, DRINK: A SOCIAL HISTORY 112 (Bantam Press, 1995) (1988). Barr continues:

[I]t is essential to their purposes that French wine-makers should continue to insist that all the unusual characteristics of their fine wines should be attributed, not to wine-making techniques, but to the soil of the vineyard. The French emphasis on *terroir* serves not only to combat competition from wine-makers in America and Australasia, but also to create an aura around the most famous French wines: to establish them as natural phenomena, beyond the control of man.

Id. at 116.

geographic place. The most vexing of these views are the terroir narratives that insist on the *incomprehensible* nature of terroir. In this vein, James E. Wilson, an American geologist, tells readers that terroir has a "spiritual aspect."[310] But it does not get the conversation very far if, when pressed, "the French winemaker would simply say terroir, and shrug his or her shoulders in that life-is-too-mysterious, Gallic way."[311] In a trade environment that demands a certain level of science, rationality, and transparency, if terroir remains "an article of faith" for some[312] but a dubious mystery to many,[313] it cannot be a useful concept for developing further international norms.

Moving baby-steps beyond simple mystery, the official website for the principal producers of *Roquefort* cheese riffs on a taxonomy we learn in childhood: "The secret of Roquefort is the meeting between the animal, the mineral, and the vegetable."[314] French oenologist Alain Carbonneau similarly defines terroir "as the interaction of the climate, grape variety, and the soil."[315] Of course, emphasis on the "vegetable" element does not support the uniqueness of terroir. The migration of grape varietals at least as far as Christianity stretched is the very foundation of the marketing problem for European winemakers.

Professor Norbert Olszak is more cautious, properly removing the vegetable element from the terroir-based justification for geographical indications protection. Professor Olszak points out that the industrial revolution made it easy for geographic names of more processed goods such as "oxford" and "eau d'Cologne," to become generic. But as to foodstuffs, he writes:

> In contrast, for agriculture products and particularly for viticultural products, it is not the same. One can transport the grape varietals, the winemakers, the presses, the casks or stills—and there effectively is a world market for all this, but one cannot replace the soil and the

---

310. WILSON, *supra* note 36, at 334.

311. ALLEN, *supra* note 34, at 31.

312. Robinson, *The Grapes of War*, *supra* note 217, at 10 (describing terroir as "an article of faith for every French vigneron").

313. OSBORNE, *supra* note 212, at 116 (winemaker Randall Grahm, "I think American babbling about their terroir is—as yet—utter bullshit. It's marketing psychobabble, okay?"); Daniel Sogg, *Sean Thackrey: Winemaking on the Edge in a Marin Eucalyptus Grove*, WINE SPECTATOR, Jan. 31–Feb. 28, 2003, at 96 ("There's one pattern he detests—the concept of *terroir*, the notion that the growing site determines the character of wines. 'You hear so much dog shit about *terroir*. It's used as such an excuse to attribute quality to real estate. You wouldn't do that with a restaurant. Every chef wants the best produce, but someone still has to cook it,' he insists.").

314. "Le secret de Roquefort, c'est le rencontre entre l'animal, le minéral, et le végétale." The website further tells us that it is a combination of "lait de brebis, cave naturelle, penicillium Roqueforti" [ewe's milk, natural cellars, and penicillium Roqueforti]. *Penicillium Roqueforti* is considered a low risk microorganism. *See* U.S. Environmental Protection Agency, Final Decision Document, Penicillium Roquefortie TSCA Section 5(h)(4) Exemption, http://www.epa.gov/biotech_rule/pubs/fra/fdoo8.htm (last visited Nov. 5, 2006).

315. OSBORNE, *supra* note 212, at 15.

climate. Certainly, there can sometimes be one region which resembles another, but there remain subtle differences, reinforced by cultural and historic particularities, that form precisely this unique combination of natural and human factors that is *le terroir.*[316]

Olszak's statement nicely captures the ambivalent, two part strategy that is the terroir-iste's response to the migration of plants, animals, and food technology: focus on geology and climate and, when that gets you in a bind, add culture, history, and human skill.

As to the first approach, explanation of terroir as geology with secondary emphasis on climate appears pretty consistently in wine narratives (and with good reason in terms of a winemaker's effort to make the best possible wine; the issue is whether these are good reasons for a robust GI law). The Chablis district is identified by thin topsoil, calcium-rich subsoil, and "inclemency of the climate."[317] Local experts in the Priorat region of Spain attribute the character of Priorat's red wines to Llicorella slate in the soil[318] as well as the combination of long hot days and cool nights claimed to present the winemaker with a different sort of raw material than vintners in other regions.[319] For Port, "[a] certain type of rock called schist is probably the factor which, in conjunction with the climate and with methods of treatment worked out over a long time, gives the wine its character."[320] A 1960s guide to wines gives a particularly memorable claim about a single crucial element of the Champagne district terroir:

> The white pebbles [in the Champagne soil] absorb the heat of the sunshine, reflecting and radiating it evenly on to the ripening fruit and holding it well after the sun has disappeared below the horizon. Without this extra source of heat, the grapes, in some years, would never ripen at all.[321]

This "heat retaining pebbles narrative" may well have some

---

316. OLSZAK, *supra* note 19, at 4 (author's translation).

317. LICHINE, *supra* note 230, at 173 ("The soil is hard, and hard to work. . . . The topsoil is thin and in many spots the white, marly, calcium-rich subsoil (a formation known as Kimmeridge Clay) shows through. . . . A further hazard is the inclemency of the climate, for Chablis is more to the north than any other fine wine district of France except Champagne and Alsace.").

318. The report from Priorat typifies this kind of narrative:

> 'Here, it is very easy to make wine,' said Jose Riera i Agustina, the winemaker at Mas Igneus. 'And the reason it is easy is this,' he said, grabbing a fistful of soil. 'The llicorella. The secret of the Priorat is this.' Llicorella is slate, and in Priorat it is so prevalent that many vineyards appear to have been planted in a bed of rubble.

Amanda Hesser, *In Spain, Old Growths and New Beginnings*, N.Y. TIMES, May 1, 2002, at F1.

319. *Id.* ("Long hot days during the summer leave the vines dry, which leads to smaller yields and grapes that are both very sweet and very concentrated in flavor. But cool nights make it difficult for tannins to develop in those grapes before the sugar content gets too high.").

320. LICHINE, *supra* note 230, at 410. When the traditions of Port were established, "the wine was made from any number of grape varieties, almost at random. To a considerable extent, this is still the case." *Id.*

321. *Id.* at 186.

foundation in geology.[322] Yet this is also where the terroir story of unique inputs runs into trouble from different directions.

First, are there really little white pebbles everywhere wine is grown in the Champagne district? *Single appellations are rarely consistent in key geology, flora, and climate.* In fact, the larger the appellation, the more variation. Geological studies have shown between ten and sixty soil types for the AOC *Alsace grand cru.*[323] Discussing "Bordeaux" as an appellation, Thierry Desseauve has noted that it "represents all forms of terroir, all kinds of microclimates, all situations, and finally all kinds of wines and prices."[324] Similarly, the larger American AVAs are probably just "too big . . . to have real viticultural meaning."[325] But this is genuinely a problem for appellations of *all* sizes. One French wine guide notes that *within* the *Le Minervois* AOC (a small region) there are four regions that are differentiated from each other by their terroir and their climate.[326] Many northern California vintners have studied soil and slope characteristics to the point of dividing individual *vineyards* into "flavor blocks," i.e., miniature terroirs that are viticulted differently.[327] This practice is undoubtedly good for superior winemaking and husbandry of the land, but undermines any consistent uniqueness to the AVA as a whole.

Just as a single appellation changes across its own geography, it also changes across time, forming another threat to the consistent uniqueness of the inputs. This happens annually with the changing grapes used in any appellation that permits at least some mixing of varietals. It also happens structurally, as when grape rootstocks and varietals are grafted. In Italy, the breed of nearly the entire cattle stock used to produce *Parmigiano-Reggiano* cheese changed from local stock to Swiss Bruna-Alpina stock to, finally, "descendants of North American Holsteins and

322. *See, e.g.*, W.H. Terry Wright, *Soil and Wine Quality: The Terroir Connection*, http://www.sonoma.edu/geology/wright/gsa.html (last visited Nov. 5, 2006) (noting that in some Sonoma vineyards "[p]ebbly clay loams developed on Franciscan Complex ophiolitic rock produces excellent red wine fruit."); *see also* OSBORNE, *supra* note 212, at 149. Mouton-Rothschild's and Pierre Siri's *Iris du Gayon* Bordeaux vineyards in France have "thin topsoil filled with white pebbles which reflect the sun and heat the grapes. At night, they give back calories to the vines." *Id.*

323. B. Burtschy, *Dix terroirs, quatre cépages, cinquante grand crus. L'équation enfin résolue*, REVUE DU VIN DE FRANCE, Mar. 2000, at 54.

324. ROUSSET-ROUARD & DESSEAUVE, *supra* note 209, at 120–21.

325. Rod Smith, *Savoring Sonoma/The Wines*, L.A. TIMES, June 1, 2005, at F5 ("The Sonoma Coast AVA was created primarily as a marketing tool for large wineries and is too big (nearly half of the county) to have real viticultural meaning.").

326. GARDAN, *supra* note 211, at 77 ("Quatre regions se différencient par leur terroir et leur climat.").

327. W.H. Terry Wright, *Diverse Geology/Soils Impact Wine Quality*, PRACTICAL WINERY & VINEYARD, Sept./Oct. 2001, at Vol. XXIII, No. 2, http://www.sonomagrapevine.org/pages/growerstoolbox/gtgeology_soils.html (noting this about Benziger Family Winery and describing "a rich smorgasbord of rock types and a complicated geological history" producing a "high diversity of soil types, each a niche with its own conditions of texture, structure, and nutrients" in Sonoma County).

Dutch Fresians."[328] Until 1984, the milk for *Parmigiano-Reggiano* cheese only came from cows grazing on fresh grass from April 1 to November 11, but that rule was abandoned with year round lactation[329] and now the cows are not allowed to graze freely and "[t]heir food, often computer-monitored, is brought to them."[330] We are told, however, that since the thirteenth century, *"le mode de fabrication n'a pas changé."*[331] A claim which might be true of the cheese-making techniques, but is not true of what are traditionally identified as the terroir inputs.

A separate challenge to the consistent unique input claim of terroir is that practically any *one* natural aspect of the region can be found somewhere else. Wine literature is full of such comparisons, whether the regions are proximate to one another or distant. In discussing wines from Cote de Duras and nearby Duras, both proximate to Bordeau, Sophie Evan writes:

> Above all, geographical considerations explain that the wines produced in the canton enjoy the same characteristics as those of the commune of Duras. The determining element here results from the fact that they are harvested from on the same ground. Consequently the wine of Duras does not offer *stricto senso* any unique characteristic.[332]

The lack of unique characteristics is easy to understand between two geographically proximate regions, but it *might* also be true when comparing regions at a greater distance. The number of wine-producing areas that make claims to having Champagne-like, hot white pebbles borders on funny.[333] An article in a 2002 British newspaper favorably compared a few sparkling wines from Sussex in southern England with Champagne sparkling wines on the grounds that the Sussex "subsoil is remarkably like the Champagne region's."[334] Winemakers in Long Island and in Connecticut credit their own region with a "maritime microclimate" not unlike Bordeaux,[335] while a French expert explained

---

328. JOHNS, *supra* note 234, at 23–24.

329. *Id.* at 25.

330. *Id.* at 24.

331. Consortium du fromage Parmigiano-reggiano, *supra* note 294, at 88.

332. Sophie Evan, *L'Appellation "Vins des Cotes De Duras" Definition Judiciare Et Administrative Entre 1917 Et 1937, in* LES TERRITOIRES DE LA VIGNE ET DU VIN 143, 152 (Féret ed., 2002).

333. Nalley, *supra* note 185, at 75 (reporting of Chateauneuf-du-Pape region, "A sizeable portion of the appellation is blanketed under smooth, glacier-deposited stones the size of softballs. . . . It may be, as is often asserted, that the rocks help boost these grapes to stratospheric ripeness by retaining the warmth of the sun."); Chateau de Beaucastel, http://www.beaucastel.com (follow "Terroir" hyperlink) (asserting that Beaucastel was formed in this manner with the "galets" contributing significantly to the quality of the wines: "they retain the heat of the day and radiate it to the vines during the night."). The cover of LES TERRITOIRES DE LA VIGNE ET DU VIN shows a close-up of soil from the Graves region of Bordeaux which is soil covered in white-ish pebbles. Evan, *supra* note 332.

334. Jancis Robinson, *Make Sure Your Fizz Is the Biz*, FIN. TIMES, Dec. 28–29, 2002, at 10 ("Champagne vintages vary enormously.").

335. Connecticut Wine Trail, Chamard Vineyards, http://www.ctwine.com/chamard.html (last

that South Australia has "the same climate" as Languedoc "except that it never rains."[336]

2. *Would Understanding Terroir Make Terroir Disappear?*

If the terroir narrative is limited to geology and climate, then in addition to the problems of consistency and uniqueness discussed above, science challenges the narrative in three ways. First, the lack of evidence about what the classical terroir inputs actually do. As British writer Andrew Barr noted in 1995, the superiority of French soil because of the presence of limestone "is not ... demonstrated by science. No expert is able adequately to explain in what way the presence of limestone might affect the flavour of the wines that have been made from the vines that grow upon it."[337] In the 1990s, one Australian winemaker opined that "[s]oil science is not well advanced. We do not yet understand the underlying principles."[338]

Second, once we believe we understand the geology, we start attempting to reproduce it. Limestone, or the appropriate mineral mix thereof, will simply be added to local land as needed. Indeed, that practice is already underway in both New World and European vineyards.[339]

Third, increased scientific precision, and reductionism, may produce an understanding that no two terroirs are truly the same, but it seems more likely to confirm what we are already learning. As discussed above, (a) at a *refined* level, single appellations (including American AVAs) contain a variety of geological and climatic conditions; and (b) at a more *gross* level, there are regions in different parts of the world that are quite similar in geological and climatic conditions. In that sense, the "earthy" narrative for terroir is likely to run aground.

One way to deflect these challenges is to add "tradition" and "custom" into the equation about what makes a single terroir unique. While some experts cleanly separate skills/traditions from the "terroir,"[340]

---

visited Nov. 5, 2006); *accord* NEW YORK WINE REFERENCE, VARIETY: CABERNET SAUVIGNON 76, *available at* http://www.newyorkwines.org/informationstation/newstouse/wine_course.pdf ("The North Fork of Long Island has a maritime climate similar to Bordeaux's; it is reasonable to expect similar success."); LongIsland.com, http://www.longisland.com/vineyard.php (last visited Nov. 5, 2006) ("Through research, soil testing and intuition, the Hargraves realized that the maritime microclimate was remarkably similar to that found in Bordeaux." (describing the founding of Long Island Winery)).

336. ROUSSET-ROUARD & DESSEAUVE, *supra* note 209, at 40 ("Le gros des vins d'Australie vient de l'Australie méridionale ... c'est même climat que dans Languedoc sauf qu'il n'y pleut jamais.").

337. BARR, *supra* note 309, at 112.

338. *Id.*

339. In the Languedoc region, Alain Roux is famous for having uprooted traditional vines, planted the varietals of Châteauneuf-du-Pape, and "resolved to plow phosphates into his soils to imitate the soil conditions at Hermitage, the great domain of the Northern Rhône." OSBORNE, *supra* note 212, at 160.

340. For example, Jérôme Quiot, former director of INAO and a Châteauneuf-du-Pape

others hedge their view of terroir as Professor Olszak does: "subtle differences, reinforced by cultural and historic particularities."[341] For example, one wine encyclopedia says of the Champagne district, "[i]t is partly soil, partly climate, partly vines, and partly labor and tradition which make Champagne what it is."[342] René Renou, president of the Wine Committee of INAO, goes further, admitting that the larger, regional appellations "correspond more to a tradition, to a 'savoir-faire,' than to a true notion of connection to the terroir."[343] Defining terroir by skill and savoir-faire has its own ironies: first, it is the very migration of savoir-faire that brought on the Old/New World competition in foodstuffs. Second, the "award" of a GI may provide "an incentive to invent tradition."[344] But we should consider at least two more charitable ways to understand the role that savoir-faire and "cultural particularities" could play in the terroir equation.

First, perhaps the diffusion of technologies means only that the savoir-faire of any one terroir (hence, one appellation) might be found, in bits and pieces, in other countries. But the single appellation might retain a unique combination of geology, climate, and a cohesive body of savoir-faire developed in relation to that geology and climate. Terroir-as-tradition would be that special, cohesive, local knowledge set: the result of finding the right varietal/soil/climate combination, a process that historically has taken a very long time. One problem with this explication of terroir is that the learning process takes considerably less time with advances in geology and biology. In discussing the Sonoma Coast, one writer noted that finding the right soils for the right grapes is "a long, vintage-by-vintage process of exploration through taste," but concludes that "while it took thousands of years for Pinot Noir to emerge as the primary red grape of Burgundy, an echo of that process in Sonoma County has taken less than half a century."[345]

But let us consider a more intriguing possibility. Instead of the simple idea that human skill and activity produce a special, local knowledge set about the land, consider the more subtle (and possibly unverifiable) idea that over time the land actually acquires additional, ineffable characteristics as it is cultivated by humans. This provides a narrative in which human skill has a significant role, but the role is not transferable through human and technological migration. No matter how skillful the European descendents in Sonoma, Stellenbosch, and

---

winemaker in ROUSSET-ROUARD & DESSEAUVE, *supra* note 209, at 49.

341. OLSZAK, *supra* note 19, at 4.

342. LICHINE, *supra* note 230, at 181.

343. *Id.* at 122.

344. Broude, *supra* note 225, at 677. Broude gives the example of an Italian coastal region awarded DOC status in 1978 with little or no local tradition or quality wines. *Id.* at 676–77.

345. Smith, *supra* note 325.

Mendoza, it will be generations, perhaps centuries, before cultivation turns the New World lands into "terroir."

This idea has adherents in the New World as well as Europe. Consider a discussion between journalist Laurence Osborne and Ellie Patterson, winemaker at the Mount Eden Vineyards in Santa Cruz:

"Is there an American terroir," I asked.

"Most Californians would be insulted even at the question. But actually it's a good question, a painful question. There's not as much American terroir as people here think. It's rarer than we think. I think we have it here because Masson and Ray brought it into being."

"So terroir expresses the legacy of fathers and sons—

"Naturally. Daughters too."[346]

We can interpret this discussion as being just terroir-as-tradition, but it is more interesting to think about terroir as "brought . . . into being" by humans working the land.[347] This is an idea we should take seriously, if only because it is a corollary of an idea we do take very seriously: that humans can make a small ecosystem *deteriorate*. If humans have the capacity to give the land new, undesirable characteristics through their presence and use, then perhaps their presence and use can also produce terroir. In fact, from a strict ecologist's perspective, terroir may be a deterioration of the indigenous environment.

3. *The Mythology of Unique Product Qualities and the Discerning-Few Theory*

Assuming that there can be genuine individuality on the input side, let us turn to the output side of the *essential land/qualities connection* claim: do appellation products really have unique, discernible qualities or, as A.J. Liebling would have said, "decided individuality"?[348] The answer is perhaps yes, but for most of us most of the time, probably not.

There is widespread agreement that within designated wine appellations like Medoc, Mendoza, Champagne, Châteauneuf-du-Pape, or Napa, there are tremendous variations in output quality.[349] Not surprisingly, the larger the appellation, the wider the swings in product characteristics.[350] There are similarly recognized output differences

---

346. OSBORNE, *supra* note 212, at 107 (emphasis added).

347. While writing from a pure historian's perspective, this seems to be how Fernand Braudel understood "terroir." *See* BRAUDEL, *supra* note 223, at 139–41 (describing how each village had a "terroir" of worked land that belonged to and defined the village).

348. A.J. LEIBLING, BETWEEN MEALS: AN APPETITE FOR PARIS 71 (1995) ("The wines of the Rhone each have a decided individuality.").

349. A proposition that seems true of most AOCs. *See, e.g.*, Nalley, *supra* note 185, at 74 (*Châteauneuf-du-Pape* wines are "all across the spectrums . . . . Some are superb, many are mediocre.").

350. ROUSSET-ROUARD & DESSEAUVE, *supra* note 209, at 97–98 (discussion between René Renou, president of Wine Committee of INAO and Thierry Desseauve on the inconsistency of wines within

among Parmigiano-Reggiano producers, even which seasons a cheese is first made, then aged.[351] But even with such variation, it would be possible for all Port or all Parmigiano-Reggiano cheese to occupy one unique zone of characteristics in which one could find no other fortified wine or cheese. In other words, although the products of a particular GI might vary from one another, there would be some unifying characteristics that they distinctly and uniquely share. Unfortunately, the evidence seems to point in the opposite direction, especially with wine, the most closely studied of foodstuffs that claim terroir.

The general comparability of New World wines to Old World vintages is both an old story and an abiding controversy. The modern era of this debate began in 1976, when Steven Spurrier organized the famed "Judgment of Paris," a blind taste test in which nine judges, all French and with unimpeachable wine-tasting credentials, judged California wines to be better than like Burgundy and Bordeaux wines.[352] For our purposes, who had the *better* wines is irrelevant. As Paul Lukacs notes, "[t]he real news was that, to a person, the experts had been unable to tell which wines came from which country."[353]

The "Judgment of Paris" that New World wines are comparable and often indistinguishable from Old World wines seems to be stable fact. A 2004 tasting of sixteen chardonnays by seven French experts, sponsored by one of France's respected wine journals, placed California chardonnays first and second, with a New Zealand wine in third place.[354]

---

an appellation).

351. JOHNS, *supra* note 234, at 32 (1997) (stating that "Mountain [*Parmesan*] cheeses from the fall season are often more robust due to the second growth of green grass available in the fall" and that "[c]heese from the same producer varies from season to season"); *see also* Robinson, *supra* note 334 ("Champagne vintages vary enormously."); Sarah Woodward, *All in the Caves of Roquefort*, FIN. TIMES, Aug. 26, 2006, at 4 (discussing the "unexpected variety" in the taste of different Roquefort cheeses).

352. The blind taste test pitted California Chardonnays against Chardonnay-based white Burgundy wines and California Cabernets against Cabernet-based wines from Bordeaux. Spurrier, an Englishman who owned a wine shop near the *Place de la Concorde*, chose the nine judges. Twelve California wines; eight French wines; nine French judges. The winning red wine was Californian. So was the winning white wine. In fact, three of the top five white wines were Californian. PAUL LUKACS, AMERICAN VINTAGE: FROM ISOLATION TO INTERNATIONAL RENOWN—THE RISE OF AMERICAN WINE 3–5 (2000) ("When the judges, led by Pierre Brejoux, chief inspector of the *Institut National des Appellations d'Origine* took their seats, they knew only that some of the wines they would be tasting came from the United States and that the others were French."); McINERNEY, *supra* note 241, at 178–79. To some French, of course, Spurrier was just another confirmation that the British have a constitutional inclination to be the European stalking horse for American interests. *See, e.g.*, LUIGI BARZINI, *supra* note 205, at 118 (1983) (attributing French opposition to British participation in Europe to Britain's "partly imaginary 'special relation'" with Americans).

353. *Id.*

354. *Dégustation Universel Chardonnay*, INT'L VINTAGE, Dec. 2004, at 22–30 (the order for scoring of all sixteen chardonnays was U.S., U.S., New Zealand, France, France, Australia, South Africa, France, U.S., Italy, France, Australia, Italy, France, France, France); *see also* Roger Morris, *California Sparkle*, SAVEUR, Mar. 2003, at 27 (explaining that in blind taste tests of Napa Valley J. Schram

Even as to the Champagne district, there is increasing evidence that other regions of the world can produce "convincing copies"[355] and "true rival(s)"[356] of Champagne's sparkling wines.[357]

One possibility remains: that there really is a difference in taste but that this difference can only be detected by the few: that the *Pont L'Eveque* cheese really does have characteristics that are not reproducible or, *at least*, have not yet been fully reproduced. While these characteristics may be discernible, they are discernible only by a very, very few people, the cognoscenti (with at least wine, these are the profound cognoscenti—because, as discussed above, the people we think are wine experts do not discern terroir differences consistently).[358] Let us call this the *discerning-few terroir narrative* and let us assume that it is absolutely true.

The discerning-few theory is, however, a thin reed on which to justify thick geographical indications law. The average American can

---

sparkling wines against "six téte-de-cuvées from Champagne," J. Schram "always finished in the top three"); Frank J. Prial, *Wines of the Times: Dodging Oak Bullets in $12 Chardonnays*, N.Y. TIMES, May 29, 2002, at F6 (describing taste test in which Californian wines and a Portugese wine placed ahead of French candidates among inexpensive chardonnays); Stimmell, *supra* note 307 (describing fourth annual "Tony Aspler Blind Taste Testing Award" in which Canadian wine buyers regularly identify and misidentify regions and types). The principle French explanation for California's victory in 1976 was that the California wines were ready to drink earlier and that, therefore, over time French wines aged better and would prevail. But the same blind taste test conducted by Spurrier ten years later produced similar results: the highest rated French red placed third behind two California wines. BARR, *supra* note 309, at 112.

355. Robinson, *supra* note 334.

356. Jonathan Ray, *American Dream: The Queen Loves it and so Do the French*, DAILY TELEGRAPH (London), Nov. 2, 2002, at 7 (reporting on Nyetimber sparkling wines from Sussex, England; made by transplanted Chicagoans, which "stunn[ed] the critics with their dazzling quality" and "came top of a blind tasting of sparkling wines in Paris—yes, Paris, France.").

357. Review after review that pits sparkling wines from Champagne against sparkling wines from other regions has the Champagne vintages generally on top, but usually with a *few* non-Champagne sparkling wines trouncing many of the Champagne products. For example, a recent taste test involved forty-four California, ninety-two Champagne wines, and four wines from other regions. *Buyline*, WINE NEWS, Dec./Jan. 2002/2003, at 89–100. One California sparkling (score 92) was only outscored by thirteen of the ninety-two Champagne wines, while nine California wines received the same score as eleven Champagne wines (88) and three California wines received the same score as eight Champagne wines (89). If one looks at the adjectives used to describe the California and Champagne wines in such reviews, there is also no significant variation. *Id.* "Pale straw hue" describes a Gloria Ferrer Sonoma County sparkler as well as a Henriot, NV Brut Souverain sparkler from Reims. *Id.* "[P]ale gold hue" describes a Korbel California "Champagne" as well as a Billecart-Salmon from the Champagne district. *Id.* Compare this with the view a few years ago. *See, e.g.*, LICHINE, *supra* note 230, at 181 ("Sparkling wines produced in other parts of the world may be good, but none will ever be Champagne—although some of them masquerade under the name.").

358. Italian winemaker Antonio Terni says that very few winemakers are actually making terroir wines and very few people have learned to taste the terroir, indicating that perhaps this is peculiar to wine. OSBORNE, *supra* note 212, at 16. One sees increasing discussion in the popular press of winemakers aiming for a "terroir wine." *See, e.g.*, Smith, *supra* note 325 (discussing Russian River Valley Pinot Noir wines, saying "[f]rom the beginning, they were *terroir*-oriented . . . .").

"hardly pass for a connoisseur of wines."[359] And she is not unlike the average Japanese, average Dutch, or average Brazilian in lack of connoisseurship across a wide range of foodstuffs. The person who can taste the *je ne sais quoi* that unifies all fortified wines from Oporto and distinguishes them from the world's other fortified wines is presumably the person who can also identify subtle differences among the tastes of *Porto* wines. The commonsensical assumption embodied in American trademark law is that a consumer who is that sophisticated is not misled by superficial similarities or immediate appearances of sameness.[360] It would be a weird model of a consumer that assumed just the opposite: that (a) she tastes the mysterious and subtle thing that unifies all fortified *Porto* wines, so much that non-Porto fortified wines are a completely different product, but (b) she is not a person who pays attention to the labeling details.

To sum up, the terroir theory is needed to justify the product-specific usurpation standard of protection presently found in TRIPS for wine and spirits that many countries would like to extend to all GIs. It is needed because phrases like "*X* style," "imitation *X*" and "*X* type" can efficiently increase consumer knowledge, *unless* X *has truly unique, consumer-desired qualities* in which case such phrases are arguably deceptive. Without the terroir theory, broad usurpation protection (as under French law) is a straightforward, additional monopoly rent penumbra attached to the otherwise legitimate purpose of a GI. Similarly, the terroir theory is needed to justify the European Union's "claw back" list in terms of "market access"—otherwise, the claw back list is also a naked monopoly rent wish list.

There is no question that soil and climate have a great impact on the production of foodstuffs, particularly those with limited processing and one central ingredient. In this regard, the concern and attention winemakers and artisanal farmers give to terroir seems completely justified; nothing here is meant to detract from that. But the lack of meaningful correlation between terroir and the GI system—whether French appellations or American AVAs—exposes the lack of any reasonable justification for granting stronger legal protection of GIs.

---

359. Taylor Wine Co. v. Bully Hill Vineyards, Inc., 569 F.2d 731, 734 (2d Cir. 1978).

360. Big Star Entm't v. NextBigStar, Inc., 105 F. Supp. 2d 185, 215–16 (S.D.N.Y. 2000) (concluding that web purchasers are less likely to be confused because the "manner in which products may be purchased on the web and the requirements imposed upon prospective buyers cannot be overlooked"); Eng'g Dynamics, Inc. v. Structural Software, 785 F. Supp. 576, 583–84 (E.D. La. 1991) (finding no confusion as to computer user interface because of technical sophistication of computer users); Michelle Brownlee, Note, *Safeguarding Style: What Protection Is Afforded to Visual Artists by the Copyright and Trademark Laws?*, 93 COLUM. L. REV. 1157, 1174 (1993) (reasoning that compared to average consumers, purchasers of fine art have considerably more expertise in discerning differences in the constituent works and would be less likely to be confused as to the origin of the works).

One potential criticism of this critique of GIs is that it overlooks that TRIPS Article 22 recognizes that protection of a GI may be justified on "reputation"[361] and that protection based only on a locality's reputation has been the basis for GI protection in Germany and forms the basis of the looser "PGI" category in the Origins Regulation. With this looser category, as one English jurist explained, "the causal link between the place of origin and the quality of the product may be a matter of reputation rather than verifiable fact,"[362] hence this entire critique of terroir is inapplicable. Indeed, this kind of "protected geographical indication" may be just a "'simple' or 'quality neutral' indication of source."[363] But this broader understanding of GIs only reinforces the overall point being made here: if the "link" between a place and a product is just a matter of reputation, then the GI functions no differently than a trademark—and there is justification neither for GI primacy over trademarks nor GI protection beyond the consumer confusion-based protection that most trademarks receive.[364]

D. OVERSELLING GIs TO EU CONSTITUENCIES AND TO DEVELOPING COUNTRIES

Those with economic interests in European geographical indications probably overstate the economic yield they would enjoy if they had complete commercial control of the word. For example, Bruno Paillard, a winemaker in the Champagne district asserts that "counterfeit" Champagne sales in the United States are "probably . . . three to four times those of 'authentic' Champagne."[365] When one looks at how few non-Champagne district sparkling wines use the word Champagne in the United States, this assertion seems reminiscent of some industry claims of losses from copyright piracy.[366]

---

361. How a "reputation . . . of the good" could be "essentially attributable to its geographical origin" without involving the good's qualities is a bit of a mystery, but technically speaking the way the Article 22 definition is constructed "goods having a certain 'reputation' but no specific quality attributable to their place of origin . . . would fulfill the TRIPS definition." DWIJEN RANGNEKAR, GEOGRAPHICAL INDICATIONS—A REVIEW OR PROPOSALS AT THE TRIPS COUNCIL: EXTENDING ARTICLE 23 TO PRODUCTS OTHER THAN WINE AND SPIRITS 16, 18 (2003), *available at* http://www.ictsd.org/pubs/ictsd_series/iprs/CS_rangnekar.pdf.

362. Consorzio del Prosciutto di Parma v. Asda Stores Limited, [2001] UKHL 7 at [8].

363. Gangjee, *supra* note 151, at 305; *see also* Friedrich-Karl Beier & Roland Knaak, *The Protection of Direct and Indirect Geographical Indications of Source in Germany and the European Community*, 25 INT'L REV. INDUS. PROP. & COPYRIGHT, 1, 2 (1994); G. Schricker, *Protection of Indications of Source, Appellations of Origin and other Geographic Designations in the Federal Republic of Germany*, 14 INT'L REV. INDUS. PROP. & COPYRIGHT 307, 308 (1998).

364. As Dev Gangjee notes, the Origins Regulation "graft[s] reputation products on to a registration system which drew its inspiration from the [*appellations d'origine*] model." Gangjee, *supra* note 151, at 308.

365. Lyn Farmer, *Abusing the C-word*, WINE NEWS, Dec./Jan. 2002/2003, at 8.

366. David Legard, *U.S. Global Piracy Losses Estimated at $9.2 Billion*, INFOWORLD, Feb. 14, 2002, *available at* http://www.infoworld.com/article/03/02/14/Hnpiracy_1.html (trade association estimate

We have only bits and pieces of empirical data. For example, we might ask what has happened since the Spanish relinquished use of Champagne and started labeling their own sparking wines *Cava*. Have Champagne district sparkling wine sales displaced Spanish sparkling wine sales in Spain? Have *Cava* sales dropped in the rest of Europe? The answer to each question looks to be no.[367] Have sales of European wines in Australia increased substantially since Australian vintners phased out use of many of Europe's cherished wine words? Apparently not.[368] But in each case, the effects of the GI-related labeling change may have been swamped by other market forces, for example rising income of Spanish consumers, increased Spanish access to the rest of the European market on entry into the European Union, the (perceived) improving quality of Australian wines, etc. We can expect that it will be hard to find examples where GI usage changed, but other significant market forces did not.

In reporting on the push for AOC designation by some apple and pear farmers in Normandy, *Le Monde* noted "the products stamped AOC could be the locomotive for new development of products from the Normandy *terroir*."[369] This is possible. Another possibility is that as the *appellations contrôlée* "space" gets more and more crowded, particularly in product categories that are rich in AOC products and in markets where consumers believe the AOC designation is important, the AOC designation simply becomes a minimum to compete. "AOC" could become de facto another bureaucratic requirement to enter a market, not a competitive advantage.

Similarly in international fora, EU officials strive to create the impression that substantially stronger GI laws will benefit countries in Africa, Asia, and Latin America. The EU argument that developing countries would benefit from substantially stronger GI law is, at best, unproven. Today's valuable geographical names are heavily concentrated in Europe and North America.[370] There are few products from

based, with some products, on assumption that every pirated copy is a lost sale).

367. Tom Carter, *Wrath of Grapes Produces Bitter French Whine*, Wash. Times, Nov. 29, 2002 ("Spain, which called its sparkling wine 'champagne' until joining the European Union, now sells more of its celebratory wine under the name of 'cava' than all the champagne from Champagne."). In fact, "Cava" seems to be having a surge in sales in northern France. *See L'Espagne effervescente en France*, Vins Mag. Winter 2002, at 16 ("[S]uccès croissant des 'cavas' (vins effervescent espagnols) dans le nord de la France.") [describing a growing success in northern France of Cava].

368. Imported sparkling wine imports have dropped recently in Australia, with only a 1% increase in red wine imports and an increase in white wine imports attributed to a shortage of domestic white wine. *Wine Sales Flat in Australia*, Wine Contact (Australian Wine and Brandy Corp.), Oct. 2002, at 2.

369. Lerosier, *supra* note 38.

370. This may be true of geographic words generally. Besides foodstuffs, consider how carmakers have used European and North American geographic names for evocative purposes in recent decades: CORDOBA, SEVILLE, BROADWAY (Renault in France), NEVADA (Renault in France), MALIBU, TAHOE, SANTE FE, YUKON, SEQUOIA, etc.

developing countries that currently have reputations with the strength of Cognac, Port, Parma ham, or Swiss chocolate.[371]

The argument that substantially stronger GI protection will benefit developing countries simply mistakes the piling up of laws for the piling up of capital investment. We want an *optimal* level of law to encourage capital formation, to promote developing world products with minimal drag from government regulation and administrative burdens. There is no evidence that stronger GI protection fills this bill. In contrast, there is at least anecdotal evidence that certification trademark law provides a legal environment in which geographical indications from developing countries can build reputational capital that can be exploited.

Some products from the developing world (tequila from Mexico, cigars from Cuba) already have reputational bases that could be further developed. However, for geographical indications to help most producers from developing countries, the same kind of initial reputational investment would be needed to build recognition of these GIs as would be needed with new trademarks. Coffee may the best example: serious coffee drinkers in North America and, more recently, Europe, would like to think they have become increasingly knowledgeable about high-end coffee producing regions (e.g., Cerrado in Brazil, San Juanillo in Costa Rica, and Yergacheffe in Ethiopia).

The oldest post-World War II development of reputational capital for a developing world GI is surely the forty year campaign by the National Federation of Coffee Growers of Colombia to convince North American coffee drinkers of the superiority of their country's coffee. Their success is measured not just by 95% of American coffee drinkers being aware that Colombia grows coffee, but also by the fact that the trademark avatar of their efforts, JUAN VALDEZ. "Juan Valdez" is a household name for 80% of Americans.[372] The Colombian coffee producers have done this successfully under certification mark law in the United States[373] and general trademark law in the European Union[374]

---

371. Admittedly, this focuses on North/South international trade and there may be significant reputational value for some geographic regions even within a developing country or a group of developing countries. For example, in Nigeria, fruits and vegetables from the region around Jos are known for their quality; in Brazil, wines from the Mendoza region of Argentina are regarded as superior to most of the local production.

372. Press Release, National Federation of Coffee Growers of Colombia, Juan Valdez Turns 40, (Sept. 14, 2000), http://www.juanvaldez.com/menu/news/Releases/Juan_Valdez_turns_40.pdf. For an online history of the Juan Valdez campaign, see National Federation of Coffee Growers, Advertising Strategy, http://www.juanvaldez.com/menu/advertising (last visited Nov. 5, 2006).

373. U.S. Trademark Registration No. 73,199,563 (filed Jan. 10, 1979) (COLOMBIAN for coffee certification mark owned by Republic of Colombia).

374. European Community Trademark No. 1185990 (filed May 26, 1999) (CAFÉ DE COLOMBIA for staple foods, light beverages, and other categories, registered to the Federación Nacional de Cafeteros de Colombia). In April 2003, the Federation also filed ECTM applications 100% CAFÉ DE COLOMBIA and JUAN VALDEZ 100% CAFÉ DE COLOMBIA.

(largely because EU law has not allowed developing countries to register EU geographical indications).

At the other extreme, coffee also provides the most recent example of the rapid reputational climb of a developing world GI, in this case, Rwandan coffee. In 2001, Rwanda's coffee crop was 100% at the lowest international grade; in 2006, 7% was sold as specialty coffee, doubling the income of 40,000 of Rwanda's 500,000 coffee farmers.[375] The specialty grade coffee sells at a 50 to 250% premium to western coffee roasters, many of whom market it as "Rwanda" coffee.[376] Thus, in the case of Rwanda (and most other coffee GIs besides Colombia), the financial investment in the regional reputations is coming from high-end coffee companies: Starbucks, Coffee Bean & Tea Leaf, Peet's Coffee & Tea, Green Mountain Coffee, Intelligentsia, etc. These companies differentiate their product from lower-end coffee through extensive promotion of geographical indications.[377] All this is happening with only the protection provided by trademark and unfair competition law.

While wealthier North Americans were becoming conditioned to purchase coffees by geographical source identification, European markets seem to lead in conditioning consumers to purchase chocolates by geographical source identification, whether from high-end chocolatiers like MICHEL CLUZIEL[378] or K-Mart-style "Monoprix" stores.[379] Godiva, perhaps the most industrial of the high-end chocolate brands, is now marketing cocoa-producing regional dark chocolates.

---

375. Laura Fraser, *Coffee, and Hope, Grow in Rwanda*, N.Y. TIMES, Aug. 6, 2006, § 3, at 1.

376. *Id.*; *see also* Laurie Goering, *A Success Story Brews in Rwanda*, CHI. TRIB., June 18, 2006, at 8; *Rwanda; USAID Funding Up By US $27 Million*, AFRICA NEWS, July 29, 2006 (quoting foreign aid representative in Rwanda as saying, "In 2000, no Specialty Coffee was exported from Rwanda. By 2005, the country was able to export 1,100 metric tons and the coffee was featured by Starbucks and Green Mountain Coffee.").

377. For example, Los Angeles-based Coffee Bean & Tea Leaf—with stores in four states and fifteen Asian and middle eastern countries—sells twenty-three unflavored coffees, of which fifteen are developing world geographical indications, either national or local (Brazil Cerrado; 100% Jamaican Blue Mountain; Java Estate; Colombia *Nariño*; Colombia; Costa Rica *La Cascada Tarrazu*; Costa Rica *La Minita Tarrazu*; Ethiopia *Yirgacheffe*; Guatemala *Antigua*; Kenya AA; Panama *Colibri Estate*; Papau New Guinea *Sigri A*; Sumatra *Mandheling*; Colombia *Nariño* Dark; and Sumatra Dark). One is a U.S. geographical indication: "Kona." *See* Press Release, The Coffee Bean & Tea Leaf Announces Inland Empire Expansion (2006), http://coffeebean.com/Inland-Empire-Expansion-W236C162.aspx; The Coffee Bean & Tea Leaf, Coffee, http://coffeebean.com/Coffees-C40.aspx (last visited Nov. 5, 2006). Vermont-based Green Mountain Coffee, principally a wholesale and catalog sale coffee company, offers eight geographical indication-based coffees, seven from the developing world and "Kona Mountain Estate." *See also* Green Mountain Coffee, Our Coffees, http://www.greenmountaincoffee.com/navDepartment.aspx?DeptName=OurCoffees (last visited Nov. 5, 2006); Peet's Coffee and Tea, http://www.peets.com/shop/coffee.asp (last visited Nov. 5, 2006).

378. Michel Cluizel markets chocolate with cocoa specified as originating in a number of locales, including Madagascar, Venezuela, and Haiti. *See* Chocolaterie Cluizel, Products, http://uk.cluizel.com/fr/The+Single+Plantation+Chocolates/5/16.html (last visited Nov. 5, 2006).

379. Monoprix "Equateur" chocolate bar. Package on file with the author and image *available at* http://www.justinhughes.net/libraries/GIs.

Again, the investment in the regional reputations is being made by companies in OECD countries. The North Americans are now following Europe in this trend with geographically-specific cocoa in chocolates marketed in high-end shops.[380]

Through years of structural prejudice in the Origins Regulation, the European Commission has inadvertently shown developing countries that an appellations system is not needed for all this investment in GI promotion. Existing laws on deceptive labeling and unfair practices appear sufficient to trigger promotion and investment by the coffee and chocolate companies. There is evidence that producers in developing countries can increase incomes by establishing geography-based reputations for quality and gaining a larger percentage of the premium retail price for their products, but there is no evidence that either process is especially aided by EU-style GI protection. Ironically, had there been any sanctions phase of the WTO's spring 2005 decision the European Commission would have been faced with a dilemma: if the European Union had argued that that lack of formal GI protection in the European Union has not really hurt U.S. and Australian products (because they could still obtain certification marks in EU member states), this would have undercut the European Union's own position that strong GI law would help developing countries in developed markets.

A final, but small point: under the French appellation concept, the stronger "designation of source" in the Origins Regulation, many if not *most* of the developing world's best known agricultural products will *not* qualify for protection. Almost *all* region-labeled coffees and chocolates would not qualify as AOCs because they are processed in developing world locations.[381] Despite being favorably mentioned by the European Commission as a GI example, the "6 million pounds of 'Antigua Coffee' ... produced around [that] region of Guatemala"[382] may not qualify for "indication of source" protection under the Origins Regulation as long as it is roasted in Seattle, Vienna, and London. Except for a few Latin American chocolatiers, high-end chocolates are also processed in developed countries. Foodstuffs grown and processed

380. *See, e.g.*, Dagoba Organic Chocolate Company, Home Page, http://www.dagobachocolate.com (last visited Nov. 5, 2006) (Ashland, Oregon company providing single source chocolates from Costa Rica, the Dominican Republic, Ecuador, and Peru); International Chocolate Company, About, http://www.chocolate4u.com/about/ (last visited Nov. 5, 2006) (Salt Lake City, Utah company providing source chocolates from the Ivory Coast and Mexico); Chocolate Santander, Home Page, http://www.chocolatesantander.com (last visited Nov. 5, 2006) (marketing Colombian "single origin" chocolates in North America); El Rey Chocolates, Wholesale Stores, http://www.chocolates-elrey.com/ wholesale.html (last visited Nov. 5, 2006) (marketing Venezuelan single source chocolates mainly to North America with a large U.S. distribution network).

381. *See* Origins Regulation, *supra* note 99, art. 2(2)(a)–(b); *see also* O'Connor, *supra* note 17, at 40.

382. *Why Do Geographical Indications Matter to Us?*, *supra* note 106, at 1.

in different regions within a single country, like some of China's most famous fermented bean curds,[383] also fall outside the stricter AOC "designation of source" definition.

This is, however, a minor point. While local processing is required for French AOC protection, it is not required for "protected geographical indication" (PGI) status under the Origins Regulation. Since a PGI enjoys the same protection as a PDO at the EU level, there is no handicap for lack of local processing. Making local processing a requirement for some monopoly-rent conferring status (as AOC labeling may be in the French market) might be justified not only on grounds of local tradition (as a needed input for the true terroir product), but simply as a means to preserve local jobs against economies of a scale that would tend to centralize processing.

V. RAMIFICATIONS AND POTENTIAL COMPROMISE IN THE DEVELOPMENT OF GEOGRAPHICAL INDICATIONS LAW

As described above, the proposals to increase international legal norms for the protection of geographical indications fall into three areas: controversies over an international registration system for GIs; the expansion of words covered by GI law through the EU demands to "re-propertize" over forty words that have become generic in much of the world; and, finally, the proposals to expand product specific "usurpation" protection that is, legal protection where there is no consumer confusion, from wine and spirit GIs to all GIs.

The European Union proposed an international GI registration system that produces binding effects in each WTO country unless that country "objects" promptly. That proposal is likely to go nowhere, if only because it is so radically different from international trademark and patent systems, in which one designates jurisdictions in which protection is sought and those jurisdictions do the actual granting of protection within their borders. This remaining Part focuses on the other two: the viability of the European Union's "re-propertization" drive and the effects of "usurpation" protection on commercial communications. As to the "claw back" list, I propose a scenario for the successful re-proprertization of "champagne," a scenario that could apply to some of the other forty-one terms. This is not a scenario that the European Commission is likely to embrace because it is lengthy and depends on private action.

Although the "claw back" list is the most blatantly aggressive effort to expand GI protection, it is the expansion of usurpation protection— legal protection of the commercial use of geographic words beyond

---

383. *See* Winnie Li, *Chinese Cheese, Wangzhihe Fermented Bean Curd*, BEIJING THIS MONTH, Aug. 2006, at 28.

consumer confusion—that poses the greater risk to disrupt efficient communication to (and among) consumers and to dampen evocative use of words that produces consumer utility. As discussed below, the EU proposal to "extend" the Article 23(1) product class usurpation standard for wines and spirits to all products may work as a stealth proposal to expand TRIPS obligations in the direction of a general usurpation standard. In other words, under that proposal, protection of Bordeaux for wine potentially might bar Pepperidge Farm's BORDEAUX cookies; once Champagne is protected for sparkling wine, some of the non-wine trademarks mentioned earlier might be at risk.

A. How to Claw Back Geographic Words

Europeans understand quite well the idea of a GI becoming generic. Camembert and Dijon mustard were declared generic by French courts decades ago, and are produced widely through the European Union and the world. The French, German, and Danish governments recently argued that "Feta" is a generic word for cheese, not an indication of Greek origin as the Greeks convincingly insisted it is.[384]

The question then becomes: if once generic, always generic? Should we be willing to allow generic words to be (re)propertized? The answer should usually be 'no,' and not by legislative fiat. But what about a situation where the private producers have been struggling to de-genericize the word? This is arguably what is happening with Champagne.

There is no question that during the nineteenth and twentieth centuries, "champagne" and its transliterations in various languages became a generic term used to describe sparkling wines. As far back as 1887, the California legislature was using "champagne" as a generic name for sparkling wine in *state statutes*.[385] The evidence of widespread generic usage, both historically and currently, is unquestionable. For example, a 1969 American title, *The Wine Book*, offered the following observation to begin its section on the Champagne district:

---

384. *See* O'Connor, *supra* note 17, at 43–44 (history of the intra-EU Feta dispute); Bernard O'Connor & Irina Kireeva, *What's in a Name? The "Feta" Cheese Saga*, 9 INT'L TRADE & L. REG. 110 (2003) (same).

385. 1887 Cal. Stat. ch. 36, § 1, pt. 47 (defining "[p]ure champagne, or sparkling wine" by natural, bottle fermentation technique). In what surely must be an irritating legal definition, California's 1934 wine regulations defined "'Champagne' [as] a light white sparkling wine identical with champagne as made in the Champagne district in France in respect to composition and basic manufacturing principle." Bronco Wine Co. v. Jolly, 95 P.3d 422, 440 n.38 (Cal. 2004) (quoting CAL. CODE REGS. tit. 17 (1936)).

> The mere word "Champagne" suggests an iridescent bubble filled with luxury, with pleasure, and with sparkling elegance. . . . The writer's pen itches with glorious epithets—but let it pause, for the word Champagne covers a vast number of wines, ranging from poor to excellent, that have nothing to do with that section of France that answers to the name Champagne.[386]

The 1973 *Webster's New Collegiate Dictionary* offers a completely generic definition of "Port" ("a fortified sweet wine of rich taste and aroma"), while defining "burgundy" and "champagne" as wines coming from those French regions or "*also*: a similar wine made elsewhere."[387] A 1971 upscale guide to California wines had no difficulty listing twenty-three California vineyards making Chablis, twenty-six making Burgundy, seven making Chianti, five making Sauternes, and a handful producing Champagne.[388] Today, Ukrainian winemakers still produce *champanskoe*[389] just as a few winemakers in California and upstate New York produce champagne,[390] Argentine winemakers produce *champaña*[391]; and at least one Brazilian winemaker offers *Champanhe Brut.*[392]

The situation of the word "champagne" is complicated by the commonly used process description, "champagne method" or "méthode champenoise"; a technical method that can be carried out in a winery, whether in Mendoza or Alsace.[393] Because control over this phrase in the European Union is now reserved to the wine producers in the Champagne region, other EU wine producers have turned to the phrase

---

386. ALEXANDER DOROZYNSKI & BIBIANE BELL, THE WINE BOOK 111 (1969).

387. WEBSTER'S NEW COLLEGIATE DICTIONARY 147, 185 (1973). The same American dictionary gives generic definitions of "camembert" ("a soft surface-ripened cheese with a thin grayish white rind and a yellow interior"), *id.* at 159, and "bourbon" ("a whiskey distilled from a mash made up of not less than 51 percent corn plus malt and rye"), *id.* at 131. By the early twentieth century, terms like "Burgundy" and "Claret" were sufficiently generic in California that the California legislature tried to mandate California labels to say "Calclaret" or "Calburgundy." *See* 1907 Cal. Stat. 127–28.

388. ROBERT S. BLUMBERG & HURST HANNUM, THE FINE WINES OF CALIFORNIA 303–05, 309 (1971).

389. For a Kiev restaurant menu listing "champanskoe" (шампанское), see Kiev2000.com, http://kiev2000.com/poster/menu.asp?IdPart=21&Id=624 (last visited Nov. 5, 2006).

390. Among American producers who still use "Champagne" to describe their sparkling wines are Korbel (Napa and Sonoma) and André (a "bulk" processor). Farmer, *supra* note 365. One of the most highly rated California sparkling wines, Gloria Ferrer from Sonoma County, does not label the wine itself "Champagne," although the vinter still calls itself—and appears on the label as—"Gloria Ferrer Champagne Caves." *Id.* For New York producers of champagne, see DrFrankWines.com, http://www.drfrankwines.com/drf2_order.taf (follow "Chateau Frank Brut Champagne (2000)" hyperlink) (last visited Nov. 5, 2006) (discussing Chateau Frank Champagne from upstate New York); New York Wine Store, New York Vineyards, http://ny-wine.com/winerylist.htm (last visited Nov. 5, 2006) (listing upstate New York wineries, including "The Regent Champagne Cellars").

391. For an Argentine restaurant menu listing "champaña," see San Babila Ristorante, Carta de Vinos, http://www.sanbabilaristorante.com.ar/champagne.htm (last visited Nov. 5, 2006).

392. *See* Cave de Pedra, http://www.cavedepedra.com.br (follow "Pedidos" hyperlink) (last visited Nov. 5, 2006).

393. LICHINE, *supra* note 230, at 188 ("The Champagne process is the name for the traditional method of making a wine sparkle by allowing it to ferment a second time in the bottle.").

"méthode traditionnelle." In a 2001 survey of sparkling wines, *Gault-Millau*, one of France's leading gastronomic publications, described "méthode champenoise," then turned to define "méthode traditionnelle": "It conforms exactly to the méthode champenoise, step by step. Only the name was changed because of European legislation that limits the adjective 'Champagne' to that which is uniquely from Champagne."[394]

At least as recently as 1991 a French wine book described sparkling wine from Languedoc and Alsace as being made with the "méthode champenoise."[395] Many of the French-owned California wine houses continue to use the phrase "méthode champenoise"[396] to label California sparkling wine, even French vintners when unencumbered by regulation continue to identify "méthode champenoise" as a general technique.[397]

Yet the situation for "champagne" is (slowly) changing. New World winemakers are increasingly abandoning the word "champagne." For example, California's finest sparkling wines, from the Schramsberg Vineyards "are no longer labeled 'champagne,' as they were for decades."[398] But the evidence is certainly equivocal: after telling us that, the same writer christens Jamie Davis, carrying on the Schramsberg sparkling wine tradition she and her late husband started, as "Napa Valley's own 'champagne widow.'"[399] For example, a December 2002 *New York Times* survey of sparkling wines from the Champagne district wrote, "[o]nce it was common to use Champagne on wines made anywhere from California to Crimea, but the European Union cracked

---

394. Anselme Selosse, *Ces vins qui bullent . . .*, GAULT-MILLAU, Dec.2001/Jan.2002, at 65, 67. Books printed for the EU market continue to define the process as *méthode champenoise*. *See, e.g.*, ALLEN, *supra* note 34, at 101 (sparkling wines in Australia, the U.S., and New Zealand made "using the so-called *méthode champenoise*, or 'Champagne method'").

395. GARDAN, *supra* note 211, at 76, 101 (describing *La Blanquette de Limoux* from Languedoc as "[c]es raisins sont suffisamment acides pour subir les manipulations de la méthode champenoise" [these grapes are sufficiently acidic to submit to the manipulations of the champagne method]; and *Crémant d'Alsace* as "élaboré selon la méthode champenoise" [made according to the champagne method]).

396. Farmer, *supra* note 365.

397. The "Méthode Champenoise" or "Méthode Traditionelle" introduces carbonation to the champagne through a second fermentation in the bottle (after a first round of fermentaiton in a vat or tank), sugar and yeast are added to the bottle along with a small plastic device called a "bidule." *See* Domaine Chandon, Artisan Winemaking, http://www.chandon.com/vineyards/artisan.html (last visited Nov. 5, 2006). The bottles are then subjected to "riddling," a process whereby they are rotated several times a day while being slowly elevated. *Id.* Once the riddling is complete, the sediment is allowed to settle and it is removed from the bottle in a process known as disgorging. *Id.* The result is a sparkling wine. *Id.* This process can be contrasted with the non-traditional method whereby carbon dioxide is simply passed through the wine to create the sparkling effect. *See* Dave Zuchowski, *Make Your Holidays Sparkle: Tiny Bubbles Help Make Pennsylvania Champagne a Festive Holiday Beverage*, PA. WINE & WINERIES, Oct. 28, 2003, http://pennsylvaniawine.com/news/news_article1.asp?articleID=60.

398. Morris, *supra* note 354, at 26.

399. *Id.* at 25.

down."[400] A restaurant critic in the same month wrote, "in the American wine industry, Champagne is almost a generic term for sparkling wine, much like we call any photocopy a Xerox, or facial tissue a Kleenex."[401] In fact, the term is even used to refer to beverages that are not sparkling wine at all: Miller Highlife refers to itself as the "Champagne of Beers"[402] and Brazilian soft drink ANTARTICA Guarana also calls itself champagne.[403]

It seems fair to say that we are in a gray period when the meaning of "champagne" appears to be shifting. Exemplary of this is some 2002 commentary by Jay McInerney, novelist and wine columnist for *House and Garden*.[404] McInerney has no question in his own mind about the meaning of "Champagne," but he clearly does not expect his readers to be as discriminating.[405] After describing champagne as "one of the most potent and venerable of all luxury brands—a universal synecdoche for the good life," he adds, "[b]y *champagne*, of course, we mean the sparkling wine produced in the Champagne region of north-central France."[406]

Even in France there are frequent echoes of the word's generic meaning. When a leading gastronomic publication ran a series of "Champagne" articles at the beginning of 2002, the second article was about sparkling wines from other regions and countries. Entitled *Ces vins qui bullent . . .* ("The wines that bubble . . . "), the editors printed "Champagne" in large letters at the top of each page, although the article was expressly about sparkling wines *not* from the Champagne district.[407]

At the same time, producers in the Champagne region have been working to re-propertize "Champagne." A 2003 advertising campaign was launched in English language publications to convince high-end consumers that "Champagne" designates only sparkling wines from the Champagne district. In one version, the advertisement asks "Alaskan Salmon From Florida?," then educates readers that if the sparkling wine

---

400. Frank J. Prial, *The Wine Panel Sips Champagnes for $40 or Less*, N.Y. TIMES, Dec. 11, 2002, at F1. The article continues on to describe the EU crackdown on "champagne" and "*méthode champenoise*" as "an understandable but slightly holier-than-thou attitude." *Id.*

401. Farmer, *supra* note 365, at 8 ("Yet its casual usage really riles the French, even more than labels such as Gallo's Hearty Burgundy and Almaden's Golden Sauterne.").

402. Miller   High   Life,   About   High   Life: The   Beer, http://www.millerhighlife.com/Millerhighlife/default.aspx (verify age, then follow the "About High Life" hyperlink) (last visited Nov. 5, 2006).

403. *See*   Soda   Pop   Stop,   Antarctica   Guarana   Champagne, http://www.sodapopstop.com/products/detail.cfm?link=340 (last visited Nov. 5, 2006).

404. MCINERNEY, *supra* note 241, at 61 (emphasis in original).

405. *Id.*

406. *Id.*

407. Selosse, *supra* note 394, at 68. The writers and editorial staff demonstrated, in other subtle ways, their view of control of the word "Champagne" including praising an Alsatian wine as better than one from Champagne ("il étonne plus d'un champenois"). *Id.* at 67.

"[is] not from Champagne, it's simply not true Champagne."[408] But the ad campaign's magazine placements speak to how much work the Champagne district producers have to do: they have placed the same ad campaign in *Vanity Fair, The New Yorker, Saveur,* and *Wine Spectator.*[409] In these publications, the articles almost never mistakenly use "champagne" or "Bordeaux" or "burgundy" for non-French wines; arguably the readers of such publications are the people who should *already* be informed.

If, over time, the generic meaning of "Champagne" is suppressed, should the Champagne regional producers regain global control of the word? Students of American trademark law may immediately answer that a word once generic remains generic. But there are at least a few cases of generic words being successfully repropertized, including SINGER for sewing machines and GOODYEAR for rubber products.

In 1896, the U.S. Supreme Court held that SINGER had become a generic term for sewing machines,[410] yet half a century later the Fifth Circuit concluded that the Singer company had successfully "recaptured" the word from the public domain.[411] McCarthy reports at least three district court decisions going back as early as 1939 that enforced trademark rights in SINGER and, therefore, were premised on the principle that the trademark had been reclaimed from its generic status.[412] In describing the "SINGER saga," McCarthy writes, "[I]t must be recognized that SINGER has gone back to being a valid trademark only by 'educating' buyers into not using the term as the name of a class of sewing machines, but as a symbol indicating products coming only from one source."[413]

A similar story surrounded the GOODYEAR trademark. In 1888, the U.S. Supreme Court ruled that GOODYEAR RUBBER could not be appropriated by one company because the phrase described a good produced by Charles Goodyear's previously patented vulcanizing

---

408. Advertisement, Economist, Jan. 18–24, 2003, at 39, 41.

409. Advertisement, Saveur, Mar. 2003 at 19–21 ("Gulf Shrimp From Nebraska?" reads the teaser on page 19; "Champagne Not From Champagne?" reads the full page on page 21); Advertisement, Wine Spectator, Jan. 31–Feb. 28, 2003, at 137–39 ("Monterey Jack From Alaska?" reads the tag on page 137; "Champagne Not From Champagne?" reads the full page on page 139). *See generally* Press Release, Office of Champagne USA, European Winemakers Launch 'Questionable Origins' Ad Campaign Highlighting the Importance of Wine Appellations (Jan. 13, 2003) (on file with author).

410. Singer Mfg. Co. v. June Mfg. Co., 163 U.S. 169, 185 (1896).

411. Singer Mfg. Co. v. Briley, 207 F.2d 519, 522 & n.3 (5th Cir. 1953) (affirming district court conclusion that Singer "has by the constant and exclusive use of the name 'Singer' in designating sewing machines . . . and in advertising the same continuously and widely recaptured from the public domain the name 'Singer'").

412. McCarthy, *supra* note 43, § 12:31. The Fifth Circuit's decision was followed, in 1970, by a ruling by the Court of Customs and Patent Appeals ruling that SINGER had valid trademark rights in relation to sewing machines. *See* Singer Co. v. Unishops, Inc., 421 F.2d 1371, 1372 (C.C.P.A. 1970).

413. McCarthy, *supra* note 43, § 12:31.

process.[414] The Court used equivocal language, sometimes saying "Goodyear" is a descriptive term, sometimes a generic term,[415] but their doctrinal description seems to favor genericity.[416] Yet a few decades later, the Goodyear Tire & Rubber Company began an ultimately successful effort to recover GOODYEAR. In the 1965 *Goodyear Tire & Rubber v. Rosenthal* case, a Minnesota district court found that the company had (re)established secondary meaning in GOODYEAR via hundreds of millions of dollars in advertising,[417] explaining away the 1888 opinion as concerning descriptiveness only. A few years earlier, the Federal Trade Commission (at the behest of Goodyear Tire & Rubber) had forced a consent decree to make raincoat importers stop using the name GOODYEAR by itself,[418] a result premised on the word now referring, at least partially, to a particular source.[419]

The lesson of SINGER and GOODYEAR is not that *any* generic words may be propertized.[420] Each started as a proper trade name (indeed a surname), identifying a single source of goods. In each case, a trademark migrated into the generic realm and migrated back into trademark protection through consumer conditioning (advertising).[421] In

---

414. Goodyear's India Rubber Glove Mfg. Co. v. Goodyear Rubber Co., 128 U.S. 598, 604 (1888).

415. *Id.* at 603–04 ("Nor can a generic name, or a name merely descriptive of an article of trade . . . be employed as a trademark."); *id.* at 602 ("[T]he name 'Goodyear Rubber Company' is not one capable of exclusive appropriation. 'Goodyear Rubber' are terms descriptive of well-known classes of goods produced by the process known as Goodyear's invention. Names which are thus descriptive of a class of goods cannot be exclusively appropriated by any one.").

416. Rettinger v. FTC, 392 F.2d 454, 455 n.2 (2d Cir. 1968) ("[I]n 1888, the Supreme Court held 'Goodyear Rubber' to be generic and in the public domain.").

417. Goodyear Tire & Rubber Co. v. H. Rosenthal Co., 246 F. Supp 724, 727 (D. Minn. 1965) (finding that "[b]etween 1952 and 1961 the advertising expenditures of the plaintiff exceeded 230 million dollars" and was then spending more than $30 million a year on advertising); *accord* McCARTHY, *supra* note 43, § 12:30 (stating that GOODYEAR was reclaimed from the public domain).

418. *In re* Rettinger Raincoat Mfg., 53 F.T.C. 132 (1956). Rettinger subsequently entered into a consent decree with Goodyear Tire & Rubber to stop using GOODYEAR completely if and when the company succeeded in getting a court order against one of Rettinger competitors. Rettinger v. F.T.C., 392 F.2d 454, 455 (2d Cir. 1968). *But see* Goodyear Tire & Rubber v. Topps of Hartford, 247 F. Supp. 899 (D. Conn. 1965) (refusing to issue preliminary injunction against raincoat makers using GOODYEAR because secondary meaning was not established and company may have been equitably estopped from action).

419. While this is an important doctrinal difference for American trademark law, note that the standard in TRIPS Article 24(6) permit for a state to refuse trademark protection to certain words is triggered when those words are "the term[s] customary in common language as the common name for such good[s] or services" without specifying "generic," "descriptive," or any other precise doctrinal category from national trademark laws. Thus, Professor Olszak's criticism of the BATF's "semi-generic" category is misplaced. *See* OLSZAK, *supra* note 19, at 22–23. American trademark law has, for example, had a category of "highly descriptive" words that, while not being generic, have been treated as outside the potential range of trademarkable words, slogans, and symbols. *See* McCARTHY, *supra* note 43, § 12:20.

420. *See also* Harley-Davidson, Inc. v. Grottanelli, 164 F.3d 806 (2d Cir. 1999) (finding "hog" was originally generic word for large motorcycle and could not become trademark of Harley-Davidson).

421. The same may have occurred with the word "opry" in relationship to Nashville country music

this sense, American law is compatible with one French commentator's observation that "it is not impossible to think of restoring the situation by 'regenerating' the geographical meaning of a [generic] word."[422] The Singer and Goodyear stories are not so different from what wine producers in Champagne are trying to do.

The main difference between the SINGER situation and the situation with Champagne is that the wine producers of the Champagne district are playing on the international stage, where the political and economic clout of the European Union is used to persuade countries to surrender previously generic words. This is similar to when Australia agreed in a 1993 Australian-EU accord to phase out twenty-three generic wine words and allow their re-propertization by Europeans.[423]

At what point should we consider the migration of meaning adequately complete to permit re-propertization? In the *Goodyear v. Rosenthal* case, the defendant pointed to four other parties in the rubber industry that were still using the word "Goodyear."[424] The court found that these other users were not relevant to plaintiff having established secondary meaning because of the scale of the plaintiff's operations: total employment of the four firms was less than 1200 people compared to the 103,000 employed by the plaintiff.[425] We might similarly require that the Champagne district producers become the "relatively exclusive" users of the word in relation to sparkling wines.

B. "Usurpation" Protection, American Law, and Preserving Space for Evocative Uses

While the claw back list is politically unworkable because of some of its high profile entries, it is "usurpation" protection of GIs that poses the real danger for both efficient commercial communication as well as evocative and aesthetic speech in commercial communications. We will first consider how Article 23(1)'s product specific usurpation protection for wines and spirits already reduces efficient communications to consumers, and how it would further crimp commercial communications if extended in a straightforward manner to all products. Second, we will look at how the European Union's proposal for an apparently minor

---

and/or the services of the Grand Old Opry in Nashville. In 1984, an Eighth Circuit panel ruled that "opry" was a generic term for country western shows, WSM, Inc. v. Hilton, 724 F.2d 1320, 1326 (8th Cir. 1984), but eight years later a panel of the Federal Circuit held for the plaintiffs before it could prove that the term had been reclaimed from the public domain, *see* Opryland USA, Inc. v. The Great American Music Show, Inc., 970 F.2d 847, 853 (Fed. Cir. 1992); *see also* BellSouth Corp. v. White Directory Publishers, Inc., 42 F. Supp. 2d 598, 612 (M.D.N.C. 1999) (finding BellSouth failed to prove that it had reclaimed trademark status for the generic designation of the "walking fingers" logo).

422. OLSZAK, *supra* note 19, at 16.
423. *Id.* at 22.
424. Goodyear Tire & Rubber Co. v. H. Rosenthal Co., 246 F. Supp. 724, 728 (D. Minn. 1965).
425. *Id.*

change in TRIPS language might broaden usurpation protection, with possible adverse effect on both efficient communication to consumers and evocative uses of geographic words in commercial speech.

1. What Article 23(1) Does Already—and Would Do if Extended in a Straightforward Manner

In the preceding parts, I claimed that the product class usurpation protection of Article 23(1) already curtails some forms of efficient communication to consumers. Article 23(1) expressly forbids use of a protected wine GI on wine (or spirit GI on spirits) when the respective wine or spirit does not come from that place. The bar expressly extends to use of the GI word when "accompanied by expressions such as 'kind,' 'type,' 'style,' 'imitation' or the like." Presumably this also prohibits packaging that uses phrases like "fake X" or "X-like." It is helpful to think about how this Article 23(1) prohibition on different expressions has different effects *in how much it extends the GI protection beyond consumer confusion.*

For example, labeling a product as "imitation X" strongly flags the *difference* between X and the product—at least in English. No one thinks "imitation vanilla" is real vanilla, just as no one thinks an "Elvis imitator" is the King. So a prohibition on "imitation Scotch" or "fake Cognac" needs to be justified in terms other than consumer confusion, particularly because the phrases do *inform* consumers as to general product characteristics. Knowing that something is imitation vanilla or imitation Scotch tells you a great deal about the product.

Saying that something is "X-like" or "X-style" still seems to highlight that the product is not X, but less dramatically than using the word "imitation." There is no question that at least some of these phrases can convey substantial useful information to consumers. A label that says that a cheese made in Wisconsin is "Roquefort-style" efficiently tells the consumer a great deal. If Article 23(1) protection were extended to cheeses, the phrases "Stilton-style" and "Roquefort-like" cheese would be barred, however neither seems to carry much risk of consumer confusion and both could be highly informative. Similarly, "Parmeggiano-type cheese" would be prohibited. This differs from "style" because "type" might be a less familiar word thus triggering some confusion. Of course, how much confusion is engendered by each of these phrases is an empirical question that could be studied.

Measured against the TRIPS Article 22 and 23 requirements, American trademark law may turn out to be a strange creature. On the one hand, *all* famous foodstuff GIs already enjoy broader, more general dilution protection under U.S. law as long as they function as geographically-based certification marks. In other words, famous certification marks in the United States such as ROQUEFORT,

DARJEELING, and COLOMBIAN coffee, already extend well beyond consumer confusion *without* any Article 23 limitation to wines and spirits.

On the other hand, "imitation Stilton" and "Roquefort-like" are phrases that resonate with our doctrines of comparative advertising and nominative fair use of trademarks. The Ninth Circuit has described nominative fair use situations as those "where a defendant has used the plaintiff's mark to describe the plaintiff's product, *even if the defendant's ultimate goal is to describe his own product.*"[426] In other words, the heart of nominative fair use is communicating a message not very different from "Roquefort-style" cheese or "Porto-like" fortified wine. In words that aptly apply to foodstuffs, one court has noted "[i]t has repeatedly been held that one may copy the un-patented formula of another's product and may use that product's trademark in its advertising to identify the product it has copied."[427] American courts repeatedly state that comparative advertising is to be promoted and *only* curbed in the face of likelihood of confusion, such confusion usually being dissipated by phrases like "fake" or "imposter."[428] By the lights of these comments, American courts might refuse to enjoin "imitation Cognac," "fake Scotch," or perhaps "Porto-like".

The possibility that American law may be TRIPS incompatible in this respect should only heighten our concern of possible utility loss from prohibiting these "comparative" phrases. But there are at least three reasons to think the utility loss from such a prohibition might be relatively low.

First, the truth is that most GIs convey very little useful, non-geographical information. Earlier, I argued that most of the developing world's GIs do not have significant reputational capital outside their national border. This may be true for most GIs in the developed world as well. "Pont L'Eveque-style cheese" and "Jos-quality vegetables" would give little information to most consumers.[429] If it is correct that most of the world's consumers do not know most of the world's GIs, then

---

426. Cairns v. Franklin Mint Co., 292 F.3d 1139, 1151 (9th Cir. 2002). As the court noted, "[t]his is in fact the standard case of nominative fair use: Only rarely, if ever, will a defendant choose to refer to the plaintiff's product unless that reference ultimately helps to describe the defendant's own product." *Id.* at n.8; *accord* McCarthy, *supra* note 43, § 23:11.

427. Tommy Hilfiger Licensing, Inc. v. Nature Labs, LLC, 221 F. Supp. 2d 410, 423 (S.D.N.Y. 2002).

428. Calvin Klein Cosmetics Corp. v. Parfums de Coeur, Ltd., 824 F.2d 665, 668 (8th Cir. 1987) (describing that district court considered "Parfums' prominent uses of the phrase 'Designer Imposters by Parfums de Coeur' on the store display, which it found adequately cured any likely confusion as to source").

429. Jos is a city in central Nigeria and the capital of "Plateau State," one of Nigeria's six states. The Jos Plateau is known for the quality of its produce. *See* Plateaustategov.org, Natural Resources, http://www.plateaustategov.org/gov_bus/resources.html (last visited Nov. 5, 2006).

prohibiting these "comparative" phrases may not eliminate much communicative utility, with the exception of a handful of very well-known product names. The second reason to think that utility loss would be low is the experience of European countries that do not permit a wide range of comparative advertising.

The third reason to think utility loss from prohibiting these comparative phrases would be low is that American law on comparative advertising may be less solid than we commonly believe. Comparative advertising cases in the United States usually focus on advertising, not packaging.[430] How would we feel about a soft drink whose label says "A Coca-Cola style beverage," a cookie in a package that described it as an "Oreo-like snack," or a line of clothes that noted, under its own trademark, that "These clothes are made according to the Evan Picone method"? While American courts have established extensive tests and standards for the truthfulness of comparative advertising,[431] the case law has a distinct focus on advertising with little or no case law exploring whether the same standards apply to *product labeling*. It is an open question whether "A Coca-Cola style beverage" could be put on the bottle of a competitor cola and an open question whether "Cognac-like" could be put on a competitor liquor with similar characteristics. One's intuitions on these sorts of questions reflect the difficulty even trademark lawyers have in deciding what constitutes nominative fair use and what constitutes inappropriate free-riding.

2.   The Current Proposal for Full Usurpation Protection of All GIs

In the discussion above, I have characterized Article 23(1) as providing product class usurpation protection for wines and spirits. The language is quite self-limiting in scope, as it applies the added protection for any "geographical indication identifying wines" against "wines not originating in the place indicated" and for any geographical indication "identifying spirits" against "spirits not originating in the place indicated."[432] The European Union and other countries have proposed to

---

430. *See, e.g.*, Smith v. Chanel, Inc., 402 F.2d 562, 569 (9th Cir. 1968) (product, perfume, and packaging did not refer to plaintiff's CHANEL trademarks); Saxony Products, Inc. v. Guerlain, Inc., 513 F.2d 716, 723 (9th Cir. 1975) (finding "advertising banners and displays" as the source of comparative advertising). Where product packages are at issue, the main problem is usually a combination of an "X-like" claim and similarity of the trade dress. *See, e.g.*, Charles of Ritz Group, Ltd. v. Quality King Distributors, Inc., 636 F. Supp. 433, 438 (S.D.N.Y. 1986) (enjoining "the use of the phrase 'IF YOU LIKE OPIUM YOU'LL LOVE OMNI,' or its equivalent, both on their product packaging and on their promotional or advertising materials").

431. *See, e.g.*, McCarthy, *supra* note 43, § 27:59.

432. In other words, it does not even apply the added protection *across* wines and spirits. If a Japanese company labeled a Japanese whiskey "Scotch-like," that would violate 23(1), but if they labeled a soft drink or a *wine* as "Scotch-like," there would be no 23(1) violation. It's hard to imagine why a company would do this and, if confusion resulted, there could be an independent violation of the Article 22 violation.

"extend" this protection to all GIs with the following language:

> Article 23: Additional Protection for Geographical Indications ~~for Wines and Spirits~~
>
> 1. Each Member shall provide the legal means for interested parties to prevent use of a geographical indication identifying goods ~~wines for wines not originating in the place indicated by the geographical indication in question or identifying spirits for spirits~~ for such goods not originating in the place indicated by the geographical indication in question, even where the true origin of the goods is indicated or the geographical indication is used in translation or accompanied by expressions such as "kind", "type", "style", "imitation" or the like.

The problem with this proposal is immediately apparent: "goods" and "such goods" may create a broader range of protection. Does GI protection of a wine render other alcoholic beverages as "such goods"? Does a GI for chocolate extend to chocolates? To cocoa-based desserts? To all sweets? Could "such goods" just be foodstuffs generally?[433]

Under a broad reading of this language, problems could arise, particularly if more and more countries took the EU message at face value and started declaring their own geographic terms to be protectable geographical indications. Many existing marketing practices and trademarks would be at risk, particularly those that produce consumer utility through evocative and aesthetic use of geographic words.

Consider some common uses of geographic words on products that are unquestionably evocative (because the only other alternative would be *deceptive*). In the Paris market, there are "artisanal" chocolates called *palets mexicains*, made in Nemours, about eighty kilometers from Paris. Then there is the Swiss chocolate maker Lindt, which offers boxes of chocolate selections called *Versailles*, *Pyrhennees*, and *Champs-Elysées*, all made in France, but at none of these locations. Brazil's domestic confections industry produces a vast array of good chocolates under the KOPENHAGEN brand (as well as various nuts sold under "The Nutty Bavarian" mark).[434] In South Africa, there is a TEX brand chocolate bar marketed by Nestlé, presumably to evoke how big the candy bar is.

Because cocoa is produced in a dozen countries and chocolates are made in scores of countries, if GIs (defined by the looser of Origins Regulations standards) were protected against "such goods" usurpation, any of these product names would be at risk. The manufacture of biscuits

---

433. Obviously this problem could be avoided by more careful language, i.e., it would be better to specify more expressly that this is product-class usurpation. In other words, the added protection extended should be only to geographical indication identifying a particular class of products against products in that same particular class of products.

434. For the "Kopehangen" homepage, see Kopenhagen, http://www.kopenhagen.com.br (last visited Nov. 5, 2006). For "The Nutty Bavarian" homepage, see Nutty Bavarian, http://www.nuttybavarian.com.br (last visited Nov. 5, 2006).

and cookies is even more ubiquitous, that is, virtually all place names could become GIs for this category of goods, thereby putting dozens of existing products at risk—whether it is Swiss-made JAPONAIS and FLORENTINS cookies, Malaysian-made LAUSANNE cookies, Brazilian-made CHAMPAHNE biscuits, Belgian-made BRAZIL, BIARRITZ, and CIGARE RUSSE cookies, or American-made GENEVA, BRUSSELS, and MILANO cookies.[435] These lists are the tip of the marketing and trademark iceberg in which geographic names are used for evocative and aesthetic purposes. And yet there seems to be no awareness at all on the part of strong GI advocates of this problem.

Conclusion

The battle over certain geographic words has been long and persistent. World War I was fought over Champagne, both literally—as in the bombardment of the cathedral at Rheims—and grammatically. Pursuant to the Treaty of Versailles, Germany surrendered to France the lands of Alsace-Lorraine and the words "Champagne" and "Cognac."[436] A century ago, Perrier had no problem advertising itself in Germany and France as "the champagne of mineral waters,"[437] but that same practice now would land Source Perrier on the docket anywhere in the European Union.

It is easy to understand the economic and political motives behind EU proposals to "claw back" valuable words that have become generic like "Gorgonzola" and "Chablis." As with the proposals to give protection against "usurpation" to all GIs, the goal is to secure wider, more extensive monopoly rents to the European Union's *agroalimentaire* industries. The European Union promotes these proposals as something that would benefit developing countries, but that mistakes the piling up of intellectual property laws for the piling up of investments. Investment in the reputation of developing country GIs—coffees, teas, and chocolates—is already happening, as quickly, if not more quickly, under certification law regimes.

While GI advocates usually want to distinguish GIs from

---

435. For American-made "Milano" cookies see Pepperidge Farm, Indulgent Treats: Cookies, http://www.pepperidgefarm.com/indulgent_treats_cookies.asp (for Geneva and Brussels cookies, on same page click menu bar titled "You'll love them all . . . ") (last visited Nov. 5, 2006).

436. "The appellations 'Sekt' and 'Weinbrand' became part of German commercial practice toward the beginning of this century . . . . They were originally parallel appellations to those of 'Champagner' and 'Kognak' for which they were, moreover, substituted in 1923, as from that date these two names ceased to be generic appellations and became registered designations of origin limited to French products." Case 12/74, Comm'n v. Germany, 1975 E.C.R. 181, 186. (explanation of German government). According to Olszak, the need in France to define some appellations was "urgent" because of the French desire to include these provisions in the Treaty of Versailles. *See* OLSZAK, *supra* note 19, at 8, 21.

437. OLSZAK, *supra* note 19, at 19 (describing marketing in Germany).

trademarks, the two legal tools share a common arc: each concept begins with efficient communication of information to consumers and, then, turns quickly into a system of myth maintenance and the extraction of monopoly rents from those myths. GI law does this through the notion of "terroir," a claim that geographically unique conditions cause unique products. But we have no convincing evidence of how the terroir inputs work, no convincing evidence that consumers can detect the allegedly unique outputs, and plenty of evidence that the geological and climatic factors that are important to artisanal food production do not line up with the appellations that have been created.

There is no justification for strengthening and extending the GI system beyond its present confines. Such an extension would hurt descriptive uses of geographic words, that is, uses which increase consumer welfare by informing us about non-geographic product characteristics. Perhaps most importantly, such extension would also hurt evocative and aesthetic uses of geographic words—the uses which increase consumer welfare by entertaining, pleasing, and charming us.

[6]

Volume 10 Number 1 2009/p. 36-49 esteyjournal.com

The Estey Centre Journal of
International Law and Trade Policy

The Nature and Function of Geographical Indications in Law

Erik W. Ibele

Attorney, Neider & Boucher, S.C., Madison, Wisconsin, USA, Adjunct Professor of Law, University of Wisconsin Law School

There are two basic types of legal regime for the protection of geographical indications (GIs). Some systems, notably that of the European Union, define and treat GIs as a distinct type of intellectual property. This approach is also reflected in the provisions concerning GIs in the Agreement on Trade-Related Aspects of Intellectual Property Rights (TRIPS Agreement). Other legal systems, notably those of Australia, Canada and the United States, treat GIs as a subcategory of trademarks. Like trademarks, GIs function principally as a means of providing information to consumers. EU legislation and jurisprudence, however, define GIs more expansively than do trademark-based legal systems, and see GIs as in some ways superior to trademarks. The EU is attempting to incorporate other features of its system of GI protection into the WTO/TRIPS system. But the nature of GIs is somewhat at odds with that of other types of intellectual property.

Keywords: geographical indications, intellectual property, Origin Regulation, trademarks, TRIPS, WTO

Editorial Office: 410 22ⁿᵈ St. E., Suite 820, Saskatoon, SK, Canada, S7K 5T6.
Phone (306) 244-4800; Fax (306) 244-7839; email: kerr.w@esteycentre.com

E. Ibele

Introduction

International protection of geographical indications and proposals to strengthen such protection have been among the principal topics of debate in the current round of World Trade Organization negotiations. The Doha Ministerial Declaration of 14 November 2001 states the ministers' agreement to negotiate the establishment of a multilateral system of notification and registration of geographical indications (GIs) for wines and spirits. As part of the Doha Round, the Council for the Agreement on Trade-Related Aspects of Intellectual Property Rights (TRIPS) has discussed extending the protection of TRIPS Article 23 for GIs for wine and spirits to other products. A third issue regards the proposal by the EU to restore GI protection on an international basis to a number of product names that are used by producers with no connection to the geographical area of the name, i.e., which have come to be understood in some countries as names for general kinds or types of products and which have therefore lost their geographical significance. The "claw-back" of such terms for the exclusive use of European producers is adamantly opposed by longtime non-European producers of products such as port and sherry.

The issue of protection for GIs cuts across the North-South/developed country–developing country division that has characterized debate on other issues concerning the international protection of intellectual property. One such division separates countries and regions whose laws and regulatory systems/procedures treat GIs as *sui generis*, a distinct category of industrial or intellectual property separate from trademarks, which GIs closely resemble, and those whose legal systems treat GIs as a subset of trademarks. Issues of GI protection also divide, on the one hand, countries or regions such as the EU that claim a multitude of geographical or geographically suggestive names and other identifiers for products linked to such places by long-standing traditions, methods and ingredients of cultivation and production, and on the other hand countries and regions with few such claims. Countries such as Australia, Canada and the United States have generally been skeptical of, if not opposed to, significant strengthening of international GI protection.

As with most international trade issues, the discussions regarding GIs have an economic background. From the perspective of producers and governments, GIs are a potential marketing tool. A geographical indication links the attributes of a product to its particular place of origin; the association created in the mind of the consumer may add value to products such as wine, spirits, agricultural products, cheeses and other foods. A number of recent studies claim to confirm and quantify the price premia associated with certain products marketed under GIs. One such study found that certain regional designations for Bordeaux wines commanded substantial price premia.[1] Another study found that wines with a "Napa Valley" designation were

E. Ibele

priced 61 percent higher than wines with a "California" designation.[2] Given such survey evidence, and in view of the phenomenon of an expanding global middle class with increasingly sophisticated tastes, the interest in strengthening international protection for GIs is not surprising.

By law, the beneficiaries of a GI, like the owner of a trademark, have the exclusive right to use it. GIs, like trademarks and other types of intellectual property, thus essentially confer monopoly rights on their users. This monopoly right is granted by law, and the determination whether a term is a GI and the processes of registering a GI and defending it from infringement or challenging its existence occur in a legal context. To appreciate the current debate, it is therefore essential to understand the **legal** nature and function of GIs, i.e., what, according to law, GIs **are**, and what they **do**.

The Territorial Nature of IP Law

The TRIPS Agreement establishes international criteria for the definition and protection of GIs. This treatment is an exception to the basically territorial nature of intellectual property (IP) law. Several international treaties, for example, the Paris Convention and the Madrid and Lisbon agreements, establish criteria for the international treatment of certain IP elements, or limited aspects of such elements. The influence of these agreements has been limited by both the scope of the agreements themselves and the fact that few countries have signed them. There are also numerous bilateral and multilateral trade agreements and treaties of friendship, commerce and navigation that touch on IP issues. However, IP rights are still primarily a matter of national and, in some cases, regional law. The definitions of the various types of IP, including GIs, the administrative requirements for registration and the nature and extent of substantive IP rights are first and foremost the subject of national law. Registering a patent, copyright or trademark internationally thus requires applying to register it on a country-by-country basis. Likewise, defending IP rights against infringement or challenging others' claims to IP protection requires bringing and pursuing claims under national law.

The TRIPS Agreement sets forth an explicit definition of GIs and establishes comprehensive minimum levels of GI protection. A number of countries have enacted national legislation incorporating the TRIPS definitions of GIs and the levels of protection mandated by TRIPS. The TRIPS Agreement may well achieve the recognition and protection of GIs on an international level that previous agreements failed to achieve. Even the TRIPS Agreement however, leaves the actual implementation of the protection mandated by it up to the WTO members, according to their national laws.

E. Ibele

Terroir and GI Protection

Historically, the concept of geographical indications has been closely related to the notion of *terroir*, literally, "soil" or "terrain". The term connotes a limited geographical area, whose geology, topography, local climate, flora and other factors impart distinctive qualities to products originating there. Thus the concept of *terroir* expresses the connection between the geographical location where a food or beverage is produced and the quality or other characteristics of the product. *Terroir* may also comprehend the human element of the geographical environment, i.e., the skilled exercise of techniques and knowledge acquired, developed and handed down over generations.[3] GIs are the form of industrial property protection specific to the notion of *terroir*.

The Nature of GIs in Law
(a) Sui Generis Treatment

There are essentially two approaches to the legal definition and protection of GIs. In many countries, GIs are regarded as a type of industrial property separate and distinct from trademarks, the type of intellectual property GIs most closely resemble. Such systems establish a specific regime of recognition and protection for GIs. The EU takes this approach. The TRIPS Agreement and the EU system of GI registration and protection established by Council Regulation 510/2006 (the Origin Regulation) exemplify the *sui generis* philosophy of GI protection. Other legal systems, in particular those of Australia, Canada and the United States, address GIs as a subset of trademarks. In such systems, GIs are registered according to the same procedures that apply to trademarks, and courts essentially apply trademark principles in adjudicating disputes involving GIs.[4]

The TRIPS Agreement represents the culmination of a series of attempts to establish common approaches to the protection of IP at the international level. Among TRIPS predecessors are the Paris Convention for the Protection of Industrial Property (1883); the Madrid Agreement for the Repression of False or Deceptive Indications of Source on Goods (1891); the Stresa Convention on the Use of Appellations of Origin and Denominations of Cheeses (1951); and the Lisbon Agreement for the Protection of Appellations of Origin and their International Registration (1958). Article 2 of the Lisbon Agreement defines "appellation of origin" as follows:

> The geographical name of a country, region, or locality, which serves to designate a product originating therein, the quality and characteristics of which are due exclusively or essentially to the geographic environment, including natural and human factors.

This definition expresses the essence of the GI concept and is carried over in large part into the definitions in both the Origin Regulation and the TRIPS Agreement.

E. Ibele

Prior to the establishment of the General Agreement on Tariffs and Trade (GATT 1947), provisions regarding protection for marks of origin were sometimes included in bilateral trade agreements. Article IX(6) of the GATT 1947 contains a general obligation with respect to the protection of geographical product names:

> The contracting parties shall cooperate with each other with a view to preventing the use of trade names in such a manner as to misrepresent the true origin of a product, to the detriment of such *distinctive regional or geographical names of products* of the territory of a contracting party as are protected by its legislation. [emphasis added]

Article IX(6) of the GATT 1947 does not further define the protected terms.

The TRIPS Agreement defines and establishes minimum levels of protection for all types of intellectual property. Article 22 of the TRIPS Agreement defines GIs as follows:

> (1) Geographical indications are, for purposes of this Agreement, indications which identify a good as originating in the territory of a Member, or a region or locality in that territory, where a given quality, reputation or other characteristic of the good is essentially attributable to its geographical origin.

The TRIPS Agreement definition of GI is thus broader than "appellation of origin" as defined in the Lisbon Agreement. Under the Lisbon Agreement definition, the quality and characteristics of the goods bearing the appellation of origin are due *exclusively or essentially* to the geographic environment. The TRIPS Agreement language is not as rigorous; it is sufficient under the TRIPS Agreement definition that a given quality of the good be attributable to its place of origin. More significantly, it is not even necessary that any of the product's *unique* qualities derive from/are attributable to the product's geographic origin. If the good's reputation or some "other characteristic" is essentially attributable to the place of origin, this too qualifies for a geographical indication.

In addition, a GI need not, under the TRIPS Agreement definition, be an actual geographical place name. As long as the indicating term identifies goods as originating in the territory (or region or locality contained in such territory) of a member, it will qualify as a GI. This means that iconic symbols such as the Matterhorn or the Taj Mahal may serve as GIs for products of Switzerland or India. Traditional names that connote but do not directly state the name of a place may also serve as GIs, e.g., Basmati for rice from India, and Feta for cheese from Greece. The TRIPS Agreement GI definition is important because the TRIPS Agreement imposes positive obligations on its members to bring their individual national systems of GI registration and protection in certain respects into compliance with its provisions.

The TRIPS GI provisions are in large part the result of the historical interest of individual European countries, and subsequently the efforts of the EU, in insuring

E. Ibele

protection for GIs. The coverage of GI protection in the EU, previously limited to wines and other alcoholic beverages, was expanded in 1992 to include agricultural products and foodstuffs.[5] As a result of the WTO dispute panel decisions in cases brought by Australia (WT/DSU290) and the United States (WT/DSU 174), Regulation 2081/92 has been superseded by Council Regulation 510/2006 (the Origin Regulation). Regulation 510/2006 defines two types of geographical indications: Protected Geographical Indications (PGIs), in Article 2(1)(a), and Protected Designations of Origin (PDOs), in Article 2(1)(b). Both terms are defined as the name of a region, specific place, or, in special circumstances, a country, which is used to describe an agricultural product or foodstuff. A PDO must satisfy three criteria:

- the product must originate in that geographical area;
- the quality or characteristics of the product must be essentially or exclusively due to a particular geographical environment with its inherent natural and human factors; and
- production, processing and preparation of the product must take place in the defined geographical area.

To qualify as a PGI,

- the product must originate in the geographical area;
- a specific quality, reputation or other characteristics must be attributable to that geographic origin; and
- the production and/or process and/or preparation of the product must take place in the defined geographical area.

A PDO is thus similar to an appellation of origin, as defined in the Lisbon Agreement, in that the essence of the product *as a whole* must be attributable to its place of origin. The relationship between a PGI and the product it identifies is not as close; it is sufficient that a quality, reputation, or other characteristic of the product be attributable to the product's geographic origin. Furthermore, only one of the elements of production, processing and preparation need occur in the geographical area. Council Regulation 510/2006 also creates an exception for circumstances that implicate the requirement of Article 2(1)(a) and (b) that the product "originat[e] in the region, specific place or country." Article 2(3) provides that "where the raw materials of the products concerned come from a geographical area larger than or different from the processing area" geographical designations with respect to such products will be treated as designations of origin, as long as

- the production area of the raw materials is limited;
- special conditions for the production of the raw materials exist; and
- inspection arrangements ensure compliance with such conditions.
- Such designations must also have been recognised as designations of origin in their country of origin prior to 01 May 2004. The PDO

E. Ibele

"Prosciutto di Parma" benefits from this provision. It is produced using meat from pigs born and raised in 11 sections of central-northern Italy. On its face, a product using pig meat from outside Parma does not originate in that geographical area, as required by Article 2(1)(a) of the Origin Regulation. As with the TRIPS definition of GI, a traditional, non-geographical term that denotes a region or specific place may also be registered as a PDO or PGI.

The wording of the Origin Regulation invites expansive interpretation. Under Article 2(1)(a) and (b) of Council Regulation 510/2006, GIs are geographical names. Article 2(2) however provides that certain traditional, non-geographical terms that have come to be understood to denote a geographical place may also be GIs. This is the case, for instance, with the term "Feta" for cheese. In the Feta cases, Greek makers of Feta cheese, supported by the Greek government, brought actions to prohibit the use of the term by Danish and German producers. German courts were asked to determine whether the claim to the GI "Feta" by its Greek proprietors was in fact supported by scientific evidence of a link between the characteristics or elements of the product as set forth in the specifications required by Article 2(1), and its geographic origin. The court held that a determination of the essential or exclusive link between the product and its place of origin is not based on strict scientific criteria, but on a "global evaluation of all factors including flora, and people."[6]

(b) GI Protection as Trademarks

A number of countries, including Australia, Canada and the United States, take a fundamentally different approach to the protection of GIs. In these and other legal systems, GIs are treated as a subcategory of trademark. The U.S. Trademark Act, for example, does not specifically mention GIs at all.[7] Instead, the Trademark Act establishes two categories of marks: certification marks and collective marks. A certification mark is

... any word, name, symbol or device, or any combination thereof

(1) used by a person other than its owner, ...

(2) ... to certify regional or other origin, material, mode of manufacture, quality, accuracy, or other characteristics of such person's goods ..." (Id)

A collective mark is

... a trademark ...

(1) used by the members of a cooperative, an association, or other collective group or organization ... (Id)

GIs sought to be registered in the U.S. Patent and Trademark Office will fall into one of these categories. The Trademark Act thus does not define the essential nature of GIs as do the European Origin Regulation and the TRIPS Agreement.

E. Ibele

The Canadian Trade-marks Act, R.S.C. 1985, c.T-13, contains a similar definition of certification mark. The Trade-marks Act also defines "geographical indication" in terms similar to TRIPS Article 22; this definition is limited to wines and spirits.[8]

There is comparatively little GI jurisprudence in the trademark-based systems. The principal U.S. case regarding GI protection concerned the application by a U.S. alcoholic beverage producer to register the trademark "Canadian Mist and Cognac" in the U.S. Patent and Trademark Office (USPTO).[9] The application was opposed by the Institut National Des Appellations d'Origine and the Bureau National Interprofessionel du Cognac. The former is the agency of the French Ministry of Agriculture responsible for maintaining and protecting, both in France and internationally, the French appellations of origin system. The latter is a trade organization representing wine and spirits growers, producers and merchants from France's Cognac region. The mark "Cognac" was not registered as a trademark in the USPTO. The French opposers, however, alleged that the mark had been used in the United States since 1994 and the U.S. public associated it solely with them and their members. The name was also the subject of protections afforded by international agreements, including the 1994 Distilled Spirits Agreement between the EC and the United States, which required the United States to restrict the use of the "Cognac" designation to products of that region. The French parties sought a determination that the term was a common law certification mark, i.e., a mark not registered in the USPTO, but to which certain trademark protections nevertheless attached.

Brown-Forman argued that the term "Cognac" had become generic and that, in order for the term to be a certification mark, it was necessary to show that the purchasing public was aware that the term constituted a certification of regional origin, rather than one simply identifying brandy produced in Cognac. The USPTO decided in favor of the French opposers, finding that they in fact controlled and limited the use of the designation to brandy that met certain standards of regional origin. The decision also rejected Brown-Forman's argument that the public had to be expressly aware of the certification function performed by a certification mark in order for a term to be accepted as a certification mark. The Brown-Foreman case indicates that, in U.S. law, the essential nature of a GI is its source-indicating quality – its ability to communicate the fact that a product comes from a certain place, meets certain quality or other standards or otherwise satisfies criteria established and administered by a certifying body.

The Function of GIs in Law

G Is confer monopoly rights on those allowed to use them. If a term is recognized as a GI, producers in the relevant geographic area may use it, and those outside the area may not. Obviously, on a superficial level, the *function* of GIs, in both *sui*

E. Ibele

generis and trademark-based legal systems, is exclusionary. At a deeper level of analysis, function refers to rationale, the justification for the existence of a legal concept. The most explicit statement of the policy rationale for GIs appears in the preamble to the EU Origin Regulation, which defines GIs and establishes a system for their registration and protection. Council Regulation 510/2006 sets forth 19 recitals or statements of principle, which collectively express the policy rationale for the protection of GIs. Several of these recitals are procedural references to the mandates of prior law, or to the general necessity or desirability of a European Community approach to GI protection. Recitals (2), (3) and (4), however, express the substantive rationale for GIs:

(2) The diversification of agricultural production should be encouraged so as to achieve a better balance between supply and demand on the markets. The promotion of products having certain characteristics can be of considerable benefit to the rural economy, particularly in less-favoured or remote areas, by improving the incomes of farmers and by retaining the rural population in these areas.

(3) A constantly increasing number of consumers attach greater importance to the quality of foodstuffs in their diet rather than to quantity. This quest for specific products generates a demand for agricultural products or foodstuffs with an identifiable geographical origin.

(4) In view of the wide variety of products marketed and the abundance of product information provided, the consumer should, in order to be able to make the best choices, be given clear and succinct information regarding the product origin.

The recitals to Council Regulation 510/2006 do not stand alone; they must be read together with other expressions of legislative intent in the EC Treaty, including the general purpose to establish a common market in goods and services. Still, the recitals reflect the legislators' conception of the range of the functions performed, or which could be performed by GIs, or the advantages of GI protection, including market rationalization, rural agricultural income support and consumer information.

Despite the available rationale in the recitals to the Origin Regulation, the jurisprudence of the regulation seems to take a more cautious view of the functions of GIs. The Spreewalder Gurken case in Germany involved the definition of the geographical area within which pickle producers could use this GI. The national application to register "Spreewalder Gurken" as a PGI defined a geographical area more than double the size of the area traditionally thought of as the Spreewald. The German court raised the issue whether the enlarged definition meant that pickles bearing the GI would in fact not meet consumer expectations. The European Court of Justice (ECJ) did not express an opinion on the matter, finding instead that is was for

E. Ibele

national courts to determine the validity of an application for registration of a designation.[10] In a more recent decision, however, the ECJ held that commercial distributors outside the Italian region of Parma could not slice or package Prosciutto di Parma,[11] and that commercial distributors outside the regions authorized to use the GI "Grana Padano" could not grate such cheese.[12] The ECJ found that the Italian legislation has as its purpose to guarantee the authenticity and quality of the product, and as a result, the reputation of the protected designation of origin. The ECJ thus appeared to base its decision in part on the foodstuff quality rationale expressed in recital (3) to Regulation 510/2006.

The U.S. Trademark Act expresses the function of GIs briefly and directly. The Trademark Act's definition of "certification mark" states that such marks certify geographic origin, or satisfaction of certain standards relating to the quality of materials or mode of manufacture. The jurisprudence of non–*sui generis* systems seems to focus exclusively on the informational rationale for GIs. This is consistent with the limited definitions given GIs in national legislation. The U.S. Trademark Trial and Appeal Board's ruling in the Cognac case was based exclusively on the finding that consumers understood the term to refer to brandy produced in Cognac. The function of certification marks/GIs in U.S. law thus seems to be essentially synonymous with their nature; that is, they function as indicators of source and other information.

GIs vs. Trademarks

Both GIs and trademarks are source indicators and can, whether by their association with high-quality goods, or astute marketing, or both, add value to the products they identify. Both as a result are subject to infringement, counterfeiting and other misuse. There are fundamental differences between GIs and trademarks, however. Identifying these distinctions highlights several other aspects of the nature of GIs.

Reference. A trademark is primarily a *commercial* source indicator; it points to a product's particular manufacturer or producer. A GI, in contrast, does not identify a particular business enterprise but rather the place of origin and the special quality, reputation or other characteristic of the product that derives from the place of origin.

Ownership. Trademarks are personal property; they belong to individual enterprises. GIs in contrast are, in a sense, collectively owned by the producers who have the right to use them, due to their location in the relevant geographic area. All producers in a geographic area have the right to use the GI that denotes the area, and no one outside the area does; the transfer of a GI and its use by a producer outside the area would automatically render its use deceptive. This means that GIs cannot be licensed or otherwise transferred.

E. Ibele

Term. A trademark expires when the commercial enterprise that owns it ceases to exist, whether as the result of dissolution, merger or acquisition, or bankruptcy, unless it is transferred to a successor enterprise. A trademark can also expire if it ceases to be used in commerce for the purposes set forth in the relevant trademark law. GIs by contrast are essentially everlasting. As long as the geographic place of origin exists, with the soil, climate, flora, human knowledge and other features of the place that impart special qualities to products produced there, the GI exists.

Genericism. If one accepts the notion of the uniqueness of *terroir,* one can argue that generic use of a GI is simply not possible. The fact that products bearing certain features come only from certain places means that uses of the GI for products not from that source will therefore be deceptive.[13] Yet it is indisputable that geographic terms such as "Champagne" have in fact become generic terms for a certain type of product; this is the point of the EU's "claw-back" proposal. There is always a risk that a well-known trademark may become generic. The claw-back proposal and the separate statutory treatment of GIs in the Origin Regulation and in the TRIPS Agreement seek to exempt GIs from ever becoming generic.

Rationale. The rationale for intellectual property protection, at least in the industrialised west, is incentive-based. Patents and copyrights, and the temporary monopolies they confer, are awarded in order to encourage the invention of new products and processes and the creation of new artistic works. Trademarks are more overtly commercial; they exist to distinguish the products of particular business enterprises. Because they are also to an extent the result of human inventiveness, however, they receive similar intellectual property protection. GIs, by contrast involve much less in the way of human inventiveness, at least of the sort that the IP system seeks to reward. The derivations of most GI names themselves are lost in history. The things that make up the *terroir* – the soil, climate, flora and other elements that impart unique qualities to the products of the particular geographic region – are for the most part the products of nature. To the extent that human knowledge is an aspect of the characteristics to which the GI refers, the methods, processes, techniques and other human inputs have in most cases already existed far longer than the patent lives with which even the most generous IP laws would have rewarded their inventors. Thus, what GIs encourage is arguably not innovation and the creative spirit but the opposite; the maintenance and preservation of the unchanging relationship between the place of geographic origin and the products that derive their unique characteristics from it. This fundamental difference between the ways in which GIs and trademarks come into existence raises the question of whether or not the intellectual property system is the appropriate vehicle for the protection of GIs.

The protection accorded GIs by the EU Origin Regulation and in the TRIPS Agreement exceeds in some ways that which trademarks receive. The Origin

E. Ibele

Regulation essentially prohibits the commercial use of names or terms that are protected GIs, with respect to **any** other product. It bars, for example, any "misuse, imitation or evocation" of a registered GI in connection with an unprotected product, even where the actual origin of the product is indicated or where name of the unprotected product is qualified with terms such as "style" or "type". This provision was held to forbid the use of the GI "Champagne" in the tagline *Champagner bekommen, Sekt bezahlen* (Get champagne, pay for sparkling wine) by a German computer retailer.[14] The prohibitions of the Origin Regulation, and their interpretations in such instances, suggest that GIs are in some sense superior to trademarks. In many countries, terms that are protected GIs in the EU have instead become generic for a type or category of product. The resistance of such countries to proposals to strengthen GI protection at the international level along EU lines, and to reclaim for exclusive use by European producers terms that have long been generic, is understandable.

Conclusion

The EU Origin Regulation and the U.S. Trademarks Act represent fundamentally different legal approaches to GI protection. In *sui generis* and trademark-based systems, GIs function primarily as source indicators. The definitions of GI in the Origin Regulation and the GI provisions of the TRIPS Agreement are subject to expansive interpretation, especially with respect to the notion of geography, when linked to a quality, production process or other characteristic. In addition, GIs are a somewhat uncomfortable fit with the other elements of intellectual property, particularly trademarks, with which they most frequently come in conflict. The GI-related elements of the Doha Development Round of WTO negotiations, the EU's claw-back proposal and the responses to these proposals indicate fundamental disagreement as to certain aspects of the nature of GIs.

E. Ibele

Endnotes

1. Bombrun, Helene, and Daniel A. Sumner. 2003. What Determines the Price of Wine? AIC Issues Brief 18, University of California, Davis.

2. Landon, Stuart, and Constance E. Smith. 1998. Quality Expectations, Reputation, and Price. *Southern Economic Journal* 64(3): 628-47.

3. Broude, T. 2005. Culture, Trade and Additional Protection for Geographical Indications. *BRIDGES* September-October, no. 9: 18.

4. See O'Connor, Bernard, 2004, *The Law of Geographical Indications* (London: Cameron May), for a comprehensive country-by-country survey of the legal issues with respect to registration and protection of GIs.

5. EC Council Regulation 2082/92 on the protection of geographical indications and designations of origin for agricultural products and foodstuffs.

6. Opinion of AG Colomer in joint cases G-465-02 and G-466-02 FRG and Kingdom of Denmark v. Commission of the European Communities ("Feta II") [2005] E.C.R O paras 194-196).

7. Lanham Act (1946), 15 U.S.C. 1051, et seq. The Lanham Act defines trademark as follows: "The term 'trademark' includes any word, name symbol, or device, or any combination thereof (1) used by a person ... (2) ...to identify and distinguish his or her goods, including a unique product, from those manufactured or sold by others and to indicate the source of the goods ..." (15 U.S.C. 1127).

8. The GI definition in the Trade-marks Act is a consequence of the EU-Canada Wine Agreement, which provides for special treatment of wine and spirit GIs that are notified by one party to the other. The EU has entered into similar agreements with Australia (Agreement of 1994 between the European Community and Australia on Trade in Wine [see 94/184/EC, Council Decision of 24 January 1994, concerning the conclusion of an agreement between the European Community and Australia on trade in wine, Official Journal L 86, 31/03/1994 pp. 1-2]; a revised trade in wine agreement is to come into effect in 2008); and the United States (Agreement of 2006 between the United States of America and the European Community on Trade in Wine [Agreement between the European Community and the United States of America on trade in wine, Official Journal L 87, 24/03/2006, pp. 2-74]). Under these agreements, certain wine and spirit GIs are removed from the trademark regime of registration and protection which would otherwise apply. The EU wine agreements represent a limited concession by the non–*sui generis* countries to the idea of *sui generis* protection for certain wine and spirit GIs.

9. Institut National Des Appellations d'Origine v. Brown-Forman Corp., 47 U.S.P.Q. 2d 1875 (Trademark Tr. & App. Bd., May 29, 1998) (NO. OPPOSITION 97,417).

10. Case C-269/99.

11. Case C-108/01, Consorzio del Prosciutto di Parma v. Asda Stores Ltd., 2003 E.C.R. I-5121, I-5194.

12. Case C-469/00, Ravil S.A.R.L. v. Bellon Imp. S.A.R.L., 2003 E.C.R. I-5053, I-5119.

13. See for instance P. Roubier, Le Droit de la Propriete Industrielle, 44 TMR, 1954, p. 722; and WIPO – International Bureau, Geographical Indications and the Territoriality Principle, SCT/9/5, 11 November 2002, WIPO 9th Session, Geneva.

E. Ibele

14. Bundesgerichtshof [BGH] [Federal Court of Justice] 17 January 2002, docket no. I ZR 290/99, slop op. at 3-4 (F.R.G.), available at http://www.bundesgerichtshof.de/, translated in 2002 EUR. TRADE MARK REP. 1091, 1093-4.

Part II
Functions of GIs

A
Rural Development

[7]

Food Supply Chain Approaches:
Exploring their Role in Rural Development

Terry Marsden, Jo Banks and Gillian Bristow

The creation, operation and evolution of food supply chains are one key dimension in the new patterns of rural development now emerging (see Marsden 1998). As a result this dimension – the food chain dimension – becomes a significant building block for a new theory of rural development. This paper explores some of the key aspects of the food supply chain approach, making a direct link between theory and practice. To more fully understand the role and potential of food supply chains in the process of rural development we contend that they need to be seen in tandem with greater, empirically rich, conceptualizations which move beyond description of product flows, examining how supply chains are built, shaped and reproduced over time and space. The focus here will be upon using theoretical and conceptual parameters to understand the diverse nature of 'alternative' or 'short' supply chains and, in turn, to comment upon what these bring to a more generalized theory of rural development. Reference is made to one case study, within a broader analysis of European cases. These help to build a more rigorous theoretical framework, which places food, supply chains as a significant element in broader rural development debates.

Given that under existing market conditions there is likely to be a continued and steady withdrawal of capital from the farm and rural areas, two questions need to be addressed by rural development theory. Firstly, what are the mechanisms needed to capture new forms of value added? And secondly, how relevant is the development of short food supply chains in delivering these?

The emergence of 'short food supply chains': re-valuing foods

The development of 'alternative food chains,' or networks has attracted much attention in recent years, with a new food politics beginning to fill gaps left by conventional government regulation and with the growing public concern over the provenance and manipulation of foods. From a rural development point of view, this new resurgence of interest in 'more natural' or 'more local' (also viewed as more healthy, see Nygard and Storstad 1998) types of food comes at a critical time for the land-based production sector. It offers potential for shifting the production of food commodities out of their 'industrial mode' and to develop supply chains that

Published by Blackwell Publishers,
108 Cowley Road, Oxford OX4 1JF, UK
350 Main Street, Malden, MA02148, USA

Sociologia Ruralis, Vol 40, Number 4, October 2000
©European Society for Rural Sociology
ISSN 0038–0199

can potentially 'short-circuit' the long, complex and rationally organized industrial chains (see Marsden et al. 2000) within which a decreasing proportion of total added value in food production is captured by primary producers. For the production sector this means that through developing new quality definitions associated with locality/region or speciality and nature, new associational networks can be built (or built upon) which involve radically different types of supply chain (see Murdoch et al. 2000). Critically, these supply chains *engender different relationships with consumers* and may engage different conventions and constructions of quality (Thevenot 1998).

A key characteristic of short supply chains is their capacity to re-socialize or re-spatialize food, thereby allowing the consumer to make value-judgements about the relative desirability of foods on the basis of their own knowledge, experience, or perceived imagery. Commonly such foods are defined either by the locality or even the specific farm where they are produced; and they serve to draw upon and enhance an image of the farm and/or region as a source of quality foods. 'Short' supply chains seek to redefine the producer-consumer relation by giving clear signals as to the origin of the food product. Short supply chains are also expressions of attempts (or struggles) by producers and consumers alike to match new types of supply and demand. Notable here are the additional identifiers which link price with quality criteria and the construction of quality. A common characteristic, however, is the emphasis *upon the type of relationship between the producer and the consumer in these supply chains, and the role of this relationship in constructing value and meaning, rather than solely the type of product itself.*

The term Short Food Supply Chain (SFSC) is used in this paper as an umbrella term. We identify three main types of SFSC, all of which facilitate or enable the defining characteristics of a SFSC to exist – that being the ability to engender some form of connection between food consumer and food producer. With a SFSC it is not the number of times a product is handled or the distance over which it is ultimately transported which is necessarily critical, but the fact that the product reaches the consumer embedded with information, for example printed on packaging or communicated personally at the point of retail. It is this, which enables the consumer to confidently make connections and associations with the place/space of production, *and, potentially, the values of the people involved and the production methods employed.* The successful translation of this information allows products to be differentiated from more anonymous commodities and potentially to command a premium price if the encoded or embedded information provided to consumers is considered valuable. All SFSC operate, in part at least, on the principle that the more embedded a product becomes, the scarcer it becomes in the market. It is, for example, clear that the region of Champagne can only produce so much wine. It is important to note that any one business may be involved in supplying one or more of these different food supply chains. The three main types of SFSC we identify are:

1. *Face-to-face*: consumer purchases a product direct from the producer/processor on a face-to-face basis. Authenticity and trust are mediated through personal interaction. The Internet also now presents opportunities for a variant of face-to-face contact through on-line trading and web pages.
2. *Spatial proximity*: products are produced and retailed in the specific region (or place) of production, and consumers are made aware of the 'local' nature of the product at the point of retail.

3. *Spatially extended*: where value and meaning laden information about the place of production and those producing the food is translated to consumers who are outside of the region of production itself and who may have no personal experience of that region.

Complexity and competition

The literature on the development of 'alternative foods' is already large, although still highly fragmented and untheorized. Our focus here, which bears heavily upon agriculture-based rural development, is upon the nature of these 'supply chain relations' rather than upon the particular characteristics of the foods themselves. Types of speciality, quality, region specific, or organic foods are by no means solely the preserve of the alternative mode. Indeed, near identical products may emerge from both of these modes of food supply. This is an important distinction given the intense and highly contingent competition between the industrial and alternative modes of food supply, as well as between the different retailers and processors involved in the industrial chains. This is producing some interesting mutations with regard to supply chains. For instance, corporate retailers are now developing home deliveries through Internet ordering and exploring closer links with their local suppliers (see Guy et al. 2000). Alternatively, some of the successful speciality and alternative quality chains have extended into national and international supply links and markets (see for example the case of Parmigiano Reggiano, De Roest and Menghi 2000). This means that producer-customer interfaces are becoming, and are likely to increasingly become, more and more complex and diverse; not so much in terms of the products they supply as in terms of the types of relations and organizational features they display. *In addition, and as we shall see in the following case study, these latter associational features become key influences upon the attribution and allocation of economic value across the different actors in the supply chains.* These processes are identified as a significant research gap in recent literature (see Murdoch et al. 2000; Murdoch and Miele 1999), whereby the dominance of work on the standardized/generic model of industrial food supply is matched with a paucity of understanding about the operation of specialized and dedicated supply chains (Storper 1997).[1]

From a rural development perspective we argue that to conceptualize and parameterize these emerging social and organizational characteristics becomes a major challenge; for it is through this understanding that we can better judge the extent to which rural actors – whether they are farmers, processors or retailers – can *create additional value for rural regions*. From a survey of short supply chains in Europe we now attempt to draw out some of the key features, which help to build up an improved conceptual picture of short supply chains, and their particular role in agrarian based rural development.

The dimensions and evolution of short food supply chains

Figure 1 highlights just five of twelve case studies developed within the IMPACT research programme[2] which focus upon the reconfiguration of food supply chains and the role of these supply chains in the process of rural development. To refine

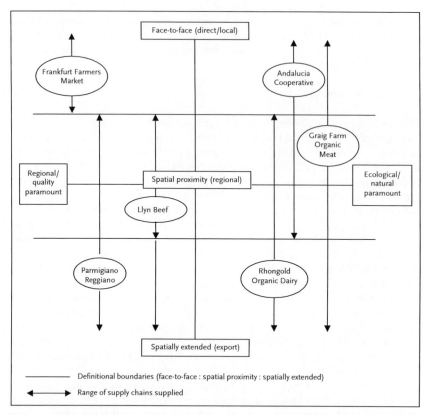

Figure 1: *Distribution of case studies according to the type of short food supply chain and the importance of ecological or regional quality criteria*

our understanding of the rural development potential of short supply chains we concentrate on their evolution and dynamic characteristics. Cases in Figure 1 range from those which derive from an ecological or regional origin to those which have been established in order to 'shorten' previous chains, or to develop alternative chains and networks which provide rural development opportunities in terms of value added. Figure 1 arranges these according to the type of short food supply chain they involve and the degree to which they focus upon an ecological or regional identity (see Table 1 for summary overviews of case studies). After analyzing all the case studies,[3] we have been able to identify some common dimensions of short food supply chains even though, as we shall see below, they are very context dependent. Nevertheless, we can begin to see some common features that help us distinguish these new and alternative patterns of rural development.

First, all of the cases are, to varying degrees, removed from the conventional chains associated with the provision of bulk food commodities to complex food chains. Second, the cases tend to display new relationships of association and institutionalization, which are located at the spatial scale of the region or locality rather than the nation. Third, the companies and actors involved in the short supply

Table 1: *Summary of impact supply chain case studies*

Frankfurt Farmers Markets (DE)	The case study 'Farmers markets in the city of Frankfurt' focuses on the establishment of short chains between producers in the Vogelsberg region and consumers in Frankfurt. Farmers are successful if they offer high quality food products and/or products with a particular regional or natural image. Also the farm households that are engaged in processing and direct marketing activities are often particularly innovative; new products are being developed and old products rediscovered.
Ecological Co-operatives in Andalusia (ES)	Farmers and consumers in Andalucia organize themselves, spurred on by a complementary generic aim: the wishes of the farmer to produce and sell ecological produce in Andalucia and the wishes of the latter to consume them at a reasonable price. Amongst the aims are the following: minimize the middlemen to assure good prices for the producers and the consumers; consumers supervise the planning and control of production to avoid fraud; promote regional production and consumption of these products; facilitate the development of local economies.
Graig Farm Organic Meat (UK)	Graig Farm is a meat processing, wholesaling, retailing and mail order business, located in mid-Wales on the border with England. The livestock used by Graig Farm are supplied by members (20) of the Graig Farm Producers Group, most of whom are based in the region. Nearly all of the products sold by Graig Farm are certified as organic.
Rhöngold Dairy (DE)	The Rhöngold case involves the establishment of a relatively large new dairy and a new product line of organic milk. Its development is linked with environmental improvements and positive socio-economic changes. The most important are the improved income prospects for dairy farmers in the region and the increased potential for the development of rural and green tourism.
Parmigiano Reggiano (IT)	The Parmigiano Reggiano production system maintains the artisanal, hence labour intensive, production techniques in cheese making, which are crucial for the final quality of the cheese. The basic formula of success is to be found in the generation of a collective agreement of the involved actors to comply with the production regulations, which differentiate the production and processing of Parmigiano Reggiano milk from milk produced and processed in industrial dairy systems.
Llyn Beef (UK)	The Llyn Beef Producer Co-operative is a registered company established in May 1997 by a group of lowland beef farmers in northwest Wales. The co-operative was established on the belief that a premium price could be secured by marketing beef produced from the area on the basis of its quality. The co-operative was also designed to enable local farmers to achieve a closer relationship with retailers and other market outlets.

chains have different relationships with the state in that they are either developing new innovations that go beyond state support, or they are resisting the negative effects of state policy. Fourth, they represent new experiments and innovations that which combine or reconfigure the natural, quality, regional and value constructions associated with food production and supply. The foods produced and supplied in this sense hold composite forms of value which go far beyond the simple commodity value form. In fact they add to this other types of value associated with natural, regional, production quality identity. Fifth, the cross section of short food supply chains examined show positive if variable value-added gains in terms of farm-level income impacts over and above those which would have been possible through the commodity-oriented mainstream 'industrial' channel. Finally, there is considerable variation in the types of associational and face-to face interactions – what Storper calls the 'interpersonal world' – which are involved in the production, 'animation' and sales of foods in these alternative short chains.

Evolutionary considerations

If such short food supply chains are able to play a significant role in the process of agrarian based rural development, it is important for us to identify and analyze any evolutionary patterns in their development. We should then question and consider their long-term impact and future potential to contribute to rural development as a genuine 'counter-movement' (Van der Ploeg et al. 2000). These questions bring us closer to an understanding of 'impacts' and the aggregation of 'little' impacts into clustered impacts – either in the region or along the supply chain. It also helps us to come to terms with the limitations and obstacles to development facing specific types of short food supply chain development.

Some food product supply chains are highly ephemeral, others endure generating long-lasting benefits to rural areas. Some supply chains remain highly localized, servicing a dedicated but small group of consumers, others expand to meet consumer demand at a national or even global scale, as has been the case with Parmigiano Reggiano, for example. Some food supply chains are highly dependent upon associational or institutional arrangements at the local, national or international level, others are less closely interwoven with socio-political structures and are the result of individualistic entrepreneurialism. We believe that there is value in examining how, why and under what conditions specific food supply chains develop. We need this for our analysis of rural development potentialities across different regions and production sectors. In so doing, we identify four key parameters of supply chain evolution. Through this categorization we argue that unlike Storper's static typology (see Figure 2) we need conceptualizations which reflect the dynamic and evolutionary nature of supply chains and the businesses they involve.

a. Temporal evolution: Reviewing the background to supply chain case studies across Europe, it was observable that two distinct periods of development had taken place. The first date from the 1950s and 1960s with case examples often receiving institutional backing and demonstrating a strong sense of regional identity. The second period began in the early 1990s, perhaps as a reaction to the crisis of the conventional agricultural system or the existence of funding and effective support structures (for example Rhöngold organic dairy, see Knickel and Renting 2000).

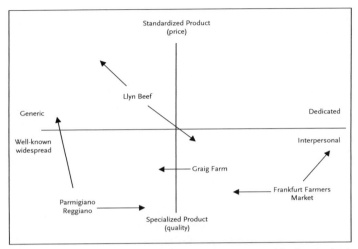

Figure 2: *Evolutionary trajectories straddling Storper's 'Four worlds of production.'*

b. Spatial evolution: Over time, the growth of demand for specific products can create conditions for the expansion (or continued viability) of certain forms of production within regions. The growth in demand for a Product of Designated Origin (PDO) may transform the economic viability of farmers in that region, especially if a high proportion of a regions productive capacity (land) is required to satisfy demand. An obvious example here is the case of Champagne in France, which is both a region and a product. Some short food supply chains will have the potential capacity to involve many farms and thereby become central to a region's agriculture. Examples here are milk production for Parmigiano Reggiano in Emilia Romagna and the champagne grape vines in Champagne. However, identifying which products are destined to capture larger markets is extremely difficult and may depend in large part upon the vagaries of the market.

c. Demand evolution: Often closely linked to spatial evolution, demand evolution encapsulates the capacity of markets and distribution channels for specific products to expand from one scale of operation to another, for example from local to regional and perhaps to international levels. Parmigiano Reggiano cheese is a good example of this process whereby a product which once had a very small level of sales outside of the region of production now because of marketing and internationalization of cuisines services a global market. Hence as short food supply chains evolve they may extend to span both generic and dedicated food markets, and may adopt 'standardized' features in product development.

Figure 2 demonstrates how different supply chain cases straddle multiple points in Storper's 'four worlds of production,' and that they do not necessarily fit neatly into simple typological frameworks. We are, after all, not talking here simply about producing nuts and bolts. We are dealing with the variable manipulation of a natural product to diversified and ever more health, quality and ecologically minded consumers. In order to maximize the potential of supply chain development, companies and agents involved may need to adopt a flexible and dynamic approach to product development and marketing, perhaps suggesting the need for a greater degree of foresight and innovation than is the case in industrialized commodity sectors. However, it may also be the case that the ability to expand (or meet) growing consumer demand does not necessarily rely upon rapid or constant product innovation or development, as is arguably the case for Parmigiano Reggiano.

d. Associational and institutional evolution: Associational interfaces (networks) are often informal but are highly significant in establishing trust, common understandings, working patterns, and forms of co-operation between different actors in a supply chain. These differ from institutional interfaces that include state regulations and the support and services offered by economic development agencies. Associational interfaces are often critical in generating and facilitating supply chain initiatives at a regional level (see Llyn case study), however, such interfaces are vulnerable to internal and externally generated disruptions. *In short, there is no inevitability that strong and mutually acceptable associational interfaces will be reproduced over time.* Furthermore, where such interfaces do not exist (or have broken down), it may take many years to rebuild relationships and trusts to a point where regional actors, or actors across a supply chain, can create the conditions necessary to effectively and efficiently meet and maximize consumer demand.

Evidence from the IMPACT programme suggests that associational interfaces are both a cause and an effect of the development of short food supply chains. Where interfaces are strong on both it usually provides a strong basis for sustainable reproduction and development over time. The case studies indicate that regional support agencies coupled with deep associational involvement and a professional form of entrepreneurship seem to be critical.

Institutional evolution may radically alter the prospects for supply chain development. For example, the decision by the state to increase support to organic food production may stimulate production and, in turn, enable both product and market development. Interestingly, many of the recent developments have occurred without significant institutional support. *The evidence would suggest that sustaining rural development through the evolution of reconfigured supply chains must be based upon both institutional support and associational development; furthermore, these relationships must alter and reconfigure over time.* Here, concerning these interactions between the farm, the institution and the associational realm, there is no one model. A key question then is the degree to which these features will need to become more widespread if aggregated rural development impacts are to be achieved, and how, if they do not exist, they might be generated? To explore these evolutionary considerations further we now present one of our case studies in more depth.

Table 2: *Average beef prices in Wales and Great Britain 1995–1997 (pence per kg)*

	Wales	UK
1995	121.55	122.96
1996	105.19	105.51
1997	95.26	96.89

Example (Wales): 600 kg cattle
December 1995: £718.08
December 1997: £548.64
Difference: £169.44

Source: Meat & Livestock Commission

The Llyn Beef Producers Co-operative

Concept and genesis: struggles of value

The Llyn Beef Producer Co-operative is a registered company which was established in May 1997 by a group of forty lowland beef farmers to market beef from the Llyn Peninsula in north-west Wales (see Figure 3). It

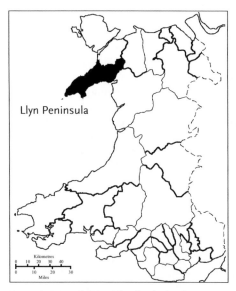

Figure 3: *Map of Wales: The Llyn Peninsula*

was established in response to the livestock crisis in Wales, which was characterized by falling prices in traditional beef commodity markets (see Table 2) and a lack of consumer confidence in the quality of the final product. The belief amongst beef farmers on the Llyn Peninsula that "something needed to be done" to secure their livelihoods[4] prompted the development of the Llyn Beef Producer Co-operative.

The Co-operative was established to try to improve the collective strength of farmers in the supply chain and thereby improve financial returns to beef farmers in the area. It was felt that a premium price could be secured by marketing the beef from the area on the basis of (I) the natural grass-based system of production, (II) the eating quality of the beef, and (III) the quality and complete traceability i.e. assurance of the origin of the product. Added value is generated by co-operation along the supply chain, supported by technical advice – particularly in matter of a new beef maturing process - and product marketing and promotion. The co-operative was also established in the belief that a closer relationship with retailers, combined with group marketing, would improve the continuity of supply and reduce the risk of retailers making unrealistic demands. Since its establishment, the co-operative has focused its efforts on securing a contract with a major wholesaler, as well as establishing premium local market outlets.

The Llyn Beef Producer Co-operative represents a response to new consumer demands for quality-assured, fully traceable, mature, lean beef of consistent eating quality. It is also a response to broader societal demands for natural methods of animal rearing, stress-free handling and transportation, and the maintenance of bio-diversity through mixed grazing, extensive management of semi-natural and unimproved grassland, and judicious use of fertilizer and animal manures. The co-operative was established on the premise that the promotion of branded Welsh beef, produced to assured standards of quality is more likely to achieve retailer and consumer support.

Evolution over time and space

Sales of Llyn Beef to local markets began with 2–3 cattle per week to an outlet through the local abattoir, Cwmni Cig Arfon, in May 1997. This quickly expanded to 6–10 cattle a week four months later. In the summer of 1998, the Llyn Beef Co-operative attracted the attention of Livestock Marketing Limited, an organization established to create marketing opportunities for farmers by setting up farmers groups to supply retail outlets. Livestock Marketing Limited subsequently acted as a facilitator for the development and expansion of the Llyn Beef Co-operative. They did this by putting the farmers in contact with both Booker Plc, the largest Cash and Carry operator in the UK, who were looking for a supply of quality, mature Welsh beef, and with the Agricultural Development and Advisory Service (ADAS), who were operating a project in support of quality Welsh beef production.

By September 1999 the Llyn Beef Producer Co-operative had around 100 members, accounting for 98 per cent of beef farmers in the area, with seven farmers acting as company directors. Farmers are required to pay a membership fee to join the scheme and must also sign up to a range of provenance, quality assurance and contractual specifications. The beef produced under these specifications is marketed as 'Extra Mature Welsh Beef' for the wholesale contract with Booker, and as 'Llyn Beef' for local butchers and the domestic, Welsh catering trade. The main difference in the specifications required to supply these two separate supply chains relate to the provenance and are set out in Table 3.

Table 3: *Specifications related to provenance for Llyn beef producers*

Extra Mature Welsh Beef	Llyn Beef
Steers & heifers born & bred in Wales	Only three-quarter bred cattle are accepted through the scheme, having spent all their lives on 'Llyn beef' farms
No more than 3 movements allowed on the cattle's passport	No more than two different addresses to be on the animals passport. The second owner may buy the cattle in any livestock market or on any farms in Wales
Cattle must have spent the last 90 days on a 'Llyn beef' members farm	All the cattle must be accompanied by a passport bearing a Welsh address

Source: Llyn Beef Producers Co-operative

The supply chain works as follows. Farmers pre-book their cattle with Farmers Marts Limited (the local auctioneer/livestock market), which acts as a procurement agent when supplying to Cwmni Cig Arfon (the abattoir). Although stock goes directly from the farm to the abattoir, grades and weights come back via Farmers Marts Ltd who undertake to pay farmers within one week. The majority of cattle currently traded through the Llyn co-operative fall into the 'Extra Mature Welsh Beef' category and are sold through Booker Plc. Only a small proportion of Llyn beef cattle – about six to eight per week – fall into the 'Llyn Beef' category for sale to local butchers, caterers and restaurants. As with the Extra Mature Welsh Beef, cattle for the production of Llyn Beef are procured through the livestock market but handled directly by the abattoir. The meat is sent out from the abattoir either in primal form (vacuum packed) or on the bone, depending on the butcher's particular preference.

Outlets are mainly in the Llyn area, although hotels further afield have begun to express an interest in stocking the product for their menus. The major selling point locally is that beef supplied in this way comes from cattle that have not left the area. This is supported by an approach that requires traceability and therefore traceability cards accompany Llyn Beef at points of sale. These cards detail the farmers name, the name of the butcher or other outlets, the length of maturation of the beef, the tag number of the animal and the carcass number. The local LEADER II group has been instrumental in both finding local retail outlets for Llyn Beef and providing financial support for the development of customer profiles and publicity and point-of-sale materials. Promotion materials make strong identification with the Llyn area, but also deliberately make use of Welsh farm-assured labels for generic marketing purposes.

The whole venture has, therefore, been based upon the development of new networks of co-operation along the beef supply chain. As a representative of Livestock Marketing Limited explained, "A number of initiatives taking place around the same time were brought together to form a model of co-operation, from primary producer to consumer, backed up by technical advice and promotion." The benefits of co-operation are felt along the supply chain (see below). According to one of the Llyn Beef farmers, "we have faced one or two difficulties along the way, but these have been overcome through the commitment of all the partners involved, and this is what has enabled us to expand. Farmers are benefiting from co-operation with one another and getting together. We have realized that we need to co-operate to survive and also to handle bulk." The Fresh Meat Controller at Booker Plc has also emphasized the benefits of co-operation: "Our customers are delighted with this product. The key has been the success we have had in developing close relationships, mutual trust and co-operation with our Welsh partners. I am convinced that there is a direct relationship between the level of co-operation and the quality of the end product."

Assessing the socio-economic impact

Table 4 illustrates that the difference between gross margins on Llyn beef farms and traditional lowland beef producers is chiefly caused by the premium price received on the final product. In other words, while costs are relatively similar, the value of output produced is significantly higher.

Table 4: *Comparison of gross margins: extra value added*

	Average from sample of Llyn beef farms (£ per head)	Traditional grass-finishing lowland beef production (average performance) (£ per head)
Output	108	84
Gross margin per head	64	37

The extra value added from Llyn beef farms can be calculated as the difference between the gross margins – £ per head of cattle - in this case £27.[5] The extra value added per farm equals the difference in gross margins per head of cattle multiplied by average size of Llyn beef herds, which equates to £5,670 per farm or £27 multiplied by 210 cattle. Multiplying this figure by the total number of farms on the Llyn involved in the Co-operative gives an indication of the total extra value added to farming in the region (£5,670 times 100 farms) of £567,000. The farmers themselves support these estimates. One farmer stated that "for a farm of my size I can secure a premium worth an extra £5,000. That is a significant mark-up on the price that could be secured elsewhere." It is also worth observing that a premium of £5,000 is very significant in the context of current beef farm incomes in Wales.

As well as the extra value-added created on Llyn beef farms, the Cig Arfon abat-toir benefits from the extra trade generated by the contract with Booker Plc. This is estimated at £2.22 million. The abattoir also estimates that sales under this con-tract could increase by a further 20% in the medium-term, indicating that there is potential for the impact of the Llyn Beef venture to increase in the future.

Overall impact : towards an evolutionary approach

Clearly the Llyn Beef case is a recent example of the development of short food supply chains prompted by the severe crisis and cost-price squeeze on the British livestock industry. It is a particularly successful case, based upon a somewhat unusual degree of co-operation between producers who do not have a tradition in this regard. The case demonstrates how significant amounts of value added have been generated at the farm level by the initiative, and that new supply chains can be successfully created, even by groups of formerly 'powerless' producers operating in the mass industrial food system. In addition, it is clear that the venture can only be sustained by encompassing other networks of actors who can assist in innovation and support and recognize new quality conventions. The case demonstrates that *synergies on the farm* through the development of economies of scope and reduc-tions in opportunity costs need to be complemented by *synergies both between farms and with the other actors in the food supply chains*. In reality two new short supply chains have been created, based on slightly different rearing and processing condi-tions, and serving different types of customers. This represents a sophisticated type of new product specialization operating in these new supply chains. This level of organizational innovation is surprising given the traditionally recognized low base level of innovation and room for manoeuvre associated with the mass industrial chains upon which the Llyn farmers were previously reliant.

The case also shows how the corporate retailing and catering sectors are also increasingly aware of the need to develop value added and 'knowledge-added' lines for their customers, supporting consumers' perception of quality. In Storper's ter-minology, this represents the development of more *dedicated* marketing based upon more specialized rather than standardized products. This can only be done, how-ever, through the emergence and evolution of new organizational structures such as the Cwmni Cig Arfon abattoir and the Farmers Marts developments *as well as* the development of new co-operative activity between the producers themselves. The development of these short supply chains is, therefore, anything but simple. It requires the building of new socio-economic relationships that operate in different spatial frameworks – in the case of Llyn beef the Llyn peninsular. Here we can see how new equations between space, nature, quality value and product come together. This does not happen automatically. It demands carefully organized action and association, which create and then *maintain* the new synergies. For them to come together elsewhere, it is likely that they would need to be reconfigured, even if there are some relevant common principles.

Clearly, the evolutionary, space-time and synergy processes involved in this case are highly specific. This is so because in such new rural development initiatives, uniqueness and distinctiveness at the place of production needs to be matched and articulated forward through to the point of consumption. The resulting supply chain relations are like unique 'forks of lightening'; they occur intensely across spaces in one vector, but by definition they are difficult to replicate in identical form elsewhere. This does not stop other groups of producers, processors or development agencies attempting to replicate the success of Llyn Beef. It does mean, however, that they will have to forge distinctive relationships and different natural and local equations with different sets of food supply chain agents including retailers and abattoirs. This suggests that as far as short food supply chains are concerned, their role in creating new forms of rural development will be to increase the distinctiveness of space and diversified agricultural relations.

Conclusion: overcoming the inherent constraints

Whilst we can see that the farm-based and local impacts of short food supply chain developments may be positive in terms of value added, what is less clear is the degree to which such rural development initiatives can be *sustained and developed both over time and space*. For this to occur we need to progress theoretically the concept of *rural development clustering*; that is, the degree to which initiatives such as Llyn Beef can be built upon through the growth of farmers' capacity to interface with other supply chain agents over time and space. This will only occur if other producers develop distinctive approaches that are partly and variably associated with the use and identity of rural space and nature in new and innovative ways. In this sense we face one of the significant paradoxes of the new rural development paradigm. *How can clusters of rural development initiatives collectively make a major spatial impact when they are all- by definition- dependent upon a distinctive evolutionary trajectory?* Unlike the old CAP-driven agro-industrial system, there are few guarantees for producers. To succeed, participants in new short food supply chains need to rely heavily upon their own knowledge and networking abilities as the Llyn case clearly testifies.

The development of short food supply chains also presents challenges to those institutions and agencies charged with supporting economic and social regeneration in rural areas. The opportunities and potential to develop local speciality products needs to be balanced against regional strategic considerations associated with more generic marketing and promotion. This is particularly significant where the value-adding potential of sub-regional identities lose their impact in export markets, and may hamper the ability to effectively supply and promote generic regional labels such as Welsh Beef rather than Llyn Beef. The wider economic region (Wales) must effectively compete in major markets, such as the United Kingdom and the European Union. Quality products should carry appropriate branding, avoiding too many sub-regional initiatives which may both intensify competition in domestic markets bringing prices down at the farm gate, and fail to engender the co-operation and co-ordination required to service major export markets.

Inside these sets of relationships identified here – and a major driving force behind their level of success – are the power struggles operating in the development of new food supply chains. Theoretically, we need to begin to assess how local ecologies, social relations, and forms of evaluation become implicated in differing production systems. Our analysis here demonstrates the significance of bringing together at least four types of evolution: temporal, spatial, demand and associational or institutional. From there we can start to specify what the most likely rural development potential generating relationships between production process and place will be. It will also enable us to question how the local social and natural resources of a particular place come to be incorporated into networks of food supply chains that were previously dominated by the industrial and commercial modes of evaluation.

In particular, we can assess how struggles around new definitions of quality can empower local producers, such that they can develop sustained levels of value from production of food products. The development of new supply chain relationships is a key mode of rural development through which this can be achieved. However it is also one that suggests a heterogeneous and diverse set of rural development outcomes rather than a clearly generalizable model of convergent spatial development.

Notes

1. As a starting point here we adopt Storper's (1997) definitions. These are ideal types of production linked to different types of market relationships (i.e. standardized, specialized, generic and dedicated; see Murdoch et al. 2000 for a more detailed commentary). While such categorizations are our descriptive starting point here, as we discuss further in the paper with reference to both the broader short supply chain analysis and the case study of the Llyn Beef Producers Co-operative, they are inadequate in capturing the evolutionary features of food supply chain construction. The analysis in this paper attempts to go beyond the rather static typological construction of supply chains, for it is only by doing this that we can begin to uncover the real social and material features that lead to the construction and development of short supply chains. Moreover, in conclusion, such explorations indicate the need for more dynamic conceptual formations that incorporate social uniqueness and difference into new rural development theory.

2. In the first phase of the Fourth Framework FAIR research programme 'The socio-economic impact of rural development policies: realities and potentials' (CT–4288) some thirty cases of rural development practices were studied. Of these fifteen cases concern food supply chain initiatives, related to the fields of organic farming, high quality production, region-specific products and product diversification.

3. The case studies developed within the IMPACT project which have been analyzed in the production of this paper are: (I) Llyn Beef Producers Co-operative – UK; (II) Marches Quality Producers Group – UK; (III) Graig Farm Organic Meat – UK; (IV) Organic Dairy Production in Wales – UK; (V) Farmers markets in the city of Frankfurt – Germany; (VI) Rhöngold dairy and organic farming – Germany; (VII) High quality food production in County Wexford – Ireland; (VIII) Producer and consumer associations of ecological produce in Andalucía: an experience of short distribution channels of quality produce – Spain; (IX) From farmer to retailer: the last frontier for the raising of beef cattle in Umbria? – Italy; (X) The production of Parmigiano-Reggiano cheese – Italy; (XI) Organic farming in Tuscany – Italy; (XII) Scalogno di Romagna – Italy.

4. In 1997 beef prices in Wales averaged 95.26p/kg compared to 121.55p/kg in 1995, a fall of 21.6% (see Table 2). Between 1996/97 and 1997/98, net farm income on lowland cattle and sheep farms in Wales fell by a dramatic 78% from £13,101 to £2,914 (Farm Business Survey 1997/98). As well as the BSE-induced crisis in confidence and the beef export ban, beef market realizations collapsed because of (a) a general trend away from consumption of red meat, (b) the appreciation of sterling (which significantly reduced the value of beef support schemes), (c) increased competition from imports, and (d) increased input costs over and above those 'normally' associated with beef production. These costs included the costs of establishing a database tracking cattle movement, and tagging.

5. At the time of the research Euro exchange rate was £0. 62 Sterling = 1 Euro

438 MARSDEN, BANKS AND BRISTOW

References

Guy, C. et al. (2000) *Pilot study of local retailer-supplier linkages in two rural areas.* (Unpublished report for Tesco Stores Ltd)

Knickel, K. and H. Renting (2000) Methodological and conceptual issue in the study of multifunctionality and rural development. *Sociologia Ruralis* 40 (4) pp. 512-528

Marsden, T.K. (1998) New rural territories: regulating the differentiated rural spaces. *Journal of Rural Studies* 14, pp. 107–117

Marsden, T.K., A. Flynn and M. Harrison (2000) *Consuming Interests: the social provision of foods* (London: UCL Press)

Murdoch, J., T.K. Marsden and J. Banks (2000) Quality, nature, and embeddedness: Some theoretical considerations in the context of the food sector. *Economic Geography* 76 (2) pp. 107–125

Murdoch, J. and M. Miele (1999) 'Back to nature': changing 'worlds of production' in the food sector. *Sociologia Ruralis* 39, pp. 465–483

Nygard, B. and O. Storstad (1998) De-globalisation of food markets? Consumer perceptions of safe food: The case of Norway. *Sociologia Ruralis* 38, pp. 35–53

Ploeg, J.D. van der et al. (2000) Rural development: From practices and policies towards theory. *Sociologia Ruralis* 40 (4) pp. 391-408

Roest, K. de and A. Menghi (2000) Reconsidering 'traditional food': the case of Parmigiano-Reggiano cheese. *Sociologia Ruralis* 40 (4) pp. 439-451

Storper, M. (1997) *The regional world* (London: Guildford Press)

Thevenot, L. (1998) Innovating in 'qualified' markets: Quality, norms and conventions. Paper presented at Systems and Trajectories of Innovation Conference, Institute of International Studies, University of California, Berkeley, April

Welsh Institute of Rural Studies (1998) *Farm business survey in Wales statistical results 1997/98* (Aberystwyth: Welsh Institute of Rural Studies)

Terry Marsden and Jo Banks
Department of City and Regional Planning
Cardiff University
Cardiff, Wales, UK

Gillian Bristow
Cardiff Business School
Cardiff University
Cardiff, Wales, UK

[8]

From Stilton to Vimto: Using Food History to Re-think Typical Products in Rural Development

Angela Tregear

Within the literature on rural development paradigms (van der Ploeg et al. 2000), culture economies (Ray 1998) and agro-food systems (Marsden et al. 2000; Murdoch et al. 2000), much has been written about agro-food products with special characteristics relating to territory. Although termed differently, for example, 'typical products' (Arfini and Mora 1998); 'origin labelled products' (Barjolle and Sylvander 1999); 'traditional foods' (Bessière 1998; Amilien 1999; de Roest and Menghi 2000), 'regional speciality products' (Tregear et al. 1998; Ilbery and Kneafsey 2000a, b), 'artisanal products' (Kupiec and Revell 1998) and 'special quality' or 'quality farm' products (Murdoch et al. 2000; Verhaegen and Van Huylenbroeck 2001), shared meanings have emerged regarding the properties of these products and their contribution to the socio-economic development of rural areas. Typical products are conceptualized as issuing from small-scale agricultural systems, with special characteristics due to the combination of local raw materials with traditional, inherited, production techniques (Bérard and Marchenay 1995; Bell and Valentine 1997; Bessière 1998): indeed, it is this conceptualization of a typical product that is enshrined in EU law, via Regulation 2081/92 (CEC 1992)[1]. The products are associated with numerous socio-economic benefits including: increased farmers' incomes in marginal areas which may, through synergies, be multiplied across whole local economic networks (Brunori and Rossi 2000); enhanced skilled employment (Ventura and Milone 2000); enhanced social vibrancy (Ray 1998); improved environmental sustainability and animal welfare, and safer, healthier food for the consumer (Nygard and Storstad 1998). In terms of their position in the wider agro-food system however, typical products are portrayed as vulnerable: predominant forces of internationalisation, industrialization and free market capitalism are perceived as threatening to the existence and integrity of small-scale, specialized agriculture (Bérard and Marchenay 1995; van der Ploeg et al. 2000; Ventura and Milone 2000), and the emergence and revalorization of such production in recent years is considered a 'countertendency' (Murdoch et al. 2000), antithetical to the predominant forces.

Critical analysis of this classic conceptualization of typical products already exists. For example, authors such as Moran (1993) and Thiedig and Sylvander (2000) demonstrate how the concept is based on 'Roman'[2] conventions regarding

Published by Blackwell Publishing,
9600 Garsington Road, Oxford OX4 2DQ, UK
350 Main Street, Malden, MA02148, USA

Sociologia Ruralis, Vol 43, Number 2, April 2003
©European Society for Rural Sociology
ISSN 0038–0199

agriculture and food, and they spell out the various political and economic problems that may arise from the concept's perpetuation in EU law. Others give cautionary insights regarding the extent to which classic typical products can bring environmental or welfare benefits, in relation to specific case examples (e.g. Edwards and Casabianca 1997; Tregear 2001a). To date however, the literature is lacking in a more fundamental examination of how food and territory are inter-related, conducted from a sufficiently broad perspective to allow alternative conceptualizations of typical products to emerge, and for the different socio-economic impacts associated with them to be assessed comparatively. This paper attempts such an analysis, via an in-depth, historical account of the production and consumption forces shaping the links between food and territory in one case study country: the UK. As well as broadening the classic conceptualization of the typical product and challenging the tacit assumptions associated with it, the paper aims to show how a broader perspective of food-territory links gives a more sophisticated reading of the relationship between typical products and forces such as industrialization, internationalization and free market capitalism. In turn, this leads to a more critical analysis of the role these products play in rural development. The next section presents the theoretical context and analytical approach of the paper in more detail.

Typical Products in Agro-Food Systems: Choice of Analytical Approach

Agro-food systems have been the subject of many studies from a wide variety of disciplines. Within sociology and geography however, the often Marxist-inspired theories on which such studies are based tend to emphasise production aspects over consumption aspects (Tovey 1997; Goodman and Dupuis 2002), and take an overly deterministic stance on the power relationships and causal forces passing between actors in the systems (Lockie and Kitto 2000). Actor Network Theory has been proposed as an alternative framework for theorising agro-food systems, as prescriptions are avoided regarding directions of causality in network relationships, as well as the importance or power of any phenomena within the networks (Murdoch et al. 2000; Goodman and Dupuis 2002). At the same time though, this neutrality can be construed as reducing the explanatory powers of ANT (Marsden 2000). In both agro-food studies (Marsden 2000) and rural development (van der Ploeg et al. 2000), the search is still on for powerful explanatory theoretical approaches, which are both transparent and grounded in careful empirical examination.

Some of these tensions and gaps are evident in extant studies of typical products in agro-food systems. As indicated in the introduction, many examinations have been made of these products within the context of rural development. These give useful insights into the dynamics of supply networks and distribution chains, but consumers often only appear as a 'shadowy presence' (Goodman and Dupuis 2002). Studies adopting conventions theory (Moran 1993; Murdoch et al. 2000) or social anthropological approaches (Bérard and Marchenay 1995; Terrio 1996; Bessière 1998), which give insights into the processes by which typical products are bestowed with meaning and value, also tend to focus on production or supply contexts rather than consumption. At the other end of the scale, the dedicated consumer studies of typical products that appear in the economics and marketing literatures tend to make only limited reference to wider social, cultural and political circumstances surrounding consumption (e.g. Gil and Sanchez 1997; Loureiro and McCluskey 2000; van der Lans et al. 2001), although they do indicate a great diversity of consumer interpretations and usage behaviours. A further overlooked dimension is that of time, with few authors setting their analyses within a well-elaborated temporal context, particularly when presenting case examples (e.g. Murdoch et al. 2000; Kneafsey et al. 2001). It may be argued that such a perspective is critical to a subject matter that incorporates explicit temporal properties, by way of heritage, tradition, etc.

The analytical approach adopted here followed the principles of the developmentalist school of food sociology (Mennell et al. 1992). For the current study, this meant tracing, over time, the key social, economic, political and cultural influences on the links between food and territory in the UK, in terms of both production and consumption. In the context of this analysis, 'production' is taken to mean aspects of agro-food systems such as labour, trade, technology, mechanisation and the behaviour and motivations of actors involved in agro-food production and supply. 'Consumption' is taken to mean size and shape of markets, user lifestyles, tastes and behaviour, and the processes and nature of social valorisation of food-territory links. Typical products themselves are conceptualised as being at the intersection of production and consumption dimensions, shaped by physical aspects such as ingredients and production techniques (the production dimension) and also perceived or symbolic aspects such as identity, branding, etc. (the consumption dimension). In application, this approach has much in common with the historical and context specific case studies of agro-food enterprises undertaken by Blundel (2002) and Bianchi (2001) in the field of small firm research, or Moran et al.'s (1996) comparative analysis of the development of agricultural policies in France and New Zealand. A key objective is to identify critical incidents in the evolution of contexts relevant to the subject matter, and to unearth unexpected or hidden forces of importance. The analysis begins with an overview of the current situation regarding UK typical products.

The Links between Food and Territory in the UK

The present day situation for typical products in the UK is characteristic of many northern European countries. Few products are PDO- or PGI-registered relative to Mediterranean countries[3] and, overall, the vast majority do not conform to the French-Roman conceptualization of products derived from indigenous, collective, agricultural systems. For example, although many have a rural production base, only a minority is actually produced on-farm, and over half of producers are 'incomers' to the area[4] (Ilbery and Kneafsey 2000a). The UK also has, in popular terms at least, a widely lamented and delocalised food culture, with higher levels of concentration in food distribution chains than Mediterranean countries. Yet a recent UK inventory of traditional foods contains almost 400 entries (Mason 1999), whilst DTZ (1999) identifies approximately 3,000 speciality food producers in the UK, many of whom employ craft-based or traditional methods. Market studies also indicate that the popularity of regional and local products is growing amongst UK consumers, as are alternative supply chains such as farmers' markets (Holloway and Kneafsey 2000). These insights imply more complex forces at play and suggest that selective indicators of the status of typical food production and consumption, such as numbers of officially registered products, must be treated with caution. This is particularly the case when such indicators are inspired by conventions exogenous to the country concerned. To understand better the present situation in the UK, key forces impacting on the links between food and territory are summarised (Table 1), drawing from the food history and food sociology literatures. For clarity, the analysis divides the evolution of food-territory links into three eras: pre-industrial, industrial and post-industrial. These correspond broadly to the development phases of 'world cuisine' described by Goody (1982) and Mennell et al. (1992). In each era, the key trends and forces are identified in both production and consumption domains.

Table 1: *Forces shaping the links between food and territoriy in the UK*

	Pre-industrial Era	Industrial Era	Post-industrial Era
Production domain	Small-scale, labour intensive systems of production, development of territorially distinctive customs of cultivation, processing, etc.	Agricultural and industrial revolutions, mechanisation, standardisation, application of science and technology to food production and processing, giving homogenising effect	Continued agricultural policy emphasis of production maximisation and efficiency, food security prioritisation
	But also international trade in agricultural commodities, periods of production intensification	But also development of explicit identities and specifications for agro-food products, linked to territory, by producers acting entrepreneurially	Creation of state monopoly marketing boards act as disincentive to small-scale, on-farm processing

Late 20th Century revalor-isation of small scale, differentiated agriculture |
| **Consumption domain** | Close geographic proximity between food production and consumption, development of territorially distinctive customs of preparation, usage | Gradual urbanisation of populations leading to loss of self-sufficiency and know-how in production: 'de-locali-sation' effect. Social elites embrace French culinary culture | Rationing continues for 13 years: loss of culinary knowledge, resptricted repertoire

Postwar social climate of convenience, reflecting changing role of women |
| | But also social hierarchies driving patterns of food distribution and usage across territorial boundaries | But also development of tastes and markets for speciality items and delica-cies, e.g. linked to rural and coastal tourist destinations | Late 20th century re-valorisation of typical foods as one trend within many, reflecting nostalgia for rural roots; alternative value system; interest in exotica |

Food Territory Links in the Pre-Industrial Era

In the pre-industrial era, it is tempting to envisage close links between food and territory and indeed, to consider typical food as the "natural order of things"(Montanari 1994, p. 160). From a production perspective, this is based on the notion of pre-industrial agrarian systems driven by needs of self-sufficiency and preservation of nutrition from locally available raw materials. Territorially differentiated foods emerge as communities in different geographic areas gradually develop their own customs for processing these raw materials. It is this vision that drives the classic view of how typical products evolve, and on this basis, it may be argued that levels of geographically distinctive food production in the British Isles would be on a par with much of continental Europe in pre-industrial times (Mennell 1996). At the same time though, food historians caution against depicting pre-industrial food production as fixed in certain modes. Periodic intensification of agricultural production is observed, for example from the 11th to the 13th centuries (Tannahill 1988; Montanari 1994). The existence of international trade from early times is also noted, introducing novel raw materials to areas that today might be considered indigenous: for example, tomatoes and pasta to Italy, (Goody 1982; Montanari 1994); olive oil to Provence (Goody 1982); and rhubarb to the British Isles (Mason 1999), all between the 15th and 17th centuries. Thus the pre-industrial era should not be envisaged as devoid of the kinds of forces – agricultural intensification, international trade – classically associated with later eras.

It may also be presumed that in a pre-industrial era, consumption tends to take place in close proximity to production, via self-sufficiency or localized trade, contributing to the development of geographically differentiated culinary habits. Yet food sociologists highlight that food usage practices are influenced by factors other than physical location of users: they are part of food culture, the dynamics of which may transcend physical local contexts. This means that although peasant based agricultural systems are associated with the development of distinctive cuisines[5], the former does not presume the latter. Indeed, Mennell (1992) attests that diets in the pre-industrial era in Europe, for the bulk of the population, were generally monotonous and homogenous. The nature of social structures is influential, such that societies with complex social hierarchies tend to evolve more differentiated food practices than egalitarian societies (Goody 1982). This may be explained by the theory of social capital (Bourdieu 1984, as discussed by Terrio 1996): as foods are visible, everyday items, they are apt vehicles for higher echelons to demonstrate social distinction. Pre-industrial food-territory links may therefore be thought of as dependent, in part, on the social strategies of powerful elites, for which politics and religion also play important roles. In circumstances where social elites prize locally derived foods, then it follows that food-territory links strengthen and classic typical production develops under aristocratic patronage (a vision presented for Parmigiano-Reggiano cheese (de Roest and Menghi 2000)). However, social elites often choose to prize extra-local products, as these demonstrate power and wealth more explicitly. Consumption of food products may therefore take place at a distance from production, stretching the distinctiveness of culinary habits beyond localized territories. This dynamic is well illustrated in Mennell's (1996) comparison of pre-industrial French and English culinary practices, where it is argued that the absolutist monarchy of the ancien regime stimulated centralist food provisioning to supply the composite cuisine of the Parisian Court, whereas in England, the relatively powerful and geographically dispersed baronetcy stimulated a greater regional differentiation of culinary practices.

Food-Territory Links in the Industrial Era

Whilst the above indicates that complex socio-cultural forces and fluctuating patterns of agricultural trade and intensification were already complicating the links between food and territory in many parts of Europe, the industrialization era is taken to be the period in which these forces and trends expand and intensify. This period is generally taken to be particularly significant for the UK typical product situation, as the agricultural and industrial revolutions here are thought to have profoundly broken previously tight food-territory links, and caused a widespread loss of typical foods in the classic sense (Ilbery and Kneafsey 2000b). This section summarises these forces, but also presents evidence, often overlooked, that the industrial era created a context in which the classic conceptualization of typical products actively developed.

In terms of agricultural production, the industrial era in Britain is associated with standardisation, mechanization, intensification, and the application of new discoveries in science and engineering to land cultivation: forces militating against the existence of small-scale, artisanal, territorially differentiated agriculture. These trends extended also to the processing level[6]. The industrial era is also associated with rural exodus, creating a 'delocalisation' effect between food production and consumption (Pelto and Pelto 1983), and a loss of inherited knowledge and skills in food production, usage and self-sufficiency. Expanding numbers of urban dwellers required an industrial provisioning process to feed them, and were thus reliant upon the products of new food processing technologies as well as collectivized distribution systems for commodities like milk (Oddy and Burnett 1992). A further consumption dynamic served to erode inherited, territorially distinctive food usage patterns. Amongst higher echelons in British society, and also the new middle classes via the first published cookbooks, French culinary practices were enthusiastically embraced, via adoption of the haute cuisine model codified by La Varenne in the Enlightenment (Mennell 1992). This culinary model echoed principles of the *ancien regime*, necessitating ingredients and 'made' dishes sourced from considerable geographic distances and also, in a British context, requiring the importation of French chefs to dispense the exogenous knowledge and skills. Several authors attest that this fashion for French cuisine (driven by desires for status and distinction – the cultural capital theory again) caused an abandonment of native culinary habits amongst upper classes in the UK (Driver 1983; Brown 1990; Montanari 1994; Mennell 1996).

Yet these trends and forces also brought forth a socio-economic context in which the concept of typicity began to be identified and acknowledged in terms akin to the present day. A key accompaniment to the improving tendencies of 19th century British agricultural revolutionists was the modernist – and entrepreneurial – desire to specify identities for the fruits of their labours. Thus, it was during the industrial era that so-called 'native' farm animal breeds (e.g. Gloucester Old Spot and Tamworth pigs, Aberdeen Angus cattle – many of which are now registered 'rare') and fruit and vegetable cultivars (e.g. Cox Orange Pippins, Jersey Royal Potatoes) were first 'invented' or given type and profile specifications[7] (Mason 1999). Many British breed societies and producer associations for typical products also have their origins in the late 19th century (e.g. Aberdeen Angus and Galloway cattle societies, the association of Stilton producers (Mason, 1999)). Permeating such activities is a concern for *authenticity*: the identification of the quintessential, genuine and 'official' embodiment of the type. Crucially, the key stimulus for both specifications and authenticity can be construed as the development of *markets* for these products. For agriculturalists, the effective branding of progeny or cultivars represented an important means of differentiating their commodities in an era of agricultural improvement and expansion. Likewise, the producers of Stilton cheese could gain competitive advantage by specifying and then assuring the product's identity (indeed, Stilton derives its name from where the cheese was originally *sold*, not produced (Mason, 1999)). The emergence and branding of rural and coastal speciality foods – baked goods, confectionary, seafood – is another example of this production-specification-marketing dynamic, in this case to cater to the tourist and leisure markets expanding with the development of the railways (Rojek 1993). Thus in the industrial era, the identification and construction of typicity developed in ways not seen in previous eras.

Food-Territory Links in the Post-Industrial Era

It is perhaps in the post-industrial era more than any other where a quite unique combination of trends and forces can be identified for the UK, giving very specific impacts on food-territory links. The drive for agricultural production efficiencies continued throughout the 20th century, given added stimulus by two world wars, which rendered food security the priority in an island nation (Tannahill 1988; Mason 1999). The creation of state marketing boards which monopolized the purchase of agricultural commodities, and heavily controlled the processing sectors, were also critical. For example, the Milk Marketing Board's position as statutory buyer and seller of all UK milk and dairy products effectively rendered small-scale, on-farm processing of milk into cheese for commercial purposes completely uneconomic (Blundel 2002), if not illegal (Mason 1999). The middle decades of the 20th century therefore witnessed a significant reduction in farm-based and artisanal food processing. Meanwhile, the government's less interventionist approach in the downstream food supply chain saw increasing concentration here – a force classically perceived as problematic to small-scale suppliers (Blundel 2002) – with the emergence of supermarkets in the 1960s.

In terms of consumption, perhaps one of the most significant forces for food-territory links was W.W.II. Not only were diets and food usage patterns severely restricted during the war years themselves, rationing continued for a full 13 years in the UK, thus a whole generation grew up with little inherited food culture to call upon and only a restricted culinary repertoire to practice (Driver 1983; Mason 1999). With the role of women altered in the post war years, items associated with the alleviation of the 'chore' of cooking became popular (e.g. convenience foods, white goods, kitchen gadgets), whilst in the 1960s, food and diet became entwined with body image (Montanari 1994; Bell and Valentine 1997). Where culinary skills were extolled, via the expanding mass media of television and magazines, these tended towards either the haute cuisine model of the industrial era, or else, via food writers such as Elizabeth David, towards an exotic vision of Mediterranean cookery (Mason 1999). Overall, the recent past presents a destructive combination of forces in terms of close food-territory links.

It is only in recent decades in the UK that forces have emerged to 'revalorise' typical products and geographic proximity between food production and consumption. In the production domain, observations have already been made in the introduction about the turn towards quality, environmental sustainability and integrated rural development, all of which might involve territorial specialisation of foods. In the consumption domain, recent decades have brought forth unprecedented food and meal options for UK consumers, set against a recent history of an eclipsed and de-racinated native food culture. In sociological terms, this leads to multiple possibilities in explaining food choice (Warde 1997): it may become more homogenous (Ritzer 1996); more fragmented and individualized (Fischler 1988); more clustered on the basis of changing special interests, e.g. vegetarianism or 'foodie'-ism (Beardsworth and Keil 1997); or more related to traditional markers like income or social class (Warde 1997). Against this background there is, however, more agreement on the consumption significance of typical products: symbolic of rurality, they represent means by which urbanites indulge nostalgic desires to return to rural roots (Montanari 1994; Bessière 1998); symbolic of craftsmanship, they represent an alternative set of production and exchange values (Terrio 1996), offering a moral and aesthetic anchor in the post-industrial world (Warde 1997; Amilien 1999). Foods associated with labour intensity also have an exotic appeal (Kupiec and Revell 1998), coinciding with a turn in fashion towards home cooking and entertaining. The shifting nature of these symbolic values is well noted by Montanari (1994) and Delamont (1995), who point out that in previous eras, foods symbolic of rusticity and artisanship (e.g. breads made from dark grains like rye) were accorded low status, whereas for the bulk of the population, refined, processed and convenience foods were prized for the liberation they represented from the tedious and often unpleasant labour entailed in making typical products. As Montanari (1994, p.159) asserts: "only a wealthy society can afford to appreciate poverty".

The preceding analysis brings forth a number of implications for the classic conceptualisation of typical products. It highlights the fallacy of conceiving of a pre-industrial era, frozen in time, that represents the cradle of typical food production: international trade, industrial production and market dynamics permeated this era, without which typical products would not have developed as they have. Neither should forces in the industrial era be conceived of as entirely antithetical to the development of typical products: the classic conceptual associations of typicity crystallised in this era. The analysis also identifies a number of cross-era forces critical to food-territory links: the role of social hierarchies in bestowing symbolic value to foods; the tendencies of entrepreneurial producers to mark identities and specifications for products in response to markets and competition; the inter-relationships and inter-dependencies between urban and rural areas with respect to the production, appreciation and usage of typical products. The next section draws on these forces to propose an alternative and broader classification of typical products, one that is grounded in a UK context and reflects its experience.

Typical Products in the UK: an Alternative Classification

Table 2 illustrates the alternative classification. The typology[8] is intended as illustrative rather than definitive: the examples presented in each category are offered as particularly 'apt' to illustrate the combination of forces in each case, but the boundaries between them should be considered as overlapping rather than mutually exclusive. A typology approach is taken here partly to retain the detailed, grounded quality of the historical analysis (more difficult under a schematic approach), and also to explicitly identify quite diverse products as manifestations of food-territory links. The five product categories all emerge from the same fundamental context of UK agro-food history, however it is the varying forces of industrialization, symbolic valuing, producer motivations, etc. that determine the distinctive features and development trajectories of each.

Table 2: *A classification of typical products in the UK*

	Pre-industrial	Industrial	Post-industrial	
1 Classic	Documented history of existence/ reputation	→ Creation of producer associations/product specifications	→ Strong reputation/ renown, PDO-eligible	eg. Stilton Cheese
2 Appropriations	Origins in widespread artisanal activity	⋯▶ Many small producers eclipsed by industrial activity; few persist through entrepreneurship	→ Remaining producers appropriate previously shared know-how	eg. Craster Kippers
3 Re-inventions	Origins in widespread artisanal activity	⋯▶ Practice dies out in face of industrialisation	→ Practices revivied in face of revalorisation ▶ Practices 'invented' in face of revalorisation	eg. Cornish Yarg, Extra Mature Welsh Beef
4 19th Century Specialities	Origins in artisanal activity	⋯▶ Branding of specific products to capture tourist/gift markets	▶ Products retain stong speciality/gift symbolism	eg. Harrogate Toffee, Morecambe Bay Potted Shrimps
5 Industrial Other	Origins in medicinal/apothecary practices	⋯▶ Products gain renown through industrial scale manufacture	▶ Products often have strong market close to local origins	eg. Vimto

Type 1. Classic Typical Products

This type refers to the classic conceptualization of typical products described at the start of the paper: small-scale, artisan-based agrarian production, organized on a collective basis, with products combining local raw materials with inherited customs of production. The preceding analysis demonstrates why so few products of this type exist currently in the UK and also why those producers who have been awarded PDO designations rarely conform to the classic model (Ilbery and Kneafsey 2000a). Industrial era forces of agricultural revolution, rural exodus, delocalisation of food production and consumption and upper class adoption of French culinary culture have combined with post-industrial era forces of agricultural efficiency drives, state marketing monopolies, supply chain concentration and post-war food policy to erode the context for classic typical foods to flourish. Stilton is one of the most apt examples of a British classic typical product: an artisanal cheese made of local materials by an association of six cheese-makers today, with a long and unbroken history of production (to at least the early 1700s), and an official specification dating back to 1910 (Mason 1999). Further research is needed to trace the particular development pathways and critical incidents of such a case example, to identify how it has persisted in the face of adverse contextual forces.

Type 2. Appropriations

This category refers to present day products with territorial associations, whose producers are the remaining small-scale operators in sectors that once contained many artisanal suppliers. Fish smoking would be an example of this: originally an artisanal activity practised widely along the north east and Scottish coasts (Brown 1990), with localized distinction in techniques, forces such as mechanisation, standardisation, supply chain concentration and changing consumption patterns reduced the number of small-scale smokehouses over the course of the 20th century. An interpretation of what happened to the remaining producers who found strategies to survive, using entrepreneurial skills, is that they effectively undertook a process of appropriation of know-how once shared collectively in the area. 'Appropriation' refers both to the status of credibility and legitimacy conferred upon the remaining producers to deliver the typical product, and also to their tendency to personify and take ownership of the territory name as their product brand name. For example, the Craster Kipper was developed in the 1840s, from the traditional methods of smoking herring on the north east coast of England, specifically to meet the demand of the Newcastle and London markets[9] (Mason 1999). Today the product is exclusively produced, and branded, by one remaining smokehouse in the village of Craster. Typical products appropriated in this way tend to have a speciality symbolic appeal, due in part to the rarity value they have developed, but also due to the effective and imaginative way in which their market-oriented producers have branded them.

Type 3. Re-inventions

This type refers to products created or re-created in recent decades, whose properties have some link to local territory either via their raw materials or the techniques of their production. Producers in this category are diverse in character, but often are not direct descendents of long-standing family enterprises in the area concerned. Small-scale cheese-making is an example. The destructive forces of the industrial era, combined with later agricultural policies, greatly reduced farm-based, artisanal cheese-making in the UK by the mid-20th century. The activity has gradually increased since the 1960s, in tandem with the 'revalorisation' forces in production and consumption domains described earlier. In some cases, products are assiduously faithful revivals which the cheese-makers themselves have inherited experience of (e.g. the traditional Lancashire cheese of Singletons Dairy (Tregear 2001b) and the traditional Cheshire cheese of Appletons (Blundel 2002)), or else, where the producers have come from other professional backgrounds, local expertise is consulted to verify authenticity (e.g. Swaledale cheese (Tregear 2001b)). Other UK artisanal cheeses are recent creations that either have only vague stylistic or identity references to an older typical product, or which are born out of completely unrelated styles and traditions. Cornish Yarg is thought to be similar to a general style of cheese formally produced in the county of Cornwall, but the product itself was invented in the 1970s and is named after its inventors: Yarg is 'Gray' backwards (Mason 1999). Other Re-invention examples would be the recent explicit territorial branding of agricultural commodities such as beef, lamb or honey (e.g. 'Extra Mature Welsh Beef' (Marsden et al. 2000)). Importantly, it is recent revalorization forces that stimulate such revivals, raising complex issues about tradition and innovation, essential and symbolic typicity, and competition and collaboration, which require much further detailed study.

Type 4. 19th Century Specialities

These products have their origins in the late 19th century, when the forces of leisure and tourism market expansion, assisted in the UK by Queen Victoria's patronage of seaside and rural resorts, stimulated a demand for speciality food items associated with these places. Small-scale operators, again acting entrepreneurially, developed or re-branded products to meet this demand. An example is Morecambe Bay potted shrimps: a tradition of shrimping on the north west coast of England dates back to at least the late 1700s, but potted shrimps – cooked in butter and mace – became a popular delicacy with visitors who began to congregate in this emerging tourist area (Mason 1999). Another example is Harrogate Toffee: based on much older traditions of confectionary production, this was a craft-produced sweet created by grocer John Farrah in the Yorkshire town of Harrogate in the 1840s, which owed its flavour (lemon) and texture (hard, like a boiled sweet) to its use as a confection for ladies to take after tasting the bitter spa waters for which this resort town was fashionable (Mason 1999). Today, the symbolic appeal of these products reflects their origins as 19th century speciality items: indeed, both of the key present day producers of Morecambe Bay shrimps and Harrogate Toffee have royal warrants of usage (Tregear 2001b). Examples in this category highlight issues of origins and myth-making in food-territory links, in addition to those of markets, entrepreneurship and patronage by social elites.

Type 5. Industrial Other

These are products with properties perhaps least akin to the classic conceptualization of typical foods. They have their origins in pre-industrial traditions, but they developed as identifiable, branded products via industrial contexts and production processes. An example is Vimto, a berry and herb-based cordial manufactured today by J. Nichols Ltd. of Warrington, north west England. Based on the medieval practice of cordial-making for restorative and medicinal purposes (Burnett 1999), the product was first formulated in 1908, from 29 fruit and herb ingredients, originally as a health tonic. Via the temperance movement, designed to encourage sobriety amongst the working class population that industrial era forces had brought to the region, the product gained popularity as a healthful leisure drink (Mason 1999). The product then became adapted into a carbonated soft drink, the bottling of which was licensed to agents in a system of small to medium scale production and distribution quite distinct to urban areas of north west England and Scotland. Other examples of this type are 'fancy' (i.e. not ship's) biscuits such as Bath Olivers or Abernethy biscuits: first developed by doctors and Quakers for medicinal use, they came to renown via industrial-scale manufacture, involving the employment of special baking machines (Goody 1982). With different symbolic values to many of the other product types in this classification, this category raises significant issues regarding degrees of industrialization in production processes and also associations of typical products with urbanity rather than rurality.

Discussion

The preceding analysis has presented an alternative classification of typical products based on the historical development of food-territory links in the UK. Cutting across the categories are common, repeated features: the balance producers strike between inheriting territorially distinctive resources and manipulating these, as symbols, to gain market advantage; the rolling out of operations across different horizontal and vertical network relationships; and the symbiosis of fluctuating scales and intensities of manufacture with the changing characteristics of consumption. Thus, it may be argued that both 'Classic' typical products like Stilton and 'Re-inventions' like Cornish Yarg represent a balance between inherited and symbolic typicity, the differences between them being incremental and temporal, rather than one being more 'authentic' than the other. The embeddedness of present day 'Re-inventions' and 'Appropriations' in networks of small firms that use regional identity as a springboard to differentiation echoes the collective systems of production in 'Classic' typical products, the difference being that the former networks are cross-sectoral rather than based on one product. Finally, different levels of production scale and intensity may be witnessed across and within the five product categories as producers choose how to engage with different consumption opportunities: some artisanal 'Re-inventions' may distribute the greater proportion of their output via national and international outlets, whilst some 'Industrial Other' firms find significant markets in their home, or neighbouring regions.

　　Echoes of these features can also be observed in classic Mediterranean typical products. For example, Casabianca and Coutron (1998) reveal the pragmatic process of negotiation undertaken by the producers of Prisutto de Corse to 'construct' their typical product, whilst Bérard and Marchenay (1995) describe the processes of myth-making surrounding the origins of Roquefort. The shifting boundaries of the production and supply networks of Parma Ham, described by Arfini and Mora (1998), illustrate the non-permanent nature of classic typical product collective systems, as does Moran's (1993) account of the licensing of the production of Bleu de Bresse in New Zealand. Modern technologies and mechanisation are characteristic of many of the most renowned Mediterranean typical products, reflecting choices made by their producers to engage with high volume urban and international markets: a balance illustrated well in de Roest and Menghi's (2000) discussion of Parmigiano-Reggiano production techniques and scales. Therefore, the classic Mediterranean concept of typical production as ancient, inherited, collective savoir-faire, whose existence is antithetical to the forces of industrialisation, internationalisation and free market capitalism, needs to be re-thought. The components of the concept themselves need to be examined in more sophisticated terms, as phenomena moving in symbiosis with changing contexts and forces. The process of re-thinking would be enhanced by acknowledgement and incorporation of other countries' experiences and conventions relating to typicity in food. After all, if typical products have a role as identity markers and celebrations of cultures, they should be representative of those cultures.

The analysis presented here also raises the need for a reassessment of the tacit assumptions regarding the rural development benefits of classic typical products. In short, products do not need to accord with the classic concept to deliver these. For example in the north of England, producers of 'Re-inventions', 'Appropriations' and '19th Century Specialities' are often key players in local rural development networks, contributing to employment, skills enhancement, localized supply chains and community vibrancy (Tregear 2001b). In north west France, Gilg and Battershill (1998) also find non-conventional farmers contribute much to their local economy. In both cases, territorial distinctiveness may be a basis upon which socio-economic benefits are brought, but they are achieved neither with production systems based on prescribed collectives, nor with centuries-old specification histories. Indeed, the freedom of individuals to develop, innovate and engage flexibly in cross-sectoral networks, drawing from diverse professional backgrounds and life experiences, may contribute positively to socio-economic enhancements and biodiversity (Bérard and Marchenay 1995).

At the same time, examples can be found amongst some of the most renowned classic typical products of production realities that somewhat belie their symbolic associations, posing challenges as well as benefits for rural development. For example, Bessière (1998) refers to the 'factory tourism' of the Roquefort consortium, whilst Edwards and Casabianca (1997) highlight the animal welfare and environmental pollution problems associated with the scale and intensity of pig production in Parma Ham (worth comparing with Murdoch and Miele's (1999, p.469) comments about "huge industrial pig farms" of North Carolina). Products produced from distinctive local ingredients with age-old production histories may have great valorisation potential in the context of rural development (Bessière 1998). However it may be argued that they do not have a monopoly on ensuing rural development benefits. Whilst much policy and academic attention is paid to such products in Mediterranean countries and elsewhere, it is probable that other categories of typical product exist that are similar to the ones identified here for the UK. However, they receive less attention and less analysis because of the general preoccupation with one conceptualisation of typicity and its assumed benefits. The result is that products, producers and firms with much to offer rural and regional development may be overlooked and undervalued. Moreover, from an academic point of view, the opportunity is missed to examine empirical cases which challenge existing theories about typical products and their benefits, and which may stimulate moves towards whole new ways of thinking about this subject area.

Conclusion

The classic concept of typical products, based on Roman conventions, pervades the academic and policy debates about food in rural development and sets up norms about how food-territory links should be understood and valued. The analysis elaborated here illustrates how, if examination is grounded in the specific contexts and conventions

104   TREGEAR

of another country, a different set of norms emerges and a more subtle and insightful picture ensues of the links between food and territory. Overall, a broadened concept of the typical product develops: the manifestation of the links between nature and culture, shaped by the actions and value systems of actors in production and consumption domains, in turn linked to macro social, economic and political forces. Thus, all typical products represent a mixture of tradition and innovation, physicality and symbolism, mechanization and craftsmanship, endogeneity and exogeneity, myths and realities. The preoccupation in some policy and academic circles of identifying, across these mixes, the products and systems that are 'more typical' than others, is distracting. Instead, a research agenda should be pursued that investigates the processes by which different mixes of properties emerge in different contexts, and that examines the consequences of these for socio-economic development. Such an agenda needs to be based on a recognition that all manifestations of food-territory links are of potential importance and relevance to rural development. Grounding investigations in the contexts and conventions of the specific geographic areas under study would be a useful basis for pursuing this agenda.

Acknowledgements

Thanks are extended to two anonymous referees for their helpful comments and suggestions. The author is also indebted to fellow participants of the European Union Concerted Action project 'DOLPHINS' ('Development of Origin Labelled Products: Humanity, Innovation and Sustainability', QLK5-2000-00593), for intellectual stimulation and inspiration on the subject of typical products. As always though, any remaining errors are the responsibility of the author.

Notes

1 Under this legislation, producers of typical products may apply to have their product names designated 'protected designation of origin' (PDO) or 'protected geographical indication' (PGI).

2 Thiedig and Sylvander (2000) use the term 'Roman' conventions to denote the particular legislative and administrative arrangements in France and Italy that regulate production and labelling of agro-food products by geographic origin. In wine for example, these countries have the *Appellation d'Origine Contrôlée* (AOC) and *Denominazione di origine controllata* (DOC) systems, respectively. The arrangements are based on a strong cultural belief – identifiable elsewhere in southern Europe – in the relationship between geographic origin and special quality in agro-food products.

3 Currently 35 in the UK compared to 127 in France and 108 in Italy.

4 Data drawn from a survey of 55 out of 100 regional speciality food producers in south west England.

5 For example Symons (1982), cited in Mennell et al. (1992) describes Australia's cuisine as one of the 'worst in the world' because the country evolved rapidly from a hunter gatherer to an industrialized mode of food provisioning, with no stable period of landed peasantry in between.

6 For example in the south west, cider-making had been conducted on a localized scale since its introduction by the Normans in the 12th century, but by the end of the 19th century production was dominated by two large firms, Bulmers and Taunton Cider, who mass-produced an homogenous product (Twiss 1999).

7 Such specifications would often be the result of years of selective breeding and intervention to arrive at an ideal type bearing little relation to naturally occurring, wild species. For

example, the Berkshire pig breed was developed with bloodlines from Chinese and East Asian stock (Mason 1999). This reinforces the point that the processes of developing and specifying typical products are guided by their role as economic, marketable objects, as much as by their status as socio-cultural symbols.

8 Strictly speaking, it is a typology rather than a classification that is presented here, in that this is a study and interpretation of types. However, for the broad purposes of this paper, the terms 'classification' and 'typology' are employed inter-changeably, to denote a range of alternative categories based on a common theme.

9 'Kipper' originally referred to either smoked salmon or herring, but today is generally taken to denote the latter.

References

Amilien, V. (1999) *Is grandmother's cuisine traditional food? A concept definition in tourism research.* Proceedings of the 8th Nordic symposium in hospitality and tourism research, 18-21 November, Alta, Norway

Arfini, F. and C. Mora eds. (1998) *Typical and traditional products: rural effect and agro-industrial problems.* Proceedings of the 52nd seminar of the European Association of Agricultural Economists, June 19-21, 1997 (Istituto de Economia Agraria e Forestale, Università di Parma: Parma, Italy)

Barjolle, D. and B. Sylvander (1999) *Some factors of success for origin labelled products in agri-food supply chains in Europe: market, internal resources and institutions.* Paper presented at the 67th seminar of the European Association of Agricultural Economists, Le Mans, France, 27-29 October

Beardsworth, A. and T. Keil (1997) *Sociology on the Menu: An Invitation to the Study of Food and Society* (London, Routledge)

Bell, D. and G. Valentine (1997) *Consuming Geographies: we are where we eat* (London, Routledge)

Bérard, L. and P. Marchenay (1995) Lieux, temps, et preuves: la construction sociale des produits de terroir. *Terrain* 24, pp. 153-164

Bessière, J. (1998) Local development and heritage: traditional food and cuisine as tourist attractions in rural areas. *Sociologia Ruralis* 38 (1) pp. 21-34

Bianchi, T. (2001) With and without co-operation: two alternative strategies in the food-processing industry in the Italian South. *Entrepreneurship and Regional Development* 13 pp. 117-145

Blundel, R. (2002) Network evolution and the growth of artisanal firms: a tale of two regional cheese makers. *Entrepreneurship and Regional Development* 14 pp. 1-30.

Bourdieu, P. (1984) *Distinction: a Social Critique of the Judgement of Taste.* Nice, R. trans. (Cambridge, MA, Harvard University Press)

Brown, C. (1990) *Broths to Bannocks: Cooking in Scotland 1690 to the present day* (London, John Murray Publishers Ltd)

Brunori, G. and A. Rossi (2000) Synergy and coherence through collective action: some insights from wine routes in Tuscany. *Sociologia Ruralis* 40(4) pp. 409-423

Burnett, J. (1999) *Liquid pleasures: a social history of drinks in modern Britain* (London, Routledge)

Casabianca, F. and C. Coutron (1998) *Relations entre caractérisation et définition d'un produit typique non industrialisé: le Prisuttu ou jambon sec corse.* Proceedings of the International Symposium on the Basis of the Quality of Typical Mediterranean Animal Products, Spain, 29 Sept-2 October, 1996

CEC (1992). Commission of the European Communities *Council Regulation (EEC) No. 2081/92 of July 14*

Delamont, S. (1995) *Appetites and Identities: An Introduction to the Social Anthropology of Western Europe* (London, Routledge)

DTZ (1999). *UK Speciality Food and Drink Sector, 1999.* Report prepared for Food from Britain and MAFF (DTZ Pieda Consulting, Edinburgh)

Edwards, S. and F. Casabianca (1997). Perception and reality of product quality from outdoor pig systems in Northern and Southern Europe. In J. Sørensen ed., *Livestock Farming Systems: More than Food Production.* Proceedings of the fourth international symposium on livestock farming systems, EAAP Publication 89 (Wageningen: EAAP)

Fischler, C. (1988) Food, self and identity. *Social Science Information* 27 (2) pp. 275-92

Gil, J. and M. Sanchez (1997) Consumer preferences for wine attributes: a conjoint approach. *British Food Journal* 99 (1) pp. 3-11

Gilg, A. and M. Battershill (1998) Quality farm food in Europe: a possible alternative to the industrialized food market and to current agri-environmental policies: lessons from France. *Food Policy* 23 (1) pp.25-40

Goodman, D. and E. M. DuPuis (2002) Knowing food and growing food: beyond the production-consumption debate in the sociology of agriculture. *Sociologia Ruralis* 42 (1) pp. 5-22

Goody, J. (1982). *Cooking, Cuisine and Class: a Study in Comparative Sociology* (Cambridge University Press)

Holloway, L. and M. Kneafsey (2000) Reading the space of the farmers' market: a case study from the United Kingdom. *Sociologia Ruralis* 40 (3) pp. 285-299

Ilbery, B. and M. Kneafsey (2000a) Producer constructions of quality in regional speciality food production: a case study from south west England. *Journal of Rural Studies* 16 pp. 217-230

Ilbery, B. and M. Kneafsey (2000b) Registering regional speciality food and drink products in the United Kingdom: the case of PDOs and PGIs. *Area* 32 (3) pp. 317-325

Kneafsey, M., B. Ilbery, and T. Jenkins (2001) Exploring the dimensions of culture economies in rural west Wales. *Sociologia Ruralis* 41 (3) pp. 296-310

Kupiec, B. and B. Revell (1998) Speciality and artisanal cheeses today: the product and the consumer. *British Food Journal* 100 (5) pp. 236-243

van der Lans, I., K. van Ittersum, A. De Cicco and M. Loseby (2001) The role of region of origin and EU certificates of origin in consumer evaluation of food products. *European Review of Agricultural Economics* 28 (4) pp. 451-477

Lockie, S. and S. Kitto (2000) Beyond the farm gate: production-consumption networks and agri-food research. *Sociologia Ruralis* 40(1) pp. 3-19

Loureiro, M. and J. McCluskey (2000) Assessing consumer response to protected geographical identification labelling. *Agribusiness* 16 (3) pp. 309-320

Marsden, T. (2000) Food matters and the matter of food: towards a new food governance? *Sociologia Ruralis* 40 (1) pp. 20-29

Marsden, T., J. Banks and G. Bristow (2000) Food supply chain approaches: exploring their role in rural development. *Sociologia Ruralis* 40 (4) pp. 424-439

Mason, L. (1999) *Traditional Foods of Britain* (Prospect Books: Totnes, Devon)

Mennell, S. (1992) Divergencies and convergencies in the development of culinary cultures. In H. Teuteberg ed., *European Food History: A Research Review* (Leicester Univeristy Press)

Mennell, S., A. Murcott and A. van Otterloo eds. (1992) *The Sociology of Food: Eating, Diet and Culture* (London, Sage Publications)

Mennell, S. (1996) *All Manners of Food: Eating and Taste in England and France from the Middle Ages to the Present* (Urbana, University of Illinois Press)

Montanari, M. (1994) *The Culture of Food* (Oxford, Blackwell)

Moran, W. (1993) Rural space as intellectual property. *Political Geography* 12 (3) pp. 263-277

Moran, W., G. Blunden, M. Workman and A. Bradly (1996) Family farmers, real regulation, and the experience of food regimes. *Journal of Rural Studies* 12 (3) pp. 245-258

Murdoch, J. and M. Miele (1999) 'Back to nature': changing 'worlds of production' in the food sector. *Sociologia Ruralis* 39 (4) pp. 465-483

Murdoch, J., T. Marsden and J. Banks (2000) Quality, nature and embeddedness: some theoretical considerations in the context of the food sector. *Economic Geography* 76 (2) pp. 107-125

Nygård, B. and O. Storstad (1998) De-globalization of food markets? consumer perceptions of safe food: the case of Norway. *Sociologia Ruralis* 38 (1) pp. 35-53

Oddy, D. and J. Burnett (1992) British diet since industrialization: a bibliographical study. Pp 19-44 in H. Teuteberg ed. *European Food History: A Research Review* (Leicester, Leicester University Press)

Pelto, G. and P. Pelto (1983) Diet and delocalisation: dietary changes since 1750. *Journal of Interdisciplinary History* XIV (2) pp. 507-528

van der Ploeg, J. D. et al. (2000) Rural development: from practice and policies towards theory. *Sociologia Ruralis* 40 (4) pp. 391-408

Ray, C. (1998) Culture, intellectual property and territorial rural development. *Sociologia Ruralis* 38 (1) pp. 3-20

Ritzer, G. (1996) *The McDonaldization of Society: an Investigation into the Changing Character of Contemporary Social Life* (California, Pine Forge Press)

de Roest, K. and A. Menghi (2000) Reconsidering 'traditional' food: the case of Parmigiano Reggiano cheese. *Sociologia Ruralis* 40 (4) pp. 439-451

Rojek, C. (1993) *Ways of Escape: Modern Transformations in Leisure and Travel* (London, The Macmillan Press)

Symons, M. (1982) *One Continuous Picnic: a History of Eating in Australia* (Adelaide, Duck Press)

Tannahill, R. (1988) *Food in History* (London, Penguin)

Terrio, S. (1996) Crafting grand cru chocolates in contemporary France. *American Anthropologist* 98 (1) pp. 67-79

Thiedig, F. and B. Sylvander (2000) Welcome to the club? An economical approach to geographic indications in the European Union. *Agrarwirtschaft* 49 (12) pp. 428-437

Tovey, H. (1997) Food, environmentalism and rural sociology: on the organic farming movement in Ireland. *Sociologia Ruralis* 37 (1) pp. 21-37

Tregear, A., S. Kuznesof and A. Moxey (1998) Policy initiatives for regional foods: some insights from consumer research. *Food Policy* 23 (5) pp. 383-394

Tregear, A. (2001a) *What is a 'typical local food'?: an examination of territorial identities in foods based on development initiatives in the agrifood and rural sectors.* Working Paper No. 58 (Centre for Rural Economy, University of Newcastle, Newcastle upon Tyne, UK)

Tregear, A. (2001b) *Speciality Regional Foods in the UK: an Investigation from the Perspectives of Marketing and Social History.* Unpublished PhD thesis, University of Newcastle

Twiss, S. (1999) *Apples: a Social History* (London: National Trust Enterprises Ltd)

Verhaegen, I. and G. Van Huylenbroeck (2001). Costs and benefits for farmers participating in innovative marketing channels for quality food products. *Journal of Rural Studies* 17 pp. 443-456

Ventura, F. and P. Milone (2000). Theory and practice of multi-product farms: farm butcheries in Umbria. *Sociologia Ruralis* 40 (4) pp. 452-465

Warde, A. (1997) *Consumption, Food and Taste* (London, Sage Publications)

Angela Tregear
School of Agriculture,
Food and Rural Development
University of Newcastle

[9]

ELSEVIER

Journal of Rural Studies 23 (2007) 12–22

JOURNAL OF
RURAL STUDIES

Regional foods and rural development: The role of product qualification

Angela Tregear[a,*], Filippo Arfini[b], Giovanni Belletti[c], Andrea Marescotti[c]

[a]*Management School and Economics, University of Edinburgh, 50 George Square, Edinburgh EH8 9JY, UK*
[b]*Faculty of Economics, Department of Economics, University of Parma, via Kennedy 8, Parma 43100, Italy*
[c]*Faculty of Economics, Department of Economics, University of Florence, via delle Pandette 9, Florence 50127, Italy*

Abstract

Qualification schemes have become popular tools for supporting regional foods, yet little is understood about the impacts they have on the rural development contribution of such foods. Qualification processes may stimulate new networks and community actions, but they may also be incompatible with strategies of extended territorial development because of their foundation in theories of competitive advantage. To explore these issues, the evolution is traced of three cases of regional food production, where local actors pursue the opportunity to qualify products under EEC Regulation 2081/92. The results reveal, in practice, the different experiences that can evolve under the same qualification mechanism, and also how the consequences for rural development can vary. The paper concludes with analysis of factors influencing the involvement and behaviour of actors in regional food qualification, and what these infer for the rural development approach pursued.
© 2006 Elsevier Ltd. All rights reserved.

1. Introduction

In recent years, much has been written about the contribution that regional foods[1] can make to rural development, and an established literature now exists on these products (Bessière, 1998; Ilbery and Kneafsey, 1999, 2000; Marsden et al., 2000; Murdoch et al., 2000; Kneafsey et al., 2001; Parrott et al., 2002), as well as on alternative and relocalised food systems (Hinrichs, 2000; Mormont and Van Huylenbroeck, 2001; Renting et al., 2003; Goodman, 2004; Ilbery et al., 2004). In this literature, regional foods are conceptualised as a form of cultural capital with the potential to leverage wider social and economic benefits to local rural areas, and several empirical studies have indicated that regional foods can indeed play this role (e.g. Ventura and Milone, 2000; Brunori and Rossi, 2000). Often, the key leverage mechanism employed

in this approach is a territorially based qualification or certification scheme, which defines standards of production and supply that are beneficial to the socio-economic status of the area, signalled clearly to buyers by way of a mark or brand. Although a number of authors have considered such qualification schemes at a macro, political economy level (Moran, 1993; Parrott et al., 2002; Barham, 2003), to date there has been much less examination of the impacts of territorial qualification schemes at the micro level. How do different types of local actor respond to them, and with what consequences? To what extent do such qualification schemes augment or constrict the rural development possibilities of regional food products? The aim of this paper is to investigate what happens in practice when actors in a local rural area pursue qualification for a regional food product, examining in particular the links between the types of actor attracted by the qualification opportunity, their motivations and interactions, and the outcomes for rural development.

The paper is structured as follows. First, the theoretical basis of qualification schemes for food products is considered, including those founded on territory or locality. Next, the literature on specialist foods and rural development is reviewed, focusing on the different approaches that actors may adopt and the implications

---

*Corresponding author. Tel.: +44 131 651 3855; fax: +44 131 668 3053.
E-mail address: angela.tregear@ed.ac.uk (A. Tregear).
[1]The foods analysed in this paper may be described as agro-food products with some special characteristics linked to local territory. We use the term 'regional food' to denote such products in preference to 'typical', 'speciality', or 'high quality' foods, as the latter contain more culturally nuanced meanings which would be contentious to use in a cross UK-Italian context.

0743-0167/$ - see front matter © 2006 Elsevier Ltd. All rights reserved.
doi:10.1016/j.jrurstud.2006.09.010

A. Tregear et al. / Journal of Rural Studies 23 (2007) 12–22 13

for how qualification schemes may be employed in this context. Then, drawing from research conducted in the United Kingdom (UK) and Italy, three cases are presented which illustrate the kinds of processes that happen in practice when actors pursue a qualification opportunity. The paper concludes with examination of the dynamics of the cases and discussion of the factors influencing the impact of territorial product qualification on rural development. Throughout the paper, the focus of analysis is on the qualification scheme associated with EEC Regulation 2081/92, which offers Protected Designations of Origin (PDOs) and Protected Geographical Indications (PGIs) to agrifood products that demonstrate special characteristics linked to territory (CEC, 1992). Although there are differences in character between the two types of designation—for PDOs, products must have quality or characteristics *essentially* due to the local area, whereas for PGIs, products have a specific quality or reputation *attributable* to the local area (CEC, 1992: Article 2.2)—application procedures and levels of protection are the same for both designations. The scheme is very appropriate for the purposes of this study not only because of its explicit rural development justification,[2] but also its pan-European coverage allows exploration of how rural development actors at the micro level interpret and engage with a policy designed at the supra-national level.

2. Qualification and agrifood products

For the purposes of this paper, qualification may be defined as the specification of production practices and/or product characteristics by an agent, which is then linked to a particular name or label. Although the branded products of individual private firms represent one example of this process, in an agrifood context qualification is often associated with schemes involving numerous producer actors who agree to meet pre-determined codes of practice, then certified or guaranteed by an independent (often non-commercial) body. For example in the UK, the Soil Association offers a qualification scheme for farmers meeting its standards of organic production, and the Royal Society for the Prevention of Cruelty to Animals (RSPCA) offers its Freedom Food scheme to producers meeting its standards of animal welfare. In Italy, examples of schemes include the Slow Food Association's *Presidium* for agrifood products of excellent quality threatened with extinction (Nosi and Zanni, 2004; Murdoch and Miele, 2004), and the Regione Toscana Administration's mark for agrifood products made from regional plant varieties

---

[2]"Whereas, as part of the adjustment of the common agricultural policy the diversification of agricultural production should be encouraged so as to achieve a better balance between supply and demand on the markets; whereas the promotion of products having certain characteristics could be of considerable benefit to the rural economy, in particular less-favoured or remote areas, by improving the incomes of farmers and by retaining the rural population in these areas." (CEC, 1992).

and rare breeds (Regional Law of Tuscany no. 64/2004, art.11). Whilst qualification processes have been theorised as representations of the shifting moral and ethical conventions of societies (Busch, 2000; Parrott et al., 2002), and as instruments constructed by powerful actors to be wielded in geopolitical negotiations (Moran, 1993; Barham, 2003), at the micro level they have their foundation, and logic, in theories of the competitive advantage of firms. Qualification labels are market mechanisms, information signals employed by producers to stimulate favourable consumer responses, particularly when consumers are faced with choosing between products within the same category (Cochoy, 2004). Specification and labelling of a product raises its market profile and distinguishes it from competing items. Qualification also offers consistent quality guarantees to consumers, leading to repeat purchasing and development of a good reputation. Qualification labels therefore allow firms to capture the added value or economic rent derived from consumer confidence in the good reputation of a firm or producer group, via the controls they impose on product quality (Shapiro, 1983; Tirole, 1988; Anania and Nisticò, 2004).

In terms of regional products, qualification schemes have a long history. For example, the present day qualification systems for wine, based on region of origin, are derived from protocols developed in the late 19th century to protect producers in prestige French wine-growing regions from fraud following the phylloxera outbreak (Moran, 1993; Allaire et al., 2005). The PDO and PGI qualification marks of EEC Regulation 2081/92 are themselves based on this wine qualification system, whereby the qualified product's character is tied to the physical (e.g. soils, climate) and/or cultural features (e.g. traditions of production and processing) of a local territory. Whilst this system may be regarded as only one convention towards food quality (Barham, 2003; Tregear, 2003), it may be argued that its logic is the same as for other agrifoods. That is, qualified producers of the regional product distinguish themselves from others by following a defined code of practice that attains certain standards or quality levels, which consumers value and are willing to pay a premium for. The qualification process effectively transforms the local knowledge and/or natural resources incorporated within the regional food (the basis of the added value) into the collective intellectual property of the actor group (Thiedig and Sylvander, 2000; Pacciani et al., 2001). Official certification resulting from the qualification process protects this intellectual property by preventing the regional food's reputation value from being usurped by competitors (Hamlin and Watson, 1997). The added value or economic rent captured by the process is then distributed within the qualified group, through a mechanism strongly influenced by the heterogeneity of the participants (e.g. their economic dimensions, access to different marketing channels) (Belletti, 2000).

14   *A. Tregear et al. / Journal of Rural Studies 23 (2007) 12–22*

3. Regional products and rural development

To consider how the qualification process described above may impact on rural development, it is first necessary to consider in more depth how regional foods can contribute to the socio-economic well-being of rural areas. Following the principles of endogenous development theory (Bryden, 1998; Ray, 1998; Terluin, 2003), regional foods represent potentially fruitful resources for development as they can incorporate, and valorise, many local assets with special or immobile characteristics linked to the area (Bessière, 1998; Nygård and Storstad, 1998; Brunori and Rossi, 2000; Marsden et al., 2000). How such assets are valorised, however, may vary according to the types of actor involved and the strategies they choose to pursue. In particular, previous studies identify two theoretical approaches which actors may adopt. The first, described as a *supply chain strategy* (Pacciani et al., 2001), involves the building of a strong network of actors in the production and processing of the regional product, focusing energies on managing production levels, improving physical product quality, and implementing effective marketing. Under this approach, the regional product contributes to socio-economic well-being through the existence of a strong producer network, increased employment opportunities within that network, and increased revenues from the effective management of the supply chain and marketing of the product.

The second approach involves a different conceptualisation of regional foods as rural development assets. Here, actors perceive such products as offering a breadth of interlinked resources including physical environmental (e.g. distinctive landscapes, local animal breeds and plant varieties), and cultural (e.g. techniques, know-how, myths, stories), as well as economic (e.g. skilled employment). Thus regional foods are seen to contribute, potentially, to a wide range of initiatives that encourage diverse activities and novel interactions between multiple types of actor (e.g. tourist trails, markets, festivals, educational initiatives, community events). This approach to the use of regional products by local actors has been described as a *territorial quality* or *extended territorial* strategy (Pacciani et al., 2001; Marescotti, 2003). Under this strategy, it is the territorial identity and associations of the product that are the bases of value generation, rather than the physical outputs of a single production network and supply chain. The identities and associations are seen to be utilisable by a broad range of actors who may apply them to a 'basket' of goods and services (Pecqueur, 2001), resulting in a wide distribution of economic rent.

Whilst debates continue about the relative merits of these approaches and their possible inter-dependencies— for example, an effective supply chain strategy may give the basis to support an extended territorial strategy—the focus of this paper is on the role played by the use of qualification mechanisms for regional products. What processes do they stimulate and do they seem to encourage

one strategy rather than another? At first glance, qualification seems logically aligned with a supply chain strategy, as it offers a mechanism for those actors with the most direct investment in a regional product (i.e. the producers) to capture and retain the added values to the exclusion of others. However, if a qualification scheme is itself based on territory, different responses and motivations may be elicited. It may encourage the creation of new partnerships and bodies through which political and financial representations can be made (Casabianca, 2003), or it may stimulate processes of community learning and cultural pride, both of which align qualification more with the extended territorial strategy. To investigate these issues, the following specific aspects of qualification must be examined:

Which actors get involved in product qualification and what are their motivations?: In the above discussion of development strategies, the assumption seems to be that the most appropriate configuration of actors assembles itself around a qualification opportunity, and that a harmonious balance ensues of private interests (i.e. those of the relevant economic groups in the supply chain and system) and civic concerns. Yet in practice, qualification processes may be dominated by one set of actors pursuing one set of interests, skewing the distribution of rent within a supply chain and/or a territory. Other actors or stakeholders may then contest the approach of the dominant actors, leading to conflicts. Whilst local institutions may play a critical role in managing the qualification process and the interests of diverse actors (Marescotti, 2003), the question arises of which institutions get involved and how they manage interests to achieve rural development benefits.

How are the codes of practice in the qualification scheme determined?: Codes of practice are important to rural development as it is through these codes that the activities most beneficial to the socio-economic well-being of an area may be assured. However, by their very nature, such codes involve processes of construction, particularly around phenomena such as tradition, heritage and local identity, which are open to different interpretations (Bérard and Marchenay, 1995; de Sainte Marie et al., 1995). The extended territorial strategy, in particular, implies that codes of practice are drawn up via a consultative process involving diverse stakeholders, arriving at a common understanding. But in practice, individual actors may disagree on codes, particularly where they are heterogenous and multi-sectoral in nature. Different actors may also promote particular constructions in order to pursue specific goals, such as the inclusion or exclusion of other types of actor (Vuylsteke et al., 2003).

Of course, in examining which actors get involved in qualification and what strategies are pursued, socio-economic context (as described by Requier-Desjardins et al., 2003) is acknowledged as playing an important role. For example, in some southern European states there are regions with long-established food quality policies linked to

A. Tregear et al. / Journal of Rural Studies 23 (2007) 12–22   15

territory and/or strong social conventions towards collective action and sharing of common resources. In these
areas, qualification processes might be expected to involve
multiple actors and a disposition towards extended
territorial strategies, in contrast to states or regions with
industrial quality policies and/or more individualistic
competition conventions, such as those popularly associated with northern Europe. On the other hand, micro
level variations may exist within national or even local
contexts, stimulating qualification processes that run
counter to expectations based on macro characteristics.
Although it is beyond the scope of the current research to
take account of all possible contextual forces and their role
in qualification processes, certain key conditions are
explored in the case studies, and their influence is reflected
upon further in the discussion.

Three cases of regional food production are now
presented, where the opportunity to qualify products under
EEC Regulation 2081/92 was pursued: Culatello di Zibello
and the Cherry of Lari (both from Italy) and Beacon Fell
Traditional Lancashire Cheese (from the UK). The
research was conducted as part of a larger EU funded
study of the socio-economic aspects of origin labelled
products.[3] The cases were chosen on the basis of three
criteria. First, to reflect diverse contextual conditions, cases
from both a northern and a southern European country
were selected. Second, in order to explore more deeply how
the same qualification mechanism can stimulate diverse
processes on the ground, the most famous, archetypal
regional products were avoided and instead cases with less
renown and more chequered production and protection
histories were identified. Third, as the main purpose of the
study was to follow how qualification processes evolve in
practice, case products were sought where actors had
responded to and pursued a PDO qualification opportunity, whether or not that process had led to the final award
of a PDO.

Data collection for the three case studies took two main
forms. First, to establish background and context, a phase
of desk research was undertaken, involving scrutiny of
trade publications and local press articles, brochures and
websites of producers and/or their representatives, plus
review of any previous studies or working papers relevant
to the case, where they existed. Second, a series of depth
interviews was conducted with the producers involved in
each case, as well as other key actors such as representatives from local institutions and/or support agencies. In
addition, in the case of the Cherry of Lari, the timing of the
research permitted participant observation of producer
meetings and association discussions, as the decisions over
whether to apply for qualification were 'live' as the study
was taking place. In the presentation that follows, each
case begins with a brief socio-economic context, followed
by a description of the key actors involved and their

---

[3]"Development of Origin Labelled Products: Humanity, Innovation and
Sustainability ('DOLPHINS'), QLK5-2000-00593.

motivations. The identification of these actors was an
inductive process, therefore different categories of key
actor appear for each case. An account is then given of
what happened as the actors responded to the opportunity
to qualify their products, finishing with a summary of the
implications for local development.

4. Case 1: Culatello di Zibello

4.1. Product and socio-economic context

Culatello is a very ancient cured ham produced in the
region of Parma (Italy). The product's origin is linked to
the characteristics of small farm households, where pigs
were bred for family consumption. Farmers would kill one
or two pigs in the winter, season them, and then preserve
them over the course of one year, moving them from the
top storey in the winter to the downstairs cantina in the
summer, to take advantage of the changing temperature
and humidity conditions. Over time, the reputation of
Culatello developed first because of the physical quality of
the product—the taste is very similar to Parma Ham—and
second, because of the product's rarity. Until recent
decades, most Culatello was produced domestically, with
only a few small restaurants and shops producing it
commercially. Industrial production of Culatello began in
1980, by a local firm. Today, per annum production of the
industrial version of the product outstrips the artisanal
version (approximately 55,000 and 18,000 pieces, respectively).

4.2. Key actors in the system and their motivations

Four sets of actors have played a role in the evolution of
the Culatello system. First, small artisan producers. In
total there are 13, of which 11 are local restaurant
businesses, leaving only two as dedicated 'cured ham
producers'. They are joined in a Consortium, with the
objective of producing high quality Culatello using only
artisan techniques, in this way differentiating themselves
from industrial competitors. The second actors are two
larger industrial producers. One of these is a renowned
international firm, operating in the market prior to the
qualification process. Initially, this firm was not interested
in joining the qualification because it was already selling
Culatello successfully under its own brand name. The other
industrial firm was created at the time of the PDO
application, by some local entrepreneurs who perceived
Culatello as a growth market opportunity compared with
the mature market of Parma Ham. The third set of actors
in this case is the local governments of Emilia-Romagna
and Provincia di Parma. Motivated by the desire to
promote development activity in the region, they assisted
in the application process for the PDO, and encouraged
other local entrepreneurs to participate in rural development initiatives based on Culatello. The final set of actors is
the intermediate institutions: the association of pig

breeders, the association of industrial slaughter (ASSICA) and local Chamber of Commerce. Their main interest was, and still is, to allow new industrial firms to get a share of the Culatello business.

4.3. The PDO qualification process—what happened?

In this case, it was one artisan producer who initiated the process. This producer, the owner of a high quality restaurant, perceived the PDO to be an opportunity to increase the value of the Culatello, and with that, his own economic activities. However, in taking forward the application process, he received help from the other artisan producers and also, notably, from the local governments. The role of the government actors became particularly significant in negotiating between the interests of the artisans and the intermediate institutions, particularly ASSICA. ASSICA contested the PDO application because it saw, in the restrictive code of practice being designed by the artisans, the possibility for industrial firms to be excluded from this very profitable market, at a time when other important markets like Parma Ham were stagnating. Of the several points of dispute in the code of practice, a key one related to processing techniques, with the artisans insisting on the long seasonal timeframe of the traditional method, whereas the intermediate institutions argued for shorter, year-round production to be allowed. In the end, the local governments arrived at a compromise whereby two designations, with different codes of practice, were applied. The first designation, "Culatello di Zibello of the Consorzio" applies to the Consortium of artisan producers and this specifies a tight code of practice highly reflective of the traditional, artisan method. This excludes industrial producers. However, by contrast, the code of practice that was finally agreed upon for the PDO designation involves a looser specification of activity, which allows the inclusion of the two industrial firms in the designation.

4.4. Qualification and rural development

As regards rural development activity linked to the qualification process, the local government actors have been instrumental in organising 'Culatello di Zibello Routes'. This initiative, which benefits from the profile-raising effect of qualification on Culatello, connects several types of firm inside the original area of production, such as restaurants, food shops and agro-tourism businesses, where consumers can find the small producers and taste Culatello. Other initiatives have also been organised by the local government actors, such as a fair, a marathon and a bike race, which are then linked to other gastronomic, cultural and environmental products of the territory. In spite of these initiatives, a lack of co-ordination exists between the producers and the other firms of the 'Routes'. Even inside the Consortium co-ordination is very weak, and all initiatives taken in the last few years have depended strongly on the artisan who began the PDO application,

and who now acts as Consortium president. Furthermore, although qualification has contributed to the reputation of the area, the economic rent derived has only been distributed amongst a certain set of firms, and there is a lack of integration of other farmers in the process. In fact, the tradition of domestic production of Culatello in farm households is still prevalent, but such actors are not involved in the Culatello 'atmosphere'. Moreover, it may be argued that the process of qualification has brought into the area of production new industrial initiatives linked to Culatello, with the associated risks of damage to the environment (due the presence of industrial pork breeding), as well as threats to small producers.

5. Case 2: Cherry of Lari

5.1. Product and socio-economic context

Cherry production is a secular tradition in the Municipality of Lari, a small village in the hilly area near Pisa (Tuscany, Italy). The tradition is demonstrated by the presence of 13 native cherry-tree varieties (Roselli and Mariotti, 1999), which, coupled with the peculiarity of the soils and the climate, form the basis of the specificity and reputation of the cherries of Lari. From the 1970s, cherry production suffered from a widespread crisis in agriculture, due to higher production costs of farmers relative to the nearby plains, and especially to the industrialisation process close to the area, resulting in a decrease in the number of farmers (especially professional ones), and in supply. Currently, although almost all farms in the Lari area grow some cherry trees, only a few are professional producers and there are few specialised orchards. Part-time farming is widespread, in which agricultural activity is treated as a contribution to the main source of income, almost always employment in industrial or service sectors, or from pensions. Only a few farms sell cherries to mass distribution firms, and a large proportion is consumed domestically or sold on local wholesale markets. Since 1957, producers based cherry promotion on the traditional annual cherry Festival, which used to attract many buyers, enhancing the product's notoriety. However, as agriculture and tree growing declined, the sales and marketing importance of the Festival decreased. At the same time, the strong identification by the Lari population of the cherry as a 'cultural marker' has made it possible to carry the annual date on, changing its meaning from a product seller to an image and traditions seller. Local consumers have a strong preference for the product, and competition from other stronger production areas does not alter its positioning.

5.2. Key actors in the system and their motivations

The first set of actors in this case is the cherry farmers themselves—predominantly part-time, non-professional growers who use agricultural activity to supplement their

A. Tregear et al. / Journal of Rural Studies 23 (2007) 12–22   17

incomes. The producers have a high degree of geographical and cultural proximity to each other, and employ homogeneous growing techniques and marketing channels. The second actors are the local consumers, who have recently shown renewed interest in traditional agrifood products. In turn this interest has been captured by the third actors, the many local agencies not part of the cherry production or supply chain: the Lari Municipality and local cultural and tourism associations, the Province of Pisa, the Tuscan Regional Administration, the local Chamber of Commerce, and Slow Food association. These actors are interested in connecting the image of the cherry to other rural amenities, such as landscape, environmental quality, art, culture and traditions, in order to promote the area. The involvement of these non-supply chain actors has increased the awareness of the cherry producers of the economic and cultural value of the cherry, strengthening their will to improve the quality image of the product. The fourth set of actors are some agents external to the local production system who have been undertaking research activities aimed at preserving the many native cherry tree varieties (National Research Council, ARSIA-Tuscan Region, Universities of Florence and Pisa). The involvement of these actors has been stimulated by a growing concern for better preservation of biodiversity.

5.3. The PDO qualification process—what happened?

Although the idea of applying for a PDO came from some local small non-professional producers, whose main aim was to stimulate the agricultural production in the area and enhance cherry-tree growing, very quickly the PDO idea was 'captured' by the other local and less local actors, in particular the public administrations of the Region, the Province of Pisa and the Municipality of Lari, who aimed to use the reputation of the cherry of Lari to strengthen the image of the village and the whole area for tourist promotion. Thus from the beginning, the interest and involvement of the producers themselves was rather low. Indeed, most were not aware of the meaning of the PDO, and were rather sceptical about its effectiveness for such a small quantity of production and short marketing channels. Nevertheless, in accordance with the requirements of Regulation 2081/92, a producers' association was set up in 2002, charged with devising the product specifications. Over the course of many meetings, the specifications were discussed, as well as problems and opportunities arising from the award of a PDO itself. In fact, consensus over the product specification was reached fairly easily, a fact that may be linked to the homogeneity of the producers, with no 'market leader' type present. Yet notwithstanding the agreement over product specification, to date, the PDO has not been applied for. This can be attributed to producer concerns over increased production costs arising from certification, as well as fears that the production area would be widened too much under the designation, due to the political pressure from public institutions, farmers'

organisations, etc. to involve the maximum number of producers even in non traditional areas (Marescotti, 2003).

5.4. Qualification and rural development

The meetings held to investigate the qualification process resulted in discussion of many problems and issues, especially those concerning the future of cherry-tree cultivation. These discussions paved the way for other collective initiatives on technical, agronomic and marketing aspects. A collective brand and a collective processing plant for producing jams has been set up, as well as some educational initiatives with local primary schools on the cherry's history. On the back of this renewed enthusiasm and producer cohesion, the local Municipality was influential in constituting a National Association of Cherry Municipalities, dedicated to reinforcing research and promotional activities for cherries across Italy. Overall therefore, although the PDO itself has not been realized, the qualification process has delivered numerous benefits. It has reinforced solidarity and cohesion between farmers by making producers meet together when no association was active in the area previously (Casabianca, 2003). Through the producer association, the interests of producers are now represented in negotiations with agencies and institutions. Finally, the qualification process, by encouraging the defence and promotion of the cherry, has acted as a catalyst for the involvement of other local and non-local actors. The qualification process has been the stimulus for collective action in this case.

6. Case 3: Beacon Fell Traditional Lancashire Cheese

6.1. Product and socio-economic context

The product is a pressed cows' milk cheese, specific to the region of Lancashire (north west England). The north of this region is well suited to pasturing, hence there is a long history of dairying and cheese-making (Mason, 1999). Today, there are nine producers of traditional Lancashire cheese, the smallest producing approximately 50 tons per annum, and the largest producing approximately 2500 tons of cheese per annum, of which about 500 tons is traditional Lancashire. Forces of industrialisation and standardisation have been strong in the UK dairy sector throughout the 20th century. These forces, combined with the existence of the Milk Marketing Board from the 1930s to the 1980s (a monopoly with statutory powers to buy and sell all UK milk) have militated against the existence of independent, on-farm milk processing, with the result that by the 1970s, only a very small number of small-scale and artisanal cheese-makers remained in the UK (Blundel, 2002). Numbers have increased in the last two decades as small-scale and speciality agrifood production have been revalorised, but production systems today tend to be driven by individual firms, with generally low levels of collective activity between producers (Tregear, 2003).

6.2. Key actors in the system and their motivations

The first actor in this case (Producer 1), the largest producer, plays a critical role in both the pursuit of the PDO application and also in the general evolution of the system. In the 1960s, the father of the present manager developed a new version of Lancashire cheese, more easily made on a large scale, but hard and acid in character. His motivation was to meet requests from local traders who sought a high yielding, relatively cheap cheese to counter the threat of competition in the most important regional urban markets. In fact, the acid version became popularised, and it is this cheese that is now regarded as 'Lancashire' in the UK, being produced on an industrial scale by large creameries. In the meantime, Producer 1 continued to make both traditional and industrial varieties, as part of a wider portfolio of cheeses. In the 1990s, the present manager of the firm initiated the PDO application, motivated by the potential marketing advantage it could bring to the traditional product, in view of the recent market growth in speciality cheeses in the UK. The second actors in this case are the other traditional cheese-makers. These are smaller in scale than Producer 1, but who also make the traditional product alongside other flavour or maturation variants, as well as other types of cheese. Marketing and distribution activities are undertaken at the individual level, with personalised branding of products. As such, the interest of these actors is in protecting the quality of their cheeses and enhancing the competitive advantage of their brand identities. The final set of actors are the regional support institutions, including the county councils and regional development agency, and also North West Fine Foods, the speciality food group for the wider north west region. This group has the aim of supporting and developing the interests of small-scale speciality food producers in the region.

6.3. The qualification process—what happened?

The PDO application process was initiated by Producer 1, who perceived a potential marketing advantage in obtaining the designation. In accordance with the group application requirements of Regulation 2081/92, Producer 1 stimulated the interest of the other producers via the reactivation of a pre-existing producer association—the Lancashire Cheesemakers Association. This had originally been set up to bargain with the Milk Marketing Board, but had effectively been disbanded since the dissolution of the MMB in the 1980s. In drawing up the code of practice, the consensus reached was helped by the fact that notwithstanding some differences in production scale and technique, none of the applicant producers was pushing for an 'industrial' specification. Moreover, as protection of the name 'Lancashire Cheese' could not be applied for (this name now being considered generic for the reasons explained earlier), other industrial producers who may have contested the application were not drawn into the

process. The issue of the protected name in fact gave rise to some creative constructions around identity. As the applicants had to find another name for the PDO, a map was consulted. A hill called Beacon Fell was identified as a relatively central geographical feature, equidistant from the location of all the applicant producers. Hence, the protected name applied for, and awarded, is 'Beacon Fell Traditional Lancashire Cheese'. The applicants also had difficulty in defining a strict geographic boundary for the production area—as Regulation 2081/92 also requires—because no precedent existed to guide this. A pragmatic approach was adopted therefore, with the final boundaries being drawn around the area of Fylde, north of the River Ribble, including the Preston and Blackpool districts of Lancashire.

6.4. Qualification and rural development

It is difficult to identify firm or direct links between qualification and rural development in this case. All the producer actors engage in some level of direct marketing and use short channels such as farmers' markets, both of which offer benefits in terms of retaining revenues within the region, generating employment, stimulating social interaction, etc. In these activities, the producers are supported by local government actors such as North West Fine Foods, that develop initiatives such as tourist trails. In addition, individual cheesemakers get involved in local communities by running courses and educational visits, although sometimes these efforts are limited by size of premises and regulations covering hygiene, safety and insurance. However, the extent to which the PDO qualification itself contributes to these activities is debatable. Only Producer 1 actually uses the PDO name and designation, and this is on products destined for supermarket outlets. Therefore the PDO is not actively contributing to the valorisation of the product. The PDO qualification may be considered to have brought more benefits in terms of reactivating a producer association and thereby encouraging more interaction and collective effort amongst the cheesemakers. Nevertheless, it should noted that even after several years of qualification, the cheesemakers still act very much as individuals, with their own sourcing, branding and marketing, not to mention community activities.

7. Discussion

7.1. Product qualification—a mechanism for a supply chain or territorial strategy?

This paper sought to examine the role that qualification schemes play in rural development activities based on regional foods, in particular, whether they are aligned with supply chain or extended territorial strategies. The results illustrate clearly how a single qualification opportunity can be captured by diverse types of actor with different

A. Tregear et al. / Journal of Rural Studies 23 (2007) 12–22   19

motivations. The experiences that ensue are quite distinct, as is the outcome for rural development, even for a qualification scheme (EEC Regulation 2081/92) which is based on territory and has an explicit rural development justification. For example, in one case (Cherry of Lari) qualification is captured by multiple, but well-coordinated actors as part of a territorial strategy. In another (Culatello di Zibello), local government intervention helps to orient a supply chain strategy towards a more territorial approach. In the third case (Lancashire Cheese), one producer dominates the entire qualification process out of perceived marketing advantage, making pragmatic use of structures (a pre-existing association) and specifications (the PDO name) to achieve the desired result (an official designation that may, in future, confer marketing benefits to one product in a portfolio). The strategy adopted in this latter case is clearly not territorial, but neither is it supply chain, as de facto, little or no collective action exists. The qualification is used as part of a marketing strategy pursued by one individual firm. Table 1 summarises these findings.

In light of these results, we now contemplate some of the features that have played an influential role in the strategic evolution of the three cases. It is emphasised that these features are specific to the cases studied and they are not put forward as definitive or generalisable. They are offered tentatively for future, larger-scale research to examine further or verify.

Socio-economic context: Earlier in the paper, socio-economic context was highlighted as important to the evolution of qualification processes. In practice, the cases reveal how such contexts can and do play a role: witness, for example, the differences between Italian and UK socio-political conventions on local institutional involvement in qualification processes (high in the case of Culatello and Cherry of Lari, low in the case of Lancashire Cheese). However, the three cases also reveal how pathways to qualification can be influenced by conditions at the local or micro level, leading to experiences that differ from those that might be expected of the nation states concerned. For example, in terms of disposition of producers towards collective action, the home region of Culatello has a well-established tradition of this, exemplified by the consortia of Parmigiano-Reggiano cheese and Parma Ham. However, this contrasts not only with the region of Lancashire Cheese, where several forces have militated against the co-operative working of small-scale producers, but also—perhaps surprisingly—with the region of the Cherry of Lari, where collective action amongst producers is also not so strong. In turn, the cases also reveal that a context such as level of collective action can have complex impacts on the type of product qualification strategy pursued. On the one hand, a tradition of collective action seems conducive to the motivation of actors to share rent, which is an important precursor to a territorial strategy. But, as the Culatello case shows, where that tradition rests only amongst supply chain actors, then the risk is that it is a sectoral, rather than a territorial strategy that develops from product qualification. On the other hand, although involvement of local institutions would seem to encourage

Table 1
Summary of how qualification was pursued in the case studies

Case	Actor involvement and motivation	Evolution of qualification process	Strategy pursued
Culatello di Zibello	Initiated by artisan producers, seeking to differentiate their product from the industrial version	• Conflict between artisan and industrial producers over code of practice • Local administration mediates • Two qualifications awarded (PDO is loose specification)	Semi supply chain, semi territorial strategy
Cherry of Lari	Initiated by part-time producer, but quickly captured by other (both public and private) actors seeking to use product reputation to strengthen whole area	• Active discussions to develop code of practice • Springboard to wider socio-economic initiatives • PDO not applied for (producers sceptical about benefits)	Territorial strategy
Beacon Fell Traditional Lancashire Cheese	Initiated and pursued by largest producer, in anticipation of marketing advantage	• Re-activation of producer association • Little conflict over code of practice • Creative constructions over product name and boundaries	(Anticipated) individual marketing strategy

20 A. Tregear et al. / Journal of Rural Studies 23 (2007) 12–22

a more cross-sectoral approach to development, the Cherry of Lari case highlights the critical role that producer actors still play in a territorial strategy—the need for their motivation and reward is essential. Therefore, the experiences in these cases suggest that for a territorial strategy to ensue from qualification opportunities, different tactics need to be employed to engage the optimal mix of actors, with their diverse tendencies and motivations.

Economic vs. cultural significance of product: A second feature of importance revealed in these cases is the extent to which the product being qualified has economic significance for individual producer actors relative to cultural significance for the local region. The Culatello case shows that producers who rely heavily on economic returns from the regional product can take a very strong interest in the way that qualification specifications are devised. The Culatello producers were most concerned that the final specifications did not disadvantage them, either by excluding them (in the case of more industrial producers), or by allowing 'new' competitors into the system (in the case of artisan producers). The actors therefore became preoccupied with how the qualification would distribute rent within the sector or supply chain, rather than approaching qualification as a tool for a territorial strategy, which is a different way of thinking about value creation and remuneration of local resources. Conversely, the Cherry of Lari case shows how cultural significance of products can contribute much to a territorial strategy because of the wealth of traditions that accompany them, touching on various aspects of community life and events. In this case, the effect was compounded by the relatively low reliance of producers on the economic value of the product, which gave greater potential for their openness to a territorial strategy. Overall, the Cherry of Lari case illustrates the evolution that can take place from a product of economic significance to one of cultural significance.

Access to, and visibility of the product in the territory: A third strategy-influencing feature revealed in these cases is the type of resource offered by the specialist regional product and the extent to which it is visible in the territory. Specifically, the Cherry of Lari case illustrates how a wide cross-section of a local population can become involved in territorial activities if the special character of the product is based on resources or techniques that are either free or easy to access: i.e., the planting of a cherry tree. In this case, the resource became a patrimonial or collectively shared good and the qualification scheme that was pursued subsequently involved the multiple actors. On the other hand, the Culatello and Lancashire Cheese cases illustrate that if the special character of a product is based on relatively inaccessible resources (e.g. the knowledge, skills and facilities required to process high quality cheese or ham), the involvement of a narrower set of actors is implied, encouraging the pursuit of a supply chain strategy. It is noteworthy that in these latter two cases, product qualification became a matter for the producer 'experts' to debate, rather than involving a wide cross-section of the

population. Related to the basis of the special character is the extent to which the production activities are visible in the territory. Highly visible activities (e.g. cherry trees growing in every small farm or orchard), lend themselves to the development of a territorial strategy linked to specific landscape and environmental features. In contrast, low-visibility resources (e.g. indoor pig units or domestic cellars in which salamis are matured) are more difficult to make the link with.

7.2. Product qualification—rural development benefits or problems?

The three cases presented here also give insights into how product qualification itself stimulates rural development problems (e.g. conflicts between actors, threats to product quality and integrity) as well as benefits (e.g. cross-sectoral interactions, enhancements of civic pride). For example, in the Cherry of Lari case, although the process activated by qualification was beneficial to development, the PDO itself was not applied for due to anticipated problems over producer costs and lack of exclusivity. In the Lancashire Cheese case, the qualification process was undertaken with little or no conflict, but the approach taken by the actors meant that the social interaction and institution creation benefits were minimal. How might one distinguish when and where product qualification offers benefits rather than problems? In the cases studied here, two key characteristics can be drawn out. As with the identification of features of importance to strategy, these characteristics are not proposed as definitive, but could be investigated in future, larger-scale research projects.

Heterogeneity of producer actors: First, the three cases reveal how conflict between producer actors pursuing qualification is linked to their heterogeneity, which refers to characteristics such as production scale and degree of industrialisation, as well as the type of marketing channel pursued. In the case of Culatello, where a high degree of production scale difference existed between producer actors, product qualification was associated with conflicts. Artisan producers resisted the inclusion of larger, more industrial producers, as the latter were seen as 'free riders' able to capture the rent accumulated via the efforts and resources already expended by the artisans. The artisan producers also feared the future loss of rent resulting from the drop in consumers' quality perceptions associated with larger producers being included in the qualification. By contrast, both the Cherry of Lari and Lancashire Cheese cases showed less conflict in the drawing up of specifications, as the producers were more homogeneous in terms of production scale. Less conflict implies more constructive and deep interactions between actors, with consequent benefits for development activities. However, as the Lancashire Cheese case has also demonstrated, lack of conflict does not necessarily imply collective action.

Local institution decisions: Following from the above, the cases also reveal the impacts of local institutions on the

A. Tregear et al. / Journal of Rural Studies 23 (2007) 12–22   21

rural development benefits of qualification, via their intervention in conflicts over qualification specifications and/or their taking responsibility for determining codes of practice, geographic boundaries, etc. In both the Culatello and Cherry of Lari cases, local institutions revealed a tendency to define rather loose codes of practice, motivated by the desire to include many actors in the qualification. These results accord with those of previous studies (e.g. Barjolle and Sylvander, 2000). The implications are that not only do such tendencies risk undermining the effective commercial operation of the qualification mark (it becomes insufficiently distinctive as a quality indicator to consumers), which threatens de-valorisation of the product and consequent problems for development activities (Carbone, 2003), if larger or more industrial producers are included within the qualification, this reduces the incentive for smaller, artisan producers to continue to engage in the environmentally or culturally significant practices that have the territorial development potential.

8. Conclusions

This paper set out to investigate the impact of territorial product qualification on the rural development potential of specialist regional foods, with particular reference to EEC Regulation 2081/92. The case study method employed means that only tentative conclusions can be drawn, based on the specific experiences of the case products analysed. The cases presented here suggest that contrary to some theoretical logic, qualification may indeed be employed as part of an extended territorial strategy, although its success is dependent upon a particular mix of actors, exhibiting a certain mix of motivations. Can qualification processes themselves bring socio-economic benefits to rural areas? Results from this study are mixed. On the one hand, the processes of interaction and debate, and setting up of interest groups can be beneficial. However, the cases presented also show that qualification can be a source of conflict between different actors, and decisions over codes of practice and exclusivity have to be made with care, if the qualification mark is to operate effectively as a market signal, and if qualified producers are to be incentivised to engage in practices with the most development potential. With this in mind, the three cases presented here suggest it may be useful to conceptualise institutional involvement in qualification processes in two phases: ex ante and ex post. In the ex ante phase (i.e. during pursuit of qualification), producer actors concern themselves over the critical issue of the codes of practice, attempting to reach the best compromise over inclusion/exclusion. Institutional intervention in this phase must strike a balance between active participation (or even leadership) on the one hand, to help stimulate producers who lack a tradition of collective action, and reticence on the other hand, so as not to upset producer negotiations and cause a loss of socio-economic cohesion. In the ex post phase however (i.e. after the award of a qualification), institutions can play a more active role,

using the qualification as part of a territorial strategy without altering, or threatening to alter, the codes of practice.

Overall, product qualification may be regarded as a mechanism for linking local and non-local actors, within the logic of the mixed exogenous/endogenous development model (Lowe et al., 1995). It is a means by which local actors can signal to, and attract revenues from, exogenous actors and institutions (Requier-Desjardins et al., 2003). But questions remain over who controls this mechanism, and how it can be managed to best effect for achieving rural development benefits.

Acknowledgements

The authors are grateful to the editor and three anonymous referees for their helpful comments on an earlier draft of this paper. The research on which this paper is based was conducted within the project Development of Origin Labelled Products: Humanity, Innovation and Sustainability ('DOLPHINS'), QLK5-2000-00593, http://www.origin-food.org. This paper draws specifically from work package 5. Thanks are extended to Mitchell Ness for help in compiling data for the Lancashire Cheese case study. The analysis presented here, and any remaining errors, are the responsibility of the authors.

References

Allaire, G., Sylvander, S., Belletti, G., Barjolle, D., Marescotti, A., Thévenod-Mottet, E., Tregear, A., 2005. Les dispositifs français et européens de protection de la qualité et de l'origine dans le contexte de l'OMC: justifications générales et contextes nationaux. Symposium international. Territoires et enjeux du développement régional, Programme transversal de l'INRA, Pour et Sur le Développement Régional, Lyon, 9–11 mars.

Anania, G., Nisticò, R., 2004. Public regulation as a substitute for trust in quality food markets: what if the trust substitute can't be fully trusted? Journal of Institutional and Theoretical Economics 160 (4), 681–701.

Barham, E., 2003. Translating terroir: the global challenge of French AOC labeling. Journal of Rural Studies 19, 127–138.

Barjolle, D., Sylvander, B., 2000. Some factors of success for origin labeled products in agri-food chains in Europe: market, internal resources and institutions. In: Sylvander, B., Barjolle, D., Arfini, F. (Eds.), The Socio-economics of Origin Labeled Products in Agro-food Supply Chains: Spatial, Institutional and Co-ordination Aspects. INRA, France.

Belletti, G., 2000. Origin labeled products, reputation and heterogeneity of firms. In: Sylvander, B., Barjolle, D., Arfini, F. (Eds.), The Socio-economics of Origin Labeled Products in Agro-food Supply Chains: Spatial, Institutional and Co-ordination Aspects. INRA, France.

Bérard, L., Marchenay, P., 1995. Lieux, temps, et preuves: la construction sociale des produits de terroir. Terrain 24, 153–164.

Bessière, J., 1998. Local development and heritage: traditional food and cuisine as tourist attractions in rural areas. Sociologia Ruralis 38 (1), 21–34.

Blundel, R., 2002. Network evolution and the growth of artisanal firms: a tale of two regional cheese makers. Entrepreneurship and Regional Development 14, 1–30.

Brunori, G., Rossi, A., 2000. Synergy and coherence through collective action: some insights from wine routes in Tuscany. Sociologia Ruralis 40 (4), 409–423.

Bryden, J., 1998. Development strategies for remote rural regions: what do we know so far? Paper presented at the OECD International Conference on Remote Rural Areas: Developing through Natural and Cultural Assets, Albarracin, Spain, 5–6 November.

Busch, L., 2000. The moral economy of grades and standards. Journal of Rural Studies 16, 273–283.

Carbone, A., 2003. The role of designation of origin in the Italian food system. In: Gatti, S., Giraud-Hraud, E., Mili, S. (Eds.), Wine in the Old World: New Risks and Opportunities. Franco Angeli, Milano, Italy, pp. 29–37.

Casabianca, F., 2003. Les produits d'origine: une aide au développement local. In: Delannoy, P., Hervieu, B. (Eds.), A Table. Peut-on encore bien manger? Editions de l'Aube, Paris, pp. 66–82.

CEC, 1992. Commission of the European Communities Council Regulation (EEC) No. 2081/92 of July 14.

Cochoy, F., 2004. Is the modern consumer a Buriden's donkey? Product packaging and consumer choice. In: Ekström, K., Bremeck, H. (Eds.), Elusive Consumption. Berg, Oxford, pp. 205–227.

de Sainte Marie, C., Prost, J.-A., Casabianca, F., Casalta, E., 1995. La construction social de la qualité: enjeux autour de l'appellation d'origin controlée broccu corse. In: Nicolas, P., Valceschini, E. (Eds.), Agro-alimentaire: une Economie de la Qualité. INRA, France, pp. 185–197.

Goodman, D., 2004. Rural Europe redux?: Reflections on alternative agro-food networks and paradigm change. Sociologia Ruralis 44 (1), 3–16.

Hamlin, R., Watson, V., 1997. The role of appellation in wine marketing—does the New Zealand wine industry know what it's getting? International Journal of Wine Marketing 9 (2/3), 52–69.

Hinrichs, C., 2000. Embeddedness and local food systems: notes on two types of direct agricultural market. Journal of Rural Studies 16, 295–303.

Ilbery, B., Kneafsey, M., 1999. Niche markets and regional speciality food products in Europe: towards a research agenda. Environment and Planning A 31 (12), 2207–2222.

Ilbery, B., Kneafsey, M., 2000. Producer constructions of quality in regional speciality food production: a case study from south west England. Journal of Rural Studies 16, 217–230.

Ilbery, B., Maye, D., Kneafsey, M., Jenkins, T., Walkey, C., 2004. Forecasting food supply chain developments in lagging rural regions: evidence from the UK. Journal of Rural Studies 20, 331–344.

Kneafsey, M., Ilbery, B., Jenkins, T., 2001. Exploring the dimensions of culture economies in rural west Wales. Sociologia Ruralis 41 (3), 296–310.

Lowe, P., Murdoch, J., Ward, N., 1995. Networks in rural development: beyond endogenous and exogenous models. In: van der Ploeg, J., van Dijk, G. (Eds.), Beyond Modernization: The Impact of Endogenous Rural Development. Van Gorcum, Assen, pp. 87–105.

Marescotti, A., 2003. Typical products and rural development: who benefits from PDO/PGI recognition? Paper presented at: Food Quality Products in the Advent of the 21st Century: Production, Demand and Public Policy. 83rd EAAE Seminar, Chania, Greece, 4–7 September.

Marsden, T., Banks, J., Bristow, G., 2000. Food supply chain approaches: exploring their role in rural development. Sociologia Ruralis 40 (4), 424–439.

Mason, L., 1999. Traditional Foods of Britain. Prospect Books, Devon.

Moran, W., 1993. Rural space as intellectual property. Political Geography 12 (3), 263–277.

Mormont, M., Van Huylenbroeck, G., 2001. A la Recherche de la Qualité. Recherches Socio-économiques sur les Nouvelles Filières Agroalimentaires. Presses de l'Université de Liège, Belgium.

Murdoch, J., Miele, M., 2004. A new aesthetic of food? Relational reflexivity in the 'alternative' food movement. In: Harvey, M., McMeekin, A., Warde, A. (Eds.), Qualities of Food. Manchester University Press, UK.

Murdoch, J., Marsden, T., Banks, J., 2000. Quality, nature and embeddedness: some theoretical considerations in the context of the food sector. Economic Geography 76 (2), 107–125.

Nosi, C., Zanni, L., 2004. Moving from 'typical products' to 'food related' services: the Slow Food case as a new business paradigm. British Food Journal 106 (10/11), 779–792.

Nygård, B., Storstad, O., 1998. De-globalization of food markets?: consumer perceptions of safe food: the case of Norway. Sociologia Ruralis 38 (1), 35–53.

Pacciani, A., Belletti, G., Marescotti, A., Scaramuzzi, S., 2001. The role of typical products in fostering rural development and the effects of Regulation (EEC) 2081/92. Paper presented at: Policy Experiences with Rural Development in a Diversified Europe. 73rd EAAE Seminar, Ancona, Italy, 28–30 June.

Parrott, N., Wilson, N., Murdoch, J., 2002. Spatializing quality : regional protection and the alternative geography of food. European Urban and Regional Studies 9 (3), 241–261.

Pecqueur, B., 2001. Qualité et développement territorial: l'hypothèse du panier de biens et de services territorialisés. Economic Rurale 261, 37–49.

Ray, C., 1998. Culture, intellectual property and territorial rural development. Sociologia Ruralis 38 (1), 3–20.

Renting, H., Marsden, T., Banks, J., 2003. Understanding alternative food networks: exploring the role of short food supply chains in rural development. Environment and Planning A 35, 393–411.

Requier-Desjardins, D., Boucher, F., Cerdan, C., 2003. Globalization, competitive advantages and the evolution of production systems: rural food processing and localized agri-food systems in Latin-American countries. Entrepreneurship and Regional Development 15, 49–67.

Roselli, G., Mariotti, P., 1999. Il Germoplasma del Ciliegio. ARSIA e CNR-Istituto sulla Propagazione delle Specie Legnose, Firenze, Italy.

Shapiro, C., 1983. Premiums for high quality products as returns to reputation. Quarterly Journal of Economics 98, 659–679.

Terluin, I., 2003. Differences in economic development in rural regions of advanced countries: an overview and critical analysis of theories. Journal of Rural Studies 19, 327–344.

Thiedig, F., Sylvander, B., 2000. Welcome to the club?: an economical approach to geographical indications in the European Union. Agrarwirtschaft 49 (12), 428–437.

Tirole, J., 1988. The Theory of Industrial Organisation. MIT Press, Cambridge, MA.

Tregear, A., 2003. From Stilton to Vimto: using food history to rethink typical products in rural development. Sociologia Ruralis 43 (2), 91–107.

Ventura, F., Milone, P., 2000. Theory and practice of multi-product farms: farm butcheries in Umbria. Sociologia Ruralis 40 (4), 452–465.

Vuylsteke, A., Collet, E., van Huylenbroeck, G., Mormont, M., 2003. Exclusion of farmers as a consequence of quality certification and standardisation. Paper presented at Food Quality Products in the Advent of the 21st Century: Production, Demand and Public Policy. 83rd EAAE Seminar, Chiana, Greece, 4–7 September.

[10]

Origin Products, Geographical Indications and Rural Development[1]

Giovanni Belletti and Andrea Marescotti

Introduction

Rural development is becoming increasingly important for populations around the world, and is finding its way on to government agendas in both developed and developing countries. Tendencies towards greater globalization, favoured by the ongoing process of trade liberalization, have led to a wide restructuring and reorganization of economic and social spaces, thus affecting territorial competitiveness. The vitality and the very survival of entire rural **regions** are sometimes endangered, particularly where local human and natural resources cannot easily be managed so as to find new bases of competitiveness (OECD, 2006).

This is particularly true in marginalized rural areas where, owing to a complex 'bundle' of factors – infrastructural, structural, geographical and cultural – it is not easy to achieve price competitiveness, and other forms of leverage are not quickly available. The crisis that many rural areas are facing may endanger their local economies, exert negative effects on the quality of the environment, threaten social relationships and livelihoods, and cause a loss of culture and traditions. Then again, the growing attention paid by consumers and citizens to 'non-commodity outputs', which is partly shifting the demand towards environmental, social and cultural goods, seems to offer new opportunities for development, even in remote rural areas.

The concept of rural development encompasses all these different economic and non-economic issues, with varying emphases according to authors and cultures. Given that the concept of rural development itself is interpreted in different ways in time and space, the links between **origin products** (OPs) and rural development should be analysed in a contextualized way: here reference is made particularly to the European Union (EU) perspective, both for the concept of rural development and for the legal **protection** tools associated with **geographical indications** (GIs).

The rural development potential of OPs comes from their strong links to their territories of origin and from the specificity of the local resources used in the production process. Consumers are looking for a reconnection to the locality where food is being produced, sometimes for reasons of identity, in other cases for food safety and quality. Given this conjuncture, GI production systems are expected to exert positive rural development effects: economic effects (both inside and outside the OP supply chain, at a local level), and social, cultural and environmental effects.

In order to explore the contributions of OPs to rural development we first need to conceptualize both OPs and rural development, and then analyse how different actors involved in OP systems mobilize these resources within their strategies. The examples of EU **protected designations of origin** (PDOs) and **protected geographical indications** (PGIs) can highlight different categories of positive effects that OP product valorization can have on rural development, as well as some ambiguous effects.

Conceptualizing Origin Products: Territory and Community

The specificity of OPs comes from their strong links to their territories of origin (Delfosse, 1996). There are three relevant dimensions in determining the **typicality** of agro-food products: the specificity of local resources used in the production process; the history of the product and of its production and consumption tradition; and the collective dimension, including presence of a shared knowledge at the local level (Barjolle *et al.*, 1998a; Bérard and Marchenay, 1995, 2004; Mollard, 2001; Pecqueur, 2001; Casabianca *et al.*, 2005).[2]

The specificity of local resources determines the peculiarities of product quality attributes, coming from the 'physical' environment where it is produced, and particularly from the pedo-climatic environmental and genetic resources. Nevertheless, the typicality is not only a matter of natural resources, as it is always through the action of people that natural resources express their potential – through the growing, breeding, handling and processing practices that result in a specialized product.

These practices are usually very specific, and transmitted through time from one generation to the next, in a process by which local actors adapt the techniques to the specific environment and culture on the basis of contextual local knowledge and scientific

progress. With time, the evolution of the techniques and know-how developed by local actors creates, modifies and adapts the specificity of OPs to the local socio-economic, environmental and cultural context. Moreover, there is also a consumption tradition specific to the place of origin: namely, knowledge of how to eat the product and when, how to prepare and cook it, how to taste it and how to evaluate its quality.

History and cultural traditions are closely connected to a third specificity of OPs, the collective dimension (Berriet, 1995; Barjolle *et al.*, 1998a; Belletti *et al.*, 2003). Actually, what clearly makes a difference between an OP and other specific **quality products** is that the link with the territorial area has been created, consolidated and modified over time, within a community of producers and consumers, in such a way that the OP becomes part of the common local patrimony, something that cannot be individually owned and managed. The process of knowledge acquisition (often contextual and non-codified), accumulation and sedimentation makes an OP the expression of a community of producers and often of the overall local community organization, values, traditions and habits. That is why we refer to a *patrimonial* dimension of OPs (Bérard and Marchenay, 1995): the product characteristics, and the way of producing, storing, marketing, consuming and appreciating an OP, are all part of the patrimony of the local community, which alone should have the right to use it to attain economic, social and cultural benefits. The link between the OP and its territory should repose in cultural aspects and local identity, especially when the OP determines the 'historical memory' of the local population, and becomes an element of identity to the point of serving as a catalyst of local community action, one that can reinforce promotion initiatives at the local level (Bérard *et al.*, 2008).

The upshot of this observation is that typicality is not built solely on production processes and product features, but mainly on relationships among actors within the system. They are the ones who interpret and give meaning to the links between the product and its environment. The specificities of an OP are, therefore, the result of a complex evolutionary process of negotiation among the local producers, between the producers and consumers in the local community, and, when the product reaches more distant **markets** and consumers, between the local system and non-local consumers and citizens. These specificities explain the particular contribution that OPs can exert on rural development.

Conceptualizing Rural Development: a Polysemous Concept

Rural development is becoming one of the most important political objectives in many countries and regions of the world. Notwithstanding its growing importance, the definitions of 'rurality' and 'rural development' are very vague, with various meanings in both the economic literature and political discourse.[3] There are many definitions of rurality, often depending on the objectives of the researchers or analyses of policy makers. The meaning of the term 'rural' changes with time, adapting itself to the prevailing general economic and social change. Especially in recent times, the concepts of 'agrarian' and 'non-urban' have been replaced by a more precise articulation that follows the social and economic changes observed in non-urban areas and the variability of situations and trends. Sectorial and territorial integration is now considered a key element of modern rurality in Europe (Basile and Cecchi, 1997).

The emerging concept of 'rurality' refers to a territory where agriculture is losing its economic leadership, but still plays, even within rural policies, a crucial role, not only in the use of the land and management of natural resources, but also by providing a basis for diversification, integration and development in rural communities. It has now been fully acknowledged that agriculture plays a significant role in meeting social requirements that can no longer be limited to accomplishing the basic function of food production, but extends to managing the environment and landscape, preserving local cultures threatened by increasing mass production and providing recreation and

services. The concept of **multifunctionality**[4] (OECD, 2001; SFER, 2003) has been built upon both the new face of agriculture and of rural areas and the new needs of society.

In fact, starting from the mid-1980s, the concept of rural development has been included more and more often in agricultural policies, especially in the EU Common Agricultural Policy (CAP), with a fairly clear definition. The rural development policy of the EU is increasingly oriented towards supporting diversification of economic and social activities in rural areas, with the goals of improving quality of life for local and external citizens, and of preserving rural resources. Other recent approaches consider rural development in an endogenous and/or neo-endogenous (Lowe *et al.*, 1995; Murdoch *et al.*, 2003) and sustainable dimension: this means that the participation of the rural community in the definition of the objectives (a bottom-up approach to policy making), the role of local resources (goods, skills, contextual knowledge) and respect for the natural and social environment all play a central role in rural development discourse.[5] The three European Conferences on Rural Development organized by the European Commission (EC, 1996 – Cork, 2003 – Salzburg and 2008 – Cyprus) provide plentiful evidence of this evolution. According to this logic, there is an increasing dependence on political spheres (Pacciani, 2002; Pecqueur, 2002; Allaire and Dupeuble, 2003), which is translated into a zoning of public action (Perraud, 2001) and a revaluation of local public administration and local actors.

Based on these new notions, alternative views of the development of rural areas and agriculture have been emerging. Thus 'new rurality' is conceptualized as a reaction to the paradigm of mass production (modernization) that has prevailed in recent decades. The new paradigm stands out both at the level of local economic systems and at the level of firms, and is no longer based solely on economies of scale and specialization, but rather on *scope economies*, diversification and new interconnections among stakeholders in rural areas (Brunori, 2003; Ventura and Milone, 2005). These changes entail a redefinition of identities, strategies, practices and networks, in which farmers no longer have a monopoly (Ploeg and Roep, 2003).

These conceptualizations of the 'new rurality' turn rural development into a complex issue based on different principles from the 'standard' model, and bring the mechanisms at work into question. Development is conceived as the result of complex social dynamics as well as a shared cognitive paradigm that guides stakeholders in their use the resources of the rural community. The multiple values of territories are rediscovered by local stakeholders, who share them and build individual and collective identities.

Rural development includes a set of different practices that are, however, interrelated: the conservation of the landscape and other values associated with the environment, agro-tourism, organic farming, the products linked to the region, etc. (Ploeg and Roep, 2003). The organization of the supply of goods and services, on the basis of a recombination of local resources, is theorized thus: there is a growth of forms of cultural economy (Moran, 1993; Ray, 1998) which are based on the capacity to link products to local resources (Mollard, 2001; Pecqueur, 2001; Di Iacovo and Ciofani, 2005). The productive vocations of regions and the products of local traditions are encompassed in this perspective, which aims both at increasing the self-esteem of local communities and promoting their visibility to the outside world.

Rural development, according to a more general view of economic development in regional studies (Storper, 1997), is now therefore based on the reinforcement of the territory as a factor of competitiveness of production systems, based on network building (consolidation of the relationship both within the rural system and between the rural system and the outside) and careful use of specific rural resources (Allaire and Sylvander, 1997). All this leads to the importance of the collective dimension and of the role of localized production systems – which some studies analyse as 'Alternative Food Networks and Short Food Supply Chains'[6] – in rural development dynamics. In this context, OP production systems are perhaps the most meaningful case to examine.

The Multifunctional Virtuous Circle: Positive Effects of Origin Products on Rural Development

The valorization of OPs, whether by means of GI special protection schemes or more informally, is increasingly seen as a powerful tool to reach private and public aims and to encourage positive dynamics in rural development, by virtue of their deep roots in the rural world. Above all, OPs are expected to exert more positive influences than other kinds of food products on a number of facets of rural development: the local economic system, the environment, landscape, biodiversity, culture, regional identity, social cohesion and the reproduction of specific local resources in rural areas. OP production systems are therefore seen as providing both local and global **public goods**. In fact, not many empirical analyses have been carried out on the positive or negative contributions that OP systems may exert on any of these dimensions. Scientific studies – both theoretical and empirical – on this subject often refer to an 'ideal type' of OP system, a sort of idealized 'virtuous OP system' (Boisseaux, 2002) that is capable of attaining a fairly high number of beneficial effects on rural development.

Owing to the above-mentioned specificities, and its deep and multiple links with its **'terroir'**, the 'ideal typical' OP system is in principle *multifunctional*. It can have multiple effects beyond the production of commodities, and thus may contribute to several societal objectives at once, thereby satisfying the market dimension while producing positive external effects and **externalities** (Belletti *et al.*, 2003). Because of these special features, OPs incorporate different values. Consumers pay a premium for quality attributes corresponding to the general food or nutritional value of a product (i.e. its hedonistic or private value). At the same time, public values are derived that are both local (the rural amenities that local actors can incorporate into their private and collective strategies) and global (the values of the environmental and cultural features that are being sustained) (Belletti, 2003).

The multifunctional virtuous OP can therefore have beneficial effects on the firms that produce it, but also side effects on the local economy through the supply of other functions (positive external effects), some part of which can be internalized by other actors, both local and non-local, via the market mechanism. This process is capable of reproducing and even increasing the stock of the resources used in the production process, thus guaranteeing the cycle's **sustainability** over time (Belletti and Marescotti, 2002; Vandecandelaere *et al.*, 2009). As shown in Fig. 6.1, the 'core' of the virtuous circle is the OP production system.

The starting point is to consider the OP as a **social construction**. On the basis of a set of local resources, the behaviour and strategies of the actors (both individual and collective) construct the OP over the course of time, setting off action that aims to give value to the local resources used in the production process by employing a specific set of tools and methods (for example, a designation of origin, or a wine route, or other tools and initiatives). The product has to be 'validated' by the outside, which is accomplished by society through the market and/or by other forms of validation (such as public support schemes), which, in this virtuous circle, leads to the remuneration of the resources used.

Thanks to its deep roots in the local context, the functioning of the OP production system implies direct economic effects connected to the marketing of the product, and also indirect effects, as it has a positive impact on the stock of other forms of capital (Bourdieu, 1987): natural capital, social capital (trust, organization, norms and codes, institutions), human capital (knowledge and techniques) and physical capital (equipment and non-renewable resources). Other local and non-local production systems may also benefit from this accumulation of capital, thus conditioning the quality of life of the local community in a way that goes beyond the actors directly involved in the OP production process.

Put another way, this 'core circle' offers opportunities for activating parallel processes in the rural area, by means of the OP itself (exploiting the reputation of the OP name) and by means of the specific local resources that the virtuous circle contributes towards its reproduction and accumulation. In the first case, the OP itself is a resource used by other actors (or by the same actors that produce it, thereby activating new production processes) in other production processes (for example,

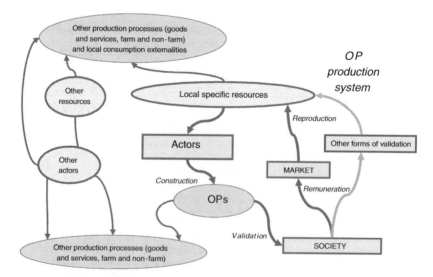

Fig. 6.1. The 'virtuous circle' of origin product (OP) valorization.

restaurants). The OP is, therefore, one of the most important elements of attraction in a 'bundle of goods and services'. In the second case, the specific resources safeguarded by the OP virtuous circle enter other production processes (for example, landscape amenities that enter the processes of tourism and are 'sold' by local tourist agencies) or consumption processes (for example, landscape amenities enjoyed by inhabitants and tourists).

We can, therefore, identify four different categories of positive effects that OP valorization is expected to exert on rural development by virtue of the specificities of those effects (Belletti *et al.*, 2008):

1. *Support to the OP supply chain*: OPs should be seen as an economic activity that is likely to improve the economy of rural areas. OP support and promotion are expected to add value to OPs on the market, allowing for the development of local enterprises (especially small and medium enterprises) and of the OP production system as a whole. Other local institutions beyond the supply chain firms are also interested in this role of OPs, with a great deal of importance given to the effects on employment and incomes and to the maintenance of agricultural and small and medium processing firms. Many studies devoted to OPs[7] deal with the analysis of the 'functioning' of OP supply chains compared with those of conventional products, based on the hypothesis that localized supply chains rely on specific organizational structures, and stressing the peculiarity of the firms, especially their relationships at a local level. The underlying hypothesis is that the proximity of economic and social activity helps to reduce transaction costs between firms thanks to the trust, norms, conventions and tacit and explicit rules existing among local actors.

2. *Support to rural economic diversification*: OPs can generate positive 'external' effects on local rural development dynamics. These effects can be integrated into strategies that go beyond the supply chain and can lead to the production of a 'territorialized basket of goods'. Therefore, these strategies develop transverse positive effects of OPs on the territory and the birth/strengthening of diversified economic activities (hospitality,

other services, handicrafts), along with strengthening farming enterprises themselves.

3. *Empowerment and activation of human resources, and the development of local social organization*: Through the sense of local identity that it fosters, the OP can be the *starting motor* of a process of reflection on local development dynamics, stimulating networking and cooperation among actors (firms inside and outside the OP supply chain, local institutions, inhabitants), which can lead to the development of new local strategies. OPs are therefore not only the 'result' of a valorization strategy, but can be simultaneously the lever of mobilization and reactivation of local resources. This approach is different from those covered by the first two concepts, and one that is potentially more far reaching. It implies the involvement of capable stakeholders, and in marginal socio-economic situations should be implemented in advance and separately from initiatives aimed directly at markets and the commercialization of the OP.

4. *Protection of the environment, amenities and local cultures*: The environment is also an important part of the 'OP virtuous circle'. By nature, OPs are more linked than other products to local (natural and built) resources and/or they are an expression of traditional farming and processing systems (Belletti, 2003). Often, the special quality of an OP is based on specific native plant varieties or breeds, and frequently these are threatened by extinction: thus, the protection of bio-diversity may contribute to supporting rural development strategies, and vice versa. Traditional production techniques often help the preservation of traditional landscape features, protecting against land and soil degradation. Traditional farming and processing systems, already adversely affected by the intensification and/or extensification of agriculture, are generally threatened by the disappearance of OPs owing to their lack of competitiveness with standardized products and production methods. The simple maintenance of farming in less favoured areas, characterized by unfavourable natural conditions and increased production costs, can also be an environmental benefit. Human know-how in traditional farming systems contributes to environmental and cultural biodiversity, and to landscape quality.

When taking into account the 'virtuous circle' and the categories of potential positive effects, the valorization of the OP should not be considered a single step, but rather as a 'process' with different phases closely connected to one another. Each of these phases requires specific tools and can be supported by specific public policies. The functioning of the OP virtuous circle may express all the potential contributions that OP production systems can give to the sustainability of rural development: economic sustainability (strengthening local supply chains and offering opportunities for the diversification and integration of economic activities in the rural areas), social sustainability (local actor cohesion, empowerment, inclusion, etc.) and environmental sustainability (biodiversity, landscape, land use, etc.).

From Theory to Practice: Actors' Strategies and Conflicts

In the real world there is not only one 'model' of OPs, but a set of differentiated situations, some of which can be quite distant from the virtuous circle. Moreover, OP production systems are not static but cover complex trajectories. They are subject to change depending on transformations taking place at both the local and global levels of the system, and also on internal actor characteristics. Effective 'performance' of the virtuous circle so that it provides the various positive contributions that OPs are capable of contributing to rural development depends on aspects of the economic organization of GI production and marketing, and on facets of the valorization process. The extent or size of the circle depends on the relative importance of the OP system in the local economy and on the relevant aspects of the local area (soil and water utilization, landscape, local food culture, etc.).

OP contributions to rural development vary according to the type of actors involved in the product's valorization and their

particular objectives and strategies. Quite often, the OP catalyses a variety of interests that go well beyond the supply chain actors themselves to include, in varying degrees, other categories of actors. These interests are linked together through the diversified 'values' incorporated into and generated by the OP, values which go beyond the economic sphere to cover the social, cultural and environmental dimension (Belletti et al., 2003). The most important group of actors are those associated with the firms producing the OP. Some are engaged in craft production processes which cannot easily be industrialized. Actors in this type of OP production system are mainly members of small and medium enterprises, not completely specialized in OP production. In other cases, the production system is based on cooperative firms that can reach scale economies in production and marketing functions, or on large private firms. The contributions made to rural development can vary according to the characteristics of the firms involved and the role they attach to the OP within their strategies. Frequently, a heterogeneous group of non-professional producers are part of the chain as well (hobby farmers, pensioners, 'amateur farmhands', etc.).

Together with more or less professional firms supporting OPs, a special role is played by local public institutions and 'intermediate institutions' (for example, **producers' associations** and **consortia**, chambers of commerce, tourist associations). These stakeholders may have converging or conflicting interests. Added to the mix are other actors external to the local production system, but who may be interested in supporting OPs. Owners of processing and distribution firms often become involved, as well as research institutes and various associations (environmental and consumer groups, etc.).

Strategies around OPs pursued by these different categories of actors are very differentiated, and normally they aim at specific categories of positive effects chosen from among those mentioned earlier in this section. Studies have identified two main approaches which actors may adopt with regard to the economic role of the OP: a supply chain strategy, or a territorial strategy (Pacciani *et al.*, 2001; Tregear *et al.*, 2007). The supply chain strategy involves the building of a strong network of actors in the production and processing of the OP, focusing energies on managing production levels, improving physical product quality and implementing effective marketing. With this approach, the OP contributes to socio-economic well-being through the existence of a strong producer network, increased employment opportunities within that network, and increased revenues from the effective management of the supply chain and marketing of the product.

The territorial strategy involves a different conceptualization of the OP as a rural development asset. Here, actors perceive OPs as offering a series of related resources, including environmental (e.g. distinctive landscapes, local animal breeds and plant varieties), cultural (e.g. techniques, know-how, local folklore and heritage), and economic (e.g. skilled employment). Thus, OPs are seen as having the potential to contribute to a wide range of initiatives that encourage diverse activities and novel inter-actions between multiple types of actors/ events (e.g. tourist trails, markets, festivals, educational initiatives, community events). In this strategy, it is territorial identity and its association with the product that are the basis of value generation, in addition to the physical output of a single supply chain. The identities and associations are seen to be utilizable by a broad range of actors who may apply them to a 'basket' of goods and services, resulting in a wide distribution of economic rent. Another less frequent strategy, which is a subset of the territorial strategy, is directly aimed at enhancing non-economic positive contri-butions to rural development using the OP product as a tool, especially for the conser-vation of culture and the environment. Public and research institutions and citizen associa-tions are normally the initiators of this type of strategy.

Actors pursuing these different strategies activate individual or collective initiatives that make use of the OP and its related assets (i.e. landscape values) to reach their specific objectives. Strategies and initiatives elaborated around the OP can conflict with one another (as in the case of the unregulated commercial exploitation of OPs, which conflicts with the protection of unique resources and local environmental equilibria). The activation of a given strategy by a group of actors can also cause losses to other OP stakeholders, which points out the fact that OP valorization can have negative effects, which should also be taken into account. The valorization of an OP activates complex dynamics within local production systems and, more generally, within the rural area that the OP occupies, and affects many different types of local actors. These dynamics lead to a modification of the organization of the system and of the values and aims of the actors, with consequent changes in the equilibrium at the basis of economic, social and environmental sustain-ability. To complicate matters further, local actors that fall outside the scope of the valorization strategy for a particular OP are, none the less, affected by the changes it brings about. The diversity of the characteristics and the aims of the actors directly or indirectly involved may cause serious problems when an agreement on collective strategies about OP valorization has to be reached, as in the case of the definition of a PDO–PGI **code of practice**.

To analyse the different contributions that OPs can make to rural development, we should focus on the mechanisms by which actors conflict or converge around a valor-ization project. How are the economic and social resources that form the basis of the OP reproduced (or not ...)? What are the institutional and governance structures brought into play to manage this process? If 'development' means that private strategies are sufficiently compatible to guarantee a collective benefit, then the point is how can different individuals and/or private valor-ization strategies make a contribution to or be a hindrance to a positive global effect on rural development, sectorial integration and social cohesion?

The functioning of the OP production system, thanks to its deep roots in the local context, exerts direct economic effects linked to strictly commercial aspects, but, indirectly, it also exerts positive and negative effects on the accumulation of the different types of capital involved (human, physical, social and natural). The valorization of OPs is, therefore, often considered through the lens of sustainability; hence, this evaluation should take into account economic, social, cultural and environmental aspects.

Equity issues are another important consideration in evaluating the impacts of an OP on rural development. OP valorization processes often modify the distribution of economic and non-economic benefits among the agents concerned. For example, a general positive outcome on incomes may be observed, but it may come from the fact that some firms improve their position at the expense of others (Barjolle and Sylvander, 2000). Two key issues in relation to the increased market value of the product created (i.e. the added value – or **value-added** – included in the price of the product) are the horizontal distribution of benefits among the various firms and categories of firms involved in a single phase of the OP supply chain, and the vertical distribution of benefits among the agents of the various stages of the supply chain (farmers who produce the raw material, and the processing and commercial firms). Often, the supply chain firms belonging to the upstream phases and furthest away from the final market are likely to be deprived of the added value of the OP, even though they contribute greatly to the construction of the OP and of its image, and also to the effects it has on the territory.

Valorization initiatives around the OP have to be analysed not only from an individual point of view (that of the actors who elaborate the strategy, based on efficiency and effectiveness criteria relative to the aims of the strategy), but also from a collective and general point of view. This means taking into account the point of view of the actors who did not take part in the valorization strategy, and the effects on different members of the rural society and region, as well as the effects on the region's collective resources (environment, landscape, social cohesion, etc.). **Interprofessional bodies/associations** and local public administrations can play an important role by stimulating convergence among the different actors and mediating the conflicts that arise from differing OP strategies.

GI Regulation Schemes and Rural Development: the Case of EU Regulation (EC) No. 510/06 (PDO/PGI)

Among the specific OP valorization tools available, the registration of GIs by means of a special legal protection scheme is the one most heavily used. The issue of whether and how to protect and regulate the use of GIs is increasing in importance all over the world (see Chapters 2 and 8). In political discourse, within producers' organizations, and more often than not in academic literature, GI special protection schemes are presented as having positive effects on supply chains (see Chapters 3 and 4). Their effects on rural development, if they are analysed, are presented in terms of the economic performance of the supply chain, in part because positive effects on other dimensions of rural development dynamics are more difficult to evaluate. In spite of this, the 'rural development justification' for GI regulations is growing in many official documents. EU Regulation (EC) No. 2081/92 (1992) and the new Regulation (EC) No. 510/06 (2006) (EC = European Commission or Council) mention rural development as one of the main motivations for EU PDOs and PGIs).[8]

Besides the characteristics of the GI product and production system, the effects of GI special protection schemes mainly depend on the legal and procedural characteristics of the schemes and on the specific way that the process of protection is constructed and managed. The analysis of EU PDO and PGI systems offers insight into some of the GI protection effects. The issue of whether and how PDOs and PGIs can reinforce the effects of GI products in rural areas and the risks inherent in their use make it necessary to define the main characteristics of these legal protection schemes. The recognition of a PDO or PGI, according to EU Regulation (EC) No. 2081/92 (now Regulation (EC) No. 510/06), proceeds from an application by a producers' association representing the local production system. The application should contain proof of the links between the quality of the OP and the territory of origin, and be accompanied by a code of practice that contains the specification of the characteristics of the raw materials, the production process and qualitative requirements of the product that limit the area in which it is possible to carry out the production process (or certain phases of it, as in the case of a PGI). Once EU protection has been obtained, the producers wanting to label their own products with the name registered under the PDO–PGI scheme must observe the rules of the code of practice.

A request for PDO–PGI protection can therefore be analysed as a collective process that leads to a codification of the production rules of the OP, aiming at validation and legitimation by an authority (in this case the EU) (Bérard *et al.*, 2000; Lassaut and Le Meur-Baudry, 2000; Allaire and Wolf, 2004). EU registration criteria for a PDO/PGI and national application procedures (Sylvander, 2004) do not require that the code of practice guarantees positive effects on rural development, but they do require that the area of production to be delimited (in order to guarantee the economic effects on supply chain phases and firms located in this area) and that the process of production be codified (in order to prevent unfair competition and as a guarantee to consumers). Potential economic effects on the supply chain are varied. They are derived in the first instance from the fact that PDO–PGI recognition and the codification of OP production rules can prevent market crises owing to the usurpation of the name. In addition, PDO–PGI recognition transforms the geographical name (and the reputation that it enjoys) into a 'club good' (Thiedig and Sylvander, 2000; Torre, 2006) which has local and selective characteristics (that is, the geographical name can be used only by firms within the codified area of production that conform to the code of practice). PDOs and PGIs are powerful tools for the qualification of an OP and they can modify the structural conditions of competition between territories of production and between the different phases of the local supply chain.

The most commonly mentioned effects of PDOs and PGIs are (i) the differentiation of OP products on the market, price increases (also due to the decrease of 'imitations' of the 'original' OP as codified in the code of practice) and/or increases in production volume and sales, (ii) strengthening of the territorialization of these effects in the area of production, and (iii) generally creating conditions for better coordination of the actors (firms and institutions) involved in the GI production system (see Chapter 4). Retaining and supporting small and artisan production units and farm-based processing in rural areas are often perceived as a goal associated with PDOs and PGIs, largely as a result of collective marketing initiatives that facilitate market access. In addition, the code of practice may include requirements which directly discourage trends towards concentration, such as limiting the supply area for raw milk for a cheese factory. While some studies stress a loss of efficiency associated with these requirements, others find them justified by an increase in the average quality of the product (Barjolle *et al.*, 1998b). The magnitude of these effects on a rural area depends on the relevance that the GI production system has for the local economy; induced social and environmental effects can come from keeping firms, population and traditional farming systems in the rural area, as well as by way of downstream effects on the supply sectors of the GI production system. Positive effects are not automatically obtained by PDO–PGI recognition, but depend on the characteristics of the OP and on how PDOs and PGIs are established. Empirical evidence is not systematic or even positive. For example, many recognized PDOs and PGIs are not used by firms because the increase in GI product prices and other benefits do not compensate them sufficiently for the increase in costs (certification costs and other types of costs connected with the use of the PDO–PGI scheme and its implementation in the firm's organization) (Belletti *et al.*, 2007).

Analysis of the distribution of economic effects among different types of firms and among the different phases of the supply chain is a crucial point, linked to sustainability and to equity issues. Even when price premiums are achieved, the extra profit (coming from the 'territorial rent') may be advantageous to larger processing and distribution firms that can sell GI products abroad and/or on modern and long marketing channels, rather than accruing to small producers. If control systems are absent or functioning poorly, the reputation acquired by the denomination may be captured and usurped by external actors. In addition, even though an increase in the price of a GI product may encourage producers to increase their production of certified quantities, it may lower the prices of unlabelled but still genuine GI products, thus discouraging producers who are incapable of complying with the official specifications. In fact, some evidence points to the difficulties faced by small–medium and/or artisanal firms in making use of PDOs/PGIs, in particular in marginal areas and when the quantities produced are small. Therefore, there seems to be a serious risk of expropriation of producer rents when official GI recognition systems are set up, especially when these systems introduce a 'modern' logic of quality assurance. In contrast, PDOs/PGIs can also stimulate firms to 'upgrade' by introducing modern quality certification systems.

The choices made in the code of practice (about the area of production, process and product characteristics) can exclude some firms from the use of the geographical name on the 'original' product, generating conflict between different firm typologies (e.g. industrial versus artisanal firms). Furthermore, the coexistence under the same quality sign (the protected geographical name) of GI products with real differences in quality levels can cause a problem of cannibalization and marginalization of the products with the highest production costs (Anania and Nisticò, 2004). The choice of which phases of the production process to link to the original territory (for instance, meat processing, but not animal breeding), which entails a choice between PDO and PGI, can exclude entire components of the territorial system of production from the benefits of name protection. Exclusion effects can also have consequences for an OP as a whole. For OPs produced in very small quantities and characterized by small or very small firm structure, the PDO–PGI registration process itself can be inaccessible. This is why PDO–PGI applications are often located in dynamic rural areas rather than in marginal and disadvantaged ones: PDOs–PGIs appear

to be more the effect than the cause of the development of the rural area,[9] but there is no agreement on this point and, in fact, some important PDOs are located in mountain areas, especially in Alpine regions.

Following the logic of endogenous rural development, it is important to discuss the impact that PDOs and PGIs can have on other categories of effects. Local socio-economic dynamics can be influenced by the very path leading to the application for the PDO/PGI, particularly during the discussion phase and the process of drawing up the code of practice. The application requires the constitution of a producers' association, and in general encourages producers to meet and discuss which, in practice, is not a frequent event in rural contexts. In effect, it encourages collective action and the establishment of cooperation mechanisms between local firms, and between firms and the local community (Casabianca, 2003; Marescotti, 2003). Writing the code of practice can stimulate reflection and self-criticism in farmers and other firms involved in the local OP production system, as well as in other local actors.[10] This can have positive effects on the capacity for planning new initiatives in the rural area. However, problems and conflicts frequently arise when identifying the boundaries of production areas, the characteristics of production techniques and the final quality of the product to be labelled. These conflicts point to the more general issue of inclusion/exclusion effects, both within the local production system and between inside and outside producers. Sometimes a group of actors applies for a PDO/PGI with the explicit aim of excluding other competitors; in other cases exclusion effects are not anticipated, but come only as a consequence of the way the PDO/PGI functions.

The rules of the recognition process, which are national rules in some EU countries, should guarantee the participation of different actors at the local level. Local institutions such as public offices and private associations can mediate between different positions and promote governance mechanisms that allow the strong participation of local actors in the PDO–PGI recognition process. PDOs and PGIs can also reinforce the effects of the OP on the environment, both natural and man-made, first because they can increase remuneration of specific local resources linked to OP systems. However, the remuneration does not automatically guarantee the reproduction of these resources. In general, there is no guarantee of the continuity of a 'traditional character', of the 'environmental friendliness' of methods of production and of the use of specific factors, bearing in mind that the techniques are flexible and that the methods of production of OPs are subject to tensions with regard to modernization. The market success of PDOs and PGIs can also have negative effects, inducing an over-exploitation of natural and local specific resources if no common rules are established.

The PDO–PGI code of practice can control unsustainable practices in the production and valorization process of the OP through the codification of rules that are more consistent with traditional farming systems and local ecological equilibria. The effective incorporation of such rules comes from actors' decision making, taking into account on the one hand the need to be competitive in production costs and on the other hand the opportunity to differentiate the OP by stressing the peculiarities of its origin. External experts, local institutions and public administrations charged with approving codes of practice may play an important role in this regard, both by forcing the producers to consider these aspects, and by providing the OP system with the necessary tools to meet the demands of the codified practices (funding, training, technical assistance, etc.).

The question is whether the burden of preserving the local ecological system can be placed on the code of practice of a GI protection scheme. The risk is that more rigid OP environmental rules may not be accompanied by effective communication to consumers so that the environmental benefits perceived by the consumer are incorporated into the product's value. In this case, the costs of imposing a new code of practice may exceed the benefits of the PDO/PGI to the producer. PDOs/PGIs per se are not necessarily relevant for environmental issues, but,

if the code of practice considers environmental impacts, the PDOs/PGIs can potentially be more effective than non-context-specific environmental schemes – such as organic agriculture.[11]

Concluding Remarks

The changes taking place in agriculture and the rural world, and the shift to a new paradigm of development, enhance the potential of OPs. Their specificities – a link with the territory, the use of traditional production processes, the collective and identity formation dimensions – are coherent with increased attention towards the multifunctionality and diversification of agricultural and rural activities, and can prove to be important levers in activating and consolidating the dynamics of sustainable rural development.

As we have seen in the previous paragraphs, the valorization of an OP is a very complex matter, one that can have very different impacts on the various actors involved in the OP system, and also on the economic, social and environmental aspects of the system itself. Valorization of OPs to reach the full development of all of their potential positive effects requires an integrated set of tools in each phase of the process, from the mobilization phase of actors and resources to that of qualification and marketing. Most of these tools imply the participation/involvement of many actors in the OP system, and these tools exert a direct influence on the actors as well. This collective aspect should be carefully taken into account in the evaluation of the effects of OPs on rural development. Several valorization tools can be used, which follow different strategies and have different aims, depending on the initiators of the valorization initiative. Each valorization tool exerts effects on different dimensions of rural development, and these effects can be conflicting (for example, positive on some economic variables and negative on other environmental variables).

Up until now there have been few empirical scientific studies or publications on the effects of OPs and PDO–PGI protection schemes on rural development, in particular with regard to social, cultural and environmental dimensions. Nevertheless, there is some truth in the fact that OPs are a more powerful tool than other possible tools, because of their (potentially) strong links (which are variable from case to case) with different dimensions of the rural areas that they come from. But products are not a 'starter': the triggering factors are always the local actors and policies that support their empowerment and coordination. Of course, most of the effects of an OP on rural development dynamics vary according to the contents of its code of practice which, in turn, depends on the strategy of the actors promoting GI recognition schemes and on the dynamics activated in the process of GI recognition. In any case, the legal protection of a GI is a means of preventing any delocalization or unfair competition from other areas that could usurp the reputation which has been collectively built on the GI.

The effects of GI schemes also depend strongly on the legal and operational characteristics of the protection schemes (see Chapters 2 and 7). Different schemes, for example, can imply different procedures for recognition (that is, different access to small and to large firms), an operational logic that is more or less formalized (consequently carrying with it different bureaucratic workloads for firms), different contents and levels of guarantee for consumers and, consequently, different certification costs.

In conclusion, recognition of a PDO/PGI cannot make an effective contribution to the different aspects of rural development processes on its own. GI recognition scheme policies should instead be a part of a more comprehensive policy which, at the relevant territorial level (municipality, region, small area ...), encompasses all the aspects relevant to maximizing the desirable effects of the OP on the rural system. GI recognition schemes are not a substitute for policies and government interventions that would support OP development-based strategies. In particular, they cannot on their own overcome structural problems at the production, processing or distribution level, problems such as lack of coordination and difficulties with access to credit, and problems with human resources and professional competence. All of these should be considered in an integrated way at the local level, which implies a search for appropriate institutions and policy coordination on a local scale.

Notes

[1] This chapter has benefited from Concerted Action DOLPHINS (Development of Origin Labelled Products: Humanity, Innovation and Sustainability) and SINER-GI (Strengthening INternational Research on Geographical Indications) EU-funded projects. The authors wish to thank the WP3 (Work Package 3) team of the DOLPHINS EU-funded project, in particular Gilles Allaire, Erwin Stucki and Stéphane Boisseaux.

[2] Although these three dimensions may be less relevant for non-local consumers, their consumption behaviour is driven by the 'reputation' of the OP, which is still built upon one or more of the three dimensions (Belletti, 2002).

[3] 'Building an "objective" or unequivocal definition of rurality appears to be an impossible task .... Member States have generally developed their own definitions of rural areas. They are often based on socio-economic criteria (such as agricultural patterns, density of inhabitants per square kilometre or population decline) and are quite heterogeneous and not universally applicable. At EU level, there is no common definition' (EC, 1996).

[4] Multifunctionality has taken over the debate on agricultural policy reform at the multinational level. But approaches to multifunctionality vary according to national positions in this debate and the OECD (Organization for Economic Cooperation and Development) has undertaken a work programme to produce a common working definition (see OECD, 2001). The issue of multifunctionality is also very controversial in the framework of international negotiations.

[5] Some authors go even further by including certain social values in rural development, particularly inclusiveness (facilitating and making possible the participation of the weakest members of society) and the equal distribution of benefits (Di Iacovo, 2003).

[6] See, for example, Ilbery and Kneafsey (1999, 2000), Leat *et al.* (2000), Marsden *et al.* (2000), Renting *et al.* (2003), Ilbery and Maye (2005).

[7] See, for example, Barjolle and Sylvander (2000),

Sylvander (2004), Arfini (2005) and Belletti and Marescotti (2006) for a review.

[8] Support for rural development is one of the most important 'justifications' for GIs that has been raised by those who defend the right to protect geographical names from usurpation and misuses, as stated in EU Regulation (EC) No. 2081/92 and confirmed by the new Regulation (EC) No. 510/06: 'Whereas, as part of the adjustment of the Common Agricultural Policy the diversification of agricultural production should be encouraged so as to achieve a better balance between supply and demand on the markets; whereas the promotion of products having certain characteristics could be of considerable benefit to the rural economy, in particular to less favoured or remote areas, by improving the incomes of farmers and by retaining the rural population in these areas'.

[9] For instance, in Italy the authorized production areas of the most important PDO products (Parmigiano Reggiano, Grana Padano, Prosciutto di Parma, Prosciutto di San Daniele ...) are located in Pianura Padana, which is one of the richest areas of the country.

[10] The creation or strengthening of intermediary institutions is not a direct effect of PDO–PGI pursuit. Indeed, EU Regulation (EC) No. 510/06 does not call for the presence of a body that represents the agents of the production system after registration. After registration, the PDO/PGI becomes a private 'affair' between the producer and the **certification body** (under the supervision of the public authority); anyway, the registration – by marking the zone and method of production – can promote the spontaneous establishment of an intermediary institution.

[11] Environmental schemes (such as organic production) are based on the codification of production rules based on technical knowledge and not on producer and contextual knowledge. Therefore, they can exert positive effects mainly on 'non-contextual' environmental goods, but not on contextual goods such as the preservation of territory-specific plant varieties or breeds.

References

Allaire, G. and Dupeuble, T. (2003) De la multifonctionnalité de l'activité agricole à la multi-évaluation de la production agricole. *Economie Rurale* 275, 51–64.

Allaire, G. and Sylvander, B. (1997) Qualité spécifique et systèmes d'innovation territoriale. *Cahiers d'Économie et Sociologie Rurales* 44, 29–59.

Allaire, G. and Wolf, S. (2004) Cognitive representations and institutional hybridity in agrofood innovation. *Science, Technology and Human Values* 29, 431–458.

Anania, G. and Nisticò, R. (2004) Public regulation as a substitute for trust in quality food markets: what if the trust substitute can't be fully trusted? *Journal of Institutional and Theoretical Economics* 160, 681–701.

Arfini, F. (2005) Prodotti tipici e sviluppo rurale: tra qualità e politiche di governance. *Progress in Nutrition* 2, 101–115.

Barjolle, D. and Sylvander, B. (2000) *Some Factors of Success for Origin Labelled Products in Agri-food Supply Chains in Europe: Market, Internal Resources and Institutions.* Working Paper for Les cahiers de l'ISMEA (Institut de Sciences Mathematiques et Économiques Appliqueés). Available at: http://www.origin-food.org/pdf/ismea1102.pdf (accessed 24 November 2010).

Barjolle, D., Boisseaux, S. and Dufour, M. (1998a) *Le lien au terroir. Bilan des travaux de recherche.* ETH (Eidgenössische Technische Hochschule Zürich) Institut d'Économie Rurale, Lausanne. Available at: http://www.origin-food.org/pdf/wp1/wp1-ch.pdf (accessed 25 November 2010).

Barjolle, D., Chappuis, J.M. and Sylvander B. (1998b) From individual competitiveness to collective effectiveness: a study on cheese with Protected Designations of Origin. In: *Proceedings of the 59th EAAE Seminar: Does Economic Theory Contribute to a Better Understanding of Competitiveness?* 22–24 April 1998, Appeldoorn, The Netherlands.

Basile, E. and Cecchi, C. (1997) Differenziazione e integrazione nell'economia rurale. *Rivista di Economia Agraria* 52, 3–28.

Belletti, G. (2002) Sviluppo rurale e prodotti tipici: reputazioni collettive, coordinamento e istituzionalizzazione. In: Romano, D. and Basile, E. (eds) *Sviluppo Rurale: Società, Territorio, Impresa.* Franco Angeli, Milan, pp. 373–397.

Belletti, G. (2003) Le denominazioni geografiche nel supporto all'agricoltura multifunzionale. *Politica Agricola Internazionale* 4, 81–102.

Belletti, G. and Marescotti, A. (2002) *WP 3. Link between Origin Labelled Products and rural development:*

Final Report, July 2002. Concerted Action DOLPHINS (Development of Origin Labelled Products: Humanity, Innovation and Sustainability). Available at: http://www.origin-food.org/pdf/wp3/wp3.pdf (accessed 25 November 2010).

Belletti, G. and Marescotti, A. (2006) *GI Social and Economic Issues.* Report, SINER-GI EU Research Project (Strengthening International Research on Geographical Indications: from research foundation to consistent policy), European Commision, Brussels/Luxembourg.

Belletti, G., Brunori, G., Marescotti, A. and Rossi, A. (2003) Multifunctionality and rural development: a multilevel approach. In: Van Huylenbroeck, G. and Durand, G. (eds) *Multifunctional Agriculture: A New Paradigm for European Agriculture and Rural Development?* Ashgate, Aldershot, UK, pp. 54–82.

Belletti, G., Burgassi, T., Marescotti, A. and Scaramuzzi, S. (2007) The effects of certification costs on the success of a PDO/PGI. In: Theuvsen, L., Spiller, A., Peupert, M. and Jahn, G. (eds) (2007) *Quality Management in Food Chains,* Wageningen Academic Publishers, The Netherlands, pp. 107–123.

Belletti, G., Marescotti, A., Paus, M. and Hauwuy, A. (2008) Evaluation des effets locaux des AOP-IGP: développement rural, organisations sociales et vie des territoires. In: Sylvander, B., Casabianca, F. and Roncin, F. (eds) Proceedings of the international symposium organized by INRA (Institut National de la Recherche Agronomique) and INAO (Institut Nationale de l'Origine et de la Qualité) *'Actes du Colloque International de Restitution des Travaux de Recherche sur les Indications et Appellations d'Origine Géographiques: Produits Agricoles et Alimentaires d'Origine: Enjeux et Acquis Scientifiques,* 17–18 Novembre 2005, Paris. INRA Editions, Paris, pp. 214–228.

Bérard, L. and Marchenay, P. (1995) Lieux, temps et preuves: la construction sociale des produits de terroir. *Terrain. Carnets du Patrimoine Ethnologique* 24, 153–164.

Bérard, L. and Marchenay, P. (2004) *Les Produits de Terroir: Entre Cultures et Règlements.* CNRS (Centre National de la Recherche Scientifiques) Editions, Paris.

Bérard, L., Beucherie, O., Fauvet, M., Marchenay, P. and Monticelli, C. (2000) Historical, cultural and environmental factors in the delimitation of PGI geographical areas. In: Sylvander, B., Barjolle, D. and Arfini, F. (eds) *The Socio-economics of Origin Labelled Products in Agrifood Supply Chains: Spatial, Institutional and Co-ordination Aspects. Proceedings of the 67th EAAE Seminar,* 28–30 October 1999, Le Mans, France. Actes et Communications No. 17(2), INRA, Paris, pp. 163–176.

Bérard, L., Marchenay, P. and Casabianca, F. (2008) Savoirs, terroirs, produits: un patrimoine biologique et culturel. In: Sylvander, B., Casabianca, F. and Roncin, F. (eds) Proceedings of the international symposium organized by INRA and INAO *'Actes du Colloque International de Restitution des Travaux de Recherche sur les Indications et Appellations d'Origine Géographiques: Produits Agricoles et Alimentaires d'Origine: Enjeux et Acquis Scientifiques,* 17–18 Novembre 2005, Paris. INRA Editions, Paris, pp. 98–105.

Berriet, M. (1995) Les interventions des collectivités locales pour le soutien des produits agricoles de qualité. In: *Séminaire 'Qualification des Produits et Territoires',* INRA, Toulouse.

Boisseaux, S. (2002) *Type de Produit, Type de Développement Rural: Est-il Possible d'Établir un Lien?* Concerted Action DOLPHINS, Barcelona Seminar, February 2002.

Bourdieu, P. (1987) The forms of capital. In: Richardson, J.G. (ed.) *Handbook of Theory and Research for the Sociology of Education.* Greenwood Press, New York, pp. 96–111.

Brunori, G. (2003) Sistemi agricoli territoriali e competitività. In: Casati, D. (ed.) *La Competitività dei Sistemi Agricoli Italiani. Atti del XXXVI Convengo di Studi della SIDEA,* 9–11 Settembre 1999, Milan. Franco Angeli, Milan, pp. 125–166.

Casabianca, F. (2003) Les produits d'origine: une aide au développement local. In: Delannoy, P. and Hervieu, B. (eds) *A table. Peut-on encore bien manger?* Editions de l'Aube, Paris, pp. 66–82.

Casabianca, F., Sylvander, B., Noël, Y., Béranger, C., Coulon, J.-B. and Roncin, F. (2005) Terroir et typicité: deux concepts-clés des appellations d'origine contrôlée. Essai de définitions scientifiques et opérationnelles. Communication pour le: *Symposium international du 'Programme de Recherche Pour et Sur le Développement Régional' (PSDR): 'Territoires et Enjeux du Développement Régional',* 9–11 March 2005, Lyon, France. Available on CD-ROM accompanying Mollard, A., Sauboua, E. and Hirczak, M. (eds) (2007) *Territoires et Enjeux du Développement Régional.* Éditions Quae, Paris.

Delfosse, C. (1996) Qualité, liens au lieu et développement local. In: Casabianca, F. and Valceschini, E. (eds) *La Qualité dans l'Agro-alimentaire: Émergence d'un Champ de Recherches.* INRA/SAD, Paris, pp. 34–40.

Di Iacovo, F. (2003) *Lo Sviluppo Sociale nelle Aree Rurali.* Franco Angeli, Milan.

Di Iacovo, F. and Ciofani, D. (2005) Le funzioni sociali dell'agricoltura: analisi teorica ed evidenze empiriche. *Rivista di Economia Agraria* 1, 78–103.

EC (European Commission) (1996) *The Cork Declaration – A Living Countryside*. Statement produced from 'The European Conference on Rural Development' held in Cork, Ireland, 7–9 November 1996. Available at: http://ec.europa.eu/agriculture/rur/cork_en.htm (accessed 19 November 2010).

EC (2003) Conclusions of Second European Conference on Rural Development in Salzburg. In: *Proceedings of The European Conference on Rural Development 'Planting Seeds for Rural Futures – Building a Policy that Can Deliver our Ambitions'*, MEMO/03/236, Agriculture Directorate-General, Brussels, 21 November 2003.

EC (2008) Europe's rural areas in action: facing the challenges of tomorrow. In: *Proceedings of the European Conference on Rural Development*, Cyprus, 16–17 October 2008.

Ilbery, B. and Kneafsey, M. (1999) Niche markets and regional speciality food products in Europe: towards a research agenda. *Environment and Planning A* 31, 2207–2222.

Ilbery, B. and Kneafsey, M. (2000) Producer constructions of quality in regional speciality food production: a case study from south west England. *Journal of Rural Studies* 16, 217–230.

Ilbery, B. and Maye, D. (2005) Food supply chains and sustainability: evidence from specialist food producers in the Scottish/English borders. *Land Use Policy* 22, 331–344.

Lassaut, B. and Le Meur-Baudry, V. (2000) The motivations of PGI's applicant groups and their interpretations of the 2081/92 rule in the case of French PGI's requests: what are the reasons of conflicts between firms and the risks of unfair competition? In: Sylvander, B., Barjolle, D. and Arfini, F. (eds) *The Socio-economics of Origin Labelled Products in Agrifood Supply Chains: Spatial, Institutional and Co-ordination Aspects. Proceedings of the 67th EAAE Seminar*, 28–30 October 1999, Le Mans, France. Actes et Communications No. 17(2), INRA, Paris, pp. 241–254.

Leat, P., Williams, F. and Brannigan, J. (2000) Rural competitiveness through quality and imagery across lagging regions of the European Union. Paper presented to: *International Conference 'European Rural Policy at the Crossroads'*, Aberdeen, Scotland.

Lowe, P., Murdoch, J. and Ward, N. (1995) Networks in rural development: beyond endogenous and exogenous models. In: Ploeg, J.D. and van Dijk, G. (eds) *Beyond Modernisation. The Impact of Endogenous Rural Development*. Van Gorcum, Assen, The Netherlands.

Marescotti, A. (2003) Typical products and rural development: who benefits from PDO/PGI recognition? In *Proceedings of 83rd EAAE Seminar 'Food Quality Products in the Advent of the 21st Century: Production, Demand and Public Policy'*, Chania-Crete, September 2003.

Marsden, T., Banks, J. and Bristow, G. (2000) Food supply chain approaches: exploring their role in rural development. *Sociologia Ruralis* 40, 424–438.

Mollard, A. (2001) Qualité et développement territorial. Un outil d'analyse: la rente. *Economie Rurale* 263, 16–34.

Moran, W. (1993) Rural space as intellectual property. *Political Geography* 12, 263–277.

Murdoch, J., Lowe, P., Ward, N. and Marsden, T. (2003) *The Differentiated Countryside*. Routledge, London.

OECD (Organization for Economic Cooperation and Development) (2001) *Multifunctionality: towards an analytical framework*. Directorate for Food, Agriculture and Fisheries, Trade Directorate, Paris.

OECD (2006) *The New Rural Paradigm: Policies and Governance*. OECD Rural Policy Reviews, Paris.

Pacciani, A. (2002) Società organizzata e istituzioni nello sviluppo rurale. In: Basile, E. and Romano, D. (eds) *Sviluppo Rurale: Società, Territorio, Impresa*. Franco Angeli, Milan, pp. 51–69.

Pacciani, A., Belletti, G. and Marescotti, A. (2001) Problemi informativi, qualità e prodotti tipici. Approcci teorici diversi. In: Fanfani, R., Montresor, E. and Pecci, F. (eds) *Il settore Agroalimentare in Italia e l'Integrazione Europea*. Franco Angeli, Milan. Available at: http://www.origin-food.org/pdf/partners/belmarpapro.pdf (accessed 25 November 2010).

Pecqueur, B. (2001) Qualité et développement territorial: l'hypothèse du panier de biens et de services territorialisés. *Economie Rurale* 261, 37–49.

Pecqueur, B. (2002) Politiques publiques, action publique et spécificités territoriales. In: Vollet, D. (ed.) *Multifonctionnalité et Territoires*. Les Cahiers de la Multifonctionnalité No. 1, INRA/CEMAGREF/CIRAD, pp. 59–70.

Perraud, D. (2001) Les politiques agricoles et rurales dans les régions: une nouvelle organisation des pouvoirs publics en Europe? *Economie Rurale* 261, 7–22.

Ploeg, J.D. and Roep, D. (2003) Multifunctionality and rural development: the actual situation in Europe. In: Van Huylenbroek, G. and Durand, G. (eds) *Multifunctional Agriculture. A New Paradigm for European Agriculture and Rural Development*. Ashgate, Aldershot, UK, pp. 37–53.

Ray, C. (1998) Culture, intellectual property and territorial rural development. *Sociologia Ruralis* 38, 3–20.

Renting, H., Marsden, T. and Banks, J. (2003) Understanding alternative food networks: exploring the role of short food supply chains in rural development. *Environment and Planning A* 35, 393–411.

SFER (Société Française d'Economie Rurale) (2003) *La Multifunctionnalité de l'Activité Agricole et sa Reconnaissance par les Politiques Publiques*. Educagri Editions, Dijon, France.

Storper, M. (1997) *The Regional World: Territorial Development in a Global Economy*. Guilford Press, New York/London.

Sylvander, B. (2004) *WP7. Final Report: Synthesis and Recommendations*. Concerted Action DOLPHINS (Development of Origin Labelled Products: Humanity, Innovation and Sustainability). Available at: http://www.origin-food.org/cadre/careport.htm (accessed 21 November 2010).

Thiedig, F. and Sylvander, B. (2000) Welcome to the club?: an economical approach to geographical indications in the European Union. *Agrarwirtschaft* 49, 428–437.

Torre, A. (2006) Collective action, governance structure and organisational trust in localised systems of production. The case of the AOC organisation of small producers,. *Entrepreneurship and Regional Development* 18, 55–72.

Tregear, A., Arfini, F., Belletti, G. and Marescotti, A. (2007) Regional foods and rural development: the role of product qualification, *Journal of Rural Studies* 23, 12–22.

Vandecandelaere, E., Arfini, F., Belletti, G. and Marescotti, A. (eds) (2009) *Linking People, Places and Products: A Guide for Promoting Quality Linked to Geographical Origin and Sustainable Geographical Indications*. FAO (Food and Agriculture Organization of the United Nations) and SINER-GI, Rome.

Ventura, F. and Milone, P. (2005) *Innovatività Contadina e Sviluppo Rurale*. Franco Angeli, Milan.

B
Certification of Product Quality

[11]

Stuart Landon and C. E. Smith
The Use of Quality and Reputation
Indicators by Consumers:
The Case of Bordeaux Wine

ABSTRACT. The absolute and relative impact of current quality and reputation variables on consumer decisions are examined using data from the market for Bordeaux wine. The estimates indicate that a model of consumer decision making which incorporates information on reputation (past quality) and collective reputation (average group quality) rejects alternative models that include current quality. The results also indicate that reputation has a large impact on the willingness to pay of consumers, that long term reputation is considerably more important than short term quality movements, and that consumers react slowly to changes in product quality. Collective reputation is shown to have an impact on consumer willingness to pay that is as large as that of individual firm reputation. If reputation and collective reputation effects are ignored, the estimated impact of current quality and short term changes in quality on consumer behaviour are overstated.

I. INTRODUCTION

Many empirical studies have found that price is not a good indicator of product quality. In a review of 90 studies, Zeithaml (1988) finds there is only "mixed evidence" of a positive correlation between price and quality while the 13 studies surveyed by Geistfeld (1988) report a mean Spearman coefficient for the price-quality correlation of only 0.19. Geistfeld (1988) argues that the low correlation between price and quality implies that markets are not operating efficiently. Alternative explanations for the low price-quality correlation stem from the costs to consumers of gathering product information. Tellis and Wernerfelt (1987) find that goods for which some information is easily available by inspection exhibit a higher price-quality correlation. Riesz (1978, 1979), Gerstner (1985), Tellis and Wernerfelt (1987), and Hanf and von Wersebe (1994) find that the correspondence between price and quality is stronger for goods for which the cost of being uninformed is greater (durable goods). Ratchford and Gupta (1990) show that a low price-quality correlation is consistent with efficient consumer behaviour if there are search costs.

Journal of Consumer Policy **20**: 289–323, 1997.
© 1997 *Kluwer Academic Publishers. Printed in the Netherlands.*

If consumers face costs of gathering information on product quality, they may rely on the quality reputation of firms to predict current quality. In this case, prices will reflect the quality of output produced by firms in the past rather than current quality. This reputation effect is likely to be particularly important for "experience" goods – many manufactured goods, services and most packaged goods – for which quality can be ascertained only after purchase and use. The importance of reputation in determining consumers' willingness to pay for a good has been recognized in the theoretical literature (Allen, 1984; Klein & Leffler, 1981; Rogerson, 1987; Shapiro, 1983). However, the size of these reputation effects, and their significance relative to the role of current quality, have received little attention in the empirical literature.

This paper provides an empirical analysis of the extent to which consumers use reputation and current quality indicators when making purchase decisions. It does this by relating prices to the information that is available to consumers. If consumers have information on current product quality, the price they are willing to pay for a product will depend on this current quality information. When consumers do not know current quality, but can observe reputation indicators which they use to form perceptions of current quality, price will reflect the value to consumers of these reputation indicator variables rather than current quality.

In order to analyze the type of information used by consumers when making consumption decisions, five models of price determination are estimated and compared. These models differ only with respect to the quality-reputation information available to consumers. In the *full-information* model, consumers have complete information on quality and, thus, current quality is the only quality-reputation factor that influences prices. The *reputation* model assumes that information on current quality is not available or is too costly to obtain and, as a result, the price of a firm's product depends on its reputation for quality, not its current quality. In the *collective reputation* model, consumers do not have information on either the current quality or reputation of an individual firm. As a result, they base their forecast of the quality of the good produced by an individual firm on the average quality of the goods produced by a group of firms with which the individual firm is identified. The final two models employ combinations of the information sets associated with these three models.

The five models described above are estimated using data from the market for Bordeaux wine. While this means that the results are based on data for only one type of good, the data set includes a large number of observations. This is in contrast to most studies of the price-quality relationship which contain relatively few observations on each type of good, such as studies which use data from *Consumer Reports* (Curry, 1985; Friedman, 1967; Geistfeld, 1982; Gerstner, 1985; Oxenfelt, 1950; Riesz, 1978, 1979; Sproles, 1977) or from similar sources such as *Runner's World* (Archibald, Haulman & Moody, 1983), *Canadian Consumer* (Bodell, Kerton, & Schuster, 1986) or the German consumer magazine *Test* and the Danish magazine *Råd og Resultater* (Hjorth-Andersen, 1991). Furthermore, as suggested by Geistfeld (1988), the use of data from another source, as is done here, may be useful in and of itself. Several of the other advantages of these data will be discussed more fully below.

The rest of the paper is organized as follows. The balance of this section reviews the empirical literature on reputation and discusses the characteristics of the Bordeaux wine industry. Section II outlines the theoretical methodology underlying the estimating equations. A description of the data, and a discussion of the advantages of the data set used, are presented in Section III. The empirical specification is described in Section IV. Section V provides an analysis of the empirical results and Section VI gives a brief summary and concluding comments.

The Empirical Literature on Reputation

In contrast to the empirical literature on price-quality correlations, the empirical reputation literature is extremely limited. Jarrell and Peltzman (1985) and Borenstein and Zimmerman (1988) analyze the importance of firm reputation by quantifying the impact on shareholder wealth of product recalls and airline crashes, respectively. Results in Mannering and Winston (1985, 1991) suggest a link, possibly a lagged reputation effect, between the decline in the quality of GM products and the fall in demand for GM cars in the 1980s. Thomas (1993) includes a previous period performance measure for the household goods motor carrier industry in a hedonic price regression, although not explicitly as a proxy for firm reputation. While these studies all examine reputation effects to some extent, none explicitly relates reputation to product prices or compares the effect of reputation and current quality on consumer behaviour.

There is also only a small empirical literature that analyzes the importance of collective reputation. Jarrell and Peltzman and Borenstein and Zimmerman examine, respectively, whether recalls or airplane crashes associated with one firm have an impact on the wealth of the shareholders of other firms in the same industry. Although Borenstein and Zimmerman find no evidence of a collective reputation effect of this type, Jarrell and Peltzman find that a recall by one US automobile or drug firm reduces its US competitors' share value, a result which suggests the possible existence of a collective reputation effect. Both studies examine relatively narrow quality indicators (recalls and crashes) and neither analyzes the impact of collective reputation on product prices.

The brand loyalty literature examines concepts similar to reputation and collective reputation. However, this literature differs from the reputation literature in that it concentrates on explaining repeat purchases, rather than prices, and examines many factors other than past quality (the number of previous purchases of the product, the cost of switching brands, brand-specific user skills and advertising) which lead customers to re-purchase specific products (Mannering & Winston, 1985, 1991). As well, brand loyalty is associated with products produced by a single firm that can internalize brand benefits. In contrast, collective reputation effects are associated with firms that are not directly related, and so imply much different information transmission and behaviour than does brand loyalty.

The Bordeaux Wine Industry

The market for red Bordeaux wine is particularly appropriate for an empirical analysis of the relationship between price, quality and reputation. For example, the Bordeaux wine industry is relatively stable in the sense that it is not rapidly expanding or contracting, there are no large changes taking place in the technology of wine making, and producers are not significantly altering the form of their existing product. In addition, most producers make only one or two wines. These factors imply that the relationship between price, quality and reputation is unlikely to be obscured by the effects of technological change, product interactions in multi-product firms or the introduction of new products or product designs.

Another advantage of Bordeaux red wine industry data is that Bordeaux wines, although differentiated products, differ in only a relatively small number of characteristics. The wines come from a fairly small region, are packaged in identical bottles (although their labels differ) and can be made from only five grape varieties. Additional regulations control grape growing methods, alcoholic strength, maximum allowable yields and the delimitation of vineyards. Thus, the measurement of quality is not likely to be obscured by difficult to quantify aesthetic or design features, post-purchase repairs and services, or a large number of models and options, factors which are typically important in analyses of other consumer goods such as automobiles and computers.

Although weather and soil are important determinants of wine quality, many of the factors which determine the quality of a wine are under the direct control of the wine producer. For example, the producer must decide which grape varieties to grow; the extent of pruning; when to pick the grapes; whether to sort the grapes by hand and the basis on which to reject grapes; whether the wine will be fermented in oak, cement, or stainless steel vats; how extensively to press the grapes following fermentation; the quantity and type of new oak barrels to use and the length of time to keep the wine in the barrels; and the extent to which the wine is filtered and clarified. Most of these decisions are made years before the wine is released. As a consequence, although quality depends on the actions of producers, it is pre-determined with respect to price and should not be contemporaneously correlated with the errors in the price equation.

Many of the wines of Bordeaux are produced in sufficient quantities to be widely available, the number of wine producing firms in Bordeaux is quite large, and there are no dominant firms in terms of production. As a result, the level of market prices does not depend significantly on the quantity produced by any single firm. In addition, the price of a bottle of Bordeaux wine (an average of $25.10 in 1985 U.S. dollars in our data set) is neither too low to make its purchase unimportant nor too high to be of critical importance to consumers.

II. THE THEORETICAL BACKGROUND

Since prices reflect the quality and reputation information used by consumers, it is necessary to specify a model of price determination that incorporates quality and reputation effects. An obvious starting point is the hedonic model of differentiated product price determination developed by Rosen (1974). In Rosen's model, each good is described by a vector of observable characteristics, $\mathbf{z}$. The interaction of consumer demand functions and firm supply functions determines the price of each product as a function, $P(\mathbf{z})$, of these characteristics. A subset of the elements of $\mathbf{z}$ represents the quality information available to and used by consumers. Therefore, the specification of the price equation will differ depending on whether consumers use current quality information, lagged quality information, or group quality information when making their purchase decisions.

The Full-Information Model

If consumers have freely available or low cost information on product quality, the $\mathbf{z}$ vector of characteristics which enters the price function, $P(\mathbf{z})$, will include a measure of current quality as one of its elements. Since reputation variables (based on lagged quality) provide no additional quality information when current quality is known, consumers will not utilize reputation information when making their consumption decisions in this case. As a consequence, past quality (reputation) will have no impact on current prices and the output price of each firm i can be described by the function:

$$P_{it} = P(\tilde{\mathbf{z}}_{it}, Q_{it}),\tag{1}$$

where Q_{it} = the quality of the good produced by firm i at time t,

$\tilde{\mathbf{z}}_{it}$ = a vector of product characteristics, at time t, other than quality and reputation variables.

The Reputation Model

For many consumer goods, product quality is imperfectly observable prior to purchase and can only be accurately determined through use. If these "experience goods" are not frequently purchased, and if full information on product quality is not available to consumers or is costly to acquire, the price equation associated with the full-information model, Equation (1) above, is inappropriate. In the absence of information on current quality, consumer demand will depend, at least in part, on predictions by consumers of product quality. The quality reputation of firms is one of the principal types of information consumers are likely to use when making these predictions. In this case, the price of each good will depend on a vector of variables reflecting the reputation for quality of the firm producing the good, $\mathbf{R}_{it}$ (along with $\tilde{\mathbf{z}}_{it}$):

$$P_{it} = P(\tilde{\mathbf{z}}_{it}, \mathbf{R}_{it}). \tag{2}$$

Theoretical models which analyze the role of firm reputation have been developed by Klein and Leffler (1981), Shapiro (1983), Allen (1984) and Rogerson (1987). In these models, a firm's reputation is assumed to depend principally on the quality of its past output. Shapiro, for example, considers reputation functions which equate reputation with one period lagged quality, Q_{it-1}, as well as more general functions in which a firm's current reputation for quality depends on both its lagged reputation and its lagged quality. This latter specification is consistent with consumers altering their assessment of a firm's reputation only gradually (perhaps because lagged quality information is initially only imperfectly observed). The key characteristic of these specifications is that each firm's reputation for quality is a function only of its past quality. It follows that price will be a function of lagged quality as well.

The Collective Reputation Model

The two models described above depend on consumers observing the current or lagged quality of the goods produced by individual firms. For some industries, particularly those with a large number of producers, it may be unrealistic to assume that either firm specific current or lagged quality information is easily available. In these industries, even though consumers are interested in the output quality of individual firms, it may only be possible (or cheaper) for them to acquire information on the quality reputation of a group of firms with which the firm producing the good being evaluated can be identified. This group information could then be used to predict or proxy the product quality of the individual firm. For example, in the automobile industry, consumers' expectations of the quality of a Japanese car may depend on the quality reputation of all Japanese cars (Ettenson, Gaeth, & Wagner, 1988). In the wine industry, consumer expectations of the quality of wine produced by an individual winery may depend on the current or past average quality of all wines from the same vintage or region. Tirole (1996) develops a theoretical framework that takes a similar approach while Rasmusen (1989) discusses the related static concept of "teams."

If consumers predict individual firm quality on the basis of the quality reputation of a group of firms with which the individual firm is identified, the price function will include indicators of the collective reputation of this group of firms, rather than the current or lagged quality of the individual firm. That is, the price function will take the form:

$$P_{it} = P(\tilde{z}_{it}, \bar{R}_{it}), \tag{3}$$

where $\bar{R}_{it}$ represents a vector of collective reputation indicators associated with the group of firms with which consumers identify firm i.

Two Extended Models

It is possible that the consumer information sets associated with the full-information and reputation models described above are too restrictive. For example, when consumers possess information on lagged quality, but not current quality, as in the reputation model, they may use collective reputation indicators to improve their forecasts of current quality. As well, even if consumers have complete current quality information, collective reputation indicator variables may affect their demand for different products because goods from some regions or countries may have snob appeal or names which are easy to pronounce. For example, Kramer (1994) argues that French wines with "a pronounceable French name" will be more successful in the U.S. market, and Berger (1994) suggests that, because "Chardonnay is easier to pronounce than Sauvignon Blanc," a Sauvignon Blanc wine will sell for a lower price than a Chardonnay of similar quality. Since consumers can easily observe many collective reputation indicators, such as nationality or region of origin, this information may have an impact on consumers' demand, and thus on price, in both the reputation and full-information models.

The incorporation of the vector of collective reputation variables in the full-information and reputation models yields the *extended full-information* and *extended reputation* models, respectively:

$$P_{it} = P(\tilde{z}_{it}, Q_{it}, \bar{R}_{it}), \tag{4}$$

$$P_{it} = P(\tilde{z}_{it}, R_{it}, \bar{R}_{it}). \tag{5}$$

Note that the full-information model, Equation (1) above, is nested in (that is, a special case of) the extended full-information model, Equation (4); the reputation model, Equation (2), is nested in the extended reputation model, Equation (5); and the collective reputation model, Equation (3), is nested in both Equations (4) and (5).

III. THE DATA

The data set consists of 559 observations on 196 different red wines from the five Bordeaux vintages (harvest years) of 1987 through 1991, although lagged quality data from the 1985 and 1986 vintages are also employed. For some of these wines current quality and price data are only available for a single year while for others the data set includes observations from all five vintages. The number of data points corresponding to each vintage varied from a low of 54 for 1987 to a high of 151 for both 1989 and 1990. Appendix I provides a detailed description of the data and data sources while data summary statistics are given in Appendix II.

Many hedonic price regressions incorporate several descriptive variables to proxy the quality of a product. For example, Kwoka (1992) uses automobile length and weight as proxies for quality while Thomas (1993) proxies the service intensity of household goods carriers with the number of man-days allocated by a carrier to each shipment. There are two problems with this type of approach. First, the products concerned are often technical and complicated and it is not clear whether the proxy variables reflect all the important characteristics of the good. Second, it may be difficult to draw definite conclusions when, as is often the case, the proxy variables used are highly multicollinear (Arguea & Hsiao, 1993).

The current study avoids these problems by employing a relatively finely gradated objective quality index. Data on this quality measure comes from the annual "Bordeaux" issue of the *Wine Spectator*, the largest circulation U.S. wine magazine, as well as from Shanken (1993). The data set includes every wine listed in the "Bordeaux" issue for which a price is reported (most of the wines) and for which two previous annual tastings by *Wine Spectator*, as well as average production information, are available. *Wine Spectator* evaluates a large number of Bordeaux wines and these are fairly representative of the Bordeaux wines available. For example, the data set includes observations on 54 of 61 of the producers included in the 1855 classification of Médoc wines and 143 of the 275 wines that belong to some type of "quality" classification.

The wine quality index (Q) reported in *Wine Spectator* rises by unit intervals from a minimum of 50 to a maximum of 100 and takes into account factors such as a wine's colour, aroma, flavour, balance, complexity and aging potential. Robert Parker, the developer of the "100 point scale," argues that "wine is no different from any consumer product. There are specific standards of quality that full-time wine professionals recognize" (quoted in Robinson, 1994, pp. 706–707).[1] The quality rankings are the result of blind tastings and much of the tasting of the wine included in the sample was conducted by the same tasters.[2]

The price (P) used as the dependent variable in all the regressions below is the per bottle price in the U.S. (the U.S. retail price provided by *Wine Spectator* at the time of the "Bordeaux" issue) divided by the U.S. CPI so that all prices are in constant 1985 U.S. dollars. These prices varied considerably across the wines in the data set (from $6.78 to $302.56). This range is far greater than in most studies which use data from *Consumer Reports* and similar sources. For example, Hjorth-Andersen (1991) uses test data on 452 products and the average ratio of the maximum to minimum price for each commodity is approximately three. Most of the data used to represent non-quality and non-reputation characteristics of the wine in the sample (the $\tilde{z}_{it}$ variables) can be found in *Bordeaux* by Robert Parker (Parker, 1991).

The data from *Wine Spectator* have several characteristics which make it preferable to data from other sources. The "100 point scale" allows for finer quality differences than in most price-quality studies, many of which use *Consumer Reports* rankings that are based on a five-point scale. Furthermore, the data set provides both quality rankings and U.S. prices for each wine, and includes a large number and variety of different wines. Finally, the tastings on which the quality rankings are based take place at the same time each year, at approximately the time the wine is released, and the quality and price data are essentially contemporaneous.

There is a large literature that relates advertising to firm quality and price (Murdock & White, 1985; Parker, 1995). The data used below do not include information on advertising by different Bordeaux wineries. However, advertising may not be important since most of the firms included in the data set are small and evidence suggests that direct advertising by these firms in the U.S. is insignificant. For example, none of the firms in the sample advertise in *Wine Spectator* (although employees and owners of the firms do make themselves available for interviews). Thus, advertising expenditures are not expected to have an important impact on, or obscure, the price-quality relationship.

IV. EMPIRICAL SPECIFICATION

Determining whether consumers rely on quality, reputation or collective reputation information involves estimating, and then comparing, the price equations associated with the five models described in Section II above. This section describes the variables used to represent individual and collective reputation, as well as the variables used to capture the non-quality and non-reputation characteristics of wine (the elements of $\bar{z}$). The methodology used to select the functional form of the estimating equations is outlined at the end of the section.

Reputation and Collective Reputation Indicators

In order to estimate the reputation and collective reputation models, it is necessary to specify variables that reflect firm reputation and collective reputation in the Bordeaux wine industry. The vector of variables representing individual firm reputation, $\mathbf{R}_{it}$, consists of the first and second lags of the summary quality index (Q_{-1}/V_{-1}, Q_{-2}/V_{-2}), where these are divided by the *Wine Spectator* overall quality rating for each vintage to normalize for differences across vintages, as well as indicators of the longer term reputation of each firm. These longer term reputation indicators are five zero-one dummy variables based on a classification of Bordeaux wine producers by Parker (1991). This classification allocates each wine to one of six groups – **R1, R2, R3, R4, R5**, and unclassified (from best to worst) – based on their quality performance between 1961 and 1990. Parker allocated 153 different wines to the top five categories and our data set includes observations from 132 of these wines.

The collective reputation variables, $\bar{\mathbf{R}}_{it}$, are represented by zero-one dummy variables which correspond to the government determined Bordeaux regional designations (appellations) and industry determined "quality" classifications.[3] Wine producers must include the regional designation on each wine's label and, if they are also entitled to a "quality" classification, they usually include this on the label as well. As a consequence, information on the regional designation and "quality" classification of each wine is easily available to consumers.

The dummy variables used to represent the Bordeaux regional designations correspond to the division of Bordeaux into ten regions: Fronsac and others (**FRON**), Haut-Médoc (**HMED**), Margaux (**MAR**), Graves (**GRA**), Listrac and Moulis (**LIS**), Pomerol (**POM**), Pauillac (**PAU**), St.-Emilion (**STEM**), St.-Julien (**STJU**), St.-Estèphe (**STES**), and the rest of the Médoc (**MED**). The "quality" classification dummy variables correspond to the following eleven designations: First-Growth (**FIRST**), Second-Growth (**SECOND**), Third-Growth (**THIRD**), Fourth-Growth (**FOURTH**), Fifth-Growth (**FIFTH**), St.-Emilion *Premier Grand Cru Classé* (**SEPGCC**), St.-Emilion *Grand Cru Classé* (**SEGCC**), Graves *Cru Classé* (**GRACC**), *Cru Grand Bourgeois Exceptionnel* (**CGBE**), *Cru Grand Bourgeois* (**CGB**) and *Cru Bourgeois* (**CB**). The base case in the estimating equations is an unclassified Médoc wine.

Non-Quality Variables

In addition to quality, reputation, and collective reputation variables, the models to be estimated include variables which reflect the other characteristics that differentiate wines (the elements of $\tilde{z}$). Since the types of grapes used to make a wine have a major impact on its taste and style, the estimating equations include the percentages grown by each producer of four of the five grape varieties that can be used to make red Bordeaux wine (Cabernet Sauvignon (**CABS**), Cabernet Franc (**CABF**), Malbec (**MAL**), and Petit Verdot (**PV**)) with the percentage of Merlot forming the base case. The inclusion of grape variety data in the price equations also controls for differences in land characteristics across firms since the grape varieties grown generally depend on soil type.

Two dummy variables were also included in the price equation to control for the effect of "second labels." These are the labels under which some wine producers market wine made from lower quality grapes (sometimes all their grapes in a bad vintage). The dummy variable (**PSEC**) indicates that a wine is produced by a firm that produces a second label, and the dummy variable (**FSEC**) identifies wines which are the first wines of firms that produce a second label. The existence of a second label may affect consumers' relative quality perception of the first and second wines of a producer and, thus, may alter the demand for both types of wine. Finally, the average number of cases produced by each producer (**CASES**) is included as an explanatory variable in each estimating equation to control for any impact the relative scarcity of a wine may have on its price (perhaps due to "snob effects" or the greater visibility of a more abundant wine).

Functional Form

The theories described in Section II above restrict the types of quality and reputation variables included in the price equation, but do not restrict its functional form. The hedonic price equation literature has employed a wide variety of different functional forms: linear, log-linear, semi-log, quadratic and various versions of the Box-Cox transformation (Cropper, Deck, & McConnell, 1988; Halvorsen & Pollakowski, 1981; Mendelsohn, 1984; Palmquist, 1984; Parker & Zilberman, 1993; Stanley & Tschirhart, 1991). Much of this literature includes estimates of quadratic versions of the hedonic price equation. Because of the large number of explanatory variables in the reputation and collective reputation models, quadratic estimation is not feasible. However, five linear-in-their-parameters functional forms – linear, semi-log, log-linear, reciprocal (or inverse) and reciprocal square root – were tested and compared with the most appropriate of these also tested against two variants of the Box-Cox model. The results of these comparisons (see Appendix III) indicate that the reciprocal square root model provides a reasonable description of the data. As a consequence, all the estimates reported below are calculated using this functional form.

V. EMPIRICAL RESULTS

Tables I and II present the parameter estimates associated with the extended full-information and extended reputation models, Equations (4) and (5), respectively, using data for each vintage and for the entire sample (with a dummy variable for each vintage). The empirical analysis begins with an examination of these two extended models

TABLE I
Extended full information model – Parameter estimates

Explanatory variables	All years	1987	1988	1989	1990	1991
Q	-0.0034**	-0.0028**	-0.0046**	-0.0041**	-0.0027**	-0.0042**
	(8.58)	(2.81)	(5.15)	(4.85)	(2.80)	(6.03)
FRON	-0.0242**	-0.0071	–	-0.0322	-0.0048	–
	(1.99)	(0.21)		(1.45)	(0.24)	
GRA	-0.0329**	-0.0612**	-0.0565**	-0.0376**	-0.0099	-0.0310**
	(3.49)	(2.76)	(2.80)	(2.21)	(0.57)	(2.26)
LIS	-0.0396**	-0.0598**	-0.0972**	-0.0280**	-0.0248**	-0.0338**
	(5.03)	(2.70)	(4.00)	(2.10)	(2.31)	(2.16)
MAR	-0.0441**	-0.0547**	-0.0777**	-0.0490**	-0.0348**	-0.0142
	(5.38)	(2.31)	(4.11)	(3.30)	(2.64)	(1.20)
PAU	-0.0470**	-0.0685**	-0.0670**	-0.0522**	-0.0381**	-0.0213*
	(5.68)	(2.93)	(3.20)	(3.37)	(2.66)	(1.79)
POM	-0.1056**	-0.0805**	-0.1120**	-0.1128**	-0.1026**	-0.0959**
	(8.59)	(2.24)	(3.88)	(4.53)	(4.98)	(5.04)
STEM	-0.0542**	-0.0182	-0.1770**	-0.0568*	-0.0243	-0.0487**
	(3.44)	(0.50)	(6.65)	(1.91)	(1.33)	(2.33)
STES	-0.0369**	-0.0377**	-0.0652**	-0.0281	-0.0374**	-0.0206*
	(4.66)	(2.23)	(3.02)	(1.61)	(3.02)	(1.74)

Quality and Reputation Indicators   303

STJU	−0.0419** (5.10)	−0.0610** (2.83)	−0.0603** (2.93)	−0.0497** (3.19)	−0.0294** (2.42)	−0.0242* (1.82)
HMED	−0.0314** (4.79)	−0.0296 (1.27)	−0.0547** (3.14)	−0.0317** (2.71)	−0.0349** (3.45)	−0.0203** (2.01)
FIRST	−0.1169** (18.55)	−0.1184** (6.43)	−0.0917** (5.64)	−0.1140** (10.94)	−0.1245** (10.47)	−0.1166** (10.03)
SECOND	−0.0591** (9.78)	−0.0638** (4.16)	−0.0525** (2.68)	−0.0634** (5.05)	−0.0575** (5.66)	−0.0556** (5.25)
THIRD	−0.0411** (7.43)	−0.0626** (5.11)	−0.0299** (2.28)	−0.0372** (3.69)	−0.0359** (3.54)	−0.0538** (4.53)
FOURTH	−0.0381** (5.64)	−0.0352 (1.65)	−0.0406** (2.15)	−0.0360** (3.01)	−0.0426** (4.41)	−0.0331** (2.58)
FIFTH	−0.0259** (4.29)	−0.0400* (1.92)	−0.0239 (1.53)	−0.0174 (1.51)	−0.0293** (2.50)	−0.0264** (2.79)
CGBE	−0.0098 (1.50)	−0.0148 (0.57)	0.0050 (0.21)	−0.0218 (1.45)	−0.0104 (1.13)	0.0035 (0.32)
CGB	0.0003 (0.05)	−0.0138 (0.86)	−0.0190 (1.44)	0.0029 (0.22)	0.0110 (1.23)	0.0086 (0.81)
CB	−0.0013 (0.22)	—	0.0159 (1.24)	0.0019 (0.15)	−0.0057 (0.59)	0.0052 (0.50)
SEPGCC	−0.0439** (3.36)	−0.1151** (5.60)	0.0500** (2.25)	−0.0357 (1.54)	−0.0638** (5.29)	0.0165 (1.01)
SEGCC	−0.0093 (0.76)	−0.0948** (6.09)	0.0884** (8.59)	0.0002 (0.01)	−0.0248** (2.11)	−0.0068 (0.41)

(continued overleaf)

Table 1 (Continued)

Explanatory variables	All years	1987	1988	1989	1990	1991
GRACC	−0.0431**	−0.0308**	−0.0447*	−0.0381**	−0.0572**	−0.0255
	(4.55)	(2.19)	(1.96)	(2.16)	(3.04)	(1.27)
#OBS	559	54	94	151	151	109
$\bar{R}^2$	0.742	0.635	0.595	0.674	0.687	0.716
RESET test (d.o.f.)	1.96	0.34	0.98	0.59	0.18	0.28
	(1,524)	(1,25)	(1,64)	(1,120)	(1,120)	(1,79)
Breusch-Pagan Heteroscedasticity test (d.o.f.)	96.45††	28.11	21.10	36.76	48.85††	36.08
	(33)	(28)	(28)	(29)	(29)	(28)
F-test that coefficients on region variables equal zero	14.05‡	12.22‡	8.42‡	3.99‡	7.66‡	3.66‡
	(10,525)	(10,25)	(9,65)	(10,121)	(10,121)	(9,80)
F-test that coefficients on classification variables equal zero	46.66‡	18.46‡	34.30‡	18.46‡	13.61‡	16.58‡
	(11,525)	(10,25)	(11,65)	(11,121)	(11,121)	(11,80)

Notes: The number in brackets under each estimated coefficient is the absolute value of the t-statistic calculated using White's (1980) heteroscedasticity consistent covariance matrix. The number in brackets below each test statistic is the degrees of freedom for that test.
** Significant at 95 percent.
* Significant at 90 percent.
† RESET test rejects at 5 percent.
†† Breusch-Pagan Heteroscedasticity test rejects homoscedasticity at 5 percent.
‡ Rejects zero restrictions at 5 percent.

Quality and Reputation Indicators 305

TABLE II

Extended reputation model – Parameter estimates

Explanatory variables	All years	1987	1988	1989	1990	1991
Q_{-1}/V_{-1}	-0.0297	0.0641	-0.0108	-0.0578	-0.0571	-0.1219**
	(1.45)	(1.05)	(0.22)	(1.59)	(1.22)	(2.28)
Q_{-2}/V_{-2}	-0.0625**	-0.3913**	-0.0804	-0.0827**	-0.0131	-0.0567
	(3.07)	(6.49)	(1.54)	(2.36)	(0.32)	(1.04)
R1	-0.0953**	-0.0901**	-0.0922**	-0.0978**	-0.0971**	-0.0889**
	(17.76)	(9.49)	(6.78)	(8.48)	(11.67)	(10.64)
R2	-0.0610**	-0.0633**	-0.0509**	-0.0649**	-0.0657**	-0.0573**
	(15.11)	(8.73)	(4.41)	(8.15)	(11.72)	(7.94)
R3	-0.0416**	-0.0410**	-0.0358**	-0.0459**	-0.0393**	-0.0352**
	(12.20)	(3.52)	(3.61)	(7.21)	(8.03)	(5.08)
R4	-0.0341**	-0.0411**	-0.0311**	-0.0317**	-0.0330**	-0.0377**
	(7.55)	(4.64)	(2.32)	(3.34)	(4.29)	(5.05)
R5	-0.0208**	-0.0494**	-0.0016	-0.0261**	-0.0168**	-0.0233**
	(7.88)	(5.64)	(0.21)	(4.54)	(4.69)	(5.64)
FRON	-0.0352**	-0.0191	–	-0.0427**	-0.0237	–
	(3.27)	(1.11)		(2.65)	(1.52)	
GRA	-0.0440**	-0.0746**	-0.0968**	-0.0541**	-0.0216	-0.0130
	(4.66)	(6.08)	(3.43)	(4.31)	(1.51)	(1.51)
LIS	-0.0482**	-0.0580**	-0.1145**	-0.0523**	-0.0285**	-0.0389**
	(5.91)	(3.68)	(3.78)	(5.09)	(2.75)	(4.52)
MAR	-0.0546**	-0.0397**	-0.0976**	-0.0661**	-0.0491**	-0.0161*
	(6.49)	(3.30)	(3.75)	(6.15)	(4.38)	(1.85)

(continued overleaf)

Table II (Continued)

Explanatory variables	All years	1987	1988	1989	1990	1991
PAU	-0.0492** (6.07)	-0.0681** (5.82)	-0.0901** (3.69)	-0.0554** (5.86)	-0.0416** (3.67)	-0.0146* (1.79)
POM	-0.1021** (9.54)	-0.0698** (3.44)	-0.1277** (4.09)	-0.1149** (7.30)	-0.0985** (6.46)	-0.0644** (4.33)
STEM	-0.0603** (4.71)	-0.0209 (0.93)	-0.1203** (3.82)	-0.0773** (5.04)	-0.0559** (2.41)	-0.0230 (1.48)
STES	-0.0422** (5.36)	-0.0383** (4.57)	-0.0816** (3.00)	-0.0395** (3.64)	-0.0448** (4.11)	-0.0156** (2.20)
STJU	-0.0455** (5.45)	-0.0669** (5.52)	-0.0745** (2.99)	-0.0582** (5.49)	-0.0339** (2.97)	-0.0151* (1.69)
HMED	-0.0376** (5.25)	-0.0718** (7.14)	-0.0606** (2.55)	-0.0429** (4.75)	-0.0346** (3.38)	-0.0244** (3.57)
FIRST	-0.0601** (9.54)	-0.0781** (8.67)	-0.0416** (2.47)	-0.0528** (4.52)	-0.0619** (6.26)	-0.0642** (5.59)
SECOND	-0.0221** (4.07)	-0.0212** (2.71)	-0.0003 (0.02)	-0.0306** (2.88)	-0.0176** (2.19)	-0.0272** (3.49)
THIRD	-0.0258** (5.59)	-0.0371** (4.33)	-0.0316** (2.48)	-0.0200** (2.15)	-0.0204** (3.82)	-0.0384** (4.38)
FOURTH	-0.0244** (4.46)	-0.0496** (6.10)	-0.0298* (1.92)	-0.0194* (1.91)	-0.0227** (2.72)	-0.0226** (2.24)
FIFTH	-0.0270** (6.02)	-0.0352** (4.72)	-0.0299** (2.21)	-0.0213** (2.46)	-0.0269** (4.51)	-0.0258** (3.55)

Quality and Reputation Indicators

307

CGBE	-0.0128** (2.25)	-0.0248 (1.66)	0.0090 (0.37)	-0.0202* (1.81)	-0.0166** (2.29)	-0.0004 (0.06)
CGB	-0.0121** (2.28)	-0.0197** (3.17)	-0.0413** (2.84)	-0.0101 (1.04)	-0.0079 (1.23)	0.0004 (0.04)
CB	-0.0134** (2.54)	—	0.0061 (0.36)	-0.0064 (0.77)	-0.0177** (2.47)	-0.0120* (1.86)
SEPGCC	-0.0361** (3.69)	-0.1043** (10.67)	-0.0236 (1.26)	-0.0224** (2.11)	-0.0359* (1.85)	0.0230** (2.02)
SEGCC	-0.0195** (2.15)	-0.1054** (7.31)	-0.0014 (0.13)	-0.0092 (0.84)	-0.0144 (0.76)	-0.0209** (2.12)
GRACC	-0.0325** (4.67)	-0.0271** (2.94)	-0.0142 (0.75)	-0.0251** (2.00)	-0.0445** (3.65)	-0.0286** (2.33)
#OBS	559	54	94	151	151	109
$\bar{R}^2$	0.860	0.916	0.728	0.839	0.877	0.855
RESET test (d.o.f.)	5.55‡ (1,518)	0.18 (1,18)	0.11 (1,58)	1.56 (1,114)	2.04 (1,114)	1.58 (1,73)
Breusch-Pagan Heteroscedasticity test (d.o.f.)	71.91†† (39)	44.40 (34)	35.33 (34)	37.68 (35)	39.20 (35)	37.64 (34)
F-test that coefficients on region variables equal zero	19.44‡ (10,519)	29.14‡ (10,19)	4.21‡ (9,59)	9.18‡ (10,115)	18.29‡ (10,115)	6.97‡ (9,74)
F-test that coefficients on classification variables equal zero	11.48‡ (11,519)	37.30‡ (10,19)	3.36‡ (11,59)	2.56‡ (11,115)	6.08‡ (11,115)	5.75‡ (11,74)
F-test that coefficients on Q_{-1} and Q_{-2} equal zero	7.10‡ (2,519)	21.40‡ (2,19)	1.80 (2,59)	4.50‡ (2,115)	0.97 (2,115)	4.23‡ (2,74)
F-test that coefficients on R1 to R5 equal zero	73.70‡ (5,519)	26.30‡ (5,19)	12.29‡ (5,59)	18.46‡ (5,115)	37.23‡ (5,115)	31.55‡ (5,74)

See notes to Table I.

308   Stuart Landon and C. E. Smith

since, as noted above, the other three models are nested in one or both of them. To conserve space and make the tables easier to read, the estimated coefficients associated with the non-quality and non-reputation variables are not reported.

In the extended full-information model (Table I), the estimated coefficient associated with current quality is significant in every case and negative indicating a positive relationship between price and current quality (since price enters the dependent variable in reciprocal form). The estimates of the extended reputation model in Table II indicate that only four of the ten estimated coefficients associated with the lagged quality variables are significant, and in only four of the six cases are these two lagged variables jointly significant. However, the long term reputation variables (**R1** to **R5**) have a positive effect on price and are jointly significant in every case. As well, 29 of the 30 estimated coefficients associated with these variables are individually significant.

The significance of current quality in Table I and the long term reputation variables in Table II suggests that both the full-information and reputation models provide potentially valid descriptions of the information used by consumers. In addition, the significant coefficients associated with the current quality and reputation variables mean that the collective reputation model is rejected by both the extended full-information and extended reputation models. This implies that consumers do not rely exclusively on collective reputation signals.

Although the simple collective reputation model is rejected by both extended models, the results in both Tables I and II show that collective reputation variables are important elements in the information sets of consumers. In both tables, an F-test rejects the hypothesis that the coefficients on the regional dummy variables are jointly zero as well as the hypothesis that the coefficients on the group classification variables are zero. These results indicate that the simple full-information and reputation models are rejected by the extended full-information and extended reputation models, respectively.

The coefficient estimates and F-tests described above suggest that both extended models provide reasonable descriptions of the data. In order to further compare these two models, their specifications were tested using RESET and heteroscedasticity tests. In addition to testing for non-constant variances, a test for heteroscedasticity can be used as a general misspecification test (White, 1980). The RESET test is a general test of a model's functional form and, in addition, it performs well as a test for omitted variables (Godfrey & Orme, 1994). As indicated by the test statistics reported in Tables I and II, the heteroscedasticity test rejects the extended full-information model in two of the six cases, but only rejects the extended reputation model when the data is aggregated across time. On the other hand, the RESET test rejects the extended reputation model when the data is aggregated across time, but does not reject the extended full-information model in any case. While these test results provide a similar level of support for both models, the adjusted R^2 statistics associated with the extended reputation model are considerably higher than those for the full-information model.

Since the extended full-information and extended reputation models are not nested, they can be further compared using a non-nested test. The test statistics for the non-nested J-test proposed by Davidson and MacKinnon (1981) are presented in Table III. These test statistics indicate that the extended full-information model can clearly be rejected by the extended reputation model in every case. In contrast, the extended reputation model is only rejected by the extended full-information model for two of the six sample definitions using a 95 percent confidence interval and only for the case in which the data are aggregated across vintages using a 99 percent confidence interval. (The results of the heteroscedasticity and RESET tests associated with the extended reputation model suggest that aggregation across vintages is probably not appropriate and, thus, it is not surprising that the extended reputation model is rejected in this case.) These test results, along with the significance of the coefficient estimates and test

TABLE III
Extended full-information and extended reputation models – Non-nested tests

	All years	1987	1988	1989	1990	1991
Test of the extended full-information model against the extended reputation model						
	22.21†	11.08†	6.77†	12.08†	14.45†	9.58†
Test of the extended reputation model against the extended full-information model						
	4.72†	1.35	1.78	2.05†	1.78	1.24

Notes: The test statistics are asymptotic t-statistics.
† the alternative model rejects the model being tested at 95 percent.

statistics reported in Table II, suggest that, of the five models considered, the extended reputation model provides the best description of the quality and reputation indicators used by consumers in the market for Bordeaux wine.

The Extended Reputation Model – Discussion of the Estimates

The results presented above indicate that both indicators of individual firm reputation and collective reputation are used by consumers when forming their purchase decisions. However, since the dependent variable in the estimating equations is in reciprocal square root form, the comparison and interpretation of the estimated coefficients is relatively complex. To make the results more transparent, the dollar values of the marginal effects associated with each of the explanatory variables in the extended reputation model are listed in Table IV. These values can be used to compare the magnitude of short run and long run reputation on price, as well as the relative impact of individual firm and collective reputation.

The dollar values in Table IV clearly reveal that the marginal impact on price of quality lagged one period is small and insignificant. While the coefficient on the twice lagged quality variable is generally larger and significant in three cases, the impact of this variable on price is still relatively small. Averaging the estimates across years, a one point increase in quality would yield an increase in the price per bottle of nine cents in the following year and an increase of 30 cents after two years (approximately one percent of the average price). In contrast, the long term reputation variables have a relatively large and significant effect on price with the reputation premium falling as the level of reputation declines. On average, a wine with the highest long term reputation (**R1**) sells for a premium of almost $10 a bottle (or almost 40 percent of the average price) over a wine without a long term reputation (one that is not classified as **R1** through **R5**) while a wine classified as **R5** sells for a premium of $3 per bottle. These results imply that consumers are much more willing to pay a higher price for a product with a long-term reputation for quality. The small and relatively insignificant coefficients on the one and two year lagged quality terms imply that consumers do not place significant value, at the margin, on short term quality movements.

The estimated coefficients associated with the regional and classification variables in the extended reputation model reflect the

Quality and Reputation Indicators 311

TABLE IV
Extended reputation model – Real dollar marginal effects

Explanatory variables	All years	1987	1988	1989	1990	1991
Q.₁	0.08	−0.12	0.04	0.22	0.17	0.15*
Q.₂	0.18*	0.75*	0.22	0.40*	0.04	0.07
R1	9.48*	8.42*	10.42*	12.13*	10.65*	5.69*
R2	7.12*	6.68*	7.05*	9.46*	8.36*	4.18*
R3	5.37*	4.83*	5.39*	7.42*	5.75*	2.84*
R4	4.58*	4.85*	4.81*	5.56*	5.01*	3.01*
R5	3.02*	5.58*	0.30	4.74*	2.81*	1.99*
FRON	4.70*	2.54	–	7.02*	3.79	–
GRA	5.60*	7.47*	10.72*	8.35*	3.51	1.17
LIS	6.01*	6.28*	11.75*	8.15*	4.44*	3.09*
MAR	6.58*	4.71*	10.77*	9.57*	6.81*	1.43
PAU	6.09*	7.02*	10.28*	8.49*	6.01*	1.30
POM	9.87*	7.14*	12.41*	13.22*	10.74*	4.56*
STEM	7.06*	2.75	12.05*	10.57*	7.48*	1.97
STES	5.42*	4.58*	9.69*	6.61*	6.37*	1.39*
STJU	5.75*	6.94*	9.15*	8.78*	5.12*	1.35
HMED	4.95*	7.28*	7.98*	7.05*	5.20*	2.07*
FIRST	7.05*	7.69*	6.07*	8.21*	8.03*	4.55*
SECOND	3.18*	2.79*	0.05	5.41*	2.93*	2.28*
THIRD	3.64*	4.47*	4.87*	3.77*	3.34*	3.05*
FOURTH	3.46*	5.60*	4.64	3.68	3.67*	1.94*
FIFTH	3.77*	4.28*	4.66*	3.99*	4.23*	2.18*
CGBE	1.94*	3.20	−1.81	3.81	2.78*	0.04
CGB	1.85*	2.61*	6.03*	2.03	1.39	−0.04
CB	2.03*	–	−1.19	1.32	2.95*	1.09
SEPGCC	4.79*	9.17*	3.82	4.16*	5.35	−2.53*
SEGCC	2.85*	9.23*	0.27	1.86	2.45	1.81*
GRACC	4.41*	3.45*	2.44	4.60*	6.33*	2.38*
Average price	25.10	20.22	25.37	31.50	27.53	15.08

Note: * the coefficient associated with the explanatory variable is significant at 95 percent.

impact on price of collective reputation holding each firm's individual reputation constant. As indicated by the dollar values provided in Table IV, the magnitude of the effect of the collective reputation variables on price can be quite large. For example, a First-Growth wine earns a premium of approximately $7 relative to an unclassified wine and, if it is from the Margaux region, it earns a further premium of approximately $6.50. Given that many wines have both a "quality" classification and a regional designation, the results in Table IV suggest that, at the margin, consumers value the information contained in collective reputation indicators as much as that in individual firm reputation.

The Bias if Reputation Effects Are Omitted

The empirical results described above indicate the important role played by reputation in consumer decisions. As noted previously, while the importance of reputation has long been recognized in the literature, the incorporation of reputation effects in empirical studies is not widespread. However, empirical studies which ignore reputation effects may greatly overestimate the impact of current quality on consumer behaviour. The magnitude of this effect is illustrated in Table V. The estimated dollar values of the marginal effect of quality on price for a model that excludes both individual and collective reputation indicators (as in the full-information model) are given in Table V.1. The model associated with the estimates in Table V.2 excludes individual reputation effects, but includes the collective reputation indicator variables. In both cases, current quality appears to have a relatively large and significant impact on price. As a consequence, the use of either of these two models, both of which were rejected by the extended reputation model, would lead to the incorrect conclusion that the purchase decisions of consumers depend significantly on current quality.

The bias in the magnitude of the impact on price of the short term

TABLE V

Real dollar marginal quality effects in the models that omit the reputation variables

Quality measure	All years	1987	1988	1989	1990	1991
1. *Full-information model (excludes individual and collective reputation variables)*						
Q	1.82*	0.73*	1.76*	2.95*	2.13*	0.85*
2. *Extended full-information model (excludes individual reputation variables)*						
Q	0.85*	0.52*	1.17*	1.43*	0.79*	0.49*
3. *Reputation model (excludes collective reputation variables)*						
Q_{-1}	0.24*	0.39	−0.10	0.46*	0.61*	0.17*
Q_{-2}	0.24*	0.78*	0.20	0.23	0.22	0.17*

* Coefficient associated with the quality variable is significant at 95 percent.

reputation effects when the collective reputation variables are not included in the reputation model are illustrated in Table V.3. These results indicate that, relative to the extended reputation model (Table IV), the basic reputation model yields more significant and larger estimates of the marginal dollar effects associated with the two-lagged quality terms. This is particularly the case for the quality variable lagged once. As a consequence, the use of the reputation model that excludes the collective reputation indicator variables would lead to the incorrect conclusion that price reacts quickly to quality changes and that consumers employ short term quality movements as indicators of current quality.

VI. SUMMARY AND CONCLUSIONS

This paper examines the extent to which consumers use current quality, reputation and collective reputation indicators. Employing data from the market for Bordeaux wine, it is shown that a model that combines reputation and collective reputation variables provides a reasonable description of the information used by consumers. Furthermore, this model rejects alternative models that include current quality. These results suggest that consumers place considerable value on mechanisms that disseminate information on the past quality performance of firms.

The results also indicate that the effect on price of short term changes in quality is relatively small. This implies that consumers primarily base their purchase decisions on persistent, rather than short run, movements in quality. As well, empirical models which include only current realizations of quality or proxies for quality, and which ignore reputation variables (such as many hedonic price studies), may overstate the impact of current quality on price.

The estimates described above reveal a very important role in consumer information sets for collective reputation variables (in particular, group designations and classification schemes) even after controlling for individual firm quality and reputation. The price premium associated with the collective reputation variables is shown to be as large as that associated with individual firm reputation. This suggests that consumers form their predictions of the quality of an individual firm's output using information on the quality of the output produced by similar firms and, thus, that they place significant value, at the margin, on group quality indicators. The high value that consumers place on the government-determined regional designations and the industry-determined "quality" classifications indicates that there may be a role for both government and industry provision of information on product characteristics. The extent of the role for government will depend on the availability of private sector sources of product information and deserves further study.

APPENDIX I. VARIABLE DEFINITIONS AND DATA SOURCES

CABF   a wine producer's average percentage of the Cabernet Franc grape variety. Source: Parker (1991) except for a small number of wines which were not included in Parker for which data from Molyneux-Berry (1990) were used. Second labels were assumed to have the same grape composition as first labels.

CABS   average percentage of grapes in the wine which are of the Cabernet Sauvignon variety. Source is the same as for CABF.

CASES   average number of cases produced by a wine producer (in thousands). Source: Parker (1991).

CB   a dummy variable which equals one if the wine was classified as a *Cru Bourgeois* in the 1978 Médoc classification and zero otherwise. Source: Parker (1991, pp. 930–931). The variable CB was excluded from the 1987 estimates because no wines included in the data set fell into this category during that year.

CGB   a dummy variable which equals one if the wine was classified as a *Cru Grand Bourgeois* in the 1978 Médoc classification and zero otherwise. Source: Parker (1991, pp. 929–930).

CGBE   a dummy variable which equals one if the wine was classified as a *Cru Grand Bourgeois Exceptionnel* in the 1978 Médoc classification and zero otherwise. Source: Parker (1991, p. 929).

FIFTH   a dummy variable which equals one if the wine was classified as a Fifth-Growth in the classification of 1855 and zero otherwise. Source: Parker (1991, p. 925).

FIRST   a dummy variable which equals one if the wine was classified as a First-Growth in the classification of 1855 and zero otherwise. Source: Parker (1991, p. 924).

FOURTH   a dummy variable which equals one if the wine was classified as a Fourth-Growth in the classification of 1855 and zero otherwise. Source: Parker (1991, p. 925).

FRON   a dummy variable which equals one if the wine has a Fronsac or Bordeaux appellation and zero otherwise. Source is the same as for Q. The FRON variable was not included in the estimating equations for 1988 and 1991 because no wines included in the data set fell into this category for those years.

FSEC   a dummy variable which equals one if the wine is a first wine that has a second label and zero otherwise. Source: Parker (1991) except for a small number of wines which were not included in Parker for which data from Molyneux-Berry (1990) was used.

Quality and Reputation Indicators 315

GRA   a dummy variable which equals one if the wine has a Graves appellation and zero otherwise. Source is the same as for Q.

GRACC   a dummy variable which equals one if the wine was classified (*Cru Classé*) in the 1959 Graves classification and zero otherwise. Chateau Haut-Brion was included in the First Growth category and not the Graves *Cru Classé* category because it is the only wine which is recognized in two categories. Source: Parker (1991, p. 926).

HMED   a dummy variable which equals one if the wine has an Haut-Médoc appellation and zero otherwise. Source is the same as for Q.

LIS   a dummy variable which equals one if the wine has a Listrac or Moulis appellation and zero otherwise. Source is the same as for Q.

MAL   average percentage of grapes in the wine which are of the Malbec variety. Source is the same as for CABF.

MAR   a dummy variable which equals one if the wine has a Margaux designation and zero otherwise. Source is the same as for Q.

P   the price per bottle of wine in 1985 US dollars. The source of the nominal prices is the same as for Q. The deflator is the quarterly average of the US CPI in the first quarter of the year in which the wine is released. This price index is reported in the International Monetary Fund's *International Financial Statistics* except for the first quarter 1994 value which was calculated using the change in the CPI from the first quarter 1993 to February 1994 with the later value being from *The Economist*, 9 April 1994, p. 114.

PAU   a dummy variable which equals one if the wine has a Pauillac designation and zero otherwise. Source is the same as for Q.

POM   a dummy variable which equals one if the wine has a Pomerol designation and zero otherwise. Source is the same as for Q.

PSEC   a dummy variable which equals one if the wine is a second wine or is the first wine of a producer that also produces a second wine and zero otherwise. Source is the same as for FSEC.

PV   average percentage of grapes in the wine which are of the Petit Verdot variety. Source is the same as for CABF.

Q   quality measure (100 point maximum, 50 point minimum). Source: 1987: Tasting the 87 Bordeaux. *Wine Spectator, 15*(3), pp. 46–49. 1988: 88 Bordeaux Tasting Notes. *Wine Spectator, 16*(2). 1989: Rating 1989 Bordeaux Reds. *Wine Spectator, 16*(21), pp. 26–32. 1990: Rating Bordeaux's Generous '90s. *Wine Spectator, 17*(22), pp. 30–39. 1991: 1991 Bordeaux in Review. *Wine Spectator, 18*(21), pp. 83–89.

Q_{-1} lagged quality. Source is the same as for Q except for the 1986 observations which come from Shanken (1993).

Q_{-2} twice lagged quality. Source is the same as for Q except for the 1985 and 1986 observations which come from Shanken (1993).

R1   a dummy variable which equals one if a wine producer is included in Parker's list of "First-Growths" and zero otherwise. Source: Parker (1991, p. 932).

R2   a dummy variable which equals one if a wine producer is included in Parker's list of "Second-Growths" and zero otherwise. Source: Parker (1991, p. 933).

R3   a dummy variable which equals one if a wine producer is included in Parker's list of "Third-Growths" and zero otherwise. Source: Parker (1991, p. 933).

R4   a dummy variable which equals one if a wine producer is included in

	Parker's list of "Fourth-Growths" and zero otherwise. Source: Parker (1991, p. 933).
R5	a dummy variable which equals one if a wine producer is included in Parker's list of "Fifth-Growths" and zero otherwise. Source: Parker (1991, pp. 933–934).
SECOND	a dummy variable which equals one if the wine was classified as a Second-Growth in the official classification of 1855 and zero otherwise. Source: Parker (1991, p. 924).
SEGCC	a dummy variable which equals one if the wine was classified as a *Grand Cru Classé* in the 1985 St. Emilion classification and zero otherwise. Source: Parker (1991, pp. 928–929).
SEPGCC	a dummy variable which equals one if the wine was classified as a *Premier Grand Cru Classé* in the 1985 St. Emilion classification and zero otherwise. Source: Parker (1991, p. 928).
STEM	a dummy variable which equals one if the wine has a St. Emilion designation and zero otherwise. Source is the same as for Q.
STES	a dummy variable which equals one if the wine has a St. Estèphe designation and zero otherwise. Source is the same as for Q.
STJU	a dummy variable which equals one if the wine has a St. Julien designation and zero otherwise. Source is the same as for Q.
THIRD	a dummy variable which equals one if the wine was classified as a Third-Growth in the official classification of 1855 and zero otherwise. Source: Parker (1991, pp. 924–925).
V_{-1}	the average quality of the previous vintage in Bordeaux. Source: Rating Bordeaux Vintages 1961–1991. *Wine Spectator, 18*(21), p. 35.
V_{-2}	the average quality of the vintage two years before. Source is the same as for V_{-1}.

APPENDIX II. DATA SUMMARY STATISTICS

	All years	1987	1988	1989	1990	1991
# Obs	559	54	94	151	151	109
Q	87.2	82.5	89.0	90.0	89.7	80.5
Q_{-1}	87.3	90.4	79.8	86.9	89.8	89.2
Q_{-2}	86.0	90.1	88.0	79.2	86.9	90.2
R1	65 (12)	10 (19)	11 (12)	15 (10)	17 (11)	12 (11)
R2	60 (11)	11 (20)	11 (12)	16 (11)	15 (10)	7 (6)
R3	87 (16)	11 (20)	15 (16)	23 (15)	21 (14)	17 (16)
R4	42 (8)	7 (13)	6 (6)	9 (6)	11 (7)	9 (8)
R5	132 (23)	12 (22)	26 (28)	37 (25)	34 (23)	23 (21)
Not R1–R5*	173 (31)	3 (6)	25 (27)	51 (34)	53 (35)	41 (38)
FIRST	23 (4)	3 (6)	5 (5)	5 (3)	5 (3)	5 (5)
SECOND	45 (8)	7 (13)	6 (6)	10 (7)	12 (8)	10 (9)
THIRD	37 (7)	3 (6)	8 (9)	11 (7)	8 (5)	7 (6)
FOURTH	30 (5)	5 (9)	5 (5)	7 (5)	6 (4)	7 (6)
FIFTH	49 (9)	4 (7)	9 (10)	14 (9)	10 (7)	12 (11)

Quality and Reputation Indicators 317

Appendix II (Continued)

	All years	1987	1988	1989	1990	1991
CGBE	39 (7)	4 (7)	5 (5)	10 (7)	10 (7)	10 (9)
CGB	46 (8)	3 (6)	8 (9)	13 (9)	13 (9)	9 (8)
CB	22 (4)	0 (0)	4 (4)	6 (4)	7 (5)	5 (5)
SEPGCC	29 (5)	4 (7)	4 (4)	10 (7)	10 (7)	1 (1)
SEGCC	43 (8)	3 (6)	9 (10)	11 (7)	12 (8)	8 (7)
GRACC	42 (8)	6 (11)	8 (9)	11 (7)	11 (7)	6 (6)
Unclassified*	154 (28)	12 (22)	23 (24)	43 (28)	47 (31)	29 (27)
FRON	11 (2)	1 (2)	0 (0)	4 (3)	6 (4)	0 (0)
GRA	65 (12)	7 (13)	12 (13)	19 (13)	16 (11)	11 (10)
LIS	25 (4)	2 (4)	5 (5)	6 (4)	7 (5)	5 (5)
MAR	74 (13)	7 (13)	14 (15)	19 (13)	19 (13)	15 (14)
PAU	74 (13)	7 (13)	14 (15)	19 (13)	16 (11)	18 (17)
POM	52 (9)	4 (7)	8 (9)	14 (9)	19 (13)	7 (6)
STEM	82 (15)	8 (15)	14 (15)	24 (16)	25 (17)	11 (10)
STES	44 (8)	5 (9)	5 (5)	11 (7)	11 (7)	12 (11)
STJU	58 (10)	9 (17)	10 (11)	12 (8)	14 (9)	13 (12)
HMED	58 (10)	3 (6)	10 (11)	18 (12)	14 (9)	13 (12)
MEDOC*	16 (3)	1 (2)	2 (2)	5 (3)	4 (3)	4 (4)
CABF	11.8	12.8	12.6	12.2	12.7	8.8
CABS	46.9	50.4	46.7	45.7	42.7	53.1
MAL	0.3	0.4	0.5	0.3	0.3	0.2
PV	1.6	1.8	1.9	1.5	1.4	1.7
Merlot*	39.4	34.7	38.4	40.3	43.0	36.2
PSEC	369 (66)	43 (80)	65 (69)	93 (62)	96 (64)	72 (66)
FSEC	347 (62)	41 (76)	61 (65)	87 (58)	91 (60)	67 (61)
CASES	16.2	17.7	16.9	15.7	15.1	16.9
V_{-1}	91.3	95	73	92	98	95
V_{-2}	88.8	95	95	73	92	98

Note: Values are averages for the period for non-dummy variables and the number of observations for which a dummy variable equals one for dummy variables. The numbers in brackets give the percentage of the sample for which the dummy variable equals one.

* These variables comprise the base case in the estimating equation.

APPENDIX III. CHOICE OF FUNCTIONAL FORM

The appropriate functional form was chosen by estimating a price equation for each of the five competing functional forms and then calculating and comparing the corresponding Breusch-Pagan heteroscedasticity and RESET test statistics. In each case, the functional form is estimated using as regressors all the explanatory variables included in the three models described in the text (38 variables including a constant). As a result, this comparison should not suffer from excluded variable bias. Table A1 reports these test statistics for estimates which combine data from all five vintages

318   Stuart Landon and C. E. Smith

as well as for each vintage separately. The hypothesis of homoscedasticity is rejected for all five functional forms when the five years of data are combined (and only the constant is allowed to differ across years), an indication that intertemporal aggregation may be inappropriate. In contrast, when data from each vintage are used separately, the hypothesis of homoscedasticity is rejected in only four of 25 cases (three of which correspond to the reciprocal model).

The RESET test rejects four of the five functional forms a minimum of three times each. The linear model is rejected in every case and the reciprocal model is rejected four times. The reciprocal square root model, in contrast, is not rejected by the RESET test for any of the six different sets of data.

Given the results of both the heteroscedasticity and RESET tests, the reciprocal square root functional form seems more appropriate than the other four specifications. To investigate this choice further, Table A2 presents the results of tests which directly compare the reciprocal square root model to several alternative specifications. The first test compares this model to the other four functional forms that are linear in their parameters using the P_E form of the non-nested test derived by MacKinnon, White, and Davidson (1983). Of the 20 non-nested test statistics reported in this Table, in only two cases is the reciprocal square root model rejected by one of the other functional forms using a 95 percent confidence interval (although in neither case would it be rejected at 99 percent). (Test statistics are not provided for the case in which data from all five vintages are combined due to the heteroscedasticity test results reported in Table A1.)

TABLE A1
Functional form tests

Model	All years	1987	1988	1989	1990	1991
Heteroscedasticity test						
Linear	$74.8^\dagger$	36.1	38.4	42.1	33.3	$55.8^\dagger$
Semi-Log	$86.8^\dagger$	42.6	32.0	44.4	40.2	46.5
Log-Linear	$82.9^\dagger$	42.1	33.1	45.0	37.0	42.7
Reciprocal	$93.3^\dagger$	$48.6^\dagger$	$49.3^\dagger$	$52.9^\dagger$	47.0	38.8
Reciprocal square root	$75.6^\dagger$	46.2	37.7	43.5	34.0	41.7
Degrees of freedom for test						
(distributed as a $\chi 2$ statistic)	35	34	34	35	35	34
RESET test						
Linear	$335.3^{\dagger\dagger}$	$6.9^{\dagger\dagger}$	$17.1^{\dagger\dagger}$	$66.7^{\dagger\dagger}$	$88.8^{\dagger\dagger}$	$10.3^{\dagger\dagger}$
Semi-Log	$81.0^{\dagger\dagger}$	1.8	0.0002	$9.3^{\dagger\dagger}$	$39.9^{\dagger\dagger}$	2.5
Log-Linear	$82.2^{\dagger\dagger}$	1.6	0.02	$8.6^{\dagger\dagger}$	$29.6^{\dagger\dagger}$	2.0
Reciprocal	$8.5^{\dagger\dagger}$	0.4	$14.0^{\dagger\dagger}$	$16.0^{\dagger\dagger}$	$6.7^{\dagger\dagger}$	0.03
Reciprocal square root	3.4	0.9	3.4	1.0	1.6	0.8
Degrees of freedom for test						
(distributed as an F-statistic)	1,522	1,18	1,58	1,114	1,114	1,73

† Rejects homoscedasticity at 95 percent.

Quality and Reputation Indicators 319

TABLE A2
Reciprocal square root model compared to other models

Alternative models	1987	1988	1989	1990	1991
P_E *non-nested test*					
Linear	0.14	1.44	0.13	2.45[†]	0.45
Semi-log	0.54	1.62	0.28	2.05[†]	0.19
Log-linear	0.54	1.28	0.25	1.49	0.55
Reciprocal	0.96	1.84	1.01	1.26	0.87
Likelihood ratio test					
Box-Cox dependent variable transformed only (1 degree of freedom)	1.98	6.40[†]	2.66	1.92	0.92
Box-Cox dependent variable and positive explanatory variables transformed by different parameters (2 degrees of freedom)	2.06	7.24[†]	4.38	2.70	0.30

[†] Reciprocal square root model is rejected by the alternative model at 95 percent. The critical value for the P_E test is 1.96 while the critical values for the likelihood ratio tests for the first and second Box-Cox alternatives are 3.84 and 5.99, respectively.

The likelihood ratio tests in the lower half of Table A2 compare the reciprocal square root functional form to two different versions of the Box-Cox transformation. The first of these is the standard Box-Cox transformation in which only the dependent variable is transformed. The second involves the usual transformation of the dependent variable as well as the transformation of the explanatory variables (only those which are always positive) by a potentially different transformation parameter than that used to transform the dependent variable. The reciprocal square root model is nested within both these transformations since it restricts the transformation parameters associated with the dependent and explanatory variables to –0.5 and 1 respectively. For only two of the 10 tests undertaken are the restrictions implied by the reciprocal square root model rejected by the more general Box-Cox transformation using a 95 percent confidence interval and in both these cases the restrictions would not be rejected using a 99 percent confidence interval. (When the explanatory variables were transformed, the likelihood function was maximized using a grid search (intervals equal to 0.1) with the explanatory variable transformation parameter allowed to vary from 1.5 to –1.0. The transformation of the explanatory variables did not have much impact on the test results relative to the transformation of the dependent variable. Linneman (1980) also finds that his results are sensitive to the dependent variable transformation, but not to the transformation of the explanatory variables.)

The test results presented in Tables A1 and A2 suggest that the reciprocal square root model provides a reasonable description of the data. It passes several basic tests and is only rejected a small percentage of the time by other linear-in-parameters functional forms or Box-Cox alternatives when a 95 percent confidence interval is used and not at all if a 99 percent confidence interval is employed.

NOTES

[1] Parker allocates points as follows: "The wine's general color and appearance merit up to 5 points . . . . The aroma and bouquet merit up to 15 points, depending on the intensity level and extract of the aroma and bouquet as well as the cleanliness of the wine. The flavor and finish merit up to 20 points, and again, intensity of flavor, balance, cleanliness, and depth and length on the palate are all important considerations . . . . Finally, the overall quality level or potential for further evolution and improvement – aging – merits up to 10 points" (Parker, 1991, p. 21).

[2] The tasting procedure used by *Wine Spectator* is as follows: "Bottles are bagged and coded. Capsules are removed and corks are substituted to ensure that the wines remain anonymous. Tasters are told only the general type of wine (varietal or region) and vintage. In scoring, price is not taken into account" (*Wine Spectator*, 31 March 1993, p. BG4). Most of the tasting for the "Bordeaux" issue takes place in January of the year of release which is approximately three years after the vintage (or harvest) year.

[3] The French government's *Appellation d'Origine Contrôlée* (AOC) system provides consumers with information on the region from which a wine's grapes originate. The most well known "quality" classification of red Bordeaux wines took place in 1855 when 61 wine makers in the Médoc and one in the Graves region were classified into five categories (from first-growth to fifth-growth) on the basis of selling price and vineyard condition. The classification was compiled by wine merchants at the request of the Bordeaux Chamber of Commerce and no provision was made for its revision. Not all current wine producers were evaluated during the 1855 classification (including those from Pomerol which today produce wines that are widely recognized as among the best in Bordeaux). In the twentieth century there have been several classifications of the lesser known wine producers. In 1932, 444 producers were classified as *Crus Bourgeois*. This classification was updated in 1966, and again in 1978, when 128 producers were classified as follows: 18 as *Crus Grands Bourgeois Exceptionnelles*, 41 as *Crus Grands Bourgeois*, and 68 as *Crus Bourgeois*. This classification was undertaken by the *Syndicat des Crus Bourgeois*, and only members of the *Syndicat* were entitled to be recognized in the classification. In 1955 the "better" St. Emilion wines were classified as *Premiers Grands Crus Classés* and *Grand Crus Classés*. This classification was revised in 1959, 1969 and, most recently, in 1985 when 73 producers were included. Thirteen wine producers in Graves were singled out for *Cru Classé* status in a 1959 classification.

REFERENCES

Allen, F. (1984). Reputation and product quality. *Rand Journal of Economics, 15,* 311–327.

Archibald, R. B., Haulman, C. A., & Moody, Jr., C. E. (1983). Quality, price, advertising, and published quality ratings. *Journal of Consumer Research, 9,* 347–356.

Arguea, N. M., & Hsiao, C. (1993). Econometric issues of estimating hedonic price functions. *Journal of Econometrics, 56,* 243–267.

Berger, D. (1994). Sauvignon Blanc sales a disaster. *Los Angeles Times*, reprinted in *The Edmonton Journal*, October 12, p. D8.

Bodell, R. W., Kerton, R. R., & Schuster, R. W. (1986). Price as a signal of quality: Canada in the international context. *Journal of Consumer Policy, 9,* 431–444.

Borenstein, S., & Zimmerman, M. B. (1988). Market incentives for safe commercial airline operation. *American Economic Review, 78*, 913–935.

Cropper, M. L., Deck, L. B., & McConnell, K. E. (1988). On the choice of functional form for hedonic price functions. *Review of Economics and Statistics, 70*, 668–675.

Curry, D. J. (1985). Measuring price and quality competition. *Journal of Marketing, 49*(2), 106–117.

Davidson, R., & MacKinnon, J. G. (1981). Several tests for model specification in the presence of alternative hypotheses. *Econometrica, 49*, 781–793.

Ettenson, R., Gaeth, G., & Wagner, J. (1988). Evaluating the effect of country of origin and the "Made in the USA" campaign: A conjoint approach. *Journal of Retailing, 64*(1), 85–100.

Friedman, M. P. (1967). Quality and price considerations in rational consumer decision making. *Journal of Consumer Affairs, 1*, 13–23.

Geistfeld, L. V. (1982). The price-quality relationship – Revisited. *Journal of Consumer Affairs, 16*, 334–346.

Geistfeld, L. V. (1988). The price quality relationship: The evidence we have, the evidence we need. In: E.S. Maynes & the ACCI Research Committee (Eds.), *The frontier of research in the consumer interest*, pp. 143–172. Columbia, MO: American Council on Consumer Interests.

Gerstner, E. (1985). Do higher prices signal higher quality? *Journal of Marketing Research, 22*, 209–215.

Godfrey, L. G., & Orme, C. D. (1994). The sensitivity of some general checks to omitted variables in the linear model. *International Economic Review, 35*, 489–506.

Halvorsen, R., & Pollakowski, H. O. (1981). Choice of functional form for hedonic price equations. *Journal of Urban Economics, 10*, 37–49.

Hanf, C.-H., & von Wersebe, B. (1994). Price, quality, and consumers' behaviour. *Journal of Consumer Policy, 17*, 335–348.

Hjorth-Andersen, C. (1991). Quality indicators in theory and in fact. *European Economic Review, 35*, 1491–1505.

Jarrell, G., & Peltzman, S. (1985). The impact of product recalls on the wealth of sellers. *Journal of Political Economy, 93*, 512–536.

Klein, B., & Leffler, K. B. (1981). The role of market forces in assuring contractual performance. *Journal of Political Economy, 89*, 615–641.

Kramer, M. (1994). Pinot Gris: California's next big white. *Wine Spectator, 19*(10), 24.

Kwoka, J. E. Jr. (1992). Market segmentation by price-quality schedules: Some evidence from automobiles. *Journal of Business, 65*, 615–628.

Linneman, P. (1980). Some empirical results on the nature of the hedonic price function for the urban housing market. *Journal of Urban Economics, 9*, 47–68.

MacKinnon, J. G., White, H., & Davidson, R. (1983). Tests for model specification in the presence of alternative hypotheses: Some further results. *Journal of Econometrics, 21*, 53–70.

Mannering, F., & Winston, C. (1985). A dynamic empirical analysis of household vehicle ownership and utilization. *Rand Journal of Economics, 16*, 215–236.

Mannering, F., & Winston, C. (1991). Brand loyalty and the decline of American automobile firms. In: *Brookings Papers: Microeconomics*, pp. 67–103. Washington: Brookings Institution.

Mendelsohn, R. (1984). Estimating the structural equations of implicit markets and household production functions. *Review of Economics and Statistics, 66*, 673–677.

Molyneux-Berry, D. (1990). *The Sotheby's guide to classic wines and their labels*. New York: Ballantine Books.

Murdock, G. W., & White, J. (1985). Does legal service advertising serve the public's interest? A study of lawyer ratings and advertising practices. *Journal of Consumer Policy, 8*, 153–165.

Oxenfelt, A. R. (1950). Consumer knowledge: Its measurement and extent. *Review of Economics and Statistics, 32*, 300–314.

Palmquist, R. B. (1984). Estimating the demand for the characteristics of housing. *Review of Economics and Statistics, 66*, 394–404.

Parker, D. D., & Zilberman, D. (1993). Hedonic estimation of quality factors affecting the farm-retail margin. *American Journal of Agricultural Economics, 75*, 458–466.

Parker, P. M. (1995). "Sweet lemons": Illusory quality, self-deceivers, advertising, and price. *Journal of Marketing Research, 32*, 291–307.

Parker, R. M. (1991). *Bordeaux*. New York: Simon & Schuster.

Rasmusen, E. (1989). *Games and information: An introduction to game theory*. Cambridge, MA: Blackwell.

Ratchford, B. T., & Gupta, P. (1990). On the interpretation of price-quality relations. *Journal of Consumer Policy, 13*, 389–411.

Riesz, P. C. (1978). Price versus quality in the marketplace, 1961–1975. *Journal of Retailing, 54* (4), 15–28.

Riesz, P. C. (1979). Price-quality correlations for packaged good products. *Journal of Consumer Affairs, 13*, 236–247.

Robinson, J. (1994). *The Oxford companion to wine*. Oxford: Oxford University Press.

Rogerson, W. P. (1987). The dissipation of profits by brand name investment and entry when price guarantees quality. *Journal of Political Economy, 95*, 797–809.

Rosen, S. (1974). Hedonic prices and implicit markets: Product differentiation in pure competition. *Journal of Political Economy, 82*, 34–55.

Shanken, M. (Ed.) (1993). *The Wine Spectator's ultimate guide to buying wine 1994 edition*. New York: Wine Spectator Press.

Shapiro, C. (1983). Premiums for high quality products as returns to reputations. *Quarterly Journal of Economics, 98*, 659–679.

Sproles, G. B. (1977). New evidence on price and product quality. *Journal of Consumer Affairs, 11*(1), 63–77.

Stanley, L. R., & Tschirhart, J. (1991). Hedonic prices for a nondurable good: The case of breakfast cereals. *Review of Economics and Statistics, 73*, 537–541.

Tellis, G. J., & Wernerfelt, B. (1987). Competitive price and quality under asymmetric information. *Marketing Science, 6*, 240–253.

Thomas, J. M. (1993). The implicit market for quality: A hedonic analysis. *Southern Economic Journal, 59*, 648–674.

Tirole, J. (1996). A theory of collective reputations (with applications to the persistence of corruption and to firm quality). *Review of Economic Studies, 63*, 1–22.

White, H. (1980). A heteroskedasticity-consistent covariance matrix estimator and a direct test for heteroskedasticity. *Econometrica, 48*, 817–838.

Zeithaml, V. A. (1988). Consumer perceptions of price, quality and value: A means-end model and synthesis of evidence. *Journal of Marketing, 52*(3), 2–22.

ZUSAMMENFASSUNG

Die Nutzung von Indikatoren für Qualität und Reputation durch Konsumenten: eine Fallstudie auf dem Markt für Bordeaux-Wein. Der Beitrag berichtet über eine Studie

Quality and Reputation Indicators   323

anhand von Daten aus den Jahren 1985 bis 1991 über den Markt für Bordeaux-Wein, deren Ziel es war, die absolute und relative Wirkung von Qualitätsvariablen auf die Entscheidungen der Kunden zu untersuchen. Verglichen wurden dabei Indikatoren der aktuellen Qualität mit solchen der Qualität in der Vergangenheit. Dabei ergab sich, daß ein Modell, das Informationen über die Reputation der Erzeuger (sowohl als Indikator der individuellen Qualität eines einzelnen Erzeugers wie auch als Indikator der kollektiven Reputation der Gemeinschaft aller Erzeuger) verwendet, solchen Modellen überlegen ist, die Indikatoren der aktuellen Qualität verwenden. Die Ergebnisse zeigen außerdem, daß die Reputation einen großen Einfluß auf die Preisbereitschaft der Konsumenten hat, daß eine längerfristig begründete Reputation eines Erzeugers wichtiger ist als kurzfristige Qualitätsveränderungen und daß Konsumenten überhaupt nur langsam auf aktuelle Qualitätsveränderungen reagieren. Die gemeinsame Reputation der Erzeuger erweist sich als genauso wichtig wie der individuelle Ruf eines einzelnen Anbieters, wenn es um die Preisbereitschaft der Verbraucher geht. Werden die Wirkungen der individuellen und gemeinschaftlichen Reputation übersehen, so führt dies zu einer Überschätzung der Wirkungen der aktuellen Qualität und ihrer Veränderungen auf das Verbraucherverhalten.

THE AUTHORS

Stuart Landon and C. E. Smith are Associate Professors in the Department of Economics, University of Alberta, 8–14 HM Tory Building, Edmonton, Canada T6G 2H4. E-mail: Landon@econ.ualberta.ca; fax +1 403 492 3300.

The authors thank Greg Dow, Robin Lindsey, Mel McMillan, Douglas West, and two anonymous referees for comments, and William M. Carter for his help in acquiring some of the data. Daisy Ho and Jessica Xu provided efficient research assistance.

[12]

European Review of Agricultural Economics Vol **28 (4)** (2001) pp. 451–477

The role of the region of origin and EU certificates of origin in consumer evaluation of food products

Ivo A. van der Lans, Koert van Ittersum

Wageningen University, Wageningen, Netherlands

Antonella De Cicco, Margaret Loseby

Università della Tuscia, Viterbo, Italy

Summary

This paper tests the hypothesis that region-of-origin cues and EU certificates of origin (PDO protection labels) influence regional food product preferences directly, and not only indirectly through perceived quality, as has sometimes been affirmed. Conjoint analysis is applied to data on Italian consumers' quality perceptions and preferences for extra virgin olive oils from the Sabina and Canino regions of Lazio, Italy. The region-of-origin cue and the PDO label were both found to influence regional product preferences through perceived quality, although the effect is limited to specific consumer segments. Furthermore, the region-of-origin cue has a direct effect on regional product preference for some consumer segments, especially those resident in the product's region of origin. No direct effect of PDO labels on product preference was found.

Keywords: certificates of origin, conjoint analysis, consumer preference, regional products, extra virgin olive oil

JEL classification: D12, L66, Q13

1. Introduction

In 1992, the European Union Regulation (EEC) 2081/92 established a harmonised set of rules and associated certificates for promoting and protecting agricultural and food products linked to a specific place of origin (PDO: Protected Designation of Origin; PGI: Protected Geographical Indication). The aim of this Regulation was (i) to encourage diversity in agricultural production, (ii) to protect product names from misuse and imitation and (iii) to help consumers by giving them information concerning the specific character of products. The third point reflects the general opinion that consumers nowadays seek variety and quality when shopping for food (Moro *et al.*, 1996; Canali, 1997; Marreiros *et al.*, 1997). The Regulation assumes that the perceived utility of food products increases for quality-seeking consumers if they are aware of the products' origin and the production methods used.

In this paper, we examine how consumers evaluate a product when they are aware of its region of origin, and when the product has a PDO certificate. In the literature on perceived quality of food products, 'country of origin' is acknowledged to signal quality to the consumers (Steenkamp, 1990; Steenkamp and Van Trijp, 1996; Becker, 1999). Here we investigate whether the region of origin might be more than a mere signal of quality, i.e. it might influence regional product preference directly and not only via perceived quality (see Verlegh and Steenkamp, 1999). Likewise, the effect of PDO certification on consumer preference is examined. The main goal of the study is to investigate whether and how the region-of-origin cue and PDO certification influence regional product preferences.

Section 2 presents the theoretical background and the hypotheses. Section 3 discusses the methods used. The results are presented in Section 4. In Section 5, conclusions are drawn and implications formulated. Finally, the limitations of this study are discussed and recommendations for future research put forward.

2. Theoretical background and hypotheses

To evaluate food products during the pre-purchase search for information, consumers use evaluative criteria, 'standards and specifications ... to compare [the product with other alternatives identified]' (Engel *et al.*, 1993: 151). These standards and specifications concern the preferred outcomes from purchase and consumption (e.g. high quality) and are determined by consumers' goals (e.g. desire for high quality). To establish whether products provide the benefits that will satisfy consumers' goals, consumers use cues. Cues are informational stimuli about or related to a product that can be judged by the consumer before consumption (Steenkamp, 1990). When a cue is perceived, consumers' associations with it are automatically evoked. Olson (1972) classifies cues as either intrinsic or extrinsic with respect to the physical product. Specifically, a cue is intrinsic if it is a part of the product itself so that manipulation of the cue changes the product (e.g. taste). Conversely, a cue is extrinsic if it is not a part of the product, i.e. manipulation of that cue does not change the product (e.g. colour of the bottle). During an encoding stage, consumers interpret and provide meaning to cues (see Olson, 1972, 1978; Schellinck, 1983). This (coded) meaning is largely a function of 'previously acquired meanings contained in the activated knowledge structures' (Olson, 1981: 74). By encoding and elaborating on cues, using pre-existing knowledge accumulated in the memory (e.g. Anderson and Bower, 1973), consumers develop an associative network related to the product. This network contains consumers' beliefs about the product and consumers' perceptions of its quality. The match between consumers' (inferential) quality beliefs and their desires forms the basis for consumers' evaluative judgements and preferences (Sheth *et al.*, 1991; Huffman and Houston, 1993). In the next section, we elaborate on the role of the region-of-origin cue and the PDO-certification cue in food product evaluation.

2.1. Region of origin

Marketing food products by using the name of the region of origin as (part of) the name of the regional product (e.g. Parma ham) can be compared with applying a branding strategy (Aaker, 1991; Keller, 1998). By using a regional indication, marketers are able to exploit consumers' associations with a region and provide their product with an image (e.g. Kapferer, 1992). When consumers encounter a regional product during the purchase decision process, the region-of-origin cue triggers consumers' associations with the region, which are then used to evaluate the product. Two conditions are, however, necessary for marketing products successfully on the basis of their region of origin.

First, a significant proportion of the target market for the regional product needs to be aware of the region: if consumers are not aware of the region, they will have no associations related to it. This explains why the use of the region-of-origin cue in international markets may be less beneficial (Keller, 1998). Nevertheless, in a way analogous to the introduction of new brands with fictitious names, promotion of regional products based on regional and product characteristics (e.g. high quality), may also be successful in foreign markets (e.g. Aaker, 1991; Keller, 1998).

Second, it is necessary that consumers have strong and favourable associations with the region, as the success of regional products increases with the strength and favourability of consumers' associations with the region (see Keller, 1998). Among others, Tregear *et al.* (1998), Van Ittersum and Candel (1998) and Van Ittersum *et al.* (2001a) show that consumers generally have a clear image of both their current and former regions of residence as well as other (domestic) regions. Consumers' awareness and image of foreign regions may be less explicit.

If consumers are aware of and have strong and favourable associations with a region, these associations will be triggered when the region-of-origin cue is encountered. Consumers' beliefs are evoked and used to evaluate the regional product. Van Ittersum *et al.* (2001a) show that consumers rely on their product-specific regional image to infer the 'true levels' of the quality of the regional product. The product-specific image of a region is defined as 'the beliefs consumers have with respect to the suitability of a region for the production of a specific product'. For example, consumers may reason that the more natural a region is, the more healthy products from that area are (Van Ittersum and Candel, 1998). Consumers thus form an inferential belief about the 'true' quality of a regional product by using their regional knowledge (see Johansson and Nebenzahl, 1986; Steenkamp, 1990; Juric and Worsley, 1998; Becker, 1999; Van Ittersum *et al.*, 2001b). Depending on how well the inferred product quality beliefs match consumers' goals, regional product preference becomes more or less favourable (Huffman and Houston, 1993). As the perceived quality of a regional product influences regional product preference (e.g. Fishbein and Ajzen, 1975), this effect is also referred to as the *indirect* effect of a product's region of origin (Johansson and Nebenzahl, 1986; Han and Terpstra, 1988; Hong and Wyer, 1989, 1990).

However, as well as triggering product-specific regional associations, the region-of-origin cue also evokes general regional beliefs (traditions, inhabitants, culture). Consumers' general regional beliefs may be an important source for their affective feelings related to the regional product (see Obermiller and Spangenberg, 1989; Verlegh and Steenkamp, 1999; Van Ittersum *et al.*, 2001a, 2001b). A specific 'class' of beliefs concerns those related to the inhabitants of the product's region of origin, their characteristics, culture and traditions. If consumers' regional beliefs relate to and are consistent with their ideal self-images (i.e. identification), *and* consumers have a strong desire for belonging, the region-of-origin cue provides them with social value (see Keller 1998). In time, the match between consumers' beliefs about the regional inhabitants, their traditions and culture, and their general desire for belonging may result in a sense of belonging to the region, which directly influences regional product preference. Likewise, regional products may acquire emotional value when associated with specific feelings or when they facilitate or perpetuate feelings (Sheth *et al.*, 1991). This might be especially true for food products. For instance, Tregear *et al.* (1998) report that 'food products would appear to embody strong associations with place because they have, by their very nature, a land-based geographical origin (Bérard and Marchenay, 1995). Moreover, there are often strong historical and symbolic links between places and foods due to the interactions between natural resource bases and peoples' lifestyles (Delamont, 1995)' (p. 385). When a consumer encounters a regional product, the region-of-origin cue automatically triggers the consumer's emotional associations with the region. The associative network model of memory and emotion (Bower, 1981) suggests that each emotion 'has its own specific node in memory, which is connected by associative links to other aspects of that emotion, as well as other proposition nodes'. 'Emotion nodes can be activated using physiological or verbal methods, and when activated, spread that excitation to nodes that are associated with it, creating excitation at the event nodes, and producing autonomic arousal' (Erevelles, 1998: 201). For instance, a product's place of origin may elicit feelings of *pleasure* and *happiness* based on consumer's experience with the region. The emotions elicited *directly* influence regional product preference (see Obermiller and Spangenberg, 1989; Li and Wyer, 1994; Verlegh and Steenkamp, 1999).

Drawing on this literature, we formulate the following hypothesis:

H1. Region of origin influences regional product preference directly, and not only indirectly via perceived quality.

2.2. Certificates of origin—PDO protection labels

Products protected by Regulation (EEC) 2081/92 are allowed to carry a certificate of origin (PDO label). Like the region of origin, this certificate of origin is an extrinsic product cue. When consumers encounter a PDO label, their associations with the label are triggered automatically. Consumers then use the beliefs evoked by the PDO label to make inferences about the

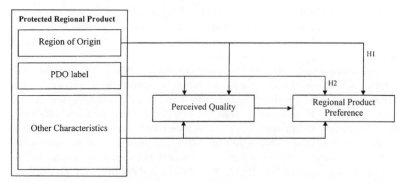

Figure 1 Effect of the region-of-origin and PDO labels on regional product preference.

true quality of the (protected) regional product. This process resembles the process applied when making inferences about product quality based on the product-specific regional image, as discussed in the previous section.

Van Ittersum *et al.* (2000) show using focus groups that consumers' beliefs related to PDO labels can be represented by two main dimensions: a quality warranty dimension and an economic support dimension. The quality warranty dimension represents consumers' beliefs about the guarantees the PDO label provides regarding the qualities of the (protected) regional product. Beliefs related to this dimension concern 'guarantee of high quality', and 'exclusivity', among others. The economic warranty dimension captures consumers' beliefs about what the PDO label does for the economic perfor-mance of the producers of the (protected) regional product. 'Increased income for farmers' and 'increased employment' in the region of origin are beliefs represented by this dimension. In a different study, Van Ittersum *et al.* (2001b) show that the quality warranty dimension merely influences pre-ference for the (protected) regional product *indirectly*, through the perceived quality of the product. The economic dimension, however, influences con-sumers' preference for the (protected) regional product *directly* (and not indirectly).

Overall, we conclude that the PDO label may influence regional product preference both directly, and indirectly, through the perceived quality. Hence, our second hypothesis:

H2. PDO labels influence regional product preference directly, and not only indirectly via perceived quality.

Figure 1 summarises our hypotheses.

3. Method

3.1. Product and sample selection

The hypotheses were tested in a conjoint study on extra virgin olive oil (EVO). The study was carried out in Italy, where most consumers buy olive oil (extra virgin or other qualities) on a regular basis. Olive oils are, moreover, often advertised on the basis of their region of origin.

Respondents were randomly sampled at shopping malls in three Italian towns: Rieti (54 respondents), Viterbo (56) and Rome (55). Rome is a metropolis where economic activity occurs mainly in the tertiary sector. Rieti and Viterbo are smaller towns, still closely linked to the local agricultural sector within which olive cultivation is a leading activity and has a strong tradition dating back to the distant past. Rieti is close to the production area of Sabina olive oil, Viterbo to that of Canino oil. Both oils have obtained a PDO certificate in recent years. In total, 165 persons were interviewed and asked to rate their overall perception of product quality and their product preference for 22 (hypothetical) EVOs. A total of 152 respondents completed both tasks. The number of respondents was balanced across combinations of two between-subjects factors: Region (Sabina versus Canino, see later section) and Place (Rieti versus Viterbo versus Rome).

The sample (70 males and 95 females) was representative of the Italian population both regarding gender ($\chi^2 = 1.74$, df $= 1$, $P > 0.10$) and regarding age ($\chi^2 = 5.03$, df $= 3$, $P > 0.10$). The sample was not representative with respect to educational level, with more highly educated respondents over-represented ($\chi^2 = 10.04$, df $= 5$, $P < 0.05$). This bias arises because less educated people were more reluctant to fill in the questionnaire as they did not feel sufficiently qualified or confident (see De Maio, 1980). The aim of our study was to explore the relationships between the region-of-origin cue and the PDO label, and constructs such as preference and perceived quality. We assume that these relationships are not significantly affected by this bias, and that our results can therefore be generalised.

3.2. Design of the conjoint study

Hypothetical EVOs

Conjoint analysis allowed us to include other attributes alongside the manipulation of the region-of-origin cue and the PDO label (referred to as the Origin attribute), thereby not unduly attracting the attention of our respondents to it (see Verlegh and Steenkamp, 1999). Three other attributes were included: Price, Colour and Appearance (see Table 1). A total of four attributes is reasonable for the application of traditional full-profile conjoint method, which was used here (Green and Srinivasan, 1978, 1990). The different hypothetical EVOs (profiles) were generated by a fractional factorial main-effects design.

Price was included in the study because it is one of the most important product attributes when purchasing food products (Steenkamp, 1997) and it adds reality to the profiles. Based on the actual price range of EVOs in the Italian market, a minimum and maximum price level were identified. In determining the price levels, besides using actual market prices, the number of price levels should be manageable and the price intervals should not be too large (Green and Srinivasan, 1978; Steenkamp and Wittink, 1994). With this in mind, the

Table 1. Attributes and levels in the conjoint study

Attribute	Level
Origin	EVO without any further indication (standard EVO)
	EVO from Sabina with indication of region of origin (Sabina ROO-EVO)
	EVO from Canino with indication of region of origin (Canino ROO-EVO)
	EVO from Sabina with PDO label (Sabina PDO-EVO)
	EVO from Canino with PDO label (Canino PDO-EVO)
Colour	Green
	Yellow
Appearance	Opaque
	Clear
Price	7,500 ITL/litre (3.87 €/litre)
	9,000 ITL/litre (4.65 €/litre)
	10,500 ITL/litre (5.42 €/litre)
	12,000 ITL/litre (6.20 €/litre)

price range was restricted to a minimum of 7,500 ITL/l[1] and a maximum of 12,000 ITL/l (with 9,000 and 10,500 ITL/l as intermediate levels). Colour and Appearance were selected as attributes describing the oil visually. These are the two organoleptic characteristics that can be assessed by the consumers before consumption and are two of the most important indicators for the quality of olive oils. Colour was either green or yellow, and Appearance was opaque or clear.

The focal attribute in the study was Origin. As mentioned above, the region of origin is used often in marketing olive oils. Five levels were selected: (i) EVO without any further specification (standard EVO); (ii) EVO from Sabina with an indication of region of origin (Sabina ROO-EVO); (iii) EVO from Canino with an indication of region of origin (Canino ROO-EVO); (iv) EVO from Sabina with a PDO label (Sabina PDO-EVO); (v) EVO from Canino with a PDO label (Canino PDO-EVO). It should be noted that profiles with a PDO label automatically carry an indication of region of origin.

Assignment of profiles to respondents
To limit the number of profiles to be evaluated by one individual, each respondent was asked to rate EVOs from either Sabina or Canino only, in addition to standard EVO. Thus each respondent was faced with only three levels of the Origin attribute (either standard EVO, Sabina ROO-EVO and Sabina PDO-EVO, or standard EVO, Canino ROO-EVO and Canino PDO-EVO). Therefore, instead of the five-level attribute Origin, we defined

---

1   1 euro = 1936.27 Italian lire (ITL).

a three-level attribute Origin2 (standard EVO versus ROO-EVO versus PDO-EVO) and a two-level between-subjects factor Region (Sabina versus Canino). In each place (Rieti, Viterbo or Rome—Place), the sample was randomly divided into two subsamples, one being interviewed on standard EVO, Sabina ROO-EVO and Sabina PDO-EVO, and the other one on standard EVO, Canino ROO-EVO and Canino PDO-EVO.

For each level of the factor Region, the same 4 (Price) × 2 (Colour) × 2 (Appearance) × 3 (Origin2) fractional factorial main-effect-only design generated a set of 16 calibration profiles. In addition, six holdout profiles were generated, so that the total number of profiles to be evaluated by each respondent was 22. Depending on the level of the factor Region, either Sabina or Canino was added to the description of the ROO- and PDO-EVOs. These profiles were presented to the respondents in a randomised order. It should be noted that we chose to use a fractional factorial main-effect-only design, again to keep the number of profiles to be evaluated by each individual respondent reasonable, and because we assume that interaction effects between the conjoint attributes are negligible.

Response scales

Respondents were asked to rate the profiles with respect both to their overall perception of quality and to their preference. The rating scale for preferences ranged from zero (low preference) to 100 (high preference) with 10-point intervals. Likewise, consumers' quality perceptions were rated on a scale from zero (low quality) to 100 (high quality).

3.3. Analysis

It is assumed that the levels of the attributes contribute in an additive way to both preference and perceived quality (see Figure 1). Furthermore, no *a priori* functional relationship is assumed among the contributions of the levels of any single attribute. That is, contributions of the levels are allowed to follow the part-worth model (Green and Srinivasan, 1978). In formulae:

$$P_{ik} = \alpha_i + \sum_{j=1}^{m} \sum_{l=1}^{L_j} x_{klj} p_{ilj} \tag{1}$$

$$Q_{ik} = \beta_i + \sum_{j=1}^{m} \sum_{l=1}^{L_j} x_{klj} q_{ilj}. \tag{2}$$

In these equations, (i) P_{ik} is the preference of respondent i for profile k, (ii) Q_{ik} is the quality of profile k, as perceived by respondent i, (iii) α_i and β_i are respondent-specific intercept terms to be estimated, (iv) m is the number of attributes (four here), (v) L_j is the number of levels of attribute j, (vi) x_{klj} is profile k's value of a dummy variable for level l of attribute j ($x_{klj} = 1$ if profile k has level l of attribute j, and $x_{klj} = 0$ otherwise), (vii) p_{ilj} is the contribution (preference part worth) of level l of attribute j to the preferences of respondent i, and (viii) q_{ilj} is the contribution (quality part worth) of level l

of attribute j to the quality perceived by respondent i. Both p_{ilj} and q_{ilj} are to be estimated.

To test the hypotheses, we followed the procedure for testing complete mediation proposed by Baron and Kenny (1986). Our hypotheses stipulate that the effects of the region-of-origin cue and the PDO label on preference are not completely mediated by perceived quality. For complete mediation to hold true in our situation, the following conditions should be satisfied (see Baron and Kenny, 1986):

(i) the ROO cue (or PDO label) has an effect on preference;

(ii) the ROO cue (or PDO label) has an effect on perceived quality;

(iii) perceived quality has an effect on preference;

(iv) the ROO cue (or PDO label) does not have an effect on preference after the effect of perceived quality on preference has been accounted for, i.e. after perceived quality has been partialled out from preference.

When we assume a linear relationship between perceived quality and preference, the four conditions can be tested by carrying out: (i) a (repeated measures) analysis of variance of the preference ratings on the conjoint attributes; (ii) a (repeated measures) analysis of variance of the quality ratings on the conjoint attributes; (iii) a linear regression of the preference ratings on the quality ratings; (iv) a (repeated measures) analysis of covariance of the preference ratings on the conjoint attributes with the quality ratings as a covariate. Significant effects of the contrasts between ROO-EVO and standard EVO, and PDO-EVO and ROO-EVO, in analyses (i), (ii) and (iv), in combination with a significant effect of the quality ratings on the preference ratings in analysis (iii), would lend support to our hypotheses. All the analyses come down to Ordinary Least Squares regression with dummy variables, which is the most common estimation method in the area of conjoint analysis using 11-point rating scales (see Green and Srinivasan, 1990; DeSarbo *et al.*, 1992; Wedel and Kamakura, 2000).

A complicating factor is that consumers are typically assumed to be heterogeneous in their preferences (Green and Srinivasan, 1978, 1990; Wedel and Kamakura, 2000). When we do not take this heterogeneity (interaction between the subjects factor and the conjoint attributes) explicitly into account, the estimate of the error mean squares can become unduly large. Taking this heterogeneity completely into account leaves a small number of degrees of freedom for the error term, which is also not desirable.[2] The amount of heterogeneity is usually assumed to be limited to some extent, and to be structured in that it is caused by the existence of a relatively small number of homogeneous segments (see Wedel and Steenkamp, 1991; DeSarbo *et al.*, 1992; Wedel and Kamakura, 2000). Therefore, in addition to analyses in which we did not take heterogeneity into account, and analyses

---

2 We thank a reviewer for pointing this out and for the suggestion to cluster our sample to model the heterogeneity.

460   *Ivo A. van der Lans* et al.

in which we took heterogeneity completely into account, we also carried out analyses in which we accounted for heterogeneity between homogeneous groups of respondents. These groups were found by regressing preference ratings on dummy variables for the conjoint attributes in a (multivariate normal) mixture regression model (DeSarbo *et al.*, 1992; Wedel and Kamakura, 2000). Differences between respondents in mean preference ratings were removed before fitting the mixture regression model, as they are irrelevant in the context of conjoint analysis. Respondents were classified into groups according to their posterior probabilities, and the resulting group-membership variable was included as a moderator in our analyses for testing the hypotheses.

Table 2. Respondent or household characteristics

Characteristic	Category
Place × Region	Viterbo–Canino (Same); Rieti–Sabina (Same); Viterbo–Sabina (Different); Rieti–Canino (Different); Rome–Canino; Rome–Sabina
Place of birth × Region	Viterbo–Canino (Same); Rieti–Sabina (Same); Viterbo–Sabina (Different); Rieti–Canino (Different); Lazio–Canino; Lazio–Sabina; outside Lazio–Canino; outside Lazio–Sabina
Place of residence × Region	Viterbo–Canino (Same); Rieti–Sabina (Same); Viterbo–Sabina (Different); Rieti–Canino (Different); Lazio–Canino; Lazio–Sabina
Consumption intensity EVO	<1 litre/month; 1–2 litres/month; 2–3 litres/month; >3 litres/month
Use EVO for cooking	No; Yes
Use EVO for frying	No; Yes
Heard about PDO before	No; Yes
Usually buy EVO at supermarket	No; Yes
Usually buy EVO at mill	No; Yes
Self-production EVO	No; Yes
Gender	Male; Female
Occupation	Student; Housewife; Employee; Self-employed; Farmer; Unemployed; Teacher; Manager; Retired
Educational level	Elementary school; 3-year secondary school; High-school diploma; University degree
Income	<1.0 million ITL/month; 1.0–1.5 million ITL/month; 1.5–2.0 million ITL/month; 2.0–2.5 million ITL/month; 2.5–3.0 million ITL/month; >3.0 million ITL/month
Age	<40 years; 40–54 years; 55–64 years; >64 years
Household size	1 person; 2 persons; 3 persons; 4 persons; >4 persons
Number of children	No children; 1 child; >1 child

In addition to the above *post hoc* segmentation procedure, we also tried to model possible heterogeneity in a more *a priori* way by incorporating in the analyses, first, the between-subject factors Region and Place, and, second, a number of other respondent or household characteristics, all of which are displayed in Table 2. We cross-classified Place (of interview), Place of birth, and Place of residence with Region, as we thought there may be a different effect when respondents come from the same region as the ROO/PDO-EVO rather than another region (see below).

4. Results

We first describe the way in which we arrived at our *post hoc* segmentation of the sample. Multivariate normal mixture regression models with one to 10 classes were fitted. On the basis of the minimum of the Consistent Akaike Information Criterion (CAIC),[3] we selected the five-class solution. The number of respondents in the segments was respectively 16 (10.5 per cent), 27 (17.8 per cent), 52 (34.2 per cent), 33 (21.7 per cent) and 24 (15.8 per cent). The parameter estimates of the mixture regression model are not reported. Instead, segment-level mean part-worth estimates from standard conjoint analysis are displayed in Figure 2 (see below).

Table 3. Fit and internal validity of conjoint analyses

	Mean fit (Pearson correlation)	Mean internal predictive validity (Kendall's τ)
Preference (individual)	0.87	0.47
Preference (segment-level)	0.62	0.42
Quality (individual)	0.88	0.46
Quality (segment-level)	0.60	0.36
Affective preference (individual)	0.73	0.20
Affective preference (segment-level)	0.31	0.21

Conjoint analyses were carried out at the individual level as well as at the *post hoc* segment level, and on the preference ratings, as well as on the quality ratings and the affective preferences. The latter were obtained by partialling out the quality ratings from the preference ratings at the individual level. Effects of the conjoint attributes on these affective preferences represent their direct effects on preference. In Table 3, measures are given for the overall fit and the internal validity of the conjoint analyses. The overall fit has been assessed by computing the mean individual-level Pearson correlation between

---

3   The Akaike Information Criterion (AIC) did not show a minimum between one and 10 classes. Both the AIC and the CAIC make a trade-off between the fit and the number of estimated parameters, with the CAIC penalising more strongly for the number of parameters than the AIC (Wedel and Kamakura, 2000).

observed and predicted (partialled) ratings for the 16 calibration profiles, using individual-level and segment-level part-worth estimates, respectively. The internal validity has been assessed by calculating the mean Kendall's τ between observed and predicted (partialled) ratings for the six holdout profiles.

It can be seen that the average fit of the individual-level conjoint analyses is acceptable, but that the average internal predictive validity of the individual-level part-worth estimates is not so high, especially regarding the affective preferences. For both perceived quality and preference ratings, slightly more than 60 per cent of the respondents have a holdout Kendall's τ larger than 0.40. For the affective preference, this percentage is about 30 per cent only. As Colour, Appearance and Price were assumed not to have an affective aspect that might cause a direct effect of these attributes on the preference ratings, a low internal predictive validity of the part-worth estimates from the affective preferences was to be expected. The average fit and the average predictive validity are lower for the segment-level conjoint analyses than for the individual-level conjoint analyses. Also, for preference and quality ratings, a lower percentage (57 and 51 per cent, respectively) of the respondents have a holdout Kendall's τ larger than 0.40. For the affective preference, the percentage stays about the same, as compared with the individual-level analyses. With respect to the fit, this result was to be expected because with segment-level estimation fewer parameters are being estimated. The lower average predictive validity may, however, come as a surprise, as a higher average predictive validity has been found for part-worth estimates at some level of aggregation in a number of studies (see, e.g. Hagerty, 1985). In other studies, however, a lower average predictive validity has been found for segment-level estimates, as in our study[4] (see, e.g. Vriens *et al.*, 1996; Wedel and Kamakura, 2000).

Figure 2 shows mean overall- and segment-level part-worth estimates. The vertical axis of the plots gives the value of the part-worth estimates. The overall-level part-worth estimates suggest that in general the respondents prefer PDO-EVO to ROO-EVO, which is preferred over standard EVO, as was expected. Furthermore, they seem to prefer a green EVO to a yellow EVO, and a clear EVO to an opaque EVO. Finally, the respondents seem to prefer higher prices to lower prices. Probably, they associate a higher price with a higher quality, a finding that is reported more often in the literature (Hair *et al.*, 1998). Based on the mean part-worth estimates, respondents seem to attach most importance to the Price attribute, followed by Colour, Origin2 and Appearance. Examining the mean importances[5] of the attributes,

4   Even lower predictive validities were found using segment-level estimates, when the segments were based on a multivariate normal mixture regression model with dummies for the conjoint attributes and perceived quality ratings as predictors, as suggested by one of the reviewers. The CAIC indicated a three-class solution. The average Kendall's τ values of the segment-level estimates for the holdout profiles were 0.20 for preference ratings, 0.21 for quality ratings and 0.10 for affective preferences.

5   In conjoint analysis, importances of attributes are computed by taking, per individual, the range of the part-worth estimates for each attribute and by renormalising them in such a way that the sum of the renormalised ranges equals 100.

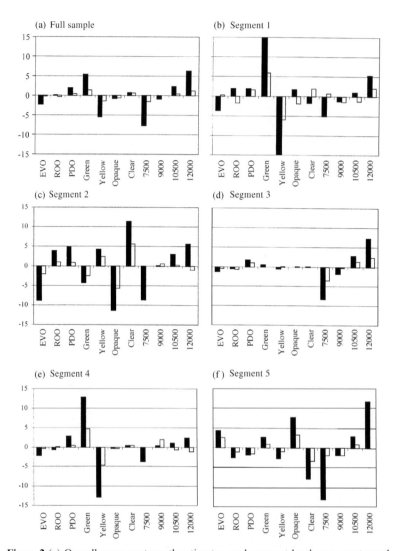

Figure 2 (a) Overall mean part-worth estimates, and segment-level mean part-worth estimates for: (b) Region-oriented quality-seekers, (c) Involved shoppers, (d) Price-oriented quality-seekers, (e) PDO-label-oriented quality-seekers and (f) ROO-averse consumers. Filled columns represent preference; open columns represent affective preference. In (b), the bars for the levels of the attribute Colour extend far beyond the boundaries of the plot. The mean part-worth estimates are 27.3 for Green and −27.3 for Yellow, respectively.

Geographical Indications I   287

464   *Ivo A. van der Lans* et al.

it turns out that Price is indeed the most important attribute with a mean importance (*w*) of 34, followed by Colour (*w* = 26), Origin2 (*w* = 22), and Appearance (*w* = 17). However, as our conjoint design has different numbers of levels per attribute, care should be taken when drawing conclusions about the relative importance of the different attributes in the evaluation process. Research has shown that the importance of an attribute tends to increase with the number of levels (see, e.g. Steenkamp and Wittink, 1994). The mean part-worth estimates based on the affective preference turn out to be much lower than their preference-based counterparts, as was to be expected because of the assumed relation between preference and perceived quality.

Comparing the segments, we find that Segments 1 and 4 both show a large difference in mean part-worth estimates for Colour, compared with differences on the other attributes. Segments 1 and 4 differ from each other in the sense that the difference for Colour is larger in Segment 1 than in Segment 4 (also on the other attributes). Focusing on the part-worth estimates for the attribute Origin2 and assuming that large differences in mean part-worth estimates for Colour and Appearance are an indication of quality-consciousness and are less relevant in the present context, we label respondents in Segment 1 as 'Region-oriented quality-seekers', and those in Segment 4 as 'PDO-label-oriented quality-seekers'. Segment 2 seems to consist of respondents who attach at least some importance to all attributes (Colour somewhat less). Therefore, we call them 'Involved shoppers'. Respondents in Segment 3 seem to be rather indifferent to the conjoint attributes, apart from the attribute Price, where they prefer higher-priced over lower-priced EVOs. Therefore, they are called 'Price-oriented quality-seekers'. Respondents in Segment 5 are much more sensitive to Price than those in Segment 3. In addition, they are sensitive to Appearance, and to a smaller extent to Origin2. It should be noted, however, that standard EVO is preferred to both ROO-EVO and PDO-EVO in this segment, which is contrary to our expectations. In the context of this study, this latter finding is most characteristic for this segment. Therefore, these respondents are called 'ROO-averse consumers'. A remarkable finding is the positive relationship between Price and preference in all segments, possibly indicating that the association of a higher price with a higher quality is pervasive for EVO in the Lazio region. Overall, the affective-preference-based part-worth estimates follow the pattern of the preference-based part-worth estimates although tending to be much smaller, suggesting the absence of direct effect of the conjoint attributes on preference.[6]

---

6   These results can be used for market segmentation purposes, if the segments are related to respondent or household characteristics. χ^2 tests have been used to test such relations. There seems to be no relation with Consumption intensity EVO, Use EVO for frying, Heard about PDO before, Usually buy EVO at supermarket, Usually buy EVO at mill, Self-production EVO, Gender, Occupation, Educational level, Income, Age, Household size and Number of children. There is a significant relation with Use EVO for cooking ($\chi^2 = 11.63$, df = 4, $P < 0.05$). The percentage of respondents that use EVO for cooking ranges from 74 per cent for 'Involved shoppers' to 100 per cent for 'Region-oriented quality-seekers' and 'ROO-averse consumers'.

As mentioned above, our hypotheses are supported when four conditions are satisfied. To test the third condition, we computed the Pearson correlation between quality and preference ratings, both corrected for individual-level means. This correlation is equal to 0.694 ($F = 2114.85$, df $= (1, 2279)$, $P < 0.01$), which indicates that perceived quality is related to preference. Although, because of the design of our study, we cannot conclude that the relationship is a causal one, the result certainly does not preclude it. In addition, the interaction between the subject-factor and the quality ratings turned out to be significant ($F = 2.93$, df $= (151, 2128)$, $P < 0.01$). Therefore, there also seems to be some heterogeneity between respondents in the slopes of the regression of preference ratings on quality ratings. Considering this heterogeneity, some analyses of covariance for testing the fourth condition were carried out both with one aggregate slope parameter as well as with individual-level slope parameters for perceived quality (the covariate). The latter basically involves partialling out quality ratings from the preference ratings at the individual level, in the same way as was done to obtain affective preferences for the conjoint analyses reported before.

Tables 4, 5 and 6 give F and P values of the repeated measures analyses of variance for testing conditions 1, 2 and 4, respectively. These values are given for two contrasts: the contrast between ROO-EVO and standard EVO, and the contrast between PDO-EVO and ROO-EVO. Results for the first contrast deal with Hypothesis 1, whereas results for the second contrast deal with Hypothesis 2. The P values correspond to two-sided tests. The F values reported for the analyses that allow for heterogeneity (between segments, or between respondents) are the F values for the combined ROO/PDO main effects, and the ROO/PDO $\times$ Segment/Subject interaction effects. Therefore, we test for the effects of ROO/PDO within segments/subjects. In

Table 4. Effect of the conjoint attribute Origin2 on preference

	ROO vs standard		PDO vs ROO	
	F value	P	F value	P
Overall (df $= 1$, 2273)	4.42	<0.05	3.45	n.s.[a]
Post hoc segments (df $= 5$, 2245)	9.73	<0.01	1.52	n.s.
Region-oriented quality-seekers	4.00	<0.05	0.00	n.s.
Involved shoppers	34.81	<0.01	0.20	n.s.
Price-oriented quality-seekers	0.27	n.s.	2.86	n.s.
PDO-label-oriented quality-seekers	0.60	n.s.	4.41	<0.05
ROO-averse consumers	8.96	<0.01	0.15	n.s.
Individual level (df $= 152$, 1216)	3.14	<0.01	1.26	<0.05

[a] A one-sided *t*-test, however, gives a significant result ($P < 0.05$). A one-sided *t*-test instead of an *F*-test is defendable in our situation (in which the *F*-test is equal to a two-sided *t*-test), as Hypothesis 2 claims that PDO certificates have a positive effect on preferences and the effect found is in the appropriate direction (see Figure 2). One-sided *t*-tests do not give significant results for any of the other not significant *F* values reported.

466   *Ivo A. van der Lans* et al.

Table 5. Effect of the conjoint attribute Origin2 on quality

	ROO vs standard		PDO vs ROO	
	F value	P	F value	P
Overall (df = 1, 2273)	10.88	<0.01	4.72	<0.05
Post hoc segments (df = 5, 2245)	7.71	<0.01	2.57	<0.05
Region-oriented quality-seekers	6.04	<0.05	1.04	n.s.
Involved shoppers	30.35	<0.01	1.19	n.s.
Price-oriented quality-seekers	1.40	n.s.	1.92	n.s.
PDO-label-oriented quality-seekers	0.31	n.s.	8.40	<0.01
ROO-averse consumers	0.43	n.s.	0.31	n.s.
Individual level (df = 152, 1216)	3.14	<0.01	1.19	n.s.

Table 6. Effect of the conjoint attribute Origin2 on affective preference (aggregate-level slope)

	ROO vs standard		PDO vs ROO	
	F value	P	F value	P
Overall (df = 1, 2272)	0.00	n.s.	0.37	n.s.
Post hoc segments (df = 5, 2244)	4.74	<0.01	0.46	n.s.
Region-oriented quality-seekers	0.82	n.s.	0.33	n.s.
Involved shoppers	13.24	<0.01	0.01	n.s.
Price-oriented quality-seekers	0.00	n.s.	1.34	n.s.
PDO-label-oriented quality-seekers	0.33	n.s.	0.60	n.s.
ROO-averse consumers	9.41	<0.01	0.02	n.s.
Individual level (df = 152, 1215)	2.20	<0.01	1.12	n.s.

addition to *F* values for all segments simultaneously, we also report *F* values for the effect of ROO/PDO within each separate segment.

At the aggregate level, the region-of-origin cue does seem to have an effect on preferences, and the PDO label does not seem to have an effect. In a one-sided test, the effect of the PDO label is, however, statistically significant (Table 4). Both the region-of-origin cue and the PDO label have an effect on the perceived quality (Table 5). Nevertheless, the direct effects of both the region-of-origin cue and of the PDO label are insignificant (Table 6), leading to a rejection of both our hypotheses.[7]

7   Similar ordered probit analyses, suggested by one of the reviewers, led to the same conclusion, as they show: (i) an effect of both the region-of-origin cue ($P < 0.05$) and the PDO label ($P < 0.05$) on preference, (ii) an effect of both the region-of-origin cue ($P < 0.01$) and the PDO label ($P < 0.05$) on perceived quality, and (iii) nonsignificant effects of both the region-of-origin cue and the PDO label on affective preference.

Allowing for heterogeneity between segments leads to the conclusion that there is a direct effect of the region-of-origin cue on preference for 'Involved shoppers' and 'ROO-averse consumers' (Table 6). For the 'Involved shoppers' there seems to be both a direct and an indirect effect (Table 5), whereas the direct effect seems to be the only effect for the 'ROO-averse consumers' (Table 5). It should be noted, however, that the effect for the 'ROO-averse consumers' is opposite to what we expected: standard EVO is preferred over ROO-EVO. On the other hand, there seems to be only an indirect effect for the 'Region-oriented quality-seekers'. The PDO label seems to have an effect only for 'PDO-label-oriented quality-seekers'. This is an indirect effect.[8] Of course, the F values from the analyses that allow for heterogeneity between segments are some kind of pseudo F values, as the segments were constructed to be as homogeneous as possible, also with respect to the effects of the region-of-origin cue and the PDO label.

Taking heterogeneity between respondents into account (results in the last row of each table) leads to the conclusion that there is a direct effect of the region-of-origin cue on preference and no direct effect of the PDO label.

Thus, Hypothesis 1 is confirmed for at least some of the respondents but Hypothesis 2 has to be rejected. As an aside, we mention that the replication of overall-level and individual-level results from Table 6, although allowing for heterogeneity in the regression slopes for the regression of preference on perceived quality, leads to the same conclusions.

The fact that we found: (i) no direct effects of the region-of-origin cue and the PDO label at the aggregate level, (ii) a direct effect of the region-of-origin cue for 'Involved shoppers' and 'ROO-averse consumers' when allowing for segment-wise heterogeneity, and (iii) a direct effect when allowing for unstructured heterogeneity, may be explained as follows. It will be recalled that a direct effect of the region-of-origin cue on regional product preference was expected to be based on consumers' sense of belonging and strong emotions related to a product's region of origin. Consumers may have a stronger sense of belonging to and emotions related to their own region of residence, whereas these may be much lower for other regions. Hence, one would expect that the direct effect of the region-of-origin cue would be larger for regional inhabitants than for respondents living outside the product's region of origin. If the 'Involved shoppers' and the 'ROO-averse consumers' consist

---

8 Similar ordered probit analyses lead to practically the same conclusion, as they show: (i) effects of the region-of-origin cue on preference for 'Involved shoppers' ($P < 0.01$) and 'ROO-averse consumers' ($P < 0.01$), and an effect of the PDO label for 'PDO-label-oriented quality-seekers' ($P < 0.05$), (ii) effects of the region-of-origin cue on perceived quality for 'Region-oriented quality-seekers' ($P < 0.05$) and 'Involved shoppers' ($P < 0.01$), and an effect of the PDO label for 'PDO-label-oriented quality-seekers' ($P < 0.01$), and (iii) effects of the region-of-origin cue on affective preference for 'Involved shoppers' ($P < 0.01$) and 'ROO-averse consumers' ($P < 0.01$), but no direct effects of the PDO label in any segment. Therefore, the only difference between the OLS and the ordered probit analyses is that in the latter analyses no indirect effect of the region-of-origin cue is found for 'Region-oriented quality-seekers'. As the differences between OLS regression and ordered probit analysis turn out to be so small, we continued with OLS regressions only in the further analyses.

of a disproportionate number of regional inhabitants, this would explain the direct effect of the ROO cue found in those segments. The same regional inhabitants may have caused the direct effect found when allowing for unstructured heterogeneity.

Likewise, the direct effect of the PDO label may be expected to differ. As described, a direct effect of the PDO label could be based on the idea that the protection may help the producers financially, and therefore the local economy. For non-regional respondents, this effect is expected to be lower. Our failure to find a direct effect of the PDO label might be caused by a segmentation that does not completely run along the line of regional inhabitants versus people from outside the region, and an individual-level analysis that consumes too many degrees of freedom in order to capture a small effect.

To test this notion, we cross-classified our *post hoc* segmentation with the combinations Place × Region, Place of birth × Region and Place of

Table 7. Effect of the conjoint attribute Origin2 on preference for different levels of the Place × Region combination

	ROO vs standard		PDO vs ROO	
	F value	*P*	*F* value	*P*
Place × Region (df = 6, 2238)	6.00	<0.01	0.81	n.s.
Viterbo–Canino (Same)	14.06	<0.01	0.01	n.s.
Rieti–Sabina (Same)	9.58	<0.01	1.15	n.s.
Viterbo–Sabina (Different)	0.21	n.s.	1.28	n.s.
Rieti–Canino (Different)	0.18	n.s.	0.41	n.s.
Rome–Canino	11.68	<0.01	1.48	n.s.
Rome–Sabina	0.31	n.s.	0.50	n.s.

Table 8. Effect of the conjoint attribute Origin2 on quality for different levels of the Place × Region combination

	ROO vs standard		PDO vs ROO	
	F value	*P*	*F* value	*P*
Place × Region (df = 6, 2238)	6.07	<0.01	0.98	n.s.
Viterbo–Canino (Same)	5.76	<0.05	0.92	n.s.
Rieti–Sabina (Same)	16.84	<0.01	0.58	n.s.
Viterbo–Sabina (Different)	3.28	n.s.	0.74	n.s.
Rieti–Canino (Different)	1.07	n.s.	0.26	n.s.
Rome–Canino	7.80	<0.01	0.27	n.s.
Rome–Sabina	1.70	n.s.	3.09	n.s.

Table 9. Effect of the conjoint attribute Origin2 on affective preference (aggregate-level slope) for different levels of the Place × Region combination

	ROO vs standard		PDO vs ROO	
	F value	P	F value	P
Place × Region (df = 6, 2237)	2.37	<0.05	0.61	n.s.
Viterbo–Canino (Same)	8.28	<0.01	0.77	n.s.
Rieti–Sabina (Same)	0.44	n.s.	0.58	n.s.
Viterbo–Sabina (Different)	0.77	n.s.	0.58	n.s.
Rieti–Canino (Different)	0.08	n.s.	0.17	n.s.
Rome–Canino	4.55	<0.05	1.30	n.s.
Rome–Sabina	0.11	n.s.	0.26	n.s.

residence × Region (see Table 2). None of the χ^2 values turned out to be significant. Therefore, we repeated the segment-wise analyses from Tables 4, 5 and 6, but instead of the *post hoc* segmentation, we used the *a priori* segmentation given by the Place × Region combination. The F and P values are reported in Tables 7–9. The mean part-worth estimates are given in Figure 3.

In line with Hypothesis 1, it was found that there is an indirect effect of the region-of-origin cue for consumers from the same region of origin as the EVO. In addition, there is a direct effect of the cue for consumers from Viterbo on their preference for the EVO from their own region (Canino). There are negative effects of the region-of-origin cue for the consumers from Rome on their preference for Canino EVO. The indirect effect of the PDO label that was found in the fourth *post hoc* segment is not found in any of the Place × Region conditions. Contrary to Hypothesis 2, no direct effect of the PDO label was found.

As the patterns of mean part-worth estimates in Figure 3 seem to be similar for consumers judging an EVO from their own region (Viterbo–Canino and Rieti–Sabina), and to be similar for consumers judging an EVO from another region (Viterbo–Sabina and Rieti–Canino), we tested for the effect of the region-of-origin cue and the PDO label within the combined Place × Region conditions, as well as for all consumers from Rome together. We therefore tested a number of contrasts within the Place × Region combination. F and P values of the contrasts are given in Tables 10–12, together with the F and P values of the overall effect of the Place × Region combination.

As can be seen, the results show only an indirect effect of the region-of-origin cue and only when consumers come from the same region as the EVO. These findings support the assumption that for a regional indication successfully to influence the performance of regional products, consumers should be aware of the region, be familiar with it and have strong, favourable associations with it. Although no significant results of the region-of-origin cue

470   *Ivo A. van der Lans* et al.

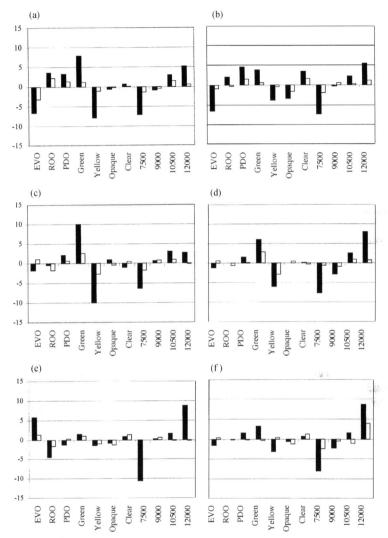

Figure 3 Mean part-worth estimates for levels of the Place × Region combination. (a) Viterbo–Canino (Same); (b) Rieti–Sabina (Same); (c) Viterbo–Sabina (Different); (d) Rieti–Canino (Different); (e) Rome–Canino; (f) Rome–Sabina. Filled columns represent preference; open columns represent affective preference.

or the PDO label were found for the Viterbo–Sabina (Different), Rieti–Canino (Different), and the Rome–Sabina conditions, the patterns of the mean part-worth estimates are similar, though less pronounced, to those for the Viterbo–Canino (Same) and Rieti–Sabina (Same), conditions. This

Table 10. Effect of the conjoint attribute Origin2 on preference for levels of the Same–Different Region-distinction and Place

	ROO vs standard		PDO vs ROO	
	F value	P	F value	P
Place × Region (df = 6, 2238)	6.00	<0.01	0.81	n.s.
Same	9.58	<0.01	1.15	n.s.
Different	0.18	n.s.	0.41	n.s.
Rome	0.31	n.s.	0.50	n.s.

Table 11. Effect of the conjoint attribute Origin2 on quality for levels of the Same–Different Region-distinction and Place

	ROO vs standard		PDO vs ROO	
	F value	P	F value	P
Place × Region (df = 6, 2238)	6.07	<0.01	0.98	n.s.
Same	17.93	<0.01	0.62	n.s.
Different	1.14	n.s.	0.28	n.s.
Rome	1.81	n.s.	3.29	n.s.

Table 12. Effect of the conjoint attribute Origin2 on affective preference (aggregate-level slope) for levels of the Same–Different Region-distinction and Place

	ROO vs standard		PDO vs ROO	
	F value	P	F value	P
Place × Region (df = 6, 2237)	2.37	<0.05	0.61	n.s.
Same	0.44	n.s.	0.58	n.s.
Different	0.08	n.s.	0.17	n.s.
Rome	0.11	n.s.	0.26	n.s.

may be because of at least some awareness of, and familiarity and favourable associations with the region of origin. The results for the Rome–Canino conditions could then be explained by assuming that Roman consumers are not so familiar with Canino, because of their distance from the olive cultivation area, or that Roman consumers have a negative image of the Canino region or of Canino EVO. Rome is a major city and usually its dwellers do not have strong links with agriculture, whereas Viterbo and Rieti are more agriculture-oriented.

472   *Ivo A. van der Lans* et al.

In addition to the *a priori* segmentation on the Place × Region combination, we analysed whether adding the respondent or household characteristics from Table 2 to the analyses of (co)variance from Tables 7–9 (i.e. adding main effects and interaction effects of these characteristics with all conjoint attributes) might reveal specific consumer segments in which direct and/or indirect effects of the region-of origin cue or the PDO label operate. It should be noted that such specific consumer segments were not found when we related the characteristics to the *post hoc* segments. Incorporating all respondent or household characteristics simultaneously in the analyses of (co)variance did not significantly improve their fit. Incorporating each characteristic separately, and thus capitalising on chance, revealed a moderating effect of gender on the direct effect of the region-of-origin cue ($P < 0.05$ for the effect on preference as well as for the effect on affective preference, and there is no significant effect on perceived quality). On closer inspection, the region-of-origin cue seems to have an effect on preferences for female respondents (mean part-worth estimates: EVO $= -3.32$, ROO $= 0.88$; $P < 0.01$). There are no significant effects on affective preference within the group of male or within the group of female respondents. Therefore, there seems to be an indirect, but not a direct effect, of the region-of-origin cue for female respondents.

5. Discussion and recommendations

First, the predictive validity of the conjoint part-worth estimates turned out to be relatively low, with both individual-level and segment-level part-worth estimates. It remains to be investigated whether the low predictive validity is due to particular groups of respondents, or to the fact that respondents had to react to both conjoint perceived quality and conjoint preference ratings.

Second, it is not clear whether the mixture regression model, which regresses preferences on conjoint attributes, is the best choice for modelling heterogeneity vis-à-vis Baron and Kenny's (1986) procedure for testing mediation. Other possible candidates seem to be mixture regression models that incorporate both regressions of preferences as well as of perceived quality. Further research, possibly using Monte Carlo studies, is called for. Also, the number of respondents may have been too small to yield really homogeneous segments between which differences are statistically detectable. With a larger number of respondents, one may obtain a larger number of homogeneous yet still well-filled segments than the five segments we found.

Third, although our sample was representative for the Italian population with respect to age and gender, it may have been less representative regarding other aspects (especially for the Rome sample), as the respondents were identified in shopping malls. For instance, some consumers may prefer shopping in smaller speciality stores, which are not always present in shopping malls. Hence, the presence of potential bias should be taken into consideration when interpreting our results and conclusions. The research should be replicated with a larger, unambiguously representative sample.

Fourth, it is assumed that the direct effect of the region-of-origin cue is primarily based on affective feelings towards the region of origin. As we did not actually measure these, some caution should be exercised. Research on the affective influence of a geographical indication on the product evaluation is currently limited.

As a fifth and final point of discussion, no direct effect of the PDO label on regional product preferences was found. This may be related to consumers' regional ethnocentric feelings. Consumer ethnocentrism has been defined as 'the beliefs consumers hold about the appropriateness, indeed morality, of purchasing foreign made products' (Shimp and Sharma, 1987: 280). A consumer's desire to support the economy of a region may depend on his degree of regional ethnocentrism. The fact that our sample contained relatively more highly educated respondents, who are generally less ethnocentric than those with a lower level of education (Shimp and Sharma, 1987), may partly explain the limited effects found. Future research should examine whether and how a direct effect of the PDO label on regional product preference depends on regional ethnocentric tendencies.

On the other hand, in the areas where the survey took place, and amongst the people who took part in the survey, particularly in Rome, the indifference to regional origin is probably explained more by lack of knowledge about the meaning of PDO certification. To understand its significance, the consumer would have to be informed about the methods of production used, the natural suitability of the producing area and the differences between the processes used for a PDO product and those for other qualities of olive oil.

If this is the case for consumers in an area so close to the producing area, clearly it is even more true in other potential but more distant markets such as the rest of Italy or the rest of the world. If the certification of origin is to realise its full potential as a marketing tool, it must be inserted into an appropriate and well-articulated marketing mix, so as to extend the direct 'affective' aspects of region of origin to aspects based on factual understanding of regional comparative advantage.

6. Conclusions and implications

The region-of-origin cue and the PDO label both influence regional product preferences indirectly, through the perceived regional product quality, but the effect is limited to (different) specific consumer segments in the market. In line with our expectations, at least some consumers thus use the cues to make inferences about the regional product quality. Furthermore, the region-of-origin cue has a direct effect on regional product preference for some consumer segments, especially among those consumers who live in the product's region of origin. This effect is probably due primarily to affective feelings consumers have regarding the region of origin. Contrary to Van Ittersum *et al.* (2001b), no direct effect of PDO labels on product preference was found. This suggests that consumers consider PDO labels merely as indicators of quality, if they consider them at all.

The findings of this study stimulate some observations on EU Reg. 2081/92. Consumers may be divided into two groups: those who appreciate the region of origin of the olive oil and those who do not. Consumers in the second group appear to focus more on other product cues, such as price, colour and appearance. Increasing the emphasis on the importance of region of origin for the quality of olive oil among these consumer segments may strengthen this cue in purchase decisions. Nevertheless, it should be recognised that intrinsic product cues, such as colour and appearance, generally are more important criteria in decision-making than extrinsic product cues such as the region of origin (Olson, 1972).

From this study, it seems that both the EU Commission and producers themselves might have overestimated the potential benefits that the PDO protection label could signal to consumers. Producers may have received the Regulation with an excessive enthusiasm: they may not have realised that a certification such as PDO or PGI must be part of a coherent marketing strategy and that an appropriate marketing mix is required.

The limited direct effect of region of origin for Roman consumers, both for Canino and for Sabina oils, may well be due not only to a lack of knowledge about production methods and the significance of the PDO certification, but also to the influence of publicity campaigns launched on TV by industrial producers of EVOs.

This publicity stresses the idea of a close association between these industrially produced oils and a countryside environment, and the consumer is usually unaware of the non-traditional refining and blending processes they have undergone. Consequently, the urban consumer may see no difference between these well-advertised EVOs and the PDO EVOs, which are hardly advertised at all. Moreover, the urban consumer may be convinced that a nationally advertised product is superior to that of a local, little-known producing area and, finally, the urban consumer may not be familiar with the taste of the EVOs produced by the PDO-certified or the traditional craft-type regional methods, and may be unwilling to experiment.

This type of reaction presents a potential threat to the category of PDO products as a whole. To ensure the survival of such traditional products, it is essential that more information be made available about the meaning of PDO and PGI certification and the guarantees it offers, so that the consumer can make an informed choice between these and other high-quality food products.

For the time being, it seems that the only goal achieved by the Regulation has been to patent the name of products, although there are some doubts also about this, as the Feta case well illustrates.[9]

---

9 Feta, a soft Greek cheese made from goats' milk, was first granted the PDO protection label by the EU Commission. Some countries fiercely opposed the recognition, claiming that 'feta' had become a 'generic name' and finally won.

Acknowledgements

The authors thank Alison Burrell, José M. Gil and two anonymous reviewers for their constructive and useful comments on earlier versions of this paper.

References

Aaker, D. A. (1991). *Managing Brand Equity: Capitalizing on the Value of a Brand Name.* New York: Free Press.

Anderson, J. R. and Bower, G. H. (1973). *Human Associative Memory.* Washington DC: Winston.

Baron, R. M. and Kenny, D. A. (1986). The mediator–moderator variable distinction in social-psychological research: conceptual, strategic, and statistical considerations. *Journal of Personality and Social Psychology* 51(6): 1173–1182.

Becker, T. (1999). 'Country of Origin' as a cue for quality and safety of fresh meat. Paper presented at the 67th EAAE Seminar: The Socio-Economics of Origin Labelled Products in Agrifood Supply Chains: Spatial, Institutional and Co-ordination Aspects, Le Mans.

Bérard, L. and Marchenay, P. (1995). Lieu, temps, et preuves: la construction sociale des produits de terroir. *Terrain* 24: 153–164.

Bower, G. H. (1981). Mood and memory. *American Psychologist* 36(2): 129–148.

Canali, G. (1997). The evolution of food distribution system and its implication on the marketing of typical products. In: F. Arfini and C. Mora (eds), *Proceedings of the 52nd EAAE Seminar: Typical and Traditional Productions: Rural Effect and Agro-Industrial Problems.* Istituto di economia agraria e forestale, Università di Parma, 303–315.

Delamont, S. (1995). *Appetites and Identities: an Introduction in the Social Anthropology of Western Europe.* London: Routledge.

De Maio, T. (1980). Refusals: who, where, and why. *Public Opinion Quarterly* 44(Summer): 223–233.

DeSarbo, W. S., Wedel, M., Vriens, M. and Ramaswamy, V. (1992). Latent class metric conjoint analysis. *Marketing Letters* 3(3): 273–288.

Engel, J. F., Blackwell, R. D. and Miniard, P. W. (1993). *Consumer Behaviour*, 7th edition. Fort Worth TX: Dryden.

Erevelles, S. (1998). The role of affect in marketing. *Journal of Business Research* 42: 199–215.

Fishbein, M. and Ajzen, I. (1975). *Beliefs, Attitude, Intention, and Behavior: an Introduction to Theory and Research.* Reading, MA: Addison Wesley.

Green, P. E. and Srinivasan, V. (1978). Conjoint analysis in consumer research: issues and outlook. *Journal of Consumer Research* 5: 103–123.

Green, P. E. and Srinivasan, V. (1990). Conjoint analysis in marketing: new developments with implications for research and practice. *Journal of Marketing* 54(October): 3–19.

Hagerty, M. R. (1985). Improving the predictive power of conjoint analysis: the use of factor analysis and cluster analysis. *Journal of Marketing Research* 22: 168–184.

Hair, J. F., Anderson, R. E., Tatham, R. L. and Black, W. C. (1998). *Multivariate Data Analysis*, 5th edn. Upper Saddle River, NJ: Prentice–Hall.

Han, C. M. and Terpstra, V. (1988). Country-of-origin effects for uni-national and bi-national products. *Journal of International Business Studies* 19(2): 235–255.

476 *Ivo A. van der Lans* et al.

Hong, S.-T. and Wyer, R. S. (1989). Effects of country-of-origin and product-attribute information on product evaluation: an information processing perspective. *Journal of Consumer Research* 16(2): 175–187.

Hong, S.-T. and Wyer, R. S. (1990). Determinants of product evaluation: effects of the time interval between knowledge of a product's country of origin and information about its specific attributes. *Journal of Consumer Research* 17(3): 277–288.

Huffman, C. and Houston, M. J. (1993). Goal-oriented experiences and the development of knowledge. *Journal of Consumer Research* 20(2): 190–207.

Johansson, J. K. and Nebenzahl, I. D. (1986). Multinational production: effect on brand value. *Journal of International Business Studies* 17(3): 101–126.

Juric, B. and Worsley, A. (1998). Consumers' attitudes towards imported food products. *Food Quality and Preference* 9(6): 431–441.

Kapferer, J. N. (1992). *Strategic Brand Management: New Approaches to Creating and Evaluating Brand Equity*. London: Kogan Page.

Keller, K. L. (1998). *Strategic Brand Management; Building, Measuring, and Managing Brand Equity*. Upper Saddle River, NJ: Prentice–Hall.

Li, W.-K. and Wyer, R. S., Jr (1994). The role of the country of origin in product evaluations: informational and standard-of-comparison effects. *Journal of Consumer Psychology* 3: 187–212.

Marreiros, C., Neto, M. C. and Carvalho, L. S. (1997). Certification of agro-food quality products: a new reality in demand and farm management. In: F. Arfini and C. Mora (eds), *Proceedings of the 52nd EAAE Seminar: Typical and Traditional Productions: Rural Effect and Agro-Industrial Problems*. Istituto di economia agraria e forestale, Università di Parma, 109–118.

Moro, D., Boccaletti, S. and Sckokai, P. (1996). Innovation and consumers' choice. In G. Galizzi and L. Venturini (eds), *Economics of Innovation: the Case of Food Industry*. Heidelberg: Physica, 23–38.

Obermiller, C. and Spangenberg, E. (1989). Exploring the effects of origin labels: an information processing framework. *Advances in Consumer Research* 16: 454–459.

Olson, J. C. (1972). Cue utilisation of the quality perception process: a cognitive model and an empirical test. Ph.D. thesis, Purdue University, West Lafayette, IN.

Olson, J. C. (1978). Inferential belief formation in the cue utilization process. *Advances in Consumer Research* 5: 706–713.

Olson, J. C. (1981). The importance of cognitive processes and existing knowledge structure for understanding food acceptance. In: J. Solms and R. L. Hall (eds), *Criteria of Food Acceptance*. Zurich: Forster, 69–80.

Schellinck, D. A. (1983). Cue choice as a function of time pressure and perceived risk. *Advances in Consumer Research* 10: 470–475.

Sheth, J. N., Newman, B. I. and Gross, B. L. (1991). Why we buy what we buy: a theory of consumption values. *Journal of Business Research* 22: 159–170.

Shimp, T. A. and Sharma, S. (1987). Consumer ethnocentrism: construction and validation of the CETSCALE. *Journal of Marketing Research* 24: 280–289.

Steenkamp, J.-B. E. M. (1990). Conceptual model of the quality perception process. *Journal of Business Research* 21: 309–333.

Steenkamp, J.-B. E. M. (1997). Dynamics in consumer behavior with respect to agricultural and food products. In: B. Wierenga, K. Grunert, J.-B.E.M. Steenkamp, M. Wedel and A. Van Tilburg (eds), *Agricultural Marketing and Consumer Behavior in a Changing*

World, Proceedings of 47th Seminar of the European Association of Agricultural Economists (EAAE). Boston, MA: Kluwer, 143–188.

Steenkamp, J.-B. E. M. and Van Trijp, J. C. M. (1996). Quality guidance: a consumer-based approach to food quality improvement using partial least squares. *European Review of Agricultural Economics* 23: 195–215.

Steenkamp, J.-B. E. M. and Wittink, D. R. (1994). The metric quality of full-profile judgments and the number-of-attribute-levels effect in conjoint analysis. *International Journal of Research in Marketing* 11: 275–286.

Tregear, A., Kuznesof, S. and Moxey, A. (1998). Policy initiatives for regional foods: some insights from consumer research. *Food Policy* 23(5): 383–394.

Van Ittersum, K. and Candel, M. J. J. M. (1998). PDO/PGI Products: Market, Supply Chain and Institutions. Qualitative Consumer Survey Report, FAIR No. 1-CT95-306. Wageningen, The Netherlands: Wageningen University.

Van Ittersum, K., Candel, M. J. J. M. and Thorelli, F. (2000). The market for PDO/PGI protected regional products: consumer attitudes and behaviour. In: B. Sylvander, D. Barjolle and F. Arfini (eds), *The Socio-Economics of Origin Labelled Products in Agri-Food Supply Chains: Spatial, Institutional and Co-ordination Aspects*. Paris: INRA–ESR, Actes et Communications No. 17-1, 209–221.

Van Ittersum, K., Candel, M. J. J. M. and Meulenberg, M. T. G. (2001a). The influence of the image of a product's region of origin on product evaluation. *Journal of Business Research* (in press).

Van Ittersum, K., Meulenberg, M. T. G., Van Trijp, J. C. M. and Candel, M. J. J. M. (2001b). Certificates of origin and regional product loyalty. Working Paper. Wageningen: Wageningen University.

Verlegh, P. and Steenkamp, J.-B. E. M. (1999). A review and meta-analysis of country-of-origin research. *Journal of Economic Psychology* 20(5): 521–546.

Vriens, M., Wedel, M. and Wilms, T. (1996). Metric conjoint segmentation methods: a Monte Carlo comparison. *Journal of Marketing Research* 33: 73–85.

Wedel, M. and Kamakura, W. A. (2000). *Market Segmentation: Conceptual and Methodological Foundations*, 2nd edn. Boston, MA: Kluwer.

Wedel, M. and Steenkamp, J.-B. E. M. (1991). A clusterwise regression method for simultaneous fuzzy market structuring and benefit segmentation. *Journal of Marketing Research* 28: 385–397.

Corresponding author: Ivo A. van der Lans, Department of Social Sciences, Wageningen University, Hollandseweg 1, 6706 KN Wageningen, The Netherlands. E-mail: ivdlans@goliath.sls.wau.nl

[13]

BFJ
104,11

898

Consumers' willingness to pay for origin labelled wine
A Greek case study

Dimitris Skuras
Department of Economics, University of Patras, Patras, Greece, and
Aleka Vakrou
*NAGREF, Agricultural Economics and Social Research Institute,
Neo Herakleio, Greece*

Keywords *Drinks industry, Country of origin, Labelling, Consumer behaviour, Pricing strategy,
Greece*

Abstract *Quality agricultural products are assuming an increasingly important role in European Union (EU) agricultural and food policies. The potential for differentiating quality products and services on a regional basis has been recognised and legislation has been introduced for protecting the geographical indications and designations of origin for agricultural products and quality foodstuffs. Today, marketing strategies for quality products attempt to explore these new opportunities, trying to build on the products' reputation and the image of their region of origin. This study employs a dichotomous choice model to identify the socio-economic characteristics that influence Greek consumers' willingness to pay for an origin labelled wine. The results indicate that wine consumers' willingness to pay varies only according to social and demographic characteristics. Furthermore, the mean willingness to pay was estimated using two alternative econometric specifications of the dichotomous choice model. We have found that non-quality wine consumers are willing to pay double the price of a bottle of normal table wine if the alternative provides for a guarantee of the place of origin of the wine. Their decision is found to be dependent only upon education and affiliation with the place of origin. The model specifications are compared and useful conclusions referring to price policy for origin labelled wines and their marketing are drawn.*

Introduction

Today agricultural producers and food enterprises have not only to anticipate the slow growth in food demand, but also to cope with severe competition existing between them, due to the globalised economy. Thus the efforts of food businesses move along two parallel directions. One is aiming to increase the quantity to be consumed by offering consumers new products to cover their needs, while the other is moving to the generation of value added for certain products that have special characteristics, that attract consumers and add to their satisfaction.

Emerald

British Food Journal,
Vol. 104 No. 11, 2002, pp. 898-912.
© MCB UP Limited, 0007-070X
DOI 10.1108/00070700210454622

This work derives from a program of collaborative research by the following: the Department of Geography at the Universities of Coventry, Leicester, Lancaster, Caen, Valencia, Galway and Trinity College Dublin; the Scottish Agricultural College (Aberdeen); Institute of Rural Studies (Aberystwyth); CEMAGREF (Clermont-Ferrand); Teagasc (Dublin); Department of Economics (University of Patras); and Seinajoki Institute for Rural Research and Training (University of Helsinki). This research project has been funded under the EU's FAIR programme (FAIR3-CT96-1827). An earlier version of this paper has been presented at the 67th EAAE conference "The socio-economics of origin labelled products in agro-food supply chains: spatial, institutional and co-ordination aspects", Le Mans 28-30 October 1999.

Under these new conditions prevailing in food markets and the requirements generated, "quality" has been accepted as a strategic element of marketing that helps sustain or improve the position of an actor in the food supply chain. The "quality" aspect is also viewed as a promising tool that can generate more value-added for a product. As a response to these new challenges and opportunities producers and businesses are moving from a product orientated marketing approach towards an approach that focuses on the satisfaction of consumers' needs and perceptions (van Trijp *et al.*, 1993), relating them with special attributes of the offered products, which can be revealed through certification, association, specification and attraction (Ilbery and Kneafsey (1998). Thus agricultural food production today bases its basic marketing strategy on the concept of a diversified produce that has in-built quality elements, which prompt consumers to identify and experience them and appreciating them by paying something more.

Still today, there is no generally agreed definition of quality products. This is mainly due to the fact that consumer perceptions of what constitutes quality vary significantly for specific products, as well as quality interpretation varies among individuals, regions and countries (Foster and Macrae, 1992; Sylvander, 1993). Although the definition of quality is fundamentally imprecise, it can be agreed that quality characteristics are positional characteristics against the standard or normal product. In other words, quality characteristics are those that lie above minimum standards and give to a product or service a competitive edge over its normal rivals. The Scottish Food Strategy Group (1993) provides a useful approach to the definition of quality products, as:

> ... a quality food and drink product is one which is differentiated in a positive manner by reason of one or more of these features from the standard product, is recognised as such by the consumer, and can therefore command a market benefit if it is effectively marketed.

Important aspects of the concept of quality are the satisfaction of consumer needs and a consistent level of performance, taste, etc., provided by the product (Vastoia, 1997). The European Commission recognises the difficulty of providing a coherent definition for quality in its official Web page for agricultural quality products and draws upon certain elements that build quality, like food safety, environmental production methods, nutritional value and product characteristics, together with region of origin and tradition in the production methods used (European Commission, 2001).

The quality guarantee is based on a variety of elements and several instruments that can be used to implement any adopted scheme. But the most important instrument is the legislative framework that supports the quality attributes and appropriate labelling that provides for the verification of the scheme and its subsequent recognition by both consumer and market. Internationally, labelling policy is least settled and developed in the areas of food safety and processing, as well as origin, while approaches to nutrition labelling are more uniform (Caswell, 1997). In EU two regulations have been introduced in 1992 (Reg. 2081/92 and 2082/92) on certificates of specific characteristics for agricultural products and foodstuffs. The aim was to promote the concept of regionally produced products that include the

Consumers' willingness to pay

899

BFJ
104,11

900

characteristics of quality, tradition and ancient production methods. The two regulations developed three distinct categories of regionally identified products, namely PDO (Products of Denominated Origin), PGI (Product of Geographic Indication) and GTS (Guaranteed Traditional Speciality) products. These products guarantee a special link with their territory, either because they are explicitly produced there, or due to other relational elements with a specific area and the local conditions prevailing in there (special recipes, typicality, etc.). The characteristics of the production area or the region of origin for quality products have been identified as important ones and have been used widely by OECD (1995). OECD provided a six-fold classification for quality products (three classes) and services (three classes) based on a region's utilisation of resources and more specifically of natural resources, tradition-culture and heritage, environment and amenity.

To further promote the idea of quality products the Commission developed an EU wide label for the inspected characteristics of quality to distinguish them from similar standard products (European Commission, 1996). This label was launched in 1998, is applicable in all 15 EU member states and assists consumers' purchasing decisions and safeguards the interests of the producers who have registered their products into the certification scheme covering all previously mentioned product types[1]. The PDO, PGI and GTS labels can apply for nearly all types of agricultural products, except for wines. Wines were actually the very first products to create quality image linked to a specific location and specific grape varieties. Particularly for grapes the distinction VQPRD exists, which indicates the quality grape varieties produced in definite regions (Reg. 2802/85) that lead to the production of quality wines. There are also the denominations AOC (Appellation d'origine Contrôlée) and the strictest AOP (Appellation d'origine Protégé), similar to the concept behind PDO and PGI products, supplemented with other indications referring simply to locality but no control procedures (*Vins de Pays*)[2].

The significance of certification schemes is gaining wider credibility, as the EU Committee of the Regions (1996) has urged the European Commission to give particular support, under the EU structural policy for the promotion and protection of local quality products. Support for regional quality products is directly linked to rural development. Thus considerable efforts have been made in this direction, which have been mainly initiated through the LEADER II program and will continue with LEADER+ (LEADER, 2000). The LEADER II (executed for the period 1994-1999) had financed projects that valorised the concept of quality and allowed for innovative promotion actions. The importance of these actions is growing, as the option for providing further measures for the promotion of local products has been reinforced by EC Reg. 1257/99. The included option has been chosen by many member states, which have included in their recently approved rural development plans (to run for the period 2000-2006) measures for the promotion and the marketing of quality agricultural products. Support for the promotion of quality products/food is viewed as a major adjustment strategy or a pathway of small enterprises or farm business development of a region (Arfini and Mora Zanetti, 1998) that can be adopted by farm households in the less favoured or lagging areas of the EU.

This paper explores further the recent quality concept as it has been built in agricultural production and focuses on one of the various quality elements that quality agricultural produce and foodstuffs explore, their origin. This study has applied a choice model to identify the socio-economic characteristics that influence Greek consumers' willingness to pay for an origin labelled wine, moschofilero, which is produced from a locally grown variety of grapes of superior quality, in the region of Arkadia, in Peloponnese. The model employed aimed to identify which consumer's characteristics and other variables related to the characteristics of the region have an influence on the values derived for willingness to pay. The identification of this information can play a decisive role in the design of appropriate marketing strategies for the particular product, but also can draw conclusions on how to market effectively origin products.

Thereafter the paper is developed as follows. The second section presents an overview of quality policies for agricultural products, focusing on the recent quality and certification schemes in EU level. It also provides a review of other research that studied how consumers understand quality and also how consumers can generate value added for these products through their willingness to pay an increased price. In the third section, the case study for the Greek quality wine moschofilero is presented and the results obtained are analysed. The paper concludes by summarising the findings of the case study and by presenting an analysis of their relevance for any future marketing strategies of quality Greek wines associated with a specific origin.

Evidence from previous studies and objectives

Whatever the objectives and the content of a policy, its acceptability by society plays one of the most crucial roles for its success. In the case of the EU quality products policy, the driving forces have been both the consumers, who demanded better, healthier products of assured quality, but also planners and policy makers. The introduction of a quality product policy as this envisaged with the PDO-PGI scheme and other origin promoting instruments has been designed as a diversification strategy to the already saturated agricultural product markets of the EU member states. Quality assurance through the adoption of specific production and processing methods, through the continuation of tradition, through the establishment of denominated production zones and the strict code of practices aimed at introducing to an EU consumer seeking quality and difference, old and new products bearing the specially developed EU logos. Region identification promotes the idea not only that there is a price differentiation between producing origins, but also that there exist intellectual property rights that govern significant productions, which stake their reputation on their origin (Moran, 1993). The concept underlying these efforts is to promote a great variety of these products as generic ones, through well-designed promotional activities and to create an umbrella for this diversified production.

Several schemes for product diversification have been used in the past and not only within the EU. Organic products, products produced using integrated pest management (IPM) techniques, environment friendly or "green" products, minimal chemical use (low pesticide fruits, acid free paper) products, are some

Consumers'
willingness
to pay

901

BFJ
104,11

902

of a wide range of products produced with new techniques. The adoption of such production techniques fits into business strategies that aim to gain market shares, probe new consumer needs, with purpose to add to firm's operations and profitability. The last issue is the one that mainly interests this study, and the most common approach to investigate it is by asking consumers to state their willingness to pay a higher price for buying these products. The premiums that consumers are willing to pay can be used as proxies for revealing the values of the additional attributes that quality adds to a product.

Lately consumers have become interested in many issues concerning food quality and their awareness has also been raised as a response to the latest food security crises deriving from the bovine spongiform encephalopathy (BSE), dioxins and foot and mouth disease (FMD) incidents. Research and surveys that have been carried out at EU level suggest that people tend to become increasingly conscious with regard to the safety of foodstuffs, the ways of production, the ingredients used, etc. Apart from issues that have received attention lately, an emerging issue is that of the origin of a product. More and more consumers ask for indications or information about the origin of the food that they purchase, although this had departed from the need to indicate the origin of specific products, like wines, mineral waters, beers, coffees and cheeses, which was derived both from marketing initiatives, and also from legislative requirements. However, it was the recent BSE crisis of the late 1980s, which through the 1990s has resulted in raising more consumer awareness about the origin of their product and most importantly has assisted in producing consumers' mental correlations for a food with a specific origin. BSE and recently the dioxins and the FMD disease have resulted more in relating food, and especially different varieties of meats, with a country of origin. However, during the 1990s, the concept of regional products/food has also been communicated to the consumers through informative campaigns, centrally directed by the relevant EU legislation, national initiatives, or local initiatives (Hoffmann, 2000; Salais and Storper, 1994).

Several studies that have been conducted for country of origin (COO) products have indicated that, in general, consumers are able to establish connotations between certain products and their origin. Food products appear to embody strong associations with place as they have by their very nature a land-based geographical origin (Bérand and Marchenay, 1995). Actually COO has been found to have a larger effect on perceived quality than on attitude towards the product or purchase intention (Verlegh and Steenkamp, 1999). Hoffmann (2000) has indicated that consumers who have been more sensitive to health issues and animal welfare and also have been aware of food security issues like salmonella bacteria and use of antibiotics have been keener on the COO concept. According to his study women and low income groups were found to be more sensitive, and their purchasing choices have been based on the COO to a greater extent than male and high income consumer groups.

Although COO research has been well established in the literature (Eroglu and Machleit, 1989) quality attributes associated with production location and unique production practices that characterise PDO and PGI products or other local produce, have not been widely studied and evaluated in full. However, several studies exploring the effects of country on regional products have indicated a strong connection between consumer's knowledge and attitude towards a region and the "favorability of consumer's affective associations" with the product's region of origin (Obermiller and Spangenberg, 1989; Verlegh and Steenkamp, 1999). Erickson *et al.* (1984) and Johansson *et al.* (1985) have found that similar products differing by their "origin" are evaluated differently. These findings can be explained by the fact that consumers use their associations with the product's origin (whether this can refer to country or region) to infer their expectations about the true levels of the attributes of products from that origin (Van Ittersum *et al.*, 2000). Based on the inferred expectations about the true attribute levels, consumers decide whether to purchase the product and on the maximum price they would be willing to pay for it.

In another study, Tregear *et al.* (1998), using focus groups, have identified that although there are not such clear indications on the exact linkages between consumer perceptions and places where the food is produced, origin relates to the delivery of quality and authenticity. Their study revealed that British consumers could produce mental associations for regional foods and specialities and that they were able to link regional foods to attributes of the physical environment and the prevailing socio-cultural practices in the region. Consumers also appeared to infer "regionality" not only from a product's physical attributes, but also from the place of purchase and communicated heritage. The aspect of authenticity of regional/origin products has received considerable attention in their study, as consumers' perceived authenticity in relation to tradition and heritage confirmed products as regional/origin products.

This study has been designed to answer two main questions. First we have tried to examine the way that a consumer exhibits preference for a quality regional wine, by identifying his willingness to pay a higher price for the regional wine. In relation to this question, we have explored the influence of socio-economic characteristics of the consumer's profile in his purchasing decision. Second, we tried to identify if a consumer's purchasing decision is connected to his or her affiliation with the region and his or her specific knowledge for the region where the wine is produced. A critical analysis of the findings deriving from these two questions, using in addition secondary data on wine prices, have further allowed us to add some additional insights to price policy for origin labelled wines and to come up with suggestions for appropriate marketing strategies.

Data and survey methodology
The consumer survey was designed and executed in the framework of a European research project financed under the FAIR research program[3]. Within this project the regional image of an area has been studied as an influential factor for the promotion of typical products of the area. The prefectures of Achaia and Arkadia, in the region of Peloponese, have been chosen, and one product specific to each respective area has been chosen, namely sultanas for Achaia together with moschofilero wine for Arkadia. Residents in the urban centers of Athens, Patras and Tripoli were selected as representatives of consumers in very large (metropolitan), large and smaller

BFJ
104,11

904

towns respectively. The survey took place from January to March 1998, while time was spent on testing the questionnaire in November and December 1997. The sample was proportionately allocated to the towns of Athens (80 percent), Patras (15 percent) and Tripoli (5 percent) respectively[4]. In order to achieve the highest possible coverage of the variance in purchasing behaviour we decided to diversify (stratify) questionnaire collection within each town, according to the place of purchase and as indicated by past marketing and wine industry surveys carried out in Greece (IIER-Messini, 1996). Thus, questionnaires were proportionately collected from regular places of purchase such as small and big supermarkets (80 percent), from restaurant and "tavernas" (type of family restaurants – bistro) (15 percent) and from specialist outlets (5 percent). Respondents were randomly selected as every tenth consumer in each of these places of purchase.

The very few consumers, less than 25, who declined to participate in our survey, were replaced. Thus, from an originally planned sample of 750 questionnaires, a total of 744 questionnaires were usable in the three study regions, of which 441 concerned quality wine consumers and 303 consumers of table wine. Data were collected using a questionnaire and a face-to-face interview of respondents with trained personnel. The questionnaire included both structured and semi-structured parts, in order to allow for the collection of both quantitative and qualitative information.

The questionnaire used was divided into several parts. One part included questions related to the consumer's perceptions of quality and attempted to identify their attitudes towards the meaning of quality for the surveyed products and the factors contributing to the purchase or not of the specific products. In the Greek questionnaire and in this part we added a question aiming to measure the willingness to pay for the product's specific properties. This set of questions enabled the execution of a formal willingness-to-pay analysis for origin goods and in this case for the moschofilero wine. Other parts included questions concerning the consumer's perceptions of regional quality products and consumer's buying behaviour, as well as consumers' perceptions of regional imagery and knowledge of other quality products and regions of the European Union. The final part of the questionnaire asked for information relevant to the consumer's individual characteristics that could add to the explanation of their purchasing behaviour. In particular, we recorded data related to the consumer's economic, social and demographic characteristics and data related to their hobbies, tastes and preferences.

The model
The contingent valuation method (CVM) has been used in previous studies for the evaluation of a consumer's willingness to pay (WTP) for different product attributes. The CVM has been applied mainly for valuation of organic agricultural products and for products produced with integrated pest management techniques (Anderson *et al.*, 1996; Bagnara, 1996). Fu *et al.* (1999) provide an extensive list of CV studies examining willingness to pay for residue free products. Alternatively, experimental auction market techniques have also been applied (Hayes *et al.*, 1995). The proportion of respondents

willing to pay a premium ranges from 60 to 70 percent in all of the aforementioned studies. However, the premium values are greatly dependent on the food under study (i.e. organic vegetables and fruits receive higher premium values than meat products) and on the issue under study (i.e. different cultivation methods, way of handling that guarantees risk minimisation, etc.).

The utility difference model, applied by Hanemann to dichotomous choice (DC) designs, is adopted in this study, because it provides a theoretical framework for deriving Hicksian compensating and equivalent surplus measures (Hanemann, 1984). Participants in the contingent valuation exercise are assumed to derive utility from income as well as the wine quality and especially denomination and geographic association or origin, while utility is assumed to be an increasing function of the consumption experience. The indirect utility function is a random variable with given parametric probability distribution with mean $v(y; s)$ and stochastic element e_j, where income is denoted by y and the individual's characteristics that influence wine consumption are denoted by s. If the difference in indirect utility from paying the offered amount is positive, respondents will maximise utility by answering "yes" to the contingent question. Thus:

$$v(1; y; s) + e_1 \geq v(0; y; s) + e_0 \tag{1}$$

where $v(1; y; s) + e_1$ is the indirect utility function when the wine is denominated and $v(0; y; s) + e_0$ is the indirect utility function of table wine and e_1 and e_0 are independently and identically distributed random variables with zero means. The WTP probability is then:

$$P_1 = F_n(dV) \tag{2}$$

where $F_n(dV)$ is the cumulative distribution function of the respondent's true maximum WTP, which is a random variable. If the probability in equation (2) is specified as the cumulative distribution function of a standard logistic variate, the indirect utility difference model function yields the logit specification:

$$Prob(Yes) = [1 + e^{-dV}]^{-1} \tag{3}$$

If, suppressing the vector s, we assume that the functional forms for the indirect utility functions are:

$$v(1; y; s) = a_1 + \beta y \text{ and } v(0; y; s) = a_0 + \beta y, \beta > 0 \tag{4}$$

then, the functional form of the difference in indirect utility is specified as:

$$dV = v(1, y - A; s) - v(0, y; s) = [\alpha_1 + \beta(y - A); s] -$$
$$[\alpha_0 + \beta y; s] = (a_1 - a_0) - \beta A; s \tag{5}$$

where A is the bid amount forgone for achieving a higher utility. Thus, the discrete choice probabilities are independent of the individual's income y and

BFJ
104,11

the model specified in equation (4) is the only utility model with the property of no "income effects".

Following the estimated difference in indirect utility, the expected WTP is calculated as (Park *et al.*, 1991):

$$E(WTP) = \int_0^\infty [1 - F_n(d\mathbf{V})]d\mathbf{V} \tag{6}$$

The mean WTP is calculated as (Park *et al.*, 1991):

$$E(WTP) = \int_0^{A_{max}} [1 - \frac{F_n(d\mathbf{V})}{F_n(A_{max})}]d\mathbf{V} \tag{7}$$

where $F(A_{max})$ is the cumulative distribution function estimated at the maximum value of the bid amount used in the survey. Alternatively, this design may be followed by a second question and a second bid contingent upon the response to the first bid. If the individual responds "yes" to the first bid, the second bid (denoted by B) is somewhat greater than the first bid; if the individual responds "no" to the first bid, the second bid is somewhat smaller than the first bid. This design results in the double-bounded contingent valuation model (Hanemann *et al.*, 1991). In this case it is assumed that a respondent's willingness to pay lies between two values, WTP_C and WTP_B, where the bid vector provides these values $WTP_C = 0$, for respondents who answered "no" to both questions and $WTP_B = \infty$ for respondents who answered "yes" to both. The log-likelihood of this model is:

$$logL = \sum_{i=1}^{n} log\left[\Theta\left(\frac{logWTP^B - \beta s}{\sigma}\right) - \Theta\left(\frac{logWTP^C - \beta s}{\sigma}\right)\right] \tag{8}$$

where Θ (.) is the standard normal cumulative density function, and β and s as before.

Cooper (1994) has demonstrated how to use the Krinsky and Robb method and Efron's percentile method, to construct confidence intervals around the welfare measure (Cooper, 1994; Efron, 1987; Krinsky and Robb, 1986). An optimal survey design for the DC question was selected to minimize the mean square error of the welfare measure and estimated using the DWEABS routine provided by Cooper (1993a) (Cooper, 1993b; Elnagheeb and Jordan, 1995). Participants were asked to value a scenario for consuming denominated wine, which translates from the original Greek as:

Assume that a standard table bottled wine costs 1,000 Greek drachmas. If the wine you consume had been a denominated product in the sense of a P.D.O or a P.G.I product. (a short explanation of the P.D.O and P.G.I quality marks followed). Would you be willing to pay an A amount more per bottle to buy this product?

_____ Yes, I would be willing to pay
_____ No, I would not be willing to pay

If you are willing to pay an A amount would you be willing to pay a B (higher than A) amount?

_____ Yes, I would be willing to pay
_____ No, I would not be willing to pay

If you are not willing to pay an A amount would you be willing to pay a C (lower than A) amount?

_____ Yes, I would be willing to pay
_____ No, I would not be willing to pay

Results and discussion

Table I shows descriptive statistics of the original (744 respondents) sample and the table wine consumers (303 respondents). The data indicate that non-quality wine consumers are older, with a lower level of education, more frequently females, unmarried and if married with larger families. They were also most frequently residents of rural areas and their stated income was lower than the one received for all consumers interviewed.

Due to the fact that only 303 non-quality consumers took part in the willingness to pay exercise, a possible selection bias could occur. Thus, the logit specification of equation (3) was tested for selection bias in a binary logit selection model. The selectivity variable was not significant and thus we may assume that the sample of non-quality wine consumers is a random sample of the original sample containing quality and non-quality wine consumers[5].

Results of fitting the single and double bounded models are shown in Table II. Although all information regarding the demographic and social variables of the respondents entered the model, only two of the respondents' characteristics were found to be statistically significant and only in the double-bounded model, namely education and place of origin. The results indicate that as education level rises so does the willingness to pay for origin labelled wine. The same holds true for origin, thus the more associated respondents are with the origin, i.e. the production area of the wine, the more they are willing to pay a premium for a guarantee of production origin.

Variable anmes	Definitions	Non-quality consumers[a]	All consumers[a]
AGE	Age of household's head in years	38.3	36.90
EDUC	Dummy variable, 1 if respondent has finished high school	0.67	0.72
MARITAL	Dummy variable, 1 if respondent is not married	0.47	0.51
FSIZE	Family size (including parents, children and other dependent members)	2.09	2.00
SEX	Dummy variable, 1 if respondent is female	0.57	0.53
RURAL	Dummy variable, 1 if respondent comes from a rural area	0.45	0.41
INCOME	Respondent's income in Euro	13,060.00	14,967.00
Number of observations		303.00	744.00

Source: Survey data

Note: [a] Figures represent mean values

Table I.
Variable definition and descriptive statistics

BFJ
104,11

908

Table II also shows the median WTP in Greek Drachmas per bottle of wine. The results indicate that the two prices do not differ very much and are laid around the price of €3.23. Taking into account the information on the average prices of the examined local wines (from wine stores and supermarkets), which reveals that prices for moschofilero wine range between €4.70 and €5.87, we can judge that the premium which non-quality wine consumers intend to pay for the guarantee of origin and variety is more or less acquired by the producers. Given the fact that although consumers usually tend to pay a little more than €2.93 for table wine and that they are willing to pay about €3.23 more for origin wine, it can be concluded that there is room for a price increase in the final consumer price of moschofilero.

The results from this study are subject to the usual limitations applied to almost any contingent valuation study and are both theoretical/conceptual, as well as statistical. Especially for this study, however, two particular limitations should be considered. First, the place of origin marketing cue is not a straightforward quality attribute; thus, it does not refer to a particular product characteristic and, as such, is subject to the consumer's subjective evaluation of the meaning of the origin. The place of origin may serve a diverse spectrum of consumer needs ranging from safe, authentic and healthy products to products of lifestyles and culinary heritage. Thus, what we measure is actually an overall level of consumer utility (total value) and not the contribution of a strictly specified marketing cue such as aroma, freshness, colour or packaging, to the consumer's utility. Second, consumers may not be totally aware of what "certification of place of origin" implies for the product's overall quality characteristics. Thus, it may be argued that, despite our effort to provide consumers with a short explanation of PDO and PGI quality labelling, a slight information bias has infringed our results.

The values calculated for the average premium that consumers wish to pay for the origin labelled wine are quite high and can exceed the average price paid for a bottle of standard table wine. Thus there are a lot of opportunities for developing a successful market for quality wines based on origin characteristics. Appropriate marketing strategies developed to appeal to specific consumer segments (i.e. consumers associated with the origin of production and more informed) can add to the market potential of origin products. Collective promotion activities can be also elaborated implementing

	Single-bounded model		Double-bounded model	
	Coefficient	*t*-ratio	Coefficient	*t*-ratio
Intercept	1.425	4.160	2.232	6.926
Bid	−0.001	−6.430	−0.002	−11.405
EDUC	0.145	0.544	0.173	1058.170
ORIGIN	0.128	0.507	0.039	379.103
Log-likelihood		−184.97		−172.39
Estimated median WTP (EURO/bottle)		3.774		2.995

Table II.
Coefficient estimates
for single- and double-
bounded models

Source: Survey data

the adopted marketing strategy built on origin characteristics, through available rural development funds. Furthermore, it has to be mentioned that additional product characteristics may play an important role in the formation of the price premium, like brand (producer) name, etc. These attributes can help in capturing an even bigger added value, but in addition to that, they can facilitate a further diversification of the market for the product.

Consumers'
willingness
to pay

909

Conclusions

The results of this survey revealed that from the factors affecting non-quality wine consumers' willingness to pay for origin labelled wine, only education and knowledge about the origin of the product were found to be significant for the choice of the bid. According to this, marketing strategies for origin products should emphasise the quality of the area and the product attributes that are generated by the characteristics of the area or by the traditional and distinctive production practices adopted in the origin.

The study indicated that it is also very probable that quality wines exemplifying origin characteristics will be more appealing to consumers with a higher educational level. Certification in the form of either a product of denominated origin (PDO) or a product of geographic indication (PGI), or the similar schemes applicable to wines (AOC and AOP), clearly targets a highly educated consumer. Given the fact that the level of education is, usually, associated with higher incomes, certification can segregate the wine market and target its upper part consisting of consumers with higher incomes and education. Consumers of the kind are more attracted to quality characteristics and generally are willing to pay a top up to average prices when other features of the product, like speciality and authenticity, add to their requests and when a corresponding label provides them a guarantee for these features. These consumers may also associate certification or place of origin with their own risk reduction consumption strategy, where the overall marketing cue of certification hedges against the risk of inferior quality wine and thus, is worth the premium. In other words, one may argue that the price premium for denominated products bears the cost of a quality assurance scheme signalling to the consumer concepts of an authentic, healthy, safe and traditional product.

The results of the study supplemented with market price observations indicate that moschofilero wine achieves a higher price than standard wines. Thus, it can be concluded that in the case of moschofilero the market for origin labelled and consequently speciality products is working. More research is needed focusing on other quality wines, in order to extend this finding to apply to a wider range of Greek origin/quality wines. There are also ways for more efficient marketing, as better communication with the consumers and efforts to further promote origin characteristics to consumers may result in a more spontaneous choice of origin wines. Supplementary activities at local level, like wine fairs and wine roots, can be proved useful marketing instruments for further building the regional image of speciality local wines and assist in the creation of mental connotations to consumers.

Labelling corresponding to the region of origin, exploration of opportunities deriving from the existing certification schemes and the price premium

BFJ
104,11

910

associated with the origin may be well utilised by businesses located in rural and lagging areas of the EU. Taking into account that certification in the form of a PDO or PGI or similar origin schemes is a strictly regulated quality cue, the supply of products bearing this quality cue may be controlled in favour of local businesses that will take advantage of the price premium over businesses located outside geographical zones of denominated production. Thus, the persistence of EU's rural development policy to establish certified quality marks and link the production of food and drink with specific localities may work in favour of rural businesses that will adopt such quality cues and create "niche" markets for their products. Of course, producers located in the remote and lagging areas are usually small and will still have to discover ways of penetrating a market with tough barriers to entry. However, initiatives that take the form of collective promotion action and marketing strategies that target specific segments of consumers, can be helpful tools in spreading the concept of origin and assist in building an additional quality characteristic for quality products based on the image of the region of origin.

Notes

1. Currently the EU list of PDO, PGI and GTS products includes over 500 products, which vary between cheeses, fruits, olive-oils, mineral waters, beers, etc. (European Commission, 2000).

2. Today Greece has 20 of its wines labelled as AOP, eight as AOC while 45 wines are recognised as locally produced, i.e. wines from grape varieties related to the production area. Recent production trends indicate an increase in the production of quality wines and a decrease in the production of table wines, which still accounts for nearly half of the Greek wine production. This is an effect of a structural adjustment to the vine farms, but also to the wine producers, which today search for quality grapes that allow them to produce better wines. The larger area cultivated with VQPRD varieties lies in the Aegean islands and Peleponese, regions with the bigger number of AOC and AOP wines. Previous analyses of the Greek viticulture and wine sector have identified that there are opportunities, which lie in the upgrade of Greek wines through the enhancement of the areas under cultivation with more VQPRD varieties (IIER-Messini, 1996). Apart from the structural measures, from the marketing side and the existing labels, either AOC or AOP, it also seems that quality wines produced by small producers, bearing the name of the producer's chateau or Cot, as well as local wines (*Vin de Pays*) offer the most appealing opportunities. Quality labelling and signalling appears to be of importance to all EU wine producing countries, but particularly for Greece and Spain, which lately observe a decline in their respective wine consumption in favour of beer and other beverages (Skurus and Vakrou, 1997; Angulo *et al.*, 2000).

3. This work arises out of a program of collaborative research between several university departments and institutes of six European countries and has been financed in the context of FAIR programmes by the European Commission, DG Research titles "Regional images and the promotion of quality products and services in the lagging regions of the European Union" (RIPPLE), run between 1997 to 1999 (FAIR3-CT96-1827). More information about this research project, its objectives, work programme and deliverables can be found at: www.ripple.upatras.gr

4. The population of the three towns according to the 1991 census was 3,072,922 inhabitants for Athens; 170,452 for Patras; and 22,463 for Tripoli.

5. More information including the distribution of first and follow-up bids, and the frequencies of "yes-yes", "yes-no" and "no-no" responses is available from the authors upon request.

References

Anderson, M.D., Hollingsworth, C.S., Van Zee, V., Coli, W.M. and Rhodes, M. (1996), "Consumer response to integrated pest management and certification", *Agriculture, Ecosystems and Environment*, Vol. 60, pp. 97-106.

Angulo, A.M., Gil, J.M., Garcia, A. and Sanchez M. (2000), "Hedonic prices for Spanish quality wine", *British Food Journal*, Vol. 102 No. 7, pp. 481-93.

Arfini, F. and Mora Zanetti, C. (1998), "Typical products and local development: the case of Parma area", *Proceedings of the 52nd EAAE Conference on Local and Traditional Products: Rural effects and Agro-industrial problems, Parma 19-22 June 1997*, Instituto di Economia Agraria e Forastrale, Universita di Parma, Parma.

Bagnara, G.L. (1996), "Brand name and added value in horticultural products: analysis of consumer perception", *Proceedings of the 5th Joint Conference on Agriculture, Food and Environment, 17-18 June, Abano Terne – Padova, Italy*, Centre for International Food and Agricultural Policy, University of Minnesota, Minneapolis, MN.

Bérand, L. and Marchenay, P. (1995), "Lieux, temps et preuves: la construction sociale des produits de terroir", *Terrain*, Vol. 24, p. 153-64.

Caswell, J.A. (1997), "Uses of food labelling regulations", *The OECD Report on Regulatory Reform, Vol. I: Sectoral Studies*, OECD, Paris.

Committee of the Regions (1996), *Promoting and Protecting Local Products – A Trump Card for the Regions*, Committee of the Regions, Brussels.

Cooper, J. (1993a), *Referendum CVM Programs*, ERS-NASS, USDA, Washington, DC.

Cooper, J. (1993b), "Optimal bid selection for dichotomous choice contingent valuation surveys", *Journal of Environmental Economics and Management*, Vol. 24, pp. 25-40.

Cooper, J. (1994), "A comparison of approaches to calculating confidence intervals for benefit measures from dichotomous choice valuation surveys", *Land Economics*, Vol. 70, pp. 111-22.

Efron, B. (1987), "Better bootstrap confidence intervals", *Journal of American Statistical Association*, Vol. 82, pp. 171-85.

Elnagheeb, A.H. and Jordan, J.L. (1995), "Comparing three approaches that generate bids for the referendum contingent valuation method", *Journal of Environmental Economics and Management*, Vol. 29, pp. 92-104.

Erickson, G.M., Johansson, J.K. and Chao, P. (1984), "Image variables in multi-attribute product evaluations: country-of-origin effects", *Journal of Consumer Research*, Vol. 11, pp. 694-9.

Eroglu, S.A. and Machleit, K.A. (1989), "Effects of individual and product-specific variables on utilizing country of origin as a product quality cue", *International Marketing Review*, Vol. 6, pp. 27-41.

European Commission (1996), "Speciality agricultural products and foodstuffs", *Green Europe, The Agricultural Situation in the EU – 1999 report/96*, EC, Brussels.

European Commission (2000), *The Agricultural Situation in the EU – 1999 Report*, Brussels.

European Commission (2001), "Food quality", Web page available at: europa.eu.int/comm./ agriculture/foodqual/ quali_en.htm. (last accessed at 20 December 2001).

Foster, A. and Macrae, S. (1992), "Food quality: what does it mean?" in National Consumer Council (Ed.), *Your Food, Whose Choice?*, HMSO, London.

Fu, T-T., Liu, J-T. and Hammitt, J. (1999), "Consumer willingness to pay for low-pesticide fresh produce in Taiwan", *Journal of Agricultural Economics*, Vol. 50, pp. 220-33.

Hanemann, W.M. (1984), "Welfare evaluations in contingent valuation experiments with discrete responses", *American Journal of Agricultural Economics*, Vol. 66, pp. 332-41.

Hanemann, W.M., Loomis, J. and Kanninen, B. (1991), "Statistical efficiency of double-bounded dichotomous choice contingent valuation", *American Journal of Agricultural Economics*, Vol. 73, pp. 1254-63.

Consumers'
willingness
to pay

911

Hayes, D.J., Shogren, J.F., Shin, S.Y. and Kliebenstein, J.B. (1995), "Valuing food safety in experimental auction markets", *American Journal of Agricultural Economics*, Vol. 77 No. 1, pp. 40-53.

Hoffmann, R. (2000), "Country of origin – a consumer perception perspective of fresh meat", *British Food Journal*, Vol. 102, pp. 211-29.

IIER (Institute for Industrial and Economic Research) – Messini, Ch. (1996), *The Wine Sector in Greece*, Athens.

Ilbery, B. and Kneafsey, M. (1998), "Product and place: promoting quality products and services in the lagging rural regions of the European Union", *European Urban and Regional Studies*, Vol. 5, pp. 329-41.

Johansson, J.K., Douglas, S.P. and Nonaka, I. (1985), "Assessing the impact of country of origin on product evaluations: a new methodological perspective", *Journal of Marketing Research*, Vol. 22, pp. 388-96.

Krinsky, I. and Robb, A. (1986), "Approximating the statistical properties of elasticities", *Review of Economics and Statistics*, Vol. 68, pp. 715-19.

LEADER European Observatory (2000), "Marketing local products. Short and long distributions channels", *Rural Innovation, Dossier No 7*, Brussels.

Moran, W. (1993), "Rural space and intellectual property", *Political Geography*, Vol. 12, pp. 263-77.

Obermiller, C. and Spangenberg, E. (1989), "Exploring the effects of origin labels: an information processing framework", *Advances in Consumer Research*, Vol. 16, pp. 454-9.

OECD (1995), *Niche Markets as a Rural Development Strategy*, OECD, Paris.

Park, T., Loomis, J.B. and Creel, M. (1991), "Confidence intervals for evaluating benefits estimates from dichotomous choice contingent valuation studies", *Land Economics*, Vol. 67, pp. 64-73.

Salais, R. and Storper, M. (1994) *Les mondes de production. Enquete sur l'indentite de la France*, Edition de l'Ecole des Hautes Etudes en Sciences Sociales, Paris.

Scottish Food Strategy Group (1993), *Scotland Means Quality*, SFSG, Edinburgh.

Skuras, D. and Vakrou, A. (1997), "Production and marketing of quality Greek wines: consumer perceptions, regional image and labels", in *Proceedings of 5th OENOMETRICS, Thessaloniki, 3-4 October*.

Sylvander, B. (1993), "Specific quality products: an opportunity for rural areas", *LEADER Magazine*, Vol. 3, pp. 8-21.

Tregear, A., Kuznesof, S. and Moxey, A. (1998), "Policy initiatives for regional foods: some insights from consumer research", *Food Policy*, Vol. 23 No. 5, pp. 383-94.

Van Ittersum, K., Candel, M.J.J.M. and Meulenberg, M.T.G. (2000), "The influence of the image of a product's region of origin on product evaluation", *Journal of Business Research*.

Van Trijp, H.J.C.M., Steenkamp, J-B.E.M. and Candel, M.J.J.M. (1993), "Quality labeling as instrument to create product equity; the case of IKB in The Netherlands", in Wierenga, B., Grunert, K., Steenkamp, J-B.E.M., Wedel, M., and Van Tilburg, A. (Eds), *Agricultural Marketing and Consumer Behavior in a Changing World*, Proceedings of 47th seminar of the European Association of Agricultural Economists (EAAE), Wageningen, pp. 201-15.

Vastoia, A. (1997), "Perceived quality and certification: the case of organic fruit", in Schiefer, G. and Helbig, R. (Eds), *Quality Management and Process Improvement for Competitive Advantage in Agriculture and Food*, Proceedings of the 49th seminar of the European Association of Agricultural Economists, Bonn.

Verlegh, P.W.J. and Steenkamp, J-B.E.M. (1999), "A review and meta-analysis of country-of-origin research", *Journal of Economic Psychology*, Vol. 20, pp. 521-46.

[14]

GEOGRAPHICAL INDICATIONS AND THE COMPETITIVE PROVISION OF QUALITY IN AGRICULTURAL MARKETS

GianCarlo Moschini, Luisa Menapace, and Daniel Pick

The economics of geographical indications (GIs) is assessed within a vertical product differentiation framework that is consistent with the competitive structure of agriculture. It is assumed that certification costs are needed for GIs to serve as (collective) credible quality certification devices, and production of high-quality product is endogenously determined. We find that GIs can support a competitive provision of quality and lead to clear welfare gains, although they fall short of delivering the (constrained) first best. The main beneficiaries are consumers. Producers may also accrue some benefit if production of the high-quality products draws on scarce factors that they own.

Key words: competitive industry, free entry/exit, geographical indications, Marshallian stability, quality certification, trademarks, welfare.

The market provision of quality is notoriously fraught with difficulties under asymmetric information: when producers cannot credibly signal the quality of their products, consumers' choices are predicated on the perceived average quality on the market, and this pooling equilibrium has undesirable welfare properties. Following Akerlof's (1970) seminal contribution, such market failures have been the object of considerable research. One possible solution has emphasized the role of firms' reputation as conveyed by their brands (Klein and Leffler 1981; Shapiro 1983). Brand names must themselves be informative, of course, and that in turns requires a credible trademark system. Trademarks thus serve as useful information tools for consumers by allowing them to more readily identify the goods of interest, thereby reducing the possibility of consumer confusion and economizing on their search costs (Landes and Posner 1987). Given that effect, trademarks also provide an incentive for firms to produce goods of consistent quality, as expected by consumers, lest they lose consumer

loyalty and suffer a loss on their investments in trademark development.[1]

Brands and trademarks are best understood in an imperfectly competitive setting. Their role in agriculture and food production, largely characterized by competitive market conditions, remains an open question. Individual firms are typically too small to credibly signal quality to consumers directly, and this is one of the justifications for specific types of government intervention such as the development of food standards and grades, a specific mandate of U.S. federal agencies (Gardner 2003; Lapan and Moschini 2007).[2] Alternatively, producers could bundle together to achieve the critical mass required for brand name and trademark development. A particularly interesting instance of such cooperation in the provision of quality is represented by the use of geographical indications (GIs). This use of geographically based labels to brand products has been in use for a long time, especially in Europe, but interest in GIs increased considerably after they were recognized as a distinct form of intellectual property (IP) rights in the TRIPS agreement of the World Trade Organization

GianCarlo Moschini is professor and Pioneer Chair in Science and Technology Policy and Luisa Menapace is a Ph.D. student, both with the Department of Economics, Iowa State University, Ames, IA. Daniel Pick is Chief of the Specialty Crops and Fiber Branch, Economic Research Service, U.S. Department of Agriculture.
The authors thank two anonymous referees, Giovanni Anania, Harvey Lapan and editor Christopher Barrett for their helpful comments. The support of the Center for Agricultural and Rural Development at Iowa State University, and of the U.S. Department of Agriculture through a cooperative research project, is gratefully acknowledged. The views expressed in this article are those of the authors and may not be attributed to the Economic Research Service or the U.S. Department of Agriculture.

[1] This standard result of reputation models was anticipated by Akerlof (1970), (p. 499), who noted that "Brand names not only indicate quality but also give the consumer a means of retaliation if the quality does not meet expectations."

[2] Two recent instances of government intervention in food and agricultural products labeling are the introduction of new organic food standards by the U.S. Department of Agriculture (USDA) in October 2002, and the new regulation for labeling genetically modified food and feed products in the European Union (EU) in April 2004.

Amer. J. Agr. Econ. 90(3) (August 2008): 794–812
Copyright 2008 American Agricultural Economics Association
DOI: 10.1111/j.1467-8276.2008.01142.x

Moschini, Menapace, and Pick   *Geographical Indications and the Provision of Quality*   795

(WTO) (Josling 2006). In the context of GIs, quality attributes of interest to consumers are presumed linked to the specific geographic origin of the good and/or particular production methods used in that region (the notion of "terroir"), and such attributes cannot be determined through inspection by the consumer prior to purchasing the good. The fundamental role of GIs in this setting, therefore, is that of providing a credible certification mechanism that solves a real-world information problem.

Some recent contributions have addressed directly some of the specific economic issues related to GIs. Zago and Pick (2004) question the desirability of GIs by showing that, with an exogenously determined supply of quality, the welfare implications of a fully credible certification system based on GIs are ambiguous. In Anania and Nisticò (2004), low-quality producers can choose to sell their product on the high-quality market (i.e., to cheat). Given an imperfect enforcement mechanism, a GI regulation might be desirable for both low- and high-quality producers. A few studies have suggested that GIs can be interpreted as "club goods" (nonrival, congestible, and excludable), as discussed in Rangnekar (2004), chapter 4, and this interpretation is adopted by Langinier and Babcock (2006). The government provides GI certification rights to high-quality producers, who are free to decide the size of the club (i.e., who among the high-quality producers has access to it). Lence et al. (2007) focus on the problem of developing new GIs. The key to developing such products is a fixed cost. Certification is implicitly free in their setting, and thus costless imitation is possible, so that some degree of supply control may be necessary to encourage geographic product differentiation.

In this article, we emphasize that the natural institutional setting for GIs is that of competitive markets. Contrary to standard trademarks, which are owned and used by a single firm, GIs are essentially public goods and are used by many firms simultaneously. Moreover, the use of a GI cannot be denied to any producer in the specified geographical area, an issue that has been overlooked by previous work. Indeed, in the European Union (EU) where GIs are widely used, there are typically no limitations on which or how many firms can use a given GI (provided that all product specifications, including the geographical origin, are met). Similarly, in the United States where GIs are mainly protected as certification marks, any firm that meets the certifying standards is entitled to use

the corresponding certification mark. Accordingly, the purpose of this article is to investigate the impacts of a credible GI certification system in a competitive market setting characterized by the possibility of free entry, and we derive and discuss the welfare effects to be expected in such a context.

Our analysis complements and adds to existing studies in this area in some novel ways. For instance, most studies discussed in the foregoing (Anania and Nisticò 2004; Zago and Pick 2004; Langinier and Babcock 2006) assume that producers are *ex ante* and exogenously identified as either of the low- or high-quality type. In particular, high-quality producers supply the high-quality product regardless of whether or not they are certified and/or receive a price premium in the market. We relax this constraining assumption and allow the (costly) provision of quality to be endogenously determined. Furthermore, in our model the production of high- and low-quality goods can coexist in equilibrium in the same area, which also captures a feature of the real world where not all producers in a given GI region take advantage of their right to supply the GI products. Finally, and perhaps most importantly, we analyze explicitly the implications of competitive entry within a coherent model of quality certification through GIs, an issue that, to date, has not been addressed.

In what follows we first review the institutional setting for GIs, with emphasis on policies implemented in the EU, a leader in the development and use of GIs. This allows us to substantiate our premise that both the letter of existing regulations and the observed practice in the predominance of cases suggest that the relevant market setting is a competitive one. In particular, entry of new firms that wish to produce GI-certified high-quality goods is possible. Based on that, we then specify a model to study how the competitive structure of agricultural production affects the supply of quality in the presence of a mechanism that mimics the nature of a GI. The model, although by necessity very stylized, captures the essential elements of the problem at hand. In particular, the demand side of the model is rooted in the economics of product differentiation, which provides an attractive formulation on how consumer preferences value quality. On the supply side, our model allows for different production costs for high- and low-quality goods and permits the supply of the high-quality (GI-certified) good to be endogenous.

796   *August 2008*   *Amer. J. Agr. Econ.*

The characterization of equilibrium centers on the competitive conditions with free entry/exit. In the benchmark case, in which all input costs are parametrically given, the need for costly certification that involves a fixed cost induces increasing returns to scale at the industry level. Consequently, the competitive equilibrium is not Pareto efficient; specifically, it underprovides the high-quality good. This equilibrium, however, does entail welfare gains relative to the absence of GI certification, and thus, it does ameliorate the information market failure that motivates interest in GIs. In this setting, some simple policies that subsidize the GI certification of quality would restore Pareto efficiency to the competitive equilibrium. Perhaps not surprisingly, given the long-run nature of the competitive equilibrium that we consider, the welfare gains due to GIs mostly take the form of increased consumer surplus. The availability of GIs benefits producers only when the production of the high-quality good draws on scarce factors owned by producers.

The Institutional Framework

Whereas recent motives of interest in GIs stem from their recognition as distinct IP rights in TRIPS and the ongoing efforts to strengthen such rights, protection of GIs has a long history in some European countries and elsewhere. GIs are protected under two similar yet distinct legal notions: appellations of origin and marks. The primary difference is that an appellation of origin requires the existence of a special tie between the quality of the product and its geographical origin, whereas in the case of a mark such a relation is not necessary.[3]

The EU framework is rooted in its Council Regulation (EEC) 2081/92, adopted in 1992, which established an EU-wide harmonized system of protection of GIs for agricultural products and foodstuffs (but excluding wines and spirits).[4] This regulation defines two types of GIs, Protected Designations of Origin (PDOs) and Protected Geographical Indications (PGIs), that differ depending on how closely a product is linked to geography (European Commission 2007). Protection under a PDO mandates the more stringent conditions, as it requires the quality or characteristics of the product must be essentially or exclusively due to natural and human factors characterizing the geographic area of origin (e.g., climate, soil quality, local production knowledge). Also, for a PDO the entire production process, including the production and processing of raw materials, must occur within the defined geographic area of origin. In contrast, the PGI merely requires that a portion of a designated product's characteristics and production occur within the specific geographical area.

PDO or PGI protection can be obtained by an association of producers and/or processors. The process requires the definition of so-called "specifications," which identify the required conditions for the GI label, including the characteristics of the product, the production method, and the geographic area of production. In addition, the association seeking protection must designate a third-party inspection body in charge of the certification and inspection along the entire supply chain. Such activities are meant to ensure that products carrying PDO or PGI labels comply with the specifications and to ensure that the information conveyed via labeling is verifiable, thus bolstering the credibility of the GIs system. It is critical to note that once a product is registered, all producers within the geographic region who comply with the product specifications, regardless of whether or not they are a member of the association that originally applied for the registration, are entitled to use the PDO or PGI label on their product (Article 8 of Regulation 510/2006).[5]

Over 700 PDO and PGI products are currently registered in the EU. Table 1 reports

---

[3] More details and discussion of the GI institutional framework may be found in OECD (2000) and Josling (2006).

[4] Regulation 2081/92 was recently updated by Council Regulation (EC) 510/2006 to comply with the TRIPS agreement. It abrogates the "reciprocity principle" and it simplifies the bureaucratic procedure for application. In particular, it simplifies the procedure for third-country parties to apply for GI registration in the EU and/or to pursue opposition against the EU registration of any GI.

[5] An example to illustrate the foregoing is the Italian cheese Asiago. The protection of the Asiago denomination under Italian law dates back to 1954, while the PDO status was obtained in 1996. The Asiago production area comprises a vast region in north-eastern Italy, encompassing four provinces (Trento, Vicenza, and parts of the lowland provinces of Padua and Treviso). Physical and sensorial characteristics as well as production procedures, from cow-feeding to the cheese ripening process, are outlined in detail in the production specifications. Local know-how and traditions (documented as far back as 1,000 AD) are deemed to be key element in the production of Asiago cheese. The "Consorzio Tutela Formaggio Asiago" is in charge of supervision, custody, promotion, and development of the denomination. Non-members are free to brand their product as Asiago PDO as long as production occurs according to the specifications and the product is certified by the appointed third-party inspection body. Control and inspection activities of Asiago producers (both consortium members and nonmembers) are performed by an independent inspection body (the "Certificazione Qualità Agroalimentare s.r.l.").

Moschini, Menapace, and Pick   *Geographical Indications and the Provision of Quality*   797

Table 1. Number of PDO and PGI Products in the European Union

	Total	Cheese	Meat-Based	Breads and Bakery	Oils	Fish	Beer	Other Drinks	Fruits and Vegetables	Fresh Meat	Other Animal Products	Table Olives	Other
Belgium	5	1	2	1	1								
Czech Republic	6			1		1	3		1				
Denmark	3	2							1				
Germany	67	4	8	4	1	2	12	31	2	3			
Greece	84	20		1	25	1			22		1	10	4
Spain	105	19	10	7	20				30	13	3		3
France	155	45	4	2	9	2		5	26	51	6	3	2
Ireland	4	1	1			1				1			
Italy	159	32	28	3	38				47	2	2	2	5
Luxemburg	4		1		1					1	1		
Netherlands	6	4							2				
Austria	12	6	2		1				3				
Poland	1	1											
Portugal	104	12	28		6				21	26	10	1	
Slovenia	1				1								
Finland	1								1				
Sweden	2	1		1									
United Kingdom	28	11				3	2	3	1	7	1		
Total	**747**	**159**	**84**	**20**	**103**	**10**	**17**	**39**	**157**	**104**	**24**	**16**	**14**

Source: Compiled by authors from EU data available at http://ec.europa.eu/agriculture/foodqual/quali1_en.htm (accessed on October 2007).

their distribution by country and by product category. The majority of these GIs come from Mediterranean countries—more than 75% of the products are registered in five southern EU states (France, Italy, Greece, Portugal, and Spain). Nevertheless, the registration of GIs by northern countries has increased over time. Of the 268 applications for new denominations that are currently being considered, more than half come from countries other than the aforementioned five southern countries (including eleven from nonmembers countries).

In most other developed countries outside the EU, the trademark system provides a legal framework for the protection of GIs. In the United States, geographical names can be registered as certification marks. Certification marks are characterized by the fact that the use of the mark is not restricted to any person or entity, as long as the attributes required for certification are met. U.S. certification marks are typically administered by a governmental body, the presumption being that such an agency is best positioned for "... preserving the freedom of all persons in the region to use the term and, second, preventing abuses or illegal uses of the mark..." (USPTO 2007, undated, p. 3).[6] Similarly to the appellations

system, the product that is labeled with a certification mark is subject to inspection. Inspection activities are in this case the responsibility of the mark's owner and not of a third-party inspection body (but the implications are analogous because the owner of the certification mark does not conduct production or commercial activity; it merely concedes the use of the mark to independent producers).

In some instances, GI protection in the United State can also be obtained through individual trademarks or collective marks. Specifically, that is possible when one can establish that the geographic term in question has acquired a "secondary meaning" to consumers. Collective marks identify the products of many firms belonging to a group (e.g., an association or cooperative). They are meant "for use only by its members..." (USPTO 2007, undated, p. 4), and as such they arguably have the nature of club goods.

TRIPS accords stronger GI protections to wines and spirits, and even in the EU wines are treated separately. "Quality wines produced in a specified region" and table wines with a "typical geographic indication," excluded from Regulation (EEC) 2081/92, are protected within the framework of the common market organization for wine (European Commission 2006). This framework limits the grape-growing potential of the EU with planting rights restrictions, including a ban on new vine plantings. These instruments have only been partially successful in trying to reduce the chronic overproduction in the EU (over the

---

[6] A well-known example of a U.S. certification mark is that of Vidalia onions, which is held by the Georgia Department of Agriculture (Clemens 2002). Producers must apply for an annual license from the Georgia Department of Agriculture to sell Vidalia onions, providing information regarding the type of onions planted, total number of acres and location. Licenses are free. The production area covers all or part of the 20 Georgia counties.

798   *August 2008*

Amer. J. Agr. Econ.

last two decades the stocks of the aforementioned protected quality wines have actually been growing at a faster rate than consumption and exports to third countries). In any event, planting rights restrictions apply to total cultivation of grapes and do allow shifting wine production into GIs, if desired. Indeed, over time, planting rights have been allocated or reallocated to higher-quality productions, increasing the incidence of GIs on total wine (European Commission 2002).

GI Product Markets and Competition

The analysis of the institutional framework for the protection of GIs in the preceding section suggests that, typically, all producers located in the relevant specified production area have the option to produce and market the corresponding GI product. Thus, it would seem that competitive entry is a feature of the supply context of GI products that is fully consistent with most current regulations governing GIs.

Despite the possibility of competitive entry/exit, of course, expanding production of a given GI may be hampered by limitations on the accessibility of relevant inputs. Given the great heterogeneity of existing GIs in this respect, no simple assessment is possible on how much such a consideration matters. For instance, if the geographic area identified by a given GI is sufficiently small, and/or the GI product accounts for much of the local agricultural production (e.g., Champagne), land and/or other factors may seriously affect potential supply response. In other cases, such as those of Greek feta cheese and Italian grappa, the appropriate geographic area encompasses virtually a whole country. The actual level of utilization of GI labels within a specified area of production also varies significantly among different GIs, and often a significant share of total production is commercialized without the GI label. For example, olive oil produced in the Italian region of Lazio involves about 130,000 producers who grow olive trees on 195,000 acres. A GI label is used on less than 10% of the olive oil that could potentially be branded with any one of the three regional GIs (Sabina PDO, Canino PDO, or Tuscia PGI) (Carbone 2003). Similarly, in the case of the Italian wine sector where a high degree of heterogeneity exists among different wines, the utilization of GIs is only about 40% (ISMEA 2005). Thus, considerable expansion of production of a number of GI wines would seem possible, even given

the overall constraint posed by EU planting rights.

If it were possible to manage GIs as privately owned labels with the power to control total supply, as in the notion of farmer-owned brands articulated in Hayes, Lence, and Stoppa (2004), that might create the potential for attractive noncompetitive returns for GI producers. The lure of noncompetitive returns in agriculture is, of course, not new; it has been of interest to farmers for a long time, as evidenced by the history of the cooperative movement and marketing orders in the United States (Crespi and Sexton 2003).[7] Producer associations with direct responsibility for managing GIs (called "consortia" in Italy) are perhaps best positioned to pursue noncompetitive goals, especially when they gather most of the producers of the relevant GI product. In fact, antitrust authorities have intervened with regard to a number of prominent GI products: the Italian Parma ham and San Daniele ham, the Italian Grana Padano, Parmigiano-Reggiano and Gorgonzola cheeses, and the French Cantal cheese (OECD 2000). The anticompetitive behavior that was investigated concerned attempts by producer associations to control total supply through the imposition of individual production quotas to their membership and through market share agreements between the consortia (OECD 2000). In all cases, after the antitrust intervention, production quota and market share agreements were abandoned, and competitive conditions were restored.[8]

A final consideration that will inform our modeling choice concerns the production technology of GI products. Whereas it is true that the geographic attributes of GIs are often critical to support their perceived higher quality, it should also be clear that there are other elements of the production technology that are part of a GI's specifications and that affect

---

[7] For example, Vidalia onions, mentioned earlier, have had a federal marketing order since 1989. The order's provisions endow growers with some supply control. The effects of the marketing order, of course, are conceptually distinct from those of the certification mark.

[8] Consortia used to carry out monitoring activities to ensure that members' production satisfies the desired specifications. After the introduction of the 1992 EU regulation on GIs, however, consortia lost any authority they might have had over the control of production, as well as the responsibility for all inspection activities (which were assigned to independent bodies). In particular, when awarded a PDO or PGI, consortia had to give up their property right over the protected name in exchange for the legal protection of the GI provided by the European regulation (Nomisma 2001). At present, consortia have custody of the collective brand identifying the GI and grant its use to producers who meet the requirements.

not only quality but also the cost of production. To illustrate, consider the example of Parmigiano-Reggiano cheese. The specifications for this PDO require production to take place in a clearly delimited region of northern Italy but also mandate a number of other production constraints. These include restrictive cow-feeding guidelines; notably, it is forbidden to feed silage to cows that produce the milk used in manufacturing Parmigiano-Reggiano (by contrast, use of silage is allowed in the production process of the other competing parmesan-type cheese, the Grana Padano). Such restrictions are deemed essential to achieve the desired cheese quality but are also known to increase considerably the cost of milk production, by approximately 20% by some estimates (de Roest and Menghi 2000). Similarly, PDO brie production requires manual techniques that may increase production costs by approximately 25% (Benitez, Bouamra-Mechemache, and Chaaban 2005).

We conclude that, for the case of most GI products, the presumption that GI producers have an effective way to control the aggregate quantity supplied of their product is not tenable. Thus, in the model that follows we will maintain the possibility of competitive entry in a setting in which producers can elect to supply either the GI product or its generic counterpart, and where the production of the GI product entails higher production costs than its generic counterpart. The implications of the fact that some necessary factors in the production of GIs may be in scarce supply will also be investigated.

A Model for the Competitive Provision of Quality Using GIs

The specification of the model that follows implements all the main features that appear to be relevant based on the foregoing review of the institutional framework and real world examples. Specifically, in the model: (a) consumers value quality as in the standard vertical product differentiation framework; (b) producers can supply quality by undertaking production processes that are costlier than those required for the alternative, low-quality product; (c) GIs can serve as (collective) quality certification devices, although for their function to be credible additional promotion and certification costs are required; and (d) producers operate in a competitive industry (with free entry and exit).

Demand: Vertical Product Differentiation

As with other studies in this area, we presume that the quality to be supplied through the use of GIs is valued by consumers within the vertical product differentiation structure of Mussa and Rosen (1978). Specifically, we consider the simple unit-demand version of the vertical product differentiation model whereby each consumer buys at most one unit of the good in question and her preferences are described by the (indirect) utility function

$$(1) \quad U = \begin{cases} \theta q - p & \text{if the good is bought} \\ 0 & \text{otherwise.} \end{cases}$$

where $q \in \mathbb{R}_{++}$ indexes the quality of the good, $p \in \mathbb{R}_{++}$ is the price of the good, and the preference parameter $\theta \in [\underline{\theta}, \bar{\theta}] \subseteq \mathbb{R}_+$ indexes consumer types. The hypothesis here is that of heterogeneous preferences for quality so that the population of consumers can be characterized by the distribution function $G(\theta)$ of the preference parameter.

More specifically, suppose that there are only two possible qualities in this market, a "low" quality q_L and a "high" quality $q_H > q_L$. If these two qualities are available at prices p_L and p_H, respectively, where $p_H > p_L > 0$, then the consumer decision problem is to select the action that yields the highest utility among the three possible options:

$$(2) \quad U = \begin{cases} \theta q_H - p_H & \text{if the high-quality} \\ & \text{good is bought} \\ \theta q_L - p_L & \text{if the low-quality} \\ & \text{good is bought} \\ 0 & \text{otherwise} \end{cases}$$

To simplify the analysis, as in related studies in this area, we put further restrictions on the distributions of consumers. That is, we postulate that the distribution $G(\theta)$ is uniform and that $\theta \in [0, 1]$. The latter condition, in particular, implies that the market will be "uncovered" (i.e., as long as prices are strictly positive, some consumers with a low enough θ will not buy anything). More specifically, let

$$(3) \quad \hat{\theta} \equiv \frac{p_H - p_L}{q_H - q_L}$$

$$(4) \quad \tilde{\theta} \equiv \frac{p_L}{q_L}.$$

800   *August 2008*   *Amer. J. Agr. Econ.*

Throughout we will consider the typical case where $0 < \tilde{\theta} \leq \hat{\theta} \leq 1$. For that parametric case, consumers with $\theta \in [\hat{\theta}, 1]$ will buy the high-quality product, consumers with $\theta \in [\tilde{\theta}, \hat{\theta}]$ will buy the low-quality product, and consumers with $\theta \in [0, \tilde{\theta}]$ will buy nothing. For the population of M consumers, market demand is readily obtained by integrating the unit demand of each consumer given the distribution of consumer types. For the uniform distribution assumption invoked earlier, the aggregate market demand functions are

$$(5) \quad X_H^D = M \left(1 - \frac{p_H - p_L}{q_H - q_L} \right)$$

$$(6) \quad X_L^D = M \left(\frac{p_H - p_L}{q_H - q_L} - \frac{p_L}{q_L} \right).$$

Sometimes it is convenient to work with the inverse demand functions. Inverting (5) and (6), for given quantities $X_i \in [0, M]$ ($i = L, H$) satisfying $X_L + X_H \leq M$, yields

$$(7) \quad p_H = q_H - \frac{(q_L X_L + q_H X_H)}{M}$$

$$(8) \quad p_L = q_L \left(1 - \frac{X_L + X_H}{M} \right).$$

Equations (7) and (8) display the market's willingness to pay for the two qualities, for given supply levels, but also implicitly define the willingness to pay for the "additional quality" that the high-quality good provides over the low-quality one. By using (7) and (8), the (inverse) derived demand for the additional quality $(q_H - q_L)$ is

$$(9) \quad p_H - p_L = (q_H - q_L) \left(1 - \frac{X_H}{M} \right).$$

Note that this (market) willingness to pay for the additional quality depends only on the quantity supplied of the high-quality good (because this quantity implicitly defines the marginal consumer that is indifferent between purchasing the high- or low-quality good).

Supply: Competitive Production of Quality

We presume a standard competitive industry populated by numerous (actual or potential) producers who behave as price takers, and each of whom can produce either the high-quality

good or the low-quality good (or zero quantity). Initially, we suppose that these producers are identical and are operating with a production technology that admits cost functions $C_H(x_H)$ and $C_L(x_L)$ for the high- and low-quality goods, respectively, where $x_i \geq 0$ ($i = H, L$) denotes the level of firm's output for either the low- or high-quality product. We assume that the cost functions $C_i(x_i)$ are strictly increasing and display standard U-shaped average cost curves. In a long-run equilibrium with free entry and exit, therefore, firms will be operating at a strictly positive efficient scale. Furthermore, we assume that $C_H(x) > C_L(x)$, $\forall x > 0$. The presumption that the high-quality good requires a costlier production process is rather intuitive, as discussed in the preceding section (e.g., more labor care, need for higher-quality inputs, need for additional inputs, restrictions on the use of some inputs, etc.).

In addition to production cost, to market the high-quality good, producers need to undertake costly activities that credibly certify, in the eyes of consumers, the claimed higher quality. Such activities may relate to marketing, promotion, and/or monitoring of production standards. In principle such activities should be open to each producer individually, as would be the case for firms marketing with individual trademarks, and we therefore allow for that possibility. But the case for GIs rests on the presumption that firms may not be able to muster the required resources to do that individually, that is, there is scope for producers to act cooperatively in this regard. Hence, we interpret GIs as a common brand whereby producers can bundle together to share the marketing, promotion, and certification costs that are necessary for a credible GI. This assumption is quite consistent with the existence of producer organizations that take an active part in the marketing of GI products, such as the consortia discussed in the preceding section. Specifically, we assume that producers share the GI promotion and certification costs via a charge per unit of output produced, so that the total cost of producing the GI-certified high-quality product is $C_H(x_H) + \alpha x_H$, where $\alpha > 0$ is the unit certification cost.[9]

---

[9] An alternative assumption might be a cost-sharing rule that takes the form of a per-firm charge. As long as firms are identical, as postulated here, the two assumptions would appear largely equivalent. The sharing rules that we follow do, however, simplify the characterization of long-run equilibrium (because the minimum efficient scale of the high-quality firms is not affected by the size of α). Also, the assumed rule might be more appealing when the model is generalized to allow for firm heterogeneity.

One of the reasons for the existence of an incentive for firms to share the costs required for a credible certification is that what these activities produce—consumer goodwill toward the product with the given GI—has the nature of a public good from the producers' perspective. Some of the required costs are largely independent of the aggregate quantity of good that is eventually produced; this would be the case, for example, for activities connected to marketing, promotion and advertising, and overhead costs of the producer organization in charge of performing such functions. We measure the cost of such activities by $F > 0$. Other costs, however, are likely to depend on the amount produced. We contend that this is the case, in particular, for the portion of certification costs that are meant to monitor production standards and prevent cheating and free riding. A credible certification system, in fact, must recognize (and deal with) the possibility that producers purporting to sell a GI product have an incentive to behave opportunistically (i.e., they may claim to sell the high-quality good while producing the low-quality good). Producer organizations have a variety of mechanisms at their disposal to monitor and limit the opportunistic behavior of members. In our context, the challenge is to represent such activities explicitly, so that their effects on equilibrium can be assessed, and to do so in a parsimonious way that is consistent with the rest of the model. To that end, the enforcement mechanism that we postulate is a sequential "auditing game" (e.g., Rasmussen 2007, pp. 85–87), as follows.

A producer who wants to supply a quantity x of certified, high-quality GI product has two strategies: to comply with the relevant GI specifications or to violate them (by producing the lower-quality good at cost $C_L(x) < C_H(x)$ instead). In the enforcement mechanism that we envision, the monitoring agency moves first by announcing an inspections policy $\{\phi, T\}$, where $\phi \in [0, 1]$ is the probability of inspection to verify that the product specifications are met (or, more precisely, ϕ is the fraction of producers that will be subject to inspection), and $T > 0$ is a finite penalty that is paid if a producer fails the inspection. The individual producer then chooses whether to comply with or to violate the production specifications. Given this enforcement mechanism, the total expected cost to the producer associated with the "comply" strategy is $C_H(x) + \alpha x$ (and the assumption, of course, of no errors at the compliance-verification stage), whereas the total expected

cost is $C_L(x) + \alpha x + \phi T$ if the "violate" strategy is used.[10] Clearly, to induce compliance the minimum penalty needs to be at least as large as the production cost difference $[C_H(x) - C_L(x)]$. Specifically, for any given $T > [C_H(x) - C_L(x)]$ there exists an inspection probability $\phi \equiv [C_H(x) - C_L(x)]/T$ that makes "comply" a best response strategy for the producer. Given that, and if the aggregate returns to producers from everyone complying (net of the cost of inspections) exceeds those of tolerating violation, then it is an equilibrium strategy for the monitoring body to adopt the policy $\{\phi, T\}$ at the initial move stage.[11]

The main point of the foregoing is that compliance is obtained with an inspection probability that is high enough, given the penalty level. But such a monitoring scheme is costly because it requires that firms be inspected with some probability. Specifically, we assume that the cost of each inspection that is carried out is proportional to the level of a firm's output, that is, βx_H, where $\beta > 0$. Thus, the expected monitoring cost for each producer to be certified is $\phi \beta x_H$.[12] Note that, in this setup, the total monitoring cost is increasing with the number of producers to be certified, an appealing feature that is lost when total certification cost is treated as a fixed cost only.

The remaining question concerns how many producer groups we should expect to see in a GI market. As stated earlier, our working assumption is that the full certification cost, as given by the fixed cost F and the variable cost of monitoring, is shared among the members of the producer organization on a per-unit-of-output basis, with the portion of total cost attributable to the certification service written as αx_H. Thus, under full cost-sharing (we will return to this issue later, in the context of possible policy implications), if there are n producers sharing such costs, it must be that $\alpha x_H = \phi \beta x_H + F/n$. Given these

---

[10] The presumption is that there is no error in the inspection/auditing activities. Anania and Nisticò (2004) also rely on a similar simple and error-free monitoring and enforcing scheme.

[11] In this Nash equilibrium, the monitoring agency must carry out the inspections even though, in equilibrium, compliance is obtained. Thus, we are assuming that the monitoring authority can credibly commit to carrying out inspections, consistent with the overall requirement of a certification system that needs to be credible in the eyes of the consumer.

[12] Because only the product ϕT matters to induce compliance, and because ϕ affects the monitoring cost whereas T does not (in equilibrium everyone complies and no penalty is assessed), ideally one would want to make T as high as possible and ϕ as small as possible. The existing legal and institutional framework (as well as firms' limited financial assets), however, likely puts bounds on how large T can be; given that level of T, the inspection frequency ϕ can in principle be calculated.

802   *August 2008*   *Amer. J. Agr. Econ.*

structural assumptions, the question of how many producer groups we should expect reduces to a simple coalition formation problem. Suppose that, in a competitive equilibrium, there are N_H producers engaged in the production of the high-quality good, each producing the same quantity x_H, and consider the possibility of there being m groups of size $n < N_H$ (so that $n \equiv N_H/m$), each independently promoting and certifying their high-quality product. Then this would be a stable coalition structure if no member can gain by switching coalitions, that is, by leaving its current group to join another group (making the latter of size $n + 1$). Thus, the hypothesized coalition structure would be stable if

$$(10) \quad \frac{F}{n} + \phi\beta x_H \le \frac{F}{(n+1)} + \phi\beta x_H.$$

But clearly this cannot hold. The larger coalition attains lower unit promotion and certification costs and pulls in new members, so that in equilibrium we are left with only one (grand) coalition of size N_H.

The other condition we need to check is the possibility that a member has of defecting from the coalition with the intention of supplying the high-quality product on its own. In such a case, the producer has to undertake the entire fixed cost F individually but saves the need for monitoring costs. This possibility is not profitable if

$$(11) \quad p_H x_1 - C_H(x_1) - F$$

$$\le p_H x_H - C_H(x_H) - \phi\beta x_H - \frac{F}{N_H}$$

where x_1 is the scale of production of the firm that incurs F individually.[13] For approximately equal production levels $(x_1 \cong x_H)$ and a reasonably large number of producers N_H, the condition is approximately $F \ge \phi\ \beta x_H$. Thus, as long as the fixed cost of certification is large enough relative to the monitoring cost, defecting to market the high-quality product with one's own trademark is not profitable.

In conclusion, a credible certification system can be supported by a GI producer association that implements a simple monitoring scheme. Assuming that (11) is satisfied, a coalition may form to supply the high-quality good, and the

process should lead to just one coalition of size N_H.[14] Whereas in equilibrium the scheme may ensure compliance by producers, it will impose additional costs on the producers of the high-quality good. In particular, the total cost function for low-quality producers is simply $C_L(x_L)$ whereas the high-quality firms have a total cost function of $C_H(x_H) + \alpha x_H$, where α is the cost of GI certification per unit of output; that is,

$$(12) \quad \alpha \equiv \frac{F}{N_H x_H} + \phi\beta.$$

Equilibrium and Welfare

In this section, we consider the long-run partial equilibrium conditions that are relevant when it is possible for firms to enter and/or exit the industry of interest (e.g., Mas-Colell, Whinston, and Green 1995, chapter 10). Initially we assume no diseconomies at the industry level; that is, the prices of all production inputs are constant and exogenous to the industry. For a given output price p_L of the low-quality good, low-quality producers choose the production level x_L that maximizes profit $p_L x_L - C_L(x_L)$. The possibility of entry/exit drives profit to zero, so that each firm will be producing at the minimum efficient scale x_L^*, that is, at the point that minimizes average cost

$$(13) \quad x_L^* = \arg\min_{x_L}\{C_L(x_L)/x_L\}.$$

Let $c_L \equiv C_L(x_L^*)/x_L^*$ denote the unit cost for the low-quality good at this efficient production scale. Then, the competitive equilibrium price for the low-quality good must satisfy[15]

$$(14) \quad p_L^* = c_L.$$

---

[13] The production level of the firm that incurs F individually would differ from that of the firm sharing costs because its cost structure is changed (it incurs a fixed certification cost instead of a unit certification cost).

[14] Note that the underlying presumption of a competitive market is maintained throughout. Taking for given the U-shaped cost structure at the farm level that we have assumed, an alternative hypothesis would be to allow the merger of several farms/plants to be run as a single firm, thereby allowing the fixed cost F to be shared over a larger (private) output that could then be marketed with a firm's own trademark. Such a hypothesis, of course, would lead to an oligopolistic market structure. We rule that out by assumption because such a strategy would raise difficult agency problems of its own. Allen and Leuck (1998) provide a convincing account of why farming has generally not changed from small family-based firms to large corporate firms. Indeed, the reasons that slant the trade-off between moral hazard and specialization in favor of small farming operation are likely to be even more compelling in the context of producing the kind of high-quality products identified by the traditional specifications of GI products.

[15] Here and in what follows, we abstract from the possible "integer" problem (technically, a nonconvexity) that arises when the firms' efficient scale is strictly positive, so that, strictly speaking, the long-run industry supply correspondence is an integer multiple of the efficient scale.

Moschini, Menapace, and Pick *Geographical Indications and the Provision of Quality* 803

As for the high-quality good, whether in equilibrium it will be supplied at all obviously depends on the level of the required certification cost, *vis-à-vis* the consumers' willingness to pay for high quality. In an equilibrium in which the high-quality good is also supplied, for a given price p_H individual producers choose the production level x_H to maximize profit $p_H x_H - C_H(x_H) - \alpha x_H$. The possibility of entry and exit, however, requires the number of producers N_H to adjust to ensure the zero-profit condition (which, in turn, affects the per-unit certification cost α). Hence, a long-run equilibrium needs to specify the equilibrium price p_H^*, the equilibrium production level x_H^* of each high-quality firm, the equilibrium number N_H^* of high-quality firms, and the equilibrium per-unit certification cost α^*. The required conditions are

$$(15) \quad p_H^* = C_H'(x_H^*) + \alpha^*$$

$$(16) \quad p_H^* x_H^* = C_H(x_H^*) + \alpha^* x_H^*$$

$$(17) \quad \alpha^* x_H^* \equiv \frac{F}{N_H^*} + \phi \beta x_H^*$$

$$(18) \quad N_H^* x_H^* = M \left(1 - \frac{p_H^* - p_L^*}{q_H - q_L}\right).$$

Equation (15) is the optimality condition for firm-level profit maximization, whereas equation (16) displays the zero-profit condition due to the assumed free entry/exit possibility. For any given per-unit certification cost, these two equations in conjunction establish that the equilibrium production level x_H^* must satisfy $C_H'(x_H^*) = C_H(x_H^*)/x_H^*$. Hence, as for the low-quality producers, each firm in equilibrium produces at its minimum efficient scale (the point that minimizes average cost). Let $c_H \equiv C_H(x_H^*)/x_H^*$ denote the unit production cost (not including the certification cost) of the high-quality product. Then by using equations (16) and (18), the equilibrium number of high-quality producers N_H^* must satisfy

$$(19) \quad (q_H - q_L)\left(1 - \frac{x_H^* N_H^*}{M}\right)$$

$$= c_H - c_L + \frac{F}{x_H^* N_H^*} + \phi \beta.$$

Thus, the equilibrium condition in (19) equates consumers' demand for the additional quality provided by the high-quality good (relative to the low-quality good), as given by equation (9) derived earlier, with the additional (industry) unit cost of producing this extra quality.[16]

It is useful to note that, at the industry level, the per-unit certification cost is declining in the number of firms that produce the GI product (because of the assumed fixed cost of promotion and certification F). The right-hand-side of equation (19) effectively defines the competitive "industry supply" function for the high-quality good. Under the usual assumption that a firm's individual production is small relative to industry output, the individual firm takes the unit cost as parametrically given. Yet, at the industry level the industry's unit cost of production is decreasing in the number of high-quality producers (i.e., decreasing in industry output). Any given firm exerts a positive externality on all other firms by sharing the fixed certification cost F but does not internalize this benefit in its decision to enter/exit the industry. This positive externality is a source of increasing returns to scale. This fact is bound to have relevant implications for an equilibrium, but it is also the case that such an instance of parametric external economies of scale are quite consistent with the existence of competitive equilibrium (Chipman 1970), although it does give rise to the possibility of multiple equilibria, as discussed next.

Rather than solving for the equilibrium number of firms, one can equivalently solve for the equilibrium aggregate quantity of the high-quality product. Define $X_H^* \equiv x_H^* N_H^*$. Then from equation (19), X_H^* must be a root of the quadratic equation

$$(20)$$
$$\frac{\Delta q}{M}(X_H^*)^2 - (\Delta q - \Delta c - \phi \beta)X_H^* + F = 0$$

where, for notational simplicity, we define $\Delta q \equiv q_H - q_L$ and $\Delta c \equiv c_H - c_L$. The roots of this equation are given by the standard formula:

$$(21)$$
$$\frac{(\Delta q - \Delta c - \phi \beta) \pm \sqrt{(\Delta q - \Delta c - \phi \beta)^2 - 4F\Delta q/M}}{2\Delta q/M}.$$

---

[16] In an equilibrium in which both the high- and the low-quality products are supplied, the zero-profit condition of course ensures that firms are indifferent as to which of the two goods they produce.

804   *August 2008*   *Amer. J. Agr. Econ.*

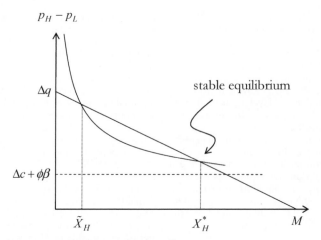

Figure 1. Equilibrium with $F < \bar{F}$

The sign of the discriminant $D \equiv (\Delta q - \Delta c - \phi \beta)^2 - 4F\Delta q/M$ determines whether we have real roots and, if so, whether we have one or two roots. Note that $dD/dF < 0$ so that, given the other parameters of the model, there exists $\bar{F} \equiv (\Delta q - \Delta c - \phi \beta)^2 (M/4\Delta q)$ such that $D = 0$ when $F = \bar{F}$. In such a case, there is only one real root to the equilibrium equation. When $F > \bar{F}$, there are no real roots, that is, certification is just too costly and the competitive equilibrium does not include production of the high-quality good. When $F < \bar{F}$, there are two distinct roots for the quadratic equation, i.e., we have two candidate equilibrium solutions $\tilde{X}_H$ and X_H^*. The case of $F < \bar{F}$ is illustrated in figure 1, where the linear downward-sloping curve represents the consumers' willingness to pay for the "additional" quality, and the nonlinear decreasing curve represents the additional (industry) unit cost of supplying the high-quality good.

To distinguish between the two candidate equilibria when $F < \bar{F}$ we appeal to stability conditions, but the choice of the relevant condition requires some care. Two concepts with a long history, conventionally labeled as Walrasian stability and Marshallian stability, differ in terms of what variable is viewed as changing in a situation of disequilibrium.[17]

Whereas the two stability concepts agree when demand and supply functions have the usual slope, they yield conflicting conclusions when the supply curve is sloping downward (in our case the equilibrium associated with $\tilde{X}_H$ is Walrasian stable, whereas the equilibrium associated with X_H^* is Marshallian stable). An important element, in such a situation, concerns why the supply function is downward sloping. When the negative slope reflects the existence of industry-wide external economies (the so-called forward-falling supply curve, as opposed to the case of individual backward-bending supply curves), Marshallian stability is arguably more appropriate, and indeed supported by strong experimental evidence (Plott and George 1992). Accordingly, in this study we rely on Marshallian stability and thus identify X_H^* as the stable equilibrium of interest. We should also note that the Marshallian stability concept, with its reliance on output adjustment, is appealing in a production context such as ours that allows for firms' entry and exit. For example, if the supply of high-quality product were to be to the left of X_H^*, then high-quality producers would be making positive profits, which would stimulate entry and thus expansion of the high-quality supply.

The competitive stable equilibrium satisfies some intuitive comparative static properties. In particular, for the case of $F < \bar{F}$, $\partial X_i^*/\partial M > 0$, $i = H, L$ (a *ceteris paribus* increase in the market size increases the

---

[17] Walrasian stability posits a price change in response to excess demand at that price, whereas Marshallian stability supposes that quantity adjusts when supply and demand prices differ at that quantity (e.g., Silberberg 1990, chapter 19).

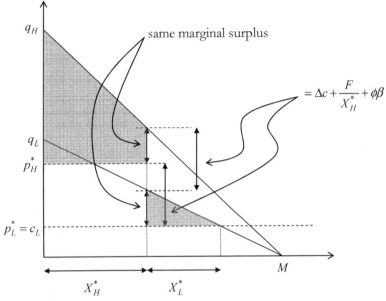

Figure 2. Consumer welfare in equilibrium

equilibrium quantities of both goods);[18] $\partial X_H^*/\partial F < 0 < \partial X_L^*/\partial F$ (e.g., a decrease in the fixed cost of certification F increases the equilibrium level of the high-quality good); $\partial X_H^*/\partial \Delta q > 0 > \partial X_L^*/\partial \Delta q$ (e.g., a larger quality markup for the GI product increases the equilibrium level of this good and decreases that of the low-quality good); and $\partial X_L^*/\partial \beta > 0 > \partial X_H^*/\partial \beta$ (e.g., a larger unit monitoring cost decreases the equilibrium quantity of the high-quality product and increases that of the low-quality product). The impact of Δc is, of course, qualitatively the same as that of the monitoring cost parameter β.

Welfare

One way to articulate the welfare implication of a GI mechanism is to suppose that the high-quality good is technologically feasible but institutional constraints (e.g., lack of legal protection for the right to use the GI) prevent the establishment of a coalition of producers that can credibly deliver the high-

quality good in a competitive fashion. Relaxing such constraints would bring about a new equilibrium with both goods being supplied. Before the introduction of a GI, only the low-quality good is supplied, with the competitive equilibrium condition $p_L^* = c_L$. After the introduction of a GI, consumers who do buy the high-quality good in equilibrium are better off, whereas consumers who continue to buy the low-quality good are unaffected. The welfare properties of the GI equilibrium can be illustrated as in figure 2, which relates the equilibrium outcome that we have characterized to the vertically differentiated demand structure of the model. The downward-sloping lines of figure 2 depict the marginal utility functions of the population of M consumers, as implied by the preference structure in (2) (along with the assumption that the preference parameter θ is uniformly distributed on $[0, 1]$). Total consumer surplus is given by the shaded areas.

Of course, to compute the gain in consumer surplus due to the GI mechanism one needs to consider that consumers who buy the high-quality good, in this equilibrium, would still enjoy some surplus if only the low-quality good were supplied. The difference between the two measures is positive whenever the GI equilibrium entails both types of goods being

---

[18] The comparative statics properties can be used to further illustrate the choice of the relevant stability concept by noting that the Walrasian-stable solution $\bar{X}_H$ would produce rather counterintuitive results. For example, $\partial \bar{X}_H/\partial M < 0$ (an increase in the market size decreases the equilibrium quantity of the high-quality good).

806   *August 2008*   *Amer. J. Agr. Econ.*

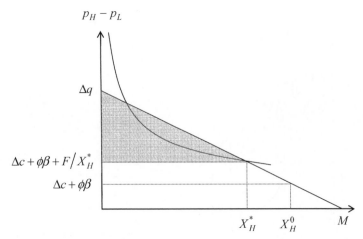

Figure 3. Gains in consumer surplus

supplied. This could be readily established analytically, given the structure of our model, but a graphical illustration can suffice. Specifically, the shaded area in figure 3 illustrates the welfare (consumer) gains from the introduction of a GI by using the demand for the additional quality of equation (9) employed earlier to characterize equilibrium.

In conclusion, the foregoing analysis has established that the following implications are derived from the model. First, there are no profits to producers in equilibrium (as one would expect in a long-run competitive model with entry). Second, consumer surplus is affected by the availability of the high-quality GI product. Any institutional change that makes GIs feasible could results in sizeable benefits to consumers (even without returns to producers). Finally, only consumers of the high-quality good derive additional welfare from the establishment of a GI.

Pareto Efficiency

Not surprisingly, given the existence of (industry) external economies in this setting, the competitive equilibrium fails to deliver the constrained first-best outcome. What we mean by the qualification "constrained" here is the choice X_H^0 that a benevolent social planner would implement, conditional on having to undertake the same certification costs as in competitive equilibrium. To derive such a first-best allocation, denote with ΔW the gain in welfare brought about by production of the

quantity X_H of the high-quality good, relative to zero quantity of this good (the no-credible-certification situation). Given the structure of this model,

$$(22) \quad \Delta W = \Delta q \left[2 - \frac{X_H}{M} \right] \frac{X_H}{2}$$

$$- (\Delta c + \phi \beta) X_H - F.$$

The optimality condition for a maximum of ΔW reduces to equating the marginal benefit of the high-quality product to its marginal cost (provided that $\Delta W \geq 0$), yielding the first-best solution

$$(23) \quad X_H^0 = \frac{(\Delta q - \Delta c - \phi \beta)}{\Delta q} M.$$

It is readily verified that, at X_H^0, $\Delta W \geq 0$ requires the fixed costs of certification to satisfy $F \leq F^0$, where

$$(24) \quad F^0 = \frac{M}{2 \Delta q} (\Delta q - \Delta c - \phi \beta)^2.$$

Hence, if the fixed certification costs are too high (i.e., $F > F^0$), provision of the high-quality good is not desirable. But for $F \leq F^0$ it is socially desirable to supply the high-quality good by the given quality-certification technology, and in that case the optimal provision of the high-quality good ought to be at the efficient level X_H^0 given by equation (23).

It is now apparent that the competitive equilibrium falls short of the first-best allocation in two ways. First, because $F^0 = 2\bar{F} > \tilde{F}$, then if the fixed cost parameter falls in the domain $F \in (\bar{F}, F^0)$, the competitive equilibrium entails $X_H^* = 0$ and yet it is strictly socially desirable to have some high-quality good supplied. Second, even when a competitive equilibrium exists with $X_H^* > 0$ because $F \le \bar{F}$, the competitive equilibrium delivers a suboptimal level of output, that is, $X_H^* < X_H^0$, as can be readily verified by comparing the solution in equation (23) with the larger of the two roots in equation (21) (see figure 3).

The failure of the competitive equilibrium to deliver the first-best outcome could be remedied by simple subsidy policies. In the domain $F \le \bar{F}$, the underprovision of the high-quality good is due to the fact that producers who pay a share F/X_H^* of the fixed costs of certification treat that as a marginal cost of production (and specifically do not internalize the contribution of their decision to enter the industry on the other firms' cost of production). One way to support the first-best outcome via the competitive equilibrium would be to provide a lump-sum subsidy to the producer association (e.g., the consortia) equal to the fixed cost F of quality promotion. Alternatively, the government could subsidize production by a unit subsidy $s \equiv F/X_H^0$, thereby offsetting the portion of certification costs due to existence of a fixed cost of certification.

The suggestion is sometimes offered that, to provide incentive for producer organizations to engage in the type of marketing and promotion required for a successful GI, it might be desirable to grant market power (i.e., the right to control supply) to producer associations in charge of GIs. In the model of Lence et al. (2007) this result arises from the assumption that a fixed cost is required to develop such products (very much as in our setting) and that there are no certification costs per se. Because costless imitation is possible in that context, some degree of supply control may be necessary (depending on the size of the required fixed cost) to encourage producers to develop a geographically differentiated agricultural product. Auriol and Schilizzi (2003), on the other hand, emphasize that certification costs are critical to achieve credibility. Our model explicitly accounts for the monitoring costs needed for credible certification, and in this context we find that market power cannot improve welfare. Specifically, if $F \le \bar{F}$, a competitive equilibrium exists, although it underproduces relative to the first best; granting market power to a club of high-quality producers would not help, and actually would make

matters worse by further reducing the quantity supply away from X_H^* (and raise the thorny question of who, among the *ex ante* identical producers, should benefit from the ensuing noncompetitive profit). Similarly, if $F > \bar{F}$, the competitive equilibrium entails $X_H^* = 0$, but in this parametric case the right to control supply is worthless to a producer association (the industry average cost is everywhere above the relevant consumer demand).

A final observation might be appropriate at this juncture. We have seen that the failure of the competitive equilibrium to deliver the first-best outcome is very much related to the existence of the fixed cost F. Insofar as this type of cost is interpreted as the cost of marketing and promotion, to convince consumers that indeed the GI product in question is a high-quality product, the public authorities' endorsement of the GI system (as with the PDOs in the EU) might be construed as a policy that attempts to lower the firms' fixed cost of promotion (by conveying relevant information to consumers) and thus can contribute to the efficient competitive provision of quality in agricultural markets.[19]

Upward-Sloping Industry Supply

The fact that there are no returns to producers in the foregoing model is predicated on two things: the assumed long-run competitive structure (i.e., with freedom of entry/exit), and the constancy of unit costs (no diseconomies at the industry level). The latter is of course questionable, and in fact we typically think of competitive aggregate supply functions in agricultural markets as being upward-sloping. Upward-sloping supply functions can arise when the inputs used by the industry are in limited supply (e.g., land) and their price is affected by the competitive demand of the industry of interest. One way to make this concept operational is to endogenize the price of the (otherwise homogeneous) input with upward-sloping supply (e.g., Hughes 1980; Lapan and

---

[19] The EU assists member countries in financing measures to promote agricultural products and food, both in the EU internal market and in third countries; see Council Regulation (EC) 2826/2000 and Council Regulation (EC) 2702/1999. These measures include information campaigns on EU quality and labeling systems, in particular on the EU system of PDOs and PGIs, and the EU system of quality wines produced in specified regions. The EU finances 50% of the cost of these measures, the remainder being met by producer organizations and/or member states. The current triennial program targeting the internal market has a total budget of €50.9 million. A third-country program targets the USA, Canada, India, Japan, and China and covers wine, fruit, meat, dairy products, olive oil, and organic product with a total budget of €18.2 million.

808   *August 2008*   *Amer. J. Agr. Econ.*

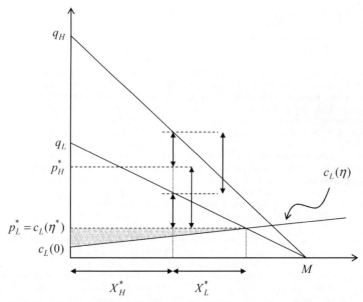

Figure 4. Upward-sloping supply and constant marginal cost of high quality

Moschini 2000). Alternatively, as in Panzar and Willig (1978), one can presume that all firms differ in their endowment of a fixed input (e.g., location or soil quality) that affects production costs and that has no alternative use outside the industry of interest.

Constant Marginal Cost of High Quality

To simplify the approach of Panzar and Willig (1978), suppose that firms either produce at an optimal efficient scale $x > 0$ (for either the low- or high-quality product) or stay out of the market, and that the firms' individual efficiency is indexed by a scalar $\eta \in [0, \infty)$. Specifically, the unit production cost for the low-quality good is written as $c_L(\eta)$, with $c'_L(\eta) \geq 0$. The industry supply curve of the low-quality good, consequently, is upward-sloping, because increased output can only come about by the production of increasingly less efficient firms. The production of the high-quality good requires additional costs, as discussed earlier, and in this case the unit cost of the high-quality good is written as

$$(25) \quad c_H(\eta) \equiv c_L(\eta) + \kappa$$

where κ is a constant. Hence, here we assume that the extra cost required to produce the high-quality good is independent of the efficiency parameter η. With this assumption, the equilibrium condition in equation (20) still applies. Specifically, to illustrate the equilibrium when the parameters of the model are such that both goods are supplied, figure 2 can be adapted as in figure 4.

Note that in this case producers do enjoy a non-zero producer surplus in equilibrium (the shaded area in figure 4). But this return to producers does not depend on the production of the high-quality GI product and would be the same even if only the low-quality good were to be supplied. The area $(p_H^* - p_L^*)X_H^*$ in equilibrium simply accounts for the additional production cost required for the high-quality product, and for the need for marketing and monitoring to deliver a credible GI certification for the high-quality good.

Increasing Marginal Cost of the High-Quality Good

More generally, one could postulate that the supply of additional quality $(q_H - q_L)$ is also upward-sloping. To make the implications of that condition more transparent, suppose that the unit production cost of the low-quality good is the same for all firms and equal to

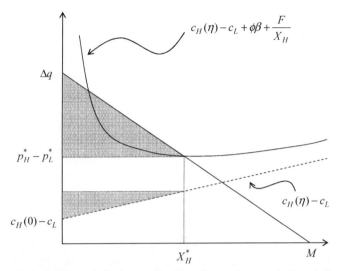

Figure 5. Upward-sloping supply due to increasing marginal cost of high quality

c_L, but the production cost of the high-quality good depends on the firm-specific efficiency parameter η, that is,

$$(26) \quad c_H(\eta) \equiv c_L + \kappa(\eta)$$

where c_L is a constant and $\kappa'(\eta) \geq 0$. In such a case, there are clearly no aggregate producer returns to producing the low-quality good, and the possibility of offering the high-quality good can bring about positive returns to producers (as well as returns to consumers).

The equilibrium determination of the high-quality production in our setting is best illustrated via the demand for quality upgrades used to characterize equilibrium. Thus, figure 3 is adapted as in figure 5, where the shaded areas denote the changes in consumer and producer surpluses brought about by the production of the high-quality GI product. Thus, it is certainly possible for the introduction of GI certification to benefit directly the producers of the high-quality product, consistent with the view of those advocating the use of GIs as a tool for rural development. Our model, however, makes clear that such an outcome is by no mean guaranteed, and it depends critically on the underlying structure of the agricultural production sector. Specifically, what is required is that production of the high-quality

products requires specialized inputs in scarce supply. Exactly how that characterizes real-world GI settings, of course, depends on the particular case at hand.

Conclusions

In this article, we have developed a model that treats GIs as an effective certification tool for high-quality products that attempts to overcome the very real information problem that consumers face when quality cannot be readily ascertained prior to purchasing. This problem is arguably particularly relevant to food products that originate from a fragmented production structure, where individual farmers are too small to muster a credible quality-signaling effort. One of our major points is the competitive structure that justifies the need for producers to act collectively, as with GIs, also carries implications for the market equilibrium that arises with a credible GI mechanism. Thus, our analysis has emphasized the implications of a competitive equilibrium with the production of GI products, including the freedom of entry/exit in the production of the high-quality good. Our model has also maintained an attractive cost structure for the case at hand (higher-quality GI products are costlier to produce than their generic counterparts),

810   *August 2008*   *Amer. J. Agr. Econ.*

and explicitly models the promotion and monitoring activities required to make the GI a credible certification system. In addition, the demand for GI products is modeled in a vertical product differentiation context. This captures the likely heterogeneity of consumer preferences *vis-à-vis* GI products but also permits generic products to interact meaningfully with GI products both in the demand and in the supply side of the model.

The main conclusions of our analysis can be summarized as follows. First, it is possible to have competitive provision of quality in agricultural markets, through certification devices similar to geographical indications. Second, although a competitive equilibrium can exist, because the GI certification entails fixed costs shared by all high-quality producers, there are external economies of scale at the industry level and the competitive equilibrium is not Pareto efficient. In particular, the competitive equilibrium underprovides the high-quality good. The failure of the competitive equilibrium to achieve a constrained first-best outcome can be corrected by policies that subsidize the certification of the high-quality good. Also, we find that measures that allows for market power (i.e., supply control) for GI producer associations in this setting are not desirable. Finally, the implications of entry in a competitive framework are critical. The possibility of entry has been neglected in many previous studies, but, as we have shown, its consideration has important implications for the welfare results that may be deduced. In particular, whereas the resolution of the "lemons" problem that the credible certification through GI makes possible clearly benefits consumers, what it does for the welfare of producers in a competitive setting ultimately depends on the presence of scarce factors that they own.

Whereas it is hoped that this article has contributed to the clarification of some basic economic effects associated with the use of GIs as quality certification devices for agricultural products, the analysis that we have proffered has some limitations. In particular, we have analyzed the case of a closed economy and considered the role of one GI system in isolation. Among the interesting additional questions that arise, one may want to consider the interaction and competition of several GIs, possibly from different geographic regions in the same country/jurisdiction, and/or the interaction of GIs and other quality labeling (e.g., organic food labels), including the issue

of possible excessive label proliferation. Also, as noted earlier, GIs are of interest in the ongoing WTO negotiation and their implementation is a question of intense disagreement among countries (Fink and Maskus 2006). Developed countries are themselves divided on this topic, with a simmering transatlantic dispute rooted in contrasting approaches to trade, IP, and agricultural policy (Josling 2006). A variety of perspectives are invoked as germane in this setting, ranging from familiar economic arguments for IP protection (Moschini 2004) to the view of GIs as a tool to safeguard cultural heritage, and to foster the preservation of traditional methods of production (Broude 2005). Thus, it may be desirable to explore the international trade implications of the expanding reach of GIs, addressing explicitly the current WTO negotiation. Such desirable extensions, which are the object of current research, should benefit from the benchmark analysis presented in this article.

[Received June 2007;
accepted December 2007.]

References

Akerlof, G.A. 1970. "The Market for Lemons: Quality Uncertainty and the Market Mechanism." *Quarterly Journal of Economics* 84:488–500.

Allen, D.W., and D. Leuck. 1998. "The Nature of the Farm." *Journal of Law and Economics* 41:343–86.

Anania G., and R. Nisticò. 2004. "Public Regulation as a Substitute for Trust in Quality Food Markets: What if the Trust Substitute cannot be Fully Trusted?" *Journal of Institutional and Theoretical Economics* 160:681–701.

Auriol, E., and S. Schilizzi. 2003. "Quality Signaling through Certification. Theory and an Application to Agricultural Seed Market." IDEI Working Paper No. 165.

Benitez, D., Z. Bouamra-Mechemache, and J. Chaaban. 2005 "Public Labeling Revisited: The Role of Technological Constraints Under Protected Designation of Origin." Working Paper, University of Toulouse, Paris.

Broude, T. 2005. "Culture, Trade and Additional Protection for Geographical Indications." *Bridges* 9(9):20–22.

Carbone, A. 2003. "The Role of Designation of Origin in the Italian Food System." In S. Gatti, E. Giraud-Héraud, and S. Mili, eds. *Wine in the Old World: New Risks and Opportunities,* p. 29–39. Franco Angeli: Milan, Italy.

Moschini, Menapace, and Pick *Geographical Indications and the Provision of Quality* 811

Chipman, J.S. 1970. "External Economies of Scale and Competitive Equilibrium." *Quarterly Journal of Economics* 84(3):347–85.

Clemens R. 2002. "Why Can't Vidalia Onion Be Grown in Iowa? Developing a Branded Agricultural Product." MATRIC Briefing Paper 02-MBF.

Crespi, J.M., and R.J. Sexton. 2003. "Competition, US Farmer Cooperatives and Marketing Orders." English translation of: "Concurrence, coopératives de producteurs et Marketing Orders aux Etats-Unis." *Économie Rurale* (277/278):135–51.

de Roest, K., and A. Menghi. 2000. "Reconsidering 'Traditional' Food: The Case of Parmigiano Reggiano Cheese." *Sociologia Ruralis* 40(4):439–51.

European Commission. 2002. "Ex-post Evaluation of the Common Market Organization for Wine." Final Report, European Commission DG-Agriculture.

——. 2006. "Wine Common Market Organization." Working Paper, European Commission, Directorate-General for Agriculture and Rural Development.

——. 2007. "European Policy for Quality Agricultural Products." Fact Sheet of the European Commission, Directorate-General for Agriculture and Rural Development.

Fink, C., and K. Maskus. 2006. "The Debate on Geographical Indications in the WTO." In R. Newfarmer, ed. *Trade, Doha, and Development: A Window into the Issues*, pp. 201–211. Washington DC: World Bank.

Gardner, B. 2003. "U.S. Food Quality Standards: Fix for Market Failure or Costly Anachronism?" *American Journal of Agricultural Economics* 85:725–30.

Hayes, D., S.H. Lence, and A. Stoppa. 2004. "Farmer-Owned Brands?" *Agribusiness* 20(3): 269–85.

Hughes, J.P. 1980. "The Comparative Statics of the Competitive, Increasing-Cost Industry." *American Economic Review* 70(3): 518–21.

ISMEA. 2005. *I vini DOCG, DOC e IGT. Aspetti normativi, economici e di mercato*, Istituto di Servizi per il Mercato Agricolo Alimentare, Rome, Italy.

Josling, T. 2006. "The War on Terroir: Geographical Indications as a Transatlantic Trade Conflict." *Journal of Agricultural Economics* 57: 337–63.

Klein, B., and K.B. Leffler. 1981. "The Role of Marker Forces in Assuring Contractual Performance." *Journal of Political Economy* 89(4):615–41.

Landes, W.M., and R.A. Posner. 1987. "Trademarks Law: An Economic Perspective." *Journal of Law and Economics* 30:265–309.

Langinier, C., and B. Babcock. 2006. "Agricultural Production Clubs: Viability and Welfare Implications." CARD Working Paper 06-WP 431.

Lapan, H., and G. Moschini. 2000. "Incomplete Adoption of a Superior Innovation." *Economica* 67:525–42.

——. 2007. "Grading, Minimum Quality Standards, and the Labeling of Genetically Modified Products." *American Journal of Agricultural Economics* 89:769–83.

Lence, S.H., S. Marette, D. Hayes, and W. Foster. 2007. "Collective Marketing Arrangements for Geographically Differentiated Agricultural Products: Welfare Impacts and Policy Implications." *American Journal of Agricultural Economics* 89:947–63.

Mas-Colell, A., M.D. Whinston, and J.R. Green. 1995. *Microeconomic Theory*. New York: Oxford University Press.

Moschini, G. 2004. "Intellectual Property Rights and the World Trade Organization: Retrospect and Prospects." In G. Anania, M. Bohman, C. Carter, and A. McCalla, eds. *Agricultural Policy Reform and the WTO: Where Are We Heading?* pp. 474–511. Cheltenham, UK: Edward Elgar.

Mussa, M., and S. Rosen. 1978. "Monopoly and Product Quality." *Journal of Economic Theory* 18(2):301–17.

Nomisma. 2001. *Prodotti tipici e sviluppo locale: Il ruolo delle produzioni di qualità nel futuro dell'agricoltura italiana*, VIII Rapporto Nomisma sull'agricoltura italiana, Edizioni Il Sole 24 ore, Milano, Italy.

OECD. 2000. "Appellations of Origin and Geographical Indications in OECD Member Countries: Economic and Legal Implications." Working Paper COM/AGR/APM/TD/WP(2000)15/FINAL, Organization for Economic Cooperation and Development, Paris.

Panzar, J.C., and R.D. Willig. 1978. "On the Comparative Statics of a Competitive Industry with Inframarginal Firms." *American Economic Review* 68(3):474–8.

Plott, C.R., and G. George. 1992. "Marshallian vs. Walrasian Stability in an Experimental Market." *Economic Journal* 102:437–60.

Rangnekar, D. 2004. *The Socio-Economics of Geographical Indications*, UNCTAD-ICTSD Project on IPRs and Sustainable Development, Issue Paper No. 8.

Rasmussen, E. 2007. *Games and Information: An Introduction to Game Theory*, 4th ed. Malden, MA: Blackwell Publishing.

Shapiro, C. 1983. "Premiums for High Quality Products as Returns to Reputation." *Quarterly Journal of Economics* 98(4):659–80.

Silberberg, E. 1990. *The Structure of Economics,* 2nd ed. New York: McGraw-Hill.

USPTO. 2007. "Geographical Indication Protection in the United States." United States Patent and Trademark Office, undated document accessed on May 2007. Available at http://www.uspto.gov/web/offices/dcom/olia/globalip/pdf/gi_system.pdf

Zago, M.A., and D. Pick. 2004. "Labeling Policies in Food Markets: Private Incentives, Public Intervention, and Welfare Effects." *Journal of Agricultural and Resource Economics* 29(1):150–65.

[15]

Volume 10 Number 1 2009/p. 111-130

esteyjournal.com

The Estey Centre Journal of
International Law
and Trade Policy

European Food Quality Policy: The Importance of Geographical Indications, Organic Certification and Food Quality Assurance Schemes in European Countries

Tilman Becker

Professor, Institute for Agricultural Policy and Markets, University of Hohenheim, Germany[1]

In the early 1990s reform of the EU's Common Agricultural Policy led to a change in emphasis away from price supports into policies to promote rural development, in part through improvements to food quality. Geographic indicators are only one of a range of EU policies designed to foster these goals. Geographic indicators are put within the context of the wider quality enhancement policies that include quality assurance schemes and organic production. There appears to be considerable regional differences within the EU when it comes to the use of the various quality-enhancing policies available. The member states of the EU can be grouped into four different clusters, each characterized by a different quality policy strategy.

Keywords: European Union, food quality, geographic indicators, regional differences

Editorial Office: 410 22nd St. E., Suite 820, Saskatoon, SK, Canada, S7K 5T6.
Phone (306) 244-4800; Fax (306) 244-7839; email: kerr.w@esteycentre.com

T. Becker

Introduction

The interest of producers, researchers, politicians and, last but not least, consumers in geographical indications has been increasing in recent decades. Geographical indications have been prominent in the Mediterranean countries for a long time. In 1992, the EU introduced a system of protection of geographical indications similar to the system already available in France. So far, the focus of the existing research in this area has been on several specific aspects of geographical indications: they have been analyzed from a marketing perspective, a legal or political and a producer perspective. One focus of the present article is the number of products registered as either Protected Designation of Origin (PDO) or Protected Geographical Indication (PGI) in the countries of the European Union. This has been analyzed already by Becker (2006); however, for a complete picture of the quality policies in the different member states, the number of quality assurance systems and the importance of organic production schemes should be examined further. Completing the analysis in this way results in some very interesting insights. To my knowledge, these insights are not available in the literature on geographical indications, quality assurance and organic production. These areas of research have been examined separately up to now. Hence, the objective of this article is to broaden the view by examining these cornerstones of EU food quality policy in an integrated fashion.

European Food Quality Policy

The reform of agricultural policy in 1992 shifted the focus of the EU's agricultural policy from price support to rural development, from the so-called first pillar of the Common Agricultural Policy (CAP) to the second pillar. Furthermore, the policy orientation changed from increasing food quantity to increasing food quality. Three regulations were adopted in 1991 and 1992, namely Regulation (EEC) No. 2081/92 on the protection of geographical indications and designations of origin for agricultural products and foodstuffs, Regulation (EEC) No. 2082/92 on certificates of specific character for agricultural products and foodstuffs, and Regulation (EEC) No. 2092/91 on organic production of agricultural products (Becker, 2000).

The objective of Regulation (EEC) No. 2081/92 is the protection of geographical indications as names for food products. The aim of Regulation (EEC) No. 2082/92 is the protection of traditional recipes for food products, and the objective of Regulation (EEC) No. 2092/91 is to explicitly define the objectives, principles and rules applicable to organic production.

Products protected by these EU quality schemes have a privileged position, not only with respect to legal protection, but also with respect to EU financial aid and the possibility of member state financial aid for their promotion.

T. Becker

Since the foundation of the CAP, EU member states have made efforts to support the promotion of national agricultural products through state aid. However, state aid might not be in accordance with the objectives of the Treaty of Rome. Two cases – Case 249/81, "Buy Irish", and Case 222/82, "Apple and Pear Development Council" – have been brought to the European Court of Justice by the European Commission, and the court concluded that state aid for promoting and advertising national food products through the means of stressing the national origin is against the treaty. The general prohibition on state aid contained in Article 87 of the treaty is applicable if the publicly funded promotion and advertising distorts or threatens to distort competition by favouring certain undertakings or the production of certain goods. Where such publicly funded promotion activities refer to the national or regional origin of the products concerned, they clearly favour certain products and therefore Article 87 may apply. As a reaction to these two cases, the European Commission laid down European Community guidelines for state aid to the agricultural sector in 1986. For the time being, the "Community guidelines for State aid for advertising of products listed in Annex I to the EC Treaty and of certain non–Annex I products (2001/C 252/03)" holds. In these guidelines the distinction is made between negative and positive criteria. National aid for promotion and advertising campaigns infringing on Article 28 of the treaty, which prohibits quantitative restrictions on imports and all measures having equivalent effects between member states, cannot in any circumstances be considered compatible with the common market within the meaning of Article 87 of the treaty. However, the situation is regarded as different in the case of products which can be clearly distinguished from other products that fall within the same category through specific characteristics concerning the raw materials used, the composition of the finished products or the production and processing methods used. This latter is regarded as being the case for products covered by Council Regulation (EEC) No. 2081/92 and Regulation (EEC) No. 2082/92 and for products covered by Regulation (EEC) No. 2092/91 (European Commission, 2001).

Regulation (EEC) No. 2081/92 distinguishes between two categories of protected names: designations of origin and geographical indications. The distinction between these two categories depends on how closely the product is linked to the specific geographical area whose name it bears. The regulation does not apply to wine sector products, except wine vinegars, or to spirit drinks. The protection of geographical indications for wine products is regulated in Regulation (EC) No. 1493/1999 on the common organisation of the market in wine.

To be eligible to use a Protected Designation of Origin(PDO), a product must meet two conditions:

- The quality or characteristics of the product must be essentially or exclusively due to the particular geographical environment of the place of origin, where the

T. Becker

geographical environment is understood to include inherent natural and human factors such as climate, soil quality and local know-how.

• The production and processing of the raw materials, up to the stage of the finished product, must take place in the defined geographical area whose name the product bears. There must therefore be an objective and very close link between the features of the product and its geographical origin.

The Protected Geographical Indication (PGI) also designates products attached to the region whose name they bear, but the link is of a different nature from that existing between a product with a PDO and its geographical area or origin. To be eligible to use a PGI a product must meet two conditions:

• It must have been produced in the geographical area whose name it bears. Unlike the protected designation of origin, it is sufficient that one of the stages of production has taken place in the defined area. For example, the raw materials used in production may come from another region.

• There must also be a link between the product and the area the product is named after. However, this feature does not have to be essential or exclusive as in the case of the protected designation of origin. It is sufficient that a specific quality, reputation or other characteristic is attributable to the geographical origin. Under the rules for PGIs, the link may simply consist of the reputation of the product, if it owes its reputation to its geographical origin. In such a case, actual characteristics of the product are not the determining factor for registration. It is enough for the name of the product to enjoy an individual reputation that is based specifically on its origin at the time the application for registration is lodged.

A system much less used is the one for traditional specialities offered under Regulation (EEC) No. 2082/92, Traditional Specialties Guaranteed (TSG). The purpose of this regulation is to take advantage of the typical features of products by granting a certificate of specific character. The regulation thus lays down two conditions for registration of a product name: the product must possess features that distinguish it from other products, and it must be a traditional product. That these conditions have been met must be proven in the documents submitted for registration.

In June 1991, the Council of the European Union adopted Regulation (EEC) No. 2092/91 on organic production of agricultural products, and indications referring thereto on agricultural products and foodstuffs. In adopting Regulation No. 2092/91, the council created a European Community framework defining in detail the requirements for agricultural products or foodstuffs that bear a reference to organic production methods. These rules are quite complex; not only do they define a method of agricultural production for crops and livestock, they also regulate the labeling, processing, inspection and marketing of organic products within the European

T. Becker

Community and the import of organic products from non-member countries. The regulation has been amended on several occasions, particularly in 1999, when the council extended its scope to cover organic livestock production. The rules were introduced as part of the reform of the CAP. By the late 1980s, the CAP had broadly achieved its original aim of generating agricultural productivity gains so as to make the European Community largely self-sufficient with regard to its food supply. The policy therefore moved towards other aims, not only to rural development and to the promotion of quality products, but also to the integration of environmental conservation into agriculture. These objectives involved major development potential for the organic farming sector, which had previously been marginal. If a product satisfies the requirements set out under Regulation (EEC) No. 2092/91, the EC organic production logo may be used in the labeling, presentation and advertising of the product. Organic production is regarded as an overall system of farm management and food production that combines best environmental practices, a high level of biodiversity, the preservation of natural resources, the application of high animal welfare standards and a production method in line with the preference of certain consumers for products produced using natural substances and processes. The organic production method is regarded as playing a dual societal role, where on the one hand it provides for a specific market, responding to a consumer demand for quality products, and on the other hand it delivers public goods, contributing to the protection of the environment and animal welfare as well as to rural development.

Community legislation merely defines a framework, an instrument producers may or may not use, where much of the responsibility is placed on the member states and producers (European Commission, 2004). In 2006, Council Regulation (EC) No. 509/2006 and Council Regulation No. 510/2006 replaced Regulation (EEC) No. 2082/92, and Regulation (EEC) No. 2081/92, respectively.

If a product is registered as PDO, PGI or TSG, the name of the product is protected against use by other producers that are not located in the geographic area. We can distinguish between statements of a certain generic nature (e.g., Emmentaler), explicit statements of geographical origin (e.g., from Bavaria), privately owned trademarks with names similar to a geographical area (e.g., Capri), privately owned trademarks where name and origin are linked together (e.g., Warsteiner), collectively owned trademarks with reference to the region, EU-protected collectively owned trademarks with reference to the region and weak links between product quality and geographical origin (PGI), and EU-protected collectively owned trademarks with reference to the region and strong links between product quality and geographical origin (PDO). The benefit for a farmer of a product registered as either PDO or PGI is the exclusive right to use of the product name. If a product is registered, the legal protection of the name is much more comprehensive than the protection for a brand name. Not only is the name protected against unfair competition, but also the mere use of the name in any other commercial context is prohibited. It is even forbidden for another product to claim that this product is produced according to the recipe of the protected product, even if this is the case. The rationale behind the granting of this very high level of legal protection to the names of registered products is the effort to contribute to rural development by erecting through law a kind of "geographical name monopoly".

However, the geographical name monopoly alone will not lead to a monopoly on profits unless it is accompanied by a corresponding product quality which differs or is perceived by consumers to differ from comparable products. In the case of the products protected by the EU system, the product specification is determined by the producer consortium registering the product, while the product specification for organic products is determined in the respective EU regulation.

The Importance of Registered Traditional Specialties in EU Member States

The number of products registered as TSGs in the EU is rather marginal. Only 16 products are thus registered. Registration as a TSG does not seem to be very attractive from the point of view of producers. The main advantage of this system is that a product bearing a certain name has to be produced according to a certain recipe.

In the case of Belgium, all 5 products registered as TSGs belong to the category beer. Italy has registered the cheese - Mozarella, and the Netherlands and Sweden each have registered a cheese as well. Further, Sweden has registered a meat-based product. Spain has registered Jamon Serrano, a meat-based product, a milk product and a bakery product. The United Kingdom has registered a fresh meat product. Finland has registered two bakery products and a beer.

Though the name of a product that is registered as a TSG is protected from misuse by products with another recipe, producers do not get the level of monopoly power as in the case of a PGI. It thus becomes obvious why so few products have been registered under this registration system.

The Importance of Collective Quality Marks in EU Member States

Collective quality marks may be regarded as possible candidates for PDO or PGI registration, and as such the number of collective quality marks in a country shows the potential for PDO or PGI registrations.

T. Becker

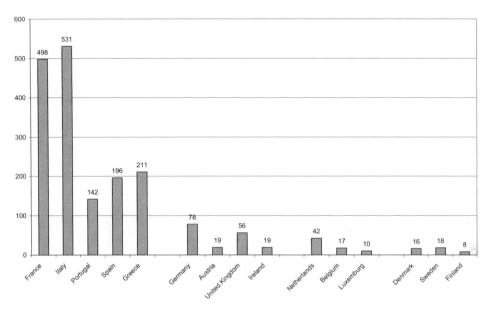

Source: own calculations according to Peri and Gaeta (1997).

Figure 1 Number of collective quality marks in 1996

As figure one shows, a large number of collective quality marks existed in Italy and France in 1996, whereas not so many existed in Greece, Spain and Portugal. There were only a few collective quality marks out on the market in Germany, Austria, the United Kingdom and Ireland. In the BeNeLux countries and the Scandinavian countries even fewer collective quality marks existed.

Italy and France in particular seem to have a high potential for registration of geographical indications. In these countries producers are already familiar with collective quality marks. The concept of collective quality marks seems to be well known in these countries, and the producers in general are well prepared for building up a consortium and registering a geographical indication.

The Importance of Products with Registered Geographical Indications in EU Member States

While TSGs have little importance, the same does not hold for origin-labeled products. The number of origin-labeled products increased from 469 in 1999 to 706 in 2007 and might reach 904 in 2010. (If mineral water is included, 31 more registered products will have to be added. Only Germany has registered mineral water, and in 2003 Regulation (EEC) No. 2081/92 was amended by Regulation (EEC)

T. Becker

692/2003 to include vinegar and exclude mineral water from the scope of the regulation. A transition period until the 31st of December 2013 is foreseen, after which mineral water names will no longer be on the register as specified in Article 6 of Regulation (EEC) No. 2081/92.)

A high number of applications for registration have been submitted. On average, it takes about three years from the time of the original submission of an application to the final registration. Therefore, the number of registrations in 2010 is estimated here by the number of applications submitted for registration in 2007.

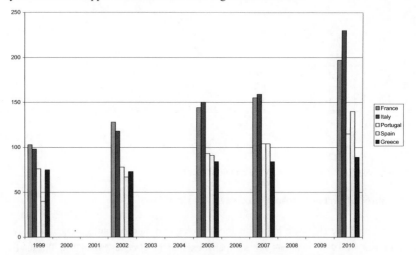

Source: own calculations using data from http://europa.eu.int/comm/dg06/qual (11/9/1999)
http://europa.eu.int/comm/agriculture/foodqual/quali1_de.htm (dg06/qua (11/24/2002)
http://europa.eu.int/comm/agriculture/foodqual/quali1_de.htm (dg06/qual (09/30/2005)
http://ec.europa.eu/ agriculture/qual/en/1bbab_en.htm (09/24/2007)

Figure 2 Number of products registered as PDO and PGI in France, Italy, Portugal, Spain and Greece

In 1999 and 2002, France was the country with the highest number of products registered. The protection of origin for foodstuffs has a long tradition in France and can be traced back to Roquefort cheese in the 14th century (OECD, 2000). The responsibility for the registration of origin labels was regarded as a task for states already in 1905. In 1919, a law on origin labeling followed. The *Appellation d'Origine Controlée* for wine and spirits was introduced by law in 1935, and an institution was founded to determine the respective production rules (OECD, 2000). This institution became the *Institut National des Appellations d'Origine* (INAO), which is still responsible for registration. In 2005, roughly 18 percent of the cheese

T. Becker

produced in France had an origin registration, and the turnover of registered-origin milk products is estimated to account for €2 billion (Becker, 2006).

In Italy, origin-labeled foods do not have such a long tradition as in France. Nevertheless, Italy has used the high potential to increase producer revenues through origin labeling. There were 26 cheeses and 2 ham products certified before 1992. The number of registered products in 2007 already totalled 159.

In Portugal, Spain and Greece, the number of products registered is lower than in Italy and France, but still higher than in the other European Union countries. A high number of meat products is registered in Portugal, and a high number of fruit and vegetable products are registered in Spain and Greece. In general, the product category with the highest number of registered products is the category cheese (Becker, 2006).

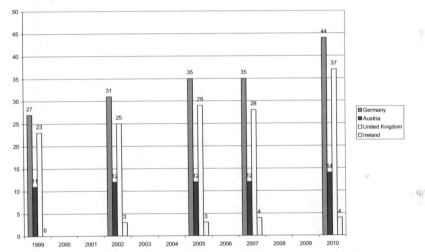

Source: own calculations using data from http://europa.eu.int/comm/dg06/qual (11/9/1999)
http://europa.eu.int/comm/agriculture/foodqual/quali1_de.htm (dg06/qua (11/24/2002)
http://europa.eu.int/comm/agriculture/foodqual/quali1_de.htm (dg06/qual (09/30/2005)
http://ec.europa.eu/ agriculture/qual/en/1bbab_en.htm (09/24/2007)

Figure 3 Number of products registered as PDO and PGI in Germany, Austria, the United Kingdom and Ireland

The second group of countries consists of Germany, Austria, the United Kingdom and Ireland. The number of products registered in these countries is far lower than in the Mediterranean countries, including Portugal. In the case of Germany, 31 mineral waters are registered, but they are not included here because mineral water will be excluded from the scope of the regulation after a transition period. In the United Kingdom, many cheese products are registered, and in Germany, many beer products are registered. If these beverages were excluded, Germany would have even fewer

T. Becker

products registered than the United Kingdom. Austria and Ireland have only a few products registered. The protection of origin labelling does not have a long tradition in Germany, Austria, the United Kingdom or Ireland. In these countries origin is not regarded as important for the quality of the product, as it is in the Mediterranean countries.

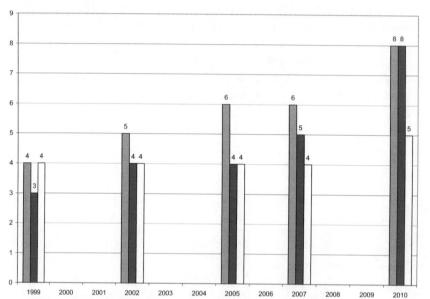

Source: own calculations using data from http://europa.eu.int/comm/dg06/qual (11/9/1999)
http://europa.eu.int/comm/agriculture/foodqual/quali1_de.htm (dg06/qua (11/24/2002)
http://europa.eu.int/comm/agriculture/foodqual/quali1_de.htm (dg06/qual (09/30/2005)
http://ec.europa.eu/ agriculture/qual/en/1bbab_en.htm (09/24/2007)

Figure 4 Number of products registered as PDO and PGI in Belgium, the Netherlands and Luxembourg

In the BeNeLux countries, only a few products are registered as PDO or PGI, and there are few efforts to alter this situation.

T. Becker

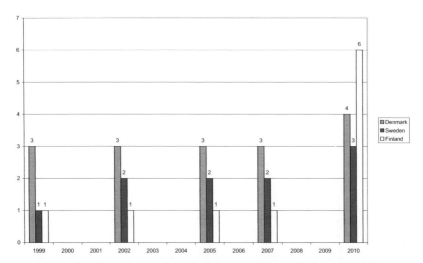

Source: own calculations using data from http://europa.eu.int/comm/dg06/qual (11/9/1999)
http://europa.eu.int/comm/agriculture/foodqual/quali1_de.htm (dg06/qua (11/24/2002)
http://europa.eu.int/comm/agriculture/foodqual/quali1_de.htm (dg06/qual (09/30/2005)
http://ec.europa.eu/ agriculture/qual/en/1bbab_en.htm (09/24/2007)

Figure 5 Number of products registered as PDO and PGI in the Scandinavian
countries

In the Scandinavian countries, very few products are registered either as PDO or
PGI. However, Finland has recently undertaken great efforts to increase the number of
registered PDO and PGI products.

T. Becker

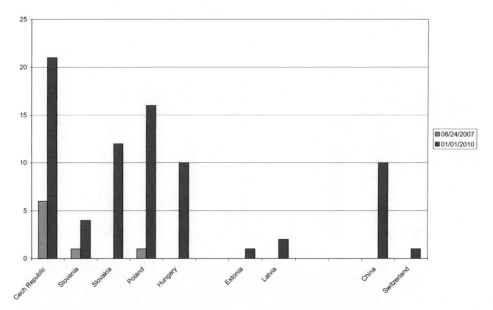

Source: own calculations using data from http://europa.eu.int/comm/dg06/qual (11/9/1999)
http://europa.eu.int/comm/agriculture/foodqual/quali1_de.htm (dg06/qua (11/24/2002)
http://europa.eu.int/comm/agriculture/foodqual/quali1_de.htm (dg06/qual (09/30/2005)
http://ec.europa.eu/ agriculture/qual/en/1bbab_en.htm (09/24/2007)

Figure 6 Number of products registered as PDO and PGI in the Eastern
European and other countries

In particular for the new member states in Eastern Europe, the EU system of origin-labeled products seems to offer opportunities. While only a few products have been registered so far, the number of applications from these countries is high. The Czech Republic has already registered 6 products and has submitted applications for 21. These products mainly belong to the categories of beer and pastries. Slovenia has registered a product in the category oil and fats, and Poland a cheese product.

Australia and the United States have brought complaints to the World Trade Organization against the European Communities' protection of trademarks and geographical indications for agricultural products and foodstuffs (DS174 and DS290, respectively). The Agreement on Trade-Related Aspects of Intellectual Property Rights (TRIPS) contains detailed provisions on the availability, acquisition, scope, maintenance and enforcement of intellectual property rights. On March 15th, 2005, the final report of the WTO panel on these complaints was published: the EU protection should be open to the geographical indications of third countries, where these are protected in their country of origin; the registration procedure should enable

T. Becker

any natural or legal person having a legitimate interest in a member state or a third country to exercise their rights by notifying their objections. The European Commission responded to the results of the WTO panel, and Council Regulation (EC) No. 510/2006 replaced Regulation (EEC) No. 2081/92 (Knaak, 2006).

In September 2007, Café de Colombia was the first non-European product registered. China and Switzerland have already submitted applications for the registration of products as well.

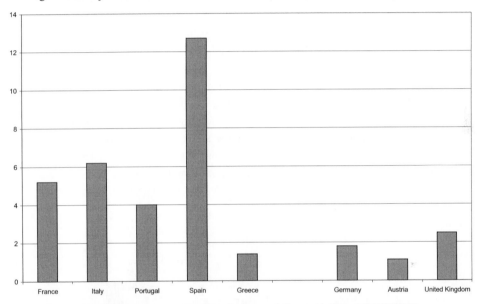

Source: own calculations using data from http://europa.eu.int/comm/dg06/qual (11/09/1999), http://ec.europa.eu/ agriculture/qual/en/1bbab_en.htm (09/24/2007)

Figure 7 Average yearly growth rate in registered products from 1999 to 2007 (%)

The EU system of geographical indications offers a very attractive opportunity not only to producers with regard to the high level of legal protection of the geographical indication, but also from the state-aid perspective. France has already been responsive to these opportunities for a long time. But other countries are currently catching up. Over the last ten years, Spain had the highest average yearly growth rate in the registration of products; during the last few years, the number of product registrations increased by 13 percent per year. While France in prior years had the highest number of registrations, Italy has caught up and left France behind. Furthermore, Italy has put great effort into registering products very recently. The average yearly growth rate was already rather high in Italy over the last ten years. Portugal also has undertaken a great effort in order to foster registered PDOs and PGIs during the last ten years. In

T. Becker

Germany, Austria and the United Kingdom, some attempts have been made in the past to increase the number of products registered. In the case of Germany, we know for sure that there are hundreds of products that are well suited to be registered either as PDO or PGI. But this potential has not been realized by the German ministries as of yet, and great obstacles are presented by the political focus on the quality marks provided by the federal states.

The Importance of Food Quality Assurance Schemes in EU Member States

Since the 1990s, quality assurance schemes have become prominent – not only in politics, but also in the agriculture and food industry as the focus has shifted from quantity to quality. This shift was supported by the abundant supply of agricultural products and the several food scares that occurred during the 1990s. The introduction of food quality assurance systems is considered one possible answer to food safety concerns. Again, this shift from emphasis on quantity to emphasis on quality was supported by political measures. Traceability was first required by law for beef and was extended to all food products with Regulation (EC) No. 178/2002. The general principles and requirements of food law were specified in Regulation 178/2002, where the European Food Safety Authority was established and procedures in matters of food safety were laid down.

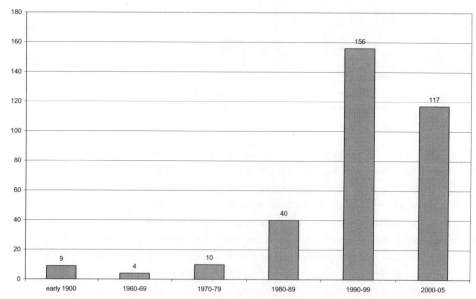

Source:http://foodqualityschemes.jrc.es/en/documents/Foodqualityconference_050207_giray.pd f (08/25/2007)

Figure 8 Number of food quality assurance schemes by initial year

T. Becker

So far, the focus of this article has been on the number of products registered either as PDO or PGI in the countries of Europe. However, for a complete picture of the quality policies in the different member states, the number of quality assurance systems should also be examined. Extending the analysis in this respect will provide some very interesting results.

These two concepts are considered jointly because under both schemes products are exempted from the general prohibition of state aid to promote the production of agricultural products in cases where these products meet standards or specifications that are clearly higher or more specific than those determined by the relevant European Community or national legislation.

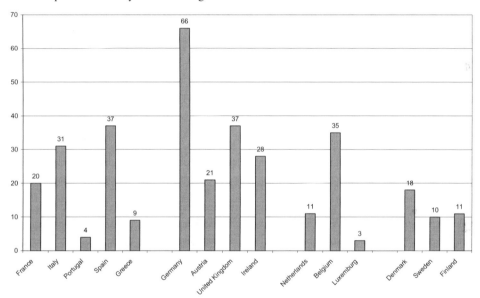

Source: own calculations using data from "Structured inventory of existing food quality assurance schemes within the EU-25" (DG JRC/IPTS), 30 November 2006, http://foodqualityschemes.jrc.es/en/outputs.html (08/25/2007)

Figure 9 Number of food quality assurance schemes by country

The number of quality assurance schemes differs across the EU member states. Germany has the highest number, followed by Spain, the United Kingdom and Belgium. The high number of quality assurance schemes in these countries, in particular in Germany, the United Kingdom and Belgium, may be regarded as indicative of endeavours by the food sector to prevent food scares. In these countries consumers are very sensitive to food scares, not least due to the experience of the BSE crisis.

T. Becker

It is very interesting to note that in some of the countries that have a low number of products registered as either PDO or PGI, the number of quality assurance schemes is rather high. This holds true not only for Germany, Austria, the United Kingdom and Ireland, but for the BeNeLux countries as well, especially Belgium.

The Importance of Organic Production in EU Member States

The picture is not complete without looking at organic production, another cornerstone of EU quality policy. The share of organic farming area as a portion of total utilized agricultural area gives some indication of the importance of its role as a cornerstone of quality policy.

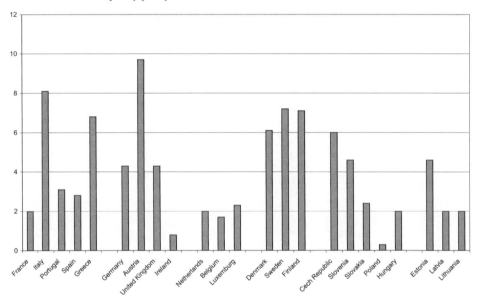

Source: own calculations using data from
http://ec.europa.eu/agriculture/qual/organic/facts_en.pdf (11/25/2007)

Figure 10 Share of organic farming area as a percentage of utilized agricultural area in 2003

Austria exhibits the highest relative share of organic farming area among all European countries. It is interesting to note that the organic farming area shares are rather high in the Scandinavian countries, too. Italy is important not only with respect to PDO and PGI products, but with respect to organic farming area as well.

T. Becker

Summary and Conclusions

The member states of the EU have a number of options when it comes food quality policies. These are

- collective quality marks,
- geographical indicators (PDOs/PGIs),
- food quality assurance schemes (FQASs),
- organic production.

These are the cornerstones of EU food quality policy. The member states have gone different ways, due to historical reasons and due to differential consumer behaviour.

France has a high number of collective quality marks, a high number of PDO/PGI products, an organic agriculture area ranging below average and a medium number of FQASs. France belongs to the group of countries that are clearly PDO/PGI oriented.

In Italy, we find a high number of collective quality marks, a high number of PDO/PGI products, a medium number of FQASs and a high proportion agricultural area devoted to organic farming. Italy is oriented to very high and diversified quality, with a focus on organic production and PDO/PGI registration. With respect to PDO/PGI products, Italy is the leading European country and will continue to lead in the future.

In Portugal, we find a moderate number of collective quality marks, a high number and medium growth rate of PDO/PGI products, a low number of FQASs and a medium percentage of agricultural land devoted to organic farming. Thus, Portugal seems to be PDO/PGI oriented.

In Spain, a moderate number of collective quality marks exists, and we find a moderate to high number of PDO/PGI products, with the growth rates for all of these very high. Spain seems to catch up with the other Mediterranean countries with respect to PDO/PGI products. The number of FQASs is rather high in Spain, and the organic share of agricultural land is average. Spain is clearly PDO/PGI oriented, with some emphasis on FQASs.

In Greece, the number of collective quality marks is moderate, but the number of PDO/PGI products is moderate to high. There is a medium growth rate of PDO/PGI registrations. The number of FQASs is rather low, but the percentage of agricultural land devoted to organic farming is high. Greece has a moderate PDO/PGI orientation and a high organic orientation.

In Germany, the number of collective quality marks is rather low, the number and growth rate of PDO/PGI products are low and the number of FQASs is very high. The percentage of agricultural area that is organic is in the average range. In the case of Germany we have a clear orientation towards food quality assurance schemes.

T. Becker

In Austria, the number of collective quality marks is low and the number and growth rate of PDO/PGI products are moderate to low, but the percentage of agricultural area that is organic is high. The number of FQASs is medial. We have a clear organic-farming orientation in the case of Austria.

In the United Kingdom, the number of collective quality marks is low, the number and growth rate of PDO/PGI products are moderate to low, the percentage of agricultural area that is organic is medial and the number of FQASs is high. Here we have a clear orientation towards food quality assurance schemes.

In Ireland, there are very few collective quality marks, very few PDO/PGI products, a very low proportion of agricultural area devoted to organic farming and a high number of FQASs. Ireland is similar to the United Kingdom and Germany in that it is oriented towards food quality assurance schemes.

In the BeNeLux countries, we find few collective quality marks, little growth in the number of PDO/PGI products, a moderate number of FQASs (except for the high number in Belgium) and a moderate proportion of agricultural area devoted to organic farming. While Belgium is clearly food-quality-assurance-scheme oriented, the other two countries have no clear quality orientation.

In the Scandinavian countries, there are hardly any collective quality marks, a low level of and hardly any growth rate in PDO/PGI registration, and few FQASs, but a large percentage of agricultural area is devoted to organic farming. In these countries we find a strong organic orientation.

The Eastern European Countries of the Czech Republic, Poland, Slovakia, Hungary and Slovenia are catching up with respect to PDO/PGI products. The Czech Republic, Slovenia and Estonia have high shares of farmland used for organic production, while Slovakia, Hungary, Latvia and Lithuania have moderate shares. In Poland, a very low percentage of farmland is used for organic production.

We can distinguish between different clusters of countries. One cluster consists of the PDO/PGI-oriented Mediterranean countries, including Portugal, with Italy being diversified and very highly quality oriented. Another cluster consists of Germany, the United Kingdom, Ireland and Belgium. These countries have a clear orientation towards food quality assurance systems. The Netherlands and Luxemburg are diversified and quality oriented. Another cluster consists of Austria and the Scandinavian countries, which are organic-farming oriented.

This analysis shows that various countries in the EU take very different approaches to improving food quality. Further, the analysis should remind researchers conducting empirical work on geographical indications that other approaches to improving food quality should also be taken into account. It would be very interesting to investigate in future research whether the different routes to food quality

T. Becker

improvement across EU countries are chosen due to differential consumer and/or producer behaviour and/or heterogeneous preferences of politicians.

T. Becker

References

Becker, T. 2000. Rechtlicher Schutz und staatliche Absatzförderung für Agrarprodukte und Lebensmittel auf dem Prüfstand. *Agrarwirtschaft* 49(12): 418-428.

Becker, T. 2006. Zur Bedeutung geschützter Herkunftsangaben. *Hohenheimer Agrarökonomische Arbeitsberichte* No. 12, 2nd edition. Hohenheim.

European Commission. 2001. Community guidelines for state aid for advertising of products listed in Annex I to the EC Treaty and of certain non–Annex I products (2001/C 252/03). Brussels.

European Commission. 2004. Protection of geographical indications, designations of origin and certificates of specific character for agricultural products and foodstuffs. Directorate General for Agricultural Food Quality Policy in the European Union, Working Document of the Commission Services Guide to Community Rules. 2nd edition. August 2004 (http://ec.europa.eu/agriculture/publi/gi/broch_en.pdf)

Knaak, R. 2006. Die EG-Verordnung Nr. 510/2006 zum Schutz von geographischen Angaben und Ursprungsbezeichnungen. *Gewerblicher Rechtsschutz und Urheberrecht Int.* 2006 (11): 893-901.

Organisation for Economic Co-operation and Development (OECD). 2000. Appellations of origin and geographical indications in OECD member countries: economic and legal implications. Final version of a study which was carried out under the Programme of Work for 1999/2000 adopted by the Committee for Agriculture and endorsed by the Trade Committee. (http://www.oecd.org/LongAbstract/0,3425,en_2649_33773_23526074_1_1_1_1, 00.html)

Peri, C., and D. Gaeta. 1997. Designations of origin and industry certification as means of valorising food products. Working paper.

Endnotes

1. I would like to thank two anonymous referees for their very helpful comments, which helped me to improve the quality of the paper.

[16]

 The current issue and full text archive of this journal is available at
www.emeraldinsight.com/0007-070X.htm

BFJ
113,7

900

Consumers' and producers' expectations towards geographical indications

Empirical evidence for a German case study

Ramona Teuber

*Institute of Agricultural Policy and Market Research,
Justus-Liebig University, Giessen, Germany*

Abstract

Purpose – This paper's objective is to investigate consumers' and producers' expectations towards geographical indications (GIs) in a German context, where this certification scheme has not been widely used so far.

Design/methodology/approach – Data for the consumer side were obtained by a structured questionnaire. A total of 741 consumers were asked online with respect to their knowledge and expectations towards geographical indications in general and Hessian apple wine in particular. The collected data were analysed by an explorative factor analysis and a binary logit model. Additionally, data for the producer side were collected via an in-depth interview with one major producer of Hessian apple wine.

Findings – The consumer side results indicate that Hessian consumers' awareness and knowledge about GIs is very limited. Moreover, it is found that the quality warranty dimension is not as important as the economic support dimension and perceived authenticity of the product. A hypothetical willingness to pay for protection is mainly driven by consumer perceptions and expectations towards the positive impacts of geographical indications on the local economy. The producer side results highlight that the most important motivation to apply for a protected G1 (PGI) is to secure the established reputation against misuse by competing producers in order to ensure the quality level of Hessian apple wine.

Practical implications – The findings indicate that a PGI is by no means a self-runner. The positive impacts of this certification scheme have to be communicated to consumers in order to be successful.

Originality/value – Empirical evidence regarding consumers' knowledge and expectations towards geographical indications in a non-Mediterranean context is limited. The present paper contributes to the existing literature by providing empirical evidence for a German case study.

Keywords Geographical indications, Cider, Germany, Consumer perceptions, Marketing strategy

Paper type Research paper

British Food Journal
Vol. 113 No. 7, 2011
pp. 900-918
© Emerald Group Publishing Limited
0007-070X
DOI 10.1108/00070701111148423

Introduction

In recent years a steadily increasing demand for regional and local foods can be observed worldwide. From the consumers' point-of-view, this growing demand for local and regional foods can be considered a countertrend against the globalisation of trade in foods with international brands and converging demand patterns (Parrott *et al.*, 2002). A growing consumer segment is concerned about food safety and food quality issues and values the origin as a useful quality cue. These ongoing developments are reflected in the growing number of products registered under regulation EC No. 510/2006 and the efforts at national and international level to foster the registration of products either as a protected geographical indication (PGI) or a protected designation of origin (PDO)[1]. This is also true for Germany, where this certification scheme has not been widely-used so far. However, several attempts have been made to promote this scheme and to encourage German producers to apply for the EU-wide protection. Some prominent examples of German PDO/PGI products are Schwarzwaelder Schinken (PGI since 1997) and Spreewaelder Gurken (PGI since 1999).

Most scientific studies on geographical indications (GIs) have been carried out in a Mediterranean context, since origin labelling has got a long tradition in countries such as France, Italy and Greece (e.g. Loureiro and McCluskey, 2000; Scarpa *et al.*, 2005). Contrarily, empirical evidence with respect to the use of PDO and PGI in a non-Mediterranean context is limited due to the rather low number of registered products originating in non-Mediterranean countries. This has changed to some extent in recent years. A growing number of agricultural producers from non-Mediterranean countries apply for registration of their products under regulation EC No. 510/2006 (Becker, 2009). However, the majority of products registered either as PDO or PGI still originate in Mediterranean countries. Becker (2009) explains this north-south divide by different policy approaches towards enhancing food quality. Whereas in Mediterranean countries the *terroir* concept is well-established and used extensively by agricultural producers, northern European countries have focused on other food quality assurance schemes (FQASs) and organic production instead. A similar reasoning is put forward by Parrott *et al.* (2002). They argue that the apparent differences between "northern" and "southern" European countries in terms of PDO/PGI-use result from notable differences in their food culture and agricultural systems. They characterize the "northern" culture as functional and commodity-driven, whereas the "southern" one is based on locality and artisanal production.

Given this background, studies investigating the establishment of geographical indications in non-Mediterranean parts of Europe are rare. Detailed knowledge about consumers' attitudes and producers' expectations towards this certification scheme is particularly limited for German consumers and producers. The present paper wants to fill this research gap by presenting empirical results for a German case study, Hessian apple wine.

Two main objectives are pursued. First, the paper addresses the awareness and perceptions of, and attitudes towards the PDO and PGI labels among Hessian consumers. This is of considerable importance, if producers want to use these labels as a successful marketing tool. Second, the paper investigates consumers' attitudes towards the product Hessian apple wine and the evaluation of a regional certification label for this specific product. Additionally, the supply side will be briefly explored by presenting findings concerning producers' motivation to apply for registration of the term "Hessischer Apfelwein" as a PGI. The expectations driving the decision to apply for a registration under regulation EC No. 510/2006 as well as possible obstacles the producer group faced during the application process shall be identified. Possible obstacles can be endogenous such as conflicts finding a consensus on the product specification or exogenous such as administrative burdens.

The paper is structured as follows. The next section highlights the main features of the cider and apple wine industry. Thereafter, a brief overview about previous empirical studies in the context of PDO and PGI products is provided, followed by a

BFJ
113,7

presentation of the empirical results with respect to Hessian apple wine. The last section discusses the obtained results and concludes.

The cider market
As in the case of wine, taste, appearance and alcohol content of cider varies across countries and regions[2]. The French cider is known for its relatively low alcohol content (3 per cent by volume), whereas the British or Irish cider normally has got an alcohol content of over 10 per cent by volume. The UK and Ireland are the main producing and consuming countries of cider. Other countries with a tradition of producing cider and possessing an established cider industry are Belgium, Finland, France, Germany and Spain. The per-capita consumption of cider across countries is presented in Figure 1.

The highest per-capita consumption of cider can be found in Ireland, the UK, and Finland with 17, 13.3 and 11 litres per annum, respectively. In all other countries, the consumption is rather low (i.e. beneath 5 litres per year). For comparison Figure 1 does also present the per-capita consumption of beer and wine.

Although the cider market is much smaller than the beer and wine market, it has experienced the highest growth rates among alcoholic beverages in some European countries in recent years. One example is the UK, where sales of cider grew by 23 per cent in 2006. According to the National Association of Cider Makers (NACM), cider is abandoning its "cheap alcohol" image and a growing share of consumers perceives cider as a quality drink (National Association of Cider Makers, 2009). A renewed interest in cider can also be observed in other European countries with a long history of cider production and consumption such as Brittany and Normandy in France and

902

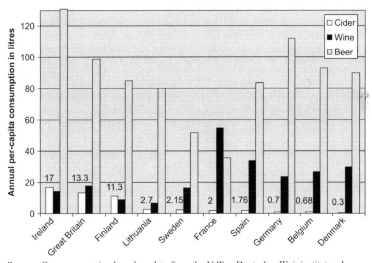

Figure 1.
Annual per-capita consumption of cider, wine and beer in selected European countries, 2004 and 2005

Source: Own presentation based on data from the VdFw, Deutsches Weininstitut and FAOStat

Northern Spain (Rowles, 2000). In these areas, cider is a central element in the local culture and most often touristic concepts are based on the local cider industry.

Moreover, the growing consumer interest in product attributes such as origin, sustainability, traceability and authenticity has fuelled the demand for regional foods and regional specialties[3]. The product cider seems to be well-suited for such a setting due to its long history and the large variety of different ciders reflecting regional differences in climate, apple varieties and local production techniques. This association between provenance and quality is sometimes denoted *terroir*. The French term *terroir* means that there is a certain link between the context of production (i.e. climate, soil, culture, tradition, local knowledge) and the quality of the produced product (Parrott *et al.*, 2002). Such a quality-origin link is a necessary condition for a product to become protected under regulation EC No. 510/2006. The increasing interest in protecting cultural heritage and promoting authentic products is possibly the underlying reason for the growing number of ciders registered either as PGI or PDO. Table I presents an overview of all currently protected ciders in Europe.

In Germany, the production and consumption of apple wine is concentrated in a few regions, namely Hesse, Bavaria, Rhineland-Palatinate and Baden-Wuerttemberg. Hesse, particularly the region around Frankfurt, is the leading producing and consuming region. In the year 2008, the production was 37 million litres, which represent around 85 per cent of total apple wine production in Germany[4]. Around 50 companies produce cider in Hesse, with the major share being small-scale producers selling their cider only locally[5]. The per-capita consumption in Hesse was six litres in 2008, ten times the average German per-capita consumption of 0.6 litre (ibidem). Of great importance is the out-of-home consumption, with only one fourth of total consumption taking place at home (Herrmann and Oberbeck, 2008).

Hessian apple wine has a long history and has been in the marketplace for decades. However, due to the steadily declining consumption in the 1990s, new ways to stimulate demand had to be found. Herrmann and Schulz (2006) analysed the Hessian apple wine market with the main objective to identify the underlying reasons for the steadily declining consumption of apple wine in Hesse in order to provide strategies for the Hessian apple wine producer association to overcome this declining trend. The results from an online-survey of 1,000 Hessian consumers conducted in 2006 highlighted that the group of regular apple wine consumers is quite satisfied with the current product. For these consumers the attributes "authenticity" and "tradition" are of great importance. They prefer a dry apple wine that is produced traditionally, which

Country	Protected product	PDO/PGI	Registered since
France	Cournaille	PDO	1999
France	Pays d'auge/Pays d'auge Cambremer	PDO	1999
France	Cidre de Bretagne	PGI	2000
France	Cidre de Normandie	PGI	2000
Spain	Sidra de Asturias	PDO	2005
UK	Gloucestershire cider	PGI	1996
UK	Herefordshire cider	PGI	1996
UK	Worcestershire cider	PGI	1996

Source: Own compilation based on the EU database on PDOs and PGIs

Table I.
Ciders protected under regulation EC No. 510/2006, August 2009

BFJ
113,7

means that it is made of Hessian apples without any additives. The Hessian origin is an important attribute for these consumers. In contrast, non-consumers often cite the harsh and bitter taste as a reason for not drinking apple wine. Thus, this consumer group, comprising mainly younger and female consumers, should be attracted by sweeter apple wine and apple wine mixed with lemonade. Several apple wine companies launched such products in recent years.

The apples used for making Hessian apple wine typically originate from so-called Streuobstwiesen. This is a traditional type of extensive grassland-orchard management system present in middle Europe. Streuobstwiesen are species-rich and offer a large biodiversity. However, this habitat is nowadays endangered and its protection is part of political and private initiatives in Germany (Suske, 2001).

The role of geographical indications in the supply chain
PDO and PGI products from a producer's point-of-view
Geographical indications like trademarks are distinctive signs that enable producers to secure their established reputation against imitation and fraud. However, trademarks are individually owned rights whilst geographical indications can be considered as club goods (Josling, 2006). The clubs owing these rights are typically producer groups or vertically integrated producer-processing associations. According to this club good nature of a PDO/PGI, Belletti *et al.* (2009) conclude that the protection of a PDO/PGI can reinforce the collective action among the participating producers.

One of the earliest studies analysing the adoption of GIs in a non-Mediterranean country is the one by Ilbery and Kneafsey (2000a) for the UK. In order to find out who applied for a PDO/PGI and why, a brief postal questionnaire was sent to 22 registered producer groups in the UK. The results point out that there is no clear pattern in terms of business type and structure among the applicants. Moreover, the PDO/PGI producer groups exhibit a large heterogeneity. With respect to the reasons for application the answers suggest that the early adopters have sought PDO/PGI status primarily to protect their named products against usurpation. The motivation to use the PDO/PGI logo as a marketing tool was not important at all. Only two of the respondents used the logo at that time on their products. Among the respondents was also one apple cider producer group, the Cider and Perry Makers. This producer group producing Gloucestershire apple cider stated that there were rumours that French cider makers wanted to enter the UK market with UK-style ciders. Consequently, cider producers in the UK applied for the protection as a PGI, because they were afraid to loose market shares if French producers were able to enter the expanding UK market with UK-style ciders. These findings are in line with the other investigated producer groups in the UK leading to the conclusion that in these cases the PDO/PGI certification scheme is primarily a mechanism to protect national producer interests rather than a marketing tool (Ilbery and Kneafsey, 2000a).

Dimara *et al.* (2004) draw a similar conclusion. They argue that regional denomination certification can be considered either as a promotion or as a protection strategy from the producers' point-of-view. In the latter case applying for registration pursues the objectives to protect an established reputation and raise barriers to entry. In the former case certification is considered a useful marketing instrument to create niche markets. The empirical analysis focused on black currant producers in Greece, who had applied for PDO status at the time the survey was carried out. The results suggest that for most producers PDO certification is not evaluated as an important marketing indicator but as a protection strategy raising barriers to entry.

PDO and PGI products from a consumer's point-of-view
Consumer studies dealing with PDO and PGI labels typically investigate the awareness and knowledge of these labels as well as consumers' perceptions and attitudes towards products carrying such a regional certification label.

The most comprehensive study with respect to consumers' appreciation and attitudes towards PDO/PGI-labelled products was conducted by Van Ittersum *et al.* (2007). In their proposed and tested model on consumers' product evaluation of protected regional products two different effects are distinguished, the effect of the region-of-origin cue and the effect of the certification label itself. The region-of-origin cue is assumed to influence consumers' attitudes towards the protected regional product through the perceived quality. The regional certification label, which guarantees that the product is the authentic product and not an imitation, is supposed to influence consumers in their purchasing behaviour through two different dimensions. The first one is the quality warranty dimension, which represents consumers' belief about the ability of the label to guarantee a higher quality level. The second dimension is the economic support dimension, which captures consumers' beliefs about the way and degree the label can support the economy in that region (Van der Lans *et al.*, 2001; Van Ittersum *et al.*, 2007). The first dimension is assumed to be relevant for all consumers of the product, whereas the second dimension is supposed to be of particular relevance for consumers located inside the production area. The model was tested based on survey data for six different PDO/PGI products from three different European countries, namely Italy, Greece and The Netherlands. The empirical results highlight that consumers have a favourable image of regional certification labels and that this image can be represented by the proposed two-dimensional construct consisting of a quality warranty and an economic support dimension. The results reveal further that the perceived higher quality of these products is the most important determinant of consumers' willingness to buy and willingness to pay for protected regional products. Moreover, Van der Lans *et al.* (2001) point out that the success of a marketing strategy based on the region of origin crucially depends on consumers' awareness and favourable image of the region. These findings are fully in line with findings from the country of origin and branding literature (Kotler and Gertner, 2004; Verlegh and Steenkamp, 1999). Accordingly, a marketing strategy based on regional certification labels resembles a branding strategy in many aspects, particularly in terms of reputation-building and promotional activities.

Another relevant study for our analysis is the one by Carpenter and Larceneux (2008). They tried to explore the decision-making process of consumers when faced with products carrying different value-based labels. Their experimental framework enabled them to compare the impact of a PGI label, when explained, to a PGI label not explained, a local terroir label and no label at all. The experiment was carried out with French consumers and two products, chicken and *foie gras*. The results highlight that the PGI label without additional information has got no positive impact on perceived quality of the product. However, if the PGI label is explained, it influences the quality perception and purchase intention positively.

BFJ
113,7

It can be summarised that the empirical evidence so far suggests that the most important factor determining the success of a PDO/PGI product is the perceived higher quality compared with non-protected products. In this context it must be stressed that quality is a social construct and may vary for specific products and between individuals (Ilbery and Kneafsey, 2000b). Moreover, quality in relation to regionally denominated foods is closely related to other socially constructed concepts such as "authenticity", "healthy" and "tradition". This notion is important in that respect, that if regionally denominated products are perceived as being of a higher quality, this higher quality can comprise many different aspects.

Empirical results
Producers' motivation and expectations
The Hessian apple wine producer association submitted the application for a registration of the term "Hessischer Apfelwein" as a protected geographical indication to the German Patent and Trade Mark Office (DPMA) in spring 2006. In August 2007, it was forwarded to the European Commission, where it is still under consideration.

In November 2008, an in-depth interview with one of the leading producers of Hessian apple wine and member of the Hessian apple wine producer association was conducted. The main research hypothesis to be tested is based on results from previous studies on the Hessian apple wine market (Herrmann and Schulz, 2006; Kubitzki and Schulz, 2007). These studies proposed using the protection of the region of origin as a marketing tool in order to stop the declining apple wine consumption in Hesse. Hence, it is hypothesised that the main motivation of Hessian apple wine producers to apply for a PGI is to use this label as a marketing tool, i.e. they primarily want to pursue a promotion instead of a protection strategy.

The Hessian apple wine producer association was founded in 1948 with the aim to represent the interests of Hessian apple wine producers in public. Hence, co-operation and bundling of interests has got a long history in the Hessian apple wine industry. This is very contrary to the case of Herefordshire, Worcestershire and Gloucestershire Cider analysed by Ilbery and Kneafsey (2000a), where a producer association was newly-founded in order to submit an application for a PGI. However, the main motivation to apply for EU-wide registration is the same in both cases. Both producer groups want to achieve protection against free-riders and imitations. The Hessian apple wine producer association considers the EU-wide registration as an important tool in securing the quality level of Hessian apple wine. In this regard the protection shall secure the recent price level and prevent price erosion due to copycat products with lower quality in the market. Moreover, the Hessian apple wine producers have got the feeling that this type of certification is somehow demanded by retailers due to a growing focus on labels and certification schemes. These results are in contrast to the hypothesis stated above that the application for protection is driven by the aim to use the EU-wide protection as an active marketing tool both in the domestic as well as in foreign markets.

Another question addressed was the decision to apply for a PGI instead of a PDO. There was no discussion on this topic among the Hessian apple wine producers, since the restriction to use only Hessian apples in the case of a PDO application would impose severe difficulties. Thus, the general consensus was to apply for a PGI with the specification to use, if possible, 100 per cent Hessian apples from Streuobstwiesen. This leads to the aspect of product specification. This is of great importance, because the product specification is the determining factor in obtaining registration (London Economics, 2008). Within the product specification, the documentation of an existing link between the product's quality or at least one characteristic and the defined geographical region is the most important part. According to the interview results, the product specification caused no problems among producers and was agreed by all participants very quickly. This can certainly be due to the long history of producing apple wine. Hence, it seems to be that endogenous obstacles were not of any importance in the application process. The same seems to be true for exogenous obstacles. No major difficulties were faced during the application process and the direct costs (e.g. application fees), were very low. This is also true for indirect costs, that is costs arising from restrictions on certain agricultural or processing practices. These costs that are often cited to be of significance in the context of geographical indications seem to be of low importance in the case of Hessian apple wine. One possible explanation is that the established way of production is the basis for the product specification.

Consumers' awareness, perceptions and attitudes towards the EU protection
At the same time the in-depth interview was carried out, an online survey with 741 Hessian consumers was conducted. The sample is representative for the population of Hesse with respect to sex, age and place of residence in the age group 15-59 years. Older consumers are clearly underrepresented while higher educated people are clearly over-represented. This is a typical bias in online surveys and should always be kept in mind while interpreting the results.

In the first part the survey addressed the level of awareness of the official EU logos (presented in Figure 2) among Hessian consumers and the associations with these labels[6]. The second part contained questions with regard to Hessian apple wine and the possible protection as a PGI. The main results are presented and discussed below.

PDO and PGI labels in general
The awareness of the official EU logos is very low among Hessian consumers. Only 9.6 per cent ($n = 71$) of all respondents claimed to know at least one of the two EU logos. This is in line with a note by the European Economic and Social Committee (EESC) issued in 2008 that the recognition of "European certification schemes and their logos and labels is still inadequate and very patchy". Moreover, due to follow-up questions it turned out that some consumers did confuse the labels with other labels. Hence, the

Figure 2.
EU Logos PGI and PDO

BFJ
113,7

908

share of consumers knowing this certification scheme and the associated labels is even overstated with 9.6 per cent.

It was investigated whether there are significant differences between consumers claiming to know at least one label and consumers not being aware of the labels ($p < 0.05$). No significant differences between these two groups were found with respect to sex, income, and household size. However, significant differences could be identified in terms of education level and age. Higher educated respondents and respondents under the age of 30 are more likely to know the labels. A significant difference was also found with respect to organic shopping behaviour. People stating to buy regularly organic products have got a significant higher awareness of the PDO/PGI label than people who buy organic products rarely or never. This can be explained by the fact that people who buy regularly organic foods are most often more interested in the foods they purchase and, hence, are generally better informed than non-organic buyers.

Of great interest is the signal effect of a label, i.e. what is transmitted by the label to the consumer. This question was investigated for consumers claiming to know at least one of the labels and consumers not being aware of these labels separately. One striking result is that among consumers declaring to have seen one of the logos before, nearly 40 per cent did not state any association with the labels. This does reflect the wide-spread lack of knowledge among Hessian consumers what these labels stand for. Among the stated associations, the statements "the label secures that the origin is the true origin", "the product is the original one", "the product is a high-quality product" and "the product is controlled" were mentioned most frequently. This group was also questioned closed-ended with respect to their expectations towards products protected either as PDO or PGI. The results are presented in Figure 3.

Consumers' agreement respectively disagreement to the presented statements was measured on a five-point Likert scale ranging from "1 = I totally disagree" to "5 = I totally agree" with an additional "I don't know"-option. Over 70 per cent of the respondents agree that geographical indications support local producers and secure

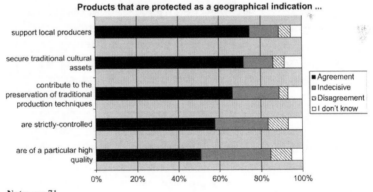

Figure 3.
Expectations towards
PDO and PGI products

Note: $n = 71$
Source: Own presentation

traditional cultural assets. On the other hand, the share of respondents associating tight controls and a particular high quality with geographical indications is 57.7 and 50.7 per cent, respectively. For these two statements the share of respondents being indecisive was highest with 25.4 and 33.8 per cent, respectively. It seems to be the case that geographical indications are tightly connected with protecting tradition and supporting the local economy, whereas around 50 per cent are not convinced that these products possess a particularly high quality. This is an important finding given the results from previous consumer studies presented above that in most cases the higher perceived quality of protected products determines the preference and WTP for these products.

Hessian apple wine and the protection as PGI
After this general part on the EU Certification labels, the second part addressed specifically Hessian apple wine. Based on their consumption frequency the respondents were classified in consumers and non-consumers.

A total of 42 per cent of respondents state to drink apple wine at no time. These consumers constitute the group of non-consumers. All other respondents comprise the group of consumers. All respondents were asked to state their associations with Hessian apple wine open-ended and closed-ended. The results for the closed-ended statements for the consumer group are presented in Figure 4 (see Table II for a complete statements list plus codes).

Figure 4 points out that the highest share of agreement can be found for statements that are related to constructs of culture, economic support and the use of traditional processing methods. The lowest degree of agreement is present for statements related to higher quality and raw material specifications such as the exclusive use of Hessian

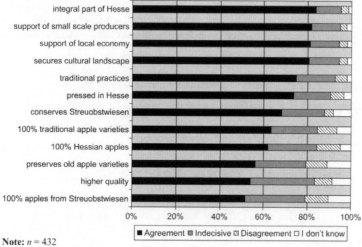

Note: *n* = 432
Source: Own presentation

Figure 4.
Associations with and
expectations towards
Hessian apple wine and
the protection as
geographical indication,
apple wine consumers

BFJ
113,7

910

Construct	Code	Statement
Economic support	Support of local economy	By buying Hessian apple wine I support the local economy
	Support of small-scale producers	Regional specialities contribute to the survival of small-scale producers
Quality and brand affinity	Higher quality	Hessian apple wine is of a higher quality than apple wine from other regions
	Brand affinity	I always buy apple wine from a certain producer
Product and processing specifications	100 per cent Hessian apples	Hessian apple wine must be produced by using exclusively Hessian apples
	100 per cent traditional apple varieties	Hessian apple wine must be produced by using exclusively traditional apple varieties
	100 per cent apples from Streuobstwiesen	Hessian apple wine must be produced by using exclusively apples from Streuobstwiesen
	Pressed in Hesse	Hessian apple wine must be pressed in Hesse
Culture and tradition	Integral part of Hesse	Hessian apple wine is an integral part of Hessian culture
	Traditional practices	Hessian apple wine must be manufactured according to traditional practices
Preservation	Secures Streuobstwiesen	The protection as geographical indication preserves Hessian Streuobstwiesen
	Secures cultural landscape	Regional specialities such as Hessian apple wine contribute to the survival of the domestic cultural landscape
	Preserves old apple varieties	The protection as geographical indication conserves endangered apple varieties

Table II.
Codeplan and detailed statements with respect to Hessian apple wine and the protection as geographical indication

Notes: The agreement to each statement is measured on a five-point Likert scale with 1 = "I don't agree at all" to 5 = "I totally agree" with an additional "I don't know" option
Source: Own presentation

apples, traditional apple varieties or apples from Streuobstwiesen. These results suggest that from the consumer point of view, Hessian apple wine is deeply rooted in the local culture and tradition, whereas detailed expectations with respect to the product specification are not very pronounced.

Furthermore, the respondents had to indicate whether they were willing to pay a higher price for a protected apple wine. A total of 48 per cent of consumers stated to be willing to pay a higher price for a protected apple wine. Hence, the question arises which factors may contribute to this hypothetical willingness to pay (WTP) for protection. Therefore, a binary logit model was estimated with the hypothetical WTP as the dependent variable. Such a model permits the examination of the marginal impact of variables on the probability of a positive WTP for protection *ceteris paribus*.

The included explanatory variables comprise socio-demographic variables as well as consumers' attitudes and expectations towards organic products, Hessian apple wine in general and the protection in particular. Before estimating the binary logit model, an explorative factor analysis (EFA) was carried out in order to reduce the large number of statements to a few independent factors that can be incorporated into the model. Several extraction (principal component, maximum likelihood) and rotation (varimax, oblimin) methods were tested, whereby the most reliable solution is a two-factor solution which is presented in Table III. Moreover, Table III presents the factor loadings on each single-item statement, as well as the mean of the single-item statement for the group of consumers stating to have a positive WTP for a protected apple wine and the group stating to have no WTP, separately.

In the binary logit model the dependent variable is a dichotomous variable, whereby in this case the top-two answers, that is "I totally agree" and "I agree" with respect to the statement "I were willing to pay a premium for an apple wine that is protected as a geographical indication", were coded as "1 = WTP for protection" and all other answers as "0 = no WTP for protection".

It is important to note that the variable WTP does only measure a hypothetical WTP, since it is derived from a hypothetical questionnaire. In hypothetical settings, researchers typically worry about two possible biases, the social desirability bias and the hypothetical bias (Lusk and Norwood, 2009; Murphy and Stevens, 2004). The social desirability bias refers to a situation where respondents provide answers they consider as being in line with social norms. This bias is assumed to be more pronounced in face-to-face interviews than in online surveys because of the presence of an interviewer in the former case (Duffy *et al.*, 2005). The hypothetical bias, which refers to a discrepancy between what people say in a hypothetical survey and how they will actually behave in a real purchase situation, typically leads to overstated WTP measures.

Whereas it is assumed that the social desirability bias is not a point of major concern in our setting due to the anonymous online survey structure), the hypothetical

Factors and the associated single-item statements[a]	Factor loading	Mean	
		WTP	No WTP
Factor 1: support dimension (percentage of variation explained: 50.8 per cent)			
Support of small-scale producers	0.874	4.45	4.05
Support of local economy	0.791	4.41	3.91
Secures cultural landscape	0.758	4.44	3.94
Factor 2: processing dimension (percentage of variation explained: 14.8 per cent)			
100 per cent apples from Streuobstwiesen	0.812	3.98	3.30
100 per cent traditional apple varieties	0.732	4.07	3.54
100 per cent Hessian apples	0.711	4.16	3.50
Protection secures old apple varieties	0.705	4.27	3.41
KMO = 0.851 ($p < 0.000$)		$n = 206$	$n = 226$

Notes: [a]The agreement to each statement is measured on a five-point Likert scale with 1 = "I don't agree at all" to 5 = "I totally agree". The "I don't know" answers were dropped; Results were obtained by using the principal component method with varimax rotation
Source: Own presentation

Table III.
Retained factors,
single-item statements,
factor loads and mean

BFJ
113,7

912

bias certainly is. In order to take this possible bias into account, the model is specified very carefully by just considering the top-two answers as a hypothetical WTP. Moreover, since the respondents were able to indicate their agreement on a five-point Likert scale with an "I don't know" option, we are quite confident that the hypothetical bias is reduced compared to the usually applied dichotomous choice. Nevertheless, the hypothetical nature of the setting must be kept in mind when drawing conclusions from the model.

The estimated model is:

$$\text{logit}(p_i) = \ln\left(\frac{p_i}{1-p_i}\right) = \alpha + \sum_j \beta_j X_{ji} \tag{1}$$

with p_i being the probability of consumer i having a positive WTP, α and β are regression coefficients and X_{ji} are explanatory variables (a detailed list of all included variables is presented in Table IV). The maximum likelihood estimates are presented in Table V.

Overall, the model fit of the comprehensive model is satisfying with a Nagelkerke R^2 of 0.268 and a correct prediction of 73.2 per cent. The impact of the independent variable is reported by the effect coefficient exp (β), which indicates the change of the odds ratio when the independent variable increases by one unit. The odd ratio is defined as

$$Odds(WTP=1) = \frac{p(WTP=1)}{1-p(WTP=1)} \tag{2}$$

This implies that an effect coefficient above unity signals a positive impact of the independent variable on the probability of having a positive WTP, whereas an effect coefficient below unity signals a negative impact.

None of the sociodemographic and socioeconomic characteristics with the exception of income is significant in explaining the hypothetical WTP for protection. It was assumed that older people, people living in rural areas and people living in southern Hesse are more likely to pay a premium for a protected apple wine. This was based on the hypothesis that these consumer groups are more closely connected with Hesse resulting in a significantly higher probability to be willing to pay a premium for protection. This could not be proven by the data. However, significant impacts are found for the constructs "economic support" and "processing methods". If consumers are convinced that geographical indications or regional specialties contribute to the local economy, they are willing to pay a price premium for a protected apple wine. The same is true for the perceptions about the way Hessian apple wine should be processed. People stating that they expect Hessian apple wine to be produced by using Hessian apples from Streuobstwiesen are also willing to pay a price premium for a protected Hessian apple wine. These results are in line with findings from previous consumer studies on perceptions and willingness to pay for regional and local foods. Sociodemographic and socioeconomic variables seem to be poor predictors of preferences for local food and regional specialties, whereas in most cases attitudes and perceptions can explain preference heterogeneity to a significant extent (Henseleit *et al.*, 2009; Zepeda and Lin, 2006).

Variables	Code	Mean	WTP	No WTP
"I would be willing to pay a premium for an apple wine that is protected as a geographical indication"[a]	WTP	0.48		
Independent variables				
Sociodemographics				
Age:				
Below 30 years (reference)			0.31	0.35
Between 30 and 49 years old	30-49 yrs		0.46	0.46
Above 49 years old	Above 49 yrs		0.23	0.19
Sex:				
Male (reference)			0.47	0.53
Female	Female		0.53	0.47
Socioeconomics				
Education:				
No qualification for university entrance (reference)			0.55	0.62
Qualification for university entrance	Higher_edu		0.45	0.38
Available monthly per-capita income:				
Below €750 (reference)			0.38	0.62
€750-€1,250	Income_medium		0.51	0.49
Above €1,250	Income_high		0.52	0.48
Size of the home town:				
Below 5,000 citizens (reference)			0.15	0.16
Above 5,000 citizens	Urban		0.85	0.84
Residence in Hesse:				
Middle and Northern Hesse (reference)			0.33	0.29
Southern Hesse	Southern Hesse		0.67	0.71
Shopping and consumption behaviour				
Place of apple wine purchase:				
Discounter (reference)			0.13	0.12
Supermarket	Supermarket		0.70	0.62
Producer	Producer		0.17	0.26
Shopping frequency of organic products:				
Never/seldom (reference)			0.29	0.46
Occasionally	Organic_occass		0.50	0.42
Regularly	Organic_regularly		0.21	0.12

Notes: $n = 432$; [a]The top-two answers, "I fully agree" and "I agree", are coded as 1, all other answers are coded as 0
Source: Own presentation

Table IV.
Variables description and descriptive statistics, apple wine consumers

Geographical indications

913

Discussion and conclusions

Previous studies on the Hessian apple wine market worked out that consumers perceive apple wine as a very region-specific product that is deeply rooted in Hesse. This result is confirmed and supported by the present study. This is an important requirement for a successful geographical indication. Barjolle and Sylvander (2000) analysed 20 PDO and PGI products with respect to the factors that are most important in determining the success of a geographical indication. They concluded that one of the most important determinants of success is the specificity of the product. Hence, the PGI

Variables	Code	Reduced model Exp(β)	Comprehensive model Exp(β)
Dependent variable: hypothetical willingness to pay (no WTP = 0, WTP = 1)			
Explanatory variables			
Constant term		0.631	0.716
		(0.361)	(0.556)
Sociodemographics			
Age	30-49 yrs	0.892	0.658
		(0.659)	(0.147)
	Above 49 yrs	1.016	0.799
		(0.963)	(0.548)
Gender	Female	1.253	1.186
		(0.327)	(0.498)
Socioeconomics			
Education income	Higher_edu	1.167	1.167
		(0.507)	(0.507)
	Income_medium	1.539	1.761[a]
		(0.147)	(0.081)
	Income_high	1.716[a]	1.794[a]
		(0.072)	(0.075)
Size of home town	Urban	1.014	1.042
		(0.966)	(0.905)
Residence in Hesse	Southern Hesse	0.899	0.962
		(0.666)	(0.886)
Shopping and consumption behaviour			
Place of apple wine purchase	Producer	0.595	0.745
		(0.218)	(0.538)
	Supermarket	0.959	0.912
		(0.910)	(0.824)
Organic foods	Organic_occass	1.525[a]	1.323
		(0.085)	(0.292)
	Organic_regularly	2.070[*]	1.566
		(0.032)	(0.237)
Psychographic factors			
Factor 1	Support dimension		2.342[***]
			(0.000)
Factor 2	Processing dimension		1.780[***]
			(0.000)
n		339	339
Percent correctly predicted (%)		56.9	73.2
LL-Value		453.05	392.45
Nagelkerke's R^2		0.059	0.268

Table V.
Results from the
estimated binary logit
model

Notes: [a], [*], [**], [***] denotes significance at the 10, 5, 1 and 0.1 per cent level, respectively
Source: Own presentation

label seems to be an appropriate tool to enforce this specificity and to promote the product at the regional and interregional level to target the growing consumer demand for traditional regional specialties.

However, a registered Hessian apple wine does not constitute its own reward. Like other labels or brands it must be promoted and advertised. This is especially relevant given the results from the consumer survey that only a very small share of consumers is familiar with this certification scheme. These findings suggest that the PGI logo itself will not boost the apple wine consumption in Hesse or in Germany. It seems rather necessary to involve the EU protection in a wider promotion campaign informing consumers about the granted protection and stressing the attributes of authenticity and typicality of Hessian apple wine. This conclusion is also strongly supported by the result that psychographic factors, that is attitudes and beliefs towards Hessian apple wine and the GI protection, do significantly influence the willingness to pay for protection. Informing consumers with respect to the impacts of a protected geographical indication seems to be indispensable. If consumers are convinced that through this certification scheme the local economy and the local culture can be supported, the protection can result in a higher willingness to pay. Hence, even if the results from the supply side indicate that the producer association primarily pursues a protection strategy, the granted protection should also be embedded in a promotion strategy. This seems to be appropriate given the increasing consumer interest in traditional and authentic products on the one hand and the lack of knowledge these labels stand for on the other hand. In promoting the protected Hessian apple wine, both traditional apple wine drinkers and potential new consumers interested in regional specialties can be attracted. However, different strategies may be pursued for different consumer segments. For local consumers the economic support dimension should come to the fore. If the protection is embedded in a broader promotion concept stressing the local support and biodiversity dimension, the PGI protection can possibly enhance the turnover in already existing marketing channels. Since out-of-home consumption is of great importance, the gastronomy must also be included. This could be accompanied by building up networks with producers of other Hessian specialty products such as Hessian Handkaes' which is typically consumed with Hessian apple wine. On the other hand, a promotion strategy targeting at new consumers that are not located in Hesse should focus on the quality warranty dimension and stress the high quality and authenticity of this product.

While targeting new marketing channels, especially long-distance distribution channels such as exports to foreign markets, the PGI label may serve as a quality standard securing authenticity and traceability. Consequently, the PGI label can reduce transaction costs if foreign retailers and/or consumers are already familiar with this certification scheme.

Even though this study provides valuable insights on consumers' perceptions and attitudes towards regional certification schemes, it has also raised several points for future research. One interesting aspect seems to be the interaction between the PGI label and individual brands. From the producers' point of view, the PGI label is considered to benefit all producers of Hessian apple wine likewise. Research on the effects of generic advertising, however, has shown that this does not necessarily be the case and that the promotion of the PGI label could affect individual producers and brands differentially (Crespi, 2007; Crespi and Marette, 2002).

BFJ
113,7

916

Notes

1. The main difference between these two instruments is the extent of the quality-origin link. In the case of a PDO all stages of production must take place in the defined region. In the case of a PGI the products' characteristics need only to be attributable to the defined area and it is sufficient that at least one production stage takes place in the defined area

2. Cider is defined as an alcoholic beverage produced by the fermentation of the juices of apples without adding distilled alcohol. Synonyms are cidre, fermente de pomme, sidra, applecider, Apfelwein, äpplecider and siider (AICV, 2009). In the following cider is used to refer to the global market, whereas apple wine is used for the German resp. Hessian market.

3. There is no clear definition of regional foods or regional specialties. In this paper regional specialties are defined as products that are protected under regulation EC No. 510/2006 and products protected under regulation EC No. 509/2006 as traditional speciality guarantees (TSG).

4. Verband der Hessischen Apfelwein- und Fruchtsaft-Keltereien e.V. Geschäftsbericht, Heusenstamm, various years.

5. In Hesse, apple wine is also produced by home-brewers for personal consumption and by small companies that are not members of the Hessian apple wine producer association. These quantities are not included in the official statistics.

6. For the survey the old PDO logo was used. The new PDO logo was introduced in July 2008 due to the claim that consumers cannot distinguish between the two labels because of the optical similarity. However, at the time the survey was carried out a large share of PDO products was still labelled with the old logo. Therefore, it was decided to use the old blue-coloured logo instead of the new red-coloured one.

References

Association des Industries des Cidres et Vins (AICV) (2009), Homepage, available at: www.aicv. org (accessed 20 July 2009).

Barjolle, D. and Sylvander, B. (2000), "Some factors of success for origin labeled products in agri-food supply chains in Europe: market, internal resources and institutions", in Sylvander, B., Barjolle, D. and Arfini, F. (Eds), *The Socio-Economics of Origin Labelled Products in Agri-Food Supply Chains: Spatial, Institutional and Coordination Aspects*, Actes et communications. No. 17/1-2, INRA, Paris, pp. 45-71.

Becker, T. (2009), "European food quality policy: the importance of geographical indications, organic certification and food quality assurance schemes in European countries", *The Estey Centre Journal of International Law and Trade Policy*, Vol. 10 No. 1, pp. 111-30.

Belletti, G., Burgassi, T., Manco, E., Marescotti, A., Pacciani, A. and Scaramuzzi, S. (2009), "The roles of geographical indications in the internationalisation process of agri-food products", in Canavari, M., Cantore, N., Castellini, A., Pignatti, E. and Spadoni, R. (Eds), *International Marketing and Trade of Quality Food Products*, Wageningen Academic Publishers, Wageningen.

Carpenter, M. and Larceneux, F. (2008), "Label equity and the effectiveness of value-based labels: an experiment with two French protected geographic indication labels", *International Journal of Consumer Studies*, Vol. 32 No. 5, pp. 499-507.

Crespi, J.M. (2007), "Generic advertising and product differentiation revisited", *Journal of Agricultural and Food Industrial Organization*, Vol. 5 No. 1, pp. 1-19.

Crespi, J.M. and Marette, S. (2002), "Generic advertising and product differentiation", *American Journal of Agricultural Economics*, Vol. 84 No. 3, pp. 691-701.

Dimara, E., Petrou, A. and Skuras, D. (2004), "Agricultural policy for quality and producers' evaluations of quality marketing indicators: a Greek case study", *Food Policy*, Vol. 29 No. 5, pp. 485-506.

Duffy, B., Smith, K., Terhanian, G. and Bremer, J. (2005), "Comparing data from online and face-to-face-surveys", *International Journal of Market Research*, Vol. 47 No. 6, pp. 615-39.

Henseleit, M., Kubitzki, S. and Teuber, R. (2009), "Determinants of consumer preferences for regional food products", in Canavari, M., Cantore, N., Castellini, A., Pignatti, E. and Spadoni, R. (Eds), *International Marketing and Trade of Quality Food Products*, Wageningen Academic Publishers, Wageningen, pp. 263-78.

Herrmann, R. and Oberbeck, C. (2008), *Die Nachfrage nach Apfelwein in Hessen: Markenimage und Geschmackspräferenzen der Verbraucher*, Interner Ergebnisbericht, Giessen.

Herrmann, R. and Schulz, W. (2006), *Determinanten der Nachfrage nach Apfelwein in Hessen*, Interner Endbericht, Giessen.

Ilbery, B. and Kneafsey, M. (2000a), "Registering regional specialty food and drink products in the UK: the case of PDOs and PGIs", *Area*, Vol. 32 No. 3, pp. 317-25.

Ilbery, B. and Kneafsey, M. (2000b), "Producer constructions of quality in regional specialty food production: a case study from South West England", *Journal of Rural Studies*, Vol. 16 No. 2, pp. 217-30.

Josling, T. (2006), "The war on terroir: geographical indications as a transatlantic trade conflict", *Journal of Agricultural Economics*, Vol. 57 No. 3, pp. 337-63.

Kotler, P. and Gertner, D. (2004), "Country as brand, product and beyond: a place marketing and brand management perspective", in Morgan, N., Pritchard, A. and Pride, R. (Eds), *Destination Branding*, 2nd ed., Elsevier, Oxford, pp. 40-56.

Kubitzki, S. and Schulz, W. (2007), "Was beeinflusst die Nachfrage nach Apfelwein?", *Jahrbuch der Absatz- und Verbrauchsforschung*, Vol. 53 No. 2, pp. 208-24.

London Economics (2008), "Evaluation of the CAP policy on protected designations of origin (PDO) and protected geographical indications (PGI)", Final Report, European Commission, Brussels.

Loureiro, M.L. and McCluskey, J.J. (2000), "Consumer preferences and willingness to pay for food labeling: a discussion of empirical studies", *Journal of Food Distribution Research*, Vol. 34 No. 3, pp. 95-102.

Lusk, J.L. and Norwood, F.B. (2009), "An inferred valuation method", *Land Economics*, Vol. 85 No. 3, pp. 500-14.

Murphy, J.J. and Stevens, T.H. (2004), "Contingent valuation, hypothetical bias and experimental economics", *Agricultural and Resource Economics Review*, Vol. 33 No. 2, pp. 182-92.

National Association of Cider Makers (2009), Homepage, available at: www.cideruk.com/nacm/about_nacm (accessed 20 July 2009).

Parrott, N., Wilson, N. and Murdoch, J. (2002), "Spatializing quality: regional protection and the alternative geography of food", *European Urban and Regional Studies*, Vol. 9 No. 3, pp. 241-61.

Rowles, K. (2000), "Processed apple product marketing analysis: hard cider and apple wine", Staff Paper SP 2000-06, Department of Agricultural Resource and Managerial Economics, Cornell University, Ithaca, New York, NY.

Scarpa, R., Philippidis, G. and Spalatro, F. (2005), "Product-country images and preference heterogeneity for Mediterranean food products: a discrete choice framework", *Agribusiness*, Vol. 21 No. 3, pp. 329-49.

BFJ
113,7

918

Suske, W. (2001), "Öffentliches Interesse 'Streuobstfläche' – Hintergründe und Beispiele der europäischen Förderungspolitik", in Umweltbundesamt GmbH (Ed.), "Beiträge zum Streuobstanbau in Europa", *Stand, Entwicklungen und Probleme*, CP-028, Vienna, pp. 14-18.

Van der Lans, I.A., van Ittersum, K., De Cicco, A. and Loseby, M. (2001), "The role of the region of origin and EU certificates of origin in consumer evaluation of food products", *European Review of Agricultural Economics*, Vol. 28 No. 4, pp. 451-77.

Van Ittersum, K., Meulenberg, M.T.G., van Trijp, H.C.M. and Candel, M.J.J. (2007), "Consumers' appreciation of regional certification labels: a pan-European study", *Journal of Agricultural Economics*, Vol. 58 No. 1, pp. 1-23.

Verlegh, P. and Steenkamp, J.-B. (1999), "A review and meta-analysis of country-of-origin research", *Journal of Economic Psychology*, Vol. 20 No. 5, pp. 521-46.

Zepeda, L. and Lin, J. (2006), "Who buys local?", *Journal of Food Distribution Research*, Vol. 37 No. 3, pp. 1-11.

Further reading

ETEPS AISBL and JRC-IPST (2006), "Economics of food quality, assurance and certification schemes managed within an integrated supply chain", Final Report, European Commission, Bruessels.

European Commission (2007), *The Common Agricultural Policy Explained*, European Communities, Brussels.

Corresponding author
Ramona Teuber can be contacted at: ramona.teuber@agrar.uni-giessen.de

[17]

The current issue and full text archive of this journal is available at
www.emeraldinsight.com/1751-1062.htm

Italian wine demand and differentiation effect of geographical indications

Antonio Stasi, Gianluca Nardone and Rosaria Viscecchia
University of Foggia, Foggia, Italy, and
Antonio Seccia
University of Bari, Bari, Italy

Received April 2009
Revised April 2009
Accepted January 2010

Abstract

Purpose – Geographical indications (GIs) provide a strong differentiation tool for firms. Whether this statement is confirmed at aggregate level in terms of market independence of different GIs is not tested yet. The purpose of this paper is to provide demand estimates and elasticities (own-price and substitution) in order to test this hypothesis and verify the differentiation effect of GIs at aggregate level.

Design/methodology/approach – The analysis consists of the application of a quadratic almost ideal demand on a four equation system. Estimates are obtained through an iterated version of a generalized method of moments, which corrects for endogeneity determined by expenditure and prices in case of promotional activities.

Findings – Estimates prove the existence of a differentiation effect of GIs in terms of magnitude of elasticities and substitution effects. GIs corresponding to higher quality generate lower price sensitiveness and product substitution, contrarily to wine without GI. Controlled origin denomination (DOC) wine demand results are price sensitive and they substitute for wines of different GI. Controlled and guaranteed origin denomination (DOCG) is the most profitable GI. In fact, because of its inelastic demand, DOCG price could be potentially increased, to a certain extent, without having significant effects on volumes consumed.

Research limitations/implications – Foreign wine should also be included in the demand system in order to understand the whole Italian wine market. Data concern retail level demand. The whole market, including hotels, restaurants and catering, should be included to offer a wider set of implications.

Practical implications – Marketers and producers could use the information provided by the estimates in order to forecast Italian wine demand. Elasticities and substitution effect provide them with a precise measure of consumers' price sensitiveness, which would be beneficial for their pricing strategies.

Originality/value – The paper provides, for the first time, estimates of a demand system relative to GI differentiated Italian wine.

Keywords Italy, Wines, Viticulture, Consumer behaviour

Paper type Research paper

1. Introduction

Geographical indications (GIs) are aimed at differentiating the origin of wines and signal quality to consumers. Empirical and theoretical analyses highlight the effects of GIs on agro-food product demand. Landes and Posner (1987) stated that GIs reduce confusion and search costs, leading consumers to express strong preferences. Gil and Sanchez (1997), Loureiro and McCluskey (2000), Skuras and Vakrou (2002), and Schamel and Anderson (2003) have concluded that consumers are willing to pay more for a differentiated and traditional/regional product, while Ribeiro and Santos (2007) confirmed that the positive image/reputation of the region of origin generates strong preferences among consumers.

International Journal of Wine
Business Research
Vol. 23 No. 1, 2011
pp. 49-61
© Emerald Group Publishing Limited
1751-1062
DOI 10.1108/17511061111121407

IJWBR
23,1

van Ittersum *et al.* (2007) concluded that consumers of regional products assign high importance to labels that contain regional certification. They reported that GI labels positively affect consumers' willingness to pay, relative to the protected regional product. Caporale and Monteleone (2001) indicated that origin information has a significantly positive impact on virgin olive oil acceptability. Lusk *et al.* (2003) found that beef consumers prefer origin labels rather than private brands.

Empirical literature on consumers' wine preferences reports similar outcomes. Ribeiro and Santos (2007) showed that region of origin is the dominant cue when consumers and retailers select a wine for purchase. Scarpa *et al.* (2006) indicated that protected denominations of origin determine positive responses from consumers and reveal their willingness to pay, rather than reactions generated by brand, seller type, and suggestions from producers and acquaintances. Bonaria and Pomarici (2006) analyzed consumers' preferences towards Sardinian wines, and results indicate that GIs are the most important attributes to Italian consumers when selecting Sardinian wines. Malorgio *et al.* (2008) studied consumers' preferences towards wine attributes and found that GIs positively affect the probability of choosing a certain wine and generates a willingness to pay. Martinez-Carrasco *et al.* (2005), Mtimet and Albisu (2006), and Perrouty *et al.* (2006) showed that the designation of origin is, in most cases, the key attribute that affects wine price and ranking among consumers.

The economic and marketing literature on the topic presents unanimous outcomes on the effectiveness of GI in orienting consumers' preferences. Obviously, cultural/national context and the type of product analyzed could be the source of the different quantitative outcomes. The literature that was reviewed in conjunction with this research, therefore, permits one to form clear expectations about the differentiation effect of GIs in the Italian wine market.

Despite the fact that GIs have been widely discussed, there is no empirical evidence nor quantitative evaluation that concerns the differentiation effect of GIs in the wine market, in terms of consumers' responsiveness to the price of GIs versus conventional products, the profitability of the GIs, or the substitutability among products of different GIs and their conventional counterparts. More specifically, the measure of substitutability indicates how much consumption would shift to another GI typology if the market price of another GI type changes. In fact, when consumption switches easily from one category to another after a price increase, a natural consequence could be a weak product differentiation.

Although latent class models are becoming popular for estimating demand due to the convenient property with which to reduce the parameters' dimensionality, they do not allow the estimation of the whole set of substitution elasticities (Berry, 1994). On the other hand, demand estimation, although it could be econometrically cumbersome, has been largely applied for this purpose.

International wine literature lacks Italian contributions in which a demand system related to wine is estimated. The only known study was conducted by Torrisi *et al.* (2006), and it analyzed Italian table wine demand by estimating a linear approximated/almost ideal demand system (LA/AIDS) brand level model. They showed that two of the main Italian brands are close substitutes, while private label and "higher" table wine quality represent differentiated product on the market. Elasticities estimates also provide information on consumers' price responsiveness, and results are lower for higher quality wines.

Wine demand estimation relative to new world wine markets is a more common topic within the international scientific context. In fact, Pompelli and Heien (1991), Buccola and Vander Zanden (1997), Seale *et al.* (2003), and Carew *et al.* (2004) estimated source- and color-differentiated wine demands. A result common to those studies is the presence of substitution effects among wines of different nationality, while red and white wines rarely substitute each another.

The analysis of the highlighted literature, which incorporates a hedonic pricing model and conjoint analysis contributions, concludes that GIs are an important element/variable for wine differentiation and quality signaling. Contrarily, the literature related to demand estimation has never considered wines of different GI and non-GI wines as competing products or separable goods. An analysis that considers that hypothesis would generate important implications for the industry and policy makers, in terms of effectiveness of GIs in differentiating the wine market and the profitability potential of various types of GIs.

The present study is contextualized in a noteworthy market situation in which the European and Italian wine markets are facing a decrease in total consumption and a modification in the preferences of consumers, who are moving towards higher quality wines compared to the past. The shift in lifestyle towards a "metropolitan stereotype", which consists of an increasing number of meals consumed out with a reduced time at each meal, wine consumed only in more relaxed meals or important occasions (not at every meal as in the Mediterranean diet) and more importance to the wine choice and matching with food, is resulting in a change in dietary habits. Wine, therefore, is perceived as an experience good rather than the typical beverage of the Mediterranean diet. These changes characterize a particular and important economic framework for analyzing wine demand and understanding how consumers' preferences are shifting among wines of different quality and different GI.

The paper is organized as follows. After the introduction that highlights the most relevant issues, reviews the literature, and proposes the objectives, Section 2 presents the Italian wine market and the institutional context of the GIs. Section 3 describes the theory of the quadratic almost ideal demand systems (QUAIDSs), while Section 4 describes the data. Section 5 illustrates the empirical analysis and the results and presents the relative discussion. Finally, implications and suggestions for further research are detailed in Section 6.

2. Italian wine market
2.1 Wine classification through geographical indications
In 1963, the Italian legislation adopted the EU wine classification through GIs. The development of GIs allowed the identity of quality wines of particular regions to be protected from fraud and facilitated commercialization through wine classification and brand recognition. In addition, the GI system is coupled with labeling regulations that allow GI wines to signal quality with a higher level of labeled information in comparison to non-GI wines (subsequently indicated as table wines).

GI categorization includes the controlled origin denomination (DOC), or *Denominazione di Origine Controllata*; the controlled and guaranteed origin denomination (DOCG), or *Denominazione di Origine Controllata e Garantita*; and the geographic and typical indication or *Indicazione Geografica Tipica* (IGT). The first two appellations are earned by adhering to a quality discipline. The designation of these appellations depends

IJWBR
23,1

on recognition criteria of the wine as a traditional product, the adherence to strict regulations that establish the production area, the grape varieties for the blend, the wine/grapes' yield, and the alcohol content (DOCG criteria include bottling rules). The third GI, the IGT, was recently introduced in order to include several high quality wines that could not be designated as DOC. The remaining wines, which are not special or sparkling wines, such as *spumante* or champagne, are designated as table wines and do not follow any "collective" quality discipline.

2.2 Italian wine production
Italian wine growing is characterized by small-size, family-owned farms. In 2005, there were approximately 600,000 farms that produced grapes, with vineyards occupying an area of approximately 772,000 hectares. Two-thirds of the wine grape area concerns the production of table wines and IGTs, while the area for DOC or DOCG wines only accounts for 36 percent. DOC and DOCG wine grapes are mainly concentrated in northern Italy, where approximately 60 percent of the area is devoted to high-quality wine production (Anderson, 2004; Table I).

2.3 Wine consumption in Italy
During the period 2000-2004, the volume of household consumption of wine has decreased, on average, 2.4 percent annually, going from 9.65 to 8.57 million of hl. Table wine consumption registered the highest decrease, approximately 3 percent, while DOC and DOCG wines only decreased by 1 percent. Special wine consumption decreased 2.4 percent. Trends in expenditures are distinct. On average, aggregate expenditures on wine increased by 1 percent per year, going from EUR 1.63 to 1.71 billion. This increase is almost entirely due to the increase in expenditures for GI wines (approximately 4 percent growth). Expenditures for table wine and special wines registered a decrease of 0.3 percent (ISMEA, 2005).

This information clearly indicates a dietary habit shift towards a more metropolitan lifestyle. Another factor that affects this modification of the market is the change in the consumption approach, which is becoming more experimental. Moreover, the increasing knowledge about wine products and the increasing awareness about the beneficial effect of the antioxidants which wine contains may have oriented consumers towards higher quality and GI products.

| Area | Wine (millions of liters) | | | | Percentage of cultivated over the total wine growing area | | | |
	DOC and DOCG	IGT	Tablewine	Total	DOC and DOCG	IGT	Tablewine	DOC and DOCG and IGT
Italy	14.79	12.59	19.72	47.11	0.31	0.27	0.42	0.58
North	8.29	7.31	4.27	19.88	0.42	0.37	0.21	0.33
Center	3.49	2.02	1.91	7.44	0.47	0.27	0.26	0.12
South	3.00	3.25	13.53	19.79	0.15	0.16	0.68	0.13

Table I.
Italian production of wine per area

Source: ISTAT (2006)

3. The model: the QUAIDS

While most of the literature that was reviewed in conjunction with this study applies the (AIDS) or its linearized version (LA/AIDS) that were originally introduced by Deaton and Muellbauer (1980), the possibility of testing for a quadratic specification oriented this research towards the use of the QUAIDS.

Arguing that, for many commodities, standard empirical demand models do not provide an accurate analysis of behavior across income or expenditure groups, Banks *et al.* (1997) elaborated a new demand model which is consistent with theory and accounts for different behaviors across income/expenditure groups. Inductively, their argument is based on the assessment of the Engel relationship. In fact, when finding a significant quadratic specification in the empirical estimation of Engel curves, they incorporated a second-order polynomial expenditure in the demand system which led to the so-called QUAIDS.

In order to construct the QUAIDS, the following general form of demand is drawn:

$$w_i = A_i(p) + B_i(p)\log x + C_i(p)g(x) \tag{1}$$

for goods $i = 1, \ldots, N$, where p is the vector of prices and A, B, and C are differentiable functions. Expenditure shares are linear in log expenditure and in another smooth function of expenditure, $g(x)$. This last term allows nonlinearities in Engel curves (Banks *et al.*, 1997). The quadratic specification begins by considering the Deaton and Muellbauer translog price index:

$$\log P^* = \alpha_0 + \sum_k \alpha_k \log p_k + 0.5 \sum_k \sum_l \gamma_{kl} \log p_k \log p_l \tag{2}$$

as well as a Cobb-Douglas price aggregator, $b(p) = \prod_{i=1}^{n} p_i^{\beta_i} \tag{3}$

Finally, the share equation system is:

$$w_i = \alpha_i + \sum_j \gamma_{ij} \log p_j \beta_i \log(x/P^*) + [\lambda_i/b(p)] \left[\log(x/p^*)\right]^2 \tag{4}$$

Such is perfectly nested with the more commonly used AIDS.

Theoretical calculation restrictions and homogeneity are imposed, as in Banks *et al.* (1997). Elasticity calculations also follow, as specified in the paper that originally proposed this approach.

Given the partial derivatives:

$$\mu_i = \partial w_i/\partial \log x = \beta_i + \left[2\lambda_i/b(p)\right]\log(x/P^*) \tag{5}$$

$$\mu_{ij} = \partial w_i/\partial \log p_i = \gamma_{ij} - \mu_i\left(\alpha_j + \sum_k \gamma_{ik}\log p_k\right) - \left[\lambda_i\beta_j/b(p)\right]\left[\log(x/p^*)\right]^2 \tag{6}$$

The expenditure elasticities are given by $e_i = \mu_i/w_i + 1 \tag{7}$

The Marshallian price elasticities are given by $e_{ij}^u = \mu_{ij}/w_i - \delta_{ij} \tag{8}$

IJWBR
23,1

54

where is the Kronecker delta, which equals 1 when $i = j$:

$$\text{The Hicksian price elasticities are calculated as } e_{if}^c = e_{ij}^u + e_i w_j \qquad (9)$$

Compared to the AIDS paradigm, the QUAIDS model presents higher flexibility, resulting in two fold implications: better performance in explaining complex Engel curve phenomena, as expected for complex products such as wine, but cumbersome estimation. In addition, endogeneity issues are expected to negatively affect the outcome of the estimation if it is not corrected. In fact, in theoretical discussions, expenditure is usually intended to be equal to income, which is assumed to be imposed on consumers from outside. On the other hand, in empirical literature, when estimating a complete system of demand equations under a two-step budgeting assumption, in which consumers first choose how to allocate their income among all the categories of goods (e.g. housing and food) and then they decide how to allocate their budget within each category (Deaton and Muellbauer, 1980), the total expenditure is intended to be the sum of prices times the quantities purchased, or the sum of the expenditure of the single goods. Clearly then, expenditure on the right-hand side is jointly endogenous with the expenditures in the denominator of the shares.

When consumers purchase products that are offered at a promotional price, or at a discounted price for club-card holders, a consumer's decision to accept the promotional activity or to use a club card does affect prices or consumer purchasing power (Torrisi *et al.*, 2006). Additionally, prices are also included in the share calculation on the left-hand side of the demand equation. These reasons lead prices to be intended as weakly endogenous. Those multiple sources of endogeneity, therefore, need to be considered in the estimation (LaFrance, 1991).

A convenient tool that allows for the consideration of all those sources of complexity is the instrumental variable estimator, such as 2SLS or 3SLS, which uses the information contained in other variables, including the instruments, in order to remove the correlation between regressors and errors and provide consistent estimates. The 2SLS and 3SLS estimators and, in general, the maximum likelihood estimator, require strong and restrictive assumptions about the distribution of the error. Contrarily, the generalized method of moment (GMM)[1]:

$$[(1/N)\sum\nolimits_n \varphi(X_i, \beta)]' W^{-1} [(1/N)\sum\nolimits_n \varphi(X_i, \beta)]$$

moves away from any sort of parametric assumptions and handles contemporarily multiple endogeneity, nonlinearity, and heteroscedasticity. For this reason, the GMM estimator, when the model is correctly specified, is asymptotically more efficient than 3SLS or FIML (Greene, 2003).

4. Data: Italian homescan wine panel data
The Italian homescan panel is the collection of weekly retail purchase records of 6,000 Italian households. The panel is stratified on demographic and geographic criteria. It is balanced on region, age of the head of the household, the age of the primary purchaser, the number of family components, income level, and the number of children. The number of households in the panel reflects the national demographic and geographic distribution. Because of the sampling design and properties, ACNielsen homescan panel data can be considered to be representative of the at-home national consumption.

Of all the products contained in the ACNielsen homescan panel, our subsample concerns only wine products. The subsample includes all the 6,000 households of the original panel. The information it contains pertains to the wine purchases of the sample from 2002 to December 2005. The total information consists of wine product characteristics, such as color, appellation, varietal characterization, organic or conventional production, region of provenience, the production firm, trademark, volume, packaging material, purchase date, retailer/shop, purchase amount, and the single-purchase expenditure amount.

5. Empirical analysis and results

The estimation of wine demand, apart from other types of beverages or goods, is feasible when a two-step budgeting procedure is assumed. In this analysis, we assumed that Italian households begin by deciding how much of their income they would allocate to wine and in the second phase, they decide the quantity of each type of wine they would purchase.

Data preparation consisted of two phases: aggregation and data-mining. As for the first phase, we aggregated households' consumption into four categories: DOC, DOCG, IGT, and table wine by calculating quantities and averaging prices by means of a weighted average in order to assign a heavier weight to those wines purchased more. Aggregation over time has also been carried out. In fact, in order not to have zero expenditure points, the original weekly data have been aggregated into two-week observations. When such a phenomenon occurs, demand estimation should consider the truncated nature of the sample. Lacking of explanatory variables in order to estimate a truncated model we have chosen to aggregate data into bi-weekly observations. Monthly aggregated data, on the other hand, would reduce enormously the variability occurring on a shorter time-period (Figure 1).

Referring to the second phase of the data preparation, the shape of the series has been checked in order to depict the seasonal patterns. Our analysis revealed that prices do not show any seasonal patterns or reflect a high variability, while quantities show a typical seasonal pattern and a high standard deviation. Since promotions are positively correlated with consumption, they have been included in terms of proportion of wines purchased at each time. They have not been considered as price shifter because not all promotions reduce the price, most of them, in fact, consist of better display on the shelves or gadgets given with a bottle of wine. Moreover, in order to account for the sawtooth behavior and the specific seasonal pattern of high values during Christmas and low

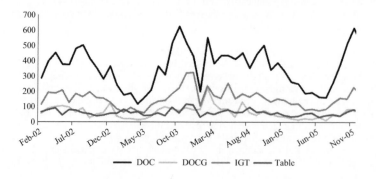

Figure 1.
Wine consumption
time series

IJWBR
23,1

56

values during the summer, the variables $\sin(\pi/13)$, the paycheck dummy at the end of each month, since Italians receive their paychecks on the 27th of each month, and the Christmas holidays dummy were also included in the model.

Data show that the most-purchased wine is the DOC, followed by the IGT. Table wine is purchased least often. The proportion of wines sold under in-store promotional activities is substantially high for DOCG and table wines. As expected, table wine shows the lower average price, while the DOCG is the most expensive (Table II).

The instruments employed in order to correct for endogeneity include the contractual level of wages; the individual price indices for all goods, food, and wine; the lag version of prices; the lag of the logarithm of prices; and the monthly index for gross domestic product and other endogenous variables uncorrelated with the error, such as the $\sin(\pi/13)$, the seasonal dummies, the stone index, and various combinations of those in terms of cross-products.

Finally, we scaled price data to the median and established the estimation. Estimation has been carried out by means of an iterated version of the GMM in which the parameters obtained at the first run serve as starting values for the second run. Estimation concludes when parameters of the last step equal those estimated in the previous step, plus or minus a tolerance values.

Estimation has required eight iterations to reach the convergence. Endogenous regressors have been significantly over-identified (e.g. the *J*-test). The auto-correlation phenomenon does not occur in any of the series, as shown by the Durbin and Watson tests. Finally, the R^2, although just indicative of a system of equations, shows that the model specification has facilitated an explanation of the data variability well above 26 percent (Table III).

Estimates of the system, although not directly interpretable for quantitative evaluations, provide a rough evaluation of wine demand differentiated by GIs through the interpretation of their signs. Price increases for IGT and table wines correspond to increases in DOC wine shares and decreases in DOCG, IGT, and table wine shares. This result confirms the strong diversification among DOCG, IGT, and table wines, but also the scarce differentiation of DOC wines, which could show strong substitution with the other categories. Substitution among GIs is expected, especially between DOC and DOCG and DOC and IGT, because they could be closely related in terms of quality.

Variable		Average	SD	Min	Max
Quantity (liters/two-week)	DOC	318.23	143.46	103.25	976.25
	DOCG	54.03	34.08	10.50	166.50
	IGT	83.82	63.79	15.00	286.50
	Table	19.49	18.28	1.50	80.00
Price (euro)	DOC	3.48	1.50	0.25	48.00
	DOCG	5.92	2.79	0.61	50.67
	IGT	2.80	1.45	0.14	16.00
	Table	1.46	0.89	0.04	21.30
Promotions (proportion of wines purchased under promotional activities)	DOC	0.31			
	DOCG	0.03			
	IGT	0.16			
	Table	0.49			

Table II.
Sample descriptive
statistics of bi-weekly
national data

| Dependent varriable | Equations (symmetry, homogeneity, and adding-up imposed) | | | | | | | |
| | DOC-share | | DOCG-share | | IGT-share | | Table-share | |
Variable	Coef.	SE	Coef.	SE	Coef.	SE	Coef.	SE
Intercept	−4.139	1.315	0.939	0.999	2.144	0.857	2.056	0.938
log DOC price	−5.872	3.222	_a		_a		_a/b	
log DOCG price	0.956	0.505	−0.074	0.011	_a		_a/b	
log IGT price	2.354	1.549	−0.465	0.538	−0.798	0.092	_a/b	
log table price	2.563	1.597	−0.417	0.228	−1.091	0.702	−1.055[b]	0.746
Expenditure term	1.349	0.331	−0.230	0.199	−0.562	0.247	−0.558[b]	0.234
Seasonality	−0.010	0.014	0.016	0.011	0.002	0.009	0.986[b]	0.020
Christmas holiday	−0.051	0.026	0.058	0.021	0.008	0.018	0.986[b]	0.020
Monthly paycheck	−0.003	0.013	−0.003	0.010	0.015	0.009	0.991[b]	0.010
Promotion	0.001	0.000	0.001	0.001	0.003	0.001	0.995[b]	0.001
Quadratic	−0.097	0.022	0.015	0.022	0.041	0.018	0.041[b]	0.014
R^2	35.010		26.710		54.210			
Durbin-Watson test	2.181		1.832		1.808			
J-test	112.675 (DF = 78)							

Notes: [a]Not estimated because of symmetry restrictions; [b]parameters retrieved through homogeneity and adding-up restrictions

Table III.
Estimation results

Substitution between DOC and table wines, on the other hand, could correspond to a reduction in DOC reputation. In fact, the increase in the number of DOC wines on the market could have influenced consumer perceptions of those wines as being niche and high-quality products.

A certain degree of consumption sensitivity to price variations was noted. Generally, demand is downward-sloping for all the four wine categories which were analyzed. This result indicates that price promotions or heavier taxation could effectively modify the level of wine consumption. In fact, there is an ongoing debate at the European level about the imposition of excises on the Italian market. Excises are volume-based taxes, so expensive wines are, in proportions, less levied than cheap wines. The taxation should reduce consumption and abuses of alcoholic beverages.

As the total expenditure for wine increases, the DOC market share increases. Contrarily, IGT and table wines are consumed less when consumers allocate more money to wine in general. This last result confirms the big scale trends that reveal an increase in total wine expenditure but also a reduction in lower quality wine consumption, opposed to the increase in DOC/DOCG wine demand.

Estimates show that, with the exception of DOC wines, consumption generally increases at Christmas. Furthermore, the monthly paychecks elicit an increase in IGT and table wine consumption. As expected, in-store promotional activities generate an increase in consumption for all of the selected categories. Finally, the significance of the quadratic term confirms that the QUAIDS is the preferred specification against the AIDS or the LA/AIDS models.

Quantitative implications could be depicted by interpreting the own- and cross-price elasticities, which are calculated using the estimated parameters and referring to a base situation[2]. Hicksian elasticities have been calculated since they provide estimates that are purified by the income/expenditure effect, compared to Marshallian elasticities[3]. Therefore, they could be considered reliable measures for drawing quantitative implications about price responsiveness of demand, substitution among the GIs, and GI-related profitability and differentiation effects.

The elements on the main diagonal presented in Table IV are own-price elasticities, which represent the percentage variation of the market share of a specific wine as a consequence of a 1 percent increase in its price. For instance, a 1 percent increase in table wine price elicits a 7.7 percent decrease in market share. Similarly, a 1 percent increase in DOCG price elicits a 0.8 percent decrease in DOCG share.

Own-price estimates show that DOC, IGT, and table wine demands are elastic, while DOCG wine demand is inelastic. Generally, own-price elasticities could be related to the quality perceived by consumers. When quality is perceived as low, a price increase would lead to many consumers reducing or ceasing to consume that product or switching to higher quality products. The demand of this kind of product would be elastic. High quality and highly differentiated products, on the other hand, satisfy specific consumers' needs. As consequence, we expect those products to show inelastic demand and generate a high level of loyalty.

DOCG wine demand, in fact, is inelastic. A price increase, in this case, would elicit a less than a proportional reduction in market shares. This result leads to the conclusion that DOCG wines are highly profitable because producers/sellers could increase their prices above marginal costs without having significant and negative effects on their market shares. Being demand-inelastic, price promotions on DOCG wines do not generate significantly higher sales. This result justifies the higher incidence of promotions for this category in order to sell out the stocks.

Contrary to DOCG wines, the demand for DOC, IGT, and table wines are own-price elastic. An increase in their price would more than proportionally reduce their consumption. In consequence, those wine categories show low margins of profitability because, in order to maintain a high level of sales/consumption, prices should be set as low as possible. Conversely, a decrease in their own-price would generate a more than proportional increase in their demand. Clearly, prices could be reduced to the extent of marginal costs being lower than prices. Among the wine categories that could be advantaged by a price reduction or a promotion, as for our results, table and DOC wines would exploit this opportunity the most because of their highly elastic demand. In fact, contrarily to DOC wines, the high level of table wine sold under promotions is a sign that producers of table wine are already using this strategy.

Looking at cross-price estimates, represented as out-of-diagonal elements in Table IV, we noticed that there are clear and significant substitution effects among DOC and other wines, especially IGT and table. Substitution indicates a scarce differentiation among DOC wines and other GIs, but also between DOC and table wine. In fact, an increase

		Price			
		DOC	DOCG	IGT	Table
Quantity	DOC	−5.418 (3.814)	_[a]	_[a]	_[a]
	DOCG	1.019 (0.026)	−0.844 (0.368)	_[a]	_[a]
	IGT	2.732 (1.369)	−2.827 (4.774)	−2.317 (1.891)	_[a]
	Table	2.722 (0.906)	−2.229 (1.743)	−2.454 (1.359)	−7.769 (2.704)

Table IV.
Hicksian/substitution elasticities at the base situation

Notes: [a]Symmetric demand at base prices consists of symmetric price responses; SE by means of delta method

in DOC price would elicit a reduction in DOC consumption and direct consumers towards other GIs or table wines. While the DOC and other GIs could effectively cause confusion among consumers which, in turn, could result in substitution effects that indicate a scare differentiation, the substitution between DOC and table wines could be associated with the ongoing loss in reputation of this typology of wines.

Complementarity, which is opposed to substitution, has been found for the DOCG, IGT, and table wine categories which result in high differentiation from one another. This outcome, contrary to the hypothesized confusion of consumers when facing different types of GIs, confirms the effectiveness of GIs as a differentiation tool and justifies the segmentation of the market into these categories for policy and managerial purposes.

Finally, the changes in consumers' tastes towards higher quality and more expensive wine products could be justified by the demand price responsiveness. As prices increase, consumers tend to keep consuming high-quality wines, such as DOCG, and avoid presumably lower quality wines, such as table varieties. For the same reason, those results are consistent with the increase in total wine expenditure that is currently happening in the market.

6. Discussion and conclusions

This study assesses that, indeed, appellations generate a strong differentiation effect. As a result, wines of competing GIs generate independent demands and consumers' preferences within the Italian wine market. Another result of the GI system is that non-GI wine demand remains differentiated from the rest of the market. The obvious conclusion concerns the effectiveness of the GI differentiation system, which allowed consumers to develop independent demands. In such a differentiated market, producers of a specific GI are able to develop their strategy without taking into account the strategies of the other wine typologies. With access to this information, producers and marketers could draw important implications because they would use at their advantage the information of operating in a differentiated market. As different wine typologies show independent demands, promotional activities could also be decided independently. When two products substitute each other, promotional activities of one player clearly negatively affect the market shares of the others.

A different behavior concerns DOC wines. The growing number of wines belonging to this group probably moved consumers to consider those wines from niche products to "quasi" commodities, with negative effects on the image/reputation of this wine typology. Policy makers, in this regard, should promote a set of activities aimed at the re-evaluation of DOC wine reputation or a reconsideration of the wines that affect the image of the DOC branding strategy into this category.

Future research should provide a more in-depth view in which wines are differentiated by price ranges and by color as well as GI. Moreover, the relationship between foreign wines and Italian GIs should be understood in order to evaluate whether domestic and imported products are differentiated from one another. More disaggregated data could be used in order to understand regional differences. Data concern retail level demand. Thus, the whole market that includes the hotel restaurant and catering sales, should be considered for providing implications relative to the entire market.

IJWBR
23,1

Notes

1. The GMM estimator follows the following specification:
   $[(1/N)\sum_n \varphi(X_i, \beta)]' W^{-1} [(1/N)\sum_n \varphi(X_i, \beta)]$

2. Promotions $= 0$; Christmas holidays dummy $= 0$; paycheck dummy $= 0$; log median scaled prices $= 0$.

3. Marshallian and expenditure elasticities are available under requests to the authors.

60

References

Anderson, K. (2004), *The World's Wine Markets: Globalization at Work*, Edward Elgar, Adelaide.

Banks, J., Blundell, R. and Lewbel, A. (1997), "Quadratic Engel curves and consumer demand", *The Review of Economics and Statistics*, Vol. 79, pp. 527-39.

Berry, S.T. (1994), "Estimating discrete-choice models of product differentiation", *The RAND Journal of Economics*, Vol. 25, pp. 242-62.

Bonaria, M. and Pomarici, E. (2006), "An evaluation of the Sardinia wine's consumers satisfaction", *Rivista di Economia Agraria*, Vol. 61 No. 2, pp. 265-92.

Buccola, S. and Vander Zanden, L. (1997), "Wine demand, price strategy, and tax policy", *Review of Agricultural Economics*, Vol. 19, pp. 428-40.

Caporale, G. and Monteleone, M. (2001), "Effect of expectations induced by information on origin and its guarantee on the acceptability of a traditional food: olive oil", *Sciences des Aliments*, Vol. 21, pp. 243-54.

Carew, R., Florkowski, W. and He, S. (2004), "Demand for domestic and imported table wine in British Columbia: a source-differentiate almost ideal demand system approach", *Canadian Journal of Agricultural Economics*, Vol. 52, pp. 183-99.

Deaton, A. and Muellbauer, J. (1980), "An almost ideal demand system", *The American Economic Review*, Vol. 70, pp. 312-26.

Gil, J.M. and Sanchez, M. (1997), "Consumer preferences for wine attributes: a conjoint approach", *British Food Journal*, Vol. 99, pp. 3-11.

Greene, W. (2003), *Econometric Analysis*, 5th ed., Prentice-Hall, Upper Saddle River, NJ.

ISMEA (2005), *Indagine acquisti domestici: vino e spumanti 2000-2004*, ISMEA, Rome.

ISTAT (2006), *Agricoltura: la produzione di uva e di vino, anno 2005*, Istituto Nazionale di Statistica, Rome.

LaFrance, J. (1991), "When is expenditure 'exogenous' in separable demand models?", *Western Journal of Agricultural Economics*, Vol. 16, pp. 49-62.

Landes, W.M. and Posner, R.A. (1987), "Trademark law: an economic perspective", *Journal of Law & Economics*, Vol. 30, pp. 265-309.

Loureiro, M.L. and McCluskey, J.J. (2000), "Assessing consumer response to protected geographical identification labeling", *Agribusiness*, Vol. 16, pp. 309-20.

Lusk, J.L., Roosen, J. and Fox, J.A. (2003), "Demand for beef from cattle administered growth hormones or fed genetically modified corn: a comparison of consumers in France, Germany, the United Kingdom, and the United States", *American Journal of Agricultural Economics*, Vol. 85, pp. 16-29.

Malorgio, G., Hertzberg, A. and Grazia, C. (2008), "Italian wine consumer behaviour and wineries responsive capacity", paper presented at 12th EAAE Congress "People, Food and Environments: Global Trends and European Strategies", Gent, 26-29 August.

Martinez-Carrasco, L., Brugalos, M. and Martinez Poveda, A. (2005), "Quality wines and wines protected by a designation of origin: identifying their consumption determinants", *Journal of Wine Research*, Vol. 16, pp. 213-32.

Mtimet, N. and Albisu, L.M. (2006), "Spanish wine consumer behavior: a choice experiment approach", *Agribusiness*, Vol. 22, pp. 343-62.

Perrouty, J.P., D'Hauteville, F. and Lockshin, L. (2006), "The influence of wine attributes on region of origin equity: an analysis of the moderating effect of consumer's perceived expertise", *Agribusiness*, Vol. 22, pp. 323-41.

Pompelli, G. and Heien, D. (1991), "Discrete/continuous consumer demand choices: an application to the US domestic and imported white wine markets", *European Review of Agricultural Economics*, Vol. 18, pp. 117-30.

Ribeiro, J.C. and Santos, J.F. (2007), "Consumer perception of Portuguese quality wine and the region-of-origin effect", paper presented at 47th Congress of the European Regional Science Association, Paris, 29 August-2 September.

Scarpa, R., Thiene, M. and Galletto, L. (2006), "Consumers WTP for wine with certified origin: latent classes based on attitudinal responses", paper presented at European Association of Agricultural Economists – 98th Seminar, 29 June-2 July, Chania.

Schamel, G. and Anderson, K. (2003), "Wine quality and varietal, regional and winery reputations: hedonic prices for Australia and New Zealand", *The Economic Record*, Vol. 79, pp. 357-69.

Seale, J., Marchant, M. and Basso, A. (2003), "Imports versus domestic production: a demand system analysis of the US red wine market", *Review of Agricultural Economics*, Vol. 25, pp. 187-202.

Skuras, D. and Vakrou, A. (2002), "Consumers' willingness to pay for origin labeled wine: a Greek case study", *British Food Journal*, Vol. 104, pp. 898-912.

Torrisi, F., Stefani, G. and Seghieri, C. (2006), "Use of scanner data to analyze the table wine demand in the Italian major retailing trade", *Agribusiness*, Vol. 22, pp. 391-403.

van Ittersum, K., Meulenberg, M.T.G., van Trijp, H.C.M. and Candel, M.J.J.M. (2007), "Consumers' appreciation of regional certification labels: a pan-European study", *Journal of Agricultural Economics*, Vol. 58, pp. 1-23.

About the authors
Antonio Stasi, MSc, PhD, is an Associate Researcher in Agriculture & Resource Economics, University of Foggia, Foggia, Italy. Antonio Stasi is the corresponding author and can be contacted at: a.stasi@unifg.it

Gianluca Nardone, MSc, PhD, is a Professor Emeritus, Agriculture & Resource Economics, University of Foggia, Foggia, Italy.

Rosaria Viscecchia, PhD, is a Researcher, Agriculture & Resource Economics, University of Foggia, Foggia, Italy.

Antonio Seccia, MSc, is an Associate Professor, Agriculture & Resource Economics, University of Bari, Bari, Italy.

Italian wine
demand and GIs

61

[18]

European Review of Agricultural Economics Vol **39** (**4**) (2012) pp. 539–566
doi:10.1093/erae/jbr053
Advance Access Publication 17 November 2011

Quality certification by geographical indications, trademarks and firm reputation

Luisa Menapace[†] and GianCarlo Moschini[‡,*]

[†]*University of Trento, Italy;* [‡]*Iowa State University, USA*

Received September 2010; final version accepted July 2011

Review coordinated by Christoph Weiss

Abstract

We develop a reputation model to study the concurrent use of trademarks and certification for food products with a geographical indication (GI). The model extends Shapiro's (1983) approach to modelling reputation to a situation in which two technologies for the production of quality are available, one of which is available only in the GI region. In this setting, trademarks capture firm-specific reputations, whereas GI certification captures a notion of collective reputation. The model shows that GI certification improves the ability of reputation to operate as a mechanism for assuring quality linked to some inherent attributes of a particular production area.

Keywords: asymmetric information, certification, geographical indications, quality, reputation, trademarks

JEL classification: D23, D82, L14, L15, Q1

1. Introduction

Some of the challenges in delivering quality products in the agricultural and food sector are rooted in the possible market failure identified by Akerlof (1970) in situations characterised by asymmetric information and moral hazard problems. An interesting market-based solution to this problem is possible when a product's quality attributes are not observable to the buyer prior to purchase but they are readily determined at consumption, and it relies on the notion of firm 'reputation,' which here refers to the buyers' beliefs about the quality associated with a firm's product. Key instruments for supporting a firm's reputation are trademarks. Specifically, when firms can identify themselves to consumers through trademarks, thereby effectively defining their

*Corresponding author: Department of Economics, Iowa State University, Ames, IA 50011, USA.
E-mail: moschini@iastate.edu

own brand of the product, they can build a reputation about their quality by consistently supplying it over time. This notion is due to the seminal treatment of Klein and Leffler (1981), with Shapiro (1983) providing an early, insightful modelling structure. The emergence of this information about quality is achieved in competitive markets through an equilibrium price structure that provides the necessary incentives for competitive firms to develop and maintain reputation for producing a given quality. It is also shown that reputation is an imperfect mechanism for assuring quality and that high-quality items can only be provided at a premium above production costs.

Trademarks are essential tools for most modern firms; their functions are well understood and supported by established legal statutes in most developed countries, and established trademarks constitute an extremely valuable intangible asset for many businesses (Landes and Posner, 2003). In agricultural and food industries, however, a related but distinct notion is that of geographical indications (GIs). Like trademarks, GIs are a form of branding, and they specifically focus on the use of names connected with the geographic origin of the product. The use of GIs has a long history in the European Union (EU), and GIs enjoy growing popularity in emerging markets and developing economies (WIPO, 2007; EU, 2008). As a form of intellectual property (IP), GIs figure prominently in the 1994 TRIPS agreement of the World Trade Organization (WTO). Unlike trademarks, which are quintessentially private goods, GIs provide common labels that are typically accessible to a large number of firms producing similar (and competing) products. Furthermore, it is very common to observe the concurrent use of GIs and trademarks for branding products of the agricultural and food industries (Bramley and Kirsten, 2007). For example, many European wines labelled with a particular GI (e.g. Chianti) are supplied by a large number of firms, each with its own distinctive trademark. But if a firm's reputation for quality can be sustained by its own private trademark, as the strand of literature following Shapiro's (1983) seminal work suggests, what exactly is the role of GIs? The public-good nature of GI labels inevitably raises the issue of a collective aspect to the reputation enjoyed by groups of like firms. In the context of reputation mechanisms, the challenge is to understand how private and public elements can profitably coexist in this setting, and to elucidate the specific informational roles of trademarks and GIs. This is the main objective of our analysis and we do so by proposing an innovative extension of Shapiro's (1983) reputation model.

In this paper we extend the theory of firm reputation as a mechanism to assure quality in competitive markets to a context in which both GI certification and trademarks are available to firms as quality indicators. We argue that our focus on quality is fully justified in the context of GIs by the presumption of a quality-geography nexus, an element that is explicitly codified in many forms of GIs and implicit in virtually all of them. The model we propose in this paper relies on Shapiro's (1983) notion of reputation, which we extend to reflect both collective and firm-specific reputations in competitive markets. By casting the analysis in such a framework, we naturally assume that quality attributes in the agricultural and food products of interest to us are best understood as experience goods. A related implication, therefore, is that consumers do not have a preference for geography *per se*, but care about the geographical attribute noted in many GIs because of their ability to signal intrinsic quality. We also note that Shapiro's (1983) modelling framework, with its insistence on competitive equilibrium conditions, is particularly suited to being extended to study GIs, as these markets are typically characterised by the presence of numerous autonomous firms that make independent business decisions and retain their own profits but share a GI label while acting in competitive conditions (Fishman *et al.*, 2008; Moschini, Menapace and Pick, 2008).

The model that we develop presumes that an initial investment via the production of high-quality product is necessary for a firm to gain private reputation. Collective reputation is obtained through certification and is determined by the conditions required for certification (e.g. minimum quality, production technology etc.). In equilibrium, quality in excess of the minimum commands a premium above marginal costs, which, as in Shapiro (1983), represents a fair return on the private investment in reputation. In our setting, GIs and trademarks turn out to be complementary means for signalling quality in agricultural and food markets. In particular, GI certification reveals some information regarding the origin (and indirectly the quality) of the product and, by constraining the moral hazard behaviour of producers, reduces the cost of building reputation and leads to lower equilibrium prices and welfare gains. The effect of the revelation of a product's geographical origin on the efficiency of the market is similar in spirit to that due to the introduction of a minimum quality standard (MQS) in Shapiro's original paper (1983).

The reputation approach to the problem of moral hazard also draws attention to the fact that the type of GI certification scheme used might matter. Specifically, our model can differentiate the two primary certification schemes currently used for GIs, the European-style *sui generis* scheme and the American-style scheme based on certification marks. These schemes differ substantially with regard to the requirements for individual firms to obtain certification. In a second-best world with asymmetric information, it turns out that these differences are relevant because they affect the collective reputation of certified products and hence the cost of providing quality.

Several instructive aspects of the role of certification in quality provision and reputation formation emerge from the model. First, we show that GI certification reduces the divergence between the reputation equilibrium and the equilibrium that would prevail under perfect information by lowering the cost of establishing reputation compared with a situation with only trademarks. Hence, GI certification improves the ability of reputation to operate as a mechanism for assuring quality, even when a fully functioning trademark system already exists. Second, the model suggests that the impact of GI certification on producers depends on whether or not they have already committed resources towards building a (private) reputation via their own trademarks. This is because GI certification raises the price that entrants can command, which reduces the cost of reputation building but also reduces the value of established reputation. Our model also has interesting implications for the current debate and negotiations over alternative forms of protection for GIs at the WTO (Fink and Maskus, 2006) and the ongoing consultations on product quality policy reform within the EU. The results we derive provide a rationale for favouring an EU-style *sui generis* scheme over certification marks.

GIs have recently attracted the interest of academics in economics, marketing, law and sociology. In particular, the economics literature on GIs has analysed various aspects of their ability to work as a certification tool in alleviating market failures due to the presence of asymmetric information when quality cannot be credibly signalled otherwise (Anania and Nisticó, 2004; Zago and Pick, 2004; Lence *et al.*, 2007; Moschini, Menapace and Pick, 2008). The role of collective reputation for agricultural goods is investigated by Winfree and McCluskey (2005) in a setting where market price depends on the industry average quality (and where, unlike the model we develop, all firms sell the same quality). To the best of our knowledge, two of the main areas of emphasis of our analysis – the concurrent use of trademarks and GIs in a reputation model, and the comparison of alternative forms of GIs – have not been investigated in any of the existing theoretical studies.[1]

In what follows, we first provide a brief review of the institutional setting for GIs and then introduce the model and the reputation formation mechanism. Next, we define and derive a long-run, rational-expectation, stationary Nash equilibrium under three different scenarios characterised by the use of trademarks and (i) the absence of a certification scheme, (ii) the presence of a *sui generis* GI certification scheme and (iii) the presence of a certification mark scheme. We characterise the equilibrium price–quality schedules that apply to the various scenarios and discuss the main economic implications and associated welfare effects.

2. Institutional framework

GIs are typically names of places or regions used to brand goods. Many GIs pertain to wines (e.g. Burgundy), agricultural products (e.g. Thai Hom Mali rice) and foods (e.g. Parmigiano-Reggiano cheese), but non-food products such as handicrafts and textiles can also be covered by GIs, particularly those from developing countries (e.g. Mysore silk).[2] The distinctive feature of GIs is that the quality attributes of the goods they identify are considered to be inherently linked to the nature of the geographic location in which production takes place (e.g. climate conditions, soil composition, local

---

1 Landon and Smith (1998), and Costanigro, McCluskey and Goemans (2010), look at collective reputation empirically.

2 Other agricultural products not intended for human consumption are ornamental plants, flowers, cork, hay, cochineal, wool, wicker and essential oils.

knowledge), i.e. to the notion of *'terroir'* (Barham, 2003; Josling, 2006).[3] GIs are considered one of the earliest instruments used to counteract market failures resulting from asymmetric information (Rangnekar, 2004), and their protection has a long tradition in Europe dating back to the fifteenth century (O'Connor, 2004). However, following the EU's Common Agricultural Policy reform in 1992, which moved EU policies progressively away from price supports towards programmes to promote food quality and rural development, GIs have taken centre stage as the 'main pillar of the EU's quality policy on agricultural products' (EU, 2003). GIs can also be viewed as a distinct form of IP rights, and as such they figure prominently in the TRIPS agreement of the WTO and have also received significant international attention outside of the EU (Moschini, 2004). In particular, significant interest in GIs has emerged recently among developing countries.[4]

As for other types of branding (e.g. trademarks), the ability of GIs to alleviate market failures due to the presence of asymmetric information rests on their credibility, thus necessitating IP protection. While trademark protection is well established and relatively harmonised across countries, the protection of GIs varies to a large degree, and its implementation is a question of intense disagreement in ongoing WTO negotiations. The TRIPS agreement requires countries to provide legal means for protecting GIs against unfair competition, but it does not specify the means by which protection should be provided.

Two primary legal notions are used to protect GIs. Perhaps most common are *sui generis* schemes originally developed and used in Roman law countries and currently adopted in the EU (OECD, 2000) and in several Asian and a few North American and Latin American countries (WIPO, 2007).[5] Examples include protected designations of origin (PDOs) and protected geographical indications (PGIs), two *sui generis* GI schemes that are used widely for agricultural and food products within the EU. Regulations concerning these schemes are harmonised across all EU member countries and, since 2008, also cover wines (EU Reg. 479/2008, Art. 34). Well-known products that are registered as PDOs include Parmigiano Reggiano cheese and Chianti wine. Tuscany extra virgin olive oil instead represents an example of a GI registered as a PGI. The distinction between these two alternative *sui generis* GI schemes is based upon the nature of the quality-geography nexus (i.e. the notion of *terroir*), in which PDOs require a stronger link between the natural environment of production and the quality attributes of the product (for additional details regarding the distinction between PDO and PGI see EU Reg. 510/2006, Art. 2).

---

3 See the definition of GIs in the TRIPS agreement (Article 22.1).
4 For example, several countries are introducing or expanding their own GI laws, regulations and promotion programmes, including China (Xiaobing and Kireeva, 2007), India (Rao, 2006), South Korea (Suh and MacPherson, 2007) and Colombia (Teuber, 2010). Noteworthy is the Kenian-Swiss ongoing project aimed at establishing a functioning GI protection scheme in Kenya and at raising awareness on GIs in the East African Community member states (see the Swiss Institute of Intellectual Property's website at https://www.ige.ch/en.html).
5 These include China, Mongolia, North Korea, Thailand, Vietnam, Colombia, Venezuela, Cuba and Costa Rica.

544   *L. Menapace and G. Moschini*

The presence of a quality-geography nexus, i.e. the requirement of a specific link between a good's qualities and its geographical origin, represents the main distinctive characteristic of any *sui generis* scheme. In other words, for a geographic name that identifies a given good to be eligible to receive this *sui generis* IP protection, evidence must be provided that the quality or characteristics of the good are due to the natural and human factors (e.g. climate, soil quality, local knowledge) characterising the geographic area of origin (e.g. EU Reg. 510/2006 Art. 2 and Art. 4.2.f). In addition to the existence of a specific quality/geography link, the European *sui generis* scheme also requires the definition of a code of rules for each GI product (commonly referred to in the literature as the 'specification'). The specification details all the product characteristics, may restrict the admissible production process and identifies the geographic area in which production takes place (EU Reg. 510/2006 Art. 4).[6] Provided these conditions are met, *sui generis* schemes are not exclusionary in the sense that usage rights over a GI are granted to all producers within a designated production area who comply with the product specification (EU Reg. 510/2006 Art. 8).

Alternatively, in common law countries, including the United States, GIs are protected within the standard trademark system and are usually registered as certification marks.[7] Certification marks simply certify that products meet given conditions and, in the case of GIs, the only such condition is the geographic area of production. In the United States, for example, the US Patent and Trademark Office (USPTO) does not scrutinise certification mark applications based on the characteristics to be certified or require the definition of quality standards. Indeed, when a certification mark includes a geographic name, it is understood that the only attribute to be certified is the origin of the good (USPTO, 2007). It is critical to emphasise that, as for *sui generis* systems, the right to use a certification mark is collective in nature. All producers who operate within the geographic area indicated by the GI have access to certification and can use (subject to obtaining certification) the GI to label their products. This contrasts sharply with usage rights over trademarks, which are private and belong to a single entity or firm.[8]

3. Model

In the model we develop the presumption that consumers' interest in the geographical origin of products is due to the implication that this origin

---

6 The product characteristics include the physical, chemical, microbiological and organoleptic characteristics of the raw materials and of the final product.

7 In the United States, certification marks used for GIs are registered with the United States Patent and Trademark Office.

8 Only under special circumstances, specifically when a geographic term has acquired a 'secondary meaning,' can a GI be registered as a trademark. When the 'secondary meaning' of a geographic name is, in the consumers' minds, a production or manufacturing source (while the primary meaning is the geographic place), then it is possible under US trademark law to register a geographic name as a trademark, a private rather than collective IP right (USPTO, 2007).

might have for the quality of the product. This view is consistent with the quality/geography nexus that is explicitly invoked to rationalise GIs in the EU but it is also implicit for many other GIs, as discussed in the previous section. In other words, consumers do not have a preference for geography *per se* (e.g. interest in Napa Valley wines is predicated on the belief that they might enjoy superior quality and not because of quality-unrelated considerations pertaining to this valley). Furthermore, our reputation modelling approach treats quality as an experience attribute (as opposed to, say, a credence attribute). The idea that food products typically ought to be treated as experience goods can be traced back to Nelson's (1970) introduction of this concept and is well established in the economics literature (e.g. Ali and Nauges, 2007).[9] As for quality, we will model it as a one-dimensional attribute. This is, admittedly, a simplification of reality. But this approach permits considerable gains in terms of analytical tractability while allowing us to provide a useful characterisation of the joint use of trademarks and GIs.

Consider the market for an experience good (e.g. parmesan cheese, sparkling wine, dry-cured ham) that can be produced in a continuum of qualities indexed by $q \in [q_0, \infty)$, where q_0 is the MQS allowed in the market (e.g. the minimum quality necessary to meet consumer safety and sanitary conditions and/or other regulatory provisions necessary for lawful marketing of the product). The presumption is that this MQS is enforced by the government and it is common knowledge that all producers meet it. We assume that there are two production areas – the GI region and the other region – and that these two regions enjoy different production technologies *vis-à-vis* the production of quality. Specifically, the production of one unit of good of quality q costs $c^G(q)$ in the GI region and $c(q)$ in the other region. The GI technology is available only in the GI region, whereas the standard technology is available in the other region.[10] These technologies satisfy standard conditions; specifically, $c^G(q)$ and $c(q)$ are assumed to be continuous, (strictly) increasing and (strictly) convex functions of quality, that is, $c_q(q) > 0$, $c_{qq}(q) > 0$, $c_q^G(q) > 0$ and $c_{qq}^G(q) > 0$. Furthermore, we assume that the GI technology $c^G(q)$ displays a cost advantage in the production of higher quality products, whereas the conventional technology $c(q)$ possesses a cost advantage in the production of lower quality products. More precisely, we assume that there

---

9 Whereas the quality attributes of interest here are best thought of as experience goods, we recognise that other attributes of food products (e.g. organic, non-genetically modified, pathogen-free) could alternatively fit Darby and Karni's (1973) notion of credence goods. Roe and Sheldon (2007) study labelling options for such goods. Whereas the existence of credence good attributes would undoubtedly expand the scope for GI labels, one of the interesting results of our model is to show that GI-certification is valuable even without assuming that consumers' value origin *per se*.

10 As will become apparent, in the context of our model it would make no difference to assume that the conventional technology $c(q)$ is available everywhere.

exists a threshold quality level $\tilde{q}$ such that

$$
\begin{aligned}
c^G(q) > c(q) \qquad &\text{for all } q < \tilde{q} \\
c^G(q) < c(q) \qquad &\text{for all } q > \tilde{q}
\end{aligned} \tag{1}
$$

and, of course, $c(\tilde{q}) = c^G(\tilde{q})$. This assumption, which mirrors the comparative advantage condition postulated by Falvey (1989) in an international context, is intended to capture the notion of *terroir*, that is, the fact that the nature and characteristics of the production conditions in GI regions facilitate the attainment of higher quality levels (the quality/geography nexus discussed earlier).

The condition in equation (1) can be supported by a number of real-world illustrations. Consider, for example, the case of some fruits and vegetables that have PDO status in the EU, such as Monteleone di Spoleto spelt and Val di Non apples. These GIs' production regions are located in mountain areas where topographic conditions drastically limit the possibilities for mechanisation, making standard mass-production unfeasible (i.e. standard qualities can be more cheaply produced elsewhere where mechanisation is possible).[11] At the same time, though, the natural environmental conditions of the production areas (e.g. including altitude, exposure, daily temperature swings etc.) favour the attainment of levels of quality that would be very costly to achieve elsewhere (e.g. in the limit one could artificially replicate the natural environmental conditions at a very high cost), making the GI technology competitive in the upper range of the quality spectrum.

We analyse a competitive setting where all producers are price-takers and where the industry (both in the conventional and GI product sectors) is characterised by free entry, consistent with the typical non-exclusionary nature of most GIs discussed earlier.[12] Each active firm is assumed to produce a fixed quantity of output per period, normalised to unity, and to choose the quality level of its product.[13] To capture the inherently dynamic nature of reputation, the model is dynamic and firms potentially operate for an infinite number of periods.

The demand side of the model arises from a population of consumers who are heterogeneous with respect to their taste for quality.[14] We assume that

---

11 Other possible explanations of why the non-GI area has a comparative advantage in producing low quality might include a greater potential to replace labour with capital (at a lower total cost) and a lower cost of less specialised labour.

12 The role of competitive markets and free entry into the GI sector is also discussed in some detail in Moschini, Menapace, and Pick (2008).

13 Fixing the size of the firm allows the model to abstract from whether there are economies or diseconomies of scale in establishing reputation. The issue of economies of scale in establishing collective reputation has been addressed by Fishman *et al.* (2008). The relationship between firm size, investment in quality and individual brand reputation is investigated by Choi (1997), Cabral (2000) and Rob and Fishman (2005).

14 It is taste heterogeneity with regard to quality that supports a range of different qualities in the market equilibrium. As noted by a reviewer, an alternative approach to the Mussa and Rosen's (1978) type of preferences used here to model the demand side would be to postulate a population of consumers with identical tastes for quality but differing income,

there is a continuum of consumer types, indexed by the parameter $\theta \in [0, \bar{\theta}]$ with distribution $F(\theta)$. Consistent with previous literature, we assume that consumers purchase one unit of the product with the quality that provides the highest positive surplus, or otherwise buy nothing, where the surplus from purchasing quality q at price p for a consumer of type θ is given by

$$U(q, \theta) - p. \tag{2}$$

For the purpose of deriving market price–quality relationships that can arise in a competitive equilibrium, we need only minimal assumptions on consumer preferences. Specifically, we postulate that $U_q > 0$ (consumers' value quality) and that $U_\theta > 0$ (consumers with higher values of θ value quality more). Note that, given this preference structure in equation (2), consumers treat brands of like quality to be perfect substitutes. Of course, as discussed earlier, the actual quality supplied to consumers is not observable prior to purchase. The assumption here, therefore, is that consumers form conjectures as to the actual quality they should expect from a given firm based on the firm's reputation.

3.1. Reputation and information structure

In the literature on the economics of information, the concept of reputation is formalised in various ways depending upon the source of the uncertainty regarding quality (Bar-Isaac and Tadelis, 2008). When quality uncertainty is due to unobservable characteristics (markets primarily characterised by adverse selection problems), reputation is commonly modelled as consumer beliefs regarding a firm's type and is assumed to evolve based on signals (e.g. the firm's performance). When, as in our case, the uncertainty regarding quality is primarily due to unobservable actions (markets characterised by moral hazard problems), reputation ultimately concerns the buyers' beliefs about a producer's equilibrium actions. Perhaps the most coherent modelling structure for that purpose is provided by the use of repeated games, where the expectation of repeated interaction between buyers and sellers provides both the means for a reputation for quality to be established and for deviation from equilibria to be punished.

It is well known that repeated games can give rise to a plethora of equilibria, and the case of reputation is no exception. Shapiro (1983), building on the earlier insight of Klein and Leffler (1981), provides an interesting equilibrium solution, and we follow his approach in what follows. The key idea is that consumers' beliefs about a seller's unobserved actions about quality are based on the producer's past quality choices, which are observed *ex post* (recall that we

---

as in Shaked and Sutton (1982). This would require an appropriate (and straightforward) re-specification of the utility function in equation (2), but the results of the paper (including those discussed in Section 5 below) would not change.

are dealing with an experience good). In principle, such a firm's reputation can be modelled as dependent on the entire history of its quality choices, but Shapiro (1983) shows that the qualitative insights to be garnered are robust to the actual mechanism of reputation formation that is postulated. Given that, we adopt the simplest form of reputation-building that captures the essence of the problem at hand and assume that the reputation for firm k at time t is given by $R_t^k = q_{t-1}^k$. In other words, at any given point in time, a firm is expected to provide the quality level that it supplied in the previous period. This naïve expectation turns out to be validated in the equilibrium that we characterise in what follows and thus, in this sense, consumers are rational. Because consumers cannot observe quality at the time of purchase and rely on reputation, by deviating from equilibrium producers could, of course, surprise consumers (for one period) with a lower quality than expected. Such a quality cut would be discovered by consumers (with a one-period delay), and consumers would punish sellers by boycotting the brand thereafter (Allen, 1984).[15]

For such a reputation to work as a mechanism for signalling a firm's quality, it is essential that consumers be able to clearly distinguish the identity of firms. Brand names, trademarks and, in our context, GI labels are tools that permit such a consumer recognition and are fundamental for reputation to arise in equilibrium.

3.2. Branding options: trademarks and GI labels

Firms use brands to clearly identify their product in the eye of consumers. In our setting, a brand can be a trademark, a combination of a trademark and a GI label, or merely a GI label. Trademarks convey firm-specific reputation, whereas the GI label alone conveys collective reputation. A combination of a trademark and a GI label, of course, mingles firm-specific and collective reputations in a way that depends on the specific nature of the GI. We assume that each producer can, at any time, adopt and use a trademark at no cost (other than that needed to establish a reputation) and that there is an infinite supply of potential trademark names. Instead, to be able to use a GI label, a producer needs to obtain certification. To obtain certification, of course, producers need to produce within the GI area and meet other specific conditions eventually spelled out by the GI. We consider two alternative GI labelling systems in turn, certification marks and the EU-style *sui generis* system. Both system make an explicit claim on geography (i.e. only the product from the specific GI area can be GI certified) but, as noted, the latter also spells out detailed specifications that constrain the production process and the GI product's attributes. In our model we interpret this additional requirement of a *sui generis* GI system as mandating a GI-specific

---

15 Because brand ownership is not observable to consumers, a producer that has cheated and has lost all his customers could re-enter the market using a different brand, which of course would require a new reputation-building investment.

MQS, labelled q_0^G. We assume that $q_0^G \geq q_0$, that is, the MQS imposed by a GI scheme is at least as strict as the baseline standard that applies to all products.

Consistent with the collective nature of GI rights, we assume that all producers who satisfy the certification requirements for a given GI are entitled to its use. Finally, we postulate an economy with a fully credible trademark system and a fully credible certification scheme for GIs (i.e. there is no counterfeit product on the market and all certified products meet the requirements established by the certification scheme). To simplify the presentation of our results, we also assume no specific costs, over and above the production costs $c(q)$ and $c^G(q)$, associated with the use of trademarks or GI certification.

4. Long-run partial equilibrium

We consider a rational-expectation, stationary Nash equilibrium in a long-run partial equilibrium setting.[16] Specifically, the reputation equilibrium we consider is a steady-state configuration with a price function across qualities, $p(q)$, and a distribution of firms, $n(q)$, such that (i) each consumer, knowing $p(q)$, chooses his most preferred quality level or decides not to purchase anything; (ii) markets clear at every level of quality [thus determining $n(q)$]; (iii) any firm with reputation R finds it optimal to produce quality $q = R$ rather than to deviate and (iv) there is no further entry or exit.

Following Shapiro (1983), we focus on the case in which all other factors of production are in perfectly elastic supply. This is, admittedly, a restrictive condition for agricultural and food products where land is constrained in the aggregate (so that its supply to any individual industry is upward sloping).[17] Whereas such an upward-sloping supply could be accommodated in our context, it would considerably complicate the analysis without affecting the qualitative insights that we wish to characterise. Specifically, the assumption of perfect competition with free entry permits us to derive equilibrium price–quality schedules that depend only on the cost-of-quality structure, and the condition that all factors of production are in perfectly elastic supply makes such costs independent of factor market supplies and of the nature and extent of market demand for the specific product under consideration. The latter means that we can derive equilibrium price–quality schedules for very general demand conditions, i.e. for all consumer preferences satisfying basic postulates: (i) consumers are indifferent between products of equal quality; (ii) utility is strictly increasing in quality and strictly decreasing in

---

16 Consumer expectations of quality are adaptive but rational in equilibrium: consumers expect firms to maintain their reputation and firms do so.

17 For a number of GIs that individually account for a small share of a region's agricultural output, the assumption that all factors of production are in perfectly elastic supply might not be unreasonable. Moschini, Menapace and Pick (2008) discuss such examples. In any event, it will be readily apparent that some of the welfare implications of the analysis are predicated on the restrictive assumption that all factors of production are in perfectly elastic supply. This point will be discussed further in the concluding section.

the price paid for quality; and (iii) consumers have heterogeneous preferences regarding quality.[18]

In what follows, we consider three IP scenarios and derive the equilibrium market price–quality schedule for each scenario. The first scenario, our benchmark case, is one in which trademarks are the only branding option. In the second and third scenarios, we consider two alternative GI certification systems, the *sui generis* scheme and the certification mark scheme, respectively.

4.1. The benchmark case with trademarks only

Although the assumption here is that only trademarks can be used to sustain reputation, either of the production technologies – the standard technology $c(q)$ and the GI technology $c^G(q)$ – can be used to produce any given quality q. But the presumption is that when only trademarks are available, consumers cannot detect which technology is used in production. In equilibrium, therefore, it must be that a given quality q is produced by the technology that carries the lowest production cost. Hence, for qualities $q \leq \tilde{q}$ the standard technology is used, and for $q \geq \tilde{q}$ the GI technology is used.[19]

Consider first a representative firm that uses the standard technology $c(q)$ and whose brand's reputation in equilibrium is equal to $q \leq \tilde{q}$. At any point in time this firm can choose between two strategies: continue to supply the quality level q or produce a lower quality than its reputation (i.e. 'cheat'). If this firm remains honest (i.e. keeps producing quality q), it earns a discounted profit equal to $[(1+r)/r][p(q) - c(q)]$, where $r > 0$ denotes the per-period interest rate. If the firm cheats by cutting quality, the most profitable avenue is to cut quality to the minimum level, thereby earning a one-period profit equal to $p(q) - c(q_0)$. The credibility constraint, which determines the range of prices for which the firm has no incentive to cheat, can therefore be written as

$$p(q) \geq c(q) + r[c(q) - c(q_0)]. \tag{3}$$

Next, consider a potential new entrant who wishes to establish a reputation for quality q. Being reputationless, this producer can only charge an entry price p_e for its product in the first (entry) period. As in Shapiro (1983), we argue that the presence of a potentially infinite supply of opportunistic (fly-by-night) sellers who could overrun the market with minimum quality q_0 implies that the entry price for a new brand is equal to the cost of producing minimum quality. Hence, $p_e = c(q_0)$. In equilibrium, a potential entrant incurs a sure

---

18 Assumptions (i) and (ii) rule out 'irrelevant' price–quality combinations. Assumption (iii) supports a range of different qualities to be exchanged in equilibrium.

19 Alternatively, because the production technology use cannot be credibly certified under a trademarks-only system, producers in the GI region wanting to sell qualities $q \leq \tilde{q}$ could outsource production to the other region while retaining their own branded trademark (and vice versa for producers in the non-GI region wanting to sell qualities $q \geq \tilde{q}$).

loss equal to $c(q_0) - c(q)$ in the entry period when the brand is still unknown and earns a profit equal to $p(q) - c(q)$ in any subsequent period. Free entry requires discounted profits of potential new brands to be non-positive, that is, $c(q_0) - c(q) + (1/r)[p(q) - c(q)] \leq 0$, and thus imposes a second restriction on the equilibrium price configuration, which can be written as

$$p(q) \leq c(q) + r[c(q) - c(q_0)]. \tag{4}$$

Together, the credibility constraint and the free-entry condition imply an equilibrium price–quality schedule for producers who use the standard technology equal to

$$A(q) \equiv c(q) + r[c(q) - c(q_0)] \quad \text{for } q_0 \leq q \leq \tilde{q}. \tag{5}$$

Similar conditions can be derived for producers who sell qualities $q \geq \tilde{q}$ using the GI technology $c^G(q)$. Here, however, because the technology of production is undetectable for consumers, and the cost of in-house production of minimum quality using the GI technology exceeds the cost of outsourcing production to firms that use the standard technology, $c^G(q_0) > c(q_0)$, the most profitable cheating option for producers who use the GI technology is outsourcing production at a cost equal to $c(q_0)$. The credibility constraint for producers who use the GI technology is then equal to

$$p(q) \geq c^G(q) + r[c^G(q) - c(q_0)]. \tag{6}$$

Being unable to detect the technology of production (recall that at this point only individual trademarks are allowed), consumers are willing to pay $c(q_0)$ for any reputationless brand independent of the actual technology used in production. The free entry condition for producers who use the GI technology is then equal to

$$p(q) \leq c^G(q) + r[c^G(q) - c(q_0)]. \tag{7}$$

Hence, for producers who use the GI technology, the credibility constraint and the free-entry condition together imply an equilibrium price–quality schedule equal to

$$B(q) \equiv c^G(q) + r[c^G(q) - c(q_0)] \quad \text{for } q \geq \tilde{q}. \tag{8}$$

Result 1
   The market price–quality schedule that prevails in equilibrium when trademarks are the only available branding option is

$$P(q) \equiv \begin{cases} A(q) & \text{for } q \in [q_0, \tilde{q}) \\ B(q) & \text{for } q \geq \tilde{q} \end{cases}. \tag{9}$$

The market schedule, $P(q)$, as given in equation (9), is represented in Figure 1 by the bold curve. This equilibrium schedule reflects the assumption that consumers are indifferent between products of equal quality regardless of the underlying production technology (hence, they would purchase only brands with the lowest price for any given quality), and the fact that consumer utility is strictly increasing in quality (hence, consumers purchase only brands with the highest quality at any given price). As discussed earlier, in this setting it must be that qualities $q < \tilde{q}$ are produced with the standard technologies and qualities $q \geq \tilde{q}$ are produced with the GI technology, where $\tilde{q}$ is the quality level that separates the two ranges over which the technologies have a cost advantage. Hence, when trademarks are the only branding option, each quality level $q \geq q_0$ is produced using the technology with the lower production cost.

4.2. The *sui generis* GI certification scheme

Two features – the product specification and the collective nature – characterise the EU-type GI *sui generis* scheme and distinguish GI labels from trademarks. As discussed earlier, the specification details all the product characteristics, including the production process and the geographic area in which production takes place. We assume that the product specification is met when the product is produced with the GI technology (i.e. we abstract from enforcement issues, which are peripheral to the central point of our model). Thus, any GI-certified product has quality $q \geq q_0^G$, where q_0^G is the GI-specific MQS under the *sui generis* scheme. Given the collective nature of GI labels, we assume that all producers who use the GI technology and meet the GI-specific MQS can use the GI label, alone or in combination with a private trademark, to brand their products.

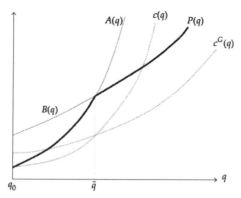

Fig. 1. Equilibrium price–quality schedule with trademarks only.

Note that a GI label alone cannot support a reputation for a quality level above $q > q_0^G$. Such a producer would be vulnerable to the competition (unrestricted, given free entry) of producers who would sell the lower (and cheaper to produce) quality q_0^G with the same label.[20] Hence, producers who want to service demand for qualities $q > q_0^G$, and thus are required to build a reputation for a quality strictly in excess of q_0^G, will need a private trademark in addition to the GI label. A firm that produces a quality in excess of q_0^G and uses a private trademark can in fact entirely capture the premium associated with the additional quality since consumers, through the trademark, can trace back the product's quality to the specific individual firm. If the firm uses only a GI label, it can only partially capture the premium associated with the additional quality (i.e. it can only capture the premium associated with the increase in the average quality of the GI labelled product) but will still bear the full cost of the additional quality. Hence, a firm is better off using a trademark in addition to the GI label whenever $q > q_0^G$. Knowing that, consumers also correctly infer that a product bearing the GI label alone is of quality q_0^G, the minimum quality that can be certified under the *sui generis* scheme.

The derivation of the equilibrium price–quality schedule for producers who certify under the *sui generis* scheme requires discussing the entry price that consumers are willing to pay for a GI-certified product when the accompanying trademark is new (i.e. it has no established reputation). We argue that the entry price for a GI-certified product with a reputationless trademark is $c^G(q_0^G)$. To this end, we note that consumers know that the quality produced by an entrant who certifies and wants to stay in business must be such that the entrant's brand is (at least weakly) preferred over alternative brands of equal quality once reputation is built and, hence, that the quality must be above a given threshold. Given this piece of information, a GI-certified product at an entry price equal to $c^G(q_0^G)$ is attractive to consumers. At the same time, any price above $c^G(q_0^G)$ would attract fly-by-night producers supplying unlimited quantity of quality q_0^G. Hence, there cannot be an equilibrium in which consumers pay more than $c^G(q_0^G)$ for an entrant's product of any quality.

In equilibrium, an entrant with a given quality q would incur a loss equal to $c^G(q_0^G) - c^G(q)$ in the (reputation-building) entry period and would earn a profit equal to $p(q) - c^G(q)$ in any subsequent period. Hence, free entry imposes the following restriction on the equilibrium price configuration for producers who use the GI technology and GI certification:

$$p(q) \le c^G(q) + r[c^G(q) - c^G(q_0^G)]. \tag{10}$$

It is critical to observe that the presence of certification constrains the moral hazard behaviour of GI-labelled producers by limiting their ability to cut

---

20 This is essentially what happens in Winfree and McCluskey's (2005) model.

costs when they reduce quality. Once a trademarked product is known to consumers and it is GI-certified, the firm must continue certifying; otherwise, consumers would anticipate that the firm is cutting quality.[21] If, in equilibrium, a firm that certifies remains honest (i.e. continues producing the same quality), it earns a discounted profit equal to $[(1 + r)/r][p(q) - c^G(q)]$. Also, conditional on certifying, the most profitable cheating avenue is to produce minimum quality q_0^G at cost $c^G(q_0^G)$, earning a one-period profit equal to $p(q) - c^G(q_0^G)$. Hence, the credibility constraint for a firm with a reputable trademark and that GI-certifies can be written as

$$p(q) \geq c^G(q) + r[c^G(q) - c^G(q_0^G)]. \tag{11}$$

The credibility constraint and free entry together imply that the price–quality schedule for certifying producers is equal to

$$G(q) \equiv c^G(q) + r[c^G(q) - c^G(q_0^G)] \quad \text{for} q \geq q_0^G. \tag{12}$$

Now suppose that a firm has built a particular reputation $R = q > q_0^G$. Could the firm maintain this reputation through the use of a trademark alone, i.e. dropping the use of the GI label? It turns out that that is not possible because if a firm were to stop certifying once its trademark is reputable, the firm's incentives to cut quality would change compared with the case in which the firm continues certifying. Without certification, the most profitable cheating avenue is to produce quality q_0 at cost $c(q_0)$, which earns a one-period profit equal to $p(q) - c(q_0)$. Hence, the credibility constraint for a firm that does not certify when its trademark is reputable is

$$p(q) \geq c^G(q) + r[c^G(q) - c(q_0)]. \tag{13}$$

It follows that, without GI certification, no price exists that would satisfy both the credibility and free entry condition (as long as $q > q_0^G$).

Producers who use the GI technology can also decide not to certify at all. In this case, the price–quality schedule for producers who use the GI technology but do not certify coincides with the schedule already derived under the benchmark case, as given by equation (8). Similarly, the presence of a *sui generis* scheme does not affect the price–quality schedule of producers who use the standard technology, for whom no certification is available under this scheme. For them, the price–quality schedule coincides with equation (5).

The equilibrium market price–quality schedule prevailing in the presence of the *sui generis* scheme corresponds to the lower envelope of the three schedules in equations (5), (8) and (12), but depending on the value of q_0^G, this schedule takes different forms. When q_0^G is suitably low, Result 2(a)

---

21 In the case of a firm using a pure GI label as a brand, discontinuing certification means selling an unbranded product, which is expected by consumers to be of baseline minimum quality q_0.

applies; for intermediate values of q_0^G, the condition in Result 2(b) is derived; and when q_0^G is large enough, Result 2(c) is obtained.

Result 2(a)

When $q_0^G \in [q_0, q']$, the market price–quality schedule that prevails in equilibrium under a *sui generis* scheme is

$$P^G(q) \equiv \begin{cases} A(q) & \text{for } q \in [q_0, \hat{q}) \\ G(q) & \text{for } q \geq \hat{q} \end{cases}, \tag{14}$$

where we define $\hat{q}$ and q' as satisfying $G(\hat{q}) = A(\hat{q})$ and $A(q') = c^G(q')$.

Thus, when the GI-specific MQS is suitably low, the equilibrium price–quality schedule that prevails under the *sui generis* scheme is continuous, just as in the benchmark case (with only trademarks) discussed earlier. Moreover, similarly to the benchmark case, it corresponds to the schedule of the producers who use the standard technology in the bottom range of the quality spectrum (here, for q smaller than $\hat{q}$) and to the schedule for certifying producers using the GI-technology in the upper range of the quality spectrum (here, for q larger than $\hat{q}$). But unlike the benchmark case, here not all qualities are produced with the production technology that has the lower production cost. Specifically, qualities $\hat{q} \leq q \leq \tilde{q}$ are produced with the GI technology even if the standard technology displays a lower cost in this quality range. What remains true, of course, is that each quality $q \geq q_0$ is produced by the firms with the lowest total cost, where the total cost includes both the production and the information cost. The market price–quality schedule that prevails under the *sui generis* scheme when the GI-specific MQS is low is represented by the bold curve in Figure 2a. It is important to note that even when GI certification does not entail any higher minimum quality than that which applies generally (i.e. $q_0^G = q_0$), the availability of GI certification does affect the equilibrium price–quality schedule because, as discussed, it affects the information cost required to establish and maintain reputation.

Note that Result 2(a) applies only when $q_0^G \leq q'$ where q' is the quality level at which the price of the standard product, $A(q)$, is equal to the production cost with the GI technology, $c^G(q)$. For this range of values of q_0^G, there exists a range of qualities $q \in [q_0^G, q']$ that are more cheaply supplied without certification, using the standard technology, than with certification [i.e. $G(q)$ is above $A(q)$]. That is, in this range the saving in production costs due to the standard technology are larger than the savings in information costs due to GI certification (because, essentially, the value of q_0^G is too close to q_0, the MQS that applies to all products). When $q_0^G > q'$, on the other hand, all qualities above the GI-specific MQS can be more cheaply supplied with certification. This is the case of Results 2(b) and 2(c).

556 *L. Menapace and G. Moschini*

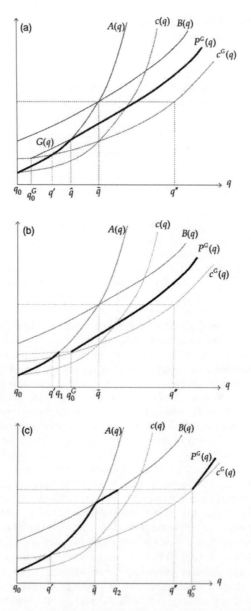

Fig. 2. (a) Price–quality schedule with trademarks and *sui generis* GI certification with $q_0^G \in [q_0, q')$. (b) Price–quality schedule with trademarks and *sui generis* GI certification with $q_0^G \in [q', q'')$. (c) Price–quality schedule with trademarks and *sui generis* GI certification with $q_0^G \geq q''$.

Result 2(b)

When $q_0^G \in [q', q'']$, the market price–quality schedule that prevails in equilibrium under a *sui generis* system is

$$P^G(q) \equiv \begin{cases} A(q) & \text{for } q \in [q_0, q_1) \\ G(q) & \text{for } q \geq q_0^G \end{cases}, \tag{15}$$

where we define q_1 and q'' as satisfying $A(q_1) = c^G(q_0^G)$ and $A(\tilde{q}) = c^G(q'')$.

Note that when the GI-specific MQS takes on a value in the given intermediate range, the market price–quality schedule under the *sui generis* scheme presents a discontinuity, i.e. we find a gap in the set of quality that can be supported by the market in equilibrium. Such a quality gap is typical in the presence of production technologies with comparative advantage over different quality ranges (e.g. Falvey and Kierzkowski, 1987 and in Flam and Helpman, 1987). Similar to the case of a low value of the GI-specific MQS, not all supplied qualities are produced by the firms with the lowest production cost: qualities $q_0^G \leq q \leq \tilde{q}$ are produced with the more expensive GI-technology instead of the cheaper standard technology.

The bold curve in Figure 2b represents the market price–quality schedule for intermediate values of the GI-specific MQS. The upper limit of this range, q'', corresponds to the quality level at which the production cost using the GI technology, $c^G(q)$, is exactly equal to the total cost (i.e. production plus information costs) of supplying quality $\tilde{q}$ (recall that $\tilde{q}$ can be produced at the same production cost with either technology). This also means that there is no quality level that can be produced with the GI technology without being certified that can be competitive on the market. When $q_0^G \geq q''$, on the other hand, there exists a quality range above $\tilde{q}$ and below q_0^G for which the GI technology that can be competitive on the market without certification (certification for this range is unavailable). This is the case of Result 2(c).

Result 2(c)

When $q_0^G \geq q''$, the market price–quality schedule that prevails in equilibrium under a *sui generis* system is

$$P^G(q) \equiv \begin{cases} A(q) & \text{for } q \in [q_0, \tilde{q}) \\ B(q) & \text{for } q \in [\tilde{q}, q_2) \\ G(q) & \text{for } q \geq q_0^G \end{cases}, \tag{16}$$

where we define q_2 as satisfying $B(q_2) = c^G(q_0^G)$.

A quality gap [over qualities $q \in [q_2, q_0^G]$] also characterises the equilibrium market price–quality schedule when the GI-specific MQS has high values, but in this case (as in the benchmark case) all supplied qualities are produced with the technology with the lower production cost. Here, we find that there exists a group of producers who use the GI technology but do not certify (i.e. they only use their own trademark), and this ends up supplying the quality range between $\tilde{q}$ and q_2. The bold curve in Figure 2c represents the market price–quality schedule for high values of the GI-specific MQS.[22]

4.3. GI certification based on certification marks

IP protection for GIs in the United States is provided through the standard trademark system, usually as certification marks. Certification marks for GIs only certify the origin of the product and provide no other quality-related claim or specification. For example, the certification mark 'Washington Apples' certifies that the apples are produced in the state of Washington, with no specific additional quality standard that needs to be met by producers (Winfree and McCluskey, 2005).

In our framework, certification under a certification mark scheme reveals to consumers the technology used in production, similar to the *sui generis* GI certification discussed in the foregoing sections. But, because certification marks do not envision any quality specification, it then follows that a certification mark system in our modelling framework is equivalent to a *sui generis* system with the minimal possible minimum quality, that is, $q_0^G = q_0$. Still, as illustrated in the foregoing analysis, the presence of such a GI certification is valuable because it curtails the moral hazard behaviour of producers by limiting their ability to cut costs were they to depart from equilibrium by supplying a quality lower than expected. The explicit graphical representation of the equilibrium market price–quality schedule with the certification mark scheme is omitted because of space limitations (it is essentially as in Figure 2a, but with $q_0^G = q_0$). Note that, again, with the certification mark scheme we find that there is a range of qualities that do not minimise production costs. Specifically, qualities $q' \leq q \leq \tilde{q}$ are produced with the GI technology despite the fact that the cost of producing them with the standard technology is lower.

5. Welfare implications

Relevant welfare questions for the problem at hand include the following: (i) What are the welfare implications of adding a GI certification scheme to a situation in which only private trademarks are used? and (ii) If GI certification is contemplated, which is best, a *sui generis* system or a certification mark system? Welfare impacts can arise for both consumers and producers. As we

---

22 As the foregoing discussion suggests, determining which of the three cases is relevant for a given real-world product would require information on the cost structure of both the GI and the standard technologies. If the matter were deemed of practical and/or policy interest, empirical work could in principle be brought to bear on these issues.

have shown, the availability of GI certification reduces the size of the reputation premium needed to support quality in the upper range of the quality spectrum, thereby taking the reputation equilibrium closer to the first best. This is illustrated in Figure 3 by the equilibrium price–quality schedule $P^G(q)$ (i.e. as Figure 2a–c shows, the equilibrium price–quality schedule moves closer to the marginal cost schedule). This reputation premium reduction is due to the revelation of some information regarding the GI-certified product to consumers. Specifically, both certification marks and certification via the *sui generis* scheme reveal the technology used in production and, in addition, certification via the *sui generis* scheme also informs consumers that the product is at least of quality q_0^G. By making these pieces of information common knowledge, certification limits the ability of producers to reduce costs by cutting quality and hence certification makes cheating a less attractive option to producers. At the lower end of the price distribution, on the other hand, the price–quality schedules with trademarks only and with trademarks plus GI certification coincide [as shown in Results 2(a)–2(c)].

For consumers, it is clear that the GI introduction effects discussed in the foregoing can only improve their welfare because they lead to a reduction in the equilibrium prices of some qualities. The welfare impacts on producers, however, are generally non-positive and depend critically on whether the introduction of GI certification is construed to happen *ex ante* (that is, before the investment in reputation-building is undertaken) or *ex post* (that is, after firms have already built up their reputation by the use of trademarks). From an *ex ante* perspective, perfect competition with free entry, coupled with the condition that all factors are in perfect elastic supply, means that, *ex ante*, the surplus of producers is nil. But the introduction of a GI system after firms have already built up their reputation by the use of trademarks can have

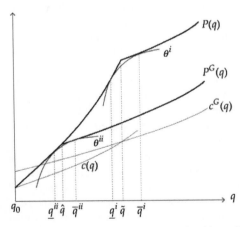

Fig. 3. Consumers' choices with trademarks only and with trademarks plus GI certification.

negative *ex post* impacts on producers' welfare. Exactly which producers (in terms of what quality they provide) are affected depends on the structure of demand. To discuss the possible welfare effects in more detail, a closer look at preferences is needed.

To put some more structure on the preference relation $U(q, \theta)$ in equation (2), assume that

$$U_q > 0, \ U_{qq} < 0, \ U_\theta > 0 \text{ and } U_{q\theta} > 0. \qquad (17)$$

Thus, in addition to the assumptions that consumers value quality and that consumers with higher θ have a higher taste for quality, discussed earlier, we also assume that utility is concave in quality and that the marginal utility of quality is larger for consumers with higher values of θ. Note that, for each θ-consumer, $U(q, \theta) - p$ defines a set of convex indifference curves in the $p \times q$ space with a southeast preference direction. The slope of such indifference curves satisfies $dp/dq = U_q$ and thus it is increasing in θ (for any give q). For each consumer, optimality requires achieving the highest feasible indifference curve, which in a competitive equilibrium is constrained by the price–quality schedules derived in the foregoing analysis (and the requirement that $U(q, \theta) \geq p$).

Depending on the particulars of the utility function, we can have either that $U(q, 0) \equiv \underline{u} \geq P(q_0)$, in which case every consumer buys the product in question (i.e. the market is covered), or that $\underline{u} < P(q_0)$, so that some consumers at the lower end of the taste distribution are not consuming the product in question (i.e. the market is uncovered). Rather than discussing all possible cases, it is instructive to consider the situation in which there exists a consumer type θ^i who, under the trademarks-only system, is indifferent between consuming quality $\underline{q}^i$ produced by the standard technology and quality $\bar{q}^i$ produced by the GI technology. This is illustrated in Figure 3 where $P(q)$ is the equilibrium price–quality schedule with trademarks only and $P^G(p)$ is the equilibrium price–quality schedule with trademarks plus GIs, and where we are essentially considering the case of Result 2(a). Prior to the introduction of GI certification, consumers with type $\theta < \theta^i$ are served by the standard technology, if they buy the good at all, and consumers with $\theta > \theta^i$ are supplied by the GI technology. In this illustration the introduction of a GI certification system results in a new consumer type $\theta^{ii} < \theta^i$ being indifferent between consuming quality $\underline{q}^{ii}$ produced by the standard technology and a quality $\bar{q}^{ii}$ produced by the GI technology.

In Figure 3, consumers with low taste for quality, specifically with $\theta \leq \theta^{ii}$, are not affected by the introduction of the GI certification. But consumers with higher taste for quality, specifically with $\theta > \theta^{ii}$ and consuming qualities $q \geq \bar{q}^{ii}$ in the new equilibrium, are strictly better off under the GI certification scheme because they can take advantage of the lower price–quality schedule. As for producers, those serving the low end of the quality spectrum, that is, producing qualities $q \leq \underline{q}^{ii}$ in the illustration of Figure 3, are not affected by the introduction of GI certification as this market segment continues to be serviced by producers who do not certify. Standard-technology producers who, prior to the introduction of GI certification, are active in the quality range $\underline{q}^{ii} < q < \underline{q}^{i}$ lose their reputation premium. Specifically, producers in the range $\underline{q}^{ii} < q < \bar{q}^{ii}$ lose their investment in reputation because these qualities disappear from the market, whereas producers in the quality range $\bar{q}^{ii} \leq q \leq \underline{q}^{i}$ lose their reputation premium because these qualities are now provided by the GI technology with the lower price–quality schedule $P^{G}(q)$.[23] Producers in the quality range $q > \bar{q}^{i}$ also partially lose their investment in reputation because, although they are still relying on the same GI technology, the advent of GI certification has reduced the reputation premium. The introduction of GI certification illustrated in Figure 3 also gives rise to new production opportunities for the quality range $\underline{q}^{i} < q < \bar{q}^{i}$, which was not serviced with the trademarks-only system but is now serviced by GI producers after the introduction of GI certification.

It is apparent that the introduction of a GI certification scheme affects consumers and producers in radically different ways. Consumers, to the extent that they prefer high quality, are clearly better off with lower prices (otherwise, if they prefer low quality, they are just as well off). As for producers, if they have already sunk the investment in reputation before the introduction of the certification scheme, they are either indifferent (at the lower end of the quality spectrum) or are negatively affected by the introduction of GI certification because the premium they can charge for their established reputation is curtailed. Note that producers using either the standard or the GI technology can lose from the introduction of GI certification.

As for aggregate welfare – the sum of consumer and producer surpluses in this model – the overall effects are more subtle and depend critically on whether one takes the *ex ante* or *ex post* perspective. With zero discounted profits for new producers, it is clear that, *ex ante*, only consumer surplus matters. From this point of view, the introduction of GI certification always increases welfare because it further improves the efficiency with which reputable brands can supply quality to consumers.[24] But if the introduction of GI certification happens after reputation has been established by all firms, the losses to producers need to be balanced against the gains to consumers. It seems that no general conclusion can be obtained in this setting without making more assumptions about the distribution of consumers $F(\theta)$. To show that, indeed, GI introduction can cause a reduction in overall welfare, consider the case in Figure 3 and suppose that θ^{ii} is the largest value in the support of $F(\theta)$, and that there

23 In this quality range one can argue that the loss of the prior investment in reputation is only partial (instead of total) if these producers can relocate production to a GI region while keeping their own private trademarks, a scenario consistent with the assumed free entry condition of the model.

24 Of course, if the distribution of consumers $F(\theta)$ is such that all consumers are bunched at the low end of quality preferences (e.g. $\bar{\theta} \leq \theta^{ii}$ in the case of Figure 3), it is possible that GIs have no effect.

is a positive mass m of consumers with this type. Prior to GI certification, all consumers are served by the standard technology, with consumers of type θ^{ii} enjoying quality $\underline{q}^{ii}$. With GI certification, however, the consumers with type θ^{ii} can now be served by the GI technology (at quality $\bar{q}^{ii}$). In such a case, by construction, there is no welfare gain to consumers. But established producers suffer a reputation premium loss of $m[P(\underline{q}^{ii}) - c(\underline{q}^{ii})]$ per period, which is not balanced by any gain to GI producers (the present value of their reputation premium is dissipated in the reputation-building stage of the entry period). Of course, it is quite possible that $F(\theta)$ is such that consumer gains from the introduction of GIs exceed producer losses, but the fact remains that it does not appear possible to derive general conclusions as to aggregate welfare impacts of the *ex post* introduction of GI certification.

Finally, we wish to discuss which GI certification scheme – the *sui generis* system or that with certification marks – is to be preferred. From the foregoing discussion, the most meaningful setting for this question is from an *ex ante* perspective, in which case the certification scheme that maximises social welfare is the one that maximises aggregate consumer surplus. Because the two GI systems in our model differ by their MQS, it will prove useful to discuss how the GI-specific MQS, q_0^G, affects consumer surplus. As is evident based on Results 2(a)–2(c), the value of the GI-specific MQS determines the shape and position of the equilibrium market price–quality schedule and hence the price–quality combinations that are available to consumers. The available price–quality combinations, in turn, determine the surplus that each consumer type can derive in the market. Hence, the specific welfare-maximising value of the GI-specific MQS will generally depend on the distribution of consumer types. Specifically, the optimal value of the GI-specific MQS has to balance the welfare losses of consumers whose quality selection is constrained by the value of q_0^G and the welfare gains to consumers who purchase the GI-certified product. By raising the value of $G(q)$, $G(q)$ is pushed down towards production costs; hence, the prices of all qualities above q_0^G decline. But, by raising q_0^G above q', some qualities are no longer supplied in the market (i.e. consumers have less quality options to choose from).

With an exogenously determined q_0^G, a comparison between the price–quality schedules under the *sui generis* and certification mark schemes reveals that (i) for any given value of $q_0^G \leq q'$ every consumer type is at least as well off with the *sui generis* scheme as with certification marks (because of lower prices in the upper end of the quality range with the *sui generis* scheme); and (ii) for any given value of $q_0^G > q'$, the scheme that provides the largest welfare depends on the distribution of consumer types. For the latter case, in fact, some qualities in an intermediate range are not supplied under the *sui generis* scheme while the same qualities would be supplied with a certification mark scheme (hence, consumers with intermediate values of θ would be better off with certification marks). But the *sui generis* scheme leads to lower prices in the upper part of the quality spectrum compared with a certification mark, and hence consumers with relatively high values of θ would be better off with the *sui generis* scheme. Finally, if the value of q_0^G can be chosen optimally so as to maximise aggregate welfare, the *sui generis* scheme is obviously unambiguously better than the technology scheme for any given distribution of consumers (because it is always possible to set $q_0^G = q_0$).

6. Conclusions

In this paper we have developed a reputation model to assess the role of certification for agricultural and food products with a regional identity, known as GIs, in a context in which firms already have access to private trademarks to establish their reputation for quality. The model nests the concept of firm reputation that provides one of the traditional justifications for trademarks, with a meaningful definition of collective reputation that can be ascribed to GI labels. We have shown that trademarks and GI certification can be viewed as complementary instruments for the purpose of credibly signalling quality to consumers in a competitive equilibrium. Thus, our model provides a rationale for the concurrent use of GI certification and trademarks, a feature that is quite common for agricultural and food products that claim superior quality because of their geographical origin.

Several instructive aspects on the role of certification in quality provision and reputation formation emerge from the model. First, we show that certification reduces the divergence between the reputation equilibrium and the equilibrium that would prevail under perfect information by lowering the cost of establishing reputation compared with a situation with only trademarks. Hence, certification improves the ability of reputation to operate as a mechanism for assuring quality. Second, in our model the welfare gains that arise from GI certification accrue to consumers, especially those with a taste for higher qualities. This is because certification, by raising the price that entrants can command, reduces the cost of building a reputation and hence the value of an established reputation. In our model, producers are either unaffected or are negatively affected by the introduction of a GI certification scheme. This observation perhaps suggests that producers' support for the introduction of new GIs might be highest at an early marketing stage, before eligible producers have already committed resources towards building a (private) reputation via their own trademarks. But we should note that what our model can say about producer welfare is limited by our assumption that all factors of production are in perfectly elastic supply. If this condition were relaxed, it is certainly possible to envision benefits to GI producers that are not accounted for in our model. For example, if land supply to the industry of interest is upward sloping, expanding production would increase the returns to land (what is typically measured as producer surplus). And, in our setting, it is clear that GI certification tends to

564   *L. Menapace and G. Moschini*

expand the output of the GI region. As production of the GI product increases, the price–quality schedule of the GI product would be pushed up towards the standard technology schedule, which represents an upper bound on equilibrium prices. Consumers would still gain (or at least be indifferent) from lower prices for some qualities due to certification, while GI producers would benefit as land owners.

Our model also considers the features of two major forms of GI certification schemes, the EU-style *sui generis* system and the US-style certification mark approach. We show that the type of GI certification matters, and that the features of the certification scheme play an important role in mitigating the informational problems connected with supplying quality for experience goods. Both of these types of GI certification work by making common knowledge some relevant information, which in turn mitigates the inherent moral hazard problem by limiting the ability of producers to operate opportunistically. In our model, a *sui generis* scheme discloses more information than a certification mark scheme and it is generally preferable to a certification mark scheme.

References

Akerlof, G. A. (1970). The market for lemons: quality uncertainty and the market mechanism. *Quarterly Journal of Economics* 84: 488–500.

Ali, H. H. and Nauges, C. (2007). The pricing of experience goods: the example of en primeur wine. *American Journal of Agricultural Economics* 89: 91–103.

Allen, F. (1984). Reputation and product quality. *The RAND Journal of Economics* 15(3): 311–327.

Anania, G. and Nisticó, R. (2004). Public regulation as a substitute for trust in quality food markets: what if the trust substitute cannot be fully trusted? *Journal of Institutional and Theoretical Economics* 160: 681–701.

Barham, E. (2003). Translating terroir: the global challenge of French AOC labeling. *Journal of Rural Studies* 19: 127–138.

Bar-Isaac, H. and Tadelis, S. (2008). Seller reputation. *Foundations and Trends in Microeconomics* 4(4): 273–351.

Bramley, C. and Kirsten, J. F. (2007). Exploring the economic rationale for protecting geographical indicators in agriculture. *Agrekon* 46(1): 69–93.

Cabral, L. (2000). Stretching firm and brand reputation. *RAND Journal of Economics* 31: 658–673.

Choi, J. P. (1997). Brand extension and information leverage. *Review of Economic Studies* 65: 655–669.

Costanigro, M., McCluskey, J. J. and Goemans, C. (2010). The economics of nested names: name specificity, reputations, and price premia. *American Journal of Agricultural Economics* 8: 1–12.

Darby, M. R. and Karni, E. (1973). Free competition and the optimal amount of fraud. *Journal of Law and Economics* 16: 67–88.

EU (2008). Geographical indications. Background Paper to the Green Paper on Agricultural Product Quality, DG Agriculture and Rural Development, Working Document October 2008.

EU (2003). Why do geographical indications matter to us? European Union Background Note No. 01/04. http://trade.ec.europa.eu/doclib/docs/2003/october/tradoc_113900.pdf. Accessed 28 May 2009.

Falvey, R. (1989). Trade, quality reputation and commercial policy. *International Economic Review* 30(3): 607–622.

Falvey, R. and Kierzkowski, H. (1987). Product quality, intra-industry trade and (im)perfect competition. In H. Kierzkowski (ed.), *Protection and Competition in International Trade*. Oxford: Basil Blackwell.

Fink, C. and Maskus, K. (2006). The debate on geographical indications in the WTO. Ch. 16. In R. Newfarmer (ed.), *Trade, Doha, and Development: A Window into the Issues*. Washington, DC: World Bank.

Fishman, A., Finkelstein, I., Simhon, A. and Yacouel, N. (2008). The economics of collective brands. SSRN Working paper. http://ssrn.com/abstract=1317262. Accessed 3 August 2011.

Flam, H. and Helpman, E. (1987). Vertical product differentiation and north-south trade. *American Economic Review* 77(5): 810–822.

Josling, T. (2006). The war on terroir: geographical indications as a transatlantic trade conflict. *Journal of Agricultural Economics* 57: 337–363.

Klein, B. and Leffler, K. B. (1981). The role of market forces in assuring contractual performance. *Journal of Political Economy* 89(4): 615–641.

Landes, W. M. and Posner, R. A. (2003). *The Economic Structure of Intellectual Property Law*. Cambridge, MA: Harvard University Press.

Landon, S. and Smith, C. E. (1998). Quality expectations, reputation, and price. *Southern Economic Journal* 64(3): 628–647.

Lence, S. H., Marette, S., Hayes, D. and Foster, W. (2007). Collective marketing arrangements for geographically differentiated agricultural products: welfare impacts and policy implications. *American Journal of Agricultural Economics* 89: 947–963.

Moschini, G. C. (2004). Intellectual Property Rights and the World Trade Organization: retrospect and prospects. In G. Anania, M. Bohman, C. Carter and A. McCalla (eds), *Agricultural Policy Reform and the WTO: Where are we Heading?* Edward Elgar Publishing.

Moschini, G. C., Menapace, L. and Pick, D. (2008). Geographical indications and the provision of quality. *American Journal of Agricultural Economics* 90(3): 794–812.

Mussa, M. and Rosen, S. (1978). Monopoly and product quality. *Journal of Economic Theory* 18: 301–317.

Nelson, P. (1970). Information and consumer behavior. *Journal of Political Economy* 78(2): 311–329.

O'Connor, B. (2004). Sui generis protection of geographical indications. *Drake Journal of Agricultural Law* 9: 359–387.

OECD (2000). Appellations of origin and geographical indication in OECD member countries: economic and legal implications. COM/AGR/APM/TD/WP(2000)15/FINAL.

566 *L. Menapace and G. Moschini*

Rangnekar, D. (2004). The socio-economics of geographical indications. UNCTAD-ICTSD Project on IPRs and Sustainable Development, Issue Paper No. 8, May 2004.

Rao, S.S. (2006). Indigenous knowledge organization: an Indian scenario. *International Journal of Information Management* 26: 224–233.

Rob, R. and Fishman, A. (2005). Is bigger better? customer base expansion through word-of-mouth reputation. *Journal of Political Economy* 113(5): 1146–1161.

Roe, B. and Sheldon, I. (2007). Credence good labeling: the efficiency and distributional implications of several policy approaches. *American Journal of Agricultural Economics* 89(4): 1020–1033.

Shaked, A. and Sutton, J. (1982). Relaxing price competition through product differentiation. *Review of Economic Studies* 49(1): 3–13.

Shapiro, C. (1983). Premiums for high quality products as returns to reputations. *The Quarterly Journal of Economics* 98(4): 659–680.

Suh, J. and MacPherson, A. (2007). The impact of geographical indication on the revitalisation of a regional economy: a case study of 'Boseong' green tea. *Area* 39(4): 518–527.

Teuber, R. (2010). Geographical indications of origin as a tool of product differentiation – the case of coffee. *Journal of International Food and Agribusiness Marketing* 22(3–4): 277–298.

USPTO (2007). Geographical indication protection in the United States. United States Patent and Trademark Office. http://www.uspto.gov/web/offices/dcom/olia/globalip/pdf/gi_system.pdf. Accessed 1 May 2007.

Winfree, J. A. and McCluskey, J. J. (2005). Collective reputation and quality. *American Journal of Agricultural Economics* 87(1): 206–213.

WIPO (2007). *Perspectives for geographical indications*. Beijing: WIPO/GEO/BEI/07, 26–28 June 2007.

Xiaobing, W. and Kireeva, I. (2007). Protection of geographical indications in China: conflicts, causes and solutions. *The Journal of World Intellectual Property* 10(2): 79–96.

Zago, M. A. and Pick, D. (2004). Labeling policies in food markets: private incentives, public intervention, and welfare effects. *Journal of Agricultural and Resource Economics* 29(1): 150–165.

C
Marketing Tool

[19]

Geographic indications, trade and the functioning of markets

Phil Evans

The issue of the interface between food policy and trade policy has been an area fraught with controversy for some considerable time. While food safety issues and their possible misuse as barriers to legitimate trade have been with us since the onset of the GATT in the late 1940s, other food issues have begun to grow in importance. One of the most interesting, and contentious, issues is that of Geographic Indications.

What is particularly interesting about the debate around GIs is that almost all the main protagonists in the argument have some form of protection for them, but none agree about how far they should go, or perhaps more importantly how they should affect trade. It would not appear to be a debate about principle but rather of degree.

What is also interesting is the degree to which the debate has avoided discussion of competition issues in agricultural markets. This is, in part, because of historical provisions excluding many agricultural markets from competition overview, most notably in the EU. The role of the Common Agricultural Policy and general 'exception' afforded agriculture in competition law is neither new nor surprising. It should be remembered that competition policy in its modern form first emerged in the USA, Canada and Australia as a rural revolt against urban 'trusts' that were seen to be doing down the farm communities.[1] This original rural revolt has affected the manner in which competition law has been framed and how it has viewed agricultural markets. In particular the role of agricultural cooperatives and farmer groups has been a difficult one for most competition bodies.

However, the restrictions that GIs impose on their members and on those that do not possess the required standard are such that a combined analytical approach is needed. If we rely solely on trade policy to analyse the GI issue we are left with little real room to question the basic structures of the systems on offer and why they emerged. This limited focus allows disputes to occur, but only insofar as issues impinge on basic trade rules. The fundamental structure of GI systems does not fall easily into trade policy analysis. Conversely competition policy allows us to question the structure of GI systems at the national or regional level. It allows us to deconstruct the incentive structures that GIs create in agricultural markets and to discuss the impact that GIs have on competition in product markets. Combining a trade and competition policy approach allows us to engineer some form of approach that could minimize trade tensions while maximizing product market competition and protecting legitimate producer interests. The only remaining piece of the puzzle lies in a socio-historical review of how current food cultures and production processes came to be. Only through seeing where food cultures came from can we hope to frame the discussion of possible ways forward for the global GI debate.

WHO DOES WHAT?

The USA has a system of certification for geographic product claims that has allowed 100 per cent Kona Coffee, Vidalia Onions and Wisconsin Real Cheese to be offered a form of trademark protection under a certification scheme. Part of that trademark protection is based on the producers of the product being within a specified geographic region. The US trademark system allows US and foreign producers to register a trademark and apply it for geographically specific products. However, it defines some products that have such protection elsewhere, such as champagne or feta cheese, as being generic terms. As such they are incapable of being granted a trademark in the USA.

The US certification scheme states that:

> A certification mark is defined as any word, name, symbol, device, or any combination, used or intended for use in commerce with the owner's permission by someone other than its owner, to certify regional or other geographic origin, material, mode of manufacture, quality, accuracy, or other characteristics of someone's goods or services, or that the work or labor on the goods or services was performed by members of a union or other organization. (Section 1127, 'Construction and Definitions,' of the Trademark Act of 1946 ('Lanham Act') as amended. US Patent and Trademark Office 2003)

The US system also has some flexibility in having state-sponsored agricultural certification programmes, such as, 'Idaho Preferred', 'A Taste of Iowa', 'Fresh from Florida', and 'Get Real Get Maine'. For example, Vidalia onions is a certification actually owned by the State of Georgia who allow it to be used in a specified area of the State. Indeed many state-owned certification schemes exist, but tend to be rather broader in nature than product-specific geographic indications, or the sort of scheme operated in Europe. However, again one is struck by an issue of degree rather than principle operating. All geographic origin labels have some defined geographic area and products; one has to ask if having a state scheme, national scheme or local scheme has a significant bearing on the product itself.

This flexibility in the US system even allows the US to protect some European GIs without formal certification. For example, Cognac is used as an example in the USA of a product that would not pass the general use test that champagne or feta would. This is justified on the basis of US consumer understanding that Cognac is inextricably linked to the Cognac region of France and nowhere else. Again the lack of ideology and persistence of pragmatism arises.

The European Union scheme also operates in addition to trademark protection. The 1992 EU Council Regulation on the Protection of Geographical Indications and Designations of Origin (2081/92) created two forms of certification: Protection of Designations of Origin (PDOs) and Protection of Geographic Indication (PGIs). To get a PDO a product must be produced, processed and prepared within a specific area and its characteristics must be 'essentially due to the area'. A PGI is accorded a product produced, processed or prepared in a specific area whose quality, reputation or other characteristics are some way attributable to that area and that area alone.

The EU scheme, unlike the US system, effectively creates collective trademarks for regions or groups of producers. While a particular company, or State, may have a certificate that it then uses, the EU scheme aims to bring together groups of producers to set quality standards for products. Each scheme has to be independently certified to gain the PDO or PDI. This is often done by governmental bodies.

The variation in schemes was of little real relevance prior to the Uruguay Round. The hybrid trademark/certification/common law system in the USA could live alongside the more rigid EU system without too many serious legal arguments. However, the incorporation of intellectual property rights rules into the WTO placed GIs firmly on the international agenda. Article 22 of the TRIPS: Geographical indications are, for the purposes of this Agreement, indications which identify a good as originating in the territory of a Member, or a region or locality in that territory, where a given quality, reputation, or other characteristic of the good is essentially attributable to its geographical origin.

The incorporation of GIs into the WTO system both highlighted the issue and focused on what were likely to be future trade disputes.

WHERE DO GIS COME FROM?

The right to know from whence a particular product has come has grown in importance as a role of consumer protection. While origin labelling is a particularly complex area of law it is less of a problem in a good deal of consumer protection labelling. The principle of such labelling has tended to be that if a product claims some form of geographic link, then that claim must not be misleading or deceptive. This motivation fits neatly into the basic consumer protection role of dealing with deceptive practices. However, how this is applied nationally has varied somewhat. In the UK, for example, the principal tended to be that if a product, such as mozzarella, was produced in a country other than Italy it had to be labelled as such. The potential deception was removed by requiring a manufacturer to place wording on the label clearly showing that the mozzarella was from Denmark, for example. Thus the consumer was not deceived, while the market was protected from potential competition problems that can arise from restricting a label to a limited number of producers.

The idea of geographic indications as a protector of consumers and its link to trade was enshrined in a number of international intellectual property treaties. For example, the Paris Convention for the Protection of Intellectual Property and the Madrid Agreement for the Repression of False or Deceptive Indications of Source of Goods both have specific provisions relating to border measures that could be used to halt trade in goods whose geographic origin was deceptively identified.

It is interesting to note that many consumer protection laws also contain provisions about what is termed 'unfair competition'. While such provisions can be controversially applied to things such as below cost selling or indeed to firms negotiating discounts on volume purchases, the form of deception that GIs seek to deal with is quite naturally aligned with such provisions.

Article 22.2(a), and Article 22.4 of The WTO Agreement on Trade Related Aspects of Intellectual Property Rights (TRIPS) specifically deal with the 'deceptive' use of GIs. The wider protection for wines and spirits enshrined in the TRIPS agreement was effectively a Trojan Horse for wider protection for all GIs. The wine provisions, most notably in Article 23.1, provided both a higher level of protection and remove motivation from deception. While the broader use of GIs involves an appeal to deception as a driver of usage, in wine an indication simply cannot be used if it does not come from a specific region.

EXEMPTIONS, EXCEPTIONS AND HISTORY

One of the greatest difficulties with the use of GIs is in cases where other producers have used them for some time, or indeed have only recently started using them. The problem is further complicated if a producer has a trademark in one country that is a GI in another. While demanders of greater protection for GIs point to such problems as evidence of their case, the reality of the differential application of GIs is more complex.

It is no coincidence that the main protagonists in the GI debate are countries that, on the one hand, experienced large-scale emigration, and those, on the other hand, that were the recipients of that emigration. In essence, on the one side is Europe and on the other former colonies of Europe. In culinary terms Europe was very much the motherland to many communities that grew up in the USA, Australia, Canada and elsewhere in the world. With emigration communities took with them the culinary traditions and recipes of their homeland. If we look at cheese as an example we find that

> (m)ost of the cheeses produced in the United States originated in another country and then traveled here with immigrants. Mozzarella, one of the most popular cheeses in the US today is an example of a cheese that emigrated; taking on a different character as cheesemakers modified the product for new markets.[2]

The tale of mozzarella exemplifies the problems that many countries have when faced with a demand from the 'homeland' that they cease calling 'their' products by the names they recognize.

Early US attempts to make Italian-style cheeses were hampered by inefficient water supplies, poor dairy quality and a simple lack of knowledge about how to make cheese. The need to make such cheese in the USA was underlined by the fact that transportation was so long and hazardous (to the cheese) that importing from the 'homeland' was prohibitively expensive and impractical. US Italian migration, particularly after the turn of the 20th century led to the development of a domestic cheese industry. The early efforts to make mozzarella in the USA centred on cow's milk mozzarella. Around the same time in Italy efforts were being made to reintroduce Buffalo milk mozzarella after they too had moved to cow's milk mozzarella. However, mozzarella cheese in the USA evolved; 'after changes in the manufacturing procedure, most mozzarella evolved into a firmer, less sour, milder flavored cheese, better suited for transport and cooking – especially pizza pies.'[3] US mozzarella increasingly was produced using part-skimmed milk. The reasons for this are unknown but are believed to be related to the premium paid for buttermilk. What is clear, however, is that mozzarella in the USA was very much a home grown variant adapted to the growth of the dairy industry in the USA. The mozzarella produced, being harder, firmer and milder than Bufala mozzarella is thus similar to Danish mozzarella in Europe. The cheese was initially formulated to be mainly used in cookery, most notably on pizzas.

One has to ask how GIs can deal with this development. Mozzarella as a product is far from alone in having different trajectories depending on where in the world the producer is. The growth of the Australian, Chilean and US wine industries shows just how imported grape varieties can develop into perfectly serviceable products. It is perfectly possible, if not likely, that the manner of protection chosen for GIs in different countries bears a close resemblance to the development of their food economies and indeed the role of food manufacturers in it.

If we accept that most countries have generally developed foodstuffs in good faith, a key number of which are imported food types brought into the country by immigrants, then we have to look to the means by which potential conflicts can be dealt with. Under the TRIPS agreement Article 24.4 allows the 'continued and similar use' of GIs for wines and spirits by 'nationals or domiciliaries who have used that geographical indication in a *continuous* manner with regard to *the same or related* goods or services'. Of course the definition of 'same or related' leaves a good deal of room for manoeuvre.

Other possible routes to conflict resolution rest on challenges to trademarks. As the GI lobby in Europe is keen to point out, a private firm has a trademark on Parma ham in Canada. Most trademark systems have options for challenge, and given the preponderance in international IP law on limiting deceptive practices one wonders why this trademark has not been challenged.

The problem of correctly defining both the production process and those firms able to meet the standard is an increasingly important one for GI producers. The initial wave of GIs appeared to be based on relatively defensible and well established standards for a specific product. However, as the net has been spread the authenticity of some standards has become questionable. The recent debate around the Melton Mowbray pie in the UK is interesting in this regard. In 1999 the Melton Mowbray Pork Pie Association (MMPPA) applied to the EU to get a GI for Melton Mowbray pies. Melton Mowbray is a small town in Leicestershire whose name has become a marketing standard for pork pies. The body sought and received backing from the UK government department responsible for applying for EU GI status, but was attacked by Northern Foods who produced pies under the Melton Mowbray name elsewhere in the country. There was great debate over whether the pie should have pink or grey meat, with the MMPPA demanding pink meat which they argued came as a side effect of pigs being fed on whey from stilton production.

The immediate problem that the MMPPA had was that there was only one firm that produced pies in Melton Mowbray, and that firm had a lot of its products produced elsewhere in the area. The solution they came to was to define Melton Mowbray to include all premises within a radius of 20 miles. Unfortunately this excluded one producer who made pies to exactly the quality and compositional standard required by the MMPPA. This producer was 40 miles away in Nottinghamshire, not Leicestershire. The response was to extend the boundary to include this producer and to include other producers that followed the production process but were nowhere near the town that bore the name.

The Melton Mowbray case illustrates the problem of differentiating recipe-based products that have a geographic designation in their name and geographic indications that also have a specific recipe component. It also indicates just how artificially restrictive a GI can be. It would be interesting to see how many GIs are awarded to bodies whose membership has a flexible boundary or whose boundary is artificial; even Parma ham is not produced in Parma, but in a valley near Parma.

GIS, TRADEMARKS, LICENSING AND COMPETITION

One of the most interesting elements of the GI 'problem' is the collective versus individual nature of the protection offered. In this respect it poses particular problems for competition analysis. While existing trademark law fits relatively neatly into competition law in terms of abusive practices and dominance issues, GIs sit in a rather awkward position. The collective nature of the GI requires members of the GI to meet and discuss 'standards' for the awarding of a label. Such a practice is normally viewed at the very least with suspicion by competition regulators. One would indeed expect any agreement that, at its core, restricts production and excludes existing producers from the market, to have to seek an exemption from competition law. Given that the most advanced system of GI protection and the authority with the majority of GIs registered and enforced is Europe, it is worth asking a few questions about the interface between GIs and competition rules.

The normal process for deciding whether an agreement is anti-competitive is to look to Article 81(1) of the Treaty Establishing the European Community (as amended by subsequent treaties) It prohibits agreements that:

1. directly or indirectly fix purchase of selling prices or any other trading conditions
2. limit or control production, markets, technical development, or investment
3. share markets or sources of supply

4. apply dissimilar conditions to equivalent transactions with other trading parties, thereby placing them at a competitive disadvantage
5. make the conclusion of contracts subject to the acceptance by other parties of supplementary obligations which, by their nature or according to commercial usage, have no connection with the subject of such contracts.

However, agreements that do breach any of these conditions can be allowed to continue provided that they meet two criteria – firstly, they can be exempted from the provisions of Article 81(1) if they meet all four criteria of Article 81(3).

Under this article the agreement must:

1. improve the production or distribution of goods or lead to a technical improvement or advance economic progress
2. offer a fair share of the benefits gained to consumers
3. have no dispensable restrictions
4. involve no substantial elimination of competition.

To receive clearance any agreement must meet all four conditions. Of course the jurisprudence spelling out how these four factors will be assessed is complex and evolutionary. However, agreements that eliminate competition, have restrictions that can be achieved in another less anti-competitive manner and that offer few obvious benefits to consumers are unlikely to pass muster.

The second set of conditions that must be met are that the agreement does not

1. 'impose on the undertakings concerned restrictions which are not indispensable to the attainment of these objectives
2. afford such undertakings the possibility of eliminating competition in respect of a substantial part of the products in question.'

Of course, agriculture is 'different'. The rules outlined above apply to 'normal' sectors of the EU economy. The EU competition regime applies to agriculture in the same sense that for many years the rules of the General Agreement on Tariffs and Trade (GATT) applied to agriculture; theoretically and in very limited circumstances. While the WTO Agreement on Agriculture (AOA) finally incorporated some coverage of agriculture into the trading system, the same cannot be said to have happened to domestic governance of European agriculture.

The position of agriculture in European regulation is of course anomalous in many ways. The encumbrance that is the Common Agricultural Policy signals the importance of a minor part of the EU economy to European rule makers. The original EC Treaty, in Articles 32 to 38 specifically, singles agriculture out for special treatment. Agriculture is essentially governed by different rules from those for non-agricultural markets, and Article 36 specifically states that competition policy will only have an impact upon agriculture in specific circumstances to be decided by the Council. The main provision excluding significant parts of European agriculture from competition regulation is Council Regulation 26 of 1962.[4]

This Regulation applies a number of conditions to the application of Articles 81 and 82 of competition law. The regulation lists a number of agricultural products in Annex II which can only be dealt with by competition law under limited conditions. The Regulation is reasonably straightforward. The first article states that competition law applies to agricultural products listed, except for Article 2 limits. Those limits are essentially of two types, although a third is used for illustrative purposes. Those two general exemptions are for activities carried out under the Common Agricultural Policy (including the desire to allow farmers a reasonable income). The second specific exemption is for activities integral to national market organizations.

While the exemption for national market organizations has been rather overtaken by events, with a large number of them disappearing, the exemption for activities in line with the CAP is both broad and very much alive. The objectives that are thus effectively exempt from Article 81 are covered by roughly five headings; increasing agricultural productivity, ensuring a fair standard of living for farmers, stabilizing markets, ensuring the availability of supplies, and ensuring that consumers get access to agricultural produce at reasonable prices.

It is fairly obvious that the five conditions laid out for the CAP are incompatible with normal competition law. The only condition that remotely approaches normal competition law conditionality is the provision on consumer interests – but even here fair prices (whatever they are) is used rather than a fair share of any benefits.

The last exception built into Article 26 is one for the activities of cooperatives. This exception covers agreements between farmers or groups of farmers that cover either production or sale of agricultural produce or provide joint facilities for storage, treatment or processing of agricultural products. Such an exemption almost exactly describes a body such as the Parma ham consortia. There are limits to the cooperative exception. These include no allowance for price fixing, it does not apply to abuse of dominance cases, and it only applies to cooperatives within a member state.

While the Director General for Competition have always tried to put a brave face on the agricultural exemption it is clear that they have managed to do little but nip at the heels of agricultural protectionism and anti-competitive behaviour. The position at the national level is, however, potentially more interesting. To take but one relevant country, Italy, activity against certain agricultural organizations has been more evident than one would assume, given the politics of food in that country. The Italian competition authority (the Autorità Garante della Concorrenza e del Mercato) have conducted a number of investigations into different agricultural groupings. These include IGOR, the consortium for producing gorgonzola cheese in 1998, the prosciutto di Parma and prosciutto di San Daniele, Parmigiano Reggiano cheese and Grana Padano in 1998 and the Grano Padano again in 2003 and 2004.

The number and focus of investigations at a national level illustrate a number of points about the potential impact of GIs administered by consortia. It is these consortia that are at the heart of the problem of the competition impact of GIs. Where trademark systems enable a single firm to register a name or designation, the GI system rewards a group of producers that can define its own borders. It should be noted that the US system, among others, allows group registrations of trademarks.

With single trademark owners there is considerable experience for competition regulators to deal with potential competition abuses. There are well tested mechanisms, such as licensing, that can be used to stop the abuse of the monopoly right that trademarks confer. However, with consortia the problem is more intractable. If one part of the European Commission wishes to use agricultural cooperatives and consortia as a means of advancing elements of the Common Agricultural Policy, then the ability of another to reform that is limited. The other major problem with consortia designed for one purpose, in this case quality regulation, is their tendency to carry out other activities. The Italian competition authority cases have tended to focus on efforts of the GIs bodies to restrict production to maintain and indeed increase prices.

The tendency of consortia to discuss matters other than quality is hardly surprising, nor is the idea new. As Adam Smith pointed out:

> People of the same trade seldom meet together, even for merriment and diversion, but the conversation ends in a conspiracy against the public, or in some contrivance to raise prices. It is impossible indeed to prevent such meetings, by any law which either could be executed, or would be consistent with liberty and justice. But though the law cannot hinder people of the same trade from sometimes assembling together, it ought to do nothing to facilitate such assemblies; much less to render them necessary.[5]

The natural scepticism of consortia is played out in the experience of the Italian authorities in which almost every case they took involved consortia members discussing matters other than quality standards. Indeed most inquiries concerned production limits imposed by GI bodies. The limits were claimed to be for 'quality' purposes.

Even where discussions do not stray beyond the quality standards that the bodies are supposed to develop, the very nature of consortia makes anti-competitive agreements more likely. Giving a group of producers a monopoly on a particular product and its composition immediately imbues them with market power. Allowing that body to discuss and set production limits makes price rises extremely likely. Any body that controls production and has a good understanding of demand can limit production to raise prices. Irrespective of the rationale for the group an anti-competitive impact is almost certain.

At such a point one would assume two sorts of action. Firstly, one would expect an investigation by a relevant competition authority and secondly, one would expect an industry to seek an exemption from normal competition law. Of course in the case of agricultural consortia the law is stacked in their favour. While price fixing is not strictly allowed, all activities that would lead to the effect of price fixing appear to be blessed. If we are to address the problem and issues of GIs it is precisely at this level that we must start.

WHERE CAN WE GO FROM HERE?

The European Commission wishes to see all WTO members adopt the EU system of Geographic Indications.[6] They want an almost exact replication of the EU system to apply everywhere; everyone will have to produce a catalogue of registered GIs. For other countries this is seen as tantamount to foodie-imperialism and will require a number of existing trademarks to be rescinded and indeed will require a number of established players to rename their existing products.

What is clear is that the manner in which the European GI regulations are structured is antithetical to normal practice in non-agricultural markets. Granting consortia of companies a monopoly on a certain product with the right to restrict entry and production is a rare beast outside agriculture. The fact that the Commission have extended the powers of these consortia to cover even how the products are retailed shows just how far from normal reality the GI standards within the EU have strayed. Of course a good deal of this depends on the market definition one uses for GI products. Here we have the GI bodies themselves to rely on. The handy rule of thumb in market analysis is that we need to look at the market that the firms are trying to monopolize before worrying about the strict market definition. The Parma ham consortia are seeking to monopolize Parma ham production, not all thinly sliced ham, which they themselves would argue is a different sort of product. The feta cheese firms are not trying to monopolize all cheese production, just feta production.

If there were no general exemption for agricultural produce under Regulation 26/1962 we would be able to test the individual requirements of the GI consortia by normal competition rules. We would be able to see whether a particular GI standard provided a fair share of benefits to consumers and whether the rule was indispensable to the attainment of the goal. In many ways it is this latter test that would be most interesting to run the GI standards by. It would not be too difficult to argue that consumers gained a fair share of benefits if product quality was maintained or improved. Of course this would need to be balanced against price rises and exclusion of existing firms. However, given the nature of the consumer share test in Article 81(3) we would not expect that to be a stumbling block.

The indispensability test would probably provide the most interesting element of any analysis of the applicability of competition law to GI consortia. This test would allow any competition authority to look closely at the rules of consortia to see if they are indispensable to attaining the goal of protecting the quality and provenance of a particular GI.

One could easily imagine that the following restrictions would not pass any indispensability test; production limits, membership or entry limits providing quality standards are met, self-regulation by existing members of a consortia, sales practice regulation or regulations that dictate where a product is cut or grated.

For example, the restriction on where Parma ham can be sliced would be hard put to pass an indispensability test. In a newspaper article following the Parma ham ECJ case a journalist from the *Sunday Telegraph* reported that: 'As he spoke, hams which had been cured for at least 12 months were being whisked into a machine which sliced each block into 60 slithers of ham, yielding 2000 packets an hour.'[7] It is difficult to believe that machine-slicing a product is an artisan skill only held in Parma or a skill that cannot be easily transferred to a venue away from Parma. Would having the ham sliced in Leeds really make Parma ham any less Parma ham; is the restriction indispensable to maintaining quality? In front of a competition regulator rather than a judge reading intellectual property law written especially for the purpose it is unlikely that such a measure would stand up.

The indispensability test would allow regulators to ensure that GIs were actually designed to protect the consumer rather than afford a small group of producers the opportunity to control a marketplace. If we could apply normal competition rules to claims for GIs then we would be some way to limiting their anti-competitive impact. If this were done then any attempts to apply such rules internationally could be received with less cynicism.

Such a system would also enable regulators to separate out products with a real geographic link and those where the link is artificially transplanted to enable producers to restrict the market. In short a means to tell Roquefort from Feta. We need, however, to address other problems; the existence of disparate national food cultures, often from the same base; and secondly, the appropriation of geographic indications by producers in countries beyond the geographic region indicated.

If we accept that different nationalities have different food cultures, and further that many of these cultures are adapted forms of food cultures exported with emigrant populations, then the need to unify global food designations appears less significant. However, it is entirely legitimate for countries and their producers to seek review of any geographic indication, no matter how registered, in a foreign country, which is misleading.

Under a number of existing consumer protection laws producers are required to place a geographic designation on their products if there is a geographic component or association with their product that they are seeking to trade on. Thus one can buy Danish mozzarella or, until recently, Yorkshire feta. Consumers were not misled and were able to distinguish the 'real' from the 'pretend'.

There are also a number of provisions in domestic trademark laws that allow challenges to occur to existing trademarks. The issue in such jurisdictions tends to rest on whether a term is generic for those countries. It is difficult to argue that for American consumers the term mozzarella or feta, or indeed champagne, is anything other than generic. The immigrant food culture for these products has since evolved on a different path to that of the 'old' country. For those consumers Wisconsin is the home of cheese, not France or Italy, or even Greece. Is it reasonable, from a US consumer point of view, for a foreign producer to demand the relabelling of all 'their' home-produced products and have them replaced under the recognized name with products they do not recognize?

A situation where different groups of consumers value products differently would tend to be one suited to a market solution, rather than a regulatory one. If Greek feta is of a higher quality than US feta, then let the US consumer decide which to value more. If they choose domestic over foreign feta, is there any real loss?

However, we still face the second problem, namely that of trademark registration or geographic claims made without qualification. One can argue that geographic claims require some form of unification across the world to encourage trade. While this argument is largely theoretical there is an argument that we need to find a means to allow easier challenge of trademarks granted to products clearly from beyond the borders of the country concerned.

If we can change the GI process to make it more consistent with competition rules and law, then we are in a stronger position to deal with our second problem of inappropriate trademark registration. However, here one has to ask the question about the relevant and appropriate tool to solve the problem. If different countries register trademarks for producers on the basis of their own food cultures, one would expect divergence. It is probably unreasonable for individual producers or consortia to police the global market for trademark registration. However, it would also appear that GIs are not a good candidate for upward harmonization (given the competition and cultural issues). It would thus appear a poor candidate for WTO inclusion. However, given the existence of the World Intellectual Property Organization (WIPO) we have a ready-made forum for registering all GIs and providing a forum for negotiation between member states regarding what may appear to be inappropriate registrations.

CONCLUSION

The claim of geographic indications for inclusion in the WTO system of trade regulation is a weak one. The initial weakness comes from the simple fact that different countries have different food cultures, complicated by the fact that many have come from the same source, Europe, but have followed different paths. The weakness is compounded by the design of EU GI regulations which eschew normal competition analysis and encourage anti-competitive behaviour by GI owners. The combined weakness is topped off by the lack of evidence of a global problem of such magnitude that a WTO solution is optimum.

If we are to reduce tension of the GI issue we must deal with each weakness in turn. The divergent food culture issues will essentially stop any global system in its tracks. The all-encompassing EU approach cannot work in other countries, and indeed it is arguable, following the feta case, that it works in the EU. The competition weakness is really the core problem that needs addressing. The current EU system encourages anti-competitive behaviour by fostering cartel behaviour. The exemption of agricultural products and cooperatives is fundamentally flawed and rests on a conception of agricultural markets that is both wrong and Panglossian. If Europe wishes to gain credibility for its system it must dismantle the blanket protection for anti-competitive behaviour in agriculture and fundamentally alter the activities of many GI-owning bodies. Removing unnecessary requirements, such as controls on where products are sliced and how they are sold, will improve the deserving GIs while removing those that are simply attempts to restrict markets.

Even if we can make the GI system more competitive we are struck with the issue of the scale of the GI 'problem', or whether we are actually dealing with the correct problem in the first place. The EU has managed to collect a small coalition of countries in favour of greater GI protection. It has done this by dangling the carrot of protection for perhaps one or two products for developing countries. In essence it has offered enhanced margins through global market restriction. It is likely that every country can find at least one product to place on a central register, alongside the many the EU have managed to develop over the years; but is this a WTO issue? The answer is yes, but not in the context the EU are arguing for it. It is not an issue of such import that the WTO should create any rules. The WIPO is far better placed to deal with the creation of a central register and the creation of a mediation process for disputed GI/trademark awards. However, the issue most definitely is a WTO one in terms of the wider agricultural trade liberalization talks. It is difficult to believe that the emergence of the GI issue is unrelated to the increasing pressure on the EU to open its market to more agricultural trade. As most GIs are by their nature higher up the value chain, the cynical could suggest that the EU is trying to sew up the higher value chain markets for its own producers by allowing other countries to provide it with agricultural produce, as long as they are low-value items. If one looks at markets such as textiles, then one clearly sees an attempt from EU producers to move up the value chain, only to be met by producers in other countries doing exactly the same thing. By creating a restrictive system of GIs that stops new entrant countries or industries producing products with recognizable names, the EU is simply trying to use regulation to restrict the higher value markets for its own producers. This is to the detriment of all agricultural exporters. Perhaps this detriment is not immediately apparent, but as their agricultural producers evolve and try to move into more high-value products then it will evidence itself more readily.

A global system that allowed the present anti-competitive nature of the GI system to impose itself globally would also be to the detriment of consumers in Europe and elsewhere. For every arguable case for a GI, like Roquefort, with a tradition of production and quality, we are lumbered with feta, claimed by Greek producers, despite its Italianized version (fetta) of the Greek word for a slice (pheta) and a product that has been produced in many countries.

The EU does not have a strong case, or indeed, almost any case for a WTO agreement on GIs. Their agenda must be resisted if we are to see European agricultural markets properly liberalized rather than balkanized. If the EU get their way they will open the low-value markets to trade while at the same time tying up almost any product name that means anything to Europe's consumers. The food imperialism of the Commission has, however, thrown light on the profoundly anti-competitive nature of the GI system and the exemptions given to agricultural markets. These agreements must be reformed and placed under the full rigour of competition regulation. Once the anti-competitive nature and effect of these rules has been dealt with, then the Commission has a case to persuade WIPO to develop a central database and registration process which allows for a low-cost arbitration system to stop inappropriate or misleading GI trademark or registration schemes at the national level.

NOTES

1. For more detail on the origins of competition policy see F.M. Scherer and David R. Ross (1993), *Industrial Market Structure and Economic Performance*, Houghton Mifflin.
2. Wisconsin Center for Dairy Research, *Dairy Pipeline*, December 2003, Vol. 15 No. 4.
3. Wisconsin Center for Dairy Research, *Dairy Pipeline*, December 2003, Vol. 15 No. 4.
4. Official Journal B 30 of 20.04.1962.
5. Adam Smith (1982), *The Wealth of Nations*, Book I, Chapter X, London: Penguin.
6. For example see Communication from Bulgaria, Cyprus, the Czech Republic, the European Communities and their Member States, Georgia, Hungary, Iceland, Malta, Mauritius, Moldova, Nigeria, Romania, the Slovak Republic, Slovenia, Sri Lanka, Switzerland and Turkey: Negotiations Relating to the Establishment of a Multilateral System of Notification and Registration of Geographical Indications. Submission to a special session of the Trips Council TN/IP/W/3.
7. *Sunday Telegraph*, 25 May, 2003. 'Victory tastes sweet to the Parma producers A court ruling on the slicing and packaging of the ham has dismayed British supermarkets but delighted the Italians', reports Bruce Johnston in Parma, 25 May, 2003, Sunday.

Chapter 2
Valuing GIs: their pros and cons

Are GIs worth pursuing?

The available evidence presented here, and in other papers reviewed but not cited for this book, indicates that GIs have clear and positive characteristics that can make them valuable assets for any country. Yet, they are not an easy achievement and in some situations, they simply are not feasible. If they are not at least a commercially viable proposition then producers will not be interested. Josling[44] and other experts caution that pursuing a GI strategy will not be the optimal answer in a number of cases.[45] In other words, resolving many business and rural development issues will require other, more basic, interventions ranging from institutional or organizational strengthening to quality or food safety practices. In some cases, the returns may not warrant the substantial investments required for a GI.

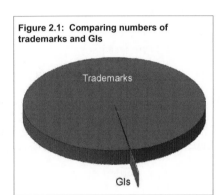

Figure 2.1: Comparing numbers of trademarks and GIs

Successful GIs, like any valuable brands, are limited in number and not easy to achieve. Like trademarks, only a small proportion of them has actually reached significant economic importance. Today's 10,000 GIs would represent less than 1% of the more than 6 million trademarks that are active worldwide.[46] GIs are clearly not an easy attainment. Creating and sustaining them is a long and resource-intensive undertaking, as noted by Kerr (2006), and confirmed by all of the Case Studies commissioned for this work.

Commercially successful GIs do not simply arise. There are some pre-conditions and they require a well-thought out strategy and resources to execute the strategy. There is no 'one-size-fits-all' approach. Protecting GIs is a vital element in this process of developing them but it is clearly not sufficient for ensuring their success. An enabling environment is also important, as Belletti and Marescotti report, the political, social, and competitive factors that can typically influence sectors will also have an impact on GIs.[47] Although protection of local names is part of a useful strategy, it may be more valuable to develop appropriate levels of quality, consistency of supply, and credible assurance systems such as those embodied in standards and traceability.[48] In the absence of the factors necessary for a successful GI (see chapter 6 for more on these), developing business or supply chain competitiveness and simply

---

44 2006b.
45 See Broude 2005 and also Rangnekar 2004.
46 Escudero 2001.
47 Belletti and Marescotti 2006.
48 Villalobos et al. 2008.

protecting their identity using collective marks or trademarks can be effective and even more flexible.[49] Sometimes, the scarce resources in many countries may be better targeted toward development strategies other than GIs.

GIs are not a magic potion, but they are certainly a powerful tool. As such, there are better ways, and worse ways, to approach and apply them. If poorly or carelessly applied, they can have negative impacts. However, if thoughtfully managed, they can deliver many benefits particularly to regions that may not otherwise easily realize the inherent potential in their latent geo-cultural assets. That, perhaps, is one of the finest features of GIs: that they are a mechanism by which a place and its people can come to realize and bring to fruition a unique and valuable asset that is already there.

Control of the GI by the owner creates value that is realized as consumer demand and preserved via certain rights.[50] GIs can manifest as private rights of an owner when protecting a specific product-place combination. However, they are also typically considered a public good because the resident persons and enterprises of a specific GI region garner multiple shared benefits – even if they are not direct producers – while consumers may also benefit from the distinction and protection of a GI. See table 2.1 for basic benefits or harm that trade partners can experience with a GI.

Table 2.1	How GIs can benefit or harm
Consumer benefits	**Owner benefits**
Higher quality and unique products for consumers available and encouraged	Higher prices for producers
Conveys messages and minimizes "search costs"	Protection of local tradition and cultural practices
Producer or manufacturer liability more easily determined and secured (traceability)	Market for differentiation and exclusivity
Can provide a means by which universal values (cultural, traditional, environmental) may be preserved via market mechanisms	Positive local externalities including better employment, rural development, governance, etc.
Consumer harm	**Owner harm**
Exclusivity may elevate costs	Higher costs of production
May reduce innovation or improvement	May reduce innovation
Public GI systems increase public costs of governance	Likely to require greater local governance and institutional capacity and costs
May reduce competition and increase protectionism	If not state-run, will elevate costs of legal protection

Understanding the costs and benefits of GIs

Producer groups or governments must first consider several economic and socio-political issues in deciding whether to undertake a GI recognition process and then which particular GI mechanisms to use or pursue. The costs of developing a GI extend far beyond the direct costs of actually filing for registration; there are greater indirect costs to consider and to weigh against the benefits. Likewise, the benefits can be more than just receiving a higher price for

---

49   Josling 2006b.
50   Cotton 2008.

the product or service. Table 2.2 offers the key categories to consider. Of course, these may or may not apply in all cases and are only indicative of the known possibilities.

Table 2.2	Typical costs and benefits of a GI	
Costs		**Benefits**
1. Establishing domestic legal structure		1. Improved market access
2. Defining exact physical boundaries		2. Increased sales
3. Establishing the criteria and standards		3. Increased value/profitability
4. Local or domestic information-education		4. Assurance of qualities or characteristics and authenticity
5. Control and certification fees		5. Traceability
6. Marketing and promoting		6. Complementary effect on other products in region
7. Assessing and applying for protection overseas		7. Elevated land values
8. Infrastructure and production investments		8. Induced tourism
9. Adaptation to rules, methods, and specifications		9. Increased employment
10. Commercial or technology limitations		10. Increased differentiation or competitiveness as a "brand"
11. Vigilance and maintaining protection		11. Coalesced local governance
12. Administrative and bureaucratic costs		12. Socio-cultural valorization

The magnitude of the costs and benefits of pursuing a GI and seeking a designation, or registration, will vary from product to product. This will be most influenced by the make-up of the producer group (especially their number and capacity), their product mix, organizational level (group coordination, legal experience, coordinated supply chains, etc.), infrastructure, public support (government or NGOs), and strategies.[51]

In Italy, Belletti et al. note that there is a considerable variety in the range of costs and benefits for three distinct producer groups with GI designations: Chianina beef cattle PGI, Pecorino Toscano cheese PDO and Olio Toscano (olive oil) PGI.[52] Many of the cost and benefit categories, though not the actual costs themselves, would be similar for any group integrating a GI. Indirect costs include: investments for necessary infrastructure adjustments; procurement of required higher-quality raw materials; reorganization of production processes; bureaucratic costs and attitudinal or psychological costs. Under benefits they include: increased sales; increased price; access to new commercial channels; and incentives or subsidies.[53]

---

51 Belletti et al. 2007c; Tregear et al. 2007.
52 Belletti et al. 2007b.
53 EU contributes funds that some states or regions provide as part of their "rural development plans" in order to cover the fixed costs for certification.

Whether it is the government introducing domestic laws, the act of defining GI boundaries, or a producer group wanting to register in another country, a sound strategy supported by specific cost-benefit analysis is imperative when determining whether to develop a GI, and which GI route to pursue. See chapter 6 for more details on such analyses.

General costs to establish and operate a GI

The costs associated with the development and adoption of a GI can be both direct and indirect, at both the individual and the collective level, and not always easy to quantify in advance.[54] Nonetheless, it is necessary to identify them in order to facilitate sound decision-making among stakeholders about whether and how to participate in a GI. This section briefly outlines all of the important categories.

Most countries have the **legal structure** to permit the domestic recognition of a GI. Yet many have very limited capacity to take advantage of GI protection.[55] This step need not be difficult but can take time. The most costly and time-consuming investments at this first stage are often in establishing the formal geographic demarcation and achieving agreement on product standards or parameters for a GI, if these are not established already.

Defining the exact boundaries of a GI can be politically and socially controversial. Some who currently participate as producers or processors may be excluded. "Free riders'" may demand to be included. Producers within the same boundaries but who follow somewhat different methods may find themselves excluded. In fact, someone will always be excluded in the demarcation and this can obviously create difficulties that must be addressed (see the case study from Nariño, Colombia).

Establishing a well-defined GI can take several years of effort, in most cases. It is not uncommon for the early stage of defining the GI to be contentious. In the Mexican state of Oaxaca, for example, the actual parameters of the Pluma Hidalgo GI are still being debated after a decade. Guatemala, one of the most successful promoters of its GIs, has invested more than US$ 1 million and nearly a decade to firmly defining and establishing its GIs (see the case study from Antigua, Guatemala).

Even the physical demarcation of an area presents a challenge, especially in the case of ecological analysis.[56] Some GIs have put considerable emphasis and investment in this. Colombia, for example, took about two years with the communities to establish the physical boundary for a distinct type of coffee and invested heavily in the science to clearly determine the specific area that met the expected quality parameters prior to formally proposing a GI. (See box 6.2 on Colombia's Café Nariño.) When this process is inclusive and successful, it can result in a product that is emblematic and very much a part of the natural and socio-cultural dimensions of its territory.

Of course, most successful GIs have good links with commercial enterprises that **market the products**. There can be a cost in terms of establishing these linkages and perhaps in providing preferential access or terms, at least initially for weaker origins. Good supply chain partners can also benefit the GI by providing valuable marketing services that few origins could ever afford to buy.

---

54 Belletti et al. 2007a and 2007c.
55 Evans 2007.
56 According to Robert Bailey, a respected expert on ecoregional geography, the only State in the United States that has demarcated regions down to the scales comparable to GI definition is Missouri (see the Missouri Resource Assessment Partnership at *http://www.ecrc.usgs.-gov/morap/*). Also, see Barham 2003 for more on this process.

Legal costs will also be incurred for most origins to **apply for protection** in relevant markets, whether domestic or abroad. In some cases, the government or producer group will need to spend a significant amount of time understanding and filling out the applications as well as compiling accurate descriptions of the methods of production and the links to geography etc. that may be necessary as part of the code of conduct, or the specifications for the application process.

Individual producers wishing to benefit from the GI designation may incur **additional costs to adapt their facilities, production methods, raw materials and overall organization** to the specified standard or code of conduct included in the designation application. Many GI regulations, including both EU designations and United States certification marks require individual producers to work with a common standard, and if necessary, to adapt their individual practices to meet that standard. The difference is a matter of timing in relation to the application. EU applicants will be required to adapt their operations prior to or shortly after making an application in order to meet European verification requirements. United States applicants have a longer period to adapt their operations, essentially until they actually sell the product in the United States, since an application in the United States can be based upon intent to conduct business, therefore possibly delaying such expenses to a later date.

Should a producer or firm wish to submit only part of their production to a GI designation, they will need to segregate their operations. This will require both separate traceability and **even investment in hard assets**, such as storage, to accommodate two production streams thus increasing the overall costs.

Reorganizing to meet a standard can be an expensive process. There is the example of Chianina beef PGI, where the code of conduct required exclusive transportation of livestock segregated from non-PGI-destined livestock being moved to slaughterhouses.[57] The need for exclusive transportation was exacerbated by the lack of high-capacity slaughterhouses, requiring livestock to be shipped to multiple locations in small numbers throughout the PGI region, thus significantly increasing transportation costs for producers.

Members of a GI group may also incur costs in adapting to **working collaboratively** as a GI group, with perhaps a new organizational logic and character, particularly given that producers are likely to be artisan-focused with small production runs and few market linkages. A change of mindset is likely to be required on the part of all the participants. Individuals may disagree on these forms of organization, leading to conflicts, particularly when the products requiere multi-sectoral cooperation.[58] There can also be a psychological effect where previously independent producers are now obliged to surrender some of their freedom in adopting a common production scheme, controls, and sometimes, common marketing. The combined costs and difficulties to generate and sustain collective action may not be warranted by the immediate economic benefit of doing so.[59] However, in some cases, joint effort can be positive and reduce the GI participants' costs of production, marketing or adaptation.

The cost of **raw materials** can also increase because producers are committed to using specific ingredients, which may or may not be readily available, or are more expensive than alternatives. For instance, the Pecorino Toscano PDO

---

57   Belletti et al. 2004.
58   Tregear et al. 2007.
59   Ramirez 2007.

must use sheep's milk from a registered breeding flock from Tuscany, Italy, rather than cheaper sheep's milk from other origins, and the milk cannot be frozen, a common practice for this form of cheese production.[60]

Similarly, the cost structure of GI producers can be significantly higher than that of non-GI producers if their **production technology** is more expensive and does not enable them to take advantage of economies of scale. In the EU, a study was carried out in 2005 comparing the non-GI and the GI production technology of French brie cheese and noted a significant cost difference.[61]

In fact, two studies suggest that some European GIs have been found to stifle **commercial efficiency**.[62] One of Mexico's few GIs has been rendered commercially unviable, reportedly due at least in part to onerous regulations required to use the GI (see the case study from Veracruz, Mexico). A preponderance of regulations pertaining to quality and origin can sometimes act as a hindrance to the activities of firms and producers by restricting their ability to innovate or experiment in the areas of technique or production.

Maintaining protection requires a measure of vigilance on the part of the GI's stakeholders to ensure that misuse of the GI name or fraud is not permitted to flourish. Many successful GI owners employ private firms as watchdogs in different markets where this risk is significant. Costs of such protection can range from a few thousand dollars to hundreds of thousands per annum, especially when the cost of monitoring is combined with the administrative and legal costs of pursuing the perpetrators in other nations. GIs that are protected by different types of trademarks must fully shoulder the burden of identifying and prosecuting any infringements of their marks. The Kona coffee GI (based in the United States State of Hawaii) has encountered considerable difficulties in defending its United States certification mark in the United States (see the case study from Kona, Hawaii). The Italian Parma-based GIs (ham, etc.) may be some of the most affected, with legal costs abroad reportedly amounting to more than US$ 1 million per year.[63] The advent of technological advances using DNA samples and genetic fingerprinting are bringing the costs of testing for fraud down to several hundred euros, but tests are still not applicable to many products.

Finally, there will also be ongoing **administrative and bureaucratic costs** incurred to meet the requirements of many GI rules, especially an EU designation or a United States certification. Registers and records must be kept for possible audit while inspection activities or certification must be regularly undertaken. These and other common costs may sometimes be distributed along the supply chain to prevent excessive loading onto smaller producers if the organizing institution is willing and able to adopt such policies.[64]

General benefits related to GIs

The popularity of GIs has increased in recent years and a host of benefits are attributed to GIs. Yet, many of these are conclusions based simply on observations and anecdotal information. Now, a growing body of research is more fully exploring the extent of these benefits.

---

60   Belletti et al. 2004.
61   Marette et al. (2007) note the study by Benitez (2005).
62   Ribaut, J.C., 2005. Peut-on encore garantir la qualité? *Le Monde*, June 17:23, and Zago and Pick (2004). Both noted in Marette et al. (2007).
63   Sebastiano Brancoli ('Prosciutto di Parma' consortium) conference presentation on "Protecting Local Uniqueness and Identity: Tools to Protect Product Distinctiveness in the Global Economy", 19 September, 2007: Washington, D.C.
64   Belletti et al. 2007.

For producer regions, GIs convey the unique characteristics that distinguish their products. The unique organoleptic properties that emerge from the *terroir*[65] and its traditional methods of production and processing may be difficult to duplicate in other regions or countries, and can thus be a valuable and lasting competitive advantage. This type of advantage is similar to that enjoyed by a successful brand in that it is not so dependent upon advantages gained from common factors of production such as labour, logistics and capital costs. The institutional structures or agreements inherent in many GIs can also contribute to competitiveness by improving collective action and reducing transaction costs along the supply chains.

> "The enduring competitive advantages in a global economy lie increasingly in local things – knowledge, relationships, motivation – that distant rivals cannot match."
>
> Michael Porter (1998)

GIs are generally aligned to the emerging trend of more stringent **standards** in global trade. Standards now set the 'rules of the game' for quality and safety assurance, and they are becoming increasingly relevant as strategic tools for market penetration, product differentiation and value-chain coordination.[66] Standards are becoming determinants of who participates in trade with the most developed markets.[67] Even in some less developed markets, the fastest growing retail channels are often managed by supermarket chains and processors, that rely on higher-than-average standards for quality, traceability and food safety.[68] Most of the GIs reviewed typically:

❑ Apply some standards;

❑ Tend to be traceable;

❑ Often implement locally appropriate processing technology;

❑ Are renowned for their particular quality.

There is an increasing demand for products and services with unique characteristics. Consumers today are making more purchasing decisions based on less tangible, or at least less verifiable, product assets such as quality standards, environmental stewardship, reputation, and social responsibility.[69] At the same time, there is much more information now available on the sources and origins of products and the nature of production processes, with the emergence of markets for such certifications as Organic, Fair Trade, GLOBALGAP, etc.[70] In many cases, GIs align with these trends and seem to convey similar attributes of reliability, quality and food safety to the consumer.

GIs have notable **developmental characteristics**. Some have demonstrated that they can generate increased and better quality employment, as elaborated further in this chapter. Ramirez claims that GIs can link entire regions to markets.[71] At least one analysis looking at the welfare associated with GIs notes that they contribute to the overall sustainability of a territory in several

GIs can be valuable mechanisms to promote local products and values.

---

65   *Terroir* is a term (French) indicating a place where the combination of a particular agro-ecology and traditional know-how yield unique quality characteristics. A GI facilitates the recognition of these characteristics for a consumer and thus enables artisan producers to thrive even in very competitive markets.

66   Giovannucci and Reardon 2000.

67   Maertens and Swinnen 2007.

68   See Reardon, Timmer and Berdegué 2003 and also Busch et al. 2007.

69   Busch et al. 2007; Giovannucci 2008.

70   A key reference standard for Good Agricultural Practices; formerly known as EUREPGAP.

71   Ramirez 2007.

important and non-economic ways.[72] For rural areas, GIs can provide part of the tangible structure for affirming and fostering the unique socio-cultural features of a particular place and the products or services it produces. The "Development" section below explores how communities benefit as GIs tend to reward the holders of indigenous knowledge or traditional and artisanal skills as valued forms of cultural expression. GIs may also provide a measure of protection for the intellectual or cultural property of a particular group or place.

Since GIs intrinsically **emphasize the local**, they value the land and its particular characteristics that are often the source of a product's unique nature. There is now increasing debate about the inherent value of local products. The arguments range from the importance of fostering local communities and maintaining rural farm space to the merit of reduced transportation (that can impact global warming) and the desire to recover authenticity and our relation to a particular cultural and agro-ecological place.[73]

More origin-labelled products are turning up in the conventional marketplace as market leading firms offer consumers increasingly more locally identified and less anonymous products.[74] In some cases popularity may be less about a specific product's flavour or uniqueness and more about the fact that it is local. Perhaps paradoxically, for some a 'local' product even when associated with a distant place, may have more value than a more anonymous and undifferentiated product. Giovannucci, Barham and Pirog suggest that, aside from personal levels of trade with familiar entities such as farmers or NGOs, there are no more effective mechanisms for credibly identifying what is truly local, than GIs.[75]

In these many ways, GIs can serve as useful conceptual frameworks to drive an integrated form of rural development that goes beyond pure economic considerations. As such, the institutional structures that are often part of successful GIs may serve to benefit local and regional governance. A large-scale EU survey in 2002 concluded that GI development had not only improved the reputation of a region as an attractive business location but also tended to enhance the **regional cooperation** between government authorities and commercial partners.[76] Together, this further facilitated the joint improvement of environmental quality and the utilization of common resources. These possible benefits are vital for the challenges many developing countries face.

There are few sound economic assessments or cost-benefit analyses available to accurately determine the financial benefit of GIs to developing regions, but the conclusions of those economic assessments that have been carried out tend to be positive overall. For many years, producers, traders and entire value chains have been able to benefit from the long-lived rents associated with a particular Geographical Indication. While it is difficult to determine direct causality between the formal GI structure and the economic benefits, the benefits do

---

72   See Zago and Pick 2002a.
73   Giovannucci, Barham and Pirog 2009.
74   One of the most successful supermarket chains (in terms of sales per square foot), Whole Foods, now actively promotes locally grown and manufactured foods in its United States and United Kingdom stores. Carrefour, one of the world's largest retailers of foods promotes regional products in nearly 40 nations including those in developing areas. The United Kingdom's largest supermarket chain, Tesco, offers an extensive range of local and regional products and intends to increase this area in both its United Kingdom and United States operations.
75   Giovannucci, Barham and Pirog 2009.
76   EC 2002.

exist. It seems clear also that while GIs can offer benefits to consumers and high-quality producers alike, there is evidence that low-quality producers may be left out.[77]

When GIs are high quality, artisan products they may also be **labour intensive** and rarely manage to achieve the size and economies of scale required to compete on a direct price basis with similar products from more industrialized processes. Nevertheless, the connection between unique quality characteristics and place (the noted *terroir* that encompasses both agro-ecology and local know-how) that GIs facilitate for a consumer, enables artisan producers to thrive even in very competitive markets. This is confirmed in the five cases studied by the team working with van de Kop, Sautier and Gerz[78] and several of the case studies covered in this publication. In the midst of the increasingly homogenized and industrial process that brings us our foods, new alternatives are emerging that reflect a desire to relate to the unique tastes and relationships embodied in local foods, and thus in many GIs.

A broad-based, multi-year research effort in the EU[79] has independently concluded that there are a number of valid reasons for undertaking the development of GIs, which include:

❑ Improving access to markets;

❑ Preserving biodiversity and preventing bio-piracy;

❑ Protecting traditional 'know-how';

❑ Supporting community or collective rural development initiatives;

❑ Reducing market price fluctuations;

❑ Improving market governance (labelling and fraud rules, standards, traceability).

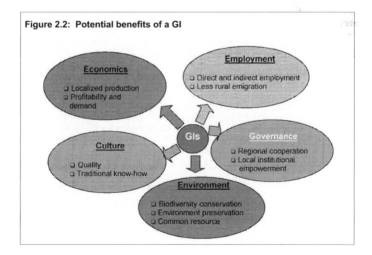

Figure 2.2: Potential benefits of a GI

---

77   Barjolle and Sylvander 1999; Zago and Pick 2002b.
78   van de Kop, Sautier and Gerz 2006.
79   See Sylvander and Allaire 2007.

Improved prices and market access for GIs

Much of the literature on GIs focuses on the policy or legal issues of protection, while less attention has been given to the economic case for GIs. Overall, the economic assessments of the impact of GIs have tended to be positive.[80] However, while a relationship undoubtedly exists, there remains only limited evidence of a direct causal link between the registration of a GI and improved prices.

It is difficult to measure the exact amount of economic impact attributable directly to a GI or to such diverse factors as the subsidies and private investments that exist in many regions, and which have an influence on GI recognition and value. In many cases, the long-standing popularity of a product is more likely to be the reason for it commanding the price premium, while the formal GI recognition acts to solidify the credibility of the value message to consumers and also to prevent or deter fraudulent use.

There are two important and related market-oriented benefits that can be gained from defining and protecting a GI. The **first** is verification of authenticity and protection from misuse or fraudulent labelling by unauthorized third parties. The **second** is the improved access to markets or the potential premium gained by the GI designation, that confirms reputation or act as a form of assurance for a desirable attribute such as quality. It should also be remembered that price premiums alone do not automatically translate into increased profitability. They must be high enough to cover the additional costs of producing, certifying and marketing high quality products.

While there have been few formal cost-benefit analyses to determine the real financial benefits of GIs, there are a number that claim improved prices. There are also some useful studies of the associated welfare effects suggesting that GIs can also contribute to the overall sustainability of a territory in other important and non-economic ways.[81]

There may be other benefits with related economic impact as well, such as a greater overall quality orientation among producers or product spin-offs and product line extensions. A potential route for expansion is to apply the GI's name recognition to other relevant local products. For example, given the success of the PGI for Chianina beef, producers in that part of Italy could reasonably expand the product range into Chianina sausage or meat pies. The famous cheese related to Parma (Parmigiano-Reggiano) and environs has helped improve the recognition of Parma ham, a related GI product.

As the success of a GI grows, so too does its identity and marketability as a brand that in turn reinforces its good reputation and recognition by purchasers. The indication of credibility provided by some GIs can be used as a foundation to market other features and attributes of the product, such as its health benefits and originality.

In the case of Viet Nam's Phu Quoc – an island where Nuoc Mam, a traditional fermented fish sauce, is made – the GI likely does make a significant economic impact. It appears that the recent legal recognition of its GI may be contributing to greater foreign demand for legitimate Nuoc Mam by reducing the estimated 80% counterfeiting of its products in Japan and the EU.[82] Domestic demand for Nuoc Mam takes more than 90% of production leaving only 500,000 litres for

---

80 See, among others, Rangnekar 2004a; Bérard et al. 2005; van de Kop, Sautier and Gerz 2006.
81 Zago and Pick 2002a.
82 UNDP report cited in presentation by C. Berger, French Embassy Attaché in the United States.

export and the new foreign demand has reportedly pushed domestic prices up considerably from ca. €0.5 to €1.5 per litre since the advent of formal GI protection.

In China, the price of Xihu Longjing tea (recognized as a GI in 2001) increased by 10% more than other teas between 2000 and 2005, reaching 100 yuan/kg as compared to 23 yuan/kg for the average price of tea in 2005.[83] Similarly, The Beijing Administration for Industry and Commerce calculates that after the Pinggu Peach was registered as a GI its market value has risen from 1.5 to 4 yuan (US$ 0.20–US$ 0.50) per kg, although the registration was also accompanied by promotional campaigns. The 20% to 30% average price increase cited for the Zhangqui Scallions GI certainly helps farmers and may also be due to the quality aspects developed and promoted by The Zhangqui Scallion Science Research Institute in China.[84]

The vast majority of existing studies focus on developed countries, and the EU in particular. For example, most likely as a result of legal protection obtained for the Lentilles Vertes du Puy GI, the local production of lentils almost quadrupled between 1990 and 2002, providing a living to increasing numbers of producers and wholesalers in the region.[85] Similarly, positive demand effects from becoming a protected GI have been experienced in the cases of Galician veal[86], Parma ham, Brunello di Montalcino wine and Vidalia onions[87]. In France, GI cheeses sell on average at a price approximately 30% higher than cheeses in general (see figure 2.3).

Figure 2.3: Relative retail value of GI and non-GI cheeses in France

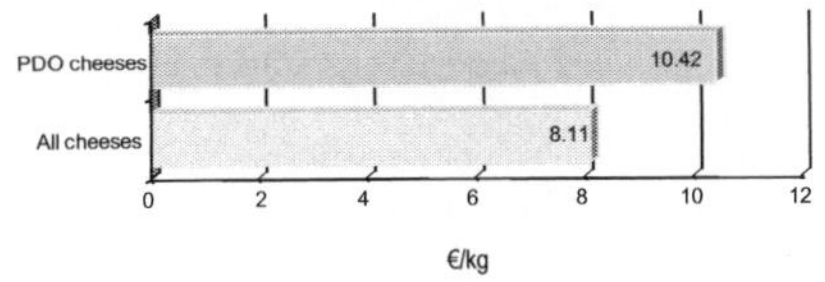

PDO cheeses   10.42

All cheeses   8.11

0   2   4   6   8   10   12

€/kg

Sources: Data from MAAPAR, ONIVINS, CFCE, INAO, and Secodip from Berger 2007.

Tuscan olive oil receives a 20% premium over similar quality oil; the market price for Bresse poultry in France is four times that of non-GI poultry meat.[88] One comparison notes that, before its protection in 1993, the price for Comté cheese was only 20% greater than that of contiguous Emmental while by 2003 this differential had risen to 46%[89] and in that period, production of Comté rose by about 3% per year on average while that of Emmental declined. Parma ham sells at prices up to 50% higher than other comparable hams, and the EC reports that cheese with designated GI status could typically claim a 30% price premium over its competitors.[90]

On a national scale, French Government statistics show that over a four-year period the total revenue from GIs grew by 6.8% per annum, comparing extremely favourably with the 0.7% average growth for the farming sector overall, 3.7% for the food industry overall, and even the 4.2% annual growth in Gross National Product for the whole French economy (see figure 2.4).

A number of studies note that the use of the PDO/PGI logo in the EU is typically perceived as an indication of high quality, capable of increasing sales and improving pricing.[91] Another study reveals that a GI for New Zealand lamb commands premiums of more than 20% in the EU and similarly Japan's Wagyu

---

83   Wallet *et al.* 2007.
84   *WIPO Magazine* 4/2007.
85   O'Connor and Company 2005.
86   Loureiro and McCluskey 2000.
87   Hayes, Lence and Stoppa 2003.
88   European Commission 2003.
89   Agency for International Trade Information and Cooperation 2005.
90   Secodip 2002 data reported in EC 2007.
91   See, for example, Belletti and Marescotti 2006; Sylvander 2004; OECD 2000.

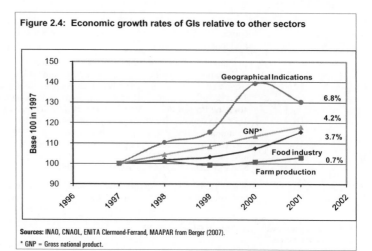

Figure 2.4: Economic growth rates of GIs relative to other sectors

Sources: INAO, CNAOL, ENITA Clermond-Ferrand, MAAPAR from Berger (2007).
* GNP = Gross national product.

beef gets 50% more.[92] The median price paid to milk producers supplying five different French cheese GIs was between 5% and 90% higher than the national average.[93] Likewise, Nyons olive oils provide about 50% more income to their producers than other high-value trademarked non-GI oils. Such effects could apply in principle to developing country products as well, but a substantial investment in market development may first be required.

Research shows that Vidalia onions consistently command a considerable price premium over the onions of other growers.[94] The prices of recently protected agave-based beverages such as Mezcal have risen dramatically (see the case study from Mezcal, Mexico). Darjeeling tea also provides clear economic benefits that go beyond premium prices to improved market access due to the widespread recognition of the origin (see the case study from Darjeeling, India).

Box 2.1   GIs can offer specific business development benefits

The literature suggests that they tend to:

❑ *Impact beyond a single product focus and can serve to promote interrelated products and services in the GI region;*

❑ *Potentially foster clustering and rural integration because not only producers, but also traders, processors, exporters and supply chains, interact at the local or regional level;*

❑ *Use fewer external intermediaries and participate in various forms of downstream "partnership" with the private firms that drive the GI recognition at the consumer level;*

❑ *Offer improved market access and increased incomes when compared to similar non-GI products.*

While there is an abundance of data supporting the case that GIs tend to command higher prices, there is very little data comparing total cost of production and marketing that are required in order to gain these higher prices. It is clear that the usually higher production and certification costs involved in many GIs are likely to erode at least some of the price benefits. Of course, a broader way of looking at this economic equation could suggest that while producer costs are higher, the local entities that provide inputs to the production process including raw materials, labour, certification and inspection services could experience positive remuneration effects. This greater distribution of income along the value chain could itself be a benefit and could feasibly contribute to improved quality and consistency.

---

92   Babcock and Clemens 2004.
93   Berger study (2007) citing data from INRA, INAO, Huile d'olive de Nyons.
94   Boyhan and Torrance 2001.

GIs as a model for development

GIs offer a particularly interesting model for development because they have the potential to provide a range of different types of benefits to the region of origin. They also represent opportunities for several different segments of the population in addition to the producers. These benefits range from having new socio-cultural values for traditional and indigenous assets to the more straightforward economic gains resulting from increased employment, higher incomes and improved market access.

> **A holistic framework for development**
>
> *It is important not to limit the idea of a GI to only its legal recognition or to only the economic development of a product. Perhaps the greatest advantage lies in the ability of a GI to offer a basket of possibilities.*

There may even be indirect benefits such as improved local governance, more tourism stemming from heightened recognition of the name and place conveyed through the GI, as well as increased land values and possible complimentary offerings such as other regional products riding on a GI's reputation, e.g. mustard from Champagne or honey from the Jamaica Blue Mountain region. At the international level, benefits can translate into unique forms of differentiation and competitive advantage that are difficult to erode.[95]

In these many ways, GIs can serve as conceptual frameworks to drive an **integrated form of multifunctional rural development**. GIs can go beyond a single product focus and facilitate progress that is multifunctional in character.[96]

An EC evaluation[97] noted that GI development amplified:

❑ Regional cooperation between municipalities, authorities, commercial and social partners;

❑ The positive identity of the regions, especially referring to culture, landscape conservation and marketing;

❑ Improvements in the general infrastructure and rural services;

❑ Profiling of the region as an attractive business location;

❑ Improvements in environmental quality and linked utilization of resources.

Many GIs are for agricultural products and reference traditional or cultural knowledge. This puts them in a category of intellectual property that theoretically should favour agricultural economies and developing countries in particular. In practice, however, only a few developing countries have taken advantage of the opportunities available to them, and most have not benefited much at all.

The GI approach to development, which intrinsically tends to integrate different functions (i.e. production, processsing, certification, governance, retail, wholesale and international trade) and different levels of action (i.e. local, regional, economic, socio-cultural and ecological) can potentially improve disconnected rural development policies. The institutional structures to manage the GI may even be beneficial to local and regional governance as

---

95   See Kaplinsky 2006; Sylvander 2004; Lewin, Giovannucci and Varangis 2004.
96   Sylvander and Allaire 2007.
97   EC 2002.

mutually reinforcing approaches.[98] GIs can certainly be a stand-alone policy tool but are likely to be more effective when structured as part of a systemic approach to rural development.

Developmental characteristics: competitiveness and economics

GIs are a potentially unique form of competitive advantage, even for smallholders. They are not easy to erode because they depend less on common factors of competition such as cost of production. Instead, GIs build on unique local factors born of tradition, know-how, and special agro-ecological endowments. A viable GI essentially leverages these assets to develop its reputation and value in much the same manner as a brand.

Indeed there are entire countries that can be viewed as GIs and consequently as **brands**. Holt, Quelcht, and Taylor in their Harvard Business Review research note that perceptions about quality and value were long tied to the countries from which the products originated.[99] Some industries, such as Italian fashion design, Japanese electronics, French wine, and various "Made in the USA" products (i.e. cigarettes, soft drinks, software) have earned reputations for their countries. The considerable premiums that accompany those reputations have persisted sometimes for decades based on consumer perceptions (not necessarily the reality) of their superior quality. The value of such positive correlations, whether at the local or the national level, can be substantial.

GIs are conceptually in alignment with **emerging trade demands** for quality, traceability, and food safety. Most apply some determined (though not always codified) standards or quality assurance schemes and several types of GIs use third-party certification as a measure of assurance. Such GIs may more easily be able to meet other fast-growing process standards such as GLOBALGAP or Organics. Nevertheless, in many cases, GIs have production limits that are less likely to expose them to the volatile supply and demand responses of commodities.[100] GIs tend to have basic traceability. This may become even easier especially with the advent of low-cost DNA tracing and related technologies. Technology helped to expose a case of "Basmati" fraud in the United Kingdom wherein only half (54%) of the bags labelled "Basmati" actually contained pure Basmati rice.[101] GIs are often the result of long-term efforts to develop a product with desirable characteristics. This implies that the methods are refined through experience and often implement appropriate processing technology that consistently delivers a measure of quality and adequate food safety.

GIs offer potentially broad **business development** benefits, since they can involve entire regions and have an impact on not only producers, but also traders, processors, exporters, etc., thereby fostering supply chain development and rural integration. The fame surrounding Kona for its sought-after coffee GI stimulates the sale of other agricultural products (e.g. beer, fruit, honey) and even bicycles that may benefit from such an association. Since GIs tend to go beyond a single product focus, and affect other products and chains in the region, they can promote clustering. Parma's well-known dairy industry that includes Parmalat is a good example. The dairy industry helped foster Parma's famous cheese-making industry that includes Parmigiano, the by-products of which are integrated into the supply chain for pigs and these, partly due to the quality of the feed, result in another well-known GI: Parma ham.

---

98 Gómez 2004.
99 Holt, Quelcht and Taylor 2004.
100 Hayes, Lence and Stoppa 2003.
101 Ravilious 2006.

In many cases, GIs tend already to have at least a rudimentary form of **supply chain management**. In developing countries, many production and supply chains are small in scale and lack resources such as capital and know-how. This makes it difficult to achieve scale economies and may limit their market access because of their inability to comply with the increasingly ubiquitous public and private standards required by more developed markets. Most GI products are already produced by small and medium enterprises.[102] GIs are at least somewhat dependent on the cooperation between producers and enterprises that may otherwise compete with each other and thus collective functions may, at least theoretically, induce new scale economies, reduce transaction costs, enhance products, and even facilitate chain governance. Related products, though not GIs, may benefit from the association with well-developed GI value chains particularly in terms of improved standards and even marketing efficiencies in the region.

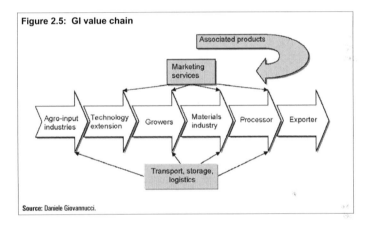

Figure 2.5: GI value chain

Source: Daniele Giovannucci.

There may be considerable returns in being able to tap into evolving consumer preferences in developed countries; preferences that simultaneously seek and recognize diversity and value the characteristic of quality assurance. A significant proportion of the economic rents from GIs may be retained locally (Kona, Darjeeling, Mongolia), although there is also evidence of GIs where multinational firms capture the majority of these rents (many alcoholic beverages and some wines – see the case study from Mezcal, Mexico). Many GI origins clearly command higher prices, although they may also incur higher costs due to investments in quality (equipment, sourcing, grading) and controls (standards development, certification, monitoring). In some cases, these costs are borne privately and in other cases they are public, with agencies managing at least some of the legal protection functions.

---

102 Barjolle and Sylvander 2000; van de Kop, Sautier and Gerz 2006 citing Barjolle et al. 2000.

Developmental characteristics: smallholders, employment, and rural enterprise

GIs offer a primary source of income for 138,000 (mostly smaller) farms in France and 300,000 Italian employees.[103] The French Government cites that 21% of French farmers are involved with the GI sector.[104] One United Kingdom analysis of origin food producers indicates that they interface tightly with the local economies and supply chains, both upstream and downstream.[105] On average, these producers source 61% of their product ingredients, 78% of their marketing services and 82% of their distribution services locally.

The Extension Service of the US State of Georgia estimates that 87% of Vidalia onions are produced on family owned and operated small farms (15 acres or less) with a farmgate value of US$ 5,833/acre or US$ 95 million overall (in 2000). Profitability is further enhanced by value-added products that trade on the reputation of the Vidalia onion GI including processed foods and tourism opportunities such as the annual Vidalia, Georgia Onion Festival that is an important source of revenue for the community.[106] In their review of United States marks for GIs, Babcock and Clemens note that certification marks are used to also promote the sale of other related agricultural products.[107]

According to the EC evaluation conducted by the LEADER project on the measures employed in four German states between 1998 and 2001, GI efforts were estimated to have directly created and sustained 1,870 regular full-time jobs, 40% of which were for women.[108] This generated an additional permanent income in the local economies of about €48 million per year counting part-time and temporary work. The evaluation gave primary credit for the success to the use of participatory development programmes with the local communities.

A comparison made in 2004 between the non-GI cheese, Emmental, and the similar GI cheese Franche-Comté, found that the less intensive Comté producers provide as much as five times more employment per litre of milk collected.[109] While Comté focuses on local development, Emmental has pursued an industrialization strategy (with no GI recognition). This has led to a shift of production by Emmental to other more intensive dairy regions and an overall decline in sales for more than a decade. Comté, on the other hand, has enjoyed a steady increase since 1992, the year of its formal EU recognition (see figure 2.6). Rural migration away from the Comté PDO region is only half that of the Emmental.[110] Part of the explanation may also lie in increased revenue from tourism on the "Routes du Comté", with 2.2 million overnight stays in 2002. This generated considerable numbers of on-site purchases direct from the producers.

GIs are at the intersection of culture, commerce and geography.

In Viet Nam's Phu Quoc GI about 90 firms that are primarily SMEs produce 10 million litres of Nuoc Mam, a traditional fermented fish sauce, and employ several thousand persons. Smaller firms have dominated the output of the GI and Unilever has signed a ten-year contract with a local consortium and agreed to invest up to US$ 1 million to upgrade production facilities as part of its deal to license the Phu Quoc appellation.[111]

---

103 EC 2003a.
104 Berger 2007.
105 Elliot et al. 2005 cited in Belletti and Marescotti 2006.
106 Boyhan and Torrance 2002.
107 2004.
108 EC 2002.
109 Dupont 2004.
110 Gerz and Dupont 2004.
111 Rangnekar 2004.

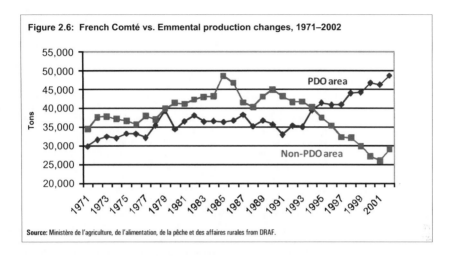

Figure 2.6: French Comté vs. Emmental production changes, 1971–2002

Source: Ministère de l'agriculture, de l'alimentation, de la pêche et des affaires rurales from DRAF.

A number of countries leverage GIs to generate national and even international tourism. France, Germany, Italy and the United Kingdom all have popular gastronomy areas or trails that are prime tourism destinations. Even the well-known GI areas of South Africa (wines), Jamaica (Blue Mountain coffee), Brazil (wines), Mexico (Tequila), Chile (fruit and wines), and Argentina (Pampas beef and wines) are now an integral part of organized holiday tourism that generates employment, income, and local pride.

Developmental characteristics: society and culture

The potential long-term value is not only at the economic level (i.e. jobs, greater income, or ancillary development such as tourism) but also at a cultural level in terms of the recognition of customary and value-adding traditions that can convey a deep sense of a people, their culture, and of their long-standing relationship to a region. This esteem can be a springboard to the recognition of assets and diverse forms of local development that can be as valuable as increased income.

As a means to foster **culture and tradition**, GIs are indeed viable tools. They value the cultural aspects and traditional methods that are intrinsic to the production and processing of a product. They are market-based and therefore likely to be more sustainable so long as they do indeed provide such benefits. Rangnekar claims that GIs are at the intersection of culture and geography.[112] While they can offer a measure of protection for both the locus of cultural or indigenous knowledge and the forms of its commercial transmission, the GIs do not protect such knowledge *per se*. Other intellectual property instruments (i.e. patents) or forms of legal protection may therefore be needed to complement GIs.

Benefits accrue to traditional communities, as GIs tend to reward the holders of indigenous knowledge.[113] For some countries, GIs are legally expected to be connected to traditional aspects. For example, Thévenod-Mottet notes that in France, the Appellations of Origin laws reference "local, fair and constant practices" and in Tunisia, the Designation of Origin law notes "methods of production must be rooted in local traditions being ancient, constant and

---

112 Rangnekar 2004a.
113 Ranaboldo and Fonte 2007.

well-known".[114] The unique nature of GIs as a somewhat collective right includes the absence of a right to assign the GI and this makes it consistent with some traditional cultural rights; if GIs are protected as trademarks they may, in some cases, legally be assigned or transferred (see chapter 4 for discussion on this). GIs can particularly help to build social equity via self-esteem and can increase valuation of local products, services and land.[115]

Cultural recognition in the marketplace facilitates the transmission of traditional and artisanal skills that are valued forms of cultural communication. GIs are an effective way for rural development to promote cultural identity even in remote areas or when cultural identity is not embodied in just a product but rather encompasses shared assets such as history and architecture that can be valued via tourism and characteristic art and crafts.[116] Such traditional and artisanal skills also imbue products with unique character that can elicit significant market premiums even for smaller producers.[117] In fact, for many larger businesses, such diversity can represent an unacceptable level of inefficiency where their business models typically require more rather than less homogenization of standards.

There is an increasing interest in whether Geographical Indications can play an important role in the development strategies of rural communities in developing countries. Though evidence is still limited regarding the most sensible ways to approach them, regions with GIs do demonstrate improved development. More positive levels of endogenous development in GI locales (as measured by the number and intensity of relations, the quality of social capital, and collective action) have been documented in Argentina, Brazil, Italy, Latvia, Portugal, South Africa, and the United Kingdom.[118] They emphasize the local but not in an insular manner since many GIs operate globally via market exchanges beyond their borders.

In many countries, there is evidence of some distinct preferences for local and traditional products that are domestically produced. This is increasingly evident even in developing countries. Beyond the international demand for such well-known products as Darjeeling tea and Basmati rice in South Asia, Peru's Pisco, Nicaragua's Chontaleño cheese and Egyptian cotton, all of them enjoy viable domestic markets. A study of Vietnamese urban consumers in 2005 found that they could identify up to 265 local or regional specialty foods and typically associate higher quality with the place of production.[119] In another 2005 study, Costa Rica coffee consumers in both supermarkets and small shops ranked 'place-of-origin' first when determining their perception of the quality of a coffee.[120]

Yet, fostering culture is not the same as protecting, and it is important to distinguish between what Broude calls "cultural protection and cultural protectionism".[121] When GIs are pulled into the service of the latter, they are likely to generate increased resistance at the international level and diminish their legitimate effectiveness. Since GIs are market-based mechanisms and are widely traded they have a vital interface with trade regimes and have been perceived by some observers as exclusionary or protectionist. Broude finds little solid evidence that GIs protect culture and more evidence that they shield it from the possibly salutary effects of change. He notes that "...markets are so

| GIs are essentially a public or collective good. |

---

114 2006.
115 Ranaboldo and Fonte 2007; Belletti and Marescotti 2006; Belletti et al. 2005.
116 Ranaboldo and Schejtman 2008.
117 Barjolle and Chappuis 2001; Villalobos et al. 2007.
118 Sylvander and Allaire 2007.
119 See Tran as cited in van de Kop, Sautier and Gerz 2006.
120 See Galland 2005.
121 2005.

pervasive that GIs cannot in and of themselves, as legal agents, prevent market influence on local culture, leading to degrees of cultural transformation and international cultural homogenization."[122]

This contrasts with the conclusions of several other case studies that GIs encourage cultural expression on a smaller community scale, and that these thrive under protection and would likely find it much more difficult to survive the challenges of large-scale commercial trade without such a mechanism for differentiation and organization.[123]

In fact, cultural diversity is not always served by GIs when they are poorly structured or managed. Researchers, note that there can be deep-seated discord between the formal legal structure of a GI and the wide-ranging and less structured aspects of culture.[124] Nevertheless, the challenge remains of how to provide adequate voice and participation to the bearers of culture. These include marginalized communities and indigenous peoples who, in commercial relations, may face the misappropriation of their culture and resources.

Developmental characteristics: environment and ecology

GIs tend to value the land and its particular agro-ecological characteristics that impart unique organoleptic aspects that may be difficult to replicate in other regions or countries. The case for GIs promoting environmental value may be valid but is less certain. The scientific literature regarding the effects of GI systems on the environment is limited but the documented observations and case studies that do cover this aspect usually point to positive and mutually reinforcing relations between the two.[125] In South Africa, for example, fostering the sustainable cultivation and control of wild harvesting for the increasingly popular Rooibos and Honeybush teas is a central issue in the debate about adopting Geographical Indications for these regions.[126]

Environmental resources, biodiversity and traditional knowledge are all areas that tend to struggle for protection under international accords. GIs are among the favoured methods used by several governments for the purpose of protecting these values.[127] There also seems to be some trend toward integrating environmental concerns into the GI codes of practice in recent years as evidenced by Brazil's Pampas Beef and the efforts of China's Agriculture Ministry.[128]

There are assumptions that the intrinsic link to place would induce better levels of environmental stewardship and this may often be the case. However, some negative examples and contradictory cases have also emerged wherein the absence of controls and the urge for greater economic benefit can result in potentially negative environmental effects such as forest clearing to increase the planted area and the introduction of large-scale monocropping in place of diversified systems. In the Mezcal Case Study, the greater demand for natural raw materials required in the GI is contributing to reduced biodiversity as wild

When GIs are poorly structured or managed, they can have negative environmental effects.

---

122 See Broude 2005 p. 26. In the same tome, Broude offers an erudite rationale for the transience of culture that illustrates, via a tour of historic wine GIs, cases where wine origins have failed to maintain the original "recipes" for GIs or have invented new ones that bear little or no relation to unique characteristics of a region. However, the narrow sample and the host of reasons available for these changes limit a plausible claim for causality and thus make the argument less convincing to some.
123 Ranaboldo and Fonte 2007 and van de Kop, Sautier and Gerz 2006.
124 Ranaboldo and Schejtman 2008.
125 Ranaboldo and Fonte 2007; Riccheri et al. 2006; Boisvert 2005; Bérard et al. 2005.
126 Belletti and Marescotti 2006.
127 Acampora and Fonte 2007 p. 208–211.
128 Cerdan et al. 2007.

plants are over-harvested. This will likely lead to environmental degradation if fragile forests and semi-arid landscapes are further transformed into mono-crops of preferred varieties.

There is evidence that environment and ecology, which are recognized as integral components in the value proposition of many GI products, are typically respected and protected within some of the EU's GIs. According to Bérard and Marchenay, the French Government is stricter in its pursuit of compliance with environmental regulation in its GIs or Controlled Appellation of Origin (AOC) areas.[129] More specifically, non-GI farms near to the Comté PDO, for example, use 40–50% more herbicides and synthetic fertilizers per hectare than do similar PDO-registered farms (see figures 2.7 and 2.8).

Figure 2.7: Fertilizer utilization in Franche-Comté (per hectare)

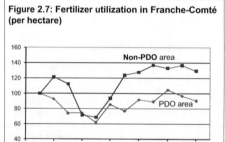

Source: Ministère de l'agriculture, de l'alimentation, de la pêche et des affaires rurales from DRAF Franche-Comté.
Base 100 in 1990.

Figure 2.8: Herbicide utilization in Franche-Comté (per hectare)

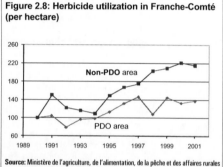

Source: Ministère de l'agriculture, de l'alimentation, de la pêche et des affaires rurales from DRAF Franche-Comté.
Base 100 in 1990.

---

129 Barham (2003) cites Laurence Bérard and Philippe Marchenay, two noted experts in the French AOC system.

[21]

ON THE DEADWEIGHT COST OF PRODUCTION
REQUIREMENTS FOR GEOGRAPHICALLY
DIFFERENTIATED AGRICULTURAL PRODUCTS

PIERRE R. MÉREL

This article investigates the welfare effects of alternate producer collusion schemes in a context where collusion is authorized in order to cover fixed costs. Using a linear equilibrium displacement model, we find evidence that, when the producer group is allowed to control quota levels, an input quota policy entails a smaller absolute deadweight loss than an output quota policy. This finding suggests that if producer groups are allowed to resort to production-distorting instruments to limit output, they will make production choices that are less costly for society than if they had been allowed to directly control output levels.

Key words: deadweight cost, fixed costs, geographical indications, input quota, production requirements, supply control, surplus transfer.

This article investigates the welfare effects of alternate collusion schemes in a context where collusion is authorized in order to cover fixed costs. We find analytical evidence that whenever producers as a group are allowed to control quota levels, an input quota policy entails a smaller absolute deadweight loss than an output quota policy. This means that in the presence of fixed costs, collusion schemes where producers collude on input use (e.g., land) may be socially preferable to arrangements where producers can directly control output. Such schemes are found in some European geographical indicator (GI) markets, where certification costs have been argued to be high (Marette, Crespi, and Schiavina 1999). This result contrasts with a conjecture by Lence et al. (2007), previously published in this *Journal*.

Recent literature on collective marketing schemes for agricultural products has identified instances where a benevolent planner may find it optimal to allow collusion among many producers in order to provide sufficient economic incentives to create new, high-valued differentiated products (Marette, Crespi, and Schiavina 1999; Marette and Crespi 2003;

Lence et al. 2007).[1] The surplus transfer is deemed necessary to compensate for nonconvexities in the production set arising from the presence of large fixed costs, typically certification costs that may be shared among producers (Marette, Crespi, and Schiavina 1999; Marette and Crespi 2003), or an investment cost incurred in the first stage of marketing the differentiated product (Lence et al. 2007).[2] Although such transfers entail efficiency losses, the benefits arising from consumption of higher-quality products may outweigh those losses and result in higher social welfare.[3]

That transfers may be desirable to provide break-even production incentives in the

___

[1] In essence, the argument parallels that underlying the restrictions in competition arising from intellectual property rights: competition is unwelcome if it annihilates economic incentives to innovate. The main difference is that, here, the argument is applied to a group of many producers sharing the initial cost, rather than to a single innovator.

[2] Giraud-Héraud, Mathurin, and Soler (2003) develop a model where the quality of the agricultural output is constrained by the quantity produced and show that, in some instances, a monopoly may set quantities in the best interest of consumers.

[3] Moschini, Menapace, and Pick (2008) examine schemes where producer groups restrict supply only to the extent necessary to exactly cover the fixed cost, by charging individual producers a well-chosen excise tax. Although such schemes are inherently more efficient than collusion in terms of social welfare, producer groups still have incentives to restrict supply beyond what is strictly necessary to cover fixed costs. Therefore, these schemes may entail large informational and enforcement costs on the part of public authorities. This is an implicit assumption in the studies of Marette, Crespi, and Schiavina (1999) and Lence et al. (2007), which focus exclusively on collusion schemes.

Pierre Mérel is assistant professor in the Department of Agricultural and Resource Economics, University of California, Davis, and a member of the Giannini Foundation of Agricultural Economics.

The author thanks Richard Sexton, Colin Carter, Daniel Sumner, Julian Alston, Walter Thurman, and an anonymous referee for helpful comments. All errors are of the author. Financial support from the French ministry of agriculture in the form of a graduate fellowship is acknowledged.

Amer. J. Agr. Econ. 91(3) (August 2009): 642–655
Copyright 2009 Agricultural and Applied Economics Association
DOI: 10.1111/j.1467-8276.2009.01272.x

presence of nonconvexities is a well-known fact in public economics. Without necessarily invoking economic justifications for such transfers, the traditional agricultural economics literature has investigated the relative efficiency of various redistribution schemes, such as government-managed subsidies and quotas (see, for instance, Wallace 1962; Floyd 1965; Gardner 1983; Gardner 1987; Gisser 1993; Bullock and Salhofer 2003). Although inspired by the same fundamental question (how to transfer economic surplus to producers efficiently), the emerging literature on collective marketing arrangements for agricultural products is novel in that it disregards traditional transfer schemes to investigate the relative efficiency of *self-administered* policies for the production sector. More specifically, policy makers are now assumed to design antitrust policies that allow for different types of collusions between producers, typically quotas on output or on an input (in particular, land), and producer groups are responsible for choosing the quota level and allocating rights among individual producers.

In a sense, this newer literature has set a bridge between traditional agricultural policy and the market power literature by considering policy instruments where producers, as a group, are allowed to influence the extent of the distortion from the competitive equilibrium. The policy question that arises is therefore more complex and can be framed within the following optimization program:

$$(1) \qquad \min_{\mathscr{P}} DWL(\mathscr{P}(\lambda^*)) \text{ subject to}$$

$$\begin{cases} \lambda^* = \arg\max_{\lambda} T(\mathscr{P}(\lambda)) \\ T(\mathscr{P}(\lambda^*)) \geq \tau \end{cases}$$

where *DWL* denotes the social cost or deadweight loss, $\mathscr{P}$ represents the policy choice (typically, the *type* of collusion that should be exempt from antitrust scrutiny, say, a quota on land), λ represents the *level* or *intensity* of collusion among producers (e.g., the number of acres in the quota), *T* represents the realized transfer to producers, and τ is a policy objective (the minimum transfer required to achieve the desired incentive). This program can be contrasted to the traditional farm policy paradigm, where the policy maker would choose both the *type* ($\mathscr{P}$) and the *intensity* (λ) of the policy to achieve any given level of transfer τ

$$(2) \qquad \min_{\mathscr{P}, \lambda} DWL(\mathscr{P}(\lambda))$$

$$\text{subject to} \quad T(\mathscr{P}(\lambda)) = \tau.$$

The recent interest in analyzing transfer policies within the framework implied by program (1) likely comes from the observation of collective marketing arrangements for so-called "geographically differentiated agricultural products" (GDAPs), also known as protected designations of origin (PDOs) or protected geographical indications (PGIs), mainly present in Europe, as well as marketing arrangements within certain U.S. marketing orders or producer cooperatives that amount to controlling supply, directly or indirectly (Carman and Alston 2005).[4] The literature has analyzed such marketing schemes from both a positive and a normative standpoint, trying to justify observed policies that may appear inefficient or providing arguments in favor of implementing them more systematically.

The Economic and Policy Significance of Lence et al.'s Conjecture

One of the most important pieces of literature in the field to date is the article by Lence et al. (2007). The authors use a general model of aggregate supply to compare the profit incentives of alternate collusion schemes in the context of geographically differentiated agricultural products and argue that allowing producers to collude on output, to restrict acreage, or to adopt cost-enhancing production requirements may have positive social welfare effects, whenever those schemes, through a rise in output price, enable producers to cover the fixed cost of developing the differentiated product.

An incidental claim in Lence et al.'s (2007) article (referred to as L's conjecture) is that, conditional on the GDAP having been developed, stronger forms of collusions (like collusion on output) may be preferable to weaker forms of collusions (like the implementation of cost-enhancing production requirements), even from a social welfare standpoint, the reason being that "legislation aimed at curtailing the market power of producer organizations may induce large technological distortions" (Lence et al. 2007, p. 962). The idea behind L's conjecture is that by preventing producer

---

[4] In the EU, PDOs and PGIs differ in that a PDO requires that each stage of production, processing, and preparation of the product be carried out in the eligible region, whereas the PGI only requires that one of those stages be carried out in the eligible region.

644 August 2009

Amer. J. Agr. Econ.

organizations from colluding on output, stringent antitrust rules only leave those organizations with indirect tools to control output, leading to inefficient production. The authors then suggest that because GDAP legislation in the United States provides producer organizations with fewer instruments to control supply than in the European Union (EU), the incentive to distort production practices to limit supply is probably larger in the United States, leading to larger overall deadweight losses. Taken literally, this conclusion could mean that unless antitrust regulations effectively prevent producer organizations from distorting production practices to restrict output, society would be better off by allowing producer organizations to directly control output levels.

Although Lence et al.'s (2007) observation that indirect ways to control output, such as input restrictions, entail additional technology-driven deadweight costs is correct, they do not explicitly recognize that this very inefficiency also affects the ability of producers to distort output price, therefore leading to a smaller consumer loss than that under output collusion. How these two opposing effects affect the overall deadweight cost comparison has not been resolved in the literature to date.

The present article investigates this question in a partial equilibrium context. Our findings cast serious doubt on the validity of L's conjecture by showing that, if producers are only allowed to resort to a production-distorting instrument to limit output (specifically, an input quota), they will, in fact, make production choices that are less costly for society as a whole than if they had been allowed to directly control the output level. Therefore, whenever both policies generate sufficient rents to cover fixed costs, an input quota is socially more desirable than an output quota.[5] The result is derived using an equilibrium displacement model and by assuming locally linear demand and input supply schedules. It is robust to whether the quasi-rent to suppliers of the unrestricted input is included in the profit maximization problem facing the colluding industry.[6]

The policy implications of our findings are potentially important. The input quota scenario that is the focus of our theoretical analysis is not limited to acreage restrictions. Rather, it covers many types of cost-enhancing production requirements such as capacity constraints or input tax schemes with redistribution of tax revenues, all of which can be recast in terms of a quota on some well-defined input. We would argue that these types of production requirements are the norm, rather than the exception, in many GDAP markets. Indeed, the adoption of production constraints by producer groups is essential to the recognition of GIs in the EU, because the stated rationale behind the PDO/PGI protection is that the registered products differ significantly from their generic counterparts due to specific geographical factors and specific production methods (Council of the European Union 2006). Therefore, unless antitrust policy effectively prevents them from doing so, there is little doubt that, in defining production standards, producer groups will try to maximize joint profits.

One recent illustrative example of the strategic adoption of cost-enhancing production requirements can be found in the French Comté cheese market. Comté is France's top-selling PDO hard cheese. In May 2007, the French government adopted a new regulation (proposed by the Comté consortium) that limits the number of basins to be used in cheese factories, the capacity of those basins, and the frequency of their use (République Française 2007).[7]

If L's conjecture were to be confirmed, antitrust authorities should start paying more attention to the definition of such production rules, because they may lead to deadweight losses that exceed even those of monopolies. In addition, European policy makers would have reasons to respond favorably to the current demands by several European PDO producer groups to implement output control more systematically (Conseil National des Appellations d'Origine Laitières 2008).[8] By doing so, they would suppress the existing incentive to distort production technologies and would,

---

[5] This result contrasts with the traditional belief that an input quota, because it leads to inefficient production, is a less efficient policy than an output quota (see, for instance, Wallace 1962). This last result is true whenever one holds the surplus transfer constant. Here, what is held constant is the ability of the production sector to choose the quota level to optimize producer profits, and therefore the surplus transfer will be different under the two policies. We require, however, that the transfer associated with either policy be large enough to cover fixed costs.

[6] A similar result was derived using constant-elasticity demand and supply schedules and a Cobb–Douglas technology. The proof is available upon request to the author.

[7] The adoption of these rules stirred controversy within the Comté industry. One firm challenged the decree before the French supreme administrative court on the basis of antitrust violations and later withdrew its complaint. With respect to land constraints, in 1998, the Comté regulations were amended to restrict the geographical area where the specialty cheese may be produced.

[8] In particular, the French and Italian associations of dairy PDOs have recently addressed a motion to the EU Commissioner for Agriculture and Rural Development, asking her to adapt competition rules to the specificity of PDOs.

by L's conjecture, reduce the associated social costs.

In contrast, our analysis suggests that artificial production requirements aimed at curtailing output are likely to be less detrimental to social welfare than pure collusion on output. Consequently, as long as they generate sufficient rents to cover fixed costs, such collective arrangements should be preferred to direct output control. Our finding has a broader industrial organization implication: somewhat reassuringly, there is no reason to suspect large deadweight losses to arise from the strategic adoption of production standards by an otherwise competitive industry.

The Model

Consider an industry composed of numerous firms that use two inputs (X_1 and X_2) to produce a single output (Q). There are markets for both inputs, and unless stated otherwise, we view the industry as also including suppliers of these inputs. In agricultural applications, the inputs could be land (X_1) and other inputs (X_2), and therefore the "industry" would include (a) suppliers of land, (b) suppliers of other inputs, and (c) farmers using these inputs to produce a commodity.[9] Although we allow both inputs to be supplied to producers of the output in a less than perfectly elastic fashion, we assume that the technology that uses these inputs displays constant returns to scale at the industry level. This does not prevent the industry's derived supply schedule from being less than perfectly elastic, because the supply of X_1 and/or X_2 may be upward sloping.

Following Lence et al. (2007), assume that production of the output entails a fixed cost (corresponding to quantity τ in program (1)) to be shared among producers. One could think of the fixed cost as the shared investment needed to first market the product, for instance, the set-up cost associated with registering a new product under the EU PDO regulation. We assume that aggregate profits under perfect competition are lower than the shared investment cost, preventing the industry from engaging in production. (Alternatively, under perfect competition, the industry may choose

to produce a generic version of the output, instead of a high-quality product.)

Consumers value the product to the extent that production is, despite the prohibitive fixed cost, socially desirable. To solve this production inefficiency, the government may decide to relax antitrust law to allow producers to set either an output quota or a quota on input X_1. The question we wish to answer is as follows: assuming that collusion on output and collusion on input both generate sufficient rents to cover the fixed costs, which of the two schemes entails the smaller social cost?[10]

Because different industry agents may be supplying the two inputs and the output, redistribution issues arise when comparing the effects of restricting the output or one of the inputs. For instance, producers of the output typically collect quota rents associated with a production quota, whereas suppliers of the restricted input would normally collect the rents associated with an input quota. For the purpose of this study, we will ignore distribution issues within the industry and assume that surplus can be redistributed costlessly among industry agents so that the input and the output quota policies can be compared solely on the basis of their economic efficiency.[11]

Given the type of quota (input or output quota), we model the final equilibrium as the outcome of a two-stage game. In the first stage, an industry board sets the quota level and allocates rights efficiently among producers to maximize aggregate profits. Equivalent to allocating a quota, the industry board could levy a tax on the restricted good and redistribute the proceeds among industry agents. As long as the quota rights are distributed efficiently among agents (or to the extent that they are tradable), the two approaches will lead to the same outcome. For instance, implementing a transferable output quota is equivalent to taxing output to the extent that agents produce exactly the same quota quantity. The corresponding tax level is then equal to the unit value of the quota right. The same can be said of an input quota. Therefore, to model the implementation of a transferable quota, we will simply assume that the industry board taxes the output or the input and then redistributes the tax proceeds to industry agents in a lump-sum fashion. Setting the tax level in the best interest of the industry will then be exactly equivalent

---

[9] This model of vertically integrated industry is quite common in agricultural PDOs, where many inputs are industry-specific. For instance, the Comté consortium (Comité Interprofessionnel du Gruyère de Comté) represents both dairy cooperatives (owned by Comté milk producers) and cheese ripeners.

[10] This question directly relates to Lence et al.'s (2007) comparison of collusion schemes *once the GDAP has been developed.*

[11] This a common assumption in the related literature.

646   *August 2009*   *Amer. J. Agr. Econ.*

to choosing the optimal quota level. In the second stage, industry agents behave competitively, taking prices and the tax as given. The tax level is set optimally in the first stage, anticipating the market outcome of the second stage.

To solve the two-stage model and identify the preferable tax scheme, we proceed as follows. In the next section, we use an equilibrium displacement model to derive the effects of a given output tax and a given input tax on producer and consumer welfare (stage 2 equilibrium). Producer welfare is defined as the sum of the quasi-rents to suppliers of both inputs and the tax revenue. (Because producers of the final output operate under constant returns to scale, their profit is zero in equilibrium). We then solve the optimization program of the industry board for both an output tax and an input tax (stage 1) and compute the associated deadweight costs. We find that the deadweight cost of the input tax, when tax levels are set to maximize producer surplus, is always smaller than that of the output tax. The result also holds when the quasi-rent to suppliers of the unrestricted input (X_2) is not accounted for in the producer surplus maximization program, provided that the cost share of the restricted input in production is not close to 1.

Welfare Effects of Output and Input Taxes (Stage 2)

An equilibrium displacement model is used to derive the welfare effects of an output or an input tax. Using such a model amounts to assuming that changes in equilibrium prices and quantities resulting from the output or input taxes can be inferred using a first-order approximation. We then compute welfare measures assuming that the demand and supply schedules are locally linear.

The model parameters are the demand elasticity ($-\eta$), the marginal cost elasticities of both inputs (ε_1 and ε_2), the elasticity of substitution between inputs (σ), the cost shares of both inputs (s_1 and s_2), and the initial value of output. All the preceding variables are evaluated at the undistorted competitive equilibrium, that is, in the absence of any output or input tax. The consumer price of the output is denoted as P^c, and the industry price as P^i. Similarly, the price of the restricted input (X_1) obtained by suppliers of this input is denoted as W_1^s, whereas the price paid by users of this input is denoted as W_1^i. The price of input X_2 is the same for suppliers and the downstream

industry and is simply denoted as W_2. In the initial state, there are no taxes, and equilibrium prices and quantities are denoted with the superscript "0". Therefore, $P^{c,0} = P^{i,0} = P^0$ and $W_1^{i,0} = W_1^{s,0} = W_1^0$. In the final state, indexed by the superscript "1", per-unit taxes are introduced. By convention, these per-unit taxes are expressed as a percentage of initial prices. Hence, an output tax rate α corresponds to a per-unit tax of αP^0, that is, $P^{c,1} - P^{i,1} = \alpha P^0$. Similarly, an input tax rate β_1 corresponds to a per-unit tax of $\beta_1 W_1^0$, that is, $W_1^{i,1} - W_1^{s,1} = \beta_1 W_1^0$. The equilibrium displacement model predicts the approximate changes in prices and quantities when either tax is introduced.

The model can be written as follows:

$$(3.1) \quad E(Q) = -\eta E(P^c)$$

$$(3.2) \quad E(Q) = s_1 E(X_1) + s_2 E(X_2)$$

$$(3.3) \quad E(W_1^i) = E(P^i) - \frac{s_2}{\sigma} E(X_1) + \frac{s_2}{\sigma} E(X_2)$$

$$(3.4) \quad E(W_2^i) = E(P^i) + \frac{s_1}{\sigma} E(X_1) - \frac{s_1}{\sigma} E(X_2)$$

$$(3.5) \quad E(X_1) = \varepsilon_1 E(W_1^s)$$

$$(3.6) \quad E(X_2) = \varepsilon_2 E(W_2)$$

$$(3.7) \quad E(P^i) = E(P^c) - \alpha$$

$$(3.8) \quad E(W_1^i) = E(W_1^s) + \beta_1$$

where $E(.)$ represents the percent change in an equilibrium variable $\frac{\Delta(.)}{(.)}$.[12] Relation (3.1) reflects the fact that changes in consumer price and quantity in the output market occur along the consumer demand schedule. Relations (3.2)–(3.4) represent profit-maximizing conditions at the industry level and are derived formally in the Appendix. Relations (3.5) and (3.6) relate to the supply schedules for each input. The last two relations link supply and demand prices to the relevant tax rates.

Using relations (3.7) and (3.8) to get rid of the variables P^c and W_1^s, the model can be reduced

———

[12] With this definition of $E(.)$, the predictions of the equilibrium displacement model are exact for linear demand and supply schedules (Alston and Wohlgenant 1990; Zhao, Mullen, and Griffith 1997). By continuity, they will be close for schedules that are close enough to being linear in the region of interest.

(4)

$$\begin{cases} E(Q) = -\eta[E(P^i) + \alpha] \\ E(Q) = s_1 E(X_1) + s_2 E(X_2) \\ E(W_1^i) = E(P^i) - \dfrac{s_2}{\sigma}E(X_1) + \dfrac{s_2}{\sigma}E(X_2) \\ E(W_2) = E(P^i) + \dfrac{s_1}{\sigma}E(X_1) - \dfrac{s_1}{\sigma}E(X_2) \\ E(X_1) = \varepsilon_1[E(W_1^i) - \beta_1] \\ E(X_2) = \varepsilon_2 E(W_2). \end{cases}$$

Model (4) can then be solved to yield the following relative changes in equilibrium variables as functions of the tax rates α and β_1

(5)

$$\begin{cases} E(Q) = -[\eta(\varepsilon_1\varepsilon_2 + \sigma(s_1\varepsilon_1 + s_2\varepsilon_2))\alpha \\ \qquad + s_1\varepsilon_1\eta(\sigma + \varepsilon_2)\beta_1]/D \\ E(P^i) = -[\eta(\sigma + s_2\varepsilon_1 + s_1\varepsilon_2)\alpha \\ \qquad - s_1\varepsilon_1(\sigma + \varepsilon_2)\beta_1]/D \\ E(X_1) = -[\eta\varepsilon_1(\sigma + \varepsilon_2)\alpha \\ \qquad + (\eta\sigma + (s_2\sigma + s_1\eta)\varepsilon_2)\varepsilon_1\beta_1]/D \\ E(X_2) = -[\eta\varepsilon_2(\sigma + \varepsilon_1)\alpha \\ \qquad - s_1(\sigma - \eta)\varepsilon_1\varepsilon_2\beta_1]/D \\ E(W_1^i) = -[\eta(\sigma + \varepsilon_2)\alpha \\ \qquad - (s_1\sigma + s_2\eta + \varepsilon_2)\varepsilon_1\beta_1]/D \\ E(W_2) = -[\eta(\sigma + \varepsilon_1)\alpha - s_1(\sigma - \eta)\varepsilon_1\beta_1]/D \end{cases}$$

where $D = \sigma(\eta + s_1\varepsilon_1 + s_2\varepsilon_2) + \eta(s_2\varepsilon_1 + s_1\varepsilon_2) + \varepsilon_1\varepsilon_2$.

Given (5), we can derive the welfare effects of an output tax and an input tax. In order to calculate changes in economic surplus measures, we assume that the demand and supply schedules are locally linear.

Welfare Effects of an Output Tax

The price and quantity effects of the output tax α in the output market are depicted in figure 1. The effects of this tax in the market for input X_1 are depicted in figure 2, and the effects on the market for input X_2 are similar. It is easy to see from these figures that the output tax will result in the following welfare changes:

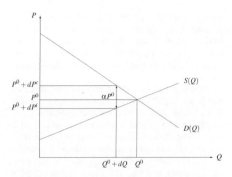

Note: $D(Q)$ denotes the inverse demand curve for the output, and $S(Q)$ the industry's inverse derived supply schedule.

Figure 1. Price and quantity effects of a per-unit output tax in the output market

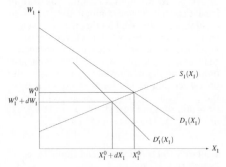

Note: $S_1(X_1)$ denotes the inverse supply curve of input 1, and $D_1(X_1)$ the industry's inverse derived demand schedule for input 1. $D_1'(X_1)$ denotes the industry's inverse derived demand schedule once the output tax has been implemented.

Figure 2. Price and quantity effects of an output tax in the market for input 1

(6)

$$\begin{cases} TR = \alpha P^0(Q^0 + dQ) \\ \qquad = P^0 Q^0 \alpha(1 + E(Q)) \\ \Delta CS = -(\alpha P^0 + dP^i)\left(Q^0 + \dfrac{1}{2}dQ\right) \\ \qquad = -P^0 Q^0(E(P^i) + \alpha)\left(1 + \dfrac{1}{2}E(Q)\right) \\ \Delta PS_1 = dW_1\left(X_1^0 + \dfrac{1}{2}dX_1\right) \\ \qquad = P^0 Q^0 s_1 E(W_1)\left(1 + \dfrac{1}{2}E(X_1)\right) \\ \Delta PS_2 = dW_2\left(X_2^0 + \dfrac{1}{2}dX_2\right) \\ \qquad = P^0 Q^0 s_2 E(W_2)\left(1 + \dfrac{1}{2}E(X_2)\right) \end{cases}$$

Amer. J. Agr. Econ.

where TR denotes the tax revenue, ΔCS denotes the change in consumer surplus, and ΔPS_1 and ΔPS_2 represent the change in the quasi-rent to suppliers of input X_1 and input X_2, respectively. Note that the superscript on W_1 has been omitted because in the absence of a tax on input X_1, the prices W_1^i and W_1^s are the same. Given the relative price changes in equation (5), these welfare changes can be expressed as

(7)

$$
\begin{cases}
TR = P^0 Q^0 \alpha \\
\quad \times \left[1 - \dfrac{\eta(\varepsilon_1 \varepsilon_2 + \sigma(s_1 \varepsilon_1 + s_2 \varepsilon_2))\alpha}{D} \right] \\[2ex]
\Delta CS = -P^0 Q^0 \\
\quad \times \left[\alpha - \dfrac{\eta(\sigma + s_2 \varepsilon_1 + s_1 \varepsilon_2)\alpha}{D} \right] \\[2ex]
\quad \times \left[1 - \dfrac{\eta(\varepsilon_1 \varepsilon_2 + \sigma(s_1 \varepsilon_1 + s_2 \varepsilon_2))\alpha}{2D} \right] \\[2ex]
\Delta PS_1 = -P^0 Q^0 s_1 \\
\quad \times \left[\dfrac{\eta(\sigma + \varepsilon_2)\alpha}{D} \right] \\[2ex]
\quad \times \left[1 - \dfrac{\eta \varepsilon_1 (\sigma + \varepsilon_2)\alpha}{2D} \right] \\[2ex]
\Delta PS_2 = -P^0 Q^0 s_2 \\
\quad \times \left[\dfrac{\eta(\sigma + \varepsilon_1)\alpha}{D} \right] \\[2ex]
\quad \times \left[1 - \dfrac{\eta \varepsilon_2 (\sigma + \varepsilon_1)\alpha}{2D} \right].
\end{cases}
$$

The resulting deadweight loss for the economy is

(8)

$$
DWL^\alpha = -P^0 Q^0 \frac{\eta}{2D^2} \big[(\varepsilon_1 \varepsilon_2 + \sigma(s_1 \varepsilon_1 + s_2 \varepsilon_2))
$$
$$
\times ((s_1 \sigma + s_2 \eta + \varepsilon_2)\varepsilon_1
$$
$$
+ (s_1 \eta + s_2 \sigma)\varepsilon_2) + \eta\sigma\{\varepsilon_1 \varepsilon_2 (s_1^2 + s_2^2)
$$
$$
+ \sigma(s_1 \varepsilon_1 + s_2 \varepsilon_2)
$$
$$
+ s_1 s_2 (\varepsilon_1^2 + \varepsilon_2^2)\} \big] \alpha^2.
$$

Note that, as expected, DWL^α is always negative. It is proportional to α^2, which implies that the marginal deadweight loss from an incremental tax on output, in the absence of a pre-existing tax, is nil.

Welfare Effects of an Input Tax

Following the same approach as in the previous section, one can show that a tax on input X_1 will result in the following welfare changes:

(9)

$$
\begin{cases}
TR = \beta_1 W_1^0 (X_1^0 + dX_1) \\
\quad = P^0 Q^0 s_1 \beta_1 (1 + E(X_1)) \\[2ex]
\Delta CS = -dP \left(Q^0 + \dfrac{1}{2} dQ \right) \\[1.5ex]
\quad = -P^0 Q^0 E(P) \left(1 + \dfrac{1}{2} E(Q) \right) \\[2ex]
\Delta PS_1 = -\left(-dW_1^i + \beta_1 W_1^0 \right) \left(X_1^0 + \dfrac{1}{2} dX_1 \right) \\[1.5ex]
\quad = P^0 Q^0 s_1 \left(E(W_1^i) - \beta_1 \right) \left(1 + \dfrac{1}{2} E(X_1) \right) \\[2ex]
\Delta PS_2 = dW_2 \left(X_2^0 + \dfrac{1}{2} dX_2 \right) \\[1.5ex]
\quad = P^0 Q^0 s_2 E(W_2) \left(1 + \dfrac{1}{2} E(X_2) \right)
\end{cases}
$$

which can be expressed as

(10)

$$
\begin{cases}
TR = P^0 Q^0 s_1 \beta_1 \\
\quad \times \left[1 - \dfrac{(\eta\sigma + (s_2 \sigma + s_1 \eta)\varepsilon_2)\varepsilon_1 \beta_1}{D} \right] \\[2ex]
\Delta CS = -P^0 Q^0 \\
\quad \times \left[\dfrac{s_1 \varepsilon_1 (\sigma + \varepsilon_2)\beta_1}{D} \right] \\[2ex]
\quad \times \left[1 - \dfrac{s_1 \varepsilon_1 \eta (\sigma + \varepsilon_2)\beta_1}{2D} \right] \\[2ex]
\Delta PS_1 = P^0 Q^0 s_1 \\
\quad \times \left[\dfrac{(s_1 \sigma + s_2 \eta + \varepsilon_2)\varepsilon_1 \beta_1}{D} - \beta_1 \right] \\[2ex]
\quad \times \left[1 - \dfrac{(\eta\sigma + (s_2 \sigma + s_1 \eta)\varepsilon_2)\varepsilon_1 \beta_1}{2D} \right] \\[2ex]
\Delta PS_2 = P^0 Q^0 s_2 \\
\quad \times \left[\dfrac{s_1 (\sigma - \eta)\varepsilon_1 \beta_1}{D} \right] \\[2ex]
\quad \times \left[1 + \dfrac{s_1 (\sigma - \eta)\varepsilon_1 \varepsilon_2 \beta_1}{2D} \right].
\end{cases}
$$

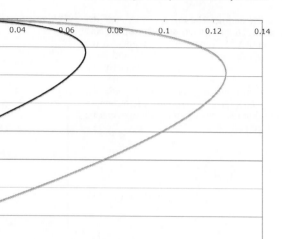

$QR+\Delta PS_1+\Delta PS_2$

···· output quota ── input quota

Note: The transfer is defined as the sum of the quota rent (QR) and the change in the quasi-rent to suppliers of inputs X_1 and X_2. The baseline parameter values are $\eta = 1, \varepsilon_1 = \varepsilon_2 = 0.5, \sigma = 0.5$, and $s_1 = 0.5$.

Figure 3. Deadweight losses of output and input quota policies as functions of the transfer to the production sector

The corresponding deadweight loss is

(11)

$$DWL^{\beta_1} = -P^0 Q^0 \frac{s_1 \varepsilon_1}{2D^2} [\sigma(\eta + s_2\varepsilon_2)D$$

$$+ \varepsilon_1\{(\eta\sigma + (s_1\eta + s_2\sigma)\varepsilon_2)(s_2\eta + \varepsilon_2)\}$$

$$+ s_1\eta\varepsilon_2(\sigma(\eta + s_2\varepsilon_2) + s_1\eta\varepsilon_2)]\beta_1^2.$$

Note that, as expected, DWL^{β_1} is always negative. It is proportional to β_1^2, which implies that the marginal deadweight loss from an incremental tax on input X_1, in the absence of any pre-existing tax, is nil.

Figure 3 represents the deadweight losses of output and input quota policies as functions of the transfer to the production sector. This is equivalent to deriving the surplus transformation curve of those policies (Gardner 1983). The transfer is defined as the sum of the quota rent and the change in the quasi-rents to suppliers of inputs X_1 and X_2. The fact that the curve for the input quota lies inside that for the output quota implies that for any *given* transfer of surplus to producers, the social cost of the

transfer will be larger for an input quota.[13] Although the two curves were derived for a given set of parameter values, changing these values does not modify the overall shape of the curves or their relative position. Making the elasticity of substitution smaller would bring the two curves closer to one another, although even for small values of σ, the two curves can be made further apart by decreasing s_1. Similarly, for any value of σ, the two curves can be made closer by increasing s_1. Note that, because the input quota is less efficient, there exists a set of transfers that are achievable through an output quota but not through an input quota. For the case shown in figure 3, surplus transfers ranging from 7% to 12.5% of the value of output are only attainable through an output quota.

Optimal Output and Input Taxes (Stage 1)

In this section, we derive optimal output and input taxes from the point of view of the industry, assuming that the revenue from taxation

---

[13] A similar comparison is made in Gardner (1987).

650   *August 2009*   *Amer. J. Agr. Econ.*

is redistributed to producers in a lump-sum fashion, and then compare the corresponding deadweight loss measures. (As argued above, this is the same as assuming that optimal output and input quotas are implemented.) The analysis is conducted under two scenarios. First, the tax level is chosen so as to maximize the sum of the tax revenue plus the quasi-rents to suppliers of both inputs. Then, it is chosen so as to maximize the tax revenue plus the quasi-rent to suppliers of input X_1.

Scenario 1: Suppliers of Inputs X_1 and X_2 Are Equally Represented in the Industry

Under this scenario, the quasi-rents to suppliers of inputs X_1 and X_2 are included in the industry's profit maximization program. This is the case, in particular, if one entity supplies both inputs and produces the output. A farming industry where farmers own farmland (input X_1) and supply family labor (input X_2) would satisfy this assumption (assuming that other inputs are supplied in a perfectly elastic fashion). The industry incorporates all suppliers of industry-specific inputs (the prices of which depend on the amount demanded by the industry) into a single entity that can achieve costless redistribution among its constituents, a model that would rather well describe several European PDO markets. (For a description of the integration and redistribution features of the Comté cheese industry, for instance, see Mérel 2007.) Note that, if we let $\varepsilon_1 \to \infty$, the

tax on input X_1 can be reinterpreted as a *purchasing* quota, with the quota rents accruing to holders of purchasing rights, and the purchase price of the restricted input being unaffected by the policy. This model could, for instance, capture restrictions on the use of particular farm inputs such as concentrated feed or silage in some European specialty cheese markets. The prices of these inputs, which are typically used by producers of generic milk as well, are unlikely to depend on the demand by a single PDO group.[14]

The optimal output tax α^* chosen by the industry under scenario 1 solves $\max_\alpha TR + \Delta PS_1 + \Delta PS_2$, where TR, ΔPS_1, and ΔPS_2 are given in (7). After multiplying the objective function by the term $\frac{D^2}{P^0 Q^0}$, the first-order condition can be obtained as

$$(12) \quad 0 = [-2\eta(\varepsilon_1 \varepsilon_2 + \sigma(s_1 \varepsilon_1 + s_2 \varepsilon_2))D$$
$$+ s_1 \varepsilon_1 \eta^2 (\sigma + \varepsilon_2)^2 + s_2 \varepsilon_2 \eta^2 (\sigma + \varepsilon_1)^2]\alpha$$
$$- (-D + s_1 \eta(\sigma + \varepsilon_2) + s_2 \eta(\sigma + \varepsilon_1))D$$

which after rearrangements yields

$$(13) \quad \alpha^* = \frac{(\sigma(s_1 \varepsilon_1 + s_2 \varepsilon_2) + \varepsilon_1 \varepsilon_2)D}{2\eta(\varepsilon_1 \varepsilon_2 + \sigma(s_1 \varepsilon_1 + s_2 \varepsilon_2))D - s_1 \varepsilon_1 \eta^2 (\sigma + \varepsilon_2)^2 - s_2 \varepsilon_2 \eta^2 (\sigma + \varepsilon_1)^2}.$$

Similarly, the optimal input tax β_1^* solves $\max_{\beta_1} TR + \Delta PS_1 + \Delta PS_2$, where TR, ΔPS_1, and ΔPS_2 are given in (10). After normalizing the objective by $\frac{D^2}{P^0 Q^0}$, the first-order condition reads

$$(14) \quad 0 = [-2(\eta\sigma + (s_2\sigma + s_1\eta)\varepsilon_2)\varepsilon_1 D$$
$$+ (D - (s_1\sigma + s_2\eta + \varepsilon_2)\varepsilon_1)$$
$$\times (\eta\sigma + (s_2\sigma + s_1\eta)\varepsilon_2)\varepsilon_1$$
$$+ s_1 s_2 (\sigma - \eta)^2 \varepsilon_1^2 \varepsilon_2]\beta_1 + D^2 - D^2$$
$$+ (s_1\sigma + s_2\eta + \varepsilon_2)\varepsilon_1 D + s_2(\sigma - \eta)\varepsilon_1 D.$$

Defining $D' = s_1\sigma + s_2\eta + \varepsilon_2$, we obtain

$$(15) \quad \beta_1^* = \frac{(\sigma + \varepsilon_2)D}{(\eta\sigma + (s_2\sigma + s_1\eta)\varepsilon_2)(D + D'\varepsilon_1) - s_1 s_2(\sigma - \eta)^2 \varepsilon_1 \varepsilon_2}.$$

To compare the deadweight losses resulting from optimization of the tax level by the industry for the two policies under consideration, expressions (13) and (15) are plugged into expressions (8) and (11), respectively. It is shown in the Appendix that the deadweight loss resulting from the optimal output quota is always larger than that resulting from the optimal input quota. For tractability purposes, we here specialize the proof to the case where $\varepsilon_1 \to \infty$ and $\varepsilon_2 \to \infty$, that is, when the gain to producers is only composed of the tax revenue. The expressions for the deadweight losses of each policy then simplify to

---

[14] Also see footnote 16.

(16)

$$\begin{cases} DWL^{\alpha}(\alpha^*) = -P^0 Q^0 \dfrac{1}{8\eta} \\[2ex] DWL^{\beta_1}(\beta_1^*) = -P^0 Q^0 \dfrac{s_1}{8} \dfrac{s_1\eta + 2s_2\sigma}{(s_1\eta + s_2\sigma)^2}. \end{cases}$$

We can write

(17)

$$\left| DWL^{\beta_1}(\beta_1^*) \right| \leq \left| DWL^{\alpha}(\alpha^*) \right|$$

$$\Leftrightarrow s_1\eta(s_1\eta + 2s_2\sigma) \leq (s_1\eta + s_2\sigma)^2.$$

It is straightforward to see that this last condition always holds. As a result, the deadweight loss of an input quota policy where producers choose the quota level is smaller than that of an output quota policy where producers choose the quota level. The result is illustrated in figure 3, where the deadweight loss corresponding to the maximum transfer to producers is always smaller (in absolute value) for the input quota than for the output quota.

Interestingly, the absolute deadweight loss $\left| DWL^{\beta_1}(\beta_1^*) \right|$ is not necessarily a monotonic function of the elasticity of substitution between inputs, at least not when $\varepsilon_2 < \infty$. More specifically, it can be shown that when $\varepsilon_2 \to \infty$, $\left| DWL^{\beta_1}(\beta_1^*) \right|$ is strictly decreasing in σ over the range $\sigma \geq 0$. But this is no longer true if we allow the supply of X_2 to be less than perfectly elastic.

Scenario 2: Only Suppliers of Input X_1 Are Represented in the Industry

Under this scenario, the profits of suppliers of input X_2 are no longer part of the industry's optimization program. This is the case, for instance, if landowners (suppliers of land and input X_1) and farm managers (owners of the output quotas) are equally represented in the industry but suppliers of hired labor (input X_2) are not. In this situation, the group composed of landowners and farm managers collects the quota rents, and farm workers are hurt by an output quota and either benefit or lose from an input quota, depending on the relative magnitudes of σ and η.[15] Because the optimization program no longer includes the quasi-rents ΔPS_2, total profits $TR + \Delta PS_1 + \Delta PS_2$ will not be maximized,

and therefore, both the industry and suppliers of input X_2 could theoretically be better off by maximizing joint profits. However, this would require costless redistribution of profits among these particular agents. Therefore, scenario 2 captures situations where institutional barriers may prohibit or hamper such a redistribution.[16]

The optimal output tax $\hat{\alpha}$ for the industry solves $\max_{\alpha} TR + \Delta PS_1$, where TR and ΔPS_1 are given in (7). After normalizing the objective by $\frac{D^2}{P^0 Q^0}$, the first-order condition reads

(18) $0 = [-2\eta(\varepsilon_1\varepsilon_2 + \sigma(s_1\varepsilon_1 + s_2\varepsilon_2))D$
$\qquad + s_1\varepsilon_1\eta^2(\sigma + \varepsilon_2)^2]\alpha$
$\qquad - (-D + s_1\eta(\sigma + \varepsilon_2))D$

which yields the optimal output tax

(19)

$\hat{\alpha} =$
$$\frac{(\sigma(s_1\varepsilon_1 + s_2\varepsilon_2) + s_2\eta(\sigma + \varepsilon_1) + \varepsilon_1\varepsilon_2)D}{2\eta(\varepsilon_1\varepsilon_2 + \sigma(s_1\varepsilon_1 + s_2\varepsilon_2))D - s_1\varepsilon_1\eta^2(\sigma + \varepsilon_2)^2}.$$

Similarly, the optimal input tax $\hat{\beta}_1$ solves $\max_{\beta_1} TR + \Delta PS_1$, where TR and ΔPS_1 are given in (10). The first-order condition reads

(20) $0 = [-2(\eta\sigma + (s_2\sigma + s_1\eta)\varepsilon_2)\varepsilon_1 D$
$\qquad + (D - (s_1\sigma + s_2\eta + \varepsilon_2)\varepsilon_1)$
$\qquad \times (\eta\sigma + (s_2\sigma + s_1\eta)\varepsilon_2)\varepsilon_1]\beta_1 + D^2$
$\qquad - D^2 + (s_1\sigma + s_2\eta + \varepsilon_2)\varepsilon_1 D.$

Rearranging the terms, we obtain

(21) $\hat{\beta}_1 = \dfrac{DD'}{(\eta\sigma + (s_2\sigma + s_1\eta)\varepsilon_2)(D + D'\varepsilon_1)}.$

To calculate the deadweight losses generated by the two alternative policies under the

---

[15] More precisely, farm workers benefit from an input quota if and only if $\sigma > \eta$, that is, inputs are gross substitutes.

[16] If we assume that suppliers of the restricted input X_1 are not represented in the industry, but suppliers of input X_2 are, and maximize $TR + \Delta PS_2$, then for $\varepsilon_1 < \infty$, the deadweight loss comparison is necessarily ambiguous. This is because when $\varepsilon_1 < \infty$, the industry may benefit not only from a higher output price but also from a lower price for input X_1 so that an input quota on X_1 may become more efficient in transferring a *given* amount of surplus to the industry than an output quota and allow larger transfers, just as an output quota is more efficient in transferring a *given* amount of surplus than an input quota when only the output price is allowed to vary. In this case, however, we are no longer comparing the two policies on the basis of their ability to transfer surplus from consumers to producers at the lowest social cost, because now producers win at the expense of two types of agents: consumers and suppliers of X_1. If we are to exclude suppliers of X_1 from the colluding industry, we therefore need to assume that $\varepsilon_1 \to \infty$.

652   *August 2009*   *Amer. J. Agr. Econ.*

assumptions of scenario 2, the optimal tax levels $\hat{\alpha}$ and $\hat{\beta}_1$ are plugged into expressions (8) and (11), respectively. It can be shown that the deadweight loss generated by the input quota policy is *almost always* smaller than that generated by the output quota policy. More precisely, it is possible to show that for values of the cost share s_1 that are smaller than 0.969, the ranking of the two deadweight loss measures is the same as in scenario 1, for all values of the parameters η, σ, ε_1, and ε_2.[17] The fact that the caveat $s_1 \leq 0.969$ needs to be considered in scenario 2 arises from the price externality in the market for input X_2. When the supply elasticity ε_2 is less than infinite, the equilibrium price W_2 changes upon implementation of the output or input taxes. Because the quasi-rent of suppliers of X_2 is no longer included in the industry surplus, this constitutes a price externality for the industry and changes its incentives in a way that may reverse the deadweight loss comparison for very large values of s_1. However, in most practical applications where s_1 is not close to 1, the ranking is the same as in scenario 1.[18]

Conclusion

In this article, we have investigated the welfare effects of two policies aimed at transferring surplus to producers, with a view to covering fixed costs that would preclude production under competitive conditions. Following the literature on collusion in GI markets, we have focused our attention on antitrust exemptions that allow producers, as a group, to collude either on output or on input use to generate rents at the expense of consumers. Even though, for a *given* transfer to producers, an input quota is less efficient than an output quota, the literature has not yet identified which policy becomes preferable when producers set the quota level in their best interest, anticipating its effect on equilibrium prices in related markets. Lence et al. (2007) have conjectured that due to technological distortions, collusion on inputs may lead to a higher total deadweight loss. Our analysis casts doubt on this conjecture. Provided that both policies

generate sufficient rents to cover fixed costs (and although the surplus transfer is necessarily larger for an output quota), we have found evidence that an input quota, the level of which is set to maximize producer surplus, is socially preferable to a producer-optimal output quota. The result was derived with the use of an equilibrium displacement model in which welfare measures were calculated by assuming that the demand and supply schedules are locally linear. A similar result, not reported in this article, was found to hold in the case of constant-elasticity demand and supply schedules and a Cobb–Douglas technology (i.e., with an elasticity of substitution equal to 1). Our finding is also robust to whether the quasi-rent to suppliers of the unrestricted input is included in the industry's profit maximization program.

The policy implications of the result are potentially large, notably in Europe, where, anticipating the likely elimination of the EU dairy quota policy, several dairy PDO consortia have recently asked member state and EU officials to extend existing antitrust exemptions to safeguard the profitability of their activity (Conseil National des Appellations d'Origine Laitières 2008). The result also has implications for countries such as the United States, where the development of GDAPs seems to have taken hold, calling for the development of standards and the possible adaptation of antitrust rules. Our finding also has a fundamental implication beyond the GDAP policy: somewhat reassuringly, there is no reason to suspect large deadweight losses to arise from the strategic adoption of production standards by an otherwise competitive industry.

*[Received February 2008;
accepted January 2009.]*

References

Alston, J.M., and M.K. Wohlgenant. 1990. "Measuring Research Benefits Using Linear Elasticity Equilibrium Displacement Models." In J.D. Mullen and J.M. Alston, eds. *The Returns to the Australian Wool Industry from Investment in R&D (Appendix 2)*. Rural and Resource Economics Report No. 10. Sydney, Australia: New South Wales Agriculture and Fisheries.

Bullock, D.S., and K. Salhofer. 2003. "Judging Agricultural Policies: A Survey." *Agricultural Economics* 28:225–43.

Carman, H.F., and J.M. Alston. 2005. "California's Mandated Commodity Programs." In H.M. Kaiser, J.M. Alston, J.M. Crespi, and R.J. Sexton, eds. *The Economics of Commodity*

---

[17] The derivation follows the same approach as that presented for scenario 1 in the appendix. However, some of the resulting polynomials in s_1 have ambiguous signs around the value $s_1 \approx 0.969$, hence, the need to add the caveat.

[18] Note also that, even when the caveat is not satisfied, the deadweight loss ranking *may* still be the same as in scenario 1. For instance, we can show analytically that as long as $\sigma < \eta$, that is, the inputs are gross complements at the undistorted equilibrium, the result of scenario 1 unambiguously extends to scenario 2.

Promotion Programs, Lessons from California. New York: Peter Lang Publishing, pp. 13–37.

Conseil National des Appellations d'Origine Laitières. 2008. *La Lettre, Industry Information Bulletin,* January 2008, Paris: Conseil National des Appellations d'Origine Laitières.

Council of the European Union. 2006. "Council Regulation (EC) No 510/2006 of 20 March 2006 on the Protection of Geographical Indications and Designations of Origin for Agricultural Products and Foodstuffs." *Official Journal of the European Union* L 93:12–25.

Floyd, J.E. 1965. "The Effects of Farm Price Supports on the Returns to Land and Labor in Agriculture." *The Journal of Political Economy* 73:148–58.

Gardner, B. 1983. "Efficient Redistribution Through Commodity Markets." *American Journal of Agricultural Economics* 65:225–34.

Gardner, B.L., ed. 1987. *The Economics of Agricultural Policies.* New York: Macmillan Publishing Company.

Giraud-Héraud, E., J. Mathurin, and L.G. Soler. 2003. "Quelle Légitimité à des Mécanismes de Régulation de l'Offre dans les Appellations d'Origine Protégée?" *Économie Rurale* 277–78:123–34.

Gisser, M. 1993. "Price Support, Acreage Controls, and Efficient Redistribution." *The Journal of Political Economy* 101:584–611.

Lence, S.H., S. Marette, D.J. Hayes, and W. Foster. 2007. "Collective Marketing Arrangements for Geographically Differentiated Agricultural Products: Welfare Impacts and Policy Implications." *American Journal of Agricultural Economics* 89:947–63.

Marette, S., and J.M. Crespi. 2003. "Can Quality Certification Lead to Stable Cartels?" *Review of Industrial Organization* 23:43–64.

Marette, S., J.M. Crespi, and A. Schiavina. 1999. "The Role of Common Labelling in a Context of Asymmetric Information." *European Review of Agricultural Economics* 26:167–78.

Mérel, P. 2007. "Three Essays on Supply Control Policies in Protected Designations of Origin." PhD dissertation, University of California, Davis.

Moschini, G., L. Menapace, and D. Pick. 2008. "Geographical Indications and the Competitive Provision of Quality in Agricultural Markets." *American Journal of Agricultural Economics* 90:794–812.

République Française. 2007. "Décret du 11 Mai 2007 Relatif à l'Appellation d'Origine Contrôlée 'Comté'." *Journal Officiel de la République Française,* 12 May 2007.

Wallace, T.D. 1962. "Measures of Social Costs of Agricultural Programs." *Journal of Farm Economics* 44:580–94.

Zhao, X., J.D. Mullen, and G.R. Griffith. 1997. "Functional Forms, Exogenous Shifts, and Economic Surplus Changes." *American Journal of Agricultural Economics* 79:1243–51.

Appendix

Derivation of Relations (3.2), (3.3), and (3.4)

Suppose that the industry-level production function, $f(X_1, X_2)$, displays constant returns to scale in the vicinity of equilibria considered. In industry equilibrium, we have the following optimality conditions:

$$(A.1) \quad Q = f(X_1, X_2)$$

$$(A.2) \quad W_1^i = P^i f_1(X_1, X_2)$$

$$(A.3) \quad W_2 = P^i f_2(X_1, X_2)$$

where f_j denotes the derivative of f with respect to the jth argument.

Total differentiation of the first equation yields $dQ = f_1 dX_1 + f_2 dX_2$, which after dividing by Q^0 and rearranging with the use of (A.2) and (A.3) yields

$$E(Q) = \frac{W_1^0 X_1^0}{P^0 Q^0} E(X_1) + \frac{W_2^0 X_2^0}{P^0 Q^0} E(X_2).$$

Using the definition of cost shares $s_j = \frac{W_j^0 X_j^0}{P^0 Q^0}$, equation (3.2) is obtained.

Total differentiation of equation (A.2) yields $dW_1^i = f_1 dP^i + P^{i,0}[f_{11} dX_1 + f_{12} dX_2]$. Dividing by $W_1^{i,0}$, and using (A.2) and (A.3), we obtain

$$E\left(W_1^i\right) = E(P^i) + \frac{P^{i,0}}{W_1^{i,0}}[f_{11} dX_1 + f_{12} dX_2].$$

Because f is homogenous of degree 1, we have that $f_{11} = -\frac{X_2^0}{X_1^0} f_{12}$, and therefore, we have

$$E\left(W_1^i\right) = E(P^i) + \frac{P^{i,0}}{W_1^{i,0}} f_{12} \left[-\frac{X_2^0}{X_1^0} dX_1 + dX_2\right]$$

$$= E(P^i) + X_2^0 \frac{f_{12}}{f_1}[-E(X_1) + E(X_2)]$$

$$= E(P^i) + \frac{f_2 X_2^0}{Q^0} \frac{f_{12} Q^0}{f_1 f_2}[-E(X_1) + E(X_2)]$$

$$= E(P^i) + \frac{W_2^0 X_2^0}{P^0 Q^0} \frac{f_{12} Q^0}{f_1 f_2}[-E(X_1) + E(X_2)]$$

$$= E(P^i) + \frac{s_2}{\sigma}[-E(X_1) + E(X_2)]$$

where the last equality makes use of the fact that $\sigma = \frac{f_1 f_2}{f_{12} Q^0}$. This proves relation (3.3). Relation (3.4) can be obtained similarly.

Deadweight Loss Comparison in Scenario 1

The deadweight loss measures $|DWL^\alpha(\alpha^*)|$ and $|DWL^{\beta_1}(\beta_1^*)|$ are compared using standard techniques. We first construct the difference $|DWL^\alpha(\alpha^*)| - |DWL^{\beta_1}(\beta_1^*)|$ and multiply by the product of the denominators, which are positive. We then replace the variable s_2 by $1 - s_1$ and factorize the resulting expression using the "Factor" command in Mathematica 6. We obtain:

$$|DWL^\alpha(\alpha^*)| - |DWL^{\beta_1}(\beta_1^*)|$$

$$\propto \eta\sigma\varepsilon_2(s_1 - 1)\mathscr{P}_1(s_1)\mathscr{P}_2(s_1)\mathscr{P}_3(s_1)$$

where $\mathscr{P}_1(s_1) = \eta\sigma + \eta\varepsilon_1 + \sigma\varepsilon_2 + \varepsilon_1\varepsilon_2 + (-\eta\varepsilon_1 + \sigma\varepsilon_1 + \eta\varepsilon_2 - \sigma\varepsilon_2)s_1$

$$\mathscr{P}_2(s_1) = \eta\sigma^2\varepsilon_2 + 3\eta\sigma\varepsilon_1\varepsilon_2 + 2\eta\varepsilon_1^2\varepsilon_2 + \sigma^2\varepsilon_2^2$$
$$+ 3\sigma\varepsilon_1\varepsilon_2^2 + 2\varepsilon_1^2\varepsilon_2^2$$
$$+ (\eta\sigma^2\varepsilon_1 + 3\eta\sigma\varepsilon_1^2 - \eta\sigma^2\varepsilon_2 - 4\eta\sigma\varepsilon_1\varepsilon_2$$
$$+ 2\sigma^2\varepsilon_1\varepsilon_2 + 3\sigma\varepsilon_1^2\varepsilon_2 + \eta\sigma\varepsilon_2^2$$
$$- 2\sigma^2\varepsilon_2^2 - 3\sigma\varepsilon_1\varepsilon_2^2)s_1$$
$$+ (-\eta\sigma\varepsilon_1^2 + \sigma^2\varepsilon_1^2 + 2\eta\sigma\varepsilon_1\varepsilon_2 - 2\sigma^2\varepsilon_1\varepsilon_2$$
$$- \eta\sigma\varepsilon_2^2 + \sigma^2\varepsilon_2^2)\,s_1^2$$

and

$$\mathscr{P}_3(s_1) = -\eta^3\sigma^4\varepsilon_2 - 4\eta^3\sigma^3\varepsilon_1\varepsilon_2 - 5\eta^3\sigma^2\varepsilon_1^2\varepsilon_2$$
$$- 2\eta^3\sigma\varepsilon_1^3\varepsilon_2 - 3\eta^3\sigma^4\varepsilon_2^2 - 12\eta^2\sigma^3\varepsilon_1\varepsilon_2^2$$
$$- 15\eta^2\sigma^2\varepsilon_1^2\varepsilon_2^2 - 6\eta^2\sigma\varepsilon_1^3\varepsilon_2^2 - 3\eta\sigma^4\varepsilon_2^3$$
$$- 12\eta\sigma^3\varepsilon_1\varepsilon_2^3 - 15\eta\sigma^2\varepsilon_1^2\varepsilon_2^3 - 6\eta\sigma\varepsilon_1^3\varepsilon_2^3$$
$$- \sigma^4\varepsilon_2^4 - 4\sigma^3\varepsilon_1\varepsilon_2^4 - 5\sigma^2\varepsilon_1^2\varepsilon_2^4 - 2\sigma\varepsilon_1^3\varepsilon_2^4$$
$$+ (-\eta^3\sigma^4\varepsilon_1 - 4\eta^3\sigma^3\varepsilon_1^2 - 4\eta^3\sigma^2\varepsilon_1^3 + \eta^3\sigma^4\varepsilon_2$$
$$+ 8\eta^3\sigma^3\varepsilon_1\varepsilon_2 - 5\eta^3\sigma^4\varepsilon_1\varepsilon_2 + 13\eta^3\sigma^2\varepsilon_1^2\varepsilon_2$$
$$- 16\eta^2\sigma^3\varepsilon_1^2\varepsilon_2 + 4\eta^3\sigma\varepsilon_1^3\varepsilon_2 - 13\eta^2\sigma^2\varepsilon_1^3\varepsilon_2$$
$$- 4\eta^3\sigma^3\varepsilon_2^2 + 6\eta^3\sigma^4\varepsilon_2^2 - 10\eta^3\sigma^2\varepsilon_1\varepsilon_2^2$$
$$+ 28\eta^2\sigma^3\varepsilon_1\varepsilon_2^2 - 6\eta\sigma^4\varepsilon_1\varepsilon_2^2 - 6\eta^3\sigma\varepsilon_1^2\varepsilon_2^2$$
$$+ 36\eta^2\sigma^2\varepsilon_1^2\varepsilon_2^2 - 18\eta\sigma^3\varepsilon_1^2\varepsilon_2^2 - \eta^3\varepsilon_1^3\varepsilon_2^2$$
$$+ 10\eta^2\sigma\varepsilon_1^3\varepsilon_2^2 - 13\eta\sigma^2\varepsilon_1^3\varepsilon_2^2 - 8\eta^2\sigma^3\varepsilon_2^3$$
$$+ 9\eta\sigma^4\varepsilon_2^3 - 20\eta^2\sigma^2\varepsilon_1\varepsilon_2^3 + 34\eta\sigma^3\varepsilon_1\varepsilon_2^3$$
$$- 3\sigma^4\varepsilon_1\varepsilon_2^3 - 12\eta^2\sigma\varepsilon_1^2\varepsilon_2^3 + 37\eta\sigma^2\varepsilon_1^2\varepsilon_2^3$$
$$- 8\sigma^3\varepsilon_1^2\varepsilon_2^3 - 2\eta^2\varepsilon_1^3\varepsilon_2^3 + 10\eta\sigma\varepsilon_1^3\varepsilon_2^3$$
$$- 5\sigma^2\varepsilon_1^3\varepsilon_2^3 - 4\eta\sigma^3\varepsilon_2^4 + 4\sigma^4\varepsilon_2^4$$
$$- 9\eta\sigma^2\varepsilon_1\varepsilon_2^4 + 12\sigma^3\varepsilon_1\varepsilon_2^4 - 4\eta\sigma\varepsilon_1^2\varepsilon_2^4$$
$$+ 10\sigma^2\varepsilon_1^2\varepsilon_2^4 + 2\sigma\varepsilon_1^3\varepsilon_2^4)\,s_1$$
$$+ (4\eta^3\sigma^3\varepsilon_1^2 - 2\eta^3\sigma^4\varepsilon_1^2 + 8\eta^3\sigma^2\varepsilon_1^3$$
$$- 4\eta^3\sigma^3\varepsilon_1^3 - 8\eta^3\sigma^3\varepsilon_1\varepsilon_2 + 5\eta^3\sigma^4\varepsilon_1\varepsilon_2$$
$$- 21\eta^3\sigma^2\varepsilon_1^2\varepsilon_2 + 24\eta^2\sigma^3\varepsilon_1^2\varepsilon_2 - 3\eta\sigma^4\varepsilon_1^2\varepsilon_2$$
$$- 4\eta^3\sigma\varepsilon_1^3\varepsilon_2 + 21\eta^2\sigma^2\varepsilon_1^3\varepsilon_2 - 6\eta\sigma^3\varepsilon_1^3\varepsilon_2$$
$$+ 4\eta^3\sigma^3\varepsilon_2^2 - 3\eta^2\sigma^4\varepsilon_2^2 + 18\eta^3\sigma^2\varepsilon_1\varepsilon_2^2$$
$$- 36\eta^2\sigma^3\varepsilon_1\varepsilon_2^2 + 12\eta\sigma^4\varepsilon_1\varepsilon_2^2 + 10\eta^3\sigma\varepsilon_1^2\varepsilon_2^2$$
$$- 54\eta^2\sigma^2\varepsilon_1^2\varepsilon_2^2 + 38\eta\sigma^3\varepsilon_1^2\varepsilon_2^2 - 3\sigma^4\varepsilon_1^2\varepsilon_2^2$$

$$+ 2\eta^3\varepsilon_1^3\varepsilon_2^2 - 10\eta^2\sigma\varepsilon_1^3\varepsilon_2^2 + 22\eta\sigma^2\varepsilon_1^3\varepsilon_2^2$$
$$- 4\sigma^3\varepsilon_1^3\varepsilon_2^2 - 5\eta^3\sigma^2\varepsilon_2^3 + 16\eta^2\sigma^3\varepsilon_2^3$$
$$- 9\eta\sigma^4\varepsilon_2^3 - 6\eta^3\sigma\varepsilon_1\varepsilon_2^3 + 38\eta^2\sigma^2\varepsilon_1\varepsilon_2^3$$
$$- 44\eta\sigma^3\varepsilon_1\varepsilon_2^3 + 9\sigma^4\varepsilon_1\varepsilon_2^3 - 2\eta^3\varepsilon_1^2\varepsilon_2^3$$
$$+ 16\eta^2\sigma\varepsilon_1^2\varepsilon_2^3 - 40\eta\sigma^2\varepsilon_1^2\varepsilon_2^3 + 16\sigma^3\varepsilon_1^2\varepsilon_2^3$$
$$+ 2\eta^2\varepsilon_1^3\varepsilon_2^3 - 4\eta\sigma\varepsilon_1^3\varepsilon_2^3 + 5\sigma^2\varepsilon_1^3\varepsilon_2^3$$
$$- 5\eta^2\sigma^2\varepsilon_2^4 + 12\eta\sigma^3\varepsilon_2^4 - 6\sigma^4\varepsilon_2^4$$
$$- 6\eta^2\sigma\varepsilon_1\varepsilon_2^4 + 18\eta\sigma^2\varepsilon_1\varepsilon_2^4 - 12\sigma^3\varepsilon_1\varepsilon_2^4$$
$$- 2\eta^2\varepsilon_1^2\varepsilon_2^4 + 4\eta\sigma\varepsilon_1^2\varepsilon_2^4 - 5\sigma^2\varepsilon_1^2\varepsilon_2^4)s_1^2$$
$$+ (-4\eta^3\sigma^2\varepsilon_1^3 + 4\eta^3\sigma^3\varepsilon_1^3 + 13\eta^3\sigma^2\varepsilon_1^2\varepsilon_2$$
$$- 16\eta^2\sigma^3\varepsilon_1^2\varepsilon_2 + 3\eta\sigma^4\varepsilon_1^2\varepsilon_2 + 4\eta^3\sigma\varepsilon_1^3\varepsilon_2$$
$$- 13\eta^2\sigma^2\varepsilon_1^3\varepsilon_2 + 10\eta\sigma^3\varepsilon_1^3\varepsilon_2 - \sigma^4\varepsilon_1^3\varepsilon_2$$
$$- 14\eta^3\sigma^2\varepsilon_1\varepsilon_2^2 + 20\eta^2\sigma^3\varepsilon_1\varepsilon_2^2 - 6\eta\sigma^4\varepsilon_1\varepsilon_2^2$$
$$- 10\eta^3\sigma\varepsilon_1^2\varepsilon_2^2 + 36\eta^2\sigma^2\varepsilon_1^2\varepsilon_2^2$$
$$- 32\eta\sigma^3\varepsilon_1^2\varepsilon_2^2 + 6\sigma^4\varepsilon_1^2\varepsilon_2^2 - \eta^3\varepsilon_1^3\varepsilon_2^2$$
$$+ 6\eta^2\sigma\varepsilon_1^3\varepsilon_2^2 - 9\eta\sigma^2\varepsilon_1^3\varepsilon_2^2 + 4\sigma^3\varepsilon_1^3\varepsilon_2^2$$
$$+ 5\eta^3\sigma^2\varepsilon_2^3 - 8\eta^2\sigma^3\varepsilon_2^3 + 3\eta\sigma^4\varepsilon_2^3$$
$$+ 8\eta^3\sigma\varepsilon_1\varepsilon_2^3 - 33\eta^2\sigma^2\varepsilon_1\varepsilon_2^3 + 34\eta\sigma^3\varepsilon_1\varepsilon_2^3$$
$$- 9\sigma^4\varepsilon_1\varepsilon_2^3 + 2\eta^3\varepsilon_1^2\varepsilon_2^3 - 12\eta^2\sigma\varepsilon_1^2\varepsilon_2^3$$
$$+ 18\eta\sigma^2\varepsilon_1^2\varepsilon_2^3 - 8\sigma^3\varepsilon_1^2\varepsilon_2^3 - 2\eta^2\sigma\varepsilon_2^4$$
$$+ 10\eta^2\sigma^2\varepsilon_2^4 - 12\eta\sigma^3\varepsilon_2^4 + 4\sigma^4\varepsilon_2^4$$
$$- \eta^3\varepsilon_1\varepsilon_2^4 + 6\eta^2\sigma\varepsilon_1\varepsilon_2^4 - 9\eta\sigma^2\varepsilon_1\varepsilon_2^4$$
$$+ 4\sigma^3\varepsilon_1\varepsilon_2^4)\,s_1^3$$
$$+ (-2\eta^3\sigma\varepsilon_1^3\varepsilon_2 + 5\eta^3\sigma^2\varepsilon_1^3\varepsilon_2 - 4\eta\sigma^3\varepsilon_1^3\varepsilon_2$$
$$+ \sigma^4\varepsilon_1^3\varepsilon_2 + 6\eta^3\sigma\varepsilon_1^2\varepsilon_2^2 - 15\eta^2\sigma^2\varepsilon_1^2\varepsilon_2^2$$
$$+ 12\eta\sigma^3\varepsilon_1^2\varepsilon_2^2 - 3\sigma^4\varepsilon_1^2\varepsilon_2^2 - 6\eta^3\sigma\varepsilon_1\varepsilon_2^3$$
$$+ 15\eta^2\sigma^2\varepsilon_1\varepsilon_2^3 - 12\eta\sigma^3\varepsilon_1\varepsilon_2^3 + 3\sigma^4\varepsilon_1\varepsilon_2^3$$
$$+ 2\eta^3\sigma\varepsilon_2^4 - 5\eta^2\sigma^2\varepsilon_2^4 + 4\eta\sigma^3\varepsilon_2^4$$
$$- \sigma^4\varepsilon_2^4)\,s_1^4.$$

It is straightforward to see that $\mathscr{P}_1(s_1) \geq 0$ for all $s_1 \in [0, 1]$. Let us show that $\mathscr{P}_2$ is also nonnegative on $[0, 1]$.

Rewrite $\mathscr{P}_2$ by rearranging like terms as follows:

Coeff.	s_1^0	s_1^1	s_1^2
$\eta\sigma^2\varepsilon_2$	1	-1	
$\eta\sigma\varepsilon_1\varepsilon_2$	3	-4	$+2$
$\eta\varepsilon_1^2\varepsilon_2$	2		
$\sigma^2\varepsilon_2^2$	1	-2	$+1$
$\sigma\varepsilon_1\varepsilon_2^2$	3	-3	
$\varepsilon_1^2\varepsilon_2^2$	2		
$\eta\sigma^2\varepsilon_1$		1	
$\eta\sigma\varepsilon_1^2$		3	-1
$\sigma^2\varepsilon_1\varepsilon_2$		2	-2
$\sigma\varepsilon_1^2\varepsilon_2$		3	
$\eta\sigma\varepsilon_2^2$		1	-1
$\sigma^2\varepsilon_1^2$			1

One can easily check that each of the polynomials above is nonnegative for $s_1 \in [0, 1]$.

Similarly, rewrite $\mathscr{P}_3$ by rearranging like terms as follows:

Coeff.	s_1^0	s_1^1	s_1^2	s_1^3	s_1^4
$\eta^3\sigma^4\varepsilon_2$	−1	+1			
$\eta^3\sigma^3\varepsilon_1\varepsilon_2$	−4	+8	−8		
$\eta^3\sigma^2\varepsilon_1^2\varepsilon_2$	−5	+13	−21	+13	
$\eta^3\sigma\varepsilon_1^3\varepsilon_2$	−2	+4	−4	+4	−2
$\eta^2\sigma^4\varepsilon_2^2$	−3	+6	−3		
$\eta^2\sigma^3\varepsilon_1\varepsilon_2^2$	−12	+28	−36	+20	
$\eta^2\sigma^2\varepsilon_1^2\varepsilon_2^2$	−15	+36	−54	+36	−15
$\eta^2\sigma\varepsilon_1^3\varepsilon_2^2$	−6	+10	−10	+6	
$\eta\sigma^4\varepsilon_2^3$	−3	+9	−9	+3	
$\eta\sigma^3\varepsilon_1\varepsilon_2^3$	−12	+34	−44	+34	−12
$\eta\sigma^2\varepsilon_1^2\varepsilon_2^3$	−15	+37	−40	+18	
$\eta\sigma\varepsilon_1^3\varepsilon_2^3$	−6	+10	−4		
$\sigma^4\varepsilon_2^4$	−1	+4	−6	+4	−1
$\sigma^3\varepsilon_1\varepsilon_2^4$	−4	+12	−12	+4	
$\sigma^2\varepsilon_1^2\varepsilon_2^4$	−5	+10	−5		
$\sigma\varepsilon_1^3\varepsilon_2^4$	−2	+2			
$\eta^3\sigma^4\varepsilon_1$		−1			
$\eta^3\sigma^3\varepsilon_1^2$		−4	+4		
$\eta^3\sigma^2\varepsilon_1^3$		−4	+8	−4	
$\eta^2\sigma^4\varepsilon_1\varepsilon_2$		−5	+5		
$\eta^2\sigma^3\varepsilon_1^2\varepsilon_2$		−16	+24	−16	
$\eta^2\sigma^2\varepsilon_1^3\varepsilon_2$		−13	+21	−13	+5
$\eta^3\sigma^3\varepsilon_2^2$		−4	+4		
$\eta^3\sigma^2\varepsilon_1\varepsilon_2^2$		−10	+18	−14	
$\eta\sigma^4\varepsilon_1\varepsilon_2^2$		−6	+12	−6	
$\eta^3\sigma\varepsilon_1^2\varepsilon_2^2$		−6	+10	−10	+6
$\eta\sigma^3\varepsilon_1^2\varepsilon_2^2$		−18	+38	−32	+12

Coeff.	s_1^0	s_1^1	s_1^2	s_1^3	s_1^4
$\eta^3\varepsilon_1^3\varepsilon_2^2$		−1	+2	−1	
$\eta\sigma^2\varepsilon_1^3\varepsilon_2^2$		−13	+22	−9	
$\eta^2\sigma^3\varepsilon_2^3$		−8	+16	−8	
$\eta^2\sigma^2\varepsilon_1\varepsilon_2^3$		−20	+38	−33	+15
$\sigma^4\varepsilon_1\varepsilon_2^3$		−3	+9	−9	+3
$\eta^2\sigma\varepsilon_1^2\varepsilon_2^3$		−12	+16	−12	
$\sigma^3\varepsilon_1^2\varepsilon_2^3$		−8	+16	−8	
$\eta^2\varepsilon_1^3\varepsilon_2^3$		−2	+2		
$\sigma^2\varepsilon_1^3\varepsilon_2^3$		−5	+5		
$\eta\sigma^3\varepsilon_2^4$		−4	+12	−12	+4
$\eta\sigma^2\varepsilon_1\varepsilon_2^4$		−9	+18	−9	
$\eta\sigma\varepsilon_1^2\varepsilon_2^4$		−4	+4		
$\eta^2\sigma^4\varepsilon_1^2$			−2		
$\eta^2\sigma^3\varepsilon_1^3$			−4	+4	
$\eta\sigma^4\varepsilon_1^2\varepsilon_2$			−3	+3	
$\eta\sigma^3\varepsilon_1^3\varepsilon_2$			−6	+10	−4
$\sigma^4\varepsilon_1^2\varepsilon_2^2$			−3	+6	−3
$\sigma^3\varepsilon_1^3\varepsilon_2^2$			−4	+4	
$\eta^3\sigma^2\varepsilon_2^3$			−5	+5	
$\eta^3\sigma\varepsilon_1\varepsilon_2^3$			−6	+8	−6
$\eta^3\varepsilon_1^2\varepsilon_2^3$			−2	+2	
$\eta^2\sigma^2\varepsilon_2^4$			−5	+10	−5
$\eta^2\sigma\varepsilon_1\varepsilon_2^4$			−6	+6	
$\eta^2\varepsilon_1^2\varepsilon_2^4$			−2		
$\sigma^4\varepsilon_1^3\varepsilon_2$				−1	+1
$\eta^3\sigma\varepsilon_2^4$				−2	+2
$\eta^3\varepsilon_1\varepsilon_2^4$				−1	.

Each of the above polynomials in s_1 is nonpositive for $s_1 \in [0, 1]$, and therefore $\mathscr{P}_3$ is also nonpositive on this interval.

Therefore, for $s_1 \in [0, 1]$, the quantity $|DWL^\alpha(\alpha^*)| - |DWL^{\beta_1}(\beta_1^*)|$ is nonnegative.   Q.E.D.

[22]

Journal of International Food & Agribusiness Marketing, 22:277–298, 2010
Copyright © Taylor & Francis Group, LLC
ISSN: 0897-4438 print/1528-6983 online
DOI: 10.1080/08974431003641612

R Routledge
Taylor & Francis Group

Geographical Indications of Origin as a Tool of Product Differentiation: The Case of Coffee

RAMONA TEUBER

Justus-Liebig University of Giessen, Giessen, Germany

An increasing interest in geographical indications of origin (GIs) as a tool of product differentiation can be observed in the so-called specialty coffee sector. Similar to the approach for wine in France and Italy, more and more coffee-producing countries try to establish appellation systems for coffee. Whereas some countries and regions such as Colombia or Jamaica have already legally protected GIs for coffee, most coffee GIs are still informal, meaning that no legal protection has been obtained so far. But the recent acceptation of the term Café de Colombia as a Protected Geographical Indication in the European Union and the Ethiopian Trademark Initiative document the increasing engagement of coffee-producing countries to achieve an appropriate legal protection for their GIs. From an economic point of view, data from U.S. online retail stores indicate that single-origin coffees receive significant higher retail prices, with 100% Kona coffee from Hawaii and Jamaican Blue Mountain coffee being the most expensive ones. Furthermore, results from a hedonic pricing model based on Internet auction data for single-origin coffees show that the country and the region of origin is already an important price determinant in the specialty coffee market.

KEYWORDS   coffee, geographical indications of origin, hedonic pricing analysis, legal regulatory systems, price premium

Received June 2007; revised October 2007; accepted March 2008.

The author thanks Dr. R. Herrmann and two anonymous referees for their constructive and very helpful comments.

Address correspondence to Ramona Teuber, Institute for Agricultural Policy and Market Research, Justus-Liebig University of Giessen, Senckenbergstr 3, Giessen 35390, Germany. E-mail: Ramona.teuber@agrar.uni-giessen.de

277

Coffee is now where wine was ten years ago.[1]

INTRODUCTION

For quite a long time the coffee market was considered a market with nearly no product differentiation at all. This picture has been changing because product and process quality are becoming more important to consumers. Especially the product origin as a proxy for product and process quality is gaining in importance in consumers' purchase decisions. As a reaction to this rising consumer demand for diversification, an increasing product differentiation based on geographical origin can also be observed in the coffee market, particularly in the so-called specialty coffee market (Kaplinski & Fitter, 2004; Lewin, Giovannucci, & Varangis, 2004).

Specialty coffees are not precisely defined but cover a wide range of somehow differentiated coffees, such as organic, fair trade, and bird-friendly coffee. Besides these kinds of coffee another type of specialty coffee called single-origin coffee or coffee with a geographical indication of origin (GI) has emerged in recent years (Daviron & Ponte, 2005; Lewin et al., 2004). Although the bulk of coffee is sold to consumers as a blend, meaning that coffees from different, mostly unidentified origins are mixed, single-origin coffees are, as the name indicates, coffees coming from only one origin. Because the term *single-origin* is not precisely defined, single-origin coffees can originate in one country, one region, or one estate or farm (Knox & Sheldon Huffaker, 1996).

Product differentiation based on geographical origin is not a new development. It has got a rather long history, especially in southern European countries. "Parmigiano Reggiano" is a well-known example of a Protected Designations of Origin (PDO) under Council Regulation (EC) No. 510/2006 with having ancient origins in the 13th century.[2] But what is new in recent years is the growing number of products labeled with GIs at the European as well as at the international level. Since the EC No. 2081/92 came into force in 1993, the number of applications per year has steadily increased. Today more than 700 products are registered either as PDO or as Protected Geographical Indication (PGI).

Moreover, geographical indications are a current topic at the international level. The Agreement on Trade-Related Aspects of Intellectual Property Rights (TRIPs), which became effective in 1995, is considered the first multilateral agreement giving an explicit definition of the term *geographical indication*. According to the TRIPs definition, geographical indications are "indications which identify a good as originating in the territory of a Member, or a region or locality in that territory, where a given quality, reputation or other characteristics of the good is essentially attributable to its geographical origin" (TRIPs, Article 22.1). Furthermore, TRIPs requires from every signatory to establish minimum standards for the protection of GIs through national law. Developed countries had to implement the TRIPs requirements by 1996, developing and transition countries by 2000, and for the least developed countries the final date for the implementation was extended to the year 2006 (Calboli, 2006, p. 183; Liebig, 2000, p. 9).

All these recent developments document the rising interest in GIs. Whereas in the past GIs have mainly been a product differentiation tool in European markets and for European producers, recently more and more developing countries have discovered this marketing instrument for their products. Some studies dealing with European GIs exist, whereas studies addressing GIs in developing countries are rare. Thus, the objective of this article is to provide insight into recent developments in the world coffee market with a particular focus on GIs. This is done from two points of view. First, the legal framework of GIs in the coffee market is explored in order to find answers to the following research questions:

- Which GIs for coffee do already exist?
- How are these GIs protected and by which legal means?
- In which markets are these GIs protected?

Second, GIs for coffee are examined from an economic point of view. Questions arising in this context are as follows:

- Which price premiums can be achieved by GIs?
- Do price premiums differ across countries and regions due to their reputation?

The article is structured as follows: The next section gives an overview about the legal situation of GIs in the coffee market. Thereafter, the economic aspects of coffees with GIs are explored. This is done in two parts. First, an overview of available coffees labeled with GIs and their retail prices in the U.S. market is given. Second, data from several Internet auctions, in which single-origin coffees are directly sold to importers and roasters, are used to estimate a hedonic pricing model. By means of this econometric tool it is elaborated how the country and region of origin influences the price for high-quality coffee controlling for other relevant product attributes such as coffee variety, sensory quality, and different certification schemes, for example, organic.

GEOGRAPHICAL INDICATIONS OF ORIGIN FOR COFFEE FROM A LEGAL POINT OF VIEW

Although TRIPs is considered the first multilateral agreement giving an explicit definition of the term *geographical indication,* there is no uniform definition of geographical indications. Moreover, regulatory systems under which GIs are protected vary strongly across different countries (Thévenod-Mottet, 2006, p. 26; World Trade Organization [WTO], 2004, p. 73). GIs may be protected through special means of protection (e.g., PDO/PGI) as trademark or by already existing laws. Laws against unfair competition or consumer protection laws are cases in point. Whereas the majority of developed countries have got rather well-developed regulatory systems, this is often not the case in developing countries. In these countries the establishment of regulatory systems to protect intellectual property in general and geographical indications in particular is often in its early stages (Josling, 2006, p. 343; Van Caenegem, 2004, p. 170). Many important coffee-producing countries belong to this group of countries.

So far no international register for GIs does exist. Therefore, an overview of already protected and registered GIs in the coffee market will be provided by surveying the literature and using data from trademark bases as well as from governments and growers' associations. Because coffee consumption is still at a low level in most producing countries, the export markets are more important in terms of income generation than the domestic market (Lewin et al., 2004, p. 59). The main export markets for single-origin coffees are Japan, the United States, and Europe. Table 1 concentrates on protected GIs in Europe and the United States as no data are available for the Japanese market.

Colombia, Ethiopia, Jamaica, Hawaii, and Mexico have already protected and registered coffee GIs in the United States and the European market. Although Colombia and Jamaica had started to rely on trademark protection in the 1980s, all other registrations were made in the last few years. Under the Ethiopian Fine Coffee Trademarking and Licensing Initiative, the government of Ethiopia has filled trademark applications in over 30 countries, including the United States and the European Union, for Harrar, Sidamo, and Yirgacheffe, three different coffee-growing regions (Ethiopian Intellectual Property Office [EIPO], 2006, October 12, November 3). This initiative has caused a dispute between the EIPO and the Specialty Coffee Association of America (SCAA)[3] about the correct way to protect geographical indications in the coffee sector. The WTO recommends the use of certification marks for the protection of geographical indications and this is also the position of the SCAA (SCAA, 2006). The Ethiopian government, however, considers trademarks the better way of protecting its coffee GIs. Whereas both concepts rely on the same economic rationale, that is, the protection of goodwill against free riding by third parties and the reduction of consumer search costs, there are substantial differences between these two legal protection schemes (Josling, 2006; World Intellectual Property Organization [WIPO], 2003). First, trademarks identify the manufacturer of a product and can be sold and licensed. Second, no reputation or quality link is necessary. In contrast, certification marks are a collective right and inform the consumer that the goods possess certain characteristics, for example, a

TABLE 1 Protected GIs for Coffee in Europe and the United States, August 2007

Name	Type of protection	Year of registration	Owner
Europe			
Café de Colombia	CTM–Figurative	2001	FNC[a]
100% Café de Colombia	CTM–Figurative	2004	FNC
Juan Valdez 100% Café de Colombia	CTM–Figurative	2005	FNC
Café de Colombia Denominacion de Origen	CTM–Figurative	2006	FNC
Café de Colombia	PGI	2006	FNC
Jamaica Blue Mountain Coffee	CTM–Figurative	2004	Coffee Marks Ltd.
Jamaica High Mountain Supreme	CTM–Word	2003	Coffee Marks Ltd.
Harrar	CTM–Word	2006	Government of Ethiopia
Sidamo	CTM–Word	—[a]	Government of Ethiopia
Yirgacheffe	CTM–Word	2006	Government of Ethiopia
United States			
Colombian	CM	1981	Republic of Colombia
Juan Valdez	TM	1969/2005	FNC
100% Kona Coffee	CM	2000	Department of Agriculture of the State of Hawaii
Jamaica Blue Mountain Coffee	CM	1986	Coffee Marks Ltd.
Jamaica High Mountain Supreme	TM	2003	Coffee Marks Ltd.
Harrar	TM	—[a]	Government of Ethiopia
Sidamo	TM	—[a]	Government of Ethiopia
Yirgacheffe	TM	2006	Government of Ethiopia
Café Veracruz	CM	2005	Consejo Regulador del Cafe-Veracruz

Note. CM = Certification Mark; CTM = Community Trade Mark; FNC = Federación Nacional de Cafeteros de Colombia; GI = Geographical Indications of Origin; PGI = Protected Geographical Indication; TM = Trademark.
[a]In these cases no final determination as to the registrability of the mark has been made.
Source: Own presentation based on CTM-Online (2007), *Official Journal of the European Union* (2006), Schulte (2005), and Trademark Electronic Search System (TESS; 2007).

specific origin. Furthermore, the owner of the right is not allowed to produce but can promote the certification mark. Thus, owners of certification marks are often governmental bodies. Contrary to trademarks, certification marks cannot be sold or licensed (Josling, 2006, p. 348). Although a detailed analysis of the advantages and disadvantages of both legal concepts lies outside the scope of this article, one important point can be derived from this dispute. GIs and their protection are not without controversies and even in the coffee sector itself the opinions about how to protect and enforce this intellectual property differ widely. This is also stressed by the point that in Europe "Harrar" is already registered as a common trademark, whereas in

282   *R. Teuber*

the United States no final decision about the registration of "Harrar" as a trademark has been made so far.

As can be seen from Table 1, both legal means, that is, trademarks and certification marks, are used for protecting coffee GIs in the U.S. market. Although trademark protection can be found both in Europe and in the United States, the protection of PGIs respectively. PDOs is only possible in the European Union. Since September 2007, "Café de Colombia" is the first non-EU product registered as a European PGI. According to the summary application, the essential characteristics of Café de Colombia among others are the soil quality; the typical climate of the country, specifically the mountainous areas of the tropics; the altitude, and the selective hand picking of the coffee bean by bean (*Official Journal of the European Union,* 2006).

To sum it up, Colombia and Ethiopia can be regarded as leading actors in the coffee sector with respect to the establishment of GIs. Although Colombia has already established a national GI, recent efforts are under way to establish regional and estate coffees besides other specialty coffees such as organic or relationship coffees (National Federation of Coffee Growers of Colombia [FNC] web site). For this purpose 86 distinct "designated microclimates" based on a set of variables, including location, rainfall, altitude, and processing methods, were currently defined (Germain, 2004). A regional approach is also followed by Costa Rica and Guatemala. Both countries have already identified seven different growing regions, every region with an individual profile (Guatemalan National Coffee Association [ANACAFÉ], 2006; Instituto del Café de Costa Rica [ICAFE], 2007). To date all these growing regions are still informal, but in all countries efforts are under way to formalize these regions through legal means.

ECONOMIC IMPLICATIONS OF GEOGRAPHICAL INDICATIONS OF ORIGIN FOR COFFEE

Data and Method

Although a number of studies deal with geographical indications from a legal point of view, economic analyses, especially empirical price or cost-benefit analyses of the impacts of geographical indications, are rather scarce (Josling, 2006; WTO, 2004). This is especially true for non-European countries and coffee. The coffee market in general is very well documented but data and analyses regarding the single-origin market are very limited (Lewin et al., 2004).

To explore the economic effects of GIs for coffee, a survey of U.S. Internet retail stores selling single-origin coffees was conducted as a first step. The U.S. market was chosen because in this market the availability of single-origin coffees is rather high compared with the European market, where this type of coffee has just emerged currently (Lewin et al., 2004). Basis of the search for online retail stores was a listing of current SCAA Wholesale Roaster members, from which roasters having an online store and selling directly to consumers were selected. Price data for different single-origin coffees from 100 online retail shops were obtained. All prices are retail prices in U.S. dollars per pound for roasted coffee covering the period August to December 2006. The prices include tax but exclude shipping costs. By considering the number of online retailers offering a certain type of coffee as a proxy for popularity, the most "popular" single-origin coffees together with their retail price were identified. These data were used to compare retail prices for single-origin coffees with the general average retail price. Additionally, available data regarding the volume of single-origin coffees sold to the various export markets were collected. Sources are individual country reports for Colombia and Indonesia and statistics from the Genuine Antigua Coffee Growers Association.

Furthermore, by using data from several Internet auctions for single-origin coffee, several hedonic pricing models were estimated. This econometric tool is used to determine the implicit value of the origin for high-quality coffee controlling for other relevant product attributes such as coffee variety, sensory quality, or certification schemes. The hedonic approach is most often applied to wine data sets in order to explore the value of different wine attributes. Some hedonic studies can also be found for European GIs such as olive oil or cheese (Santos & Ribeiro, 2005; Schamel, 2006; Schamel & Anderson, 2003). Hedonic price analyses for coffee are scarce, especially those dealing with the value of origin. Only one study has already been published investigating the effects of sensory and reputation quality attributes on specialty coffee prices based on Internet auction data (Donnet, Weatherspoon, & Hoehn, 2007). Our approach differs from the one by Donnet et al. in three crucial points. First, our data set is more comprehensive covering more recent data. Second, different explanatory variables are included in our analysis. Third, the focus of the present article is clearly on the value of the origin in order to explore the importance of reputation at the country as well as at the regional level.

The first Internet auction for specialty coffee took place in Brazil in 1999. Following from this the Cup of Excellence® (COE) competition and Internet auctions were established in eight Latin American countries.[4] The procedure is as follows: Farmers, located in the host country, can submit a coffee sample to the organization committee. These coffee samples are cupped by a national as well as an international jury and each coffee gets a score for its taste profile on a 100-point scale. This approach is very similar to the one in the wine industry, where expert quality wine ratings are widely used (Schamel & Anderson, 2003, p. 359). Only coffees scoring 84 points and above are awarded the Cup of Excellence®. In a next step these awarded coffees are sold to the highest bidder during an Internet auction (COE Homepage). Contrary to the consumer price data from the online retail shops, these prices are prices at the procurement level. This is different from most hedonic price analyses using price data at the retail level. However, the demand at the procurement level is a derived demand from the retail level.

All data regarding the awarded farms, for example, the achieved score, farm characteristics, and the achieved price in the auction, are freely available on the COE web site. Some coffee-producing countries such as Ethiopia do not take part in the COE competition but have established their own competition-auction programs. In Ethiopia this program is called ECafé Gold.

Data from COE auctions covering the period 2003–2007 were collected in order to investigate country-of-origin effects. We posit that even after controlling for quality differences between different coffee origins, the country of origin has got a significant impact on the auction price. These effects can be considered reputation effects. Our first hypothesis is that Guatemala, Costa Rica, and Colombia will achieve the highest price premiums due to their established image of high-quality coffee producers.

Additionally, data from Ethiopian and Colombian auctions for the years 2005 and 2006 were used to explore region-of-origin effects. Ethiopia and Colombia were chosen for two reasons. First, for these two countries more or less comprehensive data sets were available. Second, both approaches to establish a GI for coffee, a national and a regional one, are covered in this data set. Although Colombia has pursued a national GI strategy in the past, it has started to define regional coffees just recently. Contrarily, exporters and roasters have differentiated Ethiopian coffees by regional origin for over 100 years (SCAA, 2006). Therefore, a significant regional price differentiation based on reputation is hypothesized for Ethiopian coffee. No significant regional reputation effects are expected for Colombian coffee because the establishment of distinctive coffee regions is still in its infancy.

Descriptive statistics of the used data sets are given in Appendix A. The COE data set for investigating country-of-origin effects includes 792 observations from 27 COE auctions covering the auction years 2003 to 2007. The data set for investigating region-of-origin effects includes 111 observations for Colombian coffees sold in COE auctions and 53 observations for Ethiopian coffees sold in ECafé Gold auctions.

Results

PRICES AND QUANTITIES

Although few coffee GIs are legally protected up to now, many different single-origin coffees are available in the U.S. specialty coffee market. Taken the number of retail stores offering this kind of coffee as a proxy for popularity, the most popular single-origin coffees can be divided into three main groups: the Latin American coffees; the East African coffees; and the Island coffees, including Indonesia, Jamaica, and Hawaii. In the Latin American group Colombia Supremo was offered by 52 online shops followed by Costa

Geographical Indications of Origin 285

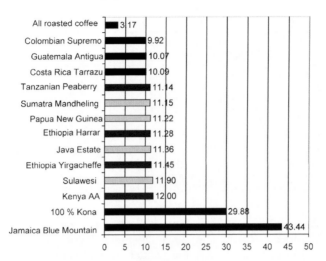

FIGURE 1 Average retail price in U.S. dollars per pound, August–December 2006. *Source.* Own presentation.

Rica Tarrazu (38) and Guatemala Antigua (33). This is consistent with the depicted picture of leading actors in Section 2. The most popular East African coffees are coffees from Kenya (77), Tanzania (41), and the Ethiopian coffees Harrar (39) and Yirgacheffe (33). The group of Island coffees comprises Sumatra Mandheling (67), Sulawesi[5] (40), Java Estate (31), 100% Kona (41), Jamaica Blue Mountain (28), and Papua New Guinea (27). The U.S. retail prices for these different single-origin coffees are presented in Figure 1.

All these coffees sell for at least 3 times the average retail price for roasted coffee. The Latin American coffees range between 9 and 10 U.S. dollars per pound. The East African and Indonesian coffees are slightly more expensive, the average retail price ranging between 11 and 12 U.S. dollars per pound. The most expensive coffees are the Hawaiian 100% Kona and the Jamaican Blue Mountain with an average retail price of 29.88 respectively. 43.44 U.S. dollars per pound.If standard deviations and coefficients of variation are calculated for all coffee prices under consideration, the two most expensive coffees are also the coffees with the highest variation in price.

Information about sold quantities of single-origin coffees is even scarcer than for prices. But some data could be collected from the sources mentioned earlier. Following from Table 2, the annual coffee bean production and export quantity of Genuine Antigua is around 3,000 metric tons (mt). Without appropriate legal protection systems and their enforcement, the incentive for free riding is quite high. This is often cited for Genuine Antigua coffee, with different sources stating that the annual volume of coffee sold as

286   *R. Teuber*

TABLE 2 Export Volume of Selected Coffees with GIs, 2002

Country	Export quantity (in metric tons)	Share in total coffee exports (in %)	Main export markets
Colombia *Regional GIs*	8,100	1.40	Japan
Guatemala *Genuine Antigua*	2,940	1.42	United States and Japan
Indonesia *Toraja, Kalosi, Mandheling*	3,644	1.13	United States and Japan

Source. Own presentation based on FAOStat (2010), Giovannucci et al. (2002), and Neilson (2005).

Genuine Antigua amounts to 23,000 mt, 7 times the amount of actual production (European Commission, 2003; Rangnekar, 2004).

In Indonesia, 3,600 mt of Arabica coffee were exported with geographical indications related to Sulawesi, constituting less than 2% of the total Indonesian coffee export volume. Besides Sulawesi, North Sumatra and East Java are the main origins of high-quality Indonesian coffee. The data in Table 2 just covers coffee exports from Sulawesi. This coffee is not labeled uniformly but either as Sulawesi, Toraja, Kalosi, Toraja Kalosi, or Mandheling depending on the export destination. In the Japanese market, the most important export market for the Indonesian high-quality coffee, the term *Toraja* is preferred. In Europe the same kind of coffee is labeled *Kalosi*. Sometimes even the term *Mandheling* is used to label coffee originating from Sulawesi. This is fraudulent because Mandheling is a coffee-growing region in North Sumatra (Neilson, 2005).

For all three listed single-origin coffees the Japanese export market is the most important one. This is especially true for Jamaica Blue Mountain, for which no reliable data on export volumes could be obtained. But it is estimated that about 85% of all Jamaica Blue Mountain coffee is sold to Japan (Lu, 2006).

HEDONIC PRICING MODEL

Because the functional specification of a hedonic pricing model is not fixed a priori, several specifications were tested to find the most appropriate one for this data set. Based on the Ramsey RESET test, which allows discriminating between alternative specifications, the following specification was chosen as the one fitting the data best:

$$\log(p_i) = \alpha + \beta_1 score_i + \beta_2 rank_i + \beta_3 \log(lotsize_i) + \beta_4 \log(coffeearea_i)$$
$$+ \beta_5 origin_i + \beta_6 variety_i + \beta_7 certification_i + \beta_8 year_i + \varepsilon_i$$

where the subscript *i* stands for the auctioned coffee i, log is the natural logarithm, and p is the price of the auctioned coffee in U.S. dollar per pound. The *score* is the achieved score in the COE competition, the *lotsize* stands for the quantity sold expressed in kilograms, and the *coffeearea* is the size of the area planted with coffee expressed in hectare. The other five variables are categorical dummy variables for the achieved rank, the coffee variety, the country of origin, possible certification schemes, and the auction year. ϵ is the stochastic error term. Unfortunately, no data with respect to altitude, precipitation, soil type, or processing methods could be included because of missing values.

The achieved score in the cupping competition can be considered a sensory quality proxy and a positive impact on the price is expected. A positive influence is also expected for the first three ranks, which are included as dummy variables, meaning the variable for first rank has the value 1 when the coffee was ranked first and 0 otherwise. Contrarily, a negative influence is expected for the *lotsize*. This is based on the idea that this variable can be interpreted as a proxy for exclusiveness. A limited availability will lead to a higher auction price and vice versa. In some hedonic studies for wine, the farm or producer size is used as a proxy for exclusiveness, limited availability, and "trendiness" (Oczkowski, 1994, p. 99). Therefore, the size of the area planted with coffee is included as another proxy for limited availability.

With regard to the origin and the coffee variety, the hypotheses are that significant reputation effects can be found for Guatemalan, Colombian, and Costa Rican coffee and for traditional coffee varieties such as *Bourbon* and *Typica*. As it is common in the wine industry to distinguish wines based on the grape variety such as Merlot or Cabernet wine, it is also possible to distinguish coffees based on the coffee variety. Because a statement was found saying that many coffee professionals favor traditional varieties, it is hypothesized that these varieties earn a price premium in comparison with modern varieties such as *Caturra*, *Catuai*, and *Pacamara*. Moreover, it is assumed that certified coffees earn higher prices than noncertified coffees of the same quality.

A problem often arising in hedonic price regressions because of the large number of product characteristics included in the analysis is multicollinearity. Multicollinearity, which is present when explanatory variables are highly correlated with each other, can lead to higher standard errors of the estimated coefficients, making them possibly insignificant (Ramanathan, 2002, p. 214). In order to explore whether multicollinearity is a problem in this data set, the pairwise correlation coefficients for all explanatory variables were calculated. The highest correlations could be observed between some country and variety dummies, for example, for Nicaragua and Caturra a correlation coefficient of 0.42 was calculated. However, all calculated correlation coefficients were smaller than 0.55 indicating that no severe problem of multicollinearity is present in the data set.

First, a comprehensive model including all available variables was estimated by using ordinary least squares robust estimation. The overall good-
ness of fit is satisfying with an adjusted R squared of 0.71. Although the
score, the ranking, the lot size, the size of the coffee-growing area, and most
of the origin and year dummies are highly significant, this is not true for the
different coffee varieties. In the group of the certification dummies only the
estimated coefficient for the organic certification is significant at the 1% level.

The score and a high-ranking influence the auction price positively. An
increase in the score by 1 point results in a price premium of 7.7%. The impact
of a good ranking is even stronger. A coffee ranked first in a competition
achieves on average a 143%[6] higher price compared with coffees ranked
fourth and below. Second- and third-ranked coffees achieve price premiums
of 38% and 29%, respectively. As hypothesized, the offered quantity has a
negative influence on the achieved auction price. Because the quantity is
expressed in logarithms, the estimated coefficient can be interpreted as the
price flexibility coefficient.[7] A 1% increase in the lot size leads to a price
decrease by 0.39%. This underlines the assumption that scarcity, which can
also be interpreted as exclusiveness, is valued by buyers. Furthermore, it
can be concluded from a price flexibility coefficient below unity that the
demand for these auctioned specialty coffees is highly price elastic (Tomek
& Robinson, 2002, p. 53). Contrarily, the size of the farm's coffee area has a significant positive influence on the price. Thus, the assumption that coffee
buyers use this information as an additional proxy for exclusiveness and "trendiness" could not be proven. However, the influence is rather marginal. A 1%
increase in the area size results in a 0.03% higher price. A certified organic
coffee receives a price premium of around 27% compared with a noncertified
coffee, whereas the coefficient for the Rainforest Alliance certification scheme
is not significant. This may be due to the fact that only very few coffees are
certified in the considered data set. Thus, the importance of certification
schemes in the high-quality segment needs further consideration.

With the exception of the coefficient for Costa Rica, all origin dummies
are highly significant. A coffee of the same quality in terms of score and
achieved rank coming from Honduras is sold at a price discount compared
with all other included countries of origin. The ranking of countries in the
hedonic pricing model confirms the picture found in the literature (Knox
& Sheldon Huffaker, 1996, p. 49). Guatemala is seen as the leading supplier
of high-quality coffee, whereas Honduras still has to establish an image of a
high-quality producer. Besides Guatemalan coffees, which receive a price
premium of around 75% compared with Honduran coffees, coffees from
Bolivia receive a price premium of 63%. Colombian and Brazilian coffees
are also higher priced than Honduran coffees but the price premium is smaller compared with coffees coming from Guatemala or Bolivia.

One shortcoming in this context is the fact that prices do not include
transportation costs. Of course, this fact could lead to a biased preference

scheme between supplier countries because of differing transportation costs. Therefore, as a first approximation the difference between the cost, insurance, and freight (CIF) prices for coffee in the U.S., German, and Japanese markets reported by the UN Comtrade database and the producer prices reported by the FAO and the International Coffee Organization for the years 2002 and 2003 were calculated. The results indicate that transportation costs calculated as the difference between CIF prices and producer prices range between 15 and 45 U.S. cent per pound, depending on the country of origin and the destination. This level is reported by other studies, too (Daviron & Ponte, 2005, p. 210). Because the important point for our analysis was not the absolute value of transportation costs but the relation between coffee-producing countries, the countries were ranked according to their amount of transportation costs. If transportation costs were an important component in the decision of the bidder, we assumed that countries receiving a price discount were countries with high transportation costs and vice versa. This could not be confirmed by the data (see Appendix B). Moreover, the results indicate that countries receiving a price premium, for example, Guatemala and Bolivia, are also countries with high transportation costs. Thus, we suppose that in the mass coffee market transportation costs are an important determinant considering producer prices of 0.50 U.S. dollars for green coffee and retail prices of around 3.25 U.S. dollars per pound for roasted coffee. But considering auction prices for specialty coffees with a mean of 3.84 U.S. dollars per pound and retail prices ranging from 15 U.S. dollars to over 50 U.S. dollars for a pound of roasted coffee, transportation costs can be seen as a more or less negligible determinant of the auction price.

With regard to the previously stated hypothesis that coffees from Guatemala, Colombia, and Costa Rica will receive the highest price premiums, the results prove this statement only for Guatemalan coffee. Colombian coffee also receives a price premium compared with Honduran coffee, but this price premium is smaller than for Bolivian and Brazilian coffee. These results are somehow surprising because Colombia has invested substantial amounts to create an image of a high-quality producer in the mass market. Even more surprising is the result for Costa Rican coffee. No significant price differentiation between Honduran and Costa Rican coffee could be proven in the analysis.

In contrast to the significant country effects, no significant variety effects were found. None of the estimated coefficients for the coffee varieties is significant, indicating that no price differentiation due to variety reputation takes place so far. To test the hypothesis, whether traditional varieties are valued more than modern hybrids by specialty buyers, a binary dummy variable called *traditional* was constructed and included in a reduced model. This variable takes the value 1 for a traditional variety and the value 0 for a nontraditional one. Additionally, the variable *coffeearea* was excluded in the reduced model because the inclusion of this variable led to a drop of

50 observations. The robust estimators of the reduced model are also listed in Table 3. Again, the estimated coefficient for the variety variable is not significant. Thus, the hypothesis that specialty buyers pay more for coffees coming from traditional varieties could not be proven.

TABLE 3 Ordinary Least Squares Estimates for the COE Auction Data Set

	Log (price)			
Dependent variable	Comprehensive model		Reduced model	
Score	0.072***	(0.000)	0.077***	(0.000)
Competition ranking				
Reference: Rank 4th and below				
1st rank	0.889***	(0.000)	0.854***	(0.000)
2nd rank	0.323***	(0.000)	0.277**	(0.000)
3rd rank	0.258***	(0.000)	0.233**	(0.000)
Log (Lot size)	−0.390***	(0.000)	−0.363***	(0.000)
Log (Coffee area)	0.028**	(0.007)	−	
Coffee variety				
Reference: Bourbon				
Catuai	0.013	(0.747)	0.019^a	(0.581)
Caturra	0.049	(0.086)		
Pacamara	0.007	(0.926)		
Typica	0.051	(0.564)		
Others	0.048	(0.366)		
Country of origin				
Reference: Honduras				
Bolivia	0.488***	(0.000)	0.458***	(0.000)
Brazil	0.409***	(0.000)	0.391***	(0.000)
Colombia	0.311***	(0.000)	0.293***	(0.000)
Costa Rica	−0.083	(0.162)	−0.095	(0.062)
El Salvador	0.226***	(0.000)	0.203***	(0.000)
Guatemala	0.559***	(0.000)	0.576***	(0.000)
Nicaragua	0.168***	(0.000)	0.194***	(0.000)
Certification				
Reference: No certification	0.237**	(0.002)	0.204**	(0.010)
Organic	−0.054	(0.203)	−0.049	(0.245)
Rainforest Alliance				
Year				
Reference: 2003				
2004	0.134**	(0.004)	0.128**	(0.004)
2005	0.113**	(0.009)	0.079	(0.057)
2006	0.275***	(0.000)	0.249***	(0.000)
2007	0.584***	(0.000)	0.562***	(0.000)
Adjusted R squared	0.71		0.70	
F statistic	92.58		99.69	
Number of observations	736		789	

Note. ***, **, *indicates significance at the 0.1%, 1%, and 5% level, respectively; p values are presented in parentheses.
^{a}This is the estimated coefficient for the new constructed variable *traditional*.
COE = Cup of Excellence®.
Source: Own computations.

Compared with the base year 2003 the prices paid in the following auction years increased. These increasing auction prices over time can possibly be due to increasing world market prices for coffee in general.

The results regarding the implicit value of the region of origin are presented in Table 4. Dummies for coffee varieties as well as for different certification schemes could not be included because of missing data (Ethiopia) or a missing variance (Colombia). Again, the achieved score is highly significant in both regressions. For Colombian coffees a 1-point increase on the 100-point scale results in a price increase of 6.6%. For Ethiopian coffees the impact is smaller with a price increase of 1.6%. The ranking variables are only significant for Colombian coffees and the implicit values are of the same magnitude than in the country-level model. That the achieved rank is not a significant price determinant for Ethiopian coffee may be due to the limited sample size and needs further investigation with a more comprehensive database. Analogue to the results at the country level, the lot size has a significant negative influence on the auction price. Nearly all regional dummies are significant with rather high impacts on the achieved price. This is especially true for Ethiopia. Coffees from the region Yirgacheffe receive a substantial price premium compared with

TABLE 4 Ordinary Least Squares Estimates for Colombian and Ethiopian Coffees

	Log (Price)			
Dependent variable	Colombia		Ethiopia	
Score	0.066***	(0.000)	0.116***	(0.000)
Competition ranking				
Reference: Rank 4th and below				
1st rank	0.811***	(0.000)	0.081	(0.653)
2nd rank	0.244**	(0.007)	−0.078	(0.693)
3rd rank	0.347	(0.254)	0.022	(0.931)
Log (Lot size)				
Region of origin	−0.270*	(0.034)	−0.393*	(−3.39)
Reference:				
Huila/Yirgacheffe				
Cauca/Sidamo	−0.280**	(0.004)	−0.228*	(0.033)
Meta	0.205**	(0.001)		
Nariño	−0.130*	(0.016)		
Tolima	−0.249***	(0.000)		
Other	−0.013	(0.853)	−0.396**	(0.004)
Year				
Reference: 2005				
2006	−0.074	(0.153)	0.011	(0.923)
Adjusted R squared	0.57		0.53	
F statistic	14.40		8.34	
Number of observations	111		53	

Source. Own computations.

Note. ***, **, *indicates significance at the 0.1%, 1%, and 5% level, respectively; *p* values are presented in parentheses.

Sidamo or other Ethiopian coffee regions. The discount for other growing regions is almost 50% compared with coffees from Yirgacheffe, other things equal. Hence, the hypothesis of a significant regional price differentiation for Ethiopian coffee can be maintained. By contrast, our hypothesis with regard to Colombian coffees is rejected by the data. The results for Colombia indicate that in the specialty coffee segment buyers already differentiate between different Colombian coffee regions. Compared with the reference region Huila, all other growing regions sell at discounts between 13% (Nariño) and 32% (Cauca).

CONCLUDING REMARKS

As data on exported quantities document, the single-origin coffee market is still a niche market. However, growth rates in this market are high and experts predict a further expansion of this segment. Many coffee-producing countries have already decided to invest in the establishment of appellation systems of coffee and are trying to formalize these regions by legal means to address the rising consumer demand for diversification and quality. Up to now Colombia, Costa Rica, Guatemala, and Ethiopia are the main actors in this field, but in other countries efforts to establish regional coffees and promote them are under way as well.

The main export markets for single-origin coffees are the United States and Japan. In Europe these coffees have just emerged. This picture is stated by the Internet auction results for single-origin coffee. In all cases half or even more than half of the coffees were bought by Japanese importers or roasters. Additionally, the results from the hedonic pricing model show that in Internet auctions for specialty coffee the most important price determinants are the sensory quality, proxied by the achieved score, and the achievement of one of the first three ranks in the cupping competition. These attributes are easy to communicate to consumers and are, thus, a valuable marketing tool.

Moreover, the results indicate that different coffee regions have already established a reputation and this is valued by buyers in the specialty segment. These findings suggest that pursuing an origin-labeling strategy can be a successful marketing tool. The reputation, however, has to be built up and this needs time as well as financial resources. Many projects in the coffee sector aim at improving the coffee quality by educating coffee farmers about the main quality-determining factors in the growing and harvesting process. This is very important because in contrast to winemakers, coffee farmers sell a semifinished product. Usually they do not know how the coffee tastes they sell. Therefore, educating coffee farmers about coffee quality is a crucial point with respect to entering the specialty coffee segment.

The results have shown that high-quality coffees earn the highest prices and offer the opportunity to create a somehow unique selling position, either for a whole country, a region, or an individual farmer. Jamaica has been very successful in creating a unique selling position, which is reflected in the tremendous price premium these coffees achieve in the U.S. retail market. What should be added in this context is that many coffee experts do not consider Jamaica Blue Mountain coffee a coffee of extraordinary quality. Consumers, however, value this exotic coffee and it does not matter for the Jamaican coffee industry whether this valuation is based on objective or perceived quality. A similar situation can be found for Colombian coffee. In the mass consumer market Colombian coffee is considered one of the best coffee origins. This is most likely a consequence of enormous marketing efforts by the FNC. However, in the specialty market Colombian coffees are not the highest valued coffees as the results from the hedonic regression document. This is also in line with statements of specialty coffee experts. In the book by Knox and Sheldon Huffaker (1996), a rating list for different single-origin coffees is presented rating Guatemala Antigua and Costa Rican coffee from the estate *La Minita* as outstanding, whereas Colombian coffee is considered only mediocre or good. The authors also state that Colombia has done a great job in marketing so that most consumers are convinced that all Colombian coffees are somehow "special." This point of view is not present in the specialty segment. Nevertheless, Knox and Sheldon Huffaker point out that there are real good Colombian coffees and these outstanding coffees are normally regionally designated coffees. This observation could possibly explain the fact that some Colombian regions have already built up a reputation reflected in the significant region-of-origin effects in the hedonic regression. Indeed, it seems that there are large differences in the valuation of coffee origins between the mass and the specialty market. Colombia was successful in the establishment of a premium image in the mass market and is now trying to enter the specialty segment with regionally designated coffees. However, Colombia is the world's third largest coffee producer and the specialty segment is just a small part of its coffee economy. Contrarily, for small coffee-producing countries such as El Salvador, Honduras, or Nicaragua, entering the specialty segment could be a valuable differentiation strategy because they cannot compete with Colombia in terms of quantity and in terms of financial investment in branding and marketing.

Finally, it should be stressed that single-origin coffees are coffees telling a story and therefore the success of a coffee GI will crucially depend on the story it tells. Such a development toward storytelling can particularly be observed in the COE Internet auctions. Whereas in the first years only very limited information about the individual coffee farm awarded the COE was provided, nowadays a whole story about the coffee, including agronomic data as well as personal data about the farmer and pictures of the farm, are available. This is often used as marketing tool for the consumer market. Consumers buying this kind of coffee do not drink a faceless product any longer; they drink a coffee grown by Isaias Cantillo Osa.[8]

NOTES

1. Statement by the chief buyer of the major United Kingdom retailer of coffee (Kaplinski & Fitter, 2004, p. 7).

2. Council Regulation (EEC) No. 2081/92 on the protection of geographical indications and designations of origin for agricultural products was replaced by Council Regulation (EC) No. 510/2006 in March 2006 as a response to a WTO Panel ruling criticizing two main components of the former regulation (European Commission, 2006).

3. SCAA was founded 1982 as a reaction to the decline in coffee quality offered by mainstream roasters. Today it is the world's largest coffee trade association with over 3,000 member companies (SCAA, 2007).

4. The countries are Bolivia, Brazil, Colombia, Costa Rica, El Salvador, Guatemala, Honduras, and Nicaragua.

5. This includes all coffees labeled Sulawesi, Celebes Kalossi, or Celebes Kalossi Toraja.

6. Because the dependent variable appears in logarithmic form, the percentage interpretation of the dummy variable has to be calculated as $100^*(\exp(\beta)-1)$ (Halvorsen & Palmquist, 1980).

7. The price flexibility is the percentage of change in the price of a good associated with a 1% change in quantity, ceteris paribus (Houck, 1965, p. 1).

8. This was the winning coffee farmer in the Colombian COE auction in 2007.

REFERENCES

Calboli, I. (2006). *Expanding the protection of geographical indications of origin under TRIPS: Old debate or new opportunity?* (Marquette University Law School Legal Studies Research Paper Series, Research Paper No. 06-19). Milwaukee, WI: Marquette University Law School.

Community Trade Mark Consultation Service (CTM-Online). (2007). Retrieved from http://oami.europa.eu/CTMOnline/RequestManager/de_SearchBasic?transition=start&source=Log-in.html&language=en&application=CTMOnline

Cup of Excellence (COE) Homepage. Retrieved from http://www.cupofexcellence.org

Daviron, B., & Ponte, S. (2005). *The coffee paradox.* London, UK: Zed Books.

Donnet, M. L., Weatherspoon, D. D., & Hoehn, J. P. (2007). What adds value in specialty coffee? Managerial implications from hedonic price analysis of Central and South American e-auctions. *International Food and Agribusiness Management Review, 10*(3), 1–16.

Ethiopian Intellectual Property Office (EIPO). (2006, October 12). [Letter to Rob Stephen, President of the Board of Directors of the Specialty Coffee Association of America]. Retrieved from http://www.ethiopianembassy.org/TradeMark Campaign/EIPO_to_Specialty_Coffee_Association_of_America.pdf

Ethiopian Intellectual Property Office (EIPO). (2006, November 3). [Letter to Jim Donald, Chief Executive Starbucks Corporation]. Retrieved from http://www.ethiopianembassy.org/TradeMarkCampaign/EIPO_to_Jim_Donald.pdf

European Commission. (2003). *Why do geographical indications matter to us?* Retrieved from http://ec.europa.eu/trade/issues/sectoral/intell_property/argu_en.htm

European Commission. (2006). *Council adopts improved rules on agricultural quality products.* IP/06/339, 03/20/2006.

FAOstat. 2010. Homepage. Retrieved from http://faostat.fao@org

Germain, S. (2004, September/October). What specialty coffee can learn from wine. *Roast Magazine* (pp. 8–10).

Giovannucci, D., Leibovich, J., Pizano, D., Paredes, G., Montenegro, S., Arevalo, H., & Varangis, P. (2002). *Colombia coffee sector study* (Report No. 24600-CO). Washington, DC: The World Bank.

Guatemalan National Coffee Association (ANACAFé). (2006). *Coffee atlas 2006/2007: Mapping hallmarks of recognition.* Retrieved from http://www.guatemalancoffees.com/GCContent/GCeng/notas_abril2006/CoffeAtlas_Eng.asp

Halvorsen, R., & Palmquist, R. (1980). The interpretation of dummy variables in semilogarithmic equations. *The American Economic Review, 70,* 474–475.

Houck, J. P. (1965). The relationship of direct price flexibilities to direct price elasticities. *Journal of Farm Economics, 47,* 789–792.

Instituto del Café de Costa Rica (ICAFE). (2007). Retrieved from http://www.icafe.go.cr/homepage.nsf

Josling, T. (2006). The war on terror. *Journal of Agricultural Economics, 57,* 337–363.

Kaplinski, R., & Fitter, R. (2004). Technology and globalisation: Who gains when commodities are de-commodified? *International Journal of Technology and Globalisation, 1*(1), 5–28.

Knox, K., & Sheldon Huffaker, J. (1996). *Coffee basics: A quick and easy guide.* New York, NY: Wiley.

Lewin, B., Giovannucci, D., & Varangis, P. (2004). *Coffee markets: New paradigms in global supply and demand* (Agriculture and Rural Development Discussion Paper No. 3). Washington, DC: The World Bank.

Liebig, K. (2000). Der Schutz geistiger Eigentumsrechte in Entwicklungsländern: Verpflichtungen, Probleme, Kontroversen [The protection of intellectual property rights in developing countries: Commitments, problems, controversies.]. Wissenschaftliches Gutachten im Auftrag der Enquete-Kommission des Deutschen Bundestages "Globalisierung der Weltwirtschaft—Herausforderungen und Antworten", Bonn, Germany.

Lu, Z. (2006, January 23). Out of the blue. *China Daily.* Retrieved from http://www.chinadaily.com.cn/english/doc/2006–01/23/content_514577.htm

National Federation of Coffee Growers of Colombia (FNC). (2007). *Cafes especiales Colombianos.* Retrieved from http://www.cafedecolombia.com/nuestrosprod/cafespeciales/pag_csc.html

Neilson, J. (2005). Geographical identities along the coffee supply chain from Toraja to Tokjo. In N. Fold & B. Pritchard (Eds.), *Cross-continental food chains* (pp. 193–216). New York, NY: Routledge.

Oczkowski, E. (1994). A hedonic price function for Australian premium table wine. *Australian Journal of Agricultural Economics, 38*(1), 93–110.

Official Journal of the European Union. Council Regulation (EC) No. 510/2006. Retrieved from http://eur-lex.europa.eu/LexUriServ/site/en/oj/2006/c_320/c_32020061228en00170020.pdf

Ramanathan, R. (2002). *Introductory econometrics with applications* (5th ed.). South-Western. Fort Worth, TX: Harcourt Brace Jovanovich College Publishers.

Rangnekar, D. (2004). *The socio-economics of geographical indications: A review of empirical evidence from Europe* (UNCTAD-ICTSD, Issue Paper No. 8). Geneva, Switzerland: UNCTAD.

Santos, J. F., & Ribeiro, J. C. (2005, August). *Product attribute saliency and region of origin: Some empirical evidence from Portugal.* Paper presented at the 99th seminar of the EAAE 'The Future of Rural Europe in the Global Agri-Food system', Copenhagen, Denmark.

Schamel, G. (2006, August). *Auction markets for specialty food products with geographical indications.* Paper presented at the 26th conference of the International Association of Agricultural Economists, Gold Coast, Queensland, Australia.

Schamel, G., & Anderson, K. (2003). Wine quality and varietal, regional and winery reputations: Hedonic prices for Australia and New Zealand. *The Economic Record, 79,* 357–369.

Schulte, C. (2005, October). Smelling the coffee? *Trademark World.* Retrieved from http://www.lovells.com/Lovells/Media Centre/Articles/Smelling+the+coffee.htm

Specialty Coffee Association of America (SCAA). (2006). *Geographic indications for the origin of coffee: Statement of the Specialty Coffee Association of America, August 8, 2006.* Retrieved from http://www.scaa.org/pdfs/news/SCAA-GI-Ethiopia-Statement0806.pdf

Specialty Coffee Association of America (SCAA). (2007). *Fact sheet about the Specialty Coffee Association of America.* Retrieved from http://www.scaa.org/pdfs/Press-About-SCAA.pdf

Thévenod-Mottet, E. (2006). *GIs legal and institutional issues* (SINER-GI, WP1 Report, Final version). Retrieved from http://www.origin-food.org/2005/upload/SIN-WP1-report-737006.pdf

Tomek, W. G., & Robinson, K. L. (2002). *Agricultural product prices* (4th ed.). Ithaca, NY, and London, UK: Cornell University Press.

Trademark Electronic Search System (TESS). (2007). Retrieved from http://tess2.uspto.gov/bin/gate.exe?f=searchss&state=vqb7vm.1.1

TRIPS. (1994). Agreement on trade-related aspects of intellectual property rights. *Annex IC of the Marrakesh Agreement Establishing the World Trade Organization.*

Van Caenegem, W. (2004). Registered GIs: Intellectual property, agricultural policy and international trade. *European Intellectual Property Review, 26,* 170–181.

World Intellectual Property Organization (WIPO). (2003). *Economic importance of trademarks and geographical indications and their use in commerce* (Document prepared by the International Bureau of WIPO Geneva, Switzerland. WIPO/TM/BEY/03/3).

World Intellectual Property Organization (WIPO). (2004, February). Intellectual property as a lever for economic growth: The Latin American and Caribbean experience. *WIPO Magazine,* 2–5.

World Intellectual Property Organization (WIPO). (2007). *Intellectual property digital library>Lisbon structured search.* Retrieved from http://www.wipo.int/ipdl/en/search/lisbon/search-struct.jsp

World Trade Organization (WTO). (2004). *World trade report 2004.* Geneva, Switzerland: Author.

CONTRIBUTOR

Ramona Teuber is a Ph.D. student and Research Assistant at the Institute for Agricultural Policy and Market Research, Justus-Liebig University, Giessen. She holds a Master's degree in food economics.

APPENDIX A Descriptive Statistics of the Data Sets

	Country		
	COE data 2003–2007	Colombia	Ethiopia
Number of observations	792	111	53
Price (in U.S. DOLLARS/Ib)	3.84	4.31	2.94
Mean	1.20	1.85	1.50
Min	49.75	19.10	10.65
Max			
Score			
Mean	86.81	86.81	87.94
Min	80.25[a]	84.05	85.03
Max	95.85	93.72	92.50
Lot Size in kg			
Mean	1,396	1,202	1,286
Min	620	980	480
Max	8,417	5,253	2,220
Origin	Bolivia, Brazil, Costa Rica, Colombia, El Salvador, Guatemala, Honduras, Nicaragua	Cauca, Huila, Meta, Nariño, Tolima, Other	Sidamo, Yirga-cheffe, Other
Variety	Bourbon, Catuai, Caturra, Pacamara, Typica, Other	Colombia	N/A
Certifications	Organic, Rainforest Alliance	None	N/A
Buyer (Mean)			
Japanese company	0.49	0.60	0.53
U.S. company	0.25	0.14	0.34
European company	0.22	0.21	0.09
Others	0.04	0.05	0.02
N/A	—	—	0.02

Source. Own computations.

Note. N/A = no data available.

[a]In the Nicaraguan COE competition 2003 the threshold was a score of 80 instead of 84. This was changed in 2004.

APPENDIX B Transportation Costs

	Difference between the U.S. CIF price and the producer price in U.S. DOLLARS/lb, 2002	Difference between the U.S. CIF price and the producer price in U.S. DOLLARS/lb, 2003
Bolivia	0.297	0.361
Brazil	0.223	0.317
Colombia	0.272	0.393
Costa Rica	0.480	0.495
El Salvador	0.329	0.379
Guatemala	0.415	0.382
Honduras	0.149	0.107
Nicaragua	0.152	0.183

Source. Own computations based on FAOSTAT, ICO Database, and UN Comtrade.

[23]

Journal of International Food & Agribusiness Marketing, 24:185–200, 2012
Copyright © Taylor & Francis Group, LLC
ISSN: 0897-4438 print/1528-6983 online
DOI: 10.1080/08974438.2012.691790

Gatekeepers' Perceptions of Thai Geographical Indication Products in Europe

RUNGSARAN WONGPRAWMAS and MAURIZIO CANAVARI

Alma Mater Studiorum–University of Bologna, Bologna, Italy

RAINER HAAS

University of Natural Resources and Life Sciences, Vienna, Austria

DANIELE ASIOLI

Alma Mater Studiorum–University of Bologna, Bologna, Italy

This study is aimed at exploring perceptions of European gatekeepers toward renowned Thai fruit and coffee products protected by geographical indication (GI) and factors influencing purchasing decision of gatekeepers toward imported food products. Sixteen qualitative interviews with distribution channel gatekeepers were administered in Austria, Italy, and Switzerland in 2010. Content analysis and concept mapping were used to analyze data. Results show that Thai GI products might be interesting for European gatekeepers, but the GI attribute alone might not be sufficient to ensure that the product is successful. Support of consistent information and promotion campaigns and fulfillment of other gatekeepers' requirements of both products and suppliers are necessary.

KEYWORDS factors influencing purchasing decision, gatekeepers, geographical indication, perception, Thai fruits and coffee

This research was performed in the framework of the project "Pro-GIs: Intellectual Property Right Extension & Geographical Indications Protection for the Benefit of EU-Thailand Trade" cofunded by the program "Thailand-EC Cooperation (TEC) Facility" of the European Union.

Address correspondence to Rungsaran Wongprawmas, Department of Agricultural Economics and Engineering, Alma Mater Studiorum–University of Bologna, Viale Giuseppe Fanin 50, I-40127, Bologna, Italy. E-mail: rungsaran.wongprawmas80@gmail.com

INTRODUCTION

Thailand is one of the main producers of agricultural products and is recognized as a producer of great unique and tasty products (Chomchalow, Somsri, & Na Songkhla, 2008). In 2007, Thailand produced 8.95 million metric tons of fruit, which is 1.61% of the world fruit production in 2007 (Food and Agriculture Organization, 2009). During the last few years Thailand has been trying to penetrate the European market because it is the largest single market with expanding demand for ethnic products and high premium prices for quality produce (Deutsche Gesellschaft für Technische Zusammenarbeit, 2010). Thai fruit export is mainly represented by tropical fruit (e.g., longans, mangoesteen, durians, rambutans, carambola, dragon fruits, pineapples, mangoes, lychees, and tamarind). The value of EU fruit importation from Thailand steadily grew over the last 8 years, from 216.64 million euro in 2002 to 274.65 million euro in 2009, now representing 1.88% of total fruit trade (European Commission, 2010b). Coffee trade between Thailand and the European Union is mainly represented by green bean coffee export to the European Union and (semi)finished coffee products import from the European Union. Thailand's share of the EU coffee imports ranged between only 0.01 and 0.26% in the period 2002–2009 (European Coffee Federation, 2009).

The Thai government is currently looking for strategies to improve quality standards and the differentiation of products so as to enhance the competitiveness of Thai exports because Thailand cannot compete on price with countries like China and Vietnam. Additionally, there is growing interest in the world market toward quality food products, in particular high-quality local and traditional food specialties, which may pave the way for specialty products from less developed countries, in order to gain access to lucrative international markets (Canavari, Galanti, Haas, & Wongprawmas, 2010). As a result, the Thai government endorsed policies and regulations—the Geographical Indication Act of B.E. 2546 (Jaovisidha, 2003) and Thai Geographical Indication Logo Approval B.E. 2008 in order to protect, foster, and promote Thai quality products and culinary recipes. It was expected that geographical indication (GI) labels will help consumers to recognize quality of the products by linking them with geographical characteristics and culinary heritage of Thailand. Thus, they aim to enhance the credibility of products, improve market access, promote typical products, and finally lead to sustainable economic and social development in a specific territory (Bramley & Kirsten, 2007).

As of June 2010, 35 product names are registered as GIs in Thailand, 29 of which are from Thailand, 5 from the European Union, and 1 from Peru. Registration is pending for 34 more products (Department of Intellectual Property, 2010). The most represented product categories are fruit (23%), handicrafts (23%), rice (20%), alcohol (17%), and coffee (6%). Furthermore, during the last few years, Thailand applied to register some Thai products under the EU regulation, namely, Thung Kula Rong-Hai Thai Hom Mali Rice, Doi Chaang Coffee, and Doi Tung Coffee (European Commission, 2010a). This motivates the belief that Thai GIs will be perceived as higher quality products and will gain a better position in the EU market if recognized by the European Union.

The Importance of GI Labels in the European Market

In the last decades, European consumers became more thoughtful about their purchasing decision, especially about product quality and food safety as well as environmental and social impacts associated with food production and marketing (Bredahl, Northen, Boecker, & Normile, 2001). One of the quality cues frequently used in the EU market, especially in wine and food products, is related to product origin. The European Union has a long history of GI labeling and currently two types of GIs are available for food products: protected designation of origin (PDO) and protected geographical indication (PGI). Producers and companies have been using GIs label to signal quality to the consumer and it is expected that they will perceive GIs as a quality attribute adding value to the product. Several studies in the literature indicated that perceived quality associated with the intrinsic attributes of PDO products have a positive and significant influence on European consumers' buying intentions (Fandos & Flavian, 2006) and they are willing to pay higher prices for PGI label in fresh meat (Loureiro & Mc Cluskey, 2000). Hence, GIs might signal quality to the consumer and create a sense of affection for consumers but only when they deal with a high-quality product and consumers recognize its superior quality (using GI labels as a brand).

GI Products From Third World Countries in the European Market

Many successful cases of GI products enhancing value are available in Europe, especially in Southern Mediterranean countries. However, most of these products are produced in small local areas inside Europe, which were already famous among consumer groups (Barjolle & Sylvander, 2000). For Thai GI products this is not the case because consumers might not be able to perceive their value due to lack of knowledge, awareness, and familiarity with products (Boccaletti, 1999). In addition, successful value-enhancement strategies for GI products depend not only upon origin but also upon effective value-adding strategies used to promote the product (Bardaji, Iraizoz, & Rapun, 2009). Vandecandelaere, Arfini, Belletti, & Marescotti (2009) highlighted that third world countries that would like to develop fruitful GI schemes should be aware of a number of requirements to be achieved in advance, such as traceability along the supply chain; responsibility and accountability of producers, processors, and marketers; and clear and sound marketing strategies.

Issues Addressed in This Study

Because introduction of Thai GIs into the EU market is still in its initial stages, products have to be chosen by European gatekeepers first. Gatekeepers are food channel members who have the power to select products to be in the market. Even though they are expected to merely select products according to their perception of consumers' demand, in many cases they may also exert a great influence on product ranges in the market due to their power to make food-buying decisions on behalf of food importing and distribution companies that supply millions of end consumers (Knight & Gao, 2005).

Hence, this research focuses on gatekeepers' perceptions toward Thai GI fruits and coffee. We aim to gain a deeper understanding of the attitudes of gatekeepers and the possibility to use GI labels to foster the competitiveness of Thai fruits and coffee products in the EU market. Given this is an exploratory qualitative study, the objectives are shown as follows:

1. Explore how European gatekeepers perceive GI fruit and coffee products from Thailand;
2. Explore potentials and barriers for GIs in fruit and coffee products from Thailand in the European markets; and
3. Explore the key factors that influence purchasing decision of European gatekeepers.

DATA AND METHODOLOGY

Exploratory research based on qualitative approach is adopted in this study. This approach makes us able to deal with complexity and rich diversities of the gatekeeper perceptions; it also leaves room to generate hypotheses for further research, although it cannot be generalized to all food chain members and channels (Myers, 2009). A semistructured interview outline was designed to serve as a nonbinding outline of the discussion with respondents following the three research aims mentioned earlier. The schedule contains a series of open-ended questions introducing wide topics and inducing the informant to raise salient issues that he or she thinks are important and relevant to the topic of interest during the conversation (Myers, 2009).

Selection of Respondents

Purposive nonstochastic sampling was applied to recruit participants in this study to retrieve information from persons who have knowledge and might be able to highlight the relevant problems or issues on a specific topic (Trochim & Donnelly, 2006). In addition, the snowball sampling procedure was applied.

A list of European operators was created on the basis that those listed are expert and professional practitioners in European food distribution (importers, wholesalers, retailers, practitioners, and experts) who already have experience dealing with Thai or Asian products in Europe. We interviewed 16 out of 35 selected contacts—10 in Italy, 5 in Austria, and 1 in Switzerland.

In the context of confidentiality, the specific names of the interviewee and the company are preserved. The characteristics of the interviewed companies were as follows: 13 respondents were importers and distributors of fruit and food products and 3 respondents were researchers and experts on agrifood marketing and European fruit markets (see Table 1). Among the importers and distributors, 6 companies were fruit and/or vegetable distributors, 4 companies were specialty shops, and the remaining were representatives of large retail companies. Among the researchers and experts, 2 were specialized in organic products only. These key informants are the main importers and distributors of Thai and Asian products in these countries so that they could provide insight and relevant information for the research. Given the limited geographical scope covered by this sample, conclusions and hypotheses drawn by means of this research are most likely to be valid only in the Austrian and Italian situations.

Interview Procedure

Sixteen semistructured interviews were administered during March–June 2010. The semistructured interview schedule was sent to respondents in advance and personal interviews ranged between 30 and 60 min in duration. They were conducted in English, in Italian, and in Thai according to respondents' preference. The interviews were structured according to a semistructured interview guideline but did not adhere strictly to them because a "conversation-like dialogue rather than asking questions that impose categorical frameworks on informants' understanding and experiences" is preferable (Arnould & Wallendorf, 1994, p. 492; Knight, Gao, Garrett, & Deans, 2008). Therefore, the core information would be collected through a series of open-ended questions introducing wide topics and inducing the informant to raise salient issues that he or she thinks are important and relevant to the topic of interest during the conversation (Myers, 2009). Thirteen interviews were face-to-face and 3 interviews were administered by telephone. Interviews were recorded if the respondent agreed, and the interviewer took note of important information and observed context-specific elements during the interview. Immediately after the interview was administered, the interviewer prepared a summary report based on notes and on the

TABLE 1 Profile of Key Informants, Companies, and Organization in Samples

No.	Company	Interviewee	Sector	Location	Activity
1	A	Communication head	Research institute	Frick, Switzerland	Researcher on organic food marketing and on Thai organic products
2	B	Executive director	Research institute	Vienna, Austria	Researcher on organic market development and capacity building
3	C	Sales manager	Specialty shop	Vienna, Austria	Importer/Distributor of Thai and Asian products
4	D	Manager	Specialty shop	Vienna, Austria	Importer/Distributor of Thai and Asian products
5	E	Senior quality manager	Large retailer	Vienna, Austria	Big supermarket chain/retailer in Austria
6	F	Owner	Specialty shop	Vienna, Austria	Importer/Distributor of Thai and Asian products
7	G	Owner	Specialty shop	Bologna, Italy	Importer/Distributor of Thai and Asian products
8	H	Trade manager	Fruits distributor	Bologna, Italy	Main exotic fruits importer and distributor in Italy
9	I	Marketing and quality manager	Wholesaler	Bologna, Italy	Major fruits and vegetables wholesaler market in Bologna
10	J	Administrator	Fruits and vegetables distributor	Bologna, Italy	Small fruits and vegetables distributor in Bologna
11	K	Purchasing manager of fruits and vegetables	Large retailer	Bologna, Italy	Big supermarket chain/retailer in Italy
12	L	Purchasing manager	Fruits and vegetables distributor	Bergamo, Italy	Main exotic fruits importer and distributor in Italy
13	M	Marketing researcher	Agrifood marketing research institute	Bologna, Italy	Marketing researcher/expert on fruits market and GI products
14	N	Purchasing manager	Fruits and vegetables distributor	Milan, Italy	Exotic fruits importer and distributor in Italy
15	O	Purchasing manager of tropical fruits	Integrated supply chain company	Bologna, Italy	Fruits and vegetables producer/importer/distributor in Italy and exporter
16	P	Category manager of fruits	Large retailer	Bologna, Italy	Big supermarket chain/retailer in Italy

Note. GI = geographical indication.
Source. Data from the survey.

recorded conversation, when available, and this report was verified by another person who collaborated in preparing the report to reduce the risk of a subjective view.

Data Analysis

Summary reports of each interview were written in English immediately after conversations. A preliminary version of summary reports was submitted to the interviewees for "checking how accurately participants' realities have been represented in the final account" (Creswell & Miller, 2000, p. 125; Knight, Holdsworth, & Mather, 2007b) in order to establish credibility of the results. Their comments and additional information were included into the final version of interview summaries. Tape-recorded interviews were transcribed and eventually translated into English. Comments were coded on the transcripts using different text colors and marginal keywords in order to identify important themes and patterns (Coffey & Atkinson, 1996; Knight et al., 2007b).

Information from the summary reports, together with available transcription and comments, were analyzed through a content summarizing procedure, aimed at describing the phenomenon and at presenting the most interesting elements arising from each interview, in order to gain an extensive overview of informants' attitudes toward the topic (Downe-Wamboldt, 1992). From the analysis and synthesis of relations among factors affecting purchasing decisions a conceptual map was created. This was in order to visually describe the concepts mentioned by key informants and connections among them (Novak & Cañas, 2008).

RESULTS

Perception of European Gatekeepers Toward Thai GI Fruit and Coffee Products

It was concluded that European consumers and gatekeepers are aware of the GI concept mainly as it relates to local or European products because GI products strongly link to territory and traditional local culture. European consumers have already developed positive perceptions toward these products and the GI label can therefore be used as a differentiation tool. However, when dealing with Thai GI products, respondents made many various comments.

Most of the gatekeepers thought that the GI label may not be able to add value to Thai fruit and coffee products because consumers do not have enough information or experience concerning these products:

> This business is too small in quantity. For me, you have to work with quality—freshness, information. Because for me, in my opinion, when

> you have many fruits, you use PGI to differentiate. This is a small market,
> so it cannot be differentiated. (Importer and distributor in Italy)

On the contrary, other gatekeepers maintain that the use of a well-known quality label such as European public brands for GIs could represent an advantage for Thai GI products because of confidence and trust that European consumers associate to them:

> If you have an origin certification of the product, it could be a way to
> enforce the knowledge, the nationality of the product. For the European
> market, I think it could be interesting, if you have this kind of certification
> between the European and Thai at the same level of quality assurance,
> origin and traceability, and so on. I think that it could be a possibility
> especially for fruits. (Marketing researcher in Italy)

Some gatekeepers and marketing researchers thought that the GI labels might be useful as a mediator of trust to assure the quality and food safety of Thai products:

> Certainly, PGI would help us to have warranties and also suppliers. They
> would enter the market more easily. It would be an advantage for con-
> sumers, too. (Importer and distributor in Italy)

Although GI certification is not a food safety guarantee, the gatekeepers argued that it could be seen as such in the eyes of the public. This is due to the fact that gatekeepers and consumers tend to be more sensitive to imported food than domestic products. Food scares and general unfamiliarity cause them to look for any form of certification for reassurance, holding them as signs of food safety and quality. Gatekeepers also mentioned that trace-ability systems are crucial for products entering the EU market.

One retail respondent stated that GI labeling would not be useful for Thai products because he gave more value to his quality private brand than to the GI certification. This inferred that GI labeling, which is one of many quality labels, might be a competitor to quality private retailer brands. There-fore large retailers might have less of an inclination to stock products with other quality labels in their stores. This could be especially true for coffee but it might not be the case for Thai fruits because they are basically totally different from fruits produced in the European Union.

Opportunities and Challenges for Thai GI Products

Information and promotion campaigns are necessary to support the Thai GI product registration efforts because European consumers and gatekeepers are unfamiliar with these products and cannot distinguish the differences between them and other similar products in terms of quality and taste.

The interviewees underlined the following conditions required for Thai GI products to be successful in the European market: (a) products must be a specialty fruit with outstanding quality; (b) exporters should provide correct information or story behind products about landscape, production area, production and work conditions; and (c) food safety certification according to the EU regulation must be provided.

> I think for some products, GI is important for merchandise as a tool if it's really a typical product from this region. But I think it has to be a well-known product so that people know that it comes from this country [Thailand]. Thai GI products have to get the image in people's mind that this product is a typical Thai product and that it's one of the best coming from Thailand. (Large retailer in Austria)

Some of the interviewees suggested that *Organic* and *Fair Trade* labels used in combination with the Thai GI labeling might be useful to enhance the competitiveness of products, although this could be costly and difficult to achieve. Furthermore, usefulness of combining GI labels with other quality labels relies upon clear consumer understanding of the separate value of product attributes communicated by each label. It is also important to synchronize the Thai GI label with the European one (mutual recognition) to maintain consistency in labeling.

Another challenge for Thai GI products mentioned by gatekeepers is consumers' attachment to own local food and culinary tradition. This is especially relevant in Mediterranean countries like Italy, where a well-defined and renowned national food culture dominates and, as a consequence, a limited demand for foreign products is present.

Factors Influencing Purchasing Decisions of European Gatekeepers

Eight major factors appear to influence European gatekeepers' decisions to purchase imported food products: quality, price, food safety, environmental aspect, social aspect, business relationship, consumer awareness, and preference and competitors (see Table 2). These factors are illustrated in the conceptual map analyzing gatekeepers' views as shown in Figure 1. However, it seems that the elements of trust and reliability are the most prominent ones with regard to deciding to import food products. In light of this, country image might influence the psychic distance between customers and exporters. Additionally, cultural distance may hinder the successful market penetration of Thai products as they may be perceived by European consumers as simply too strange, alien, and unfamiliar to be desirable.

The conceptual map of factors influencing imported food products purchasing decisions of the European gatekeepers performed in this study is a useful tool to design marketing strategy aimed at adding value to Thai fruit

TABLE 2 Overview of the Factors That Influence Gatekeepers' Purchasing Decision on Foreign Fruits and Coffee and Illustrative Quotations

Factors	Illustrative quotations
Quality	Important is quality. Price is for sure, then come the issues like pesticide and certification. (Large retailer in Austria)
Price	Price is the most important because of economic crisis. I have to sell product consumers can afford. (Importer and distributor, specialty shop in Bologna)
Food safety	Important is quality. Price is for sure, then come the issues like pesticide and certification like Global GAP certification, IFS quality certification. Low pesticide residue. I think these are the most important issues. (Large retailer in Austria)
Business relationship	For the retailer, the market is full and there are so many partners, so many suppliers to deliver the products. You have to get into this market, you have to have only very high standards and good partners for many years. (Large retailer in Austria)
Competitors	Among suppliers with similar products, I will choose the one with a better offer. (Importer and distributor, specialty shop in Bologna)
Consumer awareness and preference	Consumer preference, I think consumers' need is the most important thing. Before we import any products we have to check consumer preference and trend this year. (Importer and distributor, specialty shop in Bologna)
Environmental aspect	For the European, I think it would be the key question because of climate change and carbon footprint. It will be important; I think it will become more and more difficult to sell products that come by airplane. (Large retailer in Austria)
Social aspect	People start to say okay, we have products from country A, okay, they are good. They have good worker conditions, they have a good environment. I don't have to have a bad feeling if I'm buying it. It's good for me because it tastes good, it's good for the environment, and the people there are happy, something like that. (Large retailer in Austria)

Note. GAP = Good Agricultural Practices; IFS = International Food Standard.
Source. Authors' elaboration of survey data.

and coffee, exploiting the opportunity offered by GIs. However, given its qualitative nature, it needs to be tested in further research.

Suggested Distribution Channels for Thai GI Products

There were three potential channels suggested by gatekeepers: specialty shops, large retailers, and restaurants/spas. They explained that specialty shops are a good distribution channel because they are run by experts with similar products. These experts can be a better vehicle of information on products, methods of preparation, and consumption of consumers. Limitations of this channel include the fact that it will be only a niche market; however, the consumers in these channels tend to have a larger intention to purchase these products than other channels. Large national and international retailers are thought to be a promising channel for Thai GI products because they can move high volumes of products, have wider access to mass consumers, and

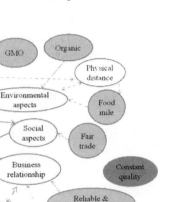

FIGURE 1 Factors influencing imported food products purchasing decision of the EU gate-keepers. *Note.* Solid arrow represents positive effect and hollow arrow represents inhibitory effect. *Source.* Authors' elaboration of survey data. (Color figure available online.)

employ better marketing strategies. However, producers and operators interested in distributing products through this channel may face difficulties in maintaining bargaining power because premium prices and stricter regulations are required. Thai restaurants and spas were mentioned as channels to display and perhaps provide a first impression of Thai products to European consumers. Agritourism markets were also mentioned as an innovative channel by one respondent.

Suggested Avenues for Further Marketing Activities to Promote Thai GI Products

Gatekeepers suggested some potential marketing activities to introduce Thai GI products in the European Union: spread of information through public relations and communication initiatives; showcasing the region of the products and telling the story behind them; assuring product safety and guaranteeing quality; demonstrating products and letting consumers try them; developing joint export platform for Thai cuisine and fruits; starting with pilot products that are typical, high quality, and without environmental and social problems; differentiating Thai GI products from other products by quality, healthiness, and packaging; offering promotion to gatekeepers; and selecting the proper distributors to channel Thai GI products. Learning lessons from the outcomes of marketing strategies used by both success and failure cases in the EU market could also be beneficial.

DISCUSSION

According to European gatekeepers Thai GI products might be interesting, but the GI attribute alone cannot enhance competitiveness of Thai GI fruit and coffee. Other attributes of products and suppliers such as quality, price, food safety, environmental aspect, social aspect, business relationship, consumer awareness and preference, and competitors also have an impact on purchasing decisions of the gatekeeper. These factors are more general for imported food products and are similar to previous literature. Skytte and Blunch (2001) found that traceability, sufficient quantities, and long-term relationships are the most prominent attributes involved with European retailer decision-making criteria. This supports the idea that the product characteristics are not the only the main factor considered by gatekeepers but supplier characteristics, business relationship, marketing strategies, and traceability are also used as key decision-making factors in evaluating foreign food products.

All respondents highlighted that information and communication are crucial issues for Thai GI products. This conforms with the study of Boccaletti (1999) that GI products from abroad should have good communication, quality indication that this product has traditional characteristics and other relevant characteristics to consumers' requirement. The originality of a typical local area can lead to a differentiation of the product only if consumers recognize its value. This highlights that niche marketing through origin labeling may require an extensive awareness campaign so as to capture the benefits associated with differentiation of products (Bramley, Bienabe, & Kirsten, 2009).

The study outcomes suggest that GIs seem to act more as a mediator of trust in the ability to assure quality and safety of Thai food products rather than as an attribute able to enhance the product image per se. This is consistent with Knight, Holdsworth, and Mather (2007a), who found that country of origin is related to confidence and trust of products rather than to country image itself. They also investigated factors influencing gatekeepers' purchasing decisions and discovered that gatekeepers are more concerned with trust issues when it comes to imported food in the product, its packaging, and in the producers and intermediaries involved in supplying that product. The explanation for this issue is that normally gatekeepers and consumers are more sensitive about imported food than domestic products due to food scares and they do not know or cannot check the real production conditions (Bredahl et al., 2001). As a result, gatekeepers tend to look for a guarantee to assure the quality and safety of products they selected (Willems, Roth, & van Roekel, 2004) and they thought that GI labels might be helpful in this aspect.

Nevertheless, GI labels might be useful as an attribute to foster the perceived quality of Thai GI products both as an intrinsic and an extrinsic cue. This may transform credence quality attributes of products into search attributes (Fandos & Flavian, 2006). Furthermore, the respondents also insisted that Thai operators and producers should improve quality control and traceability systems in order to maintain high quality of products, which will lead to the differentiation of products and better market access later. Therefore, high and consistent quality standards, well-known products, and consumers' knowledge are essential properties for GI products to be successful.

All in all, GI products' registration should not be considered the ultimate goal for Thai products in the European market but rather that it is the first step to build a clear communication strategy for high-quality and added-value products (characterized by GI labeling). Information, promotion, and proper marketing strategies should be designed and implemented to stimulate the interest of gatekeepers and to foster understanding and appreciation among consumers of the diverse array of unique and high-quality products bearing the Thai GI label.

The limitation of this research is that the qualitative research approach could not give conclusive answers to specific research questions and could not be generalized in the market directly. However, the elements that emerged could be used to arrange a subsequent analysis based on a quantitative research approach. Suggested future research based on this study is to test the relative importance of factors influencing gatekeepers' purchasing decision in order to accurately define marketing strategies to introduce these products into the market. It is also useful to test awareness and purchasing behavior among consumers who purchase products from different distribution channels because they have different knowledge and purchasing intention toward Thai GI products. This would help the operators or government to decide which distribution channels they can use to promote the product and which are proper communication actions. Finally, the only source of information used in this study is the European gatekeepers; the voice and the point of view of the Thai exporters are not taken into consideration. Therefore, further research is needed to collect information from the Thai counterparts.

REFERENCES

Arnould, E., & Wallendorf, M. (1994). Market-oriented ethnography: Interpretation building and marketing strategy formulation. *Journal of Marketing Research*, *31*(4), 484–505.

Bardaji, I., Iraizoz, B., & Rapun, M. (2009). Protected geographical indications and integration into the agribusiness system. *Agribusiness*, *25*(2), 198–214.

Barjolle, D., & Sylvander, B. (2000). Some factors of success for origin labelled products in agrifood supply chains in Europe: Market, internal resources and institutions. In B. Sylvander, D. Barjolle, & F. Arfini (Eds.), *The socio-economics of origin labelled products in agrifood supply chains: Spatial, institutional and coordination aspects* (pp. 45–71). Le Mans, France: INRA Actes et Communications.

Boccaletti, S. (1999, June). *Signaling quality of food products with designations of origin: Advantages and limitations.* Paper presented at the World Food and Agribusiness Congress, Florence, Italy.

Bramley, C., Bienabe, E., & Kirsten, J. (2009). The economics of geographical indications: Towards a conceptual framework for geographical indication research in developing countries. In *The Economics of Intellectual Property* (pp. 109–149). Geneva, Switzerland: World Intellectual Property Organization.

Bramley, C., & Kirsten, J. F. (2007). Exploring the economic rationale for protecting geographical indicators in agriculture. *Agrekon, 46*(1), 47–71.

Bredahl, M., Northen, J., Boecker, A., & Normile, M. (2001). Consumer demand sparks growth of quality assurance schemes in the European food sector. In U.S. Department of Agriculture (Ed.), *Changing structure of global food consumption and trade* (pp. 90–102). Washington, DC: U.S. Department of Agriculture, Economic Research Service.

Canavari, M., Galanti, G., Haas, R., & Wongprawmas, R. (2010). *Geographical indications: Outlook on the European and Thai systems and overview of EU gatekeepers perceptions towards GI fruit and coffee products proceeding from Thailand.* Bologna, Italy: Alma Mater Studiorum–University of Bologna, Dipartimento di Economia e Ingegneria Agrarie.

Chomchalow, N., Somsri, S., & Na Songkhla, P. (2008). Marketing and export of major tropical fruits from Thailand. *Assumption University Journal of Technology, 11*(3), 133–143.

Coffey, A., & Atkinson, P. (1996). *Making sense of qualitative data: Complementary research strategies.* Thousand Oaks, CA: Sage.

Creswell, J., & Miller, D. (2000). Determining validity in qualitative inquiry. *Theory into Practice, 39*, 124–131.

Department of Intellectual Property. (2010). *The registration of geographical indication.* Retrieved from www.ipthailand.go.th/ipthailand/index.php

Deutsche Gesellschaft für Technische Zusammenarbeit. (2010). *Thai fruit and vegetable case study.* Retrieved from www.deza.admin.ch/ressources/resource_en_164930.pdf

Downe-Wamboldt, B. (1992). Content analysis: Method, applications, and issues. *Health Care for Women International, 13*(30), 313–321.

European Coffee Federation. (2009). *European coffee report 2008.* Retrieved from http://www.ecf-coffee.org

European Commission. (2010a). *DOOR database: Agriculture and rural development.* Retrieved from http://ec.europa.eu/agriculture/quality/door/list.html

European Commission. (2010b). *EU market access database.* Retrieved from http://mkaccdb.eu.int/mkaccdb2/statistical_form.htm

Fandos, C., & Flavian, C. (2006). Intrinsic and extrinsic quality attributes, loyalty and buying intention: An analysis for a PDO product. *British Food Journal, 108*(8), 646–662.

Food and Agriculture Organization (FAO). (2009). *The FAO statistical yearbook 2009*. Retrieved from www.fao.org

Jaovisidha, S. O. H. (2003, October). *Protection of geographical indications: Thailand's perspective*. Paper presented at the EU-ASEAN Workshop on Geographical Indication: A Way Into the Market, Hanoi, Vietnam.

Knight, J. G., & Gao, H. (2005). *Country of origin and confidence in quality of imported foods in China. Marketing Working Paper Series (28)*. Retrieved from http://hdl.handle.net/10523/1569

Knight, J. G., Gao, H., Garrett, T., & Deans, K. (2008). Quest for social safety in imported foods in China: Gatekeeper perceptions. *Appetite, 50*, 146–157.

Knight, J. G., Holdsworth, D. K., & Mather, D. W. (2007a). Country-of-origin and choice of food imports: An in-depth study of European distribution channel gatekeepers. *Journal of International Business Studies, 38*(1), 107–125.

Knight, J. G., Holdsworth, D. K., & Mather, D. W. (2007b). Determinants of trust in imported food products: Perceptions of European gatekeepers. *British Food Journal, 109*(10), 792–804.

Loureiro, M. L., & Mc Cluskey, J. J. (2000). Assessing consumer response to protected geographical identification labeling. *Agribusiness, 16*(3), 309–320.

Myers, M. D. (2009). *Qualitative research in business & management*. London, UK: Sage.

Novak, J. D., & Cañas, A. J. (2008). *The theory underlying concept maps and how to construct and use them*. Pensacola, FL: Florida Institute for Human and Machine Cognition.

Skytte, H., & Blunch, N. J. (2001). Food retailers' buying behaviour: An analysis in 16 European countries. *Journal on Chain and Network Science, 1*, 133–145.

Trochim, W., & Donnelly, J. P. (2006). *The research methods knowledge base* (3rd ed.). Cincinnati, OH: Atomic Dog.

Vandecandelaere, E., Arfini, F., Belletti, G., & Marescotti, A. (2009). *Linking people, places and products: A guide for promoting quality linked to geographical origin and sustainable geographical indication*. Rome, Italy: Food and Agriculture Organization.

Willems, S., Roth, E., & van Roekel, J. (2004). *Changing European public and private food safety and quality requirements: Challenges for developing country fresh produce and fish exporters*. Washington, DC: The World Bank.

CONTRIBUTORS

Rungsaran Wongprawmas is a Ph.D. student at the Department of Agricultural Economics and Engineering at the Alma Mater Studiorum—University of Bologna. Her research fields are food safety standards and quality management systems and agri-food marketing focusing on consumer behavior, international trade and quality products.

Maurizio Canavari holds a Laurea degree in Agricultural Sciences (Bologna, 1990) and a doctorate degree in Appraisal and Land Economics (Padova, 1996). He is associate professor of Agricultural Economics and Appraisal at the Alma Mater Studiorum–University of Bologna and he lectures on agrifood marketing, strategic marketing management in agribusiness and marketing research. Current research interests regard topics in agri-food marketing and economics of quality in the agri-food chains, such as trust and quality assurance and certification in food networks, marketing and consumer behavior related to quality food products, such as organic, functional and unique specialty food.

Rainer Haas is a professor at the Institute of Marketing & Innovation. His research field is Food & Ag-Business Marketing.

Daniele Asioli is a post-doc research fellow at the Department of Agricultural Economics and Engineering at the Alma Mater Studiorum–University of Bologna, with a practical experience in food industry, specialized in agribusiness marketing, new food product development and food traceability.

[24]

Local products and geographical indications: taking account of local knowledge and biodiversity

Laurence Bérard and Philippe Marchenay

Most of the time, local agricultural products and food stuffs are linked to the animal or plant world. Whether they are raw materials or transformed, they are involved in biological processes when they are cultivated, raised, and manufactured. There is a great abundance of different practices and forms of knowledge, revealing, as if that were necessary, the inventive capacity of societies and the extreme malleability of living organisms. Certain products are based on complex systems capable of maintaining various forms of biodiversity, ranging from a landscape to a microbial ecosystem, and including plant varieties and local animal breeds. The forms of local knowledge and technical practices are the most visible factors – because they are the most directly observable ones – which influence this biological diversity. Today, geographical indications (GIs) have an international reputation (Sylvander 2005). Beyond the legal protection of the geographical name, which represents their founding principle, they can contribute to maintaining biodiversity in general and genetic resources in particular. These are good fields of study for understanding how the combination of natural factors and human factors can influence biological and cultural diversity.

Laurence Bérard and Philippe Marchenay are researchers in the eco-anthropology and ethnobiology research unit of the Centre National de la Recherche Scientifique and the Muséum national d'Histoire Naturelle. They head the "Terroir Resources – Cultures, Customs, and Societies" Department located in Bourg-en-Bresse (Ain), at the Alimentec Technopole. Their research focuses on the ethnological dimensions of local farm and food products. They work on bringing to the fore, characterising, and analysing the cultural specificity of such products. Their work emphasises the knowledge, practices, and representations implemented in the elaboration, conservation, and use of these resources.
Email: laurence.berard@ethno-terroirs.cnrs.fr; philippe.marchenay@ethno-terroirs.cnrs.fr

Space, time, and shared knowledge

The diversity of local products is omnipresent, as reflected by the impressive quantity of drinks, cheeses, meats, oils, pastries, fruits, and vegetables. It is also expressed by their social status and history, as well as in the various production techniques or methods of trade they give rise to, which are subject to great variations. Sometimes the rich foundations of a culture emerge from behind a product. In other cases the link can be much more subtle. Beyond this extreme polymorphism, these products all have a particular relationship with space. Their inscription in a place is related to their historical roots and the collective practices that produce them. In other words, they straddle space and time, and are built on shared knowledge and know-how. They all have a history, the temporal range of which varies depending on each case; however, the anteriority that gives depth to the place is indeed present, and is linked to the memory they transmit. Shared know-how constitutes the other component defining local and traditional agricultural products and foodstuffs; according to the place they occupy, these practices sometimes testify the organisation of a group or of the entire society.

Their collective dimension makes them belong to the local culture, and makes it possible to distinguish provenance from origin: the difference between merely coming from a place that does not attribute the least particularity to it, from belonging to a place that involves a relationship with a special meaning. These are the cultural criteria that link a place to a history and to a social group, and which help organise and consider this diversity and characterise the nature of this link (Bérard and Marchenay 1994, 1998, 2001, 2004, 2005).

Some of these products are designated by their place of origin, that is, the geographical name of the place where they were elaborated. This association translates the link established between the quality, the origin, and the reputation that derive from it. We speak of *beaufort* and *comté* cheeses, and *volaille de Bresse* (Bresse poultry). This practice of designation is both ancient and widespread. It is found in classical antiquity, and there is not a single country in the world in which a geographical origin is not linked to particular products. The carrots from the Ouadane oasis in Mauritania are considered to be the best in the country; the paprika from Kalocsa, in Hungary, is beyond comparison; and English Stilton refers back to the village of the same name in the county of Leicestershire. This practice is somewhat problematic, because the reputation attached to a place encourages its abusive appropriation the better to sell a product, which constitutes an unfair trading advantage for the local producers, and at the same time is a way of deceiving the consumer.

Regulations to protect origin in Europe and in the world

French law has long recognised the use of a geographical name to identify and protect against counterfeiting a product whose character is linked to a *terroir* and specific know-how. The setting up of a single market by opening up the borders and giving the producers of the various countries in the European Union the opportunity to sell their products freely has increased the risk of abusing a name. This fact raises the problem of what these products "of particular quality" will become and, more broadly speaking, of those that are specific to each country. It is in this

general context that the European Council adopted a regulation on 14 July 1992 concerning the protection of geographical indications and designations of origin, which was greatly inspired by the French model (European Economic Community 1992).

The protected designation of origin (PDO), which can be compared to the French *Appellation d'origine contrôlée* (controlled designation of origin – AOC), and the protected geographical indication (PGI), ensure protection based on a relationship to a place. Both designate "the name of a region, a specific place or, in exceptional cases, a country, used to describe an agricultural product or a foodstuff originating in that region, specific place, or country". In the case of PDOs, "the quality or characteristics are essentially or exclusively due to a particular geographical environment with its inherent human and natural factors, and the production, processing and preparation take place in the defined geographical area". In the case of PGIs, "a specific quality, reputation, or other characteristics can be attributed to this geographical origin, and the production and/or processing and/or preparation take place in the defined geographical area" (European Economic Community 2006, p. 14).

The philosophy of PDOs is to protect, with a name, a unique product that is not reproducible in another *terroir*. The entire production process must be carried out in the same zone and the coherence and influence of this zone on the characteristics of the product must be demonstrated. Meanwhile the PGI label is based on the reputation of the product, its history, linked to that of a locality, and its particular characteristics or qualities. This approach does not impose a single zone in which all the operations must take place: in particular, the raw materials can come from elsewhere. PDOs and PGIs are grouped under the more general term of geographical indicators (GI). This principle has been invoked at the international level within the framework of the Trade-Related Intellectual Property Rights Agreement established by the World Trade Organisation. In this it is stated that the geographical indications:

are, for the purposes of this Agreement, indications which identify a good as originating in the territory of a member, or a region or locality in that territory, where a given quality, reputation or other characteristic of the good is essentially attributable to its geographical origin. (TRIPS, Annex IC, article 22, p. 328).

It is obvious that this agreement contains some important weaknesses. For instance, at the time of writing, only wines and spirits are really protected. The European Union is fighting for this protection to be extended to all products and for them to be listed and protected within the framework of an international register. Nevertheless, this is only a first step, bearing witness to the increasing interest at the international level in products whose quality is linked to their origins. The creation of the association Origin (Organization for an International Geographical Indications Network) in 2003 confirms this tendency (Origin 2003). Today, Origin groups together 70 associations of producers in more than 30 countries on all the continents and is militating for better international protection of GIs and the recognition of their role in sustainable development. Developing countries show increasing interest for this new approach to their local resources, as is demonstrated by the current rallies to this trend.

Cultural biodiversity and protection of origins

Animal breeds, plant varieties, landscapes, and microbial ecosystems correspond to an accumulation of knowledge, practices, and adjustments. These vary according to the nature of the products, which are themselves dependent upon local social and environmental conditions. This combination of factors underpins and organises distinct levels of biological complexity. Biodiversity, "a set of living beings, their genetic heritage, and the ecological environments in which they evolve" (Centre National de la Recherche Scientifique 1998, p. 6), could not exist without the practices and knowledge developed by the societies that create it, and maintain or reduce it. The protection of geographical origin can encourage this cultural biodiversity to be taken account of, or even reactivated.[1] To accomplish this, it is indispensable to take into account not only the biological characteristics, but also the local knowledge and practices involved. These elements, which are an integral part of the specificity of the products,

are taken into account in the increasing elaboration of the criteria that must be respected and that constitute the specifications of GI. The delimitation of the protected zone and the definition of the conditions of production are the two major issues in the protection of a name. The French examples discussed below show how links can be established between biodiversity and protection.

Ardèche chestnuts

In the Ardèche region in the south of France, local communities were organised for centuries around chestnut groves. The management of this environment led local producers to identify, select, and then graft an impressive number of varieties, of which the size, shape, and organoleptic qualities of the fruit correspond to customs that differ according to the different areas in Ardèche. In the north, for a long time the fruit of the *combale* variety, which was eaten boiled, was part of the daily meal, in the same way as bread. In the south of the department, the *pourette* was extensively used and became a veritable subsistence foodstuff. Occupying almost the entire area, the chestnut tree shaped the landscapes and marked in a lasting way the heritage, customs, and social life of Ardèche. The traditional chestnut grove is at the same time the trace of a culture, a civilisation, and a local product intimately linked to a *terroir*. Faced with its decline, there was a proposal to introduce hybrid varieties, satisfying certain technical and commercial criteria. But this innovation, involving a very different management of the chestnut grove, moving from agroforestry to an intensive orchard system, created a great deal of tension (Dupré 2002, pp. 125–129). This led the producers to reflect upon an AOC approach that offers simultaneously the possibility of protecting the local varieties, the traditional management of trees, and the kind of landscape. The AOC *châtaigne d'Ardèche* designation has been obtained in 2006. The specifications include 19 main varieties, all of which are local.

Cider, calvados, and perry in Normandy

Cider, perry (which resembles cider but is made from pear juice), *pommeau*, and calvados are beverages, or beverages that are then distilled; the

Bleu de Termignon cheeses mature, high pastureland of Entre-Deux-Eaux, Savoie, France, August 2005.
Marchenay/Bérard, CNRS

basic ingredients of which are apples and pears. In Normandy in the west of France, their production has traditionally been based – and to a large extent still is – on the exploitation of the meadow orchard. This system of cultivating trees and grasslands over a long cycle provides on the same land various kinds of complementary products: fruit for beverages, grass, milk, and meat. A total of six cider-based products and six milk-based and cheese products have an AOC.[2]

The Norman meadow orchard corresponds to a historical and current reality which is simultaneously interesting to farming, the environment, the local economy, the cultural heritage, and biodiversity. Varietal diversity is particularly high there. Within the calvados area for example, there are 177 varieties officially listed and 477 designations (taxa) in the orchards identified by the *Institut national des appellations d'origine*.[3]

This diversity represents the production objectives: some varieties are more or less well-suited for making ciders or perries for direct consumption, for the distillation of calvados, or the production of must for *pommeau*. In effect, the final result is often linked to the subtle mixture of different varieties. The diversity is also due to a strategy of protecting against the risks of alternation in the setting of fruit, a phenomenon that is frequent in traditional orchards.

The AOC Domfront perry obtained in December 2002 is exemplary in terms of the conditions of production. On the one hand, the main variety is the *plant de blanc*, well-known locally, accompanied by complementary local varieties. On the other hand, this is the first AOC that strictly defines how the plant resources, here pear trees, must be managed and the related agroecosystem, the orchard. Plant density (less than 150 trees per hectare), standard growth trained on high stem, association with a pasture, are criteria that correspond to local customs. This consideration of local norms and plant resources introduces a landscape dimension in the cider economy and falls within the perspective of conserving cultural biodiversity. In addition, as the traditional meadow orchard is a refuge for a certain number of animals, in particular insects, mammals, and birds, it contributes to saving many species because of the resulting biodiversity (Bérard et al. 2006).

Charolais beef

Charolais beef has a particularly good reputation. The fame of the animals from this area – which gave its name to the breed – has for a long time been excellent. Two reasons for this are put forward: the local tradition of selection, which has always attached the greatest importance to the quality of the meat, and the value of the grazing, which enables exceptional finishing and is the fruit of the fatteners' skills. In effect, the know-how concerning the land and the vegetation, particular to the zone, determines the growth potential of the animals. The management of the grass is the central issue in the Charolais system (Lizet 1993). The most significant know-how resides in how the livestock farming is organised, in relation to the meadows which the stockbreeder possesses. Nearly 3500 farms specialising in the production of livestock for meat are located in the Charolais beef zone. They are characterised by a useful agricultural area that covers a minimum of 80 per cent of extensive prairie.

The AOC currently being applied for insists on the need to take account of this specific way of raising cattle, which is closely linked to the management of the grass and a breed adapted to its environment. In these conditions, the beef cattle, heifers, and cows may all be eligible for AOC status.

The Dombes carp

The fish farming practised in the ponds of the Dombes (Ain) is oriented toward raising carp. This activity is not recent; it emerged in the medieval period because of the need to find fish at a time in which food prescriptions were very strong. Today

it is based on an extensive system that alternates fish farming and grain farming on the same land. (ponds are emptied every year, to be fished, and then refilled. After around five years, the fish ponds are left to dry up, so that crops of maize or oats can be grown.) This particular form of crop rotation generates a complex set of technical and cultural practices that produce biodiversity, by conserving, in particular, a great number of wild animal and plant species, including the plankton and micro-organisms in the water and in the soil. The farming systems and the methods of appropriating the land, the great diversity in the categories of users of the environment, the specific practices, and the weight of the hunting activities constitute the main parameters that determine the functioning of these cultivated ponds (Bérard and Marchenay 1981). Here, the landscape offers the peculiarity of completely changing in appearance during the wet and dry periods. The Dombes fish is currently being considered for a protected GI label.

And, of course, cheese

At the crossroads of biology and culture, cheese products occupy a privileged position. From a raw material, milk, there is a multitude of ways of manufacturing and of variants, emerging from a great number of practices. At the heart of all of this, the interaction between living organisms and cultural entities shapes the originality of cheeses, particularly – but not always – when this concerns AOC. The cheese-making systems unite countless practices and forms of knowledge from all domains of living organisms, including plants, animals, and micro-organisms.

Grass, the primary product, is the basic resource. In addition, the cheese-making systems shape the landscapes and ensure that they are maintained, via the pastoral activity underlying their existence. There are many examples: the Chaumes fields in the Vosges mountains with *munster*; high mountain pastures in the northern Alps with *beaufort* or *abondance*; landscapes of *burons* (cheese-making structures) in the Massif central with *cantal*, *salers* or *laguiole* cheeses; the prairies of the high Jura with *comté* or the *garrigue* in the Cévennes with *pélardon*; not to forget the meadow orchards in the west of France with *livarot*, *pont l'évêque*, and *camembert*. In any case, the practices are linked to knowledge about nature and the environment.

One simply has to compare, based on photographs, the appearance of currently active cheese-making zones – which show an open landscape – with that of other zones where activity has stopped, with landscapes that are becoming closed, invaded by encroaching vegetation. Maintaining the pastures is an ongoing, long-term endeavour.

The animal is the indispensable intermediary between the grass and the finished product. Local breeds are becoming more and more important in the designations of the origins of cheeses. The breed appears to be a subtle combination of biology and culture, adapted to specific needs and conditions. For a certain number of AOCs, breeds are specified in the description of the conditions of production. For others the discussion is open, and sometimes the question is not yet on the agenda.

In the AOCs, there is a great diversity of breeds, especially bovine: *salers* for *salers*; *vosgienne* for *munster*; *normande* for *livarot*, *pont l'évêque*, or *camembert*; French *simmental* or *brune* for *époisses*; *tarine* or *abondance* for *beaufort*, *abondance*, and *reblochon*; *montbéliarde* or French *simmental* for *comté*, *mont d'or* and *bleu de Gex* and so on. These animal breeds are more or less numerous, but in no case are they endangered. On the contrary, in some cheese-making sectors, there may be the reintroduction and reactivation of local breeds threatened with extinction, such as for example the *villard-de-lans* for *bleu du Vercors Sassenage* or the *aubrac* milk branch for *laguiole*.

Micro-organisms occupy a very important place in the elaboration of cheeses. Many of them are provided by the natural inoculation of the milk. This concerns a biological capital that is an integral part of the elements of the *terroir*, even if they cannot be seen by the naked eye. Another path towards biodiversity from cheeses is the maturing process, which is an essential phase in making cheese. Mould, yeast, and bacteria evolve together in an extremely complex environment, with effects of multiplication and interaction which are themselves triggered off and controlled by the local practices and know-how.

Finally, one cannot speak of microbial biodiversity without evoking the places in which the maturing process takes place, veritable humanised ecosystems in which the temperature, humidity, and other factors are capital for the inoculation and maturing of cheeses. These are the cellars of the high Alps pastures, or those of the *terroir* of the *Causses* in the Aveyron with their natural *fleurines*, the natural caves in which certain local cheeses mature, or even the transfigured railroad tunnels.

And not forgetting . . .

Broken olives, black olives, and olive oil from the valley of Baux-of-Provence, olives from Nice, olive oil from Haute-Provence, olive oil from Aix-en-Provence, black olives and olive oil from Nyons, all of which are AOCs, mobilise many cultivars, and the list will undoubtedly continue to grow, in particular with the oils from Corsica. The four decrees concerning the Le Puy green lentil, an AOC since 1996, the Espelette red pepper (2000), the Paimpol bean (1998), and the sweet onion from the Cévennes (2003) give a description of the types of local varieties suitable for AOC labelling and indicate that producers can use the seeds produced on their farm. This is also a way to manage – at the local level – agrobiodiversity *in situ*.

A way of thinking differently about farming

Contrary to what one might think a priori, the farmers who invest in these approaches are often at the cutting edge of development. The AOC system invites a different approach to agricultural development. Distancing itself from essentially productivistic systems, it offers the opportunity to farmers to establish production schemes according to other models. Within this framework, it is the local practices and uses associated with particular natural conditions that are put forward to identify and maintain the specificity of a product, as the legal scholar Marie-Angèle Hermitte points out:

The difference between these two conceptions of progress: automatic, linear progress, deriving mechanically from technological change, and more complex progress, which can be satisfied by the conservation of memory and the maintaining of customs, which have arrived at a high degree of perfection, leads to what is perhaps the most profound originality of the designation of origin with respect to the other intellectual property rights. (Hermitte 2001, p. 205)

The approach implies the conviction of the producers. The producers themselves set the conditions of production in the specifications that are validated by the Institut national des appellations d'origine, but have the possibility of modifying them. This regulation authorises the elements within the established protocols to be reconsidered. Such a situation allows social positioning to take place by leaving open adequate room for negotiation, in particular as far as the methods of production are concerned.

Therefore, GI, and in particular the AOC, are tools making it possible to take account of this combination of cultural and biological diversity, as long as those concerned so desire. These are options that give the opportunity to initiate, then maintain the dialogue in a concrete way between scientists, managers, the agricultural world, local authorities, and other interested individuals. Paradoxically innovative, these agricultural models, which are more respectful of the environment and local resources, have become the precursors of surmodern farming, while becoming economically viable in the long term (Lamine and Roué 2005).

Protecting local products means conserving varied local ecosystems at various levels: animals, plants (breeds and local varieties), plant associations, microbial ecosystems, including the places for maturing cheeses and the landscapes. This is also a way of maintaining in a formal way shared knowledge and practices. This is all the more interesting, given that most of the products having a designation of origin label are produced in extensive systems which associate localised practices and biological diversity. However, taking account of this diversity is confronted by the effects of globalisation. Trade internationalisation associated with the unrestricted circulation of goods generates and imposes standards that are more and more constraining. These rules were conceived at the industrial scale and take very little account – or only in rare cases – of the characteristics linked to small units of production and local products. For their survival, it is important to think about standards adapted to their specificity and to small production units. While output criteria are not open to discussion – there can be no question of marketing products injurious to health – input criteria should leave room for negotiation and an enlightened and reasonable interpretation of the texts. Otherwise these products will in some cases disappear and in others be stripped of what makes them interesting, with predictable consequences for biodiversity.

Translated from French

Notes

1. A debate could take place on the ways of naming this diversity of living organisms which have been developed by human societies on the basis of quite different perspectives: agro-biodiversity, ethno-biodiversity, bio-cultural diversity, and so on.

2. Cider-based products: calvados, Pays d'Auge calvados, Domfrontais calvados, *pommeau* from Normandy, Pays d'Auge cider and Domfront perry. Cheese and milk products: camembert from Normandy, pont l'Evêque, livarot, neufchâtel, as well as butter and cream from Isigny.

3. These taxa do not necessarily constitute specific vegetal material; however, this richness in the nomenclature constitutes a good indication of cultural biodiversity. Beyond the strictly genetic aspect, the way of describing the varieties, the construction of the vernacular nomenclature, the choice of varietal collections, the representations linked to the tree and to the fruit are all interesting starting points for analysis.

References

BÉRARD, L., AND MARCHENAY, P. 1981. "Ethnologie et écologie d'un système agro-piscicole: les étangs de la Dombes", *Le monde alpin et rhodanien*, 2nd and 3rd quarter 69–102.

BÉRARD, L., AND MARCHENAY, P. 1994. "Ressources des terroirs et diversité bioculturelle: perspectives de recherche", *Journal d'agriculture traditionnelle et de botanique appliquée*, 36 (2), 87–91.

BÉRARD, L., AND MARCHENAY, P. eds 1998. "Patrimoine, montagne et biodiversité", *Revue de géographie alpine*, 86 (4).

BÉRARD, L., AND MARCHENAY, P. 2001. "A market culture. 'Produits de *terroir*' or the selling of heritage", *In*: Blowen, S., Demossier, M., and Picard, J., eds *Recollections of France. Memories, identities and heritage in contemporary France*. New York, Oxford: Berghahn, 154–167.

BÉRARD, L., AND MARCHENAY, P. 2004. *Les produits de terroir. Entre cultures et règlements*. Paris: CNRS Editions.

BÉRARD, L., AND MARCHENAY, P. 2005. "Diversity, protection and conservation: local agricultural products and foodstuffs", *In*: Sanga, G., and Ortalli, G., eds *Nature knowledge. Ethnoscience, cognition, and utility*. Oxford: Berghahn, 366–378.

BÉRARD, L., FABIAN, T., AND MARCHENAY, P. 2006. *Le pré-verger cidricole de Normandie. Un système de culture pérenne et fragile*. (Forthcoming).

BÉRARD, L., MARCHENAY, P., CEGARRA, M., DJAMA, M., LOUAFI, S., ROUSSEL, B., AND VERDEAUX, F. 2005. *Biodiversity and Local Knowledge in France*. Paris: INRA, CIRAD, IDDRI, IFB.

CENTRE NATIONAL DE LA RECHERCHE SCIENTIFIQUE 1998. *Dynamique de la biodiversité et environnement*. Paris: CNRS.

DUPRÉ, L. 2002. *Du marron à la châtaigne d'Ardèche. La relance d'un produit régional*. Paris: Éditions du CTHS.

EUROPEAN ECONOMIC COMMUNITY 1992. "Regulation (EEC) No 2081/92 on the protection of geographical indications and designations of origin for agricultural products and foodstuffs", *Official Journal of the European Communities*, No. L 208.

EUROPEAN ECONOMIC COMMUNITY 2006. "Regulation (EEC) No. 510/2006 on the protection of geographical indications and designations of origin for agricultural products and foodstuffs", *Official Journal of the European union*, No. L 93.

HERMITTE, M.-A. 2001. "Les appellations d'origine dans la genèse des droits de propriété intellectuelle", *Études et recherches sur les systèmes agraires et le développement*, 32, 195–207.

LAMINE, C., AND ROUÉ, M. 2005. "Le naturel et la qualité", *Nature, Sciences, Sociétés*, 13 (4), 383–420.

LIZET, B. 1993. "L'herbe violente", *Etudes rurales*, 129/130, 129–146.

ORIGIN (ORGANIZATION FOR AN INTERNATIONAL GEOGRAPHICAL INDICATIONS NETWORK) 2003. Available online at http://origin/technomind.be [Accessed 7 March 2006].

SYLVANDER, B. 2005. "Les produits d'origine: les enjeux du XXIe siècle", *In*: INAO ed *Le goût de l'origine*. Paris: Hachette/INAO, 60–77.

TRIPS 1994. "Agreement on trade-related aspects of intellectual property rights", Annex IC of the Marrakesh Agreement Establishing the World Trade Organization.

D
Cultural Protection

[25]

TAKING "TRADE AND CULTURE" SERIOUSLY: GEOGRAPHICAL INDICATIONS AND CULTURAL PROTECTION IN WTO LAW

TOMER BROUDE [*]

"Each bottle of American and Australian wine that lands in Europe is a bomb targeted at the heart of our rich European culture."
- A winemaker from the Languedoc, circa 2000[1]

TABLE OF CONTENTS

---

[*] Lecturer, Faculty of Law and Department of International Relations, Hebrew University of Jerusalem; BA, LLB, Hebrew University of Jerusalem; SJD, University of Toronto. The Article was presented at an international conference on "The World Trade Organization at a Crossroads," Bar Ilan University, Ramat Gan, Israel, December 12–14, 2004, and at the University of Toronto Law Faculty's Law and Economics Workshop, October 5, 2005. The author is grateful to the participants and others, and in particular Bruce Chapman, Gail Evans, Andrew Green, Aeyal Gross, Larry Helfer, Ed Iacobucci, Ariel Katz, Joel Trachtman, Michael Trebilcock, and Thomas Wälde, for their helpful comments.

[1] Quoted in WILLIAM ECHIKSON, NOBLE ROT: A BORDEAUX WINE REVOLUTION 15 (2004).

1.   *ANTIPASTI*: THE (WORLD) WAR OF THE TWO BEANS

The regulation of the relationship between international trade law and cultural protection is one of the challenges that the World Trade Organization ("WTO") will face with greater intensity in the second decade of its existence. Within the WTO, aspects of culture and its sensibilities are being raised as important non-trade considerations to be factored into trade law disciplines either in the context of Article XX of the General Agreement on Tariffs and Trade 1994 ("GATT")/Article XIV of the General Agreement on Trade in Services ("GATS") argumentation,[2] or in the promotion of *sui generis* trade-related intellectual property rights.[3]   Outside of the WTO, the trade-culture nexus appears in developments in the emerging international law of cultural diversity as promoted within the United Nations Educational, Scientific, and Cultural Organization ("UNESCO").   Such developments are little noticed today, but may in the future impact trade law on the basis of

---

[2] Cultural considerations may conceivably be cited as justifications for exceptions from World Trade Organization ("WTO") trade liberalization disciplines under Article XX(a) of the General Agreement on Tariffs and Trade 1994, Apr. 15, 1994, Marrakesh Agreement Establishing the World Trade Organization, Annex 1A, Legal Instruments—Results of the Uruguay Round, 33 I.L.M. 1125 (1994) [hereinafter GATT], or Article XIV(a) of the General Agreement on Trade in Services, Apr. 15, 1994, Marrakesh Agreement Establishing the World Trade Organization, Annex 1B, Legal Instruments—Results of the Uruguay Round, 33 I.L.M. 1125 (1994) [hereinafter GATS], if deemed "necessary to protect public morals." *See* Appellate Body Report, *United States – Measures Affecting the Cross-Border Supply of Gambling and Betting Services*, WTO Doc. WT/DS285/AB/R (Apr. 7, 2005) [hereinafter *US – Gambling II*] (modifying a panel decision and finding that U.S. federal legislation banning internet supply of gambling services is a restriction on trade in services but that it satisfies the Article XIV(a) of the General Agreement on Trade in Services ("GATS") "necessity" and "public morals" tests, although in part confirming that some of the legislation was discriminatory under the *chapeau* of GATS Article XIV); or under Article XX(f) of the General Agreement on Tariffs and Trade ("GATT") if "imposed for the protection of national treasures of artistic, historical or archeological value." For a discussion of the legal implications of a general "cultural" exception in WTO law, see *infra* Section 5.

[3] Such as the Geographical Indications ("GIs") discussed in the present Article or within the more general concept of "Traditional Knowledge." *See generally* Graham Dutfield, *Protecting Traditional Knowledge and Folklore: A Review of Progress in Diplomacy and Policy Formulation*, (UNCTAD–ICTSD Project on IPRs and Sustainable Dev., Issue Paper No. 1, 2003) (discussing recognition of traditional knowledge and folklore in the intellectual property framework).

cultural justifications.[4]

This Article approaches the problem as it is reflected in the current debate on Geographical Indications ("GIs") for food and wine products in the WTO.[5] It seeks to take "trade and culture" seriously, looking at law's effects not only on trade but on culture as well, and to examine the extent to which legal restrictions on international trade can in fact prevent the degradation of cultural diversity in a particular regulatory context. This Article's specific argument, *in nuce*, is that the conservation of local culture and cultural diversity cannot serve as an independent supporting

---

[4] *See* Universal Declaration on Cultural Diversity, annex 1, United Nations Educational, Scientific, and Cultural Organization ("UNESCO"), UNESCO Doc. 31C/Res.25, (Nov. 2, 2001), *available at* http://unesdoc.unesco.org/images/0012/001271/127160m.pdf [hereinafter UNESCO Declaration]; UNESCO, *Preliminary Draft of a Convention on the Protection of the Diversity of Cultural Contents and Artistic Expressions*, UNESCO Doc. CLT/CPD/2004/CONF-201/2, July, 2004, *available at* http://portal.unesco.org/culture/en/file_download.php/1076646d dafe81baa79c6213f7a9190eEng-PreliminaryDraftConv-conf201-2.pdf [hereinafter UNESCO First Draft Convention]; UNESCO, *Preliminary Draft Convention on the Protection and Promotion of Cultural Diversity, available in Preliminary Report by the Director-General Setting Out the Situation to Be Regulated and the Possible Scope of the Regulating Action Proposed*, annex V, UNESCO Doc. 33 C/23 (Aug. 4, 2005), http://portal.unesco.org/culture/en/file_download.php/2962532f35a06baebb19 9d30ce52956233C23_Eng.pdf [hereinafter UNESCO Second Draft Convention]. During the final editing stage of this Article, on October 20, 2005, the UNESCO Second Draft Convention was adopted by the 33rd Session of the UNESCO General Conference, as the *Convention on the Protection and Promotion of the Diversity of Cultural Expressions*. Press Release, UNESCO Bureau of Public Information, General Conference Adopts Convention on the Protection and Promotion of the Diversity of Cultural Expressions (Oct. 20, 2005), http://portal.unesco.org/culture/en/ev.php-URL_ID=29078&URL_DO=DO_TO PIC&URL_SECTION=201.html.

[5] *See* Agreement on Trade-Related Aspects of Intellectual Property Rights, Apr. 15, 1994, Marrakesh Agreement Establishing the World Trade Organization, Annex 1C, Legal Instruments—Results of the Uruguay Round, 33 I.L.M. 1125, art. 22.1 (1994) [hereinafter TRIPS Agreement] (defining GIs as "indications which identify a good as originating in the territory of a member, or a region or locality in that territory, where a given quality, reputation or other characteristic of the good is essentially attributable to its geographical origin"). This is, however, to some extent a restrictive legal definition. The concept of GIs as eligible for legal protection may be considerably broader, encompassing both "indications of source" (simply indicating the place of production), and "appellations of origin" (indicating a place of production that enjoys certain local environmental characteristics), although the meaning of "geographical indications" in the Agreement on Trade Related Aspects of Intellectual Property Rights ("TRIPS") falls between the two previous terms. BERNARD O'CONNOR, THE LAW OF GEOGRAPHICAL INDICATIONS 22–23 (2004). For this Article's purposes, GIs also include traditional non-geographical names, to which similar considerations apply, see *infra* note 12.

rationale for the expansion and strengthening of the international legal protection of GIs.[6] Historical experience and empirical evidence, especially in the area of the protection of European wine appellations, show that the national and international legal enforcement of GIs and similar measures has been ineffective in the prevention of cultural transformation and evolution. This includes enforcement brought by transnational and cross-cultural influences that have displaced preexisting traditions and to degrees of cultural homogenization. More broadly, these findings will demonstrate that trade-restrictive or otherwise economically distortive measures are not a dependable means of preserving local culture and traditions, thus casting doubts upon the validity of cultural exceptions in international trade and culture law in general.

Despite common prejudice,[7] building on food history and sociology to perform a cultural inquiry into this specific topic is neither esoteric nor frivolous. This approach directly addresses one of the underlying complexities of an ongoing trade war (that might be termed the "World War of the Two Beans"[8]), the contest

---

[6] This does not necessarily imply that other rationales for such protection, such as wealth maximization or consumer protection, do not have merit. These arguments are, however, dealt with in an extensive body of literature. *See, e.g.,* O'CONNOR, *supra* note 5, at 389–404 (exploring proposals for extending GIs and their costs and benefits). This Article aims to query only the validity of the cultural justification. Furthermore, it is argued that the extension of article 23 of TRIPS "additional protection" for GIs, as explained below, is justified in order to remove the current bias against GIs from developing countries.

[7] "Young scholars who are interested in food history are routinely advised not to go near the subject until their *second* book, *after* tenure." Warren Belasco, *Food Matters: Perspectives on an Emerging Field, in* FOOD NATIONS: SELLING TASTE IN CONSUMER SOCIETIES 3 (Warren Belasco & Philip Scranton eds., 2002).

[8] The original "War of the Two Beans" ("*La Guerre des Deux Haricots*") was a satirical editorial published in the French *Le Figaro* on September 5, 1908. It lampooned the political struggle for the legal protection of agricultural products and their geographical names in France as instigated primarily by producers of fine wines. "According to *Le Figaro*, hostilities began in the provinces of France, satirically dubbed the Kingdom of Little Peas. Two Beans, each originating from a different region, confronted each other at the market. One Bean argued that he was the superior vegetable, representative of the refined riches of the Kingdom, endowed with 'unique qualities' and heir to a rich historical legacy. His opposing legume, in the outlandish dialogue that followed, blasted these assertions by laying claim to very similar 'unique qualities.'" Kolleen M. Guy, *Wine, Champagne and the Making of French Identity in the Belle Epoque, in* FOOD, DRINK AND IDENTITY: COOKING, EATING AND DRINKING IN EUROPE SINCE THE MIDDLE AGES 163, 163 (Peter Scholliers ed., 2001); *see also* KOLLEEN M. GUY, WHEN CHAMPAGNE BECAME FRENCH: WINE AND THE MAKING OF A NATIONAL IDENTITY 144–47 (2003) (describing War of

628   *U. Pa. J. Int'l Econ. L.*   [Vol. 26:4

over the degree, nature, and scope of the international legal protection to be granted to place and place-related names associated with foods, beverages, and other products[9] (e.g., Parma ham,[10] Darjeeling tea,[11] Feta cheese,[12] and Budvar beer).[13] The

---

the Two Beans in further detail). The success of French wine and food producers to solicit legal protection at the national level has been replicated in the European Union, and in the World Trade Organization ("WTO") as well. *See infra* notes 16–17.

[9] For a particularly illuminating presentation and analysis of the GI debate, see Elizabeth Barham, *Translating Terroir: The Global Challenge of French AOC Labeling*, 19 J. RURAL STUD. 127 (2003) (focusing, *inter alia*, on the notion of *terroir* — essentially the unique connection between place and product that indeed lies at the basis of the entire GI concept). *Terroir* is undoubtedly part of the cultural justification of GIs discussed here (*see infra* Section 3), but it is not identical to it. *Terroir* also has significant non-cultural technical aspects (mainly climate and geology) and may act as the basis for the consumer protection rationale of GI rights, without requiring recourse to cultural arguments. Conversely, the cultural aspects of GIs are not contingent on the scientific validity of *terroir*. *See generally* JACQUES FANET, GREAT WINE TERROIRS (Florence Brutton trans., Univ. Cal. Press 2004) (2001) (exploring the geological basis of wine *terroirs*); JAMES E. WILSON, TERROIR: THE ROLE OF GEOLOGY, CLIMATE, AND CULTURE IN THE MAKING OF FRENCH WINES (1998).

[10] Indicative of some of the related international legal complications, Parma ham has enjoyed protection as a GI in the European Union, in line with Italian law, since the early 1990s but it has also been a registered trademark in Canada held by Maple Leaf Meats since 1964. O'CONNOR, *supra* note 5, at 101–02; *see also* Case C-108/01, Consorzio del Prosciutto di Parma v. Asda Stores Ltd., 2003 E.C.R. I-5163 (addressing the amount of intellectual property protection granted to Parma ham).

[11] Darjeeling, the name of a town in the West Bengal state of India famed for the tea it produces, is also a registered trademark in the United States. U.S. Trademark Reg. No. 2,685,923. *See* Naba Kumar Das, Chairman of the Tea Board India, Presentation to the World Intellectual Property Organization's Worldwide Symposium on GIs: Protection of Darjeeling Tea (July 9–11, 2003), WIPO/GEO/SFO/03/8, *available at* http://www.wipo.int/meetings/2003/geo-ind/en/documents/pdf/wipo_geo_sfo_03_8a.pdf (arguing for the strengthening of the Darjeeling tea GI); Niranjan Rao, *Geographical Indications in Indian Context: A Case Study of Darjeeling Tea* (Indian Council for Research on Int'l Econ. Relations, Working Paper No. 110, 2003) (discussing how the TRIPS Agreement applies to Darjeeling Tea).

[12] Feta is an example of a place-related food name that is not strictly speaking a GI since there is, in fact, no relevant geographical place called Feta, which simply means slice or slab in Greek. Under EU law, however, Feta is considered a "traditional non-geographical name" worthy of protection similar to GIs. It is therefore protected as a Protected Designation of Origin ("PDO"). *See* O'CONNOR, *supra* note 5, at 130–31 n. 33 (explaining the basis of protection of Feta under EU law). The arguments relating to food, trade and culture presented in this Article essentially apply to PDOs as well as GIs.

[13] Budvar is the Czech name for the town of Budweis, the qualitatively unlikely source for the famous commercial U.S. beer brand Budweiser, which is

weight of the business interests involved should by itself justify our awareness. The manner in which cultural rationalization has been drawn into this legal-economic field should, however, be of no less concern.

Reflecting its importance in human exchange, food and drink have acquired a special status in international trade law. In the current Doha round of trade negotiations of the WTO,[14] it has become clear that the international regulation of the production, consumption, and commercial exchange of food products (at least partially captured by the label "trade in agriculture")[15] is the ultimate deal-breaker. In disputes adjudicated in the WTO dispute settlement system, food products attract a particularly bright spotlight,[16] as they have in the European Union[17] and under the North American Free Trade Agreement ("NAFTA").[18] In these contexts, not just food itself, but also food "security" and "safety"

---

trademarked in the United States and elsewhere. The conflict between the American Budweiser and Budéjovický Budvar, the Czech manufacturer of Budweiser Budvar, has reached the WTO's dispute settlement system. Report of the Panel, *European Communities – Protection of Trademarks and Geographical Indications for Agricultural Products and Foodstuffs*, WT/DS174, ¶ 7.573 (Mar. 15, 2005) [hereinafter *EC – GIs*].

[14] I am referring to the negotiations under the 2001 Doha Declaration. World Trade Organization, Ministerial Declaration of 14 November 2001, WT/MIN(01)/DEC/1, 41 I.L.M. 746 (2002) [hereinafter DDA].

[15] Of course, agricultural trade is both broader and narrower than trade in food. On the one hand it encompasses non-food products such as cotton, while on the other hand important food products, most notably fish, have been excluded from the ambit of agricultural trade disciplines. *E.g.*, Agreement on Agriculture, annex 1, ¶ 1, Apr. 15, 1994, Marrakesh Agreement Establishing the World Trade Organization, Annex 1A, Legal Instruments – Results of the Uruguay Round, 1867 U.N.T.S. 410 (1994).

[16] By a rough count, approximately 40% of WTO disputes relate to edible products. For some of the more famous to reach Appellate Body adjudication, see Appellate Body Report, *Japan – Taxes on Alcoholic Beverages*, WT/DS8/AB/R, WT/DS10/AB/R, WT/DS11/AB/4 (Oct. 4, 1996); Appellate Body Report, *EC – Measures Concerning Meat and Meat Products (Hormones)*, WT/DS26/AB/R, WT/DS48/AB/R (Jan. 16, 1998); Appellate Body Report, *United States – Import Prohibition of Certain Shrimp and Shrimp Products*, WT/DS58/AB/R (Oct. 12, 1998).

[17] *See, e.g.*, Case 120/78, Rewe-Zentral AG v. Bundesmonopolverwaltung für Branntwein, 1979 E.C.R. 649 (the *Cassis de Dijon* case, addressing a trade dispute concerning liqueurs and spirits).

[18] One such example is the Canada–United States "beer wars" that ensued initially under GATT but were carried over to the North America Free Trade Agreement ("NAFTA") in the anti-dumping context. *See* NAFTA Binational Panel Report, *Certain Malt Beverages from the United States (Injury)*, CDA-95-1904-1 (Nov. 15, 1995) (addressing complaints over the importation of malt beverages).

630   *U. Pa. J. Int'l Econ. L.*   [Vol. 26:4

have become important terms, highlighting the additional sensitivities that accompany edible commodities.[19]

On this background, the issue of geographic indications ("GIs") has emerged on two main fronts in the WTO. First is the front of international negotiation. Paragraph 18 of the Declaration of the WTO 2001 Ministerial Conference (the Doha Development Agenda ("DDA")) places two items relating to GIs on the DDA negotiating table: (i) creating a multilateral system for notification and registration for wines and spirits, under article 23.4 of the Agreement on Trade Related Aspects of Intellectual Property Rights ("TRIPS");[20] and (ii) the extension of article 23 of TRIPS "additional protection" of GIs (i.e., protection granted even when there is no risk of misleading consumers or unfair competition) to products other than wines and spirits. The latter point, although formally designated as a DDA paragraph 12 "implementation" issue, essentially entails the potential introduction of new rights and obligations for WTO members. The outcome of these negotiations will determine the scope of statutory protection granted to GIs for years to come.

The second front is that of international litigation. The question of GIs and their protection under TRIPS has inevitably been subjected to WTO dispute settlement.[21] A WTO panel recently issued a report with regard to a challenge by Australia and the United States to the existing legislation of the European Union on GIs. The Panel Report found that significant components of the European Union's GI legislation are TRIPS-inconsistent, while other aspects have been upheld by the panel as WTO-consistent.[22]

---

[19] For a document that places both terms in the context of the right to food as a human right, see Food and Agriculture Organization Council, *Report of the 30th Session of the Committee on World Food Security, Supplement, Final Report of the Chair*, CL 127/10-Sup.1 (2004), *available at* http://www.fao.org/docrep/meeting/008/J3345e/j3345e01.htm (arguing for a voluntary set of guidelines to support the progressive realization of the right to adequate food in the context of national food security).

[20] *See* DDA, *supra* note 14, at 4 (declaring the intention to establish "a multilateral system of notification and registration of geographical indications for wines and spirits").

[21] *See, e.g., EC-GIs, supra* note 13, at 129.

[22] The dispute dealt mainly with two issues: first, whether the European Community's legislation on GI protection discriminates against non-EC GIs (by granting them less than national treatment); and second, whether a registered trademark and EC-recognized GI that are identical can coexist in EC commerce.

To be sure, in both arenas the debate has focused on technical, legal, and economic considerations that characterize much of the application of GI protection in international and domestic law. There is a distinct cultural backdrop, however, that is often ignored or taken for granted: the assumption that beyond the private interest and public welfare effects of legal protection, GIs are required for the preservation of local traditions, national culture, and cultural diversity. Arguably, this assertion is necessary to justify the inclusion of GIs in intellectual property disciplines that are usually aimed at encouraging the interests of innovation and individual creativity through the grant of a temporary monopoly.[23] GI rights do not represent these values, as they express commonly used place-names, establish permanent communal rights, and are ostensibly maintained to protect "old knowledge."[24] The notion of GIs as cultural guardians compensates for this justificatory deficiency, providing an alternative quasi-intellectual property theoretical basis.

The main proponent of this cultural rationale is the European Union, which has also broadened the cultural argument to apply to developing countries, claiming that GIs "are key to EU and developing countries cultural heritage, traditional methods of production and natural resources."[25] Indeed, the claim that GIs

---

See Report of the Panel, *European Communities — Protection of Trademarks and Geographical Indications for Agricultural Products and Foodstuffs*, WT/DS290/R (Mar. 15, 2005) (detailing Australia's claim of discrimination by the European Union against non-EU countries regarding the protection of GIs); *see also EC-GIs, supra* note 13, at 120–24 (stating that article 14(3) of the TRIPS Agreement does not prevent the registration of a GI on the basis that its use would affect any prior trademark outside a subset of trademarks which excludes trademarks with no reputation, renown, or use). Consistent with these rulings, Budweiser can coexist in EC commerce. *Id.*

[23] *See, e.g.,* Karl Shell, *Toward a Theory of Inventive Activity and Capital Accumulation,* 56 AM. ECON. REV. 62, 64 (1966) (noting that in the United States the legal concept of the patent was attached to various inventive outputs to secure its economic value and impact); Allyn A. Young, *Increasing Returns and Economic Progress,* 38 ECON. J. 527, 533 (1928) (describing how economic progress comes from changes initiating more change which "becomes progressive and propagates itself in a cumulative way").

[24] "Old Knowledge" is sometimes a euphemism for tradition and culture. *See* Dutfield, *supra* note 3, at 23 (discussing the argument that what characterizes something as traditional is not "its antiquity, but the way it is acquired and used").

[25] Delegation of the European Commission to Japan, *Why Do Geographical Indications Matter to Us?*, EU Background Note 01/04, Feb. 10, 2004, http://jpn.cec.eu.int/home/news_en_newsobj553.php [hereinafter EU Back-

can protect local culture has also been taken up by certain developing countries that are understandably interested in acquiring enhanced international GI protection for products other than wine and spirits.[26] Given that most GI wines and spirits are produced in developed countries, the current law places developing countries at a disadvantage. Moreover, the proposition that GI protection can help preserve tradition (or can be justified on this basis) is usually taken at face value.[27] Critically examining this assumption in this Article, I do not wish to argue that local culture and traditions are unworthy of protection, nor that cultural diversity should not be encouraged, but only that history as well as informed economic analysis demonstrate that GIs are a questionable way of doing so. Indeed, this will lead to more general conclusions on the legal protection of culture through trade restrictions with applications that transcend the current study of GIs.

In keeping with its subject matter, this Article will follow the path of five courses and a bit more. After this (hopefully appetizing) introduction, Section 2, titled "*Primi:* Trade Law, Culture, Food, and Wine" will expand on the more general context of the trade-culture nexus. First, I will briefly describe existing

---

ground Note].

[26] *See, e.g.,* Council for Trade-Related Aspects of Intellectual Property Rights, *Minutes of Meeting Held in the Centre William Rappard on 25–27 and 29 November, and 20 December 2002,* IP/C/M/38 at 41 (Feb. 5, 2003) (documenting intervention by the delegate from Thailand, who asserted that "[e]xtension was important because GIs were often related to culture and ancestors' traditional knowledge"); Council for Trade-Related Aspects of Intellectual Propert Rights, *Minutes of Meeting Held in the Centre William Rappard on 25-27 June 2002,* IP/C/M/36/Add.1 at 9–10 (Sept. 10, 2002) (noting that several countries have co-sponsored a proposal by India to extend GI protections to teas, coffees, rice, bananas, carpets, handicraft, and other products). Also, most of the third-parties in the *EC-GIs,* Panel proceedings were developing countries. See *EC-GIs, supra* note 13, for a review of the number of developing countries acting as third-parties in such proceedings.

[27] For example, Echols states,

> The preservation of traditions and of community values may be of such significance that it helps to define and to distinguish a neighborhood or a community. Traditions maintain a sense of community and society. Traditions made 'new' could offer a lifeline to a rural community and might offer enough cachet for a few of its young adults who otherwise would flee to the city. Communities could be beneficiaries of the use of GI's.

Marsha A. Echols, *Geographical Indications for Foods, TRIPS, and the Doha Development Agenda,* 47 J. Afr. L. 199, 201 (2003) (footnote omitted).

perceptions of the relationship between culture as a "national" or localized ideal, on one hand, and "globalization," as a universalized counter-notion, on the other hand. I will discuss the broad scope of conceivable conflicts between international trade disciplines and national or local cultural assets and policies, as expressed by and expressive of three dimensions of culture: production, consumption, and identity. Thereafter, food and wine will be drawn into the fray not merely as agents of subsistence, ingestion, or intoxication but as reflective of culture, in the specialized local/national and global diversity senses.

In Section 3, titled "*Secondi*: The Romance of Reputation—The Case for Cultural Protection Through Geographical Indications," I will present an informal, positive (yet romantic) theory of the law and economics of cultural protection through GIs, and expand on the role of cultural justification in existing perceptions of GIs. In this regard, particular attention will be granted to the previously identified cultural dimensions of production, consumption, and identity.

In Section 4, titled "*Contorni*: Markets and Tradition—Some Contrary Economic and Cultural Realities of the Food and Wine Trade" will examine specific factual aspects of the history of the wine and food trade that contradict the romantic view of GIs as possible protectors of culture. These will ultimately expose the cultural rationalization of GIs, and its underlying legal and economic theory as unpersuasive.

In Section 5, titled "*Dolci*: The Future of Cultural Protection in WTO Law," I will summarize conclusions from the investigation of the cultural aspects of GIs, and argue that GIs are inadequate cultural protectors, and that the cultural rationale should not influence the outcome of the Doha Round on these issues. More generally, I will draw some lessons for the future role to be played by cultural protection exceptions and argumentation, in three legal areas: *sui generis* trade restrictions (such as GIs), the employment and possible expansion of Article XX of GATT and Article XIV of GATS as a general "cultural exception" to trade disciplines, and the establishment of a separate international legal regime for cultural diversity, as suggested in the UNESCO Draft Convention, that would impact upon WTO law.

A short *Digestivo* will follow, offering a few thoughts on the nature of cultural diversity and culture-based protectionism.

2.   *PRIMI*: TRADE LAW, CULTURE, FOOD, AND WINE

2.1. *On Culture and Globalization*

The popular perception of the effects of globalization on world cultures is the apocalypse of a "McWorld": "[T]he onrush of economic and ecological forces that demand integration and uniformity . . . pressing nations into one commercially homogenous global network . . . ."[28]   In this vision, fragile local social and cultural structures are erased by exposure to powerful external forces.   These are brought to bear by the onslaught of electronic telecommunications (an argument first presented by Herbert Schiller, well before the advent of the internet)[29] and other enhanced transnational interactions, which promote a global culture of "consumerism."   This acculturation couples with free trade to cause local customs, products, and production methods to be vanquished by foreign, globally available alternatives.   The global proliferation of standardized products of mass culture thus threatens to stifle national and local modes of cultural expression.[30]

Beyond this stylized depiction, however, we must acknowledge the wealth of nuanced and constantly developing theorizing on globalization and culture.   Of course, the basic scenario owes much to Neo-Marxist thought, for it is often asserted that the devastation of local cultures is the product of a triumph of cultural hegemony[31] or cultural imperialism[32] on the ideological battleground of culture.[33] The result of which, in the "third world" context, is westernization or "Americanization."   These views,

---

[28] Benjamin R. Barber, *Jihad vs. McWorld*, ATLANTIC MONTHLY, Mar. 1992, at 53, 53; *see also* BENJAMIN R. BARBER, JIHAD VS. MCWORLD: HOW GLOBALISM AND TRIBALISM ARE RESHAPING THE WORLD (Ballantine Books 1996).

[29] *SEE* HERBERT I. SCHILLER, MASS COMMUNICATIONS AND AMERICAN EMPIRE 112 (1969) ("Everywhere local culture is facing submersion from the mass-produced outpourings of commercial broadcasting").

[30] *See generally* JÜRGEN HABERMAS, THE POSTNATIONAL CONSTELLATION: POLITICAL ESSAYS 72-112 (Max Pensky ed. & trans., MIT Press 2001) (1998) (analyzing the dichotomies of modern globalization).

[31] "Cultural hegemony" may grossly simplify the Gramscian term. *See, e.g.,* ANTONITO GRAMSCI, SELECTIONS FROM THE PRISON NOTEBOOKS (Quintin Hoare & Geoffrey Nowell Smith eds. & trans., Int'l Publishers 1971).

[32] For a full and critical exposition of the term, see generally JOHN TOMLINSON, CULTURAL IMPERIALISM: A CRITICAL READER (1991).

[33] Immanuel Wallerstein, *Culture as the Ideological Battleground of the Modern World-System*, 7 THEORY, CULTURE & SOCIETY 31, 31 (1990).

however, are wide open to criticism from all corners. For example, it has been argued that the notion of western cultural domination is itself a self-serving western concept, that "'[c]ultural imperialism' is a critical discourse which operates by representing the cultures whose autonomy it defends in its own (dominant) Western cultural terms."[34] Some theorists reject the danger of the domination by a western monoculture, observing instead the emergence of "global cultures in the plural."[35] Others explain how national cultures have post-modernly "reconceived themselves in order to persist in an era of intensified globalization."[36]

Though much of the following analysis may modestly contribute to the discussion, for immediate purposes it is not necessary to enter this debate. Few, if any, would argue that globalization, however conceived, does not produce *any* changes in local cultures and traditions. Indeed, signaling that there is at least some consensus on the existence of the problem, UNESCO has been exploring the loss of cultural diversity due to economic pressures for a decade.[37] The academic and at times ideological debate is thus primarily descriptive (inquiring as to the nature and extent of the changes produced) or normative (inquiring if the changes are positive or negative). The fact that the phenomena exist is not usually questioned.

---

[34] TOMLINSON, *supra* note 32, at 2.

[35] MIKE FEATHERSTONE, CONSUMER CULTURE AND POSTMODERNISM 10 (1991); *see also* Ulf Hannerz, *Cosmopolitans and Locals in World Culture, in* 7 THEORY, CULTURE & SOCIETY 237, 243-44 (1990) (noting the interaction of territorial cultures with occupationally divided, transnational cultures).

[36] FREDERICK BUELL, NATIONAL CULTURE AND THE NEW GLOBAL SYSTEM 12 (1994). *See generally* JOHN R. HALL & MARY JO NEITZ, CULTURE: SOCIOLOGICAL PERSPECTIVES (1993); CULTURE, GLOBALIZATION AND THE WORLD SYSTEM: CONTEMPORARY CONDITIONS FOR THE REPRESENTATION OF IDENTITY (Anthony D. King ed., 1997); GEORGE RITZER, THE MCDONALDIZATION THESIS (1998); 12 PUB. CULTURE (2000) (providing background material on *Globalization* (issue 12.1), *Millennial Capitalism and the Culture of Neoliberalism* (issue 12.2), and *Cosmopolitanism* (issue 12.3)).

[37] *See, e.g.,* UNESCO, OUR CREATIVE DIVERSITY: REPORT OF THE WORLD COMMISSION ON CULTURE AND DEVELOPMENT, http://kvc.minbuza.nl/uk/archive/report/intro.html (last visited Nov. 15, 2005) (establishing that, in 1993, UNESCO founded the World Commission on Culture and Development to explore the relationship between culture and development). For a more recent discussion of the effect of development on culture, see *Round Table of Ministers of Culture: Final Report, in* UNESCO, 2000-2010: CULTURAL DIVERSITY: CHALLENGES OF THE MARKETPLACE, (2000) *available at* http://www.unesco.org/culture/development/highlights/texts/html_eng/Rap portFinal-Eng.rtf.

636   *U. Pa. J. Int'l Econ. L.*   [Vol. 26:4

2.2. *Trade and Cultural Dimensions: Production, Consumption, Identity*

The "trade and culture" debate characterizes trade—or, rather, trade liberalization as enforced through the reciprocal trade obligations of the GATT/WTO and regional trade agreements—as an agent of the forces of global cultural change. Free trade brings new imported products, services, and production methods to the domestic market; each potentially a cultural influence that alters local tradition. Clearly, those who feel that their culture is at risk because of exposure to such global influences will protest and confront the international law that facilitates it.[38] In the context of trade, however, it is just as likely that those whose economic, non-cultural interests are threatened by international competition will use cultural arguments as a protectionist defense. Thus, as in many other trade-related or "trade and ——" issue areas,[39] strange bed-fellowships may form to resist change. Marxists and capitalists, cottage industries and multinational corporations, artisans and industrialists may all argue that national culture is being compromised by international trade. As in other interactions between trade and non-trade values, the problem is in drawing the line between disguised trade protectionism and bona fide cultural policy, a dilemma that clearly arises when trade disciplines and cultural interests clash.

In the existing legal and regulatory spheres, conflicts between trade liberalization and cultural policy can arise in a broad variety

---

[38] *See generally* Russell Mokhiber & Robert Weissman, *Top 10 Reasons to Shutter the WTO*, MOTHER JONES, Nov. 24, 1999, http://www.motherjones .com/news/feature/1999/11/fotc12.html (citing "prioritization of commercial over other values" as a fundamental flaw of the WTO); *Weekend Edition: Saving Slow Food in Turin by Sulvia Poggioli* (NPR radio broadcast Nov. 7, 2004) *available at* http://www.npr.org/templates/story/story.php?storyId=4157137 (documenting a "taste fair" in Turin, Italy that "grew out of a protest against the opening of the first McDonalds in Rome"); Irene McConnell, *Looking Back at the "Battle Of Seattle": Understanding the WTO, and the Roots of Civil Society's Rage*, POST, Summer 2000, *available at* http://www.ualberta.ca/PARKLAND/post/Vol-IV-No2/05mcconn ell.html ("[C]ommunal identity needs to he nurtured and protected against those who insist that culture is a commodity subject to the laws and values of the market place").

[39] For a broad perspective on the issues concerning the "trade and ——" problem, see generally Meinhard Hilf & Goetz J. Goettsche, *The Relation of Economic and Non-Economic Principles in International Law*, *in* INTERNATIONAL ECONOMIC GOVERNANCE AND NON-ECONOMIC CONCERNS: NEW CHALLENGES FOR THE INTERNATIONAL LEGAL ORDER 5 (Stefan Griller ed., 2003), and Symposium, *The Boundaries of the WTO*, 96 AM. J. INT'L L. 1 (2002).

of trade contexts. Prohibitive tariffs, import bans, quantitative restrictions, discriminatory taxation, subsidies, domestic content requirements, regulatory prohibitions, licensing restrictions, and foreign investment constraints have all been used[40] — and in some cases challenged[41] — *inter alia*, in the name of cultural protection. The propensity of trade disciplines to interfere with cultural policy is thus obvious. On the non-trade, cultural side of the coin, the question therefore arises: what is actually being protected by cultural policy? For many reasons, the "trade and culture" debate has so far centered on the film and television industries, "to the extent that the term 'culture' became synonymous with the word 'audiovisual.'"[42] Yet the recent *U.S.–Gambling* case and references to culture in broader contexts show (as should perhaps be self-evident) that culture is much more than television[43] — indeed, cultural aspects may be found in virtually any aspect of human activity. The UNESCO Declaration[44] goes so far as to state virtually all-inclusively that "culture should be regarded as the set of distinctive spiritual, material, intellectual and emotional features of society or a social group, and that it encompasses, in addition to art and literature, lifestyles, ways of living together, value systems, traditions and beliefs."[45]

It therefore seems futile to undertake the task of comprehensively defining or delimiting "culture." Instead, assuming that culture is an inherently broad and subjectively delimited concept, it would perhaps be more effective to identify the *dimensions* of culture — however defined — that may be affected by trade in *any* good or service (generally, the culture-related aspects of trade). To this end, let us simply assume that culture, generally conceived as a value, may be attached to all forms of

---

[40] *See* Mary E. Footer & Christoph B. Graber, *Trade Liberalization and Cultural Policy*, 3 J. INT'L. ECON. L. 115, 122–26 (2000) (surveying the usual measures by which WTO member countries pursue national cultural policies to regulate the trade of audiovisual media).

[41] *See, e.g.,* Appellate Body Report, *Canada – Certain Measures Concerning Periodicals*, WTO Doc. WT/DS31/AB/R (1997); *US – Gambling II, supra* note 2. *See infra* Section 5.2 (discussing *sui generis* cultural protection in greater detail).

[42] Footer & Graber, *supra* note 40, at 119.

[43] *US – Gambling II, supra* note 2.

[44] UNESCO Declaration, *supra* note 4.

[45] *Id.* at pmbl.; *see also id.* art. 1 (noting the objectives of the convention to be protection and promotion of cultural diversity; encouragement of respect, free evolution, and interaction of culture; and facilitation of the development and adoption of policies to advance such diversity, evolution, and interaction).

638 *U. Pa. J. Int'l Econ. L.* [Vol. 26:4

human exploit and existence. In the trade context, imagine a commoditized and valorized human effort, a widget, which has, in this sense, some constituent cultural value (note that a widget service, rather than good, may also qualify). The UNESCO First Draft Convention followed a similar conceptual approach (in article 4) by defining "Cultural Goods and Services" as goods, services and other activities that embody or yield "Cultural Expressions," which are in turn defined as either "Cultural Content" (the symbolic meaning or cultural values communicated or conveyed by the good, service or activity) or "Artistic Expression" (the result of creative work or aesthetic creation).[46] The relationship between Cultural Content and Artistic Expression in the UNESCO First Draft Convention is not entirely clear, but it appears that the drafters considered all creative and aesthetic work to be an expression of culture, even if it has no "Cultural Content" — i.e., it has no symbolic value or intrinsic cultural value. Moreover, in the UNESCO Second Draft Convention, reference to "Artistic Expressions" has been dropped and merged into the broader term of "Cultural Expressions," and the term "Cultural Goods and Services" has been expanded to include "Cultural Activities," which may contribute to the production of cultural goods and services or be an end in themselves.[47]

Returning to the present analysis (and departing from the sometimes awkward definitions of the UNESCO Draft Conventions), it is suggested that a widget may generally become cultural in three possible (but non-mutually exclusive) ways: through the culture of its *production*; the culture of its *consumption*; or the culture of its *identity*. More specifically:

The culture of production:[48] In this sense, it is the process of the

---

[46] UNESCO First Draft Convention, *supra* note 4, art. 4.

[47] UNESCO Second Draft Convention, *supra* note 4, art. 4.

[48] This cultural attribute superficially corresponds to the requirement in article 4(4)(a) of the UNESCO First Draft Convention that "Cultural Goods or Services" be the "outcome of human labour (industrial, artistic or artisanal) and require the exercise of human creativity for their production." UNESCO First Draft Convention, *supra* note 4, art. 4(4)(a). On one hand, however, the inclusion of the "industrial" category of labor expands the definition to include mass-produced goods and services that might otherwise have been considered of no particular value in the sense of a "culture of production" as employed here. On the other hand, the current wording of this article appears to establish this requirement as one of a series of cumulative conditions for the existence of a "Cultural Good or Service," so that mass-produced goods might not be considered "cultural" if they did not "express or convey some form of symbolic

widget's creation and/or the method of its production that ordain it with cultural value that is to be protected. A painting, a literary manuscript or a musical score would quite clearly fall into this category; but such widgets may also be cultural in the manner of their consumption, not just their production. More restrictively, a widget's culture-ness may be related to production without even being apparent in the use of the finished product. For example, a handmade kilim that will lie on the floor and be trod upon by muddy boots can hardly be said to have cultural value unless one acknowledges the artisanal craft involved in its production;[49] the same function can be fulfilled by mass-produced, synthetic rugs. In this category, the assault of globalization threatens not the commodity produced but its underlying productive culture. The loss of the product due to cultural homogenization and mass-culture is not, perhaps, the true cultural cost. Like the pottery of Cipriano Algor in Saramago's *The Cave*,[50] it is the method of production and the lifestyle that both supports it and is supported by it, that may be displaced by alternative products, industrial substitutes, and indifferently shifting consumer tastes. The consumer may be oblivious to the "make" of the product: a hand-made ceramic vase and machine-made one will do just as well; but the knowledge and culture of handicrafts will be irreparably lost in the process.

The culture of consumption:[51]   In this category, the widget

---

meaning," *id.* art. 4(4)(b), and "generate . . . intellectual property, whether or not they are protected under existing intellectual property legislation," *id.* art. 4(4)(c). This final requirement also raises several problems in the context of GIs (although not directly relevant to the current Article's subject matter and analysis). If cultural protection is granted only to goods that constitute "intellectual property," this may imply an expansion of the latter term beyond its classical definitional confines and rationales. But if for this purpose such intellectual property need not be protected by intellectual property law, how is it to be definitely recognized as intellectual property? Moreover, these issues appear to have been bypassed (if not solved) in the UNESCO Second Draft Convention, which refers to "creativity," but not to "industrial labour" or "intellectual property."

[49] *See, e.g.,* PETER DAVIES, THE TRIBAL EYE: ANTIQUE KILIMS OF ANATOLIA (1993) (discussing the tradition of Kilim weaving).

[50] JOSÉ SARAMAGO, THE CAVE (Margaret Jull Costa trans., Harcourt 2002) (2000).

[51] This is a cultural aspect that appears to have been neglected by the drafters of the UNESCO Draft Convention in defining Cultural Goods and Products, although it may be discerned in several peripheral aspects of the Second Draft Convention, *supra* note 4, art. 4, and in particular in the broad concept of "Cultural Activities."

640 *U. Pa. J. Int'l Econ. L.* [Vol. 26:4

becomes cultural by virtue of the context in which it is consumed, the way it is used. The cultural value of the production of the widget, taken on its own, is not necessarily at risk. For example, the demand for music once spawned a tradition of musical performances, expressed through the sometimes elitist culture of concert and opera attendance, but also that of the dance-hall and the folk musician. When the same performances became available, with enhanced audio quality, through mass-produced long-playing records, the social context of consumption changed, from the communal to the private. Things are more complicated; audio-visual technologies now enable a single artist to publicly perform, live, in front of tens of thousands instead of selected dozens, but here too the context of cultural consumption has changed. Much the same could be said about the shift from cinema to home-viewing via VCRs or pay-per-view video. In academia, a shift in the culture of consumption is evident as more and more primary sources, journals, and books become available online in searchable electronic format. It is no longer necessary to physically browse the bookshelves, leaf through dusty books, and even read through copious amounts of interesting (or not) but irrelevant material. Electronic databases, Google, and other search functions do the hard work. The context of consumption has thus clearly changed, even for literary works whose production cannot have changed, if only because they were produced centuries ago.[52]

The culture of identity:[53] This is perhaps the least tangible manner in which local culture may attach to a widget. In this case, there is nothing idiosyncratic in the widget's production or in its consumption, but culture is nevertheless embedded in the widget by its very existence, and through its content, such that it is

---

[52] For example, the complete works of William Shakespeare are available online in easily accessible electronic and searchable form through several websites. *See, e.g.,* William Shakespeare – Biography and Works, http://www.online-literature.com/shakespeare (last visited Dec. 2, 2005) (offering biographical information about William Shakespeare and searchable versions of all of his texts, as well as delivery of a sonnet per day via e-mail); William Shakespeare at eNotes, http://www.shakespeare.com (last visited Dec. 2, 2005) (making available the text of William Shakespeare's works as well as poetry-related games and activities).

[53] The "culture of identity" that may be attributed to a good or service was expressly acknowledged in the UNESCO First Draft Convention, *supra* note 4, at article 1(a) (identifying cultural goods as vehicles of "identity, values and meaning"), in article 4(4)(b) (using symbolic meaning as component of definition of "Cultural Goods and Services"), and in similar language in the Second Draft Convention, *supra* note 4, in articles 1(a) and 4(4)(b).

somehow representative of a cultural value that is associated with the relevant group's identity. A national flag is a concrete example, though not a very helpful one in the trade perspective. Every nation has a flag, and they are all produced and "consumed" in essentially the same way, yet the graphic content of each one is steeped in a special historiography and imagery that both express and facilitate the creation of national identity.[54]

In the context of identity, a widget becomes cultural by association with a cultural group and through symbolism. In the area of international trade, the dominant issues of audio-visual and other media services demonstrate the centrality of "identity" as a parameter of culture well. The production and consumption of magazines and television programming in Canada and the United States is in essence the same, and, yet, Canada has cited national culture in defense of its policies in these fields.[55] This is not only because Canadian media content is different from U.S. content; rather the content is particularly Canadian—the preservation of which is important for the continuation of Canadian culture. If the Canadian-ness of Canadian magazines were erased by commercial integration, an important part of Canadian identity would ostensibly be obliterated. Clearly, the culture of identity has a strong subjective element, but it cannot be ignored in the trade-culture debate; in fact, it might lie at its core.

To more or less complete this picture, the cultural charge of a widget as assumed on any of these three levels can be either positive or negative. If the traditional method of production is "positively" cultural in representing a local culture of production, the modern, international or dominant foreign method that threatens it becomes a "negatively" cultural widget and its nemesis. For example, if it is argued that local culture is

---

[54] *See, e.g.,* KIT HINRICHS & DELPHINE HIRASUNA, LONG MAY SHE WAVE: A GRAPHIC HISTORY OF THE AMERICAN FLAG (2001) (tracing the evolution of the U.S. flag and the extent to which it has become ingrained in popular U.S. culture); JOHN ROSS MATHESON, CANADA'S FLAG: A SEARCH FOR A COUNTRY (1980) (paralleling the development of the Canadian national flag with the quest for a Canadian national identity).

[55] *See,* KEITH ACHESON AND CHRISTOPHER MAULE, MUCH ADO ABOUT CULTURE: NORTH AMERICAN TRADE DISPUTES (1999) ("National culture is nurtured as a by-product of consuming cultural products."); Chi Carmody, *When 'Cultural Identity Was Not an Issue': Thinking About Canada—Certain Measures Concerning Periodicals,* 30 LAW & POL'Y INT'L. REL. 231 (1999) ("Often there is tension between freer trade and cultural autonomy, principally because of how we think and what we think about.").

642   *U. Pa. J. Int'l Econ. L.*   [Vol. 26:4]

characterized by public morals that abhor gambling or pornography, the cross-border internet services that supply them become "negatively" cultural widgets.

These three dimensions of culture—production, consumption and identity—should help us better understand the cultural basis of the arguments for increased GI protection for food and wine products. However there is first an important aside: are food and wine even remotely "culture"?

2.3. Food and Wine as Culture

There is no question that "food is important,"[56] as the source of nutrition and sustenance, on a world-wide scale. Halving the global proportion of malnutrition and hunger—those who simply do not have access to enough food—regardless of its quality or provenance, has become an internationally agreed upon policy goal.[57] But even if, and when, this target is achieved, the world's hungry will still amount to many hundred millions,[58] by all means a mind-boggling number. Yes, certainly in these terms, food *is* important.

The centrality of food in our human lives far transcends the primary physical context of nourishment, and easily takes on additional cultural or quasi-cultural dimensions. Food is a lucrative, tradable commodity, a foundation of personal and corporate income, a visibly significant component of the economy, and, not least of all, a source of human delight. "There is in fact nothing more basic. Food is the first of the essentials of life, our biggest industry, our greatest export, and our most frequently indulged pleasure."[59] Food is also an important expression of cultural practices, perceptions, and identities, both individual and collective. Brillat-Savarin's celebrated quip on the subject has rightly become a truism.[60] Indeed, following somewhat more

---

[56] Belasco, *supra* note 7, at 2.

[57] G.A. Res. 55/2, ¶ 19, U.N. Doc. A/RES/55/2 (Sept. 8, 2000).

[58] *See* UN, Department of Economic and Social Affairs, *Nutrition, Undernourished as a Percentage of Total Population*, *available at* http://millenniumindicators.un.org/unsd/mi/mi_series_results.asp?rowId=566 (last visited Dec. 2, 2005) (documenting the global toll of hunger).

[59] Belasco, *supra* note 7, at 2.

[60] *See* 1 ANSELME BRILLAT-SAVARIN, PHYSIOLOGIE DU GOUT [PHYSIOLOGY OF TASTE] 3 (Paris, Bibliotheque Nationale 1877) (1825) ("Dis-moi ce que tu manges, je te dirai ce que tu es." ["Tell me what you eat, I will tell you what you are."]). One

rigorous research, anthropologists have similarly concluded that "food is also a symbolic marker of membership (or non-membership) in practically any sort of social grouping."[61] Although not necessary for subsistence, alcoholic drinks are undoubtedly as intertwined with our social imagery as food.[62]

In the clearest historical terms, the most significant shifts in early human development have related to innovative patterns of food production and consumption, most noticeably the move from hunting-gathering to agricultural practices,[63] a harbinger of urbanization, technological progress, and ultimately, industrial production. History can also be convincingly retold through the prism of specific important foodstuffs, such as the potato[64] or chocolate.[65] Throughout considerable chronological space, each human civilization has been characterized not only by its plastic art, literature, and politics, but also — and at least as relevantly, without belaboring the point — by its cuisine and food habits. Food, in this regard, has been likened to language, as an expression of national and local culture.[66]

---

wonders what this says of the individual dignity of each of the aforementioned world's famished.

[61] Sidney W. Mintz, *Food and Eating: Some Persisting Questions*, in FOOD NATIONS: SELLING TASTE IN CONSUMER SOCIETIES, *supra* note 7, at 26.

[62] *See, e.g.*, GIOVANNI REBORA, CULTURE OF THE FORK: A BRIEF HISTORY OF FOOD IN EUROPE 153 (Albert Sonnenfeld trans., 2001) (1998) ("The vine and wine, wrote Fernand Braudel, are products of civilization . . . ."); A. Lynn Martin, *Old People, Alcohol and Identity in Europe, 1300–1700*, in FOOD, DRINK AND IDENTITY: COOKING, EATING AND DRINKING IN EUROPE SINCE THE MIDDLE AGES, *supra* note 8, at 119, 119–37 (discussing how alcohol in the 1300s–1700s was part of the identity of older people in Europe).

[63] *See generally* JARED DIAMOND, GUNS, GERMS AND STEEL: THE FATE OF HUMAN SOCIETIES (1999) (describing the critical role of agricultural endowments on social and economic progress). For a kaleidoscopic work on the interaction between food, history, and society, see REAY TANNAHILL, FOOD IN HISTORY (1973) (showing that the way in which the pursuit of more and better food has helped to direct the movement of history itself).

[64] *See generally* LARRY ZUCKERMAN, THE POTATO: HOW THE HUMBLE SPUD RESCUED THE WESTERN WORLD (1998) (revealing how western domestic and social life functioned by describing how potato achieved its influence on our life today); REDCLIFFE N. SALAMAN, THE HISTORY AND SOCIAL INFLUENCE OF THE POTATO (3rd ed. 1985) (explaining the taxonomy of the potato and its wild relatives, its archaeological background, the history of its discovery and introduction into Europe, and its social and economic history).

[65] *See* SOPHIE D. COE & MICHAEL D. COE, THE TRUE HISTORY OF CHOCOLATE (1996) (describing that, in its history, chocolate had "immense importance socially, religiously, medically, economically, and of course gastronomically").

[66] *See* Mintz, *supra* note 61, at 26 ("Imagine convincing the Russian people to

Thus, food is as an essential element of our culture as any, however defined, albeit perhaps taken for granted by many.[67] It is important at all levels of human individuality and social interaction. Scholars David Bell and Gill Valentine make this point necessarily and comprehensively — in contexts virtually extraneous to the present one — relating the role of food in the political perception of our body, home, community, city, region, nation, and global environment.[68] Indeed, at all levels of analysis, food and drink most easily lend themselves to the production-consumption-identity triad of culture presented above, as the joint crop of the earth and human inventiveness, as goods whose only use is in their physical consumption, and as representatives of significantly broader contexts of identity.

It is therefore evident that food and drink are objects of both trade relations and cultural regard, and as such are likely located at whatever intersections may exist between these two key expressions of human activity. This finding indeed is supported in the Non-Exhaustive List of Cultural Goods and Services in the UNESCO First Draft Convention, in which "culinary traditions" were included under the heading of "cultural activities"[69] (The list has been deleted from the Second Draft Convention.)[70] This approach makes food — and hence GIs for food and wine products — an appropriate focal point for the discussion of the trade-culture nexus. What, then, are the functional and cultural arguments and justifications for utilizing GIs in the regulation of the trade-culture relationship in the context of food and drink?

---

give up black bread in order to eat rice instead! Or the people of China, to give up rice to eat black bread! Such food habits are so close to the core of what culture is that they sometimes function almost like language. As with language, on many occasions people define themselves with food; at the same time, food consistently defines and redefines *them*."). Another dimension of the food-language relationship/analogy, is the role of the language *of* food as an indicator of the relative weight and characterization of food or particular foods in local culture. Those interested in this aspect will find much to explore in REBORA, *supra* note 62. For example, as noted in the translator's preface, Italian has sixty specifically named words for pork or beef sausage, where English has only *sausage* and *salami*. *Id.* at ix.

[67] Mintz, *supra* note 61, at 26.

[68] DAVID BELL & GILL VALENTINE, CONSUMING GEOGRAPHIES: WE ARE WHERE WE EAT (1997).

[69] UNESCO First Draft Convention, *supra* note 4, annex I.

[70] UNESCO Second Draft Convention, *supra* note 4.

3.   *SECONDI*: The Romance Of Reputation – The Case For Cultural Protection Through Geographical Indications

3.1. An Informal Positive Theory of the Law and Economics of Cultural Protection through GIs

Before elaborating on the cultural justifications for GI protection of food and wine products as reflected through the dimensions of production, consumption, and identity, it is helpful to examine the legal and economic functions of GIs in this cultural respect.

As already mentioned, the drive for protection of cultural assets can take virtually any form of protectionist international economic policy.[71]   This is an almost superfluous observation: insofar as trade-related policy – cultural or otherwise – and regardless of its economic merits, seeks to shelter production methods, preserve consumption patterns, and prefer "champion" products of identity, it is clearly diametrically opposed to the market logic of free trade theory.   Liberal free trade essentially sees cultural communities as groups of consumers like any other, which should be permitted to determine the market price or added-value of the cultural content of each widget, in comparison to the freely available, culturally-indifferent alternatives.   Where the community attaches sufficient economic value to the preservation of its real, alleged, or imagined cultural practices and icons, the local cultural widget will prevail.   However, where the economic value of the cultural charge of the widget is low – in terms of the worth of its production and consumption peculiarities and its impact on identity, all as determined by its local market – the market share of the widget may well decrease, enacting significant changes in production and consumption and reflecting uncompetitive "identity" values.   In some cases, the cultural widget may even be excluded entirely from the market – the economic forerunner of cultural extinction.[72]

---

[71] *See* Footer & Graber, *supra* note 40, at 122–26, and the text accompanying note 40 (listing examples of the various devices employed in the name of cultural protection).

[72] One could well conceive of cultural widgets as public goods, and of such cultural sacrifices to the market as "tragedies of the commons," in the sense that private preferences determine the demise of the "cultural" widget.   But if preferences were pooled, it would persist.   *See generally* Garrett Hardin, *The Tragedy of the Commons*, 162 Science 1243 (1968) (discussing the original

It is in these instances that economic cultural-protection measures may become relevant. Culture may be highly valued collectively, but if aggregate individual consumer demand cannot independently sustain the cultural widget in the face of non-cultural but otherwise functionally substitutable products, the widget's economic survival requires regulatory protection for its preservation.[73] In the cross-boundary context, the most obviously pursuable measures to this end are protective tariffs and discriminatory taxation designed to preserve current domestic production and consumption methods and patterns. Of course, these may likely contravene the most basic GATT/WTO non-discrimination disciplines such as Article I of GATT Most-Favored Nation Treatment and Article III of GATT National Treatment, and related rules in regional trade arrangements. This has indeed been the outcome in the relevant jurisprudence.[74] Moreover, in these leading cases cultural exceptions were not emphasized, reflecting the absence of an explicit general cultural exception in Article XX of GATT.

---

formulation of the tragedy of the commons in the context of the nuclear race).

[73] The same could be argued about public morals and negatively cultural widgets that offend them, such as gambling services. In this vein, if public morals are indeed publicly held, then arguably they do not need paternalist legislation to uphold them; but see economic analysis suggesting that cultural widgets might be particularly susceptible to market failures in Pierre Suavé & Karsten Steinfatt, *Towards Multilateral Rules on Trade and Culture: Protective Regulation or Efficient Protection?*, in ACHIEVING BETTER REGULATION OF SERVICES: CONFERENCE PROCEEDINGS 323 (Canberra, Austl., June 26–27, 2000), http://www.pc.gov.au/research/confproc/abros/abros.pdf.

[74] For example, the respective taxation schemes of Korea and Japan openly granted significant advantages to the locally distilled rice-based beverage, Soju (in Korea) and Shochu (in Japan), over alternative distilled drinks. *Japan – Taxes on Alcoholic Beverages, supra* note 16, at 34; Appellate Body Report, *Korea – Taxes on Alcoholic Beverages*, WT/DS75/AB/R, WT/DS84/AB/R., at 1 (Jan. 18, 1999). In a less overt fashion, Chile's taxation scheme set a low tax rate for the low alcohol category dominated by the local grape distillate, Pisco, and high tax categories for the higher alcohol categories of imported brandies. Appellate Body Report, *Chile – Taxes on Alcoholic Beverages*, WT/DS87/AB/R, WT/DS110/AB/R (Dec. 13, 1999). All of these taxation measures were found to be non-compliant with WTO rules. In a much earlier GATT case, the target of protection was not local production, but rather local consumption patterns of coffee (presumably for reasons related to inflationary pressures) that were to some extent described as the result of Spanish leisure and food culture. (The Spanish authorities set tariff rates that gave preference to "mild" types of coffee that had previously been purchased by the governmental coffee procurement monopoly.) Report of the Panel, *Spain – Tariff Treatment of Unroasted Coffee*, ¶ 3.14, L/5135 (June 11, 1981), GATT B.I.S.D. (28th Supp.) at 102 (1981).

GIs and their purported contribution to cultural preservation enter this arena in a different, roundabout way; they do not have the same blatantly market-restrictive effects of tariff or tax trade protectionism. It must be emphasized that the first function of GIs — indeed, their primary *raison d'etre* — is not the restriction of international trade with a view towards the safeguarding of culture. Rather, GI mechanisms have been founded on a combined quasi-intellectual property/consumer protection platform. Their initial justification is the prevention of fraud, of "passing off" a good as if it has been sourced from where it has not, ostensibly preventing the dilution of a geographical production area's reputation by low quality — or simply different-quality — produce from another region.[75] At this level of analysis, GI requirements should in theory have virtually no effect on the *intrinsic* value of the GI-protected widget, as they simply inform the consumer of its provenance. In crude neoliberal economic terms, GIs thus could actually be said to promote free trade by facilitating full information, towards perfect market conditions; a cultural widget is simply shielded from non-cultural competition that unfairly uses its GI, permitting consumers to exercise their preferences. In this sense, GI protection needs no additional cultural justification, as it runs with the grain of trade theory and the integration of intellectual property and consumer protection interests and disciplines (however controversial) therein. GI proponents have the ideals of free and informed markets, morally attributable intellectual property rights, and consumer protection on their side; GI opponents or challengers end up in the uneasy seat of protectors of the right to defraud the public unless they can show that the use of the particular GI does not risk confusing

---

[75] This is easily discernable in the language of article 22.2 of the TRIPS Agreement, wherein GIs are intended to prevent "the use of any means in the designation or presentation of a good that indicates or suggests that the good in question originates in a geographical area other than the true place of origin in a manner which misleads the public as to the geographical origin of the good" and "any use which constitutes an act of unfair competition within the meaning of Article 10*bis* of the Paris Convention (1967)." TRIPS Agreement. art 22.2. The "Paris Convention" is the Paris Convention for the Protection of Industrial Property, Mar. 20, 1883, as last revised at Stockholm, July 14, 1967, 21 U.S.T. 1583, 828 U.N.T.S. 305. The Paris Convention is complemented by the Madrid Agreement Concerning the International Registration of Marks, Apr. 14, 1891, 828 U.N.T.S. 389, and the Protocol Relating to the Madrid Agreement Concerning the International Registration of Marks, adopted June 27, 1989, WIPO Pub. No. 204(E).

648   *U. Pa. J. Int'l Econ. L.*   [Vol. 26:4

consumers.[76]

This picture is factually and economically incomplete, however, for a number of reasons. First, the basic consumer protection/perfection of information argument does not in itself justify the institution of a legal GI mechanism, whether at the national or international level. A simpler solution would have been a prohibition on misleading labeling, for example, without establishing quasi-intellectual property rights. Implicit in the GI system is the recognition that not all foods are created equal in their right to protection. Some products deserve protection and others do not; this requires a filtering norm that will allow differentiation between them. In WTO law, this norm is found in article 22.1 of TRIPS: "Geographical indications are, for the purposes of this Agreement, indications which identify a good as originating in the territory of a Member, or a region or locality in that territory, where *a given quality, reputation or other characteristic of the good* is essentially attributable to its geographical origin."[77] Here culture enters as a possible "quality, reputation, or other characteristic of the good" that justifies its GI status. GIs therefore are not just informational; they purport to say something about the specialty of the GI-protected good.

Second, and to some extent as a result, it is often argued that GIs do in fact add value to goods beyond their intrinsic value, particularly when restricted to specific goods and not accorded to all.[78] GIs thus serve a value-enhancing or premium-creating role above and beyond their informative function. It is the specialization and monopolization of the GI brand that achieves this, so that some GI-designated food and beverage products may command higher demand and higher prices than undesignated products — regardless of their actual qualitative or even GI-independent reputational merit. A mediocre product may therefore gain additional economic value simply by virtue of having a GI attached to its label. This may be true regardless of whether the GI was relatively unknown previously or widely celebrated. In any event, it is clear that regulatory and legal protection of GIs constitutes a form of governmental intervention and market manipulation that influences prices, market shares,

---

[76] This type of showing is not allowed in the case of extended GI protection to wine and spirits under article 23 of TRIPS.

[77] TRIPS Agreement art. 22.1 (emphasis added).

[78] *E.g.*, EU Background Note, *supra* note 25.

and trade flows. Trade negotiations, transnational or international litigation, and the rules they produce (including, but not limited to, the applicable filtering norm(s)) therefore determine which products will benefit from added GI-endowed value in the market—a dynamic clearly reminiscent of the War of the Two Beans.[79] Cultural protection enters this debate as an important possible justification for the *additional* value that GIs grant designated products: cultural widgets are supposedly both worth the extra cost and deserving of government intervention and regulation aimed at preserving culture that adds value. Thus, culture is protected in theory not only by distinguishing cultural widgets from the non-cultural, but by valorizing the cultural expression embodied in the widget and converting it into a commercial premium.

Third, international rules on GIs have in substance gone significantly beyond the basic intellectual property/consumer protection rationale. Specifically, GI-protected wines and spirits have, under TRIPS, been given an enhanced degree of safeguarding. GI protection is to be granted even where there is no need for consumer protection. The regular degree of protection[80] essentially establishes exclusive rights of GI use through a rebuttable presumption whereby parallel use of the same GI may cause consumer confusion. Where it can be shown that circumstances exist preventing such confusion, or that effective measures have been taken to this end, GI exclusivity may be relaxed. However, the enhanced GI protection of wines and spirits goes a step further—the risk or existence of consumer confusion is formally immaterial to the degree of protection accorded the GI. Products in this category enjoy a near-absolute degree of exclusivity that prevents the use of the GI by others, even when measures have been taken to prevent confusion, such as clear indications of the true geographical origin of the goods in question, the use of the GIs in translated form or "accompanied by expressions such as 'kind', 'type', 'style', 'imitation' or the like"[81] (such as "Port Style" or "Méthode Champenoise").

As mentioned previously, a central negotiation issue in the DDA talks on GIs is the proposed extension of this "enhanced" or

---

[79] *See supra* note 8 and accompanying text.

[80] *See* TRIPS Agreement art. 22 (describing the level of protection for GIs).

[81] *Id.* art. 23.1.

650   *U. Pa. J. Int'l Econ. L.*   [Vol. 26:4

"additional" protection beyond wines and spirits.[82]   Such an extension may have considerable economic impact on producers and consumers.   Presumably, the value of GIs that have been granted "enhanced" or "additional" protection is higher, since the general marketing costs for brand maintenance are lower under conditions of exclusivity, as are legal and litigation costs for the enforcement of the right (absent the need to confront arguments relating to consumer confusion).   Moreover, the added prestige involved in belonging to a higher category of protection may translate into market value.   Once again, culture enters the debate as a justification — this time, as a justification for the higher, indeed inflexible, degree of protection.   In the category of enhanced GI protection, consumer protection ceases to serve as a rationale[83] and therefore needs to be replaced by another justification.   Culture, among other components of reputation, fulfils this role.   Thus, in the area of enhanced GI protection, cultural concerns may act as the foundation not only of the additional degree of protection, but of the entire construct of GI protection of the relevant goods.

In sum, even taking into account the strong consumer protection motivation of the GI system *de lege lata*, the preservation of culture is a necessary (if not the most debated) component of the argument for GI protection in its existing and potentially enhanced forms.   In legal and economic theoretical terms, the cultural issue can be identified in the consumer protection argument itself.   It explains, at least in part, why the GI system has been established and the way it has been designed, and it is of critical importance in the justification of the "enhanced" level of GI protection which has disentangled itself of the original consumer protection rationale.

What, then, are the aspects of culture purportedly protected by GIs?   Let us follow the trade-related cultural dimensions previously identified,   insofar   as   they   may   be   separated: production, consumption, and identity.

---

[82] *See supra* text accompanying note 20.

[83] It might be said that the risk of consumer confusion is still the basis for enhanced GI protection, with the stricter rules applied so as to regulate the redistribution of costs between GI holders, non-GI producers, and consumers. In practice, however, the effect is to remove the consumer protection rationale of such GIs.

3.2. The Culture of Production: Terroir, *Traditional Methods of Production, and Rural Culture*

The culture of production that some GI proponents consider embedded in food and wine products is multifaceted and relates to several (mainly Eurocentric) ethos-like dimensions of common perceptions of these products' agricultural basis.

A central anchor in this respect is the difficult, mystified concept of *terroir*—a uniquely French term that has gained a following elsewhere in Europe and throughout the world. In its narrowest sense, *terroir* refers only to the physical environmental aspects of the geographical origin of a foodstuff or wine: soil, lay of the land, elevation, climate, and related factors. For *terroir* advocates, each finished agricultural or viticultural product should be a faithful expression of its geography. Better quality products will emerge from plots of land of superior quality and better endowments; in any event each product will inimitably reflect its growing conditions. It is thus necessary that different crops, cheeses, and wines be distinguishable from each other and associated with their geographical origin. (This is also a component of the "culture of consumption" that I will revisit shortly.) In this respect, the idea of *terroir* forms one of the bases for the GI legal mechanism, regardless of culture, providing a technical conceptualization of the link between food and place of cultivation. Moreover, on the production side, philosoph(iz)ers of *terroir* expand the term to include the human environment[84] or even a mental dimension—a link between producer and consumer that runs through the product and its unique *terroir*-based qualities. At minimum, this implies a noninterventionist, *terroir*-driven culture of production: less human manipulation, more respect for the earth's independent capacity to express itself through its fruits, and adequately satisfy human tastes, desires, and wants. Thinking about *terroir* on a more sophisticated level, however, just as nature and humankind have through progressive efforts established and confirmed which crops do best in which *terroir*, farmers and winegrowers have discovered the "best" winemaking practices for each area of production. *Terroir* is thus the epitomic opposite of globalization: an exemplary reflection of

---

[84] *See* FANET, *supra* note 9, at 10 (defining *terroir* as "an umbrella term for a subtle interaction of natural factors and human skills that define the characteristics of each wine-growing area").

place and people. As such, it arguably deserves protection, even enhanced protection, from commercial forces that threaten to compel homogenization and obliterate local *terroir*-ist cultures of production. GIs are ostensibly a targeted way of achieving this, since they grant each *terroir*, as officially defined and delimited, a separate, legal source of protection.

An important part of the narrative of *terroir* is the celebrated distinction between "Old World" and "New World" food production sensibilities. In much food and wine historiography, the production cultures of Europe, as a leading example, are the result of centuries (even millennia) of intimate human interaction with the earth that is absent in the Americas or Australia:

> viticultural practice in the Old World — choice of sites, growing techniques and appropriate vines — is based on a trial-and-error process dating back at least two thousand years . . . New World viticulture, by comparison is still in its infancy. It officially started 400 years ago but only really got going a century and a half ago and much more recently in some countries.[85]

This perception is most salient in the wine industry, but it also appears in the production of cheeses, oils, herbs, mushrooms, truffles, and in the culinary arts. Old World sensitivities are therefore presumed more vulnerable to global cultural tendencies, and their production peculiarities should be humored and protected. Of course, from a critical standpoint, there is something offensive about this approach — the New World is not new, and there existed a thread of indigenous traditional human interaction with its *terroir* in many locales before European domination either brutally cut it or shifted its course.

Nevertheless, *terroir*-based GI designation has gained significant support and emulation in New World countries.[86] The

---

[85] *See id.* This truism is echoed in WILSON, *supra* note 9, at 6.

[86] Appellation systems for geographical classification of wines exist in Australia, New Zealand, South Africa, Canada, the United States, Chile, and Argentina. *See* Micheal Maher, *On Vino Veritas? Clarifying the Use of Geographic References on American Wine Lables*, 89 CAL. L. REV. 1881, 1885 (2001) ("Today, every major wine-producing nation has a regulatory regime for wine labeling that incorporates geographic delimitations of grape-growing regions."). Where there is no such legal regulation, wineries in emerging wine countries (e.g., Israel) voluntarily label their produce with regional designations. *See* DANIEL ROGOV, ROGOV'S GUIDE TO ISRAELI WINES 2005, at 10–12 (2004) (discussing Israel's

EC-GIs case, although formally a dispute between Old and New World producers,[87] was not about the delimitation of the concept of GIs, but rather about the equality of New World and Old World GIs and the conditions of their legal protection. In negotiations on the extension of enhanced GI protection beyond wines and spirits, although a New/Old World dividing line is discernable, some developing countries have also adopted the rationale of the preservation of traditional cultures of production. They are asserting their Old-ness, where they might have been regarded as New World producers from a narrow European perspective.[88]

At any rate, this discussion leads to a cultural aspect of production that need not rest on acceptance of the validity of *terroir*, old or new: the preservation of traditional production practices and methods. Even if one remains skeptical of the numinous link between land, fruit, and local culture, it is indisputable as a dry fact that different regions grow different crops and varieties, and process them employing different production methods, down to the resolution of particular pieces of equipment.[89] In many cases these practices are idiosyncratic, objectively anachronistic, rooted in social, technological, or historic circumstances that once prevailed but have since disappeared. Under open market conditions they may easily vanish, without necessarily altering the qualities of the finished product,[90] although

---

voluntary regional designations).

[87] *See supra* text accompanying note 22.

[88] *See* Council for Trade-Related Aspects of Intellectual Property Rights, *Communication from Bulgaria, Cuba, Cyprus, The Czech Republic, The European Communites and Their Member States, Georgia, Hungary, Iceland, India, Kenya, Liechtenstein, Malta, Mauritius, Pakistan, Romania, The Slovak Republic, Slovenia, Sri Lanka, Switzerland, Thailand and Turkey*, ¶ 6, IP/C/W/353 (June 24, 2002) (citing traditional production methods as one of the components of a reputation relevant to GI protection in India, Kenya, Mauritius, Sri Lanka and Thailand).

[89] As a figurative example, consider *Le Têtu* ("the stubborn one"), a wine press made of 1000-year-old oak beams, erected at the historical and prestigious Burgundy vineyard Clos de Vougeot, reportedly still in operation. WILSON, *supra* note 9, at 178.

[90] For example, foot treading in lagares (open fermentation tanks) is a traditional method still used in the making of port wines in the Oporto region of Portugal, purportedly contributing to the character of the wine in a manner not replicable by regular mechanical presses. Special robotic lagares that simulate the foot treading action have recently been developed and are replacing some of the traditional foot treading. Larry Walker, *Graham's Ports Uses Robotic Lager to Crush Grapes*, WINE & VINES, Feb. 2003, *available at* http://www.findarticles.com/p/articles/mi_m3488/is_2_84/ai_98055538.

as a result the associated culture of production might be eradicated.

Hence, some production methods are regulated legally. Many national systems of GI regulation are based on the original French *Appellation d'Origine Contrôlée* ("AOC") system. In these systems, a product is eligible for GI (or similar) protection not only by virtue of its physical place of production, but also by its compliance with a set of (sometimes strict) criteria relating to content (grape varieties in wines and spirits;[91] permitted varieties of walnuts;[92] types of milk in cheeses[93]) and methods of production (yields per hectare;[94] harvesting dates and time in oak barrels for wines; detailed methods for the manufacture, aging and packaging of Balsamic Vinegar of Modena).[95] Rules such as these are to a large extent quality-oriented, aiming to set a minimum quality level for GI-worthy products. But quality here has a double meaning;

---

[91] *See e.g., Décret du 5 Mai 1982, Définissant l'Appellation d'Origine Contrôlée* [("AOC")] *"Faugères,"* Journal Officiel de la République Française [J.O.] [Official Gazette of France], May 14, 1982, p. 4609, *as modified by Décret simple du 21 juillet 2000,* Journal Officiel de la République Française [J.O.] [Official Gazette of France], July 25, 2000, p. 11451, *Décret simple du 05 février 2003,* Journal Officiel de la République Française [J.O.] [Official Gazette of France], February 12, 2003, p. 2592, and *Décret simple du 23 février 2005,* Journal Officiel de la République Française [J.O.] [Official Gazette of France], February 25, 2005, p. 3266 (defining in detail the relative part of each of the allowed varieties in the Faugères AOC red blend).

[92] Under article 4 of the *Décret n° 96-621 du 10 Juillet, 1996, Relatif à l'Appellation d'Origine Contrôlée "Noix de Grenoble,"* the AOC Noix de Grenoble for walnuts (which was established in 1939) may only apply to walnuts of the three varieties, Franquette, Mayette and Parisienne. *Décret no 96-621 du 10 juillet 1996 relatif à l'appellation d'origine contrôlée "Noix de Grenoble,"* art. 4, Journal Officiel de la République Française [J.O.] [Official Gazette of France], July 13, 1996, p. 10586. This has been recognized under EC legislation, as have the varieties that may be included in U.S. walnut mixtures and products labeled under the label "California Walnuts." Commission Regulation 80/2003, *Amending Regulation No. 175/2001 as Regards Certain Mixtures of Certain Varieties of Walnuts in Shell, Officially Defined by the Producing Country,* 2003 O.J. (L 13) preamble (2).

[93] *See, e.g.,* Paraskevi Dimou, *Les Dénominations des Fromages* (Sept. 2002) (unpublished D.E.A. dissertation, Université Robert Schuman Strasbourg III), *available at* http://www.ceipi.edu/pdf/memoires/Memoire_Demou.pdf (describing the history and practice of cheese appellations).

[94] *See, e.g., Décret du 20 octobre 1997 relatif à l'appellation d'origine contrôlée "Chinon,"* Journal Officiel de la République Française [J.O.] [Official Gazette of France], October 22, 1997, p. 15353 (describing how wines from Chinon, the land of Rabelais, can only bear the name Chinon if the wineries conform to certain hectoliter/hectare yields).

[95] For details, see the website of the *Consorzio Produttori Aceto Balsamico Tradizionale di Modena,* http://www.balsamico.it/ing/prodotto.html (last visited Dec. 3, 2005).

quality also means living up to traditional standards and reputation. Thus, GI rules also strive to preserve a certain historical purity of production.

As such they present a cultural rationale, based on traditions of production, for the maintenance of GI protection. This is a rationale that is particularly well accepted in public opinion, mainly in Europe. Reportedly, in two consumer surveys taken in 1994 and 1996 of a 16,000 EU citizen sample, 17% considered the protection of traditional methods of production to be one of the two most important functions performed by GIs/Appellations of Origin.[96]

More broadly, like other forms of agricultural protectionism, GIs may be construed as necessary for the preservation of the farm culture of production in general, without a necessary link to specifically idiosyncratic, localized production methods, or particular *terroir*. Concern for the vanishing peasant[97] and associated rural culture has accompanied western industrialization and rationalization of agricultural practices for more than a century.[98] Notably, in some cases this argument only seeks to preserve a lifestyle of agricultural productive activity as an expression of family and community culture, regardless of quality benefits.[99] Indeed, this is an argument that relates to the culture of production, but borders also on the culture of identity, linking the product whose existence may depend on GI protection with a

---

[96] Council for Trade-Related Aspects of Intellectual Property Rights, *Minutes of Meeting Held in the Centre William Rappard on 25–27 and 29 November, and 20 December 2002*, ¶ 141, IP/C/M/38 (Feb. 5, 2003).

[97] *See generally* HENRI MENDRAS, THE VANISHING PEASANT: INNOVATION AND CHANGE IN FRENCH AGRICULTURE (Jean Lerner trans., MIT Press 1970) (1967) (exploring the effects of modernization on French agriculture).

[98] *See, e.g.*, GABRIEL TARDE, FRAGMENT D'HISTORIE FUTURE [FRAGMENT OF FUTURE HISTORY] (Slatline Reprints 1980) (1896) (discussing the diminished role of rural agriculture in modern society).

[99] The epigraph of this Article quotes a winegrower in the Languedoc belligerently defending the merits of French wine culture. The truth is that the Languedoc is the largest bulk-wine producing region in France, not particularly renowned for quality (with more recent and notable exceptions). *See* KERMIT LYNCH, ADVENTURES ON THE WINE ROUTE: A WINE BUYER'S TOUR OF FRANCE 73–74 (1988) (citing ALEXIS LICHINE, ENCYCLOPEDIA OF WINE AND SPIRITS (1970 ed. and later editions)). The culture that the winegrower is adamantly trying to defend is a culture of labor, not quality or *terroir*. In 1967, it was reported that in the Languedoc "67 percent describe the good wine grower as one who knows how to work hard, while only 9 percent say he is one who has good grapevines, and 5 percent one who makes good wine." MENDRAS, *supra* note 97, at 143.

cultural way of life that ostensibly may be crushed by the wheels of global consumerism.[100]

3.3. *The Culture of Consumption: Traditions of Discrimination in Taste and Time*

In granting market advantages to particular foods and wines, GI protection may also contribute to the preservation of cultures of consumption, not just production. The most obvious such case arises when on one hand there is an equivalence or dependence between local traditions of production, and on the other hand local traditions of consumption in the same place. That is where *local* types of food or beverage are produced, as they are, primarily or even exclusively for consumption by the producers themselves and their households and immediate communities, in accordance with *local* tastes. Competitive exposure to cheaper, better, non-local alternatives might risk the survival of local production, by shifting consumption patterns and producing changes in local traditions. As much as this seems a specialized scenario, one can more generally imagine a cultural, *terroir*-minded defense for unabashed pro-local consumption traditions, in which it is argued that there exists a culture of consuming local food and beverage products, *because* they are local. This may be justified by objective quality factors (such as freshness of produce, edified as a cultural preference) or by the ethereal existence of a mental or symbolic factor of consumerism, linking place of consumption with place of production.[101] At its most abstract (and most protectionist), however, the argument would simply be that there is cultural merit in preserving the dependence of consumers on the fruits of the very land where they reside, whether they are themselves producers or not. This is, however, perhaps more appropriately an argument couched in terms of local identity, to which I will turn shortly.

Moreover, the overtly discriminatory nature of such narrow

---

[100] *See generally* Anne Tyler Calabresi, *Vin Santo and Wine in a Tuscan Farmhouse, in* CONSTRUCTIVE DRINKING: PERSPECTIVES ON DRINK FROM ANTHROPOLOGY 122, 122–25 (Mary Douglas ed., 1989) (depicting in a particularly romantic style the traditional lifestyle that centers on wine production, warts and all).

[101] This completes the trinity of the ultimate ethos of *terroir*—land, producer, consumer. *See supra* text accompanying note 84 for a discussion of a mental dimension of *terroir*.

consumption-culture arguments, however plausible (or not), make them extremely difficult to reconcile with basic GATT/WTO principles.[102] Indeed, in terms of simple economic analysis, if the preservation of such "neighborhood" production-consumption cultural networks is indeed so important to local tradition or culture, one would expect this sentiment to overcome external market pressures, even at greater cost to consumers.[103] The rejoinder would be that while these cultural arguments do not, indeed, give good reason for tariff or tax preference, they do justify accurate geographical-source labeling, permitting the public to choose between local and foreign or ex-regional produce. Thus, the informative function of GI protection may arguably serve a purpose in the context of the culture of consumption.

An additional, broader justificatory basis may be supplied, however. One also reliant on the informative function of GIs, if it is accepted that there do exist local "traditions of discrimination" — in the positive cultural sense of particularity, preference and discernment, not in the negative trade law sense — that are not chauvinistic and trade-protectionist because they do not prefer (at least not exclusively) local products. In these traditions, a local consumer-culture market preference exists for food and wine products of specific geographical sources. This preference is based on traditional perceptions of the type of production practiced at the product's source, or the quality of the finished product, and, of course, on real distinctions between different products.

For example, England produces very little wine itself, much less of viable quality or distinction.[104] Yet historically, England (or

---

[102] These principles include: the national treatment and the most favored nation principles of GATT Articles I, III, and potentially XIII; non-discrimination rules in the TRIPS Agreement and (at least with regard to distribution services) GATS; and the general exceptions of GATT Article XX and GATS Article XIV mentioned above. *See infra* Section 5.3 for more discussion of the general exception rules.

[103] But again the possibility of market failure arises, in the same way that it did with regard to the discussion of the tragedy of the commons. *See supra* note 66 and accompanying text (bemoaning the potential negative effects of private, individual preference on public goods).

[104] It is not a matter of coincidence that Ricardo's famed exposition of the principle of comparative advantage compared England's winemaking faculties unfavorably with those of Portugal. *See* DAVID RICARDO, THE PRINCIPLES OF POLITICAL ECONOMY AND TAXATION 76 (Lloyd Reynolds and William Fellner eds., Richard D. Irwin, Inc. 1963) (1817). However, in the current era one must distinguish between "British Wine," usually made from low quality grapes that must be imported from any place on earth to be vinified in Britain, and "English

658 *U. Pa. J. Int'l Econ. L.* [Vol. 26:4

more precisely, influential social classes in England) has demonstrated an independent consumption-culture of discriminating taste. The English—not the French, Germans, Portuguese, or Spanish—have been responsible for the production *cum* cultural edification and reputational establishment of some of the Old World's greatest wine regions, such as Bordeaux,[105] Oporto,[106] Jerez,[107] and the Rheingau.[108] Though individual English

---

Wine," wine made from grapes grown in England. An English specialty of repute is *Méthode Champenoise* sparkling wine of Nyetmber, a small winery in West Sussex that prides itself as being "Distinctly Anglais!", deliberately casting itself against the exclusive tradition of Champagne. For further background information, see Nyetimber Wines, http://www.nyetimber-vineyard.com (last visited Dec. 3, 2005).

[105] Bordeaux was established as an important wine region in the twelfth century with the marriage of Eleanor of Aquitaine to Henry Plantagenet, future Henry II of England. ROD PHILLIPS, A SHORT HISTORY OF WINE 87 (2001). The mouth of the Gironde, just across the channel, provided easy access to the large English fleet and made Bordeaux the ideal source of wine to satisfy the English taste for "claret." DEWEY MARKHAM, JR., 1855: A HISTORY OF THE BORDEAUX CLASSIFICATION 39-40 (1998) (recognizing English demand for Bordeaux's specialty wines and ease of access to the region by sea).

[106] The wines of Port (Oporto) flourished in the eighteenth century because of increased English demand brought on by unreliable supply from Bordeaux due to French-English strife; this was encouraged by the 1703 Treaty of Methuen, which granted Portuguese wine lower duties than those of France and Germany. *See* Phillips, *supra* note 105, at 129-30, 137 (discussing the French-English political problems that led to increased Portuguese exports of wine to England in the late 16th and early 17th centuries); *see also* TOM STEVENSON, THE SOTHEBY'S WINE ENCYCLOPEDIA: THE CLASSIC REFERENCE TO THE WINES OF THE WORLD 334 (4th ed. 2005) (noting the pro-Portuguese wine import terms of the Methuen Treaty of 1703).

[107] The truly unique wines of Jerez, known in England as Sherry, were often mentioned in Shakespearean plays and were coveted by the English even by non-peaceful means in the early seventeenth century. *See e.g.,* WILLIAM SHAKESPEARE, THE SECOND PART OF HENRY THE FOURTH act 4, sc. 3 ("Hereof comes it that Prince Harry is valiant; for the cold blood he did naturally inhereit of his father, he hath, like lean, sterile and bare land, manured, husbanded and tilled with excellent endeavour of drinking good and good store of fertile sherries, that he is become very hot and valiant."). Failure to take Cadiz in 1625, coupled with the shortage of Bordeaux wine, brought on a wave of English investment in Jerez; to this day, many of the main shippers of Jerez go under old English or Irish names, such as Garvey's, Duff & Gordon, Williams & Humbert, Sandeman and Osborne. *See generally* JULIAN JEFFS, SHERRY (5th ed. 2004) (1961) (explaining the history of sherry in more detail).

[108] The white wines of Hochheim in the Rheingau, known at all times under the colloquialism of "Hock," were held in high esteem in eighteenth and nineteenth century England. *See* STEVENSON, *supra* note 106, at 349 (noting the popularity of Hock in 19th century England). The wines' popularity was temporarily supported by a Germanic fad related to Prince Albert's heritage. *See* German Wine Notes: History, http://www.winetours.co.uk/wine-notes-

entrepreneurs facilitated these developments on the production side, arguably as early globalizers,[109] the increase in the importation of wines has been consumer-driven, propelled by English tastes and capitalizing on an English consumer culture of discrimination.[110] At least in theory, such a local culture of discrimination is the opposite of global homogenization, of "McDonaldization." The preference for products sourced from specific locations rests, of course, on a confidence in the quality and durability of the production in those locations, and on a belief that food or wine from a given location is guaranteed to reflect a certain, desirable style, or quality. The culture of consumption of one region is thus inextricably linked to the cultures of production of other regions. Moreover, it is self-evident — particularly because the qualities and characteristics of food and drink products require their consumption in order to be appreciated — that for such a culture of consumption to survive, consumers need prior accurate information on the geographical source of products, and to this end GIs may serve a positive purpose. Here, the cultural justification is in harmony with the consumer protection rationale.

Ultimately, cultures of discrimination can be generally couched in nigh post-modernist terms advocating geographical transparency: "Consumers these days want to know what they are eating, where it comes from and how it is produced."[111] However vague that argument may be, it is perhaps as relevant to the debate on genetically modified organisms as it is to the debate on the extension of GI protection.

Consumer practices may have additional supporting — some

---

germany.htm (last visited Dec. 3, 2005) (crediting Hock's popularity in England in part to Queen Victoria's marriage to Prince Albert, a native of the Rhineland).

[109] For example, the wine industry on the Portuguese island of Madeira was in fact founded virtually from scratch by the English. Madeira Wine, http://www.madeira-web.com/PagesUK/wine-uk2.html.

[110] As a historical footnote recording both geographical interest and discriminating taste, on April 10, 1663, Samuel Pepys noted in his diary that he had drunk "a sort of French wine, called *Ho Bryan*, that hath a good and most perticular [sic] taste that I never met with." 4 SAMUEL PEPYS, THE DIARY OF SAMUEL PEPYS 100 (Robert Latham & William Matthews eds., Univ. of Cal. Press 1971) (1663). Chateau Haut Brion, the wine referenced here, is still a highly prestigious first growth Bordeaux wine today. *See e.g.*, ROBERT M. PARKER, JR., THE WORLD'S GREATEST WINE ESTATES: A MODERN PERSPECTIVE 126 (2005) (referring to the history of Chateau Haut Brion as one of the "oldest and most illustrious of any vineyard").

[111] FANET, *supra* note 9, at 10.

660   *U. Pa. J. Int'l Econ. L.*   [Vol. 26:4]

might say central—aspects that focus on particular traditional habits. For example, the culture of serving meals or courses of meals with the wines that are most complementary from a sensory perspective. Some of such food-wine pairings have become staples of consumption;[112] their preservation arguably requires continued and perhaps extended accurate geographical labeling and, hence, GI protection. Traditions also sometimes match foods or wines with festive, seasonal, or other special occasions.[113] In these cases, the use of the most prestigious or desirable ingredients, or the opening of the most celebratory type of beverage may have a social meaning of cultural dimensions. Again, we are brushing with the culture of identity, but it is nevertheless an identity expressed through patterns of consumption.

3.4. The Culture of Identity: Local Champions and Cultural Landscapes

On this level of analysis, GIs arguably protect the integrity of national food icons that construct identity. Food plays an important part in defining locales, regions, and nations. Guidebooks and textbooks will normally dedicate at least a few pages to the food and drink that characterizes a particular region or country, and the shelves of the cooking sections of bookstores are often geographically categorized. A distinctive kitchen—like a flag, a currency, or a dialect—serves to distinguish one nation or region from others to the point that the development of an independent cuisine may be seen as an integral part of any nation-building project.[114]

---

[112] For example, Chablis and oysters, Rioja and lamb, Port and Stilton.

[113] *See, e.g.,* Mary Anna Thornton, Sekt *versus* Schnapps *in an Austrian Village, in* CONSTRUCTIVE DRINKING, *supra* note 94, at 100, 104-108 (discussing examples of two drinks, sekt and schnapps, that carry great social meaning, polarizing social occasions into planned versus spontaneous celebrations).

[114] For a universally acknowledged assertion of Italian culinary distinction enmeshed in the making of Italy in the last quarter of the nineteenth century, including the reclaiming of French traditions as originally Italian (e.g., *Béchamel* sauce being none other than the Italian *balsamella*, which has its origins in ancient Rome), see generally PELLEGRINO ARTUSI, LA SCIENZA IN COCINA E L'ARTE DI MANGIARE BENE [SCIENCE IN THE KITCHEN AND THE ART OF EATING WELL] (Murtha Baca trans., 2003) (1891). For a contemporary continuation of this discussion, see generally GIULIANO BUGIALLI, THE FINE ART OF ITALIAN COOKING (3d ed. 1990), which asserts Italian (or rather, Florentine) culinary supremacy by demonstrating how French cuisine was significantly influenced by Italian traditions and knowledge brought by Caterina de' Medici and her entourage from Florence when she moved to France following her political marriage to Henri II of France

Ultimately, where singular traditions are absent or incoherent, the quest for distinction may rely solely upon the use of locally sourced ingredients or products,[115] regardless of how unusual or remarkable they may be, and so these too are assimilated as components of identity.   In well-established food cultures, local produce is unabashedly put on a pedestal.   In both Piemonte and Perigord, the locals will argue the superior quality of their truffles and sneer at that of Himalayan truffles.   Some Spaniards regard their Cítricos Valencianos with national pride, just as the farmers of Prince Edward Island adulate their new potatoes, or the Italians their Chianina beef.

It is not pride alone at stake; food or drink, such as the poultry of Bresse[116] or sparkling wine of Champagne,[117] may be adopted as a national symbol or even as personifying the country, as with these products in France.[118]   The international exclusivity of usage of the geographical term is thus perceived as imperative for the preservation of a part of national identity.   The appropriation of the name of a foodstuff or beverage by a nation can even give rise to international disputes that stem from struggles for identity, such

---

in the sixteenth century. Moreover, the role of the kitchen in nation-building has many other expressions. *See, e.g.,* Richard R. Wilk, *Food and Nationalism: The Origins of 'Belizean Food', in* FOOD NATIONS: SELLING TASTE IN CONSUMER SOCIETIES 63, *supra* note 7.

[115] The creative use of local ingredients becomes, for some, the popular test for the metal of an emerging local kitchen, such as that of Canada: "The debate swirls: is there a Canadian cuisine?   One that uses local ingredients in imaginative ways to produce a distinctive, indigenous culinary style?"   Don Douloff, *Delicious Cancon Chez Metropolis,* EYE WEEKLY, Apr. 16, 1992, at 30, 30, *available at* http://www.eye.net/eye/issue/issue_04.16.92/foodanddrink/ fo0416.htm.

[116] The poultry of Bresse (Poulet de Bresse AOC) is physically recognizable as a Tricolor, with red crest, white plumage and blue feet. By law, the chickens must also wear a Tricolor badge at the base of their neck and be packed under a Tricolor etiquette.   *General Information: How to Recognize "Bresse Poultry,"* http://www.colorline.fr/pouletbresse/ang.pdf (last visited Nov. 9, 2005).

[117] "Within France, champagne has been seen as an embodiment of the national spirit . . . . 'The wine resembles us, it is made in our image: it sparkles like our intellect; it is lively like our language.'" GUY, *supra* note 8, at 1-2 (quoting Adolphe Brisson, *Preface* to ARMAND BOURGEOIS, LE CHANSONNIER DU VIN DE CHAMPAGNE EN 1890 (Chalon-sur-Marne, Martin Frères 1890)).

[118] In the French context, one might add the truncated, pyramid-shaped cheese of Valençay, by legend the result of Napoleon's rage on his unhappy return from Egypt. STEVE JENKINS, CHEESE PRIMER 92-93 (1996) (attributing the cheese's traditional shape, a pyramid with the top taken off, to the region's desire to please Napoleon, who was planning a visit after returning from an unsuccessful campaign in Egypt).

as the longstanding quarrel between Peru and Chile over Pisco, in which each party would appear to feel stripped of a national symbol if recourse to the term were not restricted.[119] GIs can therefore be seen as guardians of local identity, and as such, bulwarks against globalized homogeneity.

Identity may also underpin arguments for GI protection for foods when it is deemed necessary for the maintenance of the cultural landscape that forms part of the character of a region or nation;[120] the UNESCO Draft Convention would have policies aimed at preserving and safeguarding cultural landscapes recognized as "Cultural Policies."[121] This concept may be, as already indicated, intimately linked to the cultures of production that determine the landscape, but formulated as a separate argument. It is not the production that is being protected, but the environment that it generates.[122]

4. *CONTORNI:* MARKETS AND TRADITION — SOME CONTRARY ECONOMIC AND CULTURAL REALITIES OF THE FOOD AND WINE TRADE

4.1. Can GIs Actually Prevent Market-Induced Changes to Culture?

Against the backdrop of these seemingly compelling arguments for cultural protection through the instrument of GIs, it

---

[119] See *Pisco Liqueur Dispute between Chile and Peru,* TRADE & ENV'T DATABASE, (PISCO), http://gurukul.ucc.american.edu/TED/PISCO.HTM, ("Pisco is as Peruvian as llamas and arroz con pollo . . . . Peruvians hold a deep-seated national pride in pisco, which . . . [they] have been drinking at parties and rowdy peasant festivals for more than 400 years . . . . To make real pisco, you have to take your shoes off, crush the grapes and let it ferment in clay bottles. In Chile they make something called pisco, but it doesn't taste as it should."). This, of course, may make it impossible to draw bright-line distinctions between the culture of identity and the cultures of consumption and production, since Peru's background sentiments also relate to the role of pisco in consumption traditions.

[120] "Cultural landscape" is "a geographic area (including both cultural and natural resources and the wildlife or domestic animals therein), associated with a historic event, activity, or person or exhibiting other cultural or aesthetic values." U.S. DEP'T OF THE INTERIOR, THE SECRETARY OF THE INTERIOR'S STANDARDS FOR THE TREATMENT OF HISTORIC PROPERTIES WITH GUIDELINES FOR THE TREATMENT OF CULTURAL LANDSCAPES 4 (Charles A. Birnbaum & Christine Capella Peters eds., 1996).

[121] See UNESCO Draft Convention, *supra* note 4, annex II, ¶ 3.

[122] For a detailed study of the ways in which viticultural practices form different cultural landscapes, see generally DAN STANISLAWSKI, LANDSCAPES OF BACCHUS: THE VINE IN PORTUGAL (1970).

is not necessary to speculate about the effect of GIs on the preservation of traditions of production, consumption, and identity. In Europe, GIs have been legally regulated and enforced at varying degrees since the early decades of the twentieth century, in some cases from the mid-nineteenth century, and — in other rarer cases — even the eighteenth century,[123] particularly with regard to wine. There exists, therefore, sufficient historical as well as current empirical material to examine as a living, regulatory laboratory.

In this section I will present a (non-exhaustive) series of phenomena in particular real cases that demonstrate the contrary ways in which GIs have proven ineffective in conserving culture and safeguarding cultural diversity. Short of undertaking a comprehensive study that would overstay the welcome of this paper's menu, I would submit that these instances are in fact not exceptional but rather representative of the limits of GI-based cultural protection. If there is a general theme to these examples, it is that the market forces involved in the food and wine industries — commodity markets, production markets, labor markets, corporate markets, and indeed, as we shall see, GI markets — are so pervasive that GIs cannot in and of themselves, as legal agents, prevent the market influences on local culture that lead to degrees of cultural transformation and international cultural homogenization.

4.2. *The Culture of Production: Markets Change Cultures of Production Despite GIs, Even When Methods Are Regulated*

A first proposition along these lines is that local traditions and cultures of production that benefit from GI protection nevertheless change when markets cause them to, and remain constant when markets cause them to. The safeguarding of cultural diversity is thus at the mercy of market forces, with or without legal GI protection. This happens not only with regard to production methods that are unregulated and legally free to change with consumers' demand or producers' creative requirements, but in some cases also when production methods are stringently regulated by the laws establishing the GI itself.

A prominent example is the evolution of competing styles of winemaking in important wine appellations in Europe since the 1980s, usually demarcated along "traditional" vs. "modern" or

---

[123] *See infra* note 129 and accompanying text.

"international" lines. One aspect of this divide is the use of oak barrels in determining a wine's body, flavor, and overall character. While many national wine appellation laws set minimum periods that the wine must age in oak barrels before it may be bottled, they do not determine several additional dimensions of oak aging, such as the type of oak to be used (e.g., French, American, or Slavonian); the size of barrels (large 30 hectolitre vats or relatively small 225-litre *barriques*); the age of the barrels (new or used, and the percentage of new barrels to be employed); and the degree of toasting the oak undergoes during cooperage.[124] Each of these variables can significantly affect the organoleptic qualities of the finished wine.[125] These and other technical oenological flexibilities allow for creativity and personal stylistic expression by winemakers, as well as modernization. Moreover, they have also allowed "new wave" winemakers to depart appreciably from winemaking practices that although unregulated by statute were considered by previous generations as traditional and representative of local sensibilities.

To be sure, in many locales the innovation has been driven by quality considerations aiming at better market access and higher prices: prior traditions were sometimes the upshot of years of wine production whose unscrupulous main goal was quantity and cost-effectiveness, resulting in insipid bulk-products. Changes in production methods have in part been aimed at changing this scene. Yet in other cases, quality, as well as local typicity,[126] was achieved using the old traditional ways, albeit more dependent on unpredictable annual vintage conditions. There the more recent

---

[124] *See, e.g.,* Tom Maresca, *Spotlight on Barolo,* THE WINE NEWS, Oct.-Nov. 2002, at 30, *available at* http://www.thewinenews.com/octnov02/cover.html (showing that while new technology has created differences between Barolo winemakers over the size and age of the barrels, they are both known as Barolo wines) (last visited Nov. 16, 2005).

[125] Similarly, many wine appellation rules do determine minimum alcohol levels in the finished wine, but not maximum levels. While earliest harvest dates may be mandatory, the minimum or maximum sugar ripeness at harvest of grapes intended for dry wines is usually set by each winemaker. Duration of maceration and types of yeasts are also usually not regulated. The combination of these factors allows for considerable flexibility in the degree of alcohol in the finished wine.

[126] Typicity is a "[w]inetasting term used to indicate the degree to which a wine is typical of its origins—its variety, geography, and sometimes vintage." FOGWELL'S GUIDES, WINE GLOSSARY: TYPICITY (2001), http://www.answers.com/topic/typicity (last visited Dec. 3, 2005).

changes have aimed at producing wines of a different nature, at times meant for modern, foreign tastes.[127] Either way, the result has been a break with traditional methods of production, despite GI protection. Differences of opinion between "traditional" and "modern" winemakers can be deeply entrenched and have even been known to carry acrimonious social effects, partly on the background of economic competition, partly as a genuine divisiveness of aesthetic philosophy; case in point is the Piemonte region of northern Italy, where the traditional/modern divide is sometimes referred to as the "Barolo Wars."[128]

Market-induced changes in traditional methods of production can therefore occur working within the regulatory space of the GI/appellation legal system, which is ineffective in preventing such innovations. On the other hand, some modernization that significantly strays from traditional methods embodied in appellation rules cannot benefit from the GI. Indeed, market forces are sometimes strong enough to encourage producers to forego the GI they are legally entitled to in order to pursue new production methods. This happened in Tuscany, where innovators looking at international markets abandoned the prestigious Chianti Classico *Denominazione d'Origine Controllata e Garantita* ("DOCG"), preferring to introduce non-Tuscan grape varieties such as Cabernet Sauvignon into the blends that made up some of their best wines and to bottle them under the formally inferior Toscana *Indicazione Geografica Tipica* ("IGT"), and before the latter category's creation under the humiliating classification of *Vino da Tavola* ("VdT") (literally, table wine). These luxury wines soon became known as Super Tuscans and overtook the Chianti Classico wines in terms of international, high-end demand, but also entered low-end markets, all at the expense of traditional blends. This is an evolutionary model that has been replicated in various other

---

[127] In particular, traditionalists decry the effect of the taste of a single palate — that of the influential American wine critic Robert J. Parker, on the development of regional wines. ECHIKSON, *supra* note 1, at 89; Suzanne Goldenberg, '*I Am the Most Powerful Person in the Wine World,*' THE GUARDIAN, July 23, 2003, Food Section, at 8; *see also* MONDOVINO (Goatwork Films & Films De La Croisade 2004) (providing Nossiter's stylized depiction of the role of powerful figures such as Parker and the winemaking consultant, Michel Rolland, in the design of the modern wine trade). Interested readers can visit the critic's website. Robert Parker Online, http://www.erobertparker.com (last visited Dec. 2, 2005).

[128] *See, e.g.,* JOSEPH BASTIANICH & DAVID LYNCH, VINO ITALIANO: THE REGIONAL WINES OF ITALY 147–48 (2002).

regions in Europe. With innovators working *outside* the appellation system, in these cases GIs have been unable to forestall the erosion of what may be regarded as one of the most basic traditions of wine production: the local *cépage*, or varietal composition of local wines.

The history of the Chianti Classico DOCG also reveals that market pressures may actually bring national GI regulators to amend the traditional production requirements set out in the appellation rules themselves, making a clean break between the GI and its underlying tradition. Chianti is perhaps the world's first legally defined GI, by virtue of a Decree by Grand Duke Cosimo III de' Medici from 1716.[129] The father of modern Chianti, however, was the Baron Bettino Ricasoli, who in the 1850s defined a standard varietal blend for Chianti wine, composed mainly of the red grapes (Sangiovese and Canaiolo Nero), but also up to 30% white grapes (Malvasia and Trebbiano), the white varieties intended for freshness and accessibility in early drinking. This became the traditional composition of Chianti wine for more than a century. The Chianti region gained protected status by ministerial decree in 1932, and under legislation became a *Denominazione d'Origine Controllata* ("DOC") in 1967 which adopted the Ricasoli recipe, including the mandatory inclusion of a high minimum content of white varieties in the red wine as a binding condition for the use of the Chianti name.

Additionally, the use of white grapes in the red wine was being abused by winemakers to "stretch" or increase production quantities with little regard to quality.[130] At the same time, the Super-Tuscan breakaways were threatening the Chianti reputation. In 1984, when Chianti as a whole and the Chianti Classico sub-region were elevated to the more prestigious DOCG status, the new legislation significantly reduced the minimum content of white grapes in Chianti wines to only 2% — a proportion so small that it is safe to say that it was kept simply in order to preserve a shadow trace of the Ricasoli tradition — and allowing the inclusion of non-local varieties up to 10% of the blend. The law was changed again in 1996, eliminating entirely the requirement of white variety inclusion, now rather subjecting it to a 6% maximum, and increasing the allowed proportion of foreign varieties to 15%.

---

[129] *See id.* at 201.

[130] *Id.*

Finally, under the current production code, as of the 2006 harvest, the inclusion of the indigenous white varieties will be prohibited if the wine is to be called Chianti Classico.[131]   Thus, market requirements – the achievement of higher quality that conforms to internationally accepted tastes and standards – and pressures, notably the abandonment of the DOCG system by many producers for their highest quality wines, have stood what was previously deemed a tradition on its head: a winemaking practice that was once a mandatory legal condition for GI status is now prohibited by the successor law.[132]

Another manner in which different market pressures may detract from the integrity of cultures of production that are supposed to be protected by GIs relates to the ease with which appellation maps are drawn and redrawn. For example, the St. Joseph AOC was once "a single hillside,"[133] "a snug local appellation centered on a handful of communities on the west bank of the northern Rhône," with a vineyard area of 245 hectares."[134] In 1969 the AOC's permitted area of production was tripled, including much low quality land and causing a stampede of indiscriminate planting,[135] leading one (American) expert to write that "nothing is sacred to these officials of the INAO[136] who

---

[131] *See* Chianti Classico, http://www.chianticlassico.com/english/il-chianti-classico.htm (listing the requirements for a wine to be called Chianti Classico) (last visited Dec. 3, 2005).

[132] Less drastic though significant changes in the traditional varietal composition of regional wines have occurred elsewhere within the regulatory space of GI definitions, due to economic factors relating to production. To name two: First, very few of the current wineries of the French Southern Rhône AOC of Chateauneuf du Pape practice the somewhat mythical traditional blend that includes no less than thirteen local varieties, as allowed by AOC rules. For many decades of the twentieth century, Chateauneuf du Pape wines relied mainly on a single variety (Grenache); this "tradition" has also been supplanted, as today most domaines use the three main varieties of the region (Grenache, Syrah and Mourvedre). JOHN LIVINGSTONE–LEARMONTH, THE WINES OF THE RHÔNE 174 (3d ed. 1992). Second, in the Northern Rhône AOC of Côte Rôtie, tradition called for blending a noticeable proportion of the aromatic white variety Viognier into the red Syrah-based wine. *Id.* at 8.

[133] *See* LYNCH, *supra* note 99, at 178 ("Originally, Saint-Joseph referred to a single hillside between Mauves and Tournon which is now the property of the Chapoutier family. ").

[134] *See* LIVINGSTONE–LEARMONTH, *supra* note 132, at 104 (showing the sharp increase in total area from 97 hectares in 1971 to 245 hectares in 1982).

[135] *See id.* (explaining that the increased planting was hurting the St. Joseph's name).

[136] Institut National des Appelations d'Origine ("INAO"), is the French

continue to devalue these historic sites even though they were hired to protect them."[137] This was a change with implications for traditions of consumption (once St. Joseph's reputation declined) and of identity (expanding the "community" of winegrowers who may sell their wares under the St. Joseph GI, but eroding its quality); it should, however, be seen foremost as a shift in a culture of production, since it signaled an abandonment of the *terroir*-driven principles of winemaking. Or rather, one should say that it constituted a threat to these cultures, because in the early 1990s renewed local quality-consciousness (prompted, no doubt, also by difficulties in sales) launched an effort to redefine the St. Joseph territory, limiting its use to only worthy sites,[138] evidently with growing success.[139] Notably, in this case it was not the GI that saved the culture of production, but the producer's culture (and the decreasing value of the wines) that appeared to have saved the GI.

The same can also be said of the great classified estates of Bordeaux. They are all wine-making enterprises whose quality was ranked and classified according to their market prices in 1855. Subject to constant criticism, the 1855 classification has survived with very few changes. Yet as a prominent historiographer of the classification has noted, "[i]n theory, there is nothing to prevent a classed growth that consisted of, say, 25 hectares in 1855 from acquiring 100 hectares of neighboring vineyards that were classed lower in the hierarchy — or, for that matter, not classed at all."[140] Nevertheless, the quality rankings have been substantially preserved to this day. This can be attributed not only to the prescience of the original classifiers, but also to the care taken by successive proprietors to preserve the territory and quality to which the original ranking was granted.

---

governmental regulator of AOCs.

[137] *See* LYNCH, *supra* note 99, at 179.

[138] *See* LIVINGSTONE–LEARMONTH, *supra* note 132, at 104-106 (giving examples of how commercial success rather than quality became a driving factor in the late 1970s and 80s, and how this has changed in the 1990s).

[139] *See* Todd M. Wernstrom, *Saint-Joseph: Less Proves More in the Northern Rhône,* THE WINE NEWS, Apr.–May 2004, *available at* http://www.thewinenews.com/aprmay04/cover.asp (describing how the AOC redrew the area where St. Joseph's is grown to increase quality by removing those vineyards on the valley floor that had been included in an expansion of the appellation in the early 1970s).

[140] MARKHAM, *supra* note 105, at 184.

In sum, from the tested experiences of GIs in France and Italy (as well as in Spain), it is evident that market pressures are independently and markedly more influential than legal GI regulation with regard to patterns and practices of production, at least as far as culture is concerned. Where the market demands change, change is enacted, regardless of GI rules; where the market encourages constancy, constancy in GIs is achieved, whether directly or indirectly.

4.3. *The Culture of Consumption: Markets Change Cultures of Discriminating Consumption Despite GIs*

A second proposition regarding the ineffectiveness of GIs as agents of cultural preservation is that markets change cultures of consumption relating to GI-protected products, even those that are based on traditions of discrimination (in taste, not in trade). Not only are they not enough to conserve cultures of discrimination, GIs—or at least the way that they are legally defined and managed—may even contribute to these changes.

This is exemplified by recent trends in the British wine market, *vis-à-vis* Old World and New World wines. As has been discussed already, England is an example of a consumer market with established traditions of non-protectionist geographical discrimination in terms of tastes and preferences for food and wine.[141] Not surprisingly, France has historically been Britain's main supplier of wine; and Britain has always been an important export market for French wine. Yet sales figures for the year 2000 shockingly revealed that Australian wine exports had, by value, surpassed French wine exports for the first time ever,[142] a shift that reflected trends in other world markets as well,[143] and that has

---

[141] *See* discussion *supra* Section 3.3.

[142] It has been claimed that by volume, France's exports to Britain exceeds those from Australia. However, this only indicates that on average, the British are willing to pay more for a bottle of Australian than French wine. *See generally* Jim Budd, *CAP 2010: France Faces the Competition*, WINE BUS. MONTHLY, Dec. 3, 2002, *available at* http://www.winebusiness.com/html/PrinterVersion.cfm?dataId= 20791; *France's Wine Market Losing Global Market Share to New World Producers*, FOOD & DRINK WKLY., Aug. 20, 2001, *available at* http://www.findarticles.com/p/articles/mi_m0EUY/is_33_7/ai_77575053.

[143] Reportedly, the share of French exports in the United States wine market has dropped from over thirty-three percent in the 1990s to fifteen percent. *See* Gordon T. Anderson, *Can Anything Save French Wine?*, CNN MONEY, Aug. 23, 2004, http://money.cnn.com/2004/08/19/pf/goodlife/french_wine/ (describing the recent hits that the French wine industry has suffered).

670 *U. Pa. J. Int'l Econ. L.* [Vol. 26:4

continued since.

The severity of this finding for the French wine industry must be understood in the context of more general market trends. Wine consumption in France has decreased significantly in the post-World War II era, making export markets more important than they have been in the past. Wine consumption in non-traditional markets has grown, but so has the quantity and quality of wine products from "New World" sources. In fact, a combination of factors, not least French overproduction of low quality wine, has led to a global wine glut. The share of exports in world wine consumption is growing, although in most wine-producing countries, the majority of produce is still consumed locally.[144] In short, the loss of ground in a traditionally faithful export market served as a frightening "wake-up call" for the complacent French wine industry, leading the French Department of Agriculture to commission a report on the need for reform.[145] A key issue subsequently identified as requiring rethinking is the regulation of French AOCs and wine-labeling for export. In the debate that has ensued, proposals include scrapping the system, liberalizing it,[146] adding new high quality categories,[147] or various variations on and

---

[144] *See generally* Budd, *supra* note 142; Brian Croser, Winemaker, Petaluma Vineyards, Annual WSET Lecture 2004: Brand or Authenticity? (Feb. 23, 2004) *available at* http://www.wset.co.uk/docs/File35-2004AnnualLecture.doc (explaining the impact that the emerging Australian wine industry has on the global wine market); Andrew Inkpen & Rod Phillips, *The Wine Industry*, http://www.thunderbird.edu/pdf/about_us/case_series/a09030026.pdf (last visited Dec. 3, 2005) (detailing the history of the wine industry and its present-day state); Nicholas Le Quesne, *Vintage Advantage*, TIME EUROPE, Aug. 12, 2002, *available at* http://www.time.com/time/europe/magazine/article/0,13005 901020819336011,00.html (describing the French wine industry's response to global upstarts).

[145] *See* Jacques Berthomeau, *Comment mieux positionner les vins français sur les marchés d'exportation?* [*How Could French Wine Be Better Positioned in the Export Market?*], (2001), http://www.agriculture.gouv.fr/spip/IMG/pdf/ rappberthomeau-0.pdf (detailing the state of the French wine industry).

[146] *See* Interview by Alain Bloeykens with Jacques Berthomeau, Consultant, French Ministry of Agriculture, *The Money Flow Will Be Cut Off Without Hesitation*, *available at* http://www.underthecork.be/en/community/archief/may_02_ art1.html (arguing that drastic measures must be taken to save the French wine industry).

[147] *See* Jon Henley, *French Move the Goalposts in an Attempt to Halt Plunge in Wine Sales*, THE GUARDIAN, May 1, 2004, at 3, *available at* http://www.guardian.co.uk/france/story/0,11882,1207403,00.html (discussing the new technologies and methods the French have applied to their winemaking to halt sliding sales).

combinations of these ideas.   Thus, the future of French AOC regulation may hold many changes in mandatory methods of production within the GI system—which may yet emerge as another example of the ineffectiveness of GIs as protectors of the culture of production.

Concerned as we are in this section with traditions of consumption, however, let us focus on the British consumer market itself, not on its implications for French production. The gradual shift from French dominance to Australian (as well as North and South American) wine preference in Britain is likely the result of many combined market factors: the comparative advantage of Australia and other New World countries in the production of low-cost, successfully marketed, stereotypically gutsy wines full of ripe and vivid fruit flavors that provide easy drinking immediately upon release presents consumers with higher quality in lower price brackets and evidently panders to contemporary British consumer preferences. What is important for our purposes, however, is that underlying this market-induced change in consumption *patterns* is what may be perceived as a near-paradigmatic shift in consumption *culture*: the demise of a tradition of geographically discriminating consumption and the emergence (or rather, reinforcement) of a culture of consumption based on commercial branding. One of the distinctions between Old World and New World wine products is the system and style of their labeling and the degree of prominence accorded to their geographical designations.   In addition to the name of the producer or merchant, French wines list the name of the GI: an AOC or a lesser denomination. In France alone there exist in excess of 500 such indications, sometimes distinguishing small, adjacent plots with vastly different historical or current quality ratings and market prices.   Furthermore, quality French wine labels (with the exception of those from Alsace) are prohibited from displaying the name of the grape variety from which the wine is made. In contrast, Australian wines, like American and other New World wine labels, usually list the producer, a brand and the name of the grape variety involved—even when it is a blend.[148] There may also be a GI, but for most wines, certainly low-tier ones

---

[148] The normal rule in New World jurisdictions is that a wine may be labeled as a mono-varietal wine (e.g., Chardonnay or Cabernet Sauvignon) if a single variety constitutes 85% or more of the volume. Below that figure, the wine must be labeled as a blend (e.g., Cabernet Sauvignon-Merlot).

intended for mass-marketing, these will be very general. California or South-East Australia wines, for example, have designations that refer to territories with a size comparable to that of all of France.

In theory, the GI-intensive French system should therefore enjoy a comparative advantage in promoting its wines in a market with consumer traditions of geographical discrimination. Yet the experience in Britain shows that GIs have failed to prevent the erosion—or rather, the transformation—of consumer culture. It has simply become too difficult for the casual, nonexpert consumer to maintain a working knowledge of French appellations and their association with the kinds of wine he or she wants most. Examples of difficulties abound. If the consumer wants a Chardonnay, should she order a Pouilly-Fuisse or a Pouilly-Fume? If he likes Bourgogne, should he consider a Bourgogne-Passe-tout-grains? Is a Montrachet really so much better than a Puligny-Montrachet? If one likes Syrah, should one buy a Côtes du Rhône or a Cote Rôtie? Is a Muscadet des Coteaux de la Loire any different from a Muscadet Côtes de Grand Lieu? Similar problems of the density and intricacy of GIs surface in other "Old World" countries such as Italy, in which the palette of legally defined and protected GIs has grown and spread to new DOCs in every region, including many that will sound obscure to even the reasonably knowledgeable wine buff (e.g., Tuscany, which has Montecucco, Monteregio di Massa Maritima, Montescudaio, Candia dei Colli Apuani, Capalbio, Orcia, Sant'antimo on top of the better-known DOCs and DOCGs,[149] and Germany, which has a particularly elaborate wine law and labeling system).[150]

In comparison, it has become much easier for the general consumer to make informed assumptions on the character of a potential wine purchase on the basis of passing experience with a few grape varieties from a handful of countries and producers, not regions: "'Americans walk into a store and ask for a Chardonnay or a Cabernet . . . . They don't come in and start rattling off the

---

[149] Full listings of Italian wine *Indicazione Geografica Tipica* ("IGTs"), *Denominazione d'Origine Controllata* ("DOCs") and *Denominazione d'Origine Controllata e Garantita* ("DOCGs") are available. *E.g.*, BASTIANICH & LYNCH, *supra* note 128, at 400.

[150] *See* STEPHEN BROOK, THE WINES OF GERMANY 16–31 (2003) (detailing the wine laws of Germany and the problems encountered in reforming the vineyard classification system).

names of this or that obscure chateau.'"[151] The slipping sales of French wine in Britain indicate that the British consumer has become more "American" in this respect. Yet this cultural shift is not exclusively or even necessarily the outcome of aggressive globalization or Americanization. In fact, it is to some extent the result of the overambitious GI protection programs pursued in the legal systems of continental European countries for wine products intended for export. Quite simply, the proliferation of GIs, which in GI justificatory theory should lead to full information and to better purchasing decisions, has led to information overload that considerably obscures the consumer's view of her purchasing options and decisions. Absurdly, it might be said that free trade is at fault even here: If not for liberalization of trade, the wines of the most incomprehensible AOCs would simply not be available in foreign, "barbarian"[152] countries, leaving consumption up to the local French market.

In any event, in the field of traditions of consumption, we again see that GIs cannot withstand the cultural influence of market forces. It is not GIs that uphold culture, but rather culture that upholds GIs.[153]

---

[151] Anderson, *supra* note 143 (quoting a wine merchant).

[152] A term used in the Berthomeau Report, *supra* note 145, at 81.

[153] At least two plausible objections could be raised in relation to this admittedly stylized depiction of the changes in the British wine market. First, it is clear that the class-minded British society was not always, and never entirely, a "geographically discriminating" consumership, and so the shift is not as dramatic as it would appear. *See* Angela Tregear, *From Stilton to Vimto: Using Food History to Re-Think Typical Products in Rural Development*, 43 SOCIOLOGICA RURALIS 91 (2003) (analyzing in a highly nuanced, intelligent, and historically sensitive way the evolution of British consumption patterns in the pre-industrial, industrial, and post-industrial eras, while highlighting the influence of local raw materials and inherited, traditional production methods on food products). Building on Tregear, geographical taste in the pre-industrial era was a localized aspect of the close proximity of production and consumption (although it should be assumed that with regard to imports it applied mainly to nobility). Ever since, geographical discrimination has been restricted to the affluent classes and social elites, in the industrial era as a taste for specialty items, and in the post-industrial era as a reflection of nostalgia for rural roots and interest in "exotica." Therefore, it is possible that wealthy wine consumers have managed to overcome the complexities of ongoing geographical knowledge accumulation posed by the proliferation of GIs (increasing the gap between cognoscenti and non-geographically-minded consumers). Alternatively, they have weathered the storm by standing by the most time-tested appellations. Second, a distinction should be drawn between "super premium" wines that command high prices and may benefit from prestigious GIs at the proverbial "Grand Cru" level and low-priced market-leading brands that need to sell in the less geographically-inclined

4.4. The Culture of Identity: The Market for GIs Invents Traditions, Dilutes Culture, and Distorts Identity

A third proposition regarding the ineffectiveness of GIs as legal guardians of culture relates to their uncertain and potentially distortive effect on local identity. Much as some unique GIs do embody local cultural idiosyncrasies, reflecting a deeply inbred relationship between society and a uniquely local food and wine products, from a critical perspective many, and perhaps most of them, in fact represent legally "invented traditions"[154] and "imagined communities."[155] Even the most technically original, culturally-charged GI of all, Champagne, was legally established for primarily economic purposes: local identity and French nationalist symbolism served as rallying cries, an embellishment of reality for the purposes of a political campaign devised and pursued to ensure market protection.[156]

---

consumer market. For a discussion of the imperatives of such distinctions in modern wine markets, see Kym Anderson et al., *Globalisation and the World's Wine Markets: An Overview*, 26 WORLD ECON. 659, 661-69 (2003). The cumulative effect of these two precisions might suggest that there has not been a change in the importance of geographical discrimination. However, the increase in the average price commanded by Australian wines in relation to French wines suggests that this is not the case, and that a shift has occurred even in the more affluent — and traditionally geographically discriminating — classes of English society.

[154] According to Eric Hobsbawm:

> [Invented traditions are] "traditions" actually invented, constructed and formally instituted and those emerging in a less easily traceable manner within a brief and dateable period — a matter of a few years perhaps . . . .

> "Invented tradition" is taken to mean a set of practices, normally governed by overtly or tacitly accepted rules and of a ritual or symbolic nature, which seek to inculcate certain values and norms of behaviour by repetition, which automatically implies continuity with the past . . . . However, insofar as there is such reference to a historic past, the peculiarity of "invented" traditions is that the continuity with it is largely factitious.

Eric Hobsbawm, *Introduction: Inventing Traditions, in* THE INVENTION OF TRADITION 1-2 (Eric Hobsbawm and Terence Ranger eds., 1983).

[155] This is a phrase coined by Benedict Anderson in the context of nationalism. BENEDICT ANDERSON, IMAGINED COMMUNITIES: REFLECTIONS ON THE ORIGINS AND SPREAD OF NATIONALISM 5-7 (rev. ed., 1991).

[156] *See* Guy, *supra* note 8, at 163-73 (describing the marketing of wines that appealed to nationalist sentiment). More generally, what may be understood as the role of fantasy in the association of French national identity with wine is presented by the same author in Kolleen M. Guy, *Rituals of Pleasure in the Land of Treasures: Wine Consumption and the Making of French Identity in the Late Nineteenth Century, in* FOOD NATIONS: SELLING TASTE IN CONSUMER SOCIETIES, *supra* note 7, at

As the use of GIs spread throughout Europe, later under the canopy of international treaties and ultimately within the WTO, one of the phenomena that emerged may be described as a market for GIs, with both private and public choice aspects. On the private side, it was assumed that the consumer market assigned higher value to GI-designated products. The need for GI-have-nots to level the playing field with the GI-haves, resulted in a demand by producers for GIs—either as entirely new GIs, as breakaways from established GIs, or as GIs to be promoted in the hierarchy of GIs. On the public side, government regulators became suppliers of legally protected GIs. The pattern established in Champagne became the standard, as regional groups of producers, together with labor unions and local municipal governments, lobbied national agencies for GI recognition. Part of this lobbying process required arguments regarding the quality and singularity of the product (usually satisfied by a relatively simple demonstration of *terroir*), but GIs, as rights, have to be given to somebody—not a private entity, but a community, and one with a tradition. Thus, communities had to crystallize around the common interest of attaining GI status for local products, both for simple collective action needs and to satisfy the reputational and legal criteria for GI acquisition. This process proved self-perpetuating. Governments found it difficult and indeed politically inexpedient to refuse GI status to one region after having granted it to another, so that ultimately, the wine AOCs in France and DOCs in Italy might be said to cover virtually every viticultural area that could be associated with a locality. These market dynamics of GI acquisition have resulted in a proliferation of wine appellations in the Old World and, increasingly, in New World producing countries.

It has already been noted how the proliferation of GIs has

---

34. Much as Champagne has become perhaps the most belligerent of GIs, it has been argued that the term has been internationally used as a generic term for sparkling wine for decades. In any event, as this Article was completed, the United States and the European Union reportedly reached an agreement according to which the United States, agreed inter alia to prevent the use of "semi-generic" names, including Chamapagne, with respect to U.S. wines (without recognizing them as GIs), subject to "grandfather rights" for brands using these terms at the time of the agreement. Office of the United States Trade Representative, *Trade Facts, United States–European Communities Agreement on Trade in Wine*, Sept. 15, 2005, http://www.ustr.gov/assets/Document_Library/Fact_Sheets/2005/asset_upload_file611_7970.pdf.

676   *U. Pa. J. Int'l Econ. L.*   [Vol. 26:4

contributed to consumer confusion by eroding the consumer culture of geographical discrimination.[157] Additionally, the GI explosion has likely contributed to a general devaluation of GIs and GI-led products, thereby reducing the economic capacity of GIs to protect tradition. An advantage enjoyed by many, if not all, is not generally an advantage anymore. Furthermore, the abundance of GIs hints that, in practice, satisfying a low threshold of regional or local distinctiveness is sufficient for bestowal of GI status, including only vague references to local traditional practices—a functional dilution of the cultural rationale. In many cases, new GIs are indeed attempts to establish instant reputations through invented traditions that building a novel culture through self-reference to the distant or at least irrelevant past. Some of the more recent Tuscan DOCs listed above are cases in point,[158] as are others in several emerging regions of Italy, inasmuch as they are in fact areas that may (or may not) have had some reputation for distinctive wines more than a century ago (at best) or in the time of the Etruscans (at worst), but for generations this aspect of the land and the people has been defunct.[159] Moreover, these regions have been invigorated by some local efforts, bolstered by capital and enterprise flowing from other established areas. For example, according to popular knowledge, the coastal Tuscan Morellino di

---

[157] *See* discussion *supra* Section 4.3.

[158] *See supra* text accompanying notes 130–31.

[159] The invention or re-invention of tradition can appear in commercial contexts even when there is no GI involved. For example, the relatively new Israeli wine industry has some wineries that stress the historic roots of wine in the holy land, by depicting ancient grape presses or ruins on their labels. *See* Ella Valley Vineyards: About Us, http://www.ellavalley.com (last visited Dec. 6, 2005) ("Archaeological findings such as ancient presses and vineyards attest to Ella Valley's importance as a winemaking region thousands of years back, in the biblical Land of Israel."). In one very new project in the Negev desert, vines have been planted along terraces that are designated as archaeological relics from the Nabbatean (Byzantine) period.   *See Desert Wine*, SOURCE ISRAEL ONLINE, http://www.thesourceisrael.com/issue3/intimate.shtml (last visited Dec. 6, 2005) ("Well-versed in the agricultural successes of the Nabateans 1000 years earlier at Avdat (a few kilometers from Kibbutz Sde Boker), Ben Gurion envisioned modern vineyards that would make the desert bloom."). In another development, one sees the emergence of "borrowed traditions," as local municipalities produce maps of wine routes, and publicity material hails the Galilee or Judean Hills as an Israeli Tuscany or Provence.   *See* Tour Yoav, http://www.touryoav.org.il (Hebrew website). Indeed, in the absence of formal GIs for Israeli wines, one of the best and longest established Israeli wineries labels its wines as *"Grand Vin de Haut-Judée,"* emulating and informally assimilating the regional traditions of France. Domaine du Castel, http://www.castel.co.il.

Scansano DOC, established in 1978, can boast some positive references to its wines in the Middle Ages, and as late as 1848.[160] When the Scansano wine was granted a protected GI it had little to offer, however, in the way of quality. A handful of local wineries made good efforts, but more importantly, some of the big players in the central Tuscan wine industry recognized commercial potential in the area, bought land, planted new vines, and built wineries.

In short, in this and other cases, a DOC whose cultural foundation had little to do with present local culture reinvented itself by recalling its distant past in order to be more commercially relevant in the future. The "award" of a GI provided an incentive to invent tradition; the effects on the real tissue of local culture, however, are unknown.

Perhaps most importantly—though most difficult to substantiate on a sound anthro-sociological basis without considerable research—the invented traditions themselves, pursued for commercial purposes within the market for GIs, may ultimately emphasize the more marketable aspects of local wine and food culture, even invented ones, neglecting other less commercially attractive aspects. Again, Champagne is somehow instructive in this regard, because, until the mid-nineteenth century, local culture was more related to still wines, not *Méthode Champenoise* sparkling wines. Economic expediency produced the push for early GI protection that required an emphasis on the local and French ethos of sparkling wine. This is similar to the complex effects of tourism on communities.[161] In order to attract tourism, communities must emphasize what makes them special, and of course, agreeable from an external, market perspective, not in terms of their own self-determination of identity and aspiration. A community, real or imagined, that, for economic purposes, is interested in gaining GI status, will clearly need to emphasize those aspects of its local food or wine culture that are marketable for this purpose. As in the example of Morellino di Scansano DOC,

---

[160] *See* Italian Trade Commission http://www.italianmade.com/wines/DOC10213.cfm (noting the long-standing excellent reputation of Scansano wine).

[161] *See generally* Michel Picard & Jean Michaud, *Présentation – Tourisme et sociétés locales* [*Introduction – Tourism and Local Societies*], ANTHROPOLOGIE ET SOCIÉTÉS, 2001, at 5–13, *available at* http://www.erudit.org/revue/as/2001/v25/n2/000230ar.pdf (describing the effects of tourism on local culture and society).

above, the cost, in terms of lost, un-invented tradition, is forever unknown.

5.   DOLCI: THE FUTURE OF CULTURAL PROTECTION IN WTO LAW

5.1. *Implications for the WTO GI Debate and Beyond*

This Article could have ended here, with a simple, neat conclusion: GIs, as legal mechanisms and quasi-intellectual property rights, evidently do not have the independent capacity to protect local cultures of production, consumption or identity, or to prevent the erosion of cultural diversity. Market forces inevitably induce changes in local production methods and consumption preferences, in spite of the GIs that should, in theory, play a role in preserving them, and the proliferation of GIs has itself diluted the claims of special reputation, typicity, and cultural identity of GI-endowed locales.

For negotiators at the WTO, the consequent recommendation would, therefore, be to abandon any romantic rhetoric of cultural protection in the debate over expansion of article 23 of TRIPS "additional protection,"[162] and to recognize GIs and treat them exclusively as what they are: legal tools for granting commercial advantages to certain products, sectors and regions. GIs are instruments of trade policy, like tariffs, subsidies or service-provider regulations. GIs should, therefore, be negotiated and maintained as such: free of all overweight "cultural" baggage such as tariff concessions, subject only to reciprocal commitments and nondiscrimination obligations of WTO members relating to their respective GIs. Furthermore, since culture cannot of itself justify *any* GI protection, it should not be used as a justifying measure for selecting *some* GIs as eligible for "additional protection," or for preferring *some* GI-able products over others. There may (or may not) be plausible reasons to provide only regular protection to some GIs and "additional protection" to others, but cultural diversity is not among them. There seem to be good reasons to scrap "additional protection" entirely, but that seems politically unlikely. Given that the current legal situation clearly discriminates against developing countries—because most wine and spirits GIs are from developed countries—regardless of

---

[162] *See supra* text accompanying notes 20–21 (referring to "protection granted even when there is no risk of misleading consumers or unfair competition").

cultural justifications, article 23 of TRIPS "additional protection" should be extended to all GIs, of all members (indeed, the European Union will be the greatest single beneficiary from extension, but the viability of GIs of developing countries will be much greater than at present).

Moreover, we have endeavored to take "trade and culture" seriously, beyond the limited test case of GIs. What emerges more generally, then, from the case study of cultural protection through GIs is the following striking image: An international legal mechanism with trade restrictive effects, widely believed to have a positive effect on preserving cultural diversity, and with a plausible underlying theory of cultural protection to boot, which in practice, simply does no such thing. Cynics or uncompromising neo-liberal trade theorists might be quick to interpret this as proof that trade restrictions, in general, cannot contribute to cultural diversity and that all trade-related claims calling for cultural protection are merely disguised calls for economic protectionism. While this may be true in some or even many cases, I would instead suggest some less simplified observations, not rejecting the idea of cultural protection through trade restrictions entirely, but rather qualifying the ways in which proposed legal methods for cultural protection are to be assessed and applied.

These thoughts, laid out hereunder (in an initial way, worthy of further contemplation and discussion), relate to:

- the desirability of specific, *sui generis* cultural protection from trade liberalization;

- the viability, applicability, and mechanics of a general cultural exception in international trade law; and

- some of the problems associated with the development of a separate, UNESCO-based cultural protection regime that would impact upon rights and obligations in the WTO.

5.2. *Thinking About* Sui Generis *Cultural Protection*

Insofar as GIs represent an approach to cultural protection based upon *sui generis* legal measures in international trade law, it is apparent that the real cultural effects of such measures must be analyzed with care, if not caution (which is not always to say, with

680   *U. Pa. J. Int'l Econ. L.*   [Vol. 26:4

skepticism).

Tailor-cut, *sui generis*, case-by-case methods have the advantage of avoiding unnecessarily restrictive generalized exceptions to trade rules (an advantage significantly eroded if specialized measures are established in *addition* to general exceptions). Nevertheless, *sui generis* measures have the potential to expand trade-protectionism beyond what is necessary—or effective—for cultural protection even within their own targeted scope. Specifically, agreed upon trade-restrictive measures and mechanisms that are based upon a theory of cultural protection should therefore be defined in the strictest possible terms, on the basis of sound quantitative and qualitative research, adhering in practice and effect to their cultural rationale. This is not only necessary to mitigate the welfare-reducing economic effects of such measures, but also to maintain their coherence and, indeed, legitimacy as cultural protection mechanisms. "Culture" should not be allowed to become a euphemistic code word for protectionism.

It is probably too late to entirely undo the idea of GI protection on the mere argument that it is not conducive to cultural protection. However, proposals for similar *sui generis* trade or intellectual property disciplines that refer to a cultural protection justification[163] should be subjected to rigorous cultural—not only legal and economic—analysis, in order to discern their real effects on both trade and culture. The GI experience suggests that it is not enough to demonstrate how free trade may harm cultural diversity. Of greater importance is substantiation that the *sui generis* measure can, in fact, prevent this harm in practice. Since such proof may be difficult or, indeed, impossible to procure before the measures in question are imposed, it would appear advisable for WTO members agreeing on new specialized measures aimed at cultural protection to define a test-run or sunset review period for the measure. At the end of this period, not only could the measure's trade impact be evaluated, but a "cultural impact assessment" could be conducted, relating to predetermined criteria. This could be conducted by recognized experts, with UNESCO involvement. If these criteria are not met, the international legal measure should be abolished or modified

---

[163] Traditional knowledge may be deemed one of these cultural protection justifications; indeed, GIs are sometimes referred to as a tool for protecting traditional knowledge. *See supra* note 3.

accordingly — not because it is trade-restrictive, but because it does not promote cultural protection.

In addition, members — and in particular developing countries — who are considering adopting GIs as a suitable vehicle for the protection of rights in traditional knowledge, or who would like to see stronger specialized rules for cultural protection in the WTO and elsewhere, should be aware that although such modalities may increase the commercial value of existing cultural goods and services, their effect on cultural preservation and diversity is indeterminate at best. This is because GI protected traditions might nevertheless in the future succumb to economic pressures and international consumer preferences. GIs and other trade-related measures must be augmented by more comprehensive flanking policies and competent regulation if cultural diversity is to be preserved.

5.3. Thinking About a General GATT/GATS Cultural Exception

Our examination of the questionable practical ability of GIs to fulfill the role of cultural guardian raises several questions and suggestions relating to the viability, applicability and mechanics of a general cultural exception in international trade law. To be sure, the existing general exceptions in Article XX of GATT and Article XIV of GATS cannot be said to expressly establish a comprehensive exception for cultural policies, but some cultural legislation may be covered. The term "public morals" in Article XX(a) of GATT/ Article XIV of GATS has recently been interpreted as denoting "standards of right and wrong conduct maintained by or on behalf of a community or nation,"[164] the content of which "for [WTO] members can vary in time and space, depending upon a range of factors, including prevailing social, cultural, ethical and religious values."[165] It is not difficult to see how this exception, so defined, could apply to preventive policies (such as age limits for legal alcohol consumption, legal regulation of the sale and shipping of alcoholic beverages, and so on) that relate not only to public order but also to cultural mores, or to restrictions on the sale and importation of foodstuffs that are culturally offensive in the

---

[164] *See US — Gambling II, supra* note 2, ¶ 296 (affirming, implicitly, the definition of "public morals" in Panel Report, *United States — Measures Affecting the Cross-Border Supply of Gambling and Betting Services,* ¶ 6.487, WT/DS285/R (Nov. 10, 2004) [hereinafter *US — Gambling I*]).

[165] *US — Gambling I, supra* note 164, ¶ 6.461.

682   *U. Pa. J. Int'l Econ. L.*   [Vol. 26:4

importing state, for such reasons as religion (e.g., beef products to a Hindu region, alcohol to a Muslim state, non-kosher foods to Israel).[166]   It is, however, much more difficult to envision this language applying to import restrictions based on a positive cultural policy aimed at the preservation of a certain local craft or trade (such as artisanal wine- or cheese-making), if only because such a policy would not regularly relate to "standards of right and wrong."   Indeed, to include all cultural policies in the "public morals" exception would be tantamount to expanding its scope to include practically any legally regulated field, i.e., *reductio ad absurdum*.   (In the field of services, at least, this would be inconsistent with the strict requirement in footnote 5 of Article XIV(a) of GATS, according to which "the public order exception may be invoked only where a genuine and sufficiently serious threat is posed to one of the fundamental interests of society.")

For the same reasons, it would also be an exaggeration to allow domestic GI legislation (as an example of ostensibly cultural policy) to benefit from the public morals exception, had GIs not been specifically permitted and regulated by TRIPS as *sui generis* measures.

Thus, while culture may at times inform local morality, surely not all cultural issues are related to "public morals."

Similarly, the Article XX(f) of GATT exception is limited to the protection of "national treasures of artistic, historical or archeological value."   This should properly be read as relating to specific, physical artifacts of national importance, directed mainly to justify export rather than import restrictions.   Champagne may sincerely be regarded by the French as a national treasure,[167] as may other champion food and wine products, but it would be an abuse of this exception to interpret it as permitting trade restrictions for their preservation.   The same logic would apply to other cultural policies.   For example, each nation's language may be a national treasure of sorts, but Article XX(f) of GATT cannot be reasonably stretched to justify trade-restrictive measures based on language policies.

Moreover, WTO members could conceivably expand the meanings of these exceptions to include a broader range of cultural policies   (through   treaty   amendment   or   "authoritative

---

[166] Of course such legislation would also have to satisfy all other elements of Article XX(a) of GATT/Article XIV(a) of GATS in order to be WTO consistent.

[167] *See supra* note 117.

interpretation" under article X or article IX(2) of the WTO Agreement, respectively).[168] Regardless of the specific wording of such an expanded exception relating to cultural protection,[169] and whether through amendment or interpretation (judicial or quasi-legislative), the question would then arise regarding the conditions to be met by a trade-restrictive measure in order to benefit from the cultural exception.

Drawing from Article XX(a) of GATT/Article XIV(a) of GATS case law and otherwise analogous GATT Article XX jurisprudence, two cumulative conditions specifically addressed at "cultural protection" seem likely (in addition to the other conditions of the respective *chapeaux* of Article XX of GATT/Article XIV of GATS). First, the trade-restrictive measure must be within the scope of the "cultural protection" exception[170]; second, the measure must be "necessary" for the protection of local culture and cultural diversity.[171]

In this regard the present Article's conclusions regarding the problematic actual effect of GIs on the preservation of local tradition and cultural diversity, may cast a critical shadow on current WTO jurisprudence as applied to cultural issues. This is because panels and the Appellate Body are often receptive to the non-trade theories underlying trade-restrictive measures insofar as finding the measures to be within the scope of an exception is concerned (the first condition). They are more critical at the later

---

[168] *See* TOMER BROUDE, INTERNATIONAL GOVERNANCE IN THE WTO: JUDICIAL BOUNDARIES AND POLITICAL CAPITULATION 213–17 (2004) (discussing the legislative capacities of the WTO General Council).

[169] The language of the various sub-provisions of Article XX of GATT, and Article XIV of GATS, is not consistent, including the most frequently used and applied "necessary to" (e.g., sub-Articles XX(a), (b), (d) and also (i) GATT), "relating to," "imposed for," "undertaken in pursuance," and "essential to"). Different language has led to different interpretations, reflecting a varying "required nexus" or "degree of connection" between the measure and the protected interest. *See US – Gambling II, supra* note 2 ¶ 292 (discussing the "two-tiered analysis" under Article XIV of GATS). In the present (hypothetical) analysis, we assume that the wording "necessary to" would be applied to a general cultural exception, if applied, but this would naturally be one of the issues subject to member negotiations.

[170] *E.g., US – Gambling I, supra* note 164, ¶ 6.449 (relying on prior Appellate Body Reports, including *Korea – Various Measures on Beef*, WT/DS161/AB/R, WT/DS169/AB/R (Dec. 11, 2001) [hereinafter *Korea-Beef*], to illustrate the two-tiered analysis).

[171] *Cf. Korea-Beef, supra* note 171, ¶ 161 (discussing possible interpretations of the word "necessary" and linking the definition to "indispensable").

684   *U. Pa. J. Int'l Econ. L.*   [Vol. 26:4

analytical stages relating to the "necessity" of the challenged measures (the second condition), and the overarching requirement of the measures' conformity with the Article XX of GATT / Article XIV of GATS *chapeaux*. In the *US-Gambling* case, for example, the panel adopted a very lax test for the satisfaction of the first condition, regarding the question of the measures' inclusion within the scope of "public morals." It only briefly examined the legislative history of the challenged measures, and concluded that the record shows that their rationale was one aimed at the protection of public morals.[172] The requirement that the measure be "within the scope" of an exception has in practice been transposed into a requirement that the measure be "designed to" achieve the goal of the exception.[173] In a cultural exception, the measure would therefore be required, for example, to "be designed to protect local culture."

This may be (and with regard to other protected interests, has in practice been) constructed as a mainly subjective test (building principally on the declared intent of the legislator), ignoring the possibility of ulterior, multiple, or misguided motives for legislation. As a legal test, it does not objectively examine the actual effectiveness of the challenged measure in achieving its alleged aims. On appeal, the Appellate Body in *US – Gambling* also disposed of this issue very briefly, limiting itself to the grounds of appeal which did not include a challenge to the inclusion of the measures in question within the scope of the "public morals" exception.[174] It was "quick to justify"[175] the challenged legislation

---

[172] *US--Gambling I, supra* note 164, ¶¶ 6.479–6.487 (in particular ¶¶ 6.486–6.487). The panel referred to a 1961 Report to the House of Representatives and to a statement by the late Robert F. Kennedy, but did not require positive evidence regarding the effectiveness of the legislation in meeting its declared purposes in the four decades that had passed. The panel concluded on this point that it was satisfied that "various arms of the government of the United States consider these Acts were adopted to address concerns such as those pertaining to money laundering, organized crime, fraud, underage gambling and pathological gambling," that fall within the scope of "public morals" and/or "public order" within the meaning of GATS Article XIV(a).

[173] *Id.* ¶ 6.487.

[174] The Appellate Body seemed understatedly critical of the absence of this claim on appeal. *See US – Gambling II, supra* note 2, ¶ 297 ("Antigua contests this finding on a rather limited ground . . . .").

[175] Joost Pauwelyn, *ASIL Insight: WTO Softens Earlier Condemnation of U.S. Ban on Internet Gambling, but Confirms Broad Reach into Sensitive Domestic Regulation*, ASIL INSIGHTS, Apr. 12, 2005, http://www.asil.org/insights/2005/04/insights050412.html.

as conducive to the substantive purpose of the "public morals" exception. In general, WTO adjudicators appear to consider it more legitimacy-enhancing (and consistent with the requirement that their rulings not "add to or diminish the rights and obligations of the WTO agreements[176]") to embrace the non-trade considerations at stake, and grant national authorities considerable leeway in their delimitation, while retaining the authority to strike the contested national measures down because they are overly trade-restrictive, given the existence of alternatives. In issues relating to cultural concerns that reflect particularly sensitive national sentiments, one can only imagine that panels and the Appellate Body will be at least as permissive in accepting measures as "within the scope" of a cultural exception.

Regarding the second condition, the *US – Gambling* panel followed the established relevant jurisprudence (particularly *Korea–Beef*)[177] whereby the "necessary to" (or "necessity") test means significantly more than "making a contribution to" the protected interest, much closer to "indispensable." Consequently, and in keeping with a large mass of prior jurisprudence, the Appellate Body focused its review of this condition on an examination of the existence of viable, less trade-restrictive, substitutes for the challenged measure (a comparative, "indispensability" test), and not on the actual efficacy of the challenged measure (an absolute, objective "effectiveness" test). To be sure, one constituent element of the second, "necessity" test, is the extent to which the challenged measures "contribute to the realization of the ends respectively pursued" by them,[178] but in practice this element receives scant attention in cases where the actual effect of a measure on a protected interest is difficult to measure. Thus, in *US – Gambling* the panel (as upheld by the Appellate Body) simply concluded that since the challenged measures prohibit a form of services supply, "they must contribute, at least to some extent" to addressing the relevant

---

[176] Understanding on Rules and Procedures Governing the Settlement of Disputes, Apr. 15, 1994, Marrakesh Agreement Establishing the World Trade Organization, Annex 2, Legal Instruments—Results of the Uruguay Round, 33 I.L.M. 1125, art. 3.2 (1994) [hereinafter DSU].

[177] *Korea-Beef, supra* note 171, ¶ 161.

[178] *US – Gambling I, supra* note 164, ¶ 6.488. The other two constituent elements are the importance of the protected interest(s) and the trade impact of the measures. *Id.*

concerns.[179]

This echoes the general assumption that trade restrictions can protect cultural values, consonant with the analysis in Section 3 *supra* — an assumption and analysis shown to be incorrect in practice, in the GI context, in the subsequent Section 4.

In other words, the panel and the Appellate Body in *US – Gambling*, in practice, accepted the protective "public morals" theory underlying the measures in question with little questioning, and, on its basis, assumed that the trade restriction established by them must have a protective effect. They then proceeded to examine the extent of protection on a comparative rather than absolute basis, mainly alluding to the availability of alternatives. Thus, at no point did the panel or Appellate Body critically examine the fundamental contention that the restrictive legislation had *any* measurable positive effect on the safeguarding of public morals (or rather, that the absence of measures would have a detrimental effect upon them).[180] This approach stands in stark contrast to our current analysis of the cultural protection role of GIs, which demonstrates that some so-called cultural policies have no real effect on the protection of culture. Under current jurisprudence, evidence on the real futility of cultural protection through trade-restrictive exceptions might be ignored by WTO judicial bodies if adjudicated. This would be particularly problematic if, under the indispensability test, unworthy trade-restrictive cultural policies were sustained under an Article XX of GATT-style or GATT-stylized cultural exception because there was no readily apparent less trade-restrictive policy alternative. This would be so even though the measures themselves were not in fact effective as cultural protectors.

Furthermore, this also becomes a burden of proof issue. While it is accepted that the party invoking an Article XX of GATT/Article XIV of GATS exception (normally the respondent) bears the burden of proving the affirmative of the particular defense,[181] in practice, it is the complainant who must show that

---

[179] *Id.* at ¶ 6.494.

[180] This is even despite evidence provided by Antigua and Barbuda, the complainant in the case, whereby some U.S. military research had found that "the presence of military casinos did not have a negative effect on the morale or financial stability of the United States forces, their family members and other persons — including foreign nationals — who gambled at the government-owned facilities." *US – Gambling I, supra* note 162, at ¶ 6.480.

[181] *See* Appellate Body Report, *United States – Measure Affecting Imports of*

the challenged measure is not indispensable in terms of the necessity test by demonstrating the existence of WTO-compliant or less inconsistent alternatives. If, as in *US – Gambling* among others, the respondent is not seriously required to show that the challenged measure has a materially positive effect on culture, the burden of proof is thus effectively shifted to the complainant (while the respondent must then rebut by showing that these alternatives are not "reasonably available"),[182] and the substantive question of the absolute effectiveness of the challenged measures is bypassed. This grants both substantive and tactical advantages to the cultural consideration which, as our analysis of GIs demonstrates, may have no real empirical basis.

It is therefore evident that if "trade and culture" is to be taken seriously, the WTO dispute-settlement system should be more inquisitive regarding theories of non-trade cultural protection that are claimed to underlie trade restrictions. It should also devote more objective attention to the substantive question of whether challenged trade-restrictive measures do in fact contribute to the achievement of the protected non-trade value, such as culture and cultural diversity. This should occur well before consideration of the extent (interpreted as indispensability) of such protection. For example, if GIs had not (counterfactually) been established under specialized TRIPS rules, an investigation into the actual cultural effect of GIs might demonstrate their questionable contribution to cultural protection as presented in this Article, making unnecessary an examination of the theoretical degree of protection offered, both absolutely and in relation to conceivable alternatives.

5.4. Thinking About a Parallel UNESCO Regime

Circumventing the question of a cultural exception *in* WTO

Woven Wool Shirts and Blouses from India, WT/DS33/AB/R (Apr. 25 1997) ("It is only reasonable that the burden of establishing such a defence should rest on the party asserting it.")

182 The intricacy of the burdens of proof in Article XX, with special regard to the burden of proving the existence or absence of reasonably available alternatives is discussed by the Appellate Body in *US – Gambling II, supra* note 2, at ¶¶ 309–310. In its quest for certainty and clarity in the allocation of the burden of proof, the Appellate Body has explained its standards in this case, while in others it has merely compounded confusion, but discussion of this is for another article. Here I merely wish to point out that the tactical advantage granted to the party responding on the basis of a cultural exception by way of the "necessity" test has been construed in practice in combination with the burden of proof.

law, the UNESCO Second Draft Convention,[183] upon entering into force in the future, may establish in more ways than one, a parallel or separate legal regime for the regulation of trade and culture with significant external impacts *on* the WTO. Under article 5(1) of the Second Draft Convention, states Parties will affirm "their sovereign right to adopt measures to protect and promote the diversity of cultural expressions within their territory."[184] "Cultural expressions" are broadly defined in article 4 of the Draft Convention as including the "cultural contents" of "cultural goods and services,"[185] whose definition has already been discussed.[186]

Most importantly, under article 6(1) of the Second Draft Convention, "each [state] Party may adopt measures aimed at protecting and promoting the diversity of cultural expressions within its territory."[187] Under article 6(2) of the Second Draft Convention, such protective and/or promotive cultural measures may include (among others) the following:

(a) regulatory measures aimed at protecting and promoting diversity of cultural expressions;

(b) measures that, in an appropriate manner, provide opportunities for domestic cultural activities, goods and services among all those available within the national territory for their creation, production, dissemination, distribution and enjoyment of such domestic cultural activities, goods and services, including provisions relating to the language used for such activities, goods and services;

(c) measures aimed at providing domestic independent cultural industries and activities in the informal sector effective access to the means of production, dissemination and distribution of cultural activities, goods and services;

(d) measures aimed at providing public financial assistance;

---

[183] *See supra* note 5 (the analysis is subject to the caveat related to the adoption of the Convention, in the last sentence of the footnote).

[184] UNESCO Second Draft Convention, *supra* note 4, art. 5(1).

[185] *Id.* art. 4.

[186] *See supra* text accompanying note 47.

[187] UNESCO Second Draft Convention, *supra* note 4, art. 6(1).

(e) measures aimed at encouraging non-profit organizations, as well as public and private institutions and artists and other cultural professionals, to develop and promote the free exchange and circulation of ideas, cultural expressions and cultural activities, goods and services, and to stimulate both the creative and entrepreneurial spirit in their activities;

(f) measures aimed at establishing and supporting public institutions, as appropriate;

(g) measures aimed at nurturing and supporting artists and others involved in the creation of cultural expressions;

(h) measures aimed at enhancing diversity of the media including through public service broadcasting.[188]

The only precondition required is that these measures be "within the framework of [the State Party's] cultural policies," which are broadly defined in article 4(6) of the Second Draft Convention as "policies and measures related to culture, whether at the local, national, regional or international level that are either focused on culture as such or are designed to have a direct effect on cultural expressions of individuals, groups or societies, including on the creation, production, dissemination, distribution of and access to cultural activities, goods and services."[189]

In other words, it seems (without undertaking more detailed analysis) the UNESCO Draft Convention grants a virtual carte blanche to national discrimination in all relevant aspects of commercial activity (note the continued emphasis on "domestic" protection).   That may take the form of WTO-inconsistent quantitative restrictions and measures of equivalent effect, or the provision of actionable or prohibited direct subsidies ("public financial assistance"), or other measures, as long as these national measures can fit into a framework of "cultural policies"; and these only need be "designed to have an effect" on cultural expressions. In terms of the trade and culture debate, this approach at least seems to grant full priority to a broadly defined vision of culture over all aspects of trade (however, the UNESCO Draft Convention

---

[188] *Id.* art. 6(2).

[189] *Id.* art. 4(6).

itself includes provisions that would promote access to international cultural expressions, somewhat balancing this initial assessment).

Of course one must ask what the status would be of these proposed UNESCO obligations and rights in the WTO in case of conflict of norms. Article 19 of the First Draft Convention provided for two possibilities. Under Option B, the Draft Convention would not "affect the rights and obligations of the States Parties under any other existing international instruments,"[190] viz., when push came to shove, trade and culture issues would continue to be regulated by WTO disciplines not only in the WTO but in the entire fabric of legal relations between parties. Under the alternative Option A, however, a cultural priority was constructed. While the First Draft Convention's provisions would not affect international "intellectual property rights," existing international rights and obligations would step aside where they would "cause serious damage or threat to the diversity of cultural expressions."[191]

The relationship between the proposed UNESCO Convention and other international obligations was the focus of heated debates during 2005, and can be expected to remain so. In the UNESCO Second Draft Convention of August 2005, article 20 emphasized that the Convention is not subordinate to any other treaty and attempts to establish inter-treaty normative comity, but then provides that "[n]othing in this Convention shall be interpreted as modifying rights and obligations of the Parties under any other treaties to which they are parties."[192]

This legal construction does not seem satisfactorily meaningful for several reasons, but for present purposes suffice it to say that it does not allocate any weight to the question of whether the "cultural policies" at hand actually have any proven positive effect on cultural protection and diversity. This may lead to a significant

---

[190] UNESCO First Draft Convention, *supra* note 4, art. 19, option B.

[191] *Id.* art. 19.2, option A. For a more comprehensive blackletter analysis of the potential conflict of norms between the now superseded UNESCO First Draft Convention and WTO Agreements, from a general public international law perspective, see Jan Wouters & Bart De Meester, *UNESCO's Convention on Cultural Diversity and WTO Law: Complementary or Contradictory?* (K.U. Leuven Faculty of Law Inst. for Int'l Law, Working Paper No. 73, Apr. 2005), *available at* http://www.law.kuleuven.be/iir/nl/wp/WP/WP73e.pdf (last visited Nov. 16, 2005).

[192] UNESCO Second Draft Convention, *supra*, note 4, art. 20.

expansion of the breadth of national policies that benefit from the Draft Convention's provisions without actually making a contribution to the achievement of the Draft Convention's purposes. Thus, while the idea of a separate UNESCO cultural protection regime is certainly a worthy one, in light of this Article's conclusions regarding the dubious merits of GIs as a form cultural policy, and the potentially material adverse effect of such a regime upon trade, it appears incumbent upon such a separate cultural regime to undertake a regulatory system that would more strictly define the cultural effects it intends to achieve, and more seriously monitor and verify the achievement of these effects.

As in our discussion of *sui generis* cultural protection and of a general cultural exception in WTO law, the actual positive influence of a proposed measure, whether international or national, upon cultural protection and diversity simply cannot be taken for granted. This is so even in the face of a persuasive cultural theory and within the framework of a parallel UNESCO regime of trade and culture.

6. *DIGESTIVO*: OF CULTURAL PROTECTION AND CULTURAL PROTECTIONISM

The challenge of the "Trade and Culture" nexus lies, like in other "Trade and ——." situations, in designing workable legal mechanisms for distinguishing between genuinely cultural national regulatory measures on the one hand, and measures whose effect is merely to distort international trade on the other; between cultural protection and cultural protectionism. In this article I have endeavored to demonstrate that GIs, as *sui generis* internationally-agreed-upon legal measures, are closer to the latter than the former. Furthermore, I have argued that in drawing the boundary between cultural protection and protectionism, "trade and culture" should be taken seriously, or rather, that culture itself should be taken seriously as a non-trade consideration. As the battle cry of the disgruntled Languedoc *vigneron* in this article's epigraph illustrates, the flag of culture is all too easily unfurled on behalf of trade protectionism. If, however, culture is to be taken seriously as a justification for trade-restrictive policies, it must first be proven that these policies do indeed contribute to the protection and promotion of local culture and to the safeguarding of cultural diversity. This must be the first test of a cultural policy; only then may it be allowed to establish digressions from general international trade law disciplines, through specialized mechanisms, under the rules of a general GATT/GATS cultural exception or through a separate UNESCO cultural diversity regime. This may seem to be a "trade first" approach, but it is no less a "culture first" one, because it would not tolerate the institution of rules of international cultural diversity law that may look good on paper but have no real effects on culture in practice.

A problem that perhaps distinguishes the "trade and culture" issue from other "trade and ——" relationships lies at the core. Are trade and culture really conflicting values with opposing interests? Both trade and culture are expressions of human activity and exchange; the exchange not only of goods and services, but also of ideas. As article 7 of the UNESCO Declaration acknowledges, "[c]reation draws on the roots of cultural tradition, but flourishes in contact with other cultures."[193] Culture is not static; it flows and changes as do the individuals who create and practice it. The traditions of today are the unthinkable innovations and foreign influences of yesteryear. Without international trade and interaction, global culture might simply dry up. The UNESCO Second Draft Convention appreciates this reality in a few of its provisions, but operatively does not accord it much space.[194] As pressure mounts to establish international legal mechanisms of cultural protection that entail restrictions to trade, we must ask ourselves whether by curtailing *economic* human exchanges such mechanisms do not at the same time prevent human *cultural* exchanges in whose vibrancy lies the future of human cultural development and its diversity.

But these are thoughts best left for another meal.[195]

---

[193] UNESCO Declaration, *supra* note 4, art. 7.

[194] For definition of the concept of "interculturality," see Second Draft Convention, *supra* note 4, art. 4.8.

[195] Readers with an interest in exploring these final questions more fully must read TYLER COWEN, CREATIVE DESTRUCTION: HOW GLOBALIZATION IS CHANGING THE WORLD'S CULTURES (2002).

[26]

Analysis

Taking Local Knowledge into Account in the AOC System

Christine de Sainte Marie is an agro-economist in the SAD (science for action and development) department at INRA (National Institute for Agricultural Research). After working on the organization of supply chains for specific quality products, she now focuses on the economic analysis of the 'greening' of agriculture, especially the acknowledgement of biodiversity in the labeling of products and their production systems.

Laurence Bérard:
See page 167.

Christine de Sainte Marie, Laurence Bérard

The AOC (registered designation of origin), is a French invention designed to protect the geographical name of an agricultural or food product to which a value is attached. While it does not directly or explicitly protect local knowledge related to nature and the living world, it takes it into account whenever it proves necessary to justify the specificity linked to a particular place. For local knowledge and practices play an important role in characterizing the typicality of the designation of origin.

Examining practices in detail makes it possible to distinguish a link with biological and landscape diversity, and to cease considering this diversity as simply a positive effect of local products. But these practices imply different issues and their consideration cannot be taken for granted; it is strongly dependent on social interplay, the movement of the economy and the scale of exchanges involving local products. Consequently, to deal with the protection and exploitation of local knowledge via the French experience of designations of origin, it must first be remembered that the protection of geographical names, industrialization and globalization go hand in hand.

Designations of origin, industrialization and globalization

The protection of designations of origin is in line with late 19th century laws on industrial property. The law of 1905 on the repression of fraud and adulteration of products and services is the founding text. The AO, *appellation d'origine** (designation of origin) was introduced in 1919, at a time when urban markets and international trade in agricultural products were developing. However, lawmakers did not define the designation of origin itself, but referred to "local, loyal and constant practices" that could be opposed to third parties and that were to lead to the delimitation of an area associated with the protected geographical name.

The designation of origin was therefore based on a protectionist rationale that was to prevail until the post-war years: fighting against forgery and misappropriation of reputation.

* Glossary: See p. 261.

▶ 181

Biodiversity and Local Ecological Knowledge in France

Customs,

the basis of

protection

The law approaches local practices and know-how from the point of view of customs. It was not until 1966 that the AO received a positive definition, following close on the heels of the agricultural orientation law. Henceforth, "shall be considered a designation of origin the name of a country, a region or a specific place describing a product originating there and possessing a quality or characteristics which may be attributed to the geographical environment, including both natural and human factors". The "geographical environment" thus defined takes the knowledge of local actors into account by introducing the idea of cooperation with nature (Hermitte, 2001).

In 1990, when the field of competence of the INAO (French institute for designations of origin) was extended from wines to cheeses and other food products, the concept of the *terroir**, on which the French designation of origin system was built, was shaken. This development anticipated the creation of the single market and the radical reform of the Common Agricultural Policy. The Member States of the European Union allowed an exception to the principle of free circulation of goods in the single market when they adopted, against all expectations, a regulation on the protection of designations of origin and geographical indications on 14 July 1992.

However, the extension of the protection of local names to the European Union level also entails stricter requirements in terms of justifying the link between the quality of the product and its geographical origin, and in terms of inspection systems.

French policies, followed by European policies, enlarged the AOC protection system to include an element of exploitation by creating micro-markets for products possessing specific qualities. This development found a place in the movement involving the globalization of trade that World Trade Organization (WTO) negotiations extended to agricultural and food products.

An approach based on qualification conflicts

The recognition of a designation implies meeting three conditions. Firstly, the product must be defined, thereby setting down the characteristics and practices specifying it within a local model; these are the designation rules. Next, the geographical area associated with the product name must be defined, which draws a border that did not previously exist on the map. Finally, it is important to ensure the authorities make the product official: ministerial decree and inclusion in the register of designa-

* Glossary: See p. 261.

Promotion: Exploiting Sites and Heritage

tions in France; inclusion in the register of geographical indications of the European Communities.

Although the designation of origin is essentially an agreement — a quality agreement — experience shows that its creation is rarely consensual. Codification makes it necessary to explain knowledge that went without saying; it leads to a certain standardization, by disregarding practices or variations. Delimitation means the local name cannot be used by producers situated outside the area and by those inside the area that do not meet the requirements, even if they are local.

The contribution of AOs to the exploitation of biological and cultural diversity can be examined from the viewpoint of exemplary qualification* conflicts concerning the definition of goods and the ways in which the living world, nature and associated knowledge are treated.

Tarbais beans: privatizable genetic resource v. public food product?

Individual trademark or collective designation of origin?

There has been a good deal of talk, especially in WTO negotiations, of conflicts between trademarks and designations of origin. These conflicts revolve around the collective nature of property rights related to geographical names. Tarbais beans illustrate this rivalry between two mutually exclusive means of appropriation.

In 1996, Tarbais beans were the focus of an application for a protected geographical indication (PGI), made by a group of producers from the Hautes-Pyrénées department and a local cooperative that sorts, dries and sells the beans. At the same time a farmer from the area made an application for a plant variety certificate.

The PGI application was part of a move to revive a practice common in large areas of the south-west of France at the end of the 19th century: maize was grown in association with climbing beans. Farmers and their technicians reexamined crop techniques. Along with the traditional production of maize as stakes for beans, the specifications of the PGI permit the use of nets, thus simplifying the work without modifying the essential aspect: manual harvesting in several stages as the beans ripen. In addition to beans grown for preserving, which make up the majority of the harvest, beans harvested semi-fresh are reclassified as green vegetables. From the start, producers associated restaurant owners with this revival, in order to invent new ways of preparing a basic component of popular food. The PGI has therefore made it possible to identify and collectively plan practices associated with bean production.

* Glossary: See p. 261.

▶ 183

Biodiversity and Local Ecological Knowledge in France

As for the plant variety certificate, the applicant, an individual, was aiming to obtain ownership of this genetic resource. He had transferred his crop to large surfaces in Southern Europe, and mechanized it. The harvest was sold in France as 'Beans: Tarbais variety' in accordance with the rules for labeling vegetables. The registration of a distinct, homogeneous and stable line of beans under the name 'Tarbais' would have banned the use of this name for beans consumed as food and as a local public good. The group of Tarbais bean producers finally managed to secure the name 'Tarbais' for the PGI alone.

Raw milk v. dead milk: what importance is given to local knowledge?

The example of raw milk highlights the importance of local knowledge. The recognition of the designation and its management are assigned to a group. In France, this is often the producers' association, which represents the producers and processors involved. The association carries out inspections under the supervision of the INAO.

Debating

acceptable

innovations

Even if their interests are local, producers may belong to enterprises whose decision-making centers are located outside the designation area and may include their product in corporate strategies of national and international dimensions. This is the case of France's principal dairy group, Besnier, which became Lactalis. This configuration is the result of systematic acquisitions of dairies situated in designation areas over the last ten years or so.

The intrusion of a major industry lacking a past linked to the local area into the world of AO cheeses is linked to the demand made by Brussels to justify the link between the quality of the product and its geographical origin. This has led to a thorough reassessment of local practices and knowledge, centering on production using raw milk in a context in which international trade negotiations are making safety and hygiene standards a key issue. What knowledge is at stake?

Decrees are relatively discreet concerning the treatment of the milk used. Thus, of the 42 French AO cheeses (2004), just 12 use only raw milk. Due to the fragility of this living raw material, it is essential to leave no more than a few hours between milking and renneting, the first step in the cheese-making process.

Within the family of AO cheeses, and even within certain designations, several types of production coexist. Some use pasteurized or microfiltered milk, which must have industrial

Promotion: Exploiting Sites and Heritage

fermenting agents added to it. The producers thus work 'dead milk', and can standardize certain components of this milk by separating them. Where less demanding designations are concerned, not all of the milk collected is necessarily transformed into AO cheese: dairies rely on a range of products and as a result, producers are often unaware of the destination of their milk, as is the case in the Massif Central. Others use a raw material whose integrity is respected: the fermenting agents added do not replace the natural flora of the milk. This living material can vary depending on the herds and the season; a variability that cheese-producers must take into account, their skill being to monitor the maturing and fermenting processes.

According to those in favor of raw milk, the link between the cheese and its geographical origin is down to the farmhouse style of production, in which the key stages are as authentic as possible, and to the proximity with breeders required by this process. In fact, the AOC is a reference framework that makes it essential to decide which innovations are acceptable, and which are not, and even to reconsider previous technical choices.

Considering raw milk as a processed product that contributes to the typicality of the cheese makes it an irreplaceable factor of production. This ensures breeders in designation areas are given a say and are thus able to negotiate their role in the development of the dairy economy. In order to carry weight in negotiations concerning prices or the sharing of production rights, some breeders demand recognition of the link between the characteristics of the milk and the dairy breed. They claim local or traditional breeds are to cheese what vines are to wine.

A greater role for breeders

However, like Tarbais beans, animal breeds are easy to transfer when they are not rooted in local breeding systems that define them. Analysis of the specifications of the principal Alpine cheese designations shows that requirements concerning rearing and feeding practices are first and foremost guided by the desire to localize activities: shielding the mountain breeds from competition from the lowlands, grazing or mowing the slopes, and maintaining activity in declining rural areas. Currently, the environmental quality of the areas providing the fodder and pasture resources used to feed herds is not taken into account in the definition of the 'geographical environment'. This is an issue that cheese designations will have to address. Is the use of the emblematic sites of the cheese-producing mountain areas — the summer grazing lands and the high mountain pastures — so widespread? It is important to ensure consistency

▶ 185

Biodiversity and Local Ecological Knowledge in France

between practices and the image given of them in order to reinforce the credibility of designations of origin in international trade negotiations.

Towards a 'greening' of the geographical environment?

Certain procedures are beginning to integrate the geographical origin and the environmental quality of agrosystems. Local knowledge is no longer identified solely in terms of its effect on the expression of the potentiality of the local area in the product: the practices that define the designation implicitly refer to the production of biodiversity.

For example, the four AOC decrees concerning Puy green lentils (1996), *Piment d'Espelette* (Espelette chili peppers) (2000), Coco de Paimpol beans (1998) and Cévennes sweet onions (2003) mention the fact that producers have the possibility of using seed grown on their own farms. These farm populations, produced from local populations selected on site, are still largely dominant. Cider orchards, especially those in Normandy, are also involved in this diversity of varieties. The production conditions for Domfront perry, which has been an AOC product since December 2002, are exemplary. Firstly, the principal variety is Plant de Blanc, a well-known local variety; it is combined with other varieties, which are also local. Secondly — and this is a first in the field — the pear trees are standard size and are planted with a density of under 150 trees per hectare on a full grass surface, with all these criteria corresponding to the local practices concerning orchards of hardy trees. This acknowledgement of different varieties of pear trees and a more extensive production method, along with the restoration of a bocage network and its retinue of species providing shelter for nesting birds and small game, are part of a move to exploit ecological and cultural diversity.

Implementing varied forms of expertise

French experience in the field of designations thus highlights the diversity of ways in which local knowledge and practices can be taken into account. More broadly speaking, the idea of associating know-how and biodiversity are beginning to gain ground within the INAO and certain designation associations.

The issue of inspections

Currently under the responsibility of the producers' association and the INAO, the designation inspection system is at the center of a debate, which could seriously affect the status granted

Promotion: Exploiting Sites and Heritage

to biocultural diversity. Some people insistently call into question collusion between peers and supposedly biased inspections, arguing that an organization cannot be both judge and judged. They suggest that this role be delegated to an independent certifying organization, guaranteeing the objectivity and means required by the EN 45011 standard, without however making it the only inspection structure possible. The example of Italy shows just how much the inspection system formats the definition of the product. In addition to inspections carried out by the group in charge of the designation, based on expert appraisals by professionals of the product and on tasting, this country has created an additional inspection delegated to expert appraisal professionals, who rely on laboratory analysis and instruments.

Rather than seeking scientific proof of typicality in molecular markers, studies suggest extending the typicality inspection commission to include connoisseurs who share the cultural dimension of the local product: those who work with it, who know how to circulate it beyond its place of origin can justifiably sit on the jury (Casabianca and de Sainte Marie, 2000). Henceforth, the representation of different forms of expert appraisal in the accreditation process would be a way of objectivizing the judgment, which jurists and clinicians know well from putting it into practice.

Conclusion

Making products competitive

The designation of origin is a form of legal protection that makes it possible to ensure products and means of production are competitive where otherwise they would not be: this right creates micro-markets from production systems that would be condemned by the classical rules of competition. At the same time, to justify and exploit their specificity, designation products are integrating the global market. AOCs thus contribute to fuelling the debate on alternative techniques and the diversity of production models and economic systems.

However, this construction is not the doing of a community of people or a club of producers who reach agreements amongst themselves. The scope of local knowledge is far from limited to the local level alone. To define and justify this knowledge, it was necessary to explain what did not need explaining, being such a part of the familiar world. And to do so, a whole technical and institutional structure was required: an AOC authority, day-to-day management of the producers' association, expert scientific and technical appraisal, research programs, conservatories, and the help

Biodiversity and Local Ecological Knowledge in France

of regional authorities, etc. These initiatives are supported legally and financially within the framework of national and European public policies. But do countries that have been worn down by years of structural adjustment have the necessary institutional and financial resources to make this transfer?

Within the European Union, designations of origin are protected, but this is not the case at the international level: although AOs are recognized as indications of origin, they do not currently enjoy any formal protection.

Southern countries may well be interested in the French experience of designations of origin. But their priority is surely that Northern countries dismantle the protective measures preventing their principal products — sugar, cotton, etc. — from finding a profitable market.

To find out more:

Bérard L., Marchenay P., 2004. *Les produits de terroir, entre cultures et règlements.* Paris, CNRS Éditions, 229 p.

Casabianca F., Sainte Marie C. (de), 2000. L'évaluation sensorielle des produits typiques. Concevoir et instrumenter l'épreuve de typicité. *In 67th EAAE seminar The socio-economics of origin labelled products in agro-food supply chains: spatial, institutional and co-ordination aspects*, Le Mans (France). Paris, INRA-ESR ; Parme, Universita degli Studi di Parma, 269-276.

Hermitte M.-A., 2001. Les appellations d'origine dans la genèse des droits de la propriété intellectuelle. *In* Moity-Maïzi P., Sainte Marie C. (de), Geslin P., Muchnik J. et Sautier D. (dir.), *Systèmes agroalimentaires localisés. Terroirs, savoir-faire, innovations.* INRA-Sad, CIRAD, Cnearc, 195-206.

Protection or Privatisation of Culture? The Cultural Dimension of the International Intellectual Property Debate on Geographical Indications of Origin

RHONDA CHESMOND*

Rhonda Chesmond, Research Fellow, Australian Centre for Intellectual Property in Agriculture (ACIPA), Griffith Law School, Griffith University

17 Cultural property; Geographical indications

Introduction

"There has been too little consideration of the *cultural* nature of the actual forms that intellectual property laws protect, the social and historical contexts in which cultural proprietorship is (or is not) assumed, and the manner in which these rights are (or are not) exercised and enforced to intervene in everyday struggles over meaning."[1]

The absence of attention to the workings of law in everyday life has often been the subject of criticism. Rosemary Coombe made the above comment in the context of remonstrating with legal scholars for addressing intellectual property protections in terms of incentives to produce abstract goods at the expense of a consideration of the cultural and social nature of what was owned or protected, and how those rights were exercised.[2] A broader consideration is not only possible, but necessary.

The geographical indication of origin (GI) is a type of intellectual property right that has had a long history within Europe, but has only been in the international spotlight for a relatively short time. GIs are somewhat unique intellectual property rights because of their nature as a collective rather than an individual right, and their potentially infinite life span.

There is no doubt that the primary purpose of a GI right is inexorably linked to economics and trade. However, the protection they afford has also been justified on cultural grounds. For example, Conrad states:

"It is important to understand that those countries which have a strong tradition of recognising geographical indications are not only concerned about the economic consequences of a dilution of their geographical names, but also about part of their 'cultural heritage'."[3]

Culture is a difficult concept to convey. It is inherently sensitive and personal, yet also collective and symbolic, and often comes attached to unpredictable sentiments that lead to political and social discord. Issues of trade and economics are rarely as emotive. A cultural dimension to any issue, however, has distinct advantages, as in this era of (perceived) cultural diversity and awareness, any justification for a property right on cultural grounds is guaranteed a deal of international exposure and due consideration.

GIs provide a fascinating case study of the validity of cultural justifications for international intellectual property protection; protection which, in this case, extends much further than the better-known rights attached to patents, designs, copyright and trade marks. This cultural side of the debate appears to have been acknowledged, but largely ignored by commentators on the issue of GIs and potential expansion of existing GI rights.

However, reviewing a select cross-section of literature provides some interesting constructs within which to examine the question of whether cultural justifications for the protection afforded by the GI regime under the TRIPs Agreement,[4] and any expansion of those rights are valid justifications for protection. There are, of course, many other grounds which justify (or otherwise) the existence and expansion of GI protection (or protectionism depending on particular points of view).[5] However, in this article the author is concerned with the validity of justifications for GIs on *cultural* grounds.

This article will briefly examine the nature of GIs, their history, current proposals for expansion and

---

* The author would like to thank Professor Brad Sherman for his comments on an earlier draft of this article, and Antony Taubman (WIPO) for a helpful discussion of the original concepts.

1 R. Coombe, "Critical Cultural Legal Studies" (1998) 10 *Yale Journal of Law & the Humanities* 463 at p.470.

2 *ibid.*

3 Albrecht Conrad, "The Protection of Geographical Indications in the TRIPS Agreement" (1996) 86 *Trade Mark Reporter* 11; See also T. Broude, "Taking 'Trade and Culture' Seriously: Geographical Indications and Cultural Protection in WTO Law" (2005) 26 *University of Pennsylvania Journal of International Economic Law* 623 at p.630; European Commission, "Why do Geographical Indications matter to us?" July 2003 (updated June 2005), para.2, at *http://europa.eu.int* (last visited September 29, 2005); M. Blakeney, "Geographical Indications and Trade" [2000] Int.T.L.R. 48; Bienayme, *WIPO Symposium on Geographical Indications*, Wiesbaden, October 17–18, 1991, reported in (1991) 5 W.I.P.R. 333.

4 Agreement on Trade-related Aspects of Intellectual Property Rights [1995] A.T.S. 38 (TRIPs).

5 For good and varied discussions about GI protection arguments see J. M Cortes Martin, "TRIPS Agreement: Towards a Better Protection for Geographical Indications?" (2004) 30 *Brooklyn Journal of International Law* 117; Felix Addor and Alexandra Grazioli, "Geographical Indications beyond Wines and Spirits—A Roadmap for a Better Protection for Geographical Indications in WTO TRIPS Agreement" (2002) 5(6) *Journal of World of Intellectual Property* 865; M. Handler, "The EU's geographical indications agenda and its potential impact on Australia" (2005) 15 *Australian Intellectual Property Journal* 173; W. Van Caenegem, "Registered GIs: Intellectual Property, Agricultural Policy and International Trade" [2004] E.I.P.R. 170; S. Goldberg, "Who will Raise the White Flag? The Battle between the United States and the European Union Over the Protection of Geographical Indications" (2001) 22 *University of Pennsylvania Journal of International Economic Law* 107.

recent literature on other areas of intellectual property protection.[6] An analysis of this literature provides an opportunity to consider whether the products sought to be protected by GIs are indeed "cultural", if there is any place for cultural arguments in an essentially trade related area, and if any effective analogies can be drawn between arguments on cultural grounds for protection of traditional knowledge and enhanced anti-dilution laws for trade marks, and those for international protection of GIs.

Geographical indications

Traditionally, the two types of indication of origin recognised by law were indications of source[7] and appellations of origin.[8] The term "geographical indication" as it is used in TRIPs implies something more than an indication of source, but not necessarily meeting the requirements of an appellation of origin.[9] The GIs discussed here include those defined broadly in TRIPs which require a link between the product's place of origin[10] and its identifying characteristics, quality and reputation.[11]

It must be said that one of the most limiting characteristics of the most recent discussions concerning geographical indications in international law has been the restrictive context of TRIPs. Long before the links between trade and intellectual property rights became an international reality, GIs functioned as the prevailing designation for appropriate products and the history relating to the rights attaching to GIs, like all legal history, should not be carelessly cast aside in the quest for a single definitive international standard. Nevertheless, any discussion regarding the enhancement of international protection of GIs must inevitably take place within the international constructs now provided by TRIPs.[12]

This is because GIs took on a new significance within international intellectual property law with their inclusion in TRIPs, a situation which essentially reflects the negotiating success of the EU and its Member States.[13] The protection afforded in TRIPs is founded on a combined intellectual property/consumer protection platform, and while the notion is connected to earlier multilateral treaties[14] involving GIs, the TRIPs Agreement seeks to establish new standards and norms.[15]

Controversially, the term is defined in TRIPs with a single subject-matter definition[16] but with provisions for a hierarchy in the scope of protection based on categorisation of goods (general goods on the one hand, and wine and spirits on the other).[17] It has been suggested that two doctrines form the legal infrastructure for the general protection of GIs: protection against false and misleading[18] or deceptive use[19] of GIs; and protection against dilution of GIs,[20] which expresses a producer-protection ethos and introduces elements of unfair competition.[21] However, most commentators understand the TRIPs GI protection to focus on a limited core of unfair competition law that protects against misleading and deceptive uses, but does not extend to dilution.[22] In relation to GIs of wine and spirits, the TRIPs protection is ostensibly greater as the use of the indication is prohibited even where the true origin is stated and consumers are not misled.[23] It is important

6 Broude, above fn.3; M. Richardson, "Trade Marks and Language" (2004) 26 *Sydney Law Review* 193; J. Bosland, "The Culture of Trade Marks: An Alternative Cultural Theory Perspective" (2005) 10(2) *Media & Arts Law Review* 99; R. Coombe, "The Properties of Culture and the Politics of Possessing Identity: Native Claims in the Cultural appropriation Controversy" (1993) 6(2) *Canadian Journal of Law and Jurisprudence* 249; Coombe, "Critical Cultural Legal Studies", above fn.1.
7 A sign that indicates a product originates at a particular geographical location.
8 A sign that indicates a product originates in a specific location or region but also indicates that the characteristics or quality of the product are due to the geographical environment (which may include human and natural factors).
9 B. O'Connor, "The Legal Protection of Geographical Indications" (2004) *Intellectual Property Quarterly* 35 at p.37.
10 While GIs will commonly consist of the name of that place of origin, also included are indications that are not direct geographical names, but which identify a good from a particular region.
11 TRIPs, Art.22.1.
12 For a comprehensive discussion of the protection of geographical indications before TRIPs see Conrad, above fn.3, pp.11–22; in relation to the overall international context of GIs see WIPO, "Standing Committee on the law of Trademarks, Industrial Designs and Geographical Indications", Eighth Session, Geneva, May 27–31, 2002, WIPO document sct/8/4; see also generally WIPO, "What is a Geographical Indication" at *www.wipo.int* (last visited October 14, 2005);

and European Commission, "Why do Geographical Indications matter to us?", above fn.3. In relation to the history of geographical indications in England see Norma Dawson, "Locating Geographical Indications—Perspectives from English Law" (2000) 90 *Trademark Reporter* 590 at pp.594–600.
13 The European Union (EU) and its Member States have a large portfolio of protected GIs, totalling over 6,000 products, and as such, the EU has been the most active participant seeking the inclusion of GI protection within TRIPs. In countries such as the United States and the United Kingdom, the number of geographical indications used in international trade is negligible compared to the number of trade marks. This is also the case for those "new world" countries such as Australia, New Zealand and Canada. See generally Dwijen Rangnekar, "Geographical Indications A Review of Proposals at the TRIPS Council: Extending Article 23 to Products other than Wines and Spirits", ICTSD-UNCTAD Issue Paper No.4 (June 2003), p.15; Blakeney above fn.3, p.48; Conrad, above fn.3, p.11.
14 Madrid Agreement for the Repression of False or Deceptive Indications of Source on Goods of April 14, 1891 (as amended); Paris Convention for the Protection of Industrial Property of March 20, 1883 [1972] A.T.S. 12; Lisbon Agreement for the Protection of Appellations of Origin and their International Registration of October 31, 1958, as revised at Stockholm on July 14, 1967, and as amended on September 28, 1979: Select Documents on International Affairs No.14 (1968), p.7.
15 Rangnekar, above fn.13, p.11.
16 TRIPs Art.22.1.
17 A point often raised by supporters of increased protection: for example WTO doc IP/C/W247/ (Rev.1).
18 Art.22.2(a) TRIPs.
19 Art.22.4 TRIPs.
20 Art.22.2(b) which incorporates Art.10*bis* of the Paris Convention for the Protection of Industrial Property of March 20, 1883 [1972] A.T.S. 12.
21 Rangnekar, above fn.13, p.14.
22 See for example Christopher Wadlow, *The Law of Passing-Off* (3rd edn, London, 2004), p.66; Daniel Gervais, *The TRIPS Agreement: Drafting History and Analysis* (2nd edn, London, 2003), p.192.
23 Art.23 TRIPs.

to note that there are a number of exceptions[24] to protection which are said to considerably reduce the benefits to owners of GIs.[25] This has repercussions for those countries demanding GI extension as, if extension is achieved, it would be expected that the exceptions would apply to all GIs.[26]

The existence of the double system of protection consisting of stronger protection for wines and spirits and weaker protection for other goods is considered to be discriminatory,[27] and many countries,[28] both developed and developing, are actively working within the Word Trade Organization to have the existing TRIPs protection for wines and spirits extended to cover GIs identifying all products. The EU is the principal proponent of greater global protection for GIs, its primary ambitions being the recoupment or "clawback" of as many GIs previously lost to them (41 are currently claimed)[29] as possible; automatic global protection of all registered European GIs; and to achieve uniform high level protection for all GIs globally, whether wine or other consumables.[30] Certain developing countries also favour GI extension to cover products such as handicrafts and other forms of small localised production.[31]

The expansionist proposition openly invokes a combination of historical and cultural arguments to support the view that others should not be allowed to continue using geographical terms to describe products originating outside the relevant area simply because they have done so for some time.[32] And as Van Caenegem states, the history of protection is marked by the struggle to recapture lost GIs.[33] Accordingly, the current expansionist demands are the next logical step to repair historical wrongs.[34]

This interest in extending the current GI regime is opposed by certain new world countries,[35] which claim that use of European GIs is the result of historical accident not deliberate misappropriation, as many GIs and associated agricultural or production processes were brought by migrants to those countries. In addition,

arguments have been raised about the unconscionability of establishing a global system of registration and protection which, unlike other intellectual property regimes, is so disproportionate in its benefits to Member States.[36] Doubt has also been expressed as to whether any increased expansion would be effective.[37]

Cultural arguments for the protection of GIs

It has been noted that the controversy regarding the TRIPs GI regime has far deeper roots than the purely economic and agricultural, having become a forum for inherent historical and cultural disagreement.[38] Apart from the common view that American opposition is an example of the traditional apprehension in US trade law that agricultural co-operatives are potentially monopolistic, other potential causes of conflict have been diversely identified as including a clash of Catholic and Protestant ideals, the insufficiency of the laws which are designed to protect Western values of individualism and private property, and the conflicting aspirations of native groups to simultaneously protect and exploit their heritage and knowledge.[39]

The international arena, both inside[40] and outside[41] the trade context, is becoming increasingly influenced by aspects of culture and its associated unpredictable sentiments. This is partly because recognition of important institutions central to the individuality of a particular culture or society must necessarily strengthen arguments for its continued existence. Culture in this sense necessarily revolves around notions of tradition, heritage, history, and identity. The promotion of *sui generis* intellectual property rights relating to traditional knowledge and traditional cultural expressions is an illustration of an area very obviously influenced by cultural justifications. Similarly, there is a distinct cultural backdrop to the arguments in favour of expanding the existing GI regime under TRIPs—the requirement for the preservation of local traditions and national culture.[42] But the first question to consider is whether the products sought to be protected by either

---

24 Art.24 TRIPs.

25 Rangnekar, above fn.13, p.23.

26 *ibid.*

27 Dwijen Rangnekar, "The Pros and Cons of Stronger Geographical Indication Protection" (2002) 6 *Bridges* 3–7: *www.iprsonline.org* (last visited October 10, 2005).

28 For example the EU, Bulgaria, the Czech Republic, Egypt, Iceland, India, Kenya, Liechtenstein, Pakistan, Slovenia, Sri Lanka, Switzerland, Turkey, Cuba, Venezuela, Mauritius, Nigeria, Bangladesh, Georgia, Hungary, Jamaica, Moldova, Slovenia, Romania.

29 European Commission, "WTO talks: EU steps up bid for better protection of regional quality products", at *http://europa.eu.int* (last visited October 15, 2005).

30 For a summary of all proposals see WTO, May 18, 2005 WT/GC/W/546 TN/C/W/25; see also Van Caenegem above fn.5, p.172.

31 Van Caenegem, above fn.5, p.173.

32 See generally European Commission, "Why do Geographical Indications matter to us?" above fn.3.

33 Van Caenegem, above fn.5, p.173.

34 *ibid.*

35 Such as Australia, Argentina, Canada, Chile, Dominican Republic, El Salvador, Guatemala, New Zealand, Paraguay, the Philippines, Chinese Taipei, the United States. For a summary of all proposals see WTO (May 18, 2005) WT/GC/W/546 TN/C/W/25.

36 Van Caenegem above fn.5, p.174; and see generally WTO (May 18, 2005) WT/GC/W/546 TN/C/W/25.

37 Countries opposing GI extension have emphasised that Art.23 protection is not absolute as is often claimed by the expansionist parties. This is because to qualify for protection the indication must still meet all the conditions in Art.22.1, and be protected domestically, and the exceptions contained in Art.24 will still apply to dilute protection where applicable. See Rangnekar, above fn.13, p.33 and see IP/C/W/289 p.5 and IP/C/W/386, paras 10–12.

38 Kevin M. Murphy, "Conflict, Confusion, and Bias under TRIPS Articles 22–4" (2003–4) 19 *American University International Law Review* 1181 at pp.1206–1207.

39 See fn.38.

40 For example considerations in the context of Art.XX(a), XX(f) General Agreement on Tariffs and Trade (GATT), Marrakech Agreement establishing the World Trade Organization (WTO Agreement) [1995] A.T.S. 8; Art.XIV(a) General Agreement on Trade in Services (GATS).

41 For example, the United Nations Educational Scientific and Cultural Organization (UNESCO), Universal Declaration on Cultural Diversity, adopted by the 31st Session of the General Conference of UNESCO, Paris, November 2, 2001, *http://unesdoc.unesco.org*.

42 See generally above fn.3.

the current, or any expanded, TRIPs regime necessarily constitute a form of "culture".

Culture

"Culture is ordinary, in every society and in every mind."[43] It is arguable that there should never be a single definition of culture.[44] Rather, in the same way as "art" is now defined (or undefined), it should be anything a particular group wishes it to be.

Culture was originally[45] defined as either capital C culture, being the universal heritage of mankind, or in the sense in which different cultures lay claim to different properties.[46] Intellectual property rights over foods and wines were doubtlessly not uppermost in the minds of scholars such as John Henry Merryman[47] when defining the terms "cultural internationalism"[48] and "cultural nationalism"[49] in relation to cultural property. Cultural property, as discussed by legal scholars, cultural theorists and anthropologists, means objects that embody culture such as archeological, ethnographical and historical objects, works of art and architecture. However, as Merryman adds, the categories[50] can be changed to include "anything made or changed by man".[51] Arguably, foods, wines, spirits, handicrafts and other relevant items which embody some essence of a particular culture could conceivably be subsumed by this definition, giving rise to similar arguments about the public interest in preservation of property by GIs.

Similarly, Reaumé refers to "culture" as "the entire web of social practices, rules, beliefs and ways of doing things that constitute and structure a group's understanding of itself as a group".[52] While it has been said that "[c]ulture and intellectual property appear to have gotten a divorce during the latter decades of the twentieth century",[53] Coombe nevertheless believes that that intellectual property rights protect contemporary culture. She says:

"Intellectual property laws, which create private property rights in cultural forms, afford fertile fields of enquiry for considering the social intersections of law, culture, and interpretive agency. The rights bestowed by intellectual property regimes . . . play a constitutive role in the creation of contemporary cultures and in the social life of interpretive practice."[54]

The importance of protection of traditional culture is similarly validated, especially in the context of the longstanding debate on the protection of cultural objects,[55] traditional knowledge and cultural expressions of Indigenous communities.[56] But even within this context, commentators have suggested that the concept of "culture" is essentially contestable, and as a fluid and organic phenomenon, may continue to be an area which defies precise analysis.[57]

Ultimately, however, there should be no doubt that the "culture" sought to be protected by GI expansion is culture in the wider sense concerning elements of national history, identity, expression, traditions and beliefs. In some racial cultures, sources of food were so important to survival that they took on a spiritual meaning and an identity of their own.[58] Broude provides a thorough and interesting analysis of the issue examining the cultures of production, consumption and identity.[59] Even the more technical concept of *terroir*,[60] with its scientific and ecological context of food cultivation, can be seen to include a cultural element, as the term has been expanded to include a mental dimension or an associated human environment linking producer to consumer, and the preservation of a purity of production.[61] Similarly, consumer practices that focus on traditional habits of food preparation and consumption can be said to reinforce a cultural nexus.[62]

Arguably the most persuasive cultural protection argument in the GI debate lies with the ability of

---

43 Raymond Williams, "Moving from High Culture to Ordinary Culture", in *Convictions* (N. McKenzie ed., London, 1958).
44 It has been noted that there is no current standard definition of "culture"—see D. E. Long, "Democratizing Globalization: Practicing the Policies of Cultural Inclusion" (2002) 10 *Cardozo Journal of International and Comparative Law* 217.
45 In the 19th century.
46 Coombe, "Properties of Culture", above fn.6, pp.259–260.
47 John Henry Merryman, "Two Ways of Thinking about Cultural Property" (1986) 80 *American Journal of International Law* 831; John Henry Merryman, "The Public Interest in Cultural Property" (1989) 77 *California Law Review* 339.
48 "Cultural internationalism" embodies a commitment to the cultural heritage of all mankind where all people make their own contribution and all people have an interest.
49 See generally below.
50 See also the definitions in UNESCO, The Convention on the Means of Prohibiting and Preventing the Illicit Import, Export and Transfer of Ownership of Cultural Property, November 14, 1970 [1990] A.T.S. 2.
51 Merryman, "The Public Interest in Cultural Property", above fn.47, p.341. Similarly, Moustakas argues that the term "cultural property" is susceptible of many meanings—see John Moustakas, "Group Rights in Cultural Property: Justifying Strict Inalienability" (1989) 74 *Cornell Law Review* 1179 at p.1195.
52 Reaume, "Justice between Cultures" (1995) 29 *University of British Columbia Law Review* 117 at p.119.
53 Long, above fn.44, p.217.

54 Coombe, "Critical Cultural Legal Studies", above fn.1, p.469.
55 See generally: Coombe, "Critical Cultural Legal Studies", above fn.1; Coombe, "Properties of Culture", above fn.6; UNESCO, The Convention on the Means of Prohibiting and Preventing the Illicit Import, Export and Transfer of Ownership of Cultural Property, November 14, 1970 [1990] A.T.S. 2.
56 See generally: Graham Dutfield, "Protecting Traditional Knowledge and Folklore", UNCTAD-ICTSD Project on IPRs and Sustainable Development (June 2003); Coombe, "The Properties of Culture", above fn.6.
57 Reaumé, above fn.52, p.120.
58 For example see S. Subbiah, "Reaping What They Sow: The Basmati Rice Controversy and Strategies for Protection of Traditional Knowledge" (2004) 27 *Boston College International & Comparative Law Review* 529 at p.535 who gives instances in Asian cultures of the significance rice plays as an integral symbolic role in creating myth stories and is treated as a divine gift. In Bali, it is believed that the Hindu God caused the earth to give birth to rice, and another God taught people how to raise it; in Shinto belief, the Emperor of Japan is the living embodiment of the god of the ripened rice plant; in Burma folklore tells of people bringing the seeds of rice from the centre of the earth and were directed to the place where rice grew well.
59 Broude, above fn.3, pp.636–642. See also pp.12–14 for a most interesting account of food and wine as culture.
60 The concept of *terroir* is effectively explained in E. Barham, "Translating terroir: the global challenge of French AOC labeling" (2003) 19 *Journal of Rural Studies* 127.
61 Broude, above fn.3, pp.651–655.
62 For example, by serving particular food/wine combinations. Broude, *ibid.*, also makes this point at p.23.

food sources and products to play an important role in the construction of national identities.[63] National identity stands at the forefront of cultural expression, and its importance has been appropriately recognised. For example, Coombe notes that:

"individual and collective identities are actively created by human beings through the social forms through which they become conscious and sustain themselves as subjects in communities of similarity".[64]

Similarly, Scafidi refers to social groups' formation of cultural products through "public ceremony or private interaction, intentional design or unstudied behaviors" which over time become associated with their cultures; first internally as "the way we do things", and later externally as "the way they do things".[65] She gives examples such as Italian food, noting the perception that, while it is acceptable for non-community members to experience and enjoy a particular culture's cuisine, it is not considered acceptable for them to control or commodify it.[66]

There is no doubt that critical cultural theory as espoused by the likes of Coombe and others can provide a justification for the introduction of cultural arguments to the subject of GI protection. But can it be said that such justifications are valid in an area where international trade features so prominently?

International trade and culture nexus

Broude has recently considered the links between trade and culture, and drawing upon the problem as it is reflected in the current GI expansion debate, casts doubt upon the validity of cultural exceptions generally in international trade law.[67]

An essential point to consider when analysing the reasons given to GI protection is the theoretical basis for that right. For example, is it correct to assert that because GIs are necessary for the preservation of local traditions and national culture they are aimed at encouraging innovation and individual creativity in return for a temporary monopoly? Broude thinks not, believing a cultural argument compensates for a deficiency in meeting the traditional justifications for the grant of an intellectual property right; instead, he argues, culture provides "an alternative quasi-intellectual property theoretical basis" for GI protection.[68] He looks in detail at the "cultures" of production, consumption and identity to assist in the analysis of the cultural basis of the arguments for enhanced GI protection of food and wine products.

Broude is particularly concerned by the manner in which "alarmist" cultural rationalisation has been

drawn into the GI debate, concluding that cultural diversity and the conservation of local culture is not an effective rationale for supporting expansion of GI protection largely because GI protection itself, is an inadequate cultural protector.[69] One of the reasons for this is that market forces are strong enough to change cultures of consumption relating to products protected by GIs, even those based on cultural traditions. In effect then, it is not GIs that uphold culture but culture which upholds GIs.[70] One of Broude's most persuasive arguments is that most GIs represent "invented traditions",[71] and that the primary motive for pursuing such traditions has been an economic one.[72] He concludes that "culture" has become, in effect, a euphemism for "protectionism" and as GIs are merely instruments of trade policy they should be negotiated and regulated as such, free of cultural sensibilities.[73]

These arguments are persuasive, but is it correct to assert that the protection of culture is not, ultimately, a valid justification for the enhancement of the international protection of GIs? Broude's focus is squarely on whether and how GIs impact on the cultures of production and consumption and if claims for protection are in fact genuine. The present author prefers instead to look at the (perhaps more abstract) question of whether any genuine claim for protection is justifiable on cultural grounds. In doing so she argues that it is possible to draw analogies with arguments for the expansion of other intellectual property rights which are said to contribute to the protection of national or local culture and to the general safeguarding of cultural diversity.

Trade mark analogy

As various commentators have noted, the goals of GI registration are analogous to those of trade mark protection as registered GIs constitute proprietary protection for reputation.[74] Marks indicating the

---

63 For a more comprehensive discussion see generally *ibid.*, pp.24–25.
64 Coombe, "Critical Cultural Legal Studies", above fn.1, pp.484–485.
65 Susan Scafidi, "Intellectual Property and Cultural Products" (2003) 81 *Boston University Law Review* 793 at p.814
66 See fn.65; pp.823–824. Scafidi concludes that "Quality, authenticity, language, economic entitlement, nationalism: all of these play a role in the internal-external tug-of-war over cultural products, but their relative weights remain uncertain".
67 Broude, above fn.3.
68 *ibid*, p.631.

69 *ibid*, pp.626–633.
70 *ibid*, pp.669–673.
71 In the sense that a set of practices or traditions invented or constructed within a brief traceable period. See fn.3; p.33 where Broude relies on Eric Hobsbawm, "Introduction: Inventing Traditions", in *The Invention of Tradition* (Hobsbawm and Ranger ed., 1983).
72 Broude, above fn.3, p.674 (n.149) cites the case of the highly protected term "Champagne" where there is evidence to suggest that the term was an internationally used generic term for sparkling wines in the late 19th century.
73 See fn.72; pp.678–679. See also Joel Richard Paul, "Cultural Resistance to Global Governance" (2000) 22 *Michigan Journal of International Law* 1 at pp.8, 30–55, who concludes that arguments based on the protection of culture do not trump international norms in the area of trade . This is largely because, like Broude, he believes that they mask protectionist practices dressed up as cultural concerns. On this view, cultural arguments for increasing the scope of GIs may also be unsuccessful.
74 Van Caenegem, above fn.5, p.174; see also D. Rangnekar, "The Socio Economics of Geographical Indications", UNCTAD-ICTSD Project on IPRs and Sustainable Development (May 2004), p.9; Rangnekar, above fn.13, p.13. Stacy Goldberg comments that "geographical indications are similar to trade marks in that they function as source indicators, but the two different intellectual property rights are governed by very divergent systems of laws and bodies of beliefs"; Goldberg, above fn.5, p.109.

geographical origins of goods were, in fact, the earliest types of trade mark[75] and trade marks distinguish a trader's product in the market place. The real function of a trade mark, as noted by Schechter, is to signal the quality of goods, rather than merely their origin.[76] The same can be said of GIs.[77]

The legal means of protection may be different but the regulation of trade marks and GIs will often lead to the same ends. On this point, the monopolisation of generic names in its various forms[78] has been referred to as the "new trademark jurisprudence" and criticised for its impact, not only on international trade relations, but also language "propertisation".[79] Using the examples of protection for "catfish"[80] in the United States and "sardines"[81] in the EU, Nguyen has argued that generic names as GIs and national trade marks are protectionist practices which form the new international trade mark jurisprudence, a position which is in conflict with established trade mark jurisprudence.[82] This protectionism, he argues, is thinly veiled as being in the interests of consumers, but has more to do with the trade barrier[83] and trade manipulation.[84]

A further point to consider is whether the concept of trade mark dilution can be validly likened to the unprotected use of GIs. Schechter, whose work led to the importance of the concept of trade mark dilution, was of the view that the major value of a trade mark was its ability to create a positive association with a product even where customer confusion is absent.[85] Dilution, he said, was "the gradual whittling away or dispersion of the identity and hold upon the public mind of the mark or name by its use upon non-competing goods".[86]

This is the rationale behind arguments for expanded GI protection (and the current level of protection afforded wine and spirits under TRIPs)—protection of products referred to by their place of origin, even where consumer confusion is absent. Obviously then, comparisons and analogies can be and have been made between the rights of trade marks and GIs in relation to economic principles.[87] Similar comparisons can be drawn with respect to aspects of culture.

Trade marks—language as culture

"Ideograms that once functioned solely as signals denoting the source, origin, and quality of goods, have become products in their own right, valued as indicators of the status, preferences, and aspirations of those who use them. Some trade marks have worked their way into the English language; others provide bases for vibrant, evocative metaphors."[88]

The idea of trade marks as a form of culture is not new.[89] Megan Richardson has most recently argued that trade marks are an important component of popular culture, suggesting that as trade marks develop a cultural dimension, private rights should be granted over them with high regulation in the name of protecting the language commons kept to a minimum.[90] She argues that there is little between trade marks as signs used to distinguish goods or services in the market, and trade mark language as a socio-cultural phenomenon.[91] Relying on the work of Coombe,[92] Richardson notes that trade marks are capable of forming part of a folk culture and provide "important cultural resources for the articulation of identity and community in western societies".[93] However, trade mark law has evolved in a narrow way, traditionally regulating heavily the protection of trade marks so as to ensure that the language commons did not become overtaken by private rights.[94] It seems that the reason for such preservation[95] of the language commons was not only the hindrance of competition between traders, but also that the maintenance of a language commons was considered to be linguistically important at this point in history.[96]

Richardson suggests various reasons why the trade mark system should not continue along these historical lines and consequently why the rights of trade mark ownership should be expanded. Expansion of rights relating to the question of trade mark dilution has been on the intellectual property agenda in Commonwealth

---

75 Blakeney, above fn.3, p.48.
76 Frank Schechter, "The Rational Basis of Trademark Protection" (1927) 40 *Harvard Law Review* 813 at pp.817–818.
77 Of course, the distinction is that a trade mark can belong to an enterprise and are not limited to any territorial link. A GI is enjoyed by all enterprises in the designated geographical area.
78 Either by a GI registration system or the passing of national "exclusivity" laws such as referred to below, fn.79.
79 Xuan-Thao N. Nguyen, "Nationalizing Trademarks: A New International Trademark Jurisprudence?" (2004) 39 *Wake Forest Law Review* 729.
80 US 21 U.S.C.A. 321d (a), 343(t) (West Supp.2004), providing new label and misbranding laws for the name "catfish".
81 Council Regulation 2136/89 of June 21, 1989 Laying Down Common Marketing Standards for Preserved Sardines [1989] O.J. L212.
82 Nguyen, above fn.79, pp.732, 735.
83 Where countries are prohibited from using generic terms to describe food products for export to other countries or to be marketed and sold nationally.
84 Nguyen, above fn.79, pp.767, 771.
85 A fact also acknowledged by the High Court in *Campomar v Nike International Ltd* (2000) 202 CLR 45.
86 Schechter, above fn.76, p.825.
87 For example, Rangnekar, above fn.13, p.13.

88 Rochelle Cooper Dreyfuss, "Expressive Genericity: Trademarks as Language in the Pepsi Generation" (1989–1990) 65 Notre Dame L. Rev. 397 at p.397.
89 For example see *ibid.*; and R. Coombe, *The Cultural Life of Intellectual Properties: Authorship, Appropriation and the Law* (Duke University Press, Durham and London, 1998), p.62; and generally, Naomi Klein, *No Logo* (Picador, New York, 2000).
90 Richardson, above fn.6, p.193.
91 *ibid.*, p.194.
92 Coombe, *The Cultural Life of Intellectual Properties*, above fn.89, p.62.
93 Richardson, above fn.6, p.196.
94 See generally *ibid.*, pp.200–210. For example, Lord Herschell in the *Solio* case remarked that "[t]he vocabulary of the English Language is common property: it belongs alike to us all"—*Eastman Photographic Materials Co Ltd v Controller-General of Patents, Designs and Trade Marks* [1898] A.C. 571 at [580]. Similarly, in *Joseph Crosfield and Sons' Application* (1909) 26 R.P.C. 837 at [854], Cozens-Hardy M.R. stated that "Wealthy traders are habitually eager to enclose parts of the great commons of the English language and to exclude the general public of the present day and of the future from access to the enclosure".
95 By the high thresholds for inherent distinctiveness and infringement required for trade mark registration and protection.
96 Richardson, above fn.6, p.207, who examines the importance of the study of linguistics as a field of academic study in England in the later part of the 19th century.

countries[97] for some time,[98] and claims against dilution have appeared before courts in different guises.[99]

One of the major arguments for the expansion of anti-dilution provisions according to Richardson is the "dynamic relationship between language and culture".[100] Sociolinguistic studies apparently reveal that trade marks become language-like, crossing the threshold from commercial indicators to expressive devices, and as such, Richardson argues they become more truly intellectual property like and deserving of protection. This is because the utilitarian justification of intellectual property protection providing incentive for creation can be extended to these "new cultural items".[101] And, in Richardson's view, "traders who anticipate rewards flowing from taking on the role of cultural ambassador will do so more readily" within a trade mark and unfair competition law system which flexibly protects against dilution.[102] Richardson's argument in support of anti-dilution rights is therefore that trade mark owners would be more willing to invest in the expressive value of their marks if their rights were better protected.

The expansion of private rights over language will always, however, bring with it the associated possibility of right owners restricting and censoring the expression of others, determining what can be said or written. This point is also noted by Richardson, and, citing the example of the *Nike* case,[103] she concedes that such cases demonstrate that trade mark owners are unwilling to allow uses of their trade marks they feel may reflect badly on them or fall too far outside the scope of their activities, no matter what the overall social value.[104] Interestingly, in *Nike*, the High Court noted that notions of dilution lead to the inference that the function of trade marks "go beyond the traditional role as an identifier of origin".[105]

Any expansion of the GI provisions in TRIPs has the same effect. The European position if adopted, would take the issue of GIs far beyond their original role as identifiers of the origin of goods. The question is whether Richardson's arguments relating to the benefits of expansion of trade mark rights based on the protection of a popular culture can be applied to the issue of expansion of the GI provisions in TRIPs. It is likely that such an argument goes too far. And, as the comments by Coombe[106] at the beginning of this article suggest, it may be too simplistic merely to rely on the incentive theory of intellectual property for all subject-matter. Protection as incentive to create is difficult to apply in the case of issues of history and tradition. Protection as incentive to exploit is a different matter, but arguably the issue then becomes one of trade and economics. The expansionist position is based on a belief as to their inherent right to protect and exploit their own traditions based on a culture that is already in existence, or at least, the historical traces of one. This is not to suggest that the concept of culture is a static one, as essentially it is a living process which continues to express identity in various forms.[107]

Trade marks and cultural theory

Bosland has recently entered this debate,[108] attempting to show that trade mark rights and any potential enhancement of those rights are not harmful to culture and cultural expression, and in fact may serve culturally beneficial interests. A form of protection against trade mark dilution may ensure that the trade mark remains a valued form of "public cultural expression".[109]

One of the most interesting points raised by Bosland is whether "locking up" intangible subject-matter like intellectual property rights necessarily equals "taking it away".[110] This is an issue which applies equally to trade mark rights,[111] GIs and the protection of traditional knowledge.

In relation to trade marks, Bosland is of the view[112] that too little attention has been paid to the consumption practices of the public in assessing the impact of trade mark law on culture and that the regulation and production of meaning are quite distinct from trade mark ownership.[113] In addition, he says:

> "It might be argued that even if intellectual property rights do restrain particular expression in particular circumstances (for example, the trade mark context),

97 Note that in the United States trade mark dilution is a basis of a separate claim in the Lanham Act 1946 43–45,15 U.S.C. 1125–1127.

98 See for example the Australian Council on Intellectual Property, "Review of Enforcement of Trade Marks: Issues Paper" (2002) at *www.acip.gov.au* (last visited October 7, 2005); ACIP, *Review of Trade Mark Enforcement Report*, *www.acip.gov.au* (last visited October 7, 2005).

99 In Australia, for example, *Hogan v Koala Dundee Pty Ltd* (1988) 20 F.C.R. 314; *Twentieth Century Fox Film Corp v South Australian Brewing Co Ltd* (1996) 66 F.C.R. 451; See generally, *Lego System v Lemelstrich* [1983] F.S.R. 155; *McDonalds v Burger King* [1987] F.S.R. 112.

100 Richardson, above fn.6, pp.210–211, referring to the work of the sociolinguists Franz Boas, Edward Sapir and Lee Whorf.

101 *ibid.*, pp.212–213.

102 *ibid.*, p.214, citing the unique and expressive labels of Champagne (*Yves St Laurent Parfums SA v Institut National des Appellations d'Origin* [1994] E.C.C.C. 385), Clareyn (*Colgate Palmolive BV v NV Koninklijke Distilleerderijen Erven Lucas Bols* [1979] EEC 419) and Arthur (*LTJ Diffusion SA v Sadas Vertbaudet SA* C-291/00 (ECJ, March 20, 2003)).

103 *Campomar v Nike International Ltd* (2000) 202 C.L.R. 45. Richardson, above fn.6, p.216, also cites the US cases where dilution has been claimed in relation to "The Pink Panther Patrol" for a public safety campaign for the gay community, and "Pee Wee Scouts" as the title of a series of children's books.

104 Richardson, above fn.6, p.216.

105 *Campomar v Nike International Ltd*, above fn.103, at [53].

106 Coombe, "Critical Cultural Legal Studies", above fn.1, p.470.

107 A point made in the context of indigenous rights and culture by Coombe, "Properties of Culture", above fn.6, p.284.

108 Bosland, above fn.6, claiming to examine the issue from a "cultural theory perspective".

109 *ibid.*, p.116. But note that these conclusions do not accord with other works which employ cultural theory as an "interpretive background", where suggestions for any increase in private rights over trade marks are firmly rejected—see, e.g., generally Drefuss, above fn.93; R. Coombe, "Objects of Property and Subjects of Politics: Intellectual Property Laws and Democratic Dialogue" (1991) 69 Texas Law Rev. 1853.

110 Bosland, above fn.6, p.102.

111 Bosland refers to *San Francisco Arts & Athletics Inc v United States Olympic Committee* 483 U.S. 522 537 (1987) as an example of why such concerns are held by cultural critics.

112 Referring to the work on the anthropology of consumption by Dick Hebdige, *Subcultures: The Meaning of Style* (Routledge, New York, 1979), p.104.

113 Bosland, above fn.6, pp.103–104.

then the evolution, rejuvenation and transformation of culture often occurs just as much through restraint as it does through the freedoms that let it be put to good creative and cultural use."[114]

How does this reasoning translate to the issue of GI expansion? It is true that despite any GI expansion the right to use the expressions feta, prosciutto, and mozzarella (like Champagne, Burgundy, and Chablis) will still be available to the public at large. The property right conferred by regulation is in the use by other traders. In other words, the existence of the right to a registered GI does not take away the existence of or reference to the product itself. Rather, it is the right to use the term as a labelling mechanism in commercial trade which is the subject of the restriction created by the intellectual property right.

In addition to Richardson's incentive theory, Bosland provides a further reason why anti-dilution protection might lend support to a cultural public interest; that is "by ensuring that trade marks retain the qualities that make them such brilliant resources for cultural and critical exchange".[115] This refers to protection from tarnishment or blurring so that their capacity to facilitate speech will not be potentially undermined.[116]

This is, in fact, the central point of the argument for expansion of GIs on cultural grounds. The right to use the term indicating its origin must be protected to ensure that the term remains untarnished by inferior quality. Accordingly, if it is accepted that the cultural value of a GI, like a trade mark, is in its ability to evoke a certain connotation, then there is an argument that the law should protect against the tarnishment of those connotative associations.

Cultural theory and Indigenous rights

Some different approaches to the question of culture and property are identified by Coombe and others, and their ramifications for (arguably) protectionist practices are worth examining for any analogous application to the GI question. Several theories exist which purport to explain the value of the continued existence of distinct cultures. The importance of group membership to individuals, in particular to an individual's own culture, is thought to be essential to self-identification and individual autonomy.[117] The collective nature of the interest in culture,[118] and the intrinsic value of "groupness",[119] has also been identified as essential to the value of life itself.

In the landmark paper "The Properties of Culture and the Politics of Possessing Identity: Native Claims in the Cultural Appropriation Controversy",[120] Coombe examines the inappropriateness of Eurocentric delineations and categorisations of art and culture to the

issue of Indigenous rights and claims to their unique forms of culture. Many of the issues raised to suggest the validity of such claims, especially in relation to arguments of "identity" are also applicable (perhaps somewhat ironically in the case of European claims to protection) to the items sought to be protected under an enhanced GI system. This is reflected in the suggestions that GI rights provide at least one effective means of protection for traditional knowledge and traditional cultural expressions.[121]

Traditional knowledge is recognised as an intellectual creation of a particular community, rather than the common heritage of mankind.[122] The concept of "cultural nationalism" becomes important at this point as it supports the rights of groups to claim certain objects as part of their essential identities.[123] Coombe makes the point that the concepts embodied in cultural nationalism bear clear traces of the same logic that defines copyright, as each group or nation "is perceived as an author who originates a culture from resources that come from within and can thus lay claim to exclusive possession of the expressive works that embody its personality".[124] Concepts of culture cannot be limited to objects of property but also must extend to other forms of expression. If copyright laws protect works understood to embody the unique personality of their individual authors and the expressive component of the original is so venerated that reproduction or imitation is deemed a form of theft,[125] then it can be argued that similar justification must be available for the protection of GIs.

According to Richard Handler, each nation or group possesses a unique identity and culture constituted by its possession of property, with groups increasingly imagining themselves as individuals prizing possession of culture and history. As a result, material objects begin to epitomise collective identity.[126] This is a concept now recognised in Art.5 of the UNESCO Universal Declaration on Cultural Diversity.[127] Such arguments are used to legitimate the repatriation of objects of great importance to group identity.[128] It is arguable that

114 *ibid.*, p.104.
115 *ibid.*, p.111.
116 *ibid.*, pp.111–112.
117 A. Margalit and J. Raz, "National Self-Determination", in *The Rights of Minority Cultures* (W. Kymlicka ed., Oxford University Press, 1995), p.79.
118 Reaumé, above fn.52, p.117.
119 See generally R. Garet, "Communality and Existence: The Rights of Groups" (1983) 56 *Southern Californian Law Review* 1001.
120 Above fn.6.

121 See for example Subbiah, above fn.58, pp.546–549; Blakeney, above fn.3, p.55; Addor and Grazioli, above fn.5, pp.866, 894; D. R. Downes, "How Intellectual Property Could be a Tool to Protect Traditional Knowledge" (2000) 25 *Columbia Journal of Environmental Law* 254 at p.271. However, note the comments of Van Caenegem, above fn.5, p.181 that it is not "proven" that GIs would serve to indirectly protect traditional knowledge and technology in an efficient manner.
122 Erik B. Bluemel, "Substance without Process: Analyzing TRIPS Participatory Guarantees in Light of Protected Indigenous Rights" (2004) 86 *Journal of the Patent and Trademark Office Society* 671 at p.704.
123 Coombe, "Properties of Culture", above fn.6, p.263, referring to the work of anthropologist Richard Handler. See Richard Handler, "Who Owns the Past? History, Cultural Property, and the Logic of Possessive Individualism", in *The Politics of Culture* (Brett Williams ed., Smithsonian Press, Washington, 1991), pp.63–74.
124 Coombe, "Properties of Culture", above fn.6, p.264.
125 As stated by Coombe, *ibid.*, p.258.
126 *ibid.*, p.264. Handler argues that this is articulated by a 1976 UNESCO panel in the principle that "cultural property is a basic element of people's identity". See Handler, above fn.131, p.67.
127 Adopted by the 31st Session of the General Conference of UNESCO, Paris, November 2, 2001.
128 Coombe, "Properties of Culture", above fn.6, p.264.

CHESMOND: PROTECTION OR PRIVATISATION OF CULTURE?: [2007] E.I.P.R. 387

parallels can be drawn between calls for repatriation of cultural objects and the attempts by the EU to recoup the 41 generic terms lost to them over time.

Handler agrees with the principle of repatriation of cultural objects on the basis of fairness and equity, but casts doubts on the cultural identity argument used to support it as a global extension of Western possessive individualism. He argues that the culture groups assert as belonging to them and as embodied in particular pieces of property is not something objective which has possessed continuous meaning and identity over time, but the product of current needs and interpretations.[129] If this is correct, it arguably supports new world arguments against further GI expansion, at least on cultural grounds, as globalisation has played an important role in diluting prospective rights through years of use, and changes in consumption.

However, in relation to Indigenous claims, Coombe asserts:

"First Nations peoples are engaged in an ongoing struggle to articulate, define, exercise and assert Aboriginal Title, not only in terms of a relationship to territory, but in connection to the cultural forms that express the historical meaning of that relationship in specific communities. For Native peoples . . . culture is not a fixed and frozen entity that can be objectified in reified forms that express its identity, but an ongoing living process that cannot be severed from the ecological nexus in which it lives and grows."[130]

Without any intention to trivialise the debate regarding Indigenous claims to traditional knowledge, as that essential debate covers a broad spectrum of issues, concerns and problems which must be addressed by the international community, there are elements in common with the GI question. Comparison of those issues which relate to identity or personality of a group or nation leads to the inevitable conclusion that there are valid grounds for the justification of the use and regulation of GIs, assuming the relationship between the cultural item or process and identity itself, is valid. In other words, while the subject-matter sought to be protected by geographical indications plays a role in a given society's culture, then protection is justifiable on cultural grounds.

On a practical level, however, it must be recognised that attempts to protect traditional knowledge within the existing intellectual property rights framework (at an international level) have proven extremely difficult, with developed countries continuing to prefer discussions on protection to take place in an Intergovernmental Committee,[131] rather than incorporating any form of specific protection into their domestic IP regimes. Accordingly (and unfortunately), any attempt to cite an analogous cultural argument to support expansion of the GI regime may not succeed in being persuasive in any more than a theoretical sense.

Conclusion

There is little doubt that the international IP debate on GIs will continue unabated for some time yet,[132] and any prospective resolution will be grounded firmly in the areas of economics and trade. It is impractical to suggest that the issue could be resolved without recourse to these international realities.

However, this discussion has attempted to show that the current GI debate has an important cultural side. It has been argued that justifications for intellectual property rights are valid on cultural grounds if what is sought to be protected can be said to be credibly cultural. The protection of GIs does constitute protection of culture on the grounds of tradition, heritage, history, and identity. While well-reasoned doubts have been expressed by commentators as to the validity of cultural justifications for GIs, it is possible to make analogies with cultural justifications for other forms of intellectual property such as trade marks and traditional knowledge.

In relation to trade marks it has been shown that the rights protected are similar to GIs, but traditionally, trade marks have been highly regulated in order to protect the language commons. On this basis, commentators have argued that GIs and "national" trade marks constitute a form of language "propertisation". However, recent analysis by Richardson and Bosland has led to a conclusion that trade marks, themselves, form part of the culture of language, and greater trade mark ownership rights would enhance rather than endanger the cultural dimension of the trade mark. Analogies can be drawn with calls for greater protection against dilution of trade marks to prevent tarnishment of trade marks as cultural items, and calls for extension of the international GI protection regime.

Perhaps the most theoretically persuasive argument for the cultural justification of GI rights, particularly in relation to expansion, is by analogy with Coombe's original analysis of the issue of Indigenous rights in intellectual property based on cultural theory. The concept of the protection of cultural identity is the most genuine justification for the creation and expansion of intellectual property rights. The anthropologist Richard Handler's argument on repatriation of cultural objects may also be relevant in relation to the proposed recoupment of GIs lost to various members of the EU. While culture is a continuously evolving process, objects, goods, items and rights which are linked to that process deserve recognition.

If it can be established that cultural arguments do have a role to play in trade-related areas, the question becomes what effects this will have on the protection of GIs in practice. If greater protection is afforded, but leads to the creation of more trade-restrictive rules, then we are likely to witness even more WTO disputes between affected countries. Like all trade-related areas, the issue of balance (and compromise) will be paramount.

Globalisation has had many effects, but we must be careful to ensure that an erosion of cultural values is not one of them. Of course, no amount of protection can

---

129 *ibid.*, 265; Handler, above fn.123, p.67.
130 Coombe, "Properties of Culture", above fn.6, p.284.
131 The WIPO Intergovernmental Committee on Intellectual Property and Genetic Resources, Traditional Knowledge and Folklore was established at the 26th Session (12th Extraordinary Session) of the WIPO General assembly, held in Geneva, September 25 to October 3, 2000.

132 For the current status of the international debate, see WTO doc WT/GC/W/546 TN/C/W/25 (May 18, 2005).

388 CHESMOND: PROTECTION OR PRIVATISATION OF CULTURE?: [2007] E.I.P.R.

absolutely control the preservation of culture in a truly globalised society. A further consideration is to ensure that cultural protection is not afforded at the expense of cultural diversity. Protection should never lead to prevention of the dissemination of cultural expression.

However, ultimately, there should be no valid reason why a nation or group's culture cannot coexist with an ability to profitably market its cultural products. Culture is an essential component of a group's identity, cohesion and expression and as such, any genuine claim to protection of intellectual property rights on that basis is a valid one.

[28]

Geographical indications and traditional knowledge

Shivani Singhal*

The term 'traditional knowledge' (TK) is so broad that any attempt at defining it is necessarily incomplete. However, for the purposes of this paper, I will adopt the tentative definition proposed by WIPO: *tradition-based* literary, artistic or scientific works, performances, inventions, scientific discoveries, designs, marks, names, and symbols; undisclosed information, and all other tradition-based innovations and creations resulting from intellectual activity in the industrial, scientific, literary, or artistic fields.[1]

The operative term in this definition is 'tradition-based' which recognizes the dynamic nature of TK. TK keeps evolving and is not static. The word 'traditional' is used not because the knowledge is old but because it is created, preserved, and disseminated in the cultural traditions of particular communities.[2] It is representative of the cultural values of a community and is held collectively by it.

In recent times, protection of TK has become a major concern, given its persistent misappropriation and exploitation by outsiders. This paper examines the extent to which geographical indications (GIs) may be used to protect TK.

Need to protect TK

WIPO's fact-finding mission report identified certain concerns of the holders of TK. These included concern over lack of respect for TK and its holders, loss of traditional lifestyles, misappropriation of TK, and its usage without any benefit-sharing and the reluctance of the younger members of the community to carry traditional practices forward.[3]

Key issues

- This article discusses the circumstances under which geographical indications (GIs) can be effectively used for the protection of traditional knowledge (TK).

- The author explores the degree of protection afforded by GIs, and whether this protection measures up to the needs and expectations of the holders of TK.

- The author concludes that the protection provided by GIs is inadequate because they can neither guard against disrespectful use or misappropriation of TK, nor do they contain any explicit mechanism for benefit-sharing.

In view of these concerns, the protection sought by TK holders may be either positive or defensive. The former encompasses a situation where they seek to benefit from the commercialization of TK, whereas the latter seeks to prevent 'outsiders' from using TK, it being felt that the use of TK by 'outsiders' deprives it of its original significance and may ultimately lead to dissolution of the culture of the community. Those favouring this approach are more concerned about the cultural, social, and psychological harm caused by unauthorized use of TK than its economic implications.[4]

There has been considerable recent debate on the interface between human rights and IP rights. This interface has two dimensions. One view is that IP right is a human right.[5] As such it should be available to the

---

* National Law School of India University, Bangalore, India.
  Email: shivani@nls.ac.in

1 'Intellectual Property Needs and Expectations of Traditional Knowledge Holders' WIPO Report on Fact-Finding Missions on Intellectual Property and Traditional Knowledge (1998–1999) sourced from www.wipo.int/tk/en/tk/ffm/report/final/pdf/part1.pdf. WIPO acknowledges that a singular and exclusive definition of traditional knowledge is not possible. This is merely a working definition.

2 M Pannizon and T Cottier, 'Traditional Knowledge and Geographical Indications: Foundations, Interests and Negotiating Positions' in E-U Petersmann (ed.), *Developing Countries in the Doha Round: WTO Decision-Making Procedures and WTO Negotiations on Trade in*

Agricultural Goods and Services (Robert Schuman Centre for Advanced Studies, European University Institute, Florence, 2005).

3 Above note 1.

4 CJ Visser, 'Making Intellectual Property Laws Work for Traditional Knowledge' in JM Finger et al. (eds), *Poor People's Knowledge* (World Bank, Washington, 2004).

5 Proponents of this view rely upon instruments like UDHR. By Art 27: '(1) Everyone has the right freely to participate in the cultural life of the community, to enjoy the arts and to share in scientific advancement and its benefits. (2) Everyone has the right to the protection of the moral and material interests resulting from any scientific, literary or artistic production of which he is the author'.

holders of TK as well. The other argument is that the non-protection of TK deprives the owners, who are generally poor, of their share in the economic benefits accruing from the use of their knowledge.[6] For instance, due to misappropriation of TK, several traditional skills become economically unviable. The condition of the craftsmen deteriorates, leading to poverty and, in extreme cases, suicide.[7]

The second view also encompasses within its fold the argument that the protection of TK has enormous significance for the economic development of developing countries such as India. Since the market for goods embodying TK is substantial,[8] the need to protect TK is clear.

Suitability of GIs to protect TK

Though most of the systems of IP protection are individualized, some IP rights, such as trade marks and GIs, are based on the concept of collective rights. A GI identifies a good as originating from a particular territory, where a given quality, reputation, or other characteristic of the good is essentially attributable to its geographical origin.[9] While copyright and patents are intended to reward investments in innovation, GIs reward producers who invest in building the reputation of a product.[10]

GIs are especially suitable for use by communities because they are based upon collective traditions and a collective decision-making process. They protect and reward traditions while allowing evolution. They are designed to reward goodwill and reputation created over many years or even centuries. They reward producers who maintain a traditional high standard of quality. They do not confer a monopoly right over the use of certain information, but simply limit the class of people who can use a certain symbol. They are not freely transferable from one owner to another and can be recognized as long as the collective tradition is maintained.[11] Since they have to be periodically renewed, they can help in ensuring that the quality of the product is maintained.

It has even been argued that GIs may be better than *sui generis* systems for the protection of that TK which has been in the public domain for so long that it is difficult to assign it to a specific right holder, as in the case of kava.[12]

Further, GIs are particularly useful in cases where supply is through traditional small-scale production and products are marketed directly to consumers. GIs allow small local producers to enhance their reputations, and sell directly to final users, thus competing more effectively against large corporations. When others are excluded from using a particular name, an aura of uniqueness attaches to the product, thereby enhancing its premium.[13]

It has been observed that GIs are less appropriate where the product is a commodity traded primarily in bulk, as in the case of neem.[14] Here the commodity passes through many hands and in some cases is highly processed before reaching the consumer as an end product.[15] The consumer is then not so concerned about the raw material used because he may be influenced by other factors like the quality of processing that was involved.

Conditions under which GIs can protect TK

GI can be used to protect only certain kinds of TK. First, GI identifies a 'good'. This would exclude all intangible forms of TK such as methods of medical treatment, techniques for dyeing cloth, folk music, and dances. However, a GI may be obtained for, say, a resulting medicine or dye or the recorded versions of songs and dances.

Secondly, GI protection is of assistance only where the knowledge is associated with a defined geographical area. Thus, if the knowledge is scattered, as in the case of the Ayurvedic system of medicine, a GI cannot be used. However, there may be exceptions to this. For instance, the knowledge of 'triphala' is scattered across the country. 'Triphala' is a medicinal powder used for ailments of the stomach. The raw materials for it are

6 P Cullet, 'Human Rights, Knowledge and Intellectual Property Protection' (2006) 11 *Journal of Intellectual Property Rights* 7.

7 M Liebl and T Roy, 'Handmade in India: Traditional Craft Skills in a Changing World' in JM Finger *et al.* (eds), *Poor People's Knowledge* (World Bank, Washington, 2004).

8 id.

9 See Art 22(1) of the TRIPs Agreement. Also see section 2(1)(c) of the Geographical Indications of Goods (Registration and Protection) Act, 1999 [the 'GI Act'].

10 DR Downes and S Laird, 'Innovative Mechanisms for Sharing Benefits of Biodiversity and Related Knowledge – Case Studies on Geographical Indications and Trademarks' sourced from www.ciel.org.

11 DR Downes, 'How Intellectual Property Could be a Tool to Protect Traditional Knowledge' (2000) 25 *Columbia Journal of Environmental Law* 253.

12 Above note 2.

13 LR Nair and R Kumar, *Geographical Indications—A Search for Identity* (Butterworths, New Delhi, 2005) at 193.

14 Above note 10.

15 Above note 10.

734 | **ARTICLE** | *Journal of Intellectual Property Law & Practice*, 2008, Vol. 3, No. 11

grown in a defined geographical area.[16] It *may* be possible to treat 'triphala' as a manufactured good and argue that the activity of preparation takes place in the defined area. This is because, according to the GI Act, a GI can be obtained for a manufactured product if at least one of the activities of either the production or processing or preparation of the goods concerned takes place in the defined territory. Thus it is possible to have a GI for 'triphala'.

Thirdly, the good must enjoy a commercial reputation. This is because a GI merely signifies the true source of the good, and if the source is not important to the consumer, protection by means of a GI is immaterial. It has been suggested that the representatives of interested local communities must first survey the industry and consumer groups regarding the market demands for various indigenous products because a significant market for the product is an essential criterion for use of a GI.[17]

A large portion of TK is currently being documented, but GI cannot be used to protect all of it because most of this knowledge enjoys a reputation only in neighbouring areas, with the result that it can be easily misappropriated and marketed under a different name. A GI would be of hardly any use for such products. For example, information relating to the traditional handloom of Kinnal (Karnataka) has recently been documented.[18] The knowledge is confined to definable geographical areas and the art is organized. There is a Kinnal Handloom Co-operative Weavers' Society also, but a GI for it may not be as effective as for Kotpad Handloom Fabric because, even though both of them are traditionally established, only the latter has a reputation in the market.

Some registered GIs in India and the protection they enjoy

Textiles

Most registered GIs in India are for textiles such as Mysore Silk, Pochampally Ikat, Chanderi Sarees, Kancheepuram Silk, and Kullu Shawls.

- *Mysore Silk:* The GI application for Mysore Silk shows that its distinctiveness is due to the technique used in its production. However, there is nothing to suggest that the same quality of silk cannot be produced elsewhere. In such a case, a GI is very useful as the only factor that distinguishes Mysore

Silk and similar silk produced elsewhere is the former's reputation.

- *Chanderi Sarees:* These are famous for their transparent texture and the motifs (or *buttis*) woven on to them by hand. The application mentions that the government often organizes workshops to educate workers about these designs. Further, the skill of the workers seems to be a consequence of long experience rather than any traditional and unique technique as such. All this suggests that the product is unique to that region primarily because of its reputation.

- *Pochampally Ikat:* This is an elaborate process of tying and dyeing which involves a considerable degree of human skill because the weaver has to use his discretion in weaving. It is not a totally mechanical process, as in the case of Chanderi Sarees, and is also quite labour-intensive. If cheap substitutes were allowed to be sold under the same name, the production of ikat in Andhra Pradesh would become an economically unviable venture.

In all these cases, since the requisite knowledge is in the public domain and the distinctiveness of the product is dependent on human factors, the product may be manufactured anywhere. However, when produced in a particular area, the product enjoys a unique reputation. In such cases, a GI affords considerable protection because consumers are willing to pay a premium in the market for products manufactured in that region, and using that region's traditional methods. GI seems to be one of the best ways of protecting such products because they cannot receive patent-like protection, nor do they derive their uniqueness from any natural factor available only in that area.

A GI for such goods protects the owners of the traditional skill against competition from cheap substitutes. The skill is also preserved as there is no economic compulsion to switch over to modern methods. For instance, if traditionally natural and vegetable dyes have been used to make the product, a craftsman would not feel compelled to use cheaper synthetic dyes instead so as to make the product economically viable. When Pochampally ikat was granted a GI, it was estimated that about 100,000 weavers would benefit from it since, before then, demand for original Pochampally ikat had been falling drastically due to competition from cheaper fabrics copying their designs.

---

16 SK Soam, 'Analysis of Prospective Geographical Indications of India' (2005) 8 *The Journal of World Intellectual Property* 679.

17 Above note 11.

18 See DN Shailaja *et al.*, 'An Insight into the Traditional Handloom of Kinnal, Karnataka' (2006) 5(2) *Indian Journal of Traditional Knowledge* 173.

Such protection also encourages the new generation to learn the skills and keep them alive.

The same applies to Kancheepuram silk and Kotpad Handloom Fabric, even though these two products are not totally dependent on human factors. It is believed that the water at Kancheepuram has unique properties which impart lustre to raw silk, while the natural dye used for Kotpad Handloom Fabric is derived from the Aul trees found in the area. Since natural factors are also involved, consumers would be more willing to purchase products produced in the specified region.

Crafts

- *Aranmula Metal Mirrors* are made of certain alloys. The technique is a closely guarded secret, known only to a few families now. One piece of mirror takes almost six months to be completed. It is famous all over the world and a GI can protect it from cheap fakes. However, the protection afforded is inadequate because the process is not protected. Since the knowledge is not in the public domain even the process requires to be protected. Also, these mirrors are extremely expensive and if the same thing could be produced in a cheaper way, the demand for the original would be affected albeit not to any significant extent. Additionally, various parts of the production process are accompanied by religious rituals. In such a case, the holders of the TK may want defensive production in order to prevent unauthorized users from using it. The GI is incapable of this kind of protection.

- *Channapatna Toys and Dolls*: these are made from 'hale' wood which grows in a defined area. Thus, the finished product is not entirely dependent on human skill. The *same* kind of good may not be produced anywhere else. But substitutes may still be found, so a GI affords protection.

Embroidery

So far two kinds of embroidery have been granted a GI: Phulkari and Kasuti. Embroidery is an expression of the culture of a particular region. Phulkari is traditional Punjabi embroidery and consists mainly of floral patterns. It has religious connotations attached to it, being considered auspicious by Punjabis, so much so that the canopy over the Guru Granth Sahib is of Phulkari.[19] Kasuti meanwhile originated in Karnataka back in the period of Chalukyas.[20] Such art can benefit considerably from GIs because the consumer wants to buy the product for the skill which is associated with a particular area. The product from there reflects centuries of traditional production and development. However, GI cannot prevent offensive use of the art. Phulkari can be executed on any surface without reference to the religious sentiments of the people of that region.

Merits of some potential GIs

Efforts are being made to obtain GIs for other products, such as Khadi, Chikankari, Patan Patola, Thanjavur Paintings, and Jaipur Blue Pottery.

- *Khadi:* Mahatma Gandhi popularized the use of this fabric and projected it as something which could be produced by anyone. Since the process is common knowledge, producers can benefit from the use of a GI. It may, however, be difficult to define the area because the production is scattered across India. Further, Khadi is generally sold in bulk and is subsequently worked upon or converted into various kinds of products.

- *Chikankari and other forms of embroidery:* Chikankari involves making of delicate thread patterns on fine fabrics. The art is found primarily in and around the city of Lucknow in Uttar Pradesh. Since the art is confined to a definable area and is world-renowned, GI protection would be highly appropriate, especially since there have been instances of products being sold as 'Chinese made Lucknawi Chikan'. A similar case can be made out for other kinds of embroidery, such as Zardozi, Kantha work, and Kashmiri embroidery. They all possess distinct and unique features and are associated with particular geographical areas.

- *Patan Patola:* This is a traditional silk textile. Currently, this art is being pursued by only four families in Gujarat. The art is dying because a single patan patola saree costs about 100,000 rupees on average and is not affordable by most people. Further, it takes three to four people, working together for about six months, to finish one saree. While at present there is little incentive to produce such sarees, the grant of a GI may help the producers

---

19 Guru Granth Sahib is the holy book of the Sikhs. The tenth and last human Guru of the Sikhs, Guru Gobind Singh, designated this text as his successor, thereby elevating it from the status of a holy scripture to that of a living eternal Guru. It is housed in the Golden Temple at Amritsar, Punjab, India.

20 The Chalukyas constituted a royal dynasty that ruled large parts of Southern and Central India between the 6th and the 12th centuries.

command a better premium in the market and thus attract more workers and producers to this art.[21]

- *Thanjavur Paintings:* They are presently made by only a few hundred artists, mostly based in Tamil Nadu. Their uniqueness lies in the use of gold leaves and sparkling stones to highlight certain aspects of each painting. These paintings are now considered family heirlooms. For such art, a GI is especially beneficial, to protect a purchaser from the risk of buying a counterfeit one.

- *Jaipur Blue Pottery:* It uses quartz instead of clay as a base, and has over time become very famous even though the technique for making it did not originate in Jaipur. It may be able to obtain GI protection.

Since GIs are generally obtained for high-value products consumed by a particular sector of society, demand for those products increases and they become expensive. This is especially beneficial when the methods of production are low cost. Any extra income can be pumped back into the community inter alia for putting better systems of organization in place.[22]

Criticisms of the use of GIs

First, while a GI may sufficiently protect products such as Darjeeling tea which can only be grown in Darjeeling, it may operate unfairly in cases where protected goods are purely a product of human factors.[23] For example, a weaver of Chanderi sarees may move to another part of India. He may continue to use his skill, design base, and process in a new location, yet he is no longer a weaver of 'Chanderi' sarees. Thus, reliance on the physical location alone as a criterion for the protection of the use of a name may cause unnecessary hardship. A community is not necessarily a physical location, but a shared resource of custom and tradition, in which the expression of self remains possible.[24]

It has also been argued that the use of GI may operate unfairly when a person from outside moves into a defined geographical area.[25] He may become entitled to the benefits conferred on producers in that region, even though he is not a part of the community which traditionally practised the particular art, and has not contributed in any way to the preservation and development of the art. However, this is not a valid argument

because under Indian law a person has to be registered as an authorized user before he can use the GI for his products. The application for registration as an authorized user has to be made jointly by the producer and the registered proprietor of the GI,[26] which is the collective body in whose name the GI is registered.[27] It is highly unlikely that the registered proprietor would support the claim of an outsider. Moreover, the producer has to submit a statement explaining how he claims to be a producer of the GI. Unless he is genuinely entitled to use the GI, his application would be rejected.

Secondly, the use of a GI does not protect the knowledge about the good, but only guards against misrepresentation and unfair capitalization on the reputation of a thing. It cannot prevent offensive use of TK. Also, sometimes a similar product not using the GI may threaten to compete with the original. A GI cannot adequately protect against such cases of misappropriation. The Intergovernmental Committee on Intellectual Property and Genetic Resources, Traditional Knowledge, and Folklore has recognized that existing systems of IP protection do not adequately protect holders of TK against various kinds of misappropriation. Accordingly, the first Article of the draft provisions for the protection of TK deals with the problem of misappropriation of TK.

Thirdly, under TRIPS only the low minimum standard of protection provided under Article 22 can be required for goods embodying TK, since the higher level of protection under Article 23 is required only for wines and spirits. The lower protection under Article 22 is extended only when the use of GI results in unfair competition to producers or misleads the public. The higher protection under Article 23, on the other hand, implies that GI can be used for only those products which are actually produced in the particular region. The protection for wines and spirits is therefore absolute. The standard protection under Article 22 means that, if a product is marketed as 'Chinese made Mysore Silk' or 'American styled Kasuti embroidery' Article 22 is not violated and TRIPs members are under no obligation to take any steps to prevent this unless it results in unfair competition or misleads the public.[28]

The problem with this is that, in time, a GI may become a generic term which may result in the

---

21 'Adding life to a centuries' old dyeing art – Patan' sourced from www.nif. org.in/node/1052.

22 Above note 13 at 193.

23 Above note 7.

24 J Gibson, 'Intellectual Property Systems, Traditional Knowledge and the Legal Authority of the Community' (2004) 26 *European Intellectual Property Review* 280.

25 Above note 7.

26 See, Rule 56 of the Geographical Indications of Goods (Registration and Protection) Rules, 2002, framed under the GI Act.

27 See, section 2(n) of the GI Act which defines 'registered proprietor'.

28 See SC Srivastava, 'Geographical Indications under TRIPS Agreement and Legal Framework in India: Part I' (2004) 9(1) *Journal of Intellectual Property Rights* 9.

cancellation of the GI. Also, one of the benefits of a GI is that it can be used forever, unlike patents which are granted for a fixed period. Under Indian law, a GI has to be renewed after every 10 years. If the indication has become generic, it may not be renewed.[29] Under TRIPs too, WTO members are not required to protect GIs if they become generic.[30]

However, under section 22(2) of the GI Act, the Central Government may by special notification extend a higher level of protection to certain categories of goods. The provision does not limit the scope of the this notification to wines and spirits. Under Article 3 of TRIPs too, members are free to provide for standards higher than those required under the Agreement. Therefore, domestically India should make full use of the notification mechanism under section 22 (2)[31] to give a higher level of protection at the national level to goods other than wines and spirits.

Fourthly, GIs may be obtained by an individual, a family, a partnership, a corporation, a voluntary association, or a municipal corporation. Such producers establish the rules governing production under the GI. These rules may even be modified over time. However, there may be disagreements among the producers. What happens when there is a falling-out after the GI has been registered? For instance, even now negotiations are going on with regard to a GI application among the four Salvi families which produce *patan patola*. Even if they are able to reach an agreement now over the kind of designs to be specified, the dyes to be used and the area to be demarcated, what if there is a disagreement subsequently?

Fifthly, sometimes the GI may be granted to a single body, as in the case of Mysore silk. Only the Karnataka Silk Industries Corporation (KSIC) can produce 'Mysore silk'. This seems to be unfair to workers who reside in the area, know the skill but for some reason may have ceased working for this corporation, and who would be barred from using the GI.

Sui generis systems to protect TK

Since GIs have been found to be inadequate in many ways for the protection of TK, some countries have devised *sui generis* systems to protect their indigenous knowledge. Such systems can be adapted to the goals of protection. For instance, the Philippines have enacted an Indigenous Peoples Rights Act, which gives indigenous communities rights over their TK. These rights extend to controlling access to ancestral lands, access to biological and genetic resources, and to indigenous knowledge related to these resources. Access by other parties will be based on prior informed consent of the community obtained in accordance with customary laws. Any benefits arising from genetic resources will be equitably shared.[32]

Similarly, Costa Rica's Biodiversity Law recognizes the right of local communities and indigenous peoples to oppose any access to their resources and associated knowledge, be it for cultural, spiritual, social, economic, or other motives.[33] A similar law is found in Brazil as well.[34]

Such systems, based on restricted access to outsiders, may be beneficial for something like 'triphala', the ingredients for which can be found only in certain geographic areas. Prior informed consent would imply that the community is able to monitor the use of TK and is able to protect TK against offensive usage. Also the holders of TK will be able to reap the fruits of commercialization of TK. Such protection may be especially useful for the protection of improvements made to the existing TK which may not have become public knowledge to any significant extent.

Under the Pacific Regional Framework for the Protection of Traditional Knowledge and Expressions of Culture 2002, traditional owners have the right to authorize or prevent, among other things, the adaptation, transformation, and modification of a protected Traditional Cultural Expression (TCE). An external user must receive consent before he can make new derivative works based upon a TCE. Any IP rights in derivative works vest in the work's author. However, if the work is used for commercial purposes, the rights-holder must share benefits with the traditional owners, acknowledge the source of the TCE, and respect its moral rights.[35] Such a system may be useful for those products which are sacred to the community or are of particular religious or cultural significance.

29 V Singh, 'A Study of the Law of Geographical Indications as an IPR and Tool for Economic Development' (2005) 4 *ICFAI Journal of Intellectual Property Rights* 46.

30 Art 24.6, TRIPs.

31 S Balganesh, 'Systems of Protection for Geographical Indications of Origin' (2003) 6 *The Journal of World Intellectual Property* 191.

32 *Traditional Knowledge and Geographical Indications* sourced from www.iprcommission.org/papers/pdfs/final_reports/Ch4final.pdf.

33 D Wuger, 'Prevention of Misappropriation of Intangible Cultural Heritage' in JM Finger *et al.* (eds), *Poor People's Knowledge* (World Bank, Washington, 2004).

34 B O'Connor, 'Protecting Traditional Knowledge: An Overview of a Developing Area of Intellectual Property Law' sourced from www.oconnor-european-lawyers.com.

35 *Intellectual Property and Traditional Cultural Expressions/Folklore* sourced from www.wipo.int/freepublications/en/tk/913/wipo_pub_913.pdf.

738 | **ARTICLE**   *Journal of Intellectual Property Law & Practice*, 2008, Vol. 3, No. 11

Effective but inadequate

This paper shows that GIs can be effectively used for the protection of certain kinds of TK. But, evaluating the protection against the needs and expectations of the holders of TK, they appear to be inadequate. GIs cannot prevent disrespectful use of TK or its misappropriation; nor do they contain any explicit mechanism for benefit-sharing. The holders of TK are neither able to benefit fully from the commercialization of the knowledge nor to protect it against use by outsiders. TK is more in the nature of a service than a good. It often consists of processes which have more to do with human factors than natural factors.

GIs are unable to protect them. Even if the higher protection currently available only for wines and spirits were to be extended to TK-based goods, it would not be sufficient since the knowledge would still not be protected.

There is need for a *sui generis* system at the international level. The draft provisions of the Intergovernmental Committee are a step in that direction and may go a long way in meeting the needs and expectations of the holders of TK.

doi:10.1093/jiplp/jpn160
Advance Access Publication 2 September 2008

[29]

Int. J. Intellectual Property Management, Vol. 3, No. 4, 2009   357

Protection of Traditional Knowledge by Geographical Indications

Michael Blakeney

Faculty of Law,
University of Western Australia,
Queen Mary, University of London, UK
E-mail: m.blakeney@qmul.ac.uk
E-mail: Michael.blakeney@uwa.edu.au

Abstract: This paper considers the extent to which Geographical Indications (GIs) regimes might provide for the protection of Traditional Knowledge ('TK'), through a consideration of the debate on TK within both the WTO and WIPO. The author relates the policy objectives, identified by WIPO as ideally underpinning the legislative protection of TK, to the policy objectives of GIs protection. The paper concludes with an examination of debate within the WTO, for the extension of the special protection offered to GIs for wines and spirits to handicrafts and other products and concludes with some case studies of handicrafts as examples of GIs.

Keywords: international intellectual property law; WTO-TRIPS agreement-geographical indications; GIs; geographical indications; TK; traditional knowledge; WIPO intergovernmental committee on genetic resources.

Reference to this paper should be made as follows: Blakeney, M. (2009) 'Protection of Traditional Knowledge by Geographical Indications', *Int. J. Intellectual Property Management*, Vol. 3, No. 4, pp.357–374.

Biographical notes: Michael Blakeney is Herchel Smith Professor of Intellectual Property Law at Queen Mary, University of London and Professor of Law at the University of Western Australia. He is an arbitrator with the International Court of Arbitration. He has advised a number of international organisations on aspects of agricultural IP and on IP enforcement. He has written and edited a number of books in the fields of intellectual property, media and competition law.

1 Introduction

This paper considers the extent to which Geographical Indications (GIs) regimes might provide for the protection of Traditional Knowledge (TK).

Proposals for the protection of TK within the existing categories of intellectual property or as a sui generis subject of intellectual property protection is currently the subject of intense scrutiny in a number of international fora. Probably the most important precipitant of this scrutiny has been the impact of the WTO Agreement on Trade-Related Aspects of Intellectual Property Rights ('TRIPS Agreement'). The immediate effect of the TRIPS Agreement was to impose on all countries: LDCs, developing and

358   *M. Blakeney*

industrialised, the IP standards which were formulated in industrialised countries. The implementation of TRIPS Agreement obligations carried a tangible compliance costs.[1] Set against these costs was the promise of the TRIPS Agreement contained in Article 7 that

> "The protection and enforcement of intellectual property rights should contribute to the promotion of technological innovation and to the transfer and dissemination of technology, to the mutual advantage of producers and users of technological knowledge ..."

To test the veracity of this promise, developing country members, as part of the general review process of the Agreement, as provided in Article 71.1, have urged an analysis of the impact the TRIPS Agreement in securing the transfer and dissemination of technology (Stilwell and Monagle, 2000).[2]

This agitation for the 'operationalisation' of Article 7 was reflected in the agitation of developing country members for a development agenda both within the WTO and World Intellectual Property Organization ('WIPO'). Those countries sought to identify those IP issues which were considered to have greatest significance for their particular circumstances. In this regard, the protection of TK was identified as a negotiating priority. On 4 October, 1999 Bolivia, Columbia, Ecuador, Nicaragua and Peru specifically proposed that the Seattle Ministerial Conference establish within the framework of the Round a mandate.

a   To carry out studies, in collaboration with other relevant international organisations in order to make recommendations on the most appropriate means of recognising and protecting TK as the subject matter of intellectual property rights.

b   On the basis of the above-mentioned recommendations, initiate negotiations with a view to establishing a multilateral legal framework that will grant effective protection to the expressions and manifestations of TK.

c   To complete the legal framework envisaged in paragraph (b) above in time for it to be included as part of the results of this round of trade negotiations.[3]

A communication of 6 August, 1999 from Venezuela proposed that the Seattle Ministerial should consider the establishment

> "on a mandatory basis within the TRIPS Agreement a system for the protection of intellectual property, with an ethical and economic content, applicable to the Traditional Knowledge of local and indigenous communities, together with recognition of the need to define the rights of collective holders."[4]

The Seattle Ministerial collapsed under the pressure of anti-globalisation riots and it was not until the Doha Ministerial in November 2001, that the question of TK as an artifact of the international IP regime was resurrected. Clause 19 of the Doha Ministerial Declaration 2001, instructed

> "the Council for TRIPS, in pursuing its review programme 'to examine, *inter alia*, ... the protection of traditional knowledge' and to 'be guided by the objectives and principles set out in Articles 7 and 8 of the TRIPS Agreement and ... take fully into account the development dimension."

After the impasse of the subsequent Cancun Ministerial Meeting, which was derailed by agricultural issues, the Hong Kong Ministerial meeting on 18 December 2005 reaffirmed in clause 1 of the Declaration issued by it the Declarations and Decisions adopted at Doha and renewed the "resolve to complete the Doha Work Programme fully and to conclude the negotiations launched at Doha successfully in 2006". Clause 2 of the Hong Kong Declaration emphasised "the central importance of the development dimension in every aspect of the Doha Work Programme" and the signatories recommitted themselves "to making it a meaningful reality".

Beyond, the reference in Clause 19 of the Doha Declaration to TK, the TRIPS Council has not yet begun to address the issue of TK protection in any significant way. As is indicated below, an alternative approach for the WTO is to consider the protection of TK within the context of GIs protection.

2 TK within WIPO

The origins of the consideration of TK as an IP issue can probably be traced back to the early debates which questioned the relevance of the international copyright regime for developing countries. The Stockholm Conference for the Revision of the Berne Convention, which was convened in June 1967, witnessed the first significant agitation from developing countries for an acknowledgement of their particular circumstances. In the preparations for the Stockholm Conference, it was proposed that the concerns of developing countries could be accommodated in a separate protocol. This question was the subject of some fairly acrimonious debates at Stockholm (Ricketson, 1987).[5] The critical issues for developing countries were the definition of developing country translation rights and compulsory licensing. The establishment of a protective regime for folklore was a burgeoning consideration. Although a Protocol was grudgingly adopted by the final plenary session of the Stockholm Conference it did not come into force as it failed to secure the requisite number of ratifications.

The failure of developing countries to secure an effective protection of folklore within the regime administered by WIPO explains initiatives undertaken within other international organisations. In April 1973, the Government of Bolivia had sent a memorandum to the Director General of UNESCO requesting that the Organisation examine the opportunity of drafting an international instrument on the protection of indigenous creative works in the form of a protocol to be attached to the Universal Copyright Convention, which is administered by UNESCO. Following that request a study was prepared in 1975 by the Secretariat of UNESCO on the desirability of providing for the protection of the cultural expressions of indigenous peoples on an international scale. Because of a perception of the broad scope of this analysis, in 1977 the Director General of UNESCO convened a Committee of Experts on the Legal Protection of Folklore, which in a report in 1977 concluded that the subject required sociological, psychological, ethnological, politico-historical studies "on an interdisciplinary basis within the framework of an overall and integrated approach".[6]

Pursuant to a resolution adopted by the General Conference of the United Nations Educational, Scientific and Cultural Organization (UNESCO) in Belgrade, in September-October 1980 and a decision taken by the Governing Bodies of the World Intellectual Property Organization (WIPO) in November 1981, a Committee of Governmental Experts on the Intellectual Property Aspects of the Protection of Expressions of Folklore was convened. After a series of meetings the Committee formulated *Model Provisions for National Laws on the Protection of Expressions of*

Folklore Against Illicit Exploitation and Other Prejudicial Action which were adopted by the two organisations in 1985. Pursuant to a resolution adopted by the General Conference of the United Nations Educational, Scientific and Cultural Organization (UNESCO) in Belgrade, in September–October 1980 and a decision taken by the Governing Bodies of the World Intellectual Property Organization (WIPO) in November 1981, a Committee of Governmental Experts on the Intellectual Property Aspects of the Protection of Expressions of Folklore was convened. After a series of meetings the Committee formulated *Model Provisions for National Laws on the Protection of Expressions of Folklore Against Illicit Exploitation and Other Prejudicial Action* which were adopted by the two organisations in 1985.

As can be seen above, the first discussions about the possibility of the protection of the creativity of indigenous and traditional communities occurred within the context of folklore, which was considered to be in the area of copyright law. The first major discussion of the protection of TK, as such, occurred in the context of the joint UNESCO/WIPO World Forum on the Protection of Folklore, which was convened in Phuket in April 1997. The Forum was principally concerned with the adequacy of copyright law to protect folkloric works, such as paintings, sculptures, drama, music and magic. At the Forum, the term 'folklore' was criticised for its limited scope. For example, Mrs Mould-Idrissu, in a paper on the African Experience on the preservation and conservation of expressions of folklore,[7] observed that the western conception of folklore tended to focus on artistic, literary and performing works, whereas in Africa it was much more broad; encompassing all aspects of cultural heritage.[8] For example, she noted that under the Ghanaian Copyright Law of 1985, folklore included scientific knowledge.[8]

The particular focus of TK, which reflected the concerns of Mrs. Mould-Idrissu, were a number of incidents of 'biopiracy' in which the knowledge of traditional communities was employed in the identification and appropriation of the biological resources of developing countries (Blakeney, 1999, 2004).[9] Responding to suggestions about the potential role of IP in preventing the misappropriation of biological resources in 1999 WIPO participated in a joint study with the United Nations Environment Programme (UNEP), on the role of intellectual property rights in the sharing of benefits arising from the use of biological resources and associated TK. These matters were taken up at the third session of WIPO's Standing Committee on the Law of Patents (SCP) in September 1999. At this session the delegation of Colombia proposed the introduction into the Patent Law Treaty, which was then under negotiation, an paper which required the lawful acquisition of biological material upon which patent applications were based. This issue was deferred to the subsequent negotiations for a Substantive Patent Law Treaty. To facilitate the discussion of this matter and the related issue of the role of TK in identifying this biological material, in a Note dated September 14, 2000, the Permanent Mission of the Dominican Republic to the United Nations in Geneva submitted on behalf of the Group of Countries of Latin America and the Caribbean (GRULAC) a request for the creation of a Standing Committee on access to the genetic resources and TK of local and indigenous communities.

> "The work of that Standing Committee would have to be directed towards defining internationally recognised practical methods of securing adequate protection for the intellectual property rights in TK."[10]

At the WIPO General Assembly the Member States agreed the establishment of an Intergovernmental Committee on Intellectual Property and Genetic Resources, TK and Folklore. Three interrelated themes were identified to inform the deliberations of the Committee: intellectual property issues that arise in the context of

• access to genetic resources and benefit sharing

• protection of TK, whether or not associated with those resources

• the protection of expressions of folklore (WIPO, 2000).[11]

At the early sessions of the Intergovernmental Committee on Intellectual Property and Genetic Resources, TK and Folklore ('IGC') the Member States concentrated on

> "the development of 'guide contractual practices', guidelines, and model intellectual property clauses for contractual agreements on access to genetic resources and benefit-sharing."[12]

At its more recent sessions the IGC has reviewed key principles and objectives of TK protection "to develop an overview of policy objectives and core principles for the protection of TK".[13] The painstaking work of the IGC suggests that an international instrument providing for the sui generis protection of TK is unlikely to be promulgated in the immediate future.

3   Debates about the potential of GIs to protect TK

One reason for the delay in promulgating international sui generis legislation for the protection of TK is the suggestion that existing principles of intellectual property might be able to accommodate the concerns of the demandeurs of TK legislation. However, most of the suggestions which have been made, focus upon the role which patent law or plant breeder's rights law which might make might make in protecting TK. Not much attention has been paid to the role which GIs laws might make in protecting TK.

The leading academic study of the ways in which the existing categories of intellectual property law might be utilised to protect TK is the 2004 survey by the Max Planck Institute, led by von Lewinski (2004).[14] The Max Planck study is generally quite pessimistic about the role which GIs might make in protecting TK. The principal chapter on this subject is that by Kur and Knaak (2004, p.20)[15] on the protection of traditional names and designations. They note that

> "The indication for a product is the subject matter of this protection, not the product itself. For this reason tradition-based innovations and creations, as indicated in the WIPO Report on Fact-finding Missions on Intellectual Property and TK, cannot enjoy protection *per se* by means of geographical indications. The protection of GIs may apply only to signs indicating these innovations and creations." (Kur and Knaak, 2004, p.227)[15]

This is unquestionably the case, but all GIs whether 'Champagne' wine, 'Parma' ham, or 'Roquefort' cheese not only protect the use of the indication, but also protect the innovations which stand behind the indication.

Kur and Knaak provide no examples of how GI's might protect indications for TK, even indirectly. They reject the possibility that 'Kava' from the Pacific region and 'Rooibos' from South Africa could be protected under the Madrid Agreement stating that "they are not GIs per se as they have no direct geographical meaning" (Kur and Knaak, 2004, p.228).[15] This interpretation appears to add to the jurisprudence on GIs the concept of a "per se geographical indication". This confuses the existing jurisprudence on direct and indirect GIs. For example, the ECJ recently held 'Feta' to be a GI for cheese coming from Greece, even though there is no geographical place of that name. The ECJ did not rule that 'Feta' was not a GI per se but that it was an indirect indication, much the same way that 'Kava' and 'Rooibos' might be taken as indirect indications of the places from which they come.

Kur and Knaak are also pessimistic about the general prohibition in Article 22 of the TRIPS Agreement of the use of misleading GIs being of much assistance for the protection of TK. They explain that

> "As to geographical indications of indigenous communities, the general provisions of the TRIPS Agreement are clearly not sufficient to offer adequate protection. The general protection pursuant to the TRIPS Agreement is too limited in its scope because ... it depends on the opinions of the public in the country where protection is claimed. Under this rule GIs of indigenous communities being unknown as such to the public of certain countries are unprotected in those countries." (Kur and Knaak, 2004, pp.233, 234)[15]

This assessment makes some assumptions about the ignorance of persons about indigenous communities, although, the growth of 'ethno-marketing' suggests that there is an increasing awareness of indigenous communities and what they have to offer. However, as Kur and Knaak concede, this particular problem can be overcome by the establishment of a register for GIs.

A more optimistic assessment of the potential for GIs to protect TK is made by Marion Panizzon and Thomas Cottier in their study: "TK and GIs: Foundations, Interests and Negotiating Positions".[16] They observe that

> "Traditional Knowledge (TK) and Geographical Indications (GIs) share a common element insofar as they both protect accumulated knowledge typical to a specific locality. While TK expresses the local traditions of knowledge, GIs stand for specific geographical origin of a typical product or production method. GIs and TK relate a product (GIs), respectively a piece of information (TK), to a geographically confined people or a particular region or locality."

Similarly, in its *Review of Existing Intellectual Property Protection of* TK[17] the IGC Secretariat observed that

> "GIs as defined by Article 22.1 of the TRIPS Agreement and appellations of origin, as defined by Article 2 of the Lisbon Agreement ... rely not only on their geographical connotation but also, essentially on human and/or natural factors (which may have generated a given quality, reputation or other characteristic of the good). In practice, human and/or natural factors are the result of traditional, standard techniques which local communities have developed and incorporated into production. Goods designated and differentiated by geographical indications, be they wines, spirits, cheese, handicrafts, watches, silverware and others, are as much expressions of local cultural and community identification as other elements of traditional knowledge can be."[18]

Three examples provided by the Secretariat of TK protected by GIs are: 'Cocuy the Pecaya' liquor from Venezuela, 'Phu Quoc' fish sauce and 'Shan Tuyet Moc Chau' tea, both from Vietnam.

4 TK policy issues

For the guidance of the tenth session of the IGC (November 30–December 8, 2006) the Secretariat identified some 16 policy objectives which ought to underpin the legislative protection of TK.[19] There is a good deal of overlap between these various objectives and these have been grouped below according to their principal themes. However, from them we can see whether there might be a role for GIs in TK protection.

The first objective identified by the Secretariat of the IGC is to '*Recognise value*'. This is defined as follows:

> "(i) recognise the holistic nature of traditional knowledge and its intrinsic value, including its social, spiritual, economic, intellectual, scientific, ecological, technological, commercial, educational and cultural value, and acknowledge that traditional knowledge systems are frameworks of ongoing innovation and distinctive intellectual and creative life that are fundamentally important for indigenous and local communities and have equal scientific value as other knowledge systems."

This objective recognises the economic and commercial value of TK and that it might function as a framework for the creative life of indigenous and local communities. The economic benefits are obvious if traditional products can be protected as GIs. For example, the mark of the town of Osnabrück, the centre of the Westphalian linen industry, was held in so great respect and esteem abroad that, in England, in the middle of the 15th century, linen bearing this mark commanded a price 20% higher than other Westphalian linens (Schechter, 1925).[20] As the first preamble to recent EC Regulation on the protection of GIs and designations of origin for agricultural products and foodstuffs[21] declared: "The production, manufacture and distribution of agricultural products and foodstuffs play an important role in the Community economy" (Bently and Sherman, 2006).[22] Thus today in the EU the 640 GIs and designations of origin for foodstuffs, and over 4,200 registered designations for wines and spirits, together generate a turnover of more than €40 billion annually (O'Connor and Company, 2003).[23]

The reference to the 'holistic nature' of TK draws attention to its non-economic aspects. In this regard, promoters of GIs refer to the contribution which they can make to non-trade issues such as to the preservation of rural landscapes and rural lifestyles.

The second group of policy objectives identified by the Secretariat of the IGC concern the promotion of respect for TK systems and for meeting the needs of holders of TK. Included in the promotion of respect is a concern

> "... for the dignity, cultural integrity and intellectual and spiritual values of the traditional knowledge holders who conserve and maintain those systems; for the contribution which traditional knowledge has made in sustaining the livelihoods and identities of traditional knowledge holders; and for the contribution which traditional knowledge holders have made to the conservation of the environment, to food security and sustainable agriculture, and to the progress of science and technology."

364   *M. Blakeney*

Guided by "the aspirations and expectations expressed directly by TK holders" the Secretariat of the IGC refers to the necessity to

> "respect their rights as holders and custodians of TK … and reward the contribution made by them to their communities and to the progress of science and socially beneficial technology."

An interesting parallel with these policy objectives for TK protection can be found in the non-trade benefits that have been urged as a justification for GIs throughout their history. The attempt in 1764 to repeal the mediaeval legislation which conferred protection upon the wine marks of the Bordeaux region (Richard, 1918; van Caenegem, 2003)[24] was sought to be repelled upon the justification of the contribution made by this legislation both to rural employment and to the preservation of the continuity of the quality of rural life. Similarly, the second preamble to the EC Regulation, mentioned above, states that:

> "The diversification of agricultural production should be encouraged so as to achieve a better balance between supply and demand on the markets. The promotion of products having certain characteristics can be of considerable benefit to the rural economy, particularly in less favoured or remote areas, by improving the incomes of farmers and by retaining the rural population in these areas."

The central cluster of policy objectives identified by the Secretariat of the IGC refer to the importance of promoting the conservation and preservation of TK and protecting it from misappropriation through ensuring prior informed consent for access to genetic resources and the promotion of equitable benefit sharing. Relevant to the issue of GIs is objective (x) which urges the promotion of innovation and creativity in the following terms:

> "(x)   encourage, reward and protect tradition-based creativity and innovation and enhance the internal transmission of traditional knowledge within indigenous and traditional communities, including, subject to the consent of the traditional knowledge holders, by integrating such knowledge into educational initiatives among the communities, for the benefit of the holders and custodians of traditional knowledge."

In this regard, as Cottier and Panizzon observe:

> "TK is associated with 'niche' rather than with 'mass' production. It therefore fosters diversity and contributes to the preservation of natural resources." (Cottier and Panizzon, 2004)[25]

Plant breeding by the large life-sciences companies has been criticised for encouraging monocultures. In this context the protection of TK in the field of agricultural plant genetic resources offers the potential of 'appropriate flanking policies' (Biber-Klemm et al., 2005).[26]

A number of the policy objectives of TK legislation enumerated by the IGC Secretariat concern the preservation and development of TK systems[27] and to the safeguarding of TK "for the primary and direct benefit of TK holders in particular, and for the benefit of humanity in general".[28]

The role of traditional communities in conserving genetic resources through the perpetuation of their TK, as well as their entitlement to the sharing of benefits from the exploitation of those resources is acknowledged in a number of international instruments.

The International Treaty for the Protection of Plant Genetic Resources for Food and Agriculture acknowledges Farmer's Rights in the following terms:

> "9.1 The Contracting Parties recognise the enormous contribution that the local and indigenous communities and farmers of all regions of the world, particularly those in the centres of origin and crop diversity, have made and will continue to make for the conservation and development of plant genetic resources which constitute the basis of food and agriculture production throughout the world."

Similarly the Convention on Biological Diversity establishes the principle of equitable benefit sharing when conserved biological resources are exploited (Blakeney, 2002).[29] For example, it is estimated that about 6.5% of all genetic research undertaken in agriculture is focussed upon germplasm derived from wild species and land races (McNeely, 2001).[30] An illustration of the contribution which traditional communities have made in the conservation of biological resources is the conservation by traditional people in Mali of a blight resistant rice *O. longistaminata* s(WIPO/UNEP, 2001).[31] Although this rice was crossed into more high yielding varieties, raising PBR and patenting issues, if GIs can contribute to the preservation of traditional rural environments, then it can contribute to the preservation of useful genetic reservoirs.

A similar controversy erupted in 2000 over the patenting of the Hoodia cactus which is eaten by the San People of the Kalahari Desert as an appetite suppressant. The patent was obtained in 1995 by CSIR over the appetite-suppressing element (P57) of Hoodia. In 1998 Pfizer acquired the rights from the patentee to develop and market P57 as a potential slimming drug and cure for obesity (a market worth more than £6 billion) (UK Commission on Intellectual Property Rights, 2002).[32] The GIs implications of this case comes from the commercial appeal of marketing this product as a Hoodia extract. In other words focussing upon its 'natural' origin and its derivation from the territory of the San.

A concern for the authentication of traditional culture in the face of the economic, psychological and cultural threat from alien sources is often cited as a reason for the protection of TK (Jabbour, 1982).[33] A related concern is that expressed in a number of contemporary European GI disputes, where the producers of 'Rioja' wine,[34] 'Grano Padano' cheese[35] and 'Parma' ham[36] have successfully insisted on their exclusive right to process these products within the relevant geographic region, in order to preserve the quality and authenticity of these products.

Directly relevant to GIs is objective (xiii) which recommends the promotion of "community development and legitimate trading activities" in the following terms:

> "(xiii)   if so desired by the holders of TK, promote the use of TK for community-based development, recognising the rights of traditional and local communities over their knowledge; and promote the development of, and the expansion of marketing opportunities for, authentic products of TK and associated community industries, where TK holders seek such development and opportunities consistent with their right to freely pursue economic development."

The support, maintenance and development of TK systems is built into most national GI regimes. Various consortiums of producers have been established both to monitor and promote production in conformity with the registered GI, as well as to secure protection.

In a number of countries which are promoting the establishment of GIs as a marketing tool, the establishment of producers' consortia is being promoted.

The protection of TK is urged by the policy objectives listed by the IGC Secretariat dealing with the repression of unfair and inequitable uses[37] and precluding the grant of improper IP rights to unauthorised parties.[38]

The obligation to establish machinery to prohibit the misleading use of GIs is contained in Article 22.2 of the TRIPS Agreement. The EC Regulation on the protection of GIs and designations of origin for agricultural products and foodstuffs contains this prohibition in Article 13:

> "1. Registered names shall be protected against:
>
> (a) any direct or indirect commercial use of a registered name in respect of products not covered by the registration in so far as those products are comparable to the products registered under that name or in so far as using the name exploits the reputation of the protected name;
>
> (b) any misuse, imitation or evocation, even if the true origin of the product is indicated or if the protected name is translated or accompanied by an expression such as 'style', 'type', 'method', 'as produced in', 'imitation' or similar;
>
> (c) any other false or misleading indication as to the provenance, origin, nature or essential qualities of the product, on the inner or outer packaging, advertising material or documents relating to the product concerned, and the packing of the product in a container liable to convey a false impression as to its origin;
>
> (d) any other practice liable to mislead the consumer as to the true origin of the product."

The enforcement of GIs is a more practical way for traditional communities to secure their rights, as the expense of enforcement will be carried either by the producers' consortium or by the administrator of the GIs system.

5   International developments on GIs

Although the TRIPS Agreement makes no reference to TK, clause 19 of the Doha Declaration of 2001 requires the TRIPS Council to "examine the relationship between the TRIPS Agreement, and TK and folklore" by "fully tak[ing] into account the development dimension". In relation to GIs, Article 24.1 of TRIPS obliged Members "to enter into negotiations aimed at increasing the protection of individual geographic indications under Article 23". In order to facilitate the protection of GIs for wines, Article 23.4 provides that

> "negotiations shall be undertaken in the Council for TRIPS concerning the establishment of a multilateral system of notification and registration of geographical indications for wines eligible for protection in those Members participating in the system."

The TRIPS Council confined its initial efforts in relation to the review of GIs under Article 24 to a suggestion for a multilateral register of geographical wine indications. Prior to the Seattle Ministerial, a submission by Turkey of 9 July, 1999 proposed the extension of GIs in TRIPS beyond wines and spirits,[39] this was endorsed the African group of countries requested that the protection of GIs be extended "to other products recognisable by their geographical origins (handicrafts, agro-food products)".[40] This proposal was also taken up by Cuba, Czech Republic, Dominican Republic, Honduras, India, Indonesia, Nicaragua, Pakistan and Sri Lanka, Uganda and Venezuela.

At the TRIPS Council meetings in 2000, the President sought to separate the discussion of Article 23.2 from 24.2 to avoid confusion. A response to this suggestion was a proposal from Bulgaria, the Czech Republic, Egypt, Iceland, India, Kenya, Liechtenstein, Pakistan, Slovenia, Sri Lanka, Switzerland and Turkey that the extension of GIs to products other than wines and spirits be included as an extension of the built-in agenda.[41] This issue has also been taken up by WIPO's Standing Committee on Trademarks and Geographic Indications.

In opposition to the proposals for an extension of the protection of GIs for wines and spirits under TRIPS to all products, on 29th June 2001, a communication was sent to the TRIPS Council by Argentina, Australia, Canada, Chile, Guatemala, New Zealand, Paraguay and the USA ('the Communication'). The Communication pointed out that proposals for the extension of the TRIPS wines and spirits provisions to all products had insufficiently addressed the costs and administrative burdens of this extension. However, Clause 18 of the Doha Declaration has expressly opened the possibility of the extension of the additional protection, through a multilateral system of registration, to products other than wines and spirits and countries are currently exploring the cost impacts and other practicalities of the extension.

Clause 18 of the Declaration, states that with a view to completing the work started in the TRIPS Council, members are to negotiate the establishment of a multilateral system a register for wines and spirits, as well as the extension of GI protection beyond wines and spirits. The principal protagonists in negotiations are the European Communities, which favour an expanded international regime, and the USA, which argues that the current TRIPS and trademark protections are sufficient. The EC and its supporters would see major reform in the introduction of a multilateral system for the registration and enforcement of GIs. June 2005 saw the European Communities (EC) submit a radical proposal to amend the TRIPS Agreement to provide global protection for GIs in a multilateral system of registration.[42] This proposal seeks to bring international protection for GIs into conformity with the European Union where a Community-wide system for their registration is considered an indispensable part of agricultural policy, serving both to preserve the incomes of small to medium-size producers and to guarantee the sustainability of the rural economy. Given the fact that it possesses over 700 registered GIs,[43] sophisticated institutional infrastructure and technical prowess, the European Union is Europe is exceptionally well placed to leverage the benefits of an expanded international system of GI protection. On the other hand, the USA and its supporters largely endorse the *status quo* favouring voluntary multilateral registration and the choice of the means of protection – whether by special system or the established trade mark system – left to national discretion.

However, it would be wrong to think that the general question of whether protection should be afforded and indeed expanded is a simple North-South debate between the old industrialised and the developing worlds. Newly industrialising and leading developing countries such as India, China and Kenya are similarly well placed to take advantage of intellectual property protection afforded agricultural GIs. On the other hand, given the cost in establishing and maintaining the institutions necessary to intellectual property protection, serious doubts remain over the ability of less advanced or less advantageously placed developing nations to take advantage of GI protection. Countries such as India and

Kenya for example have GIs that are already known and the financial means and the know how to enforce their protection. Other developing countries, however, may lack either the agricultural tradition related to place or the financial means to enforce the worldwide protection of their GIs.

In as much as these differing capacities and needs have been recognised in ongoing negotiations in the WTO over the last decade, no ready solution to the further global harmonisation of GIs has been found. WTO members are divided as to their capacity to take advantage of GI protection no less than they are radically divided as to the means of regulation. Whereas the current TRIPS provisions allow Member States to choose the means by which they protect GIs, the deep transatlantic division between the major powers of the EU and the USA over the method of protection risks retarding further progress on harmonisation for the foreseeable future.

While agricultural policy remains a highly controversial issue among WTO members, we are unlikely to see any lessening of pressure by the EC and supporting WTO Members for the extension of specific GI protection for an unlimited range of agricultural commodities and foodstuffs. The text of the Doha Declaration lends support to DCs who are seeking forms of knowledge, less than high technology that they have the capacity to exploit. It recognises "the need for all our peoples to benefit from the increased opportunities and welfare gains that the multilateral trading system generates".[44] GIs, pertaining to both agriculture and handicrafts may contain TK which is capable of exploitation in sophisticated consumer markets as natural medicinal, culinary, cosmetic or lifestyle products.

Nevertheless, the USA, Australia, Canada and Argentina are among those countries who are adamantly opposed to the proposal, being of the view that international protection of GIs is adequate as it stands and that such a drastic development would only serve to undermine future gains in market access for non-European food and agricultural products.[45] Developing countries are similarly divided. On the one hand, those who support the USA and Australia have serious misgivings concerning the additional costs of implementing a distinct system of GI protection in addition to the TRIPS obligations that are outstanding. On the other hand, India and Kenya, as countries already in possession of valuable GIs, are among those who support the EC proposal.

Regrettably, the Hong Kong Ministerial Declaration of December 2005 does not record any notable progress since the last Ministerial Conference, concerning the extension of the protection of GIs to products other than wines and spirits; or the multilateral register for GIs for wines and spirits.[46] Admittedly, the momentum of negotiations was derailed by the USA and Australian requests for consultations with the European Communities concerning the discriminatory nature of the European registration system. In the aftermath, the ruling of the WTO Panel of March 2005 in the case of *EC – GIs* has done little to quell the strength of this regulatory dispute. In the result, the USA and Australia successfully challenged Council Regulation (EEC) No. 2081/92 on the protection of GIs for agricultural products (EC Regulation) as discriminatory of foreign rightholders. In fact, the decision, which nonetheless sanctioned the substantive provisions of the EC Regulation, only appears to have emboldened the EC's bid to see its system of GI protection promulgated within the TRIPS Agreement.[47]

To this end, the EC proposal of June 2005 would extend GI protection to all agricultural products as well as indigenous handicrafts and see their notification in a mandatory multilateral register.[48] The emergence of the first truly global intellectual property rights would constitute a unprecedented departure from the classical system of international intellectual property law, based as it is on the territorial principle of national systems of registration for GIs and trade marks. In addition, it would entail an erosion of the property rights of trade mark owners and the corresponding capacity of Member States to determine economic policy.

The future global regulation of GIs is now at a crossroads. The Agreement on Trade-Related Aspects of Intellectual Property Law (TRIPS) is widely recognised as having set new standards for the international protection of GIs, having succeeded at one stroke in recognising GIs as a major category of intellectual property alongside patents and copyright and trademarks (Blakeney, 2005; Evans, 1994).[49] While we may have agreement as to the fundamental principles of protection, there is a lack of precision as to legal terms and, a number of novel legal issues arising from the proposal for extended global protection, notably the extent to which legal effects at the national level should affect the registration of a GIs; and legal effect attendant upon whether Members participation in the system is on a prescriptive or voluntary basis.

6   GIs, TK and handicrafts

The international debate concerning the protection of TK is generally concerned with patent or industrial property related matters. In contrast, the protection of folklore, or Traditional Cultural Expressions (TCEs) is generally discussed in a copyright context. The inappropriateness of this bifurcation is illustrated in the debates concerning the extension of the additional protection of GIs to handicrafts. Handicrafts may be characterised equally either as aspects of TK or as TCEs. A number of commentators have noted the obvious impact of the terrain upon the availability of which raw materials for the fabrication of handicrafts (Gangjee, 2002).[50] The application of these materials for the production of handicrafts inevitably involves the application of TK. This can be seen from the Pakistani examples of GIs to protect textiles discussed by Shah (2004, p.13).[51] He refers to the production of Ajrak cloths by the people of Sindh (Shah, 2004, pp.14, 15).[51] Ajrak is usually about 2.5–3 m long, carrying geometric patterns which can be traced back to the ancient civilisations of the Indus Valley. The Ajrak may be worn as a turban or shawl or used as a bed-sheet or tablecloth. When worn out, it can be used as a hammock for a baby, covers for a bullock cart and as backing to patchwork quilts.

Shah explains that Ajrak begins life as sheets of pure cotton cloth which are washed in the river. The damp cloth is then coiled and placed on top of a copper vat, covered with a quilt to prevent steam from escaping. The vat is heated by a log fire, throughout the night into the next day. In the next stage the fabric is soaked in a mixture of camel dung, seed oil and water. The dung enables the cloth to become softer and acts as a bleaching agent. The wet cloth is then tied into an airtight bundle and kept for 5–10 days, depending upon the weather. The cloth is then dried in the sun and it goes through another oil treatment. The oil is curdled with Carbonate of Soda solution and then the cloth is soaked in this mixture to ensure that the fibres receive maximum oil. After a thorough wash in the river the next day, they are soaked in a mixture of Sakun made with Galls of Tamarisk, dried lemons, molasses, castor oil and water. The wet cloth is then dried and brought to the workshop for printing.

Shah describes that the printing is conducted through the use of wooden blocks, which are carved from the Acacia Arabica trees, indigenous to the Sindh region. The textile is first printed with a paste made with rice paste, Acacia gum and lime.

370   *M. Blakeney*

The second stage is the printing of the black areas called Kut with a mixture of Ferrous Sulphate, Fuller's earth, gum and water. For the next stage, gum is mixed with rice paste, alum, molasses, fennel, Fuller's earth and other herbs to form the mud resist-paste, called the Kharrh. This mixture is then printed on the areas that are to be protected against the indigo dye, so that the white, black and other portions become red. An indigo dye is obtained from a local plant, Neel, while a red dye is obtained from another local plant, Manjeet.

The red Ajraks are spread out to partially dry in the sun and artisans sprinkle water on the cloth. Due to the alternate drying and drenching of the cloth the white areas get bleached, whereas the coloured areas become more sharply defined. Sifted, dried, cow dung is again applied to the cloth prior to a second dying, the Ajraks receive a final washing.

The Ajrak is obviously a TCE of the Sindhis, but at the same time its production involves the application of a considerable amount of TK. At the same time the quality of the product is dependent upon a number of local ingredients rendering Ajraks.

A similar role of TK in textile production characterises the production of Shu or Chitrali Patti which is the windproof cloth woven by the women of the high mountain villages of Chitral.

7   Conclusion

Obviously, the most focussed protection for TK would be through the international adoption of a mandatory sui generis system. However, in the absence of this, other categories of intellectual property protection have to be deployed. While most of the discussion to date has focused upon the role which patent and PVP laws might play in the protection of TK, the objectives of GIs protection share a number of policy objectives with TK protection.

Both TK and GIs protection seek to preserve communal rights. GIs are a collective right owned by all producers in a geographical region who observe the specified codes for production in that region. GIs have been described as a means of "enabling people to translate their long-standing, collective, and patrimonial knowledge into livelihood and income" (Bérard and Marchenay, 1996),[53] which has been identified as one of the core IP objectives of TK protection.

GI's can be held in perpetuity, for as long as a community maintains the practices which guarantee the distinctive quality of a local product. This overcomes the limited terms of protection conferred by other forms of IP protection. On the other hand it should be noted that the proponents of TK protection emphasise its dynamism and capacity for development, which is not necessarily a characteristic of TK.

Among the strengths of GI protection is that it might provide for protection of TK which is already in the public domain. For example, in relation to Kava the USPTO granted Natrol, Inc., a US-based Company a US patent for 'kavatrol', a dietary supplement that serves as a general relaxant, composed of Kava (Downes and Laird, 1999).[53] Two German companies, William Schwabe and Krewel-Werke, obtained a patent for Kava as a prescription drug for treating strokes, insomnia and Alzheimer's disease Panizzon, 2006).[54] In (France, L'Oréal has patented the use of Kava against hair loss (Panizzon, 2006).[54] As these products are promoted on the basis of their derivation from Kava, GIs may prove to be the second best option for protecting Kava by acting as a substitute to patent protection of the TK related to the plant itself.

At all times it should be noted that GIs laws protect only the designations associated with products. Indeed, IP laws seldom protect knowledge as such. The exceptions to this are trade secrets law and patent law. However, empowering a local community or individual holder of TK with the possibility to exclude third parties from the unauthorised use of designations of its TK would not only better balance the sharing of benefits from the utilisation of that TK.

Finally, the extension of the scope of registered GIs protection under TRIPS would also provide an example for developing countries of the practical utility of an international IP regime and a justification for the implementation of the TRIPS Agreement.

References

Bently, L. and Sherman, B. (2006) *The Impact of European Geographical Indications on National Rights in Member States*, 76 TMR 1.

Bérard, L. and Marchenay, P. (1996) 'Tradition, regulation and intellectual property: local agricultural products and foodstuffs in France', in Brush, S.B. and Stabinsky, D. (Eds.): *Valuing Local Knowledge: Indigenous Peoples and Intellectual Property Rights*, Island Press, Covelo, CA, p.230 at 240.

Biber-Klemm, S., Cottier, T., Cullet, P. and Szymura-Berglas, D. (2005) 'The current law of plant genetic resources and traditional knowledge', *Traditional Knowledge on Plant Genetic Resources for Food and Agriculture*, CABI Publishing, Wallingford, Oxfordshire, pp.57–81.

Blakeney, M. (2000) 'Protection of traditional knowledge under intellectual property law', *European Intellectual Property Review*, pp.251–261.

Blakeney, M. (2002) 'Intellectual property aspects of traditional agricultural knowledge', in Evanson, R.E., Santaniello, V. and Zilberman, D. (Eds.): *Economic and Social Issues in Agricultural Biotechnology*, CABI Publishing, Oxford, pp.43–60.

Blakeney, M. (2004) 'Bioprospecting and biopiracy', in Ong, B. (Ed.): *Intellectual Property and Biological Resources*, Marshall Cavendish, Singapore, pp.393–424.

Blakeney, M. (2005) 'Stimulating agricultural innovation', in Maskus, K.E. and Reichman, J.H. (Eds.): *International Public Goods and Transfer of Technology under a Globalized Intellectual Property Regime*, Cambridge University Press, Cambridge, pp.367–390.

Blakeney, M. (Ed.) (1999) *Intellectual Property Aspects of Ethnobiology*, Sweet & Maxwell, London.

Cottier, T. and Panizzon, M. (2004) 'Legal perspectives on traditional knowledge: the case for intellectual property protection', 7 *Journal of International Economic Law*, p.371.

Downes, D.R. and Laird, S.A. (1999) *Innovative Mechanisms for Sharing Benefits of Biodiversity and Related Knowledge Case Studies on Geographical Indications and Trademarks*, UNCTAD Biotrade Initiative, Geneva, http://www.ciel.org/Publications/InnovativeMechanisms.pdf

Evans, G. (1994) 'Intellectual property as a trade issue: the making of the agreement on trade related aspects of intellectual property', *World Competition, Law and Economics Review*, Vol. 18, No. 2, pp.137–180.

Gangjee, D.S. (2002) *Geographical Indications Protection for Handicrafts under TRIPS*, MPhil Thesis, Faculty of Law, University of Oxford, Held at St Peter's College, Oxford University, p.14.

372   *M. Blakeney*

Jabbour, A. (1982) *Folklore Protection and National Patrimony: Developments and Dilemmas in the Legal Protection of Folklore*, XVII, No. 1 Copyright Bulletin 10 at 11–12, cited in Blakeney (2000).

Kur, A. and Knaak, R. (2004) *Protection of Traditional Names and Designations*, Kluwer Law Int., The Hague, London and New York, pp.221–258; and See also Roland Knaak's comments in Leistner (2004, p.90, 227, 228, 233, 234).

Leistner, M. (2004) *Analysis of Different Areas of Indigenous Resources*, Kluwer Law Int., The Hague, London and New York, p.90.

McNeely, J.A. (2001) 'Biodiversity and agricultural development: the crucial institutional issues', in Lee, D.R. and Barrett, C.B. (Eds.): *Tradeoffs or Synergies? Agricultural Intensification, Economic Development and the Environment*, Wallingford, CABI, pp.399, 404.

O'Connor and Company (2003) *Geographical Indications and the Challenges for ACP Countries*, A Discussion Paper, Brussels, CTA, 3, http://agritrade.cta.int/

Panizzon, M. (2006) *Traditional Knowledge and Geographical Indications: Foundations, Interests and Negotiating Positions*, Working Paper No. 2005/01.

Richard, A. (1918) *De la Protection des Appellation d'origine en Matièe Vinicole*, Imprimeries Gounouilhou, Bordeaux.

Ricketson, S. (1987) *The Berne Convention for the Protection of Literary and Artistic Works; 1886–1986*, London, CCLS, pp.607–620.

Schechter, I. (1925) *The Historical Foundation of the Law Relating to Trade-Marks*, Cambridge Mass, Harvard UP, pp.40–42.

Shah, S.Q. (2004) *Geographical Indications: National GIs system in Pakistan. A Country Case Study*, Islamabad, Sustainable Development Policy Institute (SDPI), p.13.

Stilwell, M. and Monagle, C. (2000) *Review of TRIPS Agreement under Article 71.1*, South Centre, Geneva, December.

UK Commission on Intellectual Property Rights (2002) *Integrating Intellectual Property Rights and Development Policy Report of the Commission on Intellectual Property Rights London CIPR*, September, ch.4.

van Caenegem, W. (2003) 'Registered geographical indications. Between intellectual property and rural policy-Part II', *JWIP*, Vol. 861, pp.699–715.

von Lewinski, S. (Ed.) (2004) *Indigenous Heritage and intellectual property. Genetic Resources, Traditional Knowledge and Folklore*, Kluwer Law Int., The Hague, London and New York.

WIPO (2000) *Matters Concerning Intellectual Property Genetic Resources Traditional Knowledge and Folklore*, WIPO Doc, WO/GA/26/6, August 25, *Protection of Traditional Knowledge by Geographical Indications* 17.

WIPO/UNEP (2001) *The Role of Intellectual Property Rights in the Sharing of Benefits Arising from the Use of Biological Resources and Associated Traditional Knowledge, Selected Case Studies*, Geneva, WIPO, p.13.

Notes

[1] A 1996 study by UNCTAD noted for example, in Chile that the additional fixed costs to upgrade the IP infrastructure were estimated at $718,000, with annual recurrent costs increasing to $837,000. In Egypt, the fixed costs were estimated at $800,000 with additional annual training costs of around $1 million. UNCTAD, *The TRIPS Agreement and the Developing Countries*, UNCTAD, Geneva, 1996.

[2] See E.g., Stilwell and Monagle (2000).

[3] Communication from Bolivia, Columbia, Ecuador, Nicaragua and Peru, "Proposal on Protection of the Intellectual Property Rights Relating to the Traditional Knowledge of Local and Indigenous Communities", World Trade Organization, WT/GC/W/362 12 October 1999.

[4]WT/GC/W/282.

[5]See E.g., Ricketson (1987).

[6]Study on the International Regulations of Intellectual Property, UNESCO/WIPO/WG.1/FOLK/3, Tunis, 11–13 July 1977.

[7]WIPO doc, UNESCO-WIPO/FOLK/PKT/97/1 (March 17, 1997).

[8]WIPO doc, UNESCO-WIPO/FOLK/PKT/97/1 (March 17, 1997, p.3).

[9]See e.g., Blakeney (1999, 2004).

[10]WIPO Doc. WO/GA/26/9, Annex I, 10.

[11]See WIPO (2000).

[12]See WIPO Doc, WIPO/GRTKF/IC/2/3, September 10, 2001, para.1.

[13]WIPO/GRTKF/IC/6/14, para.109.

[14]von Lewinski (2004).

[15]Kur, A. and Knaak, R. (2004) and See also Roland Knaak's comments in Leistner (2004, p.90, 227, 228, 233, 234).

[16]This study is part of a research project entitled "Rights to Plant Genetic Resources and Traditional Knowledge: Basic Issues and Perspectives" for the Swiss Agency for Development and Cooperation (SDC) of the Federal Department of Foreign Affairs.

[17]WIPO/GRTKF/IC/3/7 May 6, 2002.

[18]WIPO/GRTKF/IC/3/7 May 6, 2002, para.40.

[19]WIPO/GRTKF/IC/10/4, Annex, 3.

[20]Schechter (1925).

[21]Council Regulation (EC) No 510/2006 of 20 March 2006.

[22]For a recent analysis of European GIs legislation, see Bently and Sherman (2006).

[23]See O'Connor and Company (2003).

[24]The *privilège de la descente* and *privilege de la barrique* described in Richard (1918) referred to in van Caenegem (2003).

[25]Cottier and Panizzon (2004)[17] No. 6, at 8.

[26]See Biber-Klemm et al. (2005).

[27]E.g., WIPO/GRTKF/IC/10/4, Annex, 3, objective (vi).

[28]E.g., WIPO/GRTKF/IC/10/4, Annex, 3, objective (vii).

[29]See Blakeney (2002).

[30]McNeely (2001).

[31]See WIPO/UNEP (2001).

[32]Reported in UK Commission on Intellectual Property Rights (2002).

[33]Jabbour (1982).

[34]Case C-47/90.

[35]Case C-469/00.

[36]Case C-108/01.

[37]WIPO/GRTKF/IC/10/4, Annex, 3, objective (viii).

[38]WIPO/GRTKF/IC/10/4, Annex, 3, objective (xiv).

[39]WT/GC/W/249, 13 July 1999.

[40]*Preparations for the 1999 Ministerial Conference the TRIPS Agreement Communication from Kenya on Behalf of the African Group*, WT/GC/W/302, 6 August 1999.

[41]IP/C/W/204/Rev.1.

[42]In June 2005 the EC submitted a proposal for amending Section 3 of the TRIPS Agreement with a view to extending the regime of protection today available for geographical indications on wines

374   *M. Blakeney*

and spirits to geographical indications on all products ('extension') and; in addition a proposal for the inclusion of an annex to the TRIPS Agreement establishing a multilateral system of notification and registration of geographical indications (GIs). World Trade Organization, General Council, Trade Negotiations Committee, Council for Trade-Related Aspects of Intellectual Property Rights, Special Session on Geographical Indications, Communication from the European Communities 14 June 2005, WT/GC/W/547, TN/C/W/26, TN/IP/W/11. See earlier submissions of the EC, 22 June 2000, IP/C/W/107/Rev.1 with respect to the register and; submission of 2002 in respect of the extension, IP/C/W/353 24 June 2002.

[43]"Since 1993, more than 700 names, designating *inter alia* over 150 cheeses, 160 meat and meat-based products, 150 fresh or processed fruits or vegetables and 80 types of olive oil, have been registered in this context. The Commission has also received over 300 further applications for the registration of names and/or amendments to specifications from Member States and third countries". Proposal for a Council Regulation on the Protection of Geographical Indications and designations of origin for agricultural products and foodstuffs, Commission of The European Communities, Brussels, 5.1.2006, para.3.

[44]Clause 2, Doha Ministerial Declaration, 14 November 2001, WT/MIN(01)/DEC/1.

[45]See US Submissions on GIs at the WTO TRIPS Council: "Joint Proposal for a Multilateral System of Notification and Registration of Geographical Indications for Wines and Spirits", Communication from Argentina, Australia, Canada, Chile, Ecuador, El Salvador, New Zealand and the United States, TN/IP/W/9, 13 April 2004; and "Multilateral System of Notification and Registration of Geographical Indications for Wines (and Spirits)", Communication from Argentina, Australia, Canada, Chile, New Zealand and the USA, TN/IP/W/6, 29 October 2002; and "Proposal for a Multilateral System for Notification and Registration of Geographical Indications for Wines and Spirits based on Article 23.4 of the TRIPS Agreement", Communication from Argentina, Australia, Canada, Chile, Colombia, Costa Rica, Dominican Republic, Ecuador, El Salvador, Guatemala, Honduras, Japan, Namibia, New Zealand, Philippines, Chinese Taipei, and the USA, TN/IP/W/5, 23 October 2002.

[46]Clauses 29 and 39, Sixth Session, Hong Kong, 13–18 December 2005, Ministerial Declaration, adopted on 18 December 2005, WT/MIN(05)/DEC. Further see Special Session of the Council for TRIPS Report by the Chairman, Ambassador Manzoor Ahmad, to the Trade Negotiations Committee, 23 November 2005, TN/IP/14, in which Ambassador Manzoor Ahmad lament the lack of progress at para.5.

[47]Following the decision, EU Trade Commissioner Mandelson summed up the EC's position: "By confirming that geographical indications are both legal and compatible with existing trademark systems, this WTO decision will help the EU to ensure wider recognition of geographical indications and protection of regional and local product identities, which is one of our goals in the Doha Round of multilateral trade negotiations: http://www.delcan.cec.eu.int/en/press_and_information/press_releases/2005/05PR009.shtml.

[48]World Trade Organization, General Council, Trade Negotiations Committee, Council for Trade-Related Aspects of Intellectual Property Rights, Special Session on Geographical Indications, Communication from the European Communities 14 June 2005, WT/GC/W/547, TN/C/W/26, TN/IP/W/11.

[49]Blakeney (2005) and Evans (1994).

[50]See the authorities referred to in Gangjee (2002).

[51]See Shah (2004, p.13–15).

[52]Bérard and Marchenay (1996).

[53]See Downes and Laird (2004) No. 34, p.5.

[54]Panizzon (2006), No. 6, text at p.151.

[30]

Volume 11 Number 1 2010/p. 68-117   esteyjournal.com

The Estey Centre Journal of
International Law
and Trade Policy

Law and Policy on Intellectual Property, Traditional Knowledge and Development: Legally Protecting Creativity and Collective Rights in Traditional Knowledge Based Agricultural Products through Geographical Indications

Teshager Dagne

Doctoral candidate, J.S.D. Program, Schulich School of Law,

Dalhousie University, Halifax

Geographical indications emerged on the international scene at the centre of three highly debated subjects: intellectual property, international trade and agricultural policy. This article discusses the use of geographical indications in the protection of traditional knowledge–based agricultural products in the international intellectual property framework, and assesses the challenges and opportunities geographical indications present with respect to efforts to cater to the needs of indigenous people and local communities. The discussion begins with a succinct overview of the definitional aspects of geographical indications, traditional knowledge and traditional knowledge–based agricultural products. In an attempt to locate the issue of geographical indications in the current intellectual property landscape, the article examines their regulation in international and national legal frameworks, and critically appraises the attendant controversies in international negotiations. The article then broaches issues to do with the link between geographical indications and traditional knowledge, and examines the cultural, economic and environmental issues in policy debates surrounding the applicability of geographical indications to traditional knowledge–based agricultural products.

Keywords: agricultural products, geographical indications, traditional knowledge, TRIPS, WTO

Editorial Office: 410 22nd St. E., Suite 820, Saskatoon, SK, Canada, S7K 5T6. _____
Phone (306) 244-4800; Fax (306) 244-7839; email: kerr.w@esteycentre.com   68

Teshager Dagne

1. Introduction

In the wake of its emergence on the international scene, the world's major international intellectual property tool – the Agreement on Trade-Related Aspects of Intellectual Property Rights (TRIPS) – has evoked anger and dismay among indigenous people and local communities, mainly in the developing countries. Beyond the burden of setting up institutions that they previously did not have, the TRIPS expects developing countries to devote their meagre resources to the revision and introduction of legislation that provides for criminal sanctions against violations of intellectual property rights, the administration of such legislation and the enforcement of border measures.[1] The fact that most of these countries are importers of most of the intellectual property–bound products in question has resulted in high outflows of foreign currency – adding to the pressures related to the costs of compliance and making it difficult for them to satisfy the health needs of their citizens, provide educational materials and cope with the soaring price of agricultural inputs.

Despite the onerous requirements, the TRIPS Agreement does not address the concerns of the majority of the countries that are obligated to comply with it. The manner in which traditional knowledge (TK) is treated in the agreement demonstrates how the global intellectual property (IP) regime addresses the concerns of developing countries and the interests of their component indigenous peoples and local communities.[2] Generally, the relationship between TK and the IP regime incorporated in the TRIPS remains vexed due mainly to the theoretical shortcomings of the latter to accommodate the epistemological underpinnings of the former. The TRIPS requires WTO members to protect TK to the extent that such knowledge fits within the forms of intellectual property protection that the agreement recognizes.[3] The problem is that these forms of intellectual property protection tools – while they have proved instrumental to owners of technological and biotechnological knowledge and skill – do not fit well with TK and, thus, have only facilitated its misappropriation and abuse.[4]

TK plays a pivotal role in the livelihood of a large segment of the world's population in many ways.[5] The lack of protection has resulted in the unprecedented erosion of the other most important asset in most developing countries – biodiversity. The 1992 Convention on Biological Diversity (CBD) as well as subsequent agreements have widely recognized the important role of traditional knowledge systems and practices in protecting the environment and conserving biodiversity. As a result, efforts to find modes of protecting traditional knowledge have surfaced in various forums of international and national law-making, as well as in the works of public-interest groups and academicians. These efforts stem from diverse

Teshager Dagne

philosophical roots, and thus the approaches adopted and the methods proposed take varied forms. As such, the extent and mode of protection they offer as well as their effectiveness are varied.

In the efforts to protect TK through the realm of intellectual property – one of the proposed methods to protect TK – the modes of protection under consideration in the various forums usually take either of the following two forms: the protection for exploitation of TK through the use of new-fangled or extant intellectual property rights, or the protection against exploitation of this knowledge by preventing its misappropriation through the use of a similar intellectual property regime. The former is referred to as positive protection, while the latter is considered defensive protection.

The positive protection approach to TK responds to the needs of indigenous peoples and local communities who want to benefit from the commercialization of their knowledge. This system aspires to create an entitlement system through mechanisms such as sui generis legislation, contractual agreements and/or the use of existing intellectual property systems of protection that enable indigenous peoples and local communities to protect and promote their knowledge.

On the other hand, the defensive protection approach to TK responds to the needs of indigenous people and local communities who may want the preservation of cultural heritage as an end in itself, the identification and protection of TK as an element of promoting the preservation of biodiversity and the sustainable use of biological resources, and its protection in a human rights context.[6] These groups and communities may be more concerned with the cultural, social and psychological harm caused by the unauthorized use of their TK by outsiders than with economic implications.[7]

However, the distinctions between defensive and positive intellectual property protections are not watertight. The protection of TK for the purpose of exploitation by its holders also entails the protection of such knowledge against misappropriation by "outsiders."[8]

With respect to positive protection, many developing-country producers have now realized that the fruits of their "inventions" may earn them a fair share of the market.[9] This realization has coincided with the increasing awareness that rendering the knowledge bearer attentive to the value of his/her knowledge will encourage the holders to appreciate TK as "continuous and additive innovation" and thus a resource that further develops their culture.[10] Geographical indications (GIs) are touted as having the potential to offer advantages to developing-country agricultural producers along these lines.

Teshager Dagne

GIs emerged on the international scene at the centre of three highly debated subjects: intellectual property, international trade and agricultural policy. This article examines the significance of GIs in the protection of traditional knowledge–based agricultural products (TKBAPs) in the international intellectual property framework, and assesses the challenges and opportunities they present with respect to efforts to cater to the needs of indigenous people and local communities.[11] The following section provides a succinct overview of the definitional aspects of GIs, TK and TKBAPs. Section three examines the regulation of GIs in the various legal frameworks. In an attempt to locate the issue of GIs in the current intellectual property landscape, the article investigates their treatment in international and national legal frameworks, and critically appraises the attendant controversies in international negotiations.

In the rest of the article, I broach the emerging issues to do with the link between GIs and traditional knowledge and appraise the suitability of GIs to serve as modalities for protecting traditional knowledge–based agricultural products. Examined are the cultural, economic and environmental issues in the policy debates surrounding the applicability of GIs to TKBAPs. Finally, I draw conclusions regarding the circumstances under which GIs may be employed to serve the purposes sought in the context of TKBAPs.

2. Definition of Terms

2.1 Traditional Knowledge and Traditional Knowledge–Based Agricultural Products

The term "traditional knowledge" refers to a concept difficult to define and to distinguish from other knowledge.[12] Although the literature refers to this category of knowledge as "traditional knowledge," "indigenous knowledge," "local knowledge," "folk knowledge" and "community knowledge" interchangeably, I prefer to use the term "traditional knowledge" in this project to avoid the technical ambiguities associated with the other terms.[13] The conceptual bounds of "indigenous knowledge" appear to be less inclusive, due mainly to the narrow understanding of the term "indigenous people" in the current international law arena.[14]

The TRIPS Agreement is the major instrument that provides IP-based protection of modern knowledge through patents, trademarks, copyrights, industrial designs and geographical indications.[15] TRIPS does not protect TK, because TK does not fit the legal criteria for "knowledge and innovations" that form the basis for protection under modern intellectual property law. These criteria are based on a distinction between the intangible aspect of knowledge that yields "innovation" and the product to which the

Teshager Dagne

knowledge is applied. While it is widely acknowledged that the modern economic system is knowledge based, indigenous people and local communities have been considered resource based.[16] Accordingly, the extant intellectual property regimes aspire to protect "unique knowledge but not unique resources and raw materials."[17]

Although the above distinction occupies a highly specialized niche in the Western tradition, it is alien to communities outside this tradition.[18] The distinction between the material – in most cases a biological resource – and its intangible aspect is blurred in the context of indigenous people and local communities and, as such, is held to be not only "inappropriate" but also "denaturaliz[ing of] traditional knowledge," resulting in the "loss of control by indigenous peoples over the product of their intellectual effort, or over the biological resources to which it is related."[19]

In this article, I prefer to use a definition of TK that provides for the indivisibility of traditional knowledge. The definition by the African Group in its submission to the World Intellectual Property Organization (WIPO) is closer to the understanding of the concept in this article:

> knowledge which is held by members of a distinct culture and/or sometimes acquired by means of inquiry peculiar to that culture, and concerning the culture itself or the local environment in which it exists. TK is thus the totality of all knowledge and practices, whether explicit or implicit, used in the management of socio-economic and ecological facets of life.[20]

This definition covers the widest possible scope of traditional knowledge, above and beyond any of the terms used to refer to it. It accurately refers to not only "knowledge," but also "practices" of people who are members of a distinct culture. By locating the existence of the "knowledge" and "practices" within the "socio-economic and ecological facets of life" of the members of the community, the definition encompasses a wide range of knowledge across a spectrum from agricultural knowledge to ecological knowledge; medicinal knowledge; knowledge relating to medicines and remedies; knowledge of plant genetic resources; and traditional cultural expressions. As such, it provides the theoretical prism through which various components of such knowledge may be better understood. In this scenario, the phrase "traditional knowledge–based agricultural products" (TKBAPs) refers to the resources of indigenous people and local communities engaged in agricultural production who utilize traditional means of production. Agricultural products are defined as "the products of the soil, *of stock-farming and of fisheries and products of first-stage processing* directly related to these products."[21]

Teshager Dagne

2.2 Geographical Indications

S imply understood, GIs are signs used in connection with goods in order to indicate their geographical origin. Although they are part of one of the oldest intellectual property regimes addressed by the earlier international intellectual property treaties – the Paris Convention of 1883 – the literary landscape relating to GIs is heavily overcast by differences in the understanding of their nature. GIs are closely interrelated with and seemingly identical to two other varieties of intellectual property recognized in the earliest international treaties: "appellations of origin" (AOs) and "indications of source."[22]

Art. 2 of the Lisbon Agreement for the Protection of Appellations of Origin and their International Registration defines AO as "the geographical name of a country, region, or locality, which serves to designate a good originating therein, the quality and characteristics of which are due exclusively or essentially to the geographical environment, including natural and human factors."[23] The Lisbon Agreement also defines "country of origin" as "the country whose name or the country in which is situated the region or locality whose name constitutes the appellation of origin which has given the good its reputation for the quality and characteristic."[24] According to these definitions, an AO should always be a name which designates a country, region or locality. Also, it is fundamental that a good bearing the name exhibits quality and characteristics attributable to the designated area of geographical origin. Thus, an AO designates a given quality and characteristic of a good originating from a certain geographical origin, as exemplified by goods such as Champagne wine and Roquefort cheese, produced in the French districts of Champagne and Roquefort and known for their sparkling and taste/texture qualities respectively.

"Indications of source" are characterized by a link between the "indication" and the "geographical origin" of the product, which may be a certain country or a place in a country.[25] Such indications are also referred to as "country of origin" indications. The indication in an "indication of source" need not necessarily be a geographical name. Words or phrases that directly indicate geographical origin, or phrases, symbols or iconic emblems indirectly associated with the area of geographical origin, may constitute indications of source.[26] Unlike AO, an indication of source need not represent a particularly distinctive or renowned quality associated with the product's origin – although both designations refer to geographical locations.[27]

The TRIPS Agreement is the first multilateral agreement to have introduced the concept of "geographical indications" in a groundbreaking manner.[28] Art. 22.1 of the agreement provides the most extensive definition of GIs: "… indications which identify a good as originating in the territory of a Member, or a region or locality in that territory, where a given quality, reputation or other characteristic of the good is essentially attributable to its geographical origin."

GIs are similar to AOs in that both associate the quality of a good with a geographical location identified by an indication. Scope-wise, GIs are wider than "appellations of origin" because GIs are not restricted to the names of geographical locations. Other indirect references to geographical locations such as pictorial symbols may also be included under the definition of GIs, as long as they can identify a good with "a given quality, reputation or other characteristic" as originating in a territory, region or locality in the territory. For example, GIs include the use of the Eiffel Tower or the Statute of Liberty to represent France or the United States – or a place or territory in France or the United States – in association with a good.

Unlike in the case of AOs, with GIs each one of the factors – "quality," "reputation" or "other characteristic" – is on its own an adequate condition for the grant of protection, because the list in the definition of GIs under the TRIPS Agreement is in the alternative, as opposed to the cumulative listing in the earlier Lisbon Agreement.[29] The recognition of "reputation" as an independent, protectable subject in the TRIPS gives a clue to the question as to whether a GI merely denotes only a geographical location – "the sign the product points to in the eyes of the consumer" – or its connotation as well – "the penumbra of associations and qualities that ...[could be] 'usurped', 'appropriated', 'diluted' or 'imitated'."[30] It is also noted that the distinction between the denotation and connotation of GIs in this manner reveals the dichotomy in the understanding of GIs as "protection against misleading use of GIs in the consumer's interest, and a form of absolute protection as a collective right defended against all usurpation and evocation" respectively.[31]

WIPO has indicated that "reputation" with respect to GIs is mainly related to the history and historical origin of the product, an attribute more attuned to products of traditional knowledge.[32] For GIs such as "Basmati rice," for example, the quality of the rice from the region denoted is closely connected to the reputation of the product connoted by the symbolic name. As such, the protection extends not only to the term "Basmati" as denoted in reference to the region of Punjab, but also to the reputation of the product that the term connotes – the traditional method of production developed over time, and the cultural aspects of the product. This distinction is significant in that the content of the rights in the latter exhibits "many of the hallmarks of a property right," while the former grants a "mere right of action for misrepresentation – easily justified in terms of honest trade and consumer protection."[33]

"Reputation" in the protection of GIs may arise not necessarily from "physical characteristics emanating from climate or soil quality" of the product but from other

Teshager Dagne

factors in the geographical origin such as "local inventiveness."[34] Such factors must contribute to the distinctiveness of the product, i.e., its capacity to distinguish itself from other products, and the reputation must be assessed, inter alia, from the consumer's perception of the indication.[35] Although assessment of the reputation may differ depending on the systems and the products, and can be made on a local, national or international basis, WIPO suggested that a local reputation be sufficient for protection to be granted.[36]

Even when the characteristic of the product is not related to the "quality" or "reputation," GIs protect the "other characteristics" of the good. "Other characteristic" refers to any element that contributes to the typicality of the product. Natural and human factors are the most frequently used factors in determining the typicality of the product – as affirmed by WIPO.[37] Natural factors are the physical attributes of the soil, weather, geographical location and the like, as represented by the French conception of "terroir." It is noted that recognition of human factors in this respect makes it possible to protect products whose unique quality derives from traditional knowledge.[38]

Therefore, the scope of GIs as recognized by the TRIPS Agreement extends beyond a mere designation of quality. In the discussion of the subject in the international intellectual property agreements, the literature often uses the term "geographical indications" to refer to "appellations of origin" and "indications of source," and vice-versa. In such cases, WIPO has indicated that "the rights and obligations flowing from those instruments exist only in relation to the category of 'geographical indication' to which the instrument in question refers."[39] It is important to draw a distinction within the context of the international agreement that is under consideration.[40]

For the purposes of this article, geographical indications are understood within the scope and the meaning accorded to them by the TRIPS Agreement. GIs are understood in this article in such a wide scope in order to encompass the "reputation" and "other characteristics" of the goods resulting from human contribution in a geographical origin. As will be indicated below, the expansive feature of GIs under the TRIPS is an important factor that makes GIs conducive tools for the protection of TKBAPs. Before proceeding further on the link between GIs and TKBAPs, the regulation of these forms of intellectual property rights (IPRs) in international and national frameworks will first be examined, and aspects of the debate currently reigning in the TRIPS negotiations on GIs analysed.

Teshager Dagne

3. The Regulation of Geographical Indications

Generally, the protection of GIs in national and international frameworks has two major facets. First, protection in the case of GIs is understood as the right to prevent unauthorized persons from using GIs, either for goods that do not originate from the geographical place indicated or for goods that do not comply with the prescribed quality standards.[41] The second facet relates to protecting GIs against becoming generic expressions,[42] commonly referred to as genericide. Genericide is a phenomenon by which "a mark used as indication that was once highly valuable and unquestionably protectable loses its status and value and, consequently, its protection."[43]

3.1 The International Protection of Geographical Indications

Whether a GI is a generic term and void of any protection is, in the absence of an international agreement, usually determined by national legislation.[44] Accordingly, a GI protected in one country may be considered generic in another. As a result, this aspect of protection of GIs has been dealt with in the earlier international agreements on intellectual property – currently administered by WIPO – and lies at the centre of the discussions and negotiations under the current TRIPS framework in the WTO.

3.1.1 Geographical Indications in the World Trade Organization Framework and the Ongoing Negotiations

The negotiation process for the protection of GIs during the drafting of the TRIPS has generated heated arguments between the proponents for strong protection – mainly the EU – and other countries that have opted for flexible standards. In the negotiations leading up to the conclusion of the TRIPS Agreement, the EU and the United States introduced divergent treaty texts.[45] Reflecting the historical experience of national lawmaking in Europe,[46] the EU recommended the protection of all "geographical indications, including appellations of origin" through specific GI provisions to the extent that protection is accorded in the country of origin.[47] This proposal was to be applied to all goods including goods of the vine.

The United States proposed to protect GIs "that certify regional origin by providing for their registration as certification or collective marks [through the trademark regime and thus without a need for specific GI regime]."[48] In contrast, a group of developing countries led by Brazil and India called on countries "... to provide protection for geographical indications including appellations of origin against any use which is likely to confuse or mislead the public as to the true origin of the good."[49]

Teshager Dagne

A compromise between these proposals was finally presented by the then GATT director Arthur Dunkel on 20 December 1991.[50] Incorporating this version of the text, section three of the TRIPS expressly protects GIs. As a result, the agreement now provides two levels of GI protection: basic protection that sets the minimum standard of common application to all goods (Art. 22), and an additional level of protection applicable to wines and spirits only (Art. 23). Also, the agreement provided the mandate for the continuation of negotiations on the establishment of a multilateral system of notification and registration of GIs (Art. 23 (4)).

The present discussion and negotiations in the WTO regarding GIs involve two issues that stem from the TRIPS Agreement's initial treatment of GIs. The first relates to the agenda of extending the "additional protection" accorded to wines and spirits to other agricultural goods. The second relates to the establishment of a multilateral GI registration system in the WTO to ensure better protection.

On the agenda of extending the protection TRIPS provides for wines and spirits to other goods beyond wines and spirits, the debate in the WTO is effectively polarised between two camps which do not fall along the traditional WTO lines of developing countries and developed countries.[51] On the one hand are the EC and its supporters, who are seeking to achieve broad protection for a wide range of GIs for agricultural and other goods, while another group of members, led by the United States, are opposed to extending additional protection for other goods beyond wines and spirits.[52] Consensus is not expected shortly, as the EC, together with India, Thailand, Turkey and Switzerland, has been in disagreement with the Cairns Group (mainly the United States, Argentina, Canada and Australia), who consider enhanced GI protection of agricultural goods another form of agricultural protectionism.[53]

Despite the recognition that protection of GIs remains an "outstanding implementation issue"[54] of the Doha Round of negotiations, the final "July Package" did not include the agenda of extending GI protection to goods other than wines and spirits.[55] Some WTO members have even questioned whether the Doha declaration offers a sufficient negotiating mandate for extending the enhanced protection of GIs to other goods.[56] For example, the United States argued that the current WTO rules sufficiently protect GIs, and amending the rules to extend GI protection to goods other than wines and spirits and establishing a multilateral GI registry "may impose significant new costs on WTO Members, especially developing and least developed Members, which will far outweigh any potential benefits."[57] Contrary to its response to the concerns of developing countries regarding the implementation cost of the other IPR regimes contained in the TRIPS, the United States wielded the argument of

Teshager Dagne

economic efficiency to resist the pressure for the extension of GI protection to agricultural products other than wines and spirits.

Regarding the establishment of the multilateral registry, negotiations were started soon after the conclusion of the TRIPS. The agenda has also been part of the Doha declaration. The Cairns Group did not question the negotiation mandate for the establishment of the multilateral registry system, as Art. 23(4) of the TRIPS clearly provides for the "establishment of a multilateral system of notification and registration of GIs for wines eligible for protection in those Members participating in the system." However, consensus has not yet been achieved, as the Cairns Group insisted on a voluntary system of registration that includes wines and spirits only, while the EU and its supporters sought to include agricultural goods in a non-voluntary registration system among participants in the system.[58]

Despite setting out a framework of obligations to protect GIs, the TRIPS Agreement does not prescribe a particular legal means to carry out the obligations. Thus, members are at their discretion to choose the particular legal means to provide for the protection of GIs. GIs are protected through a wide range of concepts in different jurisdictions, including *sui generis* laws that protect GIs, trademark laws that take the form of collective marks or certification marks, the common law rule of passing off, unfair competition laws, consumer protection legislation and special laws that recognize individual GIs.[59]

A lot of the controversy in the WTO arises from these differences – in approach – over protecting GIs. This in turn reflects the difference in outlook – mainly between the United States and the EU – towards GIs. This difference lies at the root of trade disputes brought to WTO dispute settlement panels and the controversies in the currently stalled Doha negotiations.[60]

3.2 National Systems of Protecting Geographical Indications

Differences in the form and substance of GI protection have long been a transatlantic trade irritant.[61] The EU countries have protected GIs for a long time through a sophisticated system of *sui generis* GIs that incorporate stringent criteria. The United States, however, does not see the need for a *sui generis* legislation to protect GIs, as it regulates and protects them through its existing trademark regime. This difference has been a source of conflict in bilateral talks as well as recent negotiations and disputes in the WTO.

The transatlantic difference has wider implications, as GI regulations in the EU and the United States affect all exporters of goods that are subject to the protection. The difference will have particular implications for developing countries due to the

Teshager Dagne

increasing recognition of the significance of these forms of IPR regulation for protection of traditional knowledge–based agricultural products – as will be indicated later in this article.[62]

3.2.1 The EU System of Geographical Indications

The EU system of GIs evolved from traditions of the individual wine-producing members, mainly France. The practice of protecting GIs in France dates back to the 1800s – when Napoleon III established the Grand Crus of the Bordeaux area.[63] Initially, the protection was applied to wines, but it later evolved to include other goods with a specific brand name tied to a traditional area of production.

As part of the single economic unit that it aspired to build among its members, the EU effected a unitary system of GI protection throughout its members. The GI system introduced in 1992 allows three different forms of protection: Protected Designation of Origin (PDO), Protected Geographical Indication (PGI) and Traditional Specialty Guaranteed (TSG). The first two categories of protection are established by Council Regulation 2081/92, which was later replaced by Regulation 510/2006, while TSGs are protected by Regulation 2082/92, replaced by Regulation 509/2006.[64]

PDO is defined under Art. 2.1 (a) of the EU Regulation 510/2006 as follows:

- the name of a region, a specific place or, in exceptional cases, a country, used to describe an agricultural good or a foodstuff:
    - originating in that region, specific place or country,
    - the quality or characteristics of which are essentially or exclusively due to a particular geographical environment with its inherent natural and human factors, and
    - the production, processing and preparation of which takes place in the defined geographical area.

It can be observed that PDO is defined in a slightly different but essentially similar manner to AO, in that the indication has to be the name of "a region, a specific place or, in exceptional cases, a country" from which the good originates. In addition, there has to be a "quality or characteristic" of the good due "exclusively or essentially" to a defined geographical environment. Also, a good under PDO has to be produced, processed and prepared within the designated geographical area.

Similarly, Art. 2.1 (b) of the same regulation defines PGI. The link between the good and the attribute of the good seems loose in the case of PGI, because unlike PDO, which requires that the "quality or characteristic" of the good be "essentially or exclusively" due to the geographical origin, the requirement in PGI is that the good "possesses a specific quality, reputation or other characteristics attributable" to the geographical origin.[65] This distinction is more pronounced in the requirement that the "production, processing and preparation" of the good in the case of a PDO must take place in the defined geographical area, while in the case of a PGI "production and/or processing and/or preparation of" the good may take place in the area designated by the geographical name. Thus, a good which is produced in a designated geographical area but processed in another geographical area may be protected under PGI while the same good will not get PDO protection.

Also, while PDO protects agricultural goods or foodstuffs with "quality or characteristics" due to a geographical origin, PGI protects agricultural goods or foodstuffs that possess "... reputation or other characteristics attributable [not essentially or exclusively due to]" the geographical origin. In this regard, PGI has an expansive scope similar to the GI concept introduced by the TRIPS Agreement. Unlike GIs, however, PGIs may not be designated by indications other than geographical names.

The EU Regulation 509/2006 protects the third type of GI: TSG. Art. 2.1 (c) of the regulation defines TSG as "a traditional agricultural good or foodstuff recognised by the Community for its specific character through its registration under this regulation." It further clarifies each element of the TSG, defining the term "traditional" as "proven usage on the Community market for a time period showing transmission between generations." "Specific character" is defined as "the characteristic or set of characteristics which distinguishes an agricultural good or a foodstuff clearly from other similar goods or foodstuffs of the same category."[66] The "characteristic or set of characteristics" is described as relating to "the good's intrinsic features such as its physical, chemical, microbiological or organoleptic features, or to the good's production method or to specific conditions that pertain during its production."[67]

Unlike the criteria for PGI and PDO, the specific character that a good possesses in TSG is derived not from the geographical origin but from the "traditional raw materials or ... a traditional composition or a mode of production and/or processing reflecting a traditional type of production and/or processing."[68] However, geographical terms may be registered as TSGs under the conditions laid out in Art. 4.2–4.3, and without prejudice to the protection of PDO and PGI.[69] Thus, TSG is not employed to refer to geographical origin but rather to highlight the traditional character of a good – in either the composition or the means of production.

The EU protects wines, spirits and mineral waters through separate legislation.[70] The EU law also provides for the possibility of registering a GI as a collective mark under both the Community's Trademark Regulation and the national laws of member

Teshager Dagne

states, as long as there is no pre-existing protection for a given GI.[71] However, EU law prohibits the registration of trademarks that conflict with registered GIs, unless the trademark obtained *bona fide* protection in an EU member state prior to registration of a conflicting GI, or prior to January 1, 1996.[72]

3.2.2 Geographical Indications in the U.S. Legal Framework

The United States protects GIs in a fundamentally different manner from the EU. Policy wise, the United States does not consider GIs a separate class of intellectual property, and thus it does not have legislation especially targeted at protecting GIs. It protects GIs through specific categories of the trademark regime: certification marks, collective marks and, in some cases, ordinary trademarks.

GIs are protected through certification marks and collective marks in the United States as an exception to the general rule that individual trademarks must not be geographically descriptive without a showing of acquired distinctiveness. According to the U.S. Trademark Act, a certification mark is "any word, name, symbol, or device used by a party or parties ... to certify regional or other origin, material, mode of manufacture, quality, accuracy, or other characteristics of ... [the] goods or services or the work or labor on the goods or services ... performed by members of a union or other organization."[73] Thus, certification marks may indicate any of the following three attributes of a good: 1) regional or other origin; 2) material, mode of manufacture, quality, accuracy or other characteristics of the good/service; or 3) the performance of the work or labour on the good/service by a member of a union or other organization. Certification marks protect GIs when the marks used certify "regional ... or other origin."

Certification marks are distinguished from ordinary trademarks in many respects. In the case of a certification mark, the owner controls use of the mark, but he does not use it. The owner can not be a producer of the goods on which the mark is used. Unlike ordinary trademarks, certification marks do not indicate a commercial source, nor do they distinguish the goods and services of one person from those of another person. The owner of the mark is obliged to certify all goods or services that meet the standards he set so that consumers will be assured of the specified quality or characteristic of the goods or services. When the certification mark is employed to protect GI, such a standard specifies that the good or service originates from a specific "regional ... origin."

A collective mark is defined as "a trademark used by the members of a cooperative, an association, or other collective group or organization."[74] A collective mark is owned by a collective body, such as an agricultural cooperative, of the sellers of a good and serves to indicate that the person who uses the collective mark is a member of that collectivity.[75] The collective organization holds the title to the collectively used mark for the benefit of all members of the group, and thus no member can own the mark.[76] In the case of collective trademarks that protect GIs, membership in the association that is the owner of the collective mark is, generally speaking, subject to compliance with rules to do with the geographical area of production of the goods on which the collective mark is used.

Also, the United States protects a GI as a trademark if a geographical sign is used in such a way as to identify the source of the good/service, and, over time, consumers start to recognize it as identifying a particular company or manufacturer or group of producers in a geographical region.[77] In these circumstances, a GI is protected as an exception to the general rule in trademark law – that geographical terms or signs are not registerable as trademarks if they are geographically descriptive or geographically misdescriptive of the origin of the goods. If, through continuous usage, consumers have come to associate the geographical name with a particular manufacturer, the geographical name has acquired a "secondary meaning" in addition to the primary meaning of denoting the geographical place, and thus "acquired distinctiveness." In such a case, the GI may be registered as a trademark.

The U.S. system of protecting GIs is generally found in other common law jurisdictions too. Canada and Australia protect GIs mainly through certification and collective marks. Also, protection is offered in some cases through rules that deal with unfair competition and the common law rule of passing off.[78]

4. The Attraction of Geographical Indications for Developing Countries

As far as GIs are concerned, developing countries have long sought the amendment of the Paris Convention to require the cancellation of registration of a mark, and the prohibition of the use of a mark, "if the mark contains a GI of a country from which the associated goods do not originate and similar goods are now or later produced in the named geographical region."[79] This amendment was suggested because "the developed countries have already secured protection for their GIs to aid in their export trade, and, at the same time, have permitted the geographical names of developing countries to become registered as marks, thus effectively frustrating the use by developing countries of their geographical names."[80] In this context, the interest of developing countries with respect to GIs has traditionally been for the primacy of GIs over trademarks in order to prevent the establishment in developed countries of trademark rights to geographical names associated with places where distinctive biodiversity resources in the South are cultivated, which in effect hinders the export of goods from developing countries to larger markets.[81]

Teshager Dagne

In the latest development regarding GIs in the Doha negotiations, the major proponents of GIs – the EU and Switzerland – have managed to link the GI registry issue, which there is a clear mandate to negotiate, with two other hot-button intellectual property issues in the WTO: an amendment to the TRIPS Agreement that would require disclosure of origin on genetic materials used in patent applications, and the extension of the high-level protection enjoyed by GIs for wines and spirits to GIs for other goods.[82] In support of its proposal, the EU pointed to India as an example of a country that is in favour of GI protection because its economy is based upon its distinct culture, which it also exports in the form of saris (traditional dress worn primarily by Hindu women), specialty teas (Darjeeling, Assam) and rice varieties (such as Basmati).[83] This may signal a strategic move by the EU to join hands with the developing-country members' agenda of protecting TK through a disclosure-of-origin requirement for patent applications.[84]

The developing countries have shown keen interest in the subject of GIs in recent years.[85] GIs have been touted by some developing countries and public interest bodies acting on their behalf as useful for the protection of traditional knowledge–based goods of indigenous people and local communities. Some developing countries have increasingly shown interest in GIs as instruments that may contribute to remunerative marketing of agricultural production based upon traditional cultivation methods.[86] In a wave of interest, many developing countries – among others, Chile, Brazil, Argentina, India, Malaysia, Singapore, Thailand, Jordan and Egypt – adopted a *sui generis* system of GI legislation between 1996 and 2004 alone. In WIPO's review of the existing protection of traditional knowledge, Venezuela and Vietnam reported having protected traditional knowledge through GIs.[87] Other countries, such as India and Pakistan, have registered GI protections for diverse goods of immense export value, after widely publicized disputes involving Darjeeling tea, Basmati rice and Jasmine rice.[88]

An increasing number of academicians and organizations are actively pushing the agenda toward better protection of GIs at the international, regional and national levels as a means of protecting traditional knowledge.[89] For example, Terri Janke, the indigenous solicitor has noted that "given that indigenous peoples' cultural expression reflects their belonging to land and territories, this may allow some scope for indigenous people to use geographical indications for their clan names, and language words for regions."[90] Along the same lines, Zografos has contended that geographical indications can be a viable alternative for the protection of traditional cultural expressions.[91] Sherman and Wiseman also argued that "the regimes used to protect

Teshager Dagne

geographical indications could be used as a model for a *sui generis* scheme to protect indigenous knowledge."[92]

The foregoing discussion indicates the increasing interest in GIs in the quest for modalities for protection of TK. Unlike the other proposals for TK protection,[93] however, the promise of GIs has not been well explored to date. In the following pages, I broach issues to do with the links between IPRs and TK in general and examine the opportunities GIs may present for protecting traditional knowledge.

5. The Suitability of Geographical Indications to Protect Traditional Knowledge

A number of reasons suggest the suitability of GIs to protect TKBAPs. First, GIs – uniquely among IP regimes – are based upon collective traditions and a collective decision-making process.[94] Most existing forms of IP protection do not protect TK because the TRIPS and the notions of intellectual property incorporated therein recognize that "intellectual property rights are private rights."[95] A GI applies to an indefinite number of producers that live and produce in a geographical location that gives rise to a quality or reputation identified by the GI.[96] Of the extant IP regimes, only GIs – and in some circumstances trademarks – reward goodwill and reputation created or built up by a group of producers over many years or even centuries.[97] These types of intellectual property protection reward producers who are members of an established group or community and who adhere to traditional practices belonging to the culture of that community or group.[98] In the case of GIs, cooperative bodies and associations composed of a group of individual producers, a family, a partnership, a corporation, a voluntary association or a municipal corporation establish, monitor and modify over time the rules governing production.[99] A producer who qualifies for GI protection does not have an unqualified monopoly over the GI right, unlike other forms of IP rights where the owner acquires the exclusive right over the term during which the protection is valid. If the producer's practices fall below the defined standards, which are usually set by an association of producers in the region, the producer loses the right to use the GI.[100]

Second, GIs most often relate to old knowledge, with its attendant cultural perceptions and ways.[101] Most of the existing IP protections are unsuitable to protect TK-based products because the exclusive rights offered by those modernistic IP regimes are intended to benefit those who created new knowledge. GIs, on the other hand, do not reward "new inventions," but rather the goodwill and reputation that producers who use traditional methods have created or built up in a geographical territory.[102] It is noted that GIs protect and reward traditions while allowing evolution.[103]

Teshager Dagne

In this regard, the long-standing GI tradition in France is the best laboratory in which to test the congeniality of GIs with traditional knowledge. In France, "[w]hile production methods can evolve over time," the system of GIs reflects a strong commitment to traditional practices growing out of "long periods of empirical experience and experimentation."[104] The GI system is designed by "record[ing] and formaliz[ing]" such practices into rules; but even then the rules evolve as a result of the close and ongoing involvement of the producers themselves, for example, grape growers and winemakers.[105] In accord with indigenous people and local communities' practices, GIs emphasize the bonds among culture, ancestral lands, resources and environment.[106] The French system of GIs constitutes a combination that encompasses the physical factors specific to the geographical location and "specific human factors that pertain to the product such as vinification procedure, pruning methods, maturation, and so on."[107] As a French GI expert explained, "the notion involves the interaction between these natural and human factors, specific and peculiar to the locality, which produces the distinctive quality or character of [that region's] product."[108]

Third, GIs last for as long as the rights holders maintain the collective tradition.[109] Also, within the scope of protection, GIs allow for production methods to change over time, as protection through GIs does not relate to one specific method of production of a given product.[110] Thus, GIs reward goodwill and reputation created over many years or even centuries while allowing evolution – an attribute that makes them most suited for traditional knowledge.[111] GIs recognize the quality and reputation of cultivations by particular communities indefinitely, and prohibit others from free-riding on that reputation – as long as natural and cultural characteristics in the relevant place of cultivation are maintained.

Also, GIs "lack the typical private-property characteristic of being freely transferable."[112] In this context, GIs are beneficial in particular because the rights they confer relate to the geographical area where the product originated and they do not depend on a specific rights holder. GIs do not imply monopoly control over the knowledge embedded in the indication; rather, they simply limit the number of people who can benefit from accumulated knowledge typical to a specific locality.[113] They are not freely transferable from one owner to another, and they emphasize the relationships between human cultures and their local land and environment.[114] These characteristics make GIs better suited to protect a TK system that can no longer be assigned to a specific rights holder because it has been in the public domain for so long and, as such, may not even be covered by any of the *sui generis* systems, as, for example, in the case of kava.[115]

For these reasons, GIs have the potential to empower local communities to continue marketing their products without fearing displacement by global mass production.[116] In most cases, GIs prohibit third parties from appropriating the fruits of human labour, thereby making it possible to deter free-riding and to combat counterfeiting and piracy within a market economy.[117] In addition, GIs can create economic rewards for producers who use traditional methods developed and maintained in a designated region where the product has been traditionally produced.[118]

5.1 What Benefits Do Geographical Indications Offer to Traditional Knowledge–Based Agricultural Producers?

While most proposed systems aspire to protect TK by establishing defensive intellectual property regimes, GIs provide the opportunity for an affirmative intellectual property policy that enables TK holders to participate proactively in the global agricultural market. The most important promise GIs may offer to indigenous people and local communities relates to their potential to recognize and reward producers for their age-long cultural contribution to livelihood, conservation, lateral learning and social networking by adding premium value to their products. Therefore, a carefully designed GI-based protection of TKBAPs may – while protecting the constitutive cultural element of their knowledge – produce economic rewards for indigenous peoples and local communities. GIs would play an instrumental role in development-oriented initiatives among local communities, in accord with the increasingly strong links between "culture" and "development" in the contemporary understanding. The UN World Commission on Culture and Development has made it abundantly clear that the concepts of culture and development are inextricably intertwined in any society.[119]

The major reason for the formation of the strong link between culture and development is the fact that, since the 1990s, development has been understood in the broad terms of expanding human capabilities.[120] Following Amartya Sen's work on capacities and entitlements, development has been understood as capacitation.[121] In this view the point of development, above all, is that it be enabling.[122] "The enlargement of people's choices" is the core definition of development in the Human Development Reports of United Nations Development Program (UNDP).[123] Amartya Sen noted that "life is more than making a living, economic development is in the end about enjoying life."[124] In this understanding, development is measured based on "the capacity for many freedoms ... which range from basic needs, such as the right to life and health, to more expansive freedoms of movement, creative work, and

Teshager Dagne

participation in social, economic, and cultural institutions."[125] Along the same lines, UNESCO's focus on "capacity building" consists of "providing people with the skills and abilities for critical reception, assessment and use of information in their professional and personal lives." In this scenario, IP policy making should enable indigenous people and local communities to "recognize and market their own knowledge production ... so that they need 'not be seen primarily as passive recipients of the benefits of cunning development programs.'"[126] As Sunder observed, economic remuneration for cultural production in this manner will be "an important source of revenue and stimulus for development in the Knowledge Age."[127]

In this line, Sunder argues that the Indian GI Act "recognizes ... 'with adequate social opportunities, individuals can effectively shape their own destiny and help each other',"[128] and in providing such opportunities, GIs "[empower] local communities, which can continue to commercialize their products without fearing displacement by global mass production."[129] The income that would flow from protecting the TK component of agricultural products through the use of GIs may be one of the few resources that would have the potential to provide the greater choices that Amartya Sen shows to be a key factor in poverty alleviation.[130] Thus, GIs may be employed in the design of IP policy that responds to the call to WIPO "that intellectual property be approached in the context of broader societal interests and development-related concerns [accommodated in the framework of the cultural economy]"[131] and, as Sunder notes, "not just from the narrow lens of economic incentives for innovation [but rather to achieve just and attractive culture]."[132]

GIs create niche markets for local communities' reputable products and prohibit others from free-riding on that reputation. By doing so, GIs may contribute to the recognition of the cultural contributions and creativity of TK holders, which in turn would help in the preservation and the making of culture. The examination of GIs' contribution to development in this manner involves, among others, the examination of two main spheres: the effect of GIs in the economic sphere, and their effect with regard to environmental quality and biodiversity sustenance.

5.1.1 The Economic Benefits of GIs

As a study by the United Nations Conference on Trade and Development clearly recognizes,

> geographical indications reward producers that invest in building the reputation of a product. They are designed to reward goodwill and reputation created or built up by a producer or a group of producers over many years or even centuries. They reward producers that maintain a traditional high standard of quality, while at the same time allowing flexibility for innovation and improvement in the context of that tradition.[133]

Teshager Dagne

The reward that GIs may offer to producers arises from the "substance of the concept" of GIs, which is "to demonstrate a link between the origin of the product to which it is applied and a given quality, reputation or other characteristic that the product derives from that origin."[134] GIs carry additional information about the product, such as a traditional production method.[135] GIs signify added value and specific qualities of a product from a region by enabling producers to differentiate their products based on criteria attractive to consumers, such as the sustainability or traditional nature of production. Consumers are now looking for quality products – in other words, authentic products with a solid tradition behind them – and they are influenced by their social conscience when choosing products.[136] As Addor and Grazioli accurately pointed out, social consumers have found new purchasing criteria and have become more demanding due to the ongoing biotechnology-led transformation of the agri-food industry, which weakens the products' land-based association, and in light of "problems such as the 'mad cow' disease, as well as the burgeoning movements toward socially just trade, labour and environmental standards."[137] Given their focus on heritage, locality and "placeness," GIs have the potential to increase the price of tradition-based, reputable products, shunning the despatializing and homogenizing characteristics of contemporary globalization in the agri-food sector.[138]

In addition to signifying quality and reputation, GIs also help to halt the appropriation by outsiders of traditional knowledge–based goods that have significant market value – a concern that resonates strongly in an increasingly globalized world.[139] This sort of appropriation is illustrated by a recent dispute involving Basmati – the Indian traditional rice product. A Texas-based multinational company, RiceTec acquired a patent right that includes exclusive marketing of this rice under the brands Taxmati, Kasmati and Jasmati.[140] As Blakeney pointed out, the resolution of this dispute would have been simpler had a GI regime been in place in the countries in which protection for these brands was sought.[141] Similar traditional knowledge–based agricultural products that could be protected by GIs and have been involved similar disputes due to the establishment of IP rights in general by outsiders include Indian Neem, South Pacific Kava, South African Rooibos Tea, Mexican Enola Beans, Peruvian Yacon, Andean Nuna Beans, Amazonian Ayahausca and Bolivian Quinoa.[142]

GIs are especially important to communities engaged in traditional agricultural practices, as they provide value when they protect the common reputation of farmers who strive to improve the quality of their products.[143] The potential of GIs for rural development has been fully recognized by the EU, which links GIs directly to certification of quality and indirectly to rural development and increasing farmer

Teshager Dagne

incomes.[144] Laying groundwork for the principle of the protection of provenance as a means of protecting rural development, EC Regulation 510/2006 stated, "the promotion of products having certain characteristics could be of considerable benefit to the rural economy, in particular to less-favoured or remote areas, by improving the incomes of farmers and by retaining the rural population in these areas ...."[145] European Commission officials, such as the Commissioner responsible for Agriculture, Rural Development and Fisheries, cited rural development as one of the contributions of GIs:

> Several studies have shown that they [GIs] have an important role to play in the regeneration of the countryside since they ensure that agri-foodstuffs are produced in such a way that conserves local plant varieties, rewards local people, supports rural diversity and social cohesion, and promotes new job opportunities in production, processing and other related services. The needs of today's population are met, while natural resources and traditional skills are safeguarded for generations to come.[146]

GIs contribute to rural development due mainly to the presence of economic actors – the TK component – in the same territory, which guarantees that socio/economic benefits brought by the GI will be captured locally.[147]

5.1.2 Aspects of Environmental Protection and Biodiversity Sustenance

The standards put forth for products qualifying for GI protection ensure the sustainable use of biodiversity resources. These standards are based on traditional production practices which are of a moral, ethically based, spiritual, intuitive and holistic nature and are created through a continuous process of devising strategies for survival and group identity in the region.[148] These standards internalize "sustainability" criteria that allow for continued production over time and thus have relatively low environmental impact and preserve biodiversity.[149]

The language of Art. 8(j) of the 1992 Convention on Biological Diversity (CBD), which refers to "practices" that embody "traditional lifestyles" and that are relevant with respect to sustaining biodiversity, reflects elements common to GIs. As such, GIs may contribute to the implementation of the ecological values recognized by the convention. As Downes and Laird observe, the references under Art. 8(j) to "promoting" wider use, and "encouraging" benefit sharing, suggest that this article is intended to cover measures, such as market incentives, that influence the behaviour of civil society – GIs being important policy instruments to implement such measures.[150]

During the initial period of its introduction, the CBD proposed various strategies mostly aimed at implementing GI policy under the presumption that improved income

Teshager Dagne

for indigenous people and local communities through market incentives will ensure *in situ* conservation of the resources. For example, in an attempt to reward TK owners, the successive Conferences of Parties proposed that applicants for patent protection be required to disclose the origin of the resources utilized and that the prior informed consent of the community be secured or TK holders be given the right to challenge patents that utilize traditional knowledge, through access and benefit-sharing arrangements.[151] Thus, the CBD implements its goal of conserving biodiversity by incentivizing TK owners through benefits derived from patent rights established by third parties on their biodiversity resources.[152] The "access" aspect of the CBD's "access and benefit-sharing" strategy entirely focuses on securing access to biodiversity resources and the accompanying TK for private third parties and, in turn, benefiting the TK owners from the proceeds of patents established by the third parties. Thus, the CBD is premised on classical economic assumptions regarding the nature of conservation and the preferability of private property regimes to systems of common property.[153] As such, it aspires to achieve the goal of protecting biodiversity through a "contractual bilateral market form of regulation."[154] This may somehow respond to the quest for fair and equitable sharing of the benefits of the resources but would lead to the commercialization of biodiversity and its eventual dissipation by market forces.[155] As such, this strategy does not protect biodiversity resources and may not be in the best interest of indigenous people and local communities.[156]

Premised on an identical rationale, some environmental advocates have called for – and some countries have acted upon – the enforcement of "marks of authenticity,"[157] "ecolabels"[158] or "green marketing"[159] of products so that indigenous people and local communities would, incentivized by market gains for their products, be engaged in traditional practices. In these cases, successful marketing may increase demand for the products to the extent that existing resource management systems are put under pressure. This may result in the over exploitation of the resources and, consequently, the damaging of the ecosystem.

For example, the growth in foreign demand for the kava plant has led some farmers and harvesters in the South Pacific region to shift away from traditional methods – which frequently involve multicropping and a waiting period for the kava to reach a certain age and size – to more destructive techniques.[160] The increasing exploitation of the plant has provoked the harvesting of immature kava, thus not only jeopardizing the quality of the medicinal product but also reducing its resource base.[161] Such marketing strategies may thus lead to the eventual destruction of biological resources through the displacement of habitat by cultivated areas or the intensification of cultivation techniques, which may result in soil erosion and water

Teshager Dagne

pollution. The introduction of GIs would have facilitated the recognition and standardization of traditional cultivation methods, which would have ensured that TK holders would acquire market share for their products without the probability that marketing success would conflict with conservation of biodiversity. Thus, the successful implementation of GIs incentivizes the conservation of biodiversity resources as proposed by the CBD, albeit with a different approach than the one taken by the CBD.

As previously stated, GIs reject the notion of private property rights and are built upon collective traditions and a collective decision-making process. The economic benefits of GIs extend to all individuals and groups in the community who subscribe to the traditional practices belonging to the culture of that community. In this regard, GIs serve as a factor of "mobilisation" for local communities.[162] It is a widely held view that the mobilisation of local communities is essential in achieving the sustainable management of local resources.[163] Recognizing and protecting TK in agricultural production through the use of GIs will be important in biodiversity-rich countries where sustainable and unsustainable uses of biological resources are in competition because local people need economic incentives to select the first. The involvement and mobilisation of local communities in support of sustainable agricultural production increasingly depends on – in the context of global mass production – the existence of appropriate incentives.[164] GIs provide the incentive needed to engage in the sustainable utilization of biodiversity resources.

The promise of incentive that GIs offer for the sustainable use of biodiversity is not identical to the romantic narrative of "reward to spur innovation" that the utilitarian theorists of intellectual property advocate.[165] As indicated above, GIs will empower indigenous people and local communities to control market forces and prevent cultural appropriation by outsiders. Therefore, GIs may play a key role as a valorisation strategy which serves as incentive towards the enhancement of public goods (localness, tradition, quality, safety, biodiversity conservation, respect for the environment), creating opportunities for rural communities to undertake corresponding practices as a means of subsistence.[166] GIs thus enable TK holders to engage in an agricultural practice that yields multifunctional values beyond the acknowledged primary purpose: the supply of food, fibre and industrial products.[167]

The FAO Committee on Commodity Problems' Intergovernmental Group has summarized the positive effects of properly managed GIs as

> helping producers obtain premium prices for their products; providing guarantees to consumers regarding product quality; developing the rural economy; protecting local knowledge and strengthening local traditions; .... other wider economic and social benefits, ... for example reduction of

Teshager Dagne

rural to urban migration, and the protection of rural environments and ecologies.[168]

Generally, GIs bear advantages that make them attractive tools to farmers engaged in traditional knowledge–based agricultural practice. That GIs have a promising economic value is best demonstrated by the success story behind the Australian wine industry, which, within a short period of adopting GIs, acquired a huge share of the market that had previously been dominated by the French wine makers.[169] GIs have been an integral part of EU farm policy, and so far in the system they have fared well in protecting TK through the rewards they bring to their owners.

5.2 Limitations and Conditions of GIs in Protecting Traditional Knowledge–Based Agricultural Products

The EU's experience with GIs is immensely important to the building of successful GI strategies amongst agricultural producers in the other parts of the world; however, the potential instrumentality of GIs for the protection of TK in developing countries should be examined in light of the specific circumstances of producers in these countries. Notable differences exist between developing-country producers and EU producers, and these differences could make it difficult to argue that GIs will necessarily benefit developing-country producers just because they have been proven to do so in the EU. In this context, I examine the limitations of assigning GIs the role of protecting traditional knowledge, and the conditions under which GIs may function well in the biodiversity-rich countries of the South.

5.2.1 The Geographical Limitations of Geographical Indications

One of the foremost limitations of GIs in protecting TK arises from the geographical restriction they impose on the goods the protection covers. The definitional provision of the Lisbon Agreement provides that to qualify for protection, the "quality and characteristics" of the product should be "due exclusively or essentially to the geographical environment, with its inherent natural and human factors."[170] Under the TRIPS Agreement too, the dual requirements that "indications identify a good as originating in the territory" and that the "quality, reputation or other characteristic of the good is essentially attributable to its geographical origin" require a qualitative link between the product and the geographical environment in which it is found.[171] Due to the strong link between the product and the geographical place identified, the contemporary legal atmosphere does not allow the licensing of GIs even if similar goods are manufactured outside the designated territory.[172]

Relating to the geographical limitation, some writers also refute the suitability of GIs to protect TK on the grounds that "GI protection is of assistance only where the knowledge is associated with a defined geographical area."[173] Accordingly, "if the knowledge is scattered ..., a GI cannot be used."[174] This view takes a narrow understanding of the origin requirement for GIs as a single criterion of geographical attachment of a good to a place.

The total reliance on geographical locations for GI protection takes a narrow understanding of factors that give rise to the specific quality of the product, such as the link of "culture to land."[175] This link, which may have existed at the start of the manufacture of a good, may subsequently have been stretched to the point that its existence is difficult to prove.[176] Members of a traditional community may manufacture the GI goods in a different geographical setting due to the availability of transport, electricity, financial services and other facilities in a particular geographical setting other than the original place, but still stick to the traditional standards of production that became the basis for GI protection.

Moreover, traditions in manufacture and skilled staff can be shifted from one geographical area to another, in particular in view of the increasing mobility of human resources in all parts of the world.[177] As Soam notes, "it is a widely accepted fact that whenever people go to other places they bring along some product (such as sweets, textiles, handicrafts, artifacts, etc.) that has a specific reputation due to its association with its place of origin."[178] Due to the geographical limitation of GI protection, it is argued that related cultural practices and traditional methods of production may not be protected in the case of ex situ manufacture of an agricultural product by people who have migrated from one place to another.[179]

The exclusive emphasis on geographical territory as a basis of protection has probably to do with the age-long conception of AOs, which protect a product whose "quality and characteristics" are due "exclusively or essentially to the geographical environment, with its inherent natural and human factors." As indicated in the discussion of the definitional aspects of AOs and GIs, AOs protect goods that acquired a particular "quality and characteristic" on account of the physical factors in a geographical location. GIs, as a concept that the TRIPS introduced "in a ground-breaking manner," have an expansive scope that includes GIs that can also "highlight specific qualities of a product which are due to human factors that can be found in the place of origin of the products, such as specific manufacturing skills and traditions."[180] Thus, a GI protection can exist on the presence of purely human factors in a geographical origin – when these factors contribute to a given "reputation or other characteristic" of the good. With this understanding of GIs, where their protection is not exclusively limited to goods with "a given quality, reputation or other characteristic" from climatic, ecological and cultural factors affixed in the geographical setting, the geographical restriction of the protection is not warranted.

As a result, in the case of ex situ–manufactured GI goods whose "quality and characteristics" do not arise from the physical factors affixed to a geographical territory, indigenous people and local communities ought to be allowed to control the production of their goods and earn royalties through licensing. Licensing is defined as "the grant of permission by the owner of the IPRs to another person or legal entity to perform one or more of the acts which are covered by the exclusive rights."[181] It is a mode of assigning rights to information covered by the IP protection. Licensing will enable traditional knowledge owners to protect the traditional methods of production and related cultural practices by assigning rights associated with their GI in the relevant circumstance of ex situ manufacture by third parties. In this way, indigenous people and local communities may get the rewards for their continuous creations and ensure the perpetuity of their cultural practices and traditions through the conditions set out in the written document by which the license is granted.

The assignability of the rights to information – through licensing – distinguishes all IP protections from other forms of protection for intellectual creations, such as farmers' rights, access legislation and cultural heritage laws.[182] Nothing justifies the exclusion of traditional knowledge–protection tools from assignability through licensing while the protective tools of its epistemological counterpart – Western scientific knowledge – are assignable in all of the forms (patents, copyrights and trademarks).

Also, there are precedents where products registered for AO have been licensed by the AO rights owners – proof that the quality, reputation or special character of at least some products is not therefore exclusively or essentially attributable to the physical character of the geographical environment, but also to human intervention through traditional knowledge–based production methods. Moran gives the example of *Bleu de Bresse* cheese, where the French owners of the AO rights sold a *licence* agreement to New Zealand.[183] In this agreement, technical aspects of production are under the control of the cheese-makers from France, and the product comes out under a label that is similar to that of the French cheese but that notes the different country of origin.[184] During the time since this arrangement was made it has been argued that cheeses produced through such an arrangement are unsuitable for appellations of origin.[185] As an expansive regime introduced by the TRIPS, however, the protection of GIs can now be made operational through legislation devised in a manner that allows the licensing of ex situ manufacture in the case of certain categories of GIs, for example in cases similar to *Bleu de Bresse* cheese.

Teshager Dagne

The EU GI regime protects products whose "specific character" is not attributable to the geographical factors of a specific origin through the traditional specialty guaranteed (TSG) modality. As indicated above, the EU's PDO and PGI systems protect different types of goods based on the level of attachment that the good has to its geographical territory. As recently pointed out in the Czech Presidency High Level Conference on the Future of Agricultural Product Quality Policy, there has been strong interest in TSGs from the EU new member states due to "historical factors – forced immigration and standardization after the second world war."[186] Developing countries should adopt stratified GI regimes that will allow them to choose the appropriate modalities for specific products on a case by case basis. Thus, developing countries may devise TSG-type variations of GIs to rectify some of the shortcomings related to geographical restrictions.

In practical terms, a WIPO study noted that the wording dealing with requirement of origin in some countries states only general requirements that the product must be made in the indicated place or that the producer must be located in that area.[187] More specific requirements have also been reported, for example,[188]

- requirements that all stages of production (raw material, processing and preparation) must occur in the designated area;
- requirements that the raw material (e.g., grapes) must have originated in the area in question (except in some cases of tolerance concerning a small proportion from another area);
- requirements that the stage of production which gives a product its distinctive character must occur in the area (e.g., for spirits);
- requirements that at least one of the stages of production must occur in the area.

This variation among requirements evidences that there are no hard and fast rules on the geographical restriction of GIs. The rules are malleable enough to allow adaptability in specific circumstances. Therefore, geographical limitations should not deter the effectiveness of GIs in the relevant circumstances.

A more serious concern arises when the relevant knowledge is scattered across the national territories of two or more states. This problem was noted in a study which concluded that IP protection may not be feasible for some plant genetic resources and crops because one cannot properly trace their origins to a particular source.[189] Nevertheless, the same study confirmed that there are crops for which such determination is possible, "especially if the time-span under consideration for granting such rights is limited and accounts only for recent decades."[190] Even in cases where a good which is a likely candidate for GI protection is found across the territories of two

Teshager Dagne

or more states, the respective states have found ways to work together to allow joint registration of GI rights.[191] The presence of a resource and the accompanying knowledge in two or more than two states that have a common interest to preserve these resources will not be a problem as such if they adopt GIs as part of an overall strategy to protect traditional knowledge. The establishment of a regional or sub-regional group of developing countries that could become a focal point for interagency review with respect to the integration into domestic law of existing and evolving international legal standards affecting innovation – as Maskus and Reichman suggest – may, for example, facilitate the coordinated implementation of GIs in these circumstances.[192]

5.2.2 The Economics of Geographical Indications

Another major doubt as to the feasibility of GIs as a strategy to protect TKBAPs in developing countries arises from the cost and benefit analysis of the implementation of GIs. Some argue that a GI-based strategy may be an expensive endeavour for developing countries due to the administrative costs of GI registration and enforcement, the costs of maintaining "quality, reputation or characteristic" of the GI good, and the operative costs of marketing GI goods in the international market.

Under the TRIPS Agreement, the obligation of WTO members to protect a GI applies only if the GI is protected in the country of origin.[193] A country that adopts a GI system incurs administrative costs to establish a national system of legal and administrative frameworks for the registration and enforcement of GIs. Also, resources for the enforcement of sustainable and tradition-based production norms that gave rise to the required quality, reputation or other characteristics of the product covered by the GI are needed to protect the GI from genericide. It is argued that these costs might be prohibitively high for developing countries.[194]

Indeed, the introduction of national IP legislation such as a GI registration system involves enforcement and administration costs. However, developing countries are required at any rate to introduce implementation frameworks for IPRs, a process that creates a very considerable burden, as most of them phase in the requirements of the TRIPS. The implementation costs related to mainstream IPRs included in the TRIPS were imposed on developing countries without any suggestion of the necessity to undertake financial or economic impact studies.[195] Ironically, the same group of countries who lobbied for strong domestic enforcement of IPRs by WTO members resist the extension of enhanced GI protection to products other than wines and spirits on the grounds that GIs cause costly administrative burdens for developing countries.[196] The implementation cost of GIs is not so much of a burden as the implementation costs of other IP regimes that are not to the benefit of most developing

Teshager Dagne

countries. WIPO's effort to help countries re-orient national legal regimes in line with the TRIPS through its "Cooperation for Development Programme" should focus on IP regimes such as GIs that have real "development" implications.

Also, opponents of the extension of GIs have tended to exaggerate the cost of maintaining the "quality, reputation or other characteristics" of the good. Where TKBAP is concerned, the GI standards implemented to preserve the "quality, reputation or other characteristics" of a good are the traditional practices that have existed among the community for generations. GIs do not introduce new standards of production methods that involve intensive training and costly means of production – like the excessive environmental and sanitary standards that the industrialized countries frequently impose on developing countries' export goods. As such, the "quality, reputation or other characteristics" of a GI-protected good in a developing country may be maintained at no significant cost. Once the GI good has acquired its market price for the distinctive "quality, reputation or other characteristics," however, it is in the developing country's interest to invest in qualitative agricultural production to meet market demands through the provision of financial services as part of their development endeavour. This gives the development partners of developing countries a role to play in improving the life of the rural community.

Regarding the operative costs of GIs, it is argued that "GI is a capital intensive endeavour, requiring an elaborate structure for the control of market power to nurture, brand, and popularize susceptible local products to ensure their global reach and acceptability."[197] This view is premised on the notion that GIs are useful where consumers are willing to pay a premium on the market for products manufactured in the relevant region according to traditional methods in that region.[198] It is true that GIs provide value when they protect the common reputation of farmers who strive to improve the quality and reputation of their products to match buyers' preferences.[199] Faced with the mass production of agri-food resources that drives global food uniformity, consumers want more information about the origin of the imported product and how the imported product was produced.[200] Therefore, GIs involve the transfer of information from producers to consumers about the favourable features of a good. This is achieved through brand management initiatives that involve strong promotion and marketing. Due to the long-standing tradition of AO product marketing, EU producers have developed sizable market share and brand recognition in the agri-food industry. Therefore, effective use of GIs will require developing-country producers to invest capital to break into the market that has already been controlled by EU producers.

Teshager Dagne

However, this may not present a problem for developing-country producers in the immediate future, due mainly to the peculiar mode in which their products are made available to the market. The mode by which EU producers access the market is fundamentally different from that of producers in developing countries. For the most part, producers in the developing countries do not have direct access to the market. Their products usually pass through a long chain of wholesalers, importers, distributors, manufacturers and retailers before they reach consumers in the international market. In contrast, EU producers have niche markets which they access themselves without passing through such a complex supply chain. As Downes and Laird observe, GIs "show the greatest potential where traditional small-scale production is still present, on the supply side, and where end-use products are marketed directly to consumers ... as opposed to primary commodities that pass through many hands, and in some cases are heavily processed, before reaching the consumer as end products."[201]

Therefore, as they stand, GIs may not necessarily benefit developing-country producers on the same route as EU producers, which makes the argument about the cost of operation irrelevant, at least with respect to the majority of small farms and cooperatives in developing countries. A recent study conducted by the NGO Light Years IP reviews a number of TKBAPs from developing countries that are known worldwide for their reliably high quality within the industry but not by consumers.[202] As indicated above, the recognition of the TK component of GIs should make it possible to license their use to other parties in the industry who are aware of the quality, reputation and rich tradition behind the products they supply in the market. The establishment of GI systems in these countries gives developing-country producers bargaining power vis-à-vis wholesalers, importers, distributors, manufacturers and retailers in the determination of the prices for their high-quality products. The developing-country producers may be able to get improved income by controlling the price for their products – getting out of the commodity price determination.

Developing-country producers may also demand that wholesalers, importers, distributors, manufacturers and retailers of their products enter into licensing arrangements to take their GI-protected goods to market. Through such arrangements, the wholesalers, importers, distributors, manufacturers and retailers may be required to pay royalties for the GIs, either through commitments to establish service facilities such as farmer support centers, hospitals or schools in local communities, or direct payments to organizations, associations or government agencies who may allocate the funds in the manner they deem beneficial to society. However, financial gain from the

Teshager Dagne

royalties may not necessarily be the object of the licensing. In some cases, the licensing may be offered royalty-free to the distributors, who, in return, would invest in brand management and would actively promote the GIs to consumers.[203] Developing-country producers may, in this way, be able to make deals with the distributors of their products, who mostly have direct access to consumers and the necessary capital to invest in promoting and advertising a product "with a given quality, reputation or other characteristics," to improve its price in the market. If so designed, GIs are the most convenient IP tools to serve indigenous people and local communities for a wide list of products the aforementioned study identified, such as Kenyan tea, Sudanese cotton, Namibian marula oil, Togolese black soap, Senegalese tuna, Tanzanian blackwood, Mozambican cashews, Ugandan vanilla, Madagascan cocoa, Malian mudcloth and Ethiopian leather.[204]

However, the benefit of GIs to developing-country producers is not necessarily acquired only through cooperation with the wholesalers, importers, distributors, manufacturers and retailers in the market. In some cases, GIs would serve as marks of authenticity to protect goods that originate from developing-country producers and that already have an established reputation among consumers. Some goods are sold on the international market under the same GI names the developing-country producers are known for, but they do not actually originate from those producers. For example, the region of "Antigua" in Guatemala produces some 6 million pounds of genuine "Antigua" coffee,[205] yet some 50 million pounds of coffee are sold under the "Antigua" denomination around the world.[206] Indian "Darjeeling tea" producers export 8.5 million kg of such tea, generating some 30 million euro for the region, yet some 30 million kg of tea are traded around the world under the denomination "Darjeeling."[207] The list goes on, including products as diverse as Indian Basmati rice, Namibian Devil's Claw, South Pacific Kava, South African Rooibos, Andean Quinoa, the Neem tree and so on.[208] In all these circumstances, the domestic exporters in the respective developing countries are in a strong position to invest in the promotion and advertisement of their products, to widen and control the market they have already acquired and to prevent the sale of counterfeits of their products. They only lack the legal means to control and protect their brands to prevent the displacement of their market share through the sale of counterfeit goods that free-ride on their reputation. GIs offer an effective remedy to rectify these problems and would enable the producers to acquire an improved income.

Finally, it is worth mentioning that the effectiveness of GIs depends on understanding and acting in accordance with their limitations. GIs are not ideal instruments to protect all forms of products of TK. GIs only respond to the needs of communities that seek affirmative IP protection of their own for the products of their knowledge. As indicated in the discussion on their definitional aspects, GIs identify "goods." As such, they are applicable to products of TK that are already on the market as commercial goods.

First, this immunises GIs from the criticism generally labelled against IPRs – that they may commodify the culture of indigenous peoples and eventually annihilate their traditions through market forces. They are ideal instruments to afford positive protection (as opposed to defensive protection) for TKBAPs that already are made commercially available.

Second, they do not protect some of the intangible forms of traditional knowledge, such as methods of medical treatment, techniques for dyeing cloth, folk music, and dances. GIs do not offer a perfect solution to the "scourge of biopiracy" in circumstances where the knowledge that gives rise to the qualitative attributes of the product is imitated and the product is marketed under a different name.[209] Thus, GIs are best adopted as part of, or independent of, an overall defensive intellectual property strategy that limits patents related to TK on the various uses of biodiversity resources and prevents the misappropriation of intangible cultural heritage through inward-looking cultural protocols – as has been suggested in the WIPO global fact-finding mission report.[210]

6. Conclusion

The need to protect and recognize TK has increasingly become a critical issue of global concern. Considerable differences exist, however, as to the nature and scope of protection and the extent to which the issue may be addressed in the respective institutions entrusted with the task. There are divergent views on whether to extend the family of intellectual property to include traditional knowledge and on whether the search for a regime of TK protection should aim for a single regime to cover all types of traditional knowledge or a set of different, specific regimes, each adapted to the nature of the subject matter to be protected.[211]

The search for an appropriate modality of protecting TK transcends a single model, as the needs and expectations of traditional communities differ. Depending on the purpose and the context in which their knowledge is practised, it may be difficult to find a single strategy best suited to the practices and values of traditional communities.

The industrial countries have managed to protect diverse forms of intellectual production through different layers of IP framework. The globally entrenched, modern IP regimes offer different levels of protection to different types of Western knowledge.

Teshager Dagne

In the wake of technological revolution, for example, the industrial countries managed to expand the existing IP framework to fit different forms of computer-related inventions: patents for some categories of software inventions; copyrights for computer databases and expression of algorithm formulae; domain names in the case of web servers and networks.

Likewise, the frontiers of "invention" in the field of TK exist in varied forms. The search for an appropriate modality of traditional knowledge protection should involve identifying different regimes based on the nature and use of the knowledge in the respective category. In the context of commercially available TKBAPs, this is best achieved through the re-examination of the suitability of the established knowledge-protection tools to the needs of indigenous people and local communities.

In this regard, GIs present a unique opportunity for an affirmative protection of TKBAP that will empower the owners to participate in the global market and acquire an added price for their contribution to the development or improvement of plant varieties and for their commercially valuable information. The developing countries should take a proactive role in adopting GIs suited to the circumstances of their agricultural production, and in exploiting the flexibility inherent in the system. However, the recognition of the intellectual contributions of the farming community should involve the reforming of the system to allow GI owners to license the distribution of their goods – as do any other intellectual property owners. This is essential and appropriate in circumstances where the physical characteristics of the geographical environment do not factor in the "quality, reputation or other characteristics" of the good. This would give developing countries the opportunity to evaluate the benefits and costs of GIs as part of their economic development endeavour in the long term.

While this paper focuses on the potential of GIs – market-related instruments – to afford protection to the commercially available products of TK holders, it also recognizes that other categories of biological resources and related products of TK may be inherently inappropriate subjects for market-related tools. The development of sui generis defensive intellectual property policy built upon the inward-looking cultural protocols that already exist within a community would, as suggested by many scholars and recently advanced by WIPO and the CBD, be a major complement in responding to the needs of indigenous peoples and local communities.

Teshager Dagne

Endnotes

1. Agreement on Trade-Related Aspects of Intellectual Property Rights, 15 April 1994, 1869 U.N.T.S. 299: 33 I.L.M. 1197[TRIPS] at Arts. 41-61.

2. See definition of "traditional knowledge" *infra* note 12 and accompanying text. While the literature uses the terms "traditional knowledge," "indigenous knowledge," "local knowledge," "folk knowledge," "community knowledge" and "tribal knowledge" interchangeably, this article prefers "traditional knowledge" in order to avoid the technical ambiguities associated with other terms. For a detailed insight into the definitional problems associated with these terms and the conceptual bounds of the term "traditional knowledge," see WIPO, *Traditional Knowledge – Operational Terms and Definitions* (Intergovernmental Committee on Intellectual Property and Genetic Resources, Traditional Knowledge and Folklore, Third Session, Geneva, June 13 To 21, 2002) WIPO/GRTKF/IC/3/9; *Graham Dutfield, "TRIPS-Related Aspects of Traditional Knowledge" (2001) 33* Case Western Reserve Journal of International Law 233 at 240; Chidi Oguamanam, *International Law and Indigenous Knowledge: Intellectual Property, Plant Biodiversity, and Traditional Medicine* (Toronto: University of Toronto Press, 2006) at 21; Ikechi Mgbeoji, *Global Biopiracy: Patents, Plants, and Indigenous Knowledge* (Vancouver: UBC Press, 2005) at 10.

3. Laurence R. Helfer, "Regime Shifting: The TRIPs Agreement and New Dynamics of International Intellectual Property Lawmaking" (2004) 29 Yale Journal of International Law at nn. 120.

4. See the discussion on the "fitness question" of modern intellectual property rights and traditional knowledge in Chidi Oguamanam, "Localizing Intellectual Property in the Globalization Epoch: The Integration of Indigenous Knowledge" (2004) 11 *Indiana Journal of Global Legal Studies* 135 at 139 ff.

5. To read about "what justifies the enormous interest in and energy now being devoted to [traditional knowledge]," see Rosemary J. Coombe, "The Recognition of Indigenous Peoples' and Community Traditional Knowledge in International Law" (2001) 14 St. Thomas L. Rev. 275.

6. WIPO, *Traditional Knowledge – Operational Terms and Definitions* (Intergovernmental Committee on Intellectual Property and Genetic Resources, Traditional Knowledge and Folklore, Third Session Geneva, June 13–21, 2002) at 2, online: WIPO <http://www.wipo.int/edocs/mdocs/tk/en/wipo_grtkf_ic_3/wipo_grtkf_ic_3_9.pdf>

7. Coenraad J. Visser, "Making Intellectual Property Laws Work for Traditional Knowledge" in J.M. Finger & Philip Schuler eds., *Poor People's Knowledge: Promoting Intellectual Property in Developing Countries* (Washington: World Bank, 2004) at 212.

8. *Ibid.*

9. See for example Light Years IP, *IP in Action*, online: <http://www.lightyearsip.net/ipinaction.shtml>.

Teshager Dagne

10. Marion Panizzon, "Traditional Knowledge and Geographical Indications: Foundations, Interests and Negotiating Positions" Working Paper No. 2005/01, October 2006 at 15; see also Madhavi Sunder, "IP3" (2006) 59 Stanford Law Review 257.

11. "Traditional knowledge" encompasses very different categories of knowledge, including agricultural knowledge; technical knowledge; ecological knowledge; medicinal knowledge; knowledge relating to medicines and remedies; knowledge on plant genetic resources; and traditional cultural expressions. See Coenraad J. Visser, "Making Intellectual Property Laws Work for Traditional Knowledge" in J.M. Finger & Philip Schuler eds., *Poor People's Knowledge: Promoting Intellectual Property in Developing Countries* (Washington: World Bank, 2004) at 207. The inquiry in the paper is limited to the category of agricultural knowledge, ecological knowledge, medicinal knowledge, knowledge on genetic resources, and the practice of this category of knowledge, as it evolves to meet socio-economic and ecological challenges. Therefore, the term TKBAP is employed here to refer to traditional knowledge related to agricultural products (defined as "the variety and variability of animals, plants and micro-organisms which are necessary to sustain key functions of the agro-ecosystem") see Geoff Tansey and Tasmin Rajotte, *The Future Control of Food: A Guide to International Negotiations and Rules on Intellectual Property, Biodiversity and Food Security* (Geneva: Earthscan/IDRC 2008) at 253.

12. *United Nations Convention on Biological Diversity*, 5 June 1992, 30619 U.N.T.S. (entered into force 29 December 1993), Art. 8 (j). For the definitional difficulties involved with "traditional knowledge," see WIPO, TK – Operational Terms and Definitions (Intergovernmental Committee on Intellectual Property and Genetic Resources, TK and Folklore, Third Session, Geneva, June 13–21, 2002) WIPO/GRTKF/IC/3/9; Graham Dutfield, "TRIPS-Related Aspects of Traditional Knowledge" (2001) 33 Case Western Reserve Journal of International Law 233 at 240.

13. See Ikechi Mgbeoji, *Global Biopiracy: Patents, Plants, and Indigenous Knowledge* (Vancouver: UBC Press, 2005) at 10. Michael Blakeney, "The Protection of Traditional Cultural Expressions" online: EC-ASEAN Intellectual Property Rights Co-operation Programme <http://www.ecap-project.org/fileadmin/ecapII/pdf/en/activities/regional/aun_sept_07/traditional_cultural_ expressions_word.pdf > at 2. See UNESCO, *Recommendation on the Safeguarding of Traditional Culture and Folklore* (adopted by the General Conference at its twenty-fifth session, Paris, 15 November 198), online: < http://portal.unesco.org/en/ev.php-URL_ID=13141&URL_DO=DO_TOPIC&URL_SECTION=201.html>; also, M. Blakeney, "Protecting Expressions of Australian Aboriginal Folklore under Copyright Law" (1995) 9 E.I.P.R. 442; Chengsi, "On the Copyright Protection of Folklore and Other Legislation in China" (1996) 3 China Patents and Trade Marks 91.

14. For example, the United Nations Declaration on the Rights of Indigenous Peoples adopted by the General Assembly used the definition of "indigenous people" contained in the International Labour Organization Convention, despite the

Teshager Dagne

---

objections raised about the restrictiveness of the group of people included. See United Nations, *General Assembly Adopts Declaration on Rights of Indigenous Peoples*, 13 September 2007, online: < http://www.un.org/News/Press/docs/2007/ga10612.doc.htm>; see *Declaration on the Rights of Indigenous Peoples*, GA Res. A/61/295, 107th Plen. Mtg., (2007). The ILO Convention defines indigenous people as "those who have descended populations that inhabited a country at the time of conquest, colonization, or the establishment of present state boundaries, and who irrespective of their status, retain some or all of their own social, economic, cultural, and political institutions." See International Labour Organization Convention No. 169 Concerning Indigenous and Tribal Peoples in Independent Countries, 7 June 1989, reprinted in (1989) 28 I.L.M.1382. This definition, simple as it may appear, overly restricts the group of people to be regarded "indigenous" by limiting the criteria for indigeneity to societies subdued by conquest and colonization. Also, the requirement for the retention of the social, economic, cultural and political institutions excludes "indigenous peoples and persons whose institutional bearing and identity were disrupted by colonialism and conquest." See Chidi Oguamanam, *International Law and Indigenous Knowledge: Intellectual Property, Plant Biodiversity, and Traditional Medicine* (Toronto: University of Toronto Press, 2006) at 21. In such a narrow understanding of the term, "indigenous knowledge" is not necessarily traditional knowledge, as confirmed by WIPO. See WIPO, *Intellectual Property, TK and Genetic Resources: Policy Options for Developing Countries* (presented at International Conference on Intellectual Property, the Internet, Electronic Commerce and Traditional Knowledge, Sofia, May 29–31, 2001) at 5. See Chidi Oguamanam, "Localizing Intellectual Property in the Globalization Epoch: The Integration of Indigenous Knowledge" (2004) 11 Indiana Journal of Global Legal Studies 135 at nn 1.

15. *Agreement on Trade-Related Aspects of Intellectual Property Rights*, 15 April 1994, 1869 U.N.T.S. 299: 33 I.L.M. 1197[*TRIPS*].

16. Graham Dutfield & Uma Suthersanen, *Global Intellectual Property Law: Commentary and Materials* (Cheltenham: Edward Elgar Publishing, 2008) at 327.

17. R. Silva Repetto & M. Cavalcanti, "Art. 27.3(B): Related International Agreements (Part II)." In FAO, *Multilateral Trade Negotiations on Agriculture: A Resource Manual* (Rome: Food and Agriculture Organization of the United Nations, 2000), online:

FAO <http://www.fao.org/docrep/003/x7355e/x7355e06.htm>

18. See Angela R. Riley, *"Recovering Collectivity: Group Rights to Intellectual Property in Indigenous Communities"* (2000) 18 Cardozo Arts & Ent. L.J. 175.

19. L.M. Hurtado, *Acceso a los Recursos de la biodiversiday Pueblos Indigenas* (Edmunds Institute, 1999) cited in Brendan Tobin, "Redefining Perspectives in the Search for Protection of Traditional Knowledge: A Case Study from Peru" (2001) 10:1 R.E.C.I.E.L. at 54.

20. WIPO, *Proposal Presented by the African Group to the First Meeting of the Intergovernmental Committee on Intellectual Property and Genetic Resources, TK and Folklore* (Intergovernmental Committee on Intellectual Property and

Genetic Resources, TK and Folklore, First Session, Geneva, April 30–May 3, 2001) at paras 1.2-1.3.

21. *The Treaty Establishing the European Economic Community* (EEC) (Rome, 1957) (entered into force 1 January 1958) at Art. 38.1. This definition is more or less consistent with the definition of "agricultural products" in Article 2 and Annex I of the WTO Agreement on Agriculture, which defines "agricultural products" as products in Chapters 01 to 24 of the Harmonized System, less fish and fish products (Chapter 3), together with certain products in Chapters 29, 33, 35, 38, 41, 43, 50, 51, 52 and 53. *The Agreement on Agriculture*, Apr. 15, 1994, Marrakesh Agreement Establishing the World Trade Organization, Annex 1A, Legal Instruments – Results of the Uruguay Round vol. 31, available at http://wto.org/english/docs_e/legal_e/legal_e.htm; The "harmonized system" is the international standard that was created and is administered by the Brussels-based World Customs Organization. It is a numeric language for reporting goods to customs and other government agencies that is used by more than 180 countries worldwide, and for almost 100 percent of international trade. See http://www.wcoomd.org/home.htm.

22. The term "appellations of origin" was first introduced in the Paris Convention for the Protection of Industrial Property. See *The Paris Convention for the Protection of Industrial Property,* 1883, as revised in Stockholm on July 14, 1967, reprinted in 21 U.S.T. 1583, 828 U.N.T.S. 305 [Paris Convention].

23. *The Lisbon Agreement for the Protection of Appellations of Origin and Their International Registration*, 31 Oct. 1958, as last revised 1 Jan. 1994, at Art. 2 (1), online: <http://www.wipo.int/clea/docs/en/wo/wo012en.htm> (last visited Aug. 1, 2004) [Lisbon Agreement].

24. *Ibid*. at Art. 2 (2).

25. *The Madrid Agreement for the Repression of False or Deceptive Indications of Source of Goods*, 14 Apr. 1891, 828 U.N.T.S. 389, online: WIPO <http://www.wipo.int/treaties/en/ip/madrid/index.html> at Art. 1 (1); see Dwijen Rangnekar, *Geographical Indications: A Review of Proposals at the TRIPS Council*, UNCTAD/ICTSD Capacity Building Project on Intellectual Property Rights and Sustainable Development, June 2002, at 9.

26. *Ibid*.

27. Lori E. Simon, "Appellations of Origins: The Continuing Controversy" (1983-1984) 5 Nw. J. Int'l L. & Bus. 132, at 132.

28. Daniel Gervais, 2d ed., *The TRIPS Agreement, Drafting History and Analysis* (London: Sweet and Maxwell, 2003) at 293.

29. It is important to note that both AOs and GIs involve the protection of a reputation. (Though the definition of AO does not include "reputation" as a distinct, protectable subject matter, Art. 1(2) of the Lisbon Agreement makes a reference to "reputation.") In the case of AOs, the reputation arises from the "quality and characteristic" that the product exhibits by virtue of its geographical origin and the consumer preference associated with it, as represented by the common law concept of "goodwill." (Most in the common law jurisdiction protect AO through the law of passing off, which incorporates the element of shared

goodwill. See Daniel R. Bereskin, "Legal Protection of Geographical Indications in Canada" (paper presented at the Intellectual Property Institute of Canada's Annual Meeting, Halifax, September 18, 2003). In the case of GIs, the reputation may not necessarily relate to the "quality" of the product. Reputation is protectable subject matter in the case of GIs, independently of the "quality" of a product. It is pointed out that the specific inclusion of "reputation" in Art. 22.1 of the TRIPS Agreement did not exist in the December 1990 draft presented to the Brussels Ministerial Conference; rather, the wording is found in the consolidated text that became the basis for the final agreement. See Review of Proposals, supra note 18 referring to MTN.GG/NG11/W/76, reprinted in Daniel Gervais, *The TRIPS Agreement: Drafting History and Analysis* (London: Sweet & Maxwell, 1998). It is to be noted that the wording of the TRIPS Agreement in this regard is consistent with and closely resembles the definition of GIs in the EC's 1992 Regulation on Geographical Indications.

30. A. Taubman, "Thinking Locally, Acting Globally: How Trade Negotiations over Geographical Indications Improvise Fair Trade Rules" (2008) Intellectual Property Quarterly 231 at 238.

31. *Ibid.* at 242.

32. WIPO, *Geographical Indications* (Standing Committee on the Law of Trademarks, Industrial Designs and Geographical Indications, Tenth Session, Geneva, April 28–May 2, 2003) SCT/10/4 [Geographical Indications] at para 24.

33. William Albert Van Caenegem, "Registered Geographical Indications: Between Intellectual Property and Rural Policy", Part I (2003) 6 Journal of World Intellectual Property 699 at 702.

34. Keith E. Maskus, "Observations on the Development Potential of Geographical Indications" (paper prepared for the U.N. Millennium Project Task Force on Trade, March 2003), online: <*www.ycsg.yale.edu/documents/papers/ Maskus.doc*> *[Observation] at 1.*

35. WIPO, *Geographical Indications* (Standing Committee on the Law of Trademarks, Industrial Designs and Geographical Indications, Tenth Session, Geneva, April 28 – May 2, 2003) SCT/10/4 [Geographical Indications] at paras 23-25.

36. *Ibid.* at para 26.

37. *Ibid.* at para 27-30.

38. Matthijs Geuze, "Protection of Geographical Indications – International Legal Framework" (presentation at National Roving Seminars on Geographical Indications, Chennai, January 29–30, 2009) at 14, online: WIPO <www.wipo.int/edocs/mdocs/geoind/en/wipo_geo_in_09/ wipo_geo_in_09_geuze.ppt>.

39. WIPO, *Geographical Indications: Historical Background, Nature of Rights, Existing Systems for Protection and Obtaining Effective Protection in Other Countries* (Standing Committee on the Law of Trademarks, Industrial Designs and Geographical Indications, 6th session, March 12–16, 2001) SCT/6/3 [Historical Background] at para 8.

40. *Ibid.*

Teshager Dagne

41. WIPO, *Intellectual Property Handbook: Policy, Law and Use* (2004) WIPO Publication No. 489 (E), online: <http://www.wipo.int/export/sites/www/about-ip/en/iprm/pdf/ch2.pdf> [WIPO Handbook] at para 2.727.

42. *Ibid.* at 2.694.

43. Deven R. Desai & Sandra L. Rierson, "Confronting the Genericism Conundrum" (2007) 28 Cardozo Law Review 1789 at 1790.

44. WIPO Handbook, *supra* note 41 at 2.694.

45. Communication, *European Community – Draft Agreement on Trade-Related Aspects of Intellectual Property Rights*, MTN.GNG/NG11/W/68 (Mar. 29, 1990), reprinted & Communication, *United States – Draft Agreement on the Trade-Related Aspects of Intellectual Property Rights*, MTN.GNG/NG11/W/70 (May 11, 1990); for a detailed discussion of the negotiating history of GIs in the TRIPS, see S. Escudero, *International Protection of Geographical Indications and Developing Countries*, South Center Trade Working Paper no. 10 (2001).

46. Olufunmilayo B. Arewa, "TRIPS and Traditional Knowledge: Local Communities, Local Knowledge, and Global Intellectual Property Frameworks" (2006) 10 Marquette Intellectual Property Law Review 156 at 160.

47. *Supra* note at 23.

48. *Ibid.*

49. Art. 9 of a Group of Developing Countries proposal, Document MTN.GNG/NG11/W/71 in *ibid.*

50. *Draft Final Act Embodying the Results of the Uruguay Round of Multilateral Trade Negotiations*, 20 Dec.1991, MTN.TNC/W/FA.

51. This is because the African states have been divided on the issue. See Catherine Grant, "Geographical Indications: Implications for Africa" (2005) 6 Tralac Trade Brief at 3.

52. See *supra* note 27 at 6 ff.

53. *Ibid.*

54. WTO Ministerial Conference, *Ministerial Statement*, Fifth Session, Cancún, 10–14 September 2003, adopted 14 September 2003.

55. The "July Package," also referred to as "the General Council's post-Cancún decision," is a decision adopted by the General Council on 1 August 2004 to reformulate the Doha Round objectives in order to keep the Doha Development Round on track and to successfully wrap up the negotiations with an agreement by the end of 2005.

56. Office of the United States Trade Representative (USTR), "U.S. and Other Trade Partners Present Positions and Proposals to Prevent Unauthorized Use of Geographic Names," USTR Press Release 20 September 2002, online: < http://www.ustr.gov/Document_Library/Press_Releases/2002/September/US_Oth er_Trade_Partners_Present_Positions_Proposals_to_Prevent_Unauthorized_Use_ of_Geographic_Names.html>

57. *Ibid.*

58. See Kasturi Das, "Protection of Geographical Indications: An Overview of Select Issues with Particular Reference to India" (Center on Trade & Development

Working Paper 8, 2007); M. Echols, "Geographical Indications for Foods, TRIPS and the Doha Development Agenda" (2003) 47:2 Journal of African Law.

59. WIPO, "About Geographical Indications: How Are Geographical Indications Protected?" online:
WIPO <http://wipo.int/geo_indications/en/about.html#protec>.

60. WTO, *Protection of Trademarks and Geographical Indications for Agricultural Goods and Foodstuffs* (Complaints by the United States and Australia) WTO Doc. WT/DS174R WT/DS290R (15 March 2005) (Panel Report).

61. Tim Josling, "The War on Terroir: Geographical Indications as a Transatlantic Trade Conflict" (2006) 57 Journal of Agricultural Economics 337–363 at 338.

62. See also *supra* note 58.

63. According to the EU's memo titled "Why Do Geographical Indications Matter to Us?" GIs were used in ancient Egypt by brickmakers to indicate the origin-related resistance of bricks and stones with which pyramids were made. Geographical indications were also used as signs of quality in ancient Greece, an illustration being Thasian wine (from the island of Thasos, Macedonia region, Greece), which commanded a price premium of 20 drachmas for 20 litres. Presently used GIs such as Parmigiano or Comté date from the 13th century. European Commission, "Intellectual Property: Why Do Geographical Indications Matter to Us?" Trade Issues (30 July 2003), online:
< http://ec.europa.eu/trade/issues/sectoral/intell_property/argu_en.htm>.   Also, Hayes J. Dermot, Sergio H. Lence & Bruce Babcock, "Geographic Indications and Farmer-Owned Brands: Why Do the US and EU Disagree?" (2005) 4:2 Eurochoices 28 at 30.

64. EU, Council Regulation (EC) 2081/92 of 14 July 1992 On the Protection of Geographical Indications and Designations of Origin for Agricultural Goods and Foodstuffs, [1992] O.J. (L 208), *superseded by* Council Regulation (EC) 510/2006 of 20 March 2006 on the Protection of Geographical Indications and Designations of Origin for Agricultural Goods and Foodstuffs, [2006] O.J. (L 93/12); Council Regulation (EC) 2082/92 of 14 July 1992 on Certificates of Specific Character for Agricultural Goods and Foodstuffs, [1992] O.J. (L 208), *superseded by* Council Regulation (EC) No 509/2006 of 20 March 2006 on Agricultural Goods and Foodstuffs as Traditional Specialities Guaranteed, [2006] O.J. (L 93/1).

65. "Council Regulation" No 510/2006, *ibid.* at Art. 2 .1 (b) [*Emphasis added*].

66. "Council Regulation" (EC) No 509/2006 *supra* note 64 at Art 2.1 (a) & (b).

67. *Ibid.* at Art 2.2.

68. *Ibid.* at Art 4.1–Art. 4.2.

69. *Ibid.* at Art 5.1

70. Council Regulation 1493/99 as amended by Commission Regulation 753/2002 brings together a number of earlier regulations on the protection of wines and covers the protection of geographical indications and traditional terms, Commission Regulation (EC) No 753/2002, 2002 O.J. (L 118) 1, at Arts. 28–33, 14–18; Council Regulation 1493/1999 on the Organisation of the Market in Wine, 1999 O.J. (L 179) 1, Arts. 50–53, 27–29. For spirits, Council Regulation

Teshager Dagne

1576/89(EC), 1989 O.J. (L 160) 1, and mineral waters under Council Directive 80/777(EC), 1980 O.J. (L 229) 1, amended by Council Directive 96/70, 1996 O.J. (L 299) 26 (EC).

71. Council Regulation 40/94 on the Community Trade Mark, 1994 O.J. (L 11) 1 (EC) at Art. 66–69.

72. Council Regulation 510/2006, 2006 O.J. (L 93) at Art. 14 (2).

73. § 45 (15 U.S.C. § 1127) (2008).

74. § 45 (15 U.S.C. § 1127) (2008).

75. WIPO, *Introduction to Geographical Indications and Recent International Developments in the World Intellectual Property Organization* (Symposium on the International Protection of Geographical Indications organized by WIPO and the National Directorate for Industrial Property, Ministry of Industry, Energy and Mining of Uruguay, Montevideo, November 28–29, 2001) [Recent International] at 10.

76. United States Patent and Trademark Office, *Geographical Indication Protection in the United States*, at 3, online: USPTO
<http://www.uspto.gov/web/offices/dcom/olia/globalip/pdf/gi_system.pdf>

77. *Ibid.* at 5.

78. See the protection of GIs in Canada in *supra* note 29; also, see different methods of protecting GIs in different legal systems in Historical Background, *supra* note 39.

79. Walter R. Brookhart et al., *Current International Legal Aspects of Licensing and Intellectual Property* (Chicago: American Bar Association, 1980) at 19.

80. *Ibid.*

81. Walter R. Brookhart et al., *Current International Legal Aspects of Licensing and Intellectual Property* (Chicago, American Bar Association, 1980) at 11.

82. See WTO, Communication from Albania, Brazil, China, Colombia, Ecuador, the European Communities, Iceland, India, Indonesia, the Kyrgyz Republic, Liechtenstein, the Former Yugoslav Republic of Macedonia, Pakistan, Peru, Sri Lanka, Switzerland, Thailand, Turkey, the ACP Group and the African Group, *Draft Modalities for TRIPS Related Issues*, TN/C/W/52 (19 July 2008).

83. European Commission, *External Trade, Intellectual Property, TRIPs and Geographical Indications: EU Submits Three Communications on Geographical Indications, Brussels*, 24 June 2002, online:
http://europa.eu.int/comm/trade/issues/sectoral/intell_property/wto_nego/intel4.htm; also cited in *supra* note 89 at 29.

84. See Kaitlin Mara, "WTO: Progress on IP at Last; Consensus Still Uncertain" Intellectual Property Watch (5 December 2008), online: <http://www.ip-watch.org/weblog/2008/12/05/wto-progress-on-ip-at-last-though-consensus-elusive/>

85. See, e.g., intervention by the delegate from Thailand, WTO, Council for TRIPS, Minutes of Meeting, 5 February 2003, WTO Doc. IP/C/M/38 at 41: "Extension was important because GIs were often related to culture and ancestors' traditional knowledge"; and intervention by the delegate from India, WTO, Council for

TRIPS, Minutes of Meeting, 10 September 2002, WTO Doc. IP/C/M/36/Add. 1 at 10, relating to the role of GI extension in the protection of the cultural heritage of developing countries. It is also pointed out that most of the third parties in the EC-GIs panel proceedings were developing countries. Panel Report, European Communities – Protection of Trademarks and Geographical Indications for Agricultural Goods and Foodstuffs (EC-GIs) (15 March 2005) WTO Documents WT/DS174R WT/DS290R. See Tomer Broude, "Taking 'Trade and Culture' Seriously: Geographical Indications and Cultural Protection in WTO Law" (2005) 26 University of Pennsylvania Journal of International Economic Law at 6 ff.

86. See *supra* note 27 at 26.

87. According to the report, "Cocuy the Pecaya," a liquor made from agave, in Venezuela, and "PhuQuoc" fish, soya sauce and "Shan Tuyet Moc Chau," a variety of tea, in Vietnam, are protected as geographical indications. See WIPO, *Review of Existing Intellectual Property Protection of Traditional Knowledge*, WIPO/GRTKF/IC/3/7 (Intergovernmental Committee on Intellectual Property and Genetic Resources, Traditional Knowledge and Folklore, Third Session, Geneva, June 13–21, 2002).

88. See Teshager Dagne, "The Application of Intellectual Property Rights to Biodiversity Resources: A Technique for the Less Economically Developed Countries to Maintain Control over the Biodiversity Resources in Their Territories?" (2009) 17:1 African Journal of International and Comparative Law 150.

89. In recent times, there has been significant debate over "geographical indications" with respect to the WIPO development agenda. Also, see oriGIn, the first international network of GI producers, which now represents over one million producers of traditional products from more than 30 countries, http://origin.technomind.be/. Established under the umbrella of the Arab League in October 2008, the Arab Society for Geographical Indications (ASGI) has outlined its objectives: to "protect and promote Arab heritage and local products as well as [encourage] Arab countries to develop GI laws and regulations, and [join] international treaties related to geographical indications and [update] and [modernise] the existing geographical indications laws in the Arab countries." http://www.ip-watch.org/weblog/2008/10/27/new-arab-group-aims-at-protecting-local-products-with-geographical-origins/. Research projects financed by the EU and Switzerland have as their purpose to "strengthen international research on geographical indications": the DOLPHINS (Development of Origin Labelled Product Humanity, Innovation and Sustainability) & SINER-GI (Strengthening International Research on Geographical Indications) http://www.origin-food.org/2005/index.php?r=1&Largeur=1280& Hauteur=800.

90. Terri Janke, *Minding Culture: Case Studies on Intellectual Property and Traditional Cultural Expressions,* (Geneva: World Intellectual Property Organization, 2003) at 36, online: <http://www.wipo.int/tk/en/studies/cultural/minding-culture/studies/finalstudy.pdf >.

91. Daphne Zografos, "Can Geographical Indications Be a Viable Alternative for the Protection of Traditional Cultural Expressions?" in Fiona Macmillan and Kathy

Teshager Dagne

Bowrey eds., 3 *New Directions in Copyright Law*, (Cheltenham: Edward Elgar, 2006) at 55.

92. Brad Sherman & Leanne Wiseman, "Towards an Indigenous Public Domain?" in P. Bernt Hugenholtz and Lucie Guibault eds., *The Future of the Public Domain* (The Hague: Kluwer Law International, 2006) at 275.

93. See the various modalities for the protection of traditional knowledge in WIPO, *Intellectual Property, Traditional Knowledge and Genetic Resources Policy Options for Developing Countries* (Presented at the International Conference on Intellectual Property, the Internet, Electronic Commerce and Traditional Knowledge, Sofia, May 29–31, 2001).

94. See Shivani Singhal, "Geographical Indications and Traditional Knowledge" (2008) 11 Journal of Intellectual Property Law & Practice 732 at 733.

95. *Supra* note 1, preamble.

96. *Supra* note 27 at 349.

97. See David R. Downes, *"How Intellectual Property Could Be a Tool to Protect Traditional Knowledge"* (2000) 25 Colum. J. Envtl. L. 253 at 259.

98. Bernard O'Connor, *The Law of Geographical Indications* (London: Cameron May, 2004) at 374.

99. *Supra* note 94 at 737.

100.*Ibid.* citing Louis Lorvellec, "You've Got to Fight for Your Right to Party: A Response to Professor Jim Chen" (1996) 5 Minnesota Journal of Global Trade 65.

101.Stephen A. Hansen & Justin W. van Fleet, *A Handbook on Issues and Options for Traditional Knowledge Holders in Protecting Their Intellectual Property and Maintaining Biological Diversity* (Washington, DC: American Association for the Advancement of Science, 2003) at 201.

102.Thomas Cottier & Marion Panizzon, "Legal Perspectives on Traditional Knowledge: The Case for Intellectual Property Protection" (2004) 7 J.I.E.L. 371 at 380.

103.*Supra* note 97 at 10.

104.Warren Moran, "Rural Space as Intellectual Property" (1993) 12 Political Geography 263-277, quoted in *Ibid.*

105.*Ibid.*

106.David R. Downes & Sarah A. Laird, "Innovative Mechanisms for Sharing Benefits of Biodiversity and Related Knowledge: Case Studies on Geographical Indications and Trademarks" (paper prepared for UNCTAD Biotrade Initiative, 1999) at 11.

107.Jerome M.P.L. Agostini, Affidavit filed in *Institut National des Appellations D'Origine v. Vintners Int'l Co.,*
958 F.2d 1574 (Fed. Cir. 1992), quoted in *ibid.* at 11.

108.*Ibid.* at 11.

109.*Supra* note 97 at 269.

110.Philippe Cullet & Andrea Nascimento, "Geographical Indications" in S. Biber-Klemm and T. Cottier eds., *Rights to Plant Genetic Resources and Traditional*

Teshager Dagne

Knowledge: Basic Issues and Perspectives (London: CAB International, 2006) at page 252.

111.*Supra* note 97 at 11.

112.*Ibid.*

113.*Supra* note 10.

114.*Supra* note 97 at 269.

115.See *infra* note 147 and accompanying text; also *supra* note 27 at 32.

116.*Sunder* note 10 at 314.

117.Keith Eugene Maskus & Jerome H. Reichman, *International Public Goods and Transfer of Technology under a Globalized Intellectual Property Regime* (Cambridge: Cambridge University Press, 2005) at 579.

118.*Supra* note 27.

119.See UN-UNESCO *World Commission on Culture and Development, Our Creative Diversity* (Paris: United Nations, 1995).

120.Madhavi Sunder, "The Invention of Traditional Knowledge" UC Davis Legal Studies Research Paper Series Research Paper No. 75 (March 2006) at 26.

121.See Jan Nederveen Pieterse, *Development Theory: Deconstructions/Reconstructions* (London: Sage Publications Ltd., 2001) at 6.

122.*Ibid.*

123.*Ibid.*

124.Amartya Sen, "What's the Use of Music? The Role of the Music Industry in Africa" (Prepared for the World Bank–Policy Sciences Center, Workshop on the Development of the Music Industry in Africa, Washington, D.C., June 20–21, 2000), online: <http://www.worldbank.org/research/trade/africa_music2.htm.>.

125.*Supra* note 388 at 26.

126.*Ibid.* citing Amartya Sen, *Development as Freedom* (London: Alfred A. Knopf, 1999).

127.*Sunder, supra* note 10 at 323.

128.*Supra* note 120 at 28.

129.*Ibid.*

130.Amartya Sen, *Development as Freedom* (London: Alfred A. Knopf, 1999) at 133 ff.

131.WIPO GENERAL ASSEMBLY, "PROPOSAL BY ARGENTINA AND BRAZIL FOR THE ESTABLISHMENT OF A DEVELOPMENT AGENDA FOR WIPO" (THIRTY-FIRST (15TH EXTRAORDINARY) SESSION, SEPTEMBER 27 TO OCTOBER 5, 2004, GENEVA) AT PARA VI, ONLINE: WIPO www.wipo.int/edocs/mdocs/govbody/en/wo.../wo_ga_ 31_11.doc.

132.*Supra* note 120 at 7.

133.See *supra* note 97 at 6.

134.WIPO, *The Definition of Geographical Indications* (Standing Committee on the Law of Trademarks, Industrial Designs and Geographical Indications, Ninth Session, Geneva, November 11–15, 2002) Sct/9/4[Definition] at para 4.

Teshager Dagne

135.Dev Gangjee, "Quibbling Siblings: Conflicts between Trade Marks and GIs" (2007) 82 Chicago-Kent Law Review 1253 at 1257.

136.*Ibid.*

137.F. Addor & A. Grazioli, "Geographical Indications beyond Wines and Spirits – A Roadmap for a Better Protection for Geographical Indications in the WTO TRIPs Agreement" (2002) 5 J. *World* Intellect. *Property* 865 at 874; see also Gavin Fridell, *Fair Trade Coffee: The Prospects and Pitfalls of Market-Driven Social Justice* (Toronto: University of Toronto Press, 2007).

138.See Elizabeth Barham, "Localisation within Globalisation: Better Protecting Geographical Indications to Favour Sustainable Development" (Presentation on the 2004 Annual WTO Public Symposium: ORIGIN Round Table on Geographical Indications, 27 May 2004, Geneva).

139.Kal Raustiala & Stephen R. Munzer, "The Global Struggle over Geographic Indications" (2007) 18 E.J.I.L. 337 at 345.

140.See Jamil Uzma, "Biopiracy: The Patenting of Basmati by RiceTec," publication of the Commission on Environmental, Economic and Social Policy – South Asia & Sustainable Policy Development Institute (October 8 1998), online: www.iucn.org/themes/ceesp/publications/art-mono/basmati.doc.

141.Michael Blakeney, "Proposals for the International Regulation of Geographical Indications" (2001) 4 The Journal of World Intellectual Property 629 at 647.

142.See *Supra* note 97 at 270 ff.

143.Dev Gangjee, "Quibbling Siblings: Conflicts between Trade Marks and GIs" (2007) 82 Chicago-Kent Law Review 1253 at 1257 ff.

144.*Ibid.* at 6.

145.Council Regulation 510/2006, 2006 O.J. (L 93) at preamble.

146.Franz Fischler, *Quality Food, CAP Reform and PDO/PGI*, SPEECH/04/183, Siena (17 April, 2004).

147.Mariano Riccheri et al., *Impacts of the IPRs Rules on Sustainable Development: Assessing the Applicability of Geographical Indications as a Means to Improve Environmental Quality in Affected Ecosystems and the Competitiveness of Agricultural Products*, IPDEV Project Coordinator Final Project Workpackage 3, online:
<http://ecologic.eu/download/projekte/1800-1849/1802/wp3_final_report.pdf> at 10 ff.

148.*Supra* note 7 at 210.

149.*Supra* note 97 at 6.

150.*Ibid.* at 4–5.

151.To address the access and benefit-sharing agenda that the CBD considered important to conserve biodiversity, the fifth Conference of the Parties meeting established the Ad Hoc Open-ended Working Group on Access and Benefit-Sharing (WG-AB), which later developed the Bonn Guidelines on Access and Benefit-Sharing, adopted at the sixth COP meeting in 2002. See Conference of the Parties, "Access and benefit-sharing" in *Decisions Adopted by the Conference of the Parties to the Convention on Biological Diversity at its Fifth Meeting*, COP 5

Decision V/26 (Fifth Ordinary Meeting of the Conference of the Parties to the Convention on Biological Diversity, 15–26 May 2000, *Nairobi) at* para. 11; Conference of the Parties, Bonn Guidelines on Access to Genetic Resources and Fair and Equitable Sharing of the Benefits Arising out of their Utilization COP 6 Decision VI/24 (Sixth Ordinary Meeting of the Conference of the Parties to the Convention on Biological Diversity, the Hague, 7–19 April 2002*)*.

152.The programs of the WG-AB are more concentrated on securing access and benefit-sharing agreements for patents that utilize traditional knowledge, unlike the agenda pursued by the CBD's Working Group to Protect Traditional Knowledge – which adopted *sui generis* protection of traditional knowledge mostly through inward-looking protocols of protecting traditional knowledge. See Ad Hoc Open-Ended Inter-Sessional Working Group on Article 8(J) and Related Provisions of the Convention on Biological Diversity, *Development of Elements of* Sui Generis *Systems for the Protection of Traditional Knowledge, Innovations and Practices to Identify Priority Elements* (Fifth Meeting, 15–19 October 2007, Montreal) UNEP/CBD/WG8J/5/6 20 September 2007 at para 4, online: <http://www.cbd.int/doc/meetings/tk/wg8j-05/official/wg8j-05-06-en.pdf>.

153.Noah Zerbe, "*Biodiversity, Ownership, and* Indigenous Knowledge: Exploring Legal Frameworks for Community, Farmers, and Intellectual Property Rights in Africa" (2005) 53 Ecological Economics 493 at 500; also, Ikechi Mgbeoji, *Patents and Plants: Rethinking the Role of International Law in Relation to the Appropriation of Traditional Knowledge of the Uses of Plants (TKUP)* (Dalhousie University, unpublished J.S.D. *thesis,* 2000).

154.*Ibid.*

155.See *supra* note 101 at 4 ff.

156.See Brendan Tobin, "Redefining Perspectives in the Search for Protection of Traditional Knowledge: A Case Study from Peru" (2001)10:1 RECIEL.

157.Matthew Rimmer, "Australian Icons: Authenticity Marks and Identity Politics" (2004) 3 Indigenous Law Journal 139.

158.Niels Halberg et al. eds., *Global Development of Organic Agriculture* (Oxfordshire: CABI Publishing, 2006)

159.Stefano Pagiola et al., *Selling Forest Environmental Services* (London: Earthscan Publications, 2002).

160.*Supra* note 97 at 21.

161.*Supra* note 27 at 32.

162.*Supra* note 135 at 13.

163.*Supra* note 97 at 2 ff.

164.*Supra* note 135 at 13.

165.Contrary to the utilitarian emphasis on economic rewards to increase creation and invention, there are other incentives that encourage creation of knowledge, including honour and recognition, as evidenced and rewarded through publication, citation, academic tenure, prizes for academic achievement or demonstrations of skill in public competitions, and awards of government grants for research. Anil K. Gupta, "Accessing Biological Diversity and Associative Knowledge System:

Teshager Dagne

Can Ethics Influence Equity?" cited in *supra* note 97 at 260. Indigenous people and local communities engage in the creation, preservation and transfer of knowledge in a continual manner as a means of survival and group identity, and not for the sake of financial gain by market forces.

166.*Supra* note 135 at 15.

167.See *supra* note 135.

168.FAO Committee on Commodity Problems, *Geographical Indications for Tea* (Intergovernmental Group on Tea, Eighteenth Session, Hangzhou, 14–16 May 2008) CCP:TE 08/5 at 2, online:

< ftp://ftp.fao.org/docrep/fao/meeting/013/k2020E.pdf>.

169.Tony Battaglene, *The Australian Wine Industry Position on Geographical Indications* (Presentation to the Worldwide Symposium on Geographical Indications Jointly Organized by The World Intellectual Property Organization and the Ministry of Productive Activities of Italy under the Patronage of the Ministry of Foreign Affairs of Italy, Parma, June 27–29, 2005).

170.*Supra* note 23 at Art. 2 (1).

171.*Supra* note 41 at para 2.727.

172.Irene Calboli, *Expanding the Protection of Geographical Indications of Origin under TRIPS: Old Debate or New Opportunity?* Marquette University Law School Legal Studies Research Paper NO. 06 ‐ 19 (2006) at 187.

173.See, for example, *supra* note 97 at 737.

174.*Ibid.* at 733.

175.*Sunder, supra* note 10 at 302.

176.*Supra* note 38 at para. 2.727.

177.*Ibid.*

178.S.K. Soam, "Analysis of Prospective Geographical Indications in India" (2005) 8 J. World Intell. Prop. 679 qouted in Chidi Oguamanam, "Patents and Traditional Medicine: Digital Capture, Creative Legal Interventions, and the Dialectics of Knowledge Transformation" (2008) 15 Indiana Journal of Global Legal Studies 489 at 526.

179.See Chidi Oguamanam, "Patents and Traditional Medicine: Digital Capture, Creative Legal Interventions, and the Dialectics of Knowledge Transformation" (2008) 15 Indiana Journal of Global Legal Studies 489 at 526 [*Digital Capture*].

180.WIPO, *Geographical Indications*, online:

<http://www.wipo.int/sme/en/ip_business/collective_marks/ geographical_indications.htm>

181.WIPO, *Report on Fact-Finding Missions on Intellectual Property and Traditional Knowledge 1998–1999* (2001) at 58, online: WIPO

<http://www.wipo.int/export/sites/www/tk/en/tk/ffm/report/final/pdf/part1.pdf> at 46.

182.*Supra* note 102 at 383.

183. Warren Moran, "Rural Space as Intellectual Property" (1993) 12 Political Geography 263 in Hjalager Anne-Mette & Minho Greg Richards, Tourism and Gastronomy (London: Routledge, 2002) at 159.

184. *Supra* note 97 at 383, citing Moran *ibid*.

185. *Ibid.*

186. *Draft Conclusions of Workshop B: EU Quality Schemes* (Czech Presidency High Level Conference on the Future of Agricultural Product Quality Policy, Prague, 13 March 2009) at 4.

187. Definition, *supra* note 122 at para. 26.

188. *Ibid.*

189. The Crucible II Group, *Seeding Solutions* (Rome: IDRC, 2000).

190. *Supra* note 102 at 385.

191. For example, the archrival states India and Pakistan put aside their differences to register homonymous GIs over "Basmati rice" and "Punjabi lassi" both of which come from the Punjab State in India and the Punjab State in Pakistan. See Soam *supra* note 164 at 681.

192. Keith Eugene Maskus & Jerome H. Reichman, "The Globalization of Private Knowledge Goods and the Privatization of Global Public Goods" (2004) 7 Journal of International Economic Law 279 at 311.

193. *Supra* note 1 at Art. 24.9: "There shall be no obligation under this Agreement to protect geographical indications which are not or cease to be protected in their country of origin, or which have fallen into disuse in that country."

194. Commission on Intellectual Prop. Rights, *Integrating Intellectual Property Rights and Development Policy* (2002) at 90, online:
< http://www.iprcommission.org/papers/pdfs/final_report/Ch4final.pdf> .

195. D. Vaver, *Intellectual Property Rights: Critical Concepts in Law* (New York: Routledge, 2006) at 330.

196. Of course, both proponents and opponents of the extension of GIs to agricultural products have sought to support their positions by referring to the positive or negative impact it would have on developing-country economies. ICTSD, "TRIPS: Members Still Split on Relationship with CBD; GI Talks Going Nowhere" (22 March 2006) 10:10 Bridges Weekly Trade News Digest at 6. It is well documented that the industrialized countries, led by the United States – which is now a strong opponent of the extension of GI protection beyond wines and spirits – were the actors behind the TRIPS Agreement, which set down rules on a wide range of intellectual property norms (patents, trademarks, copyright and industrial design) mirroring norms that had been accepted in their own domestic frameworks. GIs were included in the TRIPS as part of a compromise between the EU – which boasts a strong tradition of agricultural production – and the United States. See Daniel Gervais, "Intellectual Property, Trade & Development: The State of Play" (2005) 74 Fordham L. Rev. 508–510; Daniel Gervais, *The TRIPS Agreement, Drafting History and Analysis* (London: Sweet and Maxwell, 2003).

197. Oguamanam, *Digital Capture, supra* note 165 at 525.

198. *Supra* note 97 at 260.

Teshager Dagne

199.Stéphan Marette, "Can Foreign Producers Benefit from Geographical Indications under the New European Regulation?" (2009) 10 Estey Centre Journal of International Law and Trade Policy at 69.

200.*Ibid.*

201.*Supra* note 97.

202.Light Years IP, "Distinctive Values in African Exports: How Intellectual Property Can Raise Export Income and Alleviate Poverty" (2008), online: < http: // www.lightyearsip.net/downloads/Distinctive_values_in_African_exports. pdf>.

203.For example, in an endeavour that involved a consortium of stakeholders representing farmers' cooperatives, coffee exporters and government bodies, and with financial support from the U.K.'s Department for International Development, technical advice from a Washington-based NGO – Light Years IP – and legal assistance from a U.S. law firm – Arnold and Porter – the Ethiopian Intellectual Property Office (EIPO) registered trademarks over its indigenous coffee names. The EIPO licensed the coffee names to a number of distributers royalty free with a purpose to, in the words of the director, "enlist the big companies to do what we don't have the skills or financial means for – that is, building recognition of our brands in international markets and so increasing long term demand for them." See WIPO, "Making the Origin Count: Two Coffees" (2007) 5 WIPO Magazine at 2.

204.*Ibid.*

205.EC, *supra* note 63.

206.*Ibid.*

207.*Ibid.*

208.For a case study on suggestions for the creation of IP rights on South Pacific Kava, South African Rooibos, Andean Quinoa, Neem tree and Basmati rice, see *supra* note 97 at 18 ff.

209.See Ikechi Mgbeoji, "Patents and Traditional Knowledge of the Uses of Plants: Is a Communal Patent Regime Part of the Solution to the Scourge of Biopiracy?" (2001) 9 Indiana Journal of Global Legal Studies 163.

210.The 2001 WIPO global fact-finding mission report identified the IP needs and expectations of the holders of TK and cultural expressions and suggested that informal regimes and customary protocols may be utilized to protect traditional knowledge in various areas of traditional knowledge subject matter. See WIPO, *Report on Fact-Finding Missions on Intellectual Property and Traditional Knowledge 1998–1999* (2001) at 58, online: WIPO

<http://www.wipo.int/export/sites/www/tk/en/tk/ffm/report/final/pdf/part1.pdf>.

211.See *supra* note 98 at 379.

[31]

Using Geographical Indications to Protect Artisanal Works in Developing Countries: Lessons from a Banana Republic's Misnomered Hat

*Alexandra Basak Russell**

---

* J.D. Candidate, The University of Iowa College of Law, May 2010. The author would like to thank her husband, Kane, for his unwavering patience and for sharing the transformative experiences that inspired this Note; and her mother, Camille, for her endless emotional support and keen attention to detail. She would also like to thank the attorneys at the Quito-based firm Paz Horowitz for their mentorship and expertise on the *Montecristi Case*.

I. INTRODUCTION

Since the end of World War II, many critics have faulted multilateral institutions for compelling developing countries to prioritize foreign debt reduction, foreign direct investment, and trade liberalization at the expense of community-based economic development, human rights, and cultural preservation.[1] Among the institutions most frequently faulted is the World Trade Organization ("WTO").[2] Critics from the popular press to legal academia alike assert that the WTO's prescribed financial and economic policies historically have overlooked social and equitable considerations, often to the detriment of a country's poor.[3]

This Note addresses one discipline in which trade policy, law, development, the arts, and culture converge, potentially to the benefit of a nation's poor: intellectual property ("IP"). Through IP rights, owners are "given the right to prevent others from using their inventions, designs or other creations—and to use that right to negotiate payment in return for others using them."[4] By providing authors with legal protection over, and a financial interest in, their works, society encourages them to develop

---

[1] *See, e.g.*, Sandra Blanco, *The 1960s and 1970s: The World Bank Attacks Poverty; Developing Countries Attack the IMF, in* UNIVERSITY OF IOWA CENTER FOR INTERNATIONAL FINANCE AND DEVELOPMENT E-BOOK, 9 TRANSNAT'L L. & CONTEMP. PROBS. 109 (1999), *available at* http://www.uiowa.edu/ifdebook/ebook2/contents/part1-IV.shtml; Enrique R. Carrasco, *An Introduction to the Symposium: Critical Issues Facing the Bretton Woods System: Can the IMF, World Bank, and the GATT/WTO Promote an Enabling Environment for Social Development?*, 6 TRANSNAT'L L. & CONTEMP. PROBS. 1, vii (1996); JOSEPH STIGLITZ, GLOBALIZATION AND ITS DISCONTENTS (2002); Bhagirath Lal Das, *The Steamroller Rolls On*, THIRD WORLD NETWORK, http://www.twnside.org.sg/title/roll-cn.htm [hereinafter Lal Das, *Steamroller*]; Bhagirath Lal Das, *WTO Agreements: Implications and Imbalances*, THIRD WORLD NETWORK, http://www.twnside.org.sg/title/imp-cn.htm; John W. Head, *Seven Deadly Sins: An Assessment of Criticisms Directed at the International Monetary Fund*, 52 U. KAN. L. REV. 521, 531–34 (2004).

[2] Lal Das, *Steamroller, supra* note 1. The Bretton Woods institutions and the four multilateral regional development banks are the others. In fact, since its inception, the concern International Monetary Fund ("IMF") has shown for developing countries has taken a backseat to promoting currency stability, formulating a loan repayment system, and rebuilding a war-torn European economy. Sandra Blanco & Enrique Carrasco, *The Function of the IMF and the World Bank, in* UNIVERSITY OF IOWA CENTER FOR INTERNATIONAL FINANCE AND DEVELOPMENT E-BOOK, 9 TRANSNAT'L L. & CONTEMP. PROBS. 1, 67, *available at* http://www.uiowa.edu/ifdebook/ebook2/contents/part1-II.shtml.

[3] Head, *supra* note 1, at 533–35; STIGLITZ, *supra* note 1, at IX. For an analysis of the World Bank's shifting approach toward providing aid and development assistance to developing countries, see Sophie Smyth, *World Bank Grants in a Changed World Order: How Do We Referee This New Paradigm?*, 30 U. PA. J. INT'L L. 483 (2008).

[4] World Trade Organization [WTO], Understanding the WTO: Intellectual Property: Protection and Enforcement, http://www.wto.org/english/theWTO_e/whatis_e/tif_e/agrm7_e.htm (last visited Mar. 14, 2010) [hereinafter WTO, Intellectual Property].

creatively, thus inciting further innovation and economic growth.[5] This is true regardless of the economic climate in the IP author's home country.

In recent years, some developing countries have expanded their efforts to utilize the international IP system to a greater degree. Their fruitful experiences with IP protections illustrate how it is possible for developing countries to work within the current international economic and legal systems to gain leverage against countries with advanced economies and greater trade power. Among the countries that have used IP to their benefit are India, Mexico, Kenya, Nigeria, South Africa, Pakistan, Mauritius, Sri Lanka, Egypt, Peru, and Cuba.[6] Ecuador, the primary focus of this Note, is one of the most recent countries to join that list.

The 2008 Ecuadorian case, *K. Dorfzaun v. Union de Artesanos de Paja Toquilla de Montecristi*[7] ("Montecristi Case"), serves as an international model for using IP law, specifically geographical indications ("GIs"), also called appellations of origin ("AOs") or denominations of origin ("DOs"), to boost development and trade liberalization, as well as to protect and preserve traditional arts and cultural techniques in developing countries. GIs authenticate products for consumers who are not entirely familiar with the traditional methods and standards of the product they wish to buy, or who are easily fooled by imitation versions.[8] On a broader level, IP labels combat cultural homogenization by preserving dwindling art forms and bolstering the economic development of struggling nations.[9]

---

[5] World Intellectual Property Organization [WIPO], Frequently Asked Questions About WIPO, http://www.wipo.int/about-wipo/en/faq.html (last visited Mar. 14, 2010). The World Intellectual Property Organization ("WIPO") is a U.N. agency that harmonizes IP standards by administering twenty-four international treaties relating to IP rights, and resolves IP disputes between states. *See* William T. Fryer III, *Global IP Development: A Recommendation to Increase WIPO and WTO Cooperation*, 9 U. Balt. Intell. Prop. L.J. 171, 175 (2001).

[6] Stefania Fusco, *Geographical Indications: A Discussion on the TRIPS Regulation after the Ministerial Conference of Hong Kong*, 12 Marq. Intell. Prop. L. Rev. 197, 243–44 (2008).

[7] Instituto Ecuatoriano de la Propiedad Intelectual [IEPI] [Ecuadorian Institute of Intellectual Property], 22/8/2008, K. Dorfzaun Cia. Ltda. et al. v. Union de Artesanos de Paja Toquilla de Montecristi/Intellectual Property, [Docket No. 07-306-RA-2S] (Resolution No. 98869) (Ecuador) [hereinafter Montecristi Resolution]. The cooperative was represented by attorneys Bruce Horowitz, Esteban Riofrío, and Teodoro Ribaneira, of the Ecuadorian law firm Paz Horowitz.

[8] Michelle Agdomar, *Removing the Greek from Feta and Adding Korbel to Champagne: The Paradox of Geographical Indications in International Law*, 18 Fordham Intell. Prop. Media & Ent. L.J. 541, 586 (2008); *Intellectual Property Rights Help Crafts and Visual Arts Exporters*, Int'l Trade F., Feb. 2004, *available at* http://www.tradeforum.org/news/fullstory.php/aid/664/Intellectual_Property_Rights_Help_Crafts_and_Visual_Arts_Exporters.html [hereinafter *IP Rights Help Crafts Exporters*]; WIPO, Int'l Trade Ctr., Marketing Crafts and Visual Arts: The Role of Intellectual Property: A Practical Guide 12, 15, 32–33 (2003) [hereinafter WIPO Guide], *available at* http://www.wipo.int/export/sites/www/sme/en/documents/pdf/marketing_crafts.pdf.

[9] *See* Doris Estelle Long, *Is Fame All There Is? Beating Global Monopolists at Their Own Marketing Game*, 40 Geo. Wash. Int'l L. Rev. 123 (2008); WIPO Guide, *supra* note 8, at 94.

In Ecuador, the registration of the *montecristi* hat has produced significant results, both for the weaving cooperative who filed the suit and for the greater artisan community. GI registration has allowed local artisans to raise awareness about the history and process of authentic *montecristi* hat-making and can help to preserve that craft. Locals are now empowered to curb the sales of unscrupulous hat dealers who make, sell, and export imitation hats. Ecuadorian hatmakers now can reap greater profits from their work and become competitive in the international artisanal market.

This Note posits that developing countries must follow a growing trend of utilizing GIs to protect their culture, arts, and traditional knowledge, rather than viewing GI registration as a monopolistic barrier to trade and economic development as some developed Western nations, most notably the United States, have asserted. Developing countries should grow their economies by entering artisanal products in an existing global market that applauds, and will even pay a premium for, products that are made through traditional techniques. By utilizing their rich traditions and IP rights to the fullest extent, artisans in developing countries can compete with marketing and trade heavyweights from more developed countries, and thereby shift the historic imbalance of IP protections in their favor. Such market expansion should, on a broader scale, lead to trade liberalization, enhanced economic development, and the alleviation of poverty.[10]

In Part II, this Note explains the history and techniques of the *montecristi* straw hat, which ultimately led to its acceptance as a registered GI in Ecuador. Part III then explores the role of the Agreement on Trade-Related Aspects of Intellectual Property ("TRIPS") in defining and regulating GI use in WTO member states. Part IV summarizes the Ecuadorian court's findings in the Montecristi Case, as dictated by TRIPS' Minimum Standards. Part V analyzes the international debate on TRIPS and the arguably disparate impact it has had on developing countries. The core of this Note, Part VI, demonstrates the impact that GI use has had on market expansion and the survival of traditional art forms in India and Mexico, two countries that have accepted GI use generally and as applied to traditional handicrafts. Part VII builds on the discussion and delineates reasons for developing countries to adopt GIs. The Note concludes in Part VIII by mentioning other methods of IP protection that developing countries can utilize to protect cultural practices, traditional methods of production, and traditional art forms.

---

[10] *See* OFFICE OF THE U.S. TRADE REPRESENTATIVE, DOHA DEVELOPMENT AGENDA POLICY BRIEF: EXPANDING MARKETS TO PROMOTE DEVELOPMENT AND GROWTH (2005), *available at* http://www.fas.usda.gov/ITP/WTO/hongkong/whitehouseDohafactsheet.pdf.

II.   DEVELOPMENT OF THE ISSUE: THE HISTORY AND PROCESS OF THE
MONTECRISTI "PANAMA HAT"

A.   History

Montecristi, Ecuador is a small coastal town in the Manabí province that has produced *toquilla* straw hats since the 16th Century.[11] Franklin Delano Roosevelt, Winston Churchill, Ernest Hemingway, King Edward VII, and Al Capone have all famously worn these hats over the years.[12] The term "Panama hat" is a misnomer dating back to the early 20th Century when Spaniards[13] and Ecuadorian shippers transported the hats from their place of production, Montecristi, to customers in the United States and Europe via the Isthmus of Panama.[14] They named the hats for their place of purchase rather than their place of production, and as the hats gained popularity in the United States, the misnomer flourished.[15]

B.   Technique

The Montecristi hatmaking process is time consuming and labor intensive; it requires skilled artisans and a network of other specialty laborers. First, harvesters use a machete to cut the green leaves of the *toquilla* plant.[16] They strip down the long fleshy leaves and divides them into strands barely thicker than thread, using only their fingernails as tools.[17] Next, other laborers, traditionally women, boil the fibers in iron kettles before laying them out to dry and bleach in the sun.[18] Local distributors then collect and transport batches of the split fibers for sale to master weavers

---

[11] Hal Weitzman, *The Last Straw*, FIN. TIMES, Jan. 12, 2007, *available at* http://www.ft.com/cms/s/2/c0c336fe-a181-11db-8bc1-0000779e2340.html; DANNY PALMERLEE ET AL., THE LONELY PLANET: ECUADOR AND THE GALAPAGOS ISLANDS 206, 298 (7th ed. 2006).

[12] Weitzman, *supra* note 11.

[13] PALMERLEE ET AL., *supra* note 11, at 206.

[14] TOM MILLER, THE PANAMA HAT TRAIL: A JOURNEY FROM SOUTH AMERICA 15 (1986); Tom Miller, *Shopper's World: Ecuador Is Brimful of Panama Hats*, N.Y. TIMES, Aug. 3, 1986, *available at* http://www.nytimes.com/1986/08/03/travel/shopper-s-world-ecuador-is-brimful-of-panama-hats.html [hereinafter Miller, *Brimful of Panama Hats*].

[15] Miller, *Brimful of Panama Hats*, *supra* note 14.

[16] Christian Oliver, *Panama Hats: Made in Ecuador, Undercut by China*, REUTERS, Feb. 5, 2007, http://www.reuters.com/article/email/idUSN2324082420070205?pageNumber=2&virtualBrandChannel=0; Panama Hatworks of Montecristi, How Panama Hats Are Made, http://www.panamas.biz/tour.html (last visited Mar. 14, 2010) [hereinafter Panama Hatworks]; MILLER, *supra* note 14, at 36; Ecuador.us, Montecristi, Ecuador, Panama Hats, http://www.ecuador.us/montecristi.htm (last visited Mar. 14, 2010) [hereinafter History of Hatmaking].

[17] Panama Hatworks, *supra* note 16.

[18] *Id.*

from the villages surrounding Montecristi.[19] There, expert weavers create intricate spiral patterns outward from the center of the crown of an eventual hat.[20] In order to prepare the finest hats, the weavers spend their early mornings and evenings in a darkened hut, as the afternoon sunlight, heat, and humidity can damage the delicate *toquilla* fibers.[21]

The hats do not have seams; artisans weave the edges back into the brim rather than cutting and sewing them taut like many imitation hats from other regions of the world.[22] The tightness of the weave determines the quality of the hat.[23] A true *montecristi* is woven so finely that it can hold water, can be folded for storage without damage, and is flexible enough to pass through a ring.[24] The best hats, deemed *superfinos,* have 1600 to 2000 weaves per square inch[25] and cost up to $500.[26] The weaving process can take months or years to complete for the finest *superfino montecristis.*[27]

After the weavers complete their role, a middleman transports the unfinished hats to factories, usually located in city distribution centers such as Cuenca and Quito.[28] These hatmakers, often doubling as distributors who sell to international retailers, pound the rudimentary hats into their distinctive shape and iron them smooth with old fashioned cast irons or mechanical presses.[29] Then they dye the hats, decorate them with assorted ribbons and bands, and make arrangements to ship those being exported to international retailers, such as Christie's of London.[30] A hat retailing for $500 in Ecuador can triple in value at an upscale U.S. or European department store.[31]

---

[19] History of Hatmaking, *supra* note 16.

[20] Panama Hatworks, *supra* note 16; PALMERLEE ET AL., *supra* note 11, at 206, 298.

[21] Weitzman, *supra* note 11; Panama Hatworks, *supra* note 16.

[22] PALMERLEE ET AL., *supra* note 11, at 206, 298; History of Hatmaking, *supra* note 16.

[23] Panama Hatworks, *supra* note 16.

[24] Oliver, *supra* note 16.

[25] *Id.*

[26] Weitzman, *supra* note 11.

[27] Panama Hatworks, *supra* note 16.

[28] *Id.*

[29] *Id.*

[30] *Id.*; Oliver, *supra* note 16.

[31] Weitzman, *supra* note 11.

C.　Threats to the Ecuadorian Hatmaking Industry

Two generations ago, over 2000 master weavers crafted *montecristis*.[32] Today, only about twenty master hatmakers remain in business.[33] Younger generations of coastal Ecuadorians refuse to learn the trade due to the immense patience needed and the meager profit margin.[34] They are leaving the area in search of more lucrative, steady, and fast-paced work.[35] If the international community does not support the older generation of Montecristi hatmakers and commit to preserving the art form, either through IP regulation or other channels, a distinct part of Ecuadorian culture will be lost forever.[36] As one hat historian noted, "The internet and the rise of the global market should have been the saviour of the Panama. Instead, globalisation appears about to seal its fate: most experts agree that within 20 years an Ecuadorean will weave the last-ever traditionally made Panama hat."[37]

In Ecuador, as in many developing countries, profits from skilled labor are not reaching the creators of the art form proportionately. Ecuadorian distributors (who stamp, iron, dye, and finish the hats), transportation carriers and other types of middlemen, customs officials, Western governments who collect import taxes, and retailers receive a disproportionate share of the profits from *montecristis*. While Ecuador only exports 1/10 of 1 percent of the global market for straw hats,[38] its entire economy only amounts to $107.7 billion.[39] According to these figures, about forty weavers in small villages in Ecuador are creating the hats that account for roughly 2.4 percent of the country's entire GDP, yet these weavers live in abject poverty without electricity and running water.

China is the biggest threat to Ecuadorian weavers, supplying roughly 40 percent of the worldwide "Panama hat" market.[40] As the world's top "straw" hat producer, China generates an export revenue totaling $1 billion per year from the production of *montecristi*-style hats.[41] Chinese weavers usually

---

[32] Weitzman, *supra* note 11; Panama Hatworks, *supra* note 16.

[33] Panama Hatworks, *supra* note 16.

[34] Oliver, *supra* note 16.

[35] Weitzman, *supra* note 11.

[36] *Id.*; Panama Hatworks, *supra* note 16.

[37] Weitzman, *supra* note 11.

[38] *Id.*

[39] CIA World Factbook: Ecuador, https://www.cia.gov/library/publications/the-world-factbook/geos/ec.html (last visited Jan. 31, 2010).

[40] *Id.*; Oliver, *supra* note 16.

[41] Oliver, *supra* note 16.

make their versions out of paper. However, without quality controls such as IP labels, few customers are able to discern the difference.[42]

III. EXPLANATION OF GEOGRAPHICAL INDICATIONS

A. *The Role of the WTO and TRIPS*

The WTO is an organization comprised of 153 nation states that creates international trade policy,[43] binds member states to multilateral legal trade agreements, and facilitates the registration of international intellectual property protections.[44] During the 1986–1994 Uruguay Round of the WTO, member countries led by the United States drafted TRIPS in recognition of the imbalanced IP protections available to and within WTO member states.[45] The TRIPS requires states to afford and enforce a minimum level of protection to the foreign-registered intellectual property rights within their borders through internal systems of IP.[46] Because TRIPS is a trade instrument foremost, rather than a human rights agreement, it has faced significant criticism for intensifying economic polarization and cultural homogenization.[47]

B. *Definition*

TRIPS defines geographical indications as "indications which identify a good as originating in the territory of a member state, or a region or locality in that territory, where a given quality, reputation or other characteristic of

---

[42] *Id.*

[43] *See* John W. Head, *Throwing Eggs at Windows: Legal and Institutional Globalization in the 21st Century Economy*, 50 U. KAN. L. REV. 731 (2002); Final Act Embodying the Results of the Uruguay Round of Multilateral Trade Negotiations, Apr. 15, 1994, arts. VI, IX, s. 1, 33 I.L.M. 1125 (1994) [hereinafter Final Act], *available at* http://www.wto.org/english/docs_e/legal_e/04-wto.pdf.

[44] Final Act, *supra* note 43, art. II, s. 2; WTO, Intellectual Property, *supra* note 4. Protections under TRIPS include copyright, trademarks, geographical indications, industrial designs, patents, layout-designs of integrated circuits, and trade secrets, among others. *Id.* These protections mirror the goals of WIPO, which generally allows developing countries to play a greater role and assert more control in treaty negotiations and outcomes than the WTO. *See* Fryer, *supra* note 5, at 175; WIPO, WIPO Administered Treaties, http://www.wipo.int/treaties/en/ (last visited Jan. 31, 2010).

[45] WTO, Intellectual Property, *supra* note 4; WTO, Understanding the WTO: Members and Observers, http://www.wto.org/english/thewto_e/ whatis_e/tif_e/org6_e.htm (last visited Jan. 31, 2010) [hereinafter WTO, Members and Observers]; World Health Organization [WHO], WTO and the TRIPS Agreement, http://www.who.int/medicines/areas/policy/wto_trips/en/index.html (last visited Jan. 31, 2010).

[46] WTO, Members and Observers, *supra* note 45.

[47] *See generally* Chakravarthi Raghavan, *Human Rights Experts for WTO, IMF Bank Reforms*, THIRD WORLD NETWORK, http://www.twnside.org.sg/title/experts.htm; Jagdish Bhagwati, *Reshaping the WTO*, FAR E. ECON. REV., Jan.–Feb. 2005, *available at* http://time.dufe.edu.cn/wencong/bhagwati/FEERFinal.pdf.

the good is essentially attributable to its geographical origin."[48] A stamp, logo, symbol, or other notice to the consumer is placed on the good to certify that it is from a specific geographical location, possesses certain qualities, or enjoys a certain reputation as a result of its origin or production location.[49] For example, champagne, a registered GI, is a well known example of a sparkling wine from the specific region of the same name in France.[50] Sparkling wine from Spain cannot be called champagne in the European Union, but is instead called *cava.*[51]

C.   *TRIPS Minimum Standards*

While TRIPS sets out minimum standards for its signatories, it does not mandate that WTO members enact a specific GI system in their national laws.[52] Members may utilize any one or combination of the following methods that coincide with national laws to protect GIs: *sui generis* legislation or decrees, a GI register, unfair competition laws, tort law, certification marks, and extensions of trademark law.[53] With respect to GIs, TRIPS dictates only that:

> Members shall provide the legal means for interested parties to prevent: (a) the use of any means . . . that indicates or suggests that the good in question originates in a geographical area other than the true place of origin . . .; (b) any use which constitutes an act of unfair competition . . . A Member shall . . . refuse or invalidate the registration of a trademark which contains or consists of a geographical indication with respect to goods not originating in the territory indicated, if use of the indication in the trademark for such goods in that Member is of such a nature as to mislead the public as to the true place of origin.[54]

---

[48] Agreement on Trade-Related Aspects of Intellectual Property Rights, Apr. 15, 1994, Marrakesh Agreement Establishing the World Trade Organization, Annex 1C, arts. 22–23, Legal Instruments—Results of the Uruguay Round, 33 I.L.M. 1197 (1994) [hereinafter TRIPS Agreement], *available at* http://www.wto.org/english/docs_e/legal_e/27-trips.pdf.

[49] WIPO Guide, *supra* note 8, at 85.

[50] Justin Hughes, *Champagne, Feta, and Bourbon: The Spirited Debate About Geographical Indications,* 58 Hastings L.J. 299, 369 (2006).

[51] *Id.*

[52] TRIPS Agreement, *supra* note 48.

[53] *Id.*

[54] *Id.*

Thus, Articles 22–24 of TRIPS aim to prevent unfair competition and to protect against false or misleading labels, the registration of GIs as trademarks, and passing off of generic terms as GIs.[55]

Parties who wish to register GIs in WTO member states cannot do so for generic products or products similar to those already in widespread use.[56] A term used for a well known local specialty in one country may identify a product known by a generic term in another.[57] For example, *parmigiano* cheese in Italy is generically known as parmesan cheese in Australia and the United States, resulting in limited IP protection in these countries.[58] The criteria for GI registration require that the label protect communities of producers within a given country, rather than individuals.[59] These requirements complement the community values present in many traditional cultures.

WTO developing and "least-developed" countries (thirty-two countries, mostly from Africa)[60] can self-identify to garner "special and differential treatment" under TRIPS.[61] Special treatment includes "provisions in some WTO Agreements which provide developing countries with longer transition periods before they are required to fully implement the agreement" and assistance with technology, legal counsel, and policymaking.[62] In practice, however, these benefits are not guaranteed because the preference-giving country decides which of these services will be extended.[63]

---

[55] David Snyder, *Enhanced Protections for Geographical Indications Under TRIPS: Potential Conflicts Under the U.S. Constitutional and Statutory Regimes*, 18 FORDHAM INTELL. PROP. MEDIA & ENT. L.J. 1297, 1300 (2008).

[56] Rodrigo Velasco, *Geographical Indications in Chile and Latin America*, INT'L TRADEMARK ASS'N ANN. MEETING REP. 2 (2008).

[57] WIPO, About Geographical Indications, http://www.wipo.int/geo_indications/en/about.html (last visited Jan. 31, 2009) [hereinafter About Geographical Indications]; Peter Gumbel, *Food Fight!*, TIME, Aug. 31, 2003, *available at* http://www.time.com/time/magazine/article/0,9171,48 0249-1,00.html.

[58] Gumbel, *supra* note 57, at 2.

[59] WIPO GUIDE, *supra* note 8, at 86.

[60] WTO, Grappling with 99 Proposals, http://www.wto.org/english/thewto_e/minist_e/min03_e/ brief_e/brief21_e.htm (last visited Jan. 31, 2010).

[61] *Id.*

[62] *Id.*

[63] WTO, Who Are the Developing Countries in the WTO?, http://www.wto.org/english/tratop_e/ devel_e/d1who_e.htm (last visited Jan. 31, 2010).

D.   Appellations of Origin and Denominations of Origin

While the WTO uses the GI label, the terms Appellations of Origin ("AO") and Denominations of Origin ("DO")[64] are encompassed under the concept of GI, and normally refer to a narrower geographic region than GIs.[65] These labels denote that a product's uniqueness is "exclusively or extensively attributable to a combination of human and natural factors characteristic of a geographic region."[66] As early as 1935, the French created the AO label to protect the reputation of their wine varieties.[67] The AOs, just like GIs, have most commonly been applied to agricultural products such as liquors (e.g., tequila), cheeses (e.g., feta), and cured meats (e.g., parma ham),[68] but are expanding to traditional crafts as well.

IV.   APPLYING GIS TO THE MONTECRISTI CASE

On February 15, 2005, a cooperative of *toquilla* (palmetto fiber) artisans filed a petition for GI registration with the Ecuadorian Institute of Intellectual Property ("IEPI").[69] The cooperative alleged that its style of straw hat was the product known on the international market as the "Montecristi."[70] The cooperative also claimed that the community of Montecristi was responsible for the esteemed reputation of the straw hats produced in the surrounding areas of the Manabí province since 1630 and the proliferation of the *montecristi* name worldwide.[71] As such, they argued that the cooperative and other community members from the region surrounding the Manabí province town of Montecristi should be the only parties afforded use of the label, barring its use in Ecuador by hatmakers from other provinces and from countries such as China.[72]

---

[64] "Denominación de Origen" is the actual term used by the Ecuadorian Institute of Intellectual Property in the Montecristi Case to refer to the principle of GI. *See* Montecristi Resolution, *supra* note 7. Since GI is more widely accepted in the international community, including the WTO and WIPO, it is employed throughout this Note for clarity.

[65] *See* WIPO GUIDE, *supra* note 8, at 74–75.

[66] *Geographical Indications: From Darjeeling to Doha*, WIPO MAG., July 2007 [hereinafter *From Darjeeling to Doha*], *available at* http://www.wipo.int/wipo_magazine/en/2007/04/article_00 03.html.

[67] Gumbel, *supra* note 57, at 2; About Geographical Indications, *supra* note 57.

[68] *Famous Appellations of Origin*, WIPO MAG., Dec. 2008, *available at* http://www.wipo.int/ wipo_magazine/en/2008/06/article_0009.html.

[69] Montecristi Resolution, *supra* note 7.

[70] *Id.*

[71] *Id.*

[72] *Id.*

Various hat export companies and weavers, mostly from the Ecuadorian city of Cuenca, filed oppositions to the petition based on five main points.[73] They asserted that: 1) the name "Montecristi," as used to describe the hats, was not attributable to any natural factor of the named location;[74] 2) the names "Panama Hat" and "Montecristi" are generic terms used to describe straw hats of the fedora shape and style made throughout Ecuador;[75] 3) their companies, located in the southern province of Azuay, were the major producers and exporters of the hats, and had developed the hats' reputation and worldwide demand;[76] 4) their hats were of comparable or superior quality to those from the Manabí province; and 5) IEPI should extend the AO label to all hatmakers in Ecuador rather than limiting it to those in the areas surrounding Montecristi.[77]

The IEPI laid out the test that to register a product for GI status in Ecuador, the moving party must demonstrate "a legitimate interest" in the designation and be a "natural or juridical person . . . directly engaged in the extraction, production, or manufacturing of the product sought to be protected."[78] As Ecuador is a party to the WTO, these requirements meet the WTO's standards.

After hearing the expert testimony of hatmakers who conducted an extensive physical inspection of the raw materials, manufacturing facilities, and final products from both regions, IEPI determined that the "Montecristi" met the test for a GI.[79] The *montecristi* straw hat was recognized as the first registered GI in Ecuador on August 22, 2008.[80] The IEPI ruled that human and natural factors had created a superior material and process for hatmaking unique to the area surrounding Montecristi.[81] First, the oscillating warm, humid climate, ranging between twelve and fifteen degrees Celsius during the winter and twenty and twenty-two degrees Celsius during the summer, contributes to the quality of the fibers.[82] Similarly, the Manabí region's location at 300 meters above sea level creates a fertile soil rich in salt and limestone that nurtures the *toquilla* plant.[83] Finally, the fragile leaves of

---

[73] *Id.*

[74] Montecristi Resolution, *supra* note 7.

[75] *Id.*

[76] *Id.*

[77] *Id.*

[78] *Ecuador*, 98 TRADEMARK REP. 456, 456 (2008).

[79] *Id.*; Montecristi Resolution, *supra* note 7.

[80] *See* Montecristi Resolution, *supra* note 7.

[81] *Id.*

[82] *Id.*

[83] *Id.*

the Montecristi region's *toquilla* plant, with stems over a meter long and a centimeter in diameter, are physically distinguishable from those that grow in the Cuenca region.[84] The IEPI also emphasized the importance of human factors involved in the Montecristi hatmaking process by noting that locals have passed down the time honored techniques since 1630.[85]

The law in Ecuador is surprisingly progressive in recognizing the GI label for goods other than liquor, food, and agricultural products; the IP systems of many industrialized nations have yet to widen the GI's application. Article 364 of the Ecuadorian Intellectual Property Law and Article 176 of *el Estatuto del Régimen Jurídico Administrativo de la Función Ejecutiva* both dictate that the GI label can apply to a wide array of agricultural, artisanal, and industrial products.[86] The progressive definition laid out in the statute played a major role in IEPI's decision to register the *montecristi* as the first Ecuadorian GI.

V.   THE INTERNATIONAL TRIPS DEBATE

The Ecuadorian view on GIs coincides with the current position of the WTO[87] and European Union, which recognize a wide variety of products eligible for GI protection.[88] Both perspectives diverge dramatically from the U.S. position, which restricts GI use to wine and spirits.[89] Other registered GIs in Latin America that have gained global fame, namely *tequila* and *pisco*, undoubtedly paved the way for the acceptance of the *montecristi* GI.[90] While this Note advocates for the EU position of expanding GI protections so that rich cultural traditions in developing countries can survive, it also recognizes that creative legislative solutions posed by both the European Union and United States can serve as models of how to incorporate GI protections into existing legal frameworks.

A.   The EU Position

The concept of expanded GI protection suits the European Union as a coalition of countries with distinct identities that unite for trade and currency advantages, yet retain the rich and distinct cultural heritages of individual

---

[84] Montecristi Resolution, *supra* note 7.

[85] *Id.*

[86] *Id.*

[87] Ecuador joined the WTO on January 21, 1996. WTO, Members and Observers, *supra* note 45.

[88] *See Ecuador, supra* note 78, at 456.

[89] *Id.*

[90] Velasco, *supra* note 56, at 6–11.

member states.[91] Such cultural power draws tourists to the European continent each year and fuels sales of exported products.[92] In the European Union, GI protection is an ideal means to both protect regional cultures and increase profits for local businesses.[93] It makes sense that the European Union advocates for increased GI protections because it has realized the marked economic value of protective labels for commercial goods. However, the increased GI protection it promotes may disadvantage individual countries that have less developed marketing programs and produce lesser known specialty products. This group includes many emerging economies.

TRIPS members aligned with the European Union "include Bulgaria, Guinea, India, Jamaica, Kenya, Madagascar, Mauritius, Morocco, Pakistan, Romania, Sri Lanka, Switzerland, Thailand, Tunisia, and Turkey."[94] These countries see an increased level of protection as a way to improve marketing strategies with name recognition, and object to other countries usurping their stamps and labels.[95] Rather than amend the TRIPS agreement, the group proposes that members submit GIs to a voluntary database registry.[96] This proposal requires participating countries to consult the registry before approving a GI for national protection while encouraging, but not requiring, abstaining members to consult it.[97]

B.   The U.S. Position

Curiously, transitioning and developing countries such as Argentina, Chile, Colombia, the Dominican Republic, Ecuador, El Salvador, Guatemala, Honduras, Panama, Paraguay, the Philippines, and Taiwan support the U.S. position.[98] The United States warns that providing enhanced protection would disrupt the current trademark registries of many WTO member states and would hurt the existing marketing strategies of specialty goods producers.[99] As a "melting pot" country that has used many European GIs as

---

[91] Eva Gutierrez, *Geographical Indicators: A Unique European Perspective on Intellectual Property*, 29 HASTINGS INT'L & COMP. L. REV. 29, 29 (2005).

[92] *Id.* at 39.

[93] *Id.* at 38; *see also IP Rights Help Crafts Exporters, supra* note 8; J. Sai Deepak Iyer, *GIs, Traditional Handicrafts and Incentives for Individual Innovations*, SPICY IP, Feb. 14, 2008, *available at* http://spicyipindia.blogspot.com/2008/02/gis-traditional-handicrafts-and.html.

[94] TRIPs: Geographical Indications, Background and the Current Situation, World Trade Organization, http://www.wto.org/english/tratop_e/TRIPs_e/gi_background_e.htm (last visited Jan. 31, 2010) [hereinafter GI Background].

[95] Snyder, *supra* note 55, at 1297.

[96] GI Background, *supra* note 94.

[97] *Id.*

[98] GI Background, *supra* note 94.

[99] Snyder, *supra* note 55, at 1303.

generic names for decades, the United States rejects a shift toward greater protection of GIs.[100] It cautions against the overuse of GIs, fearing that such use will lead to the dilution of the concept and the weakening of the rights that registration brings.[101] The United States also argues that GI expansion will further impede free trade and amount to unfair competition, or in extreme cases, nontariff barriers.[102] This view reflects the belief of many U.S. economists that free market economics should control all international commercial goods transactions.[103] GIs lend themselves to the concept of community property, which strongly conflicts with capitalist theory that individualized incentives drive progress.[104]

C.   *TRIPS Criticisms*

Developing countries make up two-thirds of the WTO.[105] As previously discussed, many critics of the WTO fault TRIPS for being innately biased in favor of member states and obstructing non-party developing countries from exercising their cultural rights.[106] Since developed countries and WTO member states must have trademarks registered in their home countries to apply for protections internationally, they have an unfair advantage over countries that are not members or that have not begun to utilize IP law.[107] Because of the "first in time, first in right" principle upon which the United States bases IP law, some countries strategically register a food or good to block other interested parties from future GI registration, even if they do not have a tenable interest in the name, stamp, or mark.[108]

---

[100] WTO, Intellectual Property, *supra* note 4.

[101] *See* Arun S, *GI Protection in India: A Time to Introspect?*, Fin. Express, Aug. 31, 2008, *available at* http://www.financialexpress.com/news/GI-protection-in-India-A-time-to-introspect/355400. GIs registered in India from 2007 to 2008 include "'Muga Silk' from Assam, 'Madhubani paintings' from Bihar, . . . and 'Cora Cotton' from Tamil Nadu," among others. *Id.*

[102] *See* Hughes, *supra* note 50, at 302, 334 (summarizing the different attitudes towards GI regulation).

[103] *See generally* Adam Smith, An Inquiry into the Nature and Causes of the Wealth of Nations (Edwin Cannan, ed., Methuen and Co., Ltd., 5th ed. 1904) (1776); Steven D. Levitt & Stephen J. Dubner, Freakonomics (2005).

[104] *See* Levitt & Dubner, *supra* note 103.

[105] WTO, Members and Observers, *supra* note 45.

[106] *See generally* Ian F. Fergusson, World Trade Organization Negotiations: The Doha Development Agenda (Cong. Research Serv., CRS Report for Congress Order Code RL32060, Aug. 18, 2008), *available at* http://italy.usembassy.gov/pdf/other/RL32060.pdf [hereinafter Doha Agenda]; Martin Khor, *Rethinking Liberalisation and Reforming the WTO*, Third World Network, June 28, 2000, http://www.twnside.org.sg/title/davos2-cn.htm.

[107] *See* Anup Shah, *The WTO and Free Trade*, Global Issues, http://www.globalissues.org/article/42/the-wto-and-free-trade (last visited Jan. 21, 2010).

[108] *Id.*

Another criticism of TRIPS and IP law in general is that they reallocate critical capital from developing countries to copyright, trademark, and patent owners in developed countries.[109] Critics also fault TRIPS with creating an artificial scarcity of technology and innovation, to the detriment of citizens in developing countries.[110] This is especially true of medicine that does not reach developing countries because of pharmaceutical patents.[111]

While the aforementioned criticisms of TRIPS have merit, the decision whether or not to join the WTO, and thus agree to TRIPS, is beyond the scope of this Note. Many developing countries feel that the trade benefits of WTO membership outweigh their reservations about TRIPS, and have become signatories. These countries should utilize the full benefits of TRIPS in the same way that advanced economies use it until the international community reforms the global system. When properly utilized, the GI provisions of TRIPS can be interpreted not as repressive, but instead as potentially empowering to developing countries.

As the Montecristi Case illustrates, artisans in developing countries can use GIs as a marketing tool to compete in a profitable niche market of commercial artisanal products. GIs can bring much needed capital to traditional artisans in communities around the globe "because of the intrinsic characteristics of GIs and the specific agricultural policy of some developing countries based on small-scale and traditional methods of rural production."[112] Indeed, one scholar remarked that "traditional products and names [add] value . . . and by giving international name recognition to a community, [GIs] can play a minor role but nevertheless important role in bolstering the rural areas where the majority of people live."[113]

There are few foreseeable downsides to the GI provisions of TRIPS under the present state of global wealth distribution since the buyers of cultural commercial crafts are predominantly tourists from developed countries. However, the greatest problem lies in securing the financial resources to monitor and enforce consequences for misuse of registered GIs.[114] Enhanced protection of GIs will require "the establishment, at least at the state level, of an expensive system of policing that enhances the protection to all products and of quality-control in order to guarantee the consistent quality that is the

---

[109] *Id.*

[110] *Id.*

[111] *See* DOHA AGENDA, *supra* note 106, at 17.

[112] Fusco, *supra* note 6 at 244; *see also* Marsha A. Echols, *Geographical Indications for Food, TRIPs, and the Doha Development Agenda*, 47 J. AFR. L. 1999, 211–12 (2003).

[113] Fusco, *supra* note 6, at 244 (quoting W. Can Caenegem, *Registered GIs: Intellectual Property, Agricultural Policy and International Trade*, 26 E.I.P.R. 170, 175 (2004)).

[114] *Id.*

most important element of the entire system."[115] Similarly, acquiring and defending IP rights requires access to information, legal representation, and financial resources, which may be beyond the reach of many communities in developing countries.[116] If more resources can be devoted to implementation and monitoring costs, the playing field will become fairer and the criticisms about the WTO as they relate to GIs will recede.

The growing organic food market illustrates the market impact of consumer loyalty on specialty products.[117] Consumers of organic food remain "very committed" to products despite the global recession.[118] "Even if organic products are perceived as difficult to find and expensive, most consumers judge them positively."[119] In Germany and the U.K., for example, one report indicated that consumers associate organic products with a healthy lifestyle and seek out products that reflect and promote that value.[120]

Similarly, if consumers view traditional crafts as promoting cultural preservation and craftsmanship, all else being equal, they should buy those goods over the imitation versions. Most consumers would choose to buy a slightly more expensive *montecristi* over the Chinese paper version if they knew it was a superior product and played a small role in the tradition and development of Ecuador, notwithstanding a modest price increase. The extent to which the consumer is willing to pay a premium is a crucial marketing inquiry that should be conducted by each producing community.

VI.   GI USE IN DEVELOPING COUNTRIES

A.   India

India has embraced the use of GI protection in general and for traditional artisanal products.[121] Between January and May 2008 alone, eighteen of the

---

[115] *Id.*

[116] DARRELL A. POSEY & GRAHAM DUTFIELD, BEYOND INTELLECTUAL PROPERTY: TOWARD TRADITIONAL RESOURCE RIGHTS FOR INDIGENOUS PEOPLES AND LOCAL COMMUNITIES 76 (1996).

[117] Nigel Hunt & Brad Dorfman, *How Green Is My Wallet? Organic Food Growth Slows*, REUTERS, Jan. 28, 2009, *available at* http://www.reuters.com/article/idUSTRE50R01C20090128.

[118] *Id.*

[119] Raffaele Zanoli & Simona Naspetti, *Consumer Motivations in the Purchase of Organic Food: A Means-end Approach*, BRITISH FOOD J. 1 (2002), *available at* http://www.emeraldinsight.com/Insight/viewContentItem.do?contentType=Article&contentId=870658.

[120] *Id.*

[121] Iyer, *supra* note 93; S. C. Srivastava, *Protecting the Geographical Indication for Darjeeling Tea*, *in* MANAGING THE CHALLENGES OF WTO PARTICIPATION: 45 CASE STUDIES (2005), *available at* http://www.wto.org/english/res_e/booksp_e/casestudies_e/case16_e.htm; Gladys Mirandah, *India: The Indian Perspective on GIs*, MANAGING INTELL. PROP., July/Aug. 2008, http://www.managingip.com/Article/1968978/The-Indian-perspective-on-GIs.html.

twenty-two newly registered GIs went to traditional craft products:[122] "The registration is the first milestone to begin international branding of the state handicrafts and ensuring genuine as well as superior quality of craft merchandise for the consumers. The step will ensure the good standard of these handicraft goods and would enhance their prestige in domestic and international market[s]."[123] The Indian government expected a 15 to 20 percent increase in the export market in 2008 as a result of GI registration.[124] These numbers clearly highlight the benefits of GI use.

GI registration is a marketing innovation learned from the example of Indian Darjeeling tea, which experienced global fame and skyrocketing sales after registering for GI protection in 2001.[125] Since the demand for Darjeeling Tea is now five times more than what India can supply,[126] several other countries are controversially filling the demand.[127]

The law on GIs in India, the Geographical Indications of Goods (Registration and Protection) Act, came into force on September 15, 2003.[128] Since then, eighty-three GIs have been registered and applications have been filed for thirteen more.[129] Whereas from September 2003 to March 2007 only thirty GIs were registered, thirty-one were registered from April 2007 to March 2008 alone.[130] Eighteen of twenty-two GI registrations in 2008 have gone to handicraft products.[131] The following excerpt describes how India has been using GI registration to protect and promote its exports:

> Developed nations around the world have created the infrastructure by which their intellectual property is safeguarded very well. In order to remain competitive and to prevent the loss of its own properties, India must build similarly strong systems. The nature of international agreements has created a strange beast—the trade

---

[122] Arun S, *supra* note 101.

[123] *Pashmina and Kani Shawl Accorded Registration under GI*, ONE INDIA, Oct. 19, 2008, *available at* http://news.oneindia.in/2008/10/19/pashmina-and-kani-shawl-accorded-registration-under-gi-1224412334.html.

[124] *Id.*

[125] *See generally* Sudhir Ravindran & Arya Mathew, *The Protection of Geographical Indication in India—Case Study on 'Darjeeling Tea,'* in PROPERTY RIGHTS ALLIANCE, INTERNATIONAL PROPERTY RIGHTS INDEX: 2009 REPORT 58–64 (2009), *available at* http://www.internationalpropertyrightsindex.org/atr_Final1.pdf.

[126] Arun S, *supra* note 101.

[127] *Id.*

[128] *Id.*

[129] *Id.*

[130] *Id.*

[131] Arun S, *supra* note 101.

agreements tend to define the nature of trade, rather than the other way around. Because there was a process by which the Basmati [rice] patent could be awarded to an American company, and because India had not engaged that process fully and vigorously, the export of 45,000 tonnes[sic] of Basmati was suddenly under threat. The economic security of Indians lies in identifying our rightful geographic indications, and in remaining vigilant about potential abuses of these rights by competitors.[132]

B.   Mexico

Mexico also benefits economically and culturally from GI protection.[133] The 1991 Law for the Promotion and Protection of Industrial Property enables GI protection through two complimentary concepts of IP: AOs and collective marks.[134] The AOs have been protected in Mexico in a limited capacity since 1976, but Article 156 establishes the current definition of AO to comply with WIPO's Lisbon Agreement for the Protection of Appellations of Origin and their International Registration.[135] It defines the AO as "the name of a geographical region of the country which serves to designate a product originating therein, the quality and characteristics of which are due exclusively to the geographical environment, including natural and human factors."[136] Artisans who meet these requirements and register are permitted to use the AO label. Alternatively, a collective mark is "the distinctive sign which is intended to distinguish the origin or any other common characteristic of products that have been produced or manufactured by a group of persons in a particular locality, region or country."[137] Groups of producers, manufacturers, or merchants who wish to distinguish their products from those in the greater region may register to use a collective mark.[138]

---

[132] Meena Shelgaonkar, *A Patent for Everybody,* INDIA TOGETHER, Nov. 2001, *available at* http://indiatogether.com/economy/trade/articles/gi.htm.

[133] *Id.*

[134] Esperanza Rodríguez Cisneros, Address at WIPO Symposium on the International Protection of Geographical Indications: The Protection of Geographical Indications in Mexico 2 (Nov. 28, 2001), *available at* http://www.ompi.ch/edocs/mdocs/geoind/en/wipo_geo_mvd_01/wipo_geo_mvd_01_7.pdf.

[135] *Id.*

[136] *Id.*

[137] *Id.*

[138] *Id.*

Tequila became the first registered Mexican AO in 1977.[139] Because tequila is made from the agave cactus, a plant native to only some regions of Mexico, only five states hold the right to produce this liquor.[140] A report by WIPO reveals that "the sale of tequila has seen an 83 percent increase in the past five years" because of AO use.[141] The tequila industry provides direct employment to over 36,000 Mexicans.[142]

Furthermore, two traditional handicrafts are currently registered in Mexico: *Talavera* pottery and *Olinalá* lacquered wood products.[143] *Talavera* is a type of colorful glazed ceramic earthenware manufactured using raw materials from the zone of Talavera de Puebla, Mexico.[144] *Olinalá* wood products are lacquered in layers using a centuries-old technique, and are painted in bright colors with a fine brush.[145] Based on the success of tequila and India's example, such traditional handicrafts will see increased profits in coming years as a result of AO registration.

VII. THE BENEFITS OF GIS AND OTHER IP PROTECTIONS

In their book *Beyond Intellectual Property: Toward Traditional Resource Rights for Indigenous Peoples and Local Communities*, Darrell Posey and Graham Dutfield underscore just how important IP protection can be for traditional communities:

> Traditional communities may have their own concepts of intellectual property and resource rights. However, industrializing countries are under political pressure to adopt the European and North American concepts of intellectual property, which, by guaranteeing the right of legal individuals to profit from their innovations, are widely believed to promote development. IPR laws have usually been inimical to the interests of indigenous communities, but there are ways in which these laws can serve the interests of these communities.[146]

---

[139] Gutierrez, *supra* note 91, at 45.

[140] WIPO GUIDE, *supra* note 8.

[141] Gutierrez, *supra* note 91, at 45.

[142] *Id.*

[143] Cisneros, *supra* note 134, at 3.

[144] *Id.*; May Herz, *Arts and Handicrafts: Talavera Pottery*, INSIDE MEXICO, http://www.inside-mexico.com/art1.htm (last visited Jan. 31, 2010).

[145] Crafts from Olinalá, Baalart, http://baalart.com/tienda/crafts-from-olinala-/cat_2.html (last visited Jan. 31, 2010).

[146] POSEY & DUTFIELD, *supra* note 116, at 75.

As WIPO has stated, IP law is founded partially on policy concerns for consumer protection, property rights, and economic efficiency.[147] In a world without IP protections, sellers, artists, and artisans would have little incentive to invest in quality controls or take steps to build a professional reputation.[148] WIPO contends that "any region that has a specialty associated with it, where a quality link exists or can be established between the product and the region, should consider the advantages of using a geographical indication to distinguish its products from lower-quality, non-regional competitors."[149] Thus, GIs, as a faction of IP law, both protect the artisan's investment in his or her ideas and human capital, and protect the consumer from deceptive marketing practices and inferior products.[150]

Since consumers view GI registration as an indication of quality, these labels help consumers build confidence in the product and an allegiance to it. Marketing studies show that once a craft is GI-protected, consumers' interest piques, demand increases, and consumers are likely willing to pay more for the product.[151] In addition to profits, the advantage for the producer is continued patronage and consumer loyalty.[152] A recognizable label that symbolizes a quality reputation can be the most valuable asset that a business possesses.[153]

Besides product recognition and quality, consumers often have another reason for choosing a product: the product represents a social status, style, way of life, or a set of ideas with which they want to be associated.[154] Apple Computer, Inc. is a prime example of this phenomenon.[155] For many customers, the appeal of an Apple laptop or iPod is not for the product itself, but for the association with an image and brand that "denotes a hip and modern lifestyle."[156] This same principle can be applied to GIs. When a consumer buys a product from a particular region, he or she might not only be targeting a certain type of tradition, but also the elite image that the GI

---

[147] Snyder, *supra* note 55, at 1304.

[148] Gutierrez, *supra* note 91, at 44.

[149] *Id.*

[150] Snyder, *supra* note 55, at 1305.

[151] *See generally* WIPO Guide, *supra* note 8.

[152] *Id.*; Gutierrez, *supra* note 91, at 31.

[153] *See generally* WIPO Guide, *supra* note 8.

[154] *Id.*

[155] Gutierrez, *supra* note 91, at 30; *see also* Rob Walker, *The Guts of New Machine*, N.Y. Times, Nov. 30, 2003, *available at* http://www.nytimes.com/2003/11/30/magazine/30IPOD.html?page wanted=1 (attributing the iPod's iconic status to a combination of aesthetic and structural factors of the device itself, as well as the brand's association with innovation and creativity).

[156] Gutierrez, *supra* note 91.

represents.[157] As previously mentioned, many world leaders and celebrities have worn *montecristis* throughout history. This rich history can undoubtedly contribute to the value of authentic *montecristis*.

Furthermore, GIs can fuel grassroots economic development.[158] GIs promote more than the interest of one specific seller or company—they promote the whole geographic community where a product is produced. As prosperity comes to the region due to a collective effort, the community inevitably builds cohesion. This is especially true of Montecristi hatmakers and other artisans because the process is too labor-intensive and specialized for a small group of people to complete alone. Only the combined efforts of harvesters, *toquilla* preparers, weavers, transporters, stampers, and exporters introduce hats on a global or even local scale. Through this ethos of communal cooperation, impoverished communities can work to build the local economy and preserve culture.

If governments in developing countries do not educate themselves about this emerging body of IP law and act prudently, they could lose the invaluable cultural knowledge that enriches both the countries' identity and economic stability. Registration of trademarks, copyrights, and GIs alike creates a "race to the courthouse" dynamic because IP rights are based on the principle of first in time, first in right.[159] Worse still, other countries and cultures can take credit for the traditional products, as the situation in Africa illustrates:

> The African continent is endowed with a diversity [sic] in areas of agriculture, natural resources, culture and traditions, which qualify as Geographical Indications . . . The potential though enormous has not been tapped and the custodians of such GIs languish in abject poverty. Where African products have come out distinctively in the world market, their reputation has always been abused by middlemen who ride on it and even register the products as theirs [sic] own. The geographical indication is a new concept in African countries, which if properly introduced, developed and widely published could benefit African farmers and craftsmen to market their products.[160]

---

[157] *Id.*

[158] *Id.*

[159] *See generally* INTA, Protection of Geographical Indications and Trademarks (Sept. 24, 1997), http://www.inta.org/index.php?option=com_content&task=view&id=242&Itemid=153&getcontent=3.

[160] Agnes Nyaga, VP of Origin for Africa, Presentation at the World Trade Organization Roundtable on Geographical Indications: The Geographical Indication Protection Africa Perspective (May 27, 2004), *available at* http://www.wto.org/english/tratop_e/dda_e/symp04_paper_nyaga_e.doc.

The good news for cultural handicrafts is that with globalization comes greater visibility and the opportunity to learn about foreign cultures and traditions. "According to recent WTO data, developing countries saw their share in world merchandise trade rise sharply in 2004 to 31 percent, the highest since 1950, and developing countries command now almost 20 percent of world exports."[161] The findings from a recent World Bank study "suggest that the biggest developing country winners from the Doha Round overall will be: Brazil, Argentina, other Latin American, India, Thailand and South Africa, along with some others in southern Africa. Notably, the Bank found that the rest of sub-Saharan Africa gains when . . . developing countries participate as full partners in the negotiations."[162]

Culture can be an economic asset.[163] GIs can help preserve the cultural heritage of a geographical area. Strong traditions and cultural knowledge are potentially two of developing countries' most valuable assets. Marketing commercial items that reflect these traditions is less exploitive than the sale of developing countries' other assets, such as natural resources and labor. Consumers will pay for culture, art, and the chance to own a piece of history in the form of a traditional craft. History has shown that some cultures will become extinct if developing countries do not find a way to safeguard their cultural heritage.

VIII. CONCLUSION

To preserve and fund the continuance of their priceless artisanal goods and traditional knowledge, developing countries must empower themselves through the use of IP law. GI use is one way to do so, but some countries have taken alternative routes to cultural preservation, such as Traditional Cultural Expression Law,[164] Traditional Knowledge Law, and Cultural Property Law. Whatever the method employed, IP law can help a developing country maintain its cultural and artistic integrity as it goes through stages of economic development and can actually fuel that development by garnering greater profits for artisans who often make up a disproportionate role in the GDP of their countries. GIs alone are not sufficient to maintain the cultural traditions and traditional handicrafts of developing countries in

---

[161] Facts on the Doha Round: Expanding Markets to Promote Development and Growth, Office of the United States Trade Representative (May 27, 2004), *available at* http://www.fas.usda.gov/ITP/WTO/hongkong/whitehouseDohafactsheet.pdf.

[162] *Id.*

[163] *See generally* CHRIS HAYTER & STEPHANIE CASEY PIERCE, NAT'L GOVERNORS ASS'N, CTR. FOR BEST PRACTICES, ARTS & THE ECONOMY: USING ARTS AND CULTURE TO STIMULATE STATE ECONOMIC DEVELOPMENT (2009), *available at* http://www.nga.org/Files/pdf/0901ARTSAND ECONOMY.PDF.

[164] For a more in-depth analysis of the potential relationship between traditional knowledge and GIs, see Daniel Gervais, *Traditional Knowledge: Are We Closer to the Answer(s)? The Potential Role of Geographical Indications*, 15 ILSA J. INT'L & COMP. L. 551 (2009).

the era of globalization, but they do effectively supplement other sustainable development channels and should be utilized to the greatest possible extent.

[32]

The Journal of World Intellectual Property (2010) Vol. 13, no. 2, pp. 81–93

doi: 10.1111/j.1747-1796.2009.00382.x

Incentives for and Protection of Cultural Expression: Art, Trade and Geographical Indications

Anselm Kamperman Sanders
Maastricht University

After the adoption of the Universal Declaration of Cultural Diversity, the interaction between the protection of traditional cultural expressions (TCEs) and geographical indicators (GIs) is an interesting one. The capacity of a geographical indication of origin to create a global market with local control over brand, quality and methods of production seems to make it immensely suitable for preservation of cultural diversity. Since the Agreement on Trade-Related Aspects of Intellectual Property Rights does not limit the potential causes of action for the unauthorized use of GIs, the tort of misappropriation may be applied in relation to TCEs. In order to reconcile intellectual property rights with non-Western belief systems, application of the tort of misappropriation, unjust enrichment and the remedy of restitution may make enforcement of GIs in relation to TCEs more palatable than other forms of protection.

Keywords geographical indications; culture; unfair competition; misappropriation

In the Preamble of the 2001 Universal Declaration of Cultural Diversity (UNESCO Convention), the United Nations Educational, Scientific and Cultural Organization (UNESCO) defined the concept of culture as follows:

> Culture should be regarded as the set of distinctive spiritual, material, intellectual and emotional features of society or a social group, and that it encompasses, in addition to art and literature, lifestyles, ways of living together, value systems, traditions and beliefs (UNESCO, 2001, Preamble, fn. 2).

The UNESCO Convention entered into force on 18 March 2007 and provides a framework for states to engage in protective measures to safeguard the diversity of cultural expressions against the influences of globalization and free trade.

Trade in cultural expressions is of prime importance for cultural industries that wish to export products embodying cultural expression freely across the globe, yet many states wish to reduce the influence of foreign culture and rather stimulate their own. To that end, many countries have in place, legitimately or not (Van den Bossche, 2007), systems to protect predominantly domestic cultural values against the onslaught of popular cultural goods and services, such as Hollywood movies, books, television programmes, musical recordings, video games and online content. These systems comprise direct subsidies,[1] import restrictions, tax rebates, screen quotas,[2] licensing restrictions, price fixing, limits on foreign investment and foreign

Anselm Kamperman Sanders   Incentives for and Protection of Cultural Expression

ownership, nationality requirements, domestic content requirements and intellectual property protection. Striking in this respect is the practice of siphoning off a percentage of the revenue of mandatory collecting rights societies for domestic artists and production. Copyright holders, foreign or domestic, will not receive the full proceeds of the secondary use rights of their works, but the collecting rights society rather acts as an organizer or sponsor of domestic cultural events, or "financial coach" of individual members.[3]

Unlike the protective measures for the protection of cultural expression described above, this contribution will discuss more free trade-oriented methods of stimulating and protecting localized art and cultural expression by means of the intellectual property system. The focus is on the use of geographical indications (GIs) to create a differentiated market for cultural expressions with localized characteristics and on the possibilities available under the Agreement on Trade-Related Aspects of Intellectual Property Rights (TRIPS Agreement) and Paris Convention for the Protection of Industrial Property (Paris Convention)[4] to use unfair competition law as a means to augment a GI-type protection for traditional knowledge and cultural expressions with the doctrinal basis to act against misappropriation.

GIs as a Model for Protecting Cultural Expressions?

Most commonly associated with wines, cheeses and other agricultural products, GIs are known to be powerful marketing tools that enable consumers to differentiate between goods and make rational choices about price, quality and product characteristics (Akerlof, 1970). GIs may indicate a country, region, locality, city, or even an address from which a product or service emanates. Like a trademark, GIs are signs whose function (Maniatis and Kamperman Sanders, 1993) is to provide information and protect its owner. GIs indicate the precise geographical origin and denote a quality or reputation that results from that place of origin of a product. According to Kretschmer (2003), GIs are eminently suitable for citizens from developing nations to experiment individually or collectively with accessing global markets. Asserting one's position on a global market through branding encapsulating local products and its associated knowledge on production and cultural expression may lead to self-discovery and a restatement and even preservation of traditions. The creation of value in the minds of those expressing culture and in the marketplace is conducive to the protection of cultural diversity, as market differentiation, even in purely economic terms, increases consumer welfare. Its abilities to engender collective stakeholdership, the connection to a certain place or locality, and differentiating characteristics, make GIs eminently suitable to play a role in the protection, not only of a market in traditional cultural expressions (TCEs), but also of TCEs and cultural diversity itself.

In spite of the fact that the international definition of what exactly constitutes a GI is not uniform, the question whether TCEs can be protected by GIs has been convincingly answered affirmatively by Zografos (2006). The Paris Convention covers two notions of GIs: "indications of source or appellations of origin",[5] which

Incentives for and Protection of Cultural Expression   Anselm Kamperman Sanders

are further defined by the Madrid Agreement for Repression of False and Deceptive Indications of Source of Goods (Madrid Agreement)[6] and the Lisbon Agreement for the Protection of Appellations of Origin and their International Registration (Lisbon Agreement). It is of importance to realize that the notion of "appellation" covers names, whereas "indication" also comprises drawings, photos, national emblems, flags or even symbolism.

The Madrid Agreement indicates that "indications of source" denote that a product or service originates from a certain area, country, region or locality. According to the Lisbon Agreement, "appellation of origin" covers a "geographical name of a country, region, or locality, which serves to designate a product originating therein, the quality and characteristics of which are due exclusively or essentially to the geographical environment, including natural and human factors".[7]

In the European Union (EU), GIs are protected on the basis of Council Regulation 510/2006/EC,[8] which offers protection to GIs of agricultural products and foodstuffs.[9] It employs other definitions. Whereas the definition of designation of origin[10] corresponds largely with those of the Lisbon Agreement, the definition of "geographical indication"[11] raises the threshold for appellations of origin.

The TRIPS Agreement has yet another definition in article 22, which defines GIs as "indications which identify a good as originating in the territory of a member, or locality in that territory, where a given quality, reputation or other characteristic of the good is essentially attributable to its geographic origin". Although similar to the definition in the Council Regulation, the notion of "indication" is wider than that of "name", and its overall scope is somewhat wider (Gervais, 1998, pp. 123–5; Stewart, 1993). The crucial aspect of the definition of GIs in the TRIPS Agreement is the requirement that the goods to be covered have a quality or characteristic that derives from the place of origin and cannot have been derived from another place.

Whatever the definition in various international agreements, however, it is clear that within the context of the TRIPS Agreement, GIs can be used for price discrimination, but also for the bundling of local knowledge through a localized organization of producers. Unlike a trademark, which can be transferred freely, irrespective of the locality in which production takes place, the link between the product and its geographical origin furthermore ensures that the geographical indication is tied to a locality and controlled locally.

The TRIPS Agreement does not specify by which method World Trade Organization (WTO) members have to protect GIs. This can be done through a *sui generis* GI protection regime, or through use of trademark and certification marks. Trade and certification mark systems can be relied upon for applications, registrations, oppositions, cancellations, adjudication and enforcement through national trademark regimes (Bengedkey and Mead, 1992; McCarthy, 1998–2009, pp. 19–32; Pollack, 1962). A system like this meets the requirements for national treatment and TRIPS Agreement enforcement requirements in tandem with the national trademark regime. The disadvantage, however, is clear to see. Although

Anselm Kamperman Sanders   Incentives for and Protection of Cultural Expression

such multiple registration may not be a problem for strong entities or regions which have considerable economic power,[12] smaller and poorer regions or municipalities may have greater difficulty and the cost of undertaking the task of registering in numerous countries.

The system of protection by means of a *sui generis* GI system is different in nature. GIs are territorial in the sense that they are recognized in and by the jurisdiction where the area or locality lies that they are related to. The feature of territoriality is both its strength and its weakness. Legal protection is granted in a local territory, but like any IP right, it is territorial and confined to its national jurisdiction. International conventions are commonly used to remedy this territorial feature. The key idea is that once a GI is recognized by the government in one country, other members to an international agreement will recognize the right in the GI too. The scope of protection for GIs found in the TRIPS Agreement encompasses two levels of protection that tailor for the protection of GIs as indicators of consistent quality and an enhanced protection enabling product differentiation (Kamperman Sanders, 2005). The aforementioned local control on a territorial connection explains why at the fifth session of the World Intellectual Property Organization (WIPO) Intergovernmental Committee on Intellectual Property and Genetic Resources, Traditional Knowledge and Folklore,[13] the point was made that TCE's that can be qualified as goods, such as handicraft items, can also be protected by GIs. In this instance, a GI can be affixed to a product that is made from natural resources or through knowledge held by an indigenous group. Furthermore, some TCEs consisting of names, signs or other indications can themselves serve as GIs. It is then interesting to look at the scope of protection that GIs enjoy.

Integrity of Information

The prohibited acts described in article 22(2) of the TRIPS Agreement encompass misleading use of GIs "by any means in the designation or presentation of a good that indicated that the good in question originates in a geographical area other than the true place of origin" and acts of unfair competition as defined under article 10*bis* of the Paris Convention.[14] Through this provision, article 22(2) not only covers misleading allusions to or connotations of origin by use of both words and graphics, but also covers the use of a GI on goods of low(er) quality emanating from the proper geographical area. Article 22(4) extends this protection to a case of use of GIs that, although correct, do not correspond with the geographical indication commonly understood to produce the goods with the special qualities in question, or although factually correct do not correspond with consumer expectations about origin and quality. Usually this situation arises in those cases where the same name exists in different territories, or when a description is used that is likely to confuse the consumer as to the geographical area from which the product is commonly understood to come from, like: "Parma cheese produced in America" (Baeumer, 1999, p. 17).

Article 22(2) protection is designed to safeguard that the consumer receives accurate information that enables him to differentiate between products emanating from the designated area from substitute products from outside the designated area. As indicators of quality, GIs provide information that help consumers make choices and reduce risk, or differently put: "If he [the consumer] is interested in origin, it is normally because origin imports an expectation about some quality" (Cornish and Phillips, 1982, p. 43). When the integrity of this information is tampered with, so as to render it incomplete or deceptive, this leads to market failure and welfare loss. Akerlof (1970) succinctly depicts the breakdown in the market when the consumer cannot trust the information about the product he wishes to purchase. The consumer will then prefer to buy goods of lower quality until—as in a vicious circle—the only goods available will be those of the lowest quality. Article 22(2) and 22(4) therefore also leans against allusions to a geographical indication or connotations in writing and image that distort the conveyance of correct information.

The inclusion of actions against unfair competition under article 10*bis* of the Paris Convention in GIs protection, however, means that the potential scope of protection is not limited to confusion, but also extends to concepts such as dilution, the depreciation of goodwill or reputation, or even attempts to derive an undeserved benefit from a GI. The doctrine of unfair competition may be internationally recognized by its inclusion in article 10*bis* of the Paris Convention, but a national comparison shows a wide diversity of forms of implementation (Kamperman Sanders, 1997; Ohly, 1995; de Very, 2005) albeit all with the aim to strike a balance between fairness and freedom in competition. It is this general and elastic principle that provides the courts with the possibility to award protection to the fruits of someone's ingenuity, skill, or labour on a case-by-case basis. This need for elasticity means that it is not possible to encapsulate all unfair acts in statutory provisions (Sell, 1958). Two main approaches for giving effect to the obligations of article 10*bis* of the Paris Convention can be discerned, namely protection on the basis of general provisions in a civil code, or enacted legislation on unfair competition (WIPO, 1994). Despite all examples of unfair behaviour provided for by article 10*bis* of the Paris Convention itself, or national legislation, there is always a residual category of "unfair commercial practices" that may be covered by a general clause. Here judges have to draw the line between what is fair and unfair in the marketplace (Ohly, 1995). The United Kingdom, however, has chosen to give effect to the obligations of the Paris Convention in relation to specific heads of interest under the law of passing off, injurious falsehood, or trade secrets only (Graf von Westerholt and Gysenberg, 1981), rather than "under a wide generalisation".[15] Still, once a specific head of interest can be defined, the law of passing off has shown to be flexible as well (Wadlow, 1995). In defining a head of interest for the protection of TCEs, however, one has to be conscious of the fact that indigenous peoples may have a different value system and often regard traditional knowledge and cultural heritage as "deeply personal and spiritual", a resource not subject to exploitation and misappropriation (Conway-Jones, 2005, p. 3). In the context of article 10*bis* of the Paris Convention, the concept of protection of misappropriation is

Anselm Kamperman Sanders   Incentives for and Protection of Cultural Expression

also present. It is not clearly exemplified, but is nevertheless capable of offering a protective measure against the usurpation of intellectual assets that may be considered as the property or quasi-property of another (Kamperman Sanders, 1997). In this respect, the concept of misappropriation can be used to prevent someone from passing off one's own goods as those from someone else (Cornish and Llewelyn, 2003, pp. 593 *et seq.*), but also from "reaping where he has not sown" in the sense of the landmark case *International News Service v Associated Press*.[16] This is not so much a form of assertion of an exclusive right of property, but the protection against usurpation or unjust enrichment (Callmann, 1942). When tied to and limited by geographical factors, such as land and human involvement, unjust enrichment may just be enough to create head of interest that merits protection for TCEs. If one limits the remedy for unjust enrichment to restitution of what one has gained at the expense of another, the scope of protection against misappropriation of TCEs will furthermore not be overbroad.

Product Differentiation

Article 23 of the TRIPS Agreement is limited in application to wines and spirits, but offers a wider scope of protection. There is no need for the consumer to be misled or proof that certain behaviour constitutes an act of unfair competition. The burden of proof is not as high. For wines and spirits this additional protection translates into the possibility to protect GIs even when the consumer is not confused. A prohibition of use of expressions such as "kind", "type" or "style" in relation to a GI reflects that the purpose for the protection lies in the safeguarding of a particular production technique or product characteristic and may even be used to protect a GI against the dilution of a reputation for superior quality. As such, article 23 protection may be used to facilitate product differentiation and would ideally enable producers in a designated geographical area to set higher prices, produce more, and preserve those traditional methods of production and levels of high quality that result from sustained investment, enable start-up industries to develop innovative production techniques, or enable producers to make the transformation from local to global markets.

Still, it is important to realize that there are limitations to article 23 protection. Through article 24(4), existing use of a GI is preserved and generic terms are excluded from protection. Apart from formal limitations there is also a real-life limitation in economic terms. For a GI to derive real benefit from this level of enhanced protection, investment in advertising and marketing is a must. Reputation needs time to develop. In this respect, some authors (Hausman and Rodrik, 2002) emphasize that the key to economic development is learning what one is good at producing.

Traditional Knowledge and Cultural Expressions

At an international level, the discussion on extending the protection of GIs to encompass traditional knowledge and cultural expressions has predominantly focused on biopiracy issues and the protection of genetic resources (Rafi Communique, 1994). Protection of traditional cultural expressions is, however, also part of the ongoing discussion in the context of the so-called development agenda at WIPO and the TRIPS Agreement discussions at the WTO (Kamperman Sanders, 2005; 2007). Although the discussion on these issues is often conducted in parallel, it is clear that different forms of protection for traditional knowledge need to be considered (Correa, 2001). Concerns over biopiracy, misappropriation of genetic resources and benefit sharing arrangements demand measures in the regulatory sphere of sovereignty and public international law.[17] Protection of cultural expressions calls for different measures, a private property IP regime that is shaped by local mores, endorsed by the state, recognized internationally, and one which provides incentives for innovative approaches to preservation and marketing of traditional knowledge and culture. The question then is whether to do this through *sui generis* systems or through traditional IP tools. It is here that developed and developing countries do not see eye to eye.[18]

Intellectual property law is commonly designed to provide incentives to create, rather than to preserve. For traditional cultural expressions, this means that a supportive legal regime should not exclusively focus on the act of creation. Finding novel ways of expressing traditional culture is an act of creation in and by itself, but this is different to the fostering of innovative approaches to preservation, and marketing of traditional knowledge and culture is more related to marketing and channelling revenues into traditional modes of production (Weeraworawit, 2003, p. 159). It is here that a system akin to those protecting GIs may be considered for the protection of TCEs. GIs are sustainable over a long period of time, even into perpetuity for as long as a particular method of production is maintained. A GI is also not reliant on concepts such as novelty or originality, like patent or copyright systems are. As such a GI would seem ideally suited as an example for the protection of traditional knowledge and cultural expressions. GIs serve to instil value in a sign that encapsulates locally produced goods containing unique geographical ingredients or produced with localized human knowledge. Protecting TCEs as GIs may not protect the knowledge encapsulated in the product *per se*, in fact the knowledge remains in the public domain. However, an entitlement is created that permits the holders of the right to protect not only a sign, but also a connection with or even paternity to the product that is the TCE. This is where the aforementioned concept of misappropriation may play an important role, so in the next section some practical examples will be provided. First, however, the issue of recognition of TCEs as GIs has to be further explored.

Qualifying for Protection

The issue of recognition domestically and internationally is a hotly contested issue in the area of standard GIs, so this issue will also be of concern for protection of TCEs. In essence all IP rights are territorial and it would be up to the nation state to decide whether "Cultural Expressions" would be recognized and what the criteria are. Then international protection would have to be ensured. In 2005, the EU submitted a proposal under the Doha Round at the WTO on a multilateral register for GIs, introducing a legally binding system requiring member states to report their GIs to the WTO. This multilateral register would also have to cover agricultural products and handicrafts. Recently, during the WTO Trade Negotiations Committee meetings in May and June 2008,[19] this proposal was modified to entail a register in which GI holders can publish their GIs multilaterally for notification, but would have to go through the national register of each country to obtain legal protection. The WTO registration would have the purpose of providing evidence of the claim to the GI. Most notably, this would be that the indication is not generic, for if it is, it must be excluded from protection under articles 22 and 23 of the TRIPS Agreement. Once the GI, or for that matter a "Cultural Expression", is notified to the WTO, this could lead to protection in other member states, either through an automatic recognition (like in the Lisbon Agreement system), or through a national recognition of the WTO notification.

Which TCEs should, however, qualify for protection? The combined rationale for protection of GIs, traditional knowledge and cultural expression already provides an indication for the type of requirements that should be used by national governments in order to describe which products or productions fall within the protected category, just like Parma Ham, Champagne, or Port wine, the method of production, or the form of the cultural expression. If one only looks at India one can think of folk dances like Bhangra of the Punjab, Bihu of Assam etc., or theatre like the oldest surviving theatre traditions of the world, the 2000-year-old Kutiyattam of Kerala. The advantage of a GI-type system is clear to see. Since there is no prohibition against using the Kutiyattam itself as inspiration for new development in theatre, there would be a prohibition against using the term Kutiyattam in relation to theatre that does not adhere to the prescribed "ingredients" of a Kutiyattam play. Not to be allowed to use the component parts (story line, narrative, characters, symbolism, music) of Kutiyattam would go too far for a Westerner placing value on progress and innovation. According to WIPO (2001, p. 25), traditional knowledge includes "tradition based literary, artistic and scientific works, performances, inventions, scientific discoveries, designs, marks, names and symbols, undisclosed information and all other tradition-based innovations and creations resulting from intellectual activity in the industrial, scientific, literary or artistic field". Yet when it comes to traditional knowledge, holistic notions of knowledge and indigenous expressions often sit uneasy with the liberties that modern business takes with what indigenous peoples perceive to be sacred (Antons, 2005). It is in this context that the concept of misappropriation is useful. If, for example, Maori patterns are used for tattoos of persons who have not earned the tribal right to wear them, both the tattoo artist and the wearer have misappropriated the imagery (Gray, 2005).

Incentives for and Protection of Cultural Expression   Anselm Kamperman Sanders

The remedies for misappropriation of TCEs can mostly be restitutional. Any benefit that has passed from the claimant to the enriched must then be restored. Admittedly, given the more or less permanent nature of the tattoo, this example presents problems. Financial compensation may be in order if corrective tattooing or laser-removal treatment is not deemed appropriate. In other cases of misappropriation, however, handing over infringing goods and corrections in the media may be sufficient.

Conclusion

In a globalizing world the preservation of cultural diversity has become a prime concern. Intellectual property rights, traditionally used to foster innovation, can also be used for the purpose of preservation. A GI-type protection for traditional knowledge and cultural expressions with the doctrinal basis to act against misappropriation may offer a way forward in reconciling local traditional knowledge and belief systems with Western notions of property.

About the Author

Anselm Kamperman Sanders, is a Professor of Law and Director of the Masters Intellectual Property Law and Knowledge Management (LLM/MSc) at Maastricht University, the Netherlands, and Academic Director IEEM Intellectual Property Law School, Macau SAR, China; e-mail: *a.kampermansanders@pr.unimaas.nl*

Notes

1 For Europe, Eurimages fund, Council of Europe, Resolution (88) 15 of 16 October 1988, Media Plus, Decision 2000/821/EC of the Council of 20 December 2000 on Media Plus—development, distribution and promotion; and Decisions 613/2001/EC of the European Parliament and the Council of 19 January 2001 on MEDIA training. For Canada, see the Department of Canadian Heritage website for a number of measures benefitting Canadian publishers and music, film, and multimedia producers [online]. Available at ⟨http://www.pch.gc.ca⟩ [Accessed July 2009].

2 See, for example, the quota system for foreign broadcasts in the Television Without Frontiers Directive 89/552/EEC, which was adopted in 1989, revised in 1997 by Directive 97/36/EC and in 2007 to become the Audiovisual Media Services Directive 2007/65/EC.

3 See, for example, the website of BUMA/Stemra, a Dutch collecting society for music [online]. Available at ⟨http://www.bumastemra.nl⟩ [Accessed July 2009]. The society runs a social fund that provides loans, donations, pension plans and insurance for individual music authors who are members and a cultural fund that promotes Dutch music as a product by organizing, financing and subsidizing numerous events nationally and internationally. Similar arrangements are available for authors, performing artists, music publishers, producers and distributors of music, film and interactive software, photographers, editors, translators, etc.

Anselm Kamperman Sanders   Incentives for and Protection of Cultural Expression

4 Paris Convention for the Protection of Industrial Property of 20 March 1883, as revised at Brussels, 1900, Washington, 1911, The Hague, 1925, London, 1934, Lisbon, 1958, and Stockholm, 1967, and as amended on 2 October 1979.

5 Article 10 of the Paris Convention, on False Indications of Source of Goods.

6 Madrid Agreement for the Repression of False or Deceptive Indications of Source on Goods of 14 April 1891, as revised at Washington 1911, The Hague, 1925, London, 1934, and Lisbon, 1958.

7 Article 2 of the Lisbon Agreement for the Protection of Appellations of Origin and their International Registration of 31 October 1958, as revised at Stockholm, 1967, and as amended on 28 September 1979.

8 Replacing Regulation 2081/92/EEC, as amended by Council Regulation 692/2003.

9 Regulation 510/2006/EC of 20 March 2006 on the protection of geographical indications and designations of origin for agricultural products and foodstuffs was implemented following the WTO panel reports in United States (WT/DS174) and Australia (WT/DS290), adopted by the DSB on 20 April 2005. The new Regulation extends the protection available for EU geographical indications to foreign geographical indications, without requiring an equivalent and reciprocal level of protection offered to EU geographical indications by the foreign government. Non-EU producers wishing to apply for protection of their geographical indication may furthermore apply directly to the commission, rather than having to address their own national government.

10 Regulation 2081/92/EEC, article 2(2)(a) designation of origin means the name of a region, a specific place or, in exceptional cases, a country, used to describe an agricultural product or a foodstuff:
   - originating in that region, specific place or country and
   - the quality or characteristics of which are essentially or exclusively due to a particular geographical environment with its inherent natural and human factors, and the production, processing and preparation of which take place in the defined geographical area.

11 Regulation 2081/92/EEC, article 2(2)(b) geographical indication means the name of a region, a specific place or, in exceptional cases, a country, used to describe an agricultural product or a foodstuff:
   - originating in that region, specific place or country and
   - which possesses a specific quality, reputation or other characteristics attributable to that geographical origin and the production and/or processing and/or preparation of which take place in the defined geographical area.

12 *Vide* Champagne or Roquefort.

13 See Document WIPO/GR TKF/IC/5/3, 52.

14 Paris Convention, article 10*bis*—Unfair Competition
   (1) The countries of the Union are bound to assure to nationals of such countries effective protection against unfair competition.
   (2) Any act of competition contrary to honest practices in industrial or commercial matters constitutes an act of unfair competition.
   (3) The following in particular shall be prohibited:
   1. all acts of such a nature as to create confusion by any means whatever with the establishment, the goods, or the industrial or commercial activities, of a competitor;

Incentives for and Protection of Cultural Expression   Anselm Kamperman Sanders

2. false allegations in the course of trade of such a nature as to discredit the establishment, the goods, or the industrial or commercial activities, of a competitor;

3. indications or allegations the use of which in the course of trade is liable to mislead the public as to the nature, the manufacturing process, the characteristics, the suitability for their purpose, or the quantity, of the goods.

15 *Victoria Park Racing and Recreation Grounds Co. v Taylor* (1937) 58 CLR 479; see in this respect also *Mogul Steamship Co. v McGregor Gow & Co.* (1889) 23 QBD 598 at 625–6; and *Hodgkinson & Corby Ltd and Roho Inc. v Wards Mobility Services Ltd* (1995) FSR 169 per Jacob J.: "There is no tort of copying. There is no tort of taking a man's market or customers. Neither the market nor the customers are the plaintiff's to own. There is no tort of making use of another's goodwill as such. There is no tort of competition".

16 248 US 215 (1918).

17 For a repository of articles on this issue see the website available at ⟨http://www.iprsonline.org/resources/tk.htm⟩ [Accessed July 2009].

18 See country positions submitted to the 11th Inter Governmental Conference (IGC) meeting held from 3 to 12 July 2007 in Geneva at the WIPO.

19 See Document TN/C/W/52 of 19 July 2008, available from documents online at ⟨http://www.wto.org⟩ [Accessed July 2009].

References

Akerlof, G. (1970) 'The Market for "Lemons": Quality Uncertainty and the Market Mechanism', *Quarterly Journal of Economics*, 84(3), 488–500.

Antons, C. (2005) 'Traditional Knowledge and Intellectual Property Rights in Australia and Southeast Asia', in C. Heath and A. Kamperman Sanders (eds.), *New Frontiers of Intellectual Property Law*. Hart Publishing, Oxford, pp. 37–52.

Baeumer, L. (1999) 'Protection of Geographical Indications under WIPO Treaties and Questions Concerning the Relationship between those Treaties and the TRIPS Agreement' in 'Symposium on the Protection of Geographical Indications in the Worldwide Context', WIPO publication No. 760(E), proceedings of symposium held in WIPO, Geneva, Egez, Hungary, 23–25 October 1997.

Bengedkey, L. and Mead, C. (1992) 'International Protection of Appellations of Origin and Other Geographical Designations of Regional Origin Under the Lanham Act', *Trademark Reporter*, 82, 765–792.

Callmann, R. (1942) 'He Who Reaps Where He Has Not Sown: Unjust Enrichment in the Law of Unfair Competition', *Harvard Law Review*, 55, 595–614.

Conway-Jones, D. (2005) 'Safeguarding Hawaiian Traditional Knowledge and Cultural Heritage: Supporting the Right to Self-determination and Preventing the Commodification of Culture', *Howard Law Journal*, 48, 737–762.

Cornish, W. and Llewelyn, D. (2003) *Intellectual Property: Patent, Copyright, Trade Marks and Allied Rights*, 5th edition. Thomson Sweet & Maxwell, London.

Cornish, W. and Phillips, J. (1982) 'The Economic Function of Trade Marks: An Analysis with Special Reference to Developing Countries', *International Review of Industrial Property and Copyright Law*, 13, 41–64.

Correa, C. (2001) *Traditional Knowledge and Intellectual Property—Issues and Options Surrounding the Protection of Traditional Knowledge* [online]. QUNO. Available at

⟨http://www.quno.org/geneva/pdf/economic/Discussion/Traditional-Knowledge-IP-English.pdf⟩ [Accessed April 2009].

de Very, R. (2005) *Towards a European Unfair Competition Law*. Koninklijke Brill, Leiden.

Gervais, D. (1998) *The TRIPS Agreement. Drafting History and Analysis*. Sweet & Maxwell, London.

Graf von Westerholt, H. and Gysenberg, H. (1981) 'Vereinigtes Königreich von Großbritannien und Nordirland, Part VI, in E. Ulmer (ed.), *Das Recht des unlauteren Wettbewerbs in den Mitgliedstaaten der EWG*. Carl Heymanns Verlag, Köln.

Gray, E. (2005) 'Maori Culture and Trade Mark Law in New Zealand', in C. Heath and A. Kamperman Sanders (eds.), *New Frontiers of Intellectual Property Law*. Hart Publishing, Oxford, pp. 71–96.

Hausman, R. and Rodrik, D. (2002) 'Economic Development As Self-Discovery', National Bureau of Economic Research Working Paper 8952 [online]. Available at ⟨http://ksghome.harvard.edu/ ~ .drodrik.academic.ksg/papers.html⟩[Accessed April 2009]

Kamperman Sanders, A. (1997) *Unfair Competition Law—The Protection of Intellectual and Industrial Creativity*. Clarendon Press, Oxford.

Kamperman Sanders, A. (2005) 'Future Solutions for Protecting Geographical Indications Worldwide', in C. Heath and A. Kamperman Sanders (eds.), *New Frontiers of Intellectual Property Law*. Hart Publishing, Oxford, pp. 133–48.

Kamperman Sanders, A. (2007) 'The Development Agenda for Intellectual Property', in C. Heath and A. Kamperman Sanders (eds.), *Intellectual Property and Free Trade Agreements*. Hart Publishing, Oxford, pp. 3–26.

Kretschmer, M. (2003) 'The Economics of Geographical Indications', in 'Queen Mary and Fordham University NY Joint Seminar Series', proceedings of a conference held in Barbican, London, November 2003 (unpublished).

Maniatis, S. M. and Kamperman Sanders, A. (1993) 'A Consumer Trade Mark: Protection based on Origin and Quality', *European Intellectual Property Review*, 11, 406–415.

McCarthy, J. (1998–2009) *McCarthy on Trademarks and Unfair Competition*, 4th edition. West Publishing, New York.

Ohly, A. (1995) *Richterrecht und Generalklausel im Recht des unlauteren Wettbewerbs*. Carl Heymanns Verlag, Köln.

Pollack, L. (1962) 'Roquefort—An Example of Multiple Protection for a Designation of Regional Origin Under the Lanham Act', *Trademark Reporter*, 52, 755–67.

Rafi Communique (1994), 'Bioprospecting-Biopiracy and Indigenous Peoples' [online], November. Available at ⟨http://www.rafiusa.org⟩ [Accessed July 2009].

Sell, E. (1958) 'The Doctrine of Misappropriation in Unfair Competition. The Associate Press Doctrine after Forty Years', *Vanderbilt Law Review*, 11, 483–500.

Stewart, T. (1993) *The GATT Uruguay Round, A Negotiating History*. Kluwer Law International, The Hague.

United Nations Educational, Scientific and Cultural Organization (2001) Universal Declaration on Cultural Diversity. Available at ⟨http://www.unesco.org⟩ [Accessed July 2009].

van den Bossche, P. (2007) *Free Trade and Culture: A Study of Relevant WTO Rules and Constraints on National Cultural Policy Measures*. Boekmanstudies, Amsterdam.

Wadlow, C. (1995) *The Law of Passing-off*. Sweet and Maxwell, London.

Weeraworawit, W. (2003) 'International Legal Protection for Genetic Resources, Traditional
    Knowledge and Folklore: Challenges for the Intellectual Property System', in C.
    Bellmann, G. Dutfield and R. Meléndez-Ortiz (eds.), *Trading In Knowledge:
    Development Perspectives on Trips, Trade and Sustainability*. Earthscan Publications,
    London, pp. 157–65.
World Intellectual Property Organization (1994) *Protection against Unfair Competition*.
    World Intellectual Property Organization, Geneva.
World Intellectual Property Organization (2001) *Report on Fact-Finding Missions on
    Intellectual Property and Traditional Knowledge*. World Intellectual Property
    Organization, Geneva.
Zografos, D. (2006) 'Can Geographical Indications be a Viable Alternative for the Protection
    of Traditional Cultural Expressions?', in F. Macmillan and K. Bowrey (eds.), *New
    Directions in Copyright Law*, Vol. 3, Edward Elgar, Cheltenham, pp. 37–55.

[33]

Prometheus
Vol. 29, No. 3, September 2011, 253–267

RESEARCH PAPER

The mismatch of geographical indications and innovative traditional knowledge

Susy Frankel*

Faculty of Law, Victoria University of Wellington, New Zealand

This article is about how geographical indications (GIs) cannot deliver the protection for traditional knowledge that indigenous peoples seek. There are three broad ways in which the protection of geographical indications appears to offer the possibility of providing legal mechanisms to protect traditional knowledge. These are the collective nature of the protection, the indefinite availability of the GI and the connection that GI owners perceive between their products and their land. Those seeking protection of traditional knowledge also seek a collective and an indefinite interest and frequently the relationship between their knowledge and the land is important for indigenous peoples. Yet, these similarities are superficial. GIs protect names and are used by Western farmers and sometimes rural communities to promote their products. This article concludes that GIs cannot deliver the protection that indigenous peoples seek in order to benefit from their traditional knowledge.

Introduction

There have been many suggestions that geographical indications (GIs) can and should provide some kind of protection for traditional knowledge (Downes, 2000; Blakeney, 2009; Gervais, 2011). The central rationale behind such suggestions is a view that GIs and traditional knowledge have features and even aims in common (Downes, 2000, pp.269–73). One feature that GIs and traditional knowledge share is that they have both become topics over which there is considerable debate in international intellectual property law. The two areas have become intertwined at a political level. This paper discusses the way in which the political debate has linked GIs and traditional knowledge. In addition to, and possibly as a development of, this political relationship there are thought to be several substantive similarities between the two areas. These similarities are, broadly, three. Firstly, GIs provide a potentially indefinite form of protection and those who seek protection for traditional knowledge also seek a kind of indefinite protection. Secondly, there can be a collective interest in GIs because they provide more than one trader with the right to use a GI. Indigenous peoples regard any interest in their traditional knowledge as a collective interest. Thirdly, GIs are frequently justified by a relationship between the land and the use of the GI, referred to as the *terroir*. Many traditional knowledge claimants also speak of how their knowledge comes from and is related to the land. The paper discusses these similarities and concludes that they are superficial

---

*Email: susy.frankel@vuw.ac.nz

ISSN 0810-9028 print/ISSN 1470-1030 online
© 2011 Taylor & Francis
http://dx.doi.org/10.1080/08109028.2011.629872
http://www.tandfonline.com

similarities, insufficient to support the suggestion that GIs could play a major role in the protection of traditional knowledge. In reality, GIs protect only a name, usually of geographic origin, associated with a product.[1] The static nature of GIs is explained.

The paper looks at what some proponents of traditional knowledge, particularly indigenous peoples, seek to protect and analyses how that is quite different from the rationales and aims of GIs. In particular, a major aspect of the protection that indigenous peoples seek is not necessarily exclusivity over any kind of knowledge, but some kind of control over innovative uses of traditional knowledge, in order to benefit from those uses. Even in circumstances where traditional knowledge holders seek protection of a name, a GI may not be useful unless the traditional knowledge holder has an established business. GIs, at least in Europe, function to support a particular type of agriculture. They do not function to support innovative agricultural method, but rather to preserve existing agricultural traditions and to incentivise the continuance of those traditions. Those seeking to protect traditional knowledge do not use the same approach to incentives. In contrast, traditional knowledge is often innovative and it also has the capacity to contribute to innovation. The paper considers the effects of the mismatch of GIs and traditional knowledge, and concludes that geographical indications are, therefore, the wrong vehicle to protect most traditional knowledge and particularly innovative traditional knowledge.

The international linkage between protection of traditional knowledge and geographical indications

Internationally, there is considerable disagreement over the parameters of protection of both GIs and traditional knowledge. These difficulties take different forms. The difficulty for traditional knowledge is that many are opposed to its protection altogether. Geographical indications offer a degree of internationally-agreed protection. The disagreement centres on how far this protection should expand.

The call for protection of traditional knowledge arises largely because developing countries and indigenous peoples have found that the developed world freely uses indigenous peoples' knowledge, and its associated cultural outputs or genetic resources, without any benefits necessarily flowing back to the source of that knowledge (Roht-Arriaza, 1996; Downes, 2000, pp.276–80). Additionally, the developed world's version of protection of intellectual property, exemplified in the standards of the Agreement on Trade-Related Aspects of Intellectual Property Rights (TRIPS Agreement), protects developed world knowledge assets and treats indigenous traditional knowledge as free for all to use. Global trade has exacerbated this imbalance in the protection of knowledge assets.

Some of the objections that those in the business of intellectual property make against the protection of traditional knowledge mirror general objections to aspects of intellectual property law. One concern is that the protection of traditional knowledge somehow would unduly inhibit use of the public domain. The continuous expansion of copyright and patents, for example, has been characterised as encroaching onto the public domain. When patents are granted too far up stream, research can be hampered (Dinwoodie and Dreyfuss, 2005). When copyright prevents information flows, there is a problem with copyright.

To explore fully the proposition that the protection of traditional knowledge might be deleterious to the public domain is beyond the scope of this paper, but two points should be noted. Firstly, many indigenous peoples were not necessarily aware that the sharing of their knowledge meant it would be placed in the public domain, enabling it to be used without regard for its origins or any traditions that govern its appropriate uses (Frankel and Richardson, 2009). Secondly, all intellectual property protection is a taking from what would otherwise be the public domain. What is ring-fenced from the public domain in the name of intellectual property is primarily a matter of political choice that reflects the state of development or cultural values of a state. The more developed a country, the stronger its intellectual property law is likely to be. The TRIPS Agreement has meant, however, that some developing countries have higher standards of intellectual property law than is optimal for their level of development.

There has been considerable international institutional work in framing the situations in which traditional knowledge could be protected, the use of traditional knowledge compensated through benefit sharing, and how such protection might work in conjunction with existing intellectual property rights. There are several difficulties with these international frameworks. A key difficulty is that an international framework is unlikely to achieve what is the main objective for indigenous peoples, which is the ability to utilise their traditional knowledge for their own economic and social development. A legal framework is not, on its own, a development tool. Laws cannot create development. At most, laws can support development. However, an understanding of these frameworks is relevant here because it shows the linkages between traditional knowledge and GIs.

There are two forums at the forefront of the international framework for the protection of traditional knowledge. These are the Convention on Biological Diversity (CBD) and the World Intellectual Property Organization (WIPO). The Nagoya Protocol of the CBD includes an obligation on parties to provide for measures that require, in some circumstances, prior and informed consent (PIC) of indigenous and local communities and benefit sharing with these communities (Articles 5–7). Parties to the Protocol have PIC obligations in relation to the use of traditional knowledge associated with genetic resources and in relation to genetic resources where at domestic law indigenous and local communities have rights in relation to the genetic resources. The right that attaches to traditional knowledge is not dependent on a separate right existing at domestic law in the way that a right in relation to genetic resources is dependent. There is considerable discretion in the Nagoya Protocol as to how these obligations will be enacted in domestic legal regimes. There is, for example, no definition of what 'associated with genetic resources' means, suggesting that parties may determine how strongly that association needs to be proven. Nevertheless, the Nagoya Protocol is a significant development on existing CBD rights, which tended to be aspirational in that they did not impose specific obligations.[2]

WIPO began its traditional knowledge project with a fact-finding mission to establish what the issues are. This grew into an intergovernmental committee (WIPO-IGC) that developed a series of objectives and principles in relation to traditional knowledge. Broadly, the WIPO-IGC's work is split into traditional knowledge as it relates to biological and genetic resources, and traditional knowledge as it relates to traditional cultural expressions. Traditional cultural expressions are cultural outputs, such as arts and crafts, stories and song. The principles and objectives at WIPO are quite broad and consequently controversial. The WIPO-IGC now has the authority to draft a treaty, but completion of a treaty is not likely to come about in the foreseeable future.[3]

While the work of the CBD and WIPO-IGC is not to be underestimated, the role of the World Trade Organization (WTO) in the debate over the protection of traditional knowledge is key to the success of the protection of traditional knowledge. At first blush, it may seem incongruous that the protection of traditional knowledge has a place in an organisation established to liberalise trade. However, because the WTO has a role in intellectual property law, which impacts traditional knowledge, the traditional knowledge debate has found its way into discussions at the WTO. The WTO agreements include the intellectual property agreement, known as the TRIPS Agreement. Traditional knowledge protection must in some way interface with the TRIPS Agreement, even if TRIPS does not govern the details of traditional knowledge protection. Otherwise there is the likelihood that protection will have minimal impact on unauthorised uses of traditional knowledge because TRIPS-compliant intellectual property rights will prevail. In short, however, the WTO is extremely unlikely to provide a mechanism to protect traditional knowledge or provide an interface with the protection of traditional knowledge under other international instruments. The TRIPS Council has on its agenda a discussion about the relationship between the CBD and TRIPS. This discussion developed out of a review of the part of TRIPS which allows countries to provide exceptions to the patentability of plants.[4] No progress was made in the Doha round of WTO negotiations, which stalled. Some members of the WTO dispute that the TRIPS Council has a mandate to continue the discussion and at present it is not on the agenda of meetings.[5] Even before the discussion on the relationship between the CBD and the TRIPS Agreement came off the agenda of the TRIPS Council, the CBD was not authorised to have any participation or observer rights in the TRIPS Council discussion.

The TRIPS Council also has under discussion various GI issues, including whether to expand the higher level of protection that exists for wine and spirits to other areas,[6] and the development of a multilateral register of GIs for wines and spirits.[7] The issues became strongly linked when the European Union and developing countries (including India and Brazil) supported each other in the debate. The European Union supported an amendment to the TRIPS Agreement that would require patent applicants to disclose the origin of genetic resources in patent applications.[8] Some developing countries have supported the EU's position on expanding the international framework for the protection of GIs.

Some members of the TRIPS Council took the position that the Council had no mandate to continue the traditional knowledge discussion or the extension of GIs discussion and that a mandate existed only to progress the multilateral register of wines and spirits.[9] The Chair of the TRIPS Council effectively enforced that position and created special sessions for discussion of the register issue and expressed frustration that members nonetheless brought up traditional knowledge issues in those special sessions.[10]

The United States is opposed to both the European mode of the expansion of GIs,[11] and the protection of traditional knowledge. GIs also cause much controversy although, unlike traditional knowledge, GIs have some existing protection under the TRIPS Agreement (Articles 22–24). For a considerable period there was no consensus on the protection of GIs. The TRIPS Agreement resolved aspects of that through requiring GI protection, although in whatever form the members chose

[Article 1(1)]. There remains little consensus over the form of protection for geographical indications. Primarily, the division has been over whether there needs to be separate protection, an approach heralded by the European Union, or whether trade marks are adequate, the US position. However, when compared with international protection of traditional knowledge, there is considerable agreement on the international protection of GIs.

The relative progress of international protection of GIs and their protection through the TRIPS Agreement has tended to fuel the suggestion that they may provide protection for traditional knowledge. In part this is because GIs have found support from large developing countries, such as India, which also support the protection of traditional knowledge. If GIs provide some protection for traditional knowledge, then this is a very small aspect of traditional knowledge. Yet they are held out as offering great promise. This promise is problematic because the appearance of similarity between GIs and traditional knowledge obscures a chasm of difference.

The appearance of similarity between GIs and traditional knowledge

There are ways in which GIs and the protection of traditional knowledge appear to be similar. Indeed, there may well be some instances where a GI might protect an aspect of traditional knowledge, such as a name, but that does not make GIs suitable for most claims to the protection of traditional knowledge. The purpose of protecting GIs is primarily to provide a legal means for exclusive use of the GI in relation to particular products. Even though the rationales may involve other goals, the right a registered GI gives is the right to exclude others from use of the name.

GI protection is premised on at least three rationales for protection. The first is a connection between a product and the place from which it comes. The second is to connect qualities to the product coming from a particular area. The third is that the combination of location and qualities may create some kind of evocative value of a special place (Hughes, 2006, pp.303–4). However, the protection does not give any exclusivity over that evocative value or quality – only over the name.

The primary purpose of protecting traditional knowledge is to provide its owners with some prospect of economic development and control of their knowledge and cultural identity in a globalised world. These aims of traditional knowledge are in a limited way also found in the traditions associated with products that are marketed under GIs. Because of some similarities between GIs and traditional knowledge protection, some proponents of GIs suggest they provide a good system for the protection of traditional knowledge. These similarities are, however, in many ways only skin deep. There are broadly three areas of apparent similarity:

- indefinite protection;
- collective ownership and interests; and
- relationship with the land (the *terroir*).

Indefinite protection

Those who seek protection of traditional knowledge have a range of goals. These include the protection against offensive use of their traditional knowledge and also protection from economic exploitation of their traditional knowledge where no

benefit of that exploitation is returned to the people who are the source of the traditional knowledge. The WIPO-IGC principles put a lot of detail around these goals
and, in some ways, appear broader. However, these goals are the core of most
indigenous peoples' claims to indigenous knowledge, even though (because of the
diversity of indigenous peoples) their interests in traditional knowledge are
expressed in a variety of different ways.

The supporting rationale of claims to traditional knowledge is that the knowledge derives from the community and that the knowledge is tied to the community's identity and cultural heritage. It is this link that requires an indefinite form of
protection. Identity and cultural heritage, while evolving concepts, are ideally indefinite. Struggle for survival of their cultural heritage underscores indigenous peoples'
desire for traditional knowledge protection.

Trade marks and geographical indications are potentially indefinite. Usually once
registered, indefinite protection is achieved as long as fees are paid to the registering authority. The reason that indefinite protection is part of the trade mark regime
is that trade marks protect primarily names or logos as they relate to the origin of
particular goods and services.[12] There is no economic or social policy reason that a
name associated with a business should expire for as long as the business
continues. Therefore the rational basis of trade mark protection supports indefinite
protection.[13]

A similar analogy can be applied to GIs. The association between the GI owner
and the GI does not terminate, unless the geographical term becomes generic. However, this reason for indefinite protection also reveals something of the limitations
of both trade marks and GIs. Both legal mechanisms relate to protection of a name
as applied to goods or services in trade. Neither legal mechanism protects any
knowledge that lies behind the name nor does it necessarily protect against offensive use of the name.

This idea of the indefinite protection of knowledge is often seen as the most
controversial aspect of protecting traditional knowledge. This is because all intellectual property rights purport not to protect knowledge. However, where that knowledge is embodied in an invention, patent law may provide protection for the
invention and, in theory, the knowledge is available to others to use provided that
the patent is not infringed. Where that knowledge is embodied in a creative work,
copyright law provides protection for that work. Copyright law expressly recognises
that it is only the particular expression that is protected, not the knowledge or idea,
or facts conveyed in the expression [TRIPS Agreement, Article 9(2)]. In reality,
however, the protection of intellectual property has a considerable impact on the
distribution of knowledge and knowledge assets (Drahos and Braithwaite, 2002).
This aspiration of indefinite protection appears to give rise to a head-on collision
with patents and copyright because they have finite terms, but the protection sought
is not the same as those rights. Traditional knowledge claimants do not seek indefinite copyright or patent-style protection.

Collective ownership

A GI is not usually available for any one individual. Rather, provided a producer
meets the criteria behind the GI, at least theoretically, anyone can make use of a
GI. Anyone, for example, who meets the requirement of the champagne producers,
including using grapes from a particular location and making the champagne in a

certain way, can use the GI 'champagne'. The class of those who can use the term 'Swiss chocolate' is not defined, but there must be an association with Switzerland and approval of the Swiss chocolate making authorities, known as *Chocosuisse*: Union of Swiss Chocolate Manufacturers.

Traditional knowledge holders seek a kind of collective control over their traditional knowledge. The collective nature is because no one individual owns the knowledge to the exclusion of others. Also, as knowledge has a connection to identity and cultural heritage, there is a collective interest. In common law countries where GIs are not necessarily protected as such, the interests of such entities are protectable through certification or collective trade marks. Collective trade marks can be used by people who are authorised by the owner of the trade mark.

There is, however, quite a different sort of collective ownership in the GI sense and in the traditional knowledge sense. The GI or trade mark collective owners are a group of qualified individuals who can use the GI for their independent business purposes, even though the GI has a kind of collective status. Each individual has an entitlement to the collective. The traditional knowledge collective ownership is primarily based on the view that no individual has an entitlement to the collective traditional knowledge. Rather, many indigenous peoples consider they have a responsibility to carry that traditional knowledge forward and even develop it for future generations. Also, there may be customary laws that govern which individual can make certain uses of knowledge and in what ways. Even then, however, the responsibility is collective for current uses and the benefit of future generations. In other words, the current users are guardians for appropriate current uses and development for future generations.

The relationship to the land

The concept of *terroir* is that land gives special characteristics to the products with ingredients from the land. The *terroir* justification for GIs is in addition to other reasons given for GIs: 'GIs are supposed to tell us non-geographic characteristics of the product linked to the product's geographic provenance' (Hughes, 2006, p.356). Thus, the European Union argues, a GI can only be used accurately when it is used in relation to products that are associated with a particular *terroir*. The theory is that even if, for example, *Parmigiano-Reggiano*-making methods are imitated and even improved elsewhere in the making of parmesan, that parmesan can never be the real thing because *terroir* will always be different. The same reason is used to justify non-geographical names being protected as GIs. Feta is only feta if sourced from a certain part of Greece.

While products such as wine and cheese have characteristics and flavour resulting from where their ingredients are sourced, it is debatable whether such products merit exclusive rights for that reason alone. This exclusive *terroir* argument is hotly disputed, even among those who proclaim the importance of the *terroir* (Hughes, 2006). *Terroir* is, therefore, a conveniently narrow way of defining GIs just to make sure that the European Union has a purported reason, other than blatant rent seeking, to reclaim its generic wine and cheese names.[14]

Another problem with justifying GIs on the basis of *terroir* is that it can limit their availability to those in possession of lands for a long time. Many indigenous peoples have been removed from their land and have not had access to it. Nevertheless, many indigenous peoples' claims to traditional knowledge often emphasise the importance of the relationship of the people, the knowledge, the land, and the flora and fauna of the land. The value of a connection to the land is perhaps the most convincing similarity between GIs and traditional knowledge. Traditional knowledge is closely linked to cultural identity and *terroir* is a symbol of identity (Gervais, 2011).

The comparison, however, has significant limitations. One limitation is what a GI in fact protects. It protects the name. Another limitation of the comparison is that traditional knowledge holders do not claim rights to their knowledge solely because of a connection to the land. Rather, the connection to the land explains their relationship with the knowledge, as holders and guardians of the knowledge and it is the relationship for which they seek protection. This is not to suggest that indigenous peoples do not seek to own their lands. The history of indigenous peoples is significantly about land claims. The point is that the claim to traditional knowledge is not only about the land. It is also about the indigenous peoples' relationship with the land and what lives and grows on it.[15]

The nature of GIs

A GI is sometimes a claim to traditional knowledge put in more legally recognised language (Frankel, 2008, p.453). At most, a subset of traditional knowledge includes similarities to GIs. Blakeney (2009) suggests that some of the more famous GIs, such as champagne and roquefort, protect the underlying traditions of those products. These traditions are the ways in which the products are made. However, the GI really only protects the name (see Kur & Knaak, 2004). There may be something behind the GI, such as a government agency or a trade association, which requires its members to conform to various rules in order to use the name. The French *appellations de origins controlees* system has very strict rules about what grape varieties can be grown and used in particular regions and what regions can use particular appellations. However, it is a big step from the existence of these controls to the position that GIs protect traditional knowledge. The GI protects the name for use by those whom the associated bureaucracy deems to merit its use.

Where trade mark systems are used to protect GIs, then (as with all types of trade marks) the owners may have an interest in quality control to perpetuate their brand, but quality control is not policed or enforced. In many parts of the world, GI protection does not necessarily require compliance with traditions or methods of production. Although, for instance, Australia and the United States have government agencies that determine geographical areas and viticulture areas, they do not control methods of production (Hughes, 2006, p.333). The protection of GIs, by various legal tools, in New Zealand, Australia and the United States requires compliance with the demands of local law. Certification marks certify a standard, but the certifier does not control what the standard is. When GIs are protected through the common law doctrine of passing off, what is required is a reputation in a name, not proof that that reputation is deserved because of an adherence to strict rules.[16]

It may be in the interests of the GI users to maintain quality control, but it is not a requirement of most registration systems and even those systems that do have such controls, such as the *appellations de origins controlees*, seem to be somewhat flexible when it suits them. Indeed, the large production houses of Champagne have moved a long way from their traditional roots. A claim to exclusivity of the name because of reputation may be more genuine than the claim that it is deserved because of adherence to the production methods of the seventeenth and eighteenth centuries. The idea of traditional farming has been described as a caricature in relation to champagne (Hughes, 2006, p.340).

More importantly, however, even French winemakers have extensively suggested that these intensely bureaucratic quality control systems inhibit innovation (Hughes, 2006). They cannot apply new methods of production because to do so might compromise the GI. Where the aim of protecting traditional knowledge is to support innovation, GIs are the wrong tool as they have been shown to preserve the *status quo* rather than directly enhance innovation.

Some GIs that are premised on quality standards may be supported by checks on compliance with those standards. Deviation from such standards is discouraged even when the deviation is for innovative purposes. Many French winemakers complain about the anti-innovation effects of GIs (Hughes, 2006). The clinging to tradition in the form of GIs is a static approach, which is also protectionist of the *status quo*. The nature of a GI is fixed. Because it is fixed, it is not a universal development tool. Its use for rural communities, predominantly in Western countries, does not transform the static GI into an all-purpose development tool.

In Europe, GIs also serve another protectionist purpose. They are part of European farming policy and represent a replacement for other subsidies. This policy is perhaps best described in the European Union GI Regulation of 2006, which provides that:[17]

(1) the production, manufacture and distribution of agricultural products and foodstuffs play an important role in the Community economy;

(2) the diversification of agricultural production should be encouraged so as to achieve a better balance between supply and demand on the markets. The promotion of products having certain characteristics can be of considerable benefit to the rural economy, particularly in less favoured or remote areas, by improving the incomes of farmers and by retaining the rural population in these areas; and

(3) a constantly increasing number of consumers attach greater importance to the quality of foodstuffs in their diet rather than to quantity. This quest for specific products generates a demand for agricultural products or foodstuffs with an identifiable geographical origin.

Protecting innovative traditional knowledge

The call for protection of traditional knowledge is not premised on incentives that are analogous to the above rationales behind GIs. Traditional knowledge protection is not sought only to preserve traditional knowledge in a static way. Traditional knowledge has a number of highly innovative applications. This has been demonstrated, particularly by third parties, such as pharmaceutical companies, that use traditional knowledge. Knowledge of the properties of a plant can lead to a researcher making innovative uses of the plants. Such uses can be medicinal or cosmetic. When this sort of use of traditional knowledge takes place, there is frequently a suggestion that tradition and not innovation lies with the holders of the knowledge and the innovation is that of the modern users. This is not true. First, and perhaps most obviously, something innovative must have occurred for the indigenous peoples to discover the use of the plant. Secondly, indigenous peoples can demonstrate that they have found new uses of plants to fit new circumstances (Riley, 1994). This is not to suggest that third party users do not do innovative things. They do. However, the innovation process is not solely theirs. Some examples are perhaps illustrative.

New Zealand manuka honey is renowned for its healing properties and particularly its antibacterial effects. It has been used by the Māori for many purposes and in some instances developed by the Māori for additional uses. It has also been commercialised in a range of cosmetics and antiseptic creams by both Māori and non-Māori. A university research group based in Dresden has isolated the active ingredient of manuka honey (Mavric *et al.,* 2008) and teamed up with a New Zealand company to create a standard that indicates the honey's intensity. The knowledge of manuka being effective and the importance of using it in different intensities was not dependent on the Dresden research. The contribution of this research was to pinpoint in Western terms exactly why the honey is so potent.

The manuka example is one of many where Māori knowledge about the uses of many New Zealand plants is well documented (Riley, 1994). The knowledge about plants is also reflected in many works of Māori culture and has become an integral part of Māori cultural identity. The *kowhai ngutukakau,* for instance, is found as part of the carving of many *wharenui* (meeting houses). Other examples of innovative uses of traditional knowledge include Australian Aboriginal practices used to control fires which are adapted to modern conditions (see Drahos, 2011). More broadly, indigenous peoples' ecological knowledge is used to varying degrees in a variety of environmental and conservation practices worldwide (Coombe, 2005).

What indigenous peoples seek is some control over their knowledge so that they can reap the benefits of uses of their knowledge. Unlike those who seek to expand the protection of GIs, indigenous peoples' primary aim is not to seek to confine their knowledge to make it static and thereby extract monopoly rents. Traditional knowledge is traditional because of its longevity, not because it is closed to development. There are some instances in which claims to traditional knowledge are static, but these claims are not premised on exclusive commercial rights. They are premised on respect for and preservation of cultural heritage; for example, for the protection of traditional knowledge from offensive use.

The innovative aspects of traditional knowledge are as convincing an argument for protection as any intellectual property right; and the reason that indigenous peoples should be able to reap the rewards from that innovation is because they need economic development. The protection that indigenous peoples seek will not necessarily exclude others from innovative uses of traditional knowledge; rather it aims to ensure that indigenous peoples are not excluded from the benefits of uses of this knowledge. Admittedly, this is a different model from that of mainstream intellectual property rights. However, it is perhaps analogous to the suggestion that intellectual property rights might shift focus from property to liability rules (Kur and Schovsbo, 2011). In any event, mainstream intellectual property rights are not strangers to changing boundaries. The adapting of patent laws to protect the changing needs of pharmaceutical companies is but one example.

One accusation levelled at those who seek to protect traditional knowledge is that 'indigenous activists talk about culture as if it were a fixed and corporeal thing' (Brown, 1998). To a certain extent this is true. The Declaration on the Rights of Indigenous Peoples, for example, asserts the right of indigenous peoples to the control of their culture. This approach, however, is a push-back against incursions into indigenous culture rather than a statement that culture is fixed. The push-back is in pursuit of a greater share of global wealth.

Also, the corporeal model is one that those pushing back have adopted from intellectual property law. Although (as a matter of legal definition) intellectual property rights are intangible rights, their status as property depends on a mixture of justifications for property. These include the ability to define something from which others can be excluded (Bennett Moses, 2008). The ability to define, in part, comes about because intellectual property rights manifest themselves as things that are corporeal. The book, the film and the pharmaceutical are a few examples. The GI is the ultimate legal tool that is fixed and corporeal. When claims to traditional knowledge are overstated, there is an element of the fixed and corporeal. However, it is hardly surprising when the rules of the game have been set in the fixed and corporeal manner that the people who fight for part of the action also state their claim in a fixed and corporeal manner.

When scholars discuss the difficulties of protecting traditional knowledge, a recurring theme is the difficulty of defining culture. There is a disjunction between indigenous peoples' aims and what, for example, Jeremy Waldron (2000) might call 'cosmopolitan views of culture'. This disjunction is conspicuously overstated in the name of flexibility. Many areas of intellectual property rights are expanded beyond expectations and many might say beyond reason. If there is a cosmopolitan view of culture, then intellectual property cannot claim to be premised on a utopian view of cosmopolitanism. The melting pot of cosmopolitanism is secondary to the protective aims of intellectual property rights. Although the reason that indigenous peoples seek to protect their traditional knowledge includes protection of culture, this does not necessarily mean one has to define culture. Rather, once a reason for a right is identified, the framing of the exclusive rights requires the identification of what might be excluded, in what circumstances exclusion is justified, and who has the right to exclude (Bennett Moses, 2008).

The argument against the protection of traditional knowledge that is theoretically on more solid ground is the difficulty of defining what the rights are and who they belong to. At an abstract level, this can seem difficult. However, as some domestic regimes have shown, these difficulties can be overcome. For example, if the reason for protecting traditional knowledge is the relationship between indigenous peoples and their knowledge, and those claiming the relationship can be specified, then problems of identity can be resolved. The scope of the rights can also be defined by determining the scope of the relationship. This paper does not seek to define exhaustively who indigenous peoples are or to articulate all the rights of indigenous peoples to their traditional knowledge.[18]

The effects of the mismatch of GIs and traditional knowledge

The problem with GIs being proffered as a form of protection for traditional knowledge is that GIs and traditional knowledge are, for the most part, fundamentally different. The nature and aim of GIs is not the same as the nature and aim of the protection of traditional knowledge. Geographical indications are European. This is clearly not a crime, but it is a concept that is a cultural construct of distinctive territorial origin. If people sit down to fine champagne and Bluff oysters, they can appreciate these products and might not object to GIs being applicable to them, but they are a success because there is a business and there is an infrastructure behind these products that has helped them become well known. Such products are marketed and targeted at consumers of a certain income. All successful GI stories have a product success story behind them. The GI does not make the product, the product makes the GI. GIs are a marketing tool to sell products; if there is no product, there is no marketable GI.

GIs are oversold as tools of development. They are not developmental in any innovative way, but are rather tools of maintaining the *status quo*. GIs may serve to generate wealth for some developing nations. Undoubtedly, the protection of Darjeeling and Basmati may bring greater wealth to India. However, the creation of a GI will not suddenly open new markets for the knowledge held and products produced by indigenous peoples. This oversell of GIs can be found in many places. The European Commission's website states:[19]

> Over the years European countries have taken the lead in identifying and protecting their Geographical Indications. ... However, GIs are also important for developing countries. GIs can protect and preserve intellectual property related to traditional cultures, geographical diversity and production methods. All nations have a wide range of local products that correspond to the concept of a GI – Basmati rice or Darjeeling tea – but only a few are already known as such or protected globally.

> Better protection of GIs can be a useful contribution to increasing income, in particular in rural areas. It also encourages quality production and can promote the development of tourism. GIs grant protection to a community and not to individual right holders.

> Since consumers are often ready to pay more for GI products, people from outside the region may be tempted to appropriate the GI for their own products. This not only misleads consumers, but it also dilutes the GI value as well as discourages producers from making investment decisions or launching expensive marketing campaigns.

> Consequently gains resulting from marketing GIs need to be accompanied by prevention of their loss of value through copying, or free riding. This requires intense and costly legal efforts that small rural communities can rarely afford. This is why GIs need an enhanced protection. This is something the EU has been pushing for in the ongoing Doha WTO trade negotiations.

This overstates the value of GIs to some communities. Rural communities with developed industries may benefit from GIs (Giovannucci *et al.*, 2009), but a GI without a substantive existing industry is a hollow gain. Also, as the European Commission notes, protecting a GI is costly, and therefore frequently not worth the expense if what is really needed is development. The conclusion that GIs need enhanced protection is at best an assertion.

One view is that there is no harm to traditional knowledge if GIs protect some aspects. There is no reason why the businesses of indigenous peoples should not consider GIs as any other business might. That is not the same thing, however, as holding out GIs as a model for the protection of traditional knowledge. Additionally, the holding out of GIs as protection for traditional knowledge is not necessarily benign. Rather, it obscures the needs and aspirations of traditional knowledge holders and may not make it easy for traditional knowledge proponents to gain any traction outside the GI framework. Once GIs are enacted, the reaction to traditional knowledge might be that GIs are enough. Enhancing GIs will, however, likely only enhance the prospects of the existing incumbents of the GI regime.

Conclusion

The GI has been put forward as a way to protect some traditional knowledge. While analogies can be made between GIs and the protection of traditional knowledge, these analogies are superficial in many ways and problematic in other ways. They are superficial because GIs lead to the preservation of the *status quo* whereas the protection of traditional knowledge can create a mechanism to harness innovative aspects of traditional knowledge to support the development of indigenous peoples.

Geographical indications present a one-size-fits-all mechanism for traditional knowledge, which is, in fact, a diverse concept. This is a legal danger. The practical danger is that scarce resources might be wrongly directed to GIs in the hope that they will produce wealth. However, a GI cannot create innovative opportunities. At most it can support existing businesses in some circumstances.

The GI has been held out as promising more than it is likely to deliver and distracts from the real aspirations of indigenous peoples for development. Indigenous peoples seek to protect their traditional knowledge in order to provide their communities with financial resources and to have a stake in the development of innovative uses of traditional knowledge. These aims cannot be met by GIs.

Notes

1. There are some exceptions where GIs are granted for non-geographical names, but because of an alleged geographical association. Feta is an example of a European GI for which no corresponding place can be located on any map of Greece.
2. Article 8(j) of the CBD provides that:

   Each contracting Party shall, as far as possible and as appropriate: subject to national legislation, respect, preserve and maintain knowledge, innovations and practices of indigenous and local communities embodying traditional lifestyles relevant for the conservation and sustainable use of biological diversity and promote their wider application with the approval and involvement of the holders of such knowledge, innovations and practices and encourage the equitable sharing of the benefits arising from the utilization of such knowledge innovations and practices.

   The Nagoya Protocol is aimed at making a reality of this provision. The Declaration on the Rights of Indigenous Peoples contains relevant aspirational clauses. Article 31, for example, provides that:

   Indigenous peoples have the right to maintain, control, protect and develop their cultural heritage, traditional knowledge and traditional cultural expressions, as well as the manifestations of their sciences, technologies and cultures, including human and genetic resources, seeds, medicines, knowledge of the properties of fauna and flora, oral traditions, literatures, designs, sports and traditional games and visual and performing arts. They also have the right to maintain, control, protect and develop their intellectual property over such cultural heritage, traditional knowledge, and traditional cultural expressions.

3. For the progress of talks, see the WIPO traditional knowledge website http://www.wipo.int/tk/en/ [accessed July 2011].
4. TRIPS Agreement, Article 27(3) provides that:

266   S. Frankel

Members may also exclude from patentability: (b) plants and animals other than micro-organisms, and essentially biological processes for the production of plants or animals other than non-biological and microbiological processes. However, Members shall provide for the protection of plant varieties either by patents or by an effective *sui generis* system or by any combination thereof. The provisions of this subparagraph shall be reviewed four years after the date of entry into force of the WTO Agreement.

5. For the TRIPS Council agenda see http://www.wto.org/english/tratop_e/trips_e/intel6_e.htm [accessed July 2011].
6. TRIPS Agreement, Article 23(1). GIs are also protected under a WIPO-based system known as the Lisbon Agreement.
7. TRIPS Agreement, Article 23(4) provides that:

In order to facilitate the protection of geographical indications for wines, negotiations shall be undertaken in the Council for TRIPS concerning the establishment of a multilateral system of notification and registration of geographical indications for wines eligible for protection in those Members participating in the system …

8. EU Directive 98/44/EC, 6 July 1998 provides for voluntary disclosure requirements of the origin of genetic resources in patent systems. See also WIPO (2004).
9. See submission from the United States, Australia, New Zealand and others, *Multilateral System of Notification and Registration of Geographical Indications for Wines and Spirits*, WTO Document IP/C/W/289.
10. Chairman's report, *Multilateral System of Notification and Registration of Geographical Indications for Wines and Spirits*, WTO Document TN/IP/20, 22 March 2010 and WTO Document TN/IP/21, 21 April 2011.
11. The United States has its own method for the protection of GIs, which it pushes in its free trade agreement agenda. The US negotiating text for the Trans-Pacific Partnership Agreement provides an example: 'The complete Feb 10, 2011 text of the US proposal for the TPP IPR chapter' at http://keionline.org.
12. The international standard for protection is found in the TRIPS Agreement, Article 15.
13. This can be disputed when trademarks relate to more than names or symbols, but embody expressive values, such as jingles or functional aspects, such as the shape of products.
14. Justin Hughes (2006, p.357) suggests the *terroir* claim is a response to competition from new world wines.
15. For a discussion of the Māori relationship with their *mātauranga Māori* (traditional knowledge), see the Waitangi Tribunal Report, *Indigenous Flora and Fauna and Cultural Intellectual Property*, WAI 262, chapter 2, available from http://www.waitangi-tribunal.govt.nz/news/media/wai262.asp [accessed July 2011].
16. Passing off is a judge-made doctrine that in England, Australia and New Zealand protects reputation in business goodwill from misrepresentation.
17. European Union Council Regulation No 510/2006, 20 March 2006, on the protection of geographical indications and designations of origin for agricultural products and foodstuffs.
18. For legal instruments addressing these issues, see *Nagoya Protocol on Access to Genetic Resources and the Fair and Equitable Sharing of Benefits Arising from their Utilization to the Convention on Biological Diversity*, available from http://www.cbd.int [accessed July 2011], and *UN Declaration on the Rights of Indigenous Peoples*, available from http://www.un.org/esa/socdev/unpfii/en/drip.html [accessed July 2011].
19. European Commission, Trade, *Geographical Indications*, available from http://ec.europa.eu/trade/creating-opportunities/trade-topics/intellectual-property/geographical-indications/ [accessed July 2011].

Prometheus 267

References

Bennett Moses, L. (2008) 'The applicability of property law in new contexts: from cells to cyber-space', *Sydney Law Review,* 30, pp.639–62.

Blakeney, M. (2009) 'Protection of traditional knowledge by geographical indications', *International Journal of Intellectual Property Management,* 3, pp.357–74.

Brown, M. (1998) 'Can culture be copyrighted?', *Current Anthropology,* 39, pp.193–222.

Coombe, R. (2005) 'Traditional environmental knowledge and new social movements in the Americas: intellectual property, human right or claims to an alternative form of sustainable development', *Florida Journal of International Law,* 17, pp.115–35.

Dinwoodie, G. and Dreyfuss, R. (2005) 'WTO dispute resolution and the preservation of the public domain in science' in Maskus, K. and Reichman, J. (eds) *International Public Goods and Transfer of Technology Under a Globalized Intellectual Property Regime,* Cambridge University Press, Cambridge, pp.861–83.

Downes, D. (2000) 'Intellectual property as a tool to protect traditional knowledge', *Columbia Journal of Environmental Law,* 25, pp.253–81.

Drahos, P. (2011) 'When cosmology meets property: indigenous peoples' innovation and intellectual property', *Prometheus,* 29, pp.3.

Drahos, P. with Brathwaite, J. (2002) *Information Feudalism – Who Owns the Knowledge Economy?,* Earthscan, London.

Frankel, S. (2008) 'Trade marks, traditional knowledge and cultural intellectual property' in Dinwoodie, G. and Janis, M. (eds) *Trademark Law and Theory: A Handbook of Contemporary Research,* Edward Elgar, Northampton, MA, pp.433–63.

Frankel, S. and Richardson, M. (2009) 'Cultural property and "the public domain": case studies from New Zealand and Australia' in Antons, C. (ed.) *Traditional Knowledge, Traditional Cultural Expressions and Intellectual Property Law in the Asia–Pacific Region,* Kluwer Law International, Alphen aan den Rijn, pp.275–92.

Gervais, D. (2011) 'Traditional innovation and the ongoing debate on the protection of geographical indications' in Drahos, P. and Frankel, S. (eds) *Indigenous Peoples' Innovation: IP Pathways to Development,* Australian National University epress, Canberra.

Giovannucci, D., Barham, E. and Pirog, R. (2009) 'Defining and marketing "local" foods: geographical indications for US products', *Journal of World Intellectual Property,* 12, pp.94–120.

Hughes, J. (2006) 'Champagne, feta and bourbon: the spirited debate about geographical indications', *Hastings Law Journal,* 58, pp.299–386.

Kur, A. and Knaak, P. (2004) 'Protection of traditional names and designations' in Von Lewinski, S. (ed.) *Indigenous Heritage and Intellectual Property: Genetic Resources, Traditional Knowledge and Folklore,* Kluwer Law International, Alphen aan den Rijn, pp.221–7.

Kur, A. and Schovsbo, J. (2011) 'Expropriation or fair game for all? The gradual dismantling of the IP exclusivity paradigm' in Kur, A. (ed.) *IPRs in a Fair World Trade System,* Edward Elgar, Cheltenham, pp.408–52.

Mavric, E., Wittmann, S., Barth, G. and Henle, T. (2008) 'Identification and quantification of methylglyoxal as the dominant antibacterial constituent of manuka (*leptospermum scoparium*). Honeys from New Zealand', *Molecular Nutrition and Food Research,* 52, pp.483–9.

Riley, M. (1994) *Māori Healing and Herbal,* Viking SevenSeas, Raumati South.

Roht-Arriaza, N. (1996) 'Of seeds and shamans: the appropriation of the scientific and technical knowledge of indigenous and local communities', *Michigan Journal of International Law,* 17, pp.919–65.

Waitangi Tribunal Report (2011) *Ko Aotearoa Tēnei: A Report into Claims Concerning New Zealand Law and Policy Affecting Māori Culture and Identity,* July, available from http://www.waitangi-tribunal.govt.nz/news/media/wai262.asp (WAI 262), [accessed July 2011].

Waldron, J. (2000) 'What is cosmopolitan?', *Journal of Political Philosophy,* 8, pp.227–43.

World Intellectual Property Organization (WIPO) (2004) *Technical Study on Disclosure Requirements in Patent Systems Related to Genetic Resources and Traditional Knowledge,* Study 3, UNEP/CBD/COP/7/INF/17, February.

Part III
Evaluating the Effects of GIs

[34]

THE ECONOMICS OF GEOGRAPHICAL INDICATIONS: TOWARDS A CONCEPTUAL FRAMEWORK FOR GEOGRAPHICAL INDICATION RESEARCH IN DEVELOPING COUNTRIES

CERKIA BRAMLEY*, ESTELLE BIÉNABE** AND JOHANN KIRSTEN*

1. INTRODUCTION

Over the past two decades, agrifood systems have experienced a significant move towards market differentiation and product proliferation in many parts of the world. This product proliferation and differentiation is associated with what Allaire (2003) described as "the immaterialization of food and the institutionalization of quality", which is translating into an increasing complexity of quality and new quality conventions. These institutions go beyond the neo-classical model of market pricing and quality signaling through price mechanisms, to instances where institutions that define and enforce quality standards and norms become key to the performance of market mechanisms. As stated by Sauvée and Valceschini (2003): "In the current competitive universe, the definition of quality and the information on qualities are from now on at the heart of the competitive strategies of economic actors".

The growing demand for and attention to the "qualities" of agrifood products is a result of a range of factors such as the increased awareness of food safety, the socio cultural status of consuming certain foods and renewed interest in and nostalgia for culinary heritage (Ilberry and Kneafsey (2000)). Origin-labeled products are an important example of this, as trends in the food sector over the past decade indicate that consumers are increasingly placing value on products they can associate with a certain place and/or special means of production (Ilbery and Kneafsey (1998)).

Given the global competitive environment characterized by declining agricultural commodity prices, this trend towards traditional and/or quality products with a strong cultural link provides producers of value added products with a strong link to a particular geographical origin, with the opportunity to move away from commodity markets into more lucrative niche markets through differentiation. As such, territorial origin becomes a strategic tool for differentiation in agrifood markets. However, the success of such a marketing strategy depends largely on whether there are measures in place that ensure localization of production. As a result, international rules for the regulation of origin-labeled products have become increasingly important in recent years. Geographical indication (GI) protection has, however, proved controversial with respect to the nature and the scope of the protection to be granted, as reflected by the divisive debate that ensued during the TRIPS negotiations where countries' desire to protect this IPR has largely been based on political pressures both domestically and internationally as well as the perceived economic impact of protection.

As with other distinctive signs, the economics underlying the protection of localized products is founded on the economic theories of information and reputation. These theories illustrate the

---

* Department of Agricultural Economics, Extension and Rural Development, University of Pretoria, Pretoria, South Africa. The views expressed in this paper are those of the authors and do not necessarily represent those of WIPO.

** CIRAD, UMR Innovation, Pretoria, South Africa; CIRAD, UMR Innovation, Montpellier, France; University of Pretoria, Pretoria, South Africa.

importance of (1) preventing the market distortions that arise when there is asymmetry of information between producers and consumers and (2) averting the consequences of such asymmetry of information on the level of output quality (OECD (2000)). Reputation, as used in studies of markets characterized by imperfect information (Stiglitz (1989), Tirole (1988)), aids to an extent to overcome the market failure associated with asymmetry of information. However, the successful use of reputation to restore efficiency to the market through averting the consequences of information asymmetries requires that that reputation be protected through a process which can be viewed as the "institutionalisation of reputation" (Belletti (1999)). Distinctive signs such as geographical indications can achieve this by institutionalising the relationship between the product and the region and/or tradition through the use of legal instruments that prevent the misappropriation of benefits. Geographical indications can thus be viewed as the result of a process whereby reputation is institutionalized in order to solve certain problems that arise from information asymmetry and free riding on reputation. This highlights a fundamental feature of GI protection i.e. that it functions as both a consumer protection measure (through addressing information asymmetries and quality) and a producer protection measure (through its role in protecting reputation as an asset) (OECD (2000)).

Apart from, and partly as a consequence of, the economics underlying geographical indications, both European policies and the literature emphasize the potential of geographical indications to improve rural livelihoods based on local resources (Pacciani et al (2001)) and, thus, advance rural development. Worldwide, rural communities have developed typical products based on the interaction between local know how (including selection, production and processing) and particular environmental conditions such as the soil and climate (World Bank Report (2004)). However, the market does not necessarily reward the value added to these traditional products and when it does the added value does not necessarily accrue to the producers. This is to a large extent due to a lack of a well-defined and recognized characterization of the product or to a lack of regulations and enforcement mechanisms. The legal recognition of geographical indications provides an institutional tool through which to address these problems and consequently provide rural communities with the opportunity to valorize their local production and extract rents based on local savoir faire.

These dimensions highlight the three basic objectives pursued through GI protection, i.e. consumer protection, producer protection and rural development. Various related objectives are pursued under these broader objectives and include objectives that flow from GI categorization as an IPR. The different dimensions and objectives of GI protection give an insight into the multidisciplinary nature of the subject that includes legal, economic, social and political dimensions. Despite this, geographical indications have, to date, largely been studied from a legal perspective of reconciliation between alternative ways of granting protection to producers from usurpation of names and signs (O'Connor (2004)). Much research remains to be done on the underlying economic impact of geographical indications, especially in a developing country context. The central tenet of this paper is the identification of the different economic dimensions to GI protection and the methodologies and approaches that have been used to study these. The paper starts with a typology of the institutional frameworks facilitating GI protection. This is followed in section 3 by an exposition on the economic rationale for protecting geographical indications. The paper intends to arrive at an integrative approach to studying geographical indications and/or their potential in developing countries. To this effect, section 4 of the paper provides a synopsis of the different methodologies employed to assess the different economic dimensions of geographical indications. Finally, section 5 develops a conceptual approach to studying geographical indications in developing countries.

2. THE INSTITUTIONAL LANDSCAPE

2.1 Different Legal Approaches to Geographical Indication Protection

The different dimensions of geographical indications are closely embedded in the different legal and institutional frameworks that facilitate their protection. During the TRIPS negotiations a divisive debate ensued regarding the nature and scope of protection to be granted to geographical indications. Fundamentally, two different approaches to protecting them emerged. The first relies on existing intellectual property and unfair competition laws. Certain countries, such as the US, argued that geographical indications are sufficiently protected within this framework. The second approach to protecting geographical indications is through legislation specifically designed for this purpose. The European Union, for example, argued that they are not sufficiently protected within existing trademark laws and thus demanded *sui generis* protection and the establishment of a multilateral register.

The TRIPS Agreement is not prescriptive in its approach to GI protection and requires merely that member countries provide the "legal means" by which to prevent "(a) [...] the use of any means [...] which misleads the public as to the geographical origin of the good [...] or (b) any use which constitutes an act of unfair competition [...]". Countries are thus free to regulate the protection of geographical indications at national level, provided it complies with the minimum standards set by TRIPS. As a result, countries have elected to either follow the EU approach and promulgate *sui generis* legislation or implement the US philosophy of protection under existing trademark laws. Various developing countries have moved towards the protection of geographical indications through different legal approaches. India has, for example, promulgated legislation which allows for the registration of a geographical indication *per se*. Other developing countries, including South Africa, have thus far elected to protect geographical indications under trademark laws. The divergent approaches all differ with respect to the degree of government involvement, monitoring of use and enforcement. The merits of the divergent approaches have been widely debated and will not be explored in this paper.

2.2 Organization and Control

Depending on the legal system granting protection to geographical indications, issues of control and organization are addressed differently. In contrast to trademarks, which are distinctive signs identifying goods of an enterprise and thus not limited by any territorial link, geography is at the heart of geographical indications (Marsden (1998)). This geographically intertwined nature of geographical indications has certain implications for the organization and control of origin-labeled supply chains. As Belleti and Marescotti (2002) mentioned, origin-labeled products are very often characterized by a "collective dimension" in the sense that they are linked not only with the skills of many producers and/or processors but also with locally created public goods and with the history, habits and culture of the local community. This requires the creation of collaborative networks through which many actors jointly manage the common product in the same way a single firm might do (Barjolle and Sylvander (2002)).

These actors can be highly heterogeneous in that they may or may not be directly involved with production and distribution activities. Also, they may be of an individual or collective nature and, if they are of a collective nature, they may be public institutions or producer/processor organizations (Pacciani *et al* (2001)). It is often assumed that the activities associated with producing an origin-labeled product are located within the territory. However, this disregards the many non-local actors who participate in the production of an origin-labeled product.

THE ECONOMICS OF INTELLECTUAL PROPERTY

This diversity of actors leads to a diversity of objectives which are pursued through valorization of the origin-labeled product. Often these objectives go beyond the goal of profit maximization to include other socio-cultural objectives. This diversity is well-illustrated with reference to the valorization system in place in the EU. Protection for origin-labeled products under EU Regulation No. 510/2006 is structured around three groups of participants: producers/processors, regulators and inspection agencies (Figure 1).

Figure 1. EU-Protected Designation of Origin and Protected Geographical Indications System

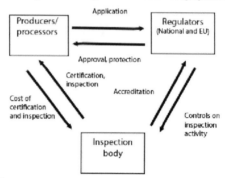

Source: Hayes *et al* (2003)

Although these actors remain economically and legally independent while producing and marketing the common good, they are linked in that their activities result in a particular origin-labeled product whose main characteristics are determined in the code of production. This peculiar manifestation of independence/interdependence between producers of the common good, each pursuing its own objectives, emphasizes the fact that origin-labeled products stem from a collective process. Menard (2000) stated that there are various advantages associated with cooperation and collective production: (1) economies of scale in the acquisition of information; (2) risk-bearing among the group when facing unanticipated contingencies; (3) mitigation of adverse selection and moral hazard; (4) increased productivity due to a more developed "sense of responsibility". However, he highlighted that there are also limits and costs to cooperation, resulting from: (1) free-riding strategies through selection of members (*ex ante*) and malingering behavior once selected (*ex post*); (2) collective decision-making that may hamper the advantages of command; (3) incentives to collude and develop side payments; (4) the high cost of processing information and communicating in a team oriented organization.

These advantages and limits associated with collective action bring to the fore the importance of co-ordination and organization in producing an origin-labeled product, a point which is reiterated throughout the research on typical products (Barjolle and Chappuis (2000)). In this regard, Chappuis and Sans (2000) identified co ordination in the supply chain as a prerequisite for the success of origin-labeled products and for the competitiveness of the firms producing and marketing them. Factors indicated by research as contributing to the need for coordination in origin-labeled supply chains include the type of product, in that they are strongly differentiated and with high value-added; the seasonal nature of a number of origin-labeled products; the location of some producers in regions where production costs may be higher. The most compelling reason seems to be the need to arrive, at the end of the processing stage, at a product with specific characteristics. In order to achieve the latter, Chappuis and Sans (2000) referred to certain activities that need to be addressed at a collective level.

One such collective activity is the need of the relevant group of producers and/or processors to define the relevant product by achieving consensus as to its characteristics and the delimitation of the production area. Definition of the product should take place in accordance with the market and differentiation objectives. Consensus on the product definition can be considered the minimum level of agreement between participating actors as it determines the product characteristics as well as those entitled to produce it. Product specification will furthermore determine the possibility of innovation and could thus limit producers regarding product development. As such, it forms an important aspect of the negotiation between participants establishing the geographical indication. The product definition is embodied in a code of practice which constitutes the first collective activity within the supply chain. A liberal code will allow for the production of a wide range of products using the same designation. This strategy, however, should be avoided as it could lead to unfair competition and could mislead consumers. In contrast, a strict code strengthens the image of a unique product and reduces differences in production techniques between firms. Defining the product necessarily raises the issue of exclusion, further necessitating collaboration and coordination between all stakeholders in defining the common good.

A further activity that highlights the collective dimension of geographical indications is that of control. Once a code of practice has been agreed upon, consensus is needed on how to ensure conformity to the product specifications. The collective nature of the production process necessitates controls to prevent free riding and opportunistic behavior. Each of the firms entitled to use the designation is dependant on the good practice of all the other firms in order to guarantee the quality and reputation of the product bearing the designation. The control function can be undertaken by external or internal institutions.

According to Barjolle and Sylvander (2002), coordination in the context of origin-labeled supply chains should be understood as the ability of firms to achieve collective and efficient product and market management. In assessing how effective coordination and cooperation is with regard to product management, Barjolle and Sylvander (2002) considered two factors: (1) the capacity to bring out the product's differentiation potential; (2) the ease with which each actor can appropriate the collective process. The latter refers specifically to the ability of the actors to adapt their individual strategies to the collective strategy. The first step to be taken in this regard is the negotiation of a code of practice. Thereafter, they must comply with the constraints imposed by the code and submit to the inspections agreed upon.

In judging coordination with reference to market management, the main issue is that of consistency. Barjolle and Sylvander (2002), for example, highlight the fact that a promotional policy will not succeed if the product is not differentiated, poorly defined or inadequately controlled. They also mention that quality grading will only be effective if payment for the raw materials is directly dependant on compliance with the quality criteria agreed upon. A further issue regarding coordination with reference to market management is the relationship between collective action and the scope left for each firm to vary product quality to suit its own strategy, as this allows firms to manage competition in segmented markets. In conclusion, it can be said that effective coordination allows producers to collectively devise a common marketing plan and to develop a competitive advantage around the product's specificity. Coordination thus becomes both a condition for and a result of the agreement between actors. As such, the capacity of producers to effectively coordinate has been identified (Barjolle and Sylvander (2002)) as one of the most important factors enabling a product to benefit from protection as a geographical indication.

3. ECONOMIC RATIONALE FOR GEOGRAPHICAL INDICATION PROTECTION

The economic rationale for protecting geographical indications fundamentally derives from the fact that place of origin may be used as a quality signal and that the resources of the region may be captured in the origin-labeled product as quality attributes (Pacciani *et al* (2001)). In the first instance, the informative meaning of the geographical name is emphasized in order to reduce information asymmetries. Where place of origin is used as an attribute, resources of the region are used to increase the value of the product. These resources could include aspects such as production techniques, varieties and species, but also resources that are general to the region such as landscape, environment and culture (Pacciani *et al* (2001)).

The added value derived from these resources leads to a differentiation based on product "qualities" and consequently to the creation of niche markets. The collective monopolies which result from the institutionalization process provide producers within origin-labeled niche markets the opportunity to protect and enhance their market and to transform the value added into an economic rent. Although this premium may be small, a geographical indication, by differentiating products by its area of origin, restricting supply and creating barriers to entry, may act as a powerful marketing tool which could improve market access.

A study by the OECD (1995) identified a number of factors that influence the success of small, rural enterprises that target niche markets. While numerous factors have an influence, two main factors emerged: market access and differentiation. The study found that one approach to addressing these factors is to work collectively in order to develop a competitive advantage. This approach is well accommodated within an origin-labeled valorization strategy confirming the economic rationale for protecting geographical indications.

Geographical indications, furthermore, may provide a strong rural development tool which has been recognized by the EU, as reflected in various policies and regulations. This rural development potential could indeed constitute a very powerful rationale for developing countries to embrace and support origin-labeled products within their territory.

In order to understand the increasing importance of geographical indications in the EU and further afield, the discussion which follows summarizes the factors which form the basis of the economic rationale for protecting geographical indications (for a more detailed discussion on the topic the reader is referred to Grant (2005)). The discussion draws on different economic theories to illustrate how the objectives of consumer and producer protection and rural development can be achieved through the use of geographical indications, in order to provide a theoretical framework which will contextualize the empirical analysis in section 4.

3.1 Information Asymmetries and the Role of Reputation

Marks indicating the geographical origin of goods were the earliest type of trademarks used by traders as a means to exploit local reputation through the use of distinctive signs to evoke a particular geographical origin (Rangnekar (2003b)). Although distinct IPRs, this association suggests similarity in the economic rationale for protecting geographical indications and trademarks. The economics underlying the protection of these distinctive signs is founded on the economic theories of information and reputation (Rangnekar (2003b)).

These theories demonstrate the importance of (1) preventing the market distortions that arise when there is asymmetry of information between producers and consumers and (2) averting the consequences of such asymmetry of information on the level of output quality (OECD (2000)).

Nelson (1970) showed that consumers do not have perfect access to information regarding the prices of goods, and even less so to the quality of the goods.

He classified goods on the basis of how information is accessed by and/or conveyed to consumers as summarized in Table 1.

Table 1, Classification of Goods Based on Access to Information

Search goods	Consumers can ascertain quality prior to purchase through inspection and/or research
Experience goods	Consumers can ascertain quality after purchase through use and experience
Credence goods	Neither prior inspection nor subsequent use is sufficient to ascertain quality

Source: Nelson (1970)

The problem of asymmetric information, thus, stems from the fact that the producer knows the product attributes while consumers do not and can only determine them through search or experience, or cannot determine them at all (OECD (2000)). This information gap leads to typical market information problems in the form of adverse selection and moral hazard, originally described by Akerlof (1970) in his work on the market for second-hand cars. The relevance of these problems in the case of agricultural products is that food products, in terms of the categorization in Table 1, display characteristics of all three types of goods (Rangnekar (2003b)). As food markets are characterized by varying qualities, only the producer is aware of the product's quality in advance, while the consumer runs the risk of buying an inferior product due to adverse selection. It is clear that information asymmetry impacts negatively on the market: the quality of total supply drops, higher-quality products are driven out of the market and some consumers will no longer be able to satisfy their preferences (OECD (2000)). Producers maintaining the quality of their products are exposed to unfair competition from producers who sell lower quality products at the same price. In order to protect themselves against such behavior, consumers adopt various strategies. These include the making of repeat purchases, developing a strong sense of brand loyalty and a willingness to pay a premium for reputation. In response, producers adopt strategies for creating reputation in their products.

The concept of reputation, as applied to studies on markets where there is imperfect information (Stiglitz (1989); Tirole (1988)), aids in overcoming the market failure associated with asymmetry of information. In his model on reputation, Shapiro (1982) and (1983) analyzed the firm's choices regarding the quality level of its production with a view to maximizing profits in a situation where it is assumed that markets are perfectly competitive but information is imperfect. He stressed the importance of the dynamics between the following three elements: firm's reputation, consumer learning and the seller's choice of product quality. If product quality cannot be observed in advance, consumers tend to use the quality of products offered by the same producer in the past as an indicator of future levels of quality. According to Shapiro (1983) reputation thus embodies expected quality in that individuals extrapolate past behavior to make inferences about likely future behavior. This value judgment develops over time creating an intangible asset whose value is given by capitalization of future price premia (Belletti (1999)).

In instances where purchase decisions are based on product reputation, producers who decide to produce for the high-end market are forced to invest in reputation. Often this period of investment requires the producer to sell his product below production costs until reputation has been established (OECD (2000)). The need to make initial investments means that, in an equilibrium scenario, high-quality goods must be sold at premium prices (OECD (2000)). This premium represents the return on the initial investment to establish the reputation (Shapiro (1983)). Given this, products which enjoy reputation earn a premium that is sustained even at equilibrium (Rangnekar (2003b)). Rangnekar (2003b) explained that the premium earned is proportional to the lags associated in consumers learning the true quality of a product. It follows from this that a producer will only be motivated to improve its product quality if consumers undergo a learning process regarding the quality of its products. The premium can thus be justified based on the role reputation plays in reducing information asymmetries as well as its role in preventing short-term compromises in quality. This allows a reduction in the actual price paid by reducing search costs for the consumer. In the context of information asymmetry, reputation thus becomes both an inducer and indicator of quality (OECD (2000)).

However, the successful use of reputation to restore efficiency to the market through averting the consequences of information asymmetries requires that reputation be protected through a process which can be viewed as the "institutionalisation of reputation" (Belletti (1999)). Distinctive signs such as geographical indications are one way of achieving this, by formalization of the relationship between the product and the region and/or tradition, achieved through the use of legal instruments that prevent the misappropriation of benefits. These signs embody reputation in that they signal a certain level of quality.

The collective nature of geographical indications as a quality signal means that use of the sign is not limited to a single producer but to all producers within the designation which adhere to the code of practice. Product reputation is thus the result of the actions of different agents active in the same area of production and is projected through tradition over a period of time (Marty (1998)). In conclusion, it could thus be said that geographical indications are the result of a process whereby collective reputation is institutionalized in order to solve certain problems that arise from information asymmetry and free riding on reputation (Belletti (1999)). As such, the above-mentioned theories of information and reputation highlight two important features of GI protection i.e. that it functions as both a consumer protection measure (through addressing information asymmetries and quality) and a producer protection measure (through its role in protecting reputation as an asset) (Rangnekar (2003b)).

3.2 Improved Market Access

Apart from its role in overcoming the detrimental effects of information asymmetries and free riding on reputation, geographical indications also reflect characteristics and values associated with a region and thus regional quality. As such, territory goes beyond its purely informative role and acquires the characteristics of an attribute (Pacciani *et al* (2001)). The resources of the region (landscape, cultural and historical resources and local savoir faire) become embedded in the origin-labeled product, thereby synthesizing the territorial attributes in the product name. It is this characteristic of territory as an attribute that translates into improved market access for products bearing a geographical indication, through the development of a sustainable competitive advantage.

As such, the economic value of geographical indications is to a large extent based on the economics of differentiation and niche marketing. This "socially constructed differentiation" allows small producers to create a competitive advantage similar to that of a trademark. However, Alavoine-Mornas (1997) warned that the originality a typical local area brings to a product can only lead to a differentiation if consumers recognize its value. This highlights the fact that in some instances niche marketing through origin-labeling may require an extensive awareness campaign in order to capture the benefits associated with differentiation. Also, it should be noted that various factors could weaken the territorial associations consumers have with a product. These factors include aspects such as packaging, processing, distribution and marketing. In certain instances technical aspects of production and/or processing can override features of the product that are intrinsically linked to its area of origin (Rangnekar (2003a)).

Geographical indications act as a strong differentiation tool through the creation of collective monopolies. Seemingly a *contradictio in terminis*, the existence of monopolies consisting of a group of firms was argued by Olsen (1962): "The concept of industry in pure competition, which is everywhere acknowledged, is based on assumptions that are perfectly parallel to those required for the concept of industry in monopolistic competition, which is often denied." (Thiedig and Sylvander (2000)). Cornes and Sandler (1996), as cited by Thiedig and Sylvander (2000), defined a club as "a voluntary group of individuals who derive mutual benefits from sharing one or more of the following: production costs, membership characteristics or a good characterized by excludable benefits".

These collectives further exhibit the characteristics of a monopoly in that they segment the production market and erect barriers on producers which limit entry at two levels. First, only producers within the demarcated area qualify for participation. This is followed by another barrier in that, within this region, only producers who comply with the code of practice fall within the collective. These institutional barriers which are created by limiting the use of the designation and defining the product and production process facilitate the formation of a monopoly which encompasses all producers within the designation who comply with the code of practice. As a result, protection of geographical indications imposes, with reference to producers outside the designation, a monopolistic market structure, given the causal link between a product and its origin which results in a proprietary right for those entitled to use it. The monopoly thus created is not unlike that which is legitimized under trademark law by allowing a "monopolistic right" to a trademark. However, for producers located within the designation, geographical indications retain local, public good characteristics of non-rivalry and non-exclusion. By limiting entry and functioning as a barrier to trade, these collective monopolies thus eliminate competition from similar products produced elsewhere, thereby improving market access for those producers entitled to use the designation. It is, however, important to bear in mind the exclusionary effects which flow from this monopoly formation. This aspect is of particular importance in the developing country context and potential difficulties associated with delimiting production areas should not be overlooked.

Various studies (e.g. Thiedig and Sylvander (2000)) allude to the fact that the collective monopolies which result from GI protection enable producers to capture a premium. That there is indeed a premium to be captured in locality is reflected by the fact that French origin-labeled cheeses earn an average of two euros per kilo more than French non-origin-labeled cheeses. French *poulet de Bresse* has a market price four times higher than regular French chicken. Producers of milk used for Comté cheese are paid 10 per cent over regular milk prices. Similarly, producers of Italian Toscano olive oil have managed to earn a premium of 20 per cent since registration as a geographical indication in 1998 (EU Background Note (2004)).

The size of the premium is dependent on a number of factors such as market size, degree of competition with substitutes, consumer perceptions about the linkage of an indication with product attributes and demand elasticity (Correa (2002)). However, in all instances the premium seems to favor authentic and distinctive products linked to a specific area (Correa (2002)). The premium captured by products displaying a geographical indication suggests that some form of value is embedded in the use of this IPR. This value is a mixture of economic, cultural and social values which derive from locality. Those actors using a geographical indication are thus pursuing a valorization strategy whereby intellectual property is harnessed in an attempt to appropriate these values which allow for the extraction of rent. It should be noted, however, that studies (Loureiro and McCluskey (2000)) indicate that some geographical indications, particularly those lesser known and of lower quality products, may earn small or insignificant price premiums and that a geographical indication does not in all instances result in a price premium.

3.3 Rural Development Potential

Apart from, and partly as a consequence of, the factors identified above, the most fundamental rationale for protecting geographical indications in the EU is found in the rural development potential of origin-labeled products. Both European policies and the literature highlight the importance of supporting origin-labeled products to achieve rural development objectives. Origin-labeled products, by definition, reflect a strict link between product and origin given that the product derives its unique characteristics from the climatic, human and technical environment of the region. As such, origin-labeled products are one of the most evident manifestations of locality and are often considered useful instruments through which to preserve local culture and traditions and to foster rural development, especially in disadvantaged areas (Pacciani *et al* (2001)).

In the developing country context, geographical indications could provide a tool by which rural producers can enter niche markets and attempt to extract a premium, thereby contributing to improving their living conditions through increased incomes. Furthermore, the link between an origin-labeled product and its territory derives not only from paedoclimatic specificities and its strong link with localized specific production assets; it also derives from local culture as it characterizes the "historical memory" of the local population and represents a catalyst of identity (Bérard and Marchenay (1995)). As such, geographical indications draw from both natural and human resources located within the territory, thereby stimulating all the components of the rural economy.

According to Pacciani *et al* (2001), the rural development impact depends on the extent to which local actors succeed in appropriating the rent with respect to actors located outside the territory. The potential of appropriating this rent is closely tied to the ability of local actors to create institutional processes that can regulate the use of these free goods (Pacciani *et al* (2001)). The possibility of enhancing rural development through the use of geographical indications is further dependent on exogenous factors such as the nature of the product as influenced by the level of elaboration, the characteristics of the production process, the marketing channels allowed by the nature of the product, the impact on the landscape and environment, the role of the product in the local culture as well as the structure of the supply chain (Pacciani *et al* (2001)). In addition, the possibility of activating sustainable rural development strategies based on an origin-labeled product depends on the strength of the link between the product and the local community. This would depend to an extent on the identity of the product and its importance in the region. Sylvander (2004) warned, however, that it is not the institutionalization of the resource origin *per se* that enhances development. Instead, the developmental impact of origin-labeled strategies is dependant on how the process is developed, and on the effectiveness of the valorization strategies built upon it (Sylvander (2004)).

In assessing the impact of origin-labeled products on rural development, a multifunctional approach should be followed, accounting also for "secondary" development objectives such as the preservation of biodiversity and traditional knowledge. As such, Sylvander (2004) advised that the assessment of the developmental impact should not be limited to the standard criteria (higher prices, increased sales and employment and income levels). Instead, the distribution of rents within the rural area, the level of participation of local actors, the sustainability and reproduction of the social system and the environmental impact are all factors which should be considered.

Finally, it should be kept in mind that the rural development potential of geographical indications is dependent on an inclusive and representative industry organization that ensures participation of local actors and an equitable distribution of rent. Of particular concern in a developing country context is the danger of large agribusiness capturing the rents embedded in the geographical indication without any benefits flowing to smaller, rural actors who are often the original custodians of the local resource. Policies around geographical indications should, therefore, provide for the potentially exclusionary effects flowing from GI protection.

4. EXISTING METHODOLOGIES TO STUDY THE ECONOMICS OF GEOGRAPHICAL INDICATIONS

The purpose of this section is to investigate the main methodologies for studying the economics of geographical indications in the context of the economic rationale for their protection. This section draws on the theoretical framework provided in section 3 and provides a discussion and review of some of the empirical studies done with respect to the economics of geographical indications.

4.1 Reputational Effects

Economic theory highlights the role of reputation in alleviating problems associated with asymmetry of information between producer and consumer. In the case of origin-labeled products, the literature makes reference to product reputation as a factor which can yield a "rent" based on the tradition and quality of the product (Belletti (1999)). A significant body of literature investigates the issues related to the establishment of a producer's reputation for quality when consumers have imperfect information. Although the theoretical literature on firm reputation is well developed, only a few empirical studies have been done. Of these, only a small number analyze the importance of collective reputation.

Belletti (1999) suggested the use of "quality premia" models of reputation developed by Klein and Leffler (1981) and Shapiro (1983) to explain the role of reputation in the case of typical products. The author departed from this frame of reference and reflected upon the mechanisms that give rise to the reputation of typical products. He investigated the importance of reputation in the process of development of typical products and addressed questions regarding instruments for protecting geographical indications under the EU Regulation. The case of Toscano extra virgin olive oil was studied and an outline provided of the process of constitution, crisis and institutionalization of the product's reputation. The limited role of individual reputation as reflected by the value of the key parameters of the "quality premia" model is highlighted. The author explained that the relevance of exogenous and social factors in determining the specificity of typical products causes reputation to assume the character of a collective asset, making it partially the outcome of a non-intentional event. This is in contrast to "quality premia" models in which reputation results exclusively from the choices of the individual firms. The analysis by means of "quality premia" models allowed the authors to go beyond the understanding of reputation as "notoriety", associating it to a set of product-specific investments sustained by the firms in the supply chain of a typical product. Analysis of the case of Toscano extra virgin olive oil demonstrates how the PGI contributes to a "recollectivization" of the reputation capital bound to the area of origin.

In their paper, Landon and Smith (1997) provided an empirical analysis of the extent to which consumers use reputation and current quality indicators when making purchasing decisions. The analysis is conducted by relating prices to the information that is available to consumers. Departing from the standard hedonic model of differentiated product price determination developed by Rosen (1974), the authors estimated and compared five models of price determination that differ only with respect to the quality-reputation information available to consumers. The authors estimated the models using data from the market for Bordeaux wine.

Collective reputation variables are based on government-determined Bordeaux regional desig-nations and industry-determined quality classifications. A limitation of this approach is the fact that the results are based on data of only one product. The data set does, however, include a large number of observations. The study concludes that a model which combines individual rep-utation and collective reputation variables provides a reasonable description of the information used by consumers, with collective reputation being based on the quality of the product pro-duced by an individual firm on the average quality of the goods produced by a group of firms with which the individual firm is identified. The result suggests that consumers place consider-able value on mechanisms that provide information on past quality. The study further indicates that the price premium associated with the collective reputation variables is as large as that associated with individual firms' reputations. The authors point out that the high value that con-sumers place on the government-determined regional designations and on the industry-deter-mined quality classifications suggests that both government and industry can meaningfully pro-vide information product characteristics.

In a further study based on the same type of model in which price is a function of current qual-ity and expected quality (where expected quality depends on reputation), Landon and Smith (1998) deepened their analysis and empirically estimated the magnitude of the impact of repu-tation and current quality on price, again using data from the market for Bordeaux wine. The analysis again distinguishes between the impact on price of both individual and collective rep-utation. In developing the model, the authors proceeded to jointly estimate the equations deter-mining price and expected quality. The results indicated that the price of Bordeaux wine depends significantly on both expected and current quality, but that the marginal impact of expected quality on price is approximately 20 times higher than that of current quality. The results further indicated that consumers consider a long-term reputation for quality as a more significant indicator of current quality than recent quality improvements. The authors deduce from this that it may take a considerable time for a firm to establish a reputation for high qual-ity that would result in a significant price premium. The results also indicate that collective rep-utation indicators play a significant role in price determination principally through their impact on expected quality. According to the authors, one explanation why both current quality and expected quality (reputation) are significant determinants of price may be that there are differ-ent types of agents in the market, some of whom are better informed about current quality than others. Alternatively, consumers may view observable quality as "noisy indicators" of actu-al quality and may thus rely to a greater extent on the accumulated evidence embodied in rep-utation.

Winfree and McCluskey (2005) equated the reputation of a product to a common property resource exclusive to the firms marketing the product. Their work is based on that of Tirole (1996) and his idea of collective reputation where it is assumed that the firms in the group share a common reputation based on the group's past average quality. Using a dynamic optimization framework that utilizes tools from differential game theory, they showed that with positive col-lective reputation and no traceability, there is an incentive to extract rents by producing at lower quality levels. The authors furthermore illustrated that the sustainable level of collective reputa-tion decreases as the number of firms in the production area increases. The authors concluded by proposing the implementation of minimum quality standards to sustain collective reputation.

4.2 Supply Chain Analysis and Transaction Cost Economics

Various aspects of geographical indications lend themselves to a transaction cost economics analysis. In particular, transaction cost economics provide insights into contractual and organi-zational issues of relevance in the GI context. Information economics (Kirmani and Rao (2000)) furthermore highlight the value of brands as a signaling device in order to reduce transaction costs, an analysis which can be fruitfully applied to the use of geographical indications.

In this respect, Raynaud *et al* (unknown) provided a transaction cost explanation of brand value. The authors explained the critical value of a brand to a firm since, from the perspective of information economics, brands are valuable assets because they economize on consumers' transaction costs. The more the brand contributes to reducing transaction costs (and with that, increasing information on product characteristics), the higher the value of the brand.

Raynaud *et al* (2002) studied the governance of transactions in the supply chain as a way to support the credibility of quality signals. It is assumed that the governance structures that are designed in the vertical chain try to guarantee the quality to the final consumer and that there is co-variation between the characteristics of a quality signal and the governance mechanisms in the supply chain. The authors set out to characterize the diversity of organizational forms found in the case studies and to explain this diversity by the heterogeneity of quality strategies. It is hypothesized that different quality signals give rise to different credibility issues and contractual hazards that in turn imply different governance structures. A structural analysis of 42 case studies in three different agrifood sectors was conducted in seven European countries. Following transaction cost economics, the study is essentially comparative and allows for comparison of the different governance methods. In particular, the authors built on Williamson's (1991) and (1996) work on governance structures to describe and compare the several bilateral governance structures observed. In order to analyze the governance of transactions in the different supply chains, the authors drew from Williamson (1996) and designed a typology of bilateral governance structures for each transaction. This method makes it possible to (1) disentangle different contractual relations and (2) to rank these relations on a market-hierarchy axis. In this study, however, the authors presented a more detailed classification to account for the diversity of situations (different sectors, different products and different quality signals, etc.). The study shows that when an agent creates a quality signal whose value can be influenced by several other agents in the supply chain, he will design the governance of transactions in order to assure product quality and improve the credibility of his signal.

Barcala *et al* (2007) studied governance aspects of the vertical chain and its impact on product quality. Different mechanisms of governance such as hierarchy, quasi-integration and geographical indications were analyzed to determine how organizational forms impact on product quality. A case study approach was used and the authors found empirical evidence in a set of international cases of quality brand names in the agrifood sector. The study found that quality problems may be ascribed to the high transaction costs, and that mechanisms of governance thus affect product quality. The results indicate that the most market-oriented mechanism of governance in the sample (quasi-integrations and geographical indications) need to introduce (1) coordination-oriented mechanisms such as norms and routines to perfectly define standards and attributes and (2) a complementary set of quality control devices based on direct supervision. Finally, the study found that the average price premium paid by consumers for quality products is much higher for geographical indications than in hierarchy-type cases. The authors concluded that the vertical chain could be more efficiently organized as a geographical indication than in the case of hierarchy in order to promote high-quality products.

Wilson *et al* (2000) conducted two case studies to examine the key factors behind the differences in market performance of two PDO products; early potatoes from the UK and from the Netherlands. They showed the influence of the differences in co-operation and co-ordination between the supply chains of the two products, which result in significant differences in product specification and traceability systems, and are associated with different consumer awareness and brand promotion efforts. The material for the supply chain analysis was based on empirical research. Semi-structured in-depth interviews were conducted with representatives from the actors within the supply chain itself and the surrounding social, economic and political system. Furthermore, qualitative consumer research was performed for both products.

4.3 Welfare Analysis

Since there will be losers and winners (domestic as well as international) in the process of introducing geographical indications, it implies that there can potentially be a redistribution of welfare that could involve conflicts. Assessing the welfare impact of geographical indications is therefore a critical area of research in this debate. A review of the literature indicates that various studies have attempted to answer the question as to whether quality assurance and certification schemes improve social welfare. Although many of the studies are not directly applicable to geographical indications, many of the proposed methodologies can be applied fruitfully in a welfare analysis on them.

The DG JRC/IPTS Analytical Framework Report (2006) describes equilibrium displacement models as models that can be used to evaluate the impact on market equilibrium (prices and quantities) of a change in an exogenous variable affecting one or several supply or demand curves. These changes in equilibrium make it possible to calculate the impact on welfare of the different factors. Thompson *et al* (2006) provided a methodological framework for the analysis of regional marketing programs which include regional origin-labeling as well as quality assurance and control measures. An equilibrium-displacement model for a segmented market with differential qualities was developed that could be applied to a variety of regional marketing programs. The objective was to model the economic implications of state-financed programs assuring both quality control at a superior level and the regional origin of an agricultural product. To assess the direct and distributional effects of such programs, the authors developed a commodity market model, segmented by both product quality and regional origin. It showed that the price impacts on high-quality and low-quality segments depend crucially on substitutive relationships between markets and the advertising elasticities. It also showed that welfare implications for producers in a program depend on the costs of participation including quality control and on the co-financing mechanism between government and producers.

In her paper, Jackson (2002) analyzed the impact of quality-based labeling on product prices, factor allocation and the resulting effects on producers within the context of an international trading system. Rather than using a partial equilibrium model, a general equilibrium model was used, calibrated to 1998 data, describing US and EU labeling regimes for genetically modified agricultural products. The results of the study indicated that the labeling choices of trade partners have large distributive impacts within national economies, as well as across countries and highlight the importance of using a general equilibrium framework to understand the system-wide impacts of segregation and quality labeling.

Zago and Pick (2004) considered the welfare impact of EU Regulation No. 92/1081 on markets where goods of different qualities are sold. A model of vertical differentiation was used showing the situation where consumers cannot distinguish between the different levels of quality from those instances where the Regulation allows consumers to recognize differing levels of quality. The authors calculated the effects on equilibrium and welfare levels by simulating consumer and producer surplus as well as the equilibrium quantities and prices that emerged. Their findings indicate that the introduction of the Regulation and the emergence of two distinct differentiated but competitive markets leave consumers and high-quality producers better off, while low-quality producers are worse off. With high costs and low quality differences, the total welfare impact of the Regulation can thus be negative. The study also considered the possible impact on market power and showed that when product differentiation increases market power, then consumers can lose even when producers gain. This highlights the need for any economic analysis of geographical indications to take into consideration the market structure, both before and after obtaining GI status. The study concluded that the impact on both consumer and producer welfare is ambiguous and depends on the characteristics of the product, on technology conditions and on the extent of market power.

Lence *et al* (2006) used a simple model to explore the incentives of individual agricultural producers located in a specific region to collectively undertake a differentiation strategy to market their products. They assessed the welfare and market effects of different producer organizations that vary with regard to the intensity of supply control and used their findings to highlight implications of their results for the EU/US debate. The authors found that as fixed and marketing costs increase and the anticipated market size falls, the producer organization's ability to control supply should be enhanced to cover the fixed costs associated with the introduction of differentiated products. Legal systems allowing for supply control favor Geographically Differentiated Agricultural Product (GDAP) development and can be welfare enhancing as long as they do not allow for more supply control than required to develop the GDAP. The authors found that stronger property right protection for producer organizations may enhance welfare even after product differentiation. Legal systems that limit the producer organizations' market power can result in large technological distortions.

Table 2. A Summary of Studies analyzing the Welfare Impact of Quality and Origin-Based Labeling

Author	Method	Findings
Thompson *et al* (2006)	Equilibrium-displacement model	• Price impacts on high-quality and low-quality segments depend crucially on substitutive relationships between markets and the advertising elasticities. • Welfare implications for producers depend heavily on advertising elasticities, costs of participation including quality control and on the co-financing mechanism between government and producers.
Jackson (2002)	General equilibrium model	• Labeling choices of trade partners have large distributive impacts within national economies.
Zago and Pick (2004)	Vertical differentiation model	• Consumers and high-quality producers are better off, while low-quality producers are worse off. • With high costs and low quality differences, the total welfare impact of the regulation can be negative. • Impact on consumer welfare is ambiguous and depends on the characteristics of the product, on technology conditions and on the extent of market power.
Lence, Marette, Hayes and Foster (2006)	Simple model to assess welfare and market effects with three periods	• Legal systems allowing for supply control favor Geographically Differentiated Agricultural Product (GDAP) development and can be welfare enhancing as long as they do not allow for more supply control than required to develop the GDAP. • Legal systems that limit the producer organizations' market power can result in large technological distortions. • Increased fixed and marketing costs of GDAP systems lead to increased need for supply control.

4.4 Measuring Willingness to Pay for Geographical Indications

From an information theory perspective, products are conceived as consisting of an array of information cues. Each cue assists consumers in evaluating the product. Cues can be classified as either extrinsic or intrinsic (Olsen, 1972). Intrinsic cues refer to characteristics such as physical features of the product (e.g. shape, size, etc.) while extrinsic cues, although related to the product, are not part of its physical description (e.g. price, brand, region of origin).

Growing attention has been paid in marketing literature to the issue of country or region of origin of foodstuffs and its effects on how consumers perceive products originating from a particular region. Several studies underline the role of the region of origin as a quality cue. According to these studies, the region of origin has an indirect impact on consumer preferences as a quality cue that stands in for other product attributes. However, geographical origin plays other more direct roles in determining consumer behavior e.g. through symbolic or cultural values attached to the region.

Various European studies have shown, through analyzing buyers' willingness to pay for specific characteristics, that consumers place value on the origin of food products. Hannemann (1991) outlines the theoretical underpinnings of willingness-to-pay studies as a utility maximization problem subject to a budget constraint. Various methods have been employed in empirical studies to measure consumers' willingness to pay.

Hedonic pricing

Hedonic pricing is a useful approach to study the relationship between price and product quality and has been widely used in consumer economics to evaluate the characteristics of agrifood products. The method uses a regression analysis of the price on the characteristics of the product. The implicit price of a characteristic is defined as the derivative of the price with respect to the product attribute. The hedonic price function captures the relationship between the observed price and the amount of each characteristic contained in the product. The partial differential of the hedonic price function shows the shadow price of the characteristic xi. This differential represents consumer preference and one can make use of the information obtained from the hedonic price to evaluate the impact of place of origin on price

Combris *et al* (1997) applied hedonic pricing to the Bordeaux wine market and estimated a hedonic price function for Bordeaux wine to include both the label characteristics and the sensory characteristics. Data was obtained from widely available wine guides. However, the authors made reference to the inadequacy of these sources for estimating hedonic price equations as they do not verify the following conditions. First, all wines that are tasted should be included in the sample, regardless of whether the wine is considered good or bad. In wine guides the wines of inferior quality are often deliberately under-represented for commercial reasons. Second, bottles that are specially prepared to participate in a wine contest must be avoided as they are not, in general, representative of the overall production of the chateau. Third, in order to ensure objectivity, the bottles must be evaluated and tasted by independent experts. Fourth, blind tasting must be carried out. Finally, all the wines in the sample must be bought under the same conditions.

In contrast to previous studies using hedonic pricing,[1] the authors' data included detailed information on the sensory characteristics of wine. With respect to their model, the dependant variable is the logarithm of the price of Bordeaux wine and in the explanatory variables the authors included all the characteristics of the bottle (both objective and sensory variables). The empirical results indicate that the market price for Bordeaux wine can be explained primarily by the objective characteristics appearing on the label of the bottle. As it is expensive to obtain information about sensory characteristics (through tasting, learning and reading wine guides) consumers may decide to make their choice primarily on the basis of the objective characteristics, thus explaining the absence of almost all sensory characteristics in the hedonic price function.

Loureiro and McCluskey (2000) analyzed the consumer's willingness to pay for PGI label veal from Galicia using a hedonic price function. Data on consumption and attitudes toward meat was collected from a representative sample of 157 families. The results indicate that the presence of the label generates a high premium only in high-quality meat cuts while in cheap cuts as well as for the highest quality cuts, the label does not generate any extra premium. The study concludes that the impact of the PGI label is significant in combination with other quality cues. The authors point out that while the PGI label is a powerful tool to promote the quality and obtain a price premium when the collective reputation is good, its use on products that are not of high quality is not an efficient marketing strategy, and they suggest that it could impact negatively on the collective reputation. The authors cite cultural identification as well as perceived quality to account for premia found using the hedonic model.

A study by Teuber (2007) explored the economic impact of GI protection for coffee. Using Internet auction data for single-origin coffees, a hedonic pricing model was estimated. The results indicate that, in the specialty coffee sector, coffees from individual coffee-growing regions receive price premia due to their reputation and that country and region of origin already play an important role in price determination. The author however, pointed out that although these findings are similar to the findings of studies on the wine market, the case of coffee differs in that it is an intermediate good which is sold, and not a product which is ready for final consumption. The author adds that this holds implications for the scope of protection a geographical indication receives and that protecting the production process from harvesting to roasting would alter the whole supply chain and trade patterns.

Table 3. Empirical Studies utilizing Hedonic Pricing

Authors	Type of data	Products	Main results
Combris *et al* (1997)	Data on sensory and labeling characteristics. Data from wine guides and price data.	Bordeaux wine	• Market explained mainly by objective characteristics on label due to cost of obtaining sensory information.
Loureiro and McCluskey (2000)	Consumer survey on consumption patterns and attitudes.	Galician veal	• PGI as a powerful marketing tool in combination with quality indicators. • Marginal diminishing returns with respect to quality.
Teuber (2007)	Internet auction data for single-origin coffee	Single-origin coffees	• Single-origin coffees receive price premia due to their reputation.

Multinomal logit models

Bonnet and Simioni (2001) suggested multinomial logit models, as first introduced by Boyd and Mellman (1980) and Cardell and Dunbar (1980), as an alternative to hedonic price models. In their opinion, multinomial logit models provide a flexible specification for representing the distribution of preferences in the population and the choices of each consumer. In contrast to hedonic price models, multinomial logit models do not exhibit the property of independence of irrelevant alternatives. The authors estimated consumers' willingness to pay for PDO labeled French Camembert cheese using scanner data on purchases of Camembert brands in the French market. They estimated mixed multinomial logit models where the parameter associated with each observed product attribute is allowed to vary randomly across consumers and which is estimated using simulation techniques. The study's results suggest that consumers do not place significant value on the PDO label and that brand appears to be more relevant in the consumer's evaluation of alternative products.

Conjoint Analysis

In addition to the afore-mentioned methods, conjoint analysis is a particularly useful technique to estimate the consumer's overall preference for a product based on its most important attributes. It is a multivariate technique that allows the quality of a good to be analyzed and the product attributes' contribution to total willingness to pay to be calculated based on the assessment of the utility that consumers attribute to individual product characteristics. Monteiro and Lucas (2001) referred to Ness (1997) and Hair *et al* (1992), and pointed out the different possible uses of conjoint analysis:

*   "To identify the combinations of the attributes which offer consumers greater utility;
*   to evaluate the relative importance of each product attribute or feature for the consumer's utility or preference;
*   to calculate the market share based on the consumer's evaluation of attributes and their respective levels in the product;
*   to segment the market through the study of consumer preferences; and
*   to evaluate market potential or opportunities by exploring unavailable attribute combinations."

Monteiro and Lucas (2001) carried out a conjoint analysis on consumer preferences for four main quality attributes of traditional cheeses: price, quality certification label, type of paste or texture and sale size unit and to identify groups of consumers with similar preference profiles according to those attributes. Data was collected from 269 consumers from six municipalities in Greater Lisbon who knew and bought PDO cheese using a stratified random sampling based on age and municipality of residence. They showed that the most important attribute for consumers of Portuguese traditional cheeses is the PDO protection, followed by price, type of paste or texture and then, sale size unit. By showing that the PDO labeling is more important to the consumer than the price, they supported the idea of a PDO benefiting from a price premium. Based on the attribute levels' utilities, they grouped consumers in three clusters, the first corresponding to the least price-sensitive with a preference for creamy cheese (28 per cent), the second to the very price-sensitive (16 per cent) and the third to include those consumers that consider both price and PDO protection as very important.

In their paper, Van der Lans *et al* (2001) tested the hypothesis that region of origin cues and PDO labeling influence regional food product preferences directly and not only indirectly through its perceived quality cue. The study was done by applying conjoint analysis to data on

Italian consumers' quality perceptions and preferences for extra virgin olive oils from Sabina and Canino, Italy. A total of 165 consumers were interviewed and asked to rate their overall perception of product quality and their product preference for 22 extra-virgin olive oils. The study concluded that the region of origin cue and the PDO label were both found to influence regional product preferences through perceived quality, although the effect was limited to specific consumer segments, especially those residents in the product's region of origin.

Fotopoulos and Krystallis (2003) set out to explore the effectiveness of PDO labeling and its acceptance by consumers through the use of conjoint analysis. The study explored whether consumers place more value on a food product with a quality label, through calculating Greek consumers' willingness to pay for PDO apples from Zagora, Central Greece. The results of the conjoint analysis indicated that the existence of the PDO label was more important than price only for certain segments of consumers.

Table 4. Empirical Studies utilizing Conjoint Analysis

Authors	Data used	Product	Results
Monteiro and Lucas (2001)	Portuguese consumer surveys	Portuguese traditional cheeses	• Between the price, the quality certification label, the type of paste or texture and the sale size unit, PDO protection is the most important attribute for consumers. • Three clusters of consumers were found based on the attribute levels.
Van der Lans *et al* (2001)	Consumer interviews on perceptions and preferences	Italian olive oil	• Region of origin cue and the PDO label both influence regional product preferences through a quality cue. • Region of origin also has direct impact on preferences of some consumers, especially those resident in the product's region of origin.
Fotopoulos and Krystallis (2003)	Full concept data collection method	Zagora apples, Greece	• Results indicate a preference for PDO-labeled apples. • Existence of PDO label is more important than price only for certain segments of consumers.

4.5 Rural Development Impact

Despite arguments supporting the rural development potential of geographical indications, few empirical studies measure whether they actually contribute to endogenous development processes. In measuring the impact of geographical indications on rural development, indicators such as increased rural incomes, market access and employment effects need to be studied. A further important impact is the potential exclusion dynamics which may arise from the institutionalization process associated with GI protection.

An attempt was made to study the link between territory-based product qualification processes and rural development by Tregear *et al* (2004). The paper aimed to investigate what happens in practice when actors in a local rural area pursue qualification for an agrifood product. A case study analysis was conducted to show how three small-scale agrifood productions evolve, examining which actors are involved, what their motivations are and what is the development impact of qualification in terms of EU Regulation No. 2081/92. The authors made use of data gathered as part of the EU DOLPHINS[2] research project and found that product qualification may be utilized as part of a territorial strategy. However, the effectiveness of this depends on the presence of various factors. The results of the study are ambiguous on whether qualification processes *per se* can bring about development. The authors pointed out that the process of interaction and debate which lead to the creation of interest groups, holds certain advantages. However, conflict may also arise between the different actors, and decisions on codes of practice and exclusivity need to be addressed with circumspection so as to encourage the different actors to engage in activities that assist development. The authors concluded that product qualification may act as a mechanism for linking local and non-local actors and that it is a means by which local actors can signal and attract revenues from exogenous actors and institutions.

Callois (2004) investigated the assumption that quality labels may act as levers for inducing economic growth. He studied the consequences of quality labels on the redistribution of income and activities between rural and urban areas. The author not only took into account the income directly generated by producing under the quality label but also looked at the effect of this agricultural differentiation. In particular, he tested the assumption that higher income for farmers positively impacts the region through the multiplier effect. To test these assumptions and to determine under which conditions a differentiation strategy based on quality labels may lead to economic growth in a rural area, the author employed a new economic geography model, based on Krugman's (1991). Despite very specific functional forms, this framework was chosen for its ability to study how positive externalities in industry may lead to situations where all economic activity becomes concentrated in one region. Furthermore, as a general equilibrium model, the framework allows one to study indirect effects between sectors. The study's results strongly qualify the potential of quality labels to induce rural development. In particular, the study alludes to the potential exclusionary effects which may arise as the income of only some farmers increases while the region as a whole does not benefit. The author cautioned, however, that the results are model specific and should not be seen as conclusive evidence that quality labels only benefit a minority of farmers.

5. A CONCEPTUAL APPROACH TO STUDYING THE ECONOMICS OF GEOGRAPHICAL INDICATIONS IN DEVELOPING COUNTRIES

Having reviewed the various methodologies that have been used to assess the economics and economic impact of geographical indications, it is now important to consider the appropriateness of the above-mentioned methodologies for the study of geographical indications in developing countries. It is evident that most economic studies of geographical indications have been done in European countries where the concept is well entrenched. Before we can consider the most appropriate ways to study the economics of origin-based products in developing countries, it is important to identify the economic issues relating geographical indications that are particularly relevant to developing countries:

(a)   Misappropriation

Many developing countries are at various stages of developing legislation for GI protection and are also considering the most suitable options for international protection for their important origin-based products such as *basmati* rice, Colombian coffee or *rooibos* tea. There is a strong international trade dimension behind the motive for 'international' protection, which may be particularly important for developing countries. The move towards greater protection of geographical indications in developing countries is attributable to an increase in instances of misappropriation and usurpation, particularly in export markets, which may prevent local actors from capturing the rents associated with their traditional products and resources.

(b)   Traditional and Indigenous Knowledge and Resources

Many developing countries are rich in traditional knowledge and often boast a large biodiversity. In this respect, concerns about "bio-piracy" have come to the fore, and developing countries could be inclined to use mechanisms such as GI protection as a way to preserve (and possibly benefit from) their national intellectual and cultural heritage as well as their biodiversity.

(c)   Improving Market Access, Niche Markets, Protection of Reputation

Many unique products originating from developing countries have strong reputations usually linked to their health benefits, high quality and other unique attributes related to the country or region of origin. Being able to protect this reputation through a GI-type system could potentially be useful for farmers and traders in improving market access.

(d)   Potential Income Effect

Preventing usurpation of origin-based products and protecting the reputation of these products could potentially have a strong developmental impact through an improved income effect. Ultimately this could contribute to increased employment and improved livelihoods. There is thus a strong argument related to the potential economic development role of protecting geographically based products in developing countries against exploitation and misappropriation by international traders. However, the possibility of effectively benefiting from potentially increased income for producers through GI protection is strongly dependent on their capacity to implement effective enforcement as highlighted by a study conducted in India (World Trade Report (2004)). This study looked at the effect of legal protection on the demand for and price of Darjeeling tea. The results suggest that GI protection increased the price of Darjeeling tea in total by less than 1 per cent in real terms over the 1986-2002 period, which indicates a very modest price premium effect as a result of GI protection (although an improvement in quality was observed that may be linked to GI protection). According to the authors, this is partly explained by a possible gap between the legal protection that has been given to Darjeeling tea in India and the quality of the enforcement procedures. This dimension appears as particularly relevant from a developing country perspective.

In the context of the current international debate on GI protection and the establishment of a multilateral register at the WTO, discussions on what might be most convenient for developing countries have attracted significant attention. Following Rangnekar (2004), the costs of developing the required domestic institutions for the effective implementation of GI protection, and for the different groups interested in acquiring and enforcing their rights, should be balanced against the increased efficiency that might be brought about by a centralized register (as opposed to multiple registrations in different countries that may not be feasible for resource-poor groups). However, another important dimension associated with this debate, which might benefit from empirical research, has been the issue of extending GI protection to a number of GIs already protected in certain markets (e.g., the "clawback list" of the European Union). In this regard, Kerr (2006) has suggested that in developing countries strong GI protection and reciprocity in protection could mean that local producers who used to market their products under a newly protected GI would have to build alternative marketing strategies. The debate, in this regard, is whether the benefits accruing to the extended group of beneficiaries of GI protection would outweigh the costs associated with the restriction over the use of some product names. According to Rangnekar (2004), domestic market disruption provoked by these restrictions will have short-term implications. On the other hand, some authors, such as Kerr (2006), argue that, to raise the benefits of GI protection, producers from developing countries would in most cases need to invest significantly in marketing campaigns with little chance of being able to sustainably capture a rent. To support his argument, Kerr (2006) referred to Cardwell (2005) which showed that the effects of marketing campaigns for products such as Washington apples require long-term resource engagement to be sustained. This question is highly dependent on product specificity and actual reputation.

Thinking about the economics of geographical indications in developing countries is rather more complicated and more multifaceted than is usually appreciated. The reasons for this are: (1) the fact that the geographical indication concept is rather foreign and new to many developing countries; (2) the institutional and legal systems are not necessarily in place to ensure sufficient domestic and international protection; (3) the economic benefits of a geographical indication system often have more of an international and market access dimension; (4) the majority of the population is rather poor and will not normally respond to the niche market concept of geographical indications, so domestic willingness-to-pay studies will not necessarily be appropriate.

Given the interest that GI protection has generated among many groups of producers of origin-based products in developing countries, it is likely that many future studies on geographical indications in developing countries will investigate the feasibility of GI protection for a number of specific products. In such cases, some *a priori* assessment of the current and future potential of the product in terms of its volumes, distinctive quality, homogeneity, pricing and cost of managing the supply chain, the existence of a market demand for the unique attributes of the product and the existence (or potential) of unfair competition will be required. Apart from these aspects, the more fundamental issue to be addressed in developing countries is to determine the economic effects of introducing a specific geographical indication and in the process to distinguish between the economic effect on producers, rural areas, livelihoods, and food security.

Linked to the process of analyzing the benefits to producers, economic studies will also be needed to compare the costs and benefits of alternatives to *sui generis* protection of geographical indications, for example, via trademarks, certification marks, collective marks or unfair competition law. These economic studies would also need to integrate legal and institutional issues to weigh up the benefits of each alternative system. The purpose of the protection or certification and the markets in which protection is required will, however, to a large extent, inform the outcome.

With the reality of developing countries in mind and having the inventory of existing methodologies related to the study of economics of geographical indications in hand, it is evident that the economic studies of geographical indications in developing countries required to investigate the feasibility of GI protection for any specific product would need to adopt an interdisciplinary approach with less of a rigorous quantitative approach in terms of testing consumers' willingness to pay. There is clearly a need for a more integrative approach to studying geographical indications in a developing country context, which would, in most cases involve the combination of law, economics, and natural sciences.

The first obvious question that would need to be asked would be: Is there a need or potential for GI protection for a specific product? In the process it is necessary to ascertain:

- the unique characteristics of the product that are linked to the geographical area or the people of the region, i.e. the product specificity (here a combination of natural sciences,

social sciences such as ethnography, anthropology as well as consumer perception surveys would be necessary);
- the quality and reputation of the product (e.g. through consumer surveys);
- the potential for a price premium or the potential loss in price and income as a result of usurpation, etc. (e.g. through economic surveys of price trends and farm incomes).

If the need for GI protection is ascertained, the second question would focus on the appropriate legal and governance system necessary to protect the reputation and the regional specificity of the product (legal and institutional analysis). One would therefore also consider the merits of alternative systems such as protection under trademark law. In this process, the focus would be on:

- the costs of the different systems (certification and inspection);
- the benefits of each alternative system; and
- the need for, and the strength of, producer and region-based collective organization.

The third set of issues that would have to be studied and addressed is the welfare, distributional and exclusionary effects of such a geographical differentiation strategy. In light of the extreme poverty and inequality in most developing countries, this aspect would have to be addressed from a political economy point of view. Ideally, studies on these issues would be undertaken using rather sophisticated and data-intensive econometric models such as equilibrium displacement models, partial and general equilibrium models, although data availability is likely to be a major constraint.

A literature review reflects virtually no examples of empirical studies on the economics of geographical indications in developing countries. This is partly due to the current limited debate on the matter, the lack of research capacity, as well as the general lack of reliable price and volume data in these countries.

However, as we are currently involved in a research project funded by the French DURAS program looking at the potential implementation of a GI-type system of protection for agricultural products in South Africa we will briefly illustrate the methodology followed in two cases to give readers a feel for the approach we followed to assess the merits for a GI system in South Africa, as relates to these two products.

6. THE APPLICATION OF ELEMENTS OF THE CONCEPTUAL FRAMEWORK: CASE STUDIES FROM SOUTH AFRICA

6.1 Karoo Lamb

Windmills, sheep, farm homesteads, endless vistas, home-baked bread, hospitable nights… these images are engrained in the minds of many South Africans when they think of the Karoo. Because of these images, and the tranquility and honesty of the Karoo way of life, the "Karoo" concept has become synonymous with quality, tradition and wholesomeness. The reputation for quality which exists in words such as "Karoo" has significant marketing potential and is sought after by producers with little or no link to the region.

The Karoo covers almost 50 per cent of the total area of South Africa and is sparsely populated, far away from major urban and distribution centers. This lonely corner of the earth is home to one of South Africa's living treasures: flocks of sheep, grazing freely amongst the scattered shrubs. Their meat has been described as "mouth-wateringly succulent, imbued with the subtle, fragrant flavors of the Karoo bush". It is not surprising – they feed on wild herbs, thousands of different species of them, where normally sheep live on one type of grass. It is a most exquisite lamb, the world-renowned free-range Karoo lamb.

Most people love Karoo lamb; it is spiced on the hoof and has a special flavor. It is argued that the bushes in the Karoo provide this taste but perhaps it is the way the farmers finish the animals in free-range environments. It is still not sure what the difference is and very few people have discovered the secret, but as some people argue "my palate knows the difference". By all accounts, most chefs agree that there is something special in Karoo lamb.

The Production Area

The great semi-arid area stretching North-eastwards from the Cape is called the Karoo. Typically, it is flat dry shrub land with grass-growth restricted to the moistness of the occasional mountain ranges. Rainfall is sporadic, less than 500 mm a year, in some places a great deal less. Periods of drought last for several years, affecting the region and its plant growth. Notable droughts occurred in the periods 1919-31, 1944-49 and 1962-73. Since 1974 it has been a relatively wet period.

Apart from Karoo lamb, the vast region of the Karoo produces little else of note. Total gross income from agriculture in the Central Karoo District Municipality (roughly representing the Karoo region) in 2002 was 147,9 million rand with sheep providing the largest share (54 per cent), followed by animal products such as wool or mohair (22 per cent).

Production Processes

The specific taste of Karoo lamb is largely due to the fact that the production is virtually organic except for minor doses for typical sheep diseases such as blue tongue. Karoo lamb is marketed straight from the field and no additional feed is provided. Sheep that are sent to a feedlot to be fattened do not have the same taste and lose the characteristic taste. It is for this reason that farmers have already agreed that fattening in feedlots is not part of the production process of Karoo lamb.

There is, however, some debate about whether the particular taste is only to be found in the Dorper breed or in the Dohne merino breed. The additional debate is whether certain bushes contribute to the specific taste which then makes the demarcation of the production region so critical. The demarcation of the region is, therefore, largely based on the vegetative and soil classifications.

The Product and its Existing Reputation (Product Exposure)

At present there is no existing scientific literature on the sensory qualities of Karoo lamb and/or mutton. As noted earlier, Karoo lamb/mutton has become associated with a unique and desirable flavor, being described as much sought after. In order to protect the geographical name of the Karoo, as well as the indigenous resources associated with Karoo lamb/mutton, the potential exists for the establishment of a geographical indication based on the reputation of quality and flavor in combination with the nostalgia generated by the perception of the Karoo region. However, it is critical to establish whether the perceived aroma and taste differences between Karoo lamb/mutton and lamb/mutton from other regions are scientifically measurable.

The product "Karoo lamb" has been part of South African culture for more than a hundred years. It is part of the Afrikaner and also Cape cuisine and many regions and towns in the Karoo market their towns, restaurants and guest houses as "the home of Karoo lamb". On the menu of most of the restaurants and guest houses in the Western Cape and Northern Cape the various dishes made from Karoo lamb can be noticed. With many Afrikaners being urbanized over the last 40 years and the connection to rural South Africa being diminished, the nostalgia around the traditional Afrikaner way of living is somehow satisfied through the association with Karoo lamb and to have a nice typical braai with a few good friends.

There is thus a strong geographical as well as cultural link in the Karoo lamb concept. However there is no insignia, no certification and no guarantee that the product truly originates form the Karoo when it is sold as Karoo lamb. Only one retail chain (Woolworths) has registered a trade mark for a Karoo lamb product: "Free Range Karoo Leg of Lamb".

In order to scientifically test the "taste" reputation of Karoo lamb and to determine whether there is a demand amongst consumers, we embarked on a number of studies (again illustrating the combination between biological and consumer sciences to verify the economic value of the product).

The primary objective of this part of our research was to compare the fatty acid profiles, sensory attributes and cooking-related properties of M. Semimembranosus (leg), cooked according to a moist heat-cooking method, of Age B mutton from fat class 3-4 of Dorper and Merino from the Karoo with that from other production areas using quantitative descriptive analyses.

The secondary research objectives were:

- to determine whether there is a sensory detectable difference between mutton produced in the Karoo region compared with mutton produced in other regions of South Africa and Namibia;
- to quantify the fatty acid profile of mutton produced in the Karoo region compared with mutton produced in other regions of South Africa and Namibia, as well as indigenous plants traditionally linked to the unique flavor compounds in mutton from the Karoo region;
- to determine whether there is a difference in consumers' degree of preference for mutton produced in the Karoo region compared with mutton produced in other regions of South Africa and Namibia in a blind evaluation experiment.

For our consumer research component of this study the main objectives were to establish consumer awareness and perception of South African mutton and to measure consumers' degree of preference for mutton linked to the geographical production origin of the meat. This was not a willingness-to-pay study but a survey to test consumer perceptions and general awareness to form an indication of the reputation of the product.

The research results are currently being processed but initial indications are that there are clear distinguishable sensory attributes of Karoo lamb – thus confirming the perceived reputation. A next step of the research is to estimate the potential premium that Karoo lamb can extract from the South African market for red meat.

6.2 Rooibos

Rooibos is an herbal tea made from Aspalathus linearis, which is an indigenous plant of the *fynbos biome* in South Africa. It only grows in the Cedarberg region of the Western Cape Province and the high-lying areas in the southern parts of the Northern Cape Province. Rooibos is also only processed in this region. *Rooibos* is the Afrikaans word for "red bush". Different qualities of *rooibos* tea are attributed to different soil and climate conditions, with some areas recognized for their superior quality.

Rooibos is known as a specific product from South Africa. It has become a popular tea worldwide, especially appreciated for its polyvalence and health benefits. Traditionally gathered in the wild, *rooibos* is nowadays mainly cultivated. It is carefully chopped, fermented and then dried and sifted. Through the fermentation process, *rooibos* gets its characteristic red color, its distinctive flavor and sweet aroma. It has a long history related to a specific territory: the processing stage still mainly relies on traditional methods, which trace back to the Khoi and San populations over 300 years ago. *rooibos* cultivation practices have been developed over the last century by the different settled populations. Its cultivation is now strongly associated with the landscape of the Cedarberg region and that is a key element of its identity. It has become a South African heritage.

Primary production involves between 300 and 450 farmers, both commercial (about 97 per cent of production) and small-scale farmers. Areas under cultivation range from a few hectares to over 5,000 hectares per farm, but these large-scale producers are in the minority. Most of the small-scale farmers are members of two cooperatives that grow, process and market *rooibos* mainly for the fair-trade market. *rooibos* processing is dominated by eight large companies mainly located in the Cedarberg production zone that collect and transform it and sell it to intermediaries who market it. Among these processors, *rooibos* Ltd[4] holds 75 per cent of market share, dominating in particular the national market through the National brands group.[5] The turnover of the *rooibos* tea industry was estimated at 180 million rand in 2004 (corresponding to 22.5 million euros). The export market represents more or less 60 per cent of the production against 40 per cent for the domestic market.

Rooibos is sold pure or in blends. The deployed qualification and certification strategies are diverse: fair trade, organic farming, "wild *rooibos* tea". These strategies can support strong differences in prices paid to the producers: in 2005, *rooibos* Ltd, whose production is mainly conventional (only 15 per cent organic) paid 1.9 euros for 1 kg of dried *rooibos* while the Wupperthal cooperative, whose production is all organic and certified through fair-trade channels, paid 3 euros per kg. However, this diversity primarily concerns the export market and is restricted to small niche markets. Most of the exporting (over 90 per cent) is done in bulk.

The Need for Protection

Rooibos is not currently produced anywhere else in the world, but with the increased international demand for *rooibos* tea, some producers feel there is a threat of possible delocalization of production outside the country. Another more immediate threat arose with the registration of trademarks on the name "*rooibos*" by different companies in different countries. This resulted in a major legal battle in the US that made *rooibos* famous. The term "*rooibos*" was registered there as a trademark in 1994 by a South African company to draw profit from its exclusive rights in marketing *rooibos* under this name in the US. In 2001, the company assigned its trademark to its US agent. Rooibos Ltd, assisted by the South African Department of Trade and Industry and the Western Cape Government, contested this registration for more than six years and had to spend almost 6 million rand (750.000 euros) in legal fees before they achieved an agreement with the agent, which recognized officially in June 2005 the canceling of its registered trademark. This was made possible because the name *rooibos* was recognized as being a descriptive generic term, commonly used to refer to the herbal tea derived from the Aspalathus linearis plant and thus cannot be used to design a trademark (TRALAC (2005), Silver (2002)).

The increased demand and lack of quality standards on *rooibos* give rise to opportunistic behaviors both from South African processors and traders – who need to create their space in a market strongly dominated by Rooibos Ltd – and from European buyers, on export tea quality. A particularly important dimension is the quantity of stick in the *rooibos* tea, which increases the volume but can degrade the quality and is used in defining different grades. However, up to now, these grades are not equally shared among the industry. The subsequent risk of degradation of quality, and thus of loss of reputation, is perceived as an important threat by some actors. Furthermore, with the dynamics of innovation in the industry and the huge product range (not only the blended herbal teas but also cosmetics, soft drinks and other products), it also becomes more important for the commercial viability of the industry to make sure that it is *rooibos* that is used. With the expansion and opening up of new markets, need for standardization becomes critical. But with more than 90 per cent of the production sold in bulk and the European market being dominated by a few international tea brokers from Germany, control on overseas markets is very difficult.

Another challenge relates to equity issues and the relations between resource-poor farmers and commercial farmers with the power in the industry captured by the elites.

Research Perspectives around GI Development in the Rooibos Industry

Following the dispute in the US, interest in developing a geographical indication for the *rooibos* tea arose both at sectoral and governmental levels. A South African Rooibos Council (SARC) grouping producers, processors and traders has been established, mainly driven by the processors. The small-scale farming community has only recently joined it. Until recently, the efforts for organizing and improving coordination among *rooibos* producers and processors concerned mainly research aspects. However, this is evolving with the increased awareness of the need to protect their product and markets and the perceived risks of quality degradation. Futhermore they are encouraged by public institutions to cooperate; and they are exploring the potential for developing a geographical indication around *rooibos*.

If interest for geographical indications was already present, actual discussions about it took place mainly as a result of the research program we have been undertaking in consultation with the industry since the end of 2005. The broad focus of the research is essentially to consider the appropriate vehicle for IP protection. At the same time, seeking a governance structure that will minimize the transaction costs in a system that will protect the industry against misuse and usurpation of the name, ensure better control over quality and combine the GI and the biodiversity strategy. The first two points have already been well explored and debated; the third will be the object of a broad consultative process with farmers from the different areas of production. The committee has been established so as to ensure representativity of the different role players in the industry and was agreed at the last general assembly meeting of the SARC.

The advanced level of differentiation inside the industry, which has up to now been managed through individual or restricted collective strategies, could be nicely complemented by GI protection. Future prospects could be to consider a geographical indication as an umbrella under which could be defined different specifications to account for the different qualities and processes of production. This could reinforce small-scale farming communities, for which market access and differentiation for their production is already well developed. Indeed, their access to market is very dependent on fair-trade trends, and communities have potential for strengthening their position in the market by benefiting from the recognition of their specific quality through geographical indications. Indeed, it is known that the areas of production of these communities offer very good conditions for producing high quality *rooibos*. They are settled in one of the best terroirs for *rooibos* production. However, it is worth mentioning that this has not yet been widely discussed inside the industry, which is first concentrating on properly establishing a geographical indication for *rooibos*.

If the GI strategy appears to offer an interesting perspective for the *rooibos* sector and is currently being defined through the consultation process based on the GI committee, it will clearly depend on the evolution of the legal framework. Two options exist: (1) relying on collective or certification marks and thus being primarily based on private strategies and initiatives from the industries, (2) GI benefiting from a *sui generis* system with public interests probably being fostered. The research program is well connected to the policy process and has been instrumental in the evolution of the policy arena from a clear lack of interest, or even a negative view on geographical indications, to a much more open attitude. In this regard, case studies such as the *rooibos* case are enriching the research process and thus the political debate.

7.   CONCLUSION

In this paper, an exposition of the economic rationale for protecting geographical indications is provided as a theoretical framework from which to start with empirical research on the topic. The discussion illustrates that providing protection for geographical indications is more than just linguistic monopolization and that the economic underpinnings of geographical indications derive from considerations of value added and market access through differentiation. The collective monopolies which result from the institutionalization process provide producers targeting origin-labeled niche markets with the opportunity to protect and enhance the potential of these markets and to transform the value added into an economic rent.

The economic arguments presented in this paper provide a strong justification for the protection of geographical indications in the developing world. In contrast to more commercialized products, indigenous products with strong links to indigenous people have an advantage in establishing a geographical indication. The stronger the connection between the product and the region, as facilitated through its link with the indigenous people, the stronger the competitive advantage. This is in line with a study which found that geographical indications show the greatest potential to benefit local producers where traditional small-scale production is still present on the supply side, and where end-use products are marketed directly to consumers. In other words, they are less likely to be appropriate when the product is a commodity traded primarily in bulk (Downes and Laird (1999)). This confirms the potential of employing the economic benefits of geographical indications to enhance development for local communities throughout the developing world.

However, from a policy perspective much empirical work remains to be done to determine the direct and indirect impact of geographical indications in the developing world. Existing empirical studies are predominantly done within the European context and do not provide for the characteristics of origin-labeled supply chains in developing countries. As a point of departure, it should be kept in mind that the motivation behind GI protection in developing countries varies from that of their developed counterparts. For one, what is emerging is that developing counties' main objective with GI protection is often the prevention of resource piracy and misappropriation. Conversely, the consumer dimension is likely to be of less importance in the domestic market. A further consideration is ensuring an inclusive and a representative industry organization which can facilitate GI protection. Without this, there exists a danger that the larger-scale farmers and agribusiness firms could capture the economic benefits without any of those benefits (higher employment and higher income) flowing to the workers and small rural enterprises. The diversity in and/or lack of supporting institutions and the impact of this on governance and coordination within the supply chain also need to be taken into consideration in empirical studies in developing countries.

Apart from the importance of contextualizing empirical research in developing countries, measurement of the contribution of geographical indications, as reflected in the theoretical arguments mentioned earlier, poses certain difficulties. According to a report of the European SINER-GI project, the main methodological difficulties are linked to (1)"The choice of reference point; (2) getting reliable data; (3) choosing between objective quantitative data methods/subjective qualitative data methods with their specific limits; and (4) separating causes (many factors are working together)."

As the research focus in GI research extends from its origins in Europe to the evolution of origin-supply chains in the developing world, these methodological challenges will no doubt be increased. However, without a collective body of empirical evidence on the impact of geographical indications, policy decisions in the developing world will remain uninformed, potentially producing unintended welfare impacts.

Notes

1   See also Nerlove (1995) and Oczkowski (1994). For a review of the literature about hedonic wine studies see Viana (2006).

2   Development of Origin-Labelled Products: Humanity, Innovation and Sustainability. European Union Concerted Action Project QLK5-2000-00593.

3   This company results from the *Rooibos* Tea Control Board, created in 1954 in order to organize the production and the marketing of *rooibos*. Until the 1990s, this state organization was the only actor in processing and marketing *rooibos*. In 1993, it was voluntarily dismantled and its assets were shared among the producers who founded Rooibos Ltd. Even now, some 200 producers hold the majority of the company's shares and are its principal suppliers through a fixed annual price system.

4   Rooibos Ltd supplies 95 per cent of the local market.

References

Akerlof, A.G., 'The Market for Lemons: Quality, Uncertainty and the Market Mechanism'. *Quarterly Journal of Economics*, 84 (August): 488-500, 1970.

Alavoine-Mornas, F., 'Fruits and Vegetables of Typical Local Areas: Consumers' Perceptions and Valorization Strategies through Distributors and Producers', in *Typical and Traditional Products: Rural Effect and Agroindustrial Problems*, F. Arfini and C. Mora (eds.), 1998, 52nd EAAE Seminar Proceedings, Parma, June19-21, 1997.

Allaire, G., 'Quality in Economics, a Cognitive Perspective', in *Theoretical Approaches to Food Quality*, M. Harvey, A. Mc Meekin and A. Warde, Manchester University Press, 2003.

Barcala, M.F., M. Gonzalez-Diaz and E. Raynaud, 'The Governance of Quality: The Case of the Agrifood Brand Names', 3rd International Conference on Economics and Management Networks, Rotterdam School of Management, Erasmus University, June 28-30, 2007.

Barjolle, D. and J.M. Chappuis, 'Transaction Costs and Artisinal Food Products', Annual Conference of ISNIE (International Society for New Institutional Economics), Tübingen, September 22-24, 2000.

138   **THE ECONOMICS OF INTELLECTUAL PROPERTY**

Barjolle, D. and B. Sylvander, 'PDO and PGI Products: Market, Supply Chains and Institutions', *Final Report, FAIR 1-CT95-0306,* European Commission, Brussels, June 2000.

Barjolle, D. and B. Sylvander, 'Some Factors of Success for "Origin Labelled Products" in Agro-Food Supply Chains in Europe: Market, Internal Resources and Institutions', *Économies et Sociétés,* 25, 9-10: 1441, 2002.

Beletti, G., 'Origin Labelled Products, Reputation and Heterogeneity of Firms', in *The Socio-Economics of Origin Labelled Products in Agro-Food Supply Chains: Spatial, Iinstitutional and Co-Ordination Aspects,* B. Sylvander, D. Barjolle and F. Arfini (eds.), 2000, Series Actes et Communications, 17, INRA, Paris, 1999.

Belleti, G. and A. Marescotti, 'OLPs and Rural Development Strategies', Dolphins Report, Introductory notes for Paris WP 3 Meeting, May 6-7, 2002.

Bérard, L. and P. Marchenay, *'Lieux, temps et preuves: la construction sociale des produits de terroir', Terrain. Carnets du patrimoine ethnologique,* 24:153-164, 1995.

Bonnet, C. and M. Simioni, 'Assessing Consumer Response to Protected Designation of Origin Labeling: A Mixed Multinomial Logit Approach', *European Review of Agricultural Economics* 28(4): 433-49, 2001.

Boyd, J. and J. Mellman, 'The Effect of Fuel Economy on the US Automobile Market: A Hedonic Demand Analysis', *Transportation Research* 14A(5-6): 367, 1980.

Buchanan, J.M., 'An Economic Theory of Clubs', *Economica,* 32:1-14, 1965.

Callois, J.M., 'Can Quality Labels Trigger Rural Development? A Micro-economic Model with Co-operation for the Production of a Differentiated Agricultural Good', *Working Paper 2004/6 CESAER,* 2004.

Cardell, N. and F. Dunbar, 'Measuring the Impact of Automobile Downsizing', Transportation Research 14A (5-6): 423, 1980.

Cardwell, R.T., 'Three Essays in Agricultural Economics: International Trade, Development and Commodity Promotion', unpublished PhD dissertation, Department of Agricultural Economics, University of Saskatchewan, 2005.

Chappuis, J.M. and P. Sans, 'Actors Coordination: Governance Structures and Institutions in Supply Chains of Protected Designation of Origin', in *The Socio-Economics of Origin Labelled Products in Agro-Food Supply Chains: Spatial, Institutional and Co ordination Aspects,* B. Sylvander, D. Barjolle and F. Arfini (eds.), Series Actes et Communications, 17(1), INRA, Paris, 2000.

Combris, P., S. Lecocq and M. Visser, 'Estimation of Hedonic Price Equation for Bordeaux Wine: Does Quality Matter?' *The Economic Journal,* 107 (441): 390, 1997.

Cornes, R. and T. Sandler, *The Theory of Externalities, Public Goods and Club Goods,* Cambridge, 1996.

Correa, C.M., 'Protection of Geographical Indications in Caricom Countries', Paper prepared for CARICOM, available at *http://www.crnm.org/documents/studies/geographical%20Indications%20-%20Correa.pdf,* 2002.

D'Aveni, R., Hypercompetition: *Managing the Dynamics of Strategic Maneuvering,* Free Press, New York, 1994.

Downes, D. and S. Laird, 'Community Registries of Biodiversity-Related Knowledge', Paper prepared for UNC-TAD Biotrade Initiative, 1999.

EU Background Note, 'Why do Geographical Indications Matter to Us?' available at *http://ljp.cec.eu.int/home/news_en_newsobj553.php,* 2004.

European Commission, 'DG JRC/IPTS Analytical Framework Report. Overview of Existing Studies', Preparatory Economic Analysis of the Value-Adding Processes within Integrated Supply Chains in Food and Agriculture, 2006.

Foutopolis, C. and A. Krystallis, 'Quality Labels as a Marketing Advantage. The Case of the "PDO Zagora" Apples in the Greek Market', *European Journal of Marketing* 37(10): 1350, 2003.

Giges, N., 'World's Product Parity Perception High', *Advertising Age,* 20 (June): 66-68, 1988.

Grossman, G.M. and C. Shapiro, 'Counterfeit-Product Trade', *American Economic Review*, 78(1): 59-75, 1988.

Hair, J., R.E. Anderson, R.L. Thatham and W.C. Black, *Multivariate Data Analysis with Readings*, 3rd ed., Maxwell Macmillan Publishing, Singapore, 1992.

Hannemann, W.M., 'Willingness to Pay and Willingness to Accept: How Much Can They Differ?' The American Economic Review 81(3): 635, 1991.

Hayes, D.J., S.H. Lence and B. Babcock, 'Geographic Indications and Farmer-Owned Brands: Why Do the US and EU disagree?' Eurochoices 4(2): 28-35, 2005.

Hayes, D.J., S.H. Lence and A. Stoppa, 'Farmer Owned Brands?' Briefing Paper 02- BP 39, Center for Agricultural and Rural Development, Iowa State University, March 2003.

Ilbery, B. and M. Kneafsey, 'Product and Place: Promoting Quality Products and Services in the Lagging Rural Regions of the European Union', *European Urban and Regional Studies*, 5(4): 329-341, 1998.

Ilbery, B. and M. Kneafsey, 'Registering Regional Speciality Food and Drink Products in the United Kingdom: The case of PDOs and PGIs', *Area*, 32(3): 317, 2000.

Jackson, L.A., 'Who Benefits from Quality Labelling? Segregation Costs, International Trade and Producer Outcomes', CIES discussion paper, available at *http://www.adelaide.edu.au*, 2002.

Kerr, W.A., 'Enjoying a Good Port with a Clear Conscience: Geographic Indicators, Rent Seeking and Development', *The Estey Centre Journal of International Law and Trade Policy*, 7 (1): 1-14, 2006.

Kirmani, A. and A.R. Rao, 'No Pain No Gain: A Critical Review of the Literature on Signaling Unobservable Product Quality', *Journal of Marketing*, 64: 66-79, 2000.

Klein, B. and K.B. Leffler, 'The Role of Market Forces in Assuring Contractual Performance', *Journal of Political Economy*, 89(4): 615, 1981.

Krugman, P., 'Increasing Returns and Economic Geography', *Journal of Political Economy*, 99: 483-499, 1991.

Landon, S. and C.E. Smith, 'The Use of Quality and Reputation Indicators by Consumers: The Case of Bordeaux Wine', *Journal of Consumer Policy*, September 20(3): 289, 1997.

Landon, S. and C.E. Smith, 'Quality Expectations, Reputation and Price', *Southern Economic Journal*, January 64(3): 628, 1998.

Lence, S., S. Marette, D.M. Hayes and W. Foster, 'Collective Marketing Arrangements for Geographically Differentiated Agricultural Products: Welfare Impacts and Policy Implications', MATRIC Working Paper 06-MWP 9, Midwest Agribusiness Trade Research and Information Center, Iowa State University, May 2006.

Loureiro, M.L. and J.J. McCluskey, 'Assessing Consumer Response to Protected Geographical Identification Labeling', Agribusiness 16 (3): 309-20, 2000.

Marty, F., 'Which are the Ways of Innovation in PDO and PGI Products?' in Typical and Traditional Products: Rural Effect and Agro-industrial Problems, F. Arfini and C. Mora (eds.), 1998, 52nd EAAE Seminar Proceedings, Parma, June 19-21, 1998.

McFadden, D. and K. Train, 'Mixed MNL Models for Discrete Response', Journal of Applied Econometrics 15: 447, 2000.

Ménard, C., 'Enforcement Procedures and Governance Structures: What Relationship?' in Institutions, Contracts and Organizations, C. Menard and E. Elgar (eds.), Cheltenham, UK, 2000.

Monteiro, D.M. and M.R. Lucas, 'Conjoint Measurement of Preferences for Traditional Cheeses in Lisbon', British Food Journal 103(6): 414, 2001.

Moran, W., 'Rural Space as Intellectual Property', Political Geography, 12(3): 263-277, 1993.

Nelson, P., 'Information and Consumer Behaviour', Journal of Political Economy, 78 (March-April): 311-329, 1970.

140 THE ECONOMICS OF INTELLECTUAL PROPERTY

Nerlove, M., 'Hedonic Price Functions and the Measurement of Preferences', European Economic Review, 39: 697, 1995.

Ness, M., 'Multivariate Analysis in Marketing Research', in Agro–Food Marketing, CAB International and CIHEAM, D.I. Padberg, C. Ritson and L.M. Albisu (eds.), Wallingford, 253, 1997.

O'Connor, B., The Law of Geographical Indications, Cameron May, London, 2004.

Oczkowski, E., 'A Hedonic Price Function for Australian Premium Table Wine', Australian Journal of Agricultural Economics, 38: 93, 1994.

OECD, 'Appellations of Origin and Geographical Indications in OECD Member Countries: Economic and Legal Implications', Working Party on Agricultural Policies and Markets of the Committee for Agriculture, Joint Working Party of the Committee for Agriculture and the Trade Committee, COM/AGR/APM/TD/WP (2000)15/FINAL, Paris, 2000.

Olsen, M., 'The Restoration of Pure Monopoly', Quarterly Journal of Economics, LXXVI: 613-631, November, 1962.

Olsen, M., 'Cue Utilization of the Quality Perception Process: A Cognitive Model and an Empirical Test', PhD Thesis, Purdue University, West Lafayette, US, 1972.

Pacciani, A., G. Belletti, A. Marescotti and S. Scaramuzzi, 'The Role of Typical Products in Fostering Rural Development and the Effects of Regulation (EEC) 2081/92', 73rd Seminar of the European Association of Agricultural Economists, Ancona, Italy, June 28-30, 2001.

Porter, M., Competitive Strategy, The Free Press, New York, 1980.

Rangnekar, D., 'Geographical Indications: A Review of Proposals at the TRIPS Council: Extending Article 23 to Products other than Wines and Spirits', Capacity Building Project on Intellectual Property Rights and Sustainable Development, UNCTAD/ICTSD, May 2003a.

Rangnekar, D, 'The Socio-Economics of Geographical Indications: A Review of Empirical Evidence from Europe', Capacity Building Project on Intellectual Property Rights and Sustainable Development, UNCTAD/ICTSD, October 2003b.

Rangnekar, D., 'The International Protection of Geographical Indications: The Asian Experience', UNCTAD/ICTSD Regional Dialogue on Intellectual Property Rights, Innovation and Sustainable Development, Hong Kong SAR, Republic of China, November 8-10, 2004.

Raynaud, E., L. Sauvée and E. Valceschini, 'Brands Value and Governance Implications: A Transaction Cost Approach', full reference unknown.

Raynaud, E., L. Sauvée and E. Valceschini, 'Governance of the Agri-Food Chains as a Vector of Credibility for Quality Signalization in Europe', 10th EAAE Congress on Exploring Diversity in the European Agri-Food System, Zaragoza, Spain, August 28-31, 2002.

Rosen, S., 'Hedonic Prices and Implicit Markets: Product Differentiation in Pure Competition', Journal of Political Economics, 82: 34-55, 1974.

Sauvée, L. and E. Valceschini, 'Agroalimentaire: la qualité au coeur des relations entre agriculteurs, industriels et distributeurs', Demeter, 2004 (10):181-226, 2003.

Shapiro, C., 'Consumer Information, Product Quality, and Seller Reputation', Bell Journal of Economics, 13: 20-25, 1982.

Shapiro, C., 'Premiums for High Quality Products as a Return to Reputations', Quarterly Journal of Economics, 98(4): 659-679, 1983.

'SINER-GI Work Paper 2', Siner GI Report on GIs Social and Economic Issues, available at http://www.origin-food.org, 2006.

Steenkamp, J.B.E.M., 'Conjoint Measurement in Ham Quality Evaluation', Journal of Agricultural Economics, 38(3): 473, 1987.

Stiglitz, J.E., 'Imperfect Information in the Product Market', in Handbook of Industrial Organization Volume 1, R. Schmalensee and R.D. Willig (eds.), Elsevier Science Publishers, Amsterdam, 1989.

Sylvander, B., 'Development of Origin Labelled Products: Humanity, Innovation and Sustainability', Dolphins WP7 Report, January 2004.

Teuber, R., 'Geographical Indications of Origin as a Tool of Product Differentiation: The Case of Coffee', Paper presented as part of the 105th EAAE Conference on International Marketing and International Trade of Food Quality Products, available at *http://www.bean-quorum.net/EAAE/pdf/EAAE105_Proceedings.pdf*, 2007.

Thiedig, F. and B. Sylvander, 'Welcome to the Club? An Economical Approach to Geographical Indications in the European Union', *Agrarwirtschaft*, 49(12): 428-437, 2000.

Thode, S.F. and J.M. Maskulka, 'Place Based Marketing Strategies, Brand Equity and Vineyard Valuation', *Journal of Product and Brand Management*, 7(5): 379-399, 1998.

Thompson, S.R., S. Anders and R. Herrmann, 'Markets Segmented by Regional – Origin Labeling with Quality Control', Contributed Paper presented at the 26th Conference of the International Association of Agricultural Economists (IAAE), Gold Coast, Australia, August 12-18, 2006.

Tirole, J., *The Theory of Industrial Organization*. MIT Press, Cambridge, 1988.

Tirole, J., 'A Theory of Collective Reputations (with Applications to the Persistence of Corruption and to Firm Quality)', *Review of Economic Studies* 63: 1-22, 1996.

Torres, A., *'Les regroupements localisés de producteurs dans le domaine agro-alimentaire: entre coopérations et règles formelles', in 'Délégation à l'agriculture, au développement et à la prospective D.A.P.P. Recherches pour et sur le développement territorial'*, Montpellier Symposium, January 11-12, 2000.

Tregear, A., F. Arfini, G. Belleti and A. Marescotti, 'The Impact of Territorial Product Qualification Processes on the Rural Development Potential of Small-Scale Food Productions', XI World Congress of Rural Sociology, Trondheim, Norway, July 25-30, 2004.

Trognon, L., J.P. Bousset, J. Brannigan and L. Lagrange, 'Consumers' Attitudes towards Regional Food Products. A Comparison between Five Different European Countries', Paper presented at the 67th EAAE Seminar, Le Mans, October 28-30, 1999.

Van des Lans, I.A., K. Van Ittersum, A. Decicco and M. Loseby, 'The Role of the Region of Origin and EU Certificates of Origin in Consumer Evaluation of Food Products', *European Review of Agricultural Economics*, 28(4): 451, 2001.

Viana, R., 'Long-Lived Port Inventories: Essays on Financial Accounting Measurement and Recognition', unpublished PhD thesis, FEP, University of Porto, Porto, 2006.

Williamson, O.E., 'Comparative Economic Organization. The Analysis of Discrete Structural Alternatives', *Administrative Science Quaterly* 36(2): 269, 1991.

Williamson, O.E., *The Mechanisms of Governance*, Oxford University Press, 1996.

Wilson, N., K. Van Ittersum and A. Fearne, 'Cooperation and Coordination in the Supply Chain: A Comparison between the Jersey Royal and the Opperdoezer Ronde Potato', in *The Socio-Economics of Origin Labelled Products in Agro-Food Supply Chains: Spatial, Institutional and Co-ordination Aspects*, B. Sylvander, D. Barjolle and F. Arfini (eds.), Series Actes et Communications, 17(1), INRA, Paris, 2000.

Winfree, J.A. and J. McCluskey, 'Collective Reputation and Quality', *American Journal of Agricultural Economics* 87: 206-213, 2005.

World Trade Organization, 'Promoting Agricultural Competitiveness through Local Know-How' Workshop on Geographical Indications for Middle Eastern and Northern African Agri-Food Products, World Bank Report, Montpellier, June 2004.

World Trade Organization, 'Exploring the Linkage between the Domestic Policy Environment and International Trade', World Trade Report, available at *http://www.wto.org/english/res_e/booksp_e/anrep_e/world_trade_report04_e.pdf*, 2004.

Zago, A. and D. Pick, 'Labeling Policies in Food Markets: Private Incentives, Public Intervention and Welfare Effects', *Journal of Agricultural and Resource Economics* 29(1): 150-165, 2004.

[35]

Evaluating the effects of protecting Geographical Indications: scientific context and case studies

Marguerite Paus, Sophie Reviron

Table of contents

Evaluation of Geographical Indications: Literature Review   Marguerite Paus & Sophie Reviron

1   Introduction

Recent research conducted in European countries has highlighted the ability of Geographical Indications (GIs) products to create economic value and to distribute a certain share of the price premium to the producers of the raw material in the rural area concerned (Barjolle et al., 2007; Desbois and Néfussi, 2007). Economic value is the driving power of development. However, most GIs have the potential to create positive social and environmental effects to the benefit of rural development. In order to assess this, it is crucial to develop reliable methods that compare the global performance (economic, social, and environmental) of GI supply chains with conventional supply chains.

Hence, encouraging GIs and their protection, as a means of promoting sustainable rural development, implies identifying the protected GIs' territorial effects. Thus, demonstrating both the concrete and probable effects is a methodological challenge to be addressed.

The following paper provides a comparison between the existing approaches in current research and aims at summarising the main lines in terms of the methodology and general results of corresponding studies.

2   Measuring impacts: a tricky exercise

Impacts are defined as being the positive and negative, intended and unintended, primary and secondary long-term effects. These effects can be economic, social, cultural, institutional, environmental, technological or of other types (OECD-DAC, 2002). In this paper, we define territorial impact as being the effect of the implementation of a GI system, or protection scheme, in the three dimensions of sustainable rural development (economic, social and environmental) on the territory concerned.

Assuming that territorialized food supply chains have territorial effects, leads to a methodological question: how to measure the supply chain's territorial impact? The impact assessment should enable the investigators to answer a question such as: "what would the situation be if no initiative had been taken and farmers had to rely on conventional patterns of development?" (Knickel and Renting, 2000).

Assessing territorial impact is a challenging exercise that needs:

- a clear research question (impact of what?, impact on what?)

- a reference point (comparisons) either diachronic (time series, before/after) and/or synchronic (cross section, with/without).

As far as GIs are concerned, it is very difficult to distinguish the impact of the supply chain itself (and the dynamic of its collective organisation) from the impact of a special

Marguerite Paus & Sophie Reviron   Evaluation of Geographical Indications: Literature Review

protection scheme (for instance, a PDO[1] protection) (Belletti and Marescotti, 2006). The chain of causality is difficult to establish, given that acquiring legal protection which attains a high economic performance, as well as building a strong collective organisation, are objectives that strengthen each other.

"Before/after" studies rarely measure impacts accurately. Baseline data (before the intervention) and end-line data (after the intervention) give facts about the development over time and describe what is factual for the supply chain (not what is counterfactual) (Leeuw and Vaessen, 2009). The differential observed by comparing before/after data is rarely caused by the intervention alone, since other factors and processes influence development, both in time and space (Leeuw and Vaessen, 2009). For example, in evaluating the impact of GI initiatives, we must control the influence of changing market conditions or agricultural policy.

The "with/without" approach aims at comparing the situation observed with "what would have happened in the absence of the intervention" (the without, or counterfactual). Such a comparison is challenging since it is not possible to observe how the situation would have been. It has to be constructed by the evaluator (Leeuw and Vaessen, 2009).

Randomisation of intervention is considered to be the best way to create an equivalent (other things being equal) (Duflo and Kremer, 2005; Leeuw and Vaessen, 2009). Random assignment to the participant and control group guarantees that the two groups will have similar average characteristics. Unfortunately, it is hardly possible to design such an experimental approach in the case of GIs' territorial impact evaluation, since GIs are based on voluntary participation and since the evaluation concerns various territorial effects on a delimited territory. This leads to difficulties in identifying an area outside the GI geographical limits, all things being equal, and in quantifying spill-over effects.

However, a recent study made a significant methodological contribution to this approach. Jena and Grote (2010) designed a stratified random sampling and analysed the GI impact of Basmati rice producers in terms of income and welfare. The study clearly identified a counterfactual element (non-GI rice producers in the same area) and paves the way for further econometrics research (see below for the results of the study).

In parallel to the comparative design, a relevant set of indicators must be selected. In technical terms, indicators are statistical variables which transform data into useful information (OECD, 1994). Regarding the selection of indicators, the challenge is to choose a set of indicators which best reflects the holistic assessment that is needed

---

[1]   PDO means Protected Designation of Origin. It corresponds to the legal regime of sui generis protection as implemented in the European Union for agricultural products and foodstuffs (European regulation 510/06). For more detail see Thévenod-Mottet (2006).

Evaluation of Geographical Indications: Literature Review   Marguerite Paus & Sophie Reviron

when dealing with development and sustainability. Moreover, official data of sufficient reach and quality is scarce at the supply chain level. Additionally, a question challenging the researchers is whether it is appropriate to aggregate indicators or to compare profiles of supply chains.

Some criteria are measured with *objective quantitative data*. "Objective methods" provide a snapshot of the impact differential between two states, permitting the comparison between farms, regions or supply chains. This differential can either be calculated for two different moments in time (diachronic evaluation, the reference is the object "before") or for two objects "other things being equal" (synchronic evaluation, the reference must be defined by the evaluator). These methods are based on a comparison of indicators which can be directly measured (hard data such as numbers, prices, and percentages). The main sources are statistical data, accounts data, surveys and field observations. Nevertheless, more qualitative indicators can also be introduced (for example educational level). Often, researchers establish a ranking system based on expert and stakeholder interviews. Several scales of analysis are possible.

However, methodologies developed to assess territorial effects cannot be purely objective. The selection of the comparison point(s) and the indicators, though seeking objectivity, results from a process that implies some subjective points of view (van der Ploeg et al., 2000). "Objective methods" are valuable since they rely on sound statistical data (*hard data*). However, due to lack of data, they do not ensure a systematic analysis of the whole territorial influence of a GI system.

Some criteria cannot be measured directly (such as landscape aesthetics), and the system of indicators might become too complex, due to a high number of variables that are difficult to measure. New methods have been developed to overcome these limits. Contrary to "objective" methods, "subjective" ones allow the systematic measurement of numerous indicators. These surveys provide *subjective quantitative data*. They measure stakeholders' acknowledgment of the effects of a PDO initiative on rural territories as compared to the main competing supply chains. They also highlight diverging opinions or, on the contrary, consensus regarding the contribution of such initiatives to rural development.

Despite these methodological difficulties, various studies on GIs in Europe conclude that in most cases the existence of positive effects can be shown. They identify key factors, in the ways in which these initiatives are organized, which may reinforce their capacity to provide economic, social and environmental positive externalities (Barjolle and Sylvander, 2002; Barjolle et al., 2007).

Marguerite Paus & Sophie Reviron   Evaluation of Geographical Indications: Literature Review

3   GIs' territorial impact assessment: a review of main studies

The early works that explored the potential of GIs to improve rural livelihoods (based on local resources), and thus advance rural development were simultaneously developed in France, Italy and Switzerland a decade ago. The DOLPHINS[2] team developed a conceptual framework that links characteristics of a GI archetype to potential effects on the territory (Belletti and Marescotti, 2002). Pacciani et al. (2001) developed the typology of GI governance in relation with territorial effects, whilst the GIS[3] Alpes du Nord (France) started to develop assessment methods. In order to analyse the territorial impact, synchronic comparisons were applied in the framework of the Pressures-State-Response (PSR) model (traditionally used in environmental sciences) (Larbouret, 2000; Paus, 2001; Paus, 2003). Frayssignes (2001) worked on the elaboration of assessment grids, and Barjolle and Thévenod-Mottet (2004) used a diachronic comparison to assess the effects of the recognition of a PDO for the Abondance cheese. An attempt at a participatory approach was made through the commitment of local stakeholders to select and measure relevant indicators (hard data) in the case of the Raclette du Valais (Paus, 2003).

Studies dealing with economic performance are more popular in the field of agro-food initiatives than in those dealing with the two other pillars of sustainable development. Numerous studies on GIs investigate their economic performance (with emphasis on producers' price premium, generally in comparison to their industrially-produced counterparts) (Babcock and Clemens, 2004; Barjolle et al., 2007; Desbois and Néfussi, 2007; Bramley et al., 2009). It is worth mentioning the recent extensive review carried out by Bramley et al. (2009) where prices and welfare analysis are discussed (see also Anders et al., 2009; Mérel, 2009) and the willingness to pay for GIs in the light of different methods (e.g., hedonic pricing, conjoint analysis). The relationship between environmental values and GI systems, which includes ecosystem pollution, biodiversity, landscape etc., is the least studied dimension. Nevertheless, researchers have started exploring it with great interest (see for example Gauttier, 2006; Bowen and Gerritsen, 2007; Garcia et al., 2007; Riccheri et al., 2007; Cavrois, 2009).

In 2006, in the framework of the SINER-GI[4] project, a first review of studies was provided (Reviron and Paus, 2006). The following paragraph is an extended and up-dated version of this review.

---

[2]   Development of Origin Labeled products: humanity, innovation and sustainability. European Union concerted action QLK-2000-00593 financed by the fifth framework of the European Community for the research, technological development and demonstration activities (1998-2002).

[3]   GIS is the acronym of "Groupement d'Intérêt Scientifique", a French framework for research programs based on collaboration between research and/or development partners. The GIS Alpes du Nord became the present GIS Alpes Jura.

[4]   SINER-GI - Strengthening International Research on Geographical Indications: from research foundation to consistent policy. European research project funded by the European Commission and the Swiss Government.

Evaluation of Geographical Indications: Literature Review   Marguerite Paus & Sophie Reviron

3.1 Measuring impacts

3.1.1 "Objective" methods

Many research studies base their assessment on "objective methods". The first five studies presented hereafter are diachronic evaluations ("before/after historical approach"). The last studies presented are synchronic ("with/without approach") ones.

- *Simulation of changes in the code of practice.* Hauser (1997) simulated the evolution of the rural territory after a modification of the code of practice of Saint-Marcellin PDO cheese that would oblige the producers to use less than 50% of maize silage in the winter feed ration. The study shows that this new limitation would reduce the risk of land abandonment.

- *Transaction costs theory.* Barjolle and Thévenod-Mottet (2004) used the transaction costs theory to evaluate the impacts of the PDO registration of Abondance cheese on the spatial distribution of the supply chain and the type of production (on-farm vs. dairy production). The study shows that among all the different explanatory factors, three are directly linked to the PDO registration: the delimitation of the area of origin, the notoriety of the product and the possibility to distinguish the labelling according to the different types of production (on-farm processing vs. processing in dairy units). On the one hand, the registration did not help to keep traditional cheese dairies in the area where the cheese was first produced and it did not slow down the industrial concentration of cheese production. On the other hand, the PDO did play a role in the increase of farm production.

- *Statistics on volumes and sales.* Suh and MacPherson (2007) analysed, with a diachronic approach, the impact of the registration of the Korean GI "Boseong green tea" on production volume and sales. Production increased from 500 tons in 1997 to 1200 tons in 2005 and the market price increased by 90% between 2002 and 2006, whereas prices for domestic tea grown elsewhere in Korea hardly changed at all. These results highlight the effectiveness of the GI in a context of rising import competition through trade liberalisation. Moreover, the authors emphasised the impact of the GI on tourism and the preservation of regional cultural heritage (green tea festival, train tours).

- *Semi-structured interviews and surveys of farmers.* Bowen and Valenzuela Zapata (2009) examined the social, economic and ecological impacts that the agave-tequila industry has had on one community in tequila's region of origin. They show that two main factors, the cycles of surplus and shortage of agave and the changing production relations in the agave-tequila industry have led to negative effects in terms of sustainability. According to the authors, economic insecurity among farm households increased the use of chemical additives and the overall decline in fertilizer application is due to the failure of the GI code of practices for tequila to value the ways in which the *terroir* of tequila's region of origin have contributed to its specific properties.

- *Evolution of added value.* Based on a comparison between a study realised in 2000 (Zaugg, 2001), which aimed at calculating the creation of added value within the Tête de Moine PDO supply chain, Isler (2007) extended the study to 2006 data. The comparison shows job creation in the region at each level of the supply chain (linked to the production as well as to the promotion of the product), despite a negative trend at national level in the same sector. It is assessed that 60% of the added value remains in the region. It highlights the importance of job creation – however small in quantitative terms – in remote areas.

- *Economic concept of the territorial rent.* Hirczak et al. (2005) used this concept to determine whether a bundle of local products can have a positive impact on the territory in terms of attractiveness and image and can be part of a strategy for local development. The study shows that the basket of goods can be an interesting and efficient tool for regional development and that a PDO product may be the leading product in the basket.

- *Comparison between PDO supply chains and the national supply chain.* Coutre-Picart (1999) compared several PDO cheese supply chains of the northern Alps in France with the national cheese supply chain in order to determine whether the PDO supply chains have a positive economic impact in the region. The study highlights a clear economic performance of the PDO cheese supply chains, with effects on the territory in terms of added value, employment and investments. Chatellier and Delattre (2003) used the same method and found that the PDO cheese supply chains of the northern Alps have the same income per work unit (compared with the national cheese supply chain) despite lower subsidies.

  Desbois and Néfussi (2007) compared PDO and non-labelled products with the data of the Farm Accountancy Data Network (FADN), an instrument for evaluating the income of agricultural holdings and the impact of the Common Agricultural Policy. Regarding the French dairy production, the authors highlighted a significant difference in the prices paid to producers, in favour of the PDO. Moreover, they stated that this added value is not totally absorbed by higher production costs.

- *Comparison between a PDO and an industrial supply chain within the same area or in similar administrative areas.* De Roest and Menghi (2002) compared the PDO Parmigiano Reggiano cheese supply chain to the industrial milk supply chain with regard to economic and environmental performance. The milk price, the farm structure, the employment per head of cattle and the balance of nitrogen were used as indicators. The results show that the PDO supply chain generates higher employment levels both on dairy farms and in the cheese dairies

Evaluation of Geographical Indications: Literature Review   Marguerite Paus & Sophie Reviron

because of labour-intensive practices. Moreover, the results show a lower loss of nitrogen per hectare due to a specific farming system (different cow feeding regimes). Furthermore, the study illustrates the importance of strong links between the actors and local culture and history for the success of a quality product.

Dupont (2003) used the same method and compared the PDO Comté cheese with the industrialised French Emmental cheese. In a combined diachronic/synchronic approach, the study highlights various positive effects of the PDO supply chain: increase in production, higher premiums to the producers, higher farmer incomes, slowdown of rural exodus, preservation of an outstanding landscape, development of agro-tourism.

Paus (2003) conducted a study in which she researched on indicator weighting and aggregation issues for a better communication of global impacts of PDO supply chains. In that perspective, she compared the Raclette du Valais cheese supply chain (in the process of being registered as a PDO) and the consumption milk supply chain (in the nearby valley) with regard to the different dimensions of sustainability. She found that the Raclette cheese supply chain favoured the upkeep of land and helped maintain local knowledge and regional specificity through the production of typical cheese in many small dairies. No significant differences were found in terms of environmental impact. This result might be explained by the fact that the Swiss agricultural policy is very demanding with regard to environmental requirements.

Hauwuy et al. (2006) combined this method and the one mentioned above (comparison with the national supply chain) to find out whether the PDO cheeses in the northern Alps have impacts in terms of agricultural dynamics, use of space, environmental performance and social relations. They found that the PDO cheese supply chains have a positive impact on agricultural dynamics in the production areas, that the incomes are similar to the French average, despite the smaller farm sizes (milk quotas), that the annual worker units employed are higher and the direct subsidies lower. On the other hand, the presence of a PDO supply chain does not seem to reinforce the direct participation of the farms in tourist activities, such as direct sales or agri-tourism. These activities are stimulated, but mostly carried out by non-farmers.

Vakoufaris (2010) stressed that "the impact of Laotyri Mytilinis PDO cheese is, on one hand, very important for the island of Lesvos but, on the other hand, not radically different when compared to the impact of Graviera, a close substitute and non-PDO cheese, which is also produced in the area by the same actors". Nevertheless, he mentioned an increase in production of more than 100% between 1998 and 2005 (to 626 tons) for the PDO cheese, whilst during the same period, the production of the substitute dropped from 957 to 696 tons. However, no price premium at producers' levels was observed.

Jena and Grote (2010) recently developed a procedure following a stratified random sampling to analyse the economic benefits of a GI in the example of Basmati rice. The authors surveyed 300 farmer households. The findings show that, despite higher production costs, Basmati rice is more profitable than the non-GI rice varieties. However, it is less profitable than the sugarcane, which is not a staple food, contrary to rice, that provides food security to the farmers. The results confirm an increment of net income from GI rice cultivation and support the hypothesis that GI adoption enhances the welfare of the households. The authors, nevertheless, are careful not to generalise the findings, as the studied product presents two particularities: it is an old well-known GI that has reached a significant value on export markets.

- *Overlay of environmental indicators and the number of PDO products in the same territory.* Hirczak and Mollard (2004) used this method of space overlays to determine whether the PDO differentiation offers a significant increase of environmental quality in the geographical areas concerned. The results show that a positive correlation can be observed between the PDO cheeses and the environmental quality. The density of producers is one of the favourable factors; however this link is neither univalent, nor systematic.

- *Benchmarking of PDOs.* Barjolle et al. (2007) studied the economic performance of PDO cheese supply chains in order to determine whether a PDO protection is a guarantee for creating and sharing added value with producers. The comparisons of quantitative data, regarding prices at different levels of the supply chain of various PDO cheeses in France and Switzerland, show that the PDO cheese organisations can obtain a premium at the consumer level and distribute this extra value to the producers. However, this performance is not guaranteed by the PDO registration and is the result of collective action.

Frayssignes (2005) compared French PDO cheese supply chains and analysed their contribution in terms of territorial development. He introduced two concepts: the concept of territorial anchoring and the concept of "PDO pole" (*pôle AOC*) that corresponds to a juxtaposition of several PDO supply chains and cooperation on the same territory. He found that the PDO supply chains only had a relatively small impact on the local economy. Nevertheless, he highlighted positive effects, such as price premium and valorisation of the profession of farmer.

Williams and Penker (2009) compared two case studies, the PGI Welsh Lamb and the PDO Jersey Royal Potato. The authors could not identify profound direct links associating the two products with ecological, economic and social effects. However, they found many indirect links. The GIs evaluated were more strongly tied to economic and social values than to ecological considerations. Moreover, the authors stressed that no significant territorial disadvantages were revealed.

- *Analysis of the environmental components of the code of practice of the Swiss PDO/PGI products.* Thévenod-Mottet and Klingemann (2007) analysed the code of practice of the Swiss PDO/PGI products in order to identify the rules with potential positive direct or indirect effects on the environment. The results show that, even though the Swiss ordinance on PDOs and PGIs does not require more environmentally friendly production methods than for standard Swiss products, some rules included in the code of practice could have positive external impacts on the environment. For instance, biodiversity could be enhanced by the obligation to use rare or ancient varieties or homemade leaven and the requirement to feed the cows with grass.

3.1.2 "Subjective" methods

Some research studies base their assessment on "subjective methods". The idea is to ask informed people to grade initiatives regarding various items in order to evaluate their perception of the positive or negative external effects on the marketing of a product.

- *Benchmarking and Likert scale between the PDO and its competing supply chains.* Lehmann et al. (2000) studied the side-effects on the territory of various regional agro-food supply chains in the canton of Valais (Switzerland), using the Likert scale method. Paus and Reviron (2010) used the same method to compare the effects of Rye Bread of Valais PDO on rural development with its main competitors. The study highlights the excellent grades obtained by the PDO supply chain for the economic, social and environmental dimensions and shows the positive effects of a well-positioned PDO initiative, with a good consensus among the persons interviewed.

- *Benchmarking between GI supply chains.* Chapados and Sautier (2009) established a benchmarking between the Rooibos (South Africa), the Pico Duarte coffee (Dominican Republic), the Tequila (Mexico) and the Pampa Gaúcho da Campanha Meridional (Brazil). As the economic performance, as well as the territorial process, strongly vary from one case to another, the authors studied the mechanisms that might induce territorial effects (e.g. the specification of the product and the definition of the production area). The results show how the decisions taken by the actors have impact on potential and recognised economic, environmental, social and cultural effects. They also highlight the need to identify potentially negative effects.

- *Analysis of the practices linked to sustainable development in PDO and PGI organisations.* Ollagnon and Touzard (2007) conducted a survey to characterise practices linked to sustainable development in PGI and PDO organisations in France. The results of the 141 PDOs and PGIs investigated show that the organisations predominantly conduct economic activities (mostly collective promotion, fairs and websites). However, they also claim to conduct actions linked

Marguerite Paus & Sophie Reviron   Evaluation of Geographical Indications: Literature Review

to the environment (most frequently mentioned actions: reduction of pollution through changes in the code of practice, soil preservation, setting up of good practices), actions linked to heritage and culture (e.g. festive events), and actions linked to social cohesion and solidarity (e.g., training, participation in the social life of the territory). The results show that the investigated GI organisations undertake numerous and various voluntary actions in the fields of sustainable development and management of resources.

There are more and more studies regarding non-European GI systems. However, most of them are descriptive analyses, and do not follow a comparative approach, nor do they focus on the specific effects of the GI protection (one noteworthy exception is the paper by Jena and Grote, 2010). There is a another valuable contribution which should be mentioned here: the diachronic study undertaken by Lybbert et al. (2010) that analyses the impact of the Argan oil boom (but not the GI) on households and the Argan forest between 1999 and 2007, revealing a slight improvement in the household income, and no improvement in terms of forest conservation.

Indeed, in emergent markets, the effects of the GI protection are even harder to distinguish from the other elements in the development of the supply chain. Additionally, it is worth noting that new topics emerged regarding territorial effects in comparison with European cases (El Benni and Reviron, 2009): biodiversity conservation (e.g. Argan oil, Coorg honey, Timiz pepper, Rooibos) (Lybbert et al., 2004; Garcia et al., 2007; Barlagne et al., 2009; Fournier et al., 2009; Leclercq et al., 2009; Simenel and Michon, 2009; Lybbert et al., 2010), and the status of unprivileged individuals (women in the case of Argan oil, coloured people in the case of Rooibos) (Leclercq, 2010; Lybbert et al., 2010).

3.2   Measure of expectations

For GI systems in progress but not yet established, as is the case in many non-European countries as mentioned above, it is not possible to assess their effective impacts. It is only possible to identify and assess factors on which the GI system or protection scheme could potentially have an impact. These expectations of potential impacts are often related to the main motivations of initiators, facilitators or backers (e.g. foreign aid agencies) of GI systems and protection schemes.

- Fournier et al. (2010) analysed the case of the shallot from the Dogon Plateau (Mali), and discussed the potential impact of the GI registration on the supply chain as well as on the territory. Higher prices for the shallot, as well as access to new markets, are expected. Moreover, the authors stress the need for coordination and collective organisation amongst local actors to obtain positive territorial effects. The authors depict ambivalent progress with regard to the collective initiative and warn against a registration that would not be coupled with territorial benefits.

Evaluation of Geographical Indications: Literature Review   Marguerite Paus & Sophie Reviron

- In the framework of the SINER-GI (2005-2008) project, a measure of expectations of GI buildings was established for the fourteen investigated case studies. A common methodological framework has been developed to analyse GI impacts with regard to expectations (Barjolle et al., 2009). Barjolle et al. (2009) established the following typology for "GIs in progress":

  - "enthusiastic": the most important expected impacts are market stabilisation or increase, the value added in the region, but also the preservation of local breeds or varieties. The expectations are high for the three dimensions of sustainability;

  - "socio-environmentalist": the expectations on economic issues are less important than the social and the environmental ones. The initiatives mainly stem from a demand for recognition of specific farming practices. Indeed, these extensive and traditional farming practices are well adapted to the area;

  - "undecided": the highest scores are given to the expected economic impacts. Nevertheless, for certain products, key actors consider the food safety and hygienic rules as being important drivers. Indeed, the evolution of general standards might put GI products under pressure. In general, issues related to the environment or society are considered as less important for the local stakeholders.

The authors concluded that for the products considered, there are clearly more expectations in terms of economic effects from GIs. The other dimensions are nevertheless also important but in diverse ways, depending on special concerns in the local context. For the local actors or the external initiators of the GI initiatives, the consensus concerning the potential impact is a good starting point as it leads to common objectives. The role of an external facilitator can be precisely to shed some light on the conflicts of interests or the common perceptions of the stakes, in order to facilitate the compromise regarding the delimitation of a geographical area or the definition of the conditions of production (Paus, 2010).

4   Conclusion

Impact assessment might concern a GI system (supply chain and network), the protection scheme (legal framework) or a cooperation project or programme aiming at implementing GI regulations. These evaluations require different perspectives and methods.

The literature review presented above provides interesting methods and strong results and shows that the assessment of effects of GI systems or protection schemes has become an important research topic. Case studies investigated mainly come from southern Europe, where the culture of protecting GIs is historically embedded. As for example, France has a century of history in promoting official origin-based quality signs

Marguerite Paus & Sophie Reviron   Evaluation of Geographical Indications: Literature Review

(Sylvander et al., 2007). Nevertheless, a growing interest in impact evaluation appeared in countries that recently established GIs' policies.

As more and more cooperation programmes are being launched in transition and developing countries (Barjolle and Salvadori, 2010), there is a need for a more robust and systematic methodology to assess the effects of both the GI framework and the registration of products. The general methodology presented hereafter is a valuable contribution to this objective.

4.1 Regarding the results

The literature review shows that the protection cannot by itself guarantee benefits for rural development. GI registration does not guarantee a fair distribution of value to producers nor positive environmental and social effects. These effects depend strongly on the quality of the supply chain governance and on the elements of the code of practices. In the EU, collective organization has been identified as a crucial success factor.

The research studies clearly identify the ability of GI production systems to create or reinforce positive effects on rural development, which are very welcome in marginal areas. These benefits come from differentiation: a special quality linked to the territory is acknowledged by consumers in the country and outside. This Unique Selling Proposition is defined by a written code of practices and guaranteed by certification. GIs' production often has the potential to obtain positive environmental and social side effects, which often justify external support from public authorities and NGOs. But the commercial idea and value creation process should not be hampered by too many external objectives.

4.2 Regarding the methods

Many methodological difficulties arise, such as the choice of a reference point for the synchronic approach, the collection of reliable data, the choice between objective or subjective methods, the sampling procedure adopted in the subjective method, and the separation of causes, as many factors work together. No single well-established method for measuring the impact of the implementation of a GI system or protection scheme exists.

Each method has its limitations: the specific point of view of the analysis, the size of the territory, the dimensions taken into account for the impacts (economic, social, and environmental), the number of indicators investigated and their prioritisation and aggregation, the size of the survey sample, the level of participation of external or internal stakeholders.

To overcome some of these limitations, participative approaches in the case of GIs' impact assessment have recently been applied to measure the territorial performance of two French PDO cheese initiatives (Reboul, 2010). Originating from the evaluation

Evaluation of Geographical Indications: Literature Review   Marguerite Paus & Sophie Reviron

toolbox of development projects, this approach has an interesting potential in non-European countries, in particular in situations of data scarcity.

Given that the building of GIs relies on the objectives of diverse actors (e.g., processors, farmers, donors, initiators), participatory evaluations enable the investigators to measure the achievement of objectives and evaluate the commitment of local actors. Moreover, participative approaches re-check interpretations with local actors and ensure a better determination of the causality chain. Finally, they contribute to ensure that political decisions are based on real needs of the population concerned.

Besides quantitative methods, qualitative analyses are also necessary to deal with important aspects, such as potential conflict(s) within the supply chain, exclusion of actors, and capacity to mobilise effective networks.

Indeed, beyond usual socio-economic and environmental indicators, such as farmer's income and use of pesticide, it is worth noting that impacts of GI implementation encompass processes that are difficult to measure. Partnership, participation, ownership, and empowerment are results that are particularly difficult to assess quantitatively. As Leeuw and Vaessen (2009) stressed, these aspects are promoted in policy, and are hardly reflected in evaluation practices. However, studies showed that partnership is a result which is crucial in the early stage of a GI-building process (Paus, 2010).

The participative approach developed in the methodology presented hereafter is a precious contribution to this research development field.

5   References

Anders, S., S. R. Thompson and R. Herrmann (2009). "Markets segmented by regional-origin labelling with quality control." Applied Economics 41(3): 311-321.

Babcock, B. A. and R. Clemens (2004). Geographical Indications and Property Rights: Protecting Value-added Agricultural Products. MATRIC Briefing Paper. Ames, Iowa, Midwest Agribusiness Trade Research and Information Center, Iowa State University. 04-MBP 7: 51 p. Available at http://www.card.iastate.edu/publications/dbs/pdffiles/04mbp7.pdf.

Barjolle, D., M. Paus and A. Perret (2009). Impacts of Geographical Indications, Review of Methods and Empirical Evidences. International Association of Agricultural Economists, Beijing, China. Available at http://ageconsearch.umn.edu/bitstream/51737/2/PaperIAAE2009_85.pdf.

Barjolle, D., S. Reviron and B. Sylvander (2007). "Création et distribution de valeur économique dans les filières de fromages AOP." Economie et Sociétés Série: "Systèmes agroalimentaires", AG, 29 (9/2007): 1507-1524.

Barjolle, D. and M. Salvadori (2010). Geographical Indications and International Cooperation in Developing Countries: an exploratory analysis of projects and institutions. Expert meeting on technical cooperation programs related to origin-linked products and geographical indications, Pergny-Geneva, AGRIDEA, FAO, OriGIn.

Barjolle, D. and B. Sylvander (2002). "Some Factors of Success for Origin Labelled Products in Agri-Food Supply Chains in Europe: Market, Internal Resources and Institutions." Economie et Sociétés, Cahiers de l'ISMEA, Série Développement Agroalimentaire(25): 21 p.

Barjolle, D. and E. Thévenod-Mottet (2004). Ancrage territorial des systèmes de pro-duction: le cas des Appellations d'Origine Contrôlée. Industries Alimentaires et Agricoles. 6: 19-27.

Barlagne, C., L. Bérard, C. Garcia and D. Marie-Vivien (2009). Miel, indication géographique et biodiversité. Des liens émergents complexes. Localiser les pro-duits: une voie durable au service de la diversité naturelle et culturelle des Suds?, Paris, UNESCO. Available at http://www.mnhn.fr/colloque/localiserlesproduits/5_Paper_BARLAGNE_C.pdf.

Belletti, G. and A. Marescotti (2002). OLPs and rural development. WP3, Concerted Action DOLPHINS – Development of Origin Labelled Products: Humanity, innovation and sustainability.

Belletti, G. and A. Marescotti (2006). GI social and economic issues. WP2 report, Strengthening International Research on Geographical Indications: from research foundation to consistent policy SINER-GI Project, European Commission, Sixth framework programme: 54 p.

Bowen, S. and P. R. W. Gerritsen (2007). "Reverse leasing and power dynamics among blue agave farmers in western Mexico." Agriculture and Human Values 24: 473-488.

Bowen, S. and A. Valenzuela Zapata (2009). "Geographical indications, *terroir*, and socioeconomic and ecological sustainability: The case of tequila." Journal of Rural Studies 25(1): 108-119.

Bramley, C., E. Biénabe and J. Kirsten (2009). The economics of geographical indi-cations: towards a conceptual framework for geographical indication reserach in developing countries. The economics of Intellectual Property. W. I. P. Organi-zation: 109-141. Available at http://www.wipo.int/ip-development/en/economics/pdf/wo_1012_e_cover.pdf.

Cavrois, A. (2009). Biodiversité et signes de reconnaissance agricoles. Quelles prise en compte de la biodiversité dans les marques, labels et certifications de productions agricoles? Paris, Comité français de l'UICN:173 p. Available at http://www.uicn.fr/IMG/pdf/Rapport_Biodiversite_signes_reconnaissance_agricol es.pdf.

Chapados, A. and D. Sautier (2009). De la qualification des produits agroalimentaires à la diversité culturelle et biologique: une analyse comparée de quatre expériences d'indications géographiques dans les pays du Sud. Localiser les produits: une voie durable au service de la diversité naturelle et culturelle des Suds?, Paris, UNESCO. Available at http://www.mnhn.fr/colloque/localiserlesproduits/10_Paper_CHAPADOS_A.pdf.

Chatellier, V. and F. Delattre (2003). "La production laitière dans les montagnes françaises: une dynamique particulière pour les Alpes du Nord." INRA Pro-ductions Animales 16(1): 61-76. Available at http://granit.jouy.inra.fr/productions-animales/2003/Prod_Anim_2003_16_1_06.pdf.

Coutre-Picard, L. (1999). "Impact économique des filières fromagères AOC savoy-ardes." Revue Purpan 191: 135-153.

de Roest, K. and A. Menghi (2002). The production of Parmigiano Reggiano cheese. Living Countrysides: Rural Development Processes in Europe - The State of the Art. J. D. van der Ploeg, A. Long and J. Banks. Doetinchem, Elsevier bedrijfsinformatie BV: 73-82.

Desbois, D. and J. Néfussi (2007). Signes de qualité : quels résultats économiques pour le producteur? Demeter 2008: 49-96.

Duflo, E. and M. Kremer (2005). Use of Randomization in the Evaluation of Devel-opment Effectiveness. Evaluating Development Effectiveness. G. Pitman, O. Feinstein and G. Ingram. New Brunswick, NJ: Transaction Publishers: 205-232.

Dupont, F. (2003). Impact de l'utilisation d'une indication géographique sur l'agriculture et le développement rural - France - Fromage de Comté. Paris, Ministère de l'agriculture (MAAPAR).

El Benni, N. and S. Reviron (2009). Geographical Indications: review of seven case studies worldwide. NCCR Trade Regulation Working Paper No 2009/15. Available at http://82.220.2.60/images/stories/publications/IP5/GI_Case-studies_2009.pdf.

Fournier, S., D. Chabrol, H. de Bon and A. Meyer (2010). La construction de ressources territoriales: l'échalote du plateau dogon (Mali) face à la mondialisation du marché des alliacées. International EAAE-SYAL Seminar - Spatial Dynamics in Agro-food Systems, Parma. Available at http://ageconsearch.umn.edu/bitstream/95495/2/paper%20completo%20190.pdf.

Fournier, S., F. Verdeaux, M. Avril and C. Durand (2009). Le développement des indications géographiques au sud: attentes des acteurs locaux et fonctions jouées. Etudes de cas en Indonésie et en Ethiopie. Localiser les produits: une voie durable au service de la diversité naturelle et culturelle des Suds? Paris, UNESCO. Available at http://www.mnhn.fr/colloque/localiserlesproduits/15_Paper_FOURNIER_S.pdf.

Frayssignes, J. (2001). "L'ancrage territorial d'une filière fromagère d'AOC – l'exemple du système Roquefort." Economie Rurale 264-265: 89-103.

Frayssignes, J. (2005). Les AOC dans le développement territorial. Une analyse en termes d'ancrage appliquée aux cas français des filières fromagères. Toulouse, INPT, ENSAT, Ecole doctorale TESC. Thèse de Géographie: 2 volumes, 469 p.

Garcia, C., D. Marie-Vivien, C. Kushalappa, P. G. Chengappa and K. M. Nanaya (2007). "Geographical Indications and Biodiversity in the Western Ghats, India. Can Labeling Benefit Producers and the Environment in a Mountain Agroforestry Landscape?" Mountain Research and Development 27(3): 206-210.

Gauttier, M. (2006). Appellations d'Origine Contrôlée et paysages. Paris, Institut National des Appellations d'Origine Contrôlée: 76 p. Available at http://agriculture.gouv.fr/IMG/pdf/inaoetpaysage_0207.pdf.

Hauser, S. (1997). Qualification d'un produit agricole et conséquences possibles sur la gestion de l'espace. Le cas des AOC Saint-Marcellin. Paris, Institut National Agronomique Paris-Grignon. Rapport de diplôme et de DEA.

Hauwuy, A., F. Delattre, D. Roybin and J.-B. Coulon (2006). "Conséquences de la présence de filières fromagères bénéficiant d'une Indication Géographique sur l'activité agricole des zones considérées: l'exemple des Alpes du Nord." INRA Productions Animales 19(5): 371-380. Available at http://granit.jouy.inra.fr/productions-animales/2006/Prod_Anim_2006_19_5_05.pdf.

Hirczak, M., M. Moalla, A. Mollard, B. Pecqueur, M. Rambonilaza and D. Vollet (2005). Du panier de biens à un modèle plus général des biens complexes territorialisés: concepts, grille d'analyse et questions. Actes du Colloque SFER: Au nom de la Qualité. Quelle(s) qualité(s) demain, pour quelle(s) demande(s)?, Clérmont-Ferrand, Enita Clérmont-Ferrand.

Hirczak, M. and A. Mollard (2004). "Qualité des produits agricoles et de l'environnement: le cas de Rhône-Alpes." Revue d'Economie Régionale et Urbaine 5: 845-868.

Isler, O. (2007). Etude Tête de Moine. Importance socio-économique de la fabrication de fromage décentralisée pour une région. Euromontana, Piatra Neamt.

Jena, P. R. and U. Grote (2010). Does Geographical Indication (GI) Reduce Vulnerability to Poverty? A Case Study of Basmati Rice from Northern India. Advancing Sustainability in a Time of Crisis, International Society for Ecological Economics Conference, Oldenburg, Bremen.

Knickel, K. and H. Renting (2000). "Methodological and Conceptual issues in the study of multifunctionality and rural development." Sociologia Ruralis 40(4): 512-528.

Larbouret, P. (2000). Evaluation de l'impact d'une filière AOC sur son territoire: conception d'une méthodologie, ENGREF, SUACI Montagne Alpes du Nord: 39 p.

Leclercq, M. (2010). Le rooibos: dynamiques locales autour d'un produit marchand à succès, révélatrices d'une société sud-africaine plurielle. Paris, Muséum national d'Histoire Naturelle. PhD: 203 p. Available at http://tel.archives-ouvertes.fr/docs/00/57/05/97/PDF/Rooibos_These_Maya_Leclercq.pdf.

Leclercq, M., E. Biénabe and P. Caron (2009). The case of the South African Rooibos: Biodiversity conservation as a collective consensus. Localiser les produits: une voie durable au service de la diversité naturelle et culturelle des Suds? Paris, UNESCO. Available at http://www.mnhn.fr/colloque/localiserlesproduits/20_Paper_LECLERCQ_M.pdf.

Leeuw, F. and J. Vaessen (2009). Impact Evaluations and Development. NONIE Guidance on Impact Evaluation, Network of Networks on Impact Evaluation: 115 p.

Lehmann, B., E. W. Stucki, N. Claeymann, V. Miéville-Ott, S. Reviron and P. Rognon (2000). Vers une agriculture valaisanne durable. Lausanne, Antenne Romande de l'Institut d'Economie Rurale, ETH Zurich: 306 p.

Lybbert, T., N. Magnan and A. Aboudrare (2010). "Household and Local Forest Impacts of Morocco's Argan Oil Bonanza." Environment & Development Economics 15: 439-464.

Lybbert, T. J., C. B. Barrett and H. Narjisse (2004). "Does Resource Commercialization Induce Local Conservation? A Cautionary Tale From Southwestern Morocco." Society and Natural Resources 17(5): 413-430.

Mérel, P. (2009). "Measuring market power in the French Comté cheese market." European Review of Agricultural Economics 36(1): 31-51.

OECD (1994). "Creating rural indicators for shaping territorial policy." Paris, OECD.

OECD-DAC (2002). Glossary of Key Terms in Evaluation- and Results-based Management. Paris, OECD-DAC.

Ollagnon, M. and J.-M. Touzard (2007). Indications géographiques et développement durable: enquête nationale sur les actions des organisations de gestion locale des Indications Géographiques. Projet PRODDIG. Montpellier, INRA Montpellier - UMR Innovation: 65 p.

Pacciani, A., G. Belletti, A. Marescotti and S. Scaramuzzi (2001). The role of typical products in fostering rural development and the effects of regulation (EEC) 2081/92. 73rd Seminar of the EAAE. Policy experiences with rural development in a diversified Europe, Ancona, Italy.

Paus, M. (2001). Evaluation de l'impact territorial d'une filière A.O.C.: Contribution à la mise en place d'une méthodologie. Cas de la filière bovin lait dans les Alpes du Nord françaises et suisses. Institut National Agronomique de Paris-Grignon.

Paus, M. (2003). Test de faisabilité de la méthode d'évaluation de l'impact territorial d'une filière de qualité: application à la filière raclette au lait cru. Une comparaison entre le Val d'Illiez et le district d'Entremont, Valais. 2003/1. Zurich, Institut d'Economie Rurale, ETH Zurich: 107 p.

Paus, M. (2010). Collective agro-food initiatives and sustainable rural development: articulation between internal governance and rural governance. Illustrated by geographical indications from Switzerland and Serbia. Zurich, Swiss Federal Institute of Technology Zurich. PhD thesis. Available at http://e-collection.library.ethz.ch/eserv/eth:2625/eth-2625-02.pdf

Paus, M. and S. Reviron (2010). "Mesure de l'impact territorial d'initiatives agro-alimentaires: enseignement de deux cas suisses." Economie Rurale 315: 28-45.

Reboul, N. (2010). Contribution à la construction de grilles d'évaluation de la durabilité de filières fromagères sous AOC. Etudes de cas sur les filières Beaufort et Bleu du Vercors Sassenage. Montpellier, Montpellier SupAgro. Diplôme d'ingénieur de spécialisation en agronomie des régions chaudes de l'IRC-SUPAGRO: 79 p.

Reviron, S. and M. Paus (2006). Impact analysis methods - Special Report WP2, Social and Economic Issues. Strengthening International Research on Geographical Indications: from research foundation to consistent policy SINER-GI Project, European Commission - Sixth framework programme: 35 p.

Riccheri, M., B. Görlach, S. Schlegel, H. Keefe and A. Leipprand (2007). Assessing the Applicability of Geographical Indications as a Means to Improve Environmental Quality in Affected Ecosystems and the Competitiveness of Agricultural Products. WP3, IPDEV Project, Impacts of the IPR Rules on Sustainable Development, European Commission, Sixth framework programme: 125 p.

Simenel, R. and G. Michon (2009). "Secret de femme, secret de nature": l'huile d'argan ou la fabrication du mythe moderne des produits du terroir au sud. Localiser les produits: une voie durable au service de la diversité naturelle et culturelle des Suds? Paris, UNESCO. Available at http://www.mnhn.fr/colloque/localiserlesproduits/30_Paper_SIMENEL_R.pdf.

Suh, J. and A. MacPherson (2007). "The impact of geographical indication on the revitalisation of a regional economy: a case study of "Boseong" green tea." Area 39(4): 518-527.

Sylvander, B., L. Lagrange and C. Monticelli (2007). "Les signes officiels de qualité et d'origine européens. Quelle insertion dans une économie globalisée?" Economie Rurale 299: 7-23.

Thévenod-Mottet, E. (2006). WP1 report: GI Legal and Institutional Issues. Strengthening International Research on Geographical Indications: from research foundation to consistent policy SINER-GI Project, European Commission - Sixth framework programme. Available at http://www.origin-food.org/2005/upload/SIN-WP1-report-131006.pdf.

Thévenod-Mottet, E. and A. Klingemann (2007). Dimensions environnementales et paysagères des AOC-IGP en Suisse et territorialisation des promesses de durabilité agro-alimentaires. Joint Congress of the European Regional Science Association (ERSA), 47th Congress and Association de Science Régionale de Langue Française (ASRDLF), 44th Congress, Paris/ Cergy-Pontoise.

Vakoufaris, H. (2010). "The impact of Ladotyri Mytilinis PDO cheese on the rural development of Lesvos island, Greece." Local Environment 15(1): 27-41.

van der Ploeg, J. D., H. Renting, G. Brunori, K. Knickel, J. Mannion, T. Marsden, K. de Roest, E. Sevilla-Guzmàn and F. Ventura (2000). "Rural Development: from Practices and Policies towards Theory." Sociologia Ruralis 40(4): 391-408.

Williams, R. and M. Penker (2009). "Do Geographical Indications Promote Sustainable Rural Development?" Jahrbuch der Österreichischen Gesellschaft für Agrarökonomie 18(3): 147-156.

Zaugg, U. (2001). Die regionale Wertschöpfung am Beispiel Tête de Moine. Tätigkeitsbericht der Schweizerischen Hochschule für Landwirtschaft 1999/2000. Zollikofen, Swiss College of Agriculture SHL.

[36]
Assessing the Economic Impact of GI Protection

Thierry Coulet

Based on a short synthesis of the economic theory of GIs, this chapter proposes a pragmatic methodology for assessing the potential economic impact of GI protection. After a brief review of the economic literature, it will thus try to identify the major benefits and costs that are most usually attributed to GI protection and will finally detail the quantitative and qualitative methods that can be implemented in order to assess these benefits and costs.

The Economic Analysis of GI Protection

Looking at what the economic theory says about the GI protection is a prerequisite to the understanding of the potential effects – positive or negative – of introducing a GI. Conceptually, a geographical indication can be considered as a club asset shared by firms acting on a specific territory in the production of a given and specified good (see Benavente 2010). The following synthesis largely relies on the literature review included in this article.

A club good is characterized by partial excludability, no or partial rivalry of benefits and congestion phenomena (Buchanan 1965). On the other hand, a club can be defined as a voluntary group deriving mutual benefit from sharing one or more of the following: production costs, the members' characteristics or a good characterized by excludable benefits (Cornes and Sandler 1996). In addition to excludability and rivalry, club goods hence share three key features: the membership to the club is voluntary, it involves sharing of benefits, without excluding partial rivalry, and the club has an exclusion mechanism at some cost.

Building on this theoretical basis, the geographical indication can indeed be defined as an intangible asset which consists in an identifiable, non-monetary resource, not material or physical in nature, which constitutes a legal claim to future benefits (Benavente 2010). [101]

It is worth noting that the reputation of the good is at the core of the value of its geographical indication. Indeed, the value of the GI relies on a pre-existing reputation and aims at enhancing it. From this analysis stem several observations.

The immaterial asset that the GI represents can appreciate or depreciate over time and, in particular, as a consequence of the behaviour of its owners, that is the members of the GI club, which can impact the reputation of the GI-labelled good in terms of quality and/or reliability. Collective action among GI-right-holders thus appears to be critical in order to avoid problems attached to what is known in economic theory as free-riding, which consists of opportunistic behaviour by one or several members of the GI club, benefiting from the club asset without respecting the constraints attached to it and putting the reputation of the GI good, that is the value of the club asset, at risk (see Rangnekar 2003).

If this coordination is critical, another risk then nevertheless arises to see this coordination leading to anti-competitive behaviour (see OECD 2000). Under an excessive coordination scheme, the market equilibrium for a GI-labelled product could well be similar to a cartel equilibrium, characterized by a higher producer surplus, a lower consumer surplus and a substantial reduction of the overall surplus, that is the global economic welfare.

A model developed by Winfree and McCluskey (2005) on collective reputation effects can be profitably used in the analysis of the allocative, competitive and welfare effects of GIs. This model considers reputation as a common property extracted by firms and builds on the previous model of Shapiro (1982) on individual reputation, on which basis Shapiro had shown that a price premium is a return on the asset value of reputation (Shapiro 1983).

Beyond these direct impacts on the market equilibrium, introducing a GI will most probably entail long-term dynamic effects.

Building on the approaches of Shapiro (1982) and Winfree and McCluskey (2005), Benavente (2010) develops a model whose main focus is to explore the relationship between the size of the membership to the GI club, the quality of the product and, in the end, the value of the club asset that the GI protection constitutes. This analysis thus aims at assessing club reputation dynamics when quality is considered as endogenous. In other words, the equilibrium level of quality is there a function of membership. Benavente shows that there could be an inflexion point in the size of the membership to a GI club of producers, up to which the equilibrium quality increases and after which it decreases.

The model also explores the respective impacts on quality and profitability of a bottom-up, firm-driven approach to optimal membership versus those of a top-down, state-driven approach. In the first case, it shows that, as long as the use of the GI name is restricted and as long as the GI product is highly valued and differentiated, the market equilibrium will command a higher quality level and a higher profit at the industry level than that which would be observed in the absence of any GI. This means that countries would not need to impose cumbersome and expensive structures for the development of GIs for some, at least, of their potential to develop as a market outcome (see Benavente 2010: 22). On the other hand , a top-down, state-driven [102] approach to optimal membership, based on the maximization of the club profits, in contrast to the maximization of firm profits that would characterize the bottom-up approach, will lead to a greater optimal level of membership and a lower level of quality than the bottom-up approach.

This dynamic analysis is complemented by a partial equilibrium approach in which quality is considered as exogenous under no rivalry or partial rivalry conditions. This approach allows to explore the impact of state subsidization and the relation between geographical confinement and factor markets. It also explores the competition implications of GIs and, in particular, the risk of seeing a GI club evolve in a cartel-like group charaterized by oligopolistic behaviour and the risk of observing the development of a monopsonistic behaviour. It is worth noting in particular that, beyond the direct economic impact on producers and consumers, a GI may also have an indirect but important impact on land and factor prices.

To sum up, introducing the protection of a GI may, in a dynamic-static approach, have an impact on all the key factors of the market equilibrium, i.e. the prices at different stages of the value added chain, the volumes of production, the producer surplus and the consumer surplus.

All these analyses developed in the economic literature give some insights into what kind of impact can be expected from the introduction of a GI protection and, above all, into the conditions and circumstances under which such positive or negative impacts can be expected. The key features in this respect relate to the market structure of the goods considered and to the competition structure of its production sector. If some of these conditions and circumstances can be influenced or modified by a proactive policy, many of them can be considered as exogenous, at least in the short term.

Other factors, of a strategic or social nature, should also be taken into account while striving to get an overall picture of the potential impact of the introduction of a GI protection. The next section tries to give a comprehensive picture of these factors while the section that follows it tries to define quantitative and qualitative methods that can be implemented in order to assess these factors.

Potential Benefits and Costs Arising from GI Protection

It should be noted first that, as shown in the case studies in this book, a GI often has a public good dimension in the sense that a GI has a social and sometimes a cultural impact that goes beyond its purely economic effect on producers and consumers, at home or abroad.

Probably the most comprehensive analyses of the potential benefits and costs and of the broader socio-economic impacts that could arise from a GI protection have been developed by Jorge Larson (2007) and Sisule F. Musungu (2008). The following mostly elaborates on these analyses.

Potential Benefits of a GI Protection

Based on an extensive literature review, Musungu (2008) has identified the main potential advantages and benefits related to a GI protection. We should distinguish, [103] for the purpose of this economic analysis, between what constitutes a potential economic benefit of a GI protection as such and broader socio-economic advantages and benefits.

POTENTIAL ECONOMIC BENEFITS

A key aspect in this regard, which has been extensively developed in the previous section, is that a GI is constitutive of an immaterial asset, the reputation of the product, which constitutes a signal to the consumers regarding a specific quality, potentially drawing a higher price or, as it is often labelled, a premium price.

Should the producers be fully committed to preserving the value of the immaterial asset that the GI constitutes, it could even lead to transforming a sector of generic goods into an exporting process chain of high-quality agricultural and handicraft products. The question of the impact of a GI protection on quality is, as seen in the previous section, one of the most researched in the economic literature. As said in this section, there appears to be specific conditions, related in particular to the membership of the GI community of producers and its size, which strongly affect this potential impact.

Musungu, again, considers that, as GI governing bodies are most often collective entities focused on regional identity, they could bring about the type of governance needed to transform supply chains into value chains that create value added. As seen in the previous section, this value added could take shape through increased volumes of production or through higher prices (premium prices) charged to the final consumer.

The collective approach to GIs could, on the other hand, benefit small producers that would normally not be able to finance marketing and brand development activities. This advantage is intrinsic to the club asset character of the GI as it was developed in the previous section. As shown therein, the value of this club asset can still increase or decrease depending on several factors and, in particular, on the size of the GI club membership and on the behaviour of its members.

Musungu also notes that, when reputation already exists, small farmers may benefit from a GI protection coupled with niche market development. This point raises the question of the prior reputation of any good considered for a GI protection. Indeed, it seems that this prior reputation might be a critical factor in the success of the GI protection. When it already exists, the GI label could be used to strengthen this reputation, formalize its quality basis and prevent any fraudulent use of it.

GIs have in addition the potential of being associated with other market incentives, such as organic or fair trade certification. This label could hence be of particular interest for small producers of natural goods. In contrast, the convergence between a GI protection and a trademark raises some questions. Although it is conceivable that some production process related to a GI good might be patented, it is usually not the case. And since GIs are based on tradition, potential patents rights are probably forfeited or unclaimed (see Benavente 2010: 50).

Musungu (2008) also considers that a GI protection could have a kind of 'spill-over' impact that could benefit small producers at no cost. Indeed, once small producers have achieved the quality standards required to access new markets, precise use of [104] geographical information in labelling could, according to him, easily be implemented with or without GI registration.

GIs are also important to prevent the delocalization of the production and to develop the local added value content, since a GI can only be produced in a given area or locality. Still, this delocalization remains a possibility and the GI specifications clearly have to strictly define the product and the production process in order to avoid such a delocalization. A loose definition of these aspects could indeed allow some key operations, in particular those yielding the highest value added, to be delocalized while benefiting from the geographical indication.

Finally, beyond its potential impact on valuation (premium price) and quality, that is the nature of the good, a GI could also have an impact on the volume of the market. We should distinguish in this respect the impact on existing markets, in the form of an increased market share of the GI product, and the impact on other markets, in the form of penetration of new markets.

BROADER ADVANTAGES AND BENEFITS POTENTIALLY ATTACHED TO A GI PROTECTION

According to Musungu (2008), GIs, unlike patents, would require very low levels of innovation, if any, which would allow a larger number of producers to apply for a GI protection without having to endure the costs and investments that could be related to innovation. It is indeed a well-documented feature of GI products that they relate, by nature, to tradition and cultural aspects and this feature could even be considered as antinomic with innovation. According to Musungu, since GIs predominantly apply to agricultural and cultural products, African and other developing countries could, in addition, have a natural comparative advantage in this respect. If so, GIs could constitute the core of a development strategy that might have been underestimated so far.

GIs could also help prevent bio-piracy and piracy of traditional knowledge as well as helping to protect or provide recognition to traditional production methods such as seed selection and food conservation practices. This would, in many cases, permit the transformation of traditional knowledge into marketable products.

Finally, GI production systems and processes based on well-managed extractive activities would promote conservation of natural vegetation and forested areas which would, in turn, benefit ecosystem and landscape conservation. Strong links between products and culture could, in addition, benefit rural development.

Potential Costs, Disadvantages and Conditions Attached to a GI Protection and its Success

As seen above, the potential benefits and advantages of introducing a GI are numerous and important. Still, potential costs and disadvantages attached to a GI protection and conditions on its success should not be neglected.

This analysis mostly relies and elaborates on Musungu (2008) and Larson (2007). These authors identify several potential drawbacks of a GI protection, which can consist in direct costs attached to the GI protection, in difficulties associated with its [105] development, including the conditions of its success, in inherent limits and, finally, in potential negative effects of a GI protection.

DIRECT COSTS ATTACHED TO THE DEVELOPMENT AND ENFORCEMENT OF A GI PROTECTION

The direct costs attached to the development and enforcement of a GI protection are numerous and of a very uneven importance. These direct costs consist in institutional, organisational and promotional costs which have been detailed in several studies.

According to Musungu (2008), building on an analysis made by O'Connor and Company and Insight Consulting (2007), the main costs to be faced in both the domestic market and the export markets in relation with the registration and the enforcement of a GI protection are the following:

- Application fees;
- Search fees;
- Advertisement fees;
- Publication fees;
- Costs in opposition proceedings;
- Litigation costs;
- Renewal fees (mainly in cases of trademarks);
- Fees for change of address or name;
- Fees in case of assignment;

- Fees for correction of clerical or other errors;
- Charges for amendment to application or registration; and
- Attorney's fees for preparation and legalization of documents.

It should be noted that this analysis does not take into account the costs that are related with the implementation of the GI system as such and with the development of a specific geographical indication. These will be considered below.

DIFFICULTIES ASSOCIATED WITH THE DEVELOPMENT OF A GI PROTECTION AND CONDITIONS FOR ITS SUCCESS

It comes out from the literature that the development of a GI protection is in itself a complex process. This complexity means that specific conditions must be fulfilled to secure the success of a GI.

For Larson (2007), formal and well-distributed knowledge and information about biological resources and cultural practices with GI potential seems to be generally lacking in developing countries. Although these countries could – in consideration of the diversity of their agricultural and handicraft products that could potentially benefit from a GI protection – have a comparative advantage in this respect, strong capacity building and, more generally, technical as well as financial assistance would be required in order to help these countries effectively seize these opportunities. [106]

One specific problem is related to the fact that small farmers or producers cannot usually produce surpluses that would allow them to participate in market-oriented activities such as GI development. This underlines the need for a strong public, and probably international, support to such activities.

The basic economic logic of GI protection relies on a form of product differentiation. Such a differentiation is well known to have the potential to improve the situation of producers through both increased market shares and a higher value added content of their product. Still, according to Larson (2007), differentiation of production processes, qualities and markets will be difficult to achieve without operating governance structures that are respectful of local culture. The organizational and institutional aspects related to the composition and working of the GI governance body will thus have a deep impact on the real benefits that can accrue from this particular form of differentiation.

It is essential, in this respect, to take into account the fact that complying with labelling, safety and traceability regulations represents a significant organizational and technical challenge to many small organizations. Capacity building and technical assistance to small producers all along the unfolding of the GI development and implementation processes will thus, once again, be critical to their success. In the same order of ideas, it should be taken into account that a statutory declaration of GIs, without the implication of the relevant operating bodies, may fail to connect GIs to rural development policy.

More generally, he notes that GIs, especially where they are related to agricultural products, may not succeed if their development is isolated from complementary agricultural and rural development policies including economic support.

Finally, the organization and management of this support are also key to the success of the overall process. One could fear, indeed, that legal frameworks and support measures from different government arms may not be well coordinated, producing a complex scenario for GI development.

Even though all the conditions for the success of a GI, as listed above, may be fulfilled, one should be aware of the inherent limits of a GI and should not base too many hopes on its introduction.

Clearly, a GI protection will not be able, most of the time, to radically change the situation and solve all problems faced by the farmers or producers concerned. Putting too many expectations on the GI protection only and neglecting other key aspects or strategies could even constitute a risk to the development of a given branch of activity or region and to the improvement of the situation of the individual producers.

More specifically, Larson (2007) notes that small producers are vulnerable in national and export markets for economic and scale reasons that cannot be addressed solely with GI differentiation.

This means that it is necessary to proceed with a global assessment of the economic constraints facing the individual producers and to integrate the protection of a GI into a global strategy for the development of a sector. [107]

In addition, although evidence of economic benefits from GI protection can be found in developing countries, the distribution of benefits within value chains is unclear and that several cases point to a concentration of power in transformers and distributors' hands. The distributive effect of the introduction of a GI protection is an aspect of the utmost importance that has to be addressed prior to any decision on the development of such a protection. It should be underlined in particular that, in the absence of democratic governance structures, the value added brought about by a GI may not be capitalized by regional interests or small farmers.

Finally, according to Larson again, employment generated by GI may contribute to the rural economy but not necessarily generate benefits for biodiversity conservation and small farmers.

The introduction of a GI has not only a cost but, under certain circumstances, it may even have some negative or perverse effects that have to be carefully analysed and, if possible, neutralized before any move in that direction is made.

First, and as seen above, introducing a GI may lead to a concentration of power within the value added chain and there is a risk to see the value added created by the GI be captured not by local individual producers but by other stakeholders, possibly out of the region of production and even abroad.

Besides, and according to Musungu (2008) and Larson (2007), linking a GI to a specific variety, breed or sub-species as a response to productivity and market demands may in particular marginalize other genetic resources that are biologically and culturally relevant. This means that the overall impact of a GI protection on biodiversity, and more generally on ecosystem and landscape conservation, could still be questioned as some arguments play in one direction, as seen above, and others in the opposite one.

Larson (2007) points to another potential negative effect which lies in the fact that market segmentation that would attend only to high-end niches may generate economic exclusions or inhibit access to nutritious and culturally valuable resources by local or low-income populations. These exclusion impacts on the demand side are clearly to be assessed prior to any decision regarding the development of a GI protection, especially, of course, when first necessity products and low-income populations are concerned.

Beside this exclusion impact on the demand side, the introduction of a GI protection may also have an exclusion inipact on supply. In particular, it should be taken into account that formal definitions of quality imposed by external stakeholders could provoke exclusions of legitimate but culturally different producers.

Finally, the question of the ownership of the GI is a clearly very sensitive one that could condition its impact. It should be noted that ownership of culturally sensitive GIs by the state may in particular lead to conflicts with indigenous peoples.

What clearly comes out of this analysis of the potential benefits and costs associated with a GI protection is that these benefits and costs are of a very different nature, [108] some of them being strictly economical while others have a broader socio-economic content, some of them constituting direct impacts to be witnessed in a pretty short period of time, others constituting indirect impacts that could be felt later. Only the purely economical, short-term or long-term, aspects are considered below.

A Pragmatic Approach to Evaluating the Economic Benefits and Costs of a GI Protection

As seen above, the economic literature suggests that positive market and value impacts can be expected from the introduction of a GI protection. Still, these positive impacts highly depend on key characteristics of market and production structures, including features of the value added chain. These characteristics can be of a quantitative or qualitative nature. The following sections detail these features, the information required to assess them and the methods to be implemented in order to collect and treat this information.

Evaluation of Benefits

The evaluation of the benefits potentially attached to a GI protection, as identified above, be it in terms of premium price captured by local producers, of increased market shares of their product on existing export markets or of development of new markets, requires a clear and comprehensive picture of the market and production structures, as well as of the nature and characteristics of the value chain. This characterization should be primarily based on quantitative data, some qualitative information still being necessary to complement or help interpret this quantitative information. We will see successively what kind of quantitative and qualitative information on, first, the domestic sector of production and, then, the major export markets, would be required in this analysis and how this information could be produced.

THE INFORMATION REQUIRED ON THE DOMESTIC SECTOR OF PRODUCTION
As said, this information is of a quantitative and of a qualitative nature.

The quantitative information required   Quantitative information is absolutely necessary to understand the market and production structures associated with the good considered. Before gathering, or producing any figure relating to these structures, a first necessary step consists in the identification of the value chain and of all the actors of this chain. This implies, in turn, to clearly define the product, or products, to be covered by the GI protection.

As the products considered for a GI protection are, most of the time, natural products that undergo minimal transformation, this production chain may well, in most cases, consist in only one or two types of actors, i.e. primary producers (farmers, stock-owners, fishers, etc.) and transformers (craftsmen, dairy product producers, pork butchers, etc.). On each of these specific components of the value chain, a string of [109] information is required to assess the potential price and production impact of any substantive change in market configuration, such as, in particular, the one involved by the introduction of a GI protection.

For each segment of the value chain, some key data are required in order to assess the potential economic impact of a GI protection on the sector. These data can relate to individual producers or to the economic sector as a whole. They can also consist in derived indicators.

DATA REQUIRED ON INDIVIDUAL PRODUCERS AND ACTORS OF THE VALUE ADDED CHAIN:

- Turnover;
- Number of persons employed (total and full-time equivalent);
- Number of employees (total and full-time equivalent);
- Volume of production in real terms (tons, litres, m^3, etc.);
- Value of production;
- Value added; and
- Volumes and values of exports by main export market.

DATA REQUIRED ON THE ECONOMIC SECTOR AS A WHOLE

The analysis of the sector's structure is key to understanding the power relations within the value added chain and hence the potential distributive effects of a GI. This analysis requires to gather the following key data:

- Total number of producers and actors at each stage of the value added chain;
- Size structure of the sector in terms of employees and production: the production of this picture of the size structure first supposes to define significant size classes in terms of both employees (or persons employed) and production value;
- Volume of production in real terms (tons, litres, m^3, etc.);
- Value of production;
- Value added; and
- Volumes and values of exports by main export market.

DERIVED INDICATORS TO BE CALCULATED

- Concentration ratio: based on the production values collected, this concentration ratio can be calculated in several ways. First, in a simple approach, it can be calculated as a composite index based on the market shares of the single biggest producer, of the five biggest producers and of the ten biggest producers. A more sophisticated concentration ratio is made of the so-called Herfindahl-Hirschman index, which is defined as the sum of the square of the market shares of every producer, expressed as a percentage. This ratio can vary between the values 0 and 10.000, 0 corresponding to a perfectly atomistic competition structure and 10.000 to a monopolistic situation. Most important in the interpretation of this index is the possible divergence between the value of the Herfindahl-Hirschman index at one [110] stage of the value chain and its value at another stage. This divergence could indeed indicate a market power of one segment (the most concentrated one) on the other (the most atomistic one);

- Average price and price index;
- Price-elasticity, that is the relative product demand evolution in relation with a given price evolution for this product. This price elasticity measures the sensitivity of demand to a given price change and is hence a critical indicator to understand the potential impact of a GI on the price of the product concerned;
- When the product considered for a GI protection is facing substitutable products on its market, the substitution price-elasticity, that is the relative demand evolution of one product in relation with a price evolution of the other, should also be calculated. This indicator is also key to understanding the potential impact of a GI on the price of the product concerned.

In addition to these key data, further quantitative information would be useful relating in particular to the cost structure of the production unit and of the economic sector as a whole, that is, chiefly, the main components of its intermediate consumption and the share of wages and salaries in total costs.

A methodology for the production of quantitative information   The primary information detailed above should, in principle, be available at the National Statistical Office or at the ministry in charge of the sector's supervision. However, it can sometimes not be readily available or the available information can be partial or not fully reliable.

In this situation, it is highly recommended to engage in an exhaustive economic census of the producers and actors of the value added chain that could be concerned by the GI protection. Three critical steps have to be performed before this economic census can be undertaken. These prior steps are the following:

- A precise and unambiguous definition of the product(s) to be covered by the geographical indication;
- A precise definition of the area covered by the geographical identification; and
- A clear identification of the value chain: identification of all economic activities implied in the production and distribution of the product(s) that would be covered by a GI protection.

The economic census itself should allow to gather all the information identified in the section above directly from the producers. It should, in addition, allow to gather additional information regarding:

- The date of creation of the company;

- The evolution of the number of persons employed and of the number of employees of the unit since its creation;
- The evolution of the turnover and of the value added of the unit since its creation; [111]
- The whole productive activity of the unit: kinds of products produced, share of the product considered for a GI protection in this total production;
- The cost structure of the product considered for a GI: main elements of the intermediate consumption of the unit, costs associated, share of wages and salaries in the total production costs.

Once again, this exhaustive census is key to the understanding of the production structure. It should be greatly facilitated by the prior delimitation of the area to which the geographical identification would be attached. Still, a census or, at least, an identification of all the producers potentially competing with those in the GI area would also be very useful to understand the potential sideline effects of this GI.

The qualitative information required   Qualitative information is key to understanding and interpreting the quantitative information collected, both on production and on market structures. This qualitative information is also critical in order to complement the quantitative information described above and to understand, in particular, the nature of the value chain at stake.

In this respect, it is worth noting that two main kinds of value chains are usually distinguished, the so-called product driven chains and consumer driven chains. In the context of a consumer driven chain, it is likely that the ultimate benefits of a GI may not go to the small producers but rather to the supermarket chains in the export markets and changing this situation might require intervention in the value chain (Musungu 2008: 16). Still, we can consider that, in most countries, such an intervention can hardly be considered and, if possible, could only produce significant changes over a long period of time.

A methodology for the production of qualitative information   The production of a relevant qualitative information that could complement and help interpret the quantitative information defined above, should rely on the identification of the key stakeholders and on the development of specific questionnaires aimed at these different groups of stakeholders. When possible, the analysis of past experience will also be instrumental.

This qualitative analysis should thus rely on the implementation of three complementary procedures: the identification and consultation of all the stakeholders, the sharing of the information gathered in order to produce a common and consistent vision and, finally, the exploitation of the acquired experience.

The key stakeholders to be considered are first made, of course, of the producers, including both primary producers and potential transformers, but also of distributors of the products, local clients, exporters, experts of the product and its markets and national administrations in charge of the monitoring of the sector. Specific questionnaires should be used in order to collect information from these specific groups. The questionnaires developed for the production of the case studies grouped in this book are reproduced in Annex 2. [112]

The collection and synthesis of this information is essential but it might, most often, not be sufficient to produce a consistent and reliable basis for understanding and completing the quantitative information. The individual interviews allow all of the stakeholders to deliver their vision of the sector, not to agree on a comprehensive and consistent picture.

In this respect, it is necessary to complete this first step of direct individual interviews by a kind of sharing exercise which could take the form of a sector workshop and should gather all the stakeholders met in the first step with the aim of producing a comprehensive, shared and reliable picture of the activity and of the production and market structures characterizing the sector.

This workshop should also be instrumental in the decision making and in the association of all the relevant parties to the decision regarding the launch of a process aiming at introducing a GI protection. It should be based on a synthesis of the quantitative information collected as above and of the qualitative information collected through the first step of this approach as well as of relevant case studies.

Indeed, most of the time, the product considered for a GI protection may be similar to a product that is already covered by a GI protection elsewhere in the world and whose protection and its impact may already be well documented and analysed. It is of course essential that, in the process of developing a GI protection, all this information regarding similar experiences, and their impact on the main export markets considered, be researched and carefully analysed.

THE INFORMATION REQUIRED ON THE MAJOR EXPORT MARKETS

In addition to this analysis of the domestic sector of production, the assessment of the potential benefit of the introduction of a GI protection clearly makes it necessary to analyse its potential impact on the main export markets of the product. Indeed, the potential direct benefit of the introduction of a GI protection for the country as a whole mostly relies on the impact this GI protection can have on the main export market(s) of the product. Therefore, first the main current and potential export markets must be identified. The first ones should be identified through the available foreign trade statistics and the second ones through the analyses of the producers and exporters.

For each of these export markets, or at least for those for which a GI protection could be considered, it is necessary to undertake a market analysis so as to assess and quantify the following elements:

- The current size and the potential evolution of the market;
- The existing knowledge and reputation of the product on this market;
- Its existing market share;
- The price-elasticity of the product on this market, or, in other words, the premium price that the consumer on this market would be ready to pay for a differentiated product based on a GI protection; and
- The potential volume growth associated with a GI protection. [113]

This market study should also allow to assess what are the key success factors on each of these main export markets and, if possible, their relative importance. These key success factors, which can consist in price competitiveness, differentiation, quality, brand reputation and many other factors, can indeed clearly indicate whether a GI protection can yield a premium price, and to what extent, on this market.

The development of this analysis clearly requires to dispose of specific and reliable information about the main export markets of the products, that is about the values and volumes of exports by destination and their evolution over a recent period (in practice, the last decade). This information should, in principle, be available at the Customs administration or, in some cases, at the Ministry in charge of the supervision of the sector.

Finally, a real experience could also be undertaken in order to assess the potential impact of a GI protection on a given export market. The potential economic benefit of a GI protection on a specific export market could indeed be assessed based on a prior experience of GI marketing, without protection and hence without the costs attached to a formal protection. The reaction of the market, in terms of both possible premium price and increased market share, could be an indication of the value of the intangible asset that the geographical indication constitutes on this market and, hence, of the value of it protection.

Evaluation of Costs

As seen above, the main costs to be faced in both the domestic market and the export markets in relation with the registration and the enforcement of a GI protection consist in institutional, organizational and promotional costs which can be detailed as follows (see Musungu 2008: 20):

- Application fees;
- Search fees;
- Advertisement fees;
- Publication fees;
- Costs in opposition proceedings;
- Litigation costs;
- Renewal fees (mainly in cases of trademarks);
- Fees for change of address or name;
- Fees in case of assignment;
- Fees for correction of clerical or other errors;
- Charges for amendment to application or registration; and
- Attorney's fees for preparation and legalization of documents.

In the analysis of the costs associated with a GI protection, we should first distinguish between costs incurred at home and costs incurred abroad, that is in the main export market(s), the first ones including, in addition to those identified above, [114] the costs of developing a GI protection system and the costs of developing a specific geographical indication. These two kinds of costs are considered successively here below.

EVALUATION OF DOMESTIC COSTS

According to Musungu (2008), various factors may impact the cost of setting up and running a GI regime in African countries. These include whether:

- legal reforms related to GI protection are undertaken in isolation or as part of a broader IP and trade law reforms. In the latter case, the costs for a GI system are likely to be lower;

- the administration of the GI regime is integrated with overall IP administration or is distinct;
- the country is party to a regional or international registration system such as the OAPI and ARIPO systems or the Lisbon system;
- cost recovery from registration and renewal fees is feasible or not;
- the enforcement of GIs, especially through litigation, is part of the general law enforcement or is dealt with separately. The costs will inevitably be higher in the latter case.

From a pragmatic point of view, the most important costs to be considered at home probably relate to the following operations:

- the development of a legal framework;
- the development of a specific GI;
- certification of individual producers;
- inspection of producers;
- inspection of retail outlets; and
- the cost associated with a possible litigation.

It should be remembered that, in most African ACP countries that are members of either OAPI or ARIPO, the legal framework is already in place, even though this could, in some cases, be adapted and 'nationalized' in the near future. This means that no specific cost is necessarily associated with the development of this legal framework. The cost associated with the development of a specific GI clearly depends on the number of stakeholders involved and on the specificities of the product. It will thus be largely determined by both the complexity of the value chain and the number of producers at each step of this value chain. This information should be produced by the economic census described above.

This cost thus should be estimated as a function of the number of persons implied in the GI development process, its probable duration and the estimated number of days per person involved in the process over its whole duration. Case studies of past [115] and similar GI development processes could be instrumental in the evaluation of these various elements.

The cost associated with the certification of individual producers will clearly depend on the technical specifications included in the code of practice and/or product specifications associated with a particular GI registration. This means that there is probably no standard cost associated with this operation. Some indications have nevertheless been given regarding the potential costs that could be associated with the certification of individual producers in relation with the specific products analysed in the case studies grouped in this book.

The enforcement of the GI implies a regular, probably yearly, inspection of producers in order to make sure that all the producers benefiting from the geographical indication respect its technical specifications and do not develop a 'free-riding' strategy, as mentioned above, which would allow them to benefit from the commercial signal that is attached to the geographical indication without supporting the technical requirements that it entails, thus lowering the quality of the GI product and affecting, in the end, its reputation, that is the value of the intangible asset that the GI protection constitutes. The cost associated with the inspection of producers will again clearly depend on the number of producers first but also on the technical specifications attached to the GI protection and, more specifically, on the detail, or number, of these specifications as well as on their inherent complexity.

The enforcement of the GI also implies a regular, probably yearly again, inspection of retail outlets selling the product in order to make sure, in this case, that all the products sold under the GI label are effectively produced by one of the certified producers or, in other terms, that no product that is not entitled to bear the GI label is sold on the market while making a fraudulent use of this label. The cost of this inspection will clearly depend on the nature of the product, which can affect the potential for its falsification as well as the complexity of its identification, and on the number of selling points through which the product reaches the consumer.

All these inspections would probably be performed by a GI governance body, that is an association of producers including, most probably, representatives of the state and of local and regional authorities, to which a specific management cost will also be associated.

Finally, individual producers or, most often, the governance body of the GI, could have to support costs of legal actions engaged in order to enforce the respect of the GI label before the courts. Such a procedure could be considered in either of the two cases mentioned above, that is the non-respect by one producer of the GI region of the technical specifications associated with the geographical indication on one hand, or the fraudulent use of the GI label by one producer which is not entitled to use this indication. In the first case, the legal action could aim at the exclusion of the free-riding member from the GI club. In the second, it could aim at the condemnation of the fraudulent user of the label and at the financial compensation of the GI members by this fraudulent user.

The costs associated with such legal procedures clearly depend on the legal system in place in each country and on the complexities of this legal system that could be assessed by the number of possible appeals and the average duration of a legal [116] procedure at each of these levels. Still, it should be noted that this cost should be borne, in the end, by the offender, who should indemnify the defendants in case, of course, he would be found guilty of the charge put against him, even though the defendants would have to bear the advance payment for these costs.

It should be noted that the costs analysed above will not be incurred by the same entities. Some of them are to be borne by the state or other public entities, such as local or regional authorities. This is the case of the development of a legal framework and of the inspection of producers and retail outlets. Others are to be incurred by individual producers or groupings of producers; groupings that could include, in some cases, some public entities. This is the case of the costs related to certification and of those associated with a possible litigation. Finally, the cost of developing a specific GI would probably, in most instances, be shared by the public and private entities concerned.

EVALUATION OF COSTS INCURRED ABROAD

As stated above, the costs associated with the registration and the enforcement of a GI are of the same kind in the export markets and in the domestic market. These costs will obviously greatly vary from one country to another and the detailed evaluation of these should thus rely first on the identification of the major export markets of the product considered, that is of the markets on which a protection of its geographical indication would be most important.

The evaluation of these specific costs on each of these major export markets would require a specific study. Still, some data on these costs may be readily available. O'Connor and Company and Insight Consulting (2007) thus provide a comprehensive picture of the various fees detailed above in 160 countries, including 47 African countries.

In conclusion, we have seen that, according to the economic theory, a geographical indication constitutes an intangible asset shared by producers acting on a specific territory in the production of a given and specified good. This asset can appreciate or depreciate over time according to various factors and, in particular, according to the behaviour of its owners, that is the producers of the good benefiting from the GI, as reputation is at the core of this asset.

A geographical indication may induce different kinds of benefit for its owners, notably in the form of a premium price, of a larger market share on the existing markets or of access to new markets. Still, the realization and the extent of these benefits highly depend on key characteristics of the production and market structures. The configuration of the value added chain is also critical to the distribution of these potential benefits between producers, transformers, exporters and distributors.

Besides, the introduction of a GI has a cost; its development could result in a complex and protracted process and the GI may even induce negative effects, in particular on competition and factors prices. It is obviously critical to assess these potential benefits and costs from the very first stages of its development.

This analysis attempts to build on existing theoretical approaches to GIs and to propose a pragmatic methodology for assessing their potential economic impact. This pragmatic methodology can be summed up in eight steps as below: [117]

1. *Definition of the product and identification of the value added chain*: The product must be precisely defined in terms of natural and/or know-how characteristics as well as in terms of geographical area. The corresponding value added chain includes all stakeholders in the production and distribution of the product, from the primary producer to the retailer.
2. *Quantitative sector analysis*: This consists of an analysis of the composition and structure of the production sector at every stage of the value chain. This analysis is key to understanding the economic power relations that might exist within the value chain. A string of key indicators, as seen above, can be used in this exercise.
3. *Individual interviews with all stakeholders*: Based on standard questionnaires, these interviews aim at gathering all the relevant information, both quantitative and qualitative, that might be necessary to fully understand the economic dynamics of the production and distribution sectors.
4. *Sector workshop*: A sector workshop should be organized with a view to sharing the information collected and to producing a comprehensive and shared vision about the sector, the conditions of production, the markets and their evolution. Actually, very often, the individual interviews may produce different or even contradictory pieces of information that it is key to reconcile.
5. *Exploitation of acquired experience*: Most of the time, a similar product to the one under consideration may already benefit from a GI protection elsewhere in the world. In this case, it is absolutely essential to try to draw lessons from the existing experience through gathering and analysing existing case studies.
6. *Analysis of the main export markets*: The development of export markets is very often a

key objective of the introduction of a GI protection but the evaluation of the potential impact of this protection on specific markets is often complex and requires to proceed with a full market analysis, including the identification of the Key Success Factors on each of the targeted markets. In addition, a real experience consisting in the introduction of a mention of the geographical origin of a product, without any formal protection of this indication, could be made so as to measure the real reaction of a particular market to this indication.

7. *Identification of domestic and foreign costs*: These consist of institutional, organizational and promotional costs. All of them have to be precisely identified and valued so as to balance the potential benefits of a protection with its full cost.

8. *Overall assessment and decision*: Based on all the pieces of information previously mentioned, a shared decision should be reached with regard to the introduction of a GI protection. This decision should involve all stakeholders, public and private.

We believe that the systematic performance of an economic assessment based on the implementation of this methodology and on the sharing of the information produced with all stakeholders in the very first steps of a reflection about the introduction of a GI may help producers and countries have the most precise view of the potential benefits and costs that could be associated with the GI and may help maximizing the net profit to both individual producers and the country as a whole that could be reached through this strategy. [118]

References

Benavente, D. (2010) 'The Economics of Geographical Indications: GIs Modelled as Club Assets', Graduate Institute of International and Development Studies Working Paper No 10/2010, Geneva: Graduate Institute of International and Development Studies.

Buchanan, J.M. (1965) 'An Economic Theory of Clubs', *Economica*, **32**: 1–14.

Cornes, R. and Sandler, T. (1996) *The Theory of Externalities, Public Goods and Club Goods*, Cambridge: Cambridge University Press.

Larson, J. (2007) 'Relevance of Geographical Indications and Designations of Origin for the Sustainable Use of Genetic Resources', study commissioned by the Global Facilitation Unit for Underutilised Species, Rome.

Musungu, S.F. (2008) 'The Protection of the Geographical Indications and the Doha Round: Strategic and Policy Considerations for Africa', QUNO IP Issue Paper No 8, Geneva: Quaker United Nations Office.

O'Connor and Company and Insight Consulting (2007) 'Geographical Indications and TRIPS: 10 Years Later ... A Roadmap for EU GI Holders to Get Protection in Other WTO Members', report for the European Commission, available at http://trade.ec. europa.eu/ doclib/docs/2007/june/tradoc_135088. pdf, Brussels.

OECD (2000) 'Appellations of Origin and Geographical Indications in OECD Member Countries: Economic and Legal Implications', COM/AGR/APM/TD/WP(2000)15/final, Paris.

Rangnekar, D. (2003) 'The Socio-economics of Geographical Indications: A Review of Empirical Evidence from Europe', Issue Paper No 8, UNCTAD-ICTSD Project on IPRs and Sustainable Development, Geneva.

Shapiro, C. (1982) 'Consumer Information, Product Quality and Seller Reputation', *The Bell Journal of Economics*, **13** (1): 20–35.

Shapiro, C. (1983) 'Premiums for High Quality Products as Returns to Reputation', *The Quarterly Journal of Economics*, **98** (4): 659–80.

Winfree, J.A. and McCluskey, J.J. (2005) 'Collective Reputation and Quality', *American Journal of Agricultural Economics*, **87** (1): 206–13. [119]